Comparative Politics

Domestic Responses to Global Challenges

Eighth Edition

Charles Hauss
Alliance for Peacebuilding

Melissa Haussman
Carleton University

WADSWORTH
CENGAGE Learning·

Australia • Brazil • Japan • Korea • Mexico • Singapore • Spain • United Kingdom • United States

Comparative Politics: Domestic Responses to Global Challenges, **Eighth Edition**
Charles Hauss
Melissa Haussman

Senior Publisher: Suzanne Jeans

Executive Editor: Carolyn Merrill

Acquisitions Editor: Anita M. Devine

Development Editor: Rebecca Green

Assistant Editor: Laura Ross

Media Editor: Laura Hildebrand

Marketing Program Manager: Caitlin Green

Manufacturing Planner: Fola Orekoya

Art Director: Linda Helcher

Sr. Rights Specialist: Jennifer Meyer Dare

Photo Researcher: Sarah Bonner,
Bill Smith Group

Text Researcher: Karyn Morrison

Production Service/Compositor: Integra

Text Designer: Lou Ann Thesing

Cover Designer: Red Hanger Design

Cover Images: Image Source/©Getty
Images; Travel Ink/Gallo Images/©Getty
Images; M. Freeman/PhotoLink/©Getty
Images

For product information and technology assistance, contact us at
Cengage Learning Customer & Sales Support, 1-800-354-9706

For permission to use material from this text or product,
submit all requests online at **cengage.com/permissions.**
Further permissions questions can be emailed to
permissionrequest@cengage.com

Library of Congress Control Number: 2011930783

ISBN-13: 978-1-111-83255-1

ISBN-10: 1-111-83255-2

Wadsworth
20 Channel Center Street
Boston, MA 02210
USA

Cengage Learning is a leading provider of customized learning solutions with office locations around the globe, including Singapore, the United Kingdom, Australia, Mexico, Brazil, and Japan. Locate your local office at: **international.cengage.com/region**

Cengage Learning products are represented in Canada by Nelson Education, Ltd.

For your course and learning solutions, visit **www.cengage.com**

Purchase any of our products at your local college store or at our preferred online store **www.CengageBrain.com**

Printed in Canada
1 2 3 4 5 6 7 15 14 13 12 11

Brief Contents

Contents

Part 4
THE GLOBAL SOUTH

Chapter 14
IRAQ   401

Chapter 15
NIGERIA   435

Preface

The eighth edition of *Comparative Politics* incorporates many changes, but the two primary goals of the book remain the same as they were in the first edition twenty years ago.

First, Chip and now Melissa (given how similar our last names are, we will be Chip and Melissa throughout the book) live in the fascinating and confusing world of comparative politics. After years of teaching, we know that students see the confusing side before the fascinating one. We also know that few students enter our classrooms with a deep and abiding interest in comparative politics. In other words, we have to bring the subject matter to life for them by focusing in part on current issues and leaders. To cite but one example, in the six months since we finished the first draft of this edition, the Chinese Communist Party named Xi Jinping as the party's, and hence the government's, new leader, German politics was roiled by the role it will play in bailing out the Greek economy, and the Arab Spring unexpectedly broke out. In our experience, paying attention to people, places, and events in the news is a good way to grab students' attention.

We also know this because, frankly, neither of us took our first comparative politics course with any awareness of what makes comparative politics fascinating. Chip started as a physics major and switched to political science because of the Vietnam War, not to mention his lack of aptitude for advanced math. It was only as a sophomore that he took a comparative politics course and then only because it fit his schedule. Melissa's very first course at Colby was a first-year seminar in French politics through literature, which was taught in French. Chip will attest that Melissa had a strong interest in politics even then, but it took a while, including a semester in Canada, for her to become excited by comparative politics.

The book's second goal has been to use the excitement of what is happening "on the ground" today as a springboard to introduce core concepts and theories used by political scientists. As we see it, the first and second goals are by no means incompatible.

We have tried to meld these two goals of introducing theory and current-day application in at least three distinctive ways.

To begin with, we have tried to show that the often abstract ideas of our field are relevant for students. The combination of theory and practice can be an effective pedagogical tool in the classroom, but it is just as important because our readers will deal with today's issues and others we cannot foresee yet as citizens long after the course is over.

Second, we have tried to do so in ways that will avoid some of the confusion we've seen from students after all of our years in the field. Indeed, if a student can define and use the key terms listed in Chapter 1, he or she will have a solid grounding in comparative politics *and* be able to make sense of the facts and figures we will be presenting.

Finally, we hope to show readers that the "fire wall" some of our colleagues have erected between comparative politics and international relations no longer makes much sense. We do focus on domestic politics, which is the traditional core of comparative politics. But as the subtitle of the book suggests, students also have to see how the global issues that IR specialists focus on are inescapable determinants of what takes place inside a country's borders.

New to This Edition

Overall Changes

One of the reasons Melissa joined the team was to better consider gender issues. We have done this throughout the text and in chapter boxes that highlight the role of women decision makers in the state or region under discussion.

We also realized that we had to present comparative politics as an important but moving target. As we looked over the first seven editions, we realized just how much the entire field has changed and just how much it is in flux. One of Chip's professors said that comparative politics was in a pre-paradigmatic state in his first graduate seminar. He needed a dictionary to figure out what the instructor meant. Readers who make it to Chapter 17 won't need a dictionary.

We also had to change the theme used to open each chapter. In 2009, when Chip wrote the seventh edition, it made sense to focus on Barack Obama, who had just been elected and was in many ways the "star" of political science. In Brazil, a candidate does not have to run for office under his or her real name. Six changed their name to Barack Obama. Apparently, all lost. As we write in June 2011, Obama has lost a lot of his luster. He might be reelected, but he is a far weaker president than he was upon taking office. As a result, we start each chapter differently, with an examination of the great recession that began in 2008, the impact of which has varied tremendously from country to country. It has barely touched India or China but has led to the deepest budget cuts in recent British history and left Germany and the rest of the EU struggling to keep the euro afloat.

We also wrote knowing that the next two to three years would produce tremendous change. There will be new elections or leaders will change through other means in the United States, France, Germany, Russia, China, Iran, Iraq, and Mexico in the next two years. And, if the history of the first seven editions is any indication, other changes will occur that we cannot anticipate at this time. Therefore, we will be writing about a world we know is in flux. Those uncertainties have always been a key component of this book. If anything, they will be more so here.

It has also been clear from the first edition on that both teaching comparative and writing a textbook are not easy. Consider one example all authors face. No matter how it is written, a book has to include more countries than most teachers can handle in a quarter or semester. Because few readers will actually read the entire book, making comparisons within the book is difficult indeed.

But we need to do so. Therefore, we have integrated two sets of boxes. The "Looking Backward" feature explores how the information the student has already seen will be reflected in or challenged by what comes in the chapter that follows. At the end of chapters are "Looking Forward" features that help the student both pull that chapter together and use that material to anticipate what is coming next.

Finally, we totally revised Chapter 17. From the outset, we realized that it was the chapter that had changed the least in seven editions, even though its subject matter is change itself. What we ended up with is a chapter that focuses on the book's subtitle through the lenses of globalization and systems theory while building on our experience as participant observers in the women's and peacebuilding communities, respectively.

Chapter by Chapter Changes

Chapter 1—Introduction. This chapter begins our concern with current crises by briefly exploring two of them—the Great Recession and the Arab Spring. The chapter then only makes minor changes in the way the previous edition outlined the field of comparative politics with one exception. Far more attention is paid to the concept of regimes since some, especially those in the Middle East, North Africa, and perhaps Mexico, Iran, and Iraq, are in jeopardy even more than they were three years ago.

Chapter 2—Industrialized Democracies. Aside from stressing the current crises and the strength of democratic regimes, this chapter is largely the same because the core principles and practices underlying established democratic regimes have not changed much. In large part, that is the point of the chapter.

Chapter 3—The United States. This chapter was modified largely because of two related changes that affected daily political life but not the regime as a whole. President Obama inherited a major economic crisis that has only gotten more severe during his first term, as seen in slow growth rates, foreclosures, and high unemployment. The Democrats were badly beaten in the 2010 midterm elections, and the shared power between the legislature and executive is complicated by the emergence of the Tea Party movement with ties to many of the newly elected Republican members of the House. What is remarkable is how little the system as a whole (and, thus, the core of the chapter) has changed. Here and in Chapter 4, we touch on why *some* regimes can remain solidly in place despite wrenching political and economic downturns.

Chapter 4—Great Britain. The key to change in Chapter 4 is the unprecedented but not terribly surprising outcome of the 2010 election. For the first time since the 1920s, no party won a parliamentary majority, and there was no viable alternative to a coalition government between the Conservatives and the Liberal Democrats. The new government introduced massive budget cuts that hit social services particularly hard. What is most intriguing about this chapter is *how little* the conceptual core of the chapter had to be rewritten because the UK's culture and institutions keep the regime as solid as ever.

Chapter 5—France. French politics has been shaken by the recession as well. It has eroded the popularity of President Nicolas Sarkozy and leaves him behind in the polls a year before the 2012 election. Political life was shaken up as well by the attempted rape charge against Dominique

Strauss-Kahn, who was seen as the candidate with the best chance of unseating Sarkozy. The Sarkozy team did push through a lot of reforms, many of which were unpopular, including reform of the pension system and the right to wear religious ornaments and clothing. The chapter tries to come to grips with why changes that might have threatened the regime a half century ago do not do so now.

Chapter 6—Germany. As with the preceding three chapters, the changes for Germany are largely about current issues and the bind they leave Germany in 2011. On the one hand, it has largely escaped the great recession and has the highest growth rate of the countries covered in Part 2. On the other hand, as the largest and wealthiest economic force in the EU, it will have to bear the brunt of the costs of whatever the Union has to do for Greece and the other troubled economies. That has put the future of Chancellor Angela Merkel's coalition in doubt; polls show that it is now considerably behind its rivals as we look toward the next election slated for 2013. As with France and the rest of the countries in Part 2, it is remarkable how little the dissatisfaction with the current government has spilled over to the regime as a whole.

Chapter 7—The European Union. This is the one chapter filled with uncertainty in Part 2. It was finished right after the EU and the IMF agreed to a second round of loans to Greece that many felt were needed to keep the euro from collapsing. Even when we wrote, it was clear that the EU was in more trouble than it had been since the empty chairs crisis of the 1960s. That is another way of saying that it is by no means clear that institutional changes such as those laid out in the Treaty of Lisbon will be effective enough to see the EU or even the eurozone through their current difficulties.

Chapter 8—Current and Former Communist Regimes. There is no need to change two of the key premises of Chapter 8 and of Part 3 in general. First, we are highly unlikely to see a return to the kind of communist regimes Melissa and Chip experienced as young professionals. Second, nonetheless, the stakes of politics are much higher in Part 3 than in Part 2. Chapter 8 focuses on what led to the rise and then collapse of Marxism-Leninism and thus has not changed. The changes in the chapter are more subtle, anticipating the higher stakes in the two chapters that follow.

Chapter 9—Russia. The bankers at Goldman Sachs determined that Russia was one of the BRICS, as it called the newly emerging economies that could play a role on the global political stage. It may or may not have deserved that ranking, as we will discuss in Chapter 11. More important politically is the continued erosion of democratic principles under President Medvedev and Prime Minister Putin.

Obviously, that means that we spend more time on the changes in Russian political institutions than in any country in Part 2. We also do so in part through the uncertainties regarding the Duma elections planned for 2011 and the presidential contest the next year. Particularly unclear are how well opposition parties can hope to do in either one now that Putin has announced that he will run for president after his term in "exile" in the prime ministry.

Chapter 10—China. China is also one of the BRICS. Its economy is booming, making it yet another country to have escaped the recession largely unscathed. China has demonstrated its institutional stability by naming Xi Jinping as the next leader who will gradually take over the top positions over the next two years. However, we also update the central dilemma of Chinese politics, which may have deepened since the seventh edition. Can its hybrid political-economic system survive as, among other things, it becomes increasingly enmeshed in a globalizing economy?

Chapter 11—The Global South. Not only have we changed the name of Part 4, we have added two issues both of which show that the stakes of politics are higher yet in these countries. The first is the emergence and recognition of the BRICS. It seems only a matter of time before the rules regarding permanent members of the UN Security Council are updated and one or all of the BRICS earns a spot among the world's leaders with, perhaps, the G-20 supplanting the G-8. Second, we return to the upheaval of the Arab Spring that is turning into the Arab summer as we go to press. Nothing else illustrates the contradiction of decades of authoritarian rule and an increasingly demanding population than the countries that have been in turmoil in 2011. In fact, had the revolts broken out sooner, we would have included one of them as a full fledged chapter.

Chapter 12—India. Like China, India is clearly one of the BRICS and has for all intents avoided the recession. Thus, the first set of changes in this chapter explores how and why Indian political and economic life continues to change so quickly. Although little has been done to change its institutions and regime, we do emphasize the emergence of the independent private sector that is developing political clout as well.

Chapter 13—Iran. Iran may face more major changes in the relatively near future for two reasons. First, President Ahmadinejad is prohibited from running for a third term. Second, the unrest shown in the aftermath of the 2009 presidential election lurks below the surface. There are other changes afoot that do not augur well for Iranian political stability. First, there is no love lost between the president and Supreme Leader Khamenei. Second, pressure from the outside is mounting as the boycotts over the nuclear program and the government's new economic policies suggest.

There is no reason to think that anything like regime change will happen soon, but there is also no reason to believe that the current arrangements can last indefinitely.

Chapter 14—Iraq. There is as much or more uncertainty about the future of Iraq than there is for any other country featured in this book. It is emerging from its third war in a quarter century and almost a decade of occupation by the United States and its allies. The government elected in 2009 is off to a shaky start, to say the least. It has led us to make the section on the emergence of the new Iraqi state even more tentative than it was in the previous two editions.

Chapter 15—Nigeria. In the first few editions of the book, Nigeria came closest to being a failed state. With the new republic's third successive elected president, there are signs that the country may be ushering in a new period of stable and effective government. There are still ethnic issues that flare into violence all too often. Despite its oil resources, the economy remains the poorest covered in this book and does not seem likely to turn itself around quickly. So one of the subthemes of the chapter is the name of the new president, Goodluck Jonathan.

Chapter 16—Mexico. We move from a consideration of current issues facing Mexico to a deeper and more analytical question: Is Mexico on the road to becoming a failed state? Those issues were raised in the seventh edition, but with the disruptions caused by the drug cartels, uncertainty in the political economy brought on both by domestic and international (largely American) causes, and the possibility that the country will return to gridlock if the 2012 elections turn out as inconclusive as polls suggest in 2011.

Chapter 17—Domestic Responses to Global Challenges. Globalization is one of the most widely used and least understood concepts in political science and related disciplines. In Chapter 17, we define it to include all the changes that are "shrinking" the world and argue that it gives new meaning and new life to systems theory. We move back and forth between such megatrends and concrete examples. Those include not just the role of the women's movement and peacebuilders but other changes that have global political implications, from global and regional governance to the dramatic shifts in the media and information technology. It ends by suggesting to students that—if we are right—they will be called on to take part in political life for the rest of their lives.

Acknowledgments

To start with, we would like to thank four people in common. Sandy Maisel and Jon Weiss were colleagues of Chip's and taught Melissa at Colby. Sandy was the driving force in its government department and helped spark our interest in American politics despite where we ended up. Jon Weiss and Chip taught the infamous seminar in French, and more than anyone else, he got us both more interested in Canadian politics. David Rayside was Chip's housemate in graduate school, has become a good friend of both of ours, and has helped us both deal with the role of gender in our discipline and in our world. We also both thank Amy Mazur who was a student of Chip's at Colby and today works on gender issues with Melissa and French politics with Chip.

We also jointly want to thank the team at Cengage. It really is a team. Chip and Melissa put the words on their respective hard drives, but the team was responsible for helping us make those words coherent and actually finishing the book. Rebecca Green ran the day-to-day operations on their end and kept us (reasonably close) to deadlines with the gentleness we have learned to expect. Anita Devine took over the role of lead editor halfway through the process and learned quickly how best to deal with quirky authors. Josh Allen and Sue Langguth served as our production project managers. Sarah Bonner found most of the photographs. Laura Ross managed the ancillary program, for which John Mercurio from San Diego State University updated the test bank and web quizzes; Wendy Whitman Cobb from Santa Fe College updated the instructor's manual; and Edward Kwon from Northern Kentucky University updated the PowerPoint® lectures.

Chip Hauss has a lot of people to thank.

First and foremost is Melissa Haussman. She has been a student and then a colleague and always a friend since her first college class. Adding her to the writing team has obvious advantages. She is the first woman and one of the few people living outside the United States to co-author a market-leading book on comparative politics primarily for the American market. Melissa helped do everything from enhancing the role given to women in the text to getting us all to think more about the good ideas in political science.

Second, he would like to thank a number of academic colleagues who helped out more than they realize. Time after time, Chip would spend time with one or another of them just when he needed help unblocking a tough passage or chapter. Often without realizing it, they helped. In addition to Sandy, Jon, and David, they include Guilain Denoeux (Colby), Eric McGlinchey (George Mason), Cliff Bob (Duquesne), David Last (Royal Military College Canada), Val Bunce and Ron Herring (Cornell), Sharon Wolchik (George Washington), and Cindy Jebb (United States Military Academy).

Third, now that he has completed the transition from academic to activist, he has to give special thanks to the men and women he works with in the NGO and military communities. Some in the latter category cannot be named. Chic Dambach and the team at the Alliance for Peacebuilding have eased the professional transition and made it fun. Other peacebuilders who are also academics helped clarify a lot of the book, especially Chapter 17. They include Ron Fisher (American), Susan Allen Nan (George Mason), Larissa Fast, Dan Philpott, and John Paul Lederach (Notre Dame), and Bill Headley (San Diego). On the Defense Department side, special thanks to Dick O'Neill who has been a friend since nursery school and to David Ignatius, John Agoglia, Puck Mykelby, Rich Yarger, and others still in uniform.

Finally, he has to thank his family which took a major turn with this edition. As always, thanks to Gretchen Sandles who is an accomplished political scientist in her own right, having worked on the Soviet Union, Russia, Eastern Europe, and now Iran and the Middle East in a distinguished career as an analyst for the U.S. government. Her daughter, Evonne Fei, was a high school student when the first edition was published. Now, she is a clinical psychologist counseling returning veterans. In November, she and her husband,

Igor Petrovski, made us grandparents. Kiril is the joy of our lives even when he looks at manuscript pages as something he should rip up. While on a visit with our in-laws in Macedonia they gave us the crazy idea of doing an online chapter on it, which Rebecca properly nixed despite the fact that Igor's father told us that the former Yugoslavia was the only country to declare goats to be enemies of the people.

Melissa thanks her partner, the Rev. Linda Privitera. Melissa thanks those who have taught her along the way from her student days, including Chip, Sandy Maisel, and Jon Weiss; Ken McRae, Jane Jenson, and Jill Vickers while at Carleton; and Allan Kornberg and Jean O'Barr at Duke. Melissa thanks her numerous colleagues from women's and Canadian caucuses in political science and Canadian studies organizations around the world, most especially including, but not limited to, Marian Sawer (ANU), Miriam Smith (York U), Mildred Schwartz (NYU), Mary Hawkesworth (Rutgers), and Dorothy McBride (Florida Atlantic-emerita); many former RNGS and current colleagues including Petra Meier (Antwerp), Anne Maria Holli (U Helsinki), Yvonne Galligan (Queen's University Belfast), Angelika Von Wahl (Lafayette U), Birgit Sauer (University of Vienna), Laurel Weldon (Purdue U), and Allison Woodward (Free University, Brussels); Caroline Andrew (Ottawa U), Sylvia Bashevkin, (U of Toronto), Don Studlar (West Virginia U), Ray Tatalovich (Loyola Chicago); former Suffolk U colleagues Ken Cosgrove, Sebastian Royo, John Berg and Agnes Bain; and current colleagues Laura Macdonald, Lisa Mills and Pauline Rankin at Carleton.

The Cengage team and we would also like to thank the reviewers who keep feeding us with ideas. For this edition, they include:

Alex Avila, Mesa Community College
Valentine Belfiglio, Texas Woman's University
Clifford Bob, Duquesne University
Huiyun Feng, Utah State University
James Hedtke, Cabrini College
Sarah Henderson, Oregon State University
Edward Kwon, Northern Kentucky University
Shannan Mattiace, Allegheny Collge
John Mercurio, San Diego State University
Kevin Navratil, Moraine Valley Community College
Amy Risley, Rhodes College
Anca Turcu, Iowa State University
Walt Vanderbush, Miami University
Phillip Warf, Mendocino College

Wendy Whitman Cobb, Santa Fe College
Bruce Wilson, University of Central Florida

The following reviewed earlier editions:

Nozar Alaolmolki, Hiram College; Leslie Anderson, University of Florida; Yan Bai, Grand Rapids Community College; Steve D. Bollard, Western Kentucky; Alan D. Buckley, Santa Monica College; John M. Buckley, Orange Coast College; William E. Caroll, Sam Houston State University; Kristine K. Cline, Riverside Community College; Richard Deeng, Temple University; Jana Eaton, Unionville High School, Kennett Square, Pennsylvania; Larry Elowitz, Georgia College; Stacey Epifane, Saint John's University; Edward Epstein, University of Utah; Leslie Fadiga-Stewart, Delta State University; Joshua B. Forrest, University of Vermont; E. Gene Frankland, Ball State University; Susan Giaimo, Marquette University; Kristina Gilbert, Riverside Community College; Michael Gold-Biss, St. Cloud State University; Kerstin Hamann, University of Central Florida; Phil Huxtable, University of Kansas; Donna Johnson, Pace University; Ersin Kalaycioglu, Sabanci University; Amal Kawar, Utah State University; Michael Kenney, University of Florida; Stuart Krusell, Bentley University; Frank P. La Veness, St. John's University; J. Edward Lee, Winthrop University; Paul Lenze, Washington State University; David A. Lynch, St. Mary's University of Minnesota; Clinton W. Maffett, University of Memphis; Margaret Martin, University of St. Thomas; Hazel M. McFerson, George Mason University; Marian A. L. Miller, University of Akron; Richard M. Mills, Fordham University; Andrei Muntean, Drexel University; David J. Myers, Pennsylvania State University; Jeffrey R. Orenstein, Kent State University; William J. Parente, Sr., University of Scranton; Colin Ramsay, Lemon Bay High School, Englewood, FL; Steven Roach, University of South Florida; Bradley Scharf, Seattle University; Richard Stahler-Sholk, Eastern Michigan University; Pak W. Tang, Chaffey College; Hubert Tworzecki, Emory University; and Carrie Rosefsky Wickham, Emory University.

Contact Us

We also like to hear from readers with favorable or critical comments. The best way to reach us is via email.

Chip Hauss   Melissa Haussman
chiphauss@gmail.com   Melissa_haussman@carleton.ca

Supplements for Students and Instructors

PowerLecture DVD with JoinIn™ and ExamView®
ISBN-10: 1111835403 |
ISBN-13: 9781111835408

This DVD provides access to **Interactive PowerPoint® Lectures,** a **Test Bank,** and the **Instructor's Manual.** Interactive, book-specific PowerPoint® lectures make it easy for you to assemble, edit, publish, and present custom lectures for your course. The slides provide outlines specific to every chapter of *Comparative Politics,* 8th Edition and include tables, statistical charts, graphs, and photos from the book as well as outside sources. In addition, the slides are completely customizable for a powerful and personalized presentation. A test bank in Microsoft® Word and ExamView® computerized testing offers a large array of well-crafted multiple-choice and essay questions, along with their answers and page references. An Instructor's Manual includes learning objectives, chapter outlines, discussion questions, suggestions for class activities and projects, tips on integrating media into your class (including step-by-step instructions on how to create your own podcasts), suggested readings and Web resources. A section specifically designed for teaching assistants and adjuncts helps instructors get started teaching right away. **JoinIn™** offers book-specific "clicker" questions that test and track student comprehension of key concepts. Save the data from students' responses all semester—track their progress and show them how political science works by incorporating this exciting new tool into your classroom. It is available for college and university adopters only.

Companion Website
ISBN-10: 1111826404 |
ISBN-13: 9781111826406
cengagebrain.com/ISBN/1111832552

Students will find open access to learning objectives, tutorial quizzes, chapter glossaries, flashcards, and crossword puzzles, all correlated by chapter, as well as additional online chapters for Japan, Canada, South Africa, and Brazil. Instructors also have access to the Instructor's Manual and PowerPoints.

WebTutor Toolbox on WebCT IAC
ISBN-10: 0534274900 |
ISBN-13: 9780534274900
WebTutor Toolbox on Blackboard IAC
ISBN-10: 0534274919 |
ISBN-13: 9780534274917
WebTutor Toolbox on WebCT PAC
ISBN-10: 0534274889 |
ISBN-13: 9780534274887
WebTutor Toolbox on Blackboard PAC
ISBN-10: 0534274897 |
ISBN-13: 9780534274894

WebTutor Toolbox is a Web-based teaching and learning tool that integrates with your school's learning management system. It offers access to the ExamView test bank and online study tools including learning objectives, flashcards, weblinks and practice quizzes.

CourseReader: Comparative Politics

1111477604|9781111477608 CourseReader 0-30: Comparative Politics Printed Access Card

1111477620|9781111477622 CourseReader 0-30: Comparative Politics Instant Access Code

1111477612|9781111477615 CourseReader 0-30: Comparative Politics SSO

1111680507|9781111680503 CourseReader 0-60: Comparative Politics Printed Access Card

1111680493|9781111680497 CourseReader 0-60: Comparative Politics Instant Access Code

1111680485|9781111680480 CourseReader 0-60: Comparative Politics SSO

1111680531 | 9781111680534 CourseReader Unlimited: Comparative Politics Printed Access Card

1111680523 | 9781111680527 CourseReader Unlimited: Comparative Politics Instant Access Code

1111680515 | 9781111680510 CourseReader Unlimited: Comparative Politics SSO

CourseReader for Comparative Politics is a fully customizable online reader which provides access to hundreds of readings, audio, and video selections from multiple disciplines. This easy to use solution allows you to select exactly the content you need for your courses, and is loaded with convenient pedagogical features like highlighting, printing, note taking, and audio downloads. YOU have the freedom to assign individualized content at an affordable price. CourseReader: Comparative Politics is the perfect complement to any class.

CengageCompose Customized Text

 www.cengage.com/cengagecompose

Instructors can create a customized version of *Comparative Politics* using only the chapters needed for their class. In addition to the in-text chapters, choose additional coverage on Brazil, Canada, Japan, and South Africa.

Introduction

PART 1

CHAPTER 1
Seeking New Lands, Seeing with
New Eyes

AP Photo/Nader Daoud

1

CHAPTER OUTLINE

1

> *The real voyage of discovery consists of not in seeking new lands, but in seeing with new eyes.*
>
> MARCEL PROUST

Seeking New Lands, Seeing with New Eyes

THE CURRENT CRISES

As we sat down in our respective studies to write the eighth edition of *Comparative Politics: Domestic Responses to Global Challenges*, we knew we would face challenges. First, we had to adapt to coauthoring for the first time. That started with an easy decision. Because our last names are so similar, we decided to be informal and refer to ourselves as Chip and Melissa on those rare occasions when personal references are necessary.

It turns out that was the least of our problems.

While writing, we were both distracted by the conflicts sweeping the Middle East. We both work for nonviolent approaches to major political change, but what happened in Egypt and so much of the rest of the Middle East was astonishing even to us. Chip had a medical appointment on February 11, 2011. When he went in to see the doctor, President Hosni Mubarak was still in power, claiming that he would not quit. By the time the appointment was over, Mubarak had resigned and left Cairo for an undisclosed location.

Leaders, of course, change all the time. Mubarak, who had been in power for 32 years, was preparing to hand over power to his son. What was remarkable about events in Egypt, however, was that the change was the result of unprecedented protest and was accomplished in less than three weeks. Though we won't talk about Egypt much in this book, it *is* important for you to understand that big changes often occur in unpredictable ways and do so amazingly quickly.

The world's problems, of course, remain. On the day we finished this chapter, President Barack Obama introduced his budget for fiscal year 2012. As is always the case, the specifics of the funding plan were dead on arrival in Congress. That is especially true now that the House of Representatives is under Republican control and is heavily influenced by **tea party** activists who would like to cut billions from the budget.

Of course, the United States is not unique among wealthy democracies. As you will see more clearly in Chapter 4 where we discuss Great Britain, they all have massive annual deficits and staggering long-term debts. How the United States (Chip's country) or Canada (Melissa's) will work through these trials remains to be seen, but countries like Nigeria and Mexico will have a much tougher time dealing with their economic crises.

Not everything we cover warrants the term crisis or is as exciting or as mind-numbing as the events that wracked the Middle East while we should have been writing. However, most of the issues we consider in the next sixteen chapters at least come close.

Michael Tremchine/Newhouse News Service/Landov

President Obama speaks at George Mason University, Feb. 2007.

That said, this is not a book or a course about the current crises alone. Rather, we will use the issues we face today as a kind of springboard so that you can make intellectual sense of our confusing world. We certainly have in what is the eighth time that Chip, at least, has had to write or revise this book.

The word crisis is, however, important. The ancient Chinese brought two characters together to convey what we mean by this single word. The first was danger, something we all think the word entails. But they also included opportunity. Time and time again, we will see how political leaders and average citizens alike found opportunity amid danger. Time and again, we will see that they did not.

We will return to this theme in the concluding chapter.

What Is Comparative Politics?

Comparativists try to explain political life in a way that transcends time and place.

That is easier said than done. It may have been easier when we were undergraduates and the course only covered Britain, France, Germany, Italy, and the Soviet Union—and then only if the professor did not run out of time. That won't do anymore. We have to include the entire world or at least as much of it as can be crammed into five hundred pages and a semester's worth of classes.

That means focusing on a handful of concepts and a single research tool, both of which will be the subject of the rest of this chapter. For the moment, it is enough to get a glimpse at one of the concepts and at the techniques we comparativists use.

The two of us are like all academics. We disagree about a lot of specific issues. However, we agree that the American and Canadian **regimes** are both likely to survive their current difficulties over the budget and economic issues in general. We will not be able to say the same for countries covered in the second half of this book. In countries that were at least under communist rule or are part of what we will call the Global South, the regime's future is anything but assured. That conclusion may seem obvious to most readers, but its implications for countries whose regimes could be in peril are far from obvious.

We academics may well disagree about many things, but not on the importance of comparison. While we will have to explain many of the concepts (including the regime), comparison is relatively simple because we have already used it, albeit perhaps without being aware we were.

In fact, if we focused only on the controversial issues in the news today, you would have a hard time retaining the material on any one country, let alone all of the ones you will be reading about. To be sure, elections, peace-building, the rights of women, policy making, and the like are what led most of us to study politics in the first place. But if we tried to cover it all, you would be overwhelmed by a sea of data.

Kyodo/AP Images

Leaders from the G-20 major industrialized and emerging economies sit for the second day of their financial summit in London on April 2, 2009.

Therefore, we have to turn to our tool—comparative analysis. We start with a negative example from a source we both read every day. Then we turn to comparison. As much as we love it and depend on it, the *New York Times* does not have the answer. On its masthead, the *New York Times* claims that it includes "all the news that's fit to print."

Not so.

Read today's editions of the *New York Times* and the *Washington Post*. If you don't have access to the hard copies, both are available online 🌐 (**www.nytimes.com** and **www.washingtonpost.com**). It should be clear that the two most highly regarded newspapers in the United States are dramatically different. The *Times* puts international news at the beginning of its first section, before turning to national issues. The *Post* leads with U.S. domestic politics, which is followed by a briefer section on international. After all, the *Post* is the "hometown" newspaper for the most powerful capital city in the world. Even its Style section has a lot of political stories.

The *Times* masthead's statement is also misleading because all the news that's fit to print *doesn't* make it into the paper. For example, until 2006 it rarely reported on the genocide in Darfur. Indeed, the paper only has a handful of full-time correspondents in Africa, though it employs more than any of its competitors.

In fact, the rule of thumb might be that these papers include all the news that fits around the advertisements they must run to turn a profit, which is harder and harder

for them to do these days—something we will discuss in the sections on the media in the chapters that follow.

More Information Than You Require[1]

If you want a humorous look at what the *New York Times* would look like if it actually included all the news that's fit to print, look at John Hodgman's books *The Areas of My Expertise* and *More Information Than You Require.*

Hodgman is a comedian, not a political scientist. His career has included time as a literary agent and a stint on *The Daily Show.* He is, in his own words, a famous minor television personality because of his role as PC in the Macintosh television ads.

His books are almost random collections of almost random—and almost always useless—factoids, only *some* of which Hodgman made up. We would not recommend reading either book in its entirety. Fitting all of that news into your head would give you a massive headache.

We think he wants his readers to get that headache.

John Hodgman, *The Areas of My Expertise.* (New York: Dutton, 2005); John Hodgman, *More Information Than You Require.* (New York: Dutton, 2008).

[1]We need to thank Chip's son in law, Igor Petrovski, for giving him these books.

The poor job of covering international politics by even the world's most esteemed newspapers reinforces why comparative politics is important. In addition to shedding light on pressing public policy issues, it gives us a lens through which to understand the confusing array of political phenomena that befuddle even those of us who have spent our professional careers as teachers, scholars, or activists trying to come to grips with them.

On one level, comparative politics is simple. After all, we have all compared things. Which college to go to? Which car to lease? Which iPod to buy? We may not always make the best decisions. Nonetheless, the judgments that we make invariably involve comparisons.

For instance, Chip wrote this paragraph on his super light Mac Book Air. (Melissa remains loyal to her PC.) Chip has a bigger screen on his desktop computer, but it was the first warm day of the year, the deck beckoned, and Chip couldn't resist.

So first comparison: inside or outside? Second comparison: Mac or PC? In 1984, Chip bought his first computer and Melissa had just escaped being his student. Macs were a lot easier to use. Twenty some desktops and laptops later, he's never seen the need to change—his is an all-Mac family.

The logic behind comparative politics is, therefore, not hard to see. We learn more about something if we contrast it with something else of the same ilk. When we were in high school, our parents took us on tours of twenty or more college campuses each. Chip ruled out some immediately. Too big. Not co-ed. He applied to ten and was accepted by a depressingly small subset of that group. Still, he had to choose among those four colleges. In other words, he had to compare again. He ended up at Oberlin, though only because it was the best place that accepted him. He spent four years there majoring in ending the war in Vietnam. A decade later Melissa showed up in Chip's classroom at Colby as a result of a comparative process that was only slightly more rational.

Of course, here we are interested in comparing political phenomena. There is an extensive and often complicated literature on what it takes to do comparative political analysis. In practice, however, it's just about as easy to compare political phenomena as computers or colleges.

To take but one obvious example, when Obama had to choose a running mate in 2008, he compared Joe Biden with a number of other candidates and decided that someone with Biden's vast experience would give his ticket the balance a youthful nominee needed.

Similarly, consider this example from the 2010 British general election. Of all the registered voters, 66 percent cast ballots. That one fact tells us very little about Britain or its political system. But the picture changes dramatically once you add two more pieces of information. Despite a slight increase over the last two elections, it was one of lowest turnouts since the 1930s. But note by contrast that that many Americans rarely show up at the polls. Turnout reached a high in recent elections at 56 percent in 2008.

With those two pieces of comparative data, you can learn a lot more and can pose far more insightful questions about elections in general. For example, why is turnout in British elections normally higher than that in the United States? Why has it been declining in recent elections? What difference does turnout make? Did the fact that only a quarter of the people voted for the Conservative Party make it easier or harder to sweep David Cameron into power?

In sum, comparison doesn't make us brilliant, but it does allow us to put the academic and political options open to us in a broader and potentially useful perspective.

Science

We call ourselves *political scientists*. It's a pretentious title because we have little in common with physicists or chemists with their fancy labs and huge research grants.

But in two important ways we share a similar worldview.

On the first level, our job is inductive—to find general explanations for the phenomena we study. How does growing bean plants (which many of you had to do in biology lab) help us understand how plants mature? Or how do elections around the world help us understand the role average people play in political life?

Science, then, is an attempt to develop a **theory** that covers an entire discipline, something often referred to as a **paradigm.** Given the complexity of politics around the world, no single and universally accepted theory is likely to emerge in your lifetime, let alone ours. Nonetheless, designing new and better theories is something we all can do, even students in introductory classes.

In this sense, science means moving upward in what the psychologist Chris Argyris called the ladder of inference. In the pages that follow, you will read about a number of countries. Your instructor will ask you a question like this one: "Of what is Germany an instance?" We hope he or she will phrase it more eloquently. But the point of such a question is clear: How do we move from a handful of examples to regional, if not global, conclusions?

On the second level, we work deductively. From this perspective, we focus on a hypothesis or a guess that cannot be proven. Political scientists then test it using data they have gathered systematically. Such data can never prove that a theory is true; however compelling the evidence might seem, in other cases and at other times the theory may be impossible to confirm.

Rather, the most interesting thing we can do is **falsify** the theory by finding at least one example in which it does not hold true. Then, we have to try to figure out why that was the case. That usually means stepping back from the computer screen and thinking creatively.

Whether we work inductively or deductively, the goal is the same. We strive to reach general conclusions about the political world, even though we know that future events will prove us wrong. We will return to many of these themes in a very different way in Chapter 17.

THE STATE: ONE FOCUS AMONG MANY

The discussion so far must seem more than a little abstract. Therefore, the rest of this chapter will bring everything we have just discussed down to earth.

The **state** will be the focus of this book. It will not be the only concept on which we concentrate, but it is the most important.

Political scientists do not agree on what the best focus of a text or course in comparative politics should be. We decided to focus on the state because it puts one of the most important topics in political life on center stage—the way scarce resources are allocated. In our political work too, the state is the most important issue. In countries like the United States, how can we use the state to help solve the economic and other crises that seem so hard to tackle? In the case of the former Soviet Union and other former and current communist regimes, is it possible to create a state that can handle the rapid transition from communism to democracy and capitalism simultaneously? And most tragically, as those of us who work in the conflict resolution field know, how can we, in the words of Ashraf Ghani and Clare Lockhart,[2] fix too many failed states in South America, Africa, and Asia?

Concentrating on the state also means focusing on the single most important common denominator of political life, **power,** which is most often defined as the ability to get people or groups to do *what they otherwise would not do.* Those last six words are important. They suggest that the exercise of power requires coercion. People typically have to be forced to do things they don't want to do. The exercise of power does not always involve the use of physical force, but the threat of its use it is almost always there.

Politics is not exclusively about power. In the pages that follow, you will encounter plenty of people who have been driven to act politically for other reasons, including the genuine desire to help the poor or to promote social justice. There are also newer definitions of power that exclude the necessity of coercion. However, as things stand now in most countries at most times, there is no escaping the connection between power and the ability to force adversaries to comply with one's wishes.

What Is the State?

The state is the first term in this book that we need to define with some precision. Many people use the terms government, state, nation, and regime interchangeably. In some countries, like the United States, it is not all that inaccurate to do so. When we consider the former Soviet Union or Iraq, however, treating these terms as synonymous can be extremely misleading.

The **government** refers to a particular set of institutions and people authorized by formal documents, such as a **constitution,** to pass laws, issue regulations, control the police, and so on. For the moment, it is enough to note that the government rarely holds all the power in a given country and, in some cases, can be far less influential than other actors. That is certainly true of failed states, where the government lacks the ability to do much of anything, such as in a society wracked by civil war. To a lesser degree, it was true of Mexico before the 2000 election, when the long dominant party, the PRI, was far more important than any government institution.

The **state** is a broader concept that includes all the institutions and individuals that exercise power. In Russia, that will be easiest to see when we consider the role of the shadowy group of businessmen (yes, they are all men), known as the oligarchs, some of whom gained positions of influence under former President Boris Yeltsin and others of whom made their money under former President and current Prime Minister Vladimir Putin, whose apparent demotion will also be a central topic in Chapter 9. In that sense, we also talk about **governance,** which the World Bank defines as "the exercise of political authority and the use of institutional resources to manage society's problems and affairs."

The **regime** refers to the institutions and practices that typically endure from government to government or, in American terms, administration to administration. This is, of course, a concept that burst onto the political scene when President George W. Bush demanded, and later forced, a regime change in Iraq. However, it should be noted that it is a term political scientists have used for a half-century or more. As we will see in Parts 3 and 4, regime change is

[2]Former World Bank Economists who have spent much of their time since 9/11 in Afghanistan.

often on the political agenda in at least half of the world's countries.

The **nation** is a psychological rather than an institutional concept. It refers to cultural, linguistic, and other identities that tie people together. Thus, the Chechens who want to secede certainly do not think of themselves as Russians. Indeed, as we will see in several chapters, a lack of national identity often reflects deep-seated ethnic and other divisions that can undermine support for any state, whatever institutional levers it may have at its disposal.

Types of States

No two states are alike. Some, like the United States, are large, rich, stable, and powerful. Others, like Somalia, are so poor, fragile, and weak that a state can barely be said to exist. About the only thing all states have in common is that what each state does—and doesn't do—matters for its own citizens and for many others who live outside its borders.

Unfortunately, political scientists have still not reached agreement about the best way to classify states. Despite all the changes since the end of the Cold War, we have decided to stick with a traditional three-way classification:

■   Industrialized democracies.

■   Current and former communist regimes.

■   The Global South.

This way of dividing the world *is* outdated. Nonetheless, because the industrialized democracies and the once-solid communist bloc each have many historical and contemporary traits in common, it still makes sense to use this framework.

The **industrialized democracies** present us with a paradox. On the one hand, they have the most resources and, so, the greatest potential for creating and sustaining powerful states. Like Great Britain, most are wealthy and have at least reasonably effective and popular political institutions. As Table 1.1 (also on the inside front cover) shows, the citizens of industrialized democracies enjoy standards of living similar to those of most Americans. Virtually everyone can read and write, and the infant mortality figures suggest that they benefit from at least basic health care coverage.

On the other hand, these states also have the strongest built-in restraints on the use of power, primarily laid out in constitutions and major pieces of legislation. What the state can do is also determined, to some degree, by public opinion and by the results of competitive elections that determine who the leaders are.

That paradox is reversed in the current and former **communist** states. During their heyday, the communist states were extremely strong. The government controlled almost everything, from the schools to the press to the economy. Indeed, the term *totalitarianism* was coined to describe these and other states that sought total control over their societies.

TABLE 1.1 Basic Data

COUNTRY	POPULATION IN (MILLIONS OF PEOPLE IN 2010 EST)	AVERAGE POPULATION GROWTH 2010 EST (ANNUAL %)	GNP PER CAPITA (US$) (2010)	GROWTH IN GNP (2010 EST)	LITERACY (%)	INFANT MORTALITY (PER 1,000 BIRTHS)	AVERAGE LIFE EXPECTANCY
Brazil	203	7.5	10,900	5.1	93	21	73
Canada	34	0.8	39,100	−2.5	99+	5	81
China	1,336	0.6	7,400	9.1	91	16	75
France	65	0.5	33,900	−2.6	99+	3	81
Germany	82	−0.2	35,900	−4.7	99+	4	79
India	1,889	1.3	3,400	7.7	61	30	70
Iran	78	1.25	12,800	1.8	77	43	70
Iraq	30	2.4	3,600	5.5	74	42	71
Japan	127	−0.28	34,200	3.0	99+	3	82
Mexico	114	1.1	13,800	−6.5	91	17	76
Nigeria	155	1.9	2,400	5.6	68	91	47
Russia	139	−0.5	15,900	3.8	99+	10	66
South Africa	49	− 0.4	10,700	3.0	86	43	50
United Kingdom	63	0.6	35,100	1.6	99+	5	80
United States	313	0.9	36,900	−2,6	99+	6	78

For countries, CIA Factbook (www.cia.gov).

As the collapse of communism in the former Soviet Union and Eastern Europe demonstrates, however, repression and central control are not enough to ensure that such states will endure. In our discussion of the causes of this historical turning point, we will focus on the failure of Soviet-style regimes to adopt economic policies that would improve the well-being of their citizens, thereby reinforcing the hostility toward those regimes. There are many other reasons for this regime failure. At or near the top of any list would be the decision by Soviet and Eastern European leaders to give their people more freedom in an effort to reinvigorate their economies. Once that happened, these regimes could no longer rely on repression—they lost the political "glue" that kept them in power.

The Chinese have followed a different path, implementing liberal economic reforms while retaining tight control over political life. So far, this strategy has "worked" in that the Chinese Communist Party (CCP) is still in power and is presiding over one of the fastest economic growth rates in the world. However, most observers doubt that the CCP can continue stifling dissent indefinitely.

There is no agreement on how to characterize the rest of the world, those countries that do not fit neatly into the categories of industrialized democracy or communist regime. In past editions, we used terms such as the **less developed countries (LDCs).** Here we have settled on the term **Global South.**[3] It is not a surprise that we have trouble with terminology. LDCs are much harder to describe as a single group, which is hardly surprising given that there are more than 130 of them. Above all else, most of them are poor. In some, the average citizen survives on less than five hundred dollars a year. A billion people worldwide live on less than the equivalent of a dollar a day. Table 1.1 shows just how wide the gap is between the industrial democracies and the world's poorest countries. With a shortage of doctors, a large number of young people, and a high degree of illiteracy, these poorest countries face far more problems than the other two types of states. To make matters even worse, many southern countries still have not been able to forge states with functioning courts, bureaucracies, and other institutions that people in the industrialized democracies take for granted. Many have experienced military coups and other forms of political upheaval that have eroded the popular support these regimes need for long-term strength.

There are exceptions to this otherwise gloomy picture. Several **newly industrialized countries (NICs)** have made great strides in breaking out of the trap of underdevelopment. The most famous are the Asian tigers—South Korea, Singapore, Indonesia, and Malaysia—along with a few other Asian countries and, perhaps, Mexico, Brazil, and Chile. Although there is disagreement over what caused these countries to grow so rapidly since the 1970s, every list includes the way these states were able to build cooperative relationships between business and labor, albeit sometimes through force.

Strong and Weak States

We will also be asking why some states are stronger than others. Obviously, every state tries to respond to the challenges it faces. Just as obviously, there is tremendous variation in what their leaders have been able to accomplish.

The distinction between strong and weak states is one of the most controversial in comparative politics. In a textbook for an introductory course, however, we can use a fairly simple definition.

Strong states take on more responsibilities and generally carry them out more effectively than do weaker ones. Comparativists have not been able to reach many firm conclusions about the factors that determine how strong a given state is. The best we can do is to note that, when viewed over the long term, strong states are relatively wealthy, their regimes have widespread popular support, and their governing elites work reasonably effectively together. Repression can strengthen states in the short run. However, as events of the past two decades suggest, it may not be enough to sustain such states over the long term.

Basic patterns in state structure and power roughly coincide with the three types of countries outlined earlier. In particular, the former communist states could not adapt to the changing social and economic conditions they faced in the 1980s because their strength lay in their ability to maintain order, not innovate. Similarly, poverty, internal divisions, and other factors are part of the reason most LDCs have relatively weak states.

Seldom are states able to do whatever they want whenever they want. If anything, most states are losing the ability to shape their own destinies in the light of globalization, which we will consider shortly.

Finally, we will spend a lot of time on the distinction between the state and regime. In particular, we will see that industrialized democracies are able to weather most crises because they enjoy an almost total acceptance that insulates them from divisive protests, such as those of the new left of the 1960s and 1970s. We will also see that most Southern countries lack such bedrock popular support; dissatisfaction with the government can often threaten the regime and in some cases, the existence of the country itself.

---

[3]Of course, this term doesn't work either. Australia, New Zealand, and Singapore are located in the South but are by no means poor. We will return to this in Chapter 11.

Key Concepts and Questions

This course is about countries and concepts. If you want to truly understand what an introductory course in comparative politics is all about, focus on the concepts that will be highlighted in this section and others like it in each chapter.

Given the discussion of the *New York Times* and its masthead, it should already be clear that you need to focus on concepts as well as names, dates, places, and events to master comparative politics.

For this chapter, and those going forward, concentrate on the following:

▪ Historically, be thinking about how did the wrenching processes of state and nation building shape the countries covered in the rest of the book.

▪ Also consider what impact imperialism has had over the last few centuries and what impact globalization is having today.

▪ How do people and the institutions they form shape decision making? How does the structure of the state affect their efforts?

▪ You will be reading this book in the second decade of the twenty-first century. Think about how the concepts discussed in this chapter will help you understand politics in the awkwardly labeled twenty teens.

Other Core Concepts

The state will not be the only concept we focus on. Most of the others, however, are based on issues that flow out of the state and its actions. More important yet, if you do not master these concepts, you will have a hard time understanding the mass of facts in this book.

Sometimes, we will use a concept in a slightly different way than our colleagues do, which is why we are returning to three of the concepts we introduced above. For example, the government can also refer to the people in power at the moment, what Americans often call the administration. Obviously, the government is important.

In addition, we will look at countries on two other levels. First is the regime, which is the set of institutions and practices that endures when one government is replaced by another. As mentioned earlier, in an established democracy, much of the regime is defined by the constitution and other major laws. During the communist era, the constitution was an essentially meaningless document. The regime was created and controlled by the Communist Party. Second, we have to consider the **system**—another term we will use in two ways (see the section on templates that follows). In many countries, people challenge the regime as well as the government of the day. In others, they go further

and question whether the country as a whole—the system itself—should continue to exist. Thus, when the Soviet Union collapsed in 1991, it was not just the regime that disappeared; the country itself split into fifteen new independent states.

Most chapters, though not all, will examine the interplay between **democracy** and **capitalism.** Modern capitalism and democracy began to take hold at about the same time. Indeed, the American colonies declared their independence the same year that Adam Smith published *The Wealth of Nations*, the first great text on capitalist economics. As we will see, neither system emerged easily and both exist in multiple forms. Perhaps most important, we will see that countries outside of Europe and North America are still struggling to democratize and create functioning market-based economies.

Whatever its type of political system, a country's **political culture** reflects the core values of its people. Political scientists rarely consider attitudes toward current leaders or issues as part of a country's culture. Rather, they focus on enduring opinions about its institutions and political practices. In many countries, much of the culture revolved around the people's **identity** or how they define themselves in racial, linguistic, ethnic, or religious terms. Today, identity issues are among the most controversial in the most divided countries.

Countries also provide their people with vehicles for **political participation.** These opportunities vary tremendously. In established democracies, people are free to vote in competitive elections, join interest groups that lobby on their behalf, and engage in (at least) peaceful protest. In authoritarian or totalitarian regimes, such opportunities rarely exist. Instead, these regimes often goad people into forms of acceptable political behavior, most notably seen in Iran and China.

All states also make **public policy** that tries to shape how they deal with political issues. Policies can regulate what citizens can do, such as setting speed limits and the drinking age. But these examples also demonstrate that states aren't always that effective at enforcing their regulations. Policies can distribute or redistribute resources. We almost certainly pay more income tax than you do. Some of our taxes support the universities of which Virginia and Ontario are justifiably proud. Other policies shift resources from wealthier to poorer people in what are loosely known as welfare programs. Yet others transfer money and services across generational lines, something that will increasingly happen in the industrialized democracies as our generation of baby boomers retires and incurs ever higher health care costs. Put simply, your generation will pay for much of ours, even if we can solve the problems with pension and health care coverage

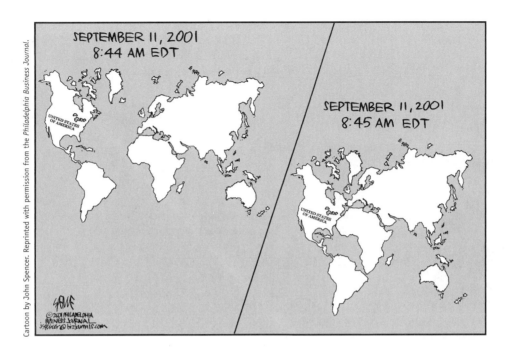

Cartoon by John Spencer. Reprinted with permission from the *Philadelphia Business Journal.*

policies that bedevil every country in the Western world. And policies can be symbolic, for instance, when political leaders only wear traditional clothing, drape themselves in flags, or drive only in cars manufactured in their own countries.

Finally, we will discuss a number of historical concepts, beginning with **imperialism.** From the end of the fifteenth century until the end of the nineteenth century, Europeans took over much of the Americas, Africa, and Asia. It is hard to overestimate the impact imperialism had on the people who were colonized. In the United States, Canada, Australia, and New Zealand, colonists and their descendants came close to destroying the indigenous populations while taking over huge amounts of land. Elsewhere, the imperial powers redrew boundaries, often putting people who had been historical antagonists in the same jurisdiction. They also imposed their religions, cultures, and forms of government on people, who found all three to be alien.

More recently, the political tensions and violence of the twentieth century continue to have a tremendous impact. One scholar estimates that as many as one hundred million people died as a result of war and other forms of political violence during those hundred years. Political scientists coined the term **totalitarianism** to describe the most vicious of those regimes, including Nazi Germany and the Soviet Union under Stalin. The **Cold War** of the second half of the last century may be over, but the consequences for those countries that were or still are under communist rule continue.

Today, one of the "hottest" and most controversial topics in political science is **globalization,** which refers to the rapid shrinking of social, economic, environmental, and political life. The world itself is not physically shrinking, of course. Nonetheless, advances in communication, travel, information technology, and much more have made it easier for people to work with—and against—each other.

There is no question that globalization is happening. But is it beneficial or harmful? It probably depends on the parts of the world and the kinds of people you focus on. Certainly, software engineers in the United States and India have done very well because of it. But textile workers in the United States have not been as lucky. Obviously, the most visible and tragic example of globalization in our world is the terrorist attacks of 2001 that destroyed the World Trade Center in New York and damaged the Pentagon in Washington, D.C. Whatever we might think about the broader implications of globalization, it is inextricably caught up with terrorism and the other threats we face at the dawn of this new millennium.

Another issue is directly tied to globalization—gender. In our lifetimes, the role of women in politics has grown dramatically. Both the UK and Germany have been run by women in recent years and women are emerging as serious candidates for office in most democracies. But it's not just gender. Lesbian, bisexual, gay, transgender, and queer (LBGTQ) issues are also on center stage. Ontario allows gay marriage. Virginia does not, but Washington, D.C. and New York City have recently legalized it. The current mayor of Paris is openly gay, so are a number of mid-career

Women protesting against and toppling Charles Taylor's dictatorial regime in Liberia.

politicians around the world. Even the Republican Party has a gay caucus.

In short, you cannot discuss globalization without considering the ever-broadening political landscape that includes everything from the conflicts currently sweeping North Africa to the global economy.

THREE TEMPLATES

The comparative method can be a powerful tool. Comparison on its own, however, is not powerful enough to lead us to the kinds of overarching conclusions we try to reach, even in an introductory course. We also have to know what to compare, what questions to ask, and which criteria to use in evaluating the evidence we uncover.

Most political scientists believe that *theories* best provide that focus. Unfortunately, comparative politics is not chemistry, physics, or microeconomics, each of which has a paradigm that structures everything from cutting-edge research to introductory textbooks. The best tools available to us are less powerful models that only allow us to see how the various components of a state are related to one another.

Think of models as the equivalent of templates designed for typical, routine tasks that computer companies provide when you buy their software. The three models that follow weave together most of the themes already discussed in this chapter and, therefore, will also help you with the concepts you will learn about in the rest of the book.

The Political System

The chapters on individual countries are organized around a model known as **systems theory** (see Figure 1.1). Although the basis for most of the natural sciences, systems theory is

FIGURE 1.1 The Political System

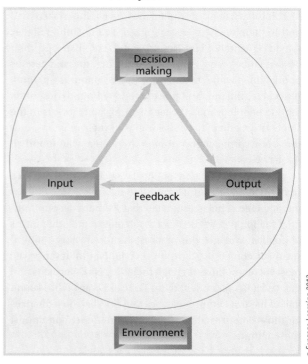

© Cengage Learning 2013

no longer very popular in political science. Nonetheless, it is more useful for our purposes than its intellectual competitors because systems theory allows us to see how a state's components interact over time and how nonpolitical and international forces shape what can and cannot be accomplished.

Systems theory revolves around five concepts: inputs, decision making, outputs, feedback, and the environment. **Inputs** are the ways in which average citizens and the groups they form engage in political life. David Easton, who adapted systems theory to political science, divided inputs into two types of activities: those that **support** and those that place **demands** on the state. Both come in many forms.

Individuals can act on their own by, for example, voting or writing a letter to the editor. However, most political activity, especially that of a demanding nature, is channeled through two types of organizations: interest groups and political parties. **Interest groups** deal with a limited range of issues and represent a narrow segment of a country's population. Examples include trade unions, business associations, and environmental groups that organize and "lobby" around specific issues and other concerns. By contrast, a **political party** tries to bring the interests of a number of groups together and to gain control over the government either on its own or as part of a coalition. A party, however, need not build its support largely, or even primarily, through elections, as was the case in the former Soviet Union or in Iraq under the Baath Party.

The conventional wisdom is that British interest groups are weaker than those in America because it is harder to lobby effectively in a parliamentary system than in a presidential system, something we will explore in the next three chapters. Nonetheless, the British Labour Party has traditionally done well at the polls because of its close ties to the Trade Unions Congress, which helped create the party in the first place and is still an integral part of its organization. On the other hand, the Conservative Party has close links to the major business and trade associations.

Sometimes demands go beyond the conventional "inside the system" activities of interest groups and political parties. Protesters, for instance, tried to disrupt the April 2009 meeting of the leading economic powers (G-20) to demonstrate their opposition to market-led plans for the recovery to the global crisis.

There is no better example of "outside the system" protest than the attacks on 9/11. Analysts will long debate what motivated the nineteen hijackers and their supporters. However, there is little doubt that their faith and their hatred of Western politics and policies led them to take not only their own lives but those of thousands of people in the World Trade Center, the Pentagon, and on the four airplanes that were the very tools of the attacks.

In a sign of how the parts of a system are interconnected, what people do is also influenced by their country's political culture. In addition to the features mentioned above, a culture reflects the impact of history on a society's beliefs. In Great Britain, the legacy of feudalism remains (albeit faintly) in the willingness of some working-class voters to trust their "social betters" who have roots in the aristocracy. The widespread support of Shiite Islam is an important value supporting the continued rule of the Islamic Republic in Iran. Russians' values today are in large part shaped by more than seventy years of communist rule. Finally, the Chechen conflict shows us that not all countries are homogeneous and that some have strikingly different subcultures.

Easton's second main concept, **decision making,** covers the same intellectual ground as that already covered in our discussion of the state and, thus, does not need much elaboration here. It is enough to note that we will examine states from two main angles: the structure of their institutions and the values, skills, and personalities of their leaders. Institutions matter more in older, established regimes like Britain's, even though it does not have a written constitution. That is less true in a country like Iran, where the ruling clerics often do political end runs around the elected institutions they created, or in Russia, where the institutions are not even two decades old and changed dramatically when the term-limited Putin left the presidency to become prime minister in 2008 in what for now must look like a confusing move.

Inputs and decision making are important in their own right. However, their importance grows when we explore what those decisions lead to—the system's **output** or public policy. We have discussed some of those outputs already, but they are important enough to revisit before we reach the end of Chapter 1.

The most common type of policy regulates the behavior of individuals or organizations. For instance, Britain is struggling to find new ways of managing constant traffic jams in its old cities by introducing tolls that drivers have to pay to enter them.

Other policies redistribute resources, sometimes to such a degree that they alter a society's basic patterns of wealth and power. That, of course, has always been the goal of Marxists and other socialists. But even with growing support for market economies, states are still heavily involved in distributional politics. We saw this in the flood of stimulus packages introduced in 2009 in countries as different as the United States and China. Under more normal circumstances, Iranian authorities have channeled billions of dollars to companies and foundations they control in order to shape the modernization of the country's economy.

Policies can also be symbolic. Under both Yeltsin and Putin, the Russian government tried to build support through symbols pegged to a new state, such as adopting a new flag and national anthem. An even more obvious example occurred in Iran in 1979, when the Islamic Republic came to power and did the same to reflect its commitment to theological orthodoxy.

Systems analysis is also the most useful model for our purposes because it incorporates **feedback,** which is the process through which people find out about public policy and the ways in which their reactions to recent political events help shape the next phase of political life. Sometimes a decision directly affects an individual or group. More often, people only learn about a policy indirectly, either through the media or by word of mouth. Most people in most countries learn about politics through the **mass media**, which is the term we will use to replace feedback because they are the main source of feedback in most systems today.

In each of the countries we will be covering in this book, the media play a powerful and frequently quite biased role in political life, either by supporting the state or by criticizing its policies. There are times, too, when people do not find out about state policies at all, which can result either from conscious attempts to keep these policies secret or from public apathy.

In the United States the media play a critical role. The UK's British Broadcasting Corporation (BBC) is renowned for the quality and impartiality of its coverage. By contrast, Putin was criticized for his decision to take away the licenses for all television stations that were not under government control. Iranian authorities, meantime, are struggling to control access to television stations run by émigrés, which hundreds of thousands of people watch on supposedly illegal satellite dishes.

The **environment** includes everything lying outside the "official" political system. Systems are defined as being *bounded* or having an autonomous identity and organization. No system, however, is completely autonomous. All politicians and citizens react to forces beyond their control and there are three types of forces that can limit—sometimes sharply—their ability to shape their own destinies.

The first is the impact of history on culture and politics in general, as discussed previously. No country's history completely shapes what happens today, however, it does partially set the political stage, determining what is and is not likely to work. Second are the limits imposed by domestic social, economic, and physical conditions, including Britain's innovative plan to force people who want to drive into central London to pay for the privilege. Finally, and today perhaps most important, are the global forces that arise outside of a country's borders. Sometimes their impact is hard to miss, as when British and American forces invaded and occupied Iraq. Other times they are far

TABLE 1.2 Factors Affecting the Development of States

	INTERNATIONAL	DOMESTIC
Historical	Imperialism	State building and nation building
Contemporary	Globalization and the end of the Cold War	Pressures from people and interest groups

harder to document, as when global media conglomerates assume control of a country's television stations and other mass communications outlets.

Historical and Contemporary Factors

Table 1.2 draws our attention to four types of forces that have largely determined the basic patterns of politics in all countries. The first row of the table highlights the historical forces that set the stage for the "dramas" of global political life today. Undoubtedly, the most important is imperialism, which led to the imposition of Western political, economic, and cultural institutions on the rest of the world. For example, although Iran was never formally colonized, the West had a profound and negative impact on its society and economy.

To this day, many former colonies are desperately poor and dependent on the policies and practices of the wealthy states and private corporations in the "north." Imperialism was also important in determining how the state itself was formed and its impact on the rest of the world. For example, prior to the 1600s, the European monarchies were weak and decentralized. But their decision to expand abroad meant that they needed more powerful states that could raise armies and feed, equip, and pay them.

State building has never occurred smoothly, and the growing power of the state has left lasting scars throughout the world. This has been particularly difficult when one or both of two problems arose. First, when a state developed too quickly, it lead to antagonism toward the government that suddenly demanded more of its people. Second, when minority ethnic, linguistic, or religious groups were incorporated into an emerging state, this tended to produce tensions that undermined its ability to govern.

To complicate matters further, when imperialist powers carved up the Southern Hemisphere, they did so largely for their own reasons, ignoring traditional boundaries and lumping together groups that had historically been antagonistic toward each other. New states, such as Angola, Afghanistan, and Nigeria, faced deeply rooted ethnic tensions, which made it all but impossible for their leaders to agree on anything.

The difficulties associated with state building have been particularly pronounced in the less-developed world. Gaining independence usually involved an intense struggle with the established imperial power. When this conflict was especially prolonged or violent, as was the case in Vietnam or Algeria, the new country's physical and economic resources were typically drained by the time it finally won independence.

As the second row in Table 1.2 suggests, you cannot understand everything about political life today by putting it into historical perspective. If you could, there would be little reason to take a course such as this one or try to change a world where the basic contours are already set!

The lingering impact of the Cold War between the United States and the former Soviet Union is an important example of contemporary factors affecting state development. The two countries emerged from World War II as the most dominant powers on earth, ushering in an unprecedented period in which a pair of superpowers shaped the destinies of almost every other country. As the United States and the Soviet Union jockeyed for position, regional problems became global problems. When the superpowers' interests directly collided, countries such as Vietnam, Nicaragua, and Afghanistan paid the price. Even for such regional powers as Japan, Britain, Poland, Hungary, and the two Germanys, the freedom to maneuver was limited by the two superpowers.

Twenty years after the collapse of communism in the former Soviet bloc, no one is sure how those international forces will continue to play out. Some observers think supranational institutions like the United Nations (UN) or the European Union (EU) will play a larger and more constructive role in finding peaceful resolutions to the conflicts that still plague international and domestic political life. Others are more skeptical. Optimists thought the global shock wave caused by the attacks of 9/11 would unite the international community and go a long way toward eradicating terrorism once and for all. Pessimists worry that the subsequent wars and the occasional upsurge in terrorist activities will only sow the seeds for more, bloodier violence in the future.

There is no doubt, however, that international political forces will remain an important determinant of domestic events around the world. Since the Organization of Petroleum Exporting Countries (OPEC) oil embargo of 1973–74 and the economic downturn that followed, we have become aware of another global force limiting what individual states can do—the **international political economy (IPE),** which is the term political scientists use to describe trade and other interactions that take place between countries. To some degree, the IPE is a legacy of imperialism, but as we are all painfully aware from the daily news reports about everything from the economic crisis to the destruction of the Brazilian rain forests, the IPE has taken on a life of its own.

The countries that are suffering as a result of globalization are indeed in a difficult bind. How can the poorest nations break out of poverty when those international dynamics are leaving them even further behind? How can countries as different as Mexico, Poland, and the United States solve their domestic problems when they owe billions of dollars to other governments and private financiers? How can a country like Brazil balance the needs of the environment with those of its impoverished citizens?

Finally, there is the traditional subject matter of comparative politics: What is happening within individual countries today? Because of what occurred in the past and what is taking place now outside their borders, few states fully control their own destinies even to the degree that they did a generation ago. Conversely, no state is completely at the mercy of globalization, although some states are better able to shape their futures than others.

State, Society, and Globalization

We can work through the third template quickly because Figure 1.2 deals with many of the phenomena it covers. What makes this template unique, however, is its focus on the causal links among three key factors, which you can use to help connect the pieces of this book.

At least since Thomas Hobbes in the seventeenth century, most political theorists have pointed out that individuals, and the groups they form, tend to seek ever more freedom and power. The more pessimistic of them have feared that people motivated by such self-interest would tear society apart if left to their own devices. Thus, like it or not, we have to create states to maintain order by keeping these centrifugal forces in check.

As a result, most political scientists believe that state and society exist in what they call an inverse relationship. For the power of one to increase, that of the other must be reduced. For example, when the Republicans took control of the House of Representatives in 2010, they were convinced that the way to give average Americans more power was to limit the jurisdiction of what they believed was a far too dominant state. Similarly, the creation of the National Health Service in Great Britain in 1948 left doctors less free to practice medicine as they saw fit and left affluent patients less able to choose their own health care options. Moreover, this inverse relationship seems to hold across all types of political systems. Giving more power to Soviet citizens in the 1980s came at the expense of the state's power and contributed to its collapse.

Figure 1.2 also draws our attention to the way globalization is reshaping political life by reducing the real

FIGURE 1.2 The Impact of Global and Domestic Forces on the State

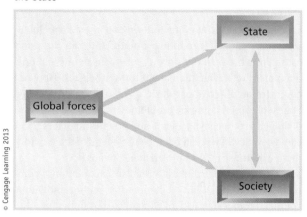

© Cengage Learning 2013

ability of states to make and implement economic policy. Although international institutions, such as the EU and the International Monetary Fund (IMF), play a critical role in this respect, rarely can we pinpoint exactly how such influence is wielded because these pressures are far subtler than those used by the United States and other major powers in fighting the wars that continue to dominate international relations. Nonetheless, they are real and important enough that they may force us to change the ways in which we view global political life, both as academics and as average citizens.

Choices

We are lucky to spend a lot of time with people who are neither political scientists nor academics. None of them has influenced Chip more than Rushworth Kidder, the founder and president of the Institute for Global Ethics. Among the things that the institute does is help everyone from third graders to top CIA managers grapple with ethical choices. Few of these choices are between right and wrong. Instead, most difficult choices must be made between ethically "good" options that are often incompatible with each other. Kidder asks us to focus on four such dilemmas, which will be at the heart of the rest of this book:

Truth versus loyalty.
Individual versus community.
Short term versus long term.
Justice versus mercy.

Rushworth M. Kidder, *How Good People Make Tough Choices.* (New York: William Morrow, 1995).

A WORLD IN CRISIS?

It should be clear already that we live in a troubled world. Every country we will discuss faces major problems, some of which could have disastrous consequences.

That is the point of view most of our students tend to take. But we also try to show them that crisis does not necessarily mean that political life is one in which you are waiting for the next disaster to happen, which is how we typically perceive things in the West.

The first sixteen chapters of this book will focus on the dangers we face. The last one will draw your attention to the opportunities. It will draw heavily on the work our colleagues do as feminists and peacebuilding practitioners and will stress the need to "think outside the box," as the cliché goes.

USING THIS BOOK

At least at first glance, you are at the beginning of what will be a typical introductory course with a typical textbook. However, to fully master the material, you will have to go beyond the typical as we pose controversial questions that do not have clear and obvious answers, but which will have a direct bearing on your life for years to come.

In short, you will have to do more than memorize the notes you take in class or the key points you highlight throughout these pages to pass this course. Courses that deal with new, complex, and controversial subjects succeed only when students stretch themselves to consider unsettling ideas, question their basic assumptions, and sift through evidence to reach their own conclusions. Therefore, if you are going to truly understand comparative politics, you have to take to heart the advice of the French novelist Marcel Proust that begins this chapter. You will be seeing new lands in Proust's terms because much of this book and your course will focus on places you do not know much about. But, if Proust is right, you will not get very far in this voyage of discovery unless you also try to see these lands through what will be the new "eyes" of comparative politics.

This book has a number of features that make the "active learning" side of the course as useful (and, we hope, as enjoyable) as possible, beginning with the structure of the book itself. The core of the book covers politics in the three kinds of states mentioned previously—industrialized democracies, current and former communist regimes, and the Global South. Each part begins with an overview chapter that explores the key trends, theories, and ideas about that type of state. The rest of the part is devoted to case studies of countries that exemplify the different aspects of that particular type of state. The countries discussed in this book were chosen because they are important in their own right and because you can use them as intellectual springboards for reaching more general conclusions about the political trends (re)shaping our world. They include:

- **Industrialized democracies:** the United States, Great Britain, France, Germany, and the EU.
- **Current and former communist regimes:** Russia and China.
- **The Global South:** India, Iran, Iraq, Nigeria, and Mexico.

Additional chapters on Canada, Japan, Brazil, and South Africa can be found at the book's companion site accessed at ᴡᴡᴡ **cengagebrain.com/ISBN/1111832552**.

Another important learning tool is the list of key terms. These terms are boldfaced in the text and can also be found in the list of key terms at the end of each chapter and in the glossaries of concepts, people, acronyms, organizations, places, and events at the end of the book.

Because this book focuses on countries and individual instructors assign various subsets of them in their classes, it is hard to build comparative analysis into the text itself. However, the boxes on core concepts will be explicitly comparative.

Critical Thinking Exercises

As you finish each chapter, ask yourself the following questions about the country you just read about:

1. Much has changed since this book was finished in 2011. Do the various assertions made in this chapter still make sense? In what ways? Why (or why not)?

2. Public opinion pollsters routinely ask whether people think the country is heading in the "right" direction or "is on the wrong track." If you were asked such a question about politics in this region, how would you answer? Why did you reach that conclusion?

3. Analyze the country using the three templates. What new insights did this exercise lead you to? What, if any, important facts, trends, or institutions were left out of the analysis?

4. Of all the concepts covered in this chapter, which do you think are the most and the least important? Why did you reach this conclusion?

5. You could interpret that this chapter is arguing that it is becoming harder for governments to govern effectively. Do you agree? Why (or why not)?

Key Terms

capitalism	globalization	less developed countries (LDCs)	regime
Cold War	Global South	nation	state
communist	governance	newly industrialized countries (NICs)	strong state
constitution	government	output	support
crisis	identity	paradigm	system
decision making	imperialism	political culture	systems theory
demand	industrialized democracy	political participation	theory
democracy	input	political party	totalitarianism
democratization	interest group	power	
environment	international political economy (IPE)	public policy	
falsify			
feedback			

ᴡᴡᴡ **Useful Websites**

The Internet has become an essential tool for students of comparative politics. Although there are not many sites dedicated to comparative politics *per se*, the Internet is filled with information on specific countries, individuals, and issues. In particular, because so many newspapers, radio and television networks, and news services have gone online, it is easy to keep up with breaking news and evolving trends around the world.

That said, the Internet is increasingly hard to use because there are so many sites; even the best search engines can catalogue only a tiny fraction of them. Therefore, we have included links to what we think are the best sites discussing the issues and countries covered in this book, updates on the countries, sources of statistical and other data, and quizzes on each chapter so you can gauge how well you have mastered the material. You can also e-mail us with questions about the book or about issues that have arisen in the course of your own class. The book's resources can be found here:

cengagebrain.com/ISBN/1111832552

You can email us directly at *chiphauss@gmail.com* **or** *Melissa_haussman@carleton.ca*

Each chapter in this book includes a section like this one with Web addresses to portals and other general sites. Specific websites will be inserted in the text the first time an institution or individual is mentioned.

There are other good resources for comparative politics. These three general sites, from the universities of Colorado, Keele, and West Virginia, respectively, divide up the field in different but useful ways.

www.polsci.colorado.edu/RES/comp.html

www.psr.keele.ac.uk/area.htm

www.polsci.wvu.edu/PolyCy/pscomp.html

The Internet also has dozens of sources providing basic data on countries that take you far beyond what can be covered in a single book and that include material on events occurring after this book was published. The CIA Factbook is a treasure trove of information about the world's countries and is updated quite frequently. Adminet and Wikipedia are the work of international "open source" teams of men and women willing to volunteer their time to provide general information about countries in general and elections in particular. Wikipedia is the best source on election results. Many academics don't like Wikipedia, but the link we are citing existed long before wikis were invented and was folded into Wikipedia because its author believes in open source documentation.

www.cia.gov/library/publications/the-world-factbook/index.html

www.adminet.com/world/gov

www.en.wikipedia.org/wiki/User:Electionworld/Electionworld

Finally, it is important to keep up with the news in any course on comparative politics and international relations. At this point, all of the world's major newspapers, news services, and broadcast media put much of their material on the Web.

Many, however, take the postings down after a week or two. The BBC and CNN have searchable databases for their coverage, including items that never made it on air. That said, their coverage on Third World issues is not great. Therefore, I also frequently look at One World, which is a good source for those parts of the planet.

www.cnn.com

www.news.bbc.co.uk

www.oneworld.net

Further Reading

Almond, Gabriel, and G. Bingham Powell. *Comparative Politics: System, Policy, and Process.* Boston: Little, Brown, 1978. Dated, but still the best presentation of the classic approach to comparative politics.

Friedman, Tom. *Hot, Flat, and Crowded.* New York: Farrar, Straus, & Giroux, 2009. The most influential and controversial book on globalization and its strengths and weaknesses.

Ghani, Ashraf, and Clare Lockhart. *Fixing Failed States.* New York: Oxford University Press, 2008. The best book on rethinking the role of government in places like Afghanistan and Iraq.

Lim, Timothy. *Doing Comparative Politics.* Boulder, CO: Lynne Reinner, 2006. A rather abstract book aimed more at grad students than undergrads but that explores three key concepts: rational choice, institutions, and culture. 2nd edition, 2010.

O'Neill, Patrick. *Essentials of Comparative Politics,* 3rd ed. New York: W. W. Norton, 2009. Like Lim's book, written for undergraduates but probably better for upper-level undergrads or grad students.

Soe, Christian, ed. *Comparative Politics: Annual Editions.* Guilford, CT: Dushkin/McGraw-Hill, published annually. A collection of recent articles from the press.

Stepan, Alfred. *Arguing Comparative Politics.* New York: Oxford University Press, 2001. A collection of essays by one of the few leading scholars in comparative politics who is willing to take on most issues and most regions.

Zahariades, Nikolaos. *Theory, Concepts, and Method in Comparative Politics.* New York: Harcourt Brace, 1996. One of the few attempts to update the ideas of comparative politics since the 1960s.

Industrialized Democracies

CHAPTER 2

The Industrialized Democracies

Democracy is the worst form of government except for all the others that have been tried.

WINSTON CHURCHILL

THE BASICS

The Industrialized Democracies

REGION	DEMOCRACIES	CONTENDERS
Europe	Austria, Belgium, Denmark, Finland, France, Germany, Great Britain, Greece, Iceland, Ireland, Italy, Luxembourg, Malta, Norway, Portugal, Spain, Sweden, Switzerland, and the Netherlands	Cyprus, Czech Republic, Estonia, Hungary, Latvia, Lithuania, Poland, Slovakia, and Turkey
The Americas	Canada and the United States	Argentina, Brazil, Chile, Costa Rica, Mexico, and most Caribbean Islands
Asia and the Pacific Islands	Australia, Japan, and New Zealand	Philippines, South Korea, and Taiwan
Africa	—	Botswana, Ghana, and South Africa

CRISIS. OR IS IT?

There is no doubt that the world's richest and most democratic countries are facing their most difficult economic times since the Great Depression of the 1930s. Banks, automobile companies, and more have collapsed. Millions of people have lost their jobs or their homes.

In fact, as we have tried to come to grips with the deep recession that began in the American financial industry in 2008, the very definition of what we mean by industrialized democracies has changed. Before 2008, most key economic decisions affecting the world as a whole were through the G-8 and other institutions that included the world's wealthiest and most stable countries—the United States, the United Kingdom, France, Germany, Japan, Italy, Canada, and Russia. When the international community came together in April 2009 to try deal with the crisis that G-8 had grown to the G-20 and included emerging economies such as Mexico, Brazil, India, and Indonesia, parts of the world we will consider in Parts 3 and 4 of this book.

Still, it is hard to miss the impact of the crisis. We live in middle class neighborhoods that should have been recession proof. Yet, we both have houses around our corners that have been empty for months. Other neighbors have tried to sell their houses and failed. In Chip's neighborhood, homes that were worth seven hundred thousand dollars in 2007 are now worth five hundred thousand dollars. Maybe less.

Throughout the world of the G-8 or the G-20, the models and templates used in Chapter 1 apply here as well. Now, we need to dig deeper and see four analytical themes that will be central to Part 2 and to the rest of the book.

First, as Table 2.1 shows, not all of the major industrialized powers (we will discuss the G-20 in the second half of the book) have dealt with the crisis in the same way. Some, like the United States, have invested many billions of dollars in "stimulus" programs to try to jump-start the economy. Indeed, when all is said and done, the United States government will probably spend a few trillion dollars on these efforts. Other governments, especially Germany and France, have concentrated on stiffening the regulation of financial institutions and other companies that are widely seen as having caused the crisis in the first place. Those differences reflect the histories, cultures, and institutions of those countries that will be on intellectual center stage in the rest of Part 2.

Second, as wrenching as the crisis has been, few economists think any of these countries are about to enter anything approaching the Great Depression. To be sure, Iceland went bankrupt in late 2008 and Greece's economy is on the brink of collapse as we write. Nonetheless, most analysts agree that the world's wealthiest countries will recover. It might take a year or two or three, but the impact on people's lives in the industrialized countries covered here is far more modest than those we will see later in less affluent and stable countries.

Third, there is also little or no doubt that the political damage of the crisis will be limited. Some incumbents—most notably Labour in the United Kingdom—have been voted out of office. They could well be joined by the Barack Obama administration in the United States in 2012. The key issue here is that the **regimes** or the institutions laid out in

constitutions and major legislation do not seem to be in jeopardy, even in countries such as Greece, Iceland and Ireland that have been hit the hardest economically.

But democracy is secure. As we will also see in Parts 3 and 4, that is not a statement one can make about other types of countries. Put simply, democracy in the industrialized world is secure. We may object to what our country's government is doing about this crisis or other issues, yet there is little evidence that more than a handful of people in the countries we are about to cover would endorse a new regime, democratic or otherwise.

Fourth, President Obama played a pivotal, but not domineering, role in the negotiations to create the G-20 summit in April 2009. On the crisis and on many other issues, he sent his cabinet members and other advisors out to listen to world leaders rather than to advocate just an American point of view, which is what many of his predecessors have done since the end of the Cold War, if not before. Far more than the administration of George W. Bush, Obama's team understands that solutions to the world's most difficult problems will require international cooperation, not American hegemony. In the case of the G-20 summit, that led to an agreement to both increase spending and strengthen regulations with individual countries on what they do best.

THINKING ABOUT DEMOCRACY

The Freedom Forum 🌐 (**www.freedomforum.org**) is one of the most important nongovernmental organizations monitoring the status of democracy around the world. As they see it, as many as two-thirds of the countries in the world today are democracies because they guarantee individual liberties and choose their rulers through reasonably free elections. However, democracy is about much more than elections and the other criteria the Freedom Forum uses. Indeed, as political scientist Fareed Zakaria, editor of *Newsweek International,* has argued, we may put too much emphasis on elections when trying to decide what makes a society democratic. As he points out, and as we will see in Parts 3 and 4, plenty of countries hold reasonably free elections but have other characteristics that make observers reluctant to call them truly democratic.[1]

In that sense, democracy is about relationships between the rulers and the ruled. That also means that democracy has proved to be anything but easy to define, let alone implement. In a literal sense, democracy means rule by the people, as the two Greek words it evolved from

TABLE 2.1 Stimulus Spending as of March 2009

COUNTRY	BILLIONS COMMITTED TO STIMULUS SPENDING (US $)
United States	841
Canada	44
United Kingdom	41
France	21
Germany	130
Italy	7
Spain	75
Japan	104
Australia	19

Source: Adapted from *The Washington Post*, 29 March 2009, A8.

---

[1] Fareed Zakaria, *The Future of Freedom.* (New York: W.W. Norton, 2003).

suggest. As such, it cannot exist because the people cannot truly rule. Even in small New England communities that still rely on town meetings, there are too many people and too many pressing issues for everyone to take part in making every decision. Instead, even they have had to follow an all but universal path by adopting a representative systems in which people select men and women to govern in their name.

In other words, democratic reality has always fallen short of the ideal. Observers acknowledge democracies compel their citizens to do things that they would rather avoid—pay taxes, serve in the military, drive at the speed limit, not drink alcohol before a certain age, and so on.

To make matters even more complicated, observers like Zakaria claim that if we equate democracy with personal liberties, like the right to vote, we can get ourselves in political as well as intellectual trouble. As we will see more clearly in the last half of the book, countries like the United States, Great Britain, France, and Germany have had more successful democratic experiences because they have blended all the characteristics covered in the next few paragraphs. For instance, any problems that we have with defining democracy by the use of free elections alone evaporate when we consider Germany between the two world wars. After its defeat in 1918, Germany adopted one of the most democratic constitutions in the world. Nonetheless, less than fifteen years later, Adolf Hitler and his Nazi Party rode the democratic process into power, allowing them to create one of the least democratic and most brutal regimes in history.

The Basics

As the discussion of the G-20 and the basic table at the beginning of this chapter suggest, there is no commonly accepted definition of democracy. In this book we define it using a conservative set of five criteria, which together will enable countries to survive the current crisis and keep their regimes intact.

Rights

Democracies guarantee basic individual freedoms of press, religion, association, and speech. Most observers are convinced that people cannot participate effectively in making the decisions that shape their lives unless those rights are guaranteed.

Countries define those rights in different ways. Many have enshrined them in their constitutions. For example, human rights are affirmed in the first paragraphs of the French Fifth Republic's constitution and in the Basic Law of Germany. Even where they are not included in a constitution, as in Great Britain (which does not have a written constitution), they are deeply ingrained in the culture.

These are not merely paper rights. There are a few restrictions placed on people's freedom, but they are very much on the margins of political life. The French still have a law that allows the government to ban organizations whose goal is to overthrow the state. The Japanese constitution has a clause that permits the government to put the "public welfare" ahead of civil liberties if it believes that national security or other key policy goals are threatened. The French and German governments can declare a state of emergency and rule in what amounts to a dictatorial manner for a limited time. All democracies have police and intelligence agencies that have infiltrated organizations their governments have deemed subversive. The important point here, however, is that these provisions are rarely used and have had little impact on political life in these countries.

Competitive Elections

At least as important as the right to civil liberties and the reliance on the rule of law is the requirement the government be chosen through regular, free, and fair elections. Simply holding elections is not enough. Mexico, for instance, has long held elections for all key offices, but few observers believe that the Institutional Revolutionary Party (PRI) would have been able to stay in power from the late 1920s until 2000 had the contests been run honestly and fairly. The former Soviet Union and its Eastern Bloc allies also held elections, but voters had were offered only a single candidate to vote for who had been handpicked by the Communist Party. Other countries, such as Nigeria in 1993 or Panama in 1989, conducted elections, only to see the military reject the outcome and seize power.

The electoral and party systems in industrialized democracies are not all alike. The United States is unique in having only two major parties, but the way Ralph Nader's candidacy affected the 2000 election shows, even a very minor candidate can determine the outcome of an election (www.ifes.org). More important, in all other democracies more than two parties have an impact at the national level. In Great Britain and Germany, two major parties vie for power, but a number of smaller ones play a pivotal role in raising issues in both countries and in forming governing coalitions in the latter. In Japan, although a single party has dominated electoral politics and governments from the 1950s through 2009, it rarely comes close to winning a majority of the popular vote. France and the Scandinavian countries have five or more parties, but they fall into two blocs, one on the Left and the other on the Right, one of which normally wins each election. Israel and the Netherlands have as many as a dozen parties with seats in the national parliament.

These differences exist in large part because the industrialized democracies are divided along lines that reflect

TABLE 2.2 Women in Parliament: Selected Countries

Sweden	Proportional	45.0%
Netherlands	Proportional	39.3%
Germany	Half proportional	32.8%
United Kingdom	First past the post	22.0%
France	Single member, two ballot	18.9%
United States	First past the post	16.0%

Sweden and the Netherlands were added to the countries covered in the book to illustrate the range of results one finds.

Source: International Parliamentary Union, www.ipu.org. Accessed 15 April 2011.

their histories, a point that will become clearer in the next four chapters. They also use different **electoral systems,** or ways of counting votes and allocating seats, that also lead to differences from country to country.

Other things being equal, **single-member districts** make it relatively easy for major-party candidates to win and to discourage the formation of new or, in American terminology, "third" parties. Under **proportional representation,** parties win roughly the same share of parliamentary seats as they received at the polls. As a result, under this system it is much easier for new parties to gain a toehold and the countries with large numbers of parties typically use electoral systems with a strong proportional element.

One of the most discussed implications of electoral law in recent years is reflected in the number of women in national legislatures. As Table 2.1 shows, women do not make up the majority of the members of the more powerful lower house of a national legislature in any industrialized democracy. They come closest in countries that use proportional representation, whereas their numbers lag in those that use any kind of single-member district system. In the latter, local party officials have the most say in determining nominations, and they tend to choose candidates who they think stand the best chance of winning. That usually means men. In proportional systems, national party elites have the most influence in choosing not only who is nominated but more important, who sits near the top of the party list on the ballot. Those are the candidates who have the greatest chance of getting elected. As a result, it is much easier for national party elites to put large numbers of women in positions to win office, especially in France where women now must make up half the ticket in most local and regional elections.

The Rule of Law

Related to civil liberties is a reliance on the **rule of law,** which means that people are governed by clear and fair rules rather than by the arbitrary, personal exercise of power. What they can and cannot do is spelled out in constitutions and in ordinary laws. As a result, people can expect to be treated fairly by the government both in their routine dealings with the state (e.g., in the way taxes are assessed) and on those rare occasions when they come up against it (e.g., after being accused of a crime). The importance of the rule of law is actually easiest to see in its absence, which will be a common theme in Parts 3 and 4.

Civil Society and Civic Culture

The pathbreaking research on the role of political culture in democracies began in the late 1950s when Gabriel Almond and Sidney Verba conducted surveys in the United States, Great Britain, Germany, Italy, and Mexico. They concluded that stable democracies have a civic culture in which people accept not just the rules of the political game but the elites who lead them. Other pollsters have found that people in the United States and Great Britain, in particular, tend to be "joiners" who belong to many social and political groups, which ties them into their community, creates a civil society, and brings them into contact with people from a variety of social, economic, and political backgrounds.

With the upsurge of protest movements in the late 1960s, academic interest in civil society and civic culture waned. However, the past few decades have seen a decline in support for politicians and in interpersonal trust in the liberal democracies. Given that trend and the dozens of attempts to build democratic regimes elsewhere in the world, these ideas have crept back toward intellectual center stage. Although we do not fully understand how they operate, all the signs indicate that a civic culture and civil society psychologically bind people to their states and make it hard for "antisystem" protest to take root, thus helping make democracies resistant to sweeping change.

Capitalism and Affluence

Most—but not all—political scientists assume that democracy can only exist alongside an affluent economy based in large part on private ownership of the means of production. There is no denying that the industrialized democracies are the richest countries in the world even given the current recession. Most of their people live in cities and almost all are literate (see the Basics table on the inside front cover). Most have access to basic health care, which translates into a low infant mortality rate and high life expectancy.

Industrialized democracies are not all equally wealthy of course. Great Britain's gross national product (GNP) is only three-fourths that of the United States. Some of the countries not included in this book (e.g., Spain, Portugal, and Greece) are only about half as well-off as Great Britain. They do not provide the same services for their people, as reflected, for instance, in the fairly high infant mortality rate in the United States, which actually surpasses that of some countries in the Global South. Nonetheless, they are all dramatically better off than the countries we will consider in Parts 3 and 4.

Scholars debate how, why, and if democracy needs affluence and capitalism. At the very least, there has been a historical connection between the rise of capitalism and the establishment of democracy. Although the causal connections are murky, it is true that, with but a handful of exceptions, only reasonably affluent and industrialized societies have been able to sustain governments that satisfy the other three criteria for an extended period of time. The examples of India and Jamaica, as well as some of the other countries in the "contenders" column of the Basics table that opens this chapter suggests that affluence, at least, may not be as important as some theorists have suggested. Nonetheless, given the political uncertainty in most of the contender countries and the historical link between capitalism and democracy, the focus in Part 2 is on countries in the industrialized world.

Key Concepts and Questions

There will be a section like this in all the chapters that follow. Each will draw your attention to variations on general concepts introduced in that chapter while also raising questions for that chapter alone.

Here, focus on the following concepts:

- Basic freedoms.
- The rule of law.
- Competitive, fair, and free elections.
- A strong civil society and civic culture.
- Capitalism and affluence.

And related questions:

- Why did democracy emerge in these countries?
- Why did democracy become so remarkably durable in the second half of the twentieth century?
- Why is there so much debate about public policy in the industrialized democracies in the first years of the twenty-first century?
- Why has that debate not gone one step further and led many people to question their regimes or democracy itself?

Which Countries Are Democracies?

Using these criteria, it is easy to identify more than twenty countries that are unquestionably democratic. Most are in Western Europe or in parts of the world Europeans colonized. The one obvious exception is Japan. All of these countries have met the five criteria for at least thirty years—which seems to be enough time for them to develop sufficient support for their democracies such that there is little chance of their regimes collapsing.

It is not easy to make judgments about the countries in the contenders column of the Basics table. Few of them meet the affluence criterion. Israel certainly is a democracy for its Jewish citizens, but it cannot be said to be one for the Arabs who live inside either its pre- or post-1967 borders. Some former communist states may well be added to this list in the future, but they cannot yet guarantee that basic freedoms will be tolerated or that elections will determine who governs. For the same reasons, most observers do not classify Chile, Argentina, Brazil, Turkey, South Korea, or Taiwan (Republic of China) as democracies yet.

That said, if the G-20 supplants the G-8 as the main vehicle for cooperation among the wealthiest countries, this definition of "who is democratic" could change sooner rather than later.

Not to mention what happens in Egypt and its neighboring countries.

The *L* Word

American students are often confused by the word *liberal*. In the United States, it refers to people who support the Left and an interventionist government. Everywhere else in the world, however, it has almost exactly the opposite meaning—opposition to government interference in the economy and any other area in which individuals can make decisions for themselves. The term will be used in this latter sense in the rest of this book.

THE ORIGINS OF THE DEMOCRATIC STATE

You cannot make sense of politics in any country without understanding its history. As we explore the origins of the industrialized democracies you will see three main conclusions, which are important not only for the countries we will cover in Part 2 but also for the ones we will consider in the rest of the book.

First, the domestic concerns listed in the table on the inside front cover of the book (state building and nation building, pressures from below) mattered far more than the international ones (imperialism, globalization) in their development. International concerns were important, of course. These countries fought countless wars, many of which strengthened their states, if not their democracies. On balance, however, the way these countries' leaders and their people handled a series of crises that were predominantly domestic in origin had a lot more to do with when, how, and why democracies emerged. That was less the case in the rest of the world, where international forces mattered more, including the impact of the countries to be discussed here.

Second, it is impossible to disentangle the history of democracy from that of Europe and North America. Thus, we cannot determine with any certainty which of the characteristics discussed here are essential to democracy anywhere and which are peculiar to the European and North American experiences.

Third, democracy in these countries took a long time to develop. Southern leaders are trying to condense something that took centuries in Europe, North America, and Japan into a few short years. History suggests they are likely to fail.

The Evolution of Democratic Thought

Modern democracy dates back only to the late eighteenth century. There were democracies in some of the ancient Greek city-states, and in medieval Poland and Switzerland, but they do not warrant consideration here because none involved states with either large populations or extensive civic responsibilities (see Table 2.3).

By the late 1700s that had been changing for the better part of two hundred years. With the rise of individualism, capitalism, and Protestantism, the scientific revolution, and the exploration of the New World, new ways of thinking, which had their roots in such diverse fields as Newtonian physics and Protestant theology, took hold. The innovative thinkers of the time believed that society is naturally composed of separate and autonomous actors who pursue their own interests and desires. For most of them, this "state of nature" was fraught with danger. They recognized that people freed of the shackles of feudalism and other social hierarchies would be more creative and productive. They also realized that these people and the groups they formed would put new demands and pressures on the weak monarchies of the feudal period.

The most important of these theorists was **Thomas Hobbes** (1586–1679). He claimed that if people were left to their own devices, the competition among them would be so intense that it would lead to the "war of all against all."

TABLE 2.3 Key Turning Points in the Development of Industrialized Democracies

CENTURY	TRENDS
Seventeenth	Emergence of the modern state
Eighteenth	First democratic revolutions
	Development of *laissez-faire* theory
Nineteenth	Industrial revolution
	Spread of voting and other democratic institutions
Twentieth	Further expansion of the vote
	Defeat of fascism and solidification of democracy in Western Europe

Therefore, to prevent anarchy, people had no choice but to give up some of their freedom to a large and powerful state, which he called the Leviathan.

During the nineteenth century, industrial capitalism became Britain's dominant economic system, which unexpectedly reinforced the shift toward more democratic government. Like the political liberals, the capitalists opposed a society still governed using feudal institutions and values. They began to demand a form of government that gave individuals free rein to pursue their economic interests. During the 1700s, their views crystallized as **laissez-faire** capitalism. Drawn from the French phrase meaning "allow to do," *laissez-faire* theory calls on government to stay out of economic life because the "invisible hand" of the market allocates resources far better.

In practice, the early liberal capitalists did not demand the abolition of government. They shared Hobbesian fears about the state of nature, especially as far as the lower classes were concerned. Most shared **John Locke's** (1632–1704) notion that the state's role was to protect "life, liberty, and property."

Thus, the capitalists and their political allies added two key ideas to democratic thought. First, the state should be limited. Second, it should no longer try to prescribe what people do in all areas of life as had been the case under feudalism. Rather, it should be like a referee whose job is to protect society from the arbitrary use of power and the excessive demands of the people who were often referred to as the "mob" or the "dangerous classes."

Given the criteria laid out in the previous section, no country could have been called democratic in the early nineteenth century. All sharply limited the **suffrage,** or the right to vote. For instance, no women and only a handful of freed African Americans could vote in the newly independent United States. In Britain, barely 5 percent of men had the franchise even after the passage of the Great Reform Act in 1832. What's more, the democratizing changes that occurred did not come quickly or easily, requiring massive protests in Britain and revolutions elsewhere.

Still, an important precedent had been set. Political power could no longer be monopolized by monarchs. Much of it had shifted into the hands of representatives who could, to some extent, hold rulers accountable and who were themselves accountable to the voters.

Even more importantly, the theorists and politicians who built the first democratic states opened a door that could not easily be shut. Over the next century, popular pressure forced the expansion of democracy in much of Europe and North America. Most countries were able to develop democracy under highly favorable international conditions. In 1815 the Congress of Vienna established a balance of power that left Europe largely free of war for the next century. The United States, Canada, Australia, and New Zealand were, if anything, even freer of outside interference.

More and more people gained the right to vote. In the United States, most white males had could vote by the 1840s. All French men gained the franchise with the creation of the Second Republic in 1848. In Britain, the right of men to vote was gradually expanded, culminating in the Reform Act of 1918, which removed all property qualifications and income restrictions.

Eventually, the vote was also granted to women. In the United States, women won it with the ratification of the Nineteenth Amendment in 1920. An Act of Parliament did the same in Britain eight years later, although women over thirty years of age had already won the right to vote in 1918. Women in France only got the vote after World War II, although there had been a female cabinet member before the war. The Swiss were the last industrialized democracy to grant women the vote in the early 1970s.

In the meantime, other opportunities for political engagement grew. Most American states passed laws enabling citizens to put proposed legislation on the ballot in a referendum. In France and Britain, laws limiting citizens' rights to form associations were abolished, permitting the growth of trade unions and other mass-based interest groups.

In much of Europe, popularly elected houses of parliament gained the all-important right to determine who governed. By the late 1870s, the two houses of the French parliament had stripped the presidency of all effective power. In 1911 the British House of Lords, which represented the hereditary nobility, lost the power to do anything more than delay the final passage of legislation. By the 1920s, cabinets everywhere in Western Europe had become responsible to parliaments, with members remaining in office only as long as they retained the support of a majority in the lower house.

Building Democracies

Democracy was not built quickly or easily anywhere. In some of today's industrialized democracies, it came about gradually and without all that much turmoil. In others, democracy was formed through a number of wrenching fits and starts that included periods of revolution and authoritarian rule in which democracy seemed a distant and often unreachable goal. That said, in Europe, and to a lesser degree, in North America, the way democracy developed was largely a result of the way countries and their rulers handled four great transformations over the last five hundred years or so:

- ■ The creation of the nation and state.
- ■ The role of religion in society and government.
- ■ The development of pressures for democracy.
- ■ The industrial revolution.

In places where democracy developed the earliest, such as Great Britain and the United States, divisions over these issues were resolved relatively easily. This happened

Museum of London/Imagestate RM/PhotoLibrary.

British women demanding the right to vote in 1909.

Democratization *and the Industrialized Democracies*

The recent wave of democratization in the rest of the world has led political scientists to reconsider democracy's emergence in Europe and North America. Their conclusions are not that encouraging for new democracies.

Depending on how we count, it took generations, if not centuries, to create the first democracies. The history of democratization stretches back to the signing of the Magna Carta in 1215 and some people are convinced that it is still going on today, given that groups such as gays and lesbians are denied what they claim to be their full civil rights. Even with a more limited definition of what it means to be democratic, it took the Anglo-American societies at least three centuries to secure basic political rights for all their citizens.

What's more, democratization was a tumultuous process. There is a tendency to look upon it as one of gradual and consensual reform. Compared to the political histories of most other countries, this may be true. However, even the United States and the United Kingdom have faced major upheavals, including civil wars and other prolonged periods of unrest, during which elites tried to hold onto their power.

We should also recognize that no real attempts were made to consciously create a democracy before the establishment of the Weimar Republic in Germany after World War I, and no successes were recorded until after World War II. Conditions may have changed enough and leaders in the new democracies may have learned enough that they can escape the problems that befell all but the most successful of the countries discussed in this chapter. ■

in part because these crises were spread out over a number of centuries and societies and their leaders were able to reach something approaching closure on one of them before the next one occurred.

The situation was very different in countries that had more trouble democratizing. The crises were not resolved in

a consensual manner and left deep **cleavages,** or social divisions. In France and Italy, conflict over the role the church should play in politics overlapped with controversies about whether the government should be democratic. Until the late 1800s, there was no unified Germany or Italy, which made it impossible for democracy to develop. Moreover, the fact that these deeply divisive issues remained unresolved meant that by the late nineteenth century the governments of the newly formed nation-states were dealing with all of them simultaneously.

Democratizers in such countries also found themselves in a more difficult position internationally. Germany, Japan, and Italy were newcomers to great power politics and found themselves lagging behind Britain and France militarily as well as economically. Desirous of power and prestige and fearful of invasion, leaders in all three countries believed that they had to catch up with the other prominent states as quickly as possible. They were also convinced that they could do so only if their governments took the lead and forced the pace of development. Each therefore imposed strict limits on political rights. Adult males did get the vote, but real political power remained in the hands of the bureaucratic and military elites, which built industrial and military machines that rivaled those of Britain and France by the time World War I broke out.

After World War I, liberal regimes were established in much of central and Eastern Europe. Japan adopted a much more democratic constitution. Most of those states, however, quickly ran into trouble, giving rise to concerns about the dangers of excessive and disruptive popular participation. Extremist parties on the Left and Right won ever larger shares of the vote. Thousands of disgruntled workers and veterans took to the streets and formed private militias. Effective democratic government became all but impossible.

One after another, the new democracies turned to authoritarian leaders and **fascism**—the most important examples are Benito Mussolini in Italy and Adolf Hitler in Germany. These men and their parties gained control in large part because they built a strong popular base and came to power as part of an elected coalition government.

World War II marked the last watershed in the evolution of democratic theory and practice for the countries covered in Part 2. The rise of fascism, the carnage of World War II, and the outbreak of the Cold War led many to question whether average citizens were capable of sustaining democracy, especially in countries with a history like Germany's or Japan's. One group of scholars argued that there was a widespread "authoritarian personality" that left people vulnerable to appeals from communists and fascists. Others stressed the uneven development in countries that had to totally reconstruct their political systems after the war. Among other things, these included measures that made it more difficult for potentially disruptive parties to elect members of parliament and for divided legislatures to hamstring governments.

A strong democratic state was in some respects a by-product of the Cold War that began as World War II ended. Early on, Europe was its main "battleground." In 1949, the communist revolution in China made Japan vitally important to the West as well. The United States sent billions of dollars of aid to help the European and Japanese economies recover from the war and thereby block the spread of communism and other authoritarian regimes.

Political scientists and historians still debate how these various forces came together. But come together they did. Within a generation, democratic regimes were securely in place in "free world" countries that had so recently opted for some of the most brutally authoritarian regimes ever.

POLITICAL CULTURE AND PARTICIPATION

Obviously the way people think and act is critical to the success—or failure—of a democracy. However, political scientists have reached some not-so-obvious conclusions about how those beliefs and actions can buttress—or undermine—democracies.

The Civic Culture?

After World War II, a number of political scientists turned their attention to the reasons for the collapse of democracy and the rise of fascism. Many of them ended up concentrating on political culture, most notably Almond and Verba in their landmark study, *The Civic Culture*. They contrasted the United States and Great Britain with Germany, Italy, and Mexico, emphasizing the importance of a culture in which democratic beliefs exist alongside a degree of political passivity. For example, they explored political efficacy or people's belief that they can do something about political decisions they disagree with. However, most of those surveyed also acknowledged that people rarely do so because they trusted their leaders to do what is right.

The massive protests of the 1960s and 1970s undermined the more simplistic arguments linking a civic culture to democracy. Today, political scientists are returning to the role of political culture, albeit in a more nuanced way. There is no consensus yet in the scholarly community, but three conclusions from recent studies will prove important throughout Part 2.

First, in successful democracies, people have a deeply felt sense of **legitimacy** and accept the "rules of the game." Critical here is the distinction between the government of

the day and the regime. As we will see in Chapter 4, even Britain had to cope with protests that reflected unprecedented anger toward the Labour government of 1974–79 and its Tory successor in the 1980s. However, there is no evidence that the protesters' ire extended beyond the James Callaghan or Margaret Thatcher governments to the British constitutional order itself. Perhaps even more important, much the same is true of protests in countries that had not developed strong democratic regimes prior to the war. Thus, despite the massive protests of May and June 1968 that almost toppled General Charles de Gaulle's government, there was little talk of scrapping the Fifth Republic, and any inclinations to do so were long gone before the socialists finally won an election thirteen years later.

Second, that feeling of legitimacy has remained despite a dramatic drop in most forms of political participation and in trust in most politicians. Only 58 percent of British voters bothered to go to the polls in 2001, the lowest figure since 1918. Turnout was particularly low in Britain's inner cities and among the young, barely a third of whom cast a ballot.

A panoramic view of the hundreds of thousands of nonviolent protesters at the 1963 March on Washington for civil rights.

Paul Schutzer/Time Life Pictures/Getty Images

The voting rate topped 60 percent in 2005 and 2009 but still remained far below the norm.

Third, more recently, scholars such as Robert Putnam and Fareed Zakaria have forced us to consider more than just the values and assumptions of a political culture. Putnam, for instance, stresses the role of social capital, which reflects the degree to which a society has networks that build trust and cooperation, especially among people and groups who typically disagree with each other. Zakaria emphasizes the importance of attitudes of tolerance and institutions that instill a respect for the views and actions of others because they can put a damper on the passions that people with strongly held views can bring to political life. Such ideas are hotly contested by other political scientists. Nonetheless, there is widespread agreement that a democratic culture consists not only of attitudes public opinion pollsters can measure but also of actions that tend to breed trust and cooperation.

Late Democracy/Strong State

There is a powerful theme lurking below the surface in this discussion that will have a tremendous bearing later on in the book. Because they eschewed democracy in favor of "top-down" development, countries like Germany continued their tradition of a strong state into the democratic period after World War II. At that time (though not earlier), in combining democracy with a strong state, they spurred unprecedented economic growth and political stability that lasted until the early 1990s.

Political Parties and Elections

Democracies are different from other countries in large part because they give their citizens a wide variety of ways to participate in political life. None of them is more important than their involvement (or lack thereof) in the competitive elections that determine who fills the top offices in the government. And, with the exception of some local races in the United States, any analysis of elections and voting has to concentrate on **political parties,** the organizations responsible for contesting elections and forming governments afterward.

There is a bewildering array of political parties in the three democracies to be covered in Part 2. Most, though, have their roots in the cleavages left by the historical transformations discussed earlier.

A few new parties have emerged in the past twenty years, which we will consider later. None of them, however, are strong enough yet to win elections or play a regular role in determining the composition of governments. In other words, if we are to understand the heart of the electoral process, we have to begin with the parties at least, in part, because of those historical upheavals.

Parties are normally thought of as lying along the traditional Left–Right spectrum. Unlike most political terms, these two do not have particularly informative meanings. Their origins lie in the seating arrangements in the French parliament after the Revolution of 1789, when deputies who favored radical change sat on the left of the speaker's rostrum and those who opposed it sat to his right. Since then, the meaning of the terms has evolved in the ways summarized in Table 2.4.

On the **Left** end are what remains of the communist parties (see Table 2.5). They were formed in the aftermath of the Russian Revolution of 1917, when members of the more radical wings of the socialist parties quit and formed new organizations to support the Bolsheviks in Moscow. For most of the time since then, the communist parties have been the most radical critics of capitalism and the strongest defenders of what they claim are the interests of the working class. Most were loyal supporters of the Soviet Union during the Cold War. Of the countries we will be covering, only France still has a significant Communist Party, and it has been in decline for years, a decline that has accelerated since the collapse of the Soviet Union.

Next are the **Social Democratic parties.** Like the Communists, they also traditionally supported the **nationalization** of industry, extensive social welfare programs, and greater equality. Unlike the Communists, however, socialists rejected revolution and were harsh critics of the Soviet Union. Most moderated their positions during the postwar years and shed all but the emptiest rhetorical references to Marxism and nationalization. Some people think that recent attempts, mainly by Tony Blair and his colleagues in the British Labour Party, to create a "third way"

TABLE 2.4 The Changing Meaning of Left and Right

PERIOD	LEFT	RIGHT
Eighteenth and early nineteenth centuries	Prodemocratic Anticlerical Promarket	Antidemocratic Proclerical Ambivalent on market
Industrial era	Prodemocratic Anticlerical For socialism or welfare state	More prodemocratic Usually proclerical Less positive about welfare state, against socialism
Postindustrial era	Egalitarian but qualms about welfare state and socialism More globalist New social issues	Promarket capitalism Traditional values More nationalistic

TABLE 2.5 Main Types of Political Parties by Country

				TYPE OF PARTY			
COUNTRY	COMMUNIST	SOCIALIST	LIBERAL	CHRISTIAN DEMOCRATIC	CONSERVATIVE	OTHER	
Great Britain	—	Labour	Liberal Democrats[a]	—	Conservative	Regional[b]	
France	PCF	PS	[c]	[c]	UPM[d]	Greens and National Front	
Germany	PDS	SPD	FDP	CDU	—	Greens	

[a]Liberal to 1983; Liberal-Social Democratic Alliance 1983–87, Liberal Democrats 1988 on.

[b]Nationalist parties of Scotland, Wales, and Northern Ireland.

[c]The French Radical and Christian Democratic parties are no longer big enough to include here.

[d]Most recent party representing the Gaullist movement.

between socialism and capitalism might breathe new ideological life into these parties, but so far their track record has been mixed at best. Only in the United States, Canada, and Japan have socialists not been serious contenders for power.

In the center are parties known as either **liberals** or **radicals.** They gained their radical label in the nineteenth century when they did stand for fundamental change—the separation of church and state, a market economy, and democracy.

The Liberals were one of the two main British parties until the 1920s, and the Radicals were France's most influential party under both the Third and Fourth Republics (1875–1958). Today, they appeal primarily to the wealthy and have no significant impact on who governs. The one major exception is the German Free Democratic Party (FDP). Although it has never done well at the polls, the FDP provided the votes either the socialists or the **Christian Democrats** needed to form a governing coalition for all but three years between the creation in 1949 of the Federal Republic and 1998 and does again now.

Countries that had deep and unresolved divisions over the relationship between church and state at one point or another have had explicitly religious, Christian Democratic parties that appealed primarily to Catholic voters. Some Catholics had qualms about democracy, whereas others advocated social reforms much like those backed by Social Democrats. With the onset of the Cold War, most Christian Democrats aligned themselves with the United States on foreign policy issues and with proponents of a capitalist economy at home. They have been extremely influential, dominating governments in Germany and Italy for most of the postwar period. Indeed, France is the only country with a large Catholic population in which the Christian Democrats have been eclipsed by other right-of-center parties.

Britain, with very few Catholics, and Japan, with very few Christians, have not had major Christian Democratic parties. Instead, the **Right** side of the political spectrum has been dominated by secular conservatives. Parties like the British Conservatives, the Japanese LDP, and the French Gaullists are not all that different from the Christian Democrats except that they do not have a religious inspiration. American readers should note that they are not conservative in the sense that the term is used in the United States because they have not traditionally opposed state intervention in the economy.

Catch-All Parties

Some observers claim that democratic party systems today are not working very well because they have such old roots. As we will see in the chapters that follow, many of these parties have had a hard time adapting to the changes of recent years, especially the rise of new social movements and the globalization of the world economy.

In part, that reflects their adoption of more moderate positions for most of the past sixty years. During the 1950s, political scientists began to notice a marked shift in public opinion toward the center. A combination of sustained economic growth, the expansion of the welfare state, and the escalation of the Cold War undermined support for radical politics. That led to the rise of **catch-all parties,** which, unlike their ideologically narrower predecessors (dubbed mass parties) tried to appeal to all voters and literally catch them all.

At first, the Left was slow to respond. The British Labour Party and the German Social Democrats (SPD) clung to their traditional socialist appeals even though their electoral fortunes continued to sag. Gradually, however, a new generation of leaders moved socialist parties toward the center and led them to victory in the 1960s.

The changes on the Right were less striking but no less significant. Conservatives, too, had to respond to the emerging consensus about the welfare state. The British Conservatives, French Gaullists, and German Christian Democrats accepted the idea that government should provide extensive social service programs and actually expanded these programs when they were in office.

The moderation was so marked during the 1950s and early 1960s that some analysts began writing about the "end of ideology." They were convinced that sharp ideological divisions were a thing of the past and that subsequent elections would be contests between similar teams of politicians.

Those ideological trends were reinforced by an even more dramatic change in the way election campaigns were conducted. By the 1960s, most people got most of their information about politics from television. Because it is impossible to say anything nuanced or detailed in a sixty-second news clip, the growing role of television accentuated the trend away from ideological appeals (see the top half of Figure 2.1).

As we are about to see, events undermined the central claims of an argument that democracies were undergoing an end of ideology. However, the technological dynamics that led to the catch-all party have, if anything, intensified. There have been instances in which parties and candidates made major breakthroughs by stressing ideological themes, most notably in the victories of Thatcher in Great Britain (1979) and Ronald Reagan in the United States (1980). Yet even their campaigns featured slogans and video clips. Polls, focus groups, and other forms of market research have led party leaders to run campaigns that "sell" to undecided voters. How much these changes have sapped parties of the ability to take strong stands and, thus, helped shape public opinion for extended periods is still very much an open question. Nonetheless, the spread of media-based campaigns has heightened the cynicism many voters feel toward politicians in democracies.

New Divisions

The image of the party system summarized in Table 2.5 is somewhat misleading because it implies that party systems were only defined by cleavages that came to the fore no later than early in the last century. The parties that have a realistic chance of winning most elections do have such old and deep roots, but important changes are occurring on the fringes of the electoral mainstream that may have more dramatic consequences in the next few years.

Most visible is the growing differences between men and women. Women used to be more conservative than men. They were less likely to work outside the home and so were less exposed to the left-leaning influence of trade unions. They were also more religious and thus deeply affected by the usually conservative clergy. As more women joined the workforce and were swept up in the feminist and new Left movements of the 1960s and 1970s, some began to question their conservative views, especially those involving reproductive rights and the family.

Many (though by no means all) women began to realize that their interests lay with progressive parties. In the United States, this has led to the "gender gap" in which the Democratic vote among women can be as much as 20 percent higher than among men. In Britain, it prompted the Labour Party to field a slate of candidates in 1997 that led to the election of over a hundred female members of parliament.

Meanwhile, many men—especially those with limited professional skills—felt that their livelihoods and positions of dominance were under threat. Some made the opposite switch, abandoning traditionally left-wing parties to become

FIGURE 2.1 Political Participation in Flux: Two Versions

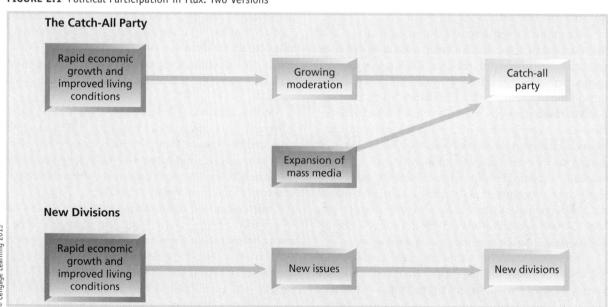

"Reagan Democrats" in the United States, Thatcherites in Britain, and supporters of the National Front in France.

The gender gap is but the tip of a much larger, but poorly understood, political iceberg. For forty years, Ronald Inglehart and his colleagues have been studying how the social and economic changes underlying **postindustrial society** are playing themselves out politically (see the bottom half of Figure 2.1). Their theoretical assumption and research methods have been the subject of much controversy; nonetheless, their empirical findings are consistent enough that it is clear that they have tapped an important trend.

Inglehart uses the same starting point as the end-of-ideology theorists—rapid economic growth and improved living conditions—but then diverges sharply from them. From his perspective, the unprecedented economic growth of the past half-century has produced a new type of middle-class, **postmaterialist** voters. They are often the third generation to be raised in affluent conditions and can realistically assume that they will have productive and rewarding careers and will not have to worry much about their economic security. As a result, they tend to focus on what Inglehart calls "higher order" values, including job and personal satisfaction, self-actualization, and international understanding. In the process, postmaterialists have become far less conservative than previous generations of affluent voters.

In American terms, postmaterialists largely overlap with the "soccer moms" (and dads) who gained so much publicity for their support of President Clinton in the 1990s and President Obama in 2008.

They are not traditional Leftists. Most have serious qualms, for instance, about the welfare state and socialism. However, they supported the peace movements of the 1980s and, more recently, environmentalism, more than any other socioeconomic group in the electorate.

They are also most likely to support the one type of new party that has had a significant impact, the **Greens.**

Greens are best known for their strong stands against nuclear weapons and power and for their support of environmental causes. Their ideology goes further to stress "deep ecology," or a worldview based on the assumption that all life is interconnected. Green parties have done rather well in most of Europe, often approaching 10 percent of the vote, most of which comes from postmaterialists. They have had the greatest impact in Germany, where they have been in parliament since 1983 and were in the governing coalition from 1998 until 2005. Before moving on, note that the Greens in the United States, as represented by the Nader campaign of 2000, are very different from what we find in Europe; they do not fully reflect the European trends either ideologically or demographically.

On the other end of the spectrum are people who have not benefited as much from economic growth. Indeed, in a high-tech world in which more and more low-skilled jobs have been either automated or outsourced, these people feel threatened by all the changes going on around them. As a result, the political priorities of these "materialists" include maintaining their own standard of living and national economic strength and security. Even though they may have been raised in left-wing

The new Sarkozy cabinet, 2011.

Franck Prevel/Getty Images.

families, many moved rightward to parties that are hostile to women's and minorities' rights and that defend economic nationalism and "traditional values." They have, in short, become the conservatives of the new millennium.

France's National Front is by far the most prominent example. It routinely wins between 10 and 20 percent of the vote in presidential elections, and its recently retired leader, Jean-Marie Le Pen, edged his way into the runoff ballot in the 2002 presidential election. Even in other countries in which the "New Right" has not fared as well at the polls, it is typically more influential than its leftist counterparts even though they get the most attention from political scientists who study new social movements.

The other important and intriguing shift in politics is the growing role women play in political life. The number of women elected to national political office is expanding, though they are yet to reach a majority anywhere other than Rwanda. Worldwide, the number of women in parliaments averages 18 percent. Nonetheless, progress is being made. There is no better example of that than the initial cabinet named by the conservative French president Nicolas Sarkozy in 2007, which included seven women among its fifteen ministers.

Realignment?

Do not read too much into the emergence of postmaterialism and parties like the Greens or the National Front. If anything, they reflect just how slowly individual parties and national party systems responded to the social and economic changes that have swept through the industrialized democracies since the 1950s.

In other times of major change, the party system eventually did respond. Existing or new parties took the lead by adopting strong positions that appealed to new segments of the electorate, producing lasting changes in basic patterns of partisanship, and, hence, the government.

Political scientists have been waiting for such a **realignment** to occur throughout the democratic world since the late 1960s. At most, two parts of it may have taken place.

First, dealignment always precedes realignment. Before they are "free" to support new parties, voters have to sever the psychological ties that bind them to the ones they have traditionally supported. A massive amount of polling evidence suggests that rates of party identification have plummeted almost everywhere and that more and more voters are skeptical about what parties and politicians can or will deliver.

Second, as implied previously, the Right has gone a long way toward redefining itself. Led by the likes of Thatcher and Reagan, it staked out new positions on the economy, racial diversity, and national security. In so doing, conservatives kept some of their traditional voters in the fold while appealing to many of the newly right-wing materialists. Nonetheless, many have moved so far to the right that

they have a hard time winning elections now that the first generation of New Right leaders have left the scene and their policies no longer have the appeal they did in the 1980s or even in the first years of the George W. Bush administration.

The Left, in contrast, has had a much harder time redefining its image and appealing to a new coalition of voters who could propel it into office with a workable ideology and majority. But that may be changing. Beginning with Clinton in the United States, more moderate politicians took over most of the leading left-of-center parties, including Blair in Britain and Gerhard Schröder in Germany. But, they, too, have left the scene, and it will take time to see whether a new generation of leftist leaders, including Obama, can make progressive politics viable again.

Interest Groups

The industrial democracies all have **interest groups** that seek to promote just about every point of view on just about every imaginable issue, to the point that it is impossible for scholars to keep track of them all. As a result, political scientists have concentrated on trade unions, business groups, and other associations that are the most visible, use the most disruptive tactics, or have the greatest apparent influence.

In most countries, trade unions are now much weaker than they used to be. There are also new groups, including hundreds of organizations working on environmental issues, both for and against expanded rights for women and minorities, and a host of foreign policy issues. Some are quite aggressive, such as the animal rights groups in England that disrupt fox-hunting parties and the export of chicken and sheep for slaughter on the continent. Others are more conventional lobbyists who operate "inside the system," trying to translate their wealth and contacts into influence.

Because there are so many interest groups, it is hard to reach many firm conclusions about them nonetheless, two seem warranted. First, business groups have more influence than unions do. Second, the nature of the relationship interest groups have with decision makers varies tremendously from country to country. In weaker states like the United States and Great Britain, civil servants and politicians try to keep their distance from interest group representatives. In Germany and France, there is a long history of open and close collaboration between interest groups and the state, which contributed heavily to the economic success of these countries from the end of World War II until the early 1990s.

Political Protest

The industrialized democracies all have protest movements that go beyond the activities of traditional interest groups. Some use violence. Some protests involve large numbers of people, as in the "events" of May and June 1968. Others involve only a handful of people, such as the vigil

LES 8 PECHES CAPITAUX
MONDIALISATION SPECULATION EXCLUSION CORRUPTION
PRIVATISATION MANIPULATION MENSONGE MEPRIS

© Antoine Serra/In Visu/Corbis.

Antiglobalization protesters marching from Annemasse, France, to Geneva, Switzerland, during the G-8 summit held in Evian, France, in June 2003. The sign reads: Eight Deadly Sins: Globalization, Speculation, Exclusion, Corruption, Privatization, Manipulation, Lying, Contempt. Protesters clashed frequently with police in normally staid Geneva and caused millions of dollars in damage.

antinuclear protesters have maintained for years across the street from the White House. Some are national in scope and others address issues of only local concern. Some come from the left, others from the right.

We will concentrate on two contrasting trends in the chapters that follow. First, protest movements often have to demonstrate to get their point of view heard. Some even feel the need to resort to violence. Top business executives, however, rarely have to take to the streets to have their views heard.

The most intriguing such group to emerge in the last few years is the Tea Party movement. Although the Tea Party, per se, is an American phenomenon, organizations that are opposed to high taxes and big government have gained a fair degree of prominence in Finland, Sweden, Germany, and Canada. Few of them have had to go "outside the system," but their anger toward the political status quo is palpable.

Second, with that said virtually no one who joins any protest movement questions the legitimacy of their regime, let alone democracy itself. There are some such opposition groups on the fringes of the political system, but the Maoists and Trotskyites on the Left and the American militias and European neo-fascists on the Right have so little influence that they will rarely appear in the next four chapters.

THE DEMOCRATIC STATE

Elections determine who the leading policy makers are, and the informal access provided by interest groups and political parties give the people in industrialized democracies more clout than their counterparts living under other kinds of regimes. But that power is by no means total. As noted previously, democratic states do impose some limits on what people can do. In other words, democratic states have not been able to avoid the trade-off between the power of the state and that of society depicted in Figure 1.2.

Presidential and Parliamentary Systems

The most important feature of the relationship between state and society in any liberal democracy is the way it handles representation between the government and the governed. To understand how that occurs and how it is reflected in public policy, we start by considering the differences between presidential and parliamentary systems. Both are based on the critical democratic principle that free and competitive elections determine who governs. However, they lead to very different kinds of outcomes.

It is misleading to speak of presidential systems in the plural because only one of them exists—the United States. As we will see in more detail in the next chapter, the drafters of the U.S. Constitution set out to create a state in which it would be very difficult for rulers to abuse their power or to act quickly and coherently. They made compromise the norm and rapid decision making difficult. By contrast, in parliamentary systems with a secure majority party or coalition, the prime minister rarely has to compromise, which allows their governments to act more quickly and decisively than any American administration.

The American president has to assume that if a bill he proposes actually is passed, the final version will be very

FIGURE 2.2 The President and Congress

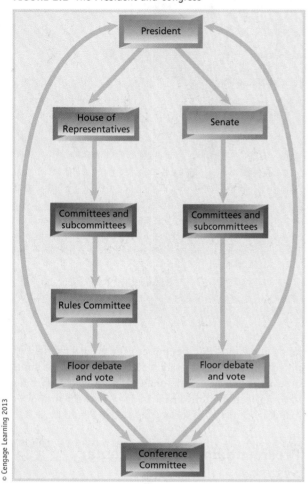

different from the one sent to Capitol Hill because he has little leverage over what senators or representatives do. Once a bill is submitted, it must pass through a number of hurdles—subcommittees, committees, floor debate, and a conference committee—before it is sent on to the White House for the president's signature or veto (see Figure 2.2). At each of those points the bill can be defeated once and for all. Even if it is not, it will almost certainly be drastically altered as members of Congress try to forge a compromise that will get the votes of a majority in each house. As that happens, the bill can be sapped of much of the coherence in the original version. There are occasional exceptions, such as the USA Patriot Act passed after the 9/11 attacks or the stimulus program adopted in early 2009.

As we write in early 2011, the United States is going through profound changes because of the results of the 2010 Congressional election. Thus, on the day we wrote this, the House of Representatives voted to abolish the United States Institute of Peace as a budget-cutting measure. This will not become law because the Senate will not pass it and President

Obama would veto it. But it reveals just how important compromise—and patience—are in the U.S. system.

Parliamentary systems operate very differently. The ones that most closely approximate the British form of government are also often called Westminster systems because many of their institutions and procedures first took shape in Westminster Palace in London. A party that wins a majority of the seats in parliament can take office and see the proposals in its program or platform passed virtually intact. Parliaments do have committees, debates, and votes. Unlike the American president, however, the prime minister has so much leverage over what happens at each of these stages that he or she can force proposed legislation through what is, for all intents and purposes, a compliant parliament.

This is the case because power in parliamentary systems is fused, not separated. After an election, the parliament selects the prime minister, who is normally the head of the majority party or coalition of parties. The prime minister has not been elected by the country as a whole and in most countries is merely a member of parliament (MP) (see Figure 2.3).

The prime minister appoints the rest of the cabinet. Unlike the United States, most ministers (the exact proportion varies from country to country) are also MPs and retain their seats in the legislature while they serve in the cabinet. Together, the prime minister and cabinet form what is known as the government.

The most important feature of a parliamentary system is the doctrine of **cabinet responsibility** to parliament. The government remains in office until the next election if *and only if* it retains the support of that majority on all major pieces of legislation. It also must keep its majority on **votes of confidence,** in which the parliament is explicitly asked to affirm its support for the government. If the government loses either of these types of votes, it must resign. At that

FIGURE 2.3 The Parliamentary System

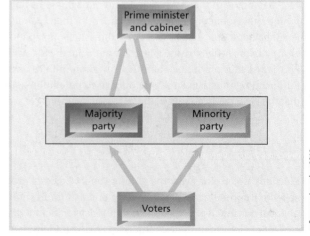

TABLE 2.6 The British General Election of 2005

	LABOUR	CONSERVATIVE	LIBERAL DEMOCRATS	OTHERS
Share of the vote (%)	35.3	32.3	22.1	11.3
Number of seats	356	198	62	30

TABLE 2.7 The French Chamber of Deputies, 1951

PARTY	NUMBER OF SEATS
Communists	101
Socialists	106
Christian Democrats	88
Radicals	76
Independents and Peasants	95
Gaullists	120
Others	40

point, either a new majority comes together within the existing parliament to form a government or the parliament is dissolved, leading to a new election within a matter of weeks.

In practice, when a prime minister has a clear majority, the government will not lose such a vote. Its members will stick together and support the government because the costs of not doing so are too high. The best a defeated government can look forward to is the uncertainty of an election. Breaking party discipline and bringing a government down can also destroy an individual member's career.

So, in a country like Great Britain, where the Labour Party won 356 out of 646 seats in the all-powerful House of Commons in 2005 (see Table 2.6), the prime minister could count on winning every key vote until the parliamentary term ended. Debates on the floor of the House of Commons are more heated than in the House of Representatives or Senate in the United States, but the legislative process rarely produces more than slight changes in the details of a bill, and then only if the government agrees.

The situation does get more complicated if no party wins a majority of the seats on its own, which is why Table 2.6 does not include the most recent British election. The Conservatives came in first but did not win a majority in 2010. They therefore had to form a coalition with the Liberal Democrats that shows every sign of surviving the five years before the next elections would have to be held (see Chapter 4).

The protracted budget stalemate Washington suffers through each year rarely occurs in a parliamentary system. Even under Britain's current coalition government, there was no doubt that Chancellor of the Treasury George Osborne's (Chancellor of the Exchequer) budget would pass intact within a matter of a few days, despite the fact that it called for the steepest spending cuts since the Great Depression.

Politicians face plenty of pressure in a parliamentary system, but to make a difference, lobbyists have to exert their influence before legislation is submitted to parliament. Otherwise, it is too late for them to have much hope of shaping a bill as it wends its way through the legislative process. Thus, because the majority party will consistently vote for legislation the government proposes, it can act quickly and coherently.

We need to add an important caveat here. If there is no clear majority in parliament, a very different situation arises. As Table 2.7 shows, six parties plus a smaller group of independents split the seats in the French Chamber of Deputies after the 1951 election. The parties held sharply different views, and their leaders disliked one another personally. Not surprisingly, they did not cooperate easily. As a result, every nine months or so, a cabinet would lose a vote of confidence or resign knowing that the next issue it had to deal with would do it in. For historical reasons, which we will discuss in Chapter 5, the premier could not dissolve the chamber and hold new elections. Every nine months or so, a cabinet would lose a vote of confidence or resign and a new majority would have to be cobbled together from the existing **members of parliament**. That new cabinet, in turn, would fall once it had to deal with its first controversial issue, and the negotiations to form a new government would start all over again.

Under such circumstances, parliamentary systems yield anything but an effective government. The Fourth Republic (1946–58) teetered from cabinet crisis to cabinet crisis and failed to meet any of the serious domestic or international challenges it faced. In the end, it lost most of its popular support and collapsed when a war of independence in colonial Algeria threatened to spill over into France itself.

In recent years, however, few parliaments have come close to being this divided. More often than not, elections have produced either a single party with a majority of its own or an enduring **coalition** of parties that are close enough to one another ideologically to stay together for the duration of a parliamentary term as has been the case in Germany or France for most of the last half-century or so. However, ideological fragmentation of this sort bedevils such countries as Israel and India today.

The Rest of the State

Governments today have to deal with highly technical issues that often call for a degree of expertise, which elected politicians rarely have. As a result, two sets of actors not included in Figure 2.2 have come to play pivotal roles in most democracies—high-level civil servants in the **bureaucracy** and leading interest group representatives.

As first discussed by Max Weber (1864–1920), modern civil services are supposed to be the epitome of efficiency.

Recruited and promoted on the basis of merit, bureaucrats are objective, scientific, and expert. Their behavior is governed not by ideology or personal whim, but by rules clearly laid out in law. They are supposed to be civil *servants*, working dispassionately for their political masters in the cabinet, whatever party happens to control it at the moment.

The realities of bureaucratic life are more complicated. In many countries, the civil service is able to attract highly educated and talented people, especially in Japan, Germany, and France, where a disproportionate number of the "best and brightest" begin their careers working for the state.

That said, most bureaucracies have rarely been able to reach the dispassionate and apolitical Weberian ideal. To varying degrees, civil servants have become important policy makers in their own right. However important their expertise may be, the bureaucrats' policy-making role is problematic from a democratic perspective because they are not elected officials and, thus, it is difficult to hold them accountable. That is especially true in countries where the business, bureaucratic, and political elites are so closely related that scholars speak of them as an **iron triangle** (see Figure 2.4).

France and the United States represent the two extremes on this score. Even before the era of the Tea Party, Americans were wary of any close cooperation among such groups. For two years after leaving government service, for example, federal bureaucrats cannot be employed by an organization that lobbies on the issues on which they worked. The doctrine of separation of powers often makes it difficult for members of Congress and their staffs to get information from civil servants. And almost everyone looks askance at close relationships between interest groups and politicians, given long-standing concerns about the possibility of corruption.

In France, cooperation among business executives, politicians, and bureaucrats is the norm. Many ambitious French students decide to start their careers as civil servants by attending one of the prestigious *grandes écoles*, which train them for bureaucratic careers. After as little as ten years in the civil service, some of them leave the government through a process nicknamed *pantouflage*, which literally means putting on soft, cushy slippers. At that point, they either become politicians in one of the major political parties or top corporate executives. In other words, current and former civil servants with similar social backgrounds, educations, and early career paths lead the key governmental and private sector institutions.

Although no single factor can explain all the variation in the ways democratic states act, there is a clear distinction to be made among them along these lines. Those with the most **integrated elite,** like France, Germany, and Japan, were among the most successful economically during the first thirty years after World War II. The countries that have resisted those trends toward interelite cooperation have had the most trouble, at least until the 1990s. Those countries' economic woes and the U.S. resurgence of the 1990s suggest that these trends may not continue. Nonetheless, they are such an important part of democratic political life over the past half-century that they will draw considerable attention in the chapters on individual countries.

The Missing Link: The Courts

Readers in the United States, in particular, may be surprised by the absence of one institution in these pages—the courts. In few countries do the courts have the sweeping powers they do in the United States (i.e., to rule on the constitutionality of laws as well as individual cases).

In the most extreme case, British courts lack any authority to practice constitutional law. This is not so in the other countries to be covered in Part 2. As we will see in Chapter 6, the German Federal Constitutional Court has made a number of important decisions, including on the legal status of a woman's right to abortion. Similarly, its French equivalent has gained power over the last twenty years or so. However, only in the United States are the courts a branch of government coequal with the legislature and the executive.

PUBLIC POLICY

The Interventionist State

Orthodox economic theorists claim that the state should keep its hands off the economy. As they see it, properly functioning markets driven by the balancing effects of supply and demand provide the maximum possible wealth and efficiency at the minimum cost.

It didn't take the current crisis to show us that markets have never worked that well in practice because two critical assumptions in economic theory have rarely been met. First, even the most ardent *laissez-faire* capitalists acknowledge

FIGURE 2.4 Elite Integration: Iron Triangles

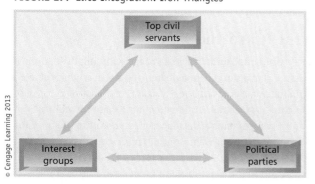

© Cengage Learning 2013

© CHRISTIAN CHARISIUS/Reuters/Corbis.

German parents picking up toys for their children at a government-funded day care center.

Challenges
to the Democratic State

There are no serious challenges to the survival of any of the major liberal democratic states. In the late 1960s and early 1970s, some observers argued that many of them were in trouble in the light of violent protests and terrorist attacks and the economic slump following the Organization of Petroleum Exporting Countries (OPEC) oil embargo. All have managed to weather those and other political storms and, with the end of the Cold War, there are no major international threats to their continued existence, either.

In other words, their regimes are secure. And, as we will see in Parts 3 and 4, the political stakes of political life are relatively low—at least compared to the rest of the world.

There is no such certainty for the rest of the world. ■

that markets cannot effectively provide collective or public goods, such as a clean environment, a national defense system, or a general education. These are services that society as a whole may want, but it is not in any individual's or firm's self-interest to provide them. Second, markets will work at their best only if a number of conditions are met, including competition and the absence of concentrated wealth and power on the part of either capitalists or workers.

To make a long and complicated story short, the social and economic changes spurred by the industrial revolution made it more and more difficult to meet those criteria. A host of problems emerged from pollution in industrial areas to failing firms to widespread poverty. Once it became clear that no one in the private or charitable sectors could handle those problems, people turned to a more **interventionist state.**

Except for the United States, all now offer a variety of social services, including:

- Basic health care and education.
- Subsidized or free education including universities.
- Unemployment compensation.
- Pensions and other programs for seniors.

The rightward drift during the past three decades has led many to question these programs. Britain and the United States, for instance, have passed welfare reform legislation that requires recipients to work or get job training. On balance, however, most of these programs remain extremely popular and have proved hard to cut back. To cite but one example, despite its antigovernment rhetoric, the George W. Bush administration actually increased federal spending above and beyond the cost of the wars against terrorism and in Iraq.

The industrialized democracies all have capitalist economies because most businesses are privately owned. That should not mask the fact that they have been going through their most wrenching transformation since the industrial revolution. The economic center of gravity has shifted away from manufacturing to the tertiary or service sector. Despite the demise of so many dot-com enterprises in the early 2000s, the computer and information technology industries in general are increasingly at the heart of postindustrial society. As they have grown, millions of jobs in the automobile, textiles, and other heavy industries have been lost to either automation or the Global South. The current recession suggests that those trends will continue.

This transition is part of the globalization of economic activity. Observers debate just how quickly and extensively globalization is occurring. But a quick glance at the products in the room you are sitting in will tell you that we increasingly buy products and consume services that originate in countries all around the world. Because so much of what we use is imported and exported, and because so many of the companies that make those products are multinational and can move their operations as market conditions warrant, no government is as able—as it was a generation ago—to enact and implement its economic policies.

We will see this most clearly in Chapter 7 when we consider the European Union (EU), which is by far the world's most powerful international organization. With the introduction of the euro as a full-fledged currency in 2002, the EU has taken on even more of the trappings of a state and is probably more influential than any of its member governments in making economic policy. At the domestic level, most governments have adopted more conservative, pro-market policies in recent years. The collapse of communism in Eastern Europe, and the consensus that Social Democrats in Europe and liberals in the United States enjoyed little success in eliminating poverty, has given "antistate" forces more clout. In particular, governments have **privatized** much of the publicly owned sector, which, in some cases, amounted to as much as 20 percent of total production at the height of what the British call the collectivist years.

Foreign Policy

Important changes have been occurring in foreign policy as well. Events since the terrorist attacks on 9/11 have had a huge but differing influence on democratic states. That said,

many of the changes began far earlier and may prove to have an even more lasting impact.

During the Cold War, most leaders in the industrialized democracies followed the lead of the United States in foreign policy. But there was one key exception to that rule. During de Gaulle's presidency (1958–69), France charted a more independent course as part of his desire to restore France's grandeur and again make it one of the world's great powers. He removed French troops from North Atlantic Treaty Organization (NATO) command, created the French nuclear arsenal, tried to serve as a broker between the superpowers, and defended what he saw as the rights of new states in the Global South. De Gaulle's successors have echoed some of his nationalist themes, but rhetoric aside, they have been far closer to the United States despite the two countries' disagreement over Iraq.

The end of the Cold War changed things to some degree. The United States is now the world's only superpower whose military might dwarfs that of its allies—and everybody else. Nonetheless, the "political space" has changed enough that it is now easier for any of the industrialized democracies to criticize and even reject Washington's initiatives on what it sees as issues of national security.

In short, however, the other industrialized democracies now chart a more autonomous course. Again, the EU, which represents all of its member states in negotiating international economic agreements, is our best example. The EU and the United States have disagreed on a number of issues, including trade in agricultural products (e.g., genetically modified food), and environmental policy, (e.g., most notably over whether the Kyoto Treaty limiting greenhouse gas emissions should be ratified).

Events following the terrorist 9/11 attacks introduced new divisions. Virtually all the democracies supported American actions during the first stages of the war against terrorism in Afghanistan. Soon thereafter, disagreements began to appear, starting with widespread opposition to the detention of prisoners at the U.S. naval base at Guantanamo Bay in Cuba. More important, France and Germany vocally opposed, and joined Russia and China to deny, American hopes to gain United Nations (UN) approval for its 2003 invasion of Iraq.

How the future of Iraq and other international crises will affect the democracies is anybody's guess. At least one thing is clear, however: Foreign policy can no longer be excluded from the study of comparative politics, as it has been for most of the field's history. What happens outside a country's borders and how it, in turn, responds to those events, are simply too important for us to ignore. Foreign policy remains the focus of another part of political science—international relations. But with events like 9/11 and broader, long-term trends such as globalization, international relations in

Economic Liberalization
in the Industrialized Democracies

Great Britain has led the way in privatizing state-owned industries. France and Germany have loosened their macro- and microeconomic coordination procedures to a lesser degree. Everywhere, tariffs and other barriers to international trade have been lowered, if not eliminated.

That said, do not assume that the free market now reigns. States and the European Union for its members remain the most powerful economic factors in all the industrialized democracies. Great Britain, for instance, still heavily regulates the privatized industries. The, albeit, weakened iron triangles of France and Japan shock most American economists. In addition, most provisions of the welfare state remain in place despite some changes in the way services are provided. ■

Globalization and the Industrialized Democracies

The liberal democracies are the strongest states in the world—especially the larger ones we will discuss in the chapters in Part 2. In this sense, the figure on the inside front cover could well have been drawn with arrows "out" from them to reflect the way that they can shape global forces, especially on geopolitical or military issues. But these countries are still affected by global forces in at least three key respects.

First, their strengths are as much a function of their wealth and the clout wielded by their corporations as of their states. Second, despite that strength international forces limit their ability to set and, even more so, implement economic policy. This is especially true for the twenty seven members of the European Union, which is increasingly responsible for their economic policies. Third because of their location and the consumption that accompanies their wealth, they are among the countries that contribute the most to environmental decay. ■

general, and foreign policy in particular, have "forced their way" onto the agenda of comparative politics.

THE MEDIA

Although the term never appeared in the classic texts, the media have always been a key feature of democratic reality. Given their importance, it is surprising to see how little research has been done on them by political scientists. Nonetheless, it does seem safe to reach two conclusions.

First, for some people, it is getting even easier, and yet more confusing, to find out about politics at home and abroad. The telecommunications revolution has brought the world's news to our homes and has done so instantaneously. Though some argue that the television networks, and even venerable newspapers such as the *New York Times* or the *Times* of London, have "dumbed down" and are nowhere near as informative as they used to be. Nonetheless, people who are interested now have access

to far more information. Cable news networks are on air twenty-four hours a day. You can buy the *New York Times* almost anyplace in the United States. In the blogosphere, and sites such as YouTube provide huge amounts of information (the accuracy of which is, however, all but impossible to verify).

Second, average citizens view the world in their own terms, which may be quite different from those of either the politicians or media moguls. At this point, one of those terms seems to be disinterest in what happens outside of their own country or region. It is no accident that American television news executives run longer local news programs than national newscasts and include less and less international news on their evening broadcasts. More and more people are tuning the political world out altogether. To some degree, this reflects what many feel is the cynical coverage by the media themselves, which has turned off millions. It may also, in part, be the result of the fact that, with the cable and satellite revolution, we can now watch reruns of *American Idol*, a soccer game from Spain, or the *Jerry Springer Show* instead of the news. But, most of all, the declining interest in politics has less to do with the media than with the general cynicism about and skepticism toward politics and politicians.

CONCLUSION: THE WORST FORM OF GOVERNMENT EXCEPT FOR ALL THE OTHERS?

Given what we have seen, it is hard not to agree with the first half of Winston Churchill's statement that begins this chapter. The industrialized democracies have obviously accomplished a lot; just as obviously, they face serious problems, some of which—for the moment—seem to be insurmountable.

The second half of the statement may be true as well, though you will have to take it as a leap of faith until you learn more about the countries covered in Parts 3 and 4. From that perspective, however serious democracy's problems may be, they pale in comparison with those in the rest of the world.

In uneven and imperfect ways, democratic regimes achieve a series of balances better than any other type of government, at least over the long haul:

- Between the governors and the governed.
- Between the political world and the rest of society.
- Between unbridled capitalism and the interests of those who do not benefit (much) from it.
- Between personal freedoms and the need to maintain order and forge coherent public policy.

Key Terms

Concepts

bureaucracy
cabinet responsibility
civic culture
civil society
cleavage
coalition
democracy
electoral system
integrated elite
interventionist state
iron triangle
laissez-faire
left
legitimacy
liberal
members of parliament (MPs)
nationalization
postindustrial society
postmaterialist
privatized
proportional representation

radical
realignment
regimes
right
rule of law
single-member district
suffrage
vote of confidence

People

Hobbes, Thomas
Locke, John

Organizations, Places, and Events

catch-all parties
Christian Democratic parties
Communist parties
fascism
Greens
Liberal parties
Social Democratic parties

Useful Websites

There are not all that many websites that deal with democracy *per se.* That's partly because theorists do not use the Internet as comparativists do. It's also because few comparativists study all democracies as a whole. Nonetheless, there are a few sites that can help sharpen your understanding of the ideas behind and the realities of democracy today.

The U.S. State Department has an excellent site that explores many of the issues raised in this chapter. Political Resources is a wonderful source for material on individual countries, whereas Election World has the most recent election results from every country in the world.

www.democ.uci.edu/resources/guide.php

www.ned.org

www.state.gov/documents/organization/55989.pdf

www.politicalresources.net

www.en.wikipedia.org/wiki/User:Electionworld/Electionworld

Further Reading

Almond, Gabriel, and Sidney Verba. *The Civic Culture.* Princeton, NJ: Princeton University Press, 1962; and Almond and Verba, eds. *The Civic Culture Revisited.* Boston: Little, Brown, 1979. The two best books on civic culture. They do, however, probably take the argument about the importance of culture a bit too far.

Barber, Benjamin. *Strong Democracy: Participatory Politics for a New Age.* Berkeley: University of California Press, 1984. A theoretical look at how to enhance participation to enhance democracy.

Dahl, Robert. *On Democracy.* New Haven, CT: Yale University Press, 1999. The most recent book by a scholar who has been studying what makes democracy "work" since the 1950s.

Dahl, Robert, Ian Shapiro, and Jose Antonio Cheibub. *The Democracy Sourcebook.* Cambridge: MIT Press, 2003. A dense book of excerpts from classic and contemporary ideas on democracy.

Fukuyama, Francis. *Trust: The Social Virtues and the Creation of Prosperity.* New York: Free Press, 1995. This book does a good job of reinforcing the importance of culture, political and otherwise. By one of the most controversial and conservative analysts of the day, though many observers find his works overstated.

Macpherson, C. B. *The Life and Times of Liberal Democracy.* New York: Oxford University Press, 1977. Like Dahl's work, a classic analysis of the way democracies work, though written from a more left-wing and democratic perspective.

Norris, Pippa, ed. *Critical Citizens: Global Support for Democratic Governance.* New York: Oxford University Press, 1999. An excellent collection of articles on the degree to which support for the regime holds in a number of democracies.

Putnam, Robert D. *Making Democracy Work.* Princeton, NJ: Princeton University Press, 1993. Ostensibly only about Italy, a controversial book that provides the best recent analysis of the role of "social capital" and political culture in general.

Reid, T. R. *The Healing of America.* New York: Penguin, 2009. A sweeping book on the politics of health care, which may itself become the most sweeping issue facing all of these countries.

Tilly, Charles. *Democracy.* New York: Cambridge University Press, 2007. A masterful compendium of almost fifty years of his writing in the field, writing that stretches back to topics almost one thousand years ago.

Zakaria, Fareed. *The Future of Freedom.* New York: W.W. Norton, 2003. A thoughtful book about liberal, as well as what he calls illiberal, democracies. Worth considering for most of the countries covered in the rest of the book.

Chicago

New York

Washington, D.C.

Los Angeles

3

The United States

Perhaps the most striking feature of the recent political history of the United States is the stability of its basic institutions despite the stress of assassinations, war, racial strife, political scandal, and economic disaffection.

ALAN ABRAMOWITZ

THE BASICS

The United States

Size	9,158,960 sq. km
Population	310 million
GNP per capita	$47,400
Ethnic composition	77.1% White, 12.9% Black, 4.2% Asian, 1.5% American Indian, 4.3% other. (Note: The United States does not keep separate statistics on Hispanic Americans, who can be of any race.)
Life expectancy	78
Religion	56% Protestant, 28% Roman Catholic, 2% Jewish, 4% other, 10% none
Capital	Washington, D.C.
Head of State	President Barack Obama (2009–)

WHAT A DIFFERENCE TWO YEARS MAKE

Senator Barack Obama swept to victory in 2008 for many reasons, which political scientists have yet to fully disentangle. One of them certainly was the recession, which seemed to get worse every day during the election campaign.

But halfway through his term, the once very popular president is in trouble. We will not even try to predict whether he will be reelected in 2012. However, it is clear that he gets much of the blame for the economic difficulties he inherited and which then got worse under his watch.

That "blame" has fueled the most intense conflict in American life since the civil rights movement and the Vietnam War. In that sense, the 2010 midterm election truly was a watershed. Not only did it give Republicans a substantial majority in the House, but it gave new momentum to the **Tea Party** movement, which wants dramatic cuts to the size of the budget. Many of the new Republican office holders have close ties to the many organizations that claim to be part of it. The newly emboldened Republicans nearly forced a government shutdown in early 2011 and threatened to do so again that summer upon a vote to raise the debt ceiling.

The Republicans only led one house of Congress, but they were clearly in the ascendant, especially given

Looking BACKWARD

GIVEN WHAT WE argued in the last chapter, our task here is simple. Make the case that the United States is unusual, if not unique. Until recently, few comparative politics books included a chapter on the United States. However, realizing that most of our readers would be Americans and that they would use the United States as a frame of reference made it clear that we had to add at least a brief chapter on the United States to dispel the notion that the country is in any way typical of the industrialized democracies.

In fact, as we will see in this chapter, the United States and the other established democracies have little in common politically. Of course, most democracies are affluent. But, politically, the United States is not part of the mainstream because of its presidential system which is, frankly, why this chapter is needed.

Covering the United States is all the more important in other countries, even Canada. Even though Melissa's students watch American television and most live within 75 miles of the U.S. border, they do not all understand American politics (or its culture) as well as they should.

In short, another reason for this chapter. Readers from outside the United States, too, tend to use the USA as a frame of reference and not always in a positive way.

the number of open—and vulnerable—Senate seats, now held by Democrats, that will be contested in 2012. Obama could well be reelected given the weakness of the likely Republican contenders. That said, divided government could become the norm again in the United States. And, especially for American readers, that almost never happens in other established democracies.

It also should be pointed out, from the beginning, that the United States falls short of other democracies on most indicators of equity, if not overall wealth and growth. Charles Blow published a remarkable article on the op-ed page of The *New York Times* on February, 19, 2011 in which

he showed that the United States ranked dead last on most indicators of well-being. It is the only major democracy that does not ensure health coverage for all, and the 2010 law that expands health coverage could well be overturned by the Supreme Court. The United States has the largest number of people in prison, and its distribution of wealth and income is among the worst in the democratic world.

We grew up in privileged homes. Melissa lived in one of the more prestigious Boston suburbs. Chip grew up in a small city but went to its best schools. Our parents could afford to send us to the best colleges—at least the best we could get into. And, we live comfortable lives today.

AP Photo/Scott Sady.

Sarah Palin on the campaign trail in 2010.

© iStockphoto.com/ contour99

But that is not the whole picture of the American political economy. The urban areas of New England where we studied and taught are for the most part an economic nightmare. Chip's home town has been especially hard hit. It lost a third of its population during the last decade, and a large number of its former businesses are shuttered.

For our purposes, however, it actually makes more sense to consider the plight of two cities in the so-called Rust Belt in the industrial Midwest—Flint, Michigan, and Youngstown, Ohio—which are in even worse shape.

Flint is the hometown of General Motors (GM), which emerged from bankruptcy in 2010 and is now making record profits, although you will not see evidence of that in Flint. Located about sixty miles northwest of Detroit, Flint used to be a boom town with 200,000 residents, most of whom worked in and around the automobile industry. By 2000, it was down to 120,000 residents and may dip below 100,000 when the 2010 census is published. Whatever happens to GM, there is and will be little left of the automobile business in Flint. A quarter of its residents are below the poverty line. The unemployment rate is almost twice the national average. Today, Flint is best known for producing star collegiate basketball players rather than cars.

Youngstown was one of the most important steel-producing cities in the United States. The American steel industry collapsed in the 1970s and Youngstown has been in trouble ever since. It is located halfway between Pittsburgh and Cleveland, themselves economically troubled cities. Like Flint, Youngstown's population is declining.

An ever-increasing proportion of its residents are below the poverty line. It has a majority minority population.

Although Youngstown used to be a steel city, it also shares GM with Flint. Just outside of the city is the Lordstown GM Assembly Plant. Opened with great fanfare in 1966 (and with great hopes for new jobs for steel workers), Lordstown was to be a model of in manufacturing efficiency and labor management relations.[1] The plant sits just off the Ohio Turnpike, which Chip drives at least twice a year to attend alumni council functions at Oberlin College. Each year, there are fewer employee cars in the parking lot and fewer new cars coming off the assembly line waiting to be shipped. There have been rumors about shutting Lordstown for years. Some of the models put together there are now made in Mexico.

Youngstown and Flint are part of the reason Obama won the 2008 election. Michigan normally votes democratic. Ohio, however, is a swing state. In fact, the high turnout of Evangelical Christians there in 2004 clinched George W. Bush's second term. The recession, however, turned Ohio into a democratic state four years later. Blaming Obama for its woes, the Republicans swept back to power in the state in 2010.

The goal of this chapter is not to explore Flint or Youngstown or Obama, *per se*, but to explore what political scientists and historians call **American exceptionalism.** As you are about to see, politics in the United States is both

---

[1]For a more skeptical view, see Stanley Aronowitz. *False Promises.* (New York: McGraw Hill, 1973).

important and unusual. You need to understand it from both perspectives.

THINKING ABOUT
THE UNITED STATES

There is nothing wrong with using the United States as a frame of reference if you keep one thing in mind: Political life in the United States is by no means the norm. In other words, to use the United States effectively as a frame of reference, you need first to take into account the ways in which it is different from other countries.

The Wrong Name

We have already misused the word *American* several times and will do so again in this box. It is a shorthand term used to describe the United States and its people. We should not do so because Canadians, Mexicans, Brazilians, Peruvians, and more are Americans, too.

Alas, our version of English has evolved in such a way that it is the only viable term we have to describe ourselves.

This chapter is designed to meet the needs of American and non-American readers. It is not as detailed as the chapters on other countries that follow. Because we assume that even non-American readers are reasonably familiar with the basics of American political life, our goal is to highlight the features that make American politics unusual, many of which would not be stressed in a course or a book that focuses on the United States alone.

To start with, the United States has a **federal** system, in which the national government shares power with states, cities, counties, and other jurisdictions. For example, states are responsible for determining how elections are held and votes counted. Washington, D.C., only gets involved in setting some basic parameters, such as the requirement that presidential and congressional elections have to be held on the first Tuesday after the first Monday in November or ensuring that voting rights and other laws are upheld.

Other countries, including Germany and Canada, also have federal systems, but by most accounts, the United States gives its states and other local governments more power than you will find in other countries—something we are seeing in fights over budgets in Wisconsin and beyond.

At the national level, the United States has a strong system of **checks and balances,** formally known as the **separation of powers.** The legislative, executive, and judicial branches all have unique powers, but it is hard for any of them to act on its own without oversight and approval from at least one of the others. However, that did happen in 2000, in Florida because the Supreme Court did not have to consult either the White House or Congress before issuing its decision that gave George W. Bush the presidency. On most policy matters, however, at least two of the three branches must reach an agreement before action can be taken.

That is one of the reasons most comparativists argue that the United States has a weak state. That statement might seem absurd at first glance. After all, the United States is the world's only superpower. However, the founders created a system that required politicians to **compromise** on almost every issue. That makes it hard for them to act in a rapid and decisive manner to enact coherent policies that systematically address pressing social and economic issues.

In addition, the United States has had an unusual history that spawned a distinctive political culture. In comparative terms, political change occurred gradually and incrementally, leaving it with widespread acceptance of the political "rules of the game." To be sure, the United States has had its share of protest, including many over the Obama administration's agenda. But when compared with the rest of the world, and even most of the other stable democracies, the United States rests on a bedrock of political stability at the regime level that is unmatched almost anywhere in the rest of the world.

We saw that most clearly in the early morning hours of November 8, 2000. The presidential election between Vice President Al Gore and Texas Governor Bush had gone down to the wire. Whoever won Florida would win the Electoral College and the White House. The exit polls and early results kept going back and forth. Little did we know that uncertainties about the way the election was conducted and the votes counted would last more than a month and reach the Supreme Court. Yet, when NBC signed off at 3:30 A.M. on election night, then-anchor Tom Brokaw was able to broadcast a picture of the calm streets of Washington, D.C., and say, "After months of bitter campaigning and a long night of partisan rhetoric, Americans can go to sleep comfortably because unlike other countries, we hold our elections with no need for the police to keep order on the streets."

On a more ambiguous front, the United States shares at least two characteristics with the other industrialized democracies. The first is a decline in civic engagement, not just in politics but in churches, community organizations, interest groups, and all the other bodies that make up **civil society**—and which, Harvard's Robert Putnam argues, are critical for a vibrant democracy.[2] The decline in such

---

[2]Robert D. Putnam, *Bowling Alone: The Collapse and Revival of American Community* (New York: Simon & Schuster, 2000).

A bleary-eyed ballot counter in Broward County trying to determine how someone has voted.

Alan Diaz/AP Photo.

Key Concepts in America Politics

The United States is unusual among established democracies in many ways.

First and foremost is its use of a presidential system with the separation and division of power. But also remember that it has had one of the least conflict-ridden histories of any democracy, which may be one of the main reasons why political scientists decided to label change in the United States as incremental. Finally, it has one of the least activist states of any democracy, which, among other things, has 45 million or more of its citizens without health care coverage until the new law goes into effect.

THE MAKING OF THE AMERICAN STATE

American exceptionalism begins with the evolution of its state. The United States was able to handle the major transitions discussed in the previous chapter with *relative* ease, although it has also faced its share of challenges, not all of which it met easily. Compared with those other countries, however, it has faced relatively few divisive issues and has been able to resolve most of those that did arise in ways that enhanced support for the regime, at least in the long run. Also, in comparative terms, the United States has been largely free of outside constraints (**www.americanhistory.about.com**).

Not everything has come smoothly. "Manifest destiny," or the expansion of the United States from coast to coast, occurred at the expense of the Native American population. North fought South in a civil war that was as bloody as any conflict up to that point. Industrialization was wrenching, too, especially because it required waves of immigrants, who ended up living in slums and working in sweatshops.

Nonetheless, compared to most countries, the United States was fortunate, which is why the word *relative* is emphasized in the first sentence of this section. Only Britain established democratic institutions as smoothly, but that country was left with far more class conflict. No other regime enjoyed the wealth, power, and political support that allowed the United States to become the world's first superpower after World War II (see Table 3.1).

By the early nineteenth century, rough agreement had been reached on the structure of the federal government and the separation of church and state. That consensus had its limits. The emerging democratic institutions did not allow women or African Americans other than a handful of freed slaves in the North to vote. Moreover, the very

involvement has probably not been as great in other countries as it has been in the United States. Most, too, have not suffered through the same kind of "culture wars" that this country has. Nonetheless, there has been some decrease in trust in politicians and in political involvement in all the industrialized democracies.

By contrast, the dissatisfaction only goes so far. Chapter 1 drew the distinction between the government and the regime. In the United States and the other industrialized democracies, virtually everyone agrees that it is perfectly legitimate for citizens to criticize incumbent politicians and their policies. However, there is such widespread acceptance of the regime that the Constitution and the institutions it created are almost never criticized. In Parts 3 and 4, you will see that one of the main differences between the industrialized democracies and the rest of the world is this powerful acceptance of regimes in the former, the absence of which dramatically raises the political stakes in most of the former communist and Global South countries.

TABLE 3.1 Key Turning Points in American History

YEAR	EVENT
1781	Victory over the British in the Revolutionary War
1787	Constitutional Convention
1861–65	Civil War
1890	Passage of first Antitrust Act
1917	Entrance into World War I
1933	Beginning of the New Deal
1941	Entrance into World War II
1945	End of World War II; start of Cold War
1964	Start of the Great Society
1974	Resignation of Richard Nixon
1980	Election of Ronald Reagan
2000	Election of George W. Bush
2008	Election of Barack Obama

existence of the republic was put in jeopardy by the Civil War, which, we often forget, the Confederacy nearly won. However, in a way, even the Civil War underscores the main point of this section. The states that seceded did not object to the type of government that had then been in existence for almost three quarters of a century. Indeed, the one they created was more like the one they left than any other state in the world at the time.

The Constitutional Order

The most important event in the creation of what Seymour Martin Lipset once called the first new nation was the adoption of the Constitution in 1787 (**www.archives. gov/exhibits/charters/constitution.html**). Events before then certainly were important. However, given this chapter's goal of providing a frame of reference, the critical starting point is the widespread acceptance of that document, which continues to shape American political institutions and culture to this day.

Before the Constitution was adopted, the new United States was in trouble. In the years after the Declaration of Independence was signed, the new country used the Articles of Confederation, which vested almost all power in the states. That should not be surprising because the thirteen colonies had staked their claim to independence on what they saw as the unjust, centralized, and arbitrary rule by King George III's England.

Quickly, however, under the Articles the new country had to deal with problems that threatened to tear it apart. States imposed tariffs on each other that all but brought interstate trade to a halt. In every state, rural and urban interests—or *factions*, as they were known—clashed, often violently.

By 1787, the state legislatures recognized that the situation had gotten out of control and sent representatives to Philadelphia to amend the Articles of Confederation. Perhaps to their own surprise, the delegates soon concluded that they could not solve the new country's problems by amending them and determined to create a new form of government altogether. They then found themselves grappling with two goals that, according to the conventional wisdom of the time, were incompatible: centralizing power to overcome squabbling and incompetent state governments, and continuing to protect against the arbitrary exercise of power. By the end of the summer, however, they had reached a series of momentous compromises and had written the Constitution. To help persuade the states to ratify the Constitution, James Madison, Alexander Hamilton, and John Jay wrote a defense of the document in the now-famous *Federalist Papers* (**www.yale.edu/lawweb/ avalon/federal/fed.htm**). Along with the diaries Madison kept during that long, hot summer and the Constitution itself, the *Federalist Papers* provide the key principles that remain at the heart of American politics to this day.

Of particular importance was the founders' novel approach to what Madison called "the evils of faction" in Federalist #10. He asserted that there was no way to avoid factions, as most democratic theorists of the time had hoped. From his perspective, they were a natural and inevitable outgrowth of an open society. The evils arose only in small units in which one group could dominate, leading to what Alexis de Tocqueville would call the "tyranny of the majority" a half-century later.

Therefore, the best thinking in either Madison or Tocqueville's day was to concentrate power in larger jurisdictions such as the national government. That way, there would be little chance that any single faction could dominate the entire system, but it would also create incentives for the smaller ones to compromise with each other.

To make that happen, the founders created institutions that are radically different from those used in all other industrialized democracies. They rejected a version of the parliamentary system, in which the legislature and executive are fused.

The American presidential system was designed to work in almost exactly the opposite manner. The founders understood that the United States would need a stronger central government to control the evils of faction. However, they were also convinced that they had to find ways to make it as difficult as possible for the people who ran the new state to abuse that power. In what is often seen as a stroke of political genius, they set out to make compromise and incremental change the normal method of policy making, through what we informally call the system of checks and balances.

Shortly after the Constitution was ratified, Congress and the states adopted the first ten amendments, the Bill of

Rights, which gave legal standing to basic civil liberties and clarified some of the ambiguities in the relationship between the state and federal governments. For our purposes, the most important were the initial sixteen words of the first amendment: "Congress shall make no law respecting an establishment of religion, or prohibiting the free exercise thereof." Prior to independence, most states had official or established churches. Massachusetts and Connecticut were Puritan, Pennsylvania was Quaker, Maryland was Catholic, and most of the South was Episcopalian. There was, thus, no way to establish a single faith as the official one nationwide. As a result, the framers decided to remove religion from formal political life, all the while guaranteeing "the free exercise thereof." The separation was never complete. Children routinely prayed in schools as recently as the 1960s. President Bush's Faith-Based Initiative, sent to Congress during his first year in office, was one of the most controversial bills of his administration. Nonetheless, disputes over the relationship between church and state have never had any real chance of undermining the regime created by the framers of the Constitution more than two hundred years ago.

Democratization
in the United States

Unlike many of the other countries we will consider, the United States did not consciously engage in democratization. In fact, most of the founders had serious doubts about democracy and the capacity of average people to make intelligent decisions about public life.

Democracy grew as part and parcel of the evolution and conflicts of American political history. To cite but one example of how difficult this transition toward democracy was, the Declaration of Independence included the statement that "all men are created equal."

Then, alas, all men did not include African Americans and poor white men, who did not have the right to vote or most other political freedoms. It would be a century and a half before "all men" came to include women and another half-century before the last racial barriers to formal political participation were removed.

And if you listen to some activists for women's, minorities, or gay-lesbian-bisexual-transsexual-queer groups, we still have a way to go. ■

Since the Founders

Even more unusual and remarkable than these ideas themselves is the fact that they continue to be the dominant ones in American political life more than two centuries later. A brief examination of some historical trends that have shaped both the continuity of, and changes in, the American system reveals that staying power.

The biggest crisis the United States has ever faced was the Civil War. After decades of grudging compromise over slavery and related issues, the Southern states no longer felt they could stay in the Union and seceded. For four years, "brother killed brother" in a war that ended with the defeat of the Confederacy and the assassination of President Abraham Lincoln.

For our purposes, it is even more important to see how the country rebuilt itself after the war. At first, the North imposed a coercive regime to "reconstruct" the defeated South. Yet, within a decade, the former Confederate states had been readmitted to the Union. Surprisingly, rather than bearing Washington the resentment many expected, white Southerners became the most patriotic and conservative segment of the population.

In the second half of the nineteenth century, in the rapidly growing cities of the North, the industrial revolution created tremendous concentrations of wealth along with a host of problems including factories and slums. With these new developments came the first significant demands for an activist or interventionist state. But even here, the American approach was unusual. Rather than enacting extensive welfare programs or taking over industries, the United States passed a series of antitrust laws designed to break up monopolies and oligopolies. The goal then—and now—was to use government as a last resort and to emphasize the preservation of competitive markets with minimal government intervention. For good or ill, that sentiment returned to center stage under the George W. Bush administration and contributed heavily to the crisis the U.S. faces today.

Much the same can be said for policies toward the poor. The United States did adopt extensive social service and welfare programs as part of Franklin Roosevelt's New Deal during the Great Depression and as part of Lyndon Johnson's Great Society in the 1960s. Whatever we may think of those programs today, they did mark a dramatic expansion of the American state at both the national and local levels. That should not keep us from seeing that these programs, however, have always been less extensive than those offered by almost all other liberal democracies and have been viewed with more skepticism by the American public than those elsewhere.

Perhaps most important of all, the United States never developed a powerful socialist party. Eugene Victor Debs did win almost a million votes in the 1912 and 1920 presidential

Economic Liberalization
in the United States

The United States has not had to adopt reforms as sweeping as those of the other countries we will be covering to liberalize the economy, because it did not institute as many, or as extensive, interventionist policies in the first place. Economic liberalism and "free market" capitalism developed hand-in-hand with many of the ideas the founders drew on during the Revolutionary War and the period of Constitution building that followed. Support for the idea that "the government that governs least governs best" has been part of American political culture from the beginning, and most Americans have turned to a more active state only when other approaches to solving problems failed. And, when Americans have done so, they have kept ideas akin to "curing the evils of faction" in mind, and created programs to safeguard against anyone amassing too much power—as shown in the penchant for antitrust and other antimonopoly legislation. This does not mean that the United States has a small state. It has grown dramatically, especially since the 1930s. However, Americans have always been reluctant to turn to the state and have been loath to give it the power to act quickly or coherently when establishing new public policies. That said, critics of the George W. Bush administration, in particular, worried that its close links to major corporations in energy, telecommunications, and other industries brought the state and private sector dangerously close to each other. ■

than one finds in any other major country, with the possible exception of Great Britain. Were the founders to rise from their graves today, they would find plenty of surprising and confusing things: television, public opinion polls, tight security at all federal buildings, and more. Yet, their basic institutions and principles, especially the separation and division of powers, remain intact and operate in ways they would easily recognize—and endorse.

THE AMERICAN PEOPLE AND POLITICS

Those historical patterns are reflected in how American citizens think and act today. However, as the global and domestic issues in the bottom row of Table 1.2 have come to play a more prominent role, there have recently been some important changes that have both increased pressures "from below" and led to declining support for politicians and some political institutions—but not the regime itself.

The American Political Culture

The echoes of that unusual past are most evident in the American political culture. Systematic research on public opinion only began in the late 1940s. Still, scholars are convinced that at least three trends in the American political culture can be traced back to the nineteenth century and the origins of the weak state.

First, with the exception of the years just before the Civil War, no more than a tiny minority of Americans has questioned the regime based on the Constitution of 1787. Americans do debate issues such as gay marriage or the war in Afghanistan as heatedly as anyone. Even before the spectacular rise of the Tea Party, distrust of politicians reached alarming levels. Yet it is political suicide to advocate rewriting the Constitution, something the French have done eleven times since the 1780s.

Second, almost all Americans accept the idea of a weak state, even those who would like to see it enact dramatic new programs such as the health care reforms passed in that began to go into effect in 2010.

Third, **individualism** remains one of Americans' most widely held beliefs. Whatever the real chances of upward mobility might be, most Americans still think anyone can "make it" through hard work. More so, too, than most Europeans, Americans are convinced that if someone "fails" it is his or her fault. Therefore, there is little need for the government to step in with extensive social service programs even though, as David Shipler has recently argued, there are 35 million people in the United States who are in poverty despite working on a regular basis.

The net impact of this has been the paradoxical nature of what Gabriel Almond and Sidney Verba called

elections. In the latter year, he campaigned from prison. Other socialists have won elections to a handful of local offices. Currently, Senator Bernard Sanders came to prominence as the self-proclaimed socialist mayor of Burlington, Vermont—he now runs as an independent. Communists gained a toehold in some parts of the labor union movement during the 1930s. However, in comparative terms, the industrial revolution did not produce the kind of divisions it did in Europe, most notably because of the way the American political culture evolved, the topic we turn to next.

Finally, despite the many twists and turns of American political life, there is far more continuity in the United States

TABLE 3.2 Declining Trust in the United States

Question: How much of the time do you think you can trust the government in Washington to do what is right: just about always, most of the time, or only some of the time?

YEAR	"ALL OR MOST OF THE TIME" (%)	"SOME OF THE TIME" (%)
1964	76	22
1968	61	36
1972	53	45
1976	33	63
1980	25	73
1984	46	51
1988	44	54
1992	23	75
1996	25	71
2000	40	59
2001	64	35
2002	46	52
2006	32	64

Source: Adapted from Steffen W. Schmidt, Mack C. Shelly, and Barbara A. Bardes, *American Government Today* (Belmont, CA: Wadsworth, 2008), 211.

a **civic culture.**[3] Polls conducted since their research was completed in the late 1950s have shown that Americans are more convinced than their European or Japanese counterparts that they could do something about a government action they objected to. Yet, even though plenty of avenues for political involvement exist, few Americans actually bother to become activists. Another team of scholars who wrote in the 1950s called this state of affairs "functional apathy" because it meant that average citizens put few pressures on their leaders, allowing them more leeway to govern than did their equivalents in France or Italy.

The political difficulties of recent decades have taken their toll on the American political culture. According to every indicator, faith in politicians and involvement in social and political life have declined dramatically. However, as Alan Abramowitz suggests in the statement that begins this chapter, that dissatisfaction has not led people to begin questioning the regime under which they live (see Table 3.2).

Parties and Elections

As in most democracies, the most common form of political participation in the United States is voting in the most important national elections: those for the presidency and Congress. And, as is the case of most of the issues covered

in this chapter, Americans act quite differently from their counterparts elsewhere.

Many American political scientists think the United States needs a two-party system to ensure that the government functions smoothly, even though none of the other democratic countries we will be covering in Part 2 have ever had as few as two parties. Whatever the link between the number of parties and the process of government, no other democracy has seen such continuity in its party system.

Americans are also unusual in their commitment to a **two-party system** (www.rnc.org and www.democrats.org). Only two parties have seriously contended for power since the end of the Civil War. There have been several challenges to the hegemony of the Democrats and Republicans, the most recent of which was launched by maverick millionaire H. Ross Perot in 1992 and 1996. Ralph Nader had a significant impact in 2000, probably denying Al Gore the presidency. Nonetheless, he was never a serious contender to win the election himself. Although the United States has had the same two dominant parties since before the Civil War, the Democrats and Republicans, it is important to understand that each of them has changed in many ways and at many times since the 1850s.

The **Democratic** Party is slightly older than the Republican Party with a history dating from the 1830s. More often than not, it has tried to present itself as the party that better represents the "little man," beginning from its support for universal suffrage in the nineteenth century, to its endorsement of the New Deal and Great Society reforms of the twentieth century, to its advocacy of women's and, to a lesser degree, gay rights in the last generation. The Democrats are more likely to propose expansion of social service programs and tax rates that tend to demand more of wealthier Americans.

The Democrats have not always been the more progressive or left-wing of the two parties. Most of the progressives of the late nineteenth and early twentieth centuries were Republicans. At that time, the base of Democratic support lay in the largely nonideological and corrupt urban machines that mobilized immigrant voters and the white, segregationist electorate of the "solid South." The New Deal and Great Society reforms of the 1930s and the 1960s changed all that. Now as many as 90 percent of African American voters routinely cast their ballots for Democratic candidates. In addition, as we will see, white Southerners, workers, and men disproportionately support the Republican Party.

The **Republicans** were created when a number of parties that opposed slavery and secession came together in the late 1850s. The first national election it contested under that name was in 1860 and brought Abraham Lincoln to power and served as the catalyst for the outbreak of the Civil War. When the war ended, Republican

---

[3]Gabriel Almond and Sidney Verba, *The Civic Culture: Political Attitudes and Democracy in Five Nations* (Princeton, NJ: Princeton University Press, 1963). Also see their *The Civic Culture Revisited* (Boston: Little, Brown, 1979).

Justin Sullivan/Getty Images.

"carpetbagger" administrations were set up in the occupied Confederate states, which went through a difficult period of Reconstruction. Those administrations won in large part because freed slaves voted for them. Most of the white voters became loyal Democrats in opposition to Reconstruction. Within a generation, almost all African Americans had lost the vote with the passage of the "Jim Crow" laws establishing segregation in the South, where almost all blacks lived at the time.

The shifts after 1865 restored the party's traditional base of support among upper and middle-class Protestants in the northern half of the country. More often than not, that meant that Republicans supported business interests. At times, however, the elite would support reform as it did in the early twentieth century by pushing for the "good government" policies of the progressive era, including the use of primary and recall elections, a merit-based civil service system, and non-partisan local government.

The Great Depression cemented the party's position on the Right. Because a Republican, Herbert Hoover, was president when the Depression broke out and he did little to improve the state of the economy, the Republicans were blamed for the wretched conditions the country was experiencing. Republicans also opposed most of the progressive reforms initiated during Roosevelt's first two terms, as they would again thirty years later under Johnson and now under Obama.

The Republicans made one more ideological turn rightward beginning in the late 1970s with the rise of the "New Right," which will be discussed in the section on social movements below. Here it is enough to note that with the emergence of Ronald Reagan, George H. W. Bush, and George W. Bush, very few moderate Republicans remain in either the House or Senate, having given way to "movement conservatives" who dominate the party's overall leadership.

Today, the two parties have very different regional and social bases (see Table 3.3). Only about fifteen Senate and thirty House seats are normally considered to be competitive. The Democrats usually do best in the industrial Northeast and Middle West as well as on the West Coast. The Republicans have a virtual stranglehold on most of the South, the agricultural Midwest, and the Rocky Mountain states. The Democrats do best among racial minorities and supporters of progressive goals that began to emerge in the 1960s, most notably civil rights and environmental protection. The Democrats also do well among people who consider themselves liberals and among people with qualms about American foreign policy since 9/11. The Republican electorate is a mirror image of the Democrats'. The Republicans win the lion's share of the votes cast by poorer, rural, white, and evangelical Christian voters. It has even made huge inroads among working-class voters, who had been one of the most solid groups behind Democrats as recently as the 1960s.

The United States is as evenly divided as at any point in recent history. The 2000 and 2004 elections went down to the wire. In 2000, Gore won a half million more votes

TABLE 3.3 The 2008 Election

DEMOGRAPHIC GROUP	VOTING FOR OBAMA (%)
WHITES	43
BLACKS	96
HISPANICS	57
MEN	49
WOMEN	56
UNDER 24	66
OVER 65	45
INCOME UNDER $15,000	73
INCOME OVER $200,000	52

Source: These figures are from the 2008 exit poll, which is a joint effort of most major newspapers and television networks. These figures are from the ABC news site. **(www.abcnews.go.com).**

than Bush but lost because of the quirks of the Electoral College and the Supreme Court's decision in Florida. Most observers expected the 2004 race to be as competitive, if not as controversial. President Bush entered the campaign with strong support for his handling of the war on terrorism after 9/11, though the American public had significant doubts about the war in Iraq. His domestic policies were also less popular. Most polls gave his opponent, Senator John Kerry, an edge on issues such as health care and education. As in 2000, the race seemed to tighten as election day neared. In the week before the vote, Senator Kerry all but erased Bush's lead in the polls and did so a few days earlier than Vice President Gore had four years previously.

The initial results from the exit polls suggested that Kerry would win. Once the final results came in, however, it had turned into a Republican night. Bush won the vast majority of the so-called "battleground states" that were deemed the key to victory for either candidate. No one knew who would win, though, until the results from Ohio came in. Turnout there was high. In the college town of Oberlin, so many students showed up at the polls in the early evening that the authorities kept the voting booths open until 11 P.M. In the end, Bush carried Ohio by more than two hundred thousand votes, probably because of the extremely large turnout of evangelical Christians who flocked to the polls to vote in what they saw as a referendum on gay marriage. Ohio's twenty electoral votes gave Bush his second term.

Bush and the Republicans viewed their victories as a mandate. After all, they not only kept the presidency but also strengthened their hold over both houses of Congress.

That the United States by no means guarantees a winner for either party was proven again in 2006 and 2008. In the first year, the Democrats regained control of the House and Senate. Two years later the surprisingly strong Obama campaign and the equally surprisingly weak McCain campaign led to a massive Electoral College victory for the

Democrats. However, the Obama-Biden ticket only beat McCain and Palin by 6 percent of the popular vote. The Democrats did pick up a number of House and Senate seats. They also gained a temporary filibuster-proof majority in the Senate after Arlen Spector switched parties and Al Franken was declared the winner of the highly contested and very close election against Norm Coleman in Minnesota.

Then came the midterm elections of 2010. Democrats lost control of the House and have to deal with the anger of many new Republican members who won with support of the various Tea Party movements. The Democrats almost lost their majority in the Senate. As we write, there are a few signs that the two parties will find a way to cooperate and, for instance, avoid the next threatened shutdown of the federal government, which they did at the last moment in early 2011. A closer look at the data reminds us that the United States remains deeply divided between what we have come to call "red" (Republican) and "blue" (Democratic) states. The exit polls from recent elections reflect the divisions among Americans (see Table 3.3). Most men, older voters, evangelical Christians, and whites cast their votes for Republicans. Younger people, women, members of minority groups, gays and lesbians, and Jews voted overwhelmingly Democratic. In 2004, eighty-five percent of the people who supported the invasion of Iraq voted for Bush, but only 12 percent of those who opposed the war opted for the president. Attitudes about the state of the economy were almost the same. Results from 2008 show that Obama's support came from opponents of the war, young people, minorities, and others who were not part of President Bush's electoral coalition.

Those divisions are increasingly important because of one other trend that has been reshaping the American electorate. For much of American history, voters have had a strong sense of party identification 🌐 (www.electionstudies.org). This meant that there were only relatively minor shifts in voting patterns from one election to the next because each party had the support of broad, yet distinct, coalitions of loyal voters. Thus, in the half-century following the New Deal, the Democrats won most of the votes of poor people and members of racial and religious minorities, and the Republicans did the same in rural areas and among the more affluent groups in the white community.

Much of that commitment and stability has evaporated since the civil rights movement and the Vietnam War. Party identification and voter turnout rates are both at an all-time low. Swings from one election to the next are bigger and more unpredictable than they used to be. One sign of that (see Table 3.4) is that four of the last eleven presidential elections have featured a "third-party" candidate who won more than 5 percent of the vote.

Soccer Moms and NASCAR Dads

Two metaphors have emerged in recent elections to represent one core constituency in each of the parties' electorates.

Soccer moms (and dads) tend to be affluent suburbanites. If they have children, they almost certainly play soccer. Soccer moms may have come from Republican families, but the fact that they tend to favor women's rights, environmentalism, and other progressive causes has contributed to the "gender gap" that has been a central feature of American political life for almost a generation.

NASCAR dads (and moms) are the soccer moms' social opposite. They tend to be white, rural, relatively poorly educated, and at most lower middle class (even though tickets for the 2012 Daytona 500 started at fifty-five dollars). Political scientists noted this demographic trend even before the "Reagan Democrats" phenomenon of the 1980s. They only got their NASCAR dads label recently because of the dramatic upsurge of interest in stock car racing as well as their tendency to support George W. Bush and other conservatives.

TABLE 3.4 Recent Presidential Elections in the United States (Percentage of the Popular Vote)

YEAR	DEMOCRAT	REPUBLICAN	MAJOR INDEPENDENTS
1964	61.1	38.5	—
1968	42.7	43.3	13.5
1972	37.3	61.3	1.4
1976	50.1	48.8	1.0
1980	41.0	51.0	7.0
1984	40.8	59.2	—
1988	46.0	54.0	—
1992	43.2	37.7	19.0
1996	49.2	42.8	8.0
2000	48.3	48.1	3.6
2004	48.0	51.0	1.0
2008	52.9	45.7	1.4

Democrats: Johnson 1964, Humphrey 1968, McGovern 1972, Carter 1976 and 1980, Mondale 1984, Dukakis 1988, Clinton 1992 and 1996, Gore 2000, Kerry 2004, Obama 2008.

Republicans: Goldwater 1964, Nixon 1968 and 1972, Ford 1976, Reagan 1980 and 1984, G. H. W. Bush 1988 and 1992, Dole 1996, G. W. Bush 2000 and 2004, McCain 2008.

Major independents: Wallace 1968, Schmitz 1972, McCarthy 1976, Anderson 1980, Perot 1992 and 1996, Nader 2000 and 2004, Nader and Barr 2008.

Again, the 2010 midterm elections show us just how volatile American politics can be. It is by no means clear that President Obama will win a second term. Prospects for Democratic senatorial candidates for 2012 do not look good.

Social Movements

There has also been a marked upsurge in protest and other "demanding" activity on the part of increasingly sullen elements of the public. Much of this activity takes place outside the traditional network of interest groups and political parties. In both the United States and the other industrialized democracies discussed in Part 2, three trends stand out.

First was the emergence of the **New Left** in the 1960s. As in most liberal democracies, the "Old Left" consisted of voters and parties that sought more economic equality and protection for the interests of the poor. The New Left introduced new issues, most notably the promotion of civil rights and opposition to the Vietnam War. Soon, other issues captured the attention of a core of mostly young activists, including the environment, feminism, and gay and lesbian rights. Throughout the industrialized world, these activists found broad support, some of which came from parts of the middle class that had never been associated with the Left before.

By the early 1970s, however, support for the protest movements began to ebb. If it remains important today it is primarily due to the "gender gap" and "soccer mom" phenomena that left the Democrats with a huge lead among women because of the party's support for abortion rights, affirmative action, and other legacies of the 1960s. We also see it from time to time in the small but often violent protests against globalization and American foreign policy initiatives since 9/11.

Second, a **New Right** has supplanted the Left as the most powerful dissenting force in American politics. It is far more diverse than its left-wing equivalent ever was. Its most visible advocates are drawn from the roughly 20 percent of the population who consider themselves fundamentalist or evangelical Christians. It includes, as well, people who oppose legalized abortion, multicultural education, same sex marriage, higher taxes, and the general undermining of what they see as traditional American values.

The New Right began with the "Reagan Democrats," who voted Republican during the 1980s and then stayed with that party. These are mostly white, working-class men and women, whose parents and grandparents were at the heart of the New Deal Democratic coalition. Turned off by the New Left and frightened by their own prospects in a rapidly changing economy, they initially shifted to the Republicans to vote for Nixon and Reagan. They made up the lion's share of the "angry white men" who gained notoriety in the aftermath of the 1994 midterm congressional elections.

This is part—but only part—of why the Tea Party movement emerged. It has only been on the scene since the aftermath of the 2008 election. Because it is so loosely organized, it is often hard to say exactly who is part of it. It does now have caucuses in the House and Senate and includes politicians such as Sarah Palin among its supporters. The Tea Party may prove to be a flash in the political pan, but we see no reason to expect that.

Third, there has been a groundswell of anger as reflected in the spread of Not In My Back Yard (NIMBY) opposition to the location of unpopular facilities. In the Washington, D.C., area, for example, opposition from people who lived near planned transportation projects has killed many of them, with the net effect of worsening a traffic flow that is so bad that the *Washington Post* runs a column three times a week called "Dr. Gridlock." In 2009, voters and politicians protested against the possible location of prisoners from Guantanamo in their states.

Although historians have a hard time quantifying such things, it does seem that the American people in general

are placing more demands on their state than ever before. To complicate matters further, this is occurring at a time, as we will soon see, when the state is having unprecedented difficulties in responding to them.

These new trends regarding parties, voting, and social movements are one area in which Americans seem rather like their counterparts in other countries. For obvious reasons, Vietnam was a more contentious issue in the United States than it was elsewhere. Similarly, of all the countries covered in Part 2, only the United States has seen the emergence of a religious Right and the "culture wars" that have come in its wake.

Of course, Al Sharpton, Sarah Palin, Newt Gingrich, Rush Limbaugh, and Jane Fonda are quintessentially American figures. However, they have their equivalents in all the other countries covered in Part 2, and these broader shifts in the political tectonic plates are having a version of the same unsettling effects everywhere.

THE WEAK AMERICAN STATE

As discussed in Chapter 2, the United States has one of the weakest states of any of the industrialized democracies. Statements like that tend to confuse nonacademic observers. After all, with the collapse of the Soviet Union, the United States became the world's only superpower, which seeks to exert its influence, seemingly, wherever and whenever it wants to.

That does not mean that the United States has a strong state for the kinds of domestic issues comparativists are most interested in. Unlike the other liberal democracies, the American government has taken on fewer social and economic responsibilities. Also, it usually takes more time and is generally less effective than those other governments when it does act.

This weakness is no accident. It is, instead, a consequence of the system the founders created in 1787. As we saw previously, they created a state in which multiple, overlapping levels of authority prevent any one person, group, or party from getting everything it wants and force all actors to seek compromise solutions to their problems.

The Legislative Process

To see the weakness of the American state, consider the way Richard Neustadt began his pathbreaking book on presidential power:

> **In the early summer of 1952, before the heat of the campaign, President [Harry S.] Truman used to contemplate the problems of the general-become-president should Eisenhower win the forthcoming election.**

Conflict
in American Politics

Examining political conflict in the United States is a good way to reveal the critical distinction between the government of the day and the regime.

The United States has seen major protest movements for civil rights for racial minorities, women, and gays on the Left, and against abortion on the Right. Although most of those efforts have been nonviolent, the United States is hardly immune from confrontation. Moreover, some of the individuals and organizers themselves have opted for violence as a strategy, as the Weathermen faction of the Students for a Democratic Society did in the 1960s, and as a small number of antiabortion activists have done more recently in bombing clinics and killing doctors.

However widespread the confrontational and violent protests may be, the protesters rarely question the legitimacy of the regime created by the founders over two hundred years ago. To be sure, some groups, such as the militias, advocate radical change in the constitutional framework. However, there are few such people, and they have virtually no support in the population as a whole. ■

"He'll sit here," Truman would remark (tapping his desk for emphasis), "and he'll say, 'Do this! Do that!' And nothing will happen. Poor Ike—it won't be a bit like the Army. He'll find it very frustrating." Eisenhower evidently found it so.[4]

Neustadt went on to show that there are very few things a president can make happen automatically. Rather, a president possesses the "power to persuade."

The president has to do more persuading than most democratic leaders because American political institutions deny him the tools that facilitate executive leadership in parliamentary systems. Instead, the president is merely the most important person in a complex decision-making process. Along the way, decisions are made at many points, and the men and women involved often have no compelling reason to go along with what the president wants.

Compared with other democratic heads of state, the president often has problems within his own administration. He makes over four thousand appointments to policy-making positions. About one thousand of them require confirmation by the Senate. It takes months before all positions are filled. In summer 2009, the administration had close to three thousand appointments to make including every political appointee at the United States Agency for International Development. By contrast, the British prime minister has barely one hundred political jobs to fill and, thus, is far more dependent on career civil servants. At first glance, this would seem to make the president extremely powerful. But if we probe just a little deeper, it is easy to see that having so many political appointees can be a mixed blessing.

To begin with, merely finding people to fill those positions is difficult and time-consuming. A number of appointments go to people who are rewarded for political service to the president and his party. As a result of the selection process, many political appointees know little about the policy areas they will be working on—certainly less than their civil servant counterparts in France or Germany.

In short, the president has something decidedly less than a unified team working for him. Coordinating an administration and its policies is made all the more difficult by the fact lines of authority are not clearly drawn. For example, three different departments and two agencies—the Departments of Defense, State, and Energy, and the Director of National Intelligence, and the Arms Control and Disarmament Agency—have direct responsibility for developing policy to stop the proliferation of nuclear weapons. The Department of Commerce is also indirectly involved because it promotes American exports, including

some technologies that could be used in a nuclear weapons program. Perhaps most telling of all, the creation of a single Department of Homeland Security required the merger of dozens of agencies housed in several different departments, ranging from Defense to the Treasury.

Once the executive branch reaches an agreement on proposed legislation, it has to overcome a far more imposing hurdle: Congress. It is in the interplay between legislators and the president that manifestations of the founders' fear of strong government are easiest to see.

The roots of congressional power lie in the multiple, independent decision-making points outlined in Figure 3.1 (http://thomas.loc.gov). When a bill is submitted, it goes through a ceremonial "first reading" and is sent to the appropriate standing committees and subcommittees in the Senate and House of Representatives, where most of the real work gets done. Many members of Congress serve on committees that deal with issues they know a lot about or that directly affect their districts. More important,

FIGURE 3.1 The President and Congress

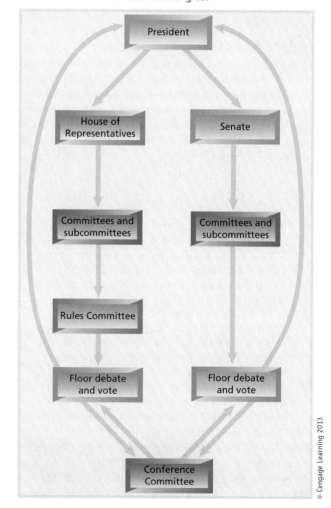

© Cengage Learning 2013

---

[4]Richard Neustadt, *Presidential Power: The Politics of Leadership* (New York: Wiley, 1960), 9.

the committees and subcommittees have large staffs with expertise on the subjects under their jurisdiction.

The first thing the committee has to do is decide whether to consider the bill at all. If it chooses not to or votes it down, it dies. If it takes a bill on, it begins by doing research that often includes extensive hearings, some of which are televised on C-SPAN. If the president is lucky, the committee then "marks up" the bill. This is not, as the words may suggest, merely an editorial task. More often than not, major portions of the proposed legislation are eliminated and replaced with entirely new provisions. Those of us who paid attention to the health care reform debate have seen the huge role a handful of influential committee members can have on legislation.

The same thing can happen to the bill when and if it reaches the full House and Senate after favorable committee "reports." Once again, amendments usually can be proposed, and once again, a negative vote can kill it outright. The latter is what has happened to all proposed legislation on immigration reform since 2007.

The House and Senate almost never pass identical versions of a bill. Therefore, their two texts go to a conference committee of members from both houses whose job is to "iron out" the differences between the two. When and if the conference committee reaches an agreement, the bill is returned to both houses, either of which has another opportunity to kill it.

In principle, the same thing can happen in parliamentary systems. All have committees, floor debates, and votes, and parliamentary approval is required for most policy initiatives. The key difference between the United States and the other industrialized democracies is the degree of party discipline in the latter. A British prime minister can be all but certain that colleagues in the House of Commons from his or her party will support the government's proposed legislation. Because prime ministers can count on that majority, legislative programs are normally passed without any significant changes or delay.

However, American members of Congress do not have to vote along party lines. Research over the past forty years has uncovered five main factors that shape the way members vote. Some reflect the levers presidents have at their disposal. On balance, however, they show why presidents rarely get what they want.

The first, of course, is the president himself. The White House Congressional Liaison Office regularly lobbies on Capitol Hill. Whenever a bill the president is especially interested in nears a final vote that might be close, the nightly news shows a parade of senators and representatives visiting the White House. The president cannot force members of the House or Senate to support him. What he can do, however, is to refuse to offer his own support for the members on other issues or even threaten to work to defeat them at the next election.

Second is the party, though it is by no means the determining important factor as it is in parliamentary systems. Both parties have "whips" who try to convince members to vote the way the leadership wants. Toeing the line can help advance a member's career and can even bring leadership support for a bill he or she is sponsoring. Nonetheless, on almost every piece of legislation, a substantial number of representatives and senators do break ranks. There are exceptions; no Republican representatives and only three Republican senators voted for Obama's stimulus passage, whereas all Democrats did. But those exceptions are rare.

Third are the members' peers. Senators and representatives cannot keep track of all the legislation pending before Congress. Consequently, especially on matters of little interest to themselves or their constituents, they often defer to their colleagues who are experts or to those whose constituents would be affected.

Fourth is what the members' constituents want. All of them use their extensive staffs to keep track of constituent mail, the press back home, and other evidence of where voters stand on the issues. Many conduct polls. Even with all this information, members can never tell exactly what their constituents want, and some critics suggest that they tend to listen not so much to the population as a whole, but to the people who donated the most money to their election campaigns. Still, there is an important link between member and constituency. Voters are not likely to elect someone who does not share their views about important local issues in the first place. In addition, members tend to keep the people back home happy both by voting the "right way" and by providing services to their communities and constituents. As a result, although Congress as an institution may not be highly respected, individual members who choose to run are almost always reelected. Even in the Democratic victory in 2008, only nineteen incumbents in the House were defeated, whereas nine open seats previously held by a Republican turned Democratic. In the Senate five Republicans lost.

Finally, there are the members' own views. Americans expect senators and representatives to exercise their judgment at least on matters that are not extremely important locally. There are, however, some examples of members voting their conscience against their constituents' wishes—as, for example, the late Senator William Fulbright (D-Ark.) did in supporting civil rights legislation during the 1960s. The most obvious recent example is former Senate Majority Leader Bill Frist (R-Tenn). Like many members of his family, Frist began his professional life as a doctor and emphasized health care throughout his political career; he even carried his medical bag with him, which he used to help people cope with emergencies on a number of occasions.

Americans derive some important benefits from a Congress whose members are willing and able to reshape

President Barack Obama and House Speaker John Boehner, R-Ohio, are on the first green as they play golf at Andrews Air Force Base, MD, on June 18, 2011.

AP Photo/Charles Dharapak.

First is the bureaucracy. Recall that the president appoints about four thousand people to policy-making and administrative positions. Some of them are experts in their field and have a wealth of experience inside and outside of government service. Well trained or not, presidential appointees have to rely on senior civil servants to provide the technical expertise needed to draft most laws. Typically, civil servants who make it to the top of the government bureaucracy are experts, and because they retain their jobs from administration to administration and provide a degree of continuity that political appointees cannot. Recent research has shown that members of the Senior Executive Service are as well trained and hardworking as their European counterparts, who play a much more central role in policy formation. There, high-level civil servants are among the most respected people in the country, and there is widespread support for their involvement in policy making. However, American bureaucrats are not widely respected because its culture views government in general, and civil servants in particular, with disdain.

Second, the United States is rare in giving its courts wide-ranging powers of **judicial review.** The Supreme Court and lower federal and state courts can rule on the constitutionality of government actions. Judicial decisions and interpretations have often marked important turning points in the evolution of American public policy. The most striking examples in recent years have to do with civil rights. It was a Supreme Court decision (*Plessy v. Ferguson*) that initially upheld Southern laws segregating blacks and whites in 1896. Another decision (*Brown v. Board of Education*), almost sixty years later, overturned the doctrine of "separate but equal" and also served as a major catalyst for the modern civil rights movement. Beginning in the 1980s, a more conservative Court has issued a series of decisions that have sharply limited affirmative action and perhaps put the *Brown* decision in jeopardy.

legislation initiated by the executive. Constituency interests are taken into account far more in the United States than they are in parliamentary systems. Congress also provides far more effective protection against the abuse of power by the executive. However, as all those diverse forces enter into the process, whatever coherence there was in the original bill typically is sacrificed.

In other words, the American state usually cannot act either quickly or coherently even when the White House and Capitol Hill are controlled by the same party. Instead, policy making tends to be slow and characterized by **incrementalism** or limited, marginal, or minor changes. It is hard to see how it could be otherwise. There are simply too many decision-making points, and a group only has to win at one of them to block change.

The Rest of the Weak State

The relationship between Congress and the presidency contributes more than anything to making the American state weak. However, there are at least three other factors that do so as well and thus deserve our attention in passing.

The Weakening American State?

No one has done a definitive study of the strengthening or weakening of the American state in recent years. However, there is a rough consensus that it is not as effective as it used to be—if by that we mean it is less able to define policies that tackle social and economic problems in a reasonably consistent manner.

Other than globalization, there are two main reasons why this is the case, reasons that reflect the domestic pressures cell of Table 1.2. First, like all states, the American government now faces more issues that tax its resources in ways no one could have imagined even fifty years ago. If the critics are right, the United States may be worse off than some other countries (see the chapters on France, Germany, and Britain) because it continues to rely on institutions and practices designed two hundred years ago, when conditions were very different. Second, it probably also faces more pressures from below and from a wider variety of groups than it did in previous generations. As research on social movements in Europe and Canada has shown, this is not unique to the United States, however, because power is so fragmented in the United States, the government has had a relatively hard time trying to respond to those demands.

Third, the United States is a federal system, which means that Washington shares power with state and local governments. Most other liberal democracies have **unitary states** in which the central government determines which powers are granted to subnational units. In the United States, state and local governments have more responsibility for education policy and have always had a lot of leeway in determining how social services programs are run. Among other things, that makes it difficult for the federal government to impose national standards.

PUBLIC POLICY

American cultural qualms about an active state and the fragmented nature of its institutions have resulted in a government that does less than those in most of the other liberal democracies. In recent years, the most widely discussed aspect of that limited coverage has been health care. Most middle-class and wealthy Americans get top-notch medical treatment because they can afford good insurance and can pay for care their policies do not cover. However, more than 45 million Americans will only get some coverage in the next few years as the provisions of the 2010 law go into effect.

It's not merely health care. Unemployment compensation and pension payments are below the norm for countries that belong to the Organisation for Economic Co-operation and Development (OECD). So, too, is the minimum wage. Publicly supported mass transit systems are almost never found outside big cities, and the passenger rail system is a shadow of its former self.

The government also does relatively little to coordinate economic policy. When it does, it usually just tries to help interest groups from a single industry and their supporters in Congress and the executive branch to cooperate. The Clinton administration started out doing more in that respect but lost momentum especially with its passage of welfare reform legislation, which limited the amount of time people can draw benefits. However, the George W. Bush administration loosened or eliminated dozens of regulations that had a lot to do with the economic crisis that Obama inherited. And in these days of the Tea Party, even the policy involvement of the Bush years seems a thing of the past.

There is also a widespread belief that when the government does act, it usually does so inefficiently and sometimes corruptly. To maintain its own control, and supposedly to guard against corruption, Congress tends to micromanage federal agencies, often determining exactly how much money they can spend on computers or even what kinds of ashtrays they could buy (in the days when civil servants could still smoke in their offices). Many members of Congress insert "earmarks" in bills, which designate funds for pet projects, usually in their home district or state. In 2009, there were more than four thousand earmarks in the budget bill passed that March. That may change with the Congress elected in 2010. It may not. As this book went to press, looming crises included the lifting of the debt ceiling and the 2012 fiscal year budget.

When applied to the private sector, such detailed and seemingly irrational legislation and regulations spawn complaints about a government that weighs too heavily "on the backs" of the people and their businesses. The Clinton administration sought to change things on this front with its "reinventing government" package of reforms designed to "steer the boat" of public policy rather than do the "rowing" or making every decision. So far, however, those proposals have done little more than provide intellectual justification for the dramatic downsizing of some federal agencies.

THE MEDIA

Of all the countries covered in this book, the United States is the one on which the most research on the media has been done. The results are mixed but worrisome, regardless of one's ideological perspective. Although there has been an explosion in the number and type of media available, there has actually been a sharp decline in the quantity and quality of the political news most Americans pay attention to.

Readership of quality newspapers and magazines is down. Most people rely primarily on television news for their political information, and the consensus among researchers is that network television does a less effective job of covering "serious" political news than it once did. To make matters even worse, fewer and fewer people are watching the news now that cable and direct satellite broadcasting give them dozens of other options during the slots the networks and local stations typically reserve for it.

Last but by no means least, American politicians are the acknowledged world masters at the art of spin doctoring, or packaging their statements and actions in ways they think people will find most attractive, often hiding the real import of the activity in the process. They do rely heavily on public opinion polls and focus groups, but one has to question how valuable these are for a public that is increasingly disinterested in political life and whose views are shaped by the spin doctors themselves.

AMERICAN EXCEPTIONALISM

There is a lot missing from this chapter, including the differences between the House of Representatives and the Senate, the Electoral College, and pressures for tax and campaign finance reform. Adding more material would take most readers—especially those who have had a course in American politics—more deeply into American political dynamics than they need to go. Doing so might obscure the key point being made here: that American exceptionalism is manifested in an unusually tranquil political history, supportive political culture, and weak or fragmented state.

LATE BREAKING NEWS

The beginning of this chapter may have suggested that Barak Obama was doomed to be a one-term president. In early May 2011, he dispelled part of the concerns about him the "birthers" had raised about his fitness to serve by issuing copies of his full birth certificate from Honolulu.

But his political fortunes also took a turn for the better in the first days of May 2011 in two respects.

First is the surprising weakness of the Republican candidates. As we write, the Republican field is filled with undeclared candidates, each with liabilities. With public opinion polls moving rightward, the Republican candidates have to move in that direction. However, it is by no means clear that a far right Republican can hope to win. On May 5, 2011, Mitt Romney, the former moderate governor of Massachusetts, topped the polls with only 18 percent support.

Second, to the surprise of many, Navy SEALs led a covert operation that killed Osama bin-Laden on May 1, 2011. That led to a huge surge in Obama's support in the poll, by as much as 20 percent in some. It also means that Republican candidates will have to address international issues as we head into the election cycle.

2012 looks to be as interesting a campaign as any in recent years.

Looking FORWARD

EARLY IN THE chapter, we stressed the idea of American exceptionalism.

Now, we will question it or at least put it under a different intellectual microscope.

What you will see is that no other country in Part 2 shares a lot with the United States other than a core commitment to democracy. Differences we will see:

- Political histories
- Cultures
- Parties
- Institutions
- Public Policy

Key Terms

American exceptionalism

checks and balances

civic culture

civil society

compromise

consensus policy making

Democratic

federal/federalism

incrementalism

individualism

judicial review

new Left

new Right

Republican

separation of powers

Tea Party

two-party system

unitary state

Useful Websites

There are literally thousands of websites on politics in the United States. The White House and Thomas (run by the Library of Congress) provide gateways to the executive and legislative branches.

www.whitehouse.gov

http://thomas.loc.gov

The Supreme Court also has its own site, but, in my opinion, the one maintained by Cornell's Law School is better.

www.law.cornell.edu/supct/index.html

Polling Report is the best online source for public opinion data. Vote Smart provides nonpartisan, unbiased information on pending issues to help voters make up their minds—and in a quirky way that my students, at least, love. The Public Agenda Foundation does much the same in analyzing policy issues themselves. Five Thirty Eight burst on the scene in 2008, its creator modeling projects based on statistical techniques that resemble baseball outcomes.

www.pollingreport.com

www.vote-smart.org

www.publicagenda.org

www.fivethirtyeight.com

Three good sites on **consensus policy making** are Search for Common Ground (where Chip worked), which has done the most work on controversial issues at the federal level; the Policy Consensus Institute, which concentrates on the states; and Public Conversations Projects, which brings average citizens together on such issues as a woman's right to choose and Mel Gibson's film, *The Passion of the Christ.*

www.sfcg.org

www.policyconsensus.org

www.publicconversations.org

Further Reading

Ambrose, Stephen, with Douglas Brinkley. *The Rise to Globalism*, 8th ed. New York: Penguin Books, 1997. The best short volume outlining global history since World War II.

Dionne, E. J. *They Only Look Dead: Why Progressives Will Dominate the Next Political Era.* New York: Simon & Schuster, 1996. By one of America's most distinguished political journalists (who also holds a Ph.D. from Harvard), an exploration of why the Left might be able to reassert itself in the new century.

Hacker, Andrew. *Two Nations: Black and White, Separate, Hostile, Unequal.* New York: Scribner, 1992. A brief but comprehensive book on the sorry state of race relations in the United States.

Halstead, Ted, and Michael Lind. *The Radical Center: The Future of American Politics.* New York: Doubleday, 2001. A provocative new book on making dramatic policy changes from the middle of the political spectrum rather than from the extremes.

Kenski, Kate, Bruce W. Hardy, and Kathleen Hall Jamieson. *The Obama Victory.* New York: Oxford University Press, 2010. The best book we've seen on why Obama won and hints at why he may not win again.

Nelson, Michael. *The Elections of 2008.* Washington: CQ Press, 2009. Edited by a great team of scholars, the most recent of a series of books published after each presidential election.

Neustadt, Richard. *Presidential Power: The Politics of Leadership.* New York: Wiley, 1960. The classic book on the presidency. It has been republished in several new editions since its initial copyright date.

Pfiffner, James. *The Modern Presidency*, 5th ed. Belmont, CA: Wadsworth, 2007. The best brief textbook on the American presidency.

Putnam, Robert D. *Bowling Alone: The Collapse and Revival of American Community.* New York: Simon & Schuster, 2000. The most thorough and most controversial book on declining civic engagement in the United States.

Reid, T. R. *The Healing of America.* New York: Penguin, 2009. The most sweeping book on the politics of health care, which may become the most important issue facing all of these countries.

Shipler, David K. *The Working Poor.* New York: Knopf, 2004. The best recent work on poverty in the United States.

Tocqueville, Alexis de. *Democracy in America.* New York: Vintage Books, 1945. The classic account of American life by a French traveler and theorist, written in the 1830s.

Wayne, Steven. *The Road to the White House 2008.* Belmont, CA: Wadsworth, 2007. The best book exploring how presidential nominations are conducted.

CHAPTER 4

The United Kingdom

The British happened to the rest of the world. Now the rest of the world happens to Britain.

ANDREW MARR

AN ENCOUNTER WITH CLEGG

On the Saturday before the British 2010 general election, Chip boarded a surprisingly crowded train and finally found a seat. A few minutes out of Reading Station, a black lab emerged from under a seat and, knowing a dog fanatic when he saw one, immediately started licking Chip, who said to the dog's "mother" that the pup would be the star of the train. She said, "No, **Nick Clegg** (1967–) is at the front of the car."

Chip was shocked that a serious candidate for prime minister would be on a commercial train with virtually no sign of a security detail. Once he realized that this was fairly common in the UK, he started talking with both of the lab's parents who had been reading *The Guardian,* which had supported **Labour** for decades but in that morning's editorial had endorsed Clegg and his **Liberal Democratic** party. Chip had read and agreed with the editorial; he found himself supporting a party other than Labour for the first time since he became interested in British politics in the 1960s.

The lab's ten-year-old "sister" went to get a snack in the next car. Passing Clegg's seat she found that he was speaking a foreign language; she rushed back to tell her family. Chip told her that Clegg's wife is Spanish and that he is actually fluent in five languages. The girl encouraged Chip

Looking BACKWARD

THE PREVIOUS TWO chapters examined the principles underlying liberal democracy and the way it is practiced in the United States. As we noted in Chapter 3, the U.S. "constitutional republic" was created in 1791 to supplant the Articles of Confederation. The American Constitutional Republic was founded on both British and French ideals and political structures. And, as we will see throughout Part 2, many other countries have developed systems that treat the separation and division of powers differently from the United States.

The reader had to take that for granted until we could explore democracies that are based on the more common parliamentary model. We will do so here and in the next three chapters. We start with the United Kingdom (UK) because it pioneered what is often called the **Westminster model,** which in one form or another is also used in Canada, Australia, and New Zealand.

One key concept to keep in mind for Britain, as for the United States, is the gradual and relative ease with which democracy developed. Otherwise, Britain and the United States are more notable for their differences, at least for the purposes of this book.

First, as noted, Britain uses a parliamentary system in which party discipline is enforced and which, in turn, makes the rapid passage of legislation in London easier than in Washington. Second, Britain has a centralized system. Despite the creation of regional assemblies in Scotland, Northern Ireland, and Wales during the last decade, none of them are constitutionally mandated. In fact, the term *federal government* makes no sense in the British context. Third, Britain and the United States both use a "first past the post" electoral system. Britain's version has not wiped out minor parties, although it has kept their representation in the House of Commons down. Fourth, Britain does not have a written constitution, and its unwritten one can be changed by a simple act of Parliament. Today, perhaps, we should add a fifth—the economic crisis that has wracked the country since at least 2008 and did more than anything else to fuel Labour's defeat in 2010.

to go meet Clegg, but Chip told her "no" because he likes to respect people's privacy. Finally, she convinced him to go.

At the front of the car, Chip started talking to a fairly thin young guy who wasn't wearing a tie. They discussed the election, in which the Liberals were likely to come in second for the first time since the 1920s. When asked why he was supporting the Liberal Democrats, Chip replied with three words: Iraq and (then-incumbent Prime Minister) **Gordon Brown** (1951–). So Chip asked what this savvy guy did for the Clegg campaign. The guy replied "I *am* Clegg." After some mortified blushing on Chip's part they talked about the campaign for another ten minutes or so. Then the journalists pounced; Chip's knowledge—and his gaffe—made it into three of the better newspapers the next day (mercifully only at the end of long articles).

Chip's brief moment of fame had absolutely no impact on the election but did give his political scientist colleagues a good laugh. Yet Clegg *was* a phenomenon. Labour had been in power for thirteen years, but ran out of political steam as a result of its highly unpopular support for the United States in Iraq (see Chapter 14) and its inability to end the recession.

There was little chance that the Liberal Democrats (often just called the Lib Dems) could win and in fact finished a strong third. However, for reasons that will be made clear later, they had no chance of winning the majority of seats in the **House of Commons,** which he would need to form a government. **David Cameron** (1966–) and his **Conservative** party had a slight lead in the polls but had next to no chance of winning a majority of the seats either.

Five days later, when the election results were reported, the Conservatives did a little better and the Liberal Democrats a little worse than the final polls had predicted. As almost everyone had forecast, there was no majority. Five days later (an eternity in British politics), **Queen Elizabeth II** officially asked Cameron and Clegg to form a coalition government, with the former as prime minister and the latter as deputy prime minister. Brown resigned as leader of the Labour party and was replaced by Ed Miliband, following one of the strangest elections ever, because the only other serious candidate was his brother David.

In three ways, this election was is part and parcel of a dramatic change in British politics, which we will be exploring in the rest of the chapter. First, this is only the first formal coalition government in Britain since the 1930s. Second, the election ushered in a generational change: Cameron and Clegg were both 42 when they were elected and replaced Brown, who at 59 often appeared older. Third, Cameron and Clegg have introduced sweeping economic reforms that are designed to streamline the government, cut some popular programs, and reduce the government's debt and deficit.

And maybe there is a fourth lesson to tease from this brief encounter. Professors make mistakes just like everyone else.

There had already been some discussion about the conservative economic policies a Tory Liberal Democratic government would follow (see the sections on the two parties below). Most observers believed Cameron would have trouble getting away with massive budget cuts that require sharp reduction in the provision of social services. He was wrong. Cameron's government has introduced the most sweeping spending cuts and tax reductions in generations, which go farther than anything imagined by earlier Conservative prime ministers **Margaret Thatcher** (1925–) and **John Major** (1943–).

THINKING ABOUT BRITAIN

Fifty years ago, Britain was included in comparative politics textbooks for four related reasons. First, it was the incubator, if not the originator, of liberal democracy. Second, its democracy evolved over a number of centuries in a process scholars call **gradualism**, which resulted in a post-World War II **collectivist consensus** with a mixed economy and an extensive welfare state. Third, Britain had been one of the world's great powers over the past 500 years and was still strong enough in 1945 to warrant a permanent seat on the United Nations Security Council. Fourth, its political system was similar in many ways to those in other English-speaking countries, which makes it an easy country to start with for most readers.

In Britain today, only the first and last of those reasons still hold. Its ranking among the world's powers has been in gradual, but constant, decline for more than a century. In short, if Britain belongs in a book like this today, it is primarily because of its historical role—in particular for what it can tell us about the ways democracies develop.

Key Concepts and Questions

This chapter will revolve around five themes that set the UK apart from most other democracies. The first is *gradualism*. It is perhaps too charitable a term to use in describing a history that stretches back to the signing of the Magna Carta in 1215. Nonetheless, in comparative terms, Britain has suffered from less unrest and has had a more consensual

history than almost any other country, which has helped smooth its transition to democracy. It did have to face the challenges of creating a nation-state, overcoming religious and class conflict, and the strife that often accompanies democratization. However, unlike the countries on the European continent, Britain was able to tackle these challenges over a number of centuries and to largely resolve each of them before it had to face the next.

Second, in some respects, Britain has had the most troubles of any of the major liberal democracies since the height of the collectivist period in the early 1960s. As Table 4.1 shows, Britain's relative economic standing declined dramatically in the second half of the twentieth century. In 1939, it was the second-wealthiest country in the world, trailing only the United States. By the 1970s, it had dropped out of the top ten, and in 2000 it ranked fourteenth. Today, it is seventh, which might be misleading because the ranking does not fully take into account the terrible toll of the great recession.

Britain is by no means a poor country, as its per capita gross national product of more than thirty-five thousand dollars a year attests. However, its economic growth has long lagged behind that of its major competitors, something British tourists are aware of whenever they visit France or Germany, where people enjoyed a noticeably higher standard of living.

More important for our purposes are the political implications of the economic decline. The recession from 2008 until the present has hit Britain particularly hard, especially in its housing market, which suffered at least as much as the one in the United States. No matter how you measure such things, the British are now less masters of their destiny than they were a half-century ago, something the British Broadcasting Company's (BBC) Andrew Marr pithily sums up in the quote that begins this chapter.

The second is the *marketization* and *privatization* of British politics, particularly in response to the EU's Maastricht Treaty, signed in 1992. However, like her Conservative counterparts in the US and Canada in the 1980s, Conservative Prime Minister Thatcher and her party led a movement to reduce welfare-state spending, often described as a "budget-killer."

TABLE 4.1 Britain's Decline in International Rank in GNP per Capita

COUNTRY	1939	1960	1974	1995	2000	2006	2009
United States	1	1	3	5	3	1	1
Great Britain	2	6	14	18	14	8	7

Source: Data for 1939, 1960, and 1974 from Walter Dean Burnham, "Great Britain: The Collapse of the Collectivist Consensus," in Louis Maisel and Joseph Cooper, eds., *Political Parties: Development and Decay* (Beverly Hills, CA: Sage, 1978), 274; data for 1995 from World Bank, *World Development Report 1996* (Oxford: Oxford University Press, 1996), 189; data for 2000 onward from www.worldbank.org.

© Robert Estall/CORBIS.

Seven estate agency boards stand in a row outside a block of flats in Camden, London.

That brings us to the third trend—the way the governments led by Conservative prime ministers Margaret Thatcher and John Major, in the 1980s and 1990s, respectively, redefined British political life and spurred the renewal of support for free-market economics that has taken hold almost everywhere. Like her Conservative counterparts in the United States and Canada in the 1980s, Thatcher and her colleagues rejected most of the premises of collectivist politics and pushed the country in a dramatically different direction. Over the seventeen years that she and Major were in office, they privatized dozens of companies, reduced spending on social services, curbed the power of the unions, opposed further British involvement in Europe, and reasserted Britain's influence in global affairs.

Thatcher (nicknamed the Iron Lady) remains controversial to this day. Her supporters are convinced that she saved the country from bankruptcy and social chaos. Her opponents claim equally vociferously that she took it to the brink of disaster and left it a far more heartless place, with a government that treats the disadvantaged with disinterest and even disdain.

Fourth, the shift to the right found its echoes on the Left. It also moved rightward as did most left-of-center parties from the 1980s onward. When Labour finally won in 1997, it produced profound changes of its own. During the Thatcher and Major years, Labour lost four consecutive elections in large part because it veered too far to the Left to have a chance of winning. After the second of those defeats in 1987, the party began an agonizing reassessment of its goals and strategies that eventually led to the selection of **Tony Blair** (1953–) as its leader in 1994.

Blair and his team embarked on a radical restructuring of the party organization and a redefinition of its goals to the point that it routinely came to be called *New Labour*, as if it were a brand new party. Most notably, Blair shed the party's commitment to nationalized industry and state-based solutions to most social problems. Instead, he endorsed some of the Thatcherite commitment to a market economy, though tempered with a greater concern for equality and a desire to forge more cooperative "partnerships" linking business, labor, and the government. However, as we saw in the introduction to the chapter, the momentum for reform evaporated with Blair's personal popularity.

The fifth is the newest and most tentative of the questions: Will the new coalition government and the reforms it expects to enact have a lasting change impact on everything from British public policy to the way the state itself operates? Writing barely a year after the 2010 election, it is hard to give a firm answer. In the pages that follow, we will offer a tentative "yes."

The Basics

Let's start with something very basic indeed. What do all the different names used to describe this country actually stand for? Technically, this chapter is about the United Kingdom. It has four parts—England, Scotland, Wales, and Nothern Ireland. The term UK is a title few people use other than in official communications. England is its historical core (see the map at the beginning of this chapter) and is where the crown gradually solidified its hold on power centuries ago. Only later did the English conquer the Celtic fringes of their island: Wales and Scotland. The three together are popularly referred to as Britain.

The UK also includes the predominantly Protestant counties of Northern Ireland. When the rest of Ireland gained its independence in 1922, Northern Ireland chose to stay in the UK. The status of Northern Ireland, or Ulster as Protestants call it, remains hotly contested, though many hope that the **Good Friday Agreement** of 1998 has paved the way toward enduring political calm there.

Although Britain is one country, the four regions can operate quite differently. It can get confusing. Scotland (but not Wales or Northern Ireland) has its own bank notes and legal system. England, Scotland, Wales, and Northern Ireland all have their own international soccer teams but play together in cricket and, sometimes, in rugby. It takes three years to get an undergraduate degree in England, but four in Scotland.

As we will see in more detail later in the chapter, the Blair government passed legislation that gave regional parliaments in Scotland, Wales, and Northern Ireland considerable power. However, the so-called devolved powers should not be confused with federalism, since those regional bodies could be eliminated by a simple act of parliament.

There are significant minorities in Wales and Scotland who want even more autonomy, if not complete independence, from England, though virtually no one there condones the use of violence to achieve their goals. The Irish, by contrast, have not relied on nonviolent protest alone. Even with the 1998 peace agreement, some Catholic and Protestant extremists carry out bombings and drive-by shootings. In fact, the worst single incident during the thirty years of "the troubles" occurred when twenty-eight people were killed by a car bomb planted by a tiny Catholic terrorist group in Omagh in August 1998, four months after the Good Friday Agreement was signed.

Regional differences also overlap with religious ones. About two-thirds of the people belong to the Church of England. As an official, or "established," church, it receives funding and other support from the state. Twenty of its top leaders serve in the **House of Lords**. Other Protestant sects are strongest in the working class and in the Celtic minority regions. About 10 percent of the people are Catholic, most of whom either live in Northern Ireland or whose families emigrated to "the mainland."

Britain also is no longer an all-white country. It is estimated that between 5 and 10 percent of the population is of African, Asian, or Caribbean origin. Racial issues have become politically significant over the past thirty years, especially among Conservative politicians, some of whom

call for an end to immigration and, at times, even the repatriation of Britain's nonwhite residents.

Since the 1991 Maastricht Treaty, "freedom of movement" of populations has become a core principle in the European Union (see Chapter 7). With the frequent downturns in the European economies since then, for good or ill, many have chosen to blame immigrants for "taking jobs away" from longer-term citizens. Curiously, the focus has shifted from people of color to those from Eastern Europe, many of whom can move to the UK as members of the European Union, and others from Africa and Asia who claim political asylum. Minority political issues became highly controversial after September 11 and the terrorist attacks in London in 2005 and in Glasgow and London in 2007. Although most immigrants and their children have no links to the terrorist networks, the public is increasingly opposed to further immigration of any sort. Thus, in a September 2008 poll, almost 60 percent of the respondents thought there were too many immigrants in the country.

Barely the size of California, the UK has just over 61 million people (compared to California's 37 million), which makes it one of the most crowded countries in the world. The congestion is actually worse than the figures might indicate because more than 70 percent of its people live in urban areas, the majority of which are located in a two-hundred-mile-wide band stretching from London in the south to Newcastle in the north. Put in other terms, almost half the country is open pastureland and home to tens of millions of sheep.

Despite deep budget cuts after 1979, and those in the pipeline now, the welfare state is still strong enough to guarantee basic health care, education, and pensions for everyone. There is very little homelessness. But other public services, most notably the country's extensive railroad system, are in need of massive investment. And in late 2010, the country faced massive protests by university students who were upset that tuition and fees will rise to something like $15,000 a year at the most selective universities.

The first years of this century did bring better times economically. Before the start of the recession in 2008, its growth rate was among the highest and its unemployment among the lowest in Europe as is reflected in the basics table on this book's inside front cover. Nonetheless, signs of the decline still exist. Most salaries are no more than two-thirds of what they would be in the United States. In the three years that Chip lived there in the late 1990s, his academic colleagues had fewer clothes, older cars, smaller personal libraries, and slower computers than his counterparts in the United States.

Perhaps the most important economic characteristic of British life is social class. More than in most countries, you can tell peoples' backgrounds by their clothing, accents, and even the sports they follow. In England, rugby union is

Profiles
Margaret Thatcher

Margaret Roberts was born in 1925 in Grantham, which has often been described as the most boring town in Britain. Her father owned a small corner grocery store and was a member of the town council. He instilled conservative values in his daughter, including self-reliance, self-discipline, and a respect for tradition, all of which were reinforced by her experiences growing up during the Great Depression and World War II.

During the war, Roberts studied chemistry at Oxford, but she soon realized she was more interested in politics than science and so became a lawyer active in Conservative politics. Marriage to the wealthy banker Denis Thatcher allowed her to turn to politics full time. In 1959, she was first elected to a safe Tory seat in suburban London. In 1970 she was named minister of education, in which position she gained the nickname "Margaret Thatcher, milk snatcher" for eliminating free milk from school lunches.

After the Conservatives lost in 1974, she and a number of her colleagues abandoned their commitment to the collectivist consensus. Two years later, she was named leader of the Conservative party and became prime minister when it won the 1979 election. Her eleven years in office made Thatcher the longest-serving prime minister in more than a hundred years. Her successor, John Major, elevated her to the House of Lords in 1993, where she will almost certainly be the last member with a hereditary peerage that can be passed on to her descendants. ■

Prime Minister Margaret Thatcher speaking in London on July 1, 1991.

© David Fowler / Shutterstock.com.

---

a middle- and upper-class sport; soccer and rugby league traditionally appealed to the working class. Many in the upper and middle classes have a degree of self-assurance that borders on arrogance, bred by generations of wealth and the educations they received at one of Britain's prestigious private schools (to make things confusing for American students, the best of them are known as public schools).

THE EVOLUTION OF THE BRITISH STATE

Chapter 2 identified four great transformations that had a tremendous impact on political life in the industrial democracies over the past several centuries:

- Building the nation-state.
- Defining the relationship between church and state.
- Establishing liberal democracy.
- Dealing with the industrial revolution.

Each had a wrenching impact. Most countries in Europe had to deal with two or more of them at the same time, never fully resolved any of them, and ended up with deeply divided populations and political instability as a result.

By contrast, the British were able to handle these crises separately. And with the exception of the industrial revolution, Britain emerged from each with a rough consensus, avoiding the lasting divisions that left France and Germany with large numbers of antagonistic political parties. The one divisive issue that was left unresolved—class—did not lead to the intense conflicts found on the continent that would pit workers demanding revolution against an upper class fearfully holding onto its property and privilege.

It was this relative gradualism that allowed the British to move from one potentially divisive issue to another without provoking the confrontations that were so common elsewhere. The evolution of the British state is all the more remarkable, because it has occurred without a written constitution. *De facto*, the UK has a constitution, but it consists simply of laws and traditions accepted by almost everyone. Furthermore, it can be changed by the passage of almost any major new legislation.

Before moving on, be sure to note the importance of the term *relative* **gradualism** here. Britain's history has by no means been tranquil. Nevertheless, as will be clearer after you read any of the remaining chapters, its evolution has been among the calmest in the world. The relative ease with which it met these challenges was a major contributor to the consensus about institutions and practices that has marked even the most tumultuous periods in its history.

The Broad Sweep of British History

The origins of the British state date at least to 1215, when a band of nobles forced King John to sign the **Magna Carta** (see Table 4.2). That historic agreement declared that the king was not an absolute monarch. He had to rule in parliament and would need the consent of the nobility before imposing taxes or spending money. The Great Council, consisting of leading nobles and churchmen—the precursor of the current House of Lords—was created. As the thirteenth century wore on, the kings found that they could not meet state expenses with their personal revenues alone and called on the council to do so. Meetings took place wherever the king happened to be. The king and his ministers sat in the front, the nobility sat on benches facing them, and the commoners knelt in the back. After they heard the king's requests, the latter two groups met separately to determine what should be done, which ultimately led to the creation of the two houses of Parliament (**europeanhistory.about.com**).

TABLE 4.2 Key Events and Trends in British History

YEAR	EVENT
1215	Magna Carta signed
1532–36	Reformation; establishment of Church of England
1642–60	Civil war and Restoration
1688	Glorious Revolution
1701	Act of Settlement
Early 1700s	Emergence of prime minister
1832	Great Reform Act
1911	Reform of House of Lords
1928	Right to vote for all adults

Over the next four centuries, a succession of kings brought most of England together in what was never more than a very loose and decentralized state. The English people did not have a sense of national identity, and the governmental institutions in London lacked the power of a modern state. Still, there was an England, which was more than one could say for Italy, Germany, or, to some extent, France at the time.

In other words, when the events listed in Table 4.2 hit in earnest during the sixteenth and seventeenth centuries, the British already had made major strides toward meeting two of the transformations that shaped modern Europe. The broad contours of the state were set, and there was a rough understanding that the king had to share power with Parliament.

The sixteenth century brought the Reformation and the split between Catholics and Protestants that tore the European continent apart. In Britain, the Reformation left nowhere near as deep a scar. In part because he wanted to divorce and remarry, King Henry VIII broke with Rome and established the Church of England. It would be centuries before the British state tolerated other religions, and the division between Anglicans and Puritans would be one of the causes of the English civil war in the 1640s. Nonetheless, Henry's actions removed religion as a deeply divisive issue by the end of the seventeenth century, even though the Church of England is still the established church and it is inconceivable that a non-Anglican could join the royal family or become Prime Minister, though Ed Miliband could throw at least some of that tradition in doubt.

England did suffer through two revolutions in the seventeenth century. They were, however, mild in comparison with those that took place on the European continent, and their resolution actually helped pave the way for parliamentary democracy.

During the civil war of the 1640s, Oliver Cromwell overthrew the monarchy and had King Charles I beheaded. In 1660, his son, Charles II, was restored to the throne on the condition that he accept an expanded role for Parliament. Charles and his successors tried to reassert royal power—and even flirted with Catholicism—which led to the Glorious Revolution of 1688 and the firm understanding that the king would henceforth be both Anglican and accountable to Parliament.

Royal prerogatives continued to disappear. In 1689, King William III (who was Dutch) agreed to a Bill of Rights with Parliament. The bill made it illegal for the monarch to impose taxes or enforce any law without the consent of Parliament. In 1701, the Act of Settlement regularized procedures for succession to the throne and asserted that the king and queen had to govern Britain in accordance with laws passed by Parliament.

In 1707, Queen Anne, who ascended to the throne following the deaths of Mary (her sister) and William, failed to give her royal assent to a bill passed by Parliament, the last time any British monarch did so. Shortly thereafter,

King George I stopped attending cabinet meetings in part because he only spoke German and could not understand what was being said. That practice has continued. People began to refer to Sir Robert Walpole, the man who chaired the cabinet, as prime minister, though it would be another two centuries before the title was mentioned in any law. By the time of the American Revolution, the king had become little more than the head of one parliamentary faction. He still appointed cabinet ministers, but they could not remain in office if they lost the confidence of Parliament.

In the nineteenth century, the rise of capitalism disrupted British life more than any of the other events discussed in this section. The industrial revolution and the imperialism that fed it brought untold wealth to the capitalists and to the country, but it was nowhere near as beneficial for the men and women who worked in the mills and mines.

Hundreds of thousands left the countryside to work in the unsafe factories and live in the filthy, overcrowded cities so powerfully described in Charles Dickens' novels. Trade unions were still illegal, but friendly societies, new denominations such as Methodism, and, most important, the great petition drives of the Chartist movement made it clear that the new working and middle classes were forces to be reckoned with. Despite these rumblings from below, political life remained the preserve of a tiny elite. No more than 1 percent of all adult males were wealthy enough to vote. Parliament overrepresented rural districts, many of which were known as "rotten boroughs" because they had so few constituents that a single lord could determine who was elected. Even the growing capitalist class chafed at being excluded from political power.

A number of movements demanding political change sprang up during the first third of the nineteenth century. Bands of workers and artisans, known as Luddites, broke into factories and smashed their machines. By 1810, the term working class was commonly used—and feared. Eventually, dissatisfaction with the status quo grew strong enough to force passage of the **Great Reform Act** of 1832. Despite its name, the reform was not all that extensive. Only about 300,000 more men gained the vote, and the aristocracy continued to dominate political life.

The small number of men added to the rolls should not lead you to underestimate the act's importance. Its passage showed that the British elite was willing to adapt to changing circumstances, ceding some of its authority rather than clinging to power and running the risk of widespread political disruption, if not revolution. It also gave the House of Commons new confidence in further curbing the power of the monarchy and the aristocracy.

A second Reform Act in 1867 increased the size of the electorate to nearly 3 million. In 1870, Parliament introduced the secret ballot. The Representation of the People Acts of 1884 and 1885 expanded the suffrage to the point that working-class men constituted the majority of the electorate. By the early twentieth century, all men had gained the right to vote. Most women won the suffrage in 1918, and the vote was extended to all women ten years later.

After the 1867 reforms, the first modern political parties were formed by parliamentary leaders who needed to win the support of the newly enfranchised voters to stay in power. The Conservative National Union did surprisingly well among the working class as well as the aristocracy, while the National Liberal Federation won disproportionate support among the middle class and in Ireland. **MPs (Members of Parliament)** were now dependent on massive party machines. Gradually, the party—that is, its leaders in Parliament—began to determine who would run for office and who would serve in cabinets. Strict party discipline was imposed on the MPs. In 1911, the House of Lords was stripped of its remaining power, marking the final step in the evolution of British parliamentary democracy.

A brief comparison with France should show just how far Britain had progressed. While Britain's parliamentary system was getting ever stronger, French democracy remained shaky at best. France had just suffered through the Dreyfus affair, in which false accusations of treason against a Jewish army officer unleashed such passionate protests that the Third Republic nearly collapsed. Significant divisions over the role of religion and the nature of the state spawned anti-regime parties that typically won a third of the seats in Parliament.

As already noted, only one of the four challenges was to have a lasting impact: the division of Great Britain into supporters of the Labour and the Conservative parties largely along class lines. But even that division paled in comparison with the class conflict taking place on the

Democratization
in Britain and the United States

Both Britain and the United States have had comparatively peaceful histories. When crises did occur, they were typically resolved before the next major transformation loomed on the political horizon. Some were quite wrenching, most notably each country's civil war. However, in Britain, they were less divisive than conflicts on the European continent and, more important for our purposes, once they were resolved, almost everyone accepted the outcome. ■

Stringer/Topical Press Agency/Getty Images.

During the 1926 general strike, workers who walked off the job did not confront the police. Instead, they played football (soccer) together.

European continent. To cite but one example, in 1926, the **Trades Union Congress (TUC)** called for a general strike and British workers walked off the job *en masse*. In France or Germany, such a strike would have been accompanied by violent clashes between police and strikers. In Britain, instead of fighting each other, many of the policemen and strikers played soccer together to pass the time.

Workers' demands were by no means fully satisfied. However, their frustrations were increasingly channeled through the TUC and the Labour Party, which were both known for their moderation. By the 1920s, Labour had surged past the Liberals and became the main competition for the Conservatives. The Great Depression that began in 1929 hit Britain as hard as any European country except Germany and had both political and economic consequences.

For most of the next decade, no party had a clear majority in Parliament and a succession of weak Conservative and Labour governments failed to ease the country's economic woes or do much to meet the dangers posed by an ever more aggressive Nazi Germany. Two changes that were to reshape British politics after the war did occur despite the uncertainty of the 1930s. First, Labour solidified itself as the main alternative to the Conservatives. Second, the liberal or free-market wing of the **Conservative party** was discredited because of its failure to solve the economic crisis brought on by the Depression. In its place rose a new generation of Tory politicians who were more willing to turn

to the state to reshape the country's economic future and meeting the needs of the poor and unemployed.

The Collectivist Consensus

The period from 1945 until the mid-1970s is often portrayed as the golden era of British politics (see Table 4.3). Leaders from both parties agreed on a variety of policy goals, including full employment, the provision of social services that

TABLE 4.3 The Collectivist Years and Beyond

YEAR	EVENT
1942	Beveridge Report published
1945	Labour elected
1948	National Health Service created
1951	Conservatives return to power
1964	Labour returns to power
1972	Heath government forced into U-turn
1974	Labour wins two elections without a working majority
1979	Thatcher elected
1990	Thatcher resigns, replaced by John Major
1997	Blair elected
2007	Brown replaces Blair as Prime Minister
2008	Onset of the economic crisis
2010	Coalition government elected

guaranteed at least subsistence-level living conditions for all, cooperation with labor unions, and government intervention to secure economic growth, the benefits of which were used to improve the living conditions of the poor.

Although the Liberal-Labour coalition government of 1906–11 did introduce limited unemployment and health insurance programs, the most important origins of the collectivist consensus lie in World War II. British fortunes had sagged during the first months of the war. Country after country fell to the Nazis. British troops were forced to withdraw from Europe. German planes by the thousands bombed London and the other major British cities. There were widespread fears of a German invasion, which would have been the first since 1066.

Finally, with defeat staring the UK in the face, Parliament called on Sir Winston Churchill to replace the ineffectual Neville Chamberlain as prime minister. Although his Conservative Party had a clear majority in the Commons, Churchill chose to head an all-party coalition. The opposition parties agreed to suspend normal politics—including elections—for the duration of the war. The Conservatives, in turn, agreed to establish a commission headed by the civil servant William Beveridge. Its task was to propose an overhaul of the social service system that would be turned into legislation after the Allied victory. When issued in 1942, the **Beveridge Report** called for a social insurance program in which every citizen would be eligible for health care, unemployment insurance, pensions, and other benefits including free tuition at the country's universities.

The election of 1945—the first in ten years—was fought largely over social and economic reform. Both major parties endorsed the broad outlines of the Beveridge Report, although Labour was committed to going further and faster in enacting its recommendations as well as in nationalizing a number of key industries.

Labour won a resounding victory, marking the first time it came to power with a parliamentary majority of its own. The new prime minister, Clement Attlee, and his government proceeded to turn the party program into legislation, which the House of Commons passed with only slight modification.

By 1949, the surge of reform had come to an end. Throughout Europe, the Cold War sapped socialist parties of their momentum. Furthermore, with economic recovery well under way, Labour decided to dismantle most of the planning boards that had brought government, the unions, and business together. Meanwhile, Labour's popular support began to wane. It barely won a majority in the 1950 elections and when Attlee dissolved Parliament the following year, the Conservatives returned to power.

One might have expected the party of capitalism to repeal the vast majority of Labour's reforms. In fact, it did not. The steel industry was privatized, and people had to pay a nominal fee for prescriptions and eyeglasses. Otherwise,

the Conservatives retained the welfare state Labour had so vastly expanded in the years after the war.

In retrospect, the Conservatives' actions should not have come as much of a surprise. The party had supported most collectivist policies in 1945. During the election campaign that year, the debate between the parties had centered on the pace and extent of reform, not on whether it should occur. In his first speech as leader of the opposition, Churchill stated:

> It is evident that not only are we two parties in the house agreed on the main essentials of foreign policy and in our moral outlook on world affairs, but we also have an immense program, prepared by our joint exertions during the coalition, which requires to be brought into law and made an inherent part of the life of the people. Here and there, there may be differences of emphasis and view but, in the main no Parliament has ever assembled with such a mass of agreed legislation as lies before us this afternoon.[1]

Electorally, the British remained divided along class lines. Normally, about 70 percent of the working class voted Labour and an even larger proportion of the middle class voted Conservative. However, ideologically, those differences were not very significant. Although the British did tend to support the party of their class, this did not lead them to hate either the other class or the other major party.

The two main parties routinely won over 90 percent of the vote and an even larger share of the seats in the House of Commons. It mattered little which party was in power. Each gradually expanded the role of the state at almost exactly the same rate year in and year out. Elections were fought over slogans such as the Conservatives' "You Never Had It So Good" in 1959 or over Labour's claim that it would bring more modern management practices to government in 1964.

Many political scientists saw the collectivist years as the natural culmination of British political history with its emphasis on class, consensus, and cooperation. Others saw them as providing a model of what modern liberal democracies could and should be like.

However, the collectivist consensus did not survive because two conditions that had made it possible did not endure, as we will also see in the discussion of Thatcher and Blair's "revolutions" later in the chapter. The consensus had existed in part because steady economic growth allowed successive governments to meet popular policy demands. In addition, British politics could be consensual only when there were not any deeply divisive issues. Both of those conditions evaporated, and the impact of the end of the collectivist consensus will be the focus of much of the rest of this chapter.

---

[1]Quoted in Allen Sked and Chris Clark, *Post-War Britain: A Political History*, 3rd ed. (London: Penguin Books, 1990), 24.

BRITISH POLITICAL CULTURE

At the height of the collectivist period in 1959, Gabriel Almond and Sidney Verba conducted about five thousand interviews in Britain and four other countries, which they drew on in writing their landmark study *The Civic Culture.*[2] They painted a picture of a harmonious and trusting British public, and concluded that any effectively functioning democracy needed a culture much like the UK's.

Critical analysis and subsequent events have led most political scientists to conclude that the British political culture is no longer as supportive as it once was and that a number of different types of cultures likely can sustain a democracy. Nonetheless, the snapshot Almond and Verba took of Britain in the collectivist years goes a long way toward explaining why the British regime and democracy were not put in jeopardy during the crisis years of the 1970s and 1980s.

The Civic Culture and the Collectivist Years

The British people were never completely satisfied with their political lot even in the 1950s. However, they probably were as content as any society in the twentieth century. There was virtually unanimous agreement that the political system based on parliamentary sovereignty and cabinet rule was legitimate. There were protests, such as those by the marchers who crossed the country to oppose nuclear weapons each year at Easter time. But, except for a tiny handful of communists and fascists, everyone acknowledged the government's right to govern.

The British were remarkably tolerant of each other and of the people who led them. Poll after poll revealed a public that trusted its politicians and institutions. At the time, most adults felt a sense of efficacy—that, as individuals, they could influence the political process. However, few people in Britain actually participated in ways that put demands on decision makers other than by voting, leading observers like Almond and Verba to conclude that democracies actually need a relatively inactive and uninvolved electorate.

The British also thought of themselves as patriotic, with flag-waving and national anthem-singing almost as widespread as in the United States. But even this patriotism was muted and rarely led to anything approaching jingoistic involvement abroad. This is most easily seen in the ease with which most people accepted the loss of Britain's colonial empire.

[2]Gabriel Almond and Sidney Verba, *The Civic Culture* (Princeton, NJ: Princeton University Press, 1962).

The Politics of Protest: Toward an Uncivic Culture?

In the 1970s, all that changed. More and more people expressed reservations about the collectivist consensus. Though the overwhelming majority of the population stayed on the sidelines, popular participation took on a decidedly confrontational tone and left many with the impression that Britain was becoming ungovernable.

Signs of dissatisfaction came from all points on the political spectrum. Northern Ireland, which had been rather peaceful, became anything but that after the introduction of British troops into the province in 1969 and "Bloody Sunday" in January 1972, when thirteen Catholics were killed by British troops. The Irish Republican Army (IRA) and various Protestant paramilitaries escalated their campaigns of violence, including an attack that nearly killed Thatcher and the rest of the Conservative leadership at the party's annual conference in 1984.

St. Ethelburga's was a medieval church and the smallest one in London. In 1993, it was leveled by an IRA bomb that killed one person and wounded more than fifty. The church has been rebuilt as a center for reconciliation where people of all faiths can find a safe place to discuss their disputes. The website is www.stethelburgas.org.

Britain also had to come to grips with widespread racism. The Conservative and, later, Ulster Unionist (Protestant) politician, Enoch Powell built a career exploiting the fear and antagonism many British men and women felt toward Asians, Africans, and Afro-Caribbeans. The National Front, whose racism was at best thinly veiled, did well in local elections in working-class white neighborhoods adjacent to others with large minority populations. White toughs repeatedly attacked blacks and Asians, which led to riots in London, Liverpool, Birmingham, and smaller cities.

Here we can concentrate on the single most important example of heightened unrest that led to worries about Britain's becoming ungovernable: the new militancy of the unions. It should come as no surprise that workers grew more dissatisfied during the crisis years. By the mid-1980s, unemployment had topped 3 million, six times what it had been during the 1950s and 1960s. Workers who still had jobs saw their standard of living eroded by inflation that regularly outpaced their annual raises.

The radicalization of the unions had begun during the 1960s and contributed heavily to the defeat of the Wilson, Heath, and Callaghan governments in the 1960s and 1970s. Strikes were larger and lasted longer. Often, workers struck without warning or the authorization of union leaders. Workers also often called "secondary" strikes against other firms that their own company dealt with, thereby spreading the disruption caused by the initial dispute. Violence at factory gates and mine pits was an all but daily occurrence.

The respective rigidities of Thatcher and the union leaders put them on a collision course that reached a peak during her second term. The government provided the pretext for such a confrontation in 1984 by passing a new Industrial Relations Act that obliged union leaders to poll their members using a secret ballot before calling a strike and held them financially responsible for illegal walkouts. On March 1, the Coal Board announced the closure of the Cortonwood mine in Yorkshire. Less than a week later, it added almost twenty more mines to a list due to be shut, which would lead to the loss of about twenty thousand jobs. The miners whose jobs were in jeopardy put down their tools, and union leaders called for a nationwide strike in violation of the new legislation. Both the striking miners and the government held firm for almost a year in a strike that was to cost the British economy about £3 billion. Finally, the miners gave up and in March 1985, they narrowly agreed to return to work.

The militancy of the unions was echoed in many other areas of political life. Many people felt that the Labour Party had been taken over by extremists, labeled the "loony Left" by the tabloid press. The peace movement opposed the deployment of American Cruise and Pershing missiles armed with nuclear warheads at the American base at Greenham Common. Thousands of women tried to stop deployment of the missiles by blocking the entrance

Environmental protestors opposing construction of a bypass around the city of Newbury in Berkshire.

to the base for more than a year. More recently, environmental activists delayed construction of a bypass around the clogged nearby city of Newbury by living in the trees that workers would have to cut down and building tunnels under the proposed path of the road.

Political scientists have discovered that the protests had a dual impact on British culture. On the one hand, the activists on the Left and Right helped create a far more polarized political system. The Left believed that the capitalists were ruthlessly exploiting the working class. The Right feared that the socialists, unions, feminists, and minorities were making Britain harder to govern and were undermining traditional values.

On the other hand, the vast majority of the populace did not take part in the protests and grew frustrated with the new confrontational politics. There was a general agreement that the Left had gone too far in its demands on both domestic and foreign policy. Even Labour supporters came to doubt the new radicalism of the unions and their own party. As the 1980s wore on, there was also was growing dissatisfaction with a Right wing that was itself perceived to be too radical.

The Civic Culture Holds

The protests also illustrate just how much British political culture did *not* change during the crisis. Indeed, in at least two respects, the British culture "held."

First, the dangers these protests posed proved rather fleeting in large part because the Thatcher government met them head on. To a large extent, it succeeded, which we can see by returning to the example of the trade unions.

The Thatcher government viewed the 1984 miners' strike as a showdown with the militant unions. Unlike previous prime ministers of both parties, Thatcher was able to play on the growing dissatisfaction with union demands and the growing split between radicals and moderates within the union movement itself to bring the miners to their knees. The defeat of the miners turned the tide. Since then, union militancy and membership have declined and most radical leaders have been replaced by moderates. The rhetoric and tactics of class war have largely disappeared despite some fears that were raised when Labour chose Ed Miliband, who does have fairly close ties to the TUC's left.

The important point here is not whether Thatcher was right or wrong. What matters is the impact her actions had on the British people. Together with the economic recovery of the mid-1980s, Thatcher's strong stance against the Left helped sharply reduce the political tensions that seemed to imperil traditional British institutions and practices.

Second, and even more important, the analysts who predicted the end of the civic culture overstated the dangers the protest movements posed. Despite what the far Left may have wanted, revolution was never on the horizon. The British public was too committed to established parliamentary institutions for that to occur.

A 1979 review of their original conclusions about the civic culture did uncover some erosion in some indicators which Almond and Verba had used to build their case twenty years earlier. To some extent, given the common perception that the government had failed to solve many of the country's problems, the increased skepticism toward politicians and their motivations was to be expected.

However, if we concentrate on the more general level that most students of political culture stress, there is much less evidence that values changed. Dissatisfaction with recent governments simply has not translated into dissatisfaction with the regime.

Will There Always Be a Britain?

There may be one way in which the civic culture is in flux. Since the late 1960s, identification with Britain as a whole has declined, especially among the Scots and the Welsh.

As we will see later in the chapter, there has been a resurgence of support for regional parties in Scotland and Wales, and the "British" parties have never fielded candidates in

Racist, right-wing protest in Britain.

REUTERS/Darren Staples /Landov.

Northern Ireland. A 2000 poll asked people about the levels of government they most identified with. Eighteen percent of the Scots said Britain, and 72 percent mentioned Scotland. The comparable figures for Wales were 27 percent for Britain and 81 percent for Wales. The English were split down the middle, with 43 percent mentioning Britain and 41 percent England. When asked about their lives twenty years in the future, 22 percent thought that the government in London would be the most important political institution in their lives—barely half that number mentioned the EU.[3]

Partially in response to those apparent shifts in public opinion, the first Blair government created regional parliaments in Northern Ireland, Scotland, and Wales. It also floated trial balloons about regional assemblies in England as well following the first direct election of the mayor of London in 1999. The creation of the regional assemblies reflects the fact many people have multiple identities, with their home region, the UK as a whole, and in a small number of cases, the EU.

Despite this new growth in regional identification and power, no one is suggesting that the UK is going to fall apart any time soon. But, many of the symbols and institutions that have held British culture together are losing their influence. There is no better example of this than the monarchy. Even though the reigning king or queen has not had any real political power for more than a century, the monarchy has been an important symbol of British unity and pride. However, much of that pride has disappeared in the wake of scandals about the personal lives of many of the "royals," which culminated in the tragic death of Princess Diana in 1997.

This "new" country is reflected in the changing physical face of Britain—and most of the other major European countries. Britain is increasingly a racially diverse nation. Most members of racial minority groups were born in the UK. Although the minority population pales in comparison with that in the United States, curry is probably the most popular food in the country, and most fish-and-chips shops are run by Chinese immigrants, who also sell egg rolls and fried rice, not to mention curry. The success of the film, *Bend It Like Beckham,* which features a racially mixed women's soccer team, is a sign of the changes that have occurred in recent years.

Still, there were overt instances of racism, especially in the grimy industrial cities in the north during the first decade of the twenty-first century where racist candidates won a handful of seats in local elections in 2009. As in the United States, young black men are more likely than their white contemporaries to be pulled over by the police "on sus" (racial profiling to Americans) and to be treated arbitrarily after an arrest. Perhaps most telling, a former cabinet member, Lord Norman Tebbit, got drew a lot of publicity when he said that citizens of Pakistani or Indian origin should not be considered truly British if they did not support the English cricket team when it played matches against their country of origin.

Last, but by no means least, the British national identity is being undermined as a side effect of its membership in the European Union. Conservative **euroskeptics** ground their qualms about Europe as much in a feared loss of national distinctiveness as on their doubts about the viability of the EU (see Chapter 7). They are probably fighting a losing battle. As more and more Europeans come to work in the UK and more and more British citizens spend time living on the continent, their concerns could abate. Satellite and cable television services carry programming in multiple languages, and British residents can get any major European daily newspaper delivered to their door the next morning.

POLITICAL PARTICIPATION

Just as important in understanding the long-term stability and short-term difficulties of any system are the ways in which people participate in political life. Over the past century or so, most of that participation in Britain has been through political parties and interest groups that pursue moderate policies and concentrate on class and economic issues.

Before the 1970s, the Labour and Conservative parties were the linchpin of British political stability. Ever since World War II, one or the other has won each general election, and the victorious party treated the result as a mandate to carry out the policies called for in its **manifesto**, or electoral platform (see Table 4.4).

With the onset of the economic crisis of the 1970s, however, the parties began to change. Both Labour and the

TABLE 4.4 British Prime Ministers since 1945

NAME	PARTY	YEARS IN OFFICE
Clement Attlee	Labour	1945–51
Winston Churchill	Conservative	1951–55
Anthony Eden	Conservative	1955–56
Harold Macmillan	Conservative	1956–63
Alec Douglas Home	Conservative	1963–64
Harold Wilson	Labour	1964–70
Edward Heath	Conservative	1970–74
Harold Wilson	Labour	1974–76
James Callaghan	Labour	1976–79
Margaret Thatcher	Conservative	1979–90
John Major	Conservative	1990–97
Tony Blair	Labour	1997–2007
Gordon Brown	Labour	2007–2010
David Cameron	Conservative	2010–

[3]Andrew Marr, *The Day Britain Died* (London: Profile Books, 2000), 2.

Conservatives ended up deeply divided, with the balance of power in each drifting toward the ideological extremes. Such polarization occurred in all of the liberal democracies, though it went further and faster in Britain than in most others. However, as in all of them, the shift toward extremism proved to be a passing phenomenon. By the end of the 1980s, Labour had joined many other social democratic parties in moderating its views, and Thatcher's retirement in 1990 and the Tory defeats in 1997, 2001, and 2005 have had the same effect on the Conservatives, although their "modernization" is still in its early phases.

In short, Labour and the Conservatives are now squarely what political scientists call brokerage or catch-all parties whose primary motivation is winning elections. Their ideological positions still differ and remain important to their grassroots activists. However, both parties' leaders have shown a willingness to sacrifice ideological purity for likely electoral gains. They are increasingly under the sway of spin doctors who, like their American counterparts, seem more like advertising executives than committed partisans.

The 2010 election may change all that, but it is impossible to tell if the Tory/Liberal Democratic coalition is a flash in the pan or a sign of lasting changes in British political life. The other dramatic change in British politics has been the rise in the number of women in the Commons and in government. In all, 22 percent of MPs are now women; in a trend that began in earnest with Blair's first victory in 1997. Notable wins by women in 2010 elections included the first two Muslim women, the second "out" lesbian, and the first Green party member elected to parliament.

Frankly, only one thing is clear after the 2010 election. The conservatives dominate a coalition government that is committed to budget cuts the likes which the UK has not seen in recent memory (see the public policy section). How Labour responds to its defeat and how the Liberal Democrats deal with being the junior partner of the coalition both remain to be seen.

The Conservatives

We start with the Conservatives, not only because they are in power today but also because they were in charge for so much of the past century and a half that they have often been seen as the "natural party of government" 🖰 (**www. conservatives.com**). They have won a majority of the elections since the late 1880s and have been in office more than half of the time since World War II.

The Conservatives have been successful for three main reasons, which began to evaporate late in the Thatcher era. First, most Conservative leaders were pragmatic politicians who were flexible enough to change their positions when circumstances warranted. For example, the early

nineteenth century Tories may well have wanted to maintain the elitist system in which only the wealthiest men could vote. However, by the time of the Chartist movement of the 1820s, they recognized that they would have to extend the suffrage. Similarly, it was the Conservative Party under Benjamin Disraeli that organized the first grassroots constituency organizations after the Reform Act of 1867 granted the vote to most working-class men.

Second, because their roots lay in the nobility, Conservative politicians tended to embody the values of noblesse oblige or the responsibility of the elite to the less fortunate. As a result, the Conservatives did not historically champion a free-market economy and unbridled capitalism. To be sure, the party always included people like Thatcher who believed market forces should be emphasized. However, the party's most influential leaders stressed its responsibility for the poor and were willing to support a substantial welfare state, to use the government to maintain the health of a capitalist economy, and to accept the collectivist consensus after World War II.

Third, the Conservatives had an elitist but effective organization. The party maintained organizations in each constituency, most of which had a full-time paid "agent." Real power, however, lay in London and, ultimately, with the leader who was also prime minister when the party was in power. There were no formal provisions for selecting the leader, who was chosen secretly by senior MPs. The leader, in turn, dominated the parliamentary party and the central office, which had veto power over local constituency organizations' nominees for Parliament.

In the mid-1970s, the Conservatives adopted more open procedures for choosing leaders that a new generation of market-oriented MPs, who were hostile to the welfare state, used to select Thatcher after Heath led the party to two defeats at the polls in 1974. Thatcher and her colleagues preferred what they called the politics of conviction to the consensus-building and pragmatism of previous periods.

Thatcherism served the Tories extremely well during the 1980s. In large part because of its own difficulties that will be discussed in the next section, Labour dumped the 1979 election into Thatcher's lap, beginning her eleven years in office. At first, she was obliged to include most of the senior party leaders in her cabinet, including many who did not share her objections to collectivist politics. Over the next few years, however, she gained more and more control over the party, forcing most of the moderates onto the sidelines and replacing them with ideological conservatives who also were personally beholden to her.

When Thatcher's popularity slipped and she was forced to resign in 1990, the challenge came not from the moderates, but from her erstwhile supporters who had come to see her as an electoral liability. They then chose her protégé, **John Major**, who proved to be a lackluster leader who neither appealed to the electorate nor coped with the party's deepening divisions, especially over Europe.

Major resigned as party leader the day after the 1997 election and was replaced by the young but experienced William Hague who is now the foreign minister. After that, the party had four leaders, the first three of whom were viewed as ineffective and resigned after yet another defeat at the polls. After its loss in 2005, the party made a bold move that few expected of it.

It turned to **David Cameron**.

At forty years old at the time of Blair's resignation, he is one of the youngest leaders of any major political party in the Western world. Cameron first entered the House of Commons in 2001. Two years later, he was part of the Tory leadership team. When his predecessor resigned, he decided to run for the leadership, portraying himself as younger and more moderate than any of the other candidates.

When Brown took office, the polls suggested that Cameron and the Tories were likely to win the next election in spring 2010. Polls ✍ (www.mori.com) suggested that they were not likely to win because they are popular, but only because Labour had done what most voters thought was a dreadful job on Iraq and the subsequent economic crisis.

Despite Cameron's popularity and Labour's descent in the polls, the key to the Tories' future probably lies elsewhere, in the way the party handles two issues. The first is European integration. Although Thatcherism was initially defined by the prime minister's promarket and antiwelfare state positions, by the 1990s most of the Tory Right came to be preoccupied with Europe. They saw such developments as the **Maastricht Treaty**, which created the EU and started plans for the euro, as serious threats to British sovereignty.

The polls, however, suggest that hard-core euroskepticism contributed heavily to the Tories' defeats after 1997 and could continue to undermine their popularity for the foreseeable future. Polls continue to show widespread doubts about adopting the euro. Nonetheless, few Britons share the degree of opposition to the EU one finds among the ardent euroskeptics who controlled the party before Cameron's ascent.

Second, and related, is its leadership and organization. As many as a third of its dues-paying members are over the age of sixty-five. What's more, the shrinking number of Conservative activists reflects the "hard Right" views of the leadership before Cameron. In other words, it had a hard time reaching out to the swing voters it will need to win on a regular basis.

Here Cameron and his de facto running mate Nick Clegg (see the section on the Lib Dems below) were a partial answer. It turns out that they were not necessarily more moderate than their rivals in the center Right nor did they want to shed the Tory commitment to Thatcherite and Euroskeptic policy and endorse other forms of conservative economic reforms to combat the recession.

Labour

For most of the past forty years, it has been Labour, not the Conservatives, that has borne the criticism for being too extreme and out of touch with the electorate. However, after four consecutive defeats and three leadership changes, the party moved back toward the center to become one of the most modern and innovative political parties in the industrialized world—at least until the mid-2000s.

The **Labour Party** ✍ (www.labour.org.uk) was formed at the beginning of the twentieth century as an alliance of trade unions, independent socialist movements, and cooperative associations. Unlike the socialist parties on the continent, Marxists had little influence on the party in its early years. Clause 4 of the original party program adopted after World War I did call for the nationalization of the "commanding heights" of British industry. Still, most observers were convinced that Labour had accepted the parliamentary system and the democratic rules of the game by the early 1900s.

This was the case in large part because the unions dominated the party, and TUC members automatically join Labour as well unless they sign a form informing the union not to send part of their dues to the party. Because the unions were more concerned with improving the lives of their members than with any doctrine, they were able to keep the party close to the center throughout most of its history. After losing three consecutive elections in the 1950s, many Labour leaders came to the conclusion that the party could never win a majority again if Clause 4 stayed in the party program. Although it did not formally repudiate Clause 4 until after Blair took over the leadership, the party conference in 1959 did make it clear that socialism was, at most, a long-term goal, not something it would implement were it to win the next election, which it did in 1964 (see Table 4.5).

The Labour government of 1964–70 was dominated by moderates. That moderation, however, would not survive the onset of the economic crisis. A new wave of union militancy pushed many in the party leftward, as did entry into the European Community (the predecessor to the EU) in 1972. Most important, the party's left wing gained support from activists first drawn to politics by the new Left in the 1960s.

The shift leftward and the party's inability to control the newly radicalized unions led to its defeat in 1979. Rather than moderating its stance, the party moved even further to the Left. It chose the radical Michael Foot to be its new leader. It also created an electoral college made up of members of Parliament, union officials, and rank-and-file activists to select new leaders, thus stripping power from the relatively moderate MPs. Meanwhile, seventeen of its most conservative MPs quit in 1981 and created the new

Profiles
David Cameron

David Cameron became leader of the Conservative Party on December 5, 2005 and was widely hailed as a breath of fresh air both because he was so young and because he was thought to be more moderate than his predecessors.

There is little in his past to indicate that he would become a reformer. He was raised about sixty miles from London where his father ran the family financial empire. His mother is the daughter of a baronet. He is also a direct descendent of King William V and one of his mistresses, which also makes him a fifth cousin of Queen Elizabeth.

Cameron had the kind of education one would expect of someone of his class. He was sent to boarding school around the corner from Windsor Castle when he was seven years old. He then went to England's most prestigious public (that is, private) school, Eton, which overlooks Windsor Castle from the other side of the Thames. He was a brilliant student, but he did have a run in with the authorities after he was caught smoking marijuana; his punishment was to copy five hundred lines of Latin prose.

After a "gap year" after his graduation from Eton, he attended Brasenose College at Oxford, where he studied in the prestigious Philosophy, Politics, and Economics program under Vernon Bogdanor, arguably the best constitutional scholar of this generation. Cameron graduated with a "first," roughly the equivalent of *summa cum laude* in the United States.

After graduation, he took a job as a researcher for the Conservative Party. He later worked for one of the earliest private television production companies before finally winning a safe conservative seat in Witney in the picturesque Cotswolds which is near his family home in 2001. It is highly unusual for a politician to rise so quickly in the United Kingdom, but within four years he was leading his party.

Although his ideological positions are not as consistently conservative a those of his predecessors.

David Cameron.

Cameron does have deep qualms about European integration, for example. However, he also voted for the Civil Partnership Act in 2004, which gave gay and lesbian couples the same benefits as heterosexual ones.

Cameron and his wife have four children. The oldest was born with cerebral palsy and epilepsy. The fourth was born during the family's first summer vacation after he was elected prime minister. He is one of the rare British politicians who talks frequently about his family in public. ■

Social Democratic Party (SDP), which we will discuss in the next section.

Control remained with the left wing, epitomized by the enigmatic Anthony Wedgwood Benn. Though from an aristocratic family (the Wedgwoods make some of Britain's finest china), Benn had gradually moved to the Left during the 1970s and was now advocating a radical break with capitalism. He, not Foot, was Labour's most visible leader during the 1983 campaign, and together they led the party to one of its worst defeats ever. The party did so poorly that many observers thought that the **Alliance**, formed between the Liberals and Social

TABLE 4.5 British General Election Results since 1945

YEAR	CONSERVATIVES		LABOUR		LIBERAL DEMOCRATS		OTHER	
	VOTES (%)	SEATS	VOTES (%)	SEATS	VOTES (%)	SEATS	VOTES (%)	SEATS
1945	39.8	213	48.3	393	9.1	12	2.7	22
1950	43.5	299	46.1	315	9.1	9	1.3	2
1951	48.0	321	46.8	295	2.5	6	0.7	3
1955	49.7	345	46.4	277	2.7	6	1.1	2
1959	49.4	365	43.8	258	5.9	6	1.0	1
1964	43.4	304	44.1	317	11.2	9	1.3	0
1966	41.9	253	47.9	363	8.5	12	1.6	2
1970	46.4	330	43.0	288	7.5	6	3.1	6
1974 (Feb)	37.8	297	37.1	301	19.3	14	5.8	23
1974 (Oct)	35.8	277	39.2	319	18.3	13	6.7	26
1979	43.9	339	37.0	269	13.8	11	5.3	16
1983	42.4	397	27.6	209	25.4	23	4.6	21
1987	42.3	376	30.8	229	22.6	22	4.3	23
1992	41.8	336	34.4	271	17.8	20	6.0	24
1997	30.6	165	43.2	419	16.7	45	9.7	30
2001	31.7	166	40.7	413	18.3	52	8.5	28
2005	32.3	198	35.3	356	22.1	62	10.3	30
2010	36.1	306	29.0	258	23.0	57	23.9	29

Note: Others consist almost exclusively of regional parties in Scotland, Wales, and Northern Ireland. Liberals includes Liberals up to 1983, Liberal–Social Democratic Alliance in 1983–87, and Liberal Democrats in 1992. The total number of seats varies from election to election, with a low of 625 in 1950 and 1951 and new highs of 659 in 1997 and 660 in 2010.

Democrats, might replace Labour as the country's second largest party.

Had Benn not lost his own seat that year, he might well have been chosen to replace the ineffectual Foot. Instead, the party turned to Neil Kinnock. Though on the left, Kinnock was willing to put the party's electoral success ahead of ideological purity. The party made up some of its lost ground in 1987, but it still found itself behind the Tories by 11.5 percent of the vote and nearly 150 seats.

Over the next five years, Labour's moderation led to increased support in the polls. Nationalization of industry all but disappeared from the party program. The party also abandoned its commitment to unilateral nuclear disarmament which had cost it dearly in 1983 and 1987. Perhaps most important, like the American Democrats in 1992, party activists and leaders had grown tired of losing. As the next elections neared, Labour found new unity rooted in a common desire to defeat the Tories, which, in turn, reinforced the belief that it had to modify its stance. At the 1991 party conference, for instance, Clare Short, a left-wing member of Parliament and part of Blair's cabinet until she quit to protest its policy on Iraq in 2003, won ringing applause for the following statement: Thatcher "should have been a short-term leader of the opposition. And that [she was not] is our fault. We have to be very grown-up, very serious and very honest about our politics. We all used to posture. This is deadly serious."

As election day neared, pollsters predicted a Labour victory or, at least, a hung Parliament in which Labour would have the most seats but not an overall majority. When the votes were counted, Labour had lost an unprecedented fourth straight election.

This time, however, defeat did not splinter the party. Kinnock immediately stepped down. Most party leaders were convinced that he had done a good job in creating a more credible image for the party and that it therefore had to continue with its more moderate policies. He was replaced by the widely respected and even more pragmatic John Smith (1938–94).

The most dramatic shift in Labour politics came after Smith's sudden death in 1994. This time, Labour took a major risk by selecting the young, dynamic Tony Blair as his successor. Blair was only forty-one at the time. He and his colleagues made it clear that they were planning to strip away all vestiges of the old Labour Left. Within a year, Clause 4 was gone. The party announced that it would keep many of the reforms of the Thatcher—Major era, including most of the privatizations of companies and the changes in the social service system. Blair even acknowledged that he had personally respected Thatcher's style, if not her policies. The power of the unions to control the party leadership was reduced, and most of the leftists were shunted onto the sidelines.

Profiles
Ed Miliband

Ed Miliband (1969–) became the new leader of the Labour party on September 25, 2010, replacing Gordon Brown after the party lost the election that May.

Miliband continues the recent trend in which major parties pick young leaders—he is actually younger than either Cameron or Clegg. He also has had a meteoric rise in political life, at least by British standards. Miliband comes from an intellectual family (his father was a renowned socialist thinker) and graduated from Oxford and the London School of Economics before becoming a researcher for Labour. There he became close with Brown who helped him get elected from a working class district in 2005 and then named him to a series of cabinet posts after Blair's resignation. Miliband also spent two years as a research and teaching fellow at Harvard.

Many see Miliband as often taking the party back to the Left. Although he wants to shed the "new Labour" label, he has also cautioned the party that it has to adopt a center left stance. The most curious thing about his selection as party leader is that he ran against and barely beat his more popular and older brother in the electoral college that chooses new leaders. Had the party members voted as a whole, it is likely that the more popular and better known David Miliband would have won.

He is also the first party leader of Jewish origins since Benjamin Disraeli launched his career in the early nineteenth century. But Disraeli had to convert to Christianity long before starting a serious political career. ∎

The Blair government's actions will be discussed in depth in the section on public policy. Here, it is enough to build on his strengths and weaknesses as a leader.

At first, Blair had moments when he was remarkably popular. He is bright, personally engaging, and maybe the most effective British politician ever at using television to get his point of view across. However, the enthusiasm for his prime ministry dissipated long before he retired.

His accomplishments were by no means trivial. Along with George Mitchell, he was the prime mover behind peace in Northern Ireland. At that point, the British economy was healthier than it had been at any point in decades, something we saw in the basics table.

On the other hand, Blair's positions on issues ranging from Iraq to university fees alienated even some of the Labour Party's staunchest supporters. His often iron-handed and seemingly arbitrary control of the party machinery had a similar effect. Finally, the scandals that brought down several of his closest colleagues and the government's failure to make inroads on such important policies as modernizing the public transit system or the National Health Service (NHS) cost it support among the moderates who had flocked to the party in 1997.

After Blair resigned, the future of the party lay in the hands of Gordon Brown. He had been a fixture in the Labour leadership for a generation. Brown lacked Blair's flair which cost him dearly during the election campaign. He also came to power in 2007, just before the great recession began, which hit Britain harder than most countries. And perhaps most importantly of all, the British people seemed to be tired of a Labour government that had been in power for thirteen years. It came as no surprise when Labour finally lost.

As we write, Miliband has been in charge of the party for a matter of months. Therefore, it is impossible to tell yet whether he will be an effective leader who could bring Labour back to power.

The Liberal Democrats

The newest major party is the **Liberal Democrats** (www.libdems.org.uk). The party is a product of a merger of the Liberals (one of the country's original parties) and the Social Democrats. Britain has never had a true two-party system, yet in the postwar period, Labour and the Conservatives have dominated political life. Although the Liberals were the largest of the other parties, they never won more than fourteen seats between 1945 and 1979.

During the 1960s, Liberal leaders struggled to define a strategy that would situate themselves between the increasingly ideological Labour and Conservative parties and provide a haven for the growing number of dissatisfied voters. Popular support for the Liberals did grow during the 1970s, although they were still only able to win a handful of constituencies.

Most of their new voters were not confirmed Liberals. Instead, they were regular Conservative or Labour supporters who felt that they could no longer support their party, but also could not bring themselves to vote for its main rival.

In 1981, four prominent leaders (known as the "gang of four") quit Labour to form the **SDP (Social Democratic Party)**. They assumed that millions of voters would follow them, and initial public opinion polls suggested they might have been right. Quickly, however, it became clear that the SDP could not win on its own. At that point, Liberal and Social Democratic leaders decided to form the **Alliance** and run a single candidate in each district. The Alliance did well, winning about 26 percent of the vote in 1983, only two percentage points less than Labour.

However, the new party fell victim to Britain's **first-past-the-post**, or winner take all, electoral system. Any number of candidates can run, and whoever wins the most votes wins the constituency even if she or he ends up far short of a majority. In other words, a minor party can win an impressive share of the vote, but if that vote is spread more or less evenly around the country, it can be all but shut out of Parliament. That is precisely what happened to the Alliance in 1983, when it only won twenty-three seats, or 3.5 percent of the total. Not surprisingly, the Lib Dems made electoral reform a key condition for joining the government in 2010. However, a referendum to adopt a more complicated electoral system was defeated by more than two-to-one in May 2011, dashing hopes for reform.

The Alliance itself proved difficult to maintain. The two parties had different traditions and different, but equally ambitious, leaders. Tensions mounted following its marginally worse results in 1987. The two leaderships decided to merge and create the Liberal Democrats. The merger was accepted by everyone except for a small faction headed by David Owen, who had been Labour's foreign minister and who would later be one of the leading negotiators seeking a solution to the civil war in Bosnia. Owen kept the SDP alive until a by-election in 1990, when it barely topped 150 votes, not even a third of the number captured by Lord David Sutch of the Raving Monster Loony Party. The SDP disbanded.

The new Liberal Democratic party and its leader, Paddy Ashdown, went into the 1992 election with high hopes. Unfortunately for them, it did even worse than the Alliance, losing 20 percent of its vote and two of its then twenty-two seats.

Over the last twenty years, the party has turned its fortunes around in two key respects. First, it capitalized on dissatisfaction with the Conservatives to build a strong base in local government, where it actually forced the Tories into third place at various times in the 1990s. Then, in the run-up to the 1997 parliamentary election, it cast itself to Labour's left on a number of issues by advocating stronger environmental policies and an income tax hike to fund increased spending on health and education. That, plus some tactical voting through which Labour supporters cast their votes for a Liberal Democrat who stood a good chance of winning, led to a doubling of its representation in Parliament despite actually losing a few votes nationwide.

In fact, the party did even better in 2001 and 2005, increasing its share of the vote by almost 6 percent and its number of MPs by seventeen over the two elections.

Profiles
Nick Clegg

JOHN GILES/PA Photos/Landov.

There is little in his early life that indicates that Nicholas William Clegg was destined to become one of the most dynamic politicians of his generation. His father's mother was from Russia and fled Bolshevik rule, finally settling in the Netherlands. His mother's family was Dutch and interned by the Japanese during World War II. They, too, left the Netherlands under a political storm. Nick's father and grandfathers were intellectuals with a strong interest in finance.

So it is hardly a surprise that young Nick grew up in an international home. He grew up at least as privileged as David Cameron, but he always had some reformist sides to his education—for example appearing in a play on HIV/AIDS while an undergraduate. It is also not surprising that he began his professional career in Brussels, not London.

Politically, he was lucky to return to the UK at a time when the Liberal Democrats were struggling to find a leader. He was first elected to the European Parliament in 2004 from the East Midlands and to Parliament in London a year later from a neighboring constituency. Two years later, he was chosen party leader.

He has been the most successful Lib Dem leader in the current era. The party gained one more percent of the vote in 2010. Despite losing six seats from its 2005 total, its votes were needed to form a majority in parliament, since both Labour and Tories fell far short of winning one on their own. ■

However, the party went through a wrenching change shortly thereafter when Charles Kennedy, its leader at the time, was forced to resign and was replaced by a senior politician who would only keep the job on an interim basis.

Nick Clegg, who champions the role of Gurkhas who fought for the UK in the colonial era, then won control of the party. He is the son of an investment banker, which left him predisposed to support traditional pro-market economic policies that had been at the heart of his party's appeals since the 1800s. Clegg had also spent most of his career working for the European Union in Brussels and was thus relatively unfamiliar with and unknown to pundits in London. Finally, as we have seen, his wife is Spanish and Clegg himself speaks five languages fluently. In short, he is both a breath of fresh air and the most unusual leader the UK has seen in generations.

As successful as Clegg has been, the Liberal Democrats still face the same problems they have since World War II. Their vote is distributed evenly around the country with only a few pockets of support giving them little more than a handful of safe seats. That means that they are not going to be serious candidates for winning a majority in the foreseeable future. In 2010, Clegg came close to leading the party to first place in total votes, but it was doomed to finish third as far as seats in Westminster are concerned.

Minor Parties

The rise in Scottish, Welsh, and Irish nationalism has also led to a modest growth in support for regional political parties. In the 1970s, Plaid Cymru (Wales) and the Scottish National Party (SNP) each won seats in the House of Commons. In 1974, the SNP leapt ahead of the Tories into second place in Scotland.

After the 1974 election, the Labour government proposed **devolution** to give Scotland and Wales limited self-government. Both proposals were put to referendum, and both were defeated.

The regional parties' fortunes have ebbed and flowed ever since. In recent general elections, they have often come in second in their regions. They were strong enough to shut the Conservatives out completely in Scotland and Wales in 1997 and to have limited them to a single seat in Scotland in 2001. However, the two parties combined won only nine or ten seats in the last four national elections. They have done better in elections for their regional parliament. In 2007, for instance, the SNP won 47 of 129 seats (one more than Labour) whereas Plaid Cymru took 15 of the 60 Welsh districts. Both did significantly better than four years earlier. Nonetheless, there is little indication that their voters take the notion of secession from the UK seriously. To the surprise of many, the SNP won a majority in the Scottish assembly in May 2011.

Regional parties have always dominated in Northern Ireland, because the "mainland" organizations never run candidates there. Therefore, parties based in the province routinely win all the seats, in the process "inflating" the number of minor party victories—eighteen of the thirty won by parties outside of the "big three" in 2010. As a result, many analysts do not include Northern Irish constituencies when covering a general election.

Britain also has a host of truly minor parties that do little more than make campaigns more enjoyable. Thus, the Natural Law Party based its 1997 campaign on the claim that the world's problems would be solved if we all learned to meditate and levitate. Somehow, it won thirty thousand votes. It disbanded in 2001. Similarly, independent cross-dresser Mrs. Moneypenny pranced around the stage while the results of the most hotly contested race in 1997—between former BBC correspondent Martin Bell and the Conservative (and corrupt) Neil Hamilton—were being announced. She/he won 128 votes.

In 2005 and in one by-election since then, minor parties have won three seats. Iraq war opponent George Galloway won one of them. The others were captured by people running on purely local issues as was the case in 2010 as well.

As picturesque as these candidates can be, they are best given little space in a book like this.

The British Electorate

During the collectivist years, the British electorate was among the easiest to understand. A single issue—social class—shaped the way most voters viewed the political world (see Table 4.6). When a sample of voters was polled in 1963, 1964, and 1966, two-thirds identified with the same party in each of the three interviews. By contrast, only

TABLE 4.6 The Changing Role of Class and Gender in British Politics (Percentage Voting Labour)

YEAR	WORKING CLASS (%)	WOMEN (%)
1974 (Oct.)	57	38
1979	50	35
1983	38	26
1987	42	32
1992	45	34
1997	58	49
2001	59	42
2005	48	38
2010	35	31

Source: Adapted from Dennis Kavanaugh, *Thatcherism and British Politics: The End of Consensus*, 2nd ed. (New York: Oxford University Press, 1990), 168; Philip Norton, *The British Polity*, 3rd ed. (New York Longman, 1994), 91–92; and David Sanders, "The New Electoral Background," in Anthony King, ed., et al, *New Labour Triumphs: Britain at the Polls*, (Chatham, NJ: Chatham House, 1997), 220. Data for 2001, 2005, and 2010 adapted from www.ipsos-mori.com, accessed August 20, 2010. Note that the measures used in the polls cited are not exactly the same. However, the differences in the questions asked do not have a huge impact on the general trends in this table.

22 percent of the French electorate did so in similar surveys. When the interviewers probed, they found that people identified with a party primarily because of the positive connection they saw between "their" party and class.

The issues of the day played a relatively minor role in determining either those long-term loyalties or the way people voted in a given election. At most, 2 or 3 percent of the electorate had clearly defined and consistent belief systems. No more than 25 percent had anything approaching a firm understanding of such central political concepts as the difference between Left and Right; 75 percent of the electorate saw these concepts in ways that were no more sophisticated (though perhaps less graphic) than those expressed by a mechanic in 1963:

> Well, when I was in the army you had to put your right foot forward, but in fighting you lead with your left. So I always think that the Tories are the right party for me and that the Labour party are fighters. I know that this isn't right really, but I can't explain it properly, and it does for me.[4]

In fact, people changed their opinions on such issues as British membership in the Common Market so frequently that pollsters wondered if voters really had opinions at all on anything but the most visible and controversial matters.

That began to change in the decade before the 1979 election. At first, observers interpreted Thatcher's first victory as a vote against the radicalism of the Labour government rather than as a first step toward a lasting realignment. There was little apparent enthusiasm for most of her policies that year, and there certainly was not the kind of support that could lead to a lasting long-term shift in how millions of people thought and acted.

Over the course of the next decade, however, a substantial number of workers and lower-middle-class voters did become loyal Tories. Nonetheless, by the early 1990s, the more marked trend was substantial dealignment from both the Tories and Labour, as voters grew disillusioned with the major parties. In other words, Blair did not win in 1997, 2001, and 2005 primarily because there was a massive and lasting increase in Labour Party identifiers. Rather, its victories can be explained better in terms of voters' "fatigue" with the Conservatives after eighteen years in office in 1997 and the extremely weak campaign run by the Tory team that year.

Labour did regain some of the support it lost among manual workers in 1997 and 2001 (see Table 4.6). However, that statistic is misleading, because the size of the working class as a whole continues to decrease. That means that Labour cannot hope to win by appealing primarily to it alone and must continue to build support in the growing middle class.

Indeed, there is evidence that Labour (as is typical in many countries) did a good a job of reaching out to some of what Ronald Inglehart called postmaterialist voters, reflected here in the second column of Table 4.6. No real gender gap has emerged in the UK, perhaps because abortion has been legal since the 1960s and has not been a serious issue. Few people want to see any change in the law.

If anything, women were historically slightly more likely to vote Tory than Labour. However, in 1997 and 2001, Labour worked hard to increase its support among women. That was clear not only in its manifesto but also in the number of young, professional women it nominated, the 106 of them who were elected in 1997, 118 in 2001, and 127 in 2005. It is also clear in the high profile a number of women have had under Labour governments. That number rose to 143 in 2010. At 22 percent of the MPs, Britain stood slightly above the European average but only fiftieth in the world. (For a global list of the number of women in national parliaments, see 🌐 www.ipu.org.)

Based on preliminary evidence, and what Chip saw in the ten days before the 2010 election, this line of reasoning still holds: Cameron and Clegg did not win because the voters agreed with them—indeed, their parties' views were distinctly different. Instead, the voters were more interested in throwing Labour out rather than in wanting to bring the erstwhile opposition in. You can see some of that in the final row of Table 4.6, which reflects the overall decline of the Blair- and Brown-led Labour Party.

Interest Groups

Britain has hundreds of interest groups, ranging from the unions discussed previously to the world's most organized group of backyard gardeners. Some of them are national. Others focus only on local concerns, as when the residents of Dover protested against a threatened French purchase of their port should the government decide to privatize it.

Because votes in the House of Commons are normally foreordained conclusions, there is little of the lobbying of the sort one finds in the United States. Groups try to maintain good relationships with members of the House of Commons, including "interested" MPs who are acknowledged agents of a union or other group. Not surprisingly, however, the groups focus their activity on the people who actually make the decisions: ministers, party leaders, and senior civil servants. In short, their influence depends on being able to shape the drafting of a bill, not on how it is

---

[4]David Butler and Donald Stokes, *Political Change in Britain*, 2nd ed. (New York: St. Martin's Press, 1976), 232.

dealt with on the floor of the House. And, in a country in which the political parties have concentrated their appeals along class lines, not all groups have had levels of influence roughly comparable to their membership or other resources. Two groups, in particular, wield disproportionate influence because of their close links to the major parties—the TUC with Labour and the **Confederation of British Industry (CBI)** with the Conservatives.

Britain actually has over three hundred trade unions that enroll about one-fourth of the workforce, down from 53 percent in 1979 and 33 percent in 1995. About 90 percent of all unionized workers are affiliated with the TUC 🖉 (**www.tuc. org.uk**). The business sector is not as monolithic. As in the United States, there are trade associations for most industries. Chambers of Commerce promote business interests in their communities. The CBI is the most important of these groups, with a membership that includes more than 250,000 companies and trade associations 🖉 (**www.cbi.org.uk**). Although most of the CBI's members are small companies, the vast majority of its income comes from the large firms with over a thousand employees which dominate it.

All governments have to consult with interest groups. They have information and expertise that civil servants have to draw on in crafting legislation. More important, the government needs their cooperation in implementing new laws, something the Heath government learned to its regret when the TUC refused to comply with the Industrial Relations Act of 1971.

During the collectivist years, the government also included the TUC and CBI when developing most economic policy in what were known as tripartite or **corporatist** arrangements. They and other groups were officially brought into the deliberations of a number of agencies, including the National Economic Development Council (NEDC), Health and Safety Executive, and Commission for Racial Equality. Relations between the state and interest groups have changed dramatically since then. The Thatcher government effectively froze the unions out of decision making. In addition, despite Labour's long-standing links to the TUC, it, too, has distanced itself from the unions and has sought, instead, to solidify its relationship with dynamic corporations, especially in the high-tech industries, since Blair took office.

THE BRITISH STATE: ENDURING MYTHS AND CHANGING REALITIES

In 1867, Walter Bagehot (1826–77) published *The English Constitution.* Much like Alexis de Tocqueville's *Democracy in America*, Bagehot's book is still read not only as a classic historical document but also as a source of useful insights into politics today for two main reasons.

TABLE 4.7 The British and American States

FEATURE	UNITED KINGDOM	UNITED STATES
Basic constitutional arrangements	Unwritten Unitary Fusion of powers Relatively strong	Written Federal Separation of Powers Relatively weak
Executive	Dominant Recruited from Parliament	Power to persuade Recruited everywhere
Legislature	Mostly debating Party voting	Making laws Coalition-based voting

First is the very fact that he analyzed the British constitution. That may not seem like a big deal to people from other liberal democracies, but it is for Britain because it does not have a written constitution. What Bagehot pointed out was that Britain indeed had a constitution composed of acts of Parliament, understandings, and traditional practices that everyone agreed to follow.

Second, Bagehot drew a distinction between what he called the "dignified" and the "real" parts of government. The dignified side included the monarchy and other institutions that no longer had much impact on day-to-day political life. Instead, he argued, the real power in the English constitutional system lay with the House of Commons (see Table 4.7).

The Monarchy and the Lords: Still Dignified?

The monarchy and the House of Lords have duties and responsibilities that give them quite a bit of visibility. However, it is safe to say that they have no real impact on what the government does.

From 1958 until 1999, there were four types of lords 🖉 (**www.parliament.uk/documents/upload/ HLLReformChronology.pdf**). Before 1958, all lords were hereditary peers or members of the senior clergy and judiciary. The hereditary peers came from the traditional nobility, whose ancestors were made lords for service—meritorious or otherwise—to the crown. Sons inherited those seats from their fathers.

In 1999, Parliament (including the Lords themselves) passed a law that stripped the hereditary peers of their membership except for a small group of ninety-two of them who were chosen by their colleagues to remain. Thus, 613 of the 731 current members of the Lords are life peers, a status that has only existed since 1958. The law authorized the monarch (but, in practice, the prime minister) to elevate people to the Lords for exemplary service in politics, business, or other walks of life. Their peerages end with their death and are thus not inherited by their children. The rest of the Lords come from two groups. The five archbishops and twenty-one other church officials are Lords. Finally, the Law Lords serve as Britain's highest court of appeal. However, unlike the Supreme Court in the United States, they cannot rule on the constitutionality of acts of Parliament.

The second Blair government outlined plans for a House of Lords that would be partially elected and partially appointed. Nothing happened during the rest of the Labour government. Although the House of Lords does have to approve all legislation, various agreements reached over the centuries have stripped it of the power to do anything more than delay enactment of a law that was proposed in the government's manifesto for up to six months.

There is no law requiring that members of the cabinet also be a member of either House of Parliament. In fact, they almost always are, which has led prime ministers to appoint members to the upper house so that they can be assured a seat.

Labour's failure to act on any of its trial balloons has given the new coalition government the initiative. All the signs are that the coalition partners prefer abolishing the Lords altogether and replacing it with a weak upper house, some of whose members would be elected and some appointed. Although Lords were not part of the 2011 referendum, the crushing defeat of electoral reform does not bode well for institutional change anywhere in the government.

FIGURE 4.1 Decision Making in Britain

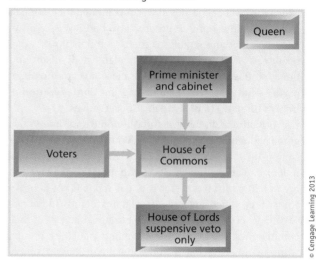

© Cengage Learning 2013

The monarchy is less powerful than ever. Theoretically, the monarch still rules "in Parliament" (see Figure 4.1). This means that Queen Elizabeth II officially names the new prime minister and the rest of the cabinet. They all kneel before her to take their oaths of office. She opens each session of Parliament by reading a speech from the throne outlining "her" policies for the upcoming term. Finally, a bill only becomes law when she gives her royal assent 🖋 (**www. royal.gov.uk**).

In practice, the monarch has no such powers. She does not determine who joins a cabinet or whether to agree to legislation. The speech from the throne is written by the prime minister. Queen Elizabeth II did play a minor role in the negotiations that led to the creation of the coalition government in 2010, however, it is safe to say that the serious work was done by the two parties and their leaders.

For many, the monarchy today is an embarrassment. The House of Windsor has been embroiled in scandals involving the failed marriages and highly publicized affairs of Prince Charles and his siblings. The tragic death of Diana, Princess of Wales, in August 1997 and the tremendous outpouring of grief it provoked only added to the royal family's woes.

That may change with the marriage of the highly popular Duke and Duchess of Cambridge in 2011.

Parliamentary Sovereignty—Sort Of

In Bagehot's eyes, the **House of Commons** 🖋 (**www. parliament.uk**) was sovereign because it determined who governed and which laws were passed. However, as critics of the British state are quick to point out, the Commons has not been a key player on most policy issues for more than a century. Instead, real influence lies with the leadership of the majority party—or now, the coalition.

KIRSTY WIGGLESWORTH/Reuters/Landov.

Gordon Brown with the Queen, taking the oath of office.

Profiles
Baroness Sayeeda Warsi

Normally, a few members of the House of Lords serve in the government. Occasionally, they are appointed to the House of Lords so that they can serve in government.

Typical is (now) Baroness Sayeedi Warsi.

She had run for parliament in 2005 and was the first candidate of Muslim origins nominated by the Tories. She lost the election but was quickly named a life peer and served in a couple of advisory roles for the party's leadership.

In May 2010 she was made deputy Tory leader in charge of cities, which made her a member of cabinet. ■

To see that, however, we have to reexamine the House of Commons and our discussion of parliamentary systems (see Chapter 2 and Figure 4.1). The House of Commons currently has 650 MPs. The exact number changes slightly each time the country is redistricted. Like members of the House of Representatives in the United States, MPs represent single-member districts and are elected in first-past-the-post elections.

But there the similarity between the two systems ends.

MPs are not expected to represent their constituencies' interests in the ways members of Congress do. They do not even have to live in their districts, and the national party organization will frequently "parachute" leading politicians into safe seats (as with Blair in 1983), all but guaranteeing that they will be reelected time and time again.

From 1995 to 1998, Chip lived just outside Henley-on-Thames, the site of the world-famous regatta in one of the most solidly conservative constituencies in the country. The member of Parliament was Michael Heseltine, long one of the most prominent Tories, who served as deputy prime minister during the last two years of the Major government. Few of his British friends knew if Heseltine lived in the district. He did not, though his mother did. Moreover, even fewer of them cared because they understood that MPs are not primarily elected to reflect the views and preferences of the "folks back home." After Heseltine retired, he was replaced by Boris Johnson who, in turn, quit when he was elected Mayor of London, where, in fact, he had always lived.

The key to the British state is the **parliamentary party**. Normally, the leader of the majority party becomes prime minister and can almost always count on the support of his or her fellow partisans. The head of the largest minority party becomes leader of the opposition and appoints the **shadow cabinet**, whose members monitor and criticize the actions of their equivalents in the government. The party leaders are senior politicians who enjoy the ideological and personal support of the other MPs in their party. As such, they are quite different from most recent American presidential candidates, who got that far because of their personal bases of support and often built careers largely outside of Washington. In Britain, there is only one road to the top—the parliamentary party.

Thatcher's and Brown's careers are typical, although the current leaders' are not.

Elected to Parliament at age thirty-three in 1959, Thatcher spent her first decade on the **backbenches**, as the seats reserved for MPs who are not part of the leadership are known. She was appointed to her first cabinet post eleven years later. Only such a veteran could seriously aspire to the leadership of a party in reasonably good shape, a post that came six years later.

Similarly, Brown was thirty-two when he was first elected. Because Labour was in disarray, young politicians like Brown could rise through the ranks more quickly. By the time John Smith died, Brown and Blair had held a number of important positions in the shadow cabinet. Still, he had spent eleven years in the House before he became one of the party's leaders and had twenty-four years' experience in the House of Commons and ten as Chancellor before moving into 10 Downing Street.[5] By contrast, the three leaders today combined had less experience than either Thatcher or Brown when they took over their parties.

The prime minister selects the rest of the cabinet most of whom are officially called secretaries of state, along with about one hundred other junior ministers. All are members of Parliament. All but two members of Cameron's cabinet were members of the House of Commons. The only exceptions are the Leader of the House of Lords (currently Lord

---

[5]10 Downing Street is the official residence of the prime minister. 11 Downing Street is the office and apartment of the Chancellor of the Exchequer, the equivalent of the American Secretary of the Treasury. As would not be the case given American street numbering systems, 10 and 11 Downing Street not only are next door to each other but share a common wall. The first two floors of the buildings are integrated into a single set of offices for the senior members of the government. The prime minister and the Chancellor live in apartments on the top floors. Intriguingly, Brown (who was single when Labour won), lived in Number 10. Blair, his wife, and four children, lived in the much larger apartment that straddled Numbers 11 and 12.

Strathclyde) and Lord Warshi who officially serves without a portfolio.

As in the United States, each cabinet minister is responsible for a department, such as foreign affairs, the Exchequer (economics), or defense. Men and women are appointed to cabinet positions that roughly correspond to their positions in the party's power structure, which are not necessarily ones that reflect their interests or talents. Consequently, they are less likely to be experts in the areas they are responsible for than their American counterparts. Each minister also has a staff of only two or three other MPs who serve as junior ministers, usually coordinating relations with the bureaucracy and Parliament.

Unlike in the United States, the cabinet is governed by the principle of **collective responsibility**, remaining in office as long as the entire government retains the support of its parliamentary majority. Moreover, individual ministers must publicly support all cabinet decisions, including those they disagree with. If not, they are expected to resign, as Clare Short and the late Robin Cook did over Iraq.

Despite the unusual circumstances after the 2010 election, little of this changed: Cameron's cabinet includes the senior leaders of both coalition partners. The one thing that did change—and which may augur reforms down the line—is that the two parties named very young leaders who agreed to govern for the length of this parliament until its term ends in 2015.

The cabinet introduces all major (government-sponsored) legislation. Debate in the House of Commons is among the most acrimonious in the world, which is reflected in the very architecture of its chamber in the Palace of Westminster. Most legislatures are laid out in a semicircle, with the speaker's podium in the center. In Britain, the government and opposition face each other on benches that, tradition has it, are separated by the distance of two drawn swords.

As in all **"Westminster" systems** patterned on the British, members hurl not only political charges but personal insults at each other. They often shout so loud that the person who has the floor cannot be heard, while the Speaker pounds the gavel and screams "order, order" to no avail. Sessions are especially heated when an important bill is being debated and when ministers come to the floor to answer whatever questions opposition MPs and their own backbenchers ask of them.

The intensity of parliamentary debate, however, should not lead you to conclude that it normally makes a difference. Because of the way parliamentary systems work as discussed in Chapter 2, as long as one party or coalition has a majority in Parliament, it is virtually assured of getting its bills passed.

During a typical parliamentary term, well over 90 percent of the legislation proposed by the majority party is passed. Backbench pressure sometimes forces the government to modify or even withdraw a bill, but that almost never happens on what it considers to be major legislation.

There are exceptions when a significant number of the government's backbenchers vote against a bill as happened in the votes on university tuition rates and Iraq. So many members defected that Labour could not realistically hope to discipline them other than blocking their promotion

David Cameron at Prime Minister's Question Time.

off the backbenches as long as it was in power. However, it should also be noted that such votes are few and far between. Even more important, there is strong, if anecdotal, evidence that many disgruntled MPs decided to vote for the government or abstain on both bills because they were not willing to put the life of the government in jeopardy.

There are "free votes" in which members can do as they choose, which governments sometimes use when their own party is divided. For instance, in 2006, the Labour government allowed a free vote on a bill that would ban smoking in most pubs and restaurants because it feared that so many Labour members would defect that the bill would be defeated. Sometimes, too, the government agrees to accept amendments from its backbenchers. However, all major legislation and even significant amendments to such bills are deemed votes of confidence, and the government wins because the majority's MPs have no real leeway in determining how they will vote.

MPs are officially notified that such a vote will take place when they receive a **three line whip**. Physically, this is a simple note from the party whips—underlined three times—stating that a vote will take place at a stated time. The MPs know what that means. When it is time for a division (the MPs literally divide and go into two rooms, one for those in favor of a bill and the other for those opposed), the prime minister can count on more than enough support for the bill to pass.

Backbenchers' influence is limited, too, by the way the House of Commons is organized. It does not have the kind of committee system in which members and their extensive staffs develop expertise in a given policy area. Members of the Commons have at most one or two full-time staffers, compared with an average of eighteen for members of the House of Representatives in the United States. Their office budgets are barely a fourth of that of an American representative.

Despite their power, British governments rarely act rashly or irresponsibly. The decision to proceed with new legislation usually comes only after an extended period of study and debate. The discussions that culminated in the 1948 act that established the National Health Service began in the mid-1930s, when major flaws in the old insurance system began to receive serious attention. It was another decade before the government **white paper** on the subject was published in 1944. Four more years elapsed before the bill was passed. More recently, Blair's welfare reform program—the highlight of his first term—did not appear out of thin air but had been under consideration for years.

Furthermore, when governments do blunder, there are ways, however imperfect, in which disgruntled MPs can respond. For example, when British and French troops occupied the Suez Canal in 1956 after it had been taken over by the Egyptian government, Conservative MPs continued to support Anthony Eden's government, which easily survived a vote of confidence. It was clear, however,

that Eden's actions had cost him the confidence of his own party. Sensing that, he resigned the following year, citing his declining health. In fact, he did not resign because of his health—he lived until 1977. Eden resigned because enough Conservative MPs had exerted behind-the-scenes pressure that he realized he had to leave.

However, on balance, the government does get what it wants. As Andrew Marr put it:

> Government backbenchers can, at rare moments, exercise some leverage on the general drift of the executive policy which can, from time to time, help change the world beyond Westminster. But most of the time, frankly, it's more like children shouting at passing aircraft.[6]

Because all important legislation originates with the cabinet, its plans and objectives are a constant source of rumor. Speeches by ministers (especially at the annual party conferences), their appearances before the House of Commons during question time, and the interviews they grant the early morning *Today* show on BBC radio or the late evening *Newsnight* on television can be moments of great political drama.

The Status of Women

The last two governments have done a lot to improve the rights of women, minorities, and people with disabilities.

Under Blair, Labour took the first steps by giving more women a real chance of winning seats, which more than 100 of them did during its three governments. With a large number of women with young children in the Commons, the government ended the practice of holding debates and votes as late as 10:00 p.m. on Thursdays so that MPs (men and women alike) could get home to their families.

The Equality Act was one of the last laws enacted under Labour. It bans and provides compensation for almost all forms of discrimination that touch on women's lives. Some of its funding will almost certainly be cut as the current economic reforms go into effect. But Theresa May, the Home Secretary and Minister for Women and Equalities under Cameron, has made it clear that the law will not be gutted.

That said, cabinet government is becoming something of a myth, too. As in most countries, British cabinet meetings

---

[6] Andrew Marr, *Ruling Britannia: The Failure and Future of British Democracy* (London: Michael Joseph, 1995), 115.

The Cabinet

The cabinet is the most important political institution in Britain for all the reasons discussed in the body of the text.

However, it is different from the American cabinet in two critical respects. All ministers and secretaries of state must also be members of the House of Commons or the House of Lords. Second, the prime minister is free to combine, break up, or create new ministries in keeping with the fact that the absence of a written constitution makes to relatively easy to redefine the structure of government. In spring 2011, twenty-four people were ministers or secretaries of state and six others who routinely attend cabinet meetings (**www.number-10.gov.uk**).

The day after he took office, Cameron named his new cabinet. Given their thirteen years in opposition, many of the ministers were new, though two of the most important posts are held by veteran politicians. William Hague (foreign ministry) and Ken Clark (Lord Chancellor) have been fixtures in Tory politics since the Thatcher years.

are held in secret and only a brief official announcement of what was decided at each one is issued at the end of the weekly session. Nonetheless, we have learned a good deal in recent years about how the cabinet operates through numerous leaks (at which British politicians seem particularly adept) and the often revealing memoirs of former ministers, most notably Richard Crossman, a political scientist and journalist who held a number of offices in the 1964–70 Labour governments.

Crossman was one of the party's leading theoreticians and hoped to head one of the major ministries. However, because of his relatively low position in the party hierarchy, he ended up as minister of housing, a position he was neither particularly interested in nor qualified to hold. Nonetheless, Crossman came to office committed to fulfilling the goal for his ministry laid out in the party's manifesto: constructing five hundred thousand new housing units during its term in office. He assumed, too, that he would simply inform his civil servants of that goal, and they would say, "Yes, minister," and begin drawing up the legislation and plans to implement it. But, as the sitcom of the same name shows (**www.yes-minister.com**), "yes, minister" often means exactly the opposite. Officially, the civil servants are there to do what their title suggests—serve their minister. In reality, they possess so much more experience and have so much more leverage over the bureaucracy

than the minister does that they often have a lot more to say about what happens. In this case, they told Crossman it was impossible to build that many new homes so quickly. Despite everything Crossman tried, he could not get them to change.

More important for Crossman, instead of experiencing the excitement and power that would come from making the "big decisions" about his country's future, he found himself preoccupied with seemingly never-ending public relations functions and paperwork. Meanwhile, Prime Minister Harold Wilson and the handful of ministers closest to him were making the important decisions and then presenting them to the cabinet as a whole as *faits accompli*s. Ministers like Crossman, who were not part of the inner circle, had a say only on issues that affected their own ministries, not on the broader issues of national policy that had drawn them into public service in the first place. If anything, that trend accelerated with Blair, who relied more heavily on personal advisers than on his cabinet. He took all but total control of the Labour Party, kept ideological rivals in the party out of the cabinet, and used his personal popularity to build support for his policy agenda. In his second and third terms, as his popularity ebbed, he seemed more prime ministerial—governing with colleagues and having to deal with disputes inside his own party, especially with his friend-turned-rival Gordon Brown. In fact, as Blair makes clear in his memoirs, he could do little without Brown's grudging support, which was not often readily forthcoming. Today, observers talk about the "presidentialization" of the cabinet through which the prime minister exerts the kind of personal influence and patronage that are so widespread in the United States.

The Rest of the State

The rest of the British state is nowhere near as important. Nonetheless, there are three areas that deserve at least some attention here.

First, is the weakness of the British bureaucracy compared to its equivalents on the European continent and in Japan. There, top civil servants believe that it is their role to help forge cooperative arrangements that allow the state to coordinate much of the economic policy making for both the public and private sectors.

Most British senior civil servants do not think of themselves as policy makers. Instead, they think they should primarily be administrators after the cabinet has defined at least the broad contours of public policy. At most, their job is to flesh out the details of proposed legislation, keep the politicians from making major mistakes, and ensure that policy is carried out once passed by Parliament.

The civil service has also long been dominated by white male "mandarins" who were recruited and promoted on the basis of their general intellectual ability and seniority. Since the 1990s, a number of reforms have been passed, most notably the creation of a Senior Civil Service in 1996. It consists of about 4,000 people and is about half the size of the American Senior Executive Service. About a third of its members are technical experts, not generalists. By 1999, 17 percent were women and almost 2 percent members of racial minorities. Senior civil service pay is determined on the basis of merit rather than time in service. It is, however, too early to tell how and if the SCS will change the way the civil service as a whole operates.

Second, during their eighteen years in office, the Tories diluted cabinet and parliamentary sovereignty by assigning more and more responsibilities to two types of nonelected bodies. First are regulatory agencies, which are supposed to oversee the newly privatized companies, most of whose names begin with "Of." Thus, Oftel deals with telecommunications, Ofwat with water, and Ofsted with standards in education.

In addition, there are now as many as 7,700 quasi-autonomous nongovernmental organizations (QUANGOs), which are roughly equivalent to independent American entities such as the Environmental Protection Agency. During the 1960s and 1970s, Conservative and Labour governments alike decided to "hive off" many regulatory, commercial, and cultural functions to these organizations. QUANGOs were set up, for example, to coordinate the development of new towns, to regulate health and safety at the workplace, and to improve human resources. Some of them, like the British Mint, were not very important politically. Others, like the Consultative Panel on Badgers and Tuberculosis, or the Welsh Office Place Names Advisory Board, rarely raise a political eyebrow. Yet, some, like the Commission for Racial Equality or the University Grants Committee (which funds universities), have some of the most controversial assignments in British politics. Though Cameron has pledged to cut the number of QUANGOs and reign in the power of those that survive, as of this writing little has happened on that front.

Third, the courts have never had a policy-making role. The settlement ending the Glorious Revolution of 1688 forbade judges from ruling on the constitutionality of an act of Parliament. Although that is still technically the case, a new generation of more activist judges is stretching that centuries-old policy to its limits. In 1991, a judge overturned the law that did not allow men to be tried for raping their wives. Two years later, another ruled that doctors do not have to keep brain-dead patients alive if their condition is irreversible. In addition, in 1995 the country's most powerful judge publicly criticized Home Secretary Michael Howard's plans to require stiffer sentences for repeat offenders.

Constitutional Reform

Change to the constitution has been on the agenda at least since the Social Democrats split with Labour. Three issues stand out, and partial steps have been taken for each of them.

- ■ Regionalization and decentralization. The Blair government did introduce regional assemblies for Wales, Scotland, and Northern Ireland. However, their powers vary, and little has been done to create similar bodies in England.

- ■ As we have seen, the House of Lords sits in limbo. The Brown government did not finish the reforms begun under Blair, although there is now widespread agreement that the structure and selection of the Lords should be reconsidered.

- ■ Electoral and parliamentary reform in general were briefly back on center stage. Labour toyed with them from 1997 until 2000, but did little. As we have seen, Clegg made it a key issue until the 2011 referendum killed the prospects for reform for now. It is likely that the number of seats at Westminster will be reduced to 600 and district boundaries redrawn so that they all contain roughly the same number of voters.

PUBLIC POLICY: FOREIGN AND ECONOMIC POLICY

Their supporters often call Margaret Thatcher's and Tony Blair's public policies revolutions. By the standards we will see in later chapters, that is certainly an overstatement. However, Thatcher used her "politics of conviction" to produce dramatic change, most notably in British economic life. Blair revitalized the social services and helped spark a decade-long economic boom, often coming with criticism from the traditional left. It is too early to determine how much Cameron's government can or will accomplish. Nonetheless, after a year in power including an emergency budget, it has at least given signs that it would go farther and faster than either its Labour or Tory predecessor.

Although the desire for change has become typical of domestic policy, continuity has been the norm internationally. Both parties have sought to maintain the "special relationship" between the UK and the United States; both have made the UK the least European of Europe's major powers.

Domestic Politics

In 1919, the Labour Party committed itself to nationalization, or state ownership, of the "commanding heights" of the economy. In addition, it planned to place much of the rest of the economy under government control through planning and to pass the benefits on to the working class and other less fortunate people, thereby creating a more just and equal society. This pledge had little impact then on public policy because Labour did not win a majority in Parliament until after World War II. After the 1945 election, Labour set up planning boards with wide-ranging authority and it nationalized dozens of key industries, especially those that provided public services but that were no longer profitable.

By the 1960s, most of the nationalized industries were performing poorly and required massive subsidies. Attempts by successive Labour governments to plan the key industrial sectors of the economy were deemed abject failures that left the unions more powerful than ever.

Economic Liberalization
in Britain

Not surprisingly, Britain is usually held up as the model of economic liberalization among the industrial democracies. When Thatcher came to power, the government owned or controlled a large part of the economy. By 1997, it had sold off more than fifty major businesses with well over a million employees. In short, the UK pursued rapid privatization more than any of its major competitors.

It also went further in adopting liberal (in the European sense) values. Sir Keith Joseph, who was the intellectual architect of privatization, once said that trying to get a state-owned firm to act like a private one was like trying to "make a mule into a zebra by painting stripes on its back."[a]

Little changed under Labour, and the first signs are that the same will hold under Cameron.

[a]Quoted in Daniel Yergin with Joseph Stanislaw, *The Commanding Heights: The Battle Between Government and the Marketplace That Is Remaking the Modern World* (New York: Simon & Schuster, 1998), 122–23. ■

The welfare state was proving increasingly expensive, especially the NHS which provided free health care to all but was terribly underfunded even though it consumed about a third of the national budget. Overall government spending grew to over 40 percent of the gross national product in the late 1970s—which is less than in most continental democracies but far more than in the United States or Japan.

Therefore, Thatcher wanted to sharply reduce the role of the state and privatize as many of the nationalized industries as possible. In her first term, eight large firms were sold, including British Petroleum (BP), British Aerospace, Cable and Wireless (Telecommunications), long-distance trucking, the sugar refineries, and the ports. During the rest of her years in power, shares in British Leyland, British Gas, British Airways, British Telecom, the jet engine division of Rolls-Royce, and the Jaguar and Rover automobile companies were sold. She also allowed most council (public) housing tenants to purchase their homes. Under Major, the water distribution system, buses, electricity generation, and even parts of the NHS and the BBC were sold to private owners.

Privatization was Thatcher's most controversial policy. To her supporters, she saved the British economy by bringing both inflation and unemployment under control and by creating a more dynamic private sector. To her detractors, she created new problems and exacerbated existing ones by widening the gap between rich and poor and by allowing public services to deteriorate. Blair's policies were no less controversial. To his supporters, he was charting a **third way** that combined the best aspects of the socialist commitment to equality with a market economy. To his detractors inside the Labour Party, he was a flashy politician who sold out the Left and created something they sneeringly refer to as "Thatcher lite."

Privatization proved extremely popular in the short term. As the council houses were gobbled up, home ownership soared to 60 percent of the total population during Thatcher's first term alone. Though most of the shares in the privatized firms were bought by institutional investors, 2.2 million citizens purchased shares in British Telecom and 4 million did the same with British Gas. In the short run, privatization gave the government a needed infusion of capital, adding £70 billion (well over $100 billion) to the British treasury by the end of 1988. More generally, the Thatcher governments tried to strengthen the role of market forces in shaping the economy. Government subsidies to industry were cut. Firms were encouraged to modernize and to reduce "redundant" labor, even though that meant the number of unemployed rose to over 3 million. Taxes that hit the wealthy the hardest were slashed to generate more money for investment. In their place, taxes were raised on cigarettes, alcohol, and gasoline, which disproportionately affected the poor.

Thatcher's and Major's privatization policies remain highly controversial. Even the Conservatives' severest critics, however, agree that they used the levers of state power quite effectively in producing one of the most dramatic policy changes in modern British history.

This is less clear for the other centerpiece of Thatcherite economic policy—rolling back the welfare state. As the critics saw it, income support and other policies put in place, usually with the support of previous Tory governments, were a waste because they handed out money without giving people the ability to pull themselves out of poverty either on their own or permanently.

Unlike the nationalized industries, most of the social services programs were quite popular, and attempts to reduce them were met with stiff resistance. Still, the government cut back programs that helped single parents, university students, and the unemployed.

More than thirty years have passed since Thatcher was driven out of office, but her policies and her legacy remains controversial. To her supporters, she saved the British economy by bringing both inflation and unemployment under control and by creating a more dynamic private sector. To her detractors, she created new problems and exacerbated existing ones by widening the gap between rich and poor and by allowing public services to deteriorate.

Blair and his colleagues had no plans to roll back Thatcher's and Major's reforms. Indeed, in some ways, they out-Thatchered Thatcher. In one of the first acts of Blair's administration, it gave the Bank of England the power to set interest rates without consulting the government. Perhaps most telling of all, government spending as a percentage of GNP actually shrank. The first Blair government pledged not to raise taxes for the life of the Parliament or to increase spending above the levels set by the Conservatives for two years. They actually privatized some more services, including failing local education authorities. The second Blair government privatized part of the London Underground to raise much-needed revenue and allow more private enterprise in the NHS to improve the quality of care.

It also took some less significant steps to transform the welfare state from a system that merely provides benefits to one that gives recipients skills to find meaningful jobs and, thus, places some responsibility on them. In one of its most controversial actions, the government agreed to retain a Conservative policy that reduces grants to lone parents (mostly single mothers) who refuse to take jobs. Its most sweeping reform did the same for unemployed people under age twenty-five who do not get either a job or job training.

Curiously, the statistics tell a very different story from Labour's and often Thatcherite rhetoric. The first Blair government was able to redirect quite a bit of money to the poor and to the public services. In part, that reflected the booming economy, which generated more tax revenues than the government had expected. But, as the following examples suggest, the government made some important policy changes.

The most impressive accomplishment involved the welfare-to-work scheme, now known as the New Deal. Of the 250,000 chronically unemployed young people, three-quarters found and kept jobs for at least three months after they finished their training. The program was then expanded to serve single mothers and older people. All in all, it cost the government about seven thousand dollars for each job created, less than it spent for a year of welfare payments.

The poorest retirees saw their incomes grow by at least 3 percent per year. The overall impact of fiscal reform was to increase the income of the bottom two-fifths of the population by 8 percent (the rich saw next to no change). Especially after the self-imposed spending limit ended, the government was able to devote significantly more money to education and the NHS, and those figures went up during the rest of Blair's tenure.

The Blair government pledged to continue reforms aimed at helping the poor and improving public services in its second term. It campaigned on a promise to add ten thousand teachers, twenty thousand nurses, and ten thousand doctors. In October 2004, it raised the minimum wage to £4.85, or nearly $8 an hour. Yet it is fair to say that the most important and potentially progressive initiatives came during the first Blair government, before the decline in his personal popularity began.

In the first three years of his second government, only two major initiatives stand out. The first is the widely unpopular tuition increase, which raised tuition fees for students from the UK and the European Union to as much as £9,000 or about $15,000 for the academic year that begins in October 2012. University tuition had been free until the late 1990s. Clearly, the rise in fees has been dramatic, but the new system leaves them below most American private colleges.

The second is far more innovative, although it is as much the work of the London city government as it is of Blair's cabinet. London was one of the most congested and polluted cities in the world. To ease that congestion, drivers entering the city center have been assessed a toll of approximately $8 since 2003. It is now almost twice that much. The scheme has already reduced traffic congestion dramatically and is now paying for itself. Within ten years it is expected to generate over $2 billion, which will be used for investment in the country's dilapidated mass transit network ✐ (**www.cfit.gov.uk/congestioncharging/ factsheets/london/index.htm**). Similar plans have been introduced in Durham and are being considered in cities like Reading, where Chip could walk the three miles from his wife's office to his own faster than he could drive it during rush hour.

Public policy has become controversial again. Because of Britain's massive deficit, Cameron introduced sweeping budget cuts that will average ten percent per department per year. It is too early to tell what the impact of the cuts would be, but economic growth all but disappeared in 2010. And some venerable institutions such as the foreign language broadcasts of the BBC World Service are disappearing.

Foreign Policy

Europe

At least for the long term, the most important foreign policy issue facing the country is Europe because its relationship with the continent will have the greatest impact on British politics in ways and for reasons that we will consider in Chapter 7. Europe is particularly important here because the British are as divided as any European society about how they should deal with their increasingly unifying continent. That ambiguity is reflected in their country's geography. It is little more than twenty miles from Dover in Kent to Calais in France, a distance that high-speed trains span in ten minutes. However, for many in Britain, the English Channel is the psychological equivalent of an ocean separating them from people on the continent who are not like them at all. The fact is, however, that Britain is a part of a European Union whose decisions have more impact on the British economy and other aspects of life than those made in London.

At this point, there are only two issues regarding Europe that seem likely to spark debate in Britain for years to come. Should it join the European Monetary Union and abandon the pound for the euro? Should it have ratified the second draft constitution for the EU that would have taken it closer to something like a united states of Europe? But even these issues may be on the backburner given the new coalition's qualms about both initiatives, despite Clegg's background in Europe.

Debate over Britain's role in Europe is nothing new. The British government decided not to join the Common Market when it was established in 1957. When it tried to join in the 1960s, France's President Charles de Gaulle twice vetoed its application. Georges Pompidou, de Gaulle's successor, was less hostile toward the British; and the UK was allowed to become a member in 1972 over the objection of many Britons, especially Labour Party activists. The first referendum in the country's history, held in 1975, determined that the UK would stay in the Common Market, and virtually all politicians came to accept that position.

However, that was about all they accepted.

Thatcher's wing of the Conservative Party consistently opposed any further expansion of the European Community's (as it was then known) powers. The British government reached compromises that allowed it to agree to the Single European Act (1986) and Maastricht Treaty (1991). However, the party's rhetoric increasingly reflected the views of the euroskeptics whenever European decisions or initiatives seemed to threaten British sovereignty.

Anti-European sentiment has grown each time the EU did something that seemed to limit British sovereignty. For instance, the EU ruled that the British violated the human rights of IRA terrorists killed in Gibraltar, and it banned the worldwide export of British beef as a result of "mad cow disease."

For the last twenty years, the most controversial issue has been the idea of a single currency. The Maastricht Treaty laid out a timetable that would bring qualifying countries into a single monetary system in 1999 and replace their currencies with the euro in 2002. But the Major government negotiated an "opt-out" clause, which meant that Britain would not have to join if the government of the day did not want to.

Most British voters opposed in both 1997 and 2001. Nonetheless, Conservative intransigence on European issues in general and internal party divisions contributed heavily to its three drubbings at the polls.

By contrast, the Labour leadership now strongly supports most aspects of the EU. Despite their early opposition to membership, most prominent Labour officials ended up supporting British membership after the 1975 referendum. By the time Blair became leader, almost everyone enthusiastically supported both adding new countries and giving new powers to the EU.

The one notable exception has been the single currency. In part because of the uncertainties about the economic logic of joining the monetary union and in part because of the state of public opinion, Labour campaigned in 1997 on a pledge not to join during the life of the Parliament elected that year. By 1999, however, Blair and his colleagues confirmed most observers' suspicions by announcing that they would make a decision during the first two years of the next Parliament. If five economic conditions were met, the government would then recommend adopting the euro and hold a referendum on it. When the new cabinet was sworn in, the best guess was that the government would try to "soften" public opinion on the euro in preparation for such a referendum. By then, there was no chance a referendum could pass. Besides, the British economy was doing so well that there would have been substantial short-term costs for adopting the euro. Thus, by the time Brown left office, the euro was at best on the back burner.

Globalization
in Great Britain

Britain probably provides the best illustration of the impact of globalization on an industrialized democracy. In most ways, the quote from Andrew Marr that begins this chapter tells it all. Britain, which once "ruled the waves," finds itself increasingly buffeted by forces from beyond its shoreline. The most obvious is the European Union, which has had a direct impact on so many areas of British life, from economic policy to the composition of its sports teams.

Perhaps most important—although hardest to pin down—is the role economic forces in other countries play in Britain. Thus, 99 percent of British automobile production is owned by companies not headquartered there. The United Kingdom is a major site for direct foreign investment, in large part because the wages of its industrial workers are so low. In addition, with the spread of satellite and cable technologies, the British increasingly watch television networks that are owned by foreigners and that run programs mostly made abroad. ∎

During the first decade of this century, the proposed EU constitution that was far more controversial than anyone expected. A commission headed by former French President Valéry Giscard d'Estaing spent years drafting a document that would formalize the powers and responsibilities of the EU, especially once the ten new members joined in 2004. Among other things, the draft called for the creation of a European president. Before the war in Iraq, it was widely assumed that the job would be offered to Blair. However, as we will see in the next section, Blair's strongly pro-American stance on Iraq made him unacceptable to colleagues who would make the selection. Moreover, it also soon became clear that most British voters had doubts about the constitution. Even though there was no legal necessity for doing so, Blair said that his government would submit the constitution to a referendum, which would almost certainly doom it to defeat. The referendum never occurred, however, because other member states rejected the constitution first. It has since been turned into a treaty (again, see Chapter 7) that is far weaker.

In the long term, however, opposition to further European integration seems like a rear-guard effort. Even though the UK does not use the euro, most of its companies conduct business in it. Citizens can be paid in euros and do their banking in them as well. And, it's more than just the currency or the constitution. When Chip taught at the University of Reading in the late 1990s, fully 20 percent of its students came from other European countries. Today, almost a third of the faculty comes from outside of the UK. In the village where we he lived, there was at least one family from all of the EU member states other than Luxembourg. His satellite television service had almost as many German as English language channels.

Iraq and Afghanistan

Unlike its glorious past, Britain today is among a handful of "second-tier" states whose influence pales in comparison with that of the United States or even the BRICS (Brazil, Russia, India, China, and South Africa) countries discussed in Parts 3 and 4. In the changed international environment since the end of World War II, Britain has seen its empire disappear and government after government has sought to redefine its global role. Far from ruling the waves, Britain has become a second tier power with limited influence. Nothing illustrates that better than Iraq and Afghanistan.

Blair took his country to war more times than any prime minister in recent British history. In the end, it was his decision—to support the American-led invasions of Iraq and Afghanistan—that drove him from office.

That Britain fought in the first Gulf War in 1991 was not surprising. After all, both the UK and the United States had conservative government at the time and Iraq's invasion of Kuwait was an unambiguous violation of international law. It was also hardly surprising that Blair supported the United States after the terrorist attacks of 9/11 given his country's experience with terrorism during the "troubles" in Northern Ireland. Last, but by no means least, the United States has stronger ties to the UK than to any other European government.

The British decision to support the United States and send the second largest contingent of troops to Iraq in 2003 was nowhere near as easy to understand. Blair and President George W. Bush had almost nothing in common. Indeed, Blair is widely known for his close relationship with former President Clinton, with whom he helped develop the idea of the third way.

Nonetheless, from the beginning of the preparation for the war with Iraq, Blair supported Bush and in so doing fortified the special relationship. The two leaders took all but identical positions on the war, including on the claims made about Iraqi weapons of mass destruction, none of

AP Photo/Charles Dharapak.

Cameron and Obama at their 2011 summit. Being England, of course it was raining.

which were accurate. The British backed the United States at the United Nations and in discussions with Germany and France, who led the European opposition to the war. Furthermore, Blair made it clear that Britain would send troops to join the so-called coalition of the willing. About fifteen thousand British troops were deployed to Iraq for the 2003 invasion; once the regime fell, they were given primary responsibility for security and reconstruction near the southern city of Basra. Britain removed the last of its troops in July 2009. (For more on the war, see Chapter 14.)

From the outset, most of the British population opposed the war, including the overwhelming majority of Labour voters. In the summer of 2003, only 32 percent of the population approved of the way Blair was handling the situation in Iraq; 56 percent opposed his policies (**www.mori.com/polls/2003/iraq4-top.shtml**). Blair was never in any danger of losing a vote of confidence over the war because the Tories supported British involvement. Nonetheless, support for Blair's policies continued to plummet. One former leader of the Liberal Democrats referred to him as "Bush's poodle." The derogatory label stuck. If Blair had allowed a free vote of Labour MPs on Iraq, he would certainly have lost the support of well over a majority of them. Anger and frustration about Iraq, and Blair's leadership style in general, helped convince him to announce before the 2005 election that he would not run

for a fourth term as Labour leader. He then accelerated his decision to leave office, resigning only two years into his third term.

One of the best books on American policy in Iraq is titled *Fiasco*.[7] Most people in Britain would use the same term to describe their involvement as well. Of course, the British suffered far fewer casualties—less than two hundred deaths by mid-2009.

Britain finally withdrew the last of its combat troops from Iraq in July 2009.

Afghanistan has proven to be a slightly different story. Britain's membership in NATO obliged it to join the United States in its campaign against al-Qaeda and the Taliban. As would be the case in Iraq, Britain sent the second largest contingent of troops to Afghanistan after the 9/11 attacks. The Afghan campaign has proved only somewhat less controversial. British troops faced some of the toughest combat of all the allied forces, most notably in Helmand province. As of November 2010, the UK had lost 386 soldiers lives there, 41 from non-combat related accidents. The UK has begun withdrawing troops from Afghanistan and expects all of them to be gone before the American target date of 2014.

---

[7]Thomas Ricks, *Fiasco*. (New York: Penguin, 2006).

THE MEDIA

As in all the industrialized democracies, most people get most of their political news from the mass media. Britain's television and radio networks and printed media, however, are quite different from those in the United States. To begin with, they are far more centralized, with most political information coming from national newspapers and television and radio stations.

England has eleven main daily newspapers, all of which are edited in London and distributed nationally. Scotland, Wales, and Northern Ireland have their own papers, but the London dailies are available there as well. Five are "quality" newspapers known as broadsheets. The *Guardian* and *Independent* usually support Labour (though neither did in 2010), the *Times* and *Telegraph* almost always endorse the Tories, and the *Financial Times* is aimed at the business community. Each has the kind of high-quality and in-depth coverage American readers find in the *Washington Post* or *New York Times*. Together, the broadsheets sell about 2 million copies a day.

The rest are tabloids whose political coverage is much more superficial and whose tone is often scandalous and even racist. The *Mirror* normally supports Labour but opposed the war in Iraq, including publishing a faked picture supposedly showing the abuse of prisoners by British soldiers. The others are traditionally Conservative. In all, the tabloids sell about 10 million copies a day.

There are local daily papers, most of which are published in the afternoon. They do not, however, cover much national news, and their political influence is largely limited to local issues.

British television news is also rather different from its American equivalent. To begin with, there is very little local news on television—in most regions local news is only on for half an hour a day. Conversely, the five networks carry their national news programs at different times, so you can watch the news at 6:00, 7:00, 8:00, 9:00, 10:00, and 10:30 p.m. every evening. BBC Radio 4's news programs are also widely listened to and have a greater impact than their equivalents on National Public Radio in the United States. Although British networks tend to be impartial, that is not necessarily true of individual journalists. Interviewers are known for the grillings they give politicians, especially those thought to be arrogant or to be withholding information. Some interviewers, including John Snow, the most popular anchor, openly display their personal views from time to time.

CONCLUSION: CAMERON'S CHALLENGE

The victory by the Conservative and Liberal Democratic coalition may not turn out to be quite as momentous as we thought in the days after May 2010 election. The problems with this coalition government, or any coalition government, are more likely to appear after four years, not one. There have already been reports of divisions between the two coalition partners. However, they publicly recommitted themselves to maintaining the government for its full five-year term.

The most dramatic step they have taken is to endorse the sweeping budget cuts mentioned above. Almost every cabinet department will be hit and hit sharply between late 2010 and 2014. The business and innovation, local government, and the environment and rural affairs budgets will be reduced by more than seven percent *a year* during that period. Some ministries—including defense and international development—will not be cut much if at all. However, they can expect no increase in spending during the life of the government.

In sum, the government is responding to the tremendous slowdown in the economy since 2008 which has bedeviled governments in all of the industrialized democracies, including the United States where it led to the crashing Democratic defeat in the 2010 mid-term election.

Looking FORWARD

IN CHAPTER 3 we asked you to take something on faith—that the United States has a unique form of democracy. Now, we do so again. What we labeled gradualism in this chapter and in the last one cannot be taken at face value given the turmoil the United States and UK have both gone through. However, we will see in the rest of Part 2, that the other key western powers have had much more difficult histories. Indeed, in France and Germany, a stable democracy was not guaranteed until well into the second half of the twentieth century.

Key Terms

Concepts

backbenchers
collective responsibility
collectivist consensus
corporatist
devolution
euroskeptic
first-past-the-post
gradualism
Magna Carta
manifesto
nationalization
Parliamentary Party
privatization
proportional representation
shadow cabinet
third way
three line whip
Westminster system
white paper

People

Blair, Tony
Brown, Gordon
Cameron, David
Clegg, Nick
Major, John
Thatcher, Margaret

Acronyms

CBI
SDP
MPs
TUC

Organizations, Places, and Events

Alliance
Beveridge Report
Confederation of British
    Industry (CBI)
Conservative Party
Good Friday Agreement
Great Reform Act
House of Commons
House of Lords
Labour Party
Liberal Democrats
Maastricht Treaty
Members of Parliament
    (MPs)
Social Democratic Party
    (SDP)
Tories
Trades Union Congress
    (TUC)

✐ Useful Websites

There are dozens of good Internet gateways on aspects of British politics. The following is the best and is hosted by the British Politics Group, which brings together American and British scholars.

www.britishpoliticsgroup.org

The most complete public opinion data are found on the site of Britain's biggest polling firm, MORI.

www.ipsos-mori.com

All of the quality British newspapers are online. However, most useful for readers of this book is the BBC's site, which has every story it has run since it went online.

news.bbc.co.uk

Direct.gov is a well-designed entry point for people seeking services and jobs from the government. You can also watch the weekly debate when the prime minister goes to the House of Commons for Question Time from C-SPAN's website. You

will have to navigate a bit around the C-SPAN site because its layout changes frequently.

www.number-10.gov.uk

www.direct.gov.uk

www.cspan.org

Further Reading

Beer, Samuel. *British Politics in the Collectivist Age* and *Britain Against Itself: The Political Contradictions of Collectivism.* New York: Norton, 1982. An examination of the origins and workings of politics during the collectivist era and the reasons it came under pressure during the crisis, respectively.

Blair, Tony. *A Journey: My Life in Politics.* New York: Knopf, 2010. A very self-reflective view of his entire career. Readers might find the analytic book by Andrew Rawnsley more useful.

The Blair Decade. PBS video. **www.shoppbs.org/sm-pbs-the-blair-decade-dvd—pi-2757530.html**. An excellent two-hour video on Blair's ten years in office.

C-SPAN. *Commons Sense: A Viewer's Guide to the British House of Commons.* Washington, D.C.: C-SPAN, 1991. A short booklet to help viewers understand the parliamentary debate that C-SPAN has regularly televised since 1990. Probably the best short source on the House of Commons.

Feigenbaum, Harvey, Jeffrey Henig, and Chris Hamnett. *Shrinking the State: The Political Underpinnings of Privatization.* Cambridge: Cambridge University Press, 1998. A thoughtful analysis of privatization in the UK, the United States, and France.

Hennessy, Peter. *The Prime Minister.* New York: Palgrave/St. Martin's, 2000. An encyclopedic but readable account of all postwar prime ministers and what made some more effective than others.

Norton, Bruce. *The Politics of Britain.* Washington: CQ Press, 2007. The best full-length text on British politics.

Rawnsley, Andrew. *The End of the Party.* (New York: Penguin, 2010). The most comprehensive book on why Labour lost, written shortly before the 2010 election.

Rentoul, John. *Tony Blair.* London: Warner Books, 1996. Though written before the 1997 election, still by far the best biography of Blair. Also gives first-rate insights into the workings of the Labour Party and British politics in general.

Toynbee, Polly, and David Walker. *Did Things Get Better? An Audit of Labour's Successes and Failures.* London: Penguin Books, 2001. A comprehensive and in some ways surprising assessment of the first Blair government's public policies, by two left-of-center journalists.

FRANCE

- Paris
- Lyons
- Bordeaux
- Marseilles

CHAPTER 5

France

My roommate's father was visiting last weekend and asked me what my major was. When I said French and Government, he told me that was a contradiction in terms.

COLLEGE STUDENT

THE BASICS

France

Size	547,030 sq. km (more than two times the size of the United Kingdom)
Climate	Mild, but much warmer along the Mediterranean coast
Population	64.5 million
GNP per capita	$32,600
Currency	1.33€ = US$1
Ethnic composition	Over 90% white, but with substantial minorities of African, Middle Eastern, Asian, and Caribbean origin
Religion	83–88% Catholics, with small minorities of Protestants, Jews, Muslims, and atheists
Capital	Paris
Form of government	Fifth Republic (1958–)
Head of state	President Nicolas Sarkozy (2007–)
Head of Government	Prime Minister François Fillon (2007–)

SARKOLAND: A ONE-TERM WONDER?

When Chip wrote the seventh edition of this book right after France's 2007 election, new President **Nicolas Sarkozy (1955–)** looked as secure in office as any leader in Europe or North America at the time. He had just defeated the Socialist candidate by six percentage points at the second ballot of the presidential election. His colleagues in the **Union for a Popular Majority** (**UMP**) won at least 320 seats (the exact number depends on how one counts the 20 seats won by independents who were allied with the UMP out of 577 members of the new and all important **National Assembly**). He soon replaced most outgoing officials in fellow-Gaullist **Jacques Chirac's (1932–)** government with people who were personally loyal to him, including the Prime Minister, the previously little known **François Fillon (1954–)**.

Sarkozy was not just personally popular. He presides over a country whose regime is as solidly supported as any. Its story will be at the heart of this chapter. For now, it is enough to note that Sarkozy became president after a generation of politicians who came on the political scene in the 1950s either died or retired. He is also not part of the larger elite that has run the country for the last half century. However different he might be from the French political

Looking BACKWARD

THIS IS ONLY the third box in this series, so it assumes you have read at least the chapter on the UK or the one on industrialized democracies.

Whichever chapters you were assigned, the "backward" themes will help you make sense of France, which students invariably find the hardest of the countries in Part 2 to understand. That is the case because it forces you to reconsider three of the questions raised so far.

- **What is democracy?** We have already seen that there are multiple models of democracy, including the one based on separation of powers used in the United States and another based on parliamentary sovereignty found in the United Kingdom and some of its former colonial offshoots. France will show us yet another one.
- **Regime vs. government of the day?** In the United States and the UK, it has been a century or more since protest against a current government also eroded support for the system as a whole or the regime. That was not the case in France. There, public support for the regime had to be built. We will see here, and in the rest of this book, that we do not understand how or

why that happens, on those rare occasions that it does. Trying to read those collective tea leaves makes comparative politics fun for introductory students and policy makers alike.

- **What should the state do?** The United States is the champion of the *laissez-faire* system that calls for minimal state intervention in the economy and tends to blame it for economic problems. What we will demonstrate in this and other chapters is that not all states—democratic or otherwise—have shied away from the kind of involvement American and some British politicians honor in principle, even if they don't always follow it in practice. Among capitalist countries, France has been a leader in using its power to help meet social goals ranging from health care to housing (but not equality of income or wealth). Looking backward, we will see why France has been different from the U.S. and the U.K. In so doing, we will also see why, until recently, an interventionist state has turned out to be so appealing in most of the rest of the world.

norm, he inherited a country that is now one of the most stable democracies on the planet and seemed likely to serve for a full two terms, if not to remake French politics in general.

To get a glimpse at what Sarkozy could have done, consider the statement that begins this chapter. Every other chapter in this book begins with a statement by an eminent politician, political scientist, or journalist. This one starts with a quip by one of Chip's students who came to his office one day almost 40 years ago to tell him about a conversation she had had with her roommate's father. When he went to college in the 1950s, her roommate's father would have been right. The average French government lasted nine months and accomplished little. The **Fourth Republic**, which had only been created in 1946, constantly seemed to be teetering and on the brink of collapse; it would not survive his undergraduate career. However, it is hard to make the case that *French* and *government* are a contradiction in terms today.

Yet, in less than three years, Sarkozy's and the UMP's majorities were in danger, to say the least. By early 2010, it seemed highly unlikely that he could defeat the Socialist candidates most likely to run in 2012. The only candidate he seemed to have a chance of beating was **Ségolène Royal (1953–)**, the same woman he had handily defeated three years earlier. We will discuss those other candidates and the issues Sarkozy faces in the second half of this chapter. For now, it is enough to note that Sarkozy made a number of policy missteps, ranging from raising doubts about his personal ethics to enacting public policies that have slowed France's recovery from the global recession.

The French public has normally not worried much about the personal lives of its leaders. Sarkozy came to office just as that toleration was diminishing. Because of this "tradition," he did not announce the end of his marriage during the campaign nor his remarriage to the Italian model and rock star, Carla Bruni, herself an heiress to a tire fortune. Since their marriage, the new Mme Sarkozy has tried to play a major role in world politics and charitable donations. There have also been rumors of extramarital affairs involving both Sarkozys.

- Several social and economic scandals came to light in summer 2010, the most serious of which involved Liliane Bettencourt, heiress to the L'Oréal cosmetics fortune, who was accused of making illegal contributions to both Sarkozy's party and his personal campaign in 2007. Complicating the relationship, Mme. Bettencourt had fallen out with her daughter and a long-time aide and friend who also accused her of evading at least $100 million in taxes per year. Bettencourt was on record for making legal contributions to both the left and the right. Sarkozy himself acknowledges dining with her at her Parisian mansion, where she is accused of giving his confidante and pension minister, Eric Woerth about $200,000. The act became even more controversial when it was revealed that Woerth's wife was also Bettencourt's accountant. This scandal would have simply blown over 15 years ago—and may do so now. However, because of the changing political climate, it may turn Sarkozyy into a one-term wonder.

- Sarkozy has been plagued by several purely public policy problems. These included his reaction to a film depicting the German takeover of a bicycle stadium in Paris, which was used to deport Jews seventy years ago. Sarkozy—whose mother was half Jewish and who himself lost at least fifty family members during the war—is also the first French President born after World War II. Sarkozy objected to the popularity of the film as part of an unending history of repenting for past wrongs at a time when many people in France still feel tremendous shame for their collaboration with the Nazis.

- Last, of course, there is the recession. Rightly or wrongly, economists put a lot of emphasis on two statistics, a national government's annual deficit between tax and other revenues and expenditures, and the national debt, which considers the same measure over many years. France does not have the worst track record in Europe. Its deficit trails those of Greece and Spain, which have been far more problematic for the EU (see Chapter 7). But its deficit is the largest among the richer EU members and its debt is projected to rise. The best prediction is that its debt will rise faster, topping those of Spain (if not Greece) by the end of 2011.

We will devote most of the first half of the chapter to why the Gaullists brought France such an unprecedented period of stability, which seems likely to endure regardless of what happens to Sarkozy and his team. In the second half we will concentrate on the social, economic, and political problems that France has faced since 1990 or so, long before Sarkozy was even a contender for national power.

THINKING ABOUT FRANCE

Key Concepts and Questions

So far, this chapter has indirectly raised a number of questions, four of which will structure the rest of it.

- How did de Gaulle's changes to the country's institutions and social, political, and economic processes contribute to the creation of an effective democratic state?

- Why is the bureaucracy at the heart of the most influential elite we will encounter in Part 2?

- Why has the French economy proven more resistant to reform over the past twenty years than the British?

- Why won't Sarkozy's gaffes (if that's what they are) undermine the long-term stability of the Fifth Republic?

But there is another overarching question that will also focus our attention in most chapters to come: why did it take so long for a stable democratic regime to take hold in France?

France's history has been quite different from that of either the United States or Great Britain something we will see was also true for Germany. It is critical, then, to understand why its deep and enduring divisions made it hard for the French to maintain a stable democracy until quite recently.

However, that is not what France is like today. To understand how France became one of the most successful European democracies in the last half century, you have to consider a series of related factors—the new constitution, the quality of its leadership, the revitalization of its political parties, the iron triangle, and more.

The Basics

France is a big country by European standards. It has almost 65 million people, just about the same number as Britain. But France has about 550,000 square miles of territory, almost two-and-a-half times that of the UK. As a result, France has more open space and less congested cities.

France has also been relatively homogeneous until the last half century. Almost everyone speaks French. There are still noticeable local accents, and some older people speak Breton, Occitan, or a regional dialect. The spread of radio and television, however, has made standard French as widely used and understood as English is in Great Britain.

Almost 90 percent of the population is at least nominally Catholic. The Catholic population, however, is not very devout. No more than 10 percent attend mass on anything approaching a regular basis. Roughly 2 percent of the population is Protestant and 1 percent is Jewish. Perhaps as much as 8 percent of the people—mostly postwar immigrants from former French colonies and their children—are Muslim. As we will see on numerous occasions, both they and the native French reaction to them have been disruptive, to say they least.

The other important factor contributing to France's homogeneity is the way Paris dominates this highly centralized country. Depending on exactly where one draws the boundaries, the Paris region contains between a quarter and a third of France's total population.

Paris is the country's cultural, political, economic, and communications hub. Almost all corporations and government agencies have their headquarters there. Road and rail systems were built with Paris as their home. Paris has long been a thriving metropolis, whereas the major provincial cities were dull and drab, leading one observer to call them the "French desert" in the 1960s. Even now, there are plenty of "turboprofs" who teach at provincial universities but refuse to move from Paris, even though they have to commute as much as eight hours each way on France's high-speed trains.

Throughout this chapter, we will encounter examples of that centralization. Here, it is enough to consider two remarkable examples. France is one of the few countries with an official agency that determines which new words can be added to its language. In recent years, it has struggled to keep foreign—mostly English—words out. People may well want to refer to a one-man show, disc jockey, or hit parade, but the High Commission for the French Language insists on *spectacle solo*, *animateur*, and *palmares*. The commission has fined American Airlines for issuing English-language boarding passes at Charles de Gaulle Airport and has hauled a furniture store owner into court for advertising his showroom rather than his *salle d'exposition*.

The second example is a tradition that has only recently been abandoned. Until the early 1990s, the government insisted that children be given the name of a saint or a figure from classical history to receive the extensive benefits it offers families. Breton, Occitan, and German names were forbidden. Richard Bernstein of the *New York Times* tells of a friend whose first and middle names were Mignon Florence, which was double trouble. Not only was Mignon not on the list of approved names, but the people at the registry office were convinced that, as a girl, she should have been Mignonne. Later, her teachers insisted that she spell her name that way. Officially, she had to be Florence, which she remained until the rules were relaxed when she was an adult.[1]

Despite a long-standing reputation as an economic backwater, France is actually one of the world's richest countries. Most French families enjoy a standard of living roughly equivalent to that in the United States. American salaries are a bit higher, but the French make up for that with guaranteed health care, university tuition that still costs about two hundred dollars a year, and a day-care system integrated into the public schools and open to all children over the age of two.

There are more French than German firms in the world's top twenty businesses. The French make the world's fastest trains, the TGV *(trains à grandes vitesses)*, which can travel comfortably at more than two hundred miles an hour. The French play a leading role in Airbus, which makes state-of-the-art jumbo jets, and Arianespace, which now surpasses the National Aeronautics and Space Administration (NASA) in commercial space ventures. The French state is a major actor in these and dozens of other firms.

Not everyone has benefited equally from what journalist John Ardagh called the "new French revolution." Three relatively disadvantaged groups, in particular, stand out. First are older people who cannot afford to move out of their isolated villages or dingy urban apartments. Second are women, who have yet to make as much political or professional progress as their counterparts in the United States. Third are members of minority groups, who are still largely stuck with the jobs whites are not willing to take and who are discriminated against in ways reminiscent of the American South before the civil rights movement.

THE EVOLUTION OF THE FRENCH STATE: CENTURIES OF TURMOIL

Transformation and Division

Comparativists typically cite Great Britain as the model of a state that evolved relatively smoothly over several centuries. They turn to France to illustrate a rather different, but far more common, historical pattern: that state building can be a long and wrenching process. That can be seen easily in the fact that France has had eleven regimes since the revolution that began in 1789. The United States and Great Britain have had one each (see Table 5.1).

To see why that was the case, it makes sense to do the same thing we did for Britain and use the top row of the table on the inside front cover to explore how France was affected by the four great transformations that shaped European history. In France, the conflicts they generated were largely left unresolved, leaving deep scars that continue to affect French politics today. France did not continually have to confront the specter of revolution. Nonetheless, in comparative terms, it had far more trouble than Great Britain

---

[1] Richard Bernstein, *Fragile Glory: A Portrait of France and the French* (New York: Penguin Books, 1900), 110ff.

TABLE 5.1 French Regimes since 1789

YEAR	REGIME
Until 1792	Bourbon Monarchy
1792–1804	First Republic
1804–15	First Empire
1815–30	Bourbon Restoration
1830–48	July Monarchy
1848–51	Second Republic
1851–70	Second Empire
1875–1940	Third Republic
1940–44	Vichy Regime
1944–46	Liberation Government
1946–58	Fourth Republic
1958–	Fifth Republic

did in dealing with the challenges it faced over the past few centuries 🖱 (**http://europeanhistory.about.com**).

Gender Issues
in France

France has long had an ambiguous track record on the role of women in politics. It was one of the last countries to give women the right to vote (1944), but women served as cabinet members a decade earlier.

A succession of French governments have done as much as any democratic government in enacting laws about families, although they have not done much to advance the role of women *per se*. Yet, it is also one of the few countries in which women have been serious candidates for national leadership positions.

But at the same time, France was one of the last countries to legalize abortion in the early 1970s.

The first transformation led to the formation of France itself. It did not leave France deeply divided, but it did give rise to one of its most powerful political traditions, **centralization**. As early as 1500, there was an entity we could identify as France. It had a government headed by a king, but its power was limited, especially the farther one travelled from Paris.

France was not as isolated as the British Isles, and it could not avoid the wars of religion and national expansion that ravaged Europe. One French response was to create a strong and centralized state, which many historians date from the reign of the "Sun King," **Louis XIV** (1643–1715).

The revolution of 1789 cemented this tradition of centralized government in Paris. Some revolutionary groups wanted to drastically scale back Paris's power. By 1792, they had lost out to the **Jacobins**, who were, if anything, more in favor of centralization than the Bourbon monarchs they

replaced. France was divided into departments controlled from Paris, which made it the most uniformly and effectively administered country in early-nineteenth-century Europe. However, it also led many to view the state as a distant and arbitrary geopolitical stone wall that frustrated them everywhere they turned.

The other three transformations left France deeply divided and also added to the alienation caused by centralization. Historically, the dispute over the role of religion and the relationship between church and state was the most disruptive, at least until very recently. Even though the overwhelming majority of French people are Catholic, this does not mean that they have deeply rooted and positive feelings about the church. The church was traditionally closely allied with the monarchy. Many of the best-known leaders of the *ancien régime*, such as Armand Jean du Plessis Richelieu, Jules Mazarin, and Jean-Baptiste Colbert, were cardinals as well as ministers to the king. The revolution of 1789, therefore, not only overturned the monarchy but also made the political power of the church a controversial issue indeed.

During the nineteenth and twentieth centuries, the religious differences divided France into an **anticlerical** Left that advocated the total separation of church and state and a **proclerical** Right that believed the church should play a leading role in a restored monarchy. In the 1890s and early 1900s, the decisions to separate church and state and thus undermine ecclesiastical wealth and power provoked such resistance from proclerical groups that the Third Republic was nearly toppled.

Disputes about the nature of the regime overlapped with those about the role of the church and slowed the spread of democracy. France does have one of the oldest and strongest democratic traditions in the world. It was in France in 1789 that a declaration of the rights of man was first included in an official government document. Subsequent constitutions expanded the definition of human rights beyond the basic political ones to include such "social" benefits as the right to a job and social security. France was also the first country to extend the right to vote to all men after the revolution of 1848.

But unlike Britain, France was unable to adopt democracy one step at a time with the acquiescence of the traditional elite. Instead, it came in lurches, many of which did not last. Prior to 1958, France always had major groups that opposed democracy in any form. Moreover, the democratic regimes it adopted were not very effective for reasons that we will discuss in more detail soon. It has only been with the widespread acceptance of the Fifth Republic that we can speak of the definitive consolidation of democracy in France.

The final transformation—the industrial revolution and the class conflict it spawned—also affected France in more complex and divisive ways than it did Britain. As with democracy and religion, social class provoked deep and lasting conflict. Many workers supported the social democrats who, like Labour in Britain, believed that fundamental change in social and economic life could be achieved by working through the parliamentary system. Others preferred more radical socialists and argued, instead, that meaningful change could only occur through a revolution. After 1920, that division was reflected in the split between a reformist Socialist Party (PS)—known as the *Section française de l'Internationale ouvrière* (SFIO) until 1969—and a **Communist Party (PCF)**, initially inspired by the Bolshevik revolution in Russia.

Also unlike in Britain, the French procapitalist forces were divided. Most small shopkeepers, merchants, and farmers had qualms about the industrial revolution. They used free-market rhetoric to help protect the traditional economic system under which they prospered. Because these business-oriented groups that resisted change were often in power, capitalists who wanted to modernize and industrialize did not endorse laissez-faire. Rather, they argued that concerted state action was needed to overcome the market's biases toward stability, a point of view that would not prevail until after World War II when it became the cornerstone of economic policy making under the Gaullists.

TRADITIONAL REPUBLICAN POLITICS: A VICIOUS CIRCLE

In trying to understand the complicated evolution of French politics, we can limit our attention to the Third and Fourth Republics and concentrate on key themes rather than historical details. Political life during those years can best be seen as a political vicious circle of four interlocking problems as summarized in Figure 5.1.

The ideological divisions left by the four transformations spawned six major "political families" of roughly equal size. The 1951 election was typical and allows us to see how the many parties reflected the conflicting points of view found in French society (see Table 5.2).

FIGURE 5.1 Traditional Republican Politics in France

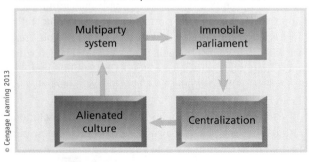

TABLE 5.2 Seats in the French Chamber of Deputies, 1951

PARTY	SEATS
PCF	101
SFIO	106
MRP	88
Radicals	76
UDSR	23
IOM	17
Independents and Peasants	95
Gaullists	120

IOM; MRP, Popular Republican Movement; PCF, Communist Party; UDSR.

As noted previously, the Socialists and Communists, which represented the two halves of the socialist tradition, had been bitter rivals ever since the PCF broke off from the SFIO. Much like the SFIO, the Catholic Popular Republican Movement (MRP) supported the welfare state and European integration, but the two found it hard to work together given their sharp disagreement over church-related issues.

The **Radicals** were formed in the nineteenth century, which meant that they believed in liberal democracy, anticlericalism, and free-market capitalism. The Independents and Peasants shared many of the Radicals' economic views but were staunchly proclerical. Neither the Radicals nor the Independents were well organized and disciplined.

Finally, the supporters of **Charles de Gaulle** or **Gaullists** were the most recent manifestation of a strand of public opinion that demanded strong leadership. Although such beliefs had their roots in monarchism and Bonapartism, the Gaullists claimed to be solid republicans. They simply wanted to replace the Fourth Republic with a better one!

The existence of so many antagonistic parties made the second component of the vicious circle—a deadlocked parliament—all but inevitable. As in most parliamentary systems, the president was little more than a figurehead. Real power was shared by the parliament and cabinet.

Unfortunately, the French were never able to achieve anything like party government as it existed in Britain. Because the parties were so divided, elections never produced a majority. Instead, cabinets had to include members of three or four parties that had little or nothing in common. Often, tiny parties like the Independents from Overseas (members of Parliament elected from then-French colonies) held the balance of power. Virtually any issue of consequence would split the coalition so that every nine months or so the government would lose its majority and resign, almost always before a formal vote of no confidence was held. The ensuing cabinet crisis would last until the parties could resolve their differences on the issues that brought the old government down and then form a new one. That cabinet, in turn, would survive until it had to confront the next difficult issue. As a result, most of France's pressing and enduring problems went unsolved.

The president and prime minister were denied the one constitutional device that might have broken the deadlock—dissolving parliament and calling for new elections. Marshal Macmahon, the first president of the Third Republic, had called for elections in 1877, hoping they would yield a monarchist majority. Instead, the republican parties won a resounding victory and forced Macmahon to resign. From then on, there was an unwritten rule that neither the president nor the prime minister could dissolve parliament before its term ended.

The Macmahon fiasco along with other episodes convinced politicians that their ambitious colleagues were dangerous. Reform-minded leaders were routinely passed over when it came to forming cabinets. The king makers preferred politicians whom they could count on, which meant those who were happy with the deadlocked system.

The effects of the ideological divisions were compounded by yet another problem—politicians' willingness to sacrifice just about everything else to advance their own careers. According to many political scientists, their ideological rhetoric was little more than a veneer to hide self-serving behavior and corruption. Many current and potential ministers were willing to sabotage any cabinet—including those in which they served—and to destroy any politician's reputation to enhance their own prestige and power.

Last, but by no means least, there was a "negative" consensus on what social and economic policy should be like, which Hoffmann called the republican synthesis that sustained a stalemate society. The dominant centrist politicians represented the most traditional elements of the population—the peasantry and the petite bourgeoisie of the small towns. Although these politicians could rarely agree on what to do about the "big issues," they had little trouble seeing eye to eye on what France should *not* do. They accepted society as it was and rejected the idea that government should be used to foster modernization.

In the absence of effective parliamentary government, what power there was devolved onto the third cog of traditional republican politics: the bureaucracy. The effects of extreme centralization and inflexibility in the bureaucratic system as a whole rippled throughout society. Educational standards, for example, were set in Paris. All schools used the same curriculum to prepare students for national examinations that determined whether they passed. Individual teachers, students, and parents had little or nothing to say about what happened in the schools.

Centralization had much to do with the final component of the vicious circle—an alienated political culture. Political scientists did not gather systematic evidence on

French values until the 1960s. Nonetheless, everything we know suggests that the French were as frustrated and ideologically divided as any mass public in the industrialized world. Unlike the British, the French frequently questioned the regime's basic structures and practices. Many were defensive individualists, convinced that they had to protect themselves from government officials and all other outsiders, who they "knew" were out to do them in. Few people believed they could redress their grievances by working through the parties or Parliament. Similarly, the bureaucracy seemed closed to input from below. Consequently, the French suppressed their anger and hostility until something triggered an explosion.

This was not merely a feature of national politics. What Michel Crozier called the "bureaucratic phenomenon" was the defining characteristic of an entire society that was built around centralized, unresponsive institutions. Students, for instance, hated the rigid rules of the national education system, but they grudgingly accepted a classroom experience they disliked as long as they felt that the teacher was doing a good job preparing them for the exams that determined their academic future. If, however, the students felt that a teacher was not doing a good job, it was a different story. Then the students might suddenly break out into a wild demonstration or *chahut* (from the words for *screaming cat*), which William Schonfeld graphically described:

> **Students might constantly talk with one another, get up and walk around the room whenever they feel like it, and if the teacher should call on them to respond to a question, they would answer disrespectfully— e.g., Teacher: "When you mix two atoms of hydrogen with one atom of oxygen, what do you get?" Pupil: "It rains," or "*merde.*" Or the students might jeer at the teacher in unison, call him nasty names and run around the classroom. In certain classes, wet wads of paper will be thrown across the room, landing and then sticking on the wall behind the teacher's desk. Or there might be a fistfight, with the winner ejecting the loser from the room, while the other pupils stand around cheering for one or the other of the pugilists. With some teachers, the students might bring small glass sulfur bombs into class, which would be simultaneously broken, creating such a stench that the teacher is usually driven into the hall while the pupils stay in class, happily suffering the odor. Finally, students might bring a tent, camping equipment, and food into their class and, during the lesson, set up the tent, prepare lunch for each other, and then eat it— the teacher being powerless to help.[2]**

---

[2] William Schonfeld, *Obedience and Revolt* (Beverly Hills, CA: Sage, 1976), 30–31.

Democratization
in France

France's difficulties in building any kind of legitimate state, let alone a democratic one, illustrate just how fortunate the United States and Great Britain have been.

By 1900, both the United States and Great Britain had states with broadly based support. The basic contours of democracy were established as well, although it would be a generation before women could vote in either country and sixty years before most American blacks could do so.

In France at that time, the Third Republic was teetering on the brink of collapse. Though it weathered the crises of the moment, it survived only because, as Georges Clémenceau put it, it was the form of government that divided the French the least. In addition, although it survived, the Third Republic accomplished very little, which is one of the reasons that France developed the reputation epitomized by the statement that begins this chapter. ∎

Ultimately, that alienation fed back into the party and parliamentary morass to complete the vicious circle. The political psychologist Nathan Leites titled one of his books about parliament under the Fourth Republic *The House Without Windows*. The main section of the Parliament building actually is windowless, but he chose the image to depict the widespread conviction that politicians did not care about the country, its problems, or its people.

The windowlessness went in both directions. As far as we can tell, the French people did not try to look in all that often either. Even though they complained about the irresponsible politicians and their ideological squabbles, they consistently reelected the members of Parliament who pushed pork barrel legislation through but could not get the bureaucracy or anyone else to move on an individual's or a community's problems. In so doing, they made it impossible for the state to govern effectively.

From the Fourth to the Fifth Republic

Though characterized by deadlock and inertia, the traditional republican system did have its share of accomplishments. The church-state issue receded from center stage.

Even though governments came and went with mind-boggling speed, there was more ministerial stability than one might expect at first glance. Cabinets were, after all, variations on the same theme because most of the same parties and politicians appeared in government after government. But none of this should obscure our basic point. All of those governments failed to meet France's pressing policy problems.

Following its liberation from German occupation in 1944, France did have one brief flirtation with effective government. The old political guard had been discredited by the depression of the 1930s, defeat by Germany, and collaboration with the Nazis. Few people wanted to go back to the *status quo ante*. The provisional government headed by de Gaulle nationalized major industrial and financial firms and established a planning commission to supervise economic recovery. Even the bureaucracy changed with the establishment of the **Ecole Nationale d'Administration** (**ENA**), a school to train civil servants, committed to democracy and modernization.

Unfortunately, the flirtation *was* brief. When the politicians finally agreed on a constitution for the Fourth Republic, it proved to be a nearly carbon copy of the one used by the Third. De Gaulle resigned in protest.

Overall, the history of the **Fourth Republic** was a sorry one indeed. The mismatch between an unchanging, ineffective government and a society with mounting unsolved problems proved to be even more serious than it had been before the war. At home, successive governments could do little to build the social infrastructure needed for a rapidly urbanizing population. Abroad, the pressures were even more intense from the colonies, which were beginning to demand their freedom.

By the mid-1950s, support for politicians was at an all-time low. Young people were so turned off that they did not even bother to learn who their leaders were. Thus, one public opinion poll showed that 95 percent of the men drafted into the army in 1956 knew who had won the Tour de France that year, but only 17 percent could identify the prime minister.

Although domestic problems received the most attention, it was a foreign policy crisis that brought the Fourth Republic's short life to an end. Throughout the postwar period, France had struggled vainly to hold onto its empire. In 1954, a revolution broke out in Algeria, where the majority Arab population demanded independence. By 1958, many of the ethnically French settlers were in revolt as well, blaming the Parisian government for failing to put down the Arab insurgency.

In spring 1958, the Fourth Republic's seventeenth prime minister resigned. It soon became clear that the little-known Pierre Pflimlin would be the next man to hold the job, and he was expected to begin negotiations with the Algerian Arabs.

That proved to be the last straw for the army and the white colonists. On the night of May 12–13, soldiers seized

Profiles
Charles de Gaulle

Charles de Gaulle (1890–1970) was one of the most prominent and influential leaders of the twentieth century. He began his career in the army, where he built a reputation as a visionary who urged his superiors (while often irritating them) to modernize their armaments to meet the growing challenge from Nazi Germany.

Despite the fact that he was largely unknown outside of military circles, de Gaulle led the resistance against Nazi occupation during World War II and headed the Liberation government from 1944 to 1946. He then retired because the politicians refused to heed his calls for a strong executive.

Brought back to power during the Algerian crisis in 1958, de Gaulle created the **Fifth Republic**. He led France for the next eleven years until he resigned following a defeat in a referendum on minor constitutional reforms. De Gaulle died the following year, but his new regime was firmly in place as the first stable and popular democracy in France's long and troubled history.

The Charles de Gaulle Institute and Foundation maintains an excellent website on the general and his legacy. Unfortunately, only a tiny portion of its material is available in English, which some would argue is to be expected of the Gaullists  (www. charles-de-gaulle.org). ∎

President Charles de Gaulle casting his ballot in the 1962 parliamentary elections at Colombey-les-deux-églises, where he lived during the Fourth Republic and where he died after resigning as the Fifth Republic's first president.

control of Algiers. Rumors quickly spread that the military was preparing to invade the mainland. Finally, on June 1, the politicians turned to de Gaulle, who agreed to become prime minister again on the condition that he would be given extraordinary powers not only to deal with the rebellion but also to revise the constitution (see Table 5.3).

Despite their agreement to these terms, most politicians expected de Gaulle to be a typical heroic leader. On several earlier occasions, the Parliament had turned to exceptional men to deal with crises and then had gotten rid of them as soon as the immediate danger passed. They had every reason to expect the same would happen with de Gaulle. He was already sixty-eight years old. Even after the 1958 elections, he had, at most, the reluctant support from the politicians in Parliament, the majority of whom were waiting for him to leave so they could return to business as usual.

De Gaulle proved them wrong. When he did leave office in 1969, a wholly new republic had been put in place, one that was strong and stable enough to confound the skeptics and survive the departure of its charismatic leader. The details of this republic and its newfound stability and resilience will be the subject of the rest of this chapter.

FRENCH POLITICAL CULTURE: FROM ALIENATION TOWARD CONSENSUS

Stereotypes about French culture abound: The French are arrogant and rude. They love to argue. Their erratic and deadly driving habits are indicative of a broader unwillingness to accept discipline and order. Somehow that lead to

TABLE 5.3 Key Events in French Politics since 1958

YEAR	EVENT
1958	Creation of the Fifth Republic
1961	End of Algerian War
1962	Referendum on direct election of president First parliamentary majority elected
1965	De Gaulle reelected
1968	Events of May and June
1969	De Gaulle's resignation
1970	De Gaulle's death
1973–74	OPEC oil embargo
1981	Mitterrand and Socialists elected
1986	First period of cohabitation
1988	Mitterrand reelected
1993	Second period of cohabitation
1995	Chirac elected
1997	Socialists' return to power
2002	First scheduled simultaneous election of Parliament and president
2007	Election of Sarkozy

the massive waves of strikes and demonstrations that have occurred on and off throughout French history.

Whatever the cause, there is no question that the French were more divided and less "civic" than the British or Americans until the 1970s. The past thirty years, however, have brought a dramatic lessening of the ideological tensions that had been so divisive and damaging. Widespread protests still occur, but, on balance, we can safely say that the success French governments have had since 1958 is now mirrored in popular attitudes and beliefs. Put in other terms, virtually no one now talks about moving on to a Sixth Republic, let alone another monarchy or empire. The alienation that remains is no worse than the dissatisfaction one encounters in the most stable of democracies.

Taming Political Protest

Return for a moment to the distinction between the government of the day and the regime as a whole, drawn in Chapters 1 and 2. Public opinion polls conducted in the United States and Great Britain since the 1950s suggest that, however intense opposition there might be to a David Cameron or Barack Obama, it stops there—at opposition to individual leaders. No more than a handful of British or American citizens would be willing to overturn the regime and the constitutional order.

By the mid-1970s, the French had come to resemble the British and Americans in that respect. Two-thirds of the population claimed to have confidence in the president's judgment, and a similar number believed that elections make politicians pay attention to what average citizens are

thinking. Trust in government has fluctuated a good bit since then and has been a bit lower since the 1990s. Still, the French public does seem to be as willing to trust its politicians and institutions as are the people in any other industrialized democracy (see Table 5.4).

The turning point, as far as support for the regime is concerned, probably occurred by the late 1960s. In May 1968, a massive wave of strikes and demonstrations paralyzed the country. Many observers (including Chip) believed that the **events of May** were evidence of a new kind of alienation that could imperil both capitalism and the Gaullist regime. We may have been right about the anger of the moment but not about its enduring implications. Table 5.4 shows just how wrong we were. Somewhere between 55 and 71 percent of the voters thought the institutions of the Fifth Republic "functioned well" during the last quarter of the twentieth century. There is no reason to believe that those statistics have changed since then. If nothing else, French pollsters think that they no longer have to ask the question!

The movement started innocently enough. Facilities at the suburban branch of the University of Paris in Nanterre were not very good. Students also chafed under strict rules regarding dormitory life at what had been billed as France's first American-style campus.

Their first significant protest occurred at the dedication of the campus swimming pool on March 22. There was nothing unusual about the demonstration other than the fact that the students threw the dean into the water. What mattered was the way the university authorities tried to discipline them. Because the administration was so centralized, the hearing on their alleged crime took place not in Nanterre, but at the Sorbonne in the Latin Quarter. During the hearing, a small group of students staged a support demonstration for what was now known as the March 22 movement in the university's medieval courtyard. For the first time in centuries, the police entered the Sorbonne. Their action provoked nightly demonstrations, which were violently repressed by the police. As the security forces

TABLE 5.4 Support for the Fifth Republic

Question: "The Constitution of the Fifth Republic went into effect in 1958. If you had to render a judgment on how its institutions have functioned since then, would you say that they have functioned well or not functioned well?"

YEAR	FUNCTIONED WELL (%)	NOT FUNCTIONED WELL (%)
1978	56	27
1983	57	25
1992	61	32
2000	71	21

Source: Adapted from Olivier Duhamel, "Confiance institutionnelle et défiance politique: la démocratie française," in *L'état de l'opinion 2001*, Olivier Duhamel and Philippe Méchet. (ed.) (Paris: Editions du Seuil, 2001), 75.

continued to overreact (at least in the eyes of most middle-class people), support for the students grew.

On the night of May 10–11, students erected barricades reminiscent of those used in previous revolutions. The police responded ever more violently. By the end of the night, leaders of the major trade unions and other left-leaning interest groups came to realize that they had the same adversary as the students: the Gaullist state. Finally, the unions and the left-wing parties decided to join in by staging a march on May 13.

After the rally, students took over the Sorbonne and other buildings in the Latin Quarter. Acting without the authorization of union leaders, workers started occupying factories around the country. Within days, France was at a standstill. By the middle of the month, approximately 8 million people were on strike, and more than 2 million had taken part in at least one demonstration.

The protesters were concerned about the centralization of power under the Gaullists. Along with personal attacks on de Gaulle (*Dix ans, ça suffit!*—Ten years, that's enough!) came demands for increased participation, freedom of speech, decentralization, labor reform, and improved quality of life. **Autogestion**, or a participatory, decentralized form of self-managed socialism, became a rallying cry for much of the noncommunist Left.

The government and the regime held, however. At the end of May, de Gaulle used one of his new powers (see the section on the state) and dissolved the National Assembly. The Gaullists, playing on growing public fear of disorder, won by a landslide in the legislative elections that finally put an end to the crisis in late June.

To some degree, the events were typical of traditional forms of protest in France. However, they were qualitatively different in many key respects that point to changes in the political culture that were probably already well underway.

The diverse groups came together in that massive movement because they could see that they had a common adversary in the state. The spontaneity and size of the protests reflect the breadth and depth of dissatisfaction that was anything but trivial or traditional. It had taken a decade, but now the "losers" had finally come to realize that the effective new regime required a new form of opposition that included criticism not just of the issues of the day but of the concentration of power under the Gaullists.

It is just as important to notice that virtually no one questioned the legitimacy of the Fifth Republic. Even the most outspoken advocates of autogestion saw it could be part and parcel of a democratic regime. Most of the veterans of the movement Chip interviewed in 1972 assumed that the sweeping policy changes they struggled for could be realized without altering the institutional arrangements of the Fifth Republic in any appreciable way.

After 1968, alienation began to abate further for a number of reasons. Mitterrand took over and rejuvenated the **Socialist Party (PS)** in 1971. It began to champion many of the themes the students and workers had raised in 1968, including autogestion, women's rights, the plight of immigrant workers, and the environment. In the process, it became one of the world's most dynamic political parties, attracting many who had been in the streets in 1968 and, in essence, channeling the conflicts growing out of the protests into conventional political life.

The Gaullists learned many of the lessons of 1968, too. Parliament passed reforms in the wake of their electoral victory in June that gave universities a degree of autonomy, raised the minimum wage by 35 percent, and expanded workers' benefits by, for instance, giving them a fifth week of paid vacation.

Perhaps most important of all was the continued rapid economic growth that contributed to a visible improvement in the standard of living of almost all French families. The improvements continued during the presidency of **Valéry Giscard d'Estaing** (1974–81), even though the rate of economic growth slowed considerably as a result of the Organization of Petroleum Exporting Countries (OPEC) oil embargo and the recession it sparked.

In the 1980s, the most important factor in the erosion of alienation undoubtedly was the election of **Francois Mitterrand** (1916–1996) and his Socialist parliamentary majority in 1981. It marked the first time there had been a real shift in who governed France since the foundation of the Fifth Republic, which is an important turning point in the history of any democratic regime. Right-wingers had worried that a PS-PCF coalition would be dangerous. Yet the smooth transition to Socialist rule further established the legitimacy of the regime. The sense that the political stakes were no longer all that high was reinforced after the 1986, 1993, and 1997 elections, when Left and Right had to cohabit and govern together, and did so with surprising ease.

By that time, doubts about the Fifth Republic had largely evaporated. As Table 5.4 shows, most French men and women thought that the institutions of the Fifth Republic were working well by the end of the 1970s, a belief that has only strengthened since then as the traditional divisions between Left and Right and between working class and bourgeoisie have declined in significance.

New Divisions

As we will see, France has its share of ideological divisions and protest movements they can spawn. Although the survival of the Fifth Republic is no longer in jeopardy, France is divided on two overlapping issues that tap the post-materialist values discussed in Chapter 2: race and Europe.

Luca Bruno/ Associated Press

The multiracial and multicultural French soccer team celebrating its victory in the 1998 World Cup. Many hoped that the victory would help ease race relations in France. In the three World Cups since then, in which France has done poorly, the diversity of the team has frequently been criticized.

As noted previously, France has a significant minority population. Until the economic downturn of the 1970s, few people objected to their presence. Rather, many welcomed the immigrants, who gladly took low-paying or unpleasant jobs the French no longer were interested in doing. That has not, however, been the case over the last twenty-five years. Many of the immigrants and their French-born children have not assimilated, sparking the resentment of traditionalists and nationalists. Although there is less immigration than there was a generation ago, many who are now entering France are doing so as political refugees at a time when, long before 9/11, terrorism led many to equate immigration with violence. More important, there is resentment against non-whites who hold jobs or receive funds from France's vast social service programs at a time when unemployment and the budget deficit have both been at near-record levels for more than a decade. The resentment toward "immigrants" undoubtedly grew after several waves of violent protests swept the working class suburbs that surround most cities. The most dramatic of these occurred in 2005 when North African and other youths burned hundreds of cars around the country after a number of teenagers were killed by the police.

The manifestations of these trends extend far beyond the 10 to 20 percent of the vote the all but openly racist **National Front (FN)** won in most elections since the 1980s. However, we should not make too much of the new French

racism. There are probably as many people who oppose all forms of racism and who welcome a more multicultural and diverse France. Many people, too, hope that the success of France's multiracial soccer team since its 1998 World Cup victory would help ease tensions. Still, such people have been far less visible and influential both on the streets and at the ballot box.

European integration became a divisive issue for the first time with the referendum on the Maastricht Treaty on European Union in 1992. It reappeared when French voters became the first to reject the proposed European constitution in 2005. Superimposed on preexisting racism, the fault lines cut across ideological camps. Similarly, opposition to further integration is concentrated in the same social and economic groups that see themselves as most threatened by competition from foreign workers. We will defer discussing these divisions until Chapter 7 on the European Union itself.

POLITICAL PARTICIPATION

Patterns of political participation in France are quite different from those in most other European countries. Although it is hard to measure such things, the French probably protest more—or at least more colorfully—than their counterparts elsewhere on the continent. In addition, their party

Conflict
in France

The evolution of conflict in France demonstrates the importance of the difference between the government and the regime more clearly than anything we have seen so far.

Before 1968, protest against the government, its leaders, and its practices easily spilled over into opposition to the regime as well. As a result, French politics had a degree of instability and fragility rarely seen in the United States or Great Britain.

Since then, however, the stakes of political life have lowered appreciably. As in most stable and effective democracies, just about everyone takes the regime and its legitimacy for granted.

Given the countries we have covered so far, this may not seem like a very important or surprising point. However, in Parts 3 and 4, we will see that such support is very much the exception rather than the rule in much of the rest of the world. ■

system has changed more often and more drastically than most. It is also going through yet another period of uncertainty and transition, as evidenced by the 2002 and 2007 elections. Nonetheless, there is little to suggest that the stability of the republic is in jeopardy.

Renewing the Party System

From the late 1960s onward, many political scientists argued that political parties had "failed." As was noted in Chapter 2, they had become catch-all organizations better suited to running slick campaigns than generating either fresh ideas or enduring electoral support.

The first signs that those arguments were somewhat overstated came in an obscure article published in 1988 on how French parties "refused to fail."[3] In it, Frank Wilson argued that over the preceding thirty years, the French

parties and party system had gotten stronger. Instead of the fragmentation reflected in Table 5.2, the party system revolved around coalitions on the Left and Right, each of which was centered on two major parties. From 1962 on, one or the other of them won a majority of seats in the National Assembly and the presidency. The parties took relatively clear stands. The major parties were led by men (the first prominent woman took on a senior leadership position only in the 1990s) who were political fixtures for a quarter century or more.

To be sure, these are catch-all parties whose spin doctors can massage the media with the best of their British or American counterparts. The governing UMPs website usually has some attacks on the Left and a brief overview of what the government is doing 🖉 (**www.u-m-p.org**). However, it also has an online shop where you can buy pens (including one that glows in the dark), t-shirts, coffee mugs, ties, and other products all adorned with the party's unusual logo of a half red and half blue tree.

Tables 5.5 and 5.6 summarize the results of legislative and presidential elections from the beginning of the Fifth Republic until 2007.

The Majority

Any analysis of the party system obviously has to start with the Gaullists. The generic term *Gaullist* is used in most of this chapter because the party has repeatedly changed its name since the 1950s. Under de Gaulle and Pompidou, its title always included the terms *union* and *republic*. After Chirac took over in 1974, it became the **Rally for the Republic (RPR)**. In 2002, it became the Union for a Presidential Majority. Afterward, it renamed itself the **Union for a Popular Movement (UMP)** and ran and won under that title five years later.

In 1958, there was no official Gaullist party. The general disliked parties and distanced himself from them after the first Gaullist organization failed to win the 1951 legislative elections. De Gaulle's disdain for parties is reflected in the fact that none of the Gaullist party's names have ever included the word *party* to this day.

In 1958, it was hard to tell what being a Gaullist meant because a wide variety of politicians ran, claiming to be an ally of the new republic's architect. By the mid-1960s, the Gaullists had created the first disciplined conservative party in French history. Since then, the Gaullists have regularly won at least a quarter of the vote, distributed fairly evenly among all segments of French society. They like to refer to themselves as the majority. Although they have never won a majority of the legislative vote, they have been in power either on their own or in coalition with the Socialists during periods of cohabitation throughout the Fifth Republic except for 1981 to 1986 and 1988 to 1993.

---

[3] Frank L. Wilson, "When Parties Refuse to Fail: The Case of France," in *The Future of Political Parties* edited by Kay Lawson (Princeton, NJ: Princeton University Press, 1988), 503–32.

TABLE 5.5 Parliamentary Elections, 1958–2007: Major Parties Only

YEAR	PCF VOTES[d] (%)	SEATS	PS[a] VOTES (%)	SEATS	CENTER[b] VOTES (%)	SEATS	GAULLISTS[c] AND ALLIES VOTES (%)	SEATS	FN VOTES (%)	SEATS
1958	19.1	10	15.5	47	41.0	215	17.6%	212	—	—
1962	21.8	41	12.5	66	26.5	84	36.4	269	—	—
1967	22.5	73	19.0	121	12.6	41	37.7	242	—	—
1968	20.0	34	16.5	49	10.3	33	43.7	354	—	—
1973	21.2	73	20.4	101	12.4	31	34.5	261	—	—
1978	20.5	86	24.7	117	—	—	43.9	274	—	—
1981	16.2	44	37.6	281	—	—	40.0	150	—	—
1986	9.7	35	31.85	210	—	—	42.0	274	9.9	35
1988	11.3	27	35.9	276	—	—	37.7	258	9.8	1
1993	9.2	23	20.3	70	—	—	39.5	460	12.4	0
1997	9.9	37	28.6	282	—	—	39.5	257	15.1	1
2002	4.8	21	24.1	140	—	—	38.5	386	11.3	0
2007	4.3	15	33.6	212	—	—	45.6	345	4.3	0

FN, National Front; PCF, Communist Party; PS, Socialist Party.

[a]SFIO before 1971. Includes parties allied with the Socialists, usually the left wing of the radicals.

[b]Includes MRP, Moderates, Radicals not allied with the SFIO, and other centrists not part of the Gaullist coalition.

[c]Includes both the Gaullist Party and, after the 1962 election, Giscard's Party, both of which kept changing their name from election to election.

[d]First-ballot vote only.

The Gaullists insist that they are above ideology. Nonetheless, three themes have stood out throughout their history. First is an unwavering commitment to the legacy of General de Gaulle. Second, of all the French political parties, the Gaullists have focused their appeal and their organization primarily around a single leader, from de Gaulle to Sarkozy. Third, of all the major European center-Right parties, the Gaullists have been the slowest to adopt the rhetoric and reality of market capitalism, something we will see in the section on public policy.

The UMP scored massive victories in 2002 and 2007, though it is the former race that tells us the most. The presidential landslide was not surprising once **Jean-Marie Le Pen** edged out **Lionel Jospin** for a spot on the runoff ballot. The UMP went into the legislative elections a month later with a lot of momentum and a surprisingly popular leader, interim Prime Minister Jean-Pierre Raffarin. Meanwhile, the PS was in shock following Jospin's defeat and immediate resignation after the first ballot and, therefore, ran a listless campaign. Together, that produced the second largest parliamentary majority in the history of the Fifth Republic.

The UMP's support fell after the election and it did poorly in European and local elections. Chirac replaced the ineffectual Raffarin with Dominique de Villepin who had been foreign minister during the run up to the invasion of Iraq. By late 2006 and early 2007, it had become clear that

there was no way the 77-year-old Chirac could win another term and he gave way to Sarkozy.

Sarkozy is a new kind of politician. He is blunt—he once called the 2005 rioters "scum." His campaign focused more on his personality than those of any of his predecessors. He raised new ideas about revitalizing the economy using market forces. Nonetheless, the continuity with the key themes of Gaullist history was clear, something he stressed in the brief speech he gave after being sworn in.

The second member of the conservative coalition that dominated the Fifth Republic during its first twenty-three years got its start when the minister of finance, Giscard, split with most moderate politicians and supported the 1962 referendum on the direct election of the president. Giscard then formed his own small party, the Independent Republicans (RI), which did well enough to provide the Gaullists with their first stable parliamentary majority in the legislative elections that followed later that fall. After Giscard's defeat for reelection in 1981, the RI merged with a number of other moderate parties to form a loose coalition known as the **Union for French Democracy (UDF)** (www.udf.org). Most UDF leaders supported Chirac in 2002 and then joined the UMP. A small rump group supported François Bayrou, who came in fourth with 6.8 percent of the vote. The party did not even reach 5 percent of the vote in the legislative elections, and its twenty-one deputies normally supported the government afterward. Bayrou did a little better in

TABLE 5.6 Presidential Elections, 1965–2007: Major Candidates Only

YEAR	COMMUNISTS[a] (%)	SOCIALISTS[b] (%)	CENTER[c] (%)	GISCARDIEN[d] (%)	GAULLIST[e] (%)	NATIONAL FRONT[f] (%)
1965						
First ballot	—	32.2	15.8	—	43.7	—
Second ballot	—	45.5	—	—	54.5	—
1969						
First ballot	21.5	5.1	23.4	—	43.8	—
Second ballot	—	—	42.4	—	57.6	—
1974						
First ballot	—	43.2	—	32.6	15.1	—
Second ballot	—	49.2	—	50.8	—	—
1981						
First ballot	15.3	25.8	—	28.3	17.9	—
Second ballot	—	51.8	—	48.2	—	—
1988						
First ballot	6.7	34.1	—	16.5	19.9	14.4
Second ballot	—	54.0	—	—	45.9	—
1995						
First ballot	8.5	23.5	—	19.0[g]	20.8	15.2
Second ballot	—	47.4	—	—	52.6	—
2002						
First ballot	3.4	16.2	—	6.8	19.9	17.8
Second ballot	—	—	—	—	82.2	17.8
2007						
First Ballot			18.6	31.2	25.9	10.0
Second ballot				53.1	46.9	

[a]Jacques Duclos in 1969, Georges Marchais in 1981, André Lajoinie in 1988, and Robert Hue in 1995 and 2002.

[b]François Mitterrand at all elections except 1969, when it was Gaston Defferre, and Lionel Jospin in 1995 and 2002, Ségolene Royale, 2007, and Marie-Georges Buffet, 2007.

[c]Jean Lecanuet in 1965 and Alain Poher in 1969.

[d]Valéry Giscard d'Estaing in 1974 and 1981, and Raymond Barre in 1988.

[e]Charles de Gaulle in 1965, Georges Pompidou in 1969, Jacques Chaban-Delmas in 1974, Jacques Chirac from 1981 to 2002, and Nicholas Sarkozy, 2007.

[f]Jean-Marie Le Pen.

[g]Raymond Balladur was actually a second Gaullist candidate.

the 2007 presidential election, but the party was reduced to three seats in the new assembly. Its future is very much in doubt.

The Left

The third and fourth major parties offer the best evidence of the success enjoyed by the party system until recently. The old SFIO had been one of France's strongest political parties during the first half of the twentieth century. However, it went into a prolonged decline after World War II, which left it with barely 5 percent of the vote in 1969 (**www.parti-socialiste.fr**).

When Mitterrand took over and renamed it the PS two years later, it underwent a remarkable recovery. It began to champion autogestion and other issues first raised in 1968 in a way that appealed to a broad cross-section of the electorate. Within a decade it was in power and has vied with the Gaullists for first place in all but one election since then.

Mitterrand succeeded in part because he broke with socialist tradition and adopted a strategy centered on an alliance with the PCF. In 1972, the two parties signed a Common Program of Government that they pledged to enact if they won the next legislative elections. Although they fell just short of victory the next year, the Left regained all of the ground it lost in 1968 and established itself as a viable alternative to the Gaullists.

Mitterrand nearly defeated Giscard in 1974. However, the Communist-Socialist coalition foundered afterward. In 1977, the parties failed to update the Common Program. The next year, their squabbling cost them what had at first seemed a sure victory in the legislative elections.

Largely because of the economic difficulties facing the Giscard and other Eurpean governments, Mitterrand finally won the presidency in 1981. The PS also won a massive majority in the National Assembly in elections held after Mitterrand dissolved parliament. But the economic difficulties did not go away, which forced the government to abandon its leftist goals. The party's standing in the country dropped dramatically. The PS went into the 1986 election knowing it was going to lose its majority. Still, it remained France's strongest party, with almost 32 percent of the vote.

During the first **cohabitation** period that followed, in which one party occupied the presidency and the other coalition controls parliament, Mitterrand was able to portray himself as a national leader above the partisan fray. He then capitalized on this in his surprisingly easy reelection in 1988. As in 1981, he immediately dissolved the National Assembly, and the PS came within a few thousand votes of winning an outright majority.

At that point, the Socialists' fortunes began to plummet again. The party had no clear policy agenda to offer voters, and nothing it tried seemed to work, especially in reducing the skyrocketing unemployment rate. Moreover, it now had a serious leadership problem. The old and terminally ill Mitterrand was little more than a lame duck. The party did badly in 1993, losing close to half its vote and three-quarters of its seats. All the signs indicated that it would do poorly in the 1995 presidential race because it had trouble even finding a candidate. Jospin, however, proved to be a more successful campaigner than anyone expected, and the party began yet another recovery that continued with the surprising victory by the PS in the snap election of 1997. However, the party has not gone through anything like the kind of renewal that we saw in the Labour Party in Britain. As noted previously, the PS was thrown into disarray by its disastrous showing in 2002.

That said, the seeming recovery of the PS was misleading, as the 2007 elections showed. It still was widely seen as having few ideas of its own for solving unemployment and France's other social and economic problems. Also, the rest of the Left was disintegrating, which means that the PS will have to come close to winning a majority of the vote on its own to win any election, something that does not seem likely for the foreseeable future other than the second ballot for the presidency. Finally, the domestic split between Hollande and Royal left the party's leadership in disarray although party stalwart Martine Aubry won the election to be leader in 2008.

Then in spring 2011, the PS underwent what could turn out to be a catastrophe for the party. On May 13, Dominique Strauss-Kahn was pulled off a Paris-bound plane in New York and arrested for allegedly attempting to rape a maid in a hotel he was staying at. DSK—as he is commonly known—was the president of the International Monetary Fund and appeared to be the Socialists' strongest candidate against Sarkozy. As we write, the case against him is unraveling, but

he almost certainly will not be a candidate. More important our purposes, his legal problems seem to have hurt all the potential PS standard bearers.

The final established party, the PCF, is the only one that existed in anything like its current form before 1958 (www.pcf.fr). It was born on Christmas night 1920, when a group of socialists who supported the Bolshevik revolution in Russia split from the SFIO. The PCF struggled until the depression, when its willingness to cooperate with the SFIO and the Radicals in the Popular Front of the mid-1930s helped swell its ranks. It gained support as well during World War II, when it spearheaded the armed resistance against the Nazis.

From then until the late 1970s, the PCF prospered, normally winning between 20 and 25 percent of the vote. However, few of its voters were committed Marxists. Rather, the PCF thrived because it gained a disproportionate share of the country's large protest vote and had a well-organized subculture within the working class.

Despite the prosperity of the postwar years, the party stuck with its traditional demand for revolution, nationalization of industry, and a sweeping redistribution of wealth. It was able to get away with its dated positions because the SFIO was in even worse shape. But when the PS began to change and the PCF did not, the party found itself in deep trouble. Its vote slipped below 10 percent in most local and national elections in the late 1980s, and its membership declined by as much as half. The collapse of communism in Europe only made matters worse. In 2002, two Trotskyist candidates outpolled the PCF's Robert Hue. In 2007, the presidential candidate it endorsed won less than 2 percent of the vote. The PCF did a bit better in the legislative elections, winning almost 5 percent of the vote and fifteen seats. Nonetheless, it is hard to see how the PCF can recover.

The National Front

Only one wholly new party has come to sustained prominence under the Fifth Republic—the National Front (FN) (www.frontnational.com). Like the UMP it also has an online store. You can buy a French flag and even a National Front flash drive for your computer. The FN is the most recent incarnation of an antidemocratic, far Right tradition in French politics that dates back to 1789. But in most respects, it is a new party whose appeal is based largely on fears of immigration, the "dilution" of French nationality and culture, and European integration.

The party was founded in the 1970s as an outgrowth of one of France's small neofascist organizations. Later in the decade, it was taken over by **Jean-Marie Le Pen** (1928–), who had briefly been a deputy in the 1950s.

The FN did poorly at the polls until 1983, when it won control of the town hall in Dreux, a city about sixty miles west of Paris with a large immigrant population. The next year, the Front won 11 percent of the vote in the elections

Profiles
Nicolas Sarkozy

Nicolas Paul Stéphane Sarközy de Nagy-Bocsa was born in Paris in 1955. His father was an exiled Hungarian aristocrat. His mother had both French and Greek Jewish roots.

As already noted, Sarkozy is the Fifth Republic's first president born after World War II and the first not to come from France's vaunted—if often hated—bureaucratic elite.

He was raised in the prestigious seventeenth *arrondissement* of Paris where his parents had a tumultuous marriage. In high school, he was a mediocre student and, thus, could not gain admission to ENA or one of the other *grandes écoles;* he "merely" studied law instead.

Like many French politicians he built his career at both the local and national level. He served in several cabinets during last years of President Chirac's administration and also served as mayor of Neuilly-sur-Seine, one of Paris's poshest suburbs.

He has been married three times, most recently to the Italian-born model and singer, Carla Bruni. ■

---

for the European Parliament. It has won between 8 and 18 percent of the vote in most elections since then. In other words, it had done well enough that its total vote in 2002 did not come as a surprise—only the fact that Le Pen came in second did.

Its share of the vote is volatile because France conducts elections differently than most Western democracies. As we will see, the electoral system used in parliamentary elections discriminates against new, small, and extremist parties like the FN. That does not happen in elections for the European Parliament or the presidency, in which the Front has done consistently well.

Le Pen himself is a colorful character who has been known to make outrageous statements, including one challenging whether the Holocaust really happened. However, on balance, the party has done a good job of presenting its racist ideas with a more acceptable profamily and patriotic veneer. As a result, it has been able to make inroads in most socioeconomic groups, especially those whose security is most threatened by the changes sweeping the Western world. Typical are the views of an unemployed twenty-five-year-old man:

When I go abroad I have no problem at all with foreigners. I respect their differences and their rules. But not all foreigners here have respect for our rules! It's a problem of integration. There should be special places for them to live—ghettos in the city which will offer everything so people can live in a community with others who speak their own language.[4]

Some thought that the FN had fallen into what they hoped would be a permanent decline in the late 1990s. For some time, Le Pen and his chief deputy, Bruno Mégret, had fought over whether the party should forge electoral alliances with the mainstream right-wing parties. The two were also rivals for control of the FN, with attention focused on what would happen once Le Pen left the political scene. The last straw came with preparations for the elections to the European parliament in 1999. Le Pen was initially banned from running as punishment for having previously hit a rival candidate. He insisted, first, that his wife, not Mégret, head the

---

[4]Mary Dejevsky, "Les évenements," *Independent Magazine*, 4 November 1994, 14.

FN's list of candidates and, then, that Charles de Gaulle, the general's grandson, be placed ahead of Mégret. Early in 1999, Mégret forced a schism and led his supporters out of the party to form a rival organization.

The split did not hurt the FN much. Mégret won only 2.3 percent of the vote in the presidential election, and his party did not even reach half that total in the legislative elections. Meanwhile, Le Pen had his best campaign ever and snuck his way into second place and a spot on the second round ballot.

The party did far worse five years later. Le Pen's vote was cut almost in half to 10.3 percent and, as usual, it did far worse in the legislative elections. In early 2011, Le Pen retired and was replaced by his 44 year old daughter, Marine, who has so little experience that it is hard to tell how she will do.

Minor Parties

France also has an ever-changing array of small parties of little political significance. For instance, it has two main groups of Greens and three small parties to the left of the Communists that regularly compete for a combined 5 or 6 percent of the vote. There are also "flash" parties that burst onto the scene for an election or two and then fade away. Some can be intriguing, such as the oddly named Extreme Center Party that ran four candidates in 1967 or Hunting, Fishing, Nature, Traditions, which has contested every election in this century.

Exploring these groups in any detail would not add much to any understanding of French politics. In 2007, minor party and independent candidates combined only won 11 percent of the first ballot vote and three seats.

Why These Changes Happened: The French Electoral System

There are many reasons why the French party system changed so dramatically in the 1960s. In all likelihood, the unusual electoral system used in all post-1958 elections except 1986 was the most important.

Under the Fourth Republic, France used a form of **proportional representation** that gave each party the same share of seats in parliament that it won at the polls. As a result, it was easy for small parties to win seats, which reinforced the fragmentation and division among them all.

The Fifth Republic uses a **single-member district, two-ballot system** (*scrutin uninominal à deux tours*). France is divided into districts, as are Britain and the United States. Any number of candidates can run at a first ballot, and if one of them wins a majority, he or she wins the seat. If not (which is usually the case), a second ballot is held one week later. Any candidate winning at least 12.5 percent of the vote at the first ballot can contest the runoff election.

A candidate who does well enough to continue, however, may decide to withdraw and support someone else he or she thinks has a better chance of winning. Therein lies the significance of this unusual electoral system. In 1958, a single candidate represented pro-Gaullist forces on the second ballot in most districts. Because Communist and Socialist candidates often both remained in the race, the Gaullists won a much higher share of the seats than their number of votes would have led one to predict. In 1962, the Communists, Socialists, and other left-wing parties realized that they were making Gaullist victory that much easier by competing with each other on the second ballot. As a result, they began cutting deals on a district-by-district basis whereby only the candidate who had the best chance of winning remained at the second ballot.

By 1967, both the Left and the Right had reached such agreements nationwide. Since then, almost all second ballot races have pitted a single left-wing candidate against a single conservative candidate.

Early on, the electoral system put the squeeze on the centrist parties that had dominated the Fourth Republic. Their voters realized that they would have to choose between Left and Right on the second ballot, and so, as early as 1962, began voting for one or the other of them in the first round as well. The centrist parties vainly tried to stem the tide, but by 1974 they had disappeared as a viable political force. Today, the same system hurts the FN and, to a lesser degree, the more radical of the Greens. There is no structural impediment against running at the first ballot. However, only candidates who are affiliated with the two broad coalitions have a reasonable chance of getting elected.

The shift toward two coalitions was reinforced by the similar system used for presidential elections. Anyone who gets a few hundred nominations from local officials can run on the first ballot. If a candidate wins a majority on the first ballot, the election is over. However, no candidate has ever come close to winning half the vote. In other words, a second ballot has always been needed. Unlike legislative elections, *only* two candidates can stay in the race, thereby magnifying the trend toward a more bipolar and consolidated party system.

As the complexity of Tables 5.5 and 5.6 suggests, the electoral system has not prevented the fragmentation of the party system at the first ballot since the 1990s. Still, second ballot contests almost always give voters a simple, single choice between Left and Right.

Parity: A Victory for Feminism?

The French municipal elections of 2001 were the first to be contested following passage of a constitutional amendment that requires parties to run slates of candidates with equal numbers of men and women in some elections—the so-called **parity law** ✎ (**www.brookings.edu/articles/2001/05france_lambert**). For some, passage of the constitutional amendment in 1999 along with enabling legislation in the two years that followed amounted to a major victory for women. For others, it was a sign of weakness because, without it, women would never have gained any meaningful political impact.

The visibility of women in politics increased in 1995 when the new Prime Minister and current foreign minister, Alain Juppé, appointed twelve women to his cabinet. But, as a sign of lingering sexism, they were immediately dubbed the *juppettes* (French for *miniskirt*). Then, in an attempt to solidify his right-wing support, Juppé dismissed half of them (referring to them as "old biddies"), in so doing inadvertently launching support for a more equitable role for women in political life.

Profiles
José Bové

The best symbol of the French tradition of outside-the-system protest today is José Bové. A veteran of the events of 1968, Bové abandoned the bourgeois professional career that awaited him and moved to a farm in southern France where he raises goats and makes Roquefort cheese.

In the 1970s, he was part of a successful protest to keep the French army from taking over the stark but beautiful Larzac plateau. In the 1980s, he participated in Greenpeace's campaign to stop French nuclear testing and led a group of his fellow farmers who plowed up part of the land near the Eiffel Tower in opposition to European Union farm pricing policies. In the 1990s, he became one of France's leading critics of globalization. That led him to the activities that got him the most notice and notoriety: vandalizing McDonald's restaurants. He labeled them symbols of American cultural imperialism, not to mention sellers of food that offended French culinary traditions.

In 2007, he got the signatures of 500 voters needed to run for president. He was never a factor in the race, however, winning but 1.3 percent of the first ballot vote. ■

The movement for parity began slowly and only received significant public attention in 1997 when activists issued the Manifesto of 577. The National Assembly has 577 members. It was therefore determined that 289 of the signatories would be women and 288 were men. Eventually, over 90 percent of the population supported the idea, at least in principle.

Then the Socialists and their allies won the 1997 National Assembly election. They already included more women in their parliamentary delegation than the right ever had. Prime Minister Jospin appointed a number of women to key positions. The government also quickly introduced the constitutional amendment on parity that went into effect two years later, after attempts to block it by the more conservative Senate failed.

France's overall track record on women and politics is mixed. It was the first country to grant the vote to all men (1848) but one of the last to give it to any women (1944). In the 1993 National Assembly election, fewer women were elected than in 1946. Even after surges in the last three elections, under 19 percent of National Assembly members are women, which leaves France in fifty-ninth place worldwide, between Tajikistan and Mauritius. The figure was that low because the parity law only applies to elections run under proportional representation, which is not used for either presidential or parliamentary contests. It has thus had its greatest impact in regional and other subnational elections in which the proportion of victorious women has grown but still not reached fifty percent. This is largely because women tend be buried near the bottom of each party's list, which makes them hard to elect for technical reasons we do not need to get into here.

Interest Groups

It is hard to reach firm conclusions about French interest groups. France was long thought to be a country in which few people joined them, although the evidence now suggests that they are as likely to do so as their counterparts in Britain or the United States.

Despite the legacy of 1968, only about 10 percent of the population belongs to an environmental group, and an even smaller percentage belongs to the antinuclear or the peace movements. France's organized women's movement is among the weakest in Europe. Racial minorities are also poorly represented in the interest group arena.

Political scientists have paid quite a bit of attention to the trade unions, perhaps because of the contentious role they have played in much of French history. The unions assert that about 25 percent of all nonagricultural workers belong to one or another of them, but most observers think that the true figure is closer to 10 percent. Moreover, there is no equivalent to the British Trades Union Congress (TUC), which brings together most individual unions into a single peak association.

Instead, French unions are fragmented. Three main unions compete for members in most factories and offices. The *Confédération Générale du Travail* **(CGT)**, the largest union for most of the twentieth century, is affiliated with the Communist Party. After the mid-1960s, however, its position was challenged by the *Confédération Française Démocratique du Travail* **(CFDT)**. The CFDT began as a Catholic union but dropped its links to the church and moved dramatically to the left during the 1970s. It now has close ties to the PS, though it has moved toward the center in recent years and even supported proposed legislation during Chirac's second term that made it harder for workers to retire early and earn a full pension. *Force ouvrière* (Workers' Force) broke away from the CGT at the beginning of the Cold War. It was then the most moderate of the three, but it has become more aggressive in recent years. It, too, has reasonably close ties with the PS.

Separate unions exist for teachers and most professional groups, including business managers. Even students have unions. France also has large and active groups representing small business owners, employers, farmers, and almost any commercial group one can imagine.

Until the 1980s, the unions were one of the most radical forces in French political life. In the 1960s, for instance, the CGT demanded the nationalization of all major industrial firms, a ban on layoffs that did not also provide for the retraining of the workers involved, and a reduction in the work week without a cut in salaries. In the early 1970s, the CFDT added support for autogestion to its list of demands. That was not mere rhetorical militancy. From 1963 through 1973 (even excluding 1968), an average of 2.5 to 3 million work days were lost to strikes each year. After the economic downturn of the mid-1970s, levels of union membership and militancy have both sagged. The CGT has dropped its demands for more nationalization and mandatory retraining. For the CFDT, autogestion has become a slogan with little or no meaning.

Since 1995, however, the unions have been more active. That year, a massive wave of strikes and demonstrations forced the government to roll back some of its plans to cut social services and raise taxes. In 1997, unions occupied some offices in opposition to the Socialist government's failure to move fast enough in creating jobs for the eighth of the workforce that was unemployed. From time to time, truck drivers engaged in wildcat strikes that brought parts of the country's commercial life to a halt for as long as a week or two. In 2010, the unions led a doomed effort to block a bill that would raise the age at which retirees could collect a full pension. However, on balance, the unions are struggling to protect the gains made for their members over the years and are, at most, a disruptive force rather than a potentially

revolutionary one. France now loses fewer days to work stoppages each year than Spain, Italy, or Great Britain.

There is one exception to this picture of divided and possibly weakening interest groups: big business. As we will see in the next section, business leaders have had such easy access to the upper levels of the civil service and to elected officials that it has often been hard to tell where the influence of one ended and that of the other began. Their impact is not exerted primarily through their main association, the **Movement of French Enterprises** (**MEDEF**), ✐ (www. medef.fr), but through those informal ties that link them to politicians and civil servants that we will be exploring in the discussion about Figure 5.3 President Sarkozy's brother is one of its senior executives.

THE FRENCH STATE

As we saw earlier, France is the home of the modern state, though it fell on hard times after the revolution of 1789. De Gaulle's return to power marked a return to the traditionally strong state. The regime he created has turned out to be both more ambitious and more effective than anything we saw in Great Britain or the United States.

In part, this reflected the adoption of a constitution that gave new powers to the president and prime minister while limiting those of parliament. In part, it also reflected something that will become clearer in the next chapter on Germany: the importance of informal but extremely close relationships between the public and private sectors in ways not spelled out in the constitution. That said, at the end of this section and in the one on public policy to follow, we will also see that the French state in the first years of the twenty-first century is not as strong—and cannot be as strong—as it was under the Fifth Republic's first presidents.

A New Constitution for a New State

Recall that the twin uprisings in Algeria left the Fourth Republic's political leaders with a tough choice: either succumb to a likely military coup or bring de Gaulle back to office. Because he understood that the politicians really had little choice in the matter, de Gaulle was able to delay and then strike a tough bargain.

He demanded emergency powers that allowed him to rule with minimal interference from parliament for six months while revising the constitution. He appointed the prominent but politically little known lawyer **Michel Debré** (1912–96) to head a commission to revise the constitution. Debré's group quickly decided not to modify the existing document but to start from scratch and create a Fifth Republic.

Debré had long been an admirer of British party government, which enables prime ministers to see their policy initiatives enacted because the government has a disciplined majority in parliament. Debré assumed, however, that the French were too divided to ever elect a British-style majority. Therefore, the drafting committee set out to write a constitution that would give the executive leverage akin to what the British cabinet gets through the election of a majority in the House of Commons. Those provisions fell into two main categories 🖉 (**www.elysee.fr**).

First, the president would be much stronger. He (so far, all have been men) could use emergency powers to rule as a de facto dictator for up to six months (Article 16) and to call a referendum (Article 11) on matters related to the "organization of governmental authority." The constitution also listed the powers of the president ahead of those of the cabinet and Parliament, thereby sending a signal that the office was to take on new importance and could even exercise the most draconian of all measures—dissolving Parliament and calling for new elections.

The stronger presidency was also evident in the way elections for the office were to be held. Under the Third and Fourth Republics, the two houses of Parliament met together to choose the president for a seven-year term. The president could not be removed by a vote of confidence and was thus beyond the reach of Parliament. Fearing a potentially strong president, the Parliament routinely chose elderly, incompetent, or unambitious men to hold what was, at most, a ceremonial position.

Now, the president was to be elected by an electoral college of more than eighty thousand voters. The members of both houses of Parliament were included in it. Their influence, however, was dwarfed by that of representatives of local and departmental councils, who made up nearly 98 percent of its delegates. But this system was used only once. Following the assassination attempt on de Gaulle's life in 1962, the electorate approved a referendum that made the president directly elected by the people.

The second set of changes was designed to strengthen the government as a whole while weakening the lower house of Parliament, the National Assembly. The framers retained the central feature of any parliamentary system: cabinet responsibility to parliament. But to reduce the likelihood that France would lapse back into "revolving-door prime ministers," the constitution included a number of provisions that strengthened the government's hand in legislative–executive relations 🖉 (**www.assemblee-nationale.fr/english/index.asp**).

For example, a new cabinet no longer had to submit to a vote of investiture, which gave it the parliament's endorsement before it formally took office. Similarly, it could not be defeated in a vote of confidence unless the opposition won an absolute majority of all members of Parliament, not a simple majority of those present and voting, as had been the case since 1875. These may seem like minor differences, but under the Fourth Republic several potential cabinets lost those initial investiture votes, and almost half were defeated by relative, not absolute, majorities.

The **incompatibility clause** (Article 23) required members of Parliament to give up their seats once appointed to a cabinet. No longer could cabinet members undermine a government in which they served, knowing they had their seats in the legislature to fall back on.

The National Assembly was not allowed to either raise the expenditures or lower the tax rates proposed in the government's budget. The government also could demand a **bloc vote** in which the National Assembly was not allowed to make any amendments to a bill but had to vote for or against the government's draft as a whole. The government could even determine when the Parliament met and what its agenda would be. Much economic and foreign policy was placed in a "domain of regulation," which meant that the government could rule by decree, without parliamentary approval.

Although the constitution clearly sought to shift the balance of power from the Parliament to the executive, it really did not make clear whether the president or prime minister would dominate. That question was resolved with de Gaulle's first act as president: appointing Debré as prime minister (see Table 5.7). Debré was neither a popular politician nor a member of the elite that had guided France for three-quarters of a century. He was never more than de Gaulle's lieutenant, always doing what the president

TABLE 5.7 French Presidents and Prime Ministers since 1958

YEAR TOOK OFFICE	PRESIDENT	PRIME MINISTER
1959	Charles de Gaulle	Michel Debré
1962	Charles de Gaulle	Georges Pompidou
1968	Charles de Gaulle	Maurice Couve de Murville
1969	Georges Pompidou	Jacques Chaban-Delmas
1972	Georges Pompidou	Pierre Messmer
1974	Valéry Giscard d'Estaing	Jacques Chirac
1976	Valéry Giscard d'Estaing	Raymond Barre
1981	François Mitterrand	Pierre Mauroy
1984	François Mitterrand	Laurent Fabius
1986	François Mitterrand	Jacques Chirac
1988	François Mitterrand	Michel Rocard
1991	François Mitterrand	Edith Cresson
1992	François Mitterrand	Pierre Bérégovoy
1993	François Mitterrand	Edouard Balladur
1995	Jacques Chirac	Alain Juppé
1997	Jacques Chirac	Lionel Jospin
2002	Jacques Chirac	Jean-Pierre Raffarin Dominique de Villepin
2007	Nicolas Sarkozy	François Fillon

wanted, including resigning when the general thought the time had come in 1962. De Gaulle and Debré appointed a number of bureaucrats and other people from outside Parliament to the first cabinet, one more action the established politicians took as an insult.

In those first years, de Gaulle used all the new powers the constitution gave him. Presidential power and autonomy from Parliament were strengthened in two referenda on Algerian independence through which de Gaulle gained popular approval for a policy he could not have gotten through the National Assembly. He invoked emergency powers after the failed coup attempt. As mentioned previously, the general went to the people in 1962 with a constitutionally questionable referendum that made the president directly elected by the people, which made his mandate far broader than that of any party or politician.

The constitution mentioned a "reserved domain" in which the president would predominate, without specifying what it included. Within the first few years, de Gaulle made it clear that the reserved domain included anything he thought was important, as he intervened in just about every policy-making area—domestic and international. From the beginning, the system functioned as de Gaulle and Debré intended. The executive dominated a National Assembly that was usually as compliant as the British House of Commons. The president's and prime minister's tasks were made much easier when the unexpected began happening in 1962 and the electorate started to regularly support a clear majority.

The president can also draw on a much larger personal staff than the British prime minister. Currently, the Elysée staff numbers over seven hundred and includes the president's closest advisers, many of whom are drawn from France's remarkable civil service, which will be discussed in the next section.

Throughout the Fifth Republic, about a third of all cabinet members have been recruited from the bureaucracy. Chirac's case is typical. He began his career as a civil servant and worked on the staff of a number of ministers in the early 1960s before being appointed agriculture minister in one of Pompidou's first governments. Only later, in 1967, did he run for electoral office.

A smaller number of ministers are recruited from outside government altogether. **Georges Pompidou** (1911–74), for instance, became prime minister after a career as an investment banker. Similarly, Bernard Kouchner joined one of the later Mitterrand governments after building a worldwide reputation as head of Doctors without Borders (*Médecins sans frontières*), a group of physicians that provides humanitarian aid in war-torn areas. In one of the more unusual twists in the history of the Fifth Republic, the conservative Sarkozy named the Socialist Kouchner his first foreign minister in 2007.

All presidents and prime ministers have used their power to issue decrees and otherwise avoid dealing with Parliament. The decisions to build the first atomic bombs in the 1950s and 1960s, as well as the one to test them in 1995, were made without parliamentary approval.

When Parliament has been involved, it has normally voted along party lines as routinely as the House of Commons. Backbench revolts have occasionally stymied governmental initiatives, but these incidents are rare and the president and prime minister almost always prevail. Indeed, the best book on economic planning through the 1970s devotes only a two-page chapter to Parliament's role because it had so little influence over one of the most important aspects of policy making in the early Fifth Republic.

The machinery worked a bit less smoothly during the three periods of cohabitation. There were some fears that the system might fall into a Fifth Republic version of parliamentary gridlock when Mitterrand first faced a Gaullist parliament in 1986. However, the two sides quickly worked out a reasonably effective *modus vivendi*, through which the parliamentary majority controlled most domestic policy, which has been the norm during all three such periods.

Finally, the **Senate** is slightly more influential than the British House of Lords, though that is not saying much. Its members are indirectly chosen by electoral colleges composed overwhelmingly of locally elected officials. Its districts are based on the departments' cantons (counties) and give small towns and rural areas a disproportionate number of seats, which means that conservatives have an overwhelming majority.

The Senate frequently objects to government proposals, especially those that conflict with the interests of the members' largely rural constituents. However, the Senate has not been, and cannot be, a serious obstacle to the

France's President Nicolas Sarkozy and Prime Minister François Fillon.

government. If the National Assembly and Senate do not agree on a bill, a joint committee is established, and if no agreement is reached, the government determines which version of the bill will prevail (see Figure 5.2).

The Integrated Elite

There is an obvious question to ask given what we have seen so far. If its legislative–executive mechanisms work in much the same way as Britain's, how can the French state be stronger?

The answer lies in the distinction between the government and the state, which we introduced in Chapter 1. Recall that the state involves all the people involved in making key decisions, not all of whom are elected officials. For France, that means extending our analysis to the bureaucracy, which has been the linchpin of the strong state since 1958. In Chapter 4, we saw that the British civil service plays a limited role in coordinating economic and other policy making. In France, however, not only are civil servants themselves powerful, but former bureaucrats dominate the political parties and big business, and serve as the glue holding a remarkably integrated elite together.

Their influence begins with their education at the ENA and other **grandes écoles**. These are specialized and highly selective institutions of higher education whose mission is to train high-level civil servants. Young men and women from France's wealthiest families tend to do best on the entrance exams because of the educational and other privileges they have enjoyed throughout their lives. Until recently, a majority of the ENA's students were graduates of a half dozen leading Parisian *lycées* (high schools), and as

many as a third come from families in which their fathers (but rarely their mothers) were themselves top-level civil servants. This has changed a bit in recent years as the top schools have added what Americans would call affirmative action programs.

The École Nationale d'Administration

There is no other school in the world quite like the *École nationale d'administration* (ENA, *www.ena.fr/en/accueil.php*).

Created after World War II, the ENA was designed to train a new generation of civil servants committed both to democracy and the use of the state to spur economic growth. Although it is a small institution that admits about a hundred students per year and has fewer than five thousand living graduates, it has cast its net over all areas of French life.

The first generation of ENArques reached the peaks of their careers at about the time de Gaulle returned to power. They thus began dominating the key branches of the civil service, orienting them toward goals of grandeur and growth—goals they shared with the Gaullists. Then they started moving out of the bureaucracy and into key positions in politics and business. Although the ENArques gained more fame—and criticism—under the Gaullists, they actually made up a larger share of officials in most Socialist governments.

From its creation until the first years of this century, the ENA was located in a building directly behind the equally influential *Institut d'études politiques* (Sciences Po) in the heart of Paris. In 2005 it merged with other schools and moved its headquarters and teaching to Strasbourg, one of the three capitals of the European Union.

FIGURE 5.2 The Legislative Process in France

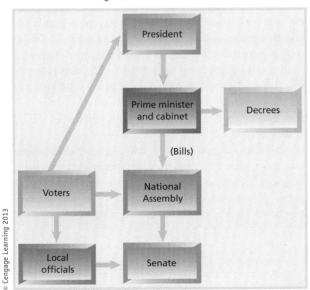

© Cengage Learning 2013

The sway of the ENArques extends far beyond the civil service. Grandes écoles graduates only owe the state ten years of service and in some cases can buy their way out sooner. Then they can resign and move into big business or politics. Thousands of them have done so in a process known as **pantouflage**—literally, "putting on soft and cushy slippers." As noted earlier, many prominent French politicians are ENA graduates. ENArques play at least as important a role in French business. Well over half of the chief executive officers of the largest French firms in both the public and private sectors are former civil servants. Because so many of them share the same background, training, and values, this integration of the elite facilitated coherent decision making throughout the first quarter-century when the Gaullists and their allies were in power.

The connections survived when the Left came to power in 1981. There is no question that the government–business links were stronger under the Gaullists. Nonetheless, the Socialists attract more than their share of ENArques, as well, including three of their six prime ministers. The Socialists also drew heavily on former ENArques for their cabinets and to head the industries they nationalized. Many of them also moved on to key positions in the private sector.

In the United States, observers often talk about an **iron triangle** of interest group lobbyists, bureaucrats, and members of Congress who dominate policy making in a given area (see Figure 5.3). The French version of the triangle is far stronger.

With the new institutions and Gaullist control of them, the Fifth Republic was able to engage in systematic planning. Paris, for example, underwent massive gentrification. Real estate speculators bought up old buildings that housed workers, small shopkeepers, and artisans, and replaced them with expensive office and apartment complexes. Businesses and families were displaced by the thousands and forced into dreary, working-class suburbs that one urban activist referred to as "people silos." Some suburban public housing complexes were so shabbily constructed that interior walls only went about three-quarters of the way to the ceiling. New suburbs with tens of thousands of inhabitants had few cafés or other public places for people to gather.

The same story was repeated in other policy areas. Immigrant workers, small merchants, farmers, students at regular universities, and the elderly fared poorly under the Gaullists. The winners did a remarkable job of turning French political and economic life around, but their way of "winning" left France an even more unequal society than it had been in 1958.

The shift toward more centralized, bureaucratic, and elitist decision making is by no means unique to France. As all industrialized societies have grown more complex and more dependent on expertise, decision-making power has moved increasingly to the upper reaches of the bureaucracy.

What is unique to France is the speed at which all this happened and the way it limited the power of those outside the integrated elite. In interviews with Ezra Suleiman, bureaucrat after bureaucrat tried to put their power in the best possible light. Most claimed that they did not have this kind of relationship with any interest groups. As three of them put it:

> **The contact with groups is mostly to inform them, to explain to them. It's true that they can't influence policy.**
>
> —*Ministry of Industry*

> **We always consult. It doesn't mean we listen, but we consult. We don't always reveal our intentions. We reveal only as much as we think it is necessary to reveal.**
>
> —*Ministry of Education*

> **First, we make out a report or draw up a text, then we pass it around discreetly within the administration. Once everyone concerned within the administration is agreed on the final version, then we pass this version around outside the administration. Of course, by then it's a fait accompli *and pressure cannot have any effect.* [emphasis added]**
>
> —*Ministry of Industry*[5]

They did not ignore people they considered "serious"—the representatives of big business and others who shared their vision of economic growth—that is, people like themselves. They just did not consider them to be interest groups. In so doing, they felt comfortable claiming that they did not consult with lobbyists in any meaningful and, in their eyes, inappropriate way. But, they were still able to work closely with those organizations and individuals who shared their conceptions of France's future. This is hardly surprising, given that the partisan and business leaders they did take seriously mostly started their careers in the civil service and shared the bureaucrats' background, training, and worldview.

Although the evidence is indirect, it certainly seems that these men and women understood that they had a choice. Either they could devote their resources to economic growth and national grandeur, or they could succumb to what they saw as the petty and selfish demands of

FIGURE 5.3 The Iron Triangle

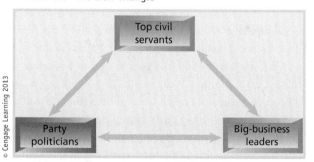

© Cengage Learning 2013

---

[5] Ezra Suleiman, *Politics, Power, and Bureaucracy in France* (Princeton, NJ: Princeton University Press, 1974), 335–36.

the "nonserious." And there was no question in their minds which they should choose.

Consequently, workers were not able to communicate to key decision makers that they were among the most exploited people in Europe. Immigrants were not able to do much about either the racism or the horrible living and working conditions they had to put up with.

The Socialists tried to address some of these issues when they first came to power in 1981. New admissions procedures were established to make it easier for underprivileged youths to get into ENA and the other grandes écoles. In the current business climate that stresses the importance of small business and entrepreneurial skills, schools like ENA have lost some of their luster. Still, on balance, one has to be struck by the continuity, not the change, in the bureaucratic impact on national government since de Gaulle's return to power.

Local Government

We can see the declining but still critical centralization of power in France by shifting our attention away from Paris and briefly exploring local government.

Two French terms tell us a lot about what that centralization was like. First, until 1981, the closest the French came to an American governor for its one hundred departments (including four in former colonies and, thus, not on French soil) was the *prefect*. Unlike an American governor, who is elected, the prefect was a civil servant, appointed by the minister of the interior. Moreover, tradition had it that prefects should not be from the department they managed and were rotated out after two or three years so they would not get too close to the local population. The second is the *tutelle*, or oversight, that the prefects and the administration as a whole exercised over local governments. Virtually all local decisions, down to the naming of schools or streets, not to mention municipal budgets, had to be approved by the prefect's office in advance.

By the 1970s, this extreme centralization had become a serious burden. There were simply too many things that had to be done locally for the central bureaucracy to control them all. Moreover, even if they did not make many decisions, local governments had grown in size because of all the policies they had to administer, which gave the mayors considerable leverage over the prefect. Local power was reinforced because of a peculiar French policy that allows people to hold more than one elected office. Mayors of most major cities were simultaneously members of parliament and even cabinet ministers.

Socialist mayors chafed under the tutelle, and they convinced the PS to make decentralization a critical plank in the party's program during the 1970s. When the Socialists finally won in 1981, decentralization was the first major reform to work its way onto the statute books. The tutelle was abolished, though it was later restored for the smallest towns, which actually needed the support services the prefectural offices provide. Among other things, cities and towns (communes) gained control of urban planning, the departments assumed jurisdiction in the administration of welfare, and the regions got responsibility for economic planning. The heads of the elected departmental and regional councils are at least as important as the prefects they replaced were. The central government now issues block grants to fund long-term investment programs and gives local authorities the revenue from the annual automobile registration fees. Communes also have the freedom to set real estate and other local tax rates.

The Courts

The Fifth Republic has a large and strong judiciary, headed by the *Cour des comptes*, which is the country's chief financial investigator, and the *Conseil d'état*, which has jurisdiction over the state and its actions. These are not, however, bodies that exercise judicial review and thus rule on the constitutionality of laws or other governmental acts. As in Britain, the Third and Fourth Republics' tradition of parliamentary sovereignty meant that the courts were not granted any such power.

The constitution of 1958 created the **Constitutional Council** (http://www.conseil-constitutionnel.fr/conseil-constitutionnel/english/homepage.14.html) with the power to supervise elections and rule on the constitutionality of bills passed by the National Assembly before they formally become law. This council is composed of nine judges who serve staggered nine-year terms. Three judges are each appointed by the president and the leaders of the two houses of Parliament. Under de Gaulle, the council was little more than a political joke. The one time it tried to assert its power by finding his decision to hold a referendum on the direct election of the president unconstitutional, de Gaulle simply ignored its judgment and forged ahead.

In the 1980s, however, the council began to play a more assertive role. For the first few years of the Mitterrand presidency, it was still dominated by judges appointed by conservatives, and it forced the Socialists to modify a number of their reforms—among other things, dramatically increasing the compensation to the former owners of nationalized firms. After 1986, the new conservative government faced a court with a Socialist majority, which overturned four of the fourteen laws that would have sold off much of the state sector. Today, the chief justice is one of the sons of Debré, the main architect of the constitution.

One should not, however, draw too many parallels between the French and the American or even the German courts, which will be covered in the next chapter. The French courts' powers are far more limited both by the constitution and by tradition.

The Changing Role of the State

It would be easy to read this chapter so far as arguing that France has had a strong and activist state for the last half century. That is partially true, as we will show in the rest of the chapter. But we also need to point out that no state can fully define or implement its own public policy.

There has been no appreciable erosion of support for the French regime, nor have its institutions changed in any significant way. In fact, the most important reform of the past generation—the reduction in the president's term from seven to five years—will probably not change the nature of the office in any meaningful way. However, the presidency and the other institutions have weakened in ways that have not reached the statute books and that often do not draw much public attention. Each is more pronounced in France than in Britain because the French state entered the last decades of the twentieth century so much stronger than its counterpart across the English Channel. Three aspects of those changes stand out.

First, France has a stronger civil society. As Vivien Schmidt put it, the traditional vision of politics in France was that "the state would lead, society would follow. [Now], the state is no longer so sure of its leadership capacity [and] society is no longer so willing to be led."[6] French interest groups are no stronger than they were thirty years ago. However, French society has changed in ways that make it hard for the state to run roughshod over a population that is more sophisticated and more skeptical about politicians and their actions.

Second, in the 1960s Arthur Schlesinger coined the term *imperial presidency* to describe the growing power of whoever occupied the White House. The term is even more appropriate for the French presidency. Much of the public policy we will cover in the next section grows out of a tradition of "heroic" decision making by an individual leader such as de Gaulle or the cohesive elite of ENArques and their allies. According to most interpretations, they were able to use the levers provided by the Fifth Republic to take bold new policy initiatives in the economy and in foreign affairs.

In recent years, however, there has been less demand or need for such heroic policy making. Instead, France has had a different and less dramatic style of leadership, most notably seen in the declining clout of the presidency since the middle of the Mitterrand years. There are several

reasons for this shift. To begin with, between 1986 and 2002, France had ten years of cohabitation in which one coalition controlled the National Assembly and had to govern with a president from the other side of the political spectrum. Under those circumstances, no one political camp could dominate. In addition, since the PS abandoned policies designed to produce a "rupture with capitalism" two years after Mitterrand was elected for the first time, neither the Left nor the Right has put forward proposals for profound change. Thus, the PS and its allies have not "modernized" themselves as much as the Labour Party has, and the Gaullists have resisted the wholesale adoption of liberal values we saw in Margaret Thatcher's and Ronald Reagan's governments. Finally, Mitterrand and Chirac were decidedly "unheroic" individuals. Like Mitterrand before him, Chirac was immensely talented. However, their ages (and Mitterrand was seriously ill for most of his second term) and the scandals that reached into the Elysée robbed both of them of any hope of leading the country in a profoundly different direction. This may change under Sarkozy but has not happened yet as his first term draws to a close.

Third, France is increasingly subject to global forces. The French interventionist state worked from the 1950s through the 1970s because it could largely control the country's economy. France was by no means autarchic. Nonetheless, it was able to enact policies that reshaped the French economic and social landscape.

This is far less true today. As we will see in more detail in the rest of the chapter, France is like other states in that it is less and less master of its own destiny. This is an outgrowth of the world's headlong shift toward globalization. National boundaries simply matter less than they used to in determining the flow of goods and services. In France, at least a third of the gross domestic product comes from foreign trade. Sometimes it is hard to see this effective loss of national sovereignty because it is at least one step removed from most people's daily lives. But, for the twenty-seven members of the European Union (EU), the decline of the state has a concrete, legal base. As we will see in Chapter 7, the EU has gradually added to its powers since it was formed in 1957. At this point, it certainly is more important than the member states as far as economic policy making is concerned, especially since the introduction of the euro in 2002.

PUBLIC POLICY: THE PURSUIT OF GRANDEUR

The 1958 constitution gives Fifth Republic leaders powers to make policy in ways that their predecessors could only have dreamed of. The emergence of the integrated elite in the 1960s gave them even more leverage, allowing the Gaullists

---

[6] Vivien Schmidt, "The Changing Nature of State-Society Relations in the Fifth Republic," in *The Changing French Political System*, edited by Robert Elgie (London: Frank Cass, 2000), 14.

to restore French power at home and abroad in pursuit of what the general called **grandeur**. Since the late 1970s, however, his successors on the Left and Right alike have enjoyed far less success, which we will see in three policy areas—the economy, assimilating the non-white part of the population, and international relations.

Economic Policy

In the eighteenth century, the French coined a word to describe state management of a capitalist economy: **dirigisme**. Between 1789 and 1958, however, republican governments were reluctant to use the policy levers at their disposal to modernize the country. The failures of the 1930s and 1940s changed all that.

Les Trentes Glorieuses

From the end of World War II until the recession sparked by the OPEC oil embargo of 1973–74, France enjoyed a period of unprecedented economic growth, which one historian called *les trentes glorieuses* (the thirty glorious years). Economists have yet to separate out the effects of the various forces that propelled France into this unexpected prosperity. However, the policies pursued by the Gaullists during their years in power after WWII and after 1958 have to be near the top of any list.

The provisional government nationalized a number of firms, including the Renault automobile company and the three largest savings banks. De Gaulle also created the General Planning Commission to speed the recovery by bringing business leaders and civil servants together to help rebuild such key industries as electricity generation, cement production, and the railroads. Meanwhile, a number of business leaders realized that they had to modernize, which they decided could best be done by cooperating with the bureaucrats.

Although economic growth continued under the Fourth Republic, the political connections between the public and private sector were not as strong. Most political leaders were either opposed to dirigisme or too weak to pursue it. That changed when de Gaulle returned to power. From 1958 until 1973, the economy, on average, grew faster each year than it did during the entire interwar period, a rate that outstripped all of its main competitors except Japan. Changes occurred most rapidly in large firms, which could become competitive in world markets for products such as automobiles, heavy durable goods, intermediate machinery, electronics, and chemicals.

During the 1960s, the government helped broker the creation of hundreds of bigger and more efficient firms. During the 1950s, several companies worth a combined 85 million francs merged with each other. By 1965, the net value of the firms that merged had leapt to 1 billion francs, and by 1970 to 5 billion francs. Typical of the change was

the consolidation of five relatively weak automobile companies into two then highly profitable giants: Renault and Citroën-Peugeot. In the late 1950s, not one of the world's most profitable hundred firms was French. By 1972, France had sixteen of them, whereas West Germany had only five.

The economic growth also had a human side that went beyond the statistical indicators. The improved standard of living was easy to see in the new houses and cars and even the changed diets that have produced a generation of taller, thinner people. The *hypermarché* (a combination supermarket and department store created a quarter century before Wal-Mart) all but wiped out the quaint but inefficient corner shops in most urban neighborhoods.

This economic growth did not appear out of thin air. The emergence of the modern French economy was in large part a result of the policies and procedures introduced by the Gaullists. De Gaulle understood that, as with everything else that could lead to grandeur, the state had to play a prominent role in managing the economy.

The Gaullists and the rest of the iron triangle were committed to long-term economic development. They hoped to create firms that would be competitive enough to withstand the threat from foreign competitors at home and to win France a larger share of markets abroad. They hoped, too, that modernizing these industries would have spillover effects throughout the economy.

They relied primarily on discretionary tax rates, investment credits, subsidies, and other state funds to encourage the formation of those larger and more competitive firms. Five giant corporations received about half of the subsidies granted in the mid-1970s, a figure that reached 80 percent by the end of the decade. In all, an average of 2.7 percent of the gross national product went to support industry. Under Giscard, the government's explicit goal became the creation of one or two large firms in each industrial sector to produce potential "national champions" that could lead in world markets.

The argument being made here is not that there was a one-to-one correspondence between elite integration and economic success, but rather that there was a strong connection between this increasingly integrated, self-conscious elite's policies and economic prosperity. Their attention was selective, focusing on high-growth industries that they assumed would make French firms leaders in global markets.

Other advanced industrialized countries enjoyed similar successes in the years after the end of World War II. That said, the countries that relied most heavily on market forces—including Great Britain and the United States—did not perform as well for most of that period. Rather, those that used the state in a concerted way to devise a reasonably coherent and consistent set of economic policies that limit the disruptive aspects of market forces did far better. Each country followed a unique path, but all involved increasing the cooperation among public and private sector elites and diminishing the role of "traditional" political forces, including legislatures and political parties.

Decline

The French economy went into a tailspin after the OPEC oil embargo. Since then, France frequently has been outperformed by its European competitors, and when compared with les trentes glorieuses, conditions seem discouraging indeed (see Table 5.8).

Industrial growth dropped to an average of 1 percent per year. Unemployment topped 10 percent for most of the 1980s and 1990s, with France losing an average of 150,000 industrial jobs per year. Inflation, too, averaged over 10 percent per year from the mid-1970s until the mid-1980s before it was finally brought under control.

Industrial disasters replaced the success stories. The shipbuilding sector all but collapsed. The steel industry was in so much trouble that the government had to restructure it in the late 1970s and was forced to take it over altogether in the 1980s. The French automobile companies saw their share of the European market cut by a third while the number of imported cars grew by more than half.

Under Giscard, the government tried to reduce state intervention so that market forces could shape the future growth of a strong economy. The recession after the first oil embargo, however, forced the government to redirect the substantial state investment to industries that they felt would most likely be national champions in a global market, especially in the Third World.

TABLE 5.8 The French Economy in Decline

YEAR	UNEMPLOYMENT (%)	GROWTH IN GDP (%)
1979	5.9	3.2
1981	7.4	1.2
1983	8.3	1.7
1986	10.4	2.5
1988	10.0	4.5
1993	11.7	2.9
1995	11.7	2.0
1998	11.5	0.3
2001	12.2	0.3
2006	9.5	2.2
2008	7.4	0.2

GDP, gross domestic product.

Source: Adapted from David Cameron, "Economic Policy in the Era of the EMS," in *Remaking the Hexagon*, Gregory Flynn (ed.), (Boulder, CO: Westview Press, 1995), 145, and *Economist*, 10 Feb 1999, 134. 2001–2008 various online sources.

Economic conditions stabilized in the mid-1980s, and there have been periods of sustained growth and improved standards of living ever since. Nonetheless, France has never again come close to achieving anything like those thirty years of profound economic change.

From Nationalization to Privatization

For the last twenty-five years, attention has shifted to government ownership rather than its management of the economy. As noted previously, the government nationalized a number of public utilities and other businesses after World War II. A second wave of nationalization occurred after the Socialists' first victory when the government bought the country's nine largest industrial firms and most of its banks. The new nationalization put the government in control of about 60 percent of France's industry and even more of its investment capital. The elite, in short, would have increased leverage in shaping the economy as a whole and, in Mitterrand's terms, in "reconquering the domestic market."

But the Socialists quickly had to abandon their goals. Within a year, France found itself facing rapidly growing unemployment and inflation rates. The budget deficit skyrocketed in large part because many of the newly nationalized firms lost money. In 1983, the Socialists did a U-turn, adopting a policy of economic austerity and abandoning all talk of further radical reform.

In the first cohabitation period, the Chirac government largely controlled economic policy. The government announced that sixty-five nationalized firms would be sold. Before the 1987 stock market crash brought those efforts to a halt, the government sold off fourteen companies, including eight large conglomerates. Subsidies for private industry were slashed. More emphasis was placed on regional economic planning and on the development of small- and medium-sized businesses.

By 1988, a rough consensus had emerged on both the Left and Right. Since then, **privatization** has been the norm. Whereas the Gaullists have sold state assets more quickly and more often, the Socialists have presided over the partial privatization of such high visibility companies as Air France and France Telecom. The new Gaullist government authorized the privatization of another seventeen companies in 1993. However, only about half of them had been sold off by the time of the 1997 election. Since then, privatization has continued on an intermittent basis, normally when international competition seemed to require it.

But we should not confuse French privatization with what happened in Great Britain under Prime Ministers Thatcher and Major. The Gaullists' rhetoric may evoke the importance of a market economy. However, their actions reflect the, albeit diminished, legacy of dirigisme. The most obvious difference is the fact that the French have not privatized most public utilities for which there is what the economists call a natural monopoly. The generation and distribution of electricity and gas, the railroads, and postal service remain publicly owned. The utilities that have been privatized, including the telephone system and airlines, faced international competition and thus had to function like conventional capitalist firms, regardless of who owned them. As of 2007, more than a quarter of the workforce was still employed by the state.

Moreover, the government or its political allies retain de facto control of many of the new privately held companies through what is called a *noyau dur* (hard core) of stock. Sometimes, the government itself retains an ownership share. Thus, the United States did not allow France Telecom to bid for the cell phone contract in postwar Iraq because the state still held more than a 5 percent stake in it. Sometimes the state made sure that "friends" in the business community gained a controlling interest. Sometimes it refused to allow foreigners to buy any stock in a privatized company, claiming doing so would jeopardize national security.

Last but by no means least, the state has intervened to influence the way some of these firms evolved. Under Jospin, the government used its traditional financial levers to try to convince three banks to merge and create a single entity that could compete with British, German, and American financial giants. In 2004, the government bailed out the industrial giant Alsthom (which, among other things, builds the high speed trains) to prevent its takeover by Siemens.

In short, the new consensus to reinforce the private sector and use the market more fell far short of the one that emerged in Britain. Thus, Harvey Feigenbaum, Jeffrey Henig, and Chris Hamnett have labeled British privatization systematic because the Thatcher and Major governments truly believed in it and sold off every nationalized firm they could. By contrast, they consider French privatization to be pragmatic, conducted not out of principle but because selling off state assets would either help an individual firm or bring in needed funds to the state's coffers.

Still, it is safe to say that the state plays a less dominant role today than it did a quarter century ago. There are at least two reasons why that is the case.

First, as in the United States and the United Kingdom, the leading force behind the growth that began in the late 1990s was the new and relatively small firms in the high-tech sector. Very few ENArques are found in that part of the business community, though a growing number of graduates of other grandes écoles are choosing to become entrepreneurs rather than work for the big companies in either the public or the private sector. At best, the government's role here is indirect, most notably in subsidizing rail service or helping to build industrial

parks, the most important of which is in the new city of Sophia Antipolis, which is rapidly becoming France's Silicon Valley.

Second, the economy is being shaped more and more by European and global financial dynamics. In 2000, there were 119 leveraged buyouts of French firms. Some of the purchasers were foreign, such as the British Candover company, which bought the giant French frozen food company Picard Surgelés. Even more frequently, the financing of these deals was arranged by European venture capitalists looking for firms that would be more dynamic and flexible. In the case of the bank merger mentioned a few paragraphs ago, the government failed in large part because the shareholders of one of them opposed the idea and began looking for a British or German bank to merge with instead. In exchange for allowing the state to subsidize Alsthom, the EU insisted that the government force the company's directors to sell some of its assets.

The bottom line is clear. France has to operate in an economy in which national borders matter less and less and a goal (like Mitterrand's) to take back control of the domestic market becomes more and more implausible. To underscore this point, since the 1990s, the French have invested almost $300 billion abroad per year, and foreigners invested about $200 billion in France.

The Politics of Headscarves

Like all of its neighbors, France has become a country of immigrants. For the last several centuries, it welcomed both political refugees and people simply looking to improve the quality of their lives. Until recently, most of those immigrants were white and, more important, quickly adopted French values and culture, including President Sarkozy's family.

The most recent immigrants are non-whites. Many have refused to "become French." Some have not even learned to speak the language. They have also arrived in far larger numbers than their predecessors.

What is important for our purposes is how the French government deals with the tensions that inevitably arise when a country's population changes so dramatically and so rapidly. That policy has been rather ambiguous, at times seeming to support the interests of immigrants and their children, at times seeming to harm them. The one common thread to them all is a firm basis in the traditions of centralization and egalitarianism that can be traced back to the revolution.

On the one hand, the French government has insisted that immigrants enjoy the same rights and privileges as native-born French men and women once they become citizens. Blatant acts of racism have been dealt with harshly by the judiciary.

Economic Liberalization
in France

France's record on liberalization is the most ambiguous of any of the industrialized democracies covered in this book.

The Right has embraced privatization rhetorically. But its actions while in office have been less clear-cut, most notably in maintaining the state's continued stake in most of the privatized corporations. The Left has not gone as far as Labour in Britain or the German Social Democratic Party in making its peace with a market-driven economy, and the Jospin government sold off only those firms it had to for international economic reasons. There are few signs that there will be major changes made under Sarkozy.

There are many reasons why this is the case. Among the most important is the role the state—with a capital S—has played not only in day-to-day political life but also as a very symbol of what it means to be French. In other words, just as "that government that governs least governs best" is an integral part of American political culture, the strong state is at the heart of France's, and, so far at least, it has proved difficult for liberals to overcome.

As one of its leading left-of-center analysts put it:

> The French are not simply afraid of losing the safety net provided by the welfare state; they fear that the retreat of the state could undermine their sense of collective purpose. Although most French people complain about the state, they are proud of its achievements and seem to accept financial burdens that in other countries, less preoccupied with their sense of "grandeur," would be considered excessive.[a]

[a]Jean-Marie Guéhenno, "The French Resistance," *Prospect* (London), June 1998, 32.n ■

people the same way. For instance, it was only in the last few years that any of the grandes écoles introduced affirmative action policies that would add more members of minority groups to their student bodies. There is currently only one non-white member of Parliament elected from France proper, and only a handful of members of minority groups have served in a cabinet during the Fifth Republic.

The often unstated goal of most policies is to encourage the immigrants and their children to assimilate fully into French society. The most telling example involves what students are allowed to wear to school. As is the case in the United States or Great Britain, Muslim girls started wearing headscarves in large numbers during the 1990s. But, what is routinely accepted in the United States and Great Britain was not tolerated in France.

The separation of church and state has been an all but universally accepted principle since 1906, when the French government cut all ties to the Catholic Church. That principle led a number of school administrators to ban girls from wearing headscarves, arguing that it brought religion into the schools. A number of girls were expelled and went instead to private Muslim academies, which are not recognized by the government. Many Muslims were, not surprisingly, incensed because no such effort was made to keep Christians from wearing crosses.

The issue came to a head on December 17, 2004 when President Chirac announced a plan to introduce legislation that would ban "conspicuous" religious symbols from the schools. Small crosses or stars of David would be allowed, but not yarmulkes or headscarves. In an attempt to gain support for the plan, Chirac made the Algerian-born deputy minister Hanifa Cherifi his spokesperson on the issue. Public opinion polls found that almost 60 percent of the public supported the ban and a similar one that already existed for civil servants. The bill on the schools easily passed the National Assembly in February, with 494 votes for it, 36 against, and 31 abstentions.

The law by no means settled the issue. Three days after Chirac's declaration, massive protests were held around the country in which, among other things, girls marched wearing red, white, and blue headscarves. The law only reinforced the anger many Muslims feel toward a society they believe treats them as second-class citizens.

Things might get more intense under Sarkozy, who thinks that immigrants need to conform to French cultural norms, just as his family did. He is not alone in this way of thinking. Unlike in many other countries, French leaders of all political stripes believe that immigrants need to become as French as native-born French men and women.

On the other hand, the French tradition of egalitarianism has kept governments on the Left and Right alike from introducing policies that would address some of the specific problems faced by non-whites precisely because politicians believe they have to treat all French

A Muslim high school student protesting the ban on wearing headscarves.

REUTERS/Charles Platiau/Landov

Foreign Policy

Nothing about France is more controversial than its foreign policy. American observers, in particular, have been critical of what many see as an irrational and unacceptable streak of independence in its international relations beginning with de Gaulle's flamboyant search for grandeur down to its refusal to support the United States in its decision to invade Iraq in 2003.

What we will try to show here, however, is that little about French foreign policy has been irrational. Rather, French presidents from de Gaulle to Sarkozy have tried to pursue what they saw as their national interest, which has periodically been at odds with that of the United States or Great Britain.

The Gaullist Years

Prior to 1914, France was one of the world's great powers. It had the largest and best-equipped army in Europe, and its empire was second only to that of Great Britain.

Over the next thirty years, France's position deteriorated rapidly. It emerged from World War II with its economy in tatters, its political leadership in disrepute, and its fate largely in American hands. Almost immediately thereafter, it faced the first in a series of colonial wars that pointed to the demise of its empire by the middle of the 1950s.

De Gaulle was able to stem that decline. His political philosophy and sense of mission were based on restoring France to its "proper" place among the world's major powers. The general believed that all countries have an inherent national interest akin to what the eighteenth-century political theorist Jean-Jacques Rousseau meant by the "general will." Grandeur was thus the successful pursuit of that national interest, thereby maximizing the country's power and prestige. Moreover, a more assertive and independent foreign policy would help restore the sense of unity and pride the French had lost under the Third and Fourth republics.

De Gaulle is frequently criticized for excessively nationalistic, bombastic, and even dangerous policy initiatives. The general, however, was neither a romantic nor a utopian. Rather, he used the available institutional levers and his own charisma in the unbending but normally pragmatic pursuit of grandeur. De Gaulle's pragmatism was not of the kind one normally expects in foreign policy. His leadership was designed to produce as much symbolic and substantive change as possible.

There is no better example of that mix of symbol and substance in Gaullist foreign policy than the decision to create the French nuclear arsenal. De Gaulle had no illusions that it would make France the equal of the United States or the former Soviet Union. He did hope that having even a small nuclear arsenal would give the country a larger role in major international decisions involving the superpowers and the countries caught between them. Most important, the bomb was to be a symbol of France's newly rediscovered influence, leading people to develop a sense of pride and unity that he was sure would spill over into other policy areas.

His desire to free France of American domination had a similar motivation. Throughout his decade in office, de Gaulle made it clear that France would no longer blindly accept American Cold War policy. He rejected proposals by Presidents Dwight Eisenhower and John Kennedy to integrate French forces more fully into the **North Atlantic Treaty Organization (NATO)** because this would have meant relinquishing part of French sovereignty. In 1964 and 1965, he responded favorably to Soviet overtures about improving Franco–Soviet relations. The next year, de Gaulle withdrew French forces from NATO control and advocated cooperative relations between France and the Soviet bloc.

That same desire to maximize French power animated policies on European integration. De Gaulle accepted the principle that the countries of Western Europe would have to cooperate if they were to meet the challenges posed by the growing American impact. Therefore, de Gaulle firmly supported the elimination of tariff barriers and the provisions of the Common Market that worked in France's interest.

There were limits, however, to how much cooperation he would tolerate. As someone interested in grandeur, he opposed a multinational, integrated, homogeneous Europe, preferring one based on sovereign states cooperating in ways beneficial to France. Consequently, he opposed British entry into the Common Market, as well as anything else he felt might lead to a loss of French influence.

If de Gaulle is seen as a visionary nationalist, Pompidou is commonly portrayed as a moderate pragmatic practitioner of realpolitik. In fact, Pompidou continued the quest for grandeur, though he did it through more conventional means. Pompidou did not engage in the kinds of flamboyant actions de Gaulle was so famous for. Because he had firmer parliamentary support than de Gaulle did in the early 1960s, and because France's position in the world had improved substantially, he did not have to.

However more cooperative and malleable Pompidou may have been, he did not compromise on the central tenets of Gaullist grandeur. He never considered integrating French forces into NATO. There was never any question of abandoning nuclear weapons or submitting them to international control. The French government continued trying to play its self-defined role as an intermediary between East and West, most notably doing what it could to settle disputes in Indochina and the Middle East.

After the OPEC Oil Embargo

President Pompidou died just months before the OPEC oil embargo of 1973–74 and the worldwide recession it helped spark. For the rest of the century, French foreign policy was noticeably less successful as the "inward" arrows of the figure on the inside front cover grew more powerful.

French rhetoric often struck the independent and anti-American tones of the Gaullist years. All parties agreed that the country should keep its nuclear arsenal. And there were areas in which it continued to go its own way, most

tragically in Rwanda, where French policy contributed to the genocide that claimed 10 percent of the country's population in 1994. Socialist officials were critical of what they saw as American cultural hegemony and have been at the forefront of efforts to limit American imports—including curved bananas, under the pretext that straight ones (grown in former French colonies) are better.

But overall, France adopted a foreign policy in line with those of the other major Western powers. Support for the EU in general, and the euro in particular, were at its core.

As we will see in Chapters 6, 8, and 9, the events that led to the end of the Cold War and the collapse of communism in Europe took almost everyone by surprise, including the French. As the Soviet Union began to change and the people of Eastern Europe mounted the movements that overthrew their regimes, France was only a bit player in that remarkable political drama.

This is most evident in the negotiations surrounding the unexpected reunification of Germany in 1990. As one of the four powers that occupied Germany after World War II, France was involved in the "four-plus-two" negotiations that led to formal approval of reunification. The emphasis, though, should be on "formal" because real decisions were made by the two superpowers and the two Germanys.

The post-Cold War period saw French leaders of the left and right trying to find their place in a world adrift in a sea of political uncertainty. The French have been actively involved in most of the international crises since the 1990s, most notably the first Gulf War (see Chapter 14), the efforts to stop the fighting in the former Yugoslavia, and the campaign to combat terrorism following the attacks on the World Trade Center and the Pentagon.

But France has not been able to play the kind of role it did at the height of the Cold War, when it wielded an influence greater than one might expect from a country with its geopolitical resources. Evidence of the strength of forces beyond French control is even more striking when it came to Europe. After de Gaulle's retirement, politicians of all ideological stripes came to see greater European involvement as crucial for France's development.

A number of critical choices were made by French governments, especially during the Mitterrand presidency, two of which stand out. Each reflects a decision made by France, but each also reveals a Europe in which decision-making power was shifting away from all national capitals.

The first was Mitterrand's decision to appoint his former finance minister, Jacques Delors, as president of the European Commission in 1984. As we will see in more detail in Chapter 7, Delors was the chief architect of the expansion of what is now the EU to then fifteen members and the leading force behind the Single European Act and the Maastricht Treaty.

The second was the broader decision to make Europe France's top foreign policy priority in the post-Cold War years. Early on, this was widely seen as an attempt to dilute the power of a unified Germany, which had emerged as both the largest and the wealthiest country in Western Europe. However, by 1991, the Socialists, many of whom had once been quite skeptical of the EU, had become its strongest supporter, seeking Europe-wide solutions to such problems as the fighting in the former Yugoslavia.

At first, all the signs were positive. France was now the strongest proponent of the efforts to deepen and broaden European institutions. It parlayed its presence in Europe into expanded markets for its goods and a vehicle to help strengthen its currency.

As the 1990s wore on, however, the European gambit failed to solve France's long-term problems, especially its high unemployment rate. More important, as support for European integration disintegrated, France found itself facing more problems no matter who was in control in Paris. What's more, some of the positions it took struck foreign observers as churlish, if not downright silly. In the negotiations for a new General Agreement on Tariffs and Trade (GATT), France insisted on protection for its farmers, who then accounted for less than 5 percent of the population, and on its right to limit the number of American movies and television shows shown in France. However, many of its problems were real. High unemployment rates were becoming the norm, especially among the young and less skilled. By contrast, despite problems of its own, which we will address in the next chapter, Germany had solidified its position as Europe's most powerful country.

Tensions reached a peak over French ratification of the Maastricht Treaty in 1992. When it was signed, all leading French politicians supported the treaty, and it was assumed it would pass easily, even after the Constitutional Council ruled that it had to be put to the people in a referendum. When the vote was held, the French came within a whisker of turning it down.

European integration turned out to be the lightning rod for the dissatisfaction with the politicians and the economy that had been building for years. Moreover, the treaty, and all the other issues eddying around it, divided the three major parties in ways reminiscent of the American debate over North American Free Trade Agreement (NAFTA) early in the Bill Clinton administration. Prominent Gaullists, Socialists, and *Giscardiens* found themselves on both sides of the issue. The opposition included not only some mainstream politicians but members of the PCF and the FN—unusual political bedfellows, to say the least.

Perhaps most important, what looks like a set of willful choices made by French governments since Pompidou's day may actually have been little more than decisions made reflecting changes that were already taking place and that would have altered French political and economic life regardless of what actions the politicians had done.

As Table 5.9 shows, international trade is a much more important part of French life today than it was even a generation ago. The table presents raw statistics, but they have real meaning for people's lives. The fact that imports and exports account for more than a quarter of French consumption and production means that more people eat McDonald's burgers, drive Nissans, and, shockingly, drink Italian or German wine. By the same token, France's prosperity is ever more dependent on its ability to sell Renaults, Airbus jets, and cheese abroad. It also means that people who lack the education or skills to shift from the dying heavy industries to more high-tech ones are losing out and, not surprisingly, are becoming increasingly dissatisfied.

Iraq

Criticisms of French foreign policy in the United States and Great Britain reached a new peak in 2002 and 2003 because of its opposition to the American-led war in Iraq. As noted previously, France had participated in the first Gulf War and supported the United States after the terrorist attacks of 9/11. But the second war with Iraq was another story.

France was by no means the only country to oppose what it saw as a rush to war by the George W. Bush administration. Russia and China joined France, which meant that three of the five permanent members of the United Nations Security Council refused to authorize the use of force in Iraq. The EU, too, was divided. Of the major members, France and Germany opposed the war, whereas Britain, Italy, and Spain supported it.

France, however, was the object of the most condemnation from the United States. Sales of French wine and

TABLE 5.9 France and the Global Economy

YEAR	EXPORTS AS PERCENTAGE OF GDP	IMPORTS AS PERCENTAGE OF GDP
1962	12	11
1974	20	22
1980	22	23
1992	23	22
1999	26	24
2002	27	25
2004	26	26
2008	22	24

GDP, gross domestic product.

Source: Data from 1962–1992 from David Cameron, "Economic Policy in the Era for the EMS," in *Remaking the Hexagon*, Gregory Flynn (ed.). (Boulder, CO: Westview Press, 1995), 121; data for 1999 from www.worldbank.org, accessed 20 July 2001; data for 2002 and 2004 www.undp.org, accessed 15 November 2004, and for 2008 from the World Bank (www.worldbank.org) accessed 20 April 2009.

cheese plummeted. Some of New York's most famous French restaurants had to close because of a diners' boycott.

On closer inspection, the French position does not seem all that irrational or, frankly, all that critical of American policy (**www.diplomatie.gouv.fr/en/**). As late as his New Year's Eve address to the French people on December 31, 2002, Chirac advised that their sons and daughters could be heading into war.

French Fries and French Toast

One of the most bizarre American reactions to France's position on Iraq was a boycott of French fries and French toast endorsed by many Republicans. It turns out that the French do not call them French fries. They refer to them as *frites* and they were most likely invented in Belgium. Likewise, what we know as French toast is *pain perdu* in French and is almost unknown there except as a dessert at Christmas dinner. Instead, rumor has it that it is called French toast in the U.S. because the dish was first introduced at French's tavern near Albany, NY, at about the time of the American revolution.

This was not the first time Americans adapted their language for political purposes. During World War I, hamburgers and frankfurters become Salisbury steak and hot dogs. The Danish do not eat Danish pastry. Russians "play" pistol roulette, not Russian roulette. The list goes on and on.

Globalization
in France

Recent French governments have taken relatively ambiguous positions on globalization. Most notably, they have tried to promote international rules that would restrict the number of foreign television programs and movies allowed into the country. But they have also been among the most resolute supporters of the European Union. In particular, they recognize that France's economic success is inextricably intertwined with that of the EU and have thus firmly supported the single currency and other attempts to deepen integration. Conversely, *public* opposition to the EU and other "foreign" influences has risen noticeably since the mid-1990s. ■

What Chirac and the other critics of American policy insisted on was allowing United Nations inspectors to finish their work and determine once and for all if Iraq had weapons of mass destruction. Of course, there were other issues involved. France had closer commercial and diplomatic ties to Iraq than did the other major Western powers, similar to those the United States had had with Baghdad during the Reagan administration. Many in France also felt insulted when Defense Secretary Donald Rumsfeld made statements that seemed to belittle France, its power, and its values.

From the beginning, France made it clear that it welcomed a regime change in Iraq. What it objected to was the way the United States managed the run up to the war and the occupation after Saddam Hussein's regime fell (again see Chapter 14).

It is not clear if Chirac would have ever endorsed an invasion; in retrospect, it seems that his government understood more clearly than the Bush administration that Iraq's weapons of mass destruction program had been all but completely shut down. The point is not to question whether the war in Iraq was appropriate or not. Rather, the key here is that the French reacted out of what they perceived to be their national interest, something they have done consistently throughout the history of the Fifth Republic. Furthermore, given the political and military quagmire since 2003, Chirac and his colleagues may well have been right!

Sarkozy is generally seen as more pro-American than Chirac. However, during the 2007 campaign, he took a more critical stance on the war. That said, his first foreign minister, Kouchner, was one of the few Socialists to support the American-led invasion and occupation. If anything, there has been more continuity than change in foreign policy under Sarkozy. His tone is different and sometimes seems more strident than what we saw under Chirac and Mitterrand. And, there are times when he seems to be torn between the French desire to a major player in Europe and his hope to be a nationalistic president.

THE MEDIA

In most respects, the French media resemble the British. The print press is dominated by Parisian-based dailies, which are sold throughout the country. Each of them has a distinctive political slant. Some are very good, especially *Le Monde*, which is widely considered to be one of the world's four or five best newspapers. Television news, too, is based primarily on national channels rather than on networks of locally owned and controlled stations. Yet, there are also some important differences.

The tabloid press has a much smaller circulation and more limited influence than that of Britain. France has three high quality weekly news magazines, each of which takes a different political line. Finally, until the early 1980s, the government routinely influenced the content and tone of television news. That changed once Giscard's government began privatizing television and radio stations and Mitterrand's administration decided to adopt a more hands-off policy. As in most countries, with the spread of cable and satellite television systems, France has seen the launch of dozens of niche program providers. A recent example is Pink TV. It is not the first gay-oriented station in the world, but it's the first one projected to turn a profit. France 24 🌀 **(www. france24.com/france24Public/en/news/world.html)** is a

largely online service that streams text and video. It also has an English version.

One of the quirks of French political life is that pollsters are not allowed to publish their findings in the week before an election. They can and do carry out surveys for parties and candidates. However, the law prevents them from making the money and getting the exposure they would otherwise obtain through contracts with the print or audiovisual media. Pollsters have always found ways to partially get around the law by publishing their results abroad; in 1997, they also began posting their findings on the Internet using foreign-based websites.

Key Terms

Concepts
anticlerical
autogestion
bloc vote
cohabitation
dirigisme
grandeur
incompatibility clause
iron triangle
pantouflage
parity law
prefect
privatization
proclerical
proportional representation
single-member district
two-ballot system
tutelle

People
Chirac, Jacques
de Gaulle, Charles
Debré, Michel
Fillon, François
Giscard d'Estaing, Valéry
Jospin, Lionel
Le Pen, Jean-Marie
Louis XIV
Mitterrand, François
Pompidou, Georges
Royal, Ségolène
Sarkozy, Nicolas

Acronyms
CFDT
CGT
ENA

FN
MEDEF
PCF
PS
RPR
UDF
UMP

Organizations, Places, and Events
Communist Party (PCF)
Confédération Française Démocratique du Travail
Confédération Générale du Travail
Constitutional Council
École nationale d'administration (ENA)
events of May
Fifth Republic
force ouvrière
Fourth Republic
Gaullist
grandes écoles
Movement of French Enterprises (MEDEF)
National Assembly
National Front (FN)
Radicals
Rally for the Republic (RPR)
Senate
Socialist Party (SP)
Union for French Democracy (UDF)
Union for a Popular Majority (UMP)

🌀 Useful Websites

There are fewer English websites on France than there are on Britain or the United States. Gradually, however, French organizations are adding English versions of their French ones. In the body of the chapter's text, I have included a few French-only sites. Those listed here are all in English.

There are two American-based sources for links to political topics in France. The first is a project run by a consortium of librarians. The second is an offshoot of H-France, a listserv for scholars working on things French.

> **wess.lib.byu.edu/index.php/French_Studies_Web**
>
> **www.h-france.net**

There are surprisingly few ways of getting news on France in English. The best source is:

> **www.French-News.biz**

The best, though still limited, English-language source on public opinion polls is run by the firm CSA.

> **www.csa-tmo.fr/accueil.asp?lang=en**

The president's office site is a good entry point for websites from most government offices and agencies.

> **www.elysee.fr**

Further Reading

Allwood, Gill, and Khursheed Wadia. *Women and Politics in France: 1958–2000*. London: Routledge, 2000. A fine overview of the role women play (and do not play) in French politics.

Ardagh, John. *France in the 1980s*. New York: Penguin Books, 1987. An encyclopedic account by a journalist fascinated with the social and economic transformations that have occurred since World War II.

De Gaulle, Charles. *Memoirs of Hope and Renewal*. New York: Scribner, 1971. A look at the postwar years and his reshaping of France.

Elgie, Robert, ed. *The Changing French Political System.* London: Frank Cass, 2000. An excellent anthology by some of the best French, British, and American academic analysts of French politics.

Feigenbaum, Harvey, Jeffrey Henig, and Chris Hamnett. *Shrinking the State: The Political Underpinnings of Privatization.* Cambridge: Cambridge University Press, 1998. A thoughtful analysis of privatization in Great Britain, the United States, and France.

Flynn, Gregory, ed. *Remaking the Hexagon: The New France in the New Europe.* Boulder, CO: Westview Press, 1995. A volume that brings together some of the best European and American authors working on France.

Hauss, Charles. *Politics in France.* Washington: CQ Press, 2008. The newest full length text on French politics. I will not claim that it is the best.

Jack, Andrew. *The French Exception: France—Still So Special?* London: Profile Books, 1999. The most thoughtful book on French politics by a journalist in recent years.

Robb, Graham. *The Discovery of France.* New York: W.W. Norton, 2007. Not the most popular book among academics, but probably the best overview of the country covering the last two hundred years. Written in the form of a travelogue by someone who toured the country on his bicycle.

Sa'adah, Anne. *Contemporary France.* Boulder, CO: Rowman and Littlefield, 2003. The best available overview of French history by a political scientist.

Tiersky, Ronald. *François Mitterrand: The Last French President.* New York: St. Martin's Press, 2000. A provocative biography that casts a broader argument about the declining power of the French president and state.

Timmerman, Kenneth R. *The French Betrayal of America.* New York: Crown, 2004. An important, but to our mind, wrong-headed view of how France has systematically undermined American interests over the years.

GERMANY

Berlin

Dresden

Bonn

Frankfurt

Munich

CHAPTER 6

Germany

Germany's resurgence as a world power has been driven by no one and no cult but by many Germans pulling together in an elaborate democracy and market economy.

NICO COLCHESTER

THE BASICS

Germany

Size	356,910 sq km (about two-thirds the size of France)
Population	82 million
GNP per capita	$34,800
Currency	1.33€ = US$1
Ethnic composition	91.5% German; of the largest remaining groups, 2.4% Turkish
Religion	34% Protestant, 34% Catholic, 3.4% Muslim, remainder unaffiliated or undeclared
Capital	Berlin
Form of government	Federal republic
Head of state	(2009–)
Head of government	Angela Merkel (2005–)

THE FIRST *OSSI*—AND THE FIRST WOMAN

On November 22, 2005, something happened that would have been unimaginable a generation earlier. **Angela Merkel** (1954–) was named chancellor of the **Federal Republic of Germany (FRG)** Not only was she the first woman to hold the most powerful office in the country, but she was also the first **ossi**, as people who grew up in the former East Germany **(German Democratic Republic— DDR)** are popularly known.

Merkel is an unusual politician. As a practicing Christian and the daughter of a Lutheran pastor, she had suffered at the hands of the former communist regime. Despite earning a Ph.D. in physics, her faith and her suspect political background made it all but impossible for her to get a university teaching position before the Berlin Wall came down in 1989.

By then, she was already active in the protest movements that would topple the DDR. Although her parents had been Social Democrats in their youth in the west, she gravitated toward what would become the East German wing of the **Christian Democratic Union (CDU)**, which merged with its western equivalent in 1990. She served as the spokesperson for the one and only democratically elected government in East Germany and then was elected

Looking BACKWARD

GERMANY POSES EVEN more trouble for our conventional wisdom on democracy than does France, assuming that is that our key assumptions are based on the British and American examples. It took longer and led to more disruption before democracy took root in Germany, and then it did so in only the western part of the country, which was jointly ruled by the United States, Britain, and France after World War II.

Democracy's troubles in Germany were based on even deeper divisions than we saw in France, let alone Britain or the United States. In addition to disputes over religion, class, and the nature of the regime, Germans had a hard time defining, where its boundaries should be drawn as well as the kind of state to put in place.

As such, Germany may tell us more about democracy's problems than any of the countries we've seen so far. And while it will not be a positive or negative role model for the countries that follow, its difficulties will allow us to get a first glimpse at why democratic regimes have not historically been the norm around the world.

In short, that is another way of saying that the political stakes in Germany—and most of the rest of the world—have been a lot higher than they have traditionally been in the United States or the United Kingdom.

to the **Bundestag** (lower house of parliament) that same year in the first postunification election.

Her first election to national office was not an easy one. Although she went into the campaign with a twenty-percentage-point lead over the outgoing **Social Democrat Party (SPD)** government and its chancellor, Gerhard Schröder, the election turned out to be even closer than the one that brought George W. Bush to power in the United States five years previously.

The CDU and its allies won a few more votes than the SPD and the other left-of-center parties. More important, in the peculiar German electoral system, which we will discuss later in this chapter, the CDU won four more seats in the Bundestag than the SPD. On paper, the SPD could have cobbled together a majority with the Greens and the former Communists, but relations had frayed among those groups because Schröder moved his party rightward during his seven years in office.

German Chancellor Angela Merkel visits French President Sarkozy in Paris on June 11, 2009.

Knud Nielsen/Shutterstock.com

There was no way the CDU could assemble a majority, either on its own or with the liberal **Free Democratic Party (FDP),** which had normally been a part of governing coalitions led by the SPD or CDU. So, after two months of negotiations, the CDU and SPD agreed to form a **grand coalition** in which they would govern together. Merkel insisted that with those four extra seats, the CDU deserved the right to head the government. She also insisted that Schröder had to leave the government because it was clear to almost all observers that the two could not work together.

Four years later, the parliament's term ended and new elections were held. Merkel's party came in first again. Support from the FDP also gave her a far more ideologically compatible coalition partner. This would allow her to introduce more of the kind of pro-market policies than had been possible with her erstwhile socialist partners.

She also returned to power just as the news broke that Germany was emerging from the global recession with the fastest growth rate in Europe, solidifying its position as one the world's strongest economies. That growth followed nearly a generation of stagnation and cannot be attributed to Merkel's policies alone, which, after all, were forged with the SPD, and those introduced with her more sympathetic FDP partners.

THINKING ABOUT GERMANY

Traditionally, introductory courses in comparative politics have not included Germany, but it is hard to leave it out today. Germany is, after all, one of the world's leading political and economic powers and it has been successful in recent years largely because it has been able to combine a functioning liberal democracy with a strong state. After unification it struggled for the better part of a decade because its vaunted approach to cooperation across class and other lines faced problems not only with integrating the DDR but in coping with globalization. For these reasons and more, it is impossible to leave Germany out of a book like this.

The Basics

Economically, Germany is the strongest country in Europe. Its eighty-two million residents make it by far Europe's most populous country—unless one counts Russia as wholly European. Its GNP per capita of roughly thirty-five thousand dollars also makes Germany one of the world's richest countries. Germans who earn substantially less than that average are covered by the most extensive social service system in Europe, which makes it all but impossible for them to have to endure the kind of poverty, homelessness, or treatable ill health that is common in many other industrialized democracies. As in all the industrialized democracies, however, the social service system has become increasingly expensive as the population ages and the economy deals with almost a generation of sluggish growth, which has only been overcome in the current decade.

Germany's wealth is all the more remarkable given World War II, which left the country in ruins. The Federal Republic turned the economy around so far and so fast that its system, dubbed ***Modell Deutschland*** (the German Model), was widely seen as an approach for other countries to emulate. The country has its share of problems. The five ***länder*** (states) inherited from East Germany remain far poorer than the rest of the country. It is there, too, that racist attacks have occurred most frequently and that neo-Nazi organizations have enjoyed the most support.

Only a country with Germany's assets could have easily taken on the challenge of unification. On the other hand, as we will see, the system of cooperative labor-management relations and extensive social services, which helped build Modell Deutschland in the first place, leaves the economy less flexible and dynamic than many of its competitors today and, therefore, more vulnerable to the crisis of the late 2000s.

Germany has done something no other industrialized democracy has even had to contemplate: incorporate sixteen million people whose standard of living was at most a quarter of its own and do so virtually overnight with minimal political or social disruption. Nevertheless, Germany's position among the three wealthiest countries in the world is not in jeopardy; instead, most observers point out that it has largely overcome the short-term difficulties brought on by unification and remains one of the world's leading political and economic powers. In addition, as we will also see, one of the keys to that success lies in the pragmatic and careful approach to political life, evoked by the late Nico Colchester in the statement that begins this chapter.

Finally, although Germany is as diverse as France or Britain, it was only in 2000 that immigrants who were not ethnic Germans could become citizens without waiting for fifteen years and that children of foreigners living in Germany could be naturalized once their parents had been in Germany legally for eight years.

Key Concepts and Questions

We could ask the same basic questions about the stability of democracy in Germany that we did for Britain and France and to some degree we will. But the discussion of an Ossi coming to power in the west gives us a first glimpse at how much higher the political stakes have been historically in Germany and how much they have been lowered since the end of World War II.

© Reuters/CORBIS

A right-wing rioter tossing a firebomb at a hostel for asylum seekers in Rostock, Germany.

Any discussion of the country, then, has to focus on what scholars call the **German question** which is really a series of questions:

- Why did it take Germany so long to unite?

- How did that delay affect German behavior once it did come together under Prussian rule in the 1870s?

- Why did Germany's first attempt at democracy give way to **Adolf Hitler** (1889–1945) and his **Nazi** regime?

- How did the division of Germany and other events after World War II help create the remarkably prosperous and stable democratic FRG in the west but also the stagnant and repressive DDR in the east?

- Why did unification occur with the end of the Cold War in Germany, and what new challenges has it posed for what is now the largest and richest country in Europe?

Because the first three questions have had such sweeping implications for Germany and much of the rest of the world, we will focus more on the historical material here than in the preceding two chapters. Once we examine how the Federal Republic was created and became a stable and legitimate regime, we will turn to the kinds of "normal" political issues we focused on for Britain and France while considering that final question, where we will see that the economic and cultural difficulties brought on by unification have been handled using the conventional tools of an established democracy.

Germany does have right-wing, antidemocratic protest movements. Since unification, most of the neo-Nazi and skinhead groups have focused their hatred on immigrants, asylum seekers, and other foreigners. However, their influence is limited, and despite an occasional breakthrough at the state level, none of them have shown any signs of breaking the 5 percent barrier parties needed to gain representation in parliament.

Put simply, democracy is as strongly established in Germany as it is anywhere. To refer again to that key distinction made in Chapter 1, its regime is as secure as any in an industrialized democracy, whatever voters think of the government of the day.

THE EVOLUTION OF THE GERMAN STATE: THE GERMAN QUESTION

In 1945, no serious observer would have dreamed that Germany would become so rich, so stable, and so democratic so quickly. The country was defeated, dismembered, and treated as a pariah by the rest of the world. Yet succeed it did. If we are to understand that turnaround and the development of a democratic Germany, we actually have to start much earlier and explore why there have been so many versions of the German question over the centuries.

Unification and the Kaiser's Reich

In Chapters 4 and 5, we saw that the state and nation developed roughly in tandem in Great Britain and in France. That was not the case in Germany. Domestic and international pressures kept Germany divided until 1871, a delay that had major political implications especially for its ability to sustain a democracy.

During the early Middle Ages, Germany had one of the most advanced political systems in Europe. It was more united than most "countries" by a single government, the Holy Roman Empire, which some Germans call the First Reich. More than most, too, Germans were unified around a common culture and language, or at least closely related dialects.

By the middle of the thirteenth century, however, any semblance of unity had disappeared when the German part of the Holy Roman Empire splintered into hundreds of principalities. The Reformation deepened those divisions as local rulers lined up on both sides of the split between Catholics and Protestants. They fought the Thirty Years' War (1618–48), the bloodiest conflict the world had ever seen until that point, but one that did not produce a clear winner or loser. As a result, Germany remained a patchwork of tiny states, some Catholic, some Protestant. The religious conflict reinforced the authoritarianism of most of the princes, Catholic and Protestant alike.

The first tentative steps toward unification occurred late in the seventeenth century in the eastern province of Brandenburg, which became the Kingdom of Prussia in 1701. Under Frederick I (ruled 1640–88), Frederick Wilhelm I (ruled 1688–1740), and Frederick the Great (ruled 1740–86), Prussia gradually gained control of more and more territory. By the end of the eighteenth century, it was one of Europe's great powers and also one of its most conservative. Lacking wealth and natural resources, the Prussians had to rely on discipline, thus strengthening authoritarian values that were under increasing pressure to the west (see Table 6.1).

Prussian expansion was brought to a temporary halt by the Napoleonic Wars. Nonetheless, by the time they ended with his capture and exile, Napoleon's campaigns had had the unintended consequence of consolidating many of the smaller states, especially in western Germany. The Congress of Vienna in 1815 continued that trend, leaving thirty-eight German states, of which only two, Prussia and Austria-Hungary, had the size and resources to conceivably unite Germany.

Under the skilled, if often ruthless, leadership of Chancellor **Otto von Bismarck** (1815–98), Prussia won wars against Denmark, Austria, and France between 1864 and 1870. At that point, Bismarck had brought all the German states, other than Austria, under Prussian control. In 1871, these states "asked" the Prussian king, Wilhelm I, to become emperor, or *Kaiser*, of a new Reich.

The new German state was very different from those in France or Britain. To begin with, it was more deeply divided. The religious disputes of the preceding three centuries had left a country split not only between clericals and anticlericals but also between Catholics and Protestants. Germany's democrats found themselves sharply at odds with the dominant Prussian elite. After the introduction of universal male suffrage in 1867, the Social Democrats became the largest party but had no real influence because the new parliament was all but powerless. Bismarck and his colleagues responded to the disruptive potential of a united Germany by extending the Prussian constitution to the entire country, thereby creating a strong, authoritarian regime. For its first twenty years, the Second Reich was dominated by Bismarck. After he left office in 1890, the government was controlled by the Kaiser and the nobility (mostly the Prussian **Junkers**) who formed the bulk of the bureaucratic, military, and civilian elite.

Although all men could vote, Germany was far from democratic. The parliament or Reichstag did not control the budget, nor were the chancellors and their cabinets responsible to it. The leadership resisted the prodemocratic forces that were gaining strength and thus laid the seeds for more intense conflict down the line.

The newly unified Germany lagged behind Britain and France economically and militarily. Although the industrial revolution was well under way in parts of the country, unification had been forged by the predominantly rural Prussians. Germany lacked an independent entrepreneurial class and the kind of heavy industry needed to produce such weapons as machine guns and massive metal warships.

The political leaders realized that they had to modernize the military and economy as rapidly as possible and could not afford the time it would take if they relied on market forces. Instead, they devised a new way of developing an industrialized capitalist economy directed by the state, sometimes called a "revolution from above." The government worked with the traditional elites in the nobility and the military to force the country to industrialize so that it could compete with its European rivals.

TABLE 6.1 German Regimes since 1871

YEAR	REGIME
1871–1918	Second Reich
1919–33	Weimar Republic
1933–45	Third Reich
1949–90	German Democratic Republic
1949–	Federal Republic

By the end of the nineteenth century, a modern army and navy had transformed it into a global power that rivaled Britain and France. Militarization, in turn, required the construction of huge industrial centers specializing in the production not only of weapons but also of manufactured goods, including railroads, chemicals, and telephone and telegraph equipment. The production of both iron and steel grew more than 700 percent between 1870 and 1910.

In Britain and, to a lesser degree, France, the impetus for the industrial revolution had come "from below," from capitalist entrepreneurs operating largely on their own, independent of the state. Both countries also took substantial, if less than complete, steps to incorporate the working class and other underprivileged groups into the political process. Perhaps most important, both reinforced parliamentary rule, thereby curbing the arbitrary power of elites not elected by the people.

Little of that happened in Germany. Instead, the Prussian-based elite clung to power. It introduced social insurance programs to try to gain the support of the working class. At the same time, it passed a series of antisocialist laws and repressed the growing union movement, which left an unusually alienated and potentially revolutionary working class. By 1890, the SPD had become Germany's largest political party, and the trade union movement affiliated with it enrolled millions of members.

As a result, imperial Germany was what scholars call a **faulted society**. On one side of the political fault line were the elites. On the other side were the powerless and increasingly angry masses. The elites pursued policies that were transforming German society, but they also resisted accepting the political consequences of those social and economic changes. Indeed, the failure of the elites to adapt to the rapidly evolving conditions of the late nineteenth and early twentieth centuries led some observers at the time to expect a civil war.

Another important fault line lay in Germany's relationship with the rest of Europe. There was no easy way to fit a newly powerful and ambitious German state into the elaborate and fragile international system created at the Congress of Vienna. Germany's imperial aspirations were mostly thwarted—at least in German eyes. It did take over a few colonies, but its empire was far smaller than those of the Netherlands, Belgium, and Portugal, let alone Great Britain and France.

Just like their geological namesakes, geopolitical fault lines ultimately produce geopolitical earthquakes. In this case, the European balance of power finally crumbled early in the twentieth century. A variety of open treaties and secret pacts pitted Germany and the weakening Austro-Hungarian and Ottoman empires against Britain, France, and Russia. Then, in 1914, a Bosnian Serb nationalist assassinated the heir apparent to the Austro-Hungarian throne.

That isolated act by a single individual acting on his own culminated in the outbreak of World War I, a war no one wanted, but that no one could prevent.

At first the war went well for Germany. Hopes for victory in a matter of weeks, however, soon disappeared as the war turned into a bloody stalemate. By the time it ended in 1918, more than 8 million people were dead, more than half of them civilians.

Germany was torn apart. The Left came to oppose the war during its final weeks. At the other end of the spectrum, nationalist groups began blaming the Left and the Jews for Germany's woes. On November 6, 1918, the military-led government initiated a program of political reforms. Three days later the Kaiser was forced into exile, and the monarchy was replaced by a hastily organized group of politicians who declared Germany a republic. Two days later, Germany surrendered.

Weimar and the Rise of Hitler

The next spring, the **Weimar Republic** (named for the city where its constitution was drafted) was created. It never had a chance.

The constitution transformed Germany from one of Europe's most authoritarian countries into one of its most democratic overnight. The traditional political and bureaucratic elites were stripped of almost all their power. Instead, authority was vested in a reformed Reichstag to which the cabinet was responsible. Elections were conducted using **proportional representation**, which gave parties a share of the seats equal to their percentage of the vote. This made it easy for extremist parties to get their foot in the parliamentary door and left Weimar with a far more fragmented and polarized party system than France's Third Republic.

Few politicians gave the new republic their wholehearted support, although most socialists did so until the very end. More radical leftists, however, wanted nothing to do with it and attempted revolutions in 1919 and 1920. Although they were put down rather easily, the revolutions drove a deep wedge between the increasingly moderate SPD and the new **Communist Party (KPD)** that was, for all intents and purposes, run by the new Soviet Union.

On the Right, many traditional elites and millions of average Germans could not accept that their country had been defeated because of its own weakness and ineptitude. Instead, they looked for scapegoats. Dozens of small, antidemocratic nationalist groups formed, laying blame for the defeat on "non-German" forces, including Jews, socialists, and the politicians who had both sued for peace and created the Weimar Republic.

In the first years after the creation of Weimar, both the left and right attempted a number of coups. All were put down easily, at least in the early going.

The terms of the Treaty of Versailles that formally ended the war magnified frustrations on the Right. American President Woodrow Wilson had called for a "just and lasting peace" sustained by a powerful League of Nations. The British and French, however, insisted on a far more vindictive settlement. The size and composition of the German army were severely restricted, and the Allies imposed a strict system of **reparations** that forced Germany to pay for the costs of the war. The payments worsened an already serious economic crisis. Inflation skyrocketed, unemployment tripled, and the purchasing power of those who kept their jobs was reduced by as much as two-thirds. Especially hard hit were the veterans who had survived four years of hell at the front only to return to a social, political, and economic hell at home.

The fact that the same politicians who had surrendered in 1918 also agreed to the treaty's terms reinforced the right-wing's hostility toward Weimar. In 1919, the three parties that most strongly supported the new republic—the SPD, the Catholic **Zentrum** (Center), and the mostly Protestant and liberal People's Party (DDP)—won over three-quarters of the vote. In the next two elections, they saw their share of the vote drop to the benefit of the Communists on the Left and the Nazis and German National People's Party (DNVP) on the antidemocratic Right.

Antitreaty protest reached a new peak in early 1923. That November, the little-known Adolf Hitler and his equally little-known party, the Nazis or **National Socialist Democratic Workers Party (NSDAP)**, attempted their first putsch. It failed miserably. Many Nazi leaders were arrested. Hitler himself spent nine months in prison, where he wrote his infamous *Mein Kampf.*

The economy rebounded temporarily and support for the extremists began to wane. Better news came from abroad, too, as the Allies agreed to a series of measures that reduced reparation payments. But the calm did not last. In 1929, the bottom fell out of the German economy after the New York stock market crash. Unemployment leapt from 6.3 percent in 1928 to 14 percent in 1930 and 30 percent two years later. No family was spared.

The Great Depression and the resulting political tensions came at a time when effective government was most needed and least likely. The three main Weimar parties had seen their share of the vote drop below 50 percent. In other words, at a time of crisis, German government fell further into the trap of political paralysis than anything we saw in France.

The parliamentary stalemate was broken in 1930, albeit not in a way that would strengthen the republic. Chancellor Heinrich Brüning knew he had no chance of gaining a parliamentary majority that would support his policies. Therefore, he convinced the aging President Paul von Hindenburg to invoke the emergency powers provision of the 1919 constitution, which allowed the government to rule by decree.

Profiles
Adolf Hitler

Adolph Hitler was born in Austria in 1889. Prior to 1914, he was a ne'er-do-well who had dreams of becoming an artist, although his biographers say he had little or no talent. He joined the German army in World War I, experienced the horrors of trench warfare, and eventually was wounded.

Hitler came back to a weakened and dispirited Germany. Like so many of his generation, he could not accept a German defeat as anything other than the result of a conspiracy. He was imprisoned after his failed 1923 putsch. By the time he got out of jail later that year, he managed to weave together an appeal that focused on frustrated nationalism and on the widespread hatred of the republic, the Jews, and the Left.

During the course of the next decade, Hitler used his impressive oratorical and organizational skills to build the Nazi Party. After it came to

Adolf Hitler, reviewing Nazi forces.

AP Photo

power, he began systematically wiping out all opposition, creating a totalitarian state, and taking the aggressive steps that would ultimately lead to World War II and the Holocaust.

Hitler died in his bunker during the final days of the war. ■

The parliamentary elections held two months later confirmed the legislative stalemate. The Weimar parties won barely 40 percent of the vote. Meanwhile, the Nazis continued their growth, earning nearly 15 percent, almost double their total from two years before.

The temporary solution of emergency rule became permanent. For three years, right-wing politicians pursued an orthodox economic strategy that emphasized fiscal responsibility and deflation. As President Herbert Hoover discovered in the United States, such policies only worsened the depression.

What happened in the streets was at least as important as events in governmental offices. As V. B. Berghahn put it, there was a "tense atmosphere of perpetual conflict."[1] The Communists, the SPD, and the Nazis all had massive organizations, which fought against each other and against the police, who were powerless to stop the violence.

Support for the regime continued to ebb. By the time elections were held again in July 1932, the antisystem parties won over 40 percent of the vote, a figure they would nearly match when Germans went back to the polls in November. The big winners in both elections were the Nazis. After the fiasco in 1923, Hitler realized it would be far easier to come to power through elections. For the next decade, he dedicated his demagogic skills and the party's organization to that effort.

The Nazis' fortunes had sagged during the relative calm of the mid-1920s, but when the depression hit, they were ready. Their popularity took off, especially among small-town and lower-middle-class Protestants. By 1932, the NSDAP had become Germany's largest party, and Hitler had made a surprisingly successful showing against President Hindenburg in that year's presidential election. Even more important, the party's influence in the streets had grown to the point that its *Sturmabteilung* (SA) was the largest and most ruthless of the partisan "armies."

By the end of the year, Germany had reached a turning point. Brüning and his successor, Franz von Papen, had accomplished next to nothing despite the continued use of emergency powers. Moreover, they were unable to maintain order in the streets as the balance of political power shifted from the moderates to the extremists on both Left and Right. Finally, the politicians had to make a choice, and on January 30, 1933, they invited Hitler to become chancellor and to form a government.

Most conservative politicians assumed that they would be able to tame Hitler by bringing him into office and then getting rid of him once the immediate crisis had ended. However, in conjunction with the more mainstream

right-wing parties, Hitler controlled a majority in the Reichstag. He used that majority to pass legislation that created one of the most repressive and reprehensible regime in history.

The Third Reich

Within weeks of taking office, Hitler began dismantling the Weimar Republic. On the night of February 7, the Reichstag building was set ablaze. Hitler blamed the Communists, even though the Nazis themselves lit the fire. The Nazi-controlled police began arresting Communists the next day. New parliamentary elections were held less than a week later. Even though the NSDAP fell short of an absolute majority, it won enough seats to allow passage of the infamous Enabling Act on March 23, which provided the legal basis for the creation of the Third Reich.

By the end of 1933, trade unions and all political parties other than the Nazis had been banned. Germany withdrew from the League of Nations. The next year, Hitler declared himself *führer* as well as chancellor, at the same time abolishing the presidency and most of the remaining Weimar institutions. Universal military service was reinstated. The infamous Nuremberg laws were passed, which removed Jews from all positions of responsibility and began the officially sanctioned anti-Semitism that would only end with the appalling "final solution" and the death of over 6 million Jews.

Hitler and his henchmen were remarkably persuasive leaders, using the new media of radio and film to reach, seduce, and mobilize millions of Germans. Nazi organizations blanketed all areas of German life. Even the 1936 Olympics were organized to show off the new Germany.

To undo the "damage" of 1918 and 1919 and restore Germany to its "rightful" place among the world's powers, the Nazis looked beyond German soil. Hitler's notion of Aryan superiority meant that all other nationalities were inferior to and therefore should be ruled by Germans. Moreover, as the world's superior race, the Germans needed more space, or living room *(lebensraum)*.

Germany rearmed and set its sights first on neighboring countries with a substantial German population and then on the rest of the world. In 1936, Hitler remilitarized the Rhineland along the French border, violating the Treaty of Versailles. Two years later Germany annexed Austria and intervened in the Spanish civil war on the side of Generalissimo Francisco Franco's neo-fascist forces. Later in the year, it laid claim to the Sudetenland, a region in the new country of Czechoslovakia that was predominantly German. Germany's actions caught Britain and France unprepared, and at the Munich conference of 1938, Prime Ministers Neville Chamberlain and Edouard Daladier acceded to Hitler's demands in what has since come to be

---

[1] V. B. Berghahn, *Modern Germany: Society, Economy, and Politics in the Twentieth Century*, 2nd ed. (New York: Cambridge University Press, 1987), 11.

called appeasement. Despite Hitler's success at Munich, German ambitions were not satisfied. In March 1939, its forces occupied the rest of Czechoslovakia. In August 1939, it signed a nonaggression pact with the Soviet Union in which the two countries pledged not to attack each other and secretly planned the dismemberment of Poland, Lithuania, Latvia, and Estonia.

Germany's aggression finally met resistance when it invaded Poland on September 1, 1939. Two days later France and Britain declared war on Germany. World War II had begun, barely twenty years after the first one ended.

For more than two years, German successes on the battlefield suggested that Hitler might have been right in proclaiming its people the master race and his a Thousand Year Reich. Poland and the rest of Eastern Europe were quickly overcome. The German blitzkrieg shifted to the west, defeating Belgium, the Netherlands, and France in a matter of weeks. Despite their pledge the Germans attacked the Soviet Union in 1941, laid siege to Leningrad, reached the outskirts of Moscow, and penetrated 1,500 miles into Soviet territory. Britain was the only major European power to avoid being invaded and then, only barely.

When the Soviet Union and the United States entered the war on the Allied side, German fortunes began to sag. At the battle of Stalingrad in the winter of 1942–43, the Soviet army finally halted the German advance and launched a counterattack that would last until the end of the war in 1945. At about the same time, Allied troops invaded Sicily and began a slow, steady drive up the Italian peninsula. Allied planes launched an air assault on the German homeland that would leave the country in ruins. The final straw came with the Allied D-day invasion of the beaches of Normandy in France on June 6, 1944. On April 30, 1945, Hitler committed suicide. Eight days later, the German general staff surrendered unconditionally.

The Thousand Year Reich was over, twelve years after it began.

Occupation and the Two Germanys

At the end of the war, the four main Allied powers occupied Germany, Italy, and Japan. Although the circumstances of the defeat and occupation varied from country to country, the Allies were committed to avoiding the "mistakes" of Versailles. Given what we have seen so far, that must have seemed a daunting, if not impossible, challenge. However, that is what happened in the three zones dominated by the western allies.

To some degree, all the defeated countries turned inward as people tried to come to grips with the values that had produced fascist governments. In so doing, some key politicians were able to draw on the less than successful, but still significant, experiments with democracy the defeated countries had had before the fascists came to power.

Germany was split into four zones, each occupied by one of the Allied nations, France, England, the United States, and the Soviet Union. The Western powers would have liked to transform Germany into a strong democratic regime right away, but they were convinced that authoritarian values were too deeply engrained. Therefore, they removed Nazis from leadership positions, and the most nefarious of them were tried and executed. Even more importantly for the long run, the Western powers realized they would be better off if they helped rebuild Germany rather than add insult to injury by imposing reparations and other policies like those of the 1920s. Food, clothing, and other forms of Western relief aid poured into the three western zones. The educational system was reformed in an attempt to forge more support for democratic values. Tentative steps were taken to reestablish the German government as well. Potential leaders who had not been tainted by involvement with the Nazis were identified and allowed to organize new parties. Limited authority over education, welfare, and other policy areas was given to the new states into which the three Western zones were subdivided.

All benefited from the occupation in three ways. First, the victorious powers helped restructure their political systems, most notably by barring former fascists from holding political office and by writing new constitutions. Just as important was the massive financial aid provided to rebuild the economy and, with it, confidence in the political system. Finally, the Cold War gave the United States and its allies all the more reason to do what they could to ensure that stable, effective, and democratic governments survived.

In 1947, the Soviets began systematically imposing Stalinist governments on the countries in their sphere of influence, marking the beginning of the Cold War. It led to a shift in Western policy particularly regarding Germany because it was divided and straddled the informal border between east and west. Strengthening recent enemies so they could become allies became more important than the long-term goals of de-Nazification and cultural change.

The purge of former Nazis came to an end. Some of them with limited involvement in the Third Reich were allowed to hold bureaucratic and teaching positions. Attempts to break up the prewar cartels that had supported Hitler and to democratize the German economy also were halted.

The Western powers sped up the political integration of their three zones. At the London Conference in January 1948, the Western powers began implementing currency reform that would bring the three economies closer together and drafting what would become the new constitution.

Pressure for the creation of a Western state increased six days after the Soviets introduced a currency reform in the east. They then imposed a land blockade on West Berlin, which was deep inside their zone of occupation. The West

TABLE 6.2 German Chancellors since 1948

YEAR	CHANCELLOR	POLITICAL PARTY
1948–63	Konrad Adenauer	CDU
1963–66	Ludwig Erhard	CDU
1966–69	Kurt Georg Kiesinger	CDU
1969–74	Willy Brandt	SPD
1974–82	Helmut Schmidt	SPD
1982–98	Helmut Kohl	SPD
1998–2005	Gerhard Schröder	SPD
2005–	Angela Merkel	CDU

responded with an airlift that kept the besieged city supplied until May 1949. During the blockade, a Constituent Assembly met to draft a constitution, which was completed three days after the blockade was lifted. Because they assumed it would be in place only until Germany was reunited, the drafters called it the **Basic Law** instead of a constitution. Bonn became the "provisional" capital city. On August 14, the first postwar elections were held. The Christian Democratic Union (CDU), the successor to the prewar Zentrum, and its leader, the anti-fascist mayor of Cologne, **Konrad Adenauer** (1876–1967), won a slim plurality of the votes (see Table 6.2).

Chancellor Adenauer then put together a coalition of the CDU, the liberal Free Democratic Party (FDP), and a number of regional parties. On September 23, 1949, his cabinet was accepted by the Allied High Command, signaling the birth of the Federal Republic.

Few expected much of it. Within weeks of the ratification of the Basic Law, the strictly Stalinist DDR was established in the East. Moreover, there was no guarantee that the economic recovery would continue, especially given the fact that the new republic had to assimilate more than 10 million refugees from countries that had come under communist rule. Everyone acknowledged, too, that there had not been enough time to progress very far in changing German values. Finally, there was little or no enthusiasm for building a democracy based on a regime that had been imposed by outsiders.

But that is precisely what happened.

Building a Democratic Germany

For fourteen years, Adenauer and the CDU gave the country strong leadership around which new political institutions and a modernized economy could be built. Moreover, the CDU and its FDP allies forged links with the business, industrial, bureaucratic, and even union elites, thereby producing the greatest period of growth Germany had ever seen, dubbed "the economic miracle."

Crucial to the renewal of German political and economic life was Adenauer himself. He had been a leader of the Catholic Zentrum Party during the Weimar Republic and had impeccable anti-Nazi credentials. That made him an obvious person for the Allies to turn to in seeking leadership for the new Germany. Adenauer was widely respected and, like his contemporary in France, Charles de Gaulle, used that reputation to gain broader support for the new regime. Under his leadership, the CDU and its allies won four elections in a row. Like most politicians of his day, he was skeptical about how democratic Germany could be in the short run. Therefore, he centralized power as much as possible in the chancellor's office, forging a system that has been called **chancellor democracy** ever since.

With his finance minister, Ludwig Erhard, Adenauer used the new institutions to help forge the unprecedented economic growth mentioned earlier. When Adenauer was finally urged into retirement at age eighty-six, he left the same kind of legacy that de Gaulle did —stability that made domestic and foreign policy success possible.

Adenauer was succeeded by Erhard who was widely credited for the economic miracle. Erhard, however, was not an effective chancellor and took the blame for the first postwar recession, which occurred during his three years in office. During the recession, the neo-Nazi **National Democratic Party (NPD)** began to make major gains and threatened to cross the 5 percent barrier, raising concerns about continued German susceptibility to right-wing extremism.

In 1966, Erhard resigned and was replaced by another Christian Democrat, Kurt Georg Kiesinger. This time, the coalition government was formed not with the FDP but with the SPD as part of a grand coalition of the two largest parties. They came together, among other things, to end the recession and, with it, the NPD threat. Moreover, with the 1967 **Law for Promoting Stability and Growth in the Economy**, the two parties committed themselves to policies designed to produce balanced growth that would benefit all of German society. In other words, a broad consensus about social and economic policy was added to the stability achieved during the Adenauer years which largely continues to this day.

After the 1969 elections, a new coalition between the SPD and FDP was formed, removing the CDU from office for the first time. Under the leadership of **Willy Brandt** and then **Helmut Schmidt**, the SPD enacted modest social reforms and opened up relations with the communist world. Far more importantly, the socialist leaders demonstrated their commitment to working within the broad consensus established during the grand coalition years. The government also was able to withstand terrorist attacks at home and the economic shock of the Organization of Petroleum Exporting Countries (OPEC) oil embargo in the 1970s with remarkable ease.

In the early 1980s, however, the Schmidt government encountered increasing difficulties. The SPD's left wing pulled it in one direction and the increasingly conservative FDP pushed it in the other. Finally, in 1982, the FDP decided to quit the center-left coalition and ally once again with the CDU. On October 1, the Schmidt government lost a vote of confidence. Because of the rules on **constructive vote of no confidence** (see the section on the state), the Bundestag immediately selected **Helmut Kohl** (1930–) to be the new chancellor. Because the Bundestag was not dissolved when the FDP switched camps, no new elections were held. Kohl agreed to early elections the next year, which the CDU-FDP team won easily, the first of its four consecutive victories.

Kohl and the new Germany

Kohl was Chancellor for more than sixteen years. One could make the case that the FRG had a stable democracy when he took power. By the time he left he had presided over years of economic malaise inside the FRG and then the shock of absorbing the DDR overnight. At that point, it would be impossible to make the case that Germany was not as firmly democratic as the UK or France.

Kohl's years in office reflected how far German politics had come since the war. We will discuss all these issues in more detail later in the chapter. However, the following examples illustrate the pragmatism and stability in German political life during the 1980s:

- Kohl's government did not follow Ronald Reagan's and Margaret Thatcher's lead and shift dramatically toward a more market-oriented economy. Rather, it retained the social market economy that reflected the consensus on balanced growth. Among other things, it ensured that workers would receive generous social benefits and encouraged the trade unions and corporate executives to cooperate with each other.

- It did not overreact to the cultural and political shock waves that occurred following the election of Green Party members to the Bundestag in 1983. Instead, Germany became an environmental leader. Tough laws mandate the recycling of 80 percent of all cardboard and plastics and 90 percent of all aluminum, glass, and tin. Germany also agreed to reduce its greenhouse gases more than it was later required to do under the provisions of the Kyoto Treaty on climate control.

- Even though he came to office without any experience in international relations, Kohl had an even greater impact on foreign policy. He skillfully guided Germany through a difficult decade that began with renewed superpower tensions but concluded with the unexpected end of the Cold War. Germany remained one of the strongest advocates of European integration and became one of the chief architects of the Single European Act, the Maastricht Treaty, and the euro. Kohl also spearheaded attempts to forge a common policy on such difficult issues as the fighting in the former Yugoslavia. Most important of all, Kohl skillfully engineered the later stages of the reunification of Germany in the months after the collapse of the Berlin Wall and then the DDR.

Democratization *in Germany*

Historians and political scientists still debate why democracy took root so much later in Germany than in the United States, Great Britain, or France. In the end, we will probably never be able to sort out all the reasons, because the causal factors overlap so much.

Indeed, there was little in German history before 1945 to suggest that it could democratize quickly. Its divided and authoritarian past, as well as the ill-fated Weimar republic, discredited democracy far more than in countries like France, where it had also had its share of troubles.

After World War II, however, a combination of international and domestic factors made effective democracy possible. The three occupying countries in the West avoided the mistakes they made after World War I, helping to rebuild rather than cripple their former enemy. More important, many Germans themselves "turned inward" and sought their own ways of avoiding the forces that had led to the creation of the Third Reich.

Just as remarkable was the smooth political integration of the DDR into the Federal Republic after 1990. Despite forty more years of authoritarian rule, people in the East had had extensive exposure to Western media and, of course, benefited from the remarkable wealth the Federal Republic could offer to ease the transition.

In other words, the German experience probably offers few guidelines for other countries to follow. None of these other countries has either the luxury of extensive outside support or the time to rethink national priorities that so aided Germany from 1949 onward. ■

We could go on and consider the details of Kohl's remarkable sixteen years in office and those of his successors. But that would add little to what should be a clear picture by now. The issues facing Germany since the 1980s are little different from those in any stable democracy. It has plenty of problems, but the durability and legitimacy of its regime are not in question.

As we will see in the rest of this chapter, Germany has had governments of almost all possible political stripes since Kohl left office in 1998. While there have been policy difference among them and economic problems at home and abroad, the most striking theme we will see in the continuity hinted at by Nico Colchester.

CREATING A DEMOCRATIC POLITICAL CULTURE

In their attempts to figure out why German politics changed so dramatically and so quickly, many political scientists focused on its political culture, where the evidence of a transformation is overwhelming. As noted earlier, at the end of the war, most analysts were convinced that the values that had made the Third Reich possible were deeply rooted in German society. According to the conventional wisdom, the Weimar Republic failed in large part because it was a "republic without republicans." Even the most sympathetic observers, who believed that the overwhelming majority of Germans had not openly supported the worst aspects of Nazism, found them guilty of having silently accepted Hitler's Reich and not having done anything about its excesses when such opportunities were open to them. No one put those sentiments more eloquently than Pastor Martin Niemöller, writing while in a concentration camp in 1944:

> **First they came for the Communists, but I didn't do anything, because I wasn't a Communist.**
> **Then they came for the Jews, but I didn't do anything, because I wasn't a Jew.**
> **Then they came for the trade unionists, but I didn't do anything, because I wasn't a trade unionist.**
> **Then they came for the Catholics, but I didn't do anything, because I wasn't a Catholic.**
> **Finally, they came for me, and there wasn't anyone left to do anything.**

In the immediate postwar years, there were ample signs that the antidemocratic and authoritarian culture persisted. Various anti-Semitic and neo-Nazi organizations appeared, and many veterans openly expressed their desire for a strong military. Early public opinion polls indicated that many Germans still preferred authoritarian governments and could conceivably support Nazi-like movements.

The first elections confirmed those fears. Turnout was low, primarily because the young *ohne mich*, or "count me out," generation wanted nothing to do with politics.

Creative artists explored the German soul, trying to discover how the nation that had produced Beethoven and Hegel could also give rise to Hitler and Goebbels. The conclusions most of them reached were hardly encouraging. In his novel *Dog Years*, for instance, Günter Grass gives 1950s German teenagers special eyeglasses that allow them to see what their parents had done during the war, which led many of them to suffer nervous breakdowns or commit suicide.

Even after the Federal republic began to take hold, skepticism remained. Observers worried that support for the system was dependent on continued economic growth and that hard times could bring new antidemocratic movements. As we will see most notably in the chapter on India, that far from being unusual, building support for democracy in general almost always is based on concrete actions from which people can extrapolate to the system as a whole.

Some of those concerns were confirmed in 1959 when pioneer political scientists Gabriel Almond and Sidney Verba found substantial differences between German and British or American values, which they thought did not augur well for German democracy.[2] Very few Germans took pride in their political institutions. They were less trusting of authority figures and felt less able to influence decision making than their British or American counterparts. In trying to explain why Germans held these views, Almond and Verba pointed to German history and to the continued authoritarian nature of their schools and families.

Twenty years later, Almond and Verba gathered a group of scholars to reevaluate their conclusions in the light of more recent data. They realized that the previous depiction of German culture no longer held. Instead, Germany now had the kind of civic culture they claimed was democracy's best attitudinal underpinning.

There are still signs of rigidity. In his wonderfully insightful study of postunification Germany, Marc Fisher described a number of them from the 1990s, most of which have been relaxed since then. Many were amazingly strict and, even more amazing, they were obeyed. Germans could not, for instance, mow their lawn between 1 and 3 P.M. because this might disturb a napping neighbor. Other rules sharply curtailed how long stores can be open in the evenings and on weekends and even how long workers could

---

[2] Gabriel Almond and Sidney Verba, *The Civic Culture: Political Attitudes and Democracy in Five Countries* (Princeton, NJ: Princeton University Press, 1962) and their edited volume, *The Civic Country Revisited* (Boston: Little, Brown, 1979).

take for their *pinkelpause*, or bathroom break. Laws even prescribed what Germans could put at the beginning of the messages on their answering machines.[3]

One should not make too much of such rules, however quaint and irksome they can be for visitors from more informal societies. The fact is that, as far as political values are concerned, Germans have more in common with their counterparts in other industrialized societies than these laws might lead one to believe.

According to a typical poll conducted in 1977, only 7 percent of the public could imagine voting for a new Nazi party. Well over 90 percent now routinely endorsed the idea that Germany needs a democratic form of government with a multiparty system. Germans are as supportive of democratic practices as citizens anywhere. Although it is hard to draw conclusions across national lines on the basis of spotty comparative research in which different questions are asked, the conclusions about Germany itself are rather striking (see Table 6.3). The German people clearly believe that the Federal Republic is legitimate. The state has the kind of strong, general support that characterizes the British and American political cultures. Moreover, Germans tend to see political participation as a way to affect decision making rather than simply as a social obligation.

There are some blemishes on the German culture. More than other Europeans, Germans do not favor an equal political role for women. There also has been a resurgence of racist, anti-Semitic, and even neo-Nazi activity since unification, especially in the east.

Obviously, any such behavior is reprehensible, but we should not overstate its importance. In 1992, authorities estimated that there were no more than 1,500 active neo-Nazis and fifty thousand sympathizers in the entire country, many of whom are better thought of as hooligans than as ideologically sophisticated extremists. Of all the people arrested for their participation in racist attacks, 70 percent are men with little education. Many seem angrier about their personal prospects as a result of unification and the influx of hundreds of thousands of immigrants than they are committed to right-wing extremism. What's more, the parties that espouse neo-Nazi themes are nowhere near as successful in Germany as the National Front is in France.

The obsession with the antidemocratic fringe kept political scientists from giving another important cultural trend its due until quite recently—the postmaterialist values discussed in Chapter 2. Polls have consistently shown that fully a third of the electorate could be classified as postmaterialists, which is far more than the European average and three times the German figure for 1970.

---

[3] Marc Fisher, *After the Wall: Germany, the Germans, and the Burden of History* (New York: Simon and Schuster, 1995).

TABLE 6.3 Germans and Democracy

	1980 (%)	1983 (%)	1989 (%)
The present national government protects our basic liberties	89.5	81.6	79.0
The political system as a whole is just and fair	87.6	86.8	77.0

Source: Adapted from Dieter Fuchs, "Trends of Political Support in the Federal Republic of Germany," in *Political Culture in Germany*, ed. Dirk Berg-Schlosser and Ralf Rytlewski (London: Macmillan, 1993), 249.

Those views are most evident in support for environmental causes. One 1991 poll showed that 87 percent of the people in the West and 82 percent of those in the East believe that the environment should be a top priority for government and industry.

Postmaterialism has also had its clearest political impact in Germany. Well over 80 percent of all postmaterialists vote for the SPD or the **Greens**, the first party in the world to gain widespread support on the basis of "new politics."

Postmaterialists are frequent participants in citizens' initiatives as well. In sharp contrast to the conventional view of a population that shuns voluntary participation, thousands of locally based, issue-oriented groups have sprung up in recent years to oppose the storage of nuclear waste, expand kindergarten space, support recycling programs, improve the conditions of immigrant workers, and more.

There is one final area in which the German political culture has changed. The overwhelming majority of Germans have come to accept their geopolitical status. Most are profoundly antimilitarist and endorse the government's leading role in the European Union, North Atlantic Treaty Organization, and other international organizations. Many scholars are convinced that Germany's new peaceful (if not pacifist) culture is one of the reasons it has not sought to assert its newfound power militarily even though it has participated in peace-keeping and peace-building operations in Kosovo and Afghanistan—actions that the Federal Constitutional Court ruled were legal in 1994.

Political scientists have pointed to three broad reasons why the political culture has changed so dramatically in barely fifty years.

The first and most obvious is that the Federal Republic has worked. As was the case with the Fifth Republic in France, the Federal Republic's success had an impact on the way people assess it and the whole idea of democracy.

Second, there has been considerable change in two of the major "agents" of political socialization. Under Allied pressure, the states began teaching civics during the occupation years and have included it in their curricula ever since. The right-wing bias of the prewar teacher corps disappeared. Similarly, the impact of the "authoritarian father" declined. Child-rearing patterns have been liberalized, and, as in all industrialized democracies, the family is less important in most people's lives in general.

Finally, and perhaps most important, we are now three generations removed from the Nazi era. Far fewer than 10 percent of those in the current electorate reached adulthood during either the Weimar or the Nazi periods, and even the current generation of political leaders experienced Nazism and World War II as teenagers if they did at all.

Political Participation

As we saw previously, the fragmented and ideologically polarized parties were a major problem in the Weimar Republic and played a substantial role in its demise. Many observers expected that to be the case in the Federal Republic as well. By the mid-1950s, however, Germany had developed what many observers have called a two-and-a-half-party system. The CDU, SPD, and FDP have been the dominant parties, never winning less than 74 percent of the vote since 1949 (see Table 6.4). During this period, the FDP has won between 5.1 percent and 12.8 percent of the vote—thus earning the half-party designation. In addition, except for the years from 1957 to 1961, the grand coalition period (1966–69), and the years of the first Merkel government, the FDP has provided either the CDU or the SPD with the seats needed to form a parliamentary majority. Only one new party, the Greens, has been able to overcome the 5 percent barrier nationwide and win seats in the Bundestag on a consistent basis. The formerly Communist PDS did so in 1998 as well with a strong showing in its eastern strongholds and then in 2005 following its merger with SPD dissidents to create the **Left Party**, but even these developments have not altered the basic logic of a system that has worked effectively since 1949.

Parties and the Electoral Process

More than is the case in any other country covered in this book, the Basic Law puts political parties in a privileged position. It gives them official status and assigns them the role of "forming the political will." The major parties play a central role in nominating judges, university professors, television and radio station managers, and directors of firms ranging from the big banks to local public transit authorities. Public funds provide about 30 percent of the $100 million or more each major party spends during each election campaign. The government also helps fund charitable foundations that each party runs to provide aid and assistance to the developing world and to help find peace between Israel and Palestine.

The most important provision of the Basic Law regarding political parties is Article 21, which created a dual system for electing the Bundestag, designed to minimize the number of new and small parties. Half the seats are elected in 299 single-member districts, as in Britain and the United States. Any number of candidates can run and whoever wins the most votes takes the seat. This makes it easy for the SPD and CDU to convince people that casting a ballot for a new, fringe, or extremist party means that they are wasting their vote. Indeed, they routinely win all the single-member districts in the old West Germany and lose only a handful of seats to the PDS in the East.

Voters also cast a second ballot in which they choose from lists of candidates representing each of the parties. Seats are then allocated proportionally to all parties that win over 5 percent of the vote. Thus, because the FDP won 14.6 percent of the vote in 2009, it got that proportion of seats in the Bundestag for a total of 93. The second ballot is also used to make any adjustments necessary from the constituency races so that each party's total Bundestag representation equals its share of the proportional vote, which meant that 315 candidates were elected on this side of the ballot in 2005. The 5 percent barrier has worked extremely effectively, dooming a number of parties that won seats in 1949 to extinction in the 1950s and keeping all claimants out ever since, other than the Greens and the PDS-Left (see Table 6.4).

The parties themselves also changed. During the Weimar era, the German parties were known for their ideological rigidity. During the 1950s, however, continued rapid growth and affluence undermined support for left-wing radicalism, while the very success of the regime did the same for the Right. In other words, divisive ideological issues disappeared and the voters flocked toward the center and away from extremist positions, Left or Right. To maintain their share of the vote, first the CDU and then the SPD had to follow suit. Each became a catch-all party (see Chapter 2) because they had to water down their ideologies to appeal to the increasingly moderate voters. The number of ideologically motivated activists diminished, forcing the parties to shift their organizational tactics and rely more on leaders who were effective campaigners on television. Because television news stories rarely last more than a couple of minutes, parties had to sacrifice the complexities of a sophisticated belief system for slogans that would fit into sound-bite journalism.

In this sense, the major parties are very different in that, instead of focusing their attention on a particular group, they literally try to "catch" all voters. The SPD no longer sees itself as primarily a working-class party, but appeals to

Conflict
in Germany

The most important conclusion to reach about conflict in Germany is that it is not very intense. Germany certainly has social movements and individuals who do not believe that the Federal Republic should continue in its current form. For the moment, the most prominent of them are the neo-Nazis on the Right. But it should be remembered that the Left spawned a number of terrorist groups in the 1960s and 1970s, the most violent of which—the Red Army Faction—disbanded in 1998.

Political scientists have not done the kind of research that would allow us to say with any precision whether extremist groups are more or less problematic in Germany than in the United States, Great Britain, or France. Still, there is nothing to suggest that they could constitute a serious threat to the legitimacy of the Federal Republic in the foreseeable future.

Critics are quick to point out that the Nazis themselves started out as a small band of hooligans that no one took seriously. However, there is one important difference between Weimar and the Federal Republic. In Germany today—as in the United States, Great Britain, and France—virtually everyone agrees that the regime is legitimate and the people as a whole will not support movements that call for radical constitutional change, democratic or otherwise. ■

progressive members of the middle class as well. The CDU no longer woos only Catholics, as the Zentrum did, but also tries to attract support from all Germans who care about religion and traditional values.

The Christian Democrats

The CDU has been by far the most powerful party in the Federal Republic, both before and after unification (www.cdu.de/en/3440.htm). It is the only German party that maintains an English-language website).

Officially, the CDU is two distinct parties. The CDU carries its banner in every state other than Bavaria, where it cooperates with a local partner, the Christian Social Union (CSU). During the 1970s and early 1980s, there was some tension between the two because the CSU was noticeably more conservative than its larger partner. After the death of the CSU's leader, Franz Joseph Strauss in 1988, however, the tensions abated, and we can treat them as if they are a single party.

After World War II, Adenauer and the other surviving Zentrum leaders chose not to recreate a party that would focus its appeal on Catholics and, thus, to less than half of the population. Instead, they decided to form a more broad-based organization that would apply basic Christian principles to political life. At first, this included a clear commitment to social justice. The Ahlen Program of 1947 called for egalitarian social reforms and even the nationalization of some industries. The CDU also agreed to the codetermination law in 1951 (see the public policy section), which gave workers' representatives seats on the boards of directors of large firms in the coal and steel industries.

The early CDU, however, was pulled in two contradictory directions. On the one hand, Catholic thought had long stressed social solidarity and, with it, programs for the poor and the otherwise disadvantaged. On the other hand, because it drew most of its support from practicing believers who tended to be rather conservative, the party had rather strong right-wing leanings and tendencies. Adenauer and his colleagues quickly resolved those tensions by forging a centrist and pragmatic party that focused more on winning elections than on ideology. As Germany came to be the flash point in the Cold War, and as the United States grew increasingly disenchanted with progressive social and economic policies, the CDU's support for conservatism at home and a pro-American foreign policy increased.

TABLE 6.4 German Election Results since 1949: Major Parties Only

PARTY	1949 (%)	1953 (%)	1957 (%)	1961 (%)	1965 (%)	1969 (%)	1972 (%)	1976 (%)	1980 (%)	1983 (%)	1987 (%)	1990 (%)	1994 (%)	1998 (%)	2002 (%)	2005 (%)	2009 (%)
CDU/CSU	31.0	45.2	50.2	45.3	47.6	46.1	44.9	48.6	44.5	48.8	44.3	43.8	41.5	35.2	38.5	35.2	33.8
FDP	11.9	9.5	7.7	12.8	9.5	5.8	8.4	7.9	10.6	7.0	9.1	11.0	6.9	6.2	7.4	9.8	14.6
SPD	29.2	28.8	31.8	36.2	39.3	42.7	45.8	42.6	42.9	38.2	37.0	33.5	36.4	40.9	38.5	34.2	23.0
Greens	—	—	—	—	—	—	—	—	1.5	5.6	8.3	3.9	7.3	6.7	8.6	8.1	10.7
PDS-Left	—	—	—	—	—	—	—	—	—	—	—	4.4	2.4	5.1	4.7	8.7	11.9

This table only includes votes cast in the proportional representation half of Bundestag elections.

CDU/CSU, Christian Democratic Union/Christian Social Union; FDP, Free Democratic Party; SPD, Social Democratic Party; PDS, Party of Democratic Socialism.

After the shift from Adenauer to Erhard in 1963 and the economic slowdown in 1965, the CDU did not fare as well. Finally, in 1969, the party lost control of the government. For much of the next thirteen years, it floundered. It had never developed either a large mass membership or

Profiles

Helmut Kohl

Helmut Kohl (1930–) is the longest-serving chancellor in the history of the Federal Republic. He was also the first to have come of age after World War II and the Third Reich. Other than that, his career was fairly typical. After graduating from university, he began his political career within the CDU organization in his home state, Rhineland-Palatinate. Following the party's loss to the SPD in 1972, Kohl was chosen leader of the party. At the time, few expected much of a man known for his pragmatism, an expectation that was reinforced by the CDU's defeat again in 1976. But, as so often happens in politics, events transformed Kohl and his career. The collapse of the SPD-FDP coalition brought him to power in 1982. At the end of the decade, he skillfully guided the Federal Republic through unification and then was a major player in the strengthening of the EU with the Maastricht Treaty two years later. Kohl is a remarkably unpretentious man, known to prefer vacationing at home, watching television while wearing his Birkenstocks. He is also an extremely large man who, with his wife, has published a cookbook of traditional (and fatty) German dishes. ■

A 1998 campaign ad by the CDU plays on Kohl's size (hence the elephant) and Lake Wolfgang (his favorite holiday spot) and tries to capitalize on the importance of continuity and stability.

a strong central organization. Instead, power within the party remained primarily in the hands of the state parties and their leaders. Following the CDU's defeat at the polls in 1972 and 1976, the party's drift was compounded by a deep ideological struggle between its right wing, headed by Strauss, and the moderates, increasingly dominated by the young Helmut Kohl, minister president of the state of Rhineland-Palatinate.

In 1978, the party broke with its pragmatic practices and issued a vague new program calling for "renewal" on the basis of more traditional values and market-oriented economic policies. In 1980, however, the party suffered its third straight defeat—this time with Strauss as its candidate for chancellor—and power within it swung back toward Kohl and the moderates.

Kohl was never as dynamic a leader as the other two great conservatives of his generation—Reagan and Thatcher. He also never supported their hopes for a radical shift toward smaller government and a more powerful market. But he did not have to. His first decade in office was marked by a dramatic economic upturn that allowed the government to maintain popular support without questioning the status quo.

From 1990 on, Kohl's support was based on his successful handling of German unification. To the surprise of many, Kohl proved an effective negotiator both with the DDR and with the victors from World War II, who had to sign off on any agreement to unify the two Germanys. He also was largely responsible for pushing through economic policies that directed hundreds of billions of dollars in aid to the former East German states.

By the middle of the 1990s, however, the costs of unification had become clearer and the CDU saw its support drop. It probably won in 1994 only because the SPD ran a lackluster campaign. Finally, as we saw previously, the CDU's and Kohl's string of successes ended in 1998.

Kohl's legacy will not be an altogether positive one. In 1999, he was implicated in a financial scandal. The CDU had accepted millions of dollars in illegal contributions, and Kohl personally acknowledged taking at least $1 million, though he refused to name the donor. Nonetheless, the CDU had to pay over $1 million in fines and forego at least $20 million in federal campaign funds. Kohl's reputation for honesty is now in tatters, and the party's image as the embodiment of traditional German values was placed in jeopardy.

To make matters worse, Kohl's designated successor, Wolfgang Schäuble, was forced to resign as party leader because he was implicated in the scandal, too. Merkel was chosen to replace him. As we saw at the start of the chapter she was the first woman and the first easterner to lead a major German party.

Unlike in Britain, being party leader does not necessarily make one its candidate for chancellor. Merkel was one of the first CDU leaders to break with Kohl once news of the illegal contributions broke. Initial reaction to her was positive, but as the 2002 election drew near, serious concerns were aired about her lack of experience, especially in economic policy making. And in April 2001, she, too, had to admit involvement in obtaining questionable funds. Therefore, in January 2002, she decided not to try for the nomination to run against Schröder that fall. Instead, the party opted for the more charismatic and more conservative premier of Bavaria, Edmund Stoiber. Despite all that, the lack of any serious western or male candidate left the field wide open for her in 2005.

The election that year led to the second grand coalition. As discussed earlier, Merkel knew she had to form a government with the SPD and was willing to do so only if it parted ways with most of its key leaders. Despite the recession that began to hit Germany hard in 2008, Merkel did not have much trouble forming a government more to her liking. She remained chancellor and was joined by Guido Westerwelle of the FDP as foreign minister and deputy chancellor.

The Social Democrats

The SPD historically has been the Federal Republic's second strongest party. Although the SPD has been in office for two extended periods (1969–82 and 1998–2005), it has only outpolled the CDU twice. The SPD has lagged behind the Christian Democrats in large part because it has not been as successful in becoming and remaining a catch-all party. To some degree, this reflects the SPD's early postwar history. It was led by men who had survived the Third Reich as prisoners, exiles, or members of the small underground resistance. Most were supporters of the prewar party's commitments. None were revolutionaries or even doctrinaire Marxists. Instead, most shared leader Kurt Schumacher's support for nationalization of major industrial firms to be achieved through legislation.

The SPD's failure to seriously threaten the CDU's lead at the polls and hold on power touched off a heated internal debate over its basic principles, much like the one over Clause 4 in Britain's Labour Party. In 1959, matters reached a head when the moderates won a majority at the annual conference at Bad Godesberg and dropped all references to Marxism and the nationalization of industry from the party's program.

At about the same time, politicians from the Schumacher generation were replaced by younger and more pragmatic leaders, most notably the mayor of West Berlin, Willy Brandt. The party made significant progress in the 1961 and 1965 elections. Its fortunes continued to improve when the CDU brought it into the Grand Coalition to help end the country's first postwar recession and thwart the far Right. Socialist ministers performed well, and the party demonstrated its acceptance of capitalism with its ringing endorsement of the 1967 law on balanced growth.

The SPD took control of the government when the FDP decided to form a coalition with it rather than the CDU after the 1969 election even though the socialists, again, had come in second. Rather than embarking on a bold program of social reform, Brandt stressed "continuity and renewal." In fact, his greatest accomplishment came not in expanding socialism but in improving relations with the Soviet bloc, for which he won the Nobel Peace Prize in 1971.

Brandt was forced out of office in 1974 because one of his key advisors was accused of spying for the DDR. He was replaced by the even more moderate Helmut Schmidt. With the exception of the codetermination system, social reform all but ground to a halt as Germany struggled to cope with the turbulent economic conditions of the post-OPEC years. Schmidt's moderation earned him the respect of leaders around the world, but it opened deep divisions within his own party. The economic problems and the ideological infighting cost the SPD 4 percent of the vote in 1980, but it was still able to form another government with the FDP. But, in the one example of a lost vote of confidence in the Federal Republic's history, the FDP put the Schmidt government out of its misery two years later. The next sixteen years spent in opposition were difficult for the SPD. Its four consecutive election losses led commentators and voters alike to begin thinking of the CDU as the "natural party of government."

Meanwhile, the socialists shot themselves in the political foot. Slow to endorse unification, some of the party's leading intellectuals actually opposed it until the last moment. Moreover, the party contested the 1994 election under a rather lackluster leader, Rudolph Scharping, who became chancellor candidate only after a scandal forced his predecessor to withdraw. The SPD did begin to turn things around in 1995. Scharping was replaced by the more dynamic, but also more left-wing, Oskar Lafontaine, the popular chief minister of Saarland. Though Lafontaine had led the party to its 1990 loss, he was widely seen as a breath of political fresh air. Under his leadership, the party began to modernize.

Then, in 1997, **Gerhard Schröder** (1944–) burst onto the political scene. Dubbing himself Germany's Tony Blair, he openly wooed the middle class and the business community and gained massive media exposure—and popular support. At that point, Lafontaine stepped aside and Schröder became the party's candidate for chancellor.

Schröder was part of the same "third way" leadership as Bill Clinton and Blair. That said, his seven years in office did not produce as much change as we saw in the United States or the United Kingdom. Although his personal views are quite similar to Blair's, traditional Social Democrats have a stronger influence in the SPD than in Labour, and the country's social service and social market economic policies are far more popular and effective than those in

Britain. Last, but by no means least, the SPD has to keep the support of its coalition partners, the environmentally oriented Greens, who we will encounter shortly.

Even before the 2002 election, which brought the SPD team back to office, it was clear that the party was in trouble. Many in its left wing found the "third way" unacceptable and announced plans to form their own party around Lafontaine. What little enthusiasm Schröder engendered disappeared, leading to the 2005 defeat that brought Merkel, a leader hardly known for her charisma, to power.

Being forced into a junior position in government did not end the SPD's problems.

A new leadership election was held less than a month after the vote, and Sigmar Gabriel was chosen to head the party. He had served in a number of positions at the national level including as the minister in charge of popular culture, which earned him the nickname "Siggy Pop." How he will do as head of the party and presumptive chancellor candidate in 2013 is anyone's guess.

The Free Democratic Party

The FDP has always run a distant but surprisingly influential third behind the CDU and SPD. Although it often comes close to falling below the 5 percent barrier, the FDP derives its strength from the fact that it has been needed to form all but four governments since 1949. That it has been frozen out of power under the SPD-Green and the CDU-SPD coalitions has more to do with broader electoral maneuverings than with its own strengths or weaknesses.

Like the CDU and SPD, the FDP had "ancestors" in Weimar, when there were a number of predominantly middle-class, Protestant parties that called themselves liberal. But these parties were marked by an economic more than a political liberalism, which left them in an ambiguous position during Hitler's rise to power.

The postwar FDP has been more consistently liberal on political issues, valuing personal responsibility, individual freedom, and respect for the rights of others over what it sees as the collectivist tendencies of the SPD and CDU. Mostly, though, the FDP carved a niche for itself as the party its two larger rivals needed to form a government. In that role, the FDP has provided the Federal Republic with a number of important leaders, including Hans-Dietrich Genscher, who was foreign minister from 1974 until 1992.

The FDP has struggled since unification and Genscher's retirement. Its standing in the polls improved somewhat since its poorest showings in 1994 and 1998, but mostly because disgruntled CDU supporters said they might vote for it out of disgust with Kohl's financial scandal, not because they supported the FDP *per se*. In an attempt to make a comeback, the party named Guido Westerwelle (1961–) its leader making him the first openly gay person to hold that high a position in German politics. There is no reason to believe that dynamic

new leadership can turn the FDP into a viable contender for power, but with a consistent 8 to 10 percent of the vote, it is also not likely to disappear.

The Greens

In 1983, the Green Party became the first new party to break the 5 percent barrier and enter the Bundestag. The Greens are Germany's most intriguing and least understood party. At first, many people considered them to be weird and, perhaps, even dangerous—an image fostered by their early deputies' insistence on wearing jeans and sporting shaggy beards. The Greens *are* different. Until 1991, for example, Greens elected to office were required to resign and be replaced by colleagues halfway through their terms so that they could never let power go to their heads.

Their offbeat image, however, belies how serious and important the Greens and their philosophy are. The success they have enjoyed in Germany and in several other European countries is no fluke. It reflects the inability of established parties to devise popular proposals to solve the new problems facing their countries. Moreover, recent research on postmaterialism indicates that there is a far larger pool of potential supporters than the Greens have yet been able to tap.

The Greens' ideology is based on deep ecology or the belief that all of life, and thus all of our problems, are interconnected. Pollution, militarism, sexism, homophobia, poverty, and the like are part of a single general crisis that can only be addressed through an equally general and radical shift to a worldview that puts the good of the planet and humanity first (see Chapter 17). The Greens scored major breakthroughs in the 1983 and 1987 elections, but were in deep trouble in the early 1990s. Even more than the SPD, they suffered because of their qualms about rapid unification. More important, the party itself was split, with the more radical *fundis* gaining influence at the expense of the more pragmatic *realos*.

After the 1994 election, however, the pragmatists gained the upper hand. The most plausible scenario for beating the CDU was a "Red-Green" coalition with the SPD. Also, frustrations that grew out of always being on the fringes led party moderates, such as **Joska Fischer** (1947–), to question their own (and the party's) more radical past. Therefore, the Greens chose a pragmatic strategy and reached an agreement with the SPD to form such a coalition, which was already in place in several state governments. It lasted for the life of the Schröder government. Fischer spent those seven years as foreign minister.

It is hard to gauge the Greens' impact on the government because they were very much the junior member of the coalition. A stiff gasoline tax undoubtedly would not have been passed had the Greens not been in government. The same may be true of the law making it easier to gain German citizenship.

More important here is the fact that the Greens have continued their moderation. In particular, like many individuals and organizations with roots in the new Left of the 1960s, the Greens reluctantly abandoned their pacifism and supported the Allied war effort in the former Yugoslavia following ethnic cleansing in Kosovo in 1999, and in Afghanistan following the attack on the World Trade Center and the Pentagon two years later. The Greens have also become staunch supporters of the EU while remaining an outspoken opponent of the war in Iraq.

The Greens lost some votes in 2009, falling into fifth place, even though in percentage terms the party had its best showing ever. Its standing in the polls actually improved during the first year of the second Merkel government. In short, like the FDP it is likely to be represented in the Bundestag for the foreseeable future but without becoming anything more than a minor force in an SPD led coalition.

The Party of Democratic Socialism/Left Party

The Greens are no longer the only "new" party to have made it into the Bundestag. The **Party of Democratic Socialism (PDS)** was created out of the ashes of the Socialist Unity Party (SED) that ruled the DDR. The SED had been one of the most rigid and out-of-date of all the communist parties in Cold War Eastern Europe. From 1949 until 1989, it controlled everything in the DDR (see Chapter 8). After the DDR collapsed, the SED tried to reform itself, among other things changing its name to the PDS. It also chose a new leader, Gregor Gysi, who was well known for defending dissidents under communist rule and who is now on the Berlin city council. He is also the most prominent German politician of Jewish origin.

In 1990, the PDS benefited from a one-time rule that allocated proportional representation seats separately in the east and west. In 1994 it survived only because it won a number of single-member districts in working-class districts in the Berlin metropolitan area. Most observers doubted the PDS could win seats again but it confounded the pundits by getting nearly 20 percent of the vote in the old DDR, thus topping 6 percent nationwide in 1998. It fell short of the 5 percent barrier in 2002 and only won two single-member seats.

Before the 2005 election, the PDS merged with a breakaway faction of the SPD, led by former party leader Oskar Lafontaine to form the Left Party. That gave it new support in the west and led to an almost 9 percent share of the vote that year. It did a bit better in 2009, winning almost 12 percent of the vote. It is hard to tell how much influence the Left can have because there is no chance in the near future that the SPD will form a coalition with its erstwhile colleagues and erstwhile Communist rivals.

The Far Right

Throughout its history, the Federal Republic has had to deal with right-wing parties that, in one way or another, appealed to some of the same traditions as the Nazis. As we saw previously, the NDP came close to breaking the 5 percent barrier in 1966.

New Life for the Left?

For more than a quarter century, two parts of the political Left have been in decline.

As we saw in Chapter 5, the French Communist Party has all but disappeared, which has also been the fate of most of its counterparts in Western Europe. The parties that grew out of the New Left of the 1960s and 1970s have not done much better. Among the most successful have been the German Greens, but even they are at most a marginal player in national decision making.

The creation of the Left Party in 2005 brings together dissident SPD members and the remnants of the East German Communist Party and was seen by many as offering the radical Left a new lease on life. The Left nosed out the Greens to finish in fourth place in the 2009 election. During the first year of the CDU/FDP government, in fact, more than 10 percent of the electorate said they would cast their ballots for the Left in the future. However, the odds of the Left replacing the SPD as the main party on the left are remote.

Double Standards

For understandable historical reasons, observers have been reluctant to label Germany or other countries such as Japan democratic and have been quick to voice concerns about incidents involving the far Right in both countries. Although there are plenty of reasons to worry about such events, we should also be careful not to use a double standard and hold these countries to higher criteria than we use for others with fewer historical blemishes. All democracies have imperfections—including Germany. But, as this chapter has suggested, Germany's are no more (or less) worrisome than those we find in the United States or Great Britain, countries that are usually portrayed as paragons of democratic virtue.

Since unification, there has been another flurry of support for the far Right, given the pressures of integrating the former DDR and immigration. A number of small parties have done reasonably well in state and local elections, including one that won over 5 percent in one of the eastern states in 1998. However, the far Right did not come close to the 5 percent barrier in the national elections that year or in any since, reinforcing the belief that it is not going to be a serious force in German politics.

The Stakes of 2013

Merkel's popularity has dropped since the 2009 election, as has that of the coalition government as a whole. As we will see in the next chapter, her support for the euro and the bailout of three currencies (so far) has garnered little support from German voters who resent paying off deficits elsewhere in the eurozone. Westerwelle has not adapted well to being foreign minister, making it clear to all that his skills and interests lie in economic policy. In the aftermath of the 2011 destruction of four nuclear power plants in Japan, she lost popular support as well, even though Germany relies on reactors for about 20 percent of its electricity, far less than France or Japan.

Polls published in January 2011 indicated that the coalition parties would not even win 40 percent of the vote. Had elections been held then, the CDU/CSU would have come in second (30 percent), but with only two percent more of the vote than the Greens. In contrast, the SPD and the Greens together were predicted to win about 45 percent. Of course, a lot may change by the time of the actual election presumably in 2013; American readers need only consider the shift in public opinion in their own country in the two years after the election of Barack Obama.

There is even talk of the coalition's collapse. However, given the history of the Federal Republic and possible breakup of the FDP, that does not appear likely.

Interest Groups

As we will see in the discussion of corporatism, German interest groups play a more important role in policy making than do their British or French equivalents. Surprisingly, however, there has not been much detailed research on them, so we cannot say for sure if it is their strength that has led them to be included or if their inclusion has, instead, contributed to their strength.

Unlike France, Germany has a large and unified labor movement. About two-thirds of all industrial workers and over 40 percent of the total workforce are unionized. The overwhelming majority of workers belong to the **Federation of German Labor (DGB)**. The DGB is an umbrella association representing seventeen unions, each of which organizes a single industrial sector. As such, it is better able to coordinate union activity or even speak with a single voice than is the more decentralized Trades Union Congress (TUC) in Britain.

The organization of the business side is a bit more complicated. The two largest groups—the Federal Association of German Employers (BDA) and the Federation of German Industry (BDI)—both represent smaller associations of business groups organized on geographical and industrial lines. Although it is harder to determine membership rates for business associations than for trade unions, a large proportion of

businesses belong to one or the other of these organizations. In addition to the BDA and BDI, quasi-public chambers of commerce and industry (DIHT) promote business and provide job training and certification services for the government.

Both business and labor have close ties with the political parties. Union officials hold important positions in the SPD and in its Bundestag group. Agricultural and business interests have a similar relationship with the CDU. Church groups also have a significant impact on the CDU and some parts of the SPD, helping to explain why West Germany banned abortion unless a doctor certified that the woman's life was in danger.

Interest groups in other areas are nowhere near as strong or as well connected politically. As noted earlier, a lot of locally based citizens' initiatives were important building blocks for the early Greens. Also, a number of protest groups emerged in East Germany in the late 1980s, but most of them have since fallen by the wayside.

Women in German Politics

Despite Merkel's prominence, women probably play a smaller role in German politics than in any other country discussed in Part 2. Women play less of a role in German politics than their counterparts in the United States.

The problem is actually more deeply rooted in corporate governance. In Germany, there are only 4 women among the 180 or more board members of the top corporations. In the United States the number is more like 15 percent of the total. Merkel and her Labor and Commerce ministers (both women) have argued that things have to change. However, Merkel has rejected a proposal from the two ministers that would require 30 percent of corporate board members be women.

That said, Germany does have an active feminist movement. Most recently, Alice Schwarzer and others have helped create a movement that is autonomous or independent of other political parties and interest groups.

THE GERMAN STATE: A SMOOTHLY FUNCTIONING DEMOCRACY

From the mid-1960s until its recent economic difficulties, observers praised what they called the "German model." Put simply, the state was built on a national consensus that stressed close cooperation between business and labor to forge consistent economic growth, the benefits of which were enjoyed by virtually everyone.

To some degree, that success reflects the formal institutions created by the Basic Law  (**www.bundesregierung.de/Webs/Breg/EN/Federal-Government/federal-government.html**). Just as important, however, are the more informal arrangements that political scientists call **corporatism**, in which the government and key interest groups work behind closed doors to forge integrated economic policies. Rarely are the supposedly vital actors in a democracy—political parties and elected officials—central players in them. Corporatist practices are never spelled out in constitutions and are rarely even mentioned in laws, but they are important because the countries that have most fully adopted corporatist practices are the ones that were the most economically successful from the end of the World War II into the 1990s.

Chancellor Democracy

Before turning to those corporatist arrangements, we first have to see how the conventional side of the state works. Any such discussion must begin with the chancellor (see Figure 6.1). As in other parliamentary systems, the chancellor started out literally as the "prime" minister, the first among what were supposed to be equally powerful members of the cabinet. During the twentieth century, however, the powers of prime ministers everywhere grew so dramatically that all notions of being first among equals disappeared.

The power of the chancellor was reinforced when the Federal Republic was created. The conflicting and overlapping jurisdictions of the chancellor and president had been among Weimar's many flaws. The framers of the Basic Law did not want to eliminate the dual executive, in which the largely ceremonial functions of a head of state (president) and the actual control of the government (chancellor) are in separate hands. At the same time, they wanted to make

it clear that the chancellor held the real executive power  (**www.bundeskanzlerin.de/Webs/BK/En/Office-and-Constitution/office-and-constitution.html**).

Executive and legislative power are fused. The chancellor and most members of the cabinet also sit in the Bundestag and remain in office either as long as they have the confidence of the parliamentary majority or until their four-year terms end. Because of the powerful link between cabinet responsibility and party discipline in parliamentary systems, German chancellors have been able to see most of their policy proposals enacted without much interference from the Bundestag (but see the section on the Bundesrat).

There are some differences between the role of the chancellor in Germany and that of the prime minister in other parliamentary systems. One is the unusual power the Basic Law grants to that office. In particular, Article 65 gives the chancellor the power "to determine the guidelines of policy" and to assume responsibility for defining the government's policy, resolving differences within the cabinet, and proposing virtually all major legislation.

The chancellor is subject to a constructive vote of no confidence. The opposition can throw a government out *only* if it simultaneously agrees on a new one to take its place. As a result, the chancellor is far less vulnerable than prime ministers in most parliamentary systems. In fact, this is one of the reasons most of the Greens who opposed German involvement in the war against terrorism did not vote no confidence in Schröder's government in November 2001.

His or her power is reinforced by a large Chancellor's Office with over five hundred employees. A staff that large gives the chancellor the opportunity to coordinate the entire executive. Indeed, each Monday, the head of the Chancellor's Office (who holds cabinet rank) meets with the top civil servants in every department to do just that.

German governments are also more streamlined than most. Although the cabinet is of average size, most departments have only the minister and one other political appointee. In all, only about 8 percent of all Bundestag members (as opposed to 17 percent in Britain's House of Commons) serve in the government, thereby giving the chancellor considerably more flexibility in choosing a leadership team.

Cabinet ministers tend to serve unusually long terms in a single department and can thus develop more expertise than their British or French counterparts. Erhard, for instance, was economics minister from 1949 until he became chancellor in 1963. Similarly, Genscher was foreign minister for nearly twenty years. The role of the cabinet is different as well. Much of the administrative work of cabinet ministers in France or Britain is conducted either by the states or by independent agencies. Cabinet ministers are thus free to spend more time crafting rather than implementing public policy.

The chancellor, however, is not as powerful as the French president. The chancellor cannot, for instance, go to

FIGURE 6.1 Policy-Making Processes in Germany

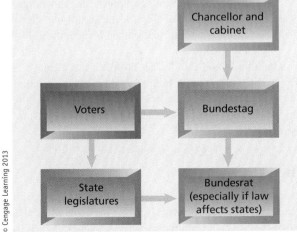

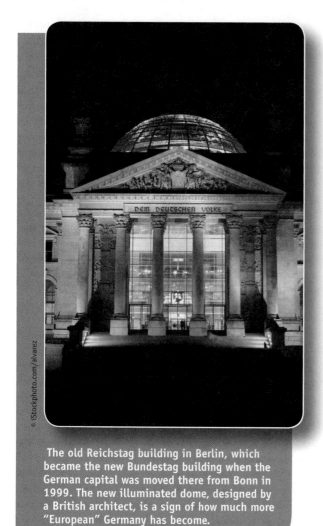

The old Reichstag building in Berlin, which became the new Bundestag building when the German capital was moved there from Bonn in 1999. The new illuminated dome, designed by a British architect, is a sign of how much more "European" Germany has become.

the public with a referendum, and the emergency powers available to the government are harder to invoke and far more limited. There is no German equivalent of the sweeping domain of regulation that allows the French government to rule by decree in many policy areas.

The chancellor's power is also less personalized. As in Britain, there is little room for an "outsider" to make it to the top on the basis of his or her personal popularity. Despite Merkel's meteoric rise after unification, chancellor candidates normally progress through their party's ranks, like British prime ministers, in careers in which negotiation and coalition building are among the most valued skills.

The Bundestag

Like most legislatures in parliamentary systems, Germany's lower house, the Bundestag, has the formal power to pass legislation and select the prime minister 🖉 (**www .bundestag.de/htdocs_e/parliament/index.html**). In practice, real power lies elsewhere. Because the chancellor

is responsible to the Bundestag, he or she can expect his majority to hold on any crucial vote, thereby minimizing the actual impact the members of Parliament can have on most legislation.

That does not mean that the Bundestag is powerless. Although the comparative evidence is sketchy, the Bundestag probably is a bit more powerful than the lower houses in Britain or France. For one thing, the Bundestag sometimes plays a pivotal role in determining who becomes chancellor. The peculiarities of the provisions of the constructive vote of no confidence have made it a significant (though not the most powerful) actor on a number of occasions when the parliamentary arithmetic was less than clear. The most important occurred in 1972, when the Brandt government lost the popular support to pursue some important domestic reforms. Polls showed that if elections were held right away the coalition's support would increase substantially. The Basic Law, however, only allows the chancellor to dissolve the Bundestag if he or she loses its confidence and no alternative majority exists to replace it. Brandt engineered that outcome by retaining the support of almost every SPD and FDP deputy, but having seventeen of the eighteen cabinet members abstain, leaving the government one vote shy of a majority.

The Bundestag also has a far more powerful committee system than either the British House of Commons or the French National Assembly. There are twenty-one standing committees, each of which has several specialized committees that consider all pending legislation. Committee members and chairs are chosen on a proportional basis from each of the parties. Because individual members' votes are not made public, party discipline is not as strict in the committees as it is on full floor votes. However, considerably less powerful than their American equivalents. For example, it is virtually impossible for them to drastically revise or kill a piece of legislation. Nonetheless, the committees propose amendments on most legislation, many of which are accepted by the government.

The third source of Bundestag power lies in its organization. As in France and Britain, the Bundestag elects a speaker (president) and, a broader leadership group, the Council of Elders, which is responsible for organizing its schedule. In the Bundestag, however, more power is given to the party groups. Individual members have larger staffs, which allow them to develop something like the experience and expertise of many American senators and representatives.

The Bundesrat

The most unusual aspect of the Federal Republic's legislative system is the **Bundesrat**, which represents the states in the national government 🖉 (**www.bundesrat.de/EN**).

Most countries' upper houses have lost any real power to affect the content of legislation. That is not the case with the Bundesrat, which gives the sixteen states direct representation in the national government. The framers of the Basic Law saw it as yet another institution that could reduce the possibility of any future Nazi-like regime emerging by limiting the power the national government could exert, whoever ran it.

Each state has between three and six votes in the Bundesrat depending on their population, and there are a total of sixty-nine members. Officially, the state governments are represented by cabinet members. In practice, the demands of running a state are so great that they normally send senior civil servants instead.

Like most upper houses, the Bundesrat has no impact on the composition of the cabinet. Similarly, it can only delay enactment of laws that would not have a direct impact on the states. However, the Bundesrat must approve all "consent" legislation that affects the länder, which accounts for more than half of all bills that come before it. When the two houses disagree, the Bundesrat convenes a Mediation Committee composed of members of both houses, which tries to iron out the differences.

The Bundesrat has vigorously defended state interests without being an exceptionally partisan or disruptive force. For most of the Federal Republic's history, the two houses have been dominated by the same coalition of parties, so there have been few ideological disputes.

Early in this century, the CDU-dominated Bundesrat often found itself at odds with the SPD/Green government. Yet even when the Bundestag and Bundesrat majorities have been at odds, it has not been a disruptive force on major legislation. In late 2010, for instance, that was not a factor because CDU-led state governments controlled 37 seats, giving it a clear majority (see Table 6.5).

The Federal System

The Bundesrat is but one part of an unusual constitutional system for a parliamentary-based government. Most other countries, including Britain and France, are unitary states in which virtually all power is legally lodged in the central government. The Basic Law, by contrast, divides responsibility between the national and state governments.

The national government has sole responsibility for matters that transcend state boundaries, including foreign policy, defense, citizenship, the economy, transportation, communication, and property rights. Everything else—including civil and criminal law, the organization of associations, broadcasting, welfare, mining, industry, banking, labor, education, highways, and health—is left to the states. The states also administer most federal law and have some leeway in determining how they do so.

But, as in other federal systems, the balance of power has long been tilting toward the national government. Most of the important policy issues, including those we will focus on in the next section, are predominantly federal in nature. And even for many of those that are not, the federal government has imposed more uniform rules and procedures from state to state than one finds in the United States.

Over the years, the most important role of state politics has been as a source of national-level leaders. Kohl, Strauss, Brandt, Schröder, and Merkel all rose to prominence first at the state level. That is quite different from the situation in France or Britain, where the careers of major national leaders are shaped almost exclusively in Paris and London. The state governments are also important because they provide opportunities to try out different types of coalitions that would not be possible at the federal level at the current time, but could prove to be so in the future.

The Civil Service

Although German legislators have larger staffs than their French or British counterparts, they, too, are ill equipped to deal with the technical issues facing most governments today. As a result, bureaucrats are playing an increasingly influential role in policy making, as well as implementation.

Upper-level civil servants have long had a powerful impact on German politics, although not always a positive one. In the early years of the Second Reich, only the chancellor was a political official. Other cabinet members were drawn from the upper ranks of the civil service. In the Weimar period, the bureaucracy remained extremely conservative and was recruited primarily from the nobility. Most senior civil servants actively and voluntarily cooperated with the Nazis.

It was hardly surprising that de-Nazifying and democratizing the bureaucracy became one of the Allies' highest priorities after the war. In all, about fifty-three thousand civil servants were purged before the British, French, and American authorities realized they needed a strong administrative service if the new republic they were creating was to get off the ground. With the onset of the Cold War, the de-Nazification and democratization programs quickly ended.

TABLE 6.5 Bundesrat Delegations: November 2010

PARTY/COALITION	STATES CONTROLLED	BUNDESRAT SEATS
CDU/FDP	6	31
CDU/FDP/Green	1	3
CDU/Green	1	3
SPD/CDR	3	11
SPD	1	4
SPD/Left	2	8
SPD/Green	2	9

As a result, there was considerable continuity in both the operations and personnel of the prewar and postwar civil service. The new bureaucracy, however, differs significantly from the old one. Most notably, it is decentralized. Only about 10 percent of the top civil servants, or *Beamten*, work directly for the federal government.

Federal bureaucrats do relatively little administrative work, most of which is the responsibility of their counterparts at the state level. Instead, federal civil servants spend most of their time drafting legislation and regulations for their partisan bosses. Most civil servants accept their political role far more readily than do their British or American counterparts. Many, in fact, are open party members or sympathizers. Some move on to political careers.

The civil service as a whole has largely escaped the daily battles of partisan politics, but there are two significant exceptions. In the aftermath of student protests and terrorist attacks in the late 1960s and early 1970s, the SPD government passed laws that severely restricted the entry of alleged radicals into the civil service at all levels, especially among the ranks of teachers and social workers. And after unification, many communist officials were purged in the East, especially in the education and foreign ministries.

The Federal Constitutional Court

Like the civil service of which they were a part, most judges before 1945 were conservatives who actively supported the Third Reich. In attempting to minimize the chances of a Nazi revival, American advisers insisted on introducing a revamped judiciary that would be more politically neutral but that could also buttress the new democracy.

The framers of the Basic Law created the **Federal Constitutional Court (FCC)**, the most important component of the judicial system. Its two chambers, or "senates," each have eight judges who serve nonrenewable twelve-year terms. Half are chosen by the Bundestag and half by the Bundesrat. In each house, a two-thirds vote is required, which means that to be elected any judge has to be acceptable to members of both major parties. In other words, although most judges have as clear a political identity as any Supreme Court justice in the United States, in order to be elected they have to have more broad-based support and thus more moderate views than many of the justices nominated by recent American administrations.

The court has wide-ranging powers. It can hear cases involving the constitutionality of state and federal law. Through the process of abstract review, an issue can go directly from the Parliament to the court without any prior legal action. The court has had a hand in almost all important policy areas involving all aspects of the Basic Law. Historically, these include:

- Ruled that the Communist Party and the neo-Nazi Reichs Party were illegal under the provisions of the Basic Law concerning political parties (1952).

- Determined that the Adenauer government could not establish a second, nationally directed television network because the Basic Law gives states responsibility for the media (1961).

- Upheld the treaty with the DDR (East Germany) that was the cornerstone of Brandt's opening of relations between the Federal Republic and the countries of the Soviet bloc (1973).

- Largely upheld the provisions designed to keep "radicals" out of the civil service and required new federal and state employees to affirm their loyalty to the Federal Republic (1975).

- Overturned the liberal abortion law passed by the SPD-FDP government (1975).

- Upheld the codetermination law that gives workers nearly half the seats on the boards of directors of large firms (1979).

- Determined that the first elections in the newly unified Germany had to be conducted using a modified version of the two-tiered electoral system with separate allocation of seats in the west and east (1990).

- Made almost all abortions illegal (1993).

A list of key recent decisions is at 🌐 **www.bundesverfassungsgericht.de/en/index.html.**

More recently, the court declared that German participation in NATO's involvement in Afghanistan was constitutional, but declared that a number of procedures that seemed to intrude on peoples' electronic privacy were not.

Although the judges have routinely acted in far more sweeping ways than their British or French counterparts, it is hard to argue that they carry the prestige or power of the U.S. Supreme Court. The way FCC judges are appointed probably makes them susceptible to the views of the current government. Because they can only serve on twelve-year term, they are also probably more open to public opinion.

Corporatism

Corporatism is the last—and perhaps most important—component of the policy-making process. It is not mentioned in the Basic Law. Nonetheless, as in many countries, such informal procedures can be more influential than any constitutional provisions in determining what actually happens in political life.

The word *corporatism* itself is one of the most controversial in modern political science. Its origins lie in nineteenth-century Catholic thought. It was later used by the fascists to describe the sham legislatures they created in which major interests or "corporations" were supposedly represented. In other words, when scholars first began using corporatism to describe close relationships between the state and interest groups, their very choice of the term conveyed the strength of their reservations about such arrangements.

Scholars have not used the term very precisely. There are dozens of definitions of corporatism, most of which revolve around the broad cooperation of highly centralized business and union organizations with the government in setting economic policy. Typically, corporatist negotiations take place behind closed doors, and neither political parties nor backbenchers have much of a role in them. Rather, cabinet members and high-level civil servants serve as brokers to help interest groups reach agreements, which are then accepted as binding by everyone involved.

Germany has used corporatist procedures more than any of the other countries covered in this book. That said, they were used on an official basis only when the SPD was first in government and helped orchestrate the **Concerted Action** meetings that brought business, government, and labor together from 1966 until 1977. Concerted Action was originally instituted by the CDU-SPD grand coalition as part of its efforts to end the Federal Republic's first recession. Over the next three years, groups met annually to reach national agreements about wage and price increases, broad macroeconomic and social policy issues, and the landmark 1967 law on balanced growth. Once the CDU went into opposition and the post-OPEC economic slump hit, the discussions became more acrimonious and less productive. They were abandoned in 1977.

Since then, there has been far less formal corporatist decision making. One should not, however, make too much of this because, on balance, the most important political decisions have always been based on informal ties between the bureaucracy and the business community. Indeed, it is often said that the Economics Ministry sees itself as the *Anwalt*, or attorney-spokesman, for industry. The ministries' planning staffs cooperate with business and labor in trying to determine what their goals could and should be for the next five years or more.

Informal corporatist arrangements also build on the consensus that exists between business and labor on basic economic priorities. At first, the DGB shared the SPD's desire for socialism. However, as the economic miracle unfolded, the unions, too, made their peace with capitalism and began concentrating on demands for a bigger share of the expanding economy for their members instead.

Labor's biggest contribution today comes through Germany's unique system of **codetermination**, which gives unions half the seats on the boards of directors of all companies with more than two thousand employees. The workers' representatives are not quite as powerful as those named by the owners. The law reserves one of the union seats for someone representing management employees and automatically gives the chair of the board to ownership.

Codetermination is but one part of a relatively peaceful system of labor-management relations that has endured throughout the postwar period. Unions traditionally have been willing to give up short-term wage gains in exchange for job security and long-term corporate growth, from which they also benefit. All firms have work councils that bring employees and management together to discuss job-related issues.

Thus, codetermination is part of a system of industrial relations that is less adversarial than that found in any other liberal democracy. Although there has been some tension between those two sides over the years, union-management relations are usually cordial and cooperative. One union official who serves on the board of a major corporation put it this way:

> **It is true that relations have become a little more conflictual nowadays, owing to lower growth and higher unemployment. But basically, we still believe that it is by cooperating with management, rather than fighting it, that we stand the best chance of securing better pay and working conditions—and the results prove it. What is more, as we see it, our obligation is not just to our own members or to other workers but to German society as a whole, where we must play an active role in upholding democracy and the rule of law. We're part of the establishment and proud of it. We're certainly not revolutionaries; we do not want to overthrow capitalism but to reform it from inside, in a more "social" direction, within the social market economy.[4]**

Finally, until changes that antedated the current crisis shook up the industry, Germany's banks helped set and coordinate economic policy. Three main private banks—Deutsche, Dresdner, and Commerz—owned about 10 percent of all the stock in Germany's biggest firms. In addition, depositors give the banks their proxies for their individual shares, leaving the banks with *de facto* control of almost all major enterprises. Thus, a relatively small number of bank officials could work with a similarly small number of colleagues in the public sector to coordinate much economic policy.

---

[4] Cited in John Ardagh, *Germany and the Germans: After Unification* (New York: Penguin Books, 1991), 125.

Many observers also argued that the **Bundesbank** was Germany's most powerful political institution until the EU's central bank took over many of its functions in 1998. Technically not part of the government, the bank worked closely with the cabinet for fifty years following its formation in 1948. In particular, it single-mindedly sought to use interest rates and other financial levers to keep inflation down and thereby help the country avoid one of the main problems that led to the collapse of the Weimar Republic.

But corporatism is a mixed blessing. Though less so than was the case under the fascists, corporatist systems underrepresent labor. Compared with what we saw in France or Britain, labor has fared rather well in Germany. Even so, it has only approached being an equal partner during the first few years the SPD was in power in the early 1970s.

Labor is not the only group to get short shrift. The consensus and the neo-corporatist arrangements are limited to issues of industrial and economic growth. Groups concerned with issues such as women's rights, immigrant workers, and the growing elderly population, which emerged with postmaterialist politics and citizens' initiatives beginning in the 1970s, are not part of the corporatist system.

Chapter 2 outlined two versions of liberal democracy. The American presidential system makes it relatively easy for organized groups to influence the decision-making process between elections. The fusion of legislature and executive in parliamentary systems provides a sharper link between party programs and the policies the government enacts, making elections themselves an effective way for a majority of the public to voice its opinions and, in turn, shape subsequent public policy making. Corporatism poses problems for either version. Decision making takes place behind closed doors and involves bureaucrats, not the elected officials over whom the voting public has some degree of control.

None of this is to say that Germany and other relatively corporatized countries are not democratic in the sense that most political scientists intend when using the term. However, the realities of corporatism reveal one of the great trade-offs of German politics today. There is little question that these cooperative arrangements have helped Germany become one of the world's leading economic and political powers, something we will see in more detail in the rest of the chapter. Yet that success has come at the cost of substantial popular participation in the setting of economic policy.

PUBLIC POLICY: *MODELL DEUTSCHLAND*

One of the key themes of this chapter is embedded in the quote that begins it. The Federal Republic has succeeded in large part because it has rarely tried to do anything rash or dramatic. Instead, its leaders have always preferred to take incremental steps based, whenever possible, on a broad national consensus. We can see this by turning to two policy areas that reflect both the success the regime has enjoyed since the late 1940s and also the challenges it faces today, which seem to put those accomplishments in some doubt.

The first, not surprisingly, is the economy, which was at the heart of Germany's rebirth after the war but is equally at the heart of its difficulties in the early twenty-first century. The second, and related, issue is the ease with which it incorporated the former DDR despite the social, political, and economic costs that came with unification.

The Social Market Economy

Germany has not always been one of the world's richest countries. In 1951, GNP per capita stood at five hundred dollars or about a fourth of what it was in the United States. By the end of the 1980s, it had drawn even with the United States on most major economic indicators. Only Japan's economy grew at a faster pace over the last sixty years. In addition, unlike during the interwar years, Germany was able to keep its inflation and unemployment rates among the lowest in the world.

As was the case with the Gaullists in France, the government's policies have not been the only cause of this remarkable track record. Germany's recovery got a needed boost from $4.4 billion in Marshall Plan aid and the influx of 14 million refugees from the East who helped keep labor costs down. Still, the state has played an extremely important role in Germany's turnaround. Since the 1950s, the government has followed remarkably consistent and successful economic policies, which were formalized in the 1967 law that obliges the state to pursue policies that maintain stable prices, full employment, adequate growth, and a positive balance of trade.

More than French policymakers, the German elite understood that the route to economic growth lay in international trade and investment more than in attempts to capture a larger share of a relatively small domestic market. As a result, Germany had Europe's most globally oriented economy well into the 1990s. It exported more goods and services than any other country in the world on a per capita basis. Its exports accounted for more than a quarter of all trade within the EU. Its currency dominated Europe for two decades and was the foundation on which the euro was built.

The key here is not so much economic performance itself, but the consistent role of the state in promoting it, which we can see by considering two alternations in power—the beginning of the Kohl, Schröder, and Merkel governments.

Thatcher, Mitterrand, and Kohl each took office in the aftermath of the second oil shock of the 1970s, which was a period of sluggish and intermittent growth. As we saw in the last two chapters, Thatcher and Mitterrand enacted sweeping reforms that they thought would help their countries cope with deteriorating economic conditions.

Under Kohl, by contrast, there was more continuity than change. Rather than embarking on a radical Thatcheresque restructuring of the economy, Kohl advocated minor reductions in government spending to make more funds available for private investment in order to recreate one of the conditions that had led to the economic miracle in the first place.

Also, unlike the British and French policies, Kohl's seemed to work. By 1986 the budget deficit had been cut by two-thirds and inflation had been all but eliminated. Industrial production increased by an average of 15 percent per year.

That economic success can perhaps best be seen in the standard of living its citizens enjoy, which, itself, is an outgrowth of corporatist policy. The average industrial worker makes about fifty dollars per hour in wages and nearly as much again in fringe benefits and social services. Most workers also earn the equivalent of another month's wages in annual Christmas bonuses. Until France passed its thirty-five-hour work week, the Germans worked the shortest hours and enjoyed the most vacation time (forty-two working days a year) in Europe. Most Germans are able to afford large cars, which they drive as fast as they want on the country's superhighways that effectively have no speed limits.

Since the early 1990s, Germany's performance has not been as impressive. In part, that reflects the economic costs of unification, which we will consider shortly. In part, too, the last two decades have seen some of Germany's past strengths turn into weaknesses.

Nonetheless, Germany's continued with its practice of consensus-drive incremental change. As most economists argue, its policy of combining a strong welfare state with fiscal responsibility could not last indefinitely in a globalizing economy. Consequently, in the last two decades some of Germany's past strengths have become weaknesses.

In response, the socialist government led by Schröder introduced programs that cut unemployment benefits and some other social service programs. Few people lost jobs. Instead, they were placed on "short work" programs in which they only worked part time. The laws on firing people were loosened, but few were actually fired. As many as 200,000 jobs were saved. The bottom line is that in 2010, the German economy grew at the fastest rate in Europe. If the summer's growth rate continued, its GNP per capita would grow by almost 9 percent that year, dwarfing modest growth in France and a shrinking economy in Greece and Spain. All the signs suggest that Germany will continue to do well, but see the next chapter.

Economic Liberalization
in Germany

Liberalization in Germany can be broken into two components. In the West, there has been little liberalization because the government owned little of the economy. Although the two main state-owned industries—Deutsche Post and Deutsche Telekom—were privatized, the key issue in western Germany is not the ownership of industry, but the intricate system of regulation, which remains largely in place.

The situation is very different in the East. There, the regime owned virtually the entire economy before it collapsed (see Chapter 8). Unlike some of the other former communist countries in Eastern Europe, however, Germany quickly reached a consensus on the need to privatize state-owned firms as soon as possible, a task that it accomplished by the middle of the 1990s. ■

The political point here is that the remarkable continuity in its economic policy has continued to somehow balance a vibrant welfare state with fiscal responsibility, perhaps because almost all political leaders view inflation as the chief threat. Germany has not even had to contemplate the massive budget cuts that we saw in the UK in Chapter 4. Although Merkel has used more free market rhetoric, the broad consensus on economic policy means that little has changed other than opening the country to more imports and exports.

There is a chance that this consensus could unravel should Merkel be able to shift economic policy dramatically rightward along the lines of David Cameron's government in the UK. She would certainly like to do so, but disagreements with the FDP, reasonably economic growth, and the possibility of losing in 2013 may well keep Germany on its now normal policy course.

The growth in the economy has not helped the Merkel government's approval rating in the polls. But, even if the coalition unravels or loses the 2013 election, it is hard to imagine a successor government doing anything dramatically different.

Unification

Most chapters in this book include a section on foreign policy as one of the ways to see the state in action. Foreign policy is certainly important in Germany, especially now that it is by far the most powerful country in Europe. However, we chose to focus on unification instead in this chapter for three reasons.

First, unification has significantly slowed Germany's economic growth for the better part of a generation. Second, even though Germany has had a hard time coping with the social and economic implications of unification, it is likely to make the country even stronger in the long run. Finally, unification provides yet another example of German adaptation to changing circumstances.

For forty years, leading politicians in the West (but not those in the DDR) consistently called for unification, but no one realistically expected it to happen until the remarkable events of 1989 unfolded. As we will see in more detail in Chapter 8, reform movements swept through Poland and Hungary that spring, culminating in the Hungarian decision to dismantle the barbed wire "iron curtain" along its border with Austria. An average of five thousand East German "vacationers" a day streamed across the border. In September, Hungary gave up even the pretense of policing the border. The DDR then closed its border with Hungary, but East Germans anxious to head West found another way out through Czechoslovakia.

On September 25, 1989, the first of what turned out to be weekly mass rallies demanding political reform took place in the East German city of Leipzig. In October, the DDR celebrated the regime's fortieth anniversary, which Soviet President Mikhail Gorbachev attended. During his visit, it became increasingly clear that the East German regime was in deep trouble and could not meet either domestic demands or Soviet pressures for a German equivalent of *perestroika* and *glasnost*, the Russian terms for economic

restructuring and political openness that became part of everyone's vocabulary in those heady days.

Shortly thereafter, the Communist Party's elite forced the aging and intransigent Erich Honecker to resign and replaced him with the younger, but still hard-line, Egon Krenz. Krenz could do nothing to stop either the protests or the flood of DDR citizens fleeing to the West. On November 9, Krenz gave in. All travel restrictions were lifted and that evening people began tearing down the Berlin Wall. Krenz resigned, and his successor, Hans Modrow, began planning free elections for the spring. The Federal Republic's parties moved into the East and took over the campaign.

Only then did Kohl seriously back rapid unification. He apparently first raised the idea in a telephone conversation with Krenz two days after the wall came down. From then on, Kohl's goal was to incorporate the DDR into the Federal Republic as five new states under Article 2 of the Basic Law rather than through Article 146, which would have required the drafting of a new constitution subject to a referendum. He also proposed that the all-but-worthless East German marks be exchanged for deutsche marks on a one-for-one basis. Finally, he insisted that newly united Germany remain in NATO and the European Community (EC).

At that point, rapid unification still seemed unlikely given Soviet objections to a unified Germany's membership in NATO. But those objections were quickly overcome. In March 1990, Kohl's supporters won an overwhelming victory in the East's first and only free election, which made negotiations with the West far easier. Meanwhile, with strong encouragement from the George H. W. Bush administration, the Soviet government agreed to join "four plus

Crowds scaling the Berlin Wall following the DDR announcement that it would no longer restrict travel to the West.

FINCK/Associated Press

two" talks, which brought the four former occupying powers and the two Germanys to the bargaining table.

In early summer 1990, the two Germanys agreed to merge their economies on July 1. In September, the Soviets agreed to German membership in NATO after the Germans formally accepted the boundaries drawn after World War II and committed themselves to spending $8 billion to send the 340,000 Soviet troops stationed in East Germany home, build housing for them, and retrain them for civilian jobs. On October 4 the two Germanys were united. In December, the Bundestag confirmed the CDU in power with strong support in both parts of the country.

Before continuing, it is worth underscoring one critical point here. Most of the steps that made unification possible were taken in East Berlin and Moscow rather than in Bonn. When the federal government acted decisively, it did so with the benefit of a broad consensus. Only the Greens and a handful of intellectuals, including the novelist Günter Grass, opposed unification. The SPD preferred a slower pace using Article 146, but it still supported the principle of unification. In short, as in domestic policy, the German government acted reactively more than proactively and took bold steps only after achieving a broad consensus.

Unification, however, presented new challenges that could not be met using the incremental policy making that German governments had followed since the 1960s. Almost everything in the East was substandard—workforce training; environmental conditions; the highway, rail, and telecommunications infrastructure; factory equipment; and housing. Only 7 percent of DDR households had a telephone, and there were only a few hundred lines that could handle international calls—including those to the Federal Republic. Per capita income in the East was a quarter that in the West, and productivity was a third that of the Federal Republic. Economists estimated that it would take up to $100 billion to modernize the rail system alone and determined that no more than 20 percent of Eastern enterprises could survive in a competitive market economy.

Therefore, the Federal Republic adopted policies to make the transition as rapid as possible, even if doing so would cause hardship in the short run. A new agency, the *Treuhandanstalt*—or **Treuhand** for short—was created to manage the privatization of East German firms. Until they could be sold, the state-owned industries were subjected to the same market forces operating in the West, including the risk of unemployment for workers and bankruptcy for the firm. All Western wage, social service, and labor laws took effect immediately, except for the granting of a year's protection from unemployment for workers in the largest factories.

The economic results were painful indeed. A year after unification, industrial production in the East was down by 70 percent. Unemployment had risen to 3.5 million in a

Globalization *in Germany*

So far, globalization has affected Germany less than the other European democracies. Despite the costs of unification, its companies and its currency (until the launch of the euro) remained the strongest in Europe. That said, Germany is by no means immune from global pressures. In particular, its high labor costs make its goods increasingly hard to sell abroad. And some of its legal restrictions have forced its companies to do some cutting-edge work abroad. For example, constitutional court decisions have made the destruction of embryos for stem cell research illegal. This does not mean that German firms do not engage in that research; they simply do it in Britain or France, where there are no such restrictions. ■

workforce of 8.5 million. The Treuhand discovered that it could not easily sell off antiquated industries even though the federal government offered a 40 percent tax credit for firms that invested in the East. Even when buyers could be found, they faced colossal challenges. BASF, for instance, bought a reasonably modern Eastern chemical firm only to discover major environmental problems, a 74,000-person workforce that would have to be cut in half, and a management filled with former Communist Party *apparatchiks*. What's more, there was no market for the factory's goods because its primary outlet had been the former Soviet Union, which could no longer pay for the chemicals it could produce.

During the 1990s, the federal government sent an average of over $100 billion a year to the East in aid and subsidies—the equivalent of 40 percent of the former DDR's GNP. This has had a tangible impact on Westerners' lifestyles because the government imposed a 7.5 percent increase in the income tax and what amounted to a fifty-five cent per liter additional tax on gasoline.

Slowly, economic conditions in the East began to improve. Having sold off all the viable companies, the Treuhand was disbanded. By 2000 unemployment had fallen to 17 percent, only 10 percent more than in the FRG. Per capita income had topped sixteen thousand dollars a year, almost twice what it was at the time of unification.

Integrating the East is not merely an economic challenge. Although most DDR citizens had been able to watch television shows and listen to radio broadcasts from the West for many years, they were largely isolated from the political and, even more, the cultural trends that remade the FRG after 1945. Most had never experienced a market economy or lived in a democracy, and many have had a hard time adapting to both (see Chapter 8). There has been a backlash against the loss of guaranteed housing, employment, and other services that were eliminated by reunification. Likewise, many West Germans are resentful of the economic costs of unification that came at the expense of their own standard of living.

Perhaps the most important long-term obstacle to effective unification, however, is what many Germans call the "wall in the mind." Other terms used to describe the difficulties in combining the *ossis* and *wessis* (people from the West) include "united but not together" and "sharing a bathroom with a stranger." Most observers are surprised by how different the two societies had grown despite having been separated for only forty-five years. One 2000 poll found that only 16 percent of the ossis felt "solidarity" with their fellow citizens in the West. Having Merkel in office has undoubtedly helped. However, the cultural gap remains and is likely to do so for some time to come.

THE MEDIA

Like their counterparts in Britain and France, Germans have access to a variety of sources of information about politics. Also like their counterparts, few take much advantage of them.

Germany's newspapers have surprisingly small circulations. The five main "quality" dailies sold only 157,000 to 405,000 copies a day at the end of 1997, a number that has declined since then. As in Britain and France, they each have clear, traditional political leanings. However, as the 1998 election neared, the *Frankfurter Allgemeine Zeitung* (known to friends and foes alike as *FAZ*) was unusually critical of the Kohl government it had long supported. The CDU has also been able to count on support from the Axel Springer media

empire, with its high-quality daily *Die Welt* and Germany's main tabloid, *Bild*. But they, too, were more critical of Kohl in 1998, perhaps sensing that their readers were ready for a change. Finally, most of the six major weeklies have been more critical of the CDU than they were in the mid-1990s.

Germans have more locally produced television options than people in Britain or France do. Subscribers to the many satellite systems (cable is much less developed in Europe) can receive more than thirty German-language stations with a "basic package." The most popular private station (SAT 1) has been more supportive of the CDU than the state-owned ones (ARD, ZDF), and it is widely believed that it played a major role in the CDU's reelection in 1994. There is an all-news channel and another channel that resembles C-SPAN, but they are not very popular. The one event that usually draws a large audience is the so-called elephant round table, or debate among the party leaders, which occurs in the last few days before a Bundestag election.

CONCLUSION: WHAT'S NEXT?

What's next in German politics is hard to disentangle for the next election will almost certainly be held in 2013. Can Merkel and CDU/FDP coalition win? The answer in mid-2011 is almost certainly not. What would the alternative be? The best guess is an SPD/Green coalition. The two parties are running neck-and-neck in recent polls with about 45 percent of the total vote. It would thus almost certainly have something short of a Bundestag majority on its own and would be dependent on the tacit support of either Left Party or the FDP.

Whoever wins will face two major issues. First, it will have to maintain the economic upswing of the last few years, which is by no means guaranteed. Second, it will still have to deal with continued fallout from the crisis in the eurozone, which we turn to next.

Looking FORWARD

WE ARE ABOUT to make the first major leap in the kinds of countries we cover.

So far, we have concentrated on relatively stable and effective democratic states. Many political scientists have long thought that the nation-state would long remain the "highest level" political organization we could achieve. That is especially true of our colleagues in international relations.

Now, we are about to see that the nation-state cannot be taken for granted from two quite different and perhaps contradictory perspectives.

First, we are beginning to see the emergence of international organizations that have taken on some

of the trappings of sovereignty from the traditional state. None is more important than the European Union, which exerts considerable autonomy over its members, though few of them admit to ceding even a part of their sovereignty.

In the rest of the book, we will consider states where sovereignty itself cannot be taken for granted. Although the term "failed state" is probably tossed around too loosely, it will be clear in Parts 3 and 4 that many governments cannot assure even the most basic services, including providing law and order, in much of their countries.

Key Terms

Concepts
Basic Law
chancellor democracy
codetermination
Concerted Action
constructive vote of no
    confidence
corporatism
faulted society
führer
German question
grand coalition
länder
Modell Deutschland
ossi
proportional representation
reparations

People
Adenauer, Konrad
Bismarck, Otto von
Brandt, Willy
Fischer, Joska
Hitler, Adolf
Kohl, Helmut
Merkel, Angela
Schmidt, Helmut
Schröder, Gerhard

Acronyms
CDU
DDR
DGB
FCC
FDP
FRG

NPD
NSDAP
PDS
SPD

Organizations, Places, and Events
Bundesbank
Bundesrat
Bundestag
Christian Democratic Union
    (CDU)
Federal Constitutional Court
    (FCC)
Federal Republic of Germany
    (FRG)
Federation of German Labor
    (DGB)
Free Democratic Party (FDP)
German Democratic
    Republic (DDR)
Greens
Law for Promoting Stability
    and Growth in the
    Economy
Left Party
National Democratic Party
    (NDP)
Nazis
Party of Democratic
    Socialism (PDS)
Social Democratic Party
    (SPD)
Treuhand
Weimar Republic

🖋 Useful Websites

There are three good entry points to German politics on the Web, though none of them are as good as the portals for most of the other countries covered in this book. WESS has an excellent site on German studies in general. The editors of H-Net, a collection of list-servs for scholars, maintain a set of links on German issues, including politics. Finally, Professor Russell Dalton of the University of California-Irvine has an excellent but brief set of links he has chosen for his own student and includes quite a few rare historical YouTube clips.

> **wessweb.info/index.php/German_Studies_Web**
> **www.h-net.org/~german/**

> **www.socsci.uci.edu/~rdalton/germany/other/**
> **weblinks.htm**

The German government provides a gateway to the chancellor's office and government agencies, most of which have material in English, as well as in German.

> **www.bundesregierung.de/Webs/Breg/EN/Homepage/**
> **home.html**

There are two good sources of news about Germany. The first is from the English language feed of Deutsche Welle, one of the country's leading radio and television broadcasters. The other is provided by the German Embassy in Washington.

> **www.dw-world.de/dw/0,1595,266,00.html**
> **www.germany.info/Vertretung/usa/en/**
> **05__Foreign__Policy__State/00/__Home.html**

Further Readings

Almond, Gabriel, and Sidney Verba. *The Civic Culture: Political Attitudes and Democracy in Five Nations*. Princeton, NJ: Princeton University Press, 1963. The classic study of political culture, including significant doubts about German commitment to democracy.

———, eds. *The Civic Culture Revisited*. Boston: Little, Brown, 1979. A volume that includes substantial data on the way German culture changed during the 1960s and 1970s and became more "civic."

Ardagh, John. *Germany and the Germans: After Unification*, rev. ed. New York: Penguin Books, 1991. An encyclopedic look at modern Germany, with an emphasis on culture and economics rather than on politics.

Ash, Timothy Garton. *The Magic Lantern: The Revolution of '89 Witnessed in Warsaw, Budapest, Berlin, and Prague*. New York: Random House, 1990. One of the best journalistic accounts of the events that swept through Eastern Europe in 1989.

———. *The File*. New York: HarperCollins, 1997. A chilling look at East Germany through Garton Ash's attempt to see his own Stasi file.

Berghahn, V. R. *Modern Germany: Society, Economy, and Politics in the Twentieth Century*, 2nd ed. New York: Cambridge University Press, 1987. A historical overview that provides the best link among political, social, and economic trends.

Bering, Henrik. *Helmut Kohl*. Washington: Regnery, 1999. The best of the few biographies on Kohl, in English, although many readers will find that it lavishes too much praise on him.

Blumenthal, W. Michael. *The Invisible Wall: Germans and Jews, a Personal Exploration*. Washington, D.C.: Counterpoint, 1998. A thoughtful volume by the former secretary of the treasury during the Jimmy Carter administration.

Bracher, Karl Dietrich. *The German Dictatorship*. New York: Praeger, 1970. Still perhaps the best and most accessible analytical study of the Hitler years.

Fisher, Marc. *After the Wall: Germany, the Germans, and the Burden of History*. New York: Simon & Schuster, 1995. An analysis of contemporary Germany by the *Washington Post*'s correspondent; especially good on ethnic issues.

Goldhagen, Donald. *Hitler's Willing Executioners*. New York: Random House, 1997. An extremely controversial book that argues that most Germans cooperated willingly with the Third Reich.

Hancock, M. Donald, and Henry Krisch, *Politics in Germany*. Washington, D.C.: CQ Press, 2008. The one up-to-date full-length textbook on Germany.

Marsh, David. *Germany and Europe: The Crisis of Unity*. London: Heineman, 1994. The most comprehensive book on the impact of unification for Germany and the EU, by the editor of the *Financial Times*. Marsh is also the author of a book on the *Bundesbank*.

Parkin, Sarah. *The Life and Death of Petra Kelly*. New York: Pandora/HarperCollins, 1994. A biography of the Greens' most prominent leader and also a solid analysis of the party itself. Written by one of the founders of the British Greens.

Roberts, Geoffrey. *Party Politics in the New Germany*. London: Pinter/Cassell, 1997. The best of the few recent academic books looking at the "big picture" of German politics.

Vanberg, Georg. *The Politics of Constitutional Review in Germany*. Cambridge: Cambridge University Press, 2005. The one English-language book on judicial review in Germany. It may go too far in stressing what the court can and cannot do.

CHAPTER 7

The European Union

Over the longer term, the institutions and powers of the (Union) will continue to expand and certain policy-making powers, heretofore vested in the member states, will be delegated or transferred to, or pooled and shared with, (Union) institutions. As a result, the sovereignty of the member states will increasingly and inevitably be eroded.

DAVID CAMERON

THE BASICS

The European Union

COUNTRY	DATE OF ACCESSION
Belgium, France, Germany, Italy Luxembourg, Netherlands	1957
Denmark, Great Britain, Ireland	1972/73
Greece	1981
Portugal, Spain	1986
Austria, Finland, Sweden	1995
Cyprus, Czech Republic, Estonia, Hungary, Latvia, Lithuania, Malta, Poland, Slovakia, Slovenia	2004
Romania, Bulgaria	2007

THE CRISIS IN THE EUROPEAN UNION?

We drafted this chapter in early 2011. We knew financial problems loomed on the horizon for the **European Union**. Some of the poorer member states had accumulated massive annual deficits and long-term debt. Greece, Ireland, and Portugal had to adopt dramatic austerity measures that make anything enacted in the UK or proposed in the U.S. seem minor. What's more, the wealthier countries in the **eurozone** found that they had to bail out their newly impoverished colleagues. We will speak later of a "multispeed" Europe as one of its lingering political problems. Since the Great Recession began, there is now also a multispeed economic Europe at its very heart, the seventeen countries that have adopted the **euro** (€). The so-called eurozone is in serious trouble. Some analysts have gone as far as to argue that many countries will abandon the currency that has only been fully in place since 2002 or that the EU itself will collapse.

Greece has gotten the most publicity, perhaps because its difficulties were the direst in 2011. Not only is it having trouble crafting an economic policy that stresses austerity, but many of its most economically vulnerable people have taken to the streets, occasionally with a modicum

Looking BACKWARD

SO FAR, THIS book has emphasized (relatively) stable and successful industrialized democracies. Now, we will shift gears in two dramatic ways, both of which illustrate that the stakes of politics are much higher elsewhere once we look at the rest of the world.

In this chapter, we will deal with assumption made by many political scientists that the nation-state is the "highest" level of political organization we can reach. The European Union is the most promising international organization to which states have gradually (and quietly) ceded some of their sovereignty. But unlike its member states, neither the success nor the democracy of the EU can be taken for granted.

The second half of this book will focus on places where the state itself has been far less successful and, in some cases, where its very existence has been and is in question.

of violence. The European Central Bank (see below) had planned to add $74 billion to the roughly $35 billion it had already pledged.

Then two things happened.

First, two days before the meeting on Greece was scheduled, the head of the International Monetary Fund, Dominique Strauss-Kahn was arrested for attempted rape and other sexual abuses at a New York City hotel. Strauss-Kahn was a firm supporter of the euro and would have played a pivotal role in the negotiations. Instead, he was forced to resign within a week of the alleged incident.

Second, the Greeks themselves could not reach an agreement on what to do about a deficit that was predicted to reach 158 percent of GDP, and the government might have to default on its debt with a pact that brought government and opposition together.

Needless to say, the financial crisis angered the relatively wealthy countries that would have to pay as well, which meant Germany above all. On the eve of the summit that Strauss-Kahn spent in jail, one of the leading German tabloids wrote, "Sell your islands, you bankrupt Greeks—and the Acropolis too!" Overall, German public opinion was almost two-to-one in opposition to the bailout. Greece agreed to sell as much as $50 billion in state-owned assets, but critics pointed out that doing so would bring in dollars and other currencies, but precious few euros.

The Portuguese and Irish bailouts proceeded more smoothly in part because they were projected to run deficits of only about 100 percent of GDP. The Irish case was unusual in that it had just emerged from a boom following an upsurge in investment from EU member states and American corporations following the Good Friday Agreement, which ended the fighting in Northern Ireland. For reasons that are too complicated for our purposes, the Irish economy collapsed. It asked for and received a loan from the EU that could total in excess of $100 billion. The funds were approved in late December 2010. Along with Greece, Portugal was the poorest of the member states before the 2004 and 2007 expansion (see below). In May 2011, the Portuguese and the EU agreed on a package of about $100 billion in aid (the details were still being worked out as we write). Unlike the Greeks, Lisbon agreed to austerity measures that would cut pensions, have the government sell off nationalized industries including its international airline, a cut or freeze in the pay of government workers, and higher sales taxes on "luxury" goods such as automobiles and tobacco. In early May, the government raised over $110 billion by issuing loans, most of which were bought by the European Central Bank and the IMF.

So the reader might be tempted to ask why we retained the more than twenty-year-old statement from David Cameron (not to be confused by the current British prime minister of the same name) to begin this chapter. As Professor Cameron suggests, the EU has had a generally positive—if uneven—track record. Its history has included relatively long periods of stagnation during which the Euroskeptics tend to come to fore. But, those periods have been followed by bursts of growth during which its number of members has grown (**broadening**) and its powers have increased (**deepening**).

We are clearly in one of those periods of stagnation. Indeed this may be the most wrenching and vexing crisis the EU has ever faced. But, given the history and institutional arrangements we are about to see, it is hard to imagine how

© BLANCHIN-LEBLEAVEC/SAGAPHOTO.COM/Alamy

Demonstrators gather in the smoke-filled streets of Athens, Greece, in 2011, protesting new labor reforms amid persisting austerity.

countries could easily or painlessly withdraw from the euro, let alone the EU itself. In places, we will refer to its *acquis communautaire* or community accomplishments in broad areas of public policy.

The EU also faces the economic crisis of the last few years in a unique way. It is not a state in the traditional sense of the term, as we will see shortly. Yet, it shares enough power with its twenty-seven members to give it state-like status, especially on economic issues.

Indeed, the situation in the EU has been so confusing that one publication has assessed it in two all but contradictory ways since 2008. The *Economist* is unquestionably the leading news weekly on European affairs. Over the years, it has normally supported the idea—if not the reality—of the EU. But in 2009, it published a book that was largely supportive of the EU, while its weekly columnist, who writes under the pseudonym Charlemagne, has been quite critical and skeptical about its future.

The crisis seems to have forestalled any serious talk about either future broadening or deepening. Nonetheless, speculation about the EU's collapse—let alone that of the euro—seems way too premature. The EU is, and continues to be, the world's most successful and most powerful international organization.

At the height of the crisis, the EU made two appointments as a result of the Treaty of Lisbon. The little known Belgian politician Herman van Rompuy was chosen to be the first president of the Union and the slightly more prominent Baroness Catherine Ashton was chosen to be the high commissioner for foreign affairs. The choice of relatively minor figures to fill its two top positions was a sign that the EU is not ready to make bold new moves in the next few years.

The EU has its problems and has evolved in fits and starts. Nonetheless, as we see every time go to Europe, the Union is clearly taking hold. It is certainly in one of its "fits" in early 2011, with a budget crisis that has all but crippled Ireland and Greece and threatens to do the same to Spain and Portugal, a topic we will return to in the policy section on the euro.

THINKING ABOUT THE EUROPEAN UNION

As was the case with Great Britain, we have to start by clarifying what and whom we will discuss in this chapter. Uncertainty over which name to use—not to mention all the accompanying acronyms—can make studying the EU confusing indeed (**http://ec.europa.eu/**). In this chapter, we will use four different names.

- The **European Economic Community (EEC)**, established by the Treaty of Rome in 1957.

- The **Common Market**, a term informally applied to the EEC and still sometimes used today.

- The **European Community (EC)**, adopted in 1965 once EEC's functions expanded beyond economics.

- The European Union, the name of all the institutions gathered under the EC's umbrella as called for in the 1992 Maastricht Treaty on European Union generally known as the Maastricht Treaty.

Key Concepts and Questions

We will go beyond the current crisis and ask other questions and raise other issues that will help us expand the scope of the book. Long ago, political scientists erected an intellectual firewall between comparative politics and international relations. The former deals with politics within states and the latter with the interactions among them.

In retrospect, it never made sense to treat the two parts of the discipline separately. States have always had to deal with problems arising outside their borders, many of which went a long way toward determining what it was like. Similarly, domestic politics has always played a major role in what a state does abroad, something that Americans could easily see as they agonized over the Iraq War during the run-up to the 2008 presidential election. In today's age of globalization, you cannot keep comparative politics out of international relations and vice versa, which is, after all, what the book's subtitle intends to convey. Nowhere is this easier to see than in the case of the EU. It has lurked just below the surface in the previous three chapters. Now we will address it directly, asking questions that are similar to those we ask about individual countries but situate them in what is, by definition, an international context that includes what some of our colleagues call **multilevel governance**:

- How and why did the EU emerge?
- What is its political culture, and how does it affect the way people participate in political life?
- What are its main decision-making bodies?
- What are its critical public policy initiatives?
- How do the European people learn about and react to that policy?

This chapter will be more than just another description of a governing body. It will also offer you a first glimpse at the trends which indicate that we might be entering a new historical period in which the nation-state may no longer be the only, or even the primary, unit we should focus on. It is very much an open question whether the EU and other **supranational** organizations will gain more power, and it is highly unlikely that they will replace the nation-state in the lifetime of any reader of this book.

In sum, do not read too much into the pages that follow. Despite its state-like attributes, the EU is far from being a state. For one thing, it lacks the monopoly over the legitimate use of force that most political scientists argue makes a state a state.

Who's In? Who's Out?

In 2007, the EU grew to twenty-seven member states. France, Germany, Italy, Belgium, the Netherlands, and Luxembourg signed the Treaty of Rome and became charter members in 1957. Britain, Ireland, and Denmark entered on New Year's Day 1973. Norway had also been invited to join, but its voters decided not to in a referendum. Greece joined in 1981 and Spain and Portugal followed suit five years later. Finland, Austria, and Sweden became members in 1995. Cyprus, the Czech Republic, Estonia, Hungary, Latvia, Lithuania, Malta, Poland, Slovakia, and Slovenia were admitted in 2004. Bulgaria and Romania joined in 2007. Applications from several more states are pending. That leaves only Norway and Switzerland among the major European countries with no current interest in "acceding" to the EU.

The member countries have almost 500 million residents, or roughly 200 million more than the United States. Their combined gross domestic product for 2011 was about the same as that of the United States, though Europeans had only about two-thirds of the average American's disposable income. Still, the EU is an economic powerhouse, generating about 30 percent of all international trade (see Table 7.1).

The EU also has many of the trappings of a state. Its flag of fifteen yellow stars on a blue background flies from official buildings. This is also a common logo in advertisements, and you can get it emblazoned on t-shirts and umbrellas (Chip has one of each). The various offices of the EU have their headquarters in its three capital cities—Brussels, Luxembourg, and Strasbourg (France). The embassies of most major powers are in Brussels and are primarily dedicated to international relations with the EU. In fact, the United States has three embassies there (Belgium, NATO, and the EU). The one to the EU is larger and more prestigious than the one to Belgium. Finally, the EU has one of the most important attributes of a state other than an army or police force: its own currency, the euro. Since its introduction, the euro has been adopted by seventeen of the member states and many of the new members are planning to use it when they meet the required financial criteria to do so.

TABLE 7.1 The European Union and the United States: 2008-2009

	EUROPEAN UNION	UNITED STATES
Population (in millions)	492	313
GDP (in trillions of US$)	14.91	14.72
Imports (in trillions of dollars)	1.69	1.90
Exports (in trillions of dollars)	1.95	1.27

Source: *CIA World Factbook* (www.cia.gov). Accessed May 20, 2011.

The New Europe

The 2004 and 2007 expansions marked the most important change in the history of European integration in at least three ways. First, if nothing else, adding twelve countries in the matter of three years forced the EU into an agonizing debate over how it should be governed. Second, before 2004, all the states that joined were established democracies with reasonably prosperous economies. Even the poorest of the fifteen—Greece, Portugal, and Spain—had gross domestic products (GDPs) of about two-thirds the EU's average. Of the twelve new members, only a handful comes close to half of that average. Finally, other than Malta and Cyprus, all had been ruled by communists and are thus making the rough transitions to democracy and capitalism that we will focus on in Part 3. In the short term, at least, the 2004 and 2007 expansions were harder politically and economically than earlier ones. But if the addition of these countries did not make things easier, it also did not bring significant new challenges, which now come from states that joined in the 1990s or before.

The expansion has also led to more discussion of what some call a "multispeed" Europe, because individual countries participate in the EU in different ways and to differing degrees. That had already begun in the 1990s when some states were allowed to opt out of social policies and of the elimination of internal border controls. Even more important, eleven of the members have chosen not to adopt the euro. Most are struggling economies in eastern Europe, but the list also includes the UK and Sweden. And, a number of policies, including the free flow of labor throughout the EU, will not apply to the new members for a number of years.

Three Pillars

As the history of its name suggests, many people mistakenly think of the EU as an economic organization. Support for European integration got new life after the horrors of World War I when a group of politicians and intellectuals resurfaced the idea. Although it is true that it began as a trading bloc, its founders always intended it to be much more than that. Since its creation, the EU has expanded to embrace other powers, together known as the **three pillars** or spheres of activity:

- The traditional involvement in trade and other economic matters.
- Cooperation in justice and home affairs.
- The desire to create a **Common Foreign and Security Policy (CFSP)**, which is the most visionary and controversial aspect of the EU today.

Functionalism

Functionalism is a theory of international organization introduced by David Mitrany in 1943. Its proponents believe that the best way to develop a body like the EU is to do so step by step or function by function.

The EU does not exactly fit functionalist theory because its growth has come more in fits and starts than Mitrany and his colleagues hoped or expected. Nonetheless, we will see later in this chapter that success in one area has "spilled over" into additional members and additional powers for the European institutions.

THE EVOLUTION OF THE EUROPEAN UNION

As we saw in Chapters 3 through 6, it took centuries of often protracted conflict to create the modern state. This has not been the case for the EU. Rather, European integration is a recent phenomenon that has been almost exclusively the handiwork of political, technical, and economic elites (www.hum.leiden.edu/history/eu-history).

Not Such a New Idea

The idea of uniting Europe has been around at least since Rome ruled most of Europe. Leaders from Julius Caesar to Adolf Hitler tried to make it happen through force but without lasting success.

When the League of Nations was created and many countries signed the Kellogg-Briand Pact, which formally abolished war, groups of young activists began organizing support for a united and peaceful Europe.

The outbreak of World War II put an abrupt end to their efforts. In the longer term, however, the war only strengthened the Europeanists' cause. People who had few ties to the discredited prewar regimes led the Resistance movements that developed in the countries the Germans occupied. They harbored hopes for change in their own countries, but they also wanted to create new European institutions because they realized that Europeans simply could not afford to keep fighting each other (see Table 7.2).

A small group of them met in neutral Switzerland in 1943 to discuss a document that called for a supranational government directly responsible to the European people. It would have its own military, which would replace the national armies. An international court would settle disputes between national governments.

By the end of the war, the Europeanists had split into two camps. Whereas the federalists wanted to create that Europe-wide government, the functionalists preferred

Profiles
Jean Monnet

Jean Monnet (1888–1979) was a remarkable man. In his long career, he was everything from a brandy salesman to the primary architect of both the French economic planning system and European integration. In a professional life that spanned two world wars (which, perhaps not coincidentally, he could not fight in because of ill health), he came to see the need to replace the carnage resulting from trench warfare and the blitzkrieg with a new kind of transnational economic cooperation.

After World War II, he dedicated his energies to reconstruction and peace through planning and integration, which he saw as inseparable parts of the same whole. Among the few official positions he held was president of the **European Coal and Steel Community (ECSC)** from its founding until 1955. He spent the next twenty years trying to create a true United States of Europe. Monnet died at age ninety (so much for ill health) without seeing his broader dream realized but having left an indelible mark on his continent and the world. ∎

Jean Monnet giving a radio address on European Union.

TABLE 7.2 Key Events in the Evolution of the European Union

YEAR	EVENT
1951	Creation of ECSC
1957	Treaty of Rome signed
1967	Creation of EC
1972	First expansion
1981	Admission of Greece
1985	Single European Act passed
1986	Portugal and Spain admitted
1991	Treaty of Maastricht signed
1995	Austria, Finland, and Sweden admitted
1997	**Treaty of Amsterdam** signed
1998	Twelve countries agree to join **European Monetary Union (EMU)**
2001	Treaty of Nice signed
2002	Euro launched
2004	Ten new members added
2007	Bulgaria and Romania admitted
2009	Treaty of Lisbon goes into effect First President and Foreign Minister appointed

between East and West magnified the need to reconstruct the war-ravaged economies and strengthen the new regimes in Germany, France, and Italy. Conventional politicians returned to center stage, eclipsing Europeanist visionaries like **Jean Monnet** in France and **Paul-Henri Spaak** in Belgium.

Nonetheless, the first important steps toward integration did occur in the late 1940s as an unintended byproduct of the early Cold War. The United States decided not to give **Marshall Plan** aid to individual governments. Instead, it chose to distribute the money through the predecessor of today's Organization for Economic Cooperation and Development (OECD).

For the rest of the 1940s, little else happened on the economic front. The Cold War and the need for military cooperation led to the creation of the North Atlantic Treaty Organization (NATO) in 1949. More important for our purposes, to the degree that attention was paid to nonmilitary integration, the assumption was that key leadership would have to come from Britain, still Europe's leading power. But it was not forthcoming.

This does not mean that the supporters of European integration gave up. In 1949, they succeeded in forming the Council of Europe that included the governments that would soon join the ECSC. It had little power because each state could veto anything the Council proposed. But it did provide an opportunity for national leaders to meet, and it began developing one of the key components of the later EU: an organization representing individual governments for both consultation and decision-making.

acting in one area at a time, building momentum for further integration along the way.

As it turned out, neither side got its way. The outbreak of the Cold War in the late 1940s made security the paramount concern on both sides of the iron curtain. The tensions

The following year, Foreign Minister Robert Schuman of France issued a plan (actually written by Monnet) for a supranational authority for the coal and steel industries. The two industries were chosen because they are critical to any modern economy, had been damaged heavily in the war, and were an obvious place to attempt more cooperative endeavors. What's more, other than Italy, the five countries that joined the ECSC bordered the Rhine river and much of their coal and iron production was located nearby.

Negotiations moved swiftly, in part because Britain was not involved and because Christian Democratic and other politicians who shared pro-European views ran most of the governments that took part in the discussions. In 1951, France, West Germany, Italy, Belgium, Luxembourg, and the Netherlands signed a treaty establishing the European Coal and Steel Community. It laid out provisions for a single market for the two products through the gradual elimination of tariffs and other barriers to trade. The treaty also created four institutions that remain at the core of the EU today in only somewhat altered form and with different names:

- A High Authority composed of representatives selected by the national governments who served as the administrative body for the ECSC at the supranational level.

- A Special Council of Ministers, consisting of cabinet members from the individual governments charged with making policy for the ECSC.

- A Court of Justice to resolve disputes arising between the ECSC and national governments or companies.

- A Common Assembly consisting of delegates chosen by the national parliaments.

The new community also had a degree of autonomy because it was funded directly from fees levied against individual companies. Having its "own resources" is something we will return to later.

It is important to underscore two things here. First, these initial steps toward European integration had more to do with the Cold War than with the purported benefits of cooperation. The United States believed that it needed an economically and politically strong Western Europe to help contain communism and, thus, supported most early efforts at European integration, including the creation of the ECSC. Second, however small and tentative these steps may have been, the creation of the ECSC did involve the transfer of some aspects of national sovereignty to a supranational body.

The ECSC was not an overnight success. Almost immediately, member governments began squabbling over which language to use and where to locate its offices. The High Authority quickly discovered that eliminating tariffs and quotas would not be enough to create a truly common market. Still, the ECSC did live up to the functionalists' most important expectation. Support for the ECSC spread to other sectors of the economy. By the middle of the decade, plans involving agriculture, the military, and transportation were on the table.

In 1955, the foreign ministers of the six member countries formed a committee headed by Spaak to explore further options. In its report the next year it called for a common market and an integrated approach to the new industry of nuclear power. Spaak's group then drafted the **Treaty of Rome**, which was signed by the six governments in 1957.

This treaty established two bodies—the EEC and the European Atomic Energy Commission (Euratom). Its most important provisions called for the elimination of all internal tariffs and the creation of common external ones over a period of twelve to fifteen years.

The EEC had essentially the same institutional structure as the ECSC. The High Authority was renamed the **Commission** and was assigned responsibility for representing supranational interests and for administering the EEC. Though given few formal powers, it was assumed that the Commission would also be the major initiator of new policies.

The **Council of Ministers** was the organ of the national governments and had to approve all policy initiatives. In those days, its members were the relevant cabinet ministers from the member states, and it met when needed. Most important, if a state decided it had a strong interest in an issue before the Council, it could veto it, thus requiring unanimity before the EEC could take any major new step. Only a few relatively minor kinds of proposals could be passed through a system of **qualified majority voting**, which is now the norm.

The treaty increased the size of the renamed **European Parliament** and gave it the power to review decisions made by the Commission and Council. Nonetheless, it remained the weakest of the four main European institutions.

The **European Court of Justice (ECJ)** had seven members, one named by each government and the seventh chosen by the other six. Like members of the Commission, the justices were no longer given instructions from their own governments. The court was responsible for seeing that the EEC itself, the member governments, and their private corporations abided by the provisions of the Treaty of Rome.

During its first decade, the EEC's primary challenge was the removal of tariffs as called for in the treaty, which it accomplished ahead of schedule. It also decided to streamline its institutions by merging the EEC and Euratom into the single EC in 1967.

European Union flags fly outside the European Commission headquarters in Brussels, Belgium.

Creating the Common Market

Even in its early years, the EEC was beset by a dilemma that has been at the heart of European integration ever since. How much power should be given to the supranational institutions, and how much should remain in national hands as represented by the Council?

The difficulties came to a head in 1963 when France vetoed Denmark's and Britain's applications for membership. At a press conference, President Charles de Gaulle announced that he was for a *Europe des patries*—a Europe based on nation-states—and that Britain was not sufficiently European to join. Then in the "empty chairs" crisis of 1965–66, the French government boycotted all decision-making sessions, which paralyzed the organization because the unanimity rule required that all countries agree to all policy decisions. De Gaulle's successor, Georges Pompidou, was a far more committed European. He did not block applications from Britain, Ireland, Denmark, and Norway, which were approved in January 1972.

The EEC followed functionalist guidelines. In 1966, the **Common Agricultural Policy (CAP)** was created. The **European Monetary System (EMS)**, with its "snake," or band, in which all member currencies floated against each other, was initiated in 1972. The EC reached a broad-based trade and aid agreement with most less developed countries. Members of the European Parliament were chosen in direct elections beginning in 1979. The workings of the Council were made more routine with the establishment of the **Committee of Permanent Representatives (COREPER)** from the member states.

In the meantime, problems began to loom on the horizon. The generation of visionary, functionalist leaders who had played such a vital role in the creation of the ECSC and the EEC left the political scene. Their replacements were far less committed to further European integration. Their hopes also ebbed as a result of the economic slump following the OPEC oil embargo of 1973–74. Because the EC proved no more able to spark continued economic growth than the individual nation-states, people began to talk about "euro-sclerosis" rather than further integration.

During those years, the EC had to overcome two major roadblocks. First, the elimination of internal tariffs was not enough to create a single, common market. The free movement of goods and services was impeded, for example, by the regulations and standards individual governments used for industrial products or by procurement policies that required state agencies to purchase goods and services from domestic sources. Second, there had been little of the spillover effect the EC's founders had expected and, thus, little new support for further economic or political integration above and beyond the expansion of its membership.

It had also become clear to a growing number of business leaders that the EC would have to become more dynamic if the European economies as a whole were to take off again. That realization began a process of consultation and negotiation that eventually led to the Single European Act and the Maastricht Treaty. The first step toward further integration came with a report prepared under the direction of Belgian Prime Minister Leo Tindemans in 1976. It called for monetary and economic union, a common defense and foreign policy, and a joint industrial development program. Though no new laws or directives came directly from the Tindemans Report, it set an agenda for the next fifteen years.

Pressures to move forward were intensified when Hans-Dietrich Genscher and Emilio Colombo, the foreign ministers of Germany and Italy, respectively, issued another report advocating the strengthening of European institutions. Progress was accelerated by the appointment of **Jacques Delors** as president of the Commission in 1985. Delors had been France's minister of finance and one of President François Mitterrand's closest advisers. The appointment of someone of his stature meant that new life was being breathed into European integration.

All those efforts culminated in the Council's passage of the **Single European Act (SEA)** in December 1985. Although the Council did not go as far as some had wanted, its actions in three areas widened the scope of the EC's powers at the expense of national governments.

- The SEA introduced provisions for the completion of what is now called the internal market. As noted earlier, the abolition of internal tariffs and quotas did not remove all barriers to trade. The Commission estimated that rules and regulations would have to be written in at least three hundred areas before there could be truly free trade of goods and services across the borders of the member states. It estimated that it would take seven years to draft and ratify all those documents, thus creating the popular image of "Europe 1992."

- It introduced a number of changes in the way the EC was run. The most important of these was a sharp cutback in the use of the **unanimity principle**. After 1985, unanimity would be required only when determining whether new members should be admitted and when embarking on wholly new policy initiatives. Otherwise, the EC would employ the easier qualified majority procedures.

- The final provisions of the SEA regularized the semiannual summit meetings of the national leaders and the links between the Council, Commission, and European Parliament. The Act also called for more cooperation in determining foreign and national security policy, though it did little to specify exactly how that would take place. The SEA by no means unified the EC. It remained primarily an economic union that had little or no authority regarding social, environmental, and political issues. In most ways, national sovereignty had not been challenged. Even in the economic arena, the all-important issue of monetary and financial integration had barely been addressed.

The impetus for further deepening occurred while the bureaucrats were filling in the details of the SEA. Delors continued to symbolize the enthusiasm many felt about Europe. The events that swept the European continent in 1989 made a strong Europe all the more desirable. Power was increasingly defined economically because Eastern Europe needed billions of dollars to make the transition from communism to capitalism. Finally, the departure of Margaret Thatcher in 1990 removed the leader who was most skeptical of any expansion of the EC's power, which she had labeled "eurononsense."

This momentum led to the signing of the **Maastricht Treaty** in December 1991. The treaty gave what was now

Profiles
Jacques Delors

Jacques Delors is generally considered the second most important person in the history of the EU, trailing only Jean Monnet.

Born in 1925 in a working-class neighborhood of Paris, Delors was unable to attend university both because of World War II and his father's demand that he go to work. He thus started his career as a clerical worker in a Parisian bank and came to politics through his Catholicism and the trade union movement.

From the 1950s on, he was involved in attempts to redefine what it meant to be on the Left. At times this led him to work with groups to the Left of the Communists, and at others to serve as an adviser to Gaullist ministers.

In 1981, President François Mitterrand appointed him minister of finance, from which position he was largely responsible for the u-turn of 1983 that ended the Socialists' radical reforms. Two years later, he went to Brussels as president of the Commission.

He retired after two terms and resisted attempts to draft him as the Socialist candidate for president of France. His daughter, Martine Aubry, was chosen to lead the French Socialist Party in late 2008.

He remains an avid soccer fan.

officially called the European Union authority to act in new areas, including monetary policy, foreign affairs, national security, fisheries, transportation, the environment, health, justice, education, consumer protection, and tourism. It also formally established the idea of the three pillars and European citizenship, which means that people can work in any member country (with the exception of some in Eastern Europe) and vote in European parliamentary and local elections. All EU nations but Britain agreed to harmonize their labor relations and social service policies. In an attempt to meet the concerns of many national politicians, the treaty also endorsed the principle of **subsidiarity**. Subsidiarity defined the EU's competence and established the principle that it would act if and only if it could make public policy better than national or regional governments (also see the discussion on multilevel governance in Chapter 17). Most important, it committed the EU to creating a single currency and a central bank.

For most of the rest of the 1990s, the EU fell on harder times. Europe suffered a serious recession, which reinforced qualms about the EU and put talk of further deepening on hold. The costs of German unification, the EU's inability to end the fighting in the former Yugoslavia, internal divisions over most major issues, and uncertainties about the euro reinforced the sense of eurosclerosis similar to that in the years before Delors moved to Brussels.

Ironically, the EU's troubles began with the Maastricht Treaty itself. At first, everyone assumed it would be ratified easily. However, the Danish voters rejected it in a referendum, and ratification debates dragged on in Britain and Germany. Despite the support of all mainstream politicians, a referendum on the treaty barely squeaked through in France. Great Britain and Denmark eventually did ratify it but only after provisions were approved that would allow them to opt out of the social chapter and single currency.

The EU also had trouble finding a leader to succeed Delors, whose second term as president of the Commission ended in 1995. After a long process that included a British veto of everyone else's first choice, the members chose a little-known former prime minister of Luxembourg, Jacques Santer. Although a committed European, Santer lacked Delors' charisma and clout, and his selection was widely seen as a sign that few major initiatives would be forthcoming under his leadership.

The leadership uncertainty was further muddied with the publication of the European Parliament's study of mismanagement and corruption among Commission members in March 1999. No commissioners were individually accused of wrongdoing. Nonetheless, all twenty decided to resign, provoking what many thought would be a major setback.

In practice, the crisis turned out to be nothing of the sort. Within days, an agreement was reached. The outgoing Commission would stay in office in a caretaker capacity, much as a cabinet that lost a vote of confidence would in any of the member states. A week later, the national governments agreed on a successor to Santer. Former Italian prime minister Romano Prodi, who would take over with a full complement of new commissioners when the outgoing one's term expired at the start of 2000.

The EU also adopted two new treaties, whose impact we will explore in more detail in the sections on governance and public policy. A 1997 treaty extended the Schengen agreement, which eliminated most border controls inside the EU and gave the EU more responsibility over legal matters, including issuing residence permits to immigrants, determining asylum procedures, and promulgating directives on judicial cooperation across borders. Most important, the Amsterdam accord acknowledged that the EU viewed NATO as the dominant security organization in Europe, while reinforcing

its desire to chart its own foreign policy in other areas, including the creation of a rapid deployment force to use in humanitarian emergencies.

At the December 2000 summit, the leaders of the member states agreed to the **Treaty of Nice**, which opened the door to the broadening of 2004 and of 2007. It also made the Treaty of Lisbon possible, which served as an alternative to a constitution as we will see in the section on the state.

POLITICAL CULTURE AND PARTICIPATION IN THE EUROPEAN UNION

All of the chapters on individual countries have extended sections on political culture and participation. This one does not simply because they are not (yet) very important to politics in the EU in at least two respects.

First, it is hard to even speak of a European political culture. There is little widespread identification with Europe. Although there is growing recognition that the EU plays an important role in people's lives, there are still very few people for whom the statement "I am a European" is anywhere near as important as "I am French" (or German, or whatever). Younger, better-educated people who have traveled extensively are the most European, but even they tend to put their national identity ahead of any transnational one.

This has only recently become a subject of serious inquiry by political scientists and other scholars. The most recent book on the subject (see the Katzenstein and Steckel reference in the further reading section) argues many, often contradictory things. Almost all of the scholars who contributed to the book acknowledge that the EU plays an increasingly important role in people's lives and that they know it. Most of the authors who focus on identification as something the EU has consciously tried to create point out that there are growing cultural divisions within Europe, especially with the addition of countries that lack anything like a democratic tradition.

Second, the key EU organizations that could link people to the state have not put down very deep roots and are largely "top down" rather than "bottom up" in nature. Parties in the European Parliament are organized along transnational lines (e.g., socialists from all twenty-seven states form a single group and sit together). Other than that, partisan life remains almost exclusively national. People tend to make up their minds about how to vote in European elections on the basis of national issues and partisan loyalties. That was never clearer than in the 2004 elections for the European Parliament, when almost every governing party suffered a huge defeat for national political reasons that had little to do with Europe. The 2009 elections, by contrast, changed little. The Christian Democratic EPP again won the most votes but again fell far short of a majority. Most interest groups, too, remain nationally oriented, even those that maintain lobbying operations in Brussels.

The lack of public involvement in the EU has given rise to what critics call its **democratic deficit**. Its citizens have at most an indirect role in determining who sits on its most important decision-making bodies. As a result, a growing number of Europeans resent the power of EU institutions and their seeming inability to hold them accountable, something we have seen in most recent national referenda in which the anti-European vote has been much higher than most analysts expected.

The lack of Europeanness is also indirectly reflected in the mass media, through which people learn about political life at the national and supranational level. Attempts have been made to create everything from Europe-wide soap operas to political newspapers. The only real success story is Eurosport, a satellite TV provider that sends out a single video feed of mostly second-tier events with audio channels in all the major languages. There are two different television systems—PAL (used in Britain, Germany, and the Netherlands, among others) and SECAM (most notably used in France and Spain). Viewers with televisions

that use one cannot watch programs on the other. Although people can get all the major European newspapers wherever they live, the fact remains that these papers are all nationally based.

One of the key causes of the lack of European identification and the failure to create European political institutions is the language gap. All official documents are published in twenty-three languages. Many Europeans speak a second or even a third, but there is no common language that more than 20 percent of them are comfortable using. Furthermore, if there were a common language, it would be English, and there is strong resistance in France and elsewhere toward adopting it or any other single tongue.

THE EUROPEAN STATE?

This section begins with a question mark, because political scientists debate whether the EU is a state. Most argue that it is not because it lacks an army and a police force to maintain order and ensure that the rule of law is enforced. That said, the EU has many other features of a state. It has institutions that do the same things as the ones we saw in the United States, Britain, France, and Germany: enact laws and issue decrees that are binding on the member states, their citizens, and their corporations.

From the perspective of mutlltilevel government, the EU has some of the characteristics of a state, but not all of them. More important, the degree to which it is "statelike"— or, conversely, the degree to which the member states retain the bulk of their power—varies from time to time and issue to issue. In particular, the EU is most like a state in exercising sovereign power in the economic pillar. However, the states still wield most of the power in major new initiatives and in the few remaining policy areas in which unanimity is required.

You Say You Want a Constitution?

The Beatles' 1968 pathbreaking *White Album* included two versions of their song "Revolution" 🎵 (www.lyricsdepot. com/the-beatles/revolution.html). It was a call to young radicals like Chip to rethink their commitment to profound political change. They chastised us for focusing on the need to reform our countries' constitutions and institutions rather than changing our ways of thinking instead.

More than forty years have passed since the *White Album* was released. Two of the Beatles have died. Meanwhile, the political revolution they worried about in Europe and North America has long since disappeared. But constitutions and institutions have not. The EU has made two attempts to draft a constitution during this decade.

In 2004, after two years of difficult negotiations, the leaders of the twenty-five members of the EU reached an

Conflict and Democratization
in the European Union

It says something about the EU, in comparison with the countries covered in Part 2, that we can treat the topics of conflict and democratization in the EU so quickly.

Thus far, the EU has been of interest primarily to elites. As a result, it kindles surprisingly little interest—and hence conflict—among its citizens. This may change as the EU becomes an inescapable part of everyone's life. Furthermore, any further deepening of the EU's powers likely will require greater involvement and more active support from rank and file voters.

It is entirely possible that the perceived lack of democracy will generate more public protests in the not so distant future like those we saw in Greece in 2010 and 2011. As the EU's powers expand, as it has to cope with the political and economic differences between its old members and the new ones, and as it tries to figure out how to create a multispeed Europe, more intense conflict between citizens and elites could emerge. ■

agreement on a draft constitution 🖳 (european-convention. eu.int). It would replace a number of treaties and other agreements the member states had reached since 1957. The more than five-hundred-page document would not have dramatically altered how the EU went about its work. What mattered most is that the leaders were using the term *consti-tution* rather than *treaty* to describe it. In the past, major steps forward for the EU had taken the form of treaties, which are agreements entered into by sovereign states which they can legally pull out of. At least symbolically, referring to a consti-tution suggested that the EU would be taking on more of the attributes of a state itself, another point we will return to later.

The member countries all had to ratify the draft. In countries such as Germany, where the parliament could cast the deciding vote, ratification came easily. That was not always the case; some governments decided they had to hold a referendum. In France and the Netherlands, the proposed constitution was defeated decisively. The same would have happened in Britain had its referendum ever occurred.

The constitution was dead.

In 2007, the member states agreed on a second attempt at institutional renewal at their summit on the wind-swept Baltic coast that June. That December, the **Treaty of Lisbon** was approved by all the member states.

It is less sweeping than a constitution. Pointedly, it is another treaty. Delicate balances were struck between big and small states, old and new members. It does keep most of the provisions of the 2004 draft, but it was easier to sell to parliaments and voters precisely because it is not labeled a constitution. Even so, the summiteers almost failed to reach an agreement, most notably when Poland insisted on main-taining voting power close to that of Germany, which is almost twice its size. It authorized a president and a foreign minister for the EU and changed the way qualified major-ity voting works. But like the constitution, the treaty would change things on the margins.

Today, it seems as if the two new offices, president of the EU and foreign minister, will be the most significant in the short term. Both of them are beginning to take root. Thus, in 2011, when the EU decided to impose tougher sanctions than the rest of the western world against Libya, in 2011, the key actor was the foreign minister, Baroness Catherine Ashton.

Despite these problems regarding governance, the EU is stable and demonstrating remarkable stability for an institution that has had to invent itself largely from scratch over the last half century. As we are about to see, the four main institutions of the European "state" have a lot in com-mon with those created for the Coal and Steel Community.

The Commission

The most "European" institution is the Commission. The word *European* is emphasized here because the Commission has been the most important body in sustaining and expanding the EU's authority. The responsibility for actually making the most important decisions lies elsewhere, but the Commission initiates most new programs and is responsible for imple-menting them once they are enacted.

Until 2004, the Commission had twenty members who served renewable five-year terms. Britain, France, Germany, Italy, and Spain each had two commissioners. Traditionally, one of them was named by the governing party or coalition, and the other by the opposition. The other ten countries had one commissioner each.

With the 2004 expansion, the Commission was expanded to twenty-five members, one from each country. With the Lisbon Treaty, the commission was reduced back to 20 members, with states nominating members on a rotat-ing basis, plus the president, vice president, and foreign minister (see Table 7.3). Commissioners are nominated by their home governments and are approved by a qualified majority vote in the Council.

On appointment to the Commission, members swear an oath of allegiance to the EU and are not supposed to take instructions from their national government. Most commissioners are prominent politicians in their home countries, and their independence from leaders there is often questioned. For example, the French commissioner in 2010, Michel Barnier, joined the Commission after a long and distinguished career in the Gaullist party and its affiliates.

The Commission is the permanent executive of the EU. It supervises the work of the twenty-two directorates general and eight services, which roughly correspond with the purview of a traditional national cabinet (see Table 7.4). Each directorate is managed by a commissioner, who is, in turn, aided by a senior European civil servant and a small personal staff.

The Commission also supervises the work of about 2,500 high-ranking civil servants and another twenty thousand staff members. Some of these men and women are on loan from their national governments, but the

TABLE 7.3 Presidents of the European Commission

START OF TERM	NAME
1958	Walter Hallstein
1967	Jean Rey
1970	Franco-Maria Malfatti
1972	Sicco Mansholt
1973	Francois-Xavier Ortoli
1977	Roy Jenkins
1981	Gaston Thorn
1985	Jacques Delors
1995	Jacques Santer
2000	Romano Prodi
2004	Jose Manuel Barroso

TABLE 7.4 Directorates-General and Services of the European Union as of 2011

Directorates-General
Agriculture and Rural Development
Budget
Climate Action
Economic and Financial Affairs
Education and Culture
Employment, Social Affairs and Inclusion
Energy
Enterprise and Industry
Environment
Health and Consumers
Home Affairs
Information, Society and Media
Internal Market and Services
Justice
Maritime Affairs and Fisheries
Mobility and Transport
Regional Policy
Research and Innovation
Other Offices
Central Library
Communication
Enlargement
Europe Aid, Development and Cooperation
European Anti-Fraud Office
Eurostat
Foreign Policy Instruments Service
Historical Archives
Humanitarian Aid
Joint Research Centre
Publications Office
Secretariat General
Trade

power to become the driving force behind initiatives that strengthened the EU's authority.

The Commission may look like a national cabinet, but we should not push that analogy too far. In particular, because its members are chosen by twenty-seven quite different governments, there is far more diversity and disagreement than we would expect in a national executive.

The Commission inevitably reflects the personality, style, and preferences of its president. Under Delors, the Commission assembled a staff of dynamic young civil servants who helped push through his agenda, often against the wishes of reluctant fellow commissioners, let alone national governments.

Perhaps in response to Delors' impact, the governments of the member states (especially Great Britain) were reluctant to choose a successor who would be anywhere near as prominent or dynamic. Neither of his first two successors, Santer and Prodi, had that kind of dramatic impact, and it is hard to tell if the current president of the Commission, **Jose Manuel Barroso** will be able to restore its prominence while it navigates the transitions brought on by the Treaty of Lisbon (**ue.eu.int**).

The Council of Ministers

If the Commission represents the supranational side of the EU, the Council of Ministers demonstrates the continued power of the states. The Council now consists of two institutions. The presidency of each rotates from country to country every six months. That government's representative chairs each Council meeting, represents the EU at diplomatic functions, and makes all of its public pronouncements.

With the Treaty of Lisbon, the presidency is officially assumed by a troika (from the Russian word for three) of countries serving eighteen months each, with one leaving every six months. It is hoped that this arrangement and the appointment of a more or less independent president and foreign minister will give more continuity to the presidency. That said, the EU has a lot still to work out, including how the president of the commission and the president of the EU should interact.

The various ministers and other representatives of the national governments meet as needed to make policy decisions. The foreign ministers meet monthly as the General Affairs Council, as do the finance ministers in the Economic and Financial Council (Ecofin). For other meetings, each government designates one of its members to attend, determined by the issue on the agenda. For instance, when the Council dealt with the mad cow disease crisis in the second half of the 1990s, the governments sent their agriculture ministers.

In addition, the national chief executives meet every six months as the European Council. Sometimes these meetings are little more than an opportunity for general

overwhelming majority are permanent EU employees on career tracks reminiscent of the French ENArques and the German *Beamten*.

The Commission is also important in the policy-making process. On a day-to-day basis, its primary job is to make rules that spell out the details of European policy, as in the more than three hundred documents it had to write to put the SEA into effect. Commission drafts immediately have the force of law in some minor and technical policy areas. Otherwise, its drafts have to be approved by the Council and the Parliament. The Commission's most important job is the initiation of proposed legislation, called directives. The Treaty of Rome and later agreements gave it the exclusive right to put new policy proposals on the EU's agenda. Although agenda setting is by no means the same as the ability to pass legislation, the Commission has used this

Jose Manuel Barroso

discussions. However, they are becoming the forum at which major new initiatives and reforms to the treaties that gave rise to the EU and its institutions are adopted.

Although the Commission initiates most EU legislation, its proposals only become law after they have been passed by the Council. Since passage of the SEA, the Council has to share most of its decision-making power with the Parliament and Commission (see Figure 7.1) and can override parliamentary objections only if it acts unanimously.

As we also saw earlier, the unanimity principle that often paralyzed the EEC early in its history has been eliminated except for the most dramatic new initiatives, including the admission of new members. Otherwise, the Council uses qualified majority voting. Each country is assigned a number of votes in rough proportion to its share of the EU population, which it casts as a bloc (see Table 7.5).

According to the Treaty of Nice, for most directives 255 of 345 votes were needed, and to create a qualified majority those had to come from countries with at least 62 percent of the European population. Therefore, 91 votes were enough to block new initiatives. The system tends to overrepresent the smaller countries to keep large states from dominating, but it is difficult to pass legislation without the support of two or three of the big countries.

This cumbersome system was one of the obstacles to the adoption of the constitution. The Treaty of Lisbon defines a majority vote in a slightly different way. Beginning in 2014, a qualified majority will consist of votes from countries encompassing 55 percent of the population if the directive is proposed by the Commission. It rises to 65 percent for actions not initiated by the Commission. And, from 2014 to 2017, countries can insist on using the procedures in the Treaty of Lisbon. In fact, neither of these changes will make much of a difference. In practice, the full European Council rarely votes, but operates by consensus instead.

The European Court of Justice

The EU has a powerful Court of Justice (ECJ). A Court of First Instance hears cases in much the way a superior court in the United States or a Crown court in the United Kingdom does. There is also a Court of Auditors that deals with the EU's finances. In addition, the Amsterdam and Nice treaties have provisions for the creation of specialized courts to deal with highly technical issues in narrow subject areas *(curia. europa.eu/jcms/jcms/Jo2_7024/)*. However, we can restrict our attention to the ECJ. Its decisions have frequently made major expansion of the EU's authority possible. Even more important, its actions have limited national sovereignty in favor of the EU's institutions. As such, it has more sweeping powers than the judiciaries in all but a handful of the world's states.

Each government appoints one member to the ECJ. The court rarely meets with all of its judges presiding. Instead, it sits in smaller "chambers" for all but the most important cases. It also has nine advocates-general who aid it in its work. No votes or dissenting opinions are published.

The ECJ hears over four hundred cases in a typical year. The Council, Commission, and Parliament can challenge

FIGURE 7.1 Decision Making in the European

European Court of Justice (jurisdiction)

Private companies

Commission proposes

if amended

National governments appoint

Parliament approves or amends

People elect

Council of Ministers

Decisions

© Cengage Learning 2013

TABLE 7.5 Size and Voting Power in the European Union: Prior to Treaty of Lisbon

COUNTRY	POPULATION IN MILLIONS	SEATS IN EUROPEAN PARLIAMENT	VOTES IN QUALIFIED MAJORITY VOTING
Germany	82.0	99	29
United Kingdom	59.4	78	29
France	59.1	78	29
Italy	57.7	7	29
Spain	39.4	54	27
Poland	38.6	54	27
Romania	21.7	35	14
Netherlands	15.8	27	13
Greece	10.6	24	12
Czech Republic	10.3	24	12
Belgium	10.2	22	12
Hungary	10.0	22	12
Portugal	9.9	22	12
Sweden	8.9	19	10
Austria	8.1	18	10
Bulgaria	7.7	18	10
Slovakia	5.4	14	7
Denmark	5.4	14	7
Finland	5.2	14	7
Ireland	3.7	13	7
Lithuania	3.7	13	7
Latvia	2.4	9	4
Slovenia	2.0	7	4
Estonia	1.4	7	4
Cyprus	0.8	6	4
Luxembourg	0.4	6	4
Malta	0.4	5	3

each other's actions. Member states can contest EU laws and regulations. Individuals and firms can sue the EU. However, states can bring cases against each other only if the claimant can show it had been directly harmed. Over the years, the court has overturned actions by all the EU institutions, all member states, and hundreds of private companies and individuals.

Early on, the ECJ decided that it practiced constitutional law, which meant that its decisions would have more clout than those of traditional international tribunals, which lack the power of judicial review. This authority is based on the court's assertion that, in ratifying the Treaty of Rome and subsequent accords, the states relinquished some of their sovereignty. The court has consistently held that European law passed by the Council and regulations issued by the Commission take precedence over national law. In other words, when the two conflict, EU law is normally upheld and enforced.

Among the most important of the court's decisions, oddly, was the Cassis de Dijon case of 1979 that opened the legal door to both the SEA and Maastricht. Cassis is a liqueur that, when combined with white wine, makes the smooth, sweet, and potent drink known as kir. It is only made near the city of Dijon, France. A German firm wanted to import cassis, but the national government banned it on the grounds that it contained too little alcohol to qualify as a liqueur but too much to be considered a wine under German law. The court found for the importer, ruling that if cassis met French standards for a liqueur it should qualify under Germany's as well and that bans based on such arbitrary differences constituted an illegal barrier to trade. The court thereby introduced the idea of "mutual recognition," which holds that, except under the most unusual of circumstances, member states must recognize the standards used by other countries. This meant that the Commission could avoid the hugely cumbersome task of harmonizing standards across national lines and simply assert that if one national government ruled that a good or service met its standards, it had to be accepted by all of them.

Another ruling with broad (if less political) ramifications came in 1995. Jean-Marc Bosman, a mediocre Belgian soccer player whose contract was expiring, wanted to move to a new team in France, much like a free agent in American sports. However, his old team and the Belgian football authorities denied him the right to do so. Bosman took his case to the ECJ, arguing that what the Europeans call transfer restrictions violated the provisions of the Maastricht Treaty regarding the free movement of labor within the EU.

The court ruled in Bosman's favor and, in one fell swoop, threw out not only the rules restricting the freedom of players to move, but also others limiting the number of foreigners who could play for a team at any one time. The wealthiest teams in England, Spain, Italy, and Germany immediately went on spending sprees, signing up players from around the EU and beyond. The impact of the decision was obvious to anyone who watched London's Chelsea play Rome's Atalanta in the 2000–2001 Champions League. Not a single player on Chelsea's starting team was born or raised in the United Kingdom; in fact, Chelsea had more Italian players (four) than did Atalanta!

The European Parliament

One reason that scholars and politicians worry about the democratic deficit is that the European Parliament is by far the weakest institution in the EU. As we saw previously, the ECSC had a Common Assembly, which was renamed the European Parliament with the formation of the EEC (www.europarl.europa.eu). Part of its weakness lies in its original composition. Until 1979, members of Parliament, or MEPs, were chosen by national governments. Thus, they tended to act as emissaries of their states, docilely voting as the leadership back home wanted.

Since then, the MEPs have been directly elected, and the powers of the Parliament have grown. The SEA also gave the Parliament more influence by creating a cooperation procedure—now known as **codecision**—for most legislation. It obliges the Council and Commission to consult the Parliament in two stages. First, when the Commission proposes a new initiative, the Parliament must give its opinion on it. If the Council agrees with the Parliament, the proposed directive is adopted. If not, the Parliament must be consulted again, at which point one of three things can occur:

■ If the Parliament agrees or takes no action within three months, the Council's bill is adopted.

■ If the Parliament proposes amendments, they must be considered by the Commission within a month.

■ If the Parliament rejects the Council's position outright, the Council can only adopt the initiative if it votes to do so unanimously.

The architects of the SEA and the Maastricht Treaty understood that the powers of the Parliament would have to be increased if the EU were to achieve widespread legitimacy. Thus, the Parliament now has the right to approve all nominees to the Commission and can remove the entire Commission if a vote of censure passes by a two-thirds margin. The Parliament also has to approve the budget.

As it did for the Council, the Treaty of Nice makes provisions for changes in the size of Parliament and spells out the number of seats each country will have. The size of the body rose to 785 seats in 2007 but will have "only" 736 after the 2009 election. Under the Treaty of Lisbon, the number could grow a bit, at least for a while.

The European Central Bank

The Maastricht Treaty created the **European Central Bank (ECB)** that replaced its national equivalents in the countries that adopted the euro. It was modeled heavily on the German *Bundesbank* that saw its job as primarily restraining inflation. Over the long term, the ECB could prove to be the most powerful European body the various treaties and directives have created since 1957 (**www.ecb.int/ecb/html/index.en.html**).

Its website defines the bank's role as follows: "The ECB's main task is to maintain the euro's purchasing power and thus price stability in the euro area." Among other things, that means it has responsibility for monitoring and setting interest rates, coordinating policies with the EU's remaining national banks, maintaining stable exchange rates, and issuing euros. It is run by a six-member governing board and representatives of the now largely powerless national banks in the eurozone. Like the Commission, its leaders are not allowed to be lobbied by their national governments. So far, that transparency seems to have worked well.

The bank is located in Frankfurt-am-Main, *de facto* giving the EU a fourth capital. Frankfurt was chosen because it was and is home to the German *Bundesbank*.

The ECB has asserted itself in the crisis affecting Greece, Italy, and Portugal that begins this chapter. Along with the IMF, it has been the most important issuer of credit and purchaser of bonds issued by these three countries.

The ECB is possible only because the EU has access to their "own resources" mentioned above. The system has changed over the years, but, by law, the EU gets a share of the tariffs charged for goods imported from outside the EU, the value added tax (more or less the equivalent of an American sales tax), and more. Unlike most other international organizations, the EU is not dependent on voluntary contributions from its members, something Americans saw in the 1980s and 1990s when the refusal by the United States to pay its dues all but hamstrung the UN.

The Complexity of European Union Decision Making

Policy making in the EU is more complex and confusing than in any of the individual countries we have considered so far for two main reasons. First, the EU has to reconcile the interests of its member states with those that transcend national boundaries. Second, the various EU institutions are even more fragmented and independent of each other than those in the United States, where the separation and division of power makes coherent decision making difficult.

The EU's growth in power has occurred when the interests of the major nations and its own institutions coincide as they did in the months leading up to the signing of the Maastricht Treaty. When those interests diverge—as has often been the case since Maastricht—it becomes more difficult for further European integration to proceed.

This complexity is also a reflection of the fact that the EU is still being built, which makes it quite different from the national states covered in the rest of Part 2. In some areas (e.g., trade), European institutions and practices are well developed; in others (e.g., defense and social policy), they are not.

Next Steps?

Turkey is the most important country with a membership application pending. However, the current signs are that it will not be admitted soon. Most objections center on Turkey's human rights record, especially regarding its Kurdish minority, and the fact that most of its territory lies in Asia. Although few people mention it publicly, the fact that Turkey is a predominantly Muslim country currently

The Eurotower headquarters of the European Central Bank and surrounding banks of the financial district on the Main River in Frankfurt, Germany.

© Oliver Hoffmann/Shutterstock.com

governed by a pro-Islamic party has not helped its case. Other countries in Eastern Europe seem even further away from joining.

Further deepening will be even more problematic given the recent constitutional difficulties and the economic crisis. There undoubtedly will be some tinkering to strengthen the internal market and perhaps reduce the Schengen provisions because of heightened immigration and asylum requests from, for instance, Libya. There is even talk of yet another treaty. But whatever happens, the changes will almost certainly be on the margins.

However, the next truly important step in building what could potentially be a "United States of Europe" would be the commitment to a common foreign and security policy—the third pillar of the post-Maastricht EU. As noted at the beginning of the chapter, the EU is committed to that on paper. However, establishing it has not been easy, to say the least.

Some progress has been made. The EU has created a rapid deployment force that could intervene in humanitarian disasters such as those that devastated the former Yugoslavia in the 1990s. It has also made great strides in determining how it can coordinate its activities with NATO, the Organization for Security and Co-Operation in Europe (OSCE), and other bodies whose membership overlaps with, but is not the same as, the EU's.

However, as the debates within Europe over the war in Iraq showed, the European states view their national interests differently. Most notably, France and Germany opposed the U.S. declaration of war on Iraq. The United Kingdom, Italy, and Spain supported the George W. Bush administration, though Spain pulled out after a socialist victory at the polls following the March 11, 2004 terrorist attack there. In other words, in areas such as foreign policy, where deepening has not progressed as far as it has with the economy, national governments and their desires are likely to trump communitywide ones for decades to come.

The European Union and National Sovereignty

In a comparative politics course, the most important question to ask about the EU is whether it could supplant the state as the primary actor determining public policy and governance in general in Europe. Here, too, the answer is ambiguous.

It is tempting to follow the lead of most international relations experts and argue that the EU has not replaced national sovereignty. This certainly is true if we focus on questions of national security and identity that have long been at the heart of that branch of political science. However, if we focus instead on economic or social policy, the EU seems a lot more powerful. In those areas, its powers certainly limit the freedom of member states to make and enforce their own policies whether or not analysts explicitly mention the declining sovereignty of the 27 member states.

The study of the EU can become quite complex and exploring its powers in many areas requires mastering a welter of acronyms and technical detail. To avoid that and yet still see the main point, consider two policy areas dealing with food. These issues may not seem all that important, but they do reveal the kinds of day-to-day power the EU can exercise over its members.

The first involves chocolate. As part of its goal of creating a single market, the EU devised common standards for thousands of goods and services. In 1973 it therefore issued Directive 73-241 on the "harmonization" of chocolate recipes. As one British observer put it:

> This directive was drawn up in the early, heady days of European integration, when European leaders believed that all products must be harmonized in every member state if the single market was to operate properly. All food had to be made to the same specification. Drawing up a European chocolate recipe meant agreeing on rules on such ingredients as vegetable and cocoa fat. Directive 73-241 declared that chocolate shall be: "the product obtained from cocoa nib, cocoa mass, cocoa powder and sucrose, with or without added cocoa butter, having, without prejudice to the definition of chocolate vermicelli, gianduja nut chocolate and converture chocolate, a minimum total dry cocoa solids content of 35 percent—at least 34 percent of nonfat cocoa solids and 18 percent of cocoa butter— these weights to be calculated after the weight of the additions provided for in paragraph five and six have been deducted.[1]

Chocolate became a problem because candy manufacturers in Britain and a few other countries did not meet those standards because British consumers liked their chocolate with less cocoa nib. After a brief tiff, the European bureaucrats allowed the British to "opt out" of these requirements, and there was something of a two-tiered chocolate market for the next twenty years.

In the mid-1990s, the chocolate controversy reared its ugly head once again. French and Belgian chocolatiers claimed that inferior and cheaper British candy was undermining their markets. They threatened to go to the ECJ and demand a ruling forcing the British companies to use the term *vegolate* instead. The court put an end to the case by invoking the mutual recognition principle, to allow the British to continue selling their products as chocolate.

[1]Sarah Helm, "The Woman from Mars," *Prospect (UK)*, March 1996, 21.

Second, in one of its most controversial moves, the EU banned the export of British beef in 1996. Over the previous decade, thousands of British cattle had come down with BSE, known to most people by its nickname— mad cow disease. In March 1996, the British government published research findings that linked BSE with Creutzfeld-Jakob disease (CJD), which is fatal to humans. The announcement touched off a furor on both sides of the English Channel. Within days the Council voted to ban the sale of British beef, first in the other fourteen EU countries, and that also meant a ban on British exports to the rest of the world. The British government was furious because no more than fifteen people had actually come down with CJD. Moreover, British agriculture minister Quentin Hogg (the pundits had great fun with his name) tried to devise a plan to slaughter up to a million cows in an attempt to eradicate the disease and the political and public reaction to it. That was not enough for the EU which insisted on a total "cull" of the herd before allowing British beef back onto the market.

Negotiations dragged on into 1999, even though there was virtually no chance that anyone could actually contract CJD. Nonetheless, politicians on the European continent, leery of public opinion at home, kept the ban in place. Finally, when the cull of the herds had been completed so that no cow born before 1996 could enter the food chain, the Commission lifted the ban later that year.

PUBLIC POLICY IN THE EUROPEAN UNION

The EU has adopted a wide range of policies, from supporting research on high technology to sponsoring student exchanges. Here, we will focus on the two that illustrate what the EU has done above and beyond the debate over chocolate or beef: the creation of an integrated internal market and the CAP. The two also highlight what are seen by most observers as the EU's greatest accomplishment and its greatest failure.

The Internal Market

The EU's most significant achievement has been the creation of what is, for all intents and purposes, a single internal market. Economics has always been a top priority for the EU because its architects assumed that economic cooperation would be the lynchpin to all their other policy goals.

The most important policy and strategy for creating the single market has been the removal of tariffs and other barriers to trade. The Treaty of Rome began a decade-long process of eliminating of all internal tariffs. The SEA did the same for the remaining obstacles to the free movement of goods and services.

Most of those barriers were technical in nature but were also very easy for the average consumer to see. Truckers, for example, could spend hours filling out paperwork or having their cargoes inspected before they were allowed to enter another country. Although it may be hard to believe, such administrative rules and regulations added as much as 10 percent to the cost of transporting goods across national borders.

Similarly, each country imposed its own standards concerning the quality of goods sold in its market, which, despite the elimination of all tariffs, frequently blocked imports from other EU countries. The same held for professional licenses, which meant that doctors, lawyers, beauticians, and so on could only work in the country in which they were trained. National governments erected barriers to free trade by following procurement policies that gave an edge to domestic firms whose sales accounted for nearly 10 percent of the EU's total production of goods and services.

The SEA was designed to resolve issues that arose because countries used widely differing standards on things far more important than soccer players or chocolate. It eliminated internal border checks, although this practice has not been fully implemented because of a few countries' fears regarding immigration and drug trafficking. Today, most goods that meet the standards of one country are assumed to meet the standards of all—as in the case of the chocolate/vegolate dispute. The same is now true for most professional licenses—though not for lawyers, reflecting the continued differences among national legal systems. Finally, financial institutions are free to invest and loan money throughout the EU.

The reasons for moving to a fully open internal market were laid out in a report the economist Paolo Cecchini prepared for the Commission in 1988. He predicted that removing the remaining barriers to trade would lead to increased private investment, higher productivity, lower costs, and reduced prices. European industry, in turn, would be more profitable, stimulating more growth, jobs, and government revenue.

In the short run, Europe fell short of those expectations. The recession of the early 1990s slowed growth everywhere. Cecchini could not have anticipated the political changes that would sweep Europe and divert billions of dollars from the EU and its member states eastward. Still, there seems to be little question that the removal of these barriers has had the kind of impact the framers of the SEA had in mind in the long term. This impact is evident in the explosion of transnational enterprises facilitated by the easing of these restrictions. The EU is not always a major actor in these endeavors, but the opening of the market itself has made the ones described here, and dozens of others, much easier to create or expand. For example, Airbus, which makes commercial jet airplanes, is a joint effort on the part of French, German, Spanish, and British companies and now is Boeing's only serious competitor. In the automobile industry, Fiat forged close links with Peugeot, and in 1999 Ford bought Volvo. In the last few years Daimler-Benz bought and abandoned Chrysler, only to be replaced by the rejuvenated Fiat. In 1985 the Commission established Eureka, a joint research and development program aimed at creating technologies to compete with Japanese and American firms in computers, telecommunications, and other high-tech areas.

The internationalization of European firms through the EU seems to have led them to be more aggressive globally as well. The most notable example is the tremendous increase in European investment in the United States. To cite but a few prominent examples, Renault bought Mack Trucks in 1990 and then sold it to Volvo in 2001, yet another European firm now owned by Ford. Michelin acquired Uniroyal Goodrich, making it the largest tire manufacturer in the world. Britain's Martin Sorrell purchased two of the largest advertising agencies in the United States, the Ogilvy Group and J. Walter Thompson, and public relations giant Hill and Knowlton.

For our purposes, though, the important thing to understand about the policies creating the single market is that they have had a tremendous impact on both European governments and their citizens. States now have far less control over what is made and sold within their borders. Of course, policy differences remain from country to country.

Economic Liberalization
in the European Union

The EU has long been a champion of liberal economic policies. It has never had to deal with privatization directly because it has never owned any businesses. Moreover, it has rarely urged member states to sell off the ones they own.

That said, it has regularly pushed for more open and competitive economies, which, of course, is in the very definition of a common market. Throughout its history, it has pursued antimonopoly policies that would be familiar to Americans who have studied their country's antitrust laws. In recent years, it has required states to cut subsidies to their companies, especially state-owned monopolies such as national airlines and telecommunications systems. ■

Britain, for example, still imposes higher taxes on liquor than France and has strict rules regarding the import of pets into the country. Such examples aside, governments have ceded much of their control over microeconomic policy.

The single market has expanded the options available to consumers. German supermarket shoppers can now purchase French wine, Italian pasta, and Spanish oranges more cheaply than before the trade barriers came down. French consumers find that Rovers, Fiats, or Volkswagens are now as affordable as Renaults, Citroëns, or Peugeots.

Monetary union proved to be the key to the further integration of the European economy. From the Treaty of Rome on, the most visionary European leaders looked to monetary union as the next big step toward a more integrated Europe. To see why, think about what the United States would be like if the states had their own currencies. It would be all but impossible for the federal government to coordinate economic policy, and it would be costly and complicated for companies to do business across state lines.

Monetary union, however, was a long time coming. The first significant steps were taken in 1979 with the creation of the European Monetary System (EMS), which had two broad features. First, it created the European Currency Unit (ECU), which was used in international business transactions. The ECU existed purely for accounting purposes and enabled companies to avoid paying commissions charged for converting funds from one currency to another. It also established the Exchange Rate Mechanism (ERM), whereby all the currencies floated together in global markets. No currency was allowed to move more than 5 percent above or below the ERM average. If a currency was heading in that direction, the national central banks would intervene in financial markets to bring it back into line.

The reforms did help. The ECU simplified business dealings and reduced the substantial costs that accompany frequent currency conversions. The ERM gave a degree of predictability to European financial markets so that, for example, Fiat in Italy could be reasonably certain how many francs or pesetas, as well as how many lire, it could get for its cars.

The creation of a single currency took another twenty years and is one of the reasons why the EU is the world's most successful international organization to date. It is by no means perfect. Not all of the eligible countries chose to join. Not all of the new members met the conditions that allowed them to join. But the fact is that the EU is the one and only international organization to have its own currency, which is a major symbol of national (or international) sovereignty.

Adoption of the euro has not been easy. National economic differences remain and were exacerbated by the great recession that began in 2008. As we saw at the start of the chapter, the richer countries have had to bail out the poorer ones in what many fear will be a never-ending transfer of funds. Consequently, anti-European sentiment grew in Germany and other creditor countries, as did resentment toward the EU in countries that received much of the aid and saw their ability to control their own economic future evaporate.

The key is not simply that many national currencies were replaced by the euro in 2002. Previously, governments determined their own fiscal and monetary policies, in particular, setting basic interest rates for lenders and savers. Now that power has been transferred almost entirely to European Central Bank, which sets a common interest rate for countries with economies as diverse as Germany's and Greece's.

So far, debate on the EMU has focused largely on whether it makes sense economically—an issue far beyond the scope of this chapter. Here, it is enough to see that it will have a tremendous impact on the balance of political power in at least two ways. First, it can strengthen the EU as a whole because the euro is already one of the world's three leading currencies along with the dollar and the yen. Second, it provides yet another area in which national governments are *de facto* ceding some of their sovereignty to a supranational body over which they have relatively little day-to-day control.

This is one of the many reasons why the euro is controversial and is seen by some observers as a "make it or break it" issue for the EU. Even before the crisis, many political leaders, especially in Britain, saw their local currency as an important symbol of national pride and abandoning it is seen as an unacceptable loss of national sovereignty. But just as important, now that the euro is in place, there may be no going back. Nothing in political life is irreversible, but it is difficult to imagine the initial members abandoning the euro and reintroducing their own currencies.

The single market has not benefited all Europeans. Increased competitive pressures have forced hundreds of inefficient firms into bankruptcy, leading to at least temporary unemployment for their workers. Nonetheless, there is little doubt that the EU has made a considerable contribution to economic growth since 1957. Among other things, a 1999 Commission report suggested that the single market was responsible for creating as many as nine hundred thousand jobs, adding as much as 1.5 percent to per-capita income, reducing inflation by a similar amount, and increasing trade in goods and direct foreign investment in the EU by about 15 percent each. Its contribution may be even more important in some less visible policy arenas, as we saw in the discussion of the Bosman ruling.

Chip was fortunate enough to live and teach in England from 1995 to 1998. Because of the EU, he was able to have any major European newspaper delivered to his door each morning. According to the owner of the corner store that

Globalization
and the European Union

The EU is one of the best vehicles we have for illustrating the impact of globalization and regionalization.

It is, of course, a major architect of both. Critics have properly pointed out that European economies and cultures would have opened up to some degree without the EU. There can be little doubt, however, that it has sped up the flow of people, information, goods, and money within its borders and has generally been a major advocate for liberalizing trade as well.

It also demonstrates that even the strongest powers are vulnerable to global pressures. ▪

delivered the papers, citizens of fourteen of the then fifteen member states were living in that village of less than three thousand residents. Because EU students pay the equivalent of in-state tuition anywhere in the EU, he had students from France, Greece, Spain, Finland, Denmark, Germany, Portugal, Ireland, Italy, and Belgium, as well as the United Kingdom, which made teaching highly enjoyable.

The Common Agricultural Policy

Not everything the EU has done has been successful. The Common Agricultural Policy (CAP), in particular, is now the subject of virtually universal criticism. *The Economist* went so far as to call it the "single most idiotic system of economic mismanagement that the rich western countries have ever devised."[2]

The CAP reflects two important political dynamics. First, it demonstrates how pressure put on member states can lead to policies that tend to impede progress toward a more united Europe. Second, we will see that some of the more recent reforms to the CAP have been forced on the EU by the Global Agreement on Trade and Tariffs (GATT) and its successor, the World Trade Organization (WTO).

But that does not mean that the CAP never made any sense. In the 1950s, there were about 15 million farmers in the six original common market members. Although

their numbers were declining rapidly, farmers were still a major political force, especially in France, where they lobbied persuasively to keep small, inefficient family farms alive. Meanwhile, countries with small agricultural populations needed to import food and wanted to keep prices as low as possible. Thus, agriculture was a divisive issue from the beginning and almost destroyed the EEC in the early 1960s. The members finally reached a compromise in 1966 and created the CAP and its two main components. First, it took steps to modernize inefficient farms so that they could be more competitive in the European market. Second, to ease the fears of farmers whose livelihood was threatened, the EC established the European Agricultural Guidance and Guarantee Fund (EAGGF), which gave them subsidies and guaranteed the purchase of surplus goods at artificially high prices.

Over the years, the modernizing side of the CAP went by the wayside. Payments to farmers consumed more than half of the EC budget. By the early 1970s, food prices in Europe were two to four times higher than they would have been had they been determined by market forces. In 1991 alone, the EC purchased 25 million tons of surplus cereal grains, eight hundred thousand tons of butter, and seven hundred thousand tons of other dairy products. Pundits joked about its butter mountains and wine lakes.

The CAP was also a major stumbling block in the Uruguay round of the GATT negotiations, which led to the creation of the WTO. American objections to the EAGGF payments almost led to a trade war between the United States and Europe in 1992 even though the United States still heavily subsidized its own farmers. In the end, the EU and the other parties reached a compromise in which the EU agreed to scale back subsidies and guaranteed payments by about a third. Nonetheless, the continued political clout of farmers' groups kept the CAP alive, leaving Europe with an extremely inefficient agricultural sector and burdening the EU's budget in the process, about 45 percent of which goes to the CAP.

As always, the CAP remains controversial. The Commission opened a debate in 2010 about its future but is not likely to reach a conclusion for a few years. It may well end subsidies to individual farmers, who get $500 million a year and, thus, oppose any change. Other reformers take a very modern stance and want to see reform to the CAP become part of a broader plan to make EU policy in general more "green."

THE MEDIA

The media in the EU illustrate the importance of things that do not happen in political life. Put simply, there is very little feedback because of the way the EU is structured and the way people participate (or do not, as the case may be) in it.

---

[2]Cited in Helen Wallace and William Wallace, eds., *Policy Making in the European Union*, 4th ed. (Oxford: Oxford University Press, 2000), 182.

How can that be for something that is this important to almost every European? It's simple. Coverage of the EU in the press is spotty and, as in most areas of political life, concentrates on its problems, not its accomplishments. There is, for instance, a mere handful of English-language newspapers that concentrate on the EU. The largest and best of them is the *European Voice,* which has about 18,000 subscribers, half of whom work for the EU. It struggles to survive. Coverage in national newspapers and television takes second place to almost everything else, such as in the British tabloid press.

When people are drawn to events in the EU, they tend to focus on the often demagogic claims about "faceless bureaucrats" in Brussels stealing their power. By contrast, as also noted previously, very few people think of themselves primarily as Europeans, even though the number of people living, working, and even marrying across national borders is growing rapidly.

This lack of media attention overlaps with the notion of the democratic deficit. Critics properly point out that the size of the EU as well as the fact that the European Parliament has relatively few—and weak—mechanisms for enforcing accountability make it difficult for average people to have much of an impact on decision making within it. In other words, the perceived lack of political clout magnifies the sense of distance and disinterest evident in most polls.

Looking FORWARD

IN THIS CHAPTER, the looking forward box has more to do with the rest of your lives than it does with the rest of this book. A number of other international organizations will be mentioned in Parts 4 and 5. However, none of them will challenge the EU as an emerging state in our professional lifetimes.

That might not be true of yours.

Think about the African Union, the Organization of American States, or ASEAN and think about what it would take for such organizations to acquire the influence that the EU has.

Key Terms

Concepts	Acronyms	Organizations, Places, and Events	
broadening	CAP	Committee of Permanent Representatives (COREPER)	European Economic Community (EEC)
codecision	CFSP	Common Agricultural Policy (CAP)	European Monetary System (EMS)
deepening	COREPER	Common Foreign and Security Policy (CFSP)	European Monetary Union (EMU)
democratic deficit	EC	Common Market	European Parliament
multilevel governance	ECJ	Council of Ministers	European Union (EU)
qualified majority voting	ECSC	euro	Maastricht Treaty
subsidiarity	EEC	European Central Bank (ECB)	Marshall Plan
supranational	EMS	European Coal and Steel Community (ECSC)	Single European Act (SEA)
three pillars	EMU	European Community (EC)	Treaty of Amsterdam
unanimity principle	EU	European Court of Justice (ECJ)	Treaty of Lisbon
People	SEA		Treaty of Nice
Barroso, Jose Manuel	**Organizations, Places, and Events**		Treaty of Rome
Delors, Jacques	Commission		
Monnet, Jean			
Spaak, Paul-Henri			

Useful Websites

The EU's website is an excellent portal to everything the Union does, and the information is available in more than twenty languages.

www.europa.eu

Many of the academic centers that focus on the EU have websites with good collections of links to other online EU material. Among the best are the European Union Studies Association and the libraries at the University of California-Berkeley, the University of Pittsburgh, and the New York University Law School.

www.eustudies.org

www.lib.berkeley.edu

www.library.pitt.edu

www.law.nyu.edu/library

european-convention.eu.int

European Voice is the only weekly newspaper on the EU and is published by *The Economist*. Its website provides the most comprehensive, up-to-date information about things European.

www.european-voice.com

There are many "euroskeptic" websites that are highly critical of the deepening and broadening of the EU. The first site listed is the most comprehensive of them. The second has links to many other similar sites.

eurofaq.freeuk.com

www.euro-sceptic.org

Further Reading

Bellamy, Richard, and Alex Warleigh. *Citizenship and Governance in the European Union*. New York: Continuum, 2002. A theorist and EU specialist look at the overlap (or lack thereof) between the way the EU is run and how average citizens respond to it.

Checkel, Jeffrey, and Peter Katzenstein, eds. *European Identity*. New York: Cambridge University Press, 2009. A bit of a tough read for undergrads, but it explores why there has been both an expansion and a contraction in support for the EU.

Dinan, Desmond. *An Ever Closer Union: An Introduction to the European Community*, 2nd ed. Boulder, CO: Lynne Rienner, 1999. The most comprehensive survey of European integration and its impact up to and beyond Maastricht.

Moravschik, Andrew. *The Choice for Europe*. Ithaca, NY: Cornell University Press, 1999. The best overview of EU history through Maastricht.

Reid, T. R. *The United States of Europe*. New York: Penguin, 2005. An extensive overview of post-Maastricht events by a very thoughtful—and very funny—former journalist at the *Washington Post*.

Rosamond, Ben. *Theories of European Integration*. Basingstoke, UK: Palgrave, 2000. A look at the EU through the lens of various theories of integration and international relations.

Ross, George. *Jacques Delors and European Integration*. New York: Oxford University Press, 1995. An insider-like account of the workings of the Commission by one of the leading American experts on French politics, to whom Delors gave unprecedented access late in his presidency. Not the easiest read, but probably the most insightful book on the EU ever written.

Sbragia, Alberta M., ed. *Euro-Politics: Institutions and Policymaking in the "New" European Community*. Washington, D.C.: Brookings Institution, 1992. An anthology that includes articles on most of the critical issues facing the EU; especially strong on the causes and consequences of the Single European Act.

Schmitter, Philippe. *How to Democratize the European Union ... and Why Bother?* Boulder, CO: Rowman & Littlefield, 2000. A fairly abstract but powerful argument by one of the leading political scientists working on democratization.

The Crisis of Communism

© Carlos Caetano/Shutterstock.com

CHAPTER OUTLINE

8

Socialism cannot exist, no matter where, contrary to the will of the people.

GEORGI ARBATOV

Current and Former Communist Regimes

THE BASICS

Current and Former Communist Regimes

COUNTRY	POPULATION IN MILLIONS	GROSS DOMESTIC PRODUCT PER CAPITA IN PURCHASING POWER PARITY - 2007 (US$)	ECONOMIC GROWTH, 2003	POPULATION FROM MINORITY GROUPS (%)
Albania	4	4,500	7	5
Armenia	3	3,500	10	7
Azerbaijan	8	3,400	11	10
Belarus	10	6,100	7	19
Bosnia	4	6,100	4	52
Bulgaria	8	7,600	4	16
Cambodia	13	1,900	5	10
China	1,300	5,000	9	8
Croatia	5	10,600	4	10
Cuba	11	2,900	3	—
Republic Czech	10	15,700	3	19
Estonia	11	2,300	5	35
Georgia	5	2,500	6	30
Hungary	10	13,900	3	10
Kazakhstan	15	6,300	9	46
Korea (North)	23	1,300	1	0
Kyrgyzstan	5	1,600	7	35
Laos	6	1,700	5	32
Latvia	2	10,200	7	42
Lithuania	4	11,400	9	20
Macedonia (FYROM)	2	6,700	3	36
Moldova	4	1,800	6	35
Mongolia	3	1,800	5	5
Poland	39	11,100	4	3
Romania	22	7,000	5	10
Russia	144	8,900	7	18
Serbia and Montenegro	11	2,200	2	32
Slovakia	5	13,300	4	14
Slovenia	2	19,000	2	8
Tajikistan	7	1,000	7	35
Turkmenistan	5	5,800	23	15
Ukraine	48	5,400	9	22
Uzbekistan	26	1,700	3	20

Source: CIA World Factbook, (www.odci.gov). Accessed November, 29, 2004.

Looking BACKWARD

WE ARE ABOUT to radically shift intellectual gears.

In Part 2, we argued that stakes of politics were not that high. Of course, people in the countries we covered have heated debates over public policy issues and candidates for election. But their regimes are not in any danger of collapse.

That was not the case in the countries that are still or used to be communist. At that time, the best we can say is that people gave their regimes grudging support. But then as the regimes failed to continue providing social services, consumer goods, and adequate housing and education and when opportunities for public expression opened up, both the governments of the day and the regimes themselves disappeared throughout what we have come to call Eurasia and used be known as the Soviet bloc.

A few countries have been able to build new regimes that could become as solid as those in France or Germany. However, as the basic table shows, a little more than twenty years after the collapse of communism, most were in dire straits and lacked the kind of outside help that both France and Germany received.

CRISIS? WHICH CRISIS?

Germans are not normally known for their comedy films, and certainly not ones about politics. Yet, in 2003, Wolfgang Becker released *Good Bye, Lenin!* The film begins in 1989 just before the wave of demonstrations brought down the Berlin Wall and took East Germany's communist regime with it.

A young man, Alex, joins one of the protests and gets arrested. His mind was diverted just at the moment of an inevitable but avoidable police charge by his desire to meet a pretty girl who was a few rows behind him among the marchers. To make matters worse, his staunchly communist mother, Christine, sees him arrested as she walks by the site of the demonstration on her way to a party. Shocked by what her son is doing, she suffers a heart attack and slips into a coma. When she regains consciousness many months later, Germany has been unified under the leadership of Chancellor Helmut Kohl as part of the Federal Republic of Germany (West Germany). To complicate matters further, her doctor tells Alex that any serious shock could kill her, including news that East Germany (DDR) is no more. The young woman from the demonstration and Alex are now a couple, and she becomes his mother's main health care provider.

As a loyal and frightened son, Alex does everything humanly possible to convince his mother—who is confined to her apartment—that East Germany still exists. He has friends make fake television and radio broadcasts, including one that seems to show disgruntled residents of West Berlin crossing the wall to move to the East. Of course,

exactly the opposite had occurred. He madly shops for her beloved brand of pickles, which are no longer made because the company went out of business. He comes up with ingenious explanations for why his mother can hear what she thinks are illegal Western broadcasts through her poorly soundproofed walls. Christine eventually wanders out of the house and sees ads for BMWs and Coke. Alex convinces her that Coca-Cola is a communist invention and that ads for BMWs are there because so many Westerners have moved to the East to avoid crime and inequality.

Of course, *Good Bye, Lenin!* is based on a preposterous plot line. That said, there is substantial *ostologie,* or nostalgia, for aspects of life in East Germany and in the other former communist countries.

Few people have any desire to return to the repression of communist rule. Nonetheless, many people miss the security the **party state** provided, including low rents, guaranteed employment, and free health care. In the former East Germany, nearly 20 percent of the population is unemployed (including Alex, whose television repair business collapsed after unification). Life is particularly hard for older people on pensions, anyone on a fixed income, and people with little education and few job skills.

Yet, reformed communist parties now do well at the polls in almost all former communist countries and have even won elections in many of them. They do well because they speak effectively to so many of the "losers" in the transition from communist rule.

There are signs that significant progress is being made in some of them. Eight former communist countries joined the

European Union (EU) in 2004; two more did three years later. Many have also seemingly turned an economic corner and are recording rapid rates of growth that are beginning to be translated into improved standards of living. Many of those same governments also joined the North Atlantic Treaty Organization (NATO). There have been very few protests against the reformed systems, particularly in the countries that have seen democratic institutions take root the most.

For people like us who grew up during the Cold War, all of this is mind boggling. Not only was the end of the Cold War unexpected, it seemed to augur amazingly well for the future of world peace. We will return to last of those topics in Part 4. Now we will focus on why virtually every communist regime collapsed between 1989 and 1991 and what has replaced them.

In many places, conditions were far worse than in the former East Germany. Bloody wars have been fought in what used to be Yugoslavia and in a number of the former Soviet republics. Central Asia remained mired in poverty, and governments there are almost as authoritarian as the communist states they replaced. In fact, most of them are led by the same men and the families who ran them before the Union of Soviet Socialist Republics (USSR) collapsed.

In short, the current and former communist countries faced multiple social, economic, and political crises before the current recession began in 2008.

THINKING ABOUT THE CURRENT AND FORMER COMMUNIST REGIMES

The Big Picture

Writing about communism in the early twenty-first century is like trying to shoot at a rapidly moving, and even more rapidly shrinking, target. Not even thirty years ago, President Ronald Reagan used American fears of communism as a major campaign theme in his landslide victory over Walter Mondale. Barely seven years later, the Soviet Union—Reagan's "focus of evil in the world"—had collapsed.

Reagan could hardly be blamed for a lack of foresight. At the time, no serious observers predicted that the Soviet Union and its allies would abandon communism in a few short years.

After World War II, the Cold War between the industrialized democracies and the Soviet bloc dominated world politics. By the 1980s, however, it had become clear that the communist regimes were neither as strong nor as ruthless as the alarmists had argued in the 1950s and 1960s. Most of the Eastern European countries had been rocked by protest movements. Even the Soviet Union had loosened

some of its more repressive policies. Factional disputes had divided the Chinese Communist Party on several occasions. Nonetheless, virtually everyone assumed that the communist regimes would remain in power and that the Cold War would continue indefinitely.

Then, the impossible happened. The unraveling of the communist world began shortly after the selection of **Mikhail Gorbachev** as **general secretary** of the Communist Party of the Soviet Union (CPSU) in March 1985. Terms like *perestroika* and *glasnost* became almost as familiar to Americans as baseball and apple pie. New York department stores sold pieces of the Berlin Wall and shoddy Soviet consumer goods as the latest trendy fads.

"Gorbymania" was not to last, however. The reforms he introduced opened a political Pandora's box. By the end of 1989, every communist regime in Eastern Europe had disintegrated. Then, less than a year after being named *Time*'s "man of the decade," Gorbachev and his Soviet Union were gone.

The transition from communist rule has been anything but smooth. Each of the Eastern European and former Soviet states declared itself a democracy. But each found that creating a regime that bore more than a fleeting resemblance to those covered in Part 2 proved easier said than done. Meanwhile, they also had to accomplish something that had never been done anywhere before: shift from a centrally planned command economy to one dominated by private ownership in a reasonably free market at the same time.

The news is not all bleak, of course. The countries that have joined NATO and the EU have made major progress on both the political and economic fronts. Poland, Hungary, the Czech Republic, Slovakia, Slovenia, Lithuania, Latvia, and Estonia have all held at least three competitive elections and seen power shift from government to the opposition, indicators most political scientists take to be signs of a strengthening democracy. Similarly, those countries have all experienced a period of sustained growth after their economies bottomed out in the middle of the 1990s until the current crisis hit in 2008. Some former communist countries voted former communists back to power, prompting *The Economist* to run the accompanying cover cartoon.

China, North Korea, Cuba, and a few others remain nominally communist. With the exception of North Korea and Cuba, however, these countries did adopt sweeping economic reforms that outstripped anything Gorbachev anticipated when he spoke of *perestroika*. To be sure, the Communist Party remains securely in control in these countries, but their societies seemingly have little in common with the socialism Karl Marx and Friedrich Engels predicted a century and a half ago. For example, despite their supposed commitment to egalitarian policies, as well as Marx's opposition to the way women were treated under capitalism, communist regimes never saw fit to promote more than a handful of women to top leadership positions.

More and more analysts are also coming to the conclusion that it will be all but impossible for these countries to remain communist. Even if their regimes survive, they almost certainly will face growing pressure from below, as evidenced, for instance, by the upsurge of interest in the Falun Gong sect in China and the authorities' stern reaction to it.

Who Are We Talking About?

As with the liberal democracies, there is some ambiguity about which countries should be considered in Part 3. The criterion used here is simple. The thirty-three countries highlighted in the map at the beginning of this chapter were all part of one of the sixteen states that employed a **Marxist-Leninist** regime. The most important of them, by far, was the USSR or Soviet Union. The first communist regime came to power there as a result of the October revolution of 1917 and the civil war that followed. Only in Mongolia did a communist government come to and stay in power between the two world wars. After World War II, the Soviet Union imposed regimes that were all but carbon copies of its own on Poland, Czechoslovakia, Romania, Bulgaria, Hungary, and the eastern part of Germany. In the West, these countries became known as **satellites** of the Soviet Union. Communist regimes came to power on their own in Yugoslavia and Albania. None of these countries has a communist regime today.

Most of the others were in Asia, as are all but one of the remaining communist countries. The settlement that ended World War II divided Korea. The northern half became the communist-run Democratic People's Republic of Korea. The Chinese Communist Party won its civil war against the Nationalists in 1949, thus bringing the world's most populous country into the communist camp. Also after World War II, a communist insurgency broke out in the French colony of Indochina. After the French were defeated in 1954, Indochina was split into four independent countries: Laos, Cambodia, and North and South Vietnam. Of the four, only North Vietnam was communist at the time. Another two decades of fighting ensued, during which half a million American troops could not defeat the communists. By 1975, Marxists were in power in Laos, Cambodia, and a united Vietnam. Laos and Vietnam still had communist regimes as of this writing.

The last country on the list is Cuba. It was granted its independence after the Spanish-American War in 1898. For the next sixty years, the United States was for all intents and purposes in charge of a country whose government was officially in the hands of a series of weak and corrupt dictators. The last of them, Fulgencio Batista, was overthrown by revolutionaries led by **Fidel Castro** in 1959. Relations with the United States quickly deteriorated, and Cuba became a Soviet ally and adopted Marxism-Leninism in 1961.

Several other countries are sometimes included in lists of communist regimes, such as Nicaragua under the Sandinistas, North Yemen, Angola, and Mozambique. All had distinctly left-wing governments at one point or another. However, they are not included here because they never fully adopted Marxist-Leninist principles.

Key Concepts and Questions

We will explore how and why the crisis of communism occurred. For now, simply note that it did happen and that it forced these countries to all but completely change political course. In other words, the stakes of political life in the current and former communist countries are much higher than anything we saw in Part 2.

The Eurasian countries are in the midst of a social, political, and economic transition for which there is no real precedent. Their leaders are simultaneously trying to build a democratic state on the ashes of the old Leninist one, a market economy based on private ownership, and a new culture stressing such values as individualism and personal initiative, which have never been prominent features in their countries either before or during communist rule.

Any one of those challenges would be difficult enough. Together, they have proved all but impossible to overcome in more than a handful of countries. Almost all highly trained people more than fifty years old were educated and forged their careers under the communists, which leaves many of them politically and socially suspect. The collapse of the

Leninist state has unleashed new political forces. Millions of people are impatient with the pace of reform. Old ethnic and other antagonisms have been rekindled. And all of this happened without as much Western economic aid as many in these countries had expected.

The stakes are different, but no lower, in the countries that still cling to the Leninist model—and *cling* is probably the most telling verb to use in describing them. All are engaged in a high-risk political balancing act. All have acknowledged the need for economic reform. However, all have resisted political reform and have tried to retain unfettered communist party rule. As we will see in Chapter 10 on China, most political scientists do not think this state of affairs can continue indefinitely. Further, they believe that if these communist parties hold on to power they will have to adopt significant democratizing reforms as well.

Studying the current and former communist countries also requires us to shift intellectual gears. We will ask many of the same questions posed in Part 2 and add some new ones. In both cases, we will end up reaching very different conclusions:

- How are decisions made in these countries?
- What role do average citizens play in policy making?
- What are their public policies?
- How is political life affected by global forces?
- How could regimes that seemed so strong collapse so quickly?
- Why have some communist systems survived? What are the political implications of economic reform in countries that have kept communism and in those that have abandoned it?
- Why are they all facing much more serious domestic and global challenges than any of the countries covered in Part 2?
- How have the current economic crisis and the election of President Obama changed life in these countries?

We will focus on these questions more in the next two chapters.

Key Characteristics

The Leninist State

The first and most important characteristic these countries had in common was a form of leadership devised by **Vladimir Lenin** for the prerevolutionary Bolshevik Party in Russia. We will explore its characteristics in detail in this chapter and the next. Here, it is enough to note two things.

First, the communist party completely controlled political life. In a few countries, other parties were allowed to

exist, but they were nothing but pawns of the communists. The party dominated the government, the media, the economy, the educational system, and most social and leisure time activities. The parties were run according to the principle of **democratic centralism**. That meant that they were democratic in name only. Little debate was allowed, and the parties were in reality ruled by a tiny group of party officials at the top of the hierarchy.

Second, until the late 1950s, the Soviet Union controlled the entire communist world. New communist regimes not only adopted Marxism-Leninism but submitted to Moscow's leadership in determining how their countries were run.

In the late 1950s, however, the communist world began to splinter. The Chinese leaders came to oppose a Soviet Union they found too moderate and complacent. The two states became bitter enemies, and their troops occasionally fired at each other along their four thousand-mile-long border. Still, most communist regimes remained loyal to Moscow until the very end, even though all experienced periods in which dissidents went public with their opposition, often capturing the attention of the rest of the world in the process.

Command Economies

Until the late 1980s, the communist countries also relied on a **command economy**, in which the government owned almost all industrial enterprises and retail sales outlets. Only in Poland and Yugoslavia was much private farming allowed to continue (see Table 8.1). The economies were managed by a party-dominated state planning committee (*Gosplan* in the Soviet Union). It devised detailed blueprints for what was to be produced, exported, and sold, typically for a five-year period. Individual enterprises, run

TABLE 8.1 The Collectively Owned Portion of the Economy in 1967

COUNTRY	AGRICULTURAL LAND (%)	INDUSTRIAL PRODUCTION (%)	RETAIL SALES (%)	NATIONAL INCOME (%)
Bulgaria	99	99	100	95
Hungary	94	99	99	96
Poland	15	100	99	76
East Germany	95	88	79	94
Romania	91	100	100	95
Czechoslovakia	90	100	100	95
Soviet Union	98	100	100	96
Yugoslavia	16	98	NA	77
Weighted average	92	99	98	95

Source: Adapted from Bernard Chavance, *The Transformation of Communist Systems: Economic Reform Since the 1950s*, trans. Charles Hauss (Boulder, CO: Westview Press, 1994), 28.

by managers appointed by the party, were then issued instructions about what to produce and how to produce it.

In the early days, central planning helped spark rapid growth. By the 1950s, some of the communist countries were among the world leaders in the production of steel, ships, and other heavy industrial goods. Major improvements were made in the average person's standard of living. Homelessness was eliminated in Eastern Europe, and starvation was done away with in China.

However, by the late 1980s, the benefits of centralized planning had evaporated, and the communist countries found themselves in deep economic trouble. Planning and coercion could help stimulate growth in the early stages of industrialization, but they were of little use when it came to the now vitally important high-tech sectors of the economy for reasons that will become clear. The macroeconomic problems were reflected in the people's poor living conditions. To be sure, most people were far better off than their parents or grandparents had been. However, everything from housing to health care was mediocre at best—a fact that was driven home to the millions of people who gained access to Western mass media or who met Western tourists visiting Eastern Europe or the USSR long before *Good Bye, Lenin!* was made.

SOCIALISM, MARXISM, AND LENINISM

As the communist regimes aged, socialism in general, and Marxism-Leninism in particular, mattered less and less to their leaders and people alike. However, both because the three doctrines gave rise to these governments and because they were so frequently misunderstood by critics in the West, it is still important to consider them here.

Socialism

Historians have traced the origins of **socialism** back to the radical Levelers of the seventeenth-century English Civil War, who advocated social, political, and economic equality. Furthermore, as you would expect with an idea that old, there are dozens of interpretations of what socialism means, making it impossible to present any single, universally accepted definition here. For the purposes of an introductory course, it is enough to think of it as having four characteristics.

First, socialists believe that capitalism and the private ownership of the **means of production** are flawed. They are convinced that private ownership leads to unacceptable levels of inequality. Not all socialists are persuaded that the central government has to control the entire economy.

Profiles
Karl Marx

Karl Marx was born in 1818 in Trier, Germany, to a family of wealthy, assimilated Jews. While a university student, Marx was exposed to the democratic and revolutionary ideas sweeping Europe at the time. In the early 1840s, Marx moved to Paris, where he worked for a number of fledgling radical journals. He started reading British capitalist economic texts as well as the philosophy that had so stimulated him while a student. He also met **Friedrich Engels**, the son of a rich industrialist and author of one of the first detailed accounts of what factory life was like.

As revolutions swept Europe in 1848, Marx and Engels began writing about a new version of socialism that was later to be called Marxism or **communism**. Their ideas were first set out in a tract, *The Communist Manifesto*, which they published that winter. Over the next forty years, the two wrote dozens of volumes, the most important of which was Marx's three-volume historical and theoretical study of capitalism, almost always referred to by its German title, *Das Kapital*. ■

A statue of Karl Marx (foreground) and Friedrich Engels overlooks the Marx-Engels Forum in Berlin, Germany.

Nonetheless, they agree that representatives of the people as a whole, and not a small group of capitalists, should determine how the economy is run.

Second, most liberals are satisfied if a society can achieve equality of opportunity, which theoretically offers everyone the same chance to succeed. Socialists go further and demand substantial equality of outcome as well. They believe that, to be truly "free to" do the things that capitalist and liberal democratic societies offer, people must also be "free from" hunger, disease, and poverty.

Third, they are convinced that democracy as practiced in a liberal, capitalist society is too limited. Most believe that the personal freedoms and competitive elections that are at the heart of liberal democratic theory are vital. However, they would extend democracy to include popular control over all decisions that shape peoples' lives, most notably at work.

Finally, socialists claim that providing for public ownership and control of a substantially more egalitarian society will improve human relations in general. In one way or another, they are all convinced that capitalism keeps most of us from reaching our potential. In other words, if we could remove the fetters of capitalism, we would all be better off.

Marxism

Since the late nineteenth century, socialists have been divided into two main camps. The first includes the various social democratic parties that play such a major role in the industrialized democracies discussed in Part 2. They believe that social and economic change can and must be achieved by working through a democratic, representative system. Here we will concentrate on the second camp, consisting of parties and politicians who believe that significant political and economic progress can occur only through revolution, based on principles derived from the writings of **Karl Marx**.

As with socialism in general, there is no universally accepted interpretation of Marxism. What follows is a brief version of the theory that stresses its key principles, most of which ended up being honored in the breach by rulers who thought of themselves as Marxists.

Like most intellectuals of his generation, Marx believed that societies passed through stages, evolving from primitive groups of hunters and gatherers, eventually culminating in the industrial society he lived in. Indeed, what set Marx apart from most socialists of his time was his understanding that industrial capitalism is but one irreversible step along the path of social development. Marx also agreed with the German philosopher Georg Hegel, who believed that societies shift from one stage to another in a wrenching process he called the *dialectic*. Societies do not change in fundamental ways because of incremental reform. Rather, major shifts occur only when their basic values and principles are challenged and new ones are adopted.

Unlike Hegel, Marx believed that progress occurs as a result of changes in the distribution of economic power, which he called *historical materialism*. Any society can be broken down into social classes determined by who owns—and who does not own—the means of production or the key institutions through which wealth is created.

Thus, according to Marx, progress occurs as a result of conflict between these classes. He was convinced that the ruling class had to exploit the rest of the population who did not control the means of production. That relationship constituted the economic **base** of any society (see Figure 8.1). Any society based on private ownership also has built-in **contradictions** because people will not long accept being exploited and will eventually rise up in opposition. To slow the rise of rebellion, the owners would create a **superstructure** of other institutions, such as the state or religion. The former runs the bureaucracy, police, and army to maintain law and order, whereas the latter offers false hopes and expectations. It is from Marx's discussion of the superstructure that we get two of his most commonly cited statements: "Religion is the opiate of the masses," and "The executive of the modern state is but a committee for managing the common affairs of the whole bourgeoisie." But, Marx wrote, with time the oppressed would be able to organize, rise up, overthrow their oppressors, and usher in a new pattern of class relations.

From Marx's perspective, capitalism was a step forward because it replaced feudalism with an economy that had capital at its core. Under feudalism, the wealthy use money primarily as a vehicle to buy the commodities—goods and services—they want (the C and M of Figure 8.2). For example, they would sell grain or wine and use the money to buy clothes or spices. In capitalism, the pursuit of money becomes the driving force. Capitalists are less interested in the goods and services they produce or can purchase than

FIGURE 8.1 Base, Superstructure, and Contradictions, According to Marx

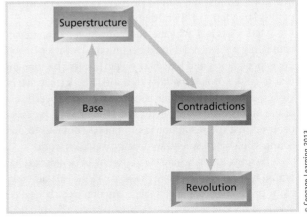

© Cengage Learning 2013

FIGURE 8.2 The Role of Money in Feudalism and Capitalism

In feudalism:
    C–M–C
In capitalism:
    M–C–M'
    M' = M + profit
But Marxist theory also holds:
    M' = total value of the labor that went into making the
        commodity
    M' = wages paid + profit
    Or, wages = labor value – profit = exploitation
Legend:
    C = commodity, M = money

© Cengage Learning 2013

FIGURE 8.3 Expansion and the Collapse of Capitalism

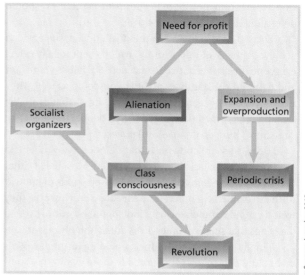

© Cengage Learning 2013

in the money they can make from a transaction M', which placed the profit motive at the heart of the economy for the first time.

This pressure to make a profit also makes capitalism exploitative by its very nature. Here Marx drew on one of his most controversial assumptions. He was convinced that the real worth of any good, as well as the price capitalists could sell it for, equaled the value of the labor that went into making it (also M in Figure 8.2). The problem was that the price capitalists set for their commodities had to include both the wages they paid their workers and their own profit. This meant that capitalists had to pay workers less than they deserved if they wanted to make money.

According to Marx, the constant need to open new markets to make more profit would, in turn, lead to alternating periods of booms and busts (see Figure 8.3). As capitalism expanded and competition intensified, more and more businesses would fail as weaker capitalists proved unable to deal with the competitive pressures of the market. As that happened, the **bourgeoisie**, or capitalist class, would grow smaller and smaller, while the working class, or **proletariat**, would swell until it included the vast majority of the population.

As in any society based on inequality, workers would resent their exploitation. Their alienation and, later, class consciousness would be enhanced by two of capitalism's own innovations: the spread of mass education and the political freedoms of liberal democracy.

Marx assumed that the contradictions of capitalism could only be resolved through revolution. However, he did not expect a long and bloody struggle. Instead, he thought that once the proletariat grew to a massive size, a wave of strikes and demonstrations would lead to the overthrow of the bourgeoisie with a minimum of violence. Marx also believed that the revolution could not be confined to one country but would spread around the capitalist world.

The revolution would be followed by a transitional period that he unfortunately chose to call the "dictatorship of the proletariat." The means of production would be taken over and run collectively, the cultural vestiges of capitalism

would be destroyed, and resources would be redistributed in an egalitarian manner.

Afterward, society would move into communism. At this point, there would be no need for government or any other part of the superstructure because people would no longer be exploiting each other. Instead, they would work voluntarily and efficiently because they were freed of the fetters of ownership and lived in a society organized by Marx's famous dictum "from each according to his abilities, to each according to his needs."

Marxism-Leninism

As an evolutionary thinker, Marx believed that socialist revolutions would first occur in advanced industrialized societies. Unfortunately for Marxists, that is not where revolutions inspired by Marx's ideas took place. Rather, they occurred in countries in which industrialization and capitalism were not very far developed. All had small working classes and socialist movements. Most had repressive governments that made the organization of broadly based socialist movements impossible. To come to power in these circumstances, Marxists had to adopt a very different strategy. Although there was considerable variation in the way Marxists won in these sixteen countries, all relied heavily on an organization and strategy first developed by Lenin to help the Marxists adapt to the poverty and repression in Russia during the first years of the twentieth century.

Even though Marx's theory seemed to rule out the possibility of Marxism taking root in countries like Russia at the time, many intellectuals there were drawn to it. At first, orthodox Marxists urged patience, arguing that no Marxist revolution was possible until Russia became industrialized and democratic. Others, led by Lenin, were unwilling to wait for history to take its "natural" course. To come to power under these circumstances, Marxists had to adopt a very different strategy initially devised by Lenin. As he saw it, Marxists could only come to power under the leadership of a highly centralized and disciplined party organized by what he called democratic centralism in a pamphlet he wrote in the first years of the twentieth century. It was democratic in name only. Lenin's leadership brooked no dissent. Rather, party members were expected to enforce decisions made by the leadership and be part of a well ordered machine.

At the time Lenin developed his ideas, they had virtually no impact because he and most of his **Bolshevik** colleagues were living in exile and had little popular support in Russia. Yet, within fifteen years, the Bolsheviks had seized power, and Lenin was convinced that they had done so because they had relied on democratic centralism.

The tactics developed to pull off a revolution in a society very different from the one that Marx envisioned became the model the Bolsheviks used to structure their new regime. Most historians now argue that Russia's adoption of Lenin's hierarchical organization and the control over society it allowed made the attainment of Marxist goals of human liberation and democracy all but impossible. Too much power was concentrated in too few hands.

Stalinism

After the Bolsheviks took power, they established a regime that they expected would preside over Marx's dictatorship of the proletariat and guide the transition from capitalism to socialism. However, something very different—and very tragic—occurred instead.

The authoritarianism of bolshevism became the regime's defining characteristic after the 1917 revolution.

TABLE 8.2 Key Events in the Evolution of Communist Regimes

YEAR	EVENT
1917	Bolshevik revolution in Russia
1924	Death of Lenin
1924	Stalin begins consolidation of power
1945–47	Start of Cold War Communists seize power in Eastern Europe
1949	Chinese communists come to power
1950	Start of Korean War
1953	Death of Stalin
1956	Secret speech and de-Stalinization
1956	Revolt in Hungary
1959	Castro comes to power in Cuba
1975	End of Vietnam War, solidification of communist rule in Indochina

To some degree, the authoritarianism, if not the totalitarianism, was an outgrowth of Lenin's democratic centralism. However, most political scientists assign the primary responsibility for the degradation of communism to **Joseph Stalin** (1879–1953) and his dictatorial control over the world communist movement from the mid-1920s until his death in 1953.

It was in studying this period that Western scholars coined the term *totalitarianism*. Stalin and his colleagues used the party, the mass media, and campaigns of terror to subjugate the population and then mobilize the people in pursuit of the leadership's goals. The party state became as close to totalitarian as imaginable.

We could go on and present statistical and other "hard" evidence about those regimes. However, as is often the case with emotionally charged material, it is easier to illustrate this point by turning to a piece of fiction, George Orwell's *Animal Farm*.

Orwell was part of a generation of young European intellectuals who were drawn to Marxism in the 1920s and 1930s. However, Orwell soon became disillusioned with Stalin's dictatorial and opportunistic policies, which he criticized in his writing for the rest of his life.

In *Animal Farm*, the animals rise up and throw off the yoke (literally and figuratively) of human oppression. Initially, they are inspired by an ideology that reads a lot like Marxism and is embodied in the anthem *Beasts of England*, which Orwell tells us was sung to a tune somewhere between *La Cucaracha* and *My Darling Clementine*. Chip once asked a group of students to sing it. He led half the group singing one tune and the rest of the class using the other. It didn't work. In fact, it produced the only moment of humor in the section of the course on Stalinism.

Soon, however, things turn sour. The old revolutionary leader dies shortly after the animals took power, just as Lenin did. The pigs, the animal Orwell not coincidentally chose to represent the Communist Party, assume more and more power over the other animals. Then a struggle for power breaks out between the two leading pigs. Snowball (based on Leon Trotsky), the more orthodox "Marxist," believes that the revolution must spread to all the farms and beasts of England. In the end, he loses out to the dictatorial Comrade Napoleon, who, like both his namesake and Stalin (on whom he is based), is more interested in power for power's sake than in any lofty goals. In the book, the subtle complexities of Marxist ideology give way first to the Seven Commandments and then to the simplistic slogan "Four legs good, two legs bad." In addition, *Beasts of England* is replaced by a new anthem, *Comrade Napoleon*, which adulates the leader. The pigs—Orwell's equivalent of what Stalin called the Communist Party *apparatchiks*—lord their power over the other animals and become more and more like their prerevolutionary oppressors: "All animals are equal, except some are more equal than others." The pigs violate the Seven Commandments by sleeping in beds and drinking alcohol. Orwell ends the novel with a scene in which the pigs are in a house drinking and playing cards with a group of men, their supposed "class" enemy. The other animals look in on the game from outside:

> As the animals outside gazed at the scene, it seemed to them that some strange thing was happening. What was it that had altered in the faces of the pigs? Clover's old dim eyes flitted from one face to another. Some of them had five chins, some had four, some had three. But what was it that seemed to be melting and changing? Then, the applause having come to an end, the company took up their cards and continued the game that had been interrupted, and the animals crept silently away.
>
> But they had not gone twenty yards when they stopped short. An uproar of voices was coming from the farmhouse. They rushed back and looked through the window again. Yes, a violent quarrel was in progress. There were shoutings, bangings on the table, sharp suspicious glances, furious denials.
>
> The source of the trouble appeared to be that Napoleon and Mr. Pilkington had each played an ace of spades simultaneously.
>
> Twelve voices were shouting in anger, and they were all alike. No question, now, what had happened to the faces of the pigs. The creatures outside looked from pig to man, and from man to pig, and from pig to man again; but already it was impossible to say which was which.[1]

Expansion

As noted earlier, Marx expected that once revolution broke out, it would soon spread. To speed up that worldwide uprising, two Workingmen's International groups were created to coordinate the actions of the world's socialist parties. During World War I, the second of them failed to keep most socialists from joining the war effort and made no contribution to the Russian Revolution of 1917.

Lenin thus felt justified in claiming that the Bolsheviks should lead the world revolutionary movement. Within months of seizing power, he and his colleagues established a **Third International**, or **Comintern**, to spread revolution, Bolshevik style. Most socialist parties split (see the discussion of the origins of the French Communist Party in Chapter 5), with the more radical wing supporting the Bolsheviks.

Nevertheless, the revolution did not spread as either Marx or Lenin had expected. A few attempts to establish Bolshevik regimes were made in 1919 and the early 1920s, but they were quickly put down. By the time Stalin had solidified his power, it was clear that no successful Marxist revolutions were likely to occur in the near future. Instead, the new, weak Soviet state was vulnerable to pressures from the hostile countries that surrounded it.

Stalin then inaugurated a new phase in Soviet policy dubbed "socialism in one country." The first and foremost goal of the Soviet government, and of all other communist parties that belonged to the Third International, was to help the world's one Marxist regime survive, even if that meant slowing the prospects for revolution in their own country.

Following the end of World War II, communism did expand, though not in the way Marx had anticipated. As the war drew to a close, resistance forces dominated by communists drove the Germans and their collaborators out of Albania and Yugoslavia and established Marxist-Leninist regimes. Between 1945 and 1947, the Soviets imposed communist regimes on the rest of Eastern Europe. In China, North Korea, Indochina, and Cuba, communist regimes were the result of domestically inspired revolutions.

No matter how they came to power, all these regimes were patterned after the Soviet party state. Even where communists came to power on their own, they acknowledged Soviet leadership and patterned their own new governments on Moscow's.

De-Stalinization

Stalin died in March 1953. He was replaced by a group of men who had been his colleagues and henchmen. Surprisingly, they ushered in a period of relaxation and, to some degree, reform that came to be known as **de-Stalinization**.

Cracks in the supposedly impenetrable totalitarian wall first came to light in **Nikita Khrushchev**'s 1956 secret speech to the Twentieth Congress of the CPSU, which documented, in gory detail, many of the atrocities committed under Stalin.

Political controls in some areas of intellectual life were loosened. Works critical of Stalin were published and widely discussed. Universities became politically and intellectually exciting places for their students, including Gorbachev, Boris Yeltsin, and most of the 1980s generation of reformers. There were, however, limits to what the reformers could openly discuss. Stalin was the only acceptable figure people were allowed to attack, and criticism of the current leadership, Lenin, or the party's monopoly on power remained strictly forbidden.

The Soviets cracked down whenever they felt that events in their own country or in Eastern Europe were

---

[1]George Orwell, *Animal Farm* (New York: Harcourt Brace, 1946), 128.

getting out of hand. In 1956, reform communists came to power in Hungary. They planned to create a multiparty system and leave the Soviet-imposed **Warsaw Pact** alliance. Meanwhile, thousands of people demonstrated in the streets of Budapest and other Hungarian cities. Finally, Soviet troops intervened, overthrowing the government of Imre Nagy and replacing it with one headed by Janos Kadar, known to be loyal to the Soviet leadership.

Problems mounted six years later in 1962 with the Soviets' humiliating defeat in the Cuban Missile Crisis. The United States discovered that the USSR was in the process of installing nuclear missiles on the island. President John F. Kennedy and his administration imposed a naval blockade on Cuba. In time, a diplomatic agreement was reached, the ships containing missiles and components turned back, and the project had to be abandoned.

In October 1964, recognizing that things had gone too far, Khrushchev's more conservative, or at least risk-averse, colleagues, forced him from office. He was replaced by a collective leadership team headed by **Leonid Brezhnev**, whose hostility toward change would not only characterize his seventeen years in power but would contribute heavily to the demise of Eurasian communism.

This point is worth underscoring. Less than half a century after the Bolshevik revolution, the Soviet Union and most other communist regimes had been taken over by an aging generation of leaders more committed to stability than to change. The new leadership could not, however, put a halt to two trends that were to become ever more prominent in the quarter-century before the crisis of communism began in earnest.

First, there was no longer a monolithic world communist movement. As early as the late 1940s, Albania and Yugoslavia had effectively broken free from Soviet control. By the 1960s, the same was true for the non-European communist regimes.

Second, although it was difficult to see at the time, Brezhnev and his colleagues had come to power at a moment when their countries needed to change—and change dramatically. That, however, was not something they were prepared to consider, as we will see.

THE MARXIST-LENINIST STATE

By the mid-1960s, governments that ruled in the name of Marx had drifted far from the egalitarian goals outlined earlier. Instead, political, economic, and other forms of power were concentrated in the hands of a few party leaders. Constitutions in the Soviet Union and elsewhere gave the party the leading role in government and society, which

meant that it, and not the government, held a monopoly on decision-making power.

The Party State

Political scientists thus emphasize what they call the *party state,* in which the former was far more powerful than the latter. The critical institutions of the party state were its **Secretariat** and **Politburo**. The exact titles varied from country to country and from time to time. The most important individuals were the general secretary and the members of the Politburo, who functioned as the equivalent of the prime minister and cabinet in a parliamentary system. Typically, the Politburo was the main decision-making body, whereas the Secretariat managed the party's internal affairs. In most countries, the top leaders were members of both bodies. There was a formal government, and most important party leaders served in both. But it was always their party "hat" that prevailed. The Parliament, cabinet, and other institutions were little more than a rubber stamp for decisions made in the party, which the government then implemented.

The party had extremely powerful leaders. Ironically, Marx had tried to downplay the role that individuals play in shaping history, stressing instead the impact of broad historical and economic forces. Lenin, too, resisted attempts to be cast in a hero's role. Yet, shortly after Lenin died, Stalin and his supporters transformed him into a symbol that some observers believe was equivalent to a god. As Orwell pointedly shows in *Animal Farm*, Stalin became the center of an even greater **cult of personality**. After Stalin, Marxist leaders maintained various forms of collective leadership in which a number of people shared power. Nonetheless, the prominence of a Castro, **Mao Zedong**, or even Gorbachev suggest that general secretaries continued to amass substantial power well into the twilight of communism.

The party always relied on democratic centralism. Leaders at one level co-opted those who served under them. Appointments to key positions, included in a list known as the **nomenklatura**, had to be approved by the Central Committee staff. People eligible for those positions were on a separate *nomenklatura* list. All real debate within the parties was forbidden, and rank-and-file members had no choice but to carry out the decisions made by leaders above them in the hierarchy.

The Communist Party was the only institution that mattered. Anyone desiring a successful career had to be a loyal and active party member. Almost every child joined the party-dominated Young Pioneers, the equivalent of the Boy Scouts and Girl Scouts in the United States. Young men and women with any ambition at all joined the Communist

Youth League, from which adult party members were recruited. The party determined where high school and university graduates were sent to work. Trade unions, women's groups, and even stamp collecting societies were under party control. Most important of all, the Communist Party presided over the command economy, which determined what goods and services would be produced, where they would be sold, and how much they would cost. It is no wonder that Western observers called these regimes totalitarian.

There was some variation from country to country. Communist control was never quite as absolute in Eastern Europe as it was in the Soviet Union. Demonstrations against communist rule broke out as early as 1953 in East Germany. Major protest movements were put down in Poland and Hungary in 1956, but they reappeared with the reform movement in and subsequent Soviet invasion of Czechoslovakia in 1968. After that, the focus turned to Poland, where a series of protest movements culminated in the rise of the independent trade union **Solidarity** in 1980–81, the first time a communist regime officially acknowledged the existence of an independent political organization. There were also some economic reforms in Eastern Europe, most notably, experiments with market mechanisms in Hungary.

China followed yet another path. Unlike most other parties, the Chinese Communist Party (CCP) had always been able to maintain a good deal of autonomy, largely because it spent the 1930s and 1940s fighting a guerrilla war and was often beyond Moscow's reach. After coming to power, the CCP followed the Soviet line until 1956. However, because Mao and the other top Chinese leaders objected to de-Stalinization and the other Soviet reforms, they began adopting their own, more revolutionary policies.

The CCP also disintegrated into factions that opposed each others' policies over the next twenty years. At times, the Left, increasingly associated with Mao himself, was dominant and led the country in what it thought of as a revolutionary direction, most notably in the chaotic and violent **Cultural Revolution**, which lasted from 1965 until the mid-1970s. When the more orthodox faction was dominant, the leadership adopted more moderate, Soviet-style policies focusing on industrial development.

Within two years of Mao's death in 1976, the moderates, led by **Deng Xiaoping**, took control. Deng and his colleagues began a program of dramatic economic reforms that we will explore in more detail in Chapter 10. Here, it is enough to note that however much economic reform they have countenanced, Chinese elites have never tolerated any changes that threatened the party's stranglehold on political power.

The Graying of Communism

It is impossible to overstate how much the Marxist-Leninists changed in the half-century following the Bolshevik revolution. Revolutionary leaders gave way to the likes of Brezhnev with his love of cowboy movies and German luxury cars. Purges were replaced by what the Soviets called "trust in cadres" that all but ensured party officials would retain their jobs as long as they did not cause trouble. Leaders who forced their countries to change were replaced by "machine" politicians intent on maintaining their own power and the perks of office. At best, the communist leaders of the 1970s and 1980s were old men like Brezhnev, desperately clinging to power (and life) as the times continued to pass them by. At worst, they were venal and corrupt, like the members of the Ceausescu family, who oppressed the impoverished Romanian people to get castles, personal armies, and Swiss bank accounts for themselves—all somehow justified in the name of Marx.

Even if they had wanted to, it is doubtful that these leaders could have used the party state to produce the kind of economic change that should have been on their agendas. Charles Lindblom likened these centralized authoritarian regimes to our thumbs.[2] If you think about it, one's thumb is best suited for crudely pushing things, whereas the other four fingers are better suited for doing more subtle, delicate, and complicated work. Lindblom suggested that in the early stages of industrial development political thumbs are good enough. At that point, a country needs more cement, railroad track, electric wire, and other relatively low-tech commodities. These can be manufactured by unskilled workers, including those who are forced to follow orders. Although most historians now doubt that the collectivization of agriculture and forced industrialization were the best ways to bring the Soviet Union into the twentieth century, there is no denying that such authoritarian mechanisms got the job done, if brutally.

However, a more modern, technologically sophisticated economy requires organizations and skills that are more like political fingers. Take, for example, a television. Unlike a tub of cement, a 1980s Soviet television had many complicated parts including everything from the remote control to the picture tube to the electronic circuitry inside the box. Workmanship and quality control are extremely important. If the frequency emitted by the remote control or the wiring or the circuitry is just a little bit off, the television will not work. This is something a thumb-based economy is not very good at.

---

[2]Charles Lindblom, *Politics and Markets* (New York: Basic Books, 1977).

Most important, moving toward fingers would undoubtedly have meant loosening many political as well as economic controls and abandoning the two defining elements of communist societies: the party state and the command economy. In this sense, the party state became an increasingly ineffective way to run a country. To be sure, the party retained its monopoly over who the decision makers were and what policies they adopted. It kept the secret police and other repressive agencies well staffed and equipped. However, leaders in all these countries found it ever more difficult to control their societies. People were better educated, and this led them to seek more control over the decisions that shaped their lives. Moreover, the influx of Western tourists and mass media made it clear to millions of people that the propaganda they heard from their own governments was wrong. People in the West were much better off than they were.

Their societies increasingly paid the cost for the lack of fingers. Growth rates dropped precipitously. The economic woes were most serious in the sectors in which fingers were most needed, such as light industry, research and development, and consumer goods production. The downturn was reflected in a poor standard of living that left everyone in the communist world lagging further and further behind people in the West. Most Soviet families, for instance, still lived in tiny, shoddily built apartments, often sharing kitchens and bathrooms with other families. People throughout the communist world had savings, but there were not enough goods to satisfy pent-up demand. The waiting list for cars was so long that used cars cost more than new ones simply because they were available.

Even the military, the most efficient sector of the Soviet economy, lagged behind. Soviet submarines were much noisier, and therefore easier to detect, than American ones. The United States developed reliable solid fuels for its missiles in the 1960s; it is not clear whether the Soviets ever did. Soviet nuclear warheads were larger than American ones because they had to be. Soviet missiles were a lot less accurate and so larger bombs were needed to get a "kill" if the missile landed considerably off target.

When Brezhnev died in 1982, communist regimes were facing ever more serious problems that imperiled the very principles on which they were based. The external problems were easiest to see. Rapid technological change, the development of global financial and commercial markets, and more rapid rates of growth, not only in the West but in some of the less developed countries, were leaving the communist countries in an ever-deepening economic bind. Meanwhile, a renewed Cold War "forced" the Soviets to spend even more on defense at a time when the costs of doing so were spiraling. The domestic challenges were harder to see, but these societies were changing, and many

people, especially the young, were chafing under continued repressive rule, as the plotline of *Good Bye, Lenin!* attests.

Half the Sky? The Role of Women in Late Communist Regimes

During the Long March (see Chapter 10) Chairman Mao extolled the role of women in revolution be saying "they hold up half the sky." Under communist rule they held up far less than half.

Very few women rose to positions of power on their own. Most who did were either the wives or widows of prominent men.

The best and worst example is Mao's widow, Jiang Qing, who essentially led the Cultural Revolution (again see Chapter 10). She rose to power—and fell from it—mostly as a result of her relationship with the Chairman. The few women who rose to political prominence in China have until recently followed a similar path. The same was true in the Soviet Union. Indeed, women were so unimportant that a book—*The Kremlin Wives*—was published about them showing that few had serious political aspirations. Leonid Brezhnev's wife spent more time choosing the food for dinner than she did on politics.

The one possible exception to this rule is Elena Ceausescu, who ran Romania with an iron fist along with her husband and was at least his political equal, if not his superior. It is not clear if Mrs. Ceausescu could have risen to prominence without her husband's backing. She was virtually illiterate but gave herself an honorary PhD. When they were overthrown, she told the accusing court, "We have the right to die the way we want." Her wish was not granted. She and her husband were both killed by a firing squad the day after Christmas in 1989.

THE CRISIS OF COMMUNISM: SUICIDE BY PUBLIC POLICY

Return now to the quote from Georgi Arbatov (1923–2010) that begins this chapter. Arbatov played a pivotal role in U.S.-Soviet relations as the Cold War ended. He was the founder and director of the U.S. and Canadian studies institute in Moscow. As such, he was a loyal *apparathik* but also someone who knew the West well. As the 1980s wore on, he became a voice for reform within the USSR, all the while maintaining his influential post. He may become little more than a footnote in history, but his statement was as good a way of understanding why the USSR collapsed as any.

What we learned in two short years was that communism in Europe and Asia died because it lost the support of its people.

Reform: Too Little, Too Late

In retrospect, it is easy to see how fragile these regimes had become as the twentieth century drew to a close. At the time, however, most observers assumed that the party state was here to stay. As evidence of its continued clout, the Soviets invaded Afghanistan in 1979, and the Polish government was able to impose martial law and drive Solidarity underground two years later.

Perhaps because they could not read the political "handwriting on the wall" in their rapidly changing societies, the party states refused to change and clung to power. The Soviets continued to select leaders from the same old generation, picking Yuri Andropov to succeed Brezhnev, and then Konstantin Chernenko when Andropov died fifteen months later. With the exception of Poland, the Eastern European countries all had general secretaries who had taken office in the 1960s. Only China was engaging in any kind of reform, but its aging leaders were carefully limiting reform to economics, not politics.

In 1985, however, European communism's final act began (see Table 8.3). When Chernenko died, the Soviet Central Committee had no choice but to turn to the next generation to find a successor and selected Gorbachev to be general secretary. Gorbachev was by no means responsible for everything that happened in the communist world afterward. Nonetheless, he was the catalyst who unleashed the forces that brought about unprecedented and unexpected change.

When Gorbachev came to power, he was known to be something of a reformer, but no one expected him to go anywhere near as far as he did. After all, he had risen through the ranks of the Soviet Communist Party and had won because he had gained the support of old-guard politicians. Quickly,

however, Gorbachev began replacing the older generation with younger men and women. Together, they introduced reforms that they hoped would revitalize communism. In the end, the political forces they unleashed killed it instead.

The four types of reforms they introduced will be discussed in detail in the next chapter:

- *Glasnost*, or more openness in the political system.
- Democratization, beginning with the introduction of a degree of competition to the way the Communist Party was run.
- *Perestroika*, or economic restructuring, including a degree of private ownership.
- New thinking in foreign policy, especially improved relations with the West.

It is important to emphasize that when the Soviet leadership initiated these reforms they certainly did not expect them to destroy communism. That they would prove fatal to communism as we knew and feared it only became clear when the spirit of reform reached Eastern Europe and hit a political roadblock. The elderly party leaders there resisted implementing *glasnost*, *perestroika*, and democratization. East Germany's Erich Honecker went so far as to forbid the press to carry stories about the changes taking place in the Soviet Union.

But Honecker and his colleagues would not be able to maintain the Brezhnevite status quo. There were pressures for change from abroad, most notably and ironically from the Soviet Union itself. Gorbachev and his supporters in the Soviet leadership had decided that they no longer had to keep an iron grip on Eastern Europe. The security value of the "buffer states" had declined in a world in which nuclear missiles could fly over Eastern Europe and strike the Soviet Union in a matter of minutes. In fact, Eastern Europe had become such a financial burden on the Soviet Union that, at the height of the popularity of the *Star Wars* films, an American political scientist titled an article on Soviet–Eastern European relations "The Empire Strikes Back."

By 1988, the Soviet Union was eager to see change in Eastern Europe, though certainly not the total collapse of communism. Gorbachev continued to push the region's recalcitrant leaders to reform. It was even clear that the Soviets were willing to consider modifications in their relationship with Eastern Europe if that would persuade them to adopt at least moderate reforms.

Changes within Eastern Europe itself were at least as important. To varying degrees, these countries were suffering from the same economic problems as the Soviet Union. More important, the cultural changes discussed previously had progressed further in the more economically advanced countries of Eastern Europe. Moreover, none of the Eastern European regimes (save, perhaps, Albania) had

TABLE 8.3 Key Events in the Crisis of Communism

YEAR	EVENT
1956	Hungarian uprising
1968	Prague Spring in Czechoslovakia
1980–81	Emergence of Solidarity in Poland and imposition of martial law
1985	Gorbachev chosen general secretary of Communist Party of the Soviet Union
1988	Opening of iron curtain in Hungary
1989	Collapse of communism in Eastern Europe; Democracy movement in China
1990	German unification
1991	Disintegration of Soviet Union

ever either succeeded in completely suppressing dissent or in achieving even the limited degree of legitimacy found in Brezhnev's Soviet Union.

1989: The Year That Changed the World

The revolutions started in Poland. In 1988, Solidarity reappeared, stronger than it had been when General Wojciech Jaruzelski imposed martial law in December 1981. His government was quickly forced into "round table" negotiations with Solidarity and other non-communist organizations. Out of those discussions came an agreement to hold elections in which some seats would be reserved for the Communist Party and others freely contested. Solidarity won a resounding victory in the competition for open seats, and in August 1989 the Communists agreed to give up power—the first time that had ever happened anywhere in the communist world. Jaruzelski stayed on temporarily as president, but the Catholic intellectual Tadeusz Mazowiecki held the more powerful position of prime minister in a Solidarity-run government that dismantled the command economy within months.

The next to fall was Hungary, where the first liberal economic reforms had been implemented in the mid-1960s. By the late 1980s, reformists within the Communist Party had grown strong enough to replace Janos Kadar, whom the Soviets had put in power in 1956. The new leaders dismantled the iron curtain along the Austrian border. They also roundly criticized the Soviet invasion of 1956 and the Hungarians who had cooperated with the USSR. They even stopped calling themselves communists. Finally, the leadership agreed to free elections in April 1990, in which anti-communists won an overwhelming majority.

Opening the border in Hungary inadvertently sparked more sweeping changes. East Germans vacationing there crossed the open border into Austria and then moved on to West Germany. Even though the Warsaw Pact required them to keep the border closed, the Hungarian government did nothing to stop the escapees, claiming that its commitment to human rights was more important than the provisions of an outdated political and military alliance. By the fall of 1990, thousands of people were fleeing to the West every day.

Meanwhile, protest movements in East Germany sprang up, and pressures continued to mount until the unthinkable happened. On November 9, 1989, jubilant Germans smashed open the Berlin Wall, and people from both sides celebrated together. The most visible sign of the Cold War disappeared.

The pace of change continued to accelerate. The East German government agreed to free elections in spring 1990, which Christian Democrats with strong ties to their colleagues in West Germany won handily. By that time,

Conflict and Democratization
in the Communist World

Some key differences between the industrialized democracies and the current and former communist regimes become easy to see by considering the role of conflict and democratization in each.

In Part 2 we saw that democracies have taken firm root—albeit often after centuries of turmoil—and that conflict is viewed as a normal part of political life. In the countries covered in Part 3, however, almost all forms of conflict were suppressed throughout the communist period. All had some dissident movements, but rarely did they grow beyond a tiny proportion of the population or threaten the regime. The collapse of communism in Eurasia and the changes in what remains of the communist world have brought much of the conflict that lurked just below the surface into the open. Indeed, in the first decade or so of the twenty-first century, many of these countries have more conflict than they can effectively handle and still build a democracy or market economy. That is especially true of countries with deep ethnic divisions, some of which broke into their constituent parts, many of which have ethnic difficulties of their own.

Thus, if there are parallels to the Western democracies, it is to France or Germany of the early 1900s, when their regimes were anything but stable and legitimate in large part because of protests coming from literally dozens of groups. ■

German unification as a part of NATO, which had seemed impossible a year before, was inevitable.

The quickest to fall was the Czechoslovak government headed by Gustav Husak, whom the Soviets had installed in power in 1968. The Soviet invasion of Czechoslovakia in August of that year was a brutal response to the peaceful reform movement dubbed the "Prague Spring." Anti-Soviet demonstrations broke out again during the late 1980s. Hundreds of thousands jammed Wenceslaus Square in Prague on a daily basis. Finally, in 1989, the previously powerless legislature reacted to public pressure and chose Vaclav Havel—who had been in jail less than a year before—to be the new president. Even more remarkably, the legislature elected the liberal communist leader of the 1968 Prague Spring, Alexander Dubcek, to be its head. When elections were finally held in June 1990, the reforms were confirmed when the Communists came in a distant third.

Only in Romania did the revolution turn violent. Under the Ceausescus, the country had been little more than a personal fiefdom since the mid-1960s. Even as the Romanian people starved so that the country could pay off its international debt, the Ceausescus built monuments to themselves. The Ceausescus also controlled the largest and most ruthless secret police in Eastern Europe, the *Securitate*.

The first protests took place in the provincial city of Timisoara on December 17, 1989. *Securitate* forces fired into the crowd, killing hundreds. A civil war broke out, with the *Securitate* and other forces loyal to the Ceausescus on one side and much of the army and armed citizens on the other. Within a week, the government had been overthrown. The Ceausescus fled but were soon captured. On Christmas Day 1989 they were executed. By the end of the

month, *Securitate* opposition was crushed, and a regime headed by the reform communist Ion Iliescu was in power.

These successful and largely nonviolent revolutions were not the only earthquakes to shake the communist world in 1989. Economic reforms in China were beginning to show some promising results. Political reform, however, was not forthcoming. In April 1989, prodemocracy protests broke out as a group led by students occupied Beijing's **Tiananmen Square**, the symbolic heart of Chinese politics.

The next month, Gorbachev became the first Soviet leader since the beginning of the Sino-Soviet split to visit Beijing. As in Eastern Europe, Gorbachev served as a lightning rod for reformers in China. Massive, adoring crowds greeted him wherever he went, giving more and more support to the prodemocracy movement. The crowds kept growing. As they did, hopes for any kind of a peaceful end to the protests evaporated. The government began assembling troops around Beijing. During the night of June 3 into June 4, the military stormed the square, killing as many as several thousand students and others who were still there. After martial law was imposed, China was widely criticized as the most repressive of the communist regimes. As we will see in Chapter 10, the crackdown and smaller ones that followed all but ended any real chance of a regime change. Instead, many Chinese pursued the ever wider opportunities for economic reform to the point that twenty years after Tiananmen Square, a largely capitalist economy coexists with a Marxist-Leninist political system.

In 1990, the focus of attention shifted back to the Soviet Union, where centrifugal forces were tearing the country apart. The Communist Party had already given up its legal monopoly on power. New organizations were cropping up at every imaginable point along the political spectrum. The new Congress of People's Deputies and Supreme Soviet were turning into real legislative bodies. Groups demanding sovereignty, and, sometimes total independence, emerged in each of the fourteen non-Russian republics. In many of them, ethnic antagonisms escalated into violence that bordered on civil war.

At the party congress in the summer of 1990, **Boris Yeltsin** led fellow radical reformers out of the Communist Party. Meanwhile, Gorbachev increasingly turned to conservative leaders within the military and security apparatus to keep himself in power even though advisers such as former foreign minister Eduard Shevardnadze kept warning of a right-wing coup. By April 1991, the Baltic republics (i.e., Lithuania, Latvia, and Estonia) were clamoring for independence. The economy was on the brink of collapse.

Finally, the most impossible of impossible events occurred. On August 19, 1991, military and security service leaders attempted a coup against Gorbachev at his villa in the Crimea. For nearly four days, Gorbachev was

One of many people who took a turn at knocking down the Berlin Wall.

© David Brauchli/Reuters/CORBIS

held hostage and his wife was apparently psychologically abused by men that he himself had put in power. In Moscow, Yeltsin—though Gorbachev's most vocal critic—led the opposition in the streets that toppled the plotters. On August 22, Gorbachev returned to Moscow and to what he thought was power.

The coup proved to be the last straw. The Baltic republics gained their independence within a few weeks. Every remaining Soviet republic declared itself sovereign and Yeltsin emerged as the most powerful politician. Finally, in December, leaders of most of the republics agreed to form the Commonwealth of Independent States. Gorbachev was not even invited to the founding meeting. On December 31, he resigned the presidency of a country that no longer existed.

The Remnants of the Communist World

In 2011, there are only five communist countries left—China, North Korea, Vietnam, Laos, and Cuba. Far less attention has been paid to the reasons why communist regimes survived in these countries than to the causes of their collapse in Eurasia. The limited research on the subject has, however, pointed to three main reasons.

First, each of their parties remained willing to use force. One of the remarkable aspects of the events in Eastern Europe and the Soviet Union was that the police and the army (that is, the party) were not willing to fire on their own people. With the exception of Romania, only a handful of people died in the revolutions, and those deaths were inadvertent. In these other countries, however, the regimes have been more willing to resort to force in order to stay in power.

Second, these countries are poorer and less open to outside influences than was the Soviet bloc. In other words, the cultural developments discussed previously had not progressed anywhere near as far in them. To be sure, as early as the 1980s, Chinese students and members of the middle class were beginning to demand "discos and democracy," as journalist Orville Schell put it, but they constituted only a tiny proportion of the total population.

Recent reports hint that some children of members of the Cuban elite have grave reservations about the regime. However, there are only a handful of these people, whereas there were thousands of young "new thinkers" beginning to build careers and exert political influence in the Soviet Union during the 1980s. Similarly, the American press has given such spectacular events as Elian Gonzalez's case and the defection of star baseball players a lot of attention, but it has probably overstated the degree to which they reflect widespread dissatisfaction with the regime. The key issue for Cuba is what will happen when the Castro brothers finally leave the scene. Their departure seems likely to occur in the near future. Fidel continues to suffer from a serious illness that has kept him from most of his presidential duties since July 2006 and led him to name his less than sprightly brother Raoul leader.

Third, these countries had been outside the Soviet Union's orbit for quite some time before 1989. Cuba and Vietnam were Soviet allies and, in many ways, were dependent on the USSR economically and militarily. However, the Soviets exerted relatively little influence on the way local communists ruled. They also had little desire or ability to force their leaders to adopt *perestroika* or *glasnost*. Thus, during his April 1989 visit to Cuba, Gorbachev had no success in convincing Castro to reform, nor were there any demonstrations in the streets of Havana as there would be throughout the rest of the communist world that spring, summer, and fall.

TRANSITIONS

There was a lot of optimism in the first heady days after the collapse of communism in Eastern Europe and the Soviet Union. Given the demonstration of "people power" in 1989, many thought it would be relatively easy for these countries to make the transition to a market economy and democratic government. Those hopes gave way to widespread pessimism following a wave of strife and civil war, weak leadership, and further economic deterioration.

Conditions have improved in most of those countries since then, as a comparison of Table 8.4 and the Basic Box at the beginning of the chapter shows. With a few exceptions, their economies hit rock bottom and began to recover by the middle or late 1990s. Some are more prosperous than they have ever been because they found market niches for their own goods or succeeded in attracting foreign investment. Many of the economically successful countries also have relatively stable and democratic governments. Nonetheless, in only a handful of cases can we safely say that major progress has been made toward either democracy or capitalism. That said, it is by no means clear that they will all survive as democracies or prosper as capitalist countries given the impact of the current economic crisis.

To see how difficult the first stages of the economic side of the transitions were, consider Table 8.4 again. It is based on data gathered and analyzed by the World Bank for the period 1989–95. None of these countries has had it easy. Groups 1 and 2 are composed mostly of the former satellite countries and Baltic republics from the Soviet Union. Though they did the best, their economies shrank and they

TABLE 8.4 Economic Change in Former Communist Countries, 1989–95

COUNTRY OR TYPE	AVERAGE GROSS DOMESTIC PRODUCT GROWTH	AVERAGE INFLATION (%)	LIBERALIZATION INDEX	CHANGE IN LIFE EXPECTANCY (YEARS)
Group 1	−1.6	106.0	6.9	0.7
Group 2	−4.2	49.2	4.7	−0.2
Group 3	−9.6	466.4	3.4	−4.4
Group 4	−6.7	809.6	2.0	−1.6
Countries affected by regional tensions	−11.7	929.7	3.9	0.5
China/Vietnam	9.4	8.4	5.5	2.1

Notes: Chinese data are for the entire reform period (1979–95) and include Vietnam for the liberalization index.

Group 1: Poland, Slovenia, Hungary, Croatia*, Macedonia*, Czech Republic, Slovakia.

Group 2: Estonia, Lithuania, Bulgaria, Latvia, Albania, Romania, Mongolia.

Group 3: Kyrgyz Republic, Russia, Moldova, Armenia*, Georgia*, Kazakhstan.

Group 4: Uzbekistan, Ukraine, Belarus, Azerbaijan*, Tajikistan*, Turkmenistan.

Countries with an asterisk (*) are among those severely affected by regional tensions. The table does not have data on Bosnia and Yugoslavia (Serbia and Montenegro) because of the continuing war there.

Source: Adapted from World Bank, *From Plan to Market: World Development Report 1996* (Washington, D.C.: World Bank, 1996), 18, 33.

suffered from an inflation rate that saw prices at least double each year through the mid-1990s.

Groups 3 and 4 consist of the other twelve former Soviet republics, including Russia. Their economies declined by as much as 10 percent per year, which meant that in 1995 some of them produced only half the goods and services they had before the collapse of the USSR. Inflation rates were typically in the 500 percent range, which meant that prices went up fivefold each year. Even more remarkable than the economic statistics are those on life expectancy. In Russia, the average man could expect to live ten fewer years than he would have before the fall of communism because of the failing social welfare, health care, and economic systems.

The World Bank also identified a subset of these four groups: countries that were severely affected by ethnic conflict. Before we proceed, note two things about that row of the table. It includes neither Russia, because the fighting in Chechnya had yet to begin, nor Bosnia, because neither the World Bank nor local authorities could gather reliable statistics at the time. The wars in those countries not only disrupted the economies, as shown in this table, but also made effective government—let alone a transition to democracy—impossible.

Finally, contrast these groups of countries to those in the final numbered row, China and Vietnam, the two remaining communist regimes that have reformed their economies the most. Instead of the decline we see for the rest of the countries in the table, the Chinese economy grew by an average of nearly 10 percent a year, which

meant that overall output doubled during that same period.

(Relative) Success: Eastern and Central Europe

All the former communist countries that have been admitted to the EU or NATO are found in the first two rows of Table 8.4. There is no commonly accepted explanation of why they have succeeded more than the others. However, a glance at the experience of Hungary gives us a good look at the kinds of trends political scientists stress the most.

First, Hungary is homogeneous. More than 90 percent of its population is ethnically Hungarian. The largest minority are the often ill-treated Roma (or gypsies), but they only make up about 2 percent of the population.

Second, Hungary's economy is doing relatively well. It grew by almost 4 percent in 2006 although its growth rate has slipped since then because of the recession. Although the gap between rich and poor is growing, gross national product (GNP) per capita is almost eighteen thousand per year, or about 60 percent of that in the United States. One indicator of Hungary's growing affluence is that 70 percent of the population already owned a cell phone by the end of 2003.

Third, and perhaps most important, the Hungarian transition occurred so smoothly, in part because many reform-minded communists and opposition leaders cooperated with each other in a process political scientists

Economic Liberalization
in the Current and Former Communist World

Liberalization in general and privatization in particular have been very popular policies since the collapse of communism in Eurasia. In fact, the process began somewhat sooner in China, Hungary, and Yugoslavia.

These countries also provide us with a classic example of how theoretical predictions and empirical realities do not always jibe. In this case, the now dominant liberal economic theory tells us that freeing markets, decentralizing control of an economy, and transferring ownership from state to private hands should do tremendous good.

However, the situation on the ground has never been quite so rosy. In countries in which **shock therapy** (an economic policy that called for as rapid a shift as possible from public to private ownership, whatever the social and political costs) has been fully implemented, we have seen tremendous growth in the disparities between the winners and losers of economic reform. In most countries, as well, political pressures forced governments to slow the pace of reform to some degree, and resentment against change sparked the limited left-wing resurgence noted at the beginning of this chapter. ■

no more intense than those between U.S. Democrats and Republicans, even when they are in the midst of post-2010 budget stalemate.

Troubled Transitions: The Former Soviet Union

The case of Russia and most of the former Soviet Republics is a different story. With the exception of the Baltic states (Latvia, Estonia, and Lithuania), these countries have had a much harder time making the political and economic transition. Like Russia, most have held several elections. However, the best we can say about these elections is that several of them have been relatively free and fair contests. However, very few of them resulted in a genuine shift in power in which a party or coalition that was once in opposition took office. All suffer from corruption because an elite of former communists has not only entrenched itself in political power but has enriched itself by gaining control of the countries' leading enterprises, whether they remain in public hands or have been officially privatized. We will defer dealing with these difficulties in any detail until the next chapter.

Ethnic Conflict

President George H. W. Bush used to enjoy noting that the forty-five years between the end of World War II and the collapse of communism marked the longest period in recorded history without a war in Europe. Unfortunately, that period lasted only forty-five years.

By the early 1990s, sporadic fighting had broken out in a number of the former Soviet republics. It began even before the USSR collapsed with the conflict between Armenia and Azerbaijan over the predominantly Armenian enclave of Nagorno-Karabakh within Azerbaijan.

For our purposes, it is most important to note two conflicts that have had a devastating impact on the peoples caught up in the fighting. The former Yugoslavia has experienced five wars since the breakup of the country in 1991. Only the first one, over the independence of Slovenia, resulted in few casualties and caused little damage. By contrast, upward of two hundred fifty thousand people were killed and millions more were turned into refugees during the struggle in Bosnia-Herzegovina, which also introduced the notion of ethnic cleansing into the world's political vocabulary.

The wars between Russia and rebels in Chechnya have been even more devastating. Antagonism toward Russians in the tiny, mostly Muslim region has existed since it was incorporated into Russia in the early nineteenth century. Bloody fighting erupted when Russia put down a first bid for independence in 1994–96. After two years of fighting,

call **pacting**. Among other things, that made it relatively easy for the former communists to turn themselves into a Western-style social democratic party, which has won two elections since 1989, and to establish something approaching a consensus on economic policy with their former opponents.

Thus, both democracy and market capitalism are taking root in Hungary and the other reasonably successful post-communist states in Eastern Europe. In Hungary's case that can be seen in the fact that the Left and the Right have each won two elections since 1989 and the transition from Left to Right and back to Left again has gone smoothly each time. Disagreements between Left and Right are still significant, but most observers think they are tens of thousands were dead, the city of Grozny had been leveled, and no settlement had been reached. The war broke out again shortly after Vladimir Putin became Russia's prime minister in 1999. This time the Russians were able to defeat the rebels more handily, but only after thousands of civilians and rebels had been killed. Sporadic fighting continues almost a decade after the war supposedly ended, including the world's deadliest terrorist attack since 9/11.

What Is Left of Marxism?

North Korea and Cuba have kept their orthodox Marxist-Leninist systems, and their people have paid the price. Their countries are among the poorest in the world. There have been reports of mass starvation in North Korea, for instance.

In contrast, the others have embraced economic reform to the point that countries such as China and Vietnam have mixed economies in which the private sector is far more dynamic than the remaining state-owned monopolies. In fact, the shift toward capitalism and the popularity of the growing consumer culture is so pronounced that there is little of Marxist egalitarianism left. Even Cuba is experimenting with private businesses, mostly in the tourism industry.

The one remaining aspect of Marxism-Leninism is the continued political monopoly enjoyed by the communist parties in these countries. As we will see in Chapter 10, the Chinese communists have cracked down whenever any signs of political dissent appeared, and, so far, most Chinese citizens have been willing to accept economic reform without political liberalization. However, many observers are convinced that it is only a matter of time before a significant number of people demand political as well as economic change.

Globalization and the Communist World

Prior to the 1980s, global trends did not affect communist countries as much as the democracies covered in Part 2. However, globalization did have a bearing on them then—and has an even more powerful impact today—in two broad ways.

First, global forces were at least indirectly responsible for the crisis of communism that is at the heart of this chapter. The communist countries certainly had their internal problems. However, they might well have survived had they not faced increased economic pressures and a renewed arms race with the West.

Second, international influences have left their current states in a weakened position, economically and otherwise. As we will see with the Russian economy in the next chapter, the triumph of capitalism has given Western bankers, industrialists, and politicians unprecedented influence over the internal affairs of most of these countries. In addition, that impact is not merely economic, as the popularity of Western cultural icons from CNN to Coca-Cola to Barbie dolls attests. To cite but one admittedly trivial example, you can buy *matroshka* dolls (multiple dolls within dolls) in Moscow's open-air markets with likenesses of the Clinton family (including Monica Lewinsky), the Simpsons, and the New York Yankees. ■

THE MEDIA

When political scientists wrote about the totalitarian nature of communist regimes, they invariably included the media in their list of characteristics. The media in the communist bloc were never like those in the West. The party controlled them hook, line, and sinker. Every newspaper, magazine, and book printed, as well as all television and radio outlets, were controlled by the party. What's more, anything printed or broadcast was subject to prior censorship. Meanwhile, the authorities kept Western media out.

That started to change in the 1980s. Advances in communication technology made it more difficult to keep Western influences out. Then, during the Gorbachev years, there was a noticeable loosening of controls in the Soviet Union and, to a lesser degree, in Eastern Europe. Since then, the printed press in Eastern Europe has been just as open as in the West and, given the nature of political and economic life, even more contentious. Even in Russia, where the state still dominates the main national television channels, viewers have little trouble finding criticism of the status quo in a dwindling number of independent newspapers, on the radio, and through the Internet at least among those who have some access to it. In 2011, about a million and a half families had broadband in their homes.

There are cracks in the party's protective armor in the countries that have kept their communist regimes. The protesters in Tiananmen Square were able to coordinate their activities in part because of faxes they received from Chinese students abroad, and the CCP is now struggling to limit access to satellite television and the Internet, which has become all the more difficult now that protesters are using social media, as we will see most clearly in Chapter 13 on Iran. Similarly, Cuba's isolation is less than complete, something American sports fans discovered when they learned that 1998 World Series star Orlando Hernandez (El Duque) of the New York Yankees had watched his half-brother Livan's exploits for the Florida Marlins on television beamed from the United States before deciding to make his own escape from the island.

Conclusion: Which Crisis Revisited

Those of us who are old enough to have lived through the height of the Cold War "knew" that the Soviet Union and its allies would be competitors with and adversaries of the West for the indefinite future. The superpower rivalry seemed to be the most important and most dangerous relationship in international political life.

But it is gone now. None of us miss it. What is not clear is what happens next.

Less than a quarter of a century ago, these countries all had Marxist-Leninist regimes and seemed destined to for the indefinite future.

And as we said on a few occasions in this chapter, the transitions are unprecedented and bring large number of crises in their wake. Analysts tend to focus on the ones that are most germane to their academic discipline. But it is hard to do so for two reasons.

First, they are unprecedented in terms of scope.

Second, post-Leninist leaders are tying to affect these changes in an amazingly short period of time. France and Germany, for instance, struggled for more than a century to establish their democracies on anything approaching a firm footing.

Given those two criteria, suspending judgment and watching as events unfold seem like a prudent academic strategy.

Of necessity, this had to be a primarily historical chapter.

Still, we should not ignore the impact that the current economic crisis can add to the pre-existing ones involving the collapse of communism in Eurasia.

The economic crisis has hit the most integrated economies the hardest. And harder than anywhere in Western Europe other than Greece, Portugal, Ireland, and Iceland (not a member of the EU). In 2009 alone, it forced the prime ministers of Hungary, the Czech Republic, and Latvia to resign. So far, none of the more stable democratic regimes seem to be in jeopardy.

But who knows what another year or two of sharp decline could lead to?

Looking FORWARD

IT SHOULD BE clear that the rest of Part 3 will bring these historical and conceptual ideas down to earth with case studies. If we are going to do two, they are obvious: Russia and China.

As we hinted at in this chapter, they represent the two, almost polar, options the communist world faced beginning in the 1980s. The Soviet Union under Gorbachev chose to open the political system in most ways without firming plans for making, let alone implementing, economic policy beforehand. By contrast, China has allowed maximum experimentation with market principles in the economy, to the point that even most state-owned companies now seek to make profits and compete with other firms based either at home or abroad. At the

same time, there has been little or no political reform. In fact, any time reforms seemed to threaten the CCP's monopoly on power, the party clamped down.

In sum, the next two chapters ask a simple pair of questions. Why did the two countries pursue such different paths? Given that, what, if any, is the future of socialism, Marxism, or Marxism-Leninism?

It would have been interesting to consider two other countries—one that made the transition to reasonable facsimiles of liberal democracy and a market economy such as Poland or Hungary and one that steadfastly clings to an ultra-authoritarian version of Marxism-Leninism such as Cuba or North Vietnam.

Alas, there just isn't room.

Key Terms

Concepts

base

bourgeoisie

command economy

communism

contradictions

cult of personality

democratic centralism

dialectic

glasnost

historical materialism

Marxist-Leninist

means of production

nomenklatura

pacting

party state

perestroika

proletariat

satellite

shock therapy

socialism

superstructure

totalitarianism

People

Brezhnev, Leonid

Castro, Fidel

Deng Xiaoping

Engels, Friedrich

Gorbachev, Mikhail

Khrushchev, Nikita

Lenin, Vladimir

Mao Zedong

Marx, Karl

Stalin, Joseph

Yeltsin, Boris

Organizations, Places, and Events

Bolsheviks

Comintern

Cultural Revolution

de-Stalinization

general secretary

Politburo

Secretariat

Solidarity

Third International

Tiananmen Square

Warsaw Pact

Useful Websites

Communism in Eurasia collapsed just as the Internet was becoming even a minor factor in our lives, therefore there are not as many good sites on it as one would like. Both Marxists.org and the Australian National University maintain archives with many of the basic documents in Marxist history.

> **www.anu.edu.au/polsci/marx/**

My colleague Bryan Caplan of George Mason University's Department of Economics runs a highly critical "Museum of Communism" website.

> **www.gmu.edu/depts/economics/bcaplan/museum/marframe.htm**

Transitions Online and Radio Free Europe/Radio Liberty both provide regular news feeds on post-communist countries.

> **www.rferl.org**

St. Francis Xavier University in Canada has an excellent program in post-communist studies, including a website with some of its scholars' own writing and a great group of lists.

> **www.stfx.ca/pinstitutes/cpcs/**

Further Reading

Ash, Timothy Garton. *The Magic Lantern.* New York: Random House, 1990. The best general account of what happened in Eastern Europe in 1989 by someone who witnessed most of it firsthand.

Chavance, Bernard. *The Transformation of Communist Systems: Economic Reform Since the 1950s.* Trans. by Charles Hauss. Boulder, CO: Westview Press, 1994. The only brief overview of communist political economy and efforts at reform that carries into the early 1990s.

Dawisha, Karen. *Eastern Europe, Gorbachev, and Reform.* New York: Cambridge University Press, 1990. The best academic treatment of domestic politics in Eastern Europe in the years before 1989.

Diamond, Larry, and Marc F. Plattner, eds. *Democracy after Communism.* Baltimore: Johns Hopkins University Press, 2002. A generally excellent collection of articles drawn from the *Journal of Democracy*, which means they were written for a general more than a scholarly audience.

Lindblom, Charles. *Politics and Markets.* New York: Basic Books, 1977. A rather dense, theoretical, and dated book, but also one of the first to identify the limits to what could be accomplished with a command economy.

Mason, David S. *Revolution in East Central Europe: The Rise and Fall of Communism and the Cold War,* 2nd ed. Boulder, CO: Westview Press, 1997. An outstanding overview of why communism came to power in Eastern Europe, why it collapsed, and why the countries in that region have had such trouble since then.

Nolan, Peter. *China's Rise/Russia's Fall.* London: Cassell/Pinter, 1997. The only good book contrasting the reforms in the two countries; makes an unusual, left-of-center argument.

Przeworski, Adam, et al. *Sustainable Democracy.* New York: Cambridge University Press, 1995. By a group of twenty-one prominent social scientists; an exploration of what we know about democratization, drawing on the experiences of southern Europe, South America, and Eurasia.

Tucker, Robert C., ed. *The Marx and Engels Reader,* 2nd ed. New York: Norton, 1984. Among the best of the many collections of Marx's and Engels' basic works.

World Bank. *World Development Report: From Plan to Market.* New York: Oxford University Press, 1997. A report on liberalization in the "transitional" economies; heavy going, but informative.

CHAPTER 9

Russia

Autocratic leadership existed in Russia for many centuries, changing only its ideological colors and method of legitimization.

LILIA SHEVTSOVA

THE BASICS

Russia

OFFICIAL NAME	RUSSIAN FEDERATION
Size	17,075,200 sq. km (roughly 1.75 times the size of the United States)
Climate	Subarctic in much of the country
Population	139 million
Currency	32 rubles = US$1
GNP per capita	$15,100
Ethnic composition	79.8% Russian, 3.8% Tatar, 2% Ukrainian, 14.4% Other
Life Expectancy	Men 60, Women 73
Capital	Moscow
President	Dmitri Medvedev (2008–)
Prime Minister	Vladimir Putin (2008–)

DÉJÀ VU ALL OVER AGAIN?

Yogi Berra was one of the greatest baseball players of all time, but he is better known today for uttering one liners that make little sense after you think about them for a second—a skill that got him a late-in-life career pitching AFLAC insurance.

One of his best quips was to say about a game that it was "déjà vu all over again," or, the repeat of the past repeating the past. Although Yogi will never become one of the world's greatest political scientists, his statement makes a lot of sense as we write during the first months of 2011.

A little more than three years earlier, President **Vladimir Putin** (1952–) had to leave office because he had served the two terms he was allowed by the constitution. He was replaced by his hand-picked successor, **Dmitri Medvedev** (1965–) who won the 2008 presidential election with a mere 71 percent of the vote. Putin was then appointed prime minister, a position from which he all but runs the country. Most analysts also assume that Putin will run for the presidency again in 2012 whether Medvedev decides to seek reelection or not. There is next to no doubt about the outcome should he run, even though we are more than two years before the vote occurs.

The political sleight of hand here would not be probable or even possible in the countries covered in Part 2.

Looking BACKWARD

WE HAVE JUST spent almost half of this book considering reasonably stable and democratic states. That does not mean that political life in those countries lacks its share of excitement. To cite but one example, we began revising this chapter on the day the United States held its mid-term congressional elections, dealing the Obama administration a major setback.

But nothing we have seen approaches the level of tensions that have been a common feature of Russian political life since the collapse of the Soviet Union in 1991. The USSR turned into fifteen sovereign states.

Russia is the largest, but it has barely half of the former Soviet Union's territory or population. It has survived a rash—and probably alcoholic—president, a half dozen wrenching economic crises, and a return toward authoritarian rule, albeit under a regime that bears little resemblance to that of the USSR which helped give rise to the term "totalitarianism."

In short, as suggested in the looking forward boxes in the previous two chapters, we will now begin considering countries in which the political stakes are a lot higher. And they will get even higher in the chapters to come.

President Bill Clinton could not pass the political baton to his Vice President, Al Gore. Gordon Brown suffered from being the successor to his friend and rival, Tony Blair. President Nicolas Sarkozy comes from a very different wing of the center-right than all of his predecessors in the Gaullist movement.

In other words, the shift to Medvedev and the inclusion of Putin in the new government in a supposedly less important role is a sign of just how much more political life is controlled by the elites in Russia than in the industrialized democracies. This is a theme that will become more and more important as we move through the second half of this book.

When Putin stepped down (or aside), two main parties competed for the presidency. One was **United Russia** and the other was **Just Russia** (one can see Yogi and the AFLAC duck trying to figure that one out). In fact, both were creations of Putin's team at the Kremlin, and therein lies the importance of the story.

Many Russian analysts are concerned that Putin and his colleagues are taking the country dangerously close to its Soviet and totalitarian past. The statement by Lilia Shevtsova that begins this chapter is almost a decade old. Even at the dawn of this new century and millennium, she understood that something important and worrisome was happening in Moscow.

All television stations, the leading radio networks, and most newspapers are again under the Kremlin's control. Political competition has been limited as a result of new laws that make it harder for opposition or even regional parties to run for office.

The new leadership, as well, came to power at the onset of the economic crisis. As we will see later in the chapter, the transition from communism to democracy and capitalism did not come easily in Russia. Nonetheless, in the late 1990s and early 2000s its economic growth rate spiked, largely as the result of sharp increases in the price of oil and gas, its only significant exports.

So, when the crisis hit shortly after Medvedev's election, the impact on Russia was greater than we have seen anywhere else so far. In particular, oil prices fell by a half or more, which cost Russia most of its earnings from international trade. Each dollar in oil price gains or losses is worth nearly $2 billion a year for Russian gross domestic

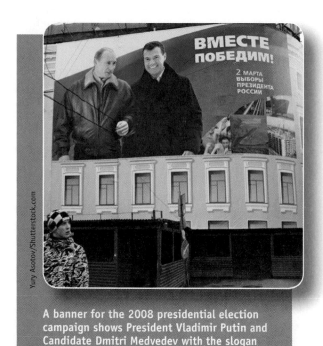

A banner for the 2008 presidential election campaign shows President Vladimir Putin and Candidate Dmitri Medvedev with the slogan "Together We Will Win."

Yury Asotov/Shutterstock.com

product. Because, as again we will see, the Russian economy was already weak on other fronts, and therefore the crisis sent shock waves throughout the country. Prices of all petrochemical goods have risen appreciably since then. And while Russia has benefited from the increase, it still has to deal with the fact that it is the only major emerging economy that is so dependent on a single export.

A couple of statistics tell it all. The Russian GDP grew by about 8 percent in 2008. It was projected to decline by almost the same amount in 2009. The inflation rate is almost 12 percent.

Foreign debt and vulnerability are at an all time high despite the boom of the previous decade and the current spike in oil prices. And given the recentralization of power since the collapse of the Soviet Union, Yogi probably had it right with one exception. There is no AFLAC duck to provide the kind of insurance he promotes on American television.

THINKING ABOUT RUSSIA

Russia's future—with or without Putin—will not be easy in ways that will reflect the raised stakes of political life that will be at the heart of both Parts 3 and 4 of this book. There is no better way to see that than in the trial and conviction of **Mikhail Khodorkovsky** (1963–), once a darling of the post-Soviet business community and one of the oligarchs who had unusual access to **Boris Yeltsin** (1931–2007). But Khodorkovsky and several of his colleagues ran afoul of Putin. He was convicted of multiple counts of fraud—including his "failure" to pay as much as $4.5 billion in taxes from his oil company, Yukos. He was also sentenced to nine years in prison. He has since been convicted of yet another "crime" and could well spend the rest of his life in jail even though the Russian Supreme Court ruled that his conviction was politically motivated on June 1, 2011. Some of his colleagues escaped jail and live in exile in Israel, England, and Cyprus.

What makes Russia important is not that some of its politicians and business leaders honor the constitution and the rule of law in the breach. That can and does occur everywhere some of the time. Rather, it is at the heart of our field because the stakes of political life are so much higher than they are today in any of the countries covered in Part 2, as Russia tries to make one of the most dramatic and difficult transitions in world history.

The Basics

Geography

The **Russian Federation** is the world's largest country, stretching across eleven time zones. Although Russia only has about half the population of the former Soviet Union,

it is still the sixth most populous country in the world, trailing only China, India, the United States, Indonesia, and Brazil.

Russia is also blessed with an abundance of natural resources, including oil, natural gas, and precious minerals, though many of these resources lie under permafrost. That is not surprising given that the Russian Federation is also one of the coldest countries on earth. Almost all its territory lies above the forty-eighth parallel, which separates the United States from Canada. St. Petersburg has six hours of dim sunlight in January. Kotlas, in the northern region of Arkhangelsk, has a growing season of about forty-five days, which makes even raising radishes difficult. If you spend time in Russia in January, the weather forecast will become boringly monotonous—*sneg ne bolshoi*—snow, but not much.

Diversity

Perhaps a more important thing to note about Russia and the other fourteen former Soviet republics is their diversity. As Table 9.1 shows, Russia's population, for instance, was only 82 percent Russian when the Union of Soviet Socialist

TABLE 9.1 Ethnic Composition of the Former Soviet Republics

COUNTRY	POPULATION (%)	TITULAR NATIONALITY (%)	MAIN MINORITIES (%)
Russia	147.0	82	Tatars 4
Ukraine	51.5	73	Russians 22
Uzbekistan	19.8	71	Russians 8
Kazakhstan	16.5	40	Russians 38
			Ukrainians 5
Belarus	10.2	78	Russians 13
Azerbaijan	7.0	83	Russians 6
			Armenians 6
Georgia	5.4	70	Armenians 8
			Russians 6
			Azeris 6
Tajikistan	5.1	62	Uzbeks 23
			Russians 7
Moldova	4.3	65	Ukrainians 14
			Russians 13
Kyrgyzstan	4.3	52	Russians 22
			Uzbeks 12
Lithuania	3.7	80	Russians 9
			Poles 7
Turkmenistan	3.5	72	Russians 9
			Uzbeks 9
Armenia	3.3	93	Azeris 2
Latvia	2.7	52	Russians 35
Estonia	1.6	62	Russians 30

Source: Based on 1989 census.

Republics (USSR) collapsed, and twelve of the others were even more ethnically diverse. All but Armenia have sizable Russian minorities, which has heightened demands from nationalists to recreate the Soviet Union in what they call the **near abroad**.

From the late 1980s onward, several of the Soviet Republics experienced ethnic fighting. In other words, the Soviet Union was anything but a melting pot. Unlike immigrants who came to the United States voluntarily (other than the slaves, of course), most Chechens or Tatars or Kazakhs were forced to join the Russian Empire prior to the communist revolution that led to the creation of the USSR.

Although most non-Russian groups retained their culture and language, the Soviet regime kept a lid on ethnic protest until the late 1980s. But the reforms launched in those years allowed minority groups to voice their dissatisfactions and by 1991 each republic had declared some form of sovereignty or independence from central rule. Most experienced substantial violence. In some places, ethnic tensions have gotten worse since the collapse of the Soviet Union. Fighting over the mostly Armenian enclave of Nagorno-Karabakh in Azerbaijan, for example, has continued on and off since 1988. The three Baltic republics passed legislation restricting the ability of ethnic Russians and other "foreigners" who lived in the republics at the time of independence to achieve Lithuanian, Latvian, or Estonian citizenship. The ethnic strife continues to this day, mostly in the on-again, off-again war between Russia and rebels who seek independence in Chechnya and as of May 2011 between Armenia and Azerbaijan.

Poverty

Russia is also much poorer than any of the countries we have covered so far. It is the only major country in the world in which life expectancy has declined in the last generation. A typical urban family lives in a three-room apartment, does not own an automobile, and may not even have a telephone. Living conditions in the countryside are worse. Household tasks take at least twice as long as in the West because stores are poorly organized and few families have washing machines, microwaves, and other laborsaving devices that are standard in Western homes. Table 9.2 summarizes statistical data from the 1990s on the declining production of basic goods most Russian citizens and corporations rely on in their daily lives. As the table at the beginning of the chapter suggests, things have improved in the last decade, but Russia remains far poorer than any industrialized democracy.

Russia is often included in the list of so-called BRICS countries that are widely viewed as the world's emerging economies. Russia belongs on the list because it is so large.

TABLE 9.2 Economic Decline in Russia, 1990–97*

PRODUCT	1990	1997
Meat	6.6	1.4
Butter	0.8	0.3
Canned goods (billions of cans)	8.2	2.2
Salt	4.2	2.1
Bread	16.2	8.9
Pasta	1.0	0.5
Footwear (millions of pairs)	385.0	32.0
Silk (millions of square yards)	1,051.0	134.0
Coats (millions; later figure is 1992)	17.2	2.3
Cement	83.0	26.6
Beer (millions of gallons)	874.0	655.0
Watches and clocks (millions of units)	60.1	5.0
Refrigerators (millions of units)	3.8	0.1
Vacuum cleaners (millions of units)	4.5	0.6

*All figures in millions of tons unless otherwise noted. Source: Adapted from the *Washington Post*, November 14, 1998, A16.

However, its rate of growth and the slow improvement of its standard of living pale in comparison of those in Brazil, India, South Africa, and China (see Chapters 10, 11, 12, and the South African and Brazilian chapters online).

The Environment

Russia is an environmental nightmare. The disaster at Chernobyl in 1986 was the worst accident ever at a nuclear power plant and devastated hundreds of square miles of farmland. Scientists predict that upward of thirty thousand people will die over the next three generations as a result of cancer and other diseases caused by radiation from the plant.

Chernobyl was only the most glaring environmental catastrophe. The Soviet and Russian governments dumped dozens of spent, leaking, and dangerous nuclear reactors from submarines into the ocean. More than 70 million people in the former Soviet Union live in cities where it is unhealthy to breathe the air. Three-quarters of the surface water is polluted. A water diversion project led to the shrinking of the Aral Sea by dozens of miles, and the salt left behind when the water evaporated has destroyed the soil that is now on the surface.

Air and water pollution in the city of Kemerevo, where the environment is probably is too dirty to be cleaned up, is all too typical. Its residents have three times the average incidence of chronic bronchitis, kidney failure, and diseases of the endocrine system. In one particularly filthy neighborhood, 7 percent of the children born in 1989 were mentally impaired, more than three times the national average. In the small city of Karabash, a foundry emits the equivalent of nine tons annually of sulfur, lead, arsenic, tellurium, and other pollutants—for each man, woman, and child.

The Stakes of Russian Politics: A Lighter View

When the Soviet Union was falling apart in late 1991, the *Economist* ran a tongue-in-cheek contest, asking its readers to suggest names for the new country that would be replacing it. Here are some of the more revealing—and humorous—answers:

RELICS—Republics Left in Total Chaos
PITS—Post-Imperial Total Shambles
COMA—Confederation of Mutual Antagonism (its people would be called Commies)
UFFR—Union of Fewer and Fewer Republics

Key Concepts and Questions

On one level, the key questions to ask about Russia are the same as those laid out in Chapter 1, including how its state evolved, what it is like today, and how it deals with domestic and international pressures. Although all of the core concepts discussed in Parts 1 or 2 are relevant here, we should focus on a few that were not terribly important until now but will be critical in the rest of the book as we deal with fragile and/or failing states. However, given the differences between Russia and the countries covered in Part 2, we will also have to spend more time on the historical material and then focus on the uncertainties and difficulties that emerged during Yeltsin's presidency, which have continued under Putin and Medvedev.

- How and why did the Soviet Union collapse?

- How did its legacy affect the way Russia has evolved?

- Will Putin and his successors be able to strengthen and stabilize the Russian state? Why has the Russian regime had so much trouble gaining legitimacy despite the widespread dislike of the Soviet Union? In so doing, will they also be able to make the regime more democratic and legitimate?

- Can they build stronger and more broadly accepted institutions now that the economy is more stable than it was in the 1990s?

- Is rapid and uncontrolled privatization the best way of responding to globalization?

- How will Russia adapt to its new international role in which it remains a major power in some military arenas but is increasingly buffeted by global economic forces beyond its control?

THE EVOLUTION OF THE RUSSIAN STATE

The Russian Federation is a new state, and it is, therefore, tempting to begin this section by discussing the events that led to its creation following the collapse of the Soviet Union. However, it would be a mistake to do so. Perhaps even more than was the case for the countries covered in Part 2, its past weighs heavily on its present. If nothing else, most leading politicians were active members of the **Communist Party of the Soviet Union (CPSU)**, and most Russian adults lived the bulk of their lives under its rule.

Therefore, this section actually has to be somewhat longer and more detailed than its equivalents in previous chapters. Not only do we have to examine the basic trends in Russian and Soviet history before 1991, we have to dig more deeply into the institutions and power bases of the once-powerful state that collapsed so quickly and so unexpectedly 🌐 (**www.departments.bucknell.edu/russian**).

The Broad Sweep of Russian History

Accounts of Russian history normally begin with the ninth-century Kievan Rus, which was centered in today's Ukraine. The Kievans were but one of many Slavic tribes that occupied a wide arc stretching from the former Yugoslavia (which literally means "land of the southern Slavs") northward and eastward to Siberia, which the Kievans and their Russian successors gradually took over.

Russia's evolution was not as easy or as peaceful as that last sentence might suggest. Time and time again, Russia was invaded and overrun. However, by the early nineteenth century, it had solidified itself as one of Europe's major powers and had occupied most of the lands that would become part of the Soviet Union a century later.

This does not mean that Russia remained one of Europe's great powers for long. It had missed out on most of the transformations that reshaped Western Europe from the 1500s onward. The tsars remained absolute monarchs. There was no Reformation, leaving Russia dominated by an Orthodox Church with strong ties to the autocracy. Individualism, the scientific revolution, and the other intellectual trends that played such a key role in the West had next to no impact on Russia.

There were periods of reform. Peter the Great (ruled 1682–1725) introduced ideas and technologies from the West, just as Mikhail Gorbachev was to do three centuries later. From then on, Russia always had Westernizers, who looked elsewhere for ways to modernize their country. Just as important, though, were the Slavophiles, who were convinced that Russian traditions were superior to anything in the West and who fought to keep foreign influences out.

TABLE 9.3   Key Events in the Origins of the Soviet State

YEAR	EVENT
1854	Start of the Crimean War
1881	Assassination of Tsar Alexander II
1904–05	Russo-Japanese War
1905	First revolution
1914	Outbreak of World War I
1917	February and October revolutions
1921	End of civil war, formal creation of Soviet Union
1924	Death of Lenin

Consequently, Russia lagged behind the other European powers. As is so often the case, the stark realities of Russia's situation were driven home by a relatively minor event: its defeat by Britain and France in the Crimean War of 1854–55. That defeat set political forces in motion, which would culminate in the revolution of 1917 (see Table 9.3).

Prelude to Revolution

As we saw in Chapter 8, Marx expected a socialist revolution to occur first in one of the industrialized capitalist countries. Instead, it took place in a Russia that had little in common with the more advanced societies Marx had in mind. Three overlapping differences between the expectations of Marxist theory and the realities of life in Russia go a long way toward explaining why the Bolshevik revolution occurred, and then why the USSR turned out as it did.

Backwardness

The term *backwardness* is value-laden and pejorative. However, it does describe Russia in the second half of the nineteenth century. At the time, Russia had a tenth of the railroad lines of Germany or France. To the degree that Russia was beginning to industrialize, its factories were owned either by the government or by foreigners, so it did not develop the class of independent capitalists Marx assumed would industrialize society and lay the groundwork for an eventual socialist revolution. As late as the 1860s, most Russians were serfs who were, for all intents and purposes, slaves of their feudal lords. At the end of the century, over 90 percent of the people still lived in the countryside. Most urban workers were illiterate and had not developed the organization and sophistication Marx expected of a mature proletariat.

Failed Reform

Russia also adopted few of the democratic reforms we saw in eighteenth and nineteenth-century France and Britain. Indeed, groups that advocated individualism or limits on the autocracy had no choice but to be revolutionaries. There were no "inside the system" ways of effectively pressing for change.

In the aftermath of Russia's defeat in the Crimean War, the new tsar, Alexander II (ruled 1855–81), realized that Russia was lagging too far behind the West and began a series of belated yet far too limited reforms. Serfs were liberated. Some forms of censorship were relaxed. Universities and the civil service were opened to commoners. Alexander was on the verge of introducing a constitution that would give about 5 percent of the male population the right to vote when he was assassinated in 1881.

Political reform came to a halt under his son, Alexander III (ruled 1881–94). State-led industrialization continued, but this tsar was a reactionary who reinforced the autocratic state at the same time that the power of kings and lords was disappearing in the West.

A Weak State

This does not mean that Russia had a strong state. In fact, during the reign of the last tsar, Nicholas II (ruled 1894–1917), the state grew weaker and weaker in every respect other than its ability to infiltrate revolutionary movements.

Russia's weakness was especially evident in its dealings with the rest of the world. The Russian elite continued to think of their country as a great power. The fact that it was not was driven home as a result of the disastrous Russo-Japanese War and World War I. In 1904, Russia attacked Japan, in part to quell dissent at home. The Russians assumed they would win easily, but they were routed by the Japanese. Any remaining pretenses to great power status were shattered in World War I, when Russian troops on horseback were mowed down by the dramatically better-trained and better-equipped forces of Germany and its allies.

Lenin and the (Wrong?) Revolution

Not surprisingly, a growing number of Russians found their political and economic situation to be intolerable. Because the state maintained its secret police and banned all reformist groups, the ranks of revolutionaries swelled with dissidents of all stripes, many of whom were forced into exile.

By the 1890s, these dissidents included small groups of Marxists. They were actually among the least revolutionary because, as orthodox Marxists, they assumed that Russia would have to first go through capitalism before a socialist revolution was possible.

Early in the 1900s, however, one of the exiled Marxists, **V. I. Lenin** (1870–1924), reached a conclusion that was to define Russian politics until the Soviet Union collapsed. As he saw it, the situation in Russia was so bad that the country could not wait until the conditions for a Marxist revolution were ripe.

In the pamphlet *What Is to Be Done?* (**www.fordham .edu/halsall/mod/1902lenin.html**), Lenin outlined plans for a new type of revolutionary organization. He argued that only a small, secretive, hierarchical party of professional revolutionaries could hope to succeed. To thwart the secret police, the party would have to be based on what he called **democratic centralism**. Discussion and debate would be allowed before the party decided to act. However, once a decision was made, everyone had to obey it without question. Leaders at the top would co-opt officials to run lower-level organizations, which, in turn, would not be allowed to communicate with each other. Party members would all use pseudonyms. All of these measures were designed to make it hard for the secret police to infiltrate what Lenin expected would be an efficient machine.

At a congress of the Social Democratic Party held in 1903, there was a spirited debate over Lenin's ideas, which led to the famous split between the **Mensheviks** and **Bolsheviks**. The former, advocating a more orthodox Marxist approach, barely lost on the key vote to Lenin's supporters, who came to be called Bolsheviks—a term that simply meant they were the larger faction.

Like the party itself, their disagreements had little practical impact because most socialist leaders were living in exile and had minimal support at home. Nonetheless, the Bolsheviks' prospects improved dramatically over the next fifteen years, not so much because of anything they did but because the tsarist regime continued to weaken. A spontaneous revolution broke out in 1905 in the wake of the Japanese debacle. Although the tsar was able to put it down and solidify his power in the short run, the state turned out to be even more vulnerable than it had been before the war began.

The autocracy finally collapsed in 1917 as Russia staggered toward defeat in World War I. The tsar was replaced by a **provisional government** that, in turn, found itself unable to withstand a counterrevolution by tsarist forces without the help of the Bolsheviks. Finally, in the fall, Lenin decided that the time had come. On the night of November 7, 1917, Bolshevik troops overthrew the provisional government. For the first time anywhere, Marxists had succeeded in taking over a government. But the revolution was by no means over. Although the Bolsheviks quickly took control of most cities, they had little support in the countryside and faced opposition from dozens of other groups. In the Constituent Assembly elected on November 25, they won only 168 of the 703 seats.

Despite the Bolsheviks' lack of popular support, Lenin was not prepared to yield. He allowed the assembly to meet once in January 1918 and then closed it for good, dashing hopes for a democratic outcome. Meanwhile, the Bolsheviks accepted the Brest-Litovsk Treaty with Germany, which cost revolutionary Russia 32 percent of its arable land, 26 percent of its railroads, 33 percent of its factories, and 75 percent of its coal mines. As industrial production dropped to a third of its 1913 level, thousands of workers fled the cities. No one knows how many people froze or starved to death.

Profiles
V. I. Lenin

Lenin was the chief architect of the Bolshevik revolution and the first leader of the Soviet Union.

He was born Vladimir Ulyanov in 1870. His father was a successful bureaucrat, and young Vladimir seemed destined for a prominent career himself until his brother was arrested and hanged for his involvement in a plot to assassinate the tsar. Vladimir entered university shortly thereafter and began studying law but was quickly expelled and sent into exile for his own political activities. He spent those years near the Lena River, from which he derived his pseudonym. While in his first period of exile, he became a Marxist. He finished his studies independently and was admitted to the bar in 1891. Lenin spent the rest of the 1890s organizing dissidents in St. Petersburg and was in and out of jail until he was sent into exile again in 1900, this time outside of Russia.

V. I. Lenin addressing communist activists and soldiers in Red Square, 1919.

Lenin returned to Russia after the tsar was overthrown and led the Bolsheviks' seizure of power in the October revolution. But he never fully recovered from an assassination attempt that left him with a bullet in his shoulder and another in his lung. He suffered three strokes between 1922 and 1923 and died in 1924. ■

Civil war broke out in 1918. A poorly organized group of forces loyal to the tsar and the provisional government joined with other revolutionary factions in an attempt to topple the new Bolshevik regime. The Bolsheviks responded by reinforcing democratic centralism, laying the groundwork for the CPSU's domination. They created the **Cheka**, their first secret police, to enforce discipline within the party. At the same time, the Bolsheviks had to bring back members of the old elite to run the factories and the new Red Army. Because the Bolsheviks did not trust them, they assigned loyal political commissars to oversee what the officers and bureaucrats did.

In 1921, the Bolsheviks gained control of the entire country. Once their rule was secure, they formally created the USSR. The Communist Party was given the leading role in policy making and supervised everything that happened in the new country. The overlapping party and state hierarchies from the civil war were maintained along with democratic centralism.

In the early 1920s, the Soviet Union was not yet the totalitarian dictatorship it would become under Stalin. There were still open debates within the party. There were also lively cultural and artistic communities in which dissenting views were frequently raised. Stringent wartime economic measures were relaxed under the New Economic Policy (NEP), which encouraged peasants, merchants, and even some industrialists to pursue private businesses.

Terror and the Modernization of the Soviet Union

Before he died in 1924, Lenin wrote a political "testament" in which he criticized the Bolshevik leadership. He singled out Leon Trotsky (1879–1940) and **Joseph Stalin** (1879–1953), warning that neither should be allowed to take over the party.

To make a long and complicated story short, Lenin's wishes were not heeded. After an intense factional fight, Stalin won control of the party—and, hence, the country. Few people had expected him to replace Lenin. He was not part of the group of exiled intellectuals who led the Bolsheviks before the revolution. Instead, he stayed at home to work with the underground party, among other things robbing banks to raise money for it. After the revolution, Stalin was put in charge of the party organization. From that position, he was able to surpass his more visible rivals because, in a party in which all leaders are co-opted, he determined who was appointed to which positions.

The quarter-century that Stalin ruled the Soviet Union was one of the most painful periods in all of history (see Table 9.4). In what is often called the second revolution, as many as 20 million Soviet citizens lost their lives—far too often for little or no reason.

Industrialization

Stalin is typically—and accurately—portrayed as one of the most vicious men ever to lead a country. There was,

TABLE 9.4 Key Events in the Evolution of the Soviet State

YEAR	EVENT
1927	Solidification of power by Stalin
	Socialism in one-country speech
1929	Beginning of collectivization campaign
1934	First major purges and show trials
1939	Nonaggression pact with Germany
1941	German invasion of Soviet Union
1945	End of World War II; Beginning of Cold War
1953	Death of Stalin
1956	Twentieth Party Congress and Khrushchev's secret speech
1964	Ouster of Khrushchev
1982	Death of Brezhnev

however, a degree of macabre rationality to some of what he did. The Soviet Union was in trouble. Hopes of global revolution had given way to a resurgence of right-wing governments in countries surrounding the USSR, something that Stalin called "capitalist encirclement." Whoever was in charge, the world's first socialist state had to respond decisively. To see that, consider this excerpt from one of his speeches:

> To slacken the tempo would mean falling behind. And those who fall behind get beaten. But we do not want to be beaten. No, we refuse to be beaten. One feature of the history of old Russia was the continual beatings she suffered because of her backwardness. She was beaten by the Mongol Khans. She was beaten by the Swedish feudal rulers. She was beaten by the Polish and Lithuanian gentry. She was beaten by British and French capitalists. She was beaten by Japanese barons. All beat her because of her backwardness. We are fifty or a hundred years behind the advanced countries. We must make good this distance in ten years. Either we do it or we shall go under.[1]

Stalin forced his beleaguered country to industrialize. In so doing, he committed some of the worst excesses of his rule. That said, a plausible case can be made that if Stalin had not pursued something like the policies described here, the Soviet Union would not have survived.

Before turning to the issue of forced industrialization, we should acknowledge that no country has ever been able to painlessly create a modern industrial economy. This is especially true of states that lag far behind their competitors and want to close that gap quickly. Adopting a *laissez-faire* approach seems to condemn these countries

---

[1]J. V. Stalin, *Problems of Leninism* (Moscow: International Publishers, 1953), 454.

to decades of "catch-up economics." Therefore, they often conclude—and perhaps rightfully so—that their only option is to force their society to industrialize as quickly as possible (see also Chapter 6 on Germany and the online chapter on Japan).

Stalin adopted a two-pronged strategy. First, because the Soviet Union only had one real resource—human labor, which was concentrated in the countryside—Stalin decided to restructure rural life. Farmers were herded onto gigantic, supposedly more efficient, collective and state farms. The peasants who were no longer needed in the countryside were relocated to the cities to work in the factories that were being built at breakneck speed. The government planned to sell the surplus food the new factory-like farms produced abroad to raise desperately needed hard currency. The government accomplished this with violence the likes of which this country with a long history of violence had never seen. In a matter of months, more than 9 million peasants were forced to move to the cities. At least that many more who resisted collectivization were sent to forced labor camps, where most of them perished. An unknown number were killed on the spot.

Second, the agricultural surplus and other resources were used to spark the industrialization and modernization of the Soviet economy. Stalin introduced an ambitious **five-year plan** that called for at least doubling the production of such goods as coal, oil, pig iron, steel, electricity, and cloth between 1928 and 1932. The Central State Planning Commission *(Gosplan)* set goals for the entire economy. Individual ministries then turned them into specific quotas for each factory and farm to fulfill. As in the rural areas, people who resisted the state's plans were treated brutally. Although the plan fell short of its most ambitious goals, the Soviet Union industrialized as rapidly as any country in history, though at a tremendous human cost.

Foreign Policy

There was a similar pattern to Soviet foreign policy under Stalin. Lenin had created the **Third International**, or **Comintern**, to spearhead what he expected to be a worldwide revolution, Soviet style. By the time Stalin solidified his power, however, the revolutionary tides had ebbed. Instead, capitalist forces seemed to threaten the very existence of the world's first socialist state. Therefore, in the late 1920s, Stalin reversed the course of Soviet foreign policy and called for "socialism in one country," something no orthodox Marxist would have dreamed possible.

Over the next twenty-five years, he led the Soviet Union and the global communist movement through what must seem like a contradictory series of shifts. At first, Stalin prohibited communist parties elsewhere from participating in anti-fascist coalitions that might, for instance,

Profiles
Joseph Stalin

Josif Dzhugashvili was born in the Georgian town of Gori in 1879. Unlike Lenin, he was of humble origins. His mother was a maid and his father an alcoholic and abusive shoemaker. As an adolescent, he entered a seminary, but he abandoned his studies in 1899 to become a full-time revolutionary.

Stalin followed Lenin into the Bolshevik wing of the Social Democratic Party, but unlike most of his influential colleagues, he spent the years before 1917 in Russia, organizing the party underground. During those years he took the pseudonym Stalin, for "man of steel."

During the revolution and civil war period, Stalin was given more and more responsibility for the "nationality question" and for party organization. Despite alienating Lenin because of his "rude" behavior, Stalin was able to outmaneuver his competitors and seize all but complete control of the country by 1927.

Most historians are convinced that Stalin suffered from a series of psychological problems that contributed to making his regime one of the most brutal in history. He died in 1953. ■

Joseph Stalin in 1929, shortly after he had consolidated power and begun the brutal collectivization campaign.

Hulton Archive/Getty Images

have kept the Nazis from taking power in Germany. But once he realized how serious the fascist threat was, Stalin switched direction in 1934, endorsing popular or united fronts in which communists cooperated with just about anyone who opposed fascism. In 1939, the Soviets reversed course once again, signing the infamous nonaggression pact with Nazi Germany. It was to last less than two years. In 1941, the Germans invaded the Soviet Union at which point Moscow joined the British-led Allies, which would include the United States after the attack on Pearl Harbor. Even before the war ended, however, tensions between the Soviet Union and the West escalated into what became the Cold War, prompting yet another u-turn in Soviet policy. To cite but one example, President Franklin Roosevelt decided not to share American plans for building a nuclear weapon. It didn't matter because the laboratory at Los Alamos which took the lead in designing the bomb had its share of Soviet spies.

The Purges

Stalin's economic and foreign policies made some kind of tragic sense. Obviously, millions of people suffered because of them, but the Soviet Union did industrialize, and it did survive. In fact, by the time Stalin died, the Soviet Union had become one of the world's first two superpowers.

It is impossible, however, to find any such logic behind the **purges**. In the 1920s, the party conducted limited ones to eliminate opportunists and others who joined in the aftermath of the revolution. Later in the decade, Stalin forced Trotsky and most of his other rivals out of the party. From the early 1930s on, the pace of the purges accelerated. They had no credible link, however twisted, to the country's economic development.

In 1933, the party held a Congress, which Stalin called the "Congress of Victors," to celebrate the completion of the collectivization campaign. At that meeting, Sergei Kirov, the young party leader in Leningrad, actually won more votes than Stalin in the election of the new Central Committee. In December 1934, Kirov was assassinated at his office, apparently on Stalin's orders. Nonetheless, Stalin ordered the arrest of anyone "involved" in Kirov's assassination, which set off a wave of torture, show trials, and executions that touched the lives of millions of innocent Soviet citizens. By the end of the decade, five of the nine Politburo members, 98 of 139 Central Committee members, 1,108 of the 1,966 delegates to the 1933 party congress, and half the army officer corps had been killed. A series of show trials took place at which most of the old Bolshevik leaders confessed to crimes they had not committed and then were summarily executed.

The purges and executions were carried out all the way up and down the party hierarchy. They drained the party of many of its enthusiastic members and qualified leaders, including in the secret police, many of whose own leaders found themselves on trial for their lives.

In this nightmarish environment, virtually the only way people could express their feelings was through humor. Consider, here, one "report" of a conversation between two prisoners that sums up just how absurd and horrible the purges were:

> **Prisoner One: What's your sentence?**
> **Prisoner Two: Twenty-five years.**
> **Prisoner One: What for?**
> **Prisoner Two: Nothing.**
> **Prisoner One: Don't lie. You only get five years for nothing in our country.**

In the larger prisons, the authorities executed an average of seventy people per day. Millions of innocent people were sent to the gulag, as the network of concentration camps was known. Many were given five-to-eight-year sentences merely for having a "socially dangerous" relative. Very few survived that long.

Khrushchev, Brezhnev, and the Politics of Decline

In March 1953, Stalin suffered a fatal stroke. Like Lenin, he died without designating a successor, and a number of men jockeyed for control. This time the dozen or so top party leaders apparently agreed that no one should be allowed to amass the kind of power Stalin had and that the Soviet Union should, instead, be governed by some form of collective leadership. Within two years, **Nikita Khrushchev** (1894–1971) emerged as the most influential of them. Khrushchev was a typical communist of his generation. Drawn to the party by the revolution, he had risen to the top during Stalin's rule and was involved in some of the regime's most brutal activities.

Under his leadership, the basic institutions of the party state remained intact. Nonetheless, Khrushchev proved to be a reformer both at home and abroad. He brought the worst excesses of Stalinism to a halt. The first clear sign that politics was changing came on the night of February 24 to 25, 1956, when Khrushchev called the delegates to the CPSU's **Twentieth Party Congress** back for a special session. For three hours, he held his audience spellbound with his now famous **secret speech** in which he detailed many of Stalin's crimes. After the speech, which did not remain secret for very long, censorship and other political controls were loosened. More open political debate made university campuses exciting places and left an indelible mark on that generation of students, which included Gorbachev and Yeltsin. Khrushchev also sought to decentralize economic decision making and to revitalize the flagging agricultural sector. The Soviet Union retained its Cold War hostility toward the West but also sought to relax tensions through a policy he called "peaceful coexistence."

Always controversial, Khrushchev barely survived an attempt to oust him in 1957 in which his colleagues objected to what they later called his "harebrained schemes," few of which worked. Many of Khrushchev's colleagues believed that his reforms went too far in eroding central party control and Soviet prestige. As social and economic problems mounted, so did opposition to his rule.

For many Soviet leaders, the Cuban missile crisis of 1962 proved to be the last straw. That August, American reconnaissance planes discovered that the Soviets were preparing to deploy nuclear missiles in Cuba, a country ninety miles south of Florida that had recently passed into the Soviet camp. Two months later, President John F. Kennedy imposed a naval blockade to prevent the ships carrying the missiles and other material from reaching Cuba. World War III was a very real possibility. Eventually, the ships turned around, and the Soviets dismantled their bases.

Khrushchev's critics in Moscow saw Cuba as a humiliating defeat and as yet another example of what they branded his "harebrained schemes." Two years later, they succeeded in removing him from office.

Khrushchev was replaced by a group of leaders, many of whom had been his protégés. The most important of them was **Leonid Brezhnev** (1906–82), who served as general secretary of the Communist Party until his death. Under Brezhnev the reforms ended, and the leadership took as few risks as possible in both domestic and foreign affairs.

By the time Brezhnev and his colleagues took power, the Soviet Union already faced serious economic problems (see the discussion of "thumbs" and "fingers" in Chapter 8). In the years that followed, things only got worse. By the early 1980s, economic growth slipped to 3 percent per year or barely 60 percent of the goal laid out in the Tenth Five-Year Plan (1976–80). In some sectors, the figures were worse— only a fifth of planned increases were reached in coal and chemicals, barely a third in steel and consumer goods, and only half in agriculture.

The Brezhnev leadership did introduce some limited economic reforms. However, little progress was made because anything more than piecemeal change would have threatened the two central elements of the Soviet system that dated back to Lenin's time: the party's monopoly on political power and the centrally controlled economy. The Brezhnev generation was not willing to modify either.

Instead, it clung to power. By the beginning of the 1980s, the average age of Politburo members was about seventy. When Brezhnev finally died in 1982, power was transferred to other members of the old guard—Yuri Andropov and Konstantin Chernenko—both of whom died within months of taking office.

Economic conditions continued to deteriorate. Even though people had more disposable income, there were not enough consumer goods to meet pent-up demand and those goods that were available were shoddily made. To cite but one example, the few people fortunate enough to own cars took their windshield wipers with them when they parked. Otherwise, they would be stolen.

The *Economist* summed up this period brilliantly in its rather snide obituary on Brezhnev:

> The death of Leonid Brezhnev was the only major innovation he ever introduced into Soviet political history. In life, he stood for the status quo—as firmly as a man can stand when he is in fact walking slowly backward on a conveyor belt that is moving slowly forward beneath his feet. Brezhnev, a solid machine man, was put in to reassure the frightened hierarchs that the experimenting would stop. In this he was remarkably successful. He did not just stop the clocks, but turned some of them back. Defying Marx, he virtually halted the evolution of Soviet society in its tracks. But the country, which was intended to be ruled by the Brezhnev men after Brezhnev's death, presumably with the aim of immortalizing his immobilism, had been changing under them despite all their efforts; and the world in which it must live has been changing too. His legacy in foreign as in domestic policy is a set of concepts which were old when his reign began eighteen years ago. In Brezhnev's Russia, only one thing was kept entirely up to date: its military hardware. The most appropriate monument for him would be a multiwarhead nuclear missile linked to a stopped clock.[2]

When Chernenko died in March 1985, there was no one left from the Brezhnev generation. Someone younger had to take over, and Gorbachev was the obvious choice.

Although there were signs that he was not cut from the same political cloth as members of the Brezhnev-Andropov-Chernenko generation, no one expected change to come as quickly as it did. In 1984, Serge Schmeman of the *New York Times* reported an incident that hinted at just how uncertain things were. That December Gorbachev was sent on a mission to London. He was already in line to replace Chernenko, who was obviously in failing health. The assumption was that the trip would provide some insight into the next leader of the Soviet Union.

Schmeman began his report with Gorbachev's departure from Moscow. Gorbachev, dressed in a somber gray suit, shook the hands of his equally somberly dressed colleagues who had come to see him off. His wife, Raisa, went

[2]"Brezhnev's Legacy," *The Economist*, November 13, 1982, 7–8.

up the back ramp onto the plane, out of public view. When they arrived in London, however, they emerged from the airplane together, wearing colorful Western-style clothes, and enthusiastically greeted the crowd.

Which, Schmeman wondered, was the real Gorbachev?

The Collapse of the Soviet State: The Gorbachev Years

Schmeman's question was answered quickly. **Mikhail Gorbachev** (1931–) proved to be a dedicated reformer and one of the twentieth century's most influential leaders. In the end, however, he failed in large part because he was either unwilling or unable to take on the party state. Because his reforms went a lot further than those of the Khrushchev years, he provoked fierce opposition within the party hierarchy. However, his reforms probably could never have sparked the revitalization of the Soviet society and economy he sought because they did not go far enough in challenging the party's stranglehold on power. The end result was the rapid polarization of Soviet politics and, with it, the country's demise.

The Party State

The Soviet Union that Gorbachev inherited was dominated by the CPSU and its massive organization, whose membership numbered about 10 percent of the adult population. It was for all intents and purposes the same as the state. It was, therefore, the only political body that mattered.

Until 1988, all important decisions were made by senior party leaders. Party officials were responsible for overseeing the actions of every individual and institution. For all but those at the very top, the party was a massive bureaucratic machine whose primary task was to ensure that the policies made by the elite were carried out. Most leading journalists, military officers, factory managers, teachers, and even athletes were required to be party members. Few, however, joined out of a sense of commitment to building a society based on Marxist ideals. Rather, most entered one of the four hundred thousand or so primary party organizations for a far more pragmatic reason. The CPSU was the only route to success in almost every sector of Soviet society.

Until the late 1980s, the party structure remained the same as it had been since the 1920s (see Figure 9.1). The

FIGURE 9.1 The Communist Party of the Soviet Union

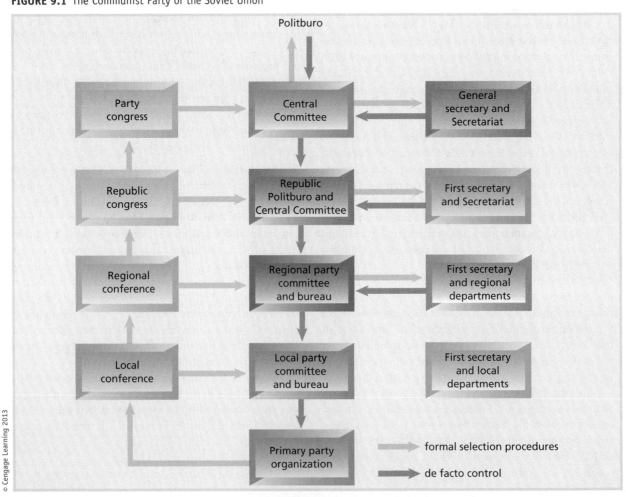

primary party organizations reported to city or regional committees that, in turn, reported to provincial units. Fifteen union republic party organizations were above the provincial units.

Atop it all were the national party organs. In principle, the most important—but in practice the least influential—was the party congress, which was normally held every four years. Until the final one in 1990, however, party congresses were little more than rubber stamps that ratified decisions made by the party elite. Much the same could be said of the **Central Committee**, which had about three hundred members, many of whom lived and worked outside of Moscow.

Instead, power was concentrated in two small groups that the Central Committee officially appointed but that were actually self-perpetuating bodies. The **Politburo** (normally twelve to fifteen members, with another five to six nonvoting, candidate members) acted much like a cabinet in a parliamentary system. The **Secretariat** (usually about twenty-five members and a staff of 1,500) oversaw the work of the party apparatus. There was considerable overlap in the membership of these two bodies, and the general secretary served both as head of the Secretariat and chair of the Politburo.

The continued reliance on democratic centralism meant that leaders at one level determined who ran things at the level below them. This allowed the elite to perpetuate itself by choosing people it could count on for all important positions. Its control over the entire organization was exercised through the **nomenklatura** lists of important positions and people qualified to fill them, both of which were maintained by the Secretariat. As a result, the arrows in Figure 9.1 that suggest "upward" influence are misleading. Because of this continued use of the system Lenin created to wage and win a revolution, the leadership maintained

TABLE 9.5 Key Events in the Gorbachev Years

YEAR	EVENT
1985	Gorbachev becomes general secretary of CPSU
1986	Chernobyl; first summit with President Ronald Reagan
1987	Intermediate nuclear forces agreement; Boris Yeltsin removed from office
1988	Special party conference; Reagan visits Moscow
1989	First somewhat competitive elections; collapse of communism in Eastern Europe
1990	Final CPSU congress; Yeltsin resigns from party
1991	Failed coup attempt; collapse of USSR

CPSU, Communist Party of the Soviet Union; USSR, Union of Soviet Socialist Republics.

total control over who was appointed to official positions and, therefore, also over the decisions it cared most about.

Reform

Gorbachev and his colleagues came to power understanding that the Soviet Union had to change. Economic growth had all but ground to a halt, and the country was falling behind the West in almost every way imaginable. Therefore, they introduced four sets of reforms designed to reinvigorate Soviet society. What the reforms actually did, however, was polarize both the elite and the country as a whole (see Figure 9.2). They dramatically expanded both the number of people trying to influence decision making and the range of opinions voiced in those debates. As the 1980s wore on, Gorbachev found himself trying to govern from an ever-shrinking center. That would have been a challenge under the best of circumstances, but Gorbachev also became quite tentative in his own decision making, especially once it became clear that the party itself was the major roadblock (see Table 9.5).

FIGURE 9.2 The Changing Soviet Political Landscape

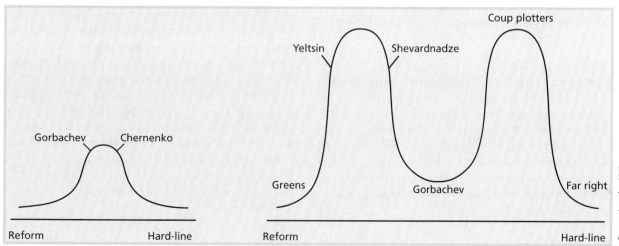

Glasnost

Gorbachev and his colleagues understood that they could not breathe new life into Soviet institutions without changing the country's political culture. At most, Soviets granted the party state a grudging sense of legitimacy. A country that would be more innovative and take more risks economically would have to start by creating a culture that stressed similar values.

The first of the reforms, *glasnost*, turned out to be the most counterproductive. The term is derived from the Russian word for voice and is best translated as *openness*. It had occasionally been used by earlier Soviet leaders but only made it onto political center stage after the 1986 Chernobyl nuclear power plant disaster. After a few days of typical Soviet secrecy, the government began making everything about the accident public and even allowed foreign experts in to care for people who had been exposed to radiation.

From then on, the system opened up dramatically. The old Soviet aphorism—"Everything that isn't explicitly permitted is forbidden"—was turned on its head. Censors stopped reviewing most works before they were published. The heavy-handed control of the mass media was lifted. Some conservative newspapers and magazines remained, but the press and airwaves were filled with material that was critical not only of the Soviet past but also of the current leadership.

Glasnost did not, however, create the kind of tolerant, Western-style political culture Gorbachev had in mind. Instead, it allowed people to vent seventy years' worth of frustrations. Rather than produce a more energized and enthusiastic population, the Soviet Union faced ever larger and more radical protests on a number of fronts. Workers struck against low pay and poor working conditions. Women and environmentalists added their voices to shaping the political agenda. An independent peace movement urged the party to move even faster in its rapprochement with the United States and to end its crippling invasion of Afghanistan. Most important of all, nationalist movements among the country's minority groups challenged the legitimacy of the Soviet state itself.

Democratization

The reformers also realized that they could not pursue *glasnost* without introducing a degree of democracy. They never planned to turn the Soviet Union into a Western-style liberal democracy. This is hardly surprising, given that even the most radical reformers were products of the system and that most of them—including Gorbachev himself—thought of themselves as committed Marxists. Therefore, movement on democratization came more slowly but included two important steps.

First, the reformers removed Article 6 from the Soviet constitution, which had defined the party as "the leading and guiding force of Soviet society and the nucleus of its political system, of all state organizations and political organizations." As early as January 1987, Gorbachev hinted that there could be changes in the party's monopoly on power. Formal proposals were made in June 1988 at a special party conference called to discuss democratization and economic reform. Plans were announced to strengthen the presidency, a position Gorbachev assumed that September.

Second, Gorbachev announced that there would be a new Parliament, the Congress of People's Deputies, which would be chosen through partially free elections. When the elections were held, many of the liberal reformers received a lot of publicity. However, people concerned that Gorbachev was moving too fast and too far won more of the seats.

In short, Gorbachev did make the regime a bit more democratic. He did not, however, mount a frontal assault on the CPSU. If anything, he was hoping to strengthen it by forcing it to reform and modernize. Nonetheless, the main consequence of his actions was to intensify apprehension and opposition from party members to his right.

Perestroika

When he took office, Gorbachev inherited a rapidly deteriorating economy. Soviet factories were archaic and were rendered even less productive by a workforce that neither worked very hard nor cared about the quality of goods it produced. The service industries were in shambles, and people who could afford to do so turned to the black market to get their cars repaired or to obtain decent food. The massive state and collective farms were so poorly run that a third of the harvest spoiled or simply disappeared between harvest and market. Last, but not least, the peculiar nature of the Soviet currency and the country's arcane foreign trade laws kept the USSR from participating in the increasingly important international economy.

At first, there were few signs that Gorbachev contemplated radical economic reform. In his first two years in office, he tried to make improvements within the party state system by increasing the discipline of Soviet workers—for instance clamping down on the sale of alcohol. As the crisis deepened and his incremental reforms failed to bear fruit, Gorbachev and his advisers decided that nothing short of *perestroika*, or a total restructuring of the economy, would restore the Soviet Union to world prominence or improve the living conditions of its citizens. They realized that such a restructuring would require relinquishing much of the party state's economic power to the market and promoting private ownership, individual initiative, and decentralized decision making.

Profiles
Mikhail Gorbachev

Mikhail Gorbachev was born in 1931 near Stavropol in the Crimea. His father was a tractor driver, and Gorbachev himself worked on a collective farm as a teenager. At eighteen, he was already a committed and respected member of the Komsomol, the Communist Youth League, when he enrolled at Moscow State University to study law. Like many of his generation, he was deeply affected by de-Stalinization, which, some say, convinced him as early as the 1950s of the need for reform.

Gorbachev returned to the Stavropol region, where he quickly moved up the party ranks. He was no radical. But like many of his colleagues in out-of-the-way parts of the country, he implemented some innovative reforms—in his case in agricultural administration—that earned him national attention and a seat on the Politburo in 1980.

Gorbachev was never willing or able to wholly break with the traditional party state, which ultimately led to his and his country's undoing. Since 1991, he has headed the Gorbachev Institute, which works for human rights and world peace along the lines of the "new thinking" he championed while in office. He made an attempt at a political comeback in the 1996 presidential election but won less than 1 percent of the vote (www.gorby.ru/en). ▪

Mikhail Gorbachev speaking at George Mason University in March 2009.

Nicolas Tan/George Mason University

Although much of *perestroika* never made it onto the statute books, by the late 1980s the leadership had undertaken five broad initiatives:

- Proposing a law on state enterprises to introduce market mechanisms into the parts of the economy that would remain under state ownership.

- Passing the law on cooperatives authorizing the existence of some small, privately owned companies, mostly in the service industries.

- Initiating agricultural reforms that would eventually allow farmers to lease, if not own, their land outright.

- Introducing price reforms so that people paid market value for goods and services.

- Easing restrictions on joint ventures with foreign firms.

As with democratization, they faced resistance from much of the party hierarchy, whose power they threatened. Moreover, the ever more indecisive Gorbachev team never even got to the point of proposing a full-fledged package of reforms. By the time they came close to doing so, it may have already been too late to satisfy the demands of an increasingly impatient population.

Foreign Policy

Gorbachev will be remembered most positively for his role in ending the Cold War. One of his first acts as leader was to declare a unilateral moratorium on nuclear testing, which was followed by more dramatic initiatives. There was a strong dose of self-interest behind those proposals from a leader who understood that his country was overburdened by defense expenditures that consumed at least a quarter of its gross national product (GNP).

Gorbachev was the most visionary international leader of his time. Thus, in his remarkable speech to the United Nations General Assembly in December 1988, he talked hopefully about interdependence and a new world order of countries able to solve their differences peacefully. This is not the place to review those actions in any detail because they fall more in the domain of international relations. It is enough to note that they also provoked considerable opposition at home from people who feared that they would undermine the Soviet Union's position as one of the two most powerful countries in the world.

Crisis and Collapse

By the time communism collapsed in Eastern Europe, the Soviet Union was already a political tinderbox. In the two years between the fall of the Berlin Wall and the disintegration of the Soviet Union, the state grew weaker and its society more divided. Rumors of an impending coup were rife. In response, Gorbachev strengthened presidential powers and elevated hard-liners to prominent posts in the military and security apparatus.

On June 12, 1991, Yeltsin was elected president of the Russian Republic, enabling him to claim that he had a broader mandate and that his rule was more legitimate than Gorbachev's. Five days later, the head of the **KGB** issued an ominous warning against carrying out liberal reforms "dreamed up across the ocean." On July 24, Gorbachev reached an agreement with the presidents of ten of the fifteen republics that would have given them considerable autonomy in most areas of domestic policy making. The Union Treaty was to be signed on August 20, the day after Gorbachev returned from vacation.

At 6 A.M. on August 19, 1991, the Soviet press agency announced that Gorbachev was ill and had been replaced by Vice President Gennadi Yanayev, who, along with seven other hard-liners, had seized power. Gorbachev and his family were taken into custody. Troops occupied critical positions in Moscow and other cities.

Most politicians were slow to respond. Yeltsin, however, opposed the coup from the outset. He immediately went to the White House in Moscow (the headquarters of the Russian government), which was surrounded by troops. Overnight, he galvanized the opposition. Within forty-eight hours, it had become clear that the coup was poorly planned by desperate leaders who knew that the signing of the Union Treaty would mean the end of the Soviet Union as they knew it. The coup collapsed and Gorbachev returned to Moscow, claiming he would continue to rule as before.

In fact, business as usual could not continue. The Union Treaty was put on hold indefinitely as the Soviet Union continued to disintegrate. By September, the Baltic republics had broken away, and in December the leaders of eleven of the remaining twelve republics agreed to form the Commonwealth of Independent States. By the end of the month, Gorbachev had resigned his position as president of a country that no longer existed.

BETWEEN DICTATORSHIP AND DEMOCRACY

One of the best recent books on Russian politics bears the apt title, *Between Dictatorship and Democracy*.[3] At first, many people were hopeful that the new country would make a rapid and smooth transition to democracy. That is not what happened. The rest of the 1990s were traumatic times, as epitomized by Yeltsin's troubled presidency. Yeltsin resigned on the very last day of the twentieth century. Since then, political life has stabilized considerably under the leadership of Russia's second president, current prime minister, and still de facto leader, Putin. However, Putin has achieved that stability by undermining most of

---

[3]Michael McFaul, Nikolai Petrov, and Andrei Ryabov, *Between Dictatorship and Democracy: Russian Post-Communist Political Reform* (Washington: Carnegie Endowment for International Peace, 2004).

Boris Yeltsin, standing on an armored personnel carrier and rallying the crowd opposing the coup against Mikhail Gorbachev in 1991.

AP Images

the tentative steps Russia had taken toward democracy in the first decade after the breakup of the Soviet Union.

Birth Pangs

Most of the post-Soviet republics got off to a shaky start. To begin with, they did not make a clean break from the old order. They began their lives using Soviet-era institutions and most were led by politicians who had built their careers as communists. In Russia, Yeltsin's team had to govern with a parliament that had been elected in 1989 and was still dominated by men and women who had been loyal party activists.

The Russian people had never lived under a democracy. In contrast, although Germany and Japan had hardly been successful in their first attempts at democracy, they had "untainted" politicians to call on, established organizations that could serve as the starting point for new political parties and interest groups, and millions of individuals who had voted in competitive elections. Russia did not (see Table 9.6).

What's more, economic conditions sank to a level no one could have imagined under the communists. Ethnic conflict, which had been bad enough before 1991, intensified after the Soviet collapse. Russians also had to deal with the humiliating reality that they were no longer a superpower and, even worse, had been stripped of territories and peoples—some of which they had controlled for centuries. Even more humiliating and contentious for some was the fact that the Russian government seemed to have to beg for

aid from the same Western governments that so recently had feared Soviet military power.

The hard-line holdovers turned into the new regime's conservatives. They obviously did not advocate free market capitalism along the lines of conservatives in Great Britain or the United States. Rather, they were conservative in the sense that they resisted the reforms proposed by the Yeltsin administration, preferring instead to reestablish the old system and possibly to reintegrate the lost republics back into Russia or to recreate the USSR itself.

Meanwhile, the old Communist Party reinvented itself as the **Communist Party of the Russian Federation (CPRF).** New political groupings, most notably the **Liberal Democrats**, led by **Vladimir Zhirinovsky**, sprang up as well, defending various versions of traditional, Soviet-style geopolitical and economic goals. On the other end of the spectrum, radical reformers, most of whom started off in the Yeltsin camp, formed an opposition and clamored for **shock therapy** in the economy. This Western-inspired policy emphasized the **privatization** of state-owned industry and macroeconomic policies designed to bring the rampant inflation under control.

Throughout 1993, tensions continued to mount. By summer, Yeltsin's team apparently realized that it had made a mistake in trying to implement meaningful economic and political reforms under a communist-era political system. Therefore, it proposed a new constitution, which met stiff resistance from many parliamentary and regional leaders. On September 21, Yeltsin issued Decree 1400, which dissolved the Congress of People's Deputies and announced new legislative elections for December 12.

This proved to be the last straw for his opponents, who took the decree as "proof" that the president was trying to create a personal dictatorship. For the next two weeks, hundreds of people, including many parliamentary leaders, occupied the White House. Yeltsin countered by sending troops to surround the building. He also cut off its heat, water, and electricity.

In sharp contrast to what he had done in 1991, Yeltsin ordered the troops to attack the White House on October 3. The occupiers proved no match for the soldiers and soon surrendered, but not before at least a hundred people were killed and the White House was heavily damaged. The leaders were hustled out of the building and arrested.

At that point, Yeltsin decided to add a new draft constitution to the ballot for December. The constitution was approved, but to his embarrassment conservative parties won by far the most seats in the **State Duma**, the lower house of the new parliament.

In other words, despite removing the coup's plotters from active politics and gaining support for the new constitution, Yeltsin faced the same kind of political deadlock as Gorbachev. For the next two-and-a-half years,

TABLE 9.6 Key Events in Russian Politics since 1991

YEAR	EVENTS
1991	Boris Yeltsin elected Russian president Failed coup Collapse of USSR
1992	New state called Russian Federation
1993	Referendum supports most reforms Coup attempt First parliamentary elections New constitution
1994	Drift rightward accelerates Outbreak of war in Chechnya
1995	Yeltsin's second heart attack Second parliamentary election
1996	Presidential election
1997	Expansion of NATO
1998	Economic collapse Two prime ministers sacked
2000	Vladimir Putin assumes presidency
2004	Putin reelected
2008	End of Putin presidency, new elections
2012	Next presidential election

Profiles
Boris Yeltsin

Boris Yeltsin was born in Siberia in 1931. Like most Soviet leaders of his generation, he was well educated, beginning his career as a civil engineer. He soon turned to full-time party work and rose through the ranks in the city of Sverdlovsk, which has since returned to its pre-communist name of Ekaterinburg.

Yeltsin was brought to Moscow in 1985 and put in charge of the Moscow party organization (a prize position) and made a member of the Politburo. He soon became one of the country's most outspoken and radical reformers. For instance, he openly criticized party leaders for their privileged and lavish lifestyles. In 1988, Gorbachev felt he had gone too far and Yeltsin was stripped of all his major party and state posts. In 1990, Yeltsin quit the Communist Party at what turned out to be its final congress. The next year, he was elected president of the Russian Republic, which had previously not been a particularly important post. But with his personal popularity and the position he took in opposition to the August 1991 coup, Yeltsin soon became the most powerful politician in the USSR as it collapsed and then in the new Russian Federation.

He was less successful as president. His years in office were marred by economic difficulties, ethnic unrest, corruption, and, of course, questions about his own health and sobriety.

Yeltsin died in 2007. ▪

the president and Parliament remained at loggerheads. If anything, the conservatives grew stronger and obliged the president to drop more and more of his reformist goals and advisers. Meanwhile, Yeltsin's declining personal popularity and deteriorating health sapped the presidency of its strength. The pace of economic and other reform slowed. Intense fighting broke out between the central government and separatists in the southern republic of Chechnya. More important for the long term were the preparations for the legislative and presidential elections that were to be held in December 1995 and June 1996, respectively.

For good or ill, those elections did little to resolve the differences between Yeltsin and the Duma, which remained under opposition control. The president had

had to bring former general Alexander Lebed and other conservatives into his coalition. In short, the high-stakes political stalemate continued in only slightly modified form.

Conditions deteriorated for the rest of Yeltsin's abbreviated second term. As we will see in more detail, the bottom fell out of the economy in 1998, and there was growing concern about the political and economic clout of the "family"—the people in Yeltsin's inner circle. As a result, there was something approaching a collective sigh of relief when Yeltsin quit.

Putin and Stability

Yeltsin's surprise resignation made Putin acting president. When Yeltsin named him prime minister that August, Putin was a virtual unknown. He had spent the bulk of his career in the KGB and had then served in the mayor's office in St. Petersburg after the collapse of the Soviet Union. Putin's personal popularity soared that fall because of what seemed like the successful prosecution of the second war in Chechnya. It soon became clear that Yeltsin was grooming him to be his successor. Putin also proved to be an effective politician, steering the newly found Unity Party to a victory in the 1999 parliamentary elections and then winning the presidency the following March without even having to go through a runoff election.

Putin has had a much greater impact on Russian politics than anyone expected, which we will consider in detail in the rest of this chapter. The turmoil many expected after the erratic Yeltsin retired did not materialize. Instead, Putin drew on colleagues from the security services and Yeltsin's inner circle to solidify his own power. After his first meeting with George W. Bush, the American president claimed that he had looked into Putin's eyes and seen someone the United States could work with.

Putin's reputation, however, soon lost its luster. He clamped down on the freedom of the press, eliminated the ability of rival political parties to realistically win elections, and forced a number of Yeltsin's business colleagues, or **oligarchs**, either into prison or exile. As prime minister, Putin is still the dominant leader, even if his position makes him nominally subservient to President Medvedev. There are rumors that Medvedev might step aside, which would make it easy for Putin to run for president again in 2012; both men have denied that they have any such plans.

At this point, it is most important to see that Yeltsin and especially Putin have personalized the regime. Whatever democratic principles are enshrined in the constitution and the protests that led up to it have been honored in the breach, at best. Do not take this line of reasoning too far,

Profiles
Vladimir Putin

Vladimir Putin was born in Leningrad (now St. Petersburg) in 1952. His family was not well off, and Putin describes himself as having had a troubled youth until he started competing in judo, which has been a passion of his ever since.

In 1975, he graduated from Leningrad State University with a degree in law. He then joined the KGB where he held a number of posts in Germany and the Soviet Union until he left to work for the Leningrad city government in 1990.

In 1996, Putin was brought to Moscow to help run the Kremlin's administrative office. There, he captured the attention of Yeltsin's "family," his inner circle of politicians, including his powerful daughter, Tatyana Dyachenko. In March 1999, Putin effectively was given control of the Federal Security Bureau (FSB), the successor to the Soviet era KGB. On August 9, 1999, he was named prime minister and automatically became acting president when Yeltsin resigned.

He won the next two elections. When his second full term ended he stepped down from the presidency as required by the constitution and became prime minister. From that post, he has continued to run the country. His period in power has been marked by a sharp erosion in what democratic rights and values existed when he took power. As we write, there is widespread speculation that he will run for president again in 2012. ◼

Vladimir Putin and George W. Bush at their first summit in Crawford, Texas, in November 2001.

however. Today's Russia is not a totalitarian state, but some observers fear it is heading that way.

We are little more than a year away from the election, and no one knows who will run or win. It is not at all like the U.S. Republican race for the 2012 presidential nomination. In Russia, only Putin and Medvedev have any chance of winning. And if Putin chooses to run, he will almost certainly win. If he doesn't, Mevedev will undoubtedly win.

POLITICAL CULTURE AND PARTICIPATION

Evidence about Russian political culture and participation is difficult to assess for two reasons. First, all forms of open and voluntary political participation are new, and it is often difficult to determine what peoples' intentions are when they get involved. Second, there are fewer and fewer honest politicians. Elections are generally rigged and the media are almost all under state control. To cite but one example, more than fifteen dissident journalists have been killed since Putin came to power, although no one has been able to find a direct link between that violence and the regime. Third, public opinion polling is also quite new, so we have relatively little reliable data about what average Russians think and do politically.

Nonetheless, the available evidence points to a pair of largely paradoxical conclusions. On the one hand, there is reason to believe that most Russians want a democratic regime. On the other, their voting patterns and other political behavior suggest that they are not happy with the way their regime is working (**www.russiavotes.org**).

Political Culture

As is the case with most aspects of Russian politics, its political culture forces us to shift gears because it has so little in common with those in liberal democracies. Most people there believe that their regimes are legitimate, which contributes to political stability and helps sustain the system during tough times.

This is not the case for Russia. To the degree that we understand it, Russian political culture is shaped by widespread frustration and hostility.

It could hardly be otherwise. Russians have never been governed by a regime that enjoyed widespread legitimacy. When people were finally given the opportunity to participate somewhat freely and to express their views in the late 1980s, it was the anger built up over centuries of imperial rule and seventy years of Soviet control that burst to the surface.

TABLE 9.7 Percentage of Population Citing Improvement: 1993–2004

QUESTION	1993	1998	2000	2004
Everybody has freedom of choice in religious matters.	71	79	84	84
Everybody has the right to say what they think.	65	73	81	81
One can join any organization one likes.	63	75	77	83
Everyone can decide individually whether or not to take an interest in politics.	57	66	70	76
Compared to the political system before *perestroika*.	62	72	73	65
Our present system of governing.	36	70	72	63
The system of government will have in five years.	52	49	64	88

Source: *Levada Center*, www.russiavotes.org, accessed 28 July 28, 2007

The shift to the new regime did not mean that the underlying culture changed. There is no question that most Russian voters think that their system is better than the one it replaced, as noted in Table 9.7 which is based on polls conducted between 1993 and 2004 by the Levada Center. The first four questions asked if the situation has gotten better or worse; the last three asked whether the respondent has a positive, neutral, or negative attitude toward the institutions. For the first four, the shift in the positive direction was at least 13 percent between 1993 and 2004. For the others, the evidence is more mixed. For both sets of the questions, most of the change occurred before Putin was elected in 2000. Less reliable polls (not included in Table 9.7) have shown that three quarters of all Russians typically tell pollsters that the regime is better than the old communist one as far as respecting individual rights is concerned and that they prize that freedom. In addition, voter turnout is reasonably high. Only 50.6 percent of eligible voters participated in the 1993 Duma election following the failed coup attempt. But turnout in national elections since then has only once dropped below 60 percent, which is 10 percent higher than the rate of participation in a typical American presidential contest.

There is also some evidence that a number of values that are not particularly conducive to democracy have carried over from the Soviet—and in some cases the tsarist—past. There is, for instance, widespread suspicion of those in positions of authority. Most Russians, especially those who did relatively well under the old system, still seem to want the state to provide critical services, hand down directives, and take the initiative in important social, political, and economic issues

More recent polls do not paint a much more flattering picture. In a poll of 1,600 Russians conducted in 2010, Levada found that 65 percent of them had a hard time defining democracy. About a quarter of them said that their country had never been a democracy, although a third of them believed that Russia was a democracy at the time. More than ninety percent of them thought they had no control over the government; almost as many felt little or no responsibility for what happened in the country. Three in five believed the government was above the law. Almost the same number thought that the judiciary should be controlled by state. Only four percent felt that private property was secure.

Important demographic changes are occurring that indicate that Russian culture may become more democratic over time. In particular, young, urban, and well-educated people support liberal values far more than do their older, rural, and poorly educated counterparts. But if such a shift occurs, it will take place over the course of the next generation or two, not the next year or two.

Far less hopeful is a trend not seen in public opinion polls and which is even harder to pin down empirically: the

Conflict
in Russia

As in most of the formerly communist countries, there is much conflict in Russia and has been since Gorbachev removed the political lid with *glasnost* in the late 1980s. Unlike in the industrialized democracies, however, much of the protest is aimed not just at individual politicians and their policies but at the regime as well.

There is surprisingly little violence in the conflict at the mass level other than in Chechnya. However, dozens of politicians, journalists, human rights activists, and business leaders have been assassinated. In the most blatant attack in recently years, Andrei Litvinenko was attacked in London on November 1, 2006 in London and died three weeks later. Litvinenko had been an agent for the KGB. He was poisoned with a radioactive chemical in an attack that was widely believed to have been authorized and carried out by the state security service in Moscow. Other politicians and journalists have been killed under suspicious circumstances inside of Russia. ■

weakness of Russia's civil society. As we have seen in other chapters, a strong civil society is important because it helps build legitimacy *and* the belief that people can have an impact on the policy decisions that have to be made by elites.

One of the best indicators of the strength of a civil society is the status of its interest groups. Here, the signs are not encouraging. Russia has the same kinds of interest groups and other social organizations we found in Part 2. However, they tend to be weaker and less independent of the state. If anything, the regime has made it harder for groups to organize or try to exert their influence. The most glaring example of this is the way the state has used cumbersome registration procedures to deny legal status to as many as half of the existing environmental, religious, and regional organizations. Indeed, the situation is so bleak that Michael McFaul (who was recently named ambassador to Russia) and Elina Treyger concluded, "Civil society's ability to influence political outcomes on a national scale seems to have been greater during the last years of the Soviet era than it is today. Russian civil society is weak, atomized, apolitical, and heavily dependent on Western assistance for support."[4] The one possible exception to this trend toward alienation is the growing number of strikes among miners, teachers, industrial workers, and others who often go months without getting paid. Even here, however, the unions that supposedly represent the interests of those workers are small and have had at best a limited impact on economic policy making.

A 2006 law made this situation worse. The Kremlin had been worried about the role nongovernmental organizations (NGOs) had played in nonviolent protests that produced political change in a number of countries in the near abroad. That year, the Duma passed a law requiring all NGOs to register with the state so that their activities could be approved, monitored, and controlled by it. Particularly vulnerable are NGOs whose funding largely comes from the West, including such respected organizations as Human Rights Watch.

Dissatisfaction with the government became increasingly hard to avoid in early 2009. Tens of thousands of workers staged strikes and demonstrations, starting in the Pacific seaport of Vladivostok. Some were organized by the Communist Party (see the next section) and drew widespread support just as the economic crisis was having a major impact after nearly a decade of economic growth. Vladivostok was particularly hard hit because it is the port where most imported cars arrive; the economic slump slashed demand for automobiles and with it jobs at the shipyards.

---

[4]Michael McFaul and Elina Treyger, "Civil Society," in McFaul, Petrov, and Ryabov, *Between Dictatorship and Democracy*, 135–36.

Women in Russian Politics

In Chapter 8, we argued that few women forged prominent political careers on their own in communist countries. For good or ill, the same is true in post-communist Russia. As one journalist put it almost a decade ago, women are "breadwinners at home, outcasts in politics."

Most Russian women accept a degree of inequality compared to men. But they have a hard time avoiding "gender inequality." They are more likely to be employed, perform almost all the household chores, and usually hand over their paychecks to their husbands.

There is a small women's movement. For instance, a small but unknown number of Russian women participated in a demonstration protesting violence against women in November 2010, an event that is held annually as part of a United Nations campaign.

The proportion of women in the State Duma declined by about half until 2007, when it rebounded to 14 percent. Nonetheless, Russia only ranks 82nd out of the 188 countries ranked by the International Parliamentary Union.

A number of prominent dissident women have been assassinated, almost certainly by the authorities. The most prominent of them was Anna Politkovskaya. She was a crusading investigative journalist for one of the few newspapers that didn't fall under Kremlin control. On October 7, 2006, she was shot while taking the elevator to her apartment. It was only on June 1, 2011 that someone was arrested for being the gunman.

Political Parties and Elections

Perhaps even more worrisome is the status of Russia's electoral and party systems. As we saw in Chapter 2, both are vital to the health and stability of any democratic regime. Russia's situation is problematic on two very different levels.

First, through the post-communist period, Russia has had what the scholars conducting the New Russia Barometre (NRB) polls call a "floating" party system. In most stable democracies, voters choose from essentially the same parties from election to election. And because the individual parties do not change their positions all that much from one ballot to the next, most voters develop loyalties to one or another of them in what political scientists call "party identification." Enduring identification with political parties allows them to play a vital role in linking people's preferences to the parties' actions as they organize governments and make policy decisions.

There are few signs that any such pattern of partisan and electoral behavior is developing in Russia. Instead, as the tables in this section will show, there is little continuity in either the parties that contest elections or in the voters' reactions to them. Indeed, the Russian party system is more fluid than any other we will consider in this book except perhaps for India's. This fluidity, in turn, contributes to the broader uncertainties about Russian politics and the fact that the tables are far more complicated than those we have seen in any other chapter so far.

Second, it is now obvious that Putin reshaped the party system so that it can be more easily manipulated, if not controlled outright, from the center. There are no indications that he has any desire to end a limited version of competitive elections, and there is little evidence of the kind of voting fraud that we will see, for instance, in Chapter 16 on Mexico.

Nonetheless, since he came to power in 1999, the government has taken effective control of all the television stations, which it has used to assiduously promote Putin and his policies. Before the 2003 legislative election, he forced a law through the Duma which made it all but impossible for small parties without nationwide support to even get on the ballot. In 2005, he forced through a new law that eliminated single-member districts, making it harder for regional parties and independents to run, and raised the minimum threshold a party needs to get Duma seats from 5 to 7 percent of the vote. In 2010, Putin and Medvedev forced the popular and long-time mayor of Moscow to resign, only to replace him with someone who was more clearly under the Kremlin's control.

Elections

Russians' first opportunity to vote in a reasonably free election came in the referendum of 1993. Early that year, the conflict between the still-reformist administration and the increasingly conservative Congress of People's Deputies came to a head. Yeltsin invoked special powers and called for a referendum in which the people were asked if they supported his rule and economic reforms and if they favored early elections for president and the Parliament.

Yeltsin got clear but not overwhelming majorities in support of his presidency and his economic policies. Voters rejected early presidential elections but supported them for the legislature. However, the turnout was so low that Yeltsin did not get the absolute majority he needed to call new legislative elections. Moreover, only about a third of the eligible voters actually supported either Yeltsin or his policies. In short, the referendum results did little more than set the stage for the events that culminated in the unsuccessful coup attempt that fall.

Russians' next opportunity to vote was a referendum on the new constitution held simultaneously with State Duma elections in December 1993. As in the spring, barely half the voters turned out and barely half of those voting supported the government's initiative. Since then, Russians have voted in nine national elections—five for the Duma (1993, 1995, 1999, 2003, and 2007) and four for the presidency (1996, 2000, 2004, and 2008).

Until 2007, Duma elections were run under the same basic system used in Germany. There were 450 seats, half of which were elected by proportional representation and half in single-member districts. In the proportional half of the ballot, seats only went to parties that won at least 5 percent of the vote nationwide. In the single-member district half, whoever got the most votes in a district won it.

Presidential elections follow the French pattern. Any number of candidates can run on a first ballot, and if no one wins a majority in that first round of voting, the top two vote-getters compete in a runoff two weeks later.

The dual system for choosing Duma members worked very differently from the one in Germany. There, in every election in the past fifty years, the major parties have won just about all of the single member districts and the proportional side of the ballot is used, in part, to make certain that that the parliamentary delegations accurately reflect the parties' overall support. In Russia, anywhere from 60 to 110 independents were elected from the single-member districts, most of whom were beyond the control of national party leaders before 2003. Herein lies the importance of the elimination of those districts, which went into effect for the 2007 election. Now, all 450 seats are chosen on a proportional basis and allotted only to parties winning 7 percent of the vote. In the end, only four parties won at least 7 percent, and three of them were controlled by Putin.

As also noted previously, there is nothing stable about Russian parties and elections (see Tables 9.8 and 9.9). Indeed, the most striking thing is that only three parties have run candidates in every Duma election and they saw their share of the vote slip from nearly half in 1993 to barely a quarter in 2003.

The presidential elections do not show much more stability (see Tables 9.10 through 9.13). To be sure, some of the same candidates have run in more than one election, and some of them are easily identified as members of one of the national political parties. Nonetheless, each presidential campaign from the beginning has been less competitive than the one before it. Only the first election required two ballots to determine a winner. In contrast, France has always needed two ballots, as have most of the other Eastern European countries that have adopted a similar system for choosing a president. The 2004 election was particularly problematic. Putin's obvious strength coming out of the Duma elections made the results a foregone conclusion. As a result, other potentially serious candidates withdrew from the contest. The Communists ran an unknown who came in a very distant second. The late but rarely lamented Rodina

TABLE 9.8 The 1993, 1995, and 1999 State Duma Elections

PARTY	PERCENTAGE OF LIST VOTE			SEATS ON PARTY LIST			SEATS IN SINGLE-MEMBER DISTRICTS		
	1993	1995	1999	1993	1995	1999	1993	1995	1999
Communists	12.35	22.30	24.29	32	99	67	32	58	55
Women of Russia	8.1	—	—	21	—	4	3	—	—
Liberal Democrats	22.79	11.18	5.98	59	50	17	11	1	2
Our Home is Russia	—	1.13	—	—	45	—	—	10	7
Unity	—	—	22.32	—	—	64	—	—	9
Yabloko	7.82	6.89	5.93	20	31	17	13	14	5
Russia's Democratic Choice	15.38	—	—	40	—	—	56	9	—
Union of Right Forces	—	—	8.52	—	—	24	—	—	5
Fatherland All Russia	—	—	13.33	—	—	—	—	—	32
Party of Russian Unity and Accord	6.76	—	—	18	—	—	9	1	—
Democratic Party of Russia	5.5	—	—	14	—	—	7	—	—
Others and independents	—	—	—	—	—	—	60	103	110
Against all	4.36	3.60	—	—	—	—	—	—	—

Note: Major parties only. Others were all elected from single-member districts. Many have since rallied to United Russia.

TABLE 9.9 The 2003 and 2007 State Duma Elections

PARTY	VOTE, 2003 (%)	SEATS 2003	VOTE 2007 (%)	SEATS 2007
United Russia	37.6	222	64.3	315
Communists	12.6	51	11.6	57
Liberal Democrats	11.5	36	8.1	40
Other	17.3	44	—	—
Independents	21.0	94	12.0	0

TABLE 9.10 The Russian Presidential Election of 1996

CANDIDATE	FIRST BALLOT VOTE (%)	SECOND BALLOT VOTE (%)
Boris Yeltsin	35.3	53.8
Gennady Zyuganov	32.0	40.3
Alexander Lebed	14.5	—
Grigori Yavlinsky	7.5	—
Vladimir Zhirinovsky	5.7	—
Others	2.2	—
Against all	1.5	4.8

TABLE 9.11 The Russian Presidential Election of 2000

CANDIDATE	SHARE OF VOTE (%)
Vladimir Putin	52.94
Gennady Zyuganov	29.21
Grigori Yavlinski	5.80
Anan Tuleev	2.95
Vladimir Zhirinovsky	2.70
Other candidates	2.58
Against all	1.88

TABLE 9.12 Presidential Vote, 2004

CANDIDATE	SHARE OF VOTE (%)
Vladimir Putin	71.2
Nikolai Charitonov	13.7
Sergei Glaziev	4.1
Others	6.7
Against all	4.3

TABLE 9.13 Presidential Vote, 2008

CANDIDATE	SHARE OF VOTE (%)
Dmitry Medvedev	71.3
Gennady Zyuganov	18.0
Vladimir Zhirinovsky	9.5
Others	1.3

ran its founder (and reported Putin protégé) Sergei Glazev, who came in an even more distant third. Putin won with almost three-quarters of the vote.

The apparent confusion in Table 9.8 suggests just how "floating" the party system was in Russia's early years. It *did* become more stable in the last two elections. However, as we will see in the next section, that does not mean that the party system is any more democratic or that the individual parties are effective at reflecting the preferences of the people who vote for them.

The Political Parties Today

Table 9.9 presents the results of the 2003 and 2007 elections separately from the three previous ones because it is important to see just how much the system changed during the Putin administration. For the first time, a single party scored an overwhelming victory and assured the president of a massive majority in the Duma. All the signs are that that party, United Russia, will dominate political life for years to come. The only question, then, is how—or if—the other parties can restructure themselves into a viable democratic opposition.

United Russia is not like any of the political parties considered in Part 2 in that it is not defined primarily by its stance on divisive issues. Rather, it is what observers of Russian politics call a **party of power,** created not so much to defend policy proposals or ideological positions as to promote the interests of the current leadership. It is also not the first party of power. In 1995, then-Prime Minister Viktor Chernomyrdin created **Our Home Is Russia**. It, too, was short on ideology and existed largely to support Chernomyrdin and his entourage. When he was forced to resign in 1998, the party's fortunes plummeted. It won only 1.2 percent of the vote and five single-member districts in 1999. It did not survive to run in 2003.

United Russia was formed for the 1999 Duma election, when it was known as Unity. Its specific origins are shrouded in secrecy, but all signs indicate that it was put together by oligarch **Boris Berezovsky** and other members of the Yeltsin "family." It had little support in the public opinion polls until Putin's popularity began to soar because of his forceful prosecution of the war in Chechnya. Three months after its creation, Unity came within a single percentage point of the Communists, even though it won only nine single-member districts, which is to be expected for a new organization. It later merged with **Fatherland-All Russia** and took on its new name.

Early on, Putin publicly kept his distance from the party. By the time of the 2003 and 2004 campaigns, there was no longer any pretense of his staying above the political fray. In fact, the most critical observers thought he planned the party system from the top so that the middle-of-the-road United Russia could win a landslide victory in 2007 with 64 percent of the vote and 315 of the 450 seats in the Duma.

Putin has so effectively removed the democratic side of Russian politics (for instance by taking all but complete control of the media) that few observers expect the elections of 2011 and 2012 to turn out any differently. The only possibility of this happening would occur if Medvedev and Putin both run for president and the former can build an independent base of support. One typical poll showed that 55 percent of the population planned to vote for United Russia in 2011. In summer 2010, only the Communists seemed likely to get the 7 percent needed to win seats in the Duma.

Until 2003, the CPRF had been the most effective party in the country. It was the only one to have a viable organization, which allowed it to do such things as conduct door-to-door campaigns in most of the country. More important, its support steadily increased until it earned nearly a quarter of the vote in the proportional half of the election in 1999. Its leader and presidential candidate, **Gennady Zyuganov**, came in second in the first two presidential elections.

Like the reformed communist parties in Eastern Europe, the CPRF is not a carbon copy of the old Stalinist machine. The new party counts few prominent communists from the old days among its leaders. Zyuganov comfortably plays his role as leader of the parliamentary opposition and has tried to portray the party more in Social Democratic terms as an organization that wants to protect the social and economic interests of Russia's poor.

Nonetheless, the party is far less reformist than its counterparts in Eastern Europe. Zyuganov was a staunch opponent of Gorbachev-era reforms and headed a shady "national salvation front" that seemed to want to restore the Soviet Union after it fell apart. He also was quoted as saying that the army should combat "the destructive might of rootless democracy," and he served on the editorial board of a conservative and often anti-Semitic newspaper. Like many former communists, Zyuganov and his colleagues have adopted nationalistic positions that include sometimes not-so-veiled references to expanding the Russian Federation's border into the near abroad. In the 1996 campaign, Zyuganov and the CPRF took a harder line against economic reform than before, advocating a return to more state ownership and central planning. They have also called for the retention of the collective and state farms created under Stalin. During the 1998 economic crisis, the CPRF advocated a slowdown in the pace of economic reform and the breakup of the monopolies and oligopolies created since 1991, which we will discuss in the public policy section.

The Communists still are the best-organized party in Russia. This is the case because they can draw on the thousands of middle and lower-level party officials from the old CPSU. One asset they do not have, however, is the property formerly owned by the CPSU, which was all transferred to the state.

The CPRF's influence probably peaked in 1995 when, along with other antireform factions, it held enough seats to have de facto control of the Duma and block many of Yeltsin's legislative measures. The CPRF and those other groups lost support in 1999, and Zyuganov's inability to win more than a third of the vote suggested that the party was in trouble.

The 2003 and 2004 elections brought even more bad news. It saw its share of the Duma vote cut almost in half. No prominent Communist was willing to run in a campaign everyone knew would lead to a landslide victory for Putin. The lackluster candidate who filled in for Zyuganov won little more than a third of the votes the Communists tallied four years previously. It is the only opposition party to pass the 7 percent threshold in 2007, but the CPRF has not been able to win even a fifth of the vote in recent national polls. Like all other opposition parties, the Communists seem unlikely to pose a viable threat to United Russia for the foreseeable future. By 2010, its support was cut by about two-thirds from its peak, and it could be entering a period of permanent decline.

Russia also has two parties that are usually considered reformist because they have been reasonably consistent supporters of efforts to forge a democratic state and a market economy. Together, they once accounted for close to a quarter of the electorate. Both are currently in their death throes.

Yabloko is the most consistent and persistent of the reformist parties. Yabloko (Russian for *apple*) is an acronym for its three founding leaders, Grigori Yavlinsky, Yuri Boldyrev, and Vladimir Lukin. Only two of these leaders, Yavlinsky and Lukin, are still with the party. Of the reformist parties, it has taken the strongest stand not only in support of democracy but also for the retention of some form of welfare state, which makes it most like the Social Democratic parties considered in Part 2. It is also the party that does the best among intellectuals who were prominent supporters

of Gorbachev's reforms. Yabloko's vote dropped by one percentage point in each of the Duma elections. Its leader, Yavlinsky, announced that if the party did not win at least 6 percent of the vote in 1999 he would not run for president in 2000. It did not win 6 percent, but he ran anyway—coming in a disappointing third, further harming his own reputation and that of the party. Later in the decade, Yabloko all but disappeared.

The **Union of Right Forces** was created by another group of reformers who were more firmly committed to promarket policies than Yabloko. The most prominent of them, Yegor Gaidar and **Anatoly Chubais**, had been key architects of privatization and economic policy in general in the early Yeltsin years. When their previous party, Russia's Choice, failed to break the 5 percent barrier in 1995, Gaidar realized that he had to build a broader coalition. The new Union of Right Forces hinted that Putin supported its economic plans and therefore it was able to score a respectable 8.5 percent of the proportional vote in 1999. The party's use of the word *right* in its name does not mean it is right-wing. Rather, the Russian term it uses, *pravikh*, has the same root as *pravda*, or *truth*. Thus, *right* is used by Gaidar and his colleagues to suggest that they have the right or correct answers to Russia's political and economic problems.

Both parties face uncertain futures, at best. Their leaders have failed to find a durable audience outside the

An angry woman confronting Liberal Democratic Party leader Vladimir Zhirinovsky during a Duma debate on Russia's relationship with North Atlantic Treaty Organization (NATO) in September 1995.

AP Images

intellectual communities in the big cities. It is hard to see how either can survive their drubbing in 2007.

Finally, Russia has a number of political parties that can only be viewed as antidemocratic—or worse. The most prominent of them has been the **Liberal Democrats**, headed by the enigmatic, and some say dangerous, **Vladimir Zhirinovsky**. Almost everything about him is murky. Despite his frequently anti-Semitic ravings, he is of Jewish origin. Some think he was once a KGB agent and paid to infiltrate Jewish and dissident organizations during the 1970s and 1980s.

There is no debating one thing. Zhirinovsky is a loose cannon whose often-frightening rhetoric struck a chord with a significant proportion of Russia's most alienated voters. Since he burst onto the scene in 1993, he has, among other things:

- Hinted that he would use nuclear weapons on Japan.

- Advocated expanding the Russian border all the way to the Indian Ocean.

- Invited the racist French politician Jean-Marie Le Pen to a ceremony marking his twenty-fifth wedding anniversary.

- Blamed Western governments and businessmen (in his case, it is always men) for the collapse of the Soviet Union.

- Attacked just about every reformist politician in Russia (for instance, alleging that Yeltsin was in power only because of the Central Intelligence Agency).

The Liberal Democrats have no local organization to speak of, which is the main reason the party was able to capture only one single-member constituency in 1995. The party's fortunes have declined since then because Russians have grown tired of Zhirinovsky's positions and antics. The party was technically ruled unconstitutional for the 1999 election and had to reformulate itself as the Zhirinovsky Bloc. It saw its vote decline to a bare 6 percent in 1999, and then Zhirinovsky did not win even half of that in 2000. He rebounded to nearly 12 percent four years later. His party won forty seats in 2007, and it lost most of its autonomy because it came to be widely seen as the right wing of the Putin-Medvedev coalition. In early 2011 the polls showed that the Liberal Democrats would only win 5 percent of the next Duma vote.

A Balance Sheet

The Russian party system is likely to remain in flux. Given the impermanence of the parties and the fragmentation of the system, it is hard to imagine how Russia could develop a system anything like those we saw in Britain, France, or Germany in the foreseeable future unless United Russia can

establish itself as a strong centrist party and allow serious opposition parties to compete with it.

The difficulties go far beyond election returns or party platforms. To illustrate this, consider the following television ads that aired during the 1995 Duma campaign. Only Our Home Is Russia had anything ads that approached being slick, Western-style commercials with rapidly changing and reassuring images backed by neutral-but-not-bland synthesized music. The other ads ranged from unprofessional to incompetent—to the degree that it was often hard to tell which party the ad was promoting. Some simply showed "talking heads," and even they were unable to keep within the time allotted to them. Some of the less-than-serious parties, of course, had less-than-serious ads. An ad for the Beer Lovers' Party (0.62 percent of the vote) started with two old women looking disapprovingly at a drunken man staggering along a muddy path, a bottle of vodka sticking out of his pocket. One woman said to the other: "This is not an acceptable way to drink." Immediately the scene shifted to three men at a picnic on a sunny day, drinking beer. One of the women said to the others: "This is an acceptable way to drink." The Ivan Rybkin Bloc (Rybkin was the outgoing speaker of the Duma, although his party only won 1.11 percent of the vote) ran an ad showing a conversation between two cows in which one cow (Ivan) tried to explain justice to the other by asking if (s)he had ever seen or eaten butter. It ended with the first cow eating a slice of bread covered with butter and saying that they would all have butter with their bread if Rybkin was reelected. The Communists ran a simplistic piece in which they showed horror scenes from the Russian past and asked: "Who will stop this?" The answer was obvious. Yabloko had one of Isaac Newton (though the ad said it was Lord Byron) getting hit by an apple falling from a tree.

The two most bizarre ads were made by the Liberal Democrats. The first showed a couple watching television in bed. Former Soviet leader Brezhnev came on; they said he was boring. Then came Gorbachev, and they said they had seen all that before. Finally it was Zhirinovsky's turn, and this time they said that this was more interesting even as their body language made it clear that watching more television was not on their agenda for the rest of the evening. The second ad took place in an upscale nightclub. After the singer finished her act, she was lured back onstage for an encore that was a much more upbeat song with the refrain, "Without you, this would be boring; Vladimir Wolfovich [as Zhirinovsky is commonly known], you turn me on."

The quality of television ads has improved noticeably since then. However, the state's all but complete control of the mass media has kept the opposition parties weak and strengthened Putin's hand in ways that cannot be considered favorable to democracy.

THE RUSSIAN STATE

Each of the countries examined in the remainder of this book has one major difference from those discussed in Part 2.

All have constitutions specifying how offices are structured, bills are passed, rights are ensured, and the like. However, those constitutions matter less than they do in any of the industrialized democracies. In the case of Russia, as in the other countries we will consider, it is just as important to recognize that certain institutions, some of which are not mentioned in the constitution, probably wield more power than the State Duma, cabinet, or any other legally authorized body. Russia has a more fluid kind of power, determined as much by who holds which offices and what resources they have at their disposal as by the rules laid out in the constitution or any other legal document, which we saw when Putin was "demoted" to prime minister in 2008 but still holds more power than anyone in the country by far (**www.constitution.ru/en/10003000-01.htm**).

The Presidency

Given Russian traditions and the rocky relations between President Yeltsin and what was then still the Supreme Soviet, it came as no surprise that he wrote a constitution in 1993 for the new regime based on a strong presidency, much like the one in France. Indeed, there was every reason to believe that, were it to have adopted a conventional parliamentary system, Russia would have been even more divided and difficult to govern than France's Fourth Republic (**www.eng.kremlin.ru**).

As we have already seen, the president is directly elected for a four-year term in a two-ballot system. Any candidate who gets a million signatures (which could be bought for a dollar apiece in 2004) can run on the first ballot. If a candidate gains a majority at the first ballot, he or she wins outright, as has been the case in the last three elections. If, however, no one wins more than half of the votes cast, the first and second-place candidates meet in a runoff two weeks later.

The president is all but completely independent of the Duma. There are provisions for impeaching the president, but it is extremely difficult to do so, as Yeltsin's opponents learned when they tried to remove him shortly after the constitution was adopted. The president appoints the prime minister and the other cabinet members (see Table 9.14). The Duma can reject the president's choice, but if it does so three times, the president can dissolve the Duma and call for new elections. Thus, in 1998, Yeltsin fired Prime Minister Sergei Kiriyenko and tried to bring Viktor Chernomyrdin back to replace him. The Duma voted the former prime minister down twice. It took the threat of new elections before the deputies and president agreed on a compromise candidate, Yevgeni Primakov.

TABLE 9.14 Russian Presidents and Prime Ministers

PRESIDENT	PRIME MINISTER
Boris Yeltsin (1991–99)	Boris Yeltsin (1991–92)
	Yegor Gaidar (Acting 1992–93)
	Viktor Chernomyrdin (1993–98)
	Sergei Kiriyenko (1998)
	Yevgeni Primakov (1998–99)
	Sergei Stepashin (1999)
	Vladimir Putin (1999)
Vladimir Putin (2000–)	Mikhail Kasyanov (2000–04)
	Mikhail Fradkov (2004–07)
	Viktor Zubkov (2007–08)
Dmitri Medvedev (2008–)	Vladimir Putin (2008–)

The president can issue decrees that have the force of law in many policy areas. More important, the president runs an administration that is extremely centralized. Since the mid-1990s, authority has been concentrated in the **power ministries**—defense, foreign affairs, interior (including the police), the State Security Bureau (FSB), and an informal body known as the Security Council.

After Chernomyrdin was replaced, the prime minister exercised little independent authority until Putin assumed the office in 2008. As we saw above, he only took the job because the constitution did not allow him run for a third consecutive terms, but he still essentially runs the country from what was designed to be a second-tier position. The roles will be reversed if Putin runs in and wins the next election. If not, all bets are off about the relative power of the two offices.

Government ministries are free to act more or less on their own as far as implementing policy is concerned. Nonetheless, for reasons that will become clear when we look behind the scenes, they are not very effective at initiating policy.

The Oligarchs

Some people think that the real power in Russia is held by a tiny group of tycoons who have profited immensely from privatization and who have used their wealth to gain political leverage. The power of these oligarchs became clear toward the end of Yeltsin's first term in office when analysts began criticizing what they thought was the undue influence of what they came to call the family—a small circle of relatives and advisers who controlled access to and had tremendous influence over the president (**www.cdi.org /russia/johnson/7033-4.cfm**).

The most important member of the family undoubtedly was Tatyana Dyachenko, Yeltsin's daughter. And there is no doubt as well that Yeltsin's family made millions of dollars through shady deals, if not outright corruption, which led Putin to grant them all amnesty from possible prosecution in one of his first steps as acting president.

Although the Yeltsins have left the scene, some of the oligarchs remain. No one outside the Kremlin knows exactly how many of them there are, how they made their money, or how much influence they have. Nonetheless, no one thought it was an outrageous overstatement when Boris Berezovsky declared in 1997 that he and six other businessmen controlled over half of Russia's GNP. Like Yeltsin's family, the oligarchs undoubtedly gained much of their wealth through suspicious deals, if not outright corruption. They also have sent much of their wealth abroad; in fact, they may have exported more capital from Russia than has been invested there by foreign businesses since 1991. What's more, they all have close, if not well-documented, ties to the Russian mafia.

Berezovsky's case is typical. Born in 1946 to a Jewish family that was part of Moscow's intellectual elite, Berezovsky earned a PhD in mathematics and electronics and then joined the prestigious Academy of Sciences, where he specialized in developing computerized management systems. He used his contacts to launch his first business during the Gorbachev years, and by the time the USSR collapsed, he was a major trader in automobiles, oil, gas, and the nationalized airline Aeroflot. As we will see in the section on public policy, the Yeltsin government virtually gave away shares in the nationalized industries it inherited. Berezovsky and the other oligarchs capitalized on this odd form of privatization to gain control over thousands of companies. Berezovsky ran companies in dozens of sectors but exercised the most influence through his media holdings, including two of the most respected newspapers and the most widely watched television network, ORT.

It is no exaggeration to say that Yeltsin owed his reelection in 1996 to Berezovsky and the other oligarchs. Not only did they contribute vast sums of money, they controlled all the major media outlets, whose campaign coverage was extremely biased. They also are largely responsible for the creation of United Russia and for Putin's meteoric rise.

However, Putin's relationship with some of the oligarchs has been extremely bumpy, and three have had dramatic clashes with the president. First was Vladimir Gusinsky. After his television network, NTV, openly condemned Putin, Gusinsky was arrested for corruption and control of NTV was handed over to the still state-owned natural gas monopoly, Gazprom. After being released on bail, Gusinsky moved abroad. Berezovsky, too, ran afoul of Putin and joined Gusinsky in exile in late 2001.

Finally, there is Khodorkovsky, who probably was the richest of the oligarchs, and he apparently thought it was safe for him to remain in Russia. Perhaps to his surprise, he was arrested by state security forces on tax evasion charges while his plane was being refueled in Siberia on October 25, 2003. Two years later he was convicted and sentenced to eight years in prison, which he is currently serving at a particularly bleak, Soviet-era prison in Siberia. In 2010, he was tried again and sentenced to another seven-year term. Barring unpredictable changes in Moscow, the best bet is that Khodorkovaky will spend the rest of his life in prison.

TATYANA MAKEYEVA/AFP/Getty Images

Mikhail Khodorkovsky in the cage he was kept in during his trial.

In May 2011, the Supreme Court ruled that the authorities had violated his civil rights but denied that any political intention lay behind the prosecution.

The downfall of these three oligarchs does not mean that political or economic power has been more widely distributed. Rather, they have been replaced by other oligarchs who head other massive corporations, such as the petrochemical giants Lukoil and Sibneft. The top ten are worth about $20 billion each. Most maintain residences outside of the country, including Roman Abramovich, owner of London's Chelsea soccer team who, while living in London, also somehow managed to be the provincial governor of the Chukotka region, which is the northern-most part of Siberia, for eight years. One wonders how often he had to go to his region, one of the country's poorest, with under sixty thousand residents. He has, however, invested $1 billion there, creating jobs and providing direct aid to its impoverished residents. In 2009, he bought a controlling interest in Russia's largest steel manufacturer and was ranked as the fifty-first richest person in the world.

The only difference between the old and new oligarchs is that this second generation is loyal to Putin.

The Parliament

Until 1999, the Parliament was the main counterweight to the presidency and, as such, frequently was a lightning rod in the intense divisions of the Yeltsin years. That does not mean, however, that the Parliament has ever been all that powerful. In fact, the 1993 constitution was written to minimize its likely impact.

As is the case in most of the democratic world, the Parliament consists of two houses. The upper house, the **Federation Council**, has two members from each republic and region for a total of 168 members. Like most upper houses, however it can do little more than delay the passage of legislation. If anything, its power has diminished further when its members became by all intents and purposes presidential appointees in 2004.

The lower house, the State Duma, is elected by proportional representation. The Duma itself is a fairly wild place by Western standards. Deputies scream at each other and walkouts are common. So are fistfights. By 1995, eighty-seven candidates had either been convicted of felonies or were under indictment.

More important for our purposes is the fact that the State Duma does not have much real power. It cannot, for example, force the executive to enforce the laws it passes, and it has only limited influence over the budget. In theory, the Duma has to approve presidential appointments, but Yeltsin was known to keep nominees in "acting" positions for more than a year. Furthermore, the Duma has no effective ability to cast a vote of no confidence and force a prime minister and cabinet out of office. It also can do little to remove a president.

As Table 9.9 implied, the Communists and other opponents of reform controlled the Duma following the first two elections. They used that base to block many policy proposals requiring legislative approval and to keep reformist nominees from taking or holding onto office. With the emergence of United Russia, however, the role of the Duma has changed. Putin, and now Medvedev, have had the kind of disciplined parliamentary majority we find in Britain's House of Commons. In practice, the majority is much larger than that table suggests because almost 90 percent of the members elected in 2007 are loyal to the dual executive. That means that the Duma now eagerly passes all of their major legislative initiatives, including laws that reduced the power of the republics and regions, restructured the party system, and reduced taxes (see Figure 9.3).

Democratization *in Russia*

Although institutions matter, focusing on them can obscure the most important point about Russia's fledgling democracy. Constitutional provisions and the rule of law pale in comparison with what political scientists call the "personalization of leadership" around Boris Yeltsin, Vladimir Putin, and other top leaders.

Perhaps it should not come as a surprise that a man who spent the first thirty-five years of his professional life clawing his way up the Communist Party hierarchy would find it natural to create a "top-down" style of leadership when the going got rough. Nonetheless, by the time of the 1996 election, it was clear that neither Yeltsin nor any of his leading rivals could be said to be committed democrats. Indeed, all the major candidates favored maintaining the personalization of power around a strong presidency in ways that are not likely to strengthen democratic institutions or the rule of law. There is little evidence that things on this extremely important but hard-to-measure front changed appreciably during Putin's time as president nor in his years as prime minister when he acted as if he were president. ■

FIGURE 9.3 Decision Making in Russia

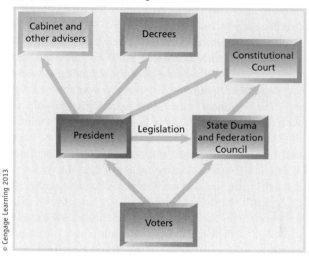

The Bureaucracy

The Yeltsin team would have preferred purging the bureaucracy of the officials who had been the glue in the old communist system, especially those in policy-making and security positions. In practice, however, they could not do so because the country lacked trained personnel to replace them.

Consider education. The old regime had relied heavily on the schools in its attempts to shape public opinion and create a docile population. Teachers were expected to support the party line. The curriculum and textbooks presented official party positions not only in the mandatory courses in Marxism-Leninism but also in the examples used by textbook writers to teach first-graders reading or arithmetic. As much as they might have liked to have done so, government officials lacked the resources to replace all those teachers and books.

In areas such as the Foreign Ministry and the various agencies that replaced the KGB, many top officials did lose their jobs. However, even in those organizations, there are many people from the old days whose loyalties are by no means certain and who can, therefore, be used to fill the plots of post-Cold War spy novels.

There is some concern today about the impact of the security services, most notably the Federal Security Bureau (FSB), which is the main body that replaced the Soviet-era KGB. This is the case because of Putin's background. He spent his entire career in the KGB during the Soviet era, was brought to Moscow in part to run the FSB, and has appointed a number of security officials to top posts in his government. The security services also may be influential because it has *kompromat*, or compromising evidence, on all leading officials—including Putin.

The Judiciary

Prior to 1991, the Soviet judiciary was little more than a cog in the party machine. The situation was not as bleak as it had been under Stalin. Nonetheless, the legal system lacked the provisions that sustain an independent and impartial judicial system and the rule of law.

The new Russian republic has tried to rebuild a judicial system that used to invariably find defendants guilty and historically relied on "show" trials in high-profile cases. Most notably, it established a Constitutional Court to deal with cases involving legal principle. Similarly, there is now a Supreme Court that serves as a final court of appeal in criminal, civil, and administrative cases. Both have been reasonably active. The Constitutional Court, for example, played a major role in determining how the 1993 referendum was conducted. More important, both courts have been highly politicized because their judges are named by the president and by the heads of the two houses of Parliament, respectively, each of whom is reluctant to appoint anyone he cannot count on.

In the long run, what happens in everyday judicial life—given the many abuses that occurred during the Soviet years—may prove to be more important. Despite the difficulty in retraining the entire legal profession or recruiting a new generation of attorneys, considerable progress has been made. Although sixty-five thousand people claimed they were illegally detained in 1994, fully a third of them were released from jail on the basis of a court order. A few defendants who were falsely accused have won cash settlements from the state prosecutor's office. There have even been a few thousand jury trials—the first since 1918. Still, the Russian government faces an uphill struggle on this and many other fronts. To cite but one example, in 1995 there were only twenty-eight thousand prosecutors and twenty thousand independent attorneys, most of whom were trained under the very different Soviet legal system (www.supcourt.ru/catalog.php?c1=English). Putin's government passed major reforms of the judiciary in 2001 and 2005, but their net impact seems to have been to bring the courts under ever tighter political control.

Most important of all is the degree to which the judiciary can contribute to the rule of law, which is still frequently violated. That begins with the spectacular examples, such as the way Khodorkovsky's arrest and trial were handled, but it goes even deeper. Basic civil liberties are by no means guaranteed, especially outside the major cities. Even everyday interactions between the people and the state are often conducted outside the law with, for instance, the widespread expectation that bribes are needed or the still pervasive underpayment of taxes. The most important recent example has been the courts' banning almost all internationally led NGOs.

The Federation

On paper, the Soviet Union was a federal system composed of fifteen union republics that supposedly had joined it voluntarily. The constitutions adopted over the years guaranteed certain political and cultural rights to the republics. There were even provisions outlining procedures for seceding from the USSR.

But those rights existed only on paper. Until the Gorbachev years, party leaders in Moscow determined policy for the subnational units, just as they did for everything else. This changed, however, in the late 1980s. Pent-up hostilities in the non-Russian republics, and then in Russia itself, erupted and proved to be among the forces that led to the Soviet collapse.

Some observers thought that the creation of fifteen new countries would ease ethnic tensions. However, because none of the new republics is anywhere near homogeneous, most have faced serious internal difficulties. The Russian Federation is no exception. In most instances, with the exception of Chechnya, the Russian government has been somewhat more successful than its Soviet predecessor in quelling ethnic unrest and defusing much of the pressure from the regions.

The minority population consists of hundreds of ethnic groups, the largest of which, the Tatars, makes up only 4 percent of the total. Russia has basically kept the complex maze of regions delineated along ethnic lines that it inherited from the Soviet Union. There are twenty-one autonomous republics and sixty-eight other bodies with various titles that are defined as "subjects of the federation," such as the autonomous *okrug* of Chukotka, previously mention because of its connection with Abramovich. All are represented in the Federation Council.

Relations between Moscow and many of the republics and regions were quite tense in 1992. Tatarstan declared itself a sovereign state. Leaders in what was then Checheno-Ingushetia refused to carry out Russian laws. Fighting in Georgia spilled over into the Russian republics in the north Caucasus. The situation was by far the worst in Chechnya, where civil wars raged from 1994 to 1997 and then from 1999 until 2009, cost well over one hundred thousand lives, and took a terrible toll on the government's legitimacy at home and abroad.

There is no doubt that Chechens suffered. They were forcibly incorporated into the Russian empire at the beginning of the nineteenth century. They did not fare any better under the Soviets. Fearful that they might collaborate with the Germans, Stalin (and here he may have been right) ordered all Chechens deported more than one thousand miles away, and they were only permitted to return as part of the reforms of the Khrushchev era. No wonder they were angry and seized on the first opportunity to show it.

Chechnya may prove to be the exception rather than the rule. In the aftermath of the 1993 coup attempt in Moscow, the overall situation began to improve. There was

MAXIM MARMUR/AFP/Getty Images

Mourners following the 2004 attack by Chechen rebels on a school in Beslan, which killed hundreds of children.

a growing awareness in most of the autonomous republics that full independence was not a viable option. Only Tatarstan and the impoverished Bashkyria had more than 3 million people; eleven had fewer than 1 million.

After the early separatist protests, the government issued a nationwide Federation Treaty and a series of bilateral agreements with eight of the republics. Komi, for example, was granted special powers to deal with its environment, which had been heavily contaminated by waste from the petrochemical industry. Yakutia won concessions allowing it to keep profits from the sale of its diamonds and other minerals. The tiny but once independent Tyva gained the right to secede. Other such agreements have been worked out to give the other forty-nine provinces more autonomy. But few could be independent. Most are in the populated west and surrounded, like Komi is, by Russia.

But there may be trouble ahead for these "subjects of the federation." Putin has also pushed through reforms designed to weaken the power of the republics' and regions' governors. Many of them had turned their jurisdictions into personal fiefdoms, all but ignoring Moscow's policies and regulations. As a result, in May 2000, Putin created seven new "federal districts" between the national government and the republics and regions, each of which is headed by a presidential representative. The Federation Council also has been weakened. Another new law gives the president the power to remove a governor if he or she refuses to harmonize local law with national policy or the constitution. Finally, Putin issued a plan to turn governors into appointed officials (by the president, of course) who would only be ratified by the regional assemblies.

The Military

In studying Russia, we also have to consider an institution that we could safely ignore in Part 2, but that will feature prominently in the rest of this book: the military. Under the Soviets, the military was not actively involved in politics, other than in trying to increase its piece of the budgetary pie.

So far, this has largely been true in post-communist Russia as well. Yeltsin survived the 1993 coup attempt because the troops he called on were loyal to the regime. They attacked the Russian White House even though one of the leading conspirators, Vice President Alexander Rutskoi, was a former air force general and one of the few heroes of the war in Afghanistan.

However, many commentators are worried that the military might not stay out of politics. Yeltsin needed support from another prominent former general, Alexander Lebed, to win in 1996. Since then, the military (unlike the intelligence services) have not been actively involved in

politics. However, there have been rumors of frustration within the military. This is hardly surprising in a country whose past influence was largely a function of its military might, which disappeared virtually overnight. Officers are worried, too, because so many of their comrades are suffering economically. Thousands of serving officers are not being paid and have been forced to moonlight in other jobs to make ends meet. Tens of thousands of them were forced to retire in 2010. More will follow suit.

Still, Russia has the fifth largest military in the world and has several thousand nuclear warheads. Much of its technology is outdated, and few observers think it could be a major fighting force in the near future. Nonetheless, the fact that Defense Minister Sergei Ivanov was initially one of the candidates most frequently touted to succeed Putin might suggest that its influence could grow.

Public Policy

Not surprisingly, the Yeltsin and Putin governments struggled to define and implement public policy. Although this has been the case in all the former communist countries, Russia has had a particularly hard time, as we saw, for instance, in Table 9.4.

The Economy

By far the most important, and the most problematic, policy area is the economy. To see why, simply recall how economic deterioration contributed to the collapse of the Soviet Union.

The new Russian leaders faced a dual challenge. First, how would they shift from a centrally planned economy in which the state owned virtually everything to one based on private ownership and a freer market? Second, how could they ensure that the fruits of these changes—when and if they came about—would be shared by all Russians?

Yeltsin and his team were initially committed to sweeping economic reform as the only viable response to the appalling conditions they inherited. However, like everything else in the former Soviet Union, actually carrying out reform was easier said than done. To begin with, there were no historical examples of transitions from centrally planned to market economies for them to draw on. Add to that Yeltsin's own personal lack of decisiveness, perhaps magnified by his many illnesses, and the result was a government that was usually unwilling and unable to follow any consistent economic policy.

Post-communist economic policy initially revolved around the struggle between two groups. The reformers, including most professional economists, stressed the importance of a rapid and complete shift to a market economy. Their preferred policy was shock therapy, but even its strongest advocates acknowledged that it would have tremendous costs in the short term.

The conservatives wanted to proceed much more slowly. They stressed the fact that the *laissez-faire* approach has not been all that successful in the West, where all countries have had to turn to a welfare state to help cushion the impact of capitalism's uneven development on the less fortunate.

Proponents of the two approaches were not distributed randomly in Russian society. On the one hand, almost all reformers were in the Yeltsin camp and have never gained much support either in the Parliament or the country as a whole. The first Dumas, on the other hand, were dominated by the rejuvenated Communist Party and others who preferred a "go slow" approach.

Conservatives were not the only obstacle facing the reformers. Given the domination of the Communist Party over education prior to 1991, most reformist economists, like former acting Prime Minister Yegor Gaidar, were self-trained and inexperienced. Therefore, in a move that provoked criticism at home and in the West, the reformers drew on a relatively unrepresentative group of Western neoclassical economists who urged them to move rapidly to a free-market economy, whatever the costs to people and enterprises in the transition.

In 1991 and 1992, deteriorating economic conditions, the popularity of Yeltsin and his administration, and the as-yet untested but theoretically elegant predictions of the economists tilted the balance toward shock therapy. This led the first Yeltsin governments to emphasize privatization, which took two forms. The first occurred spontaneously, mostly among small firms in the service sector. About 95 percent of the restaurants, shoe repair stores, gas stations, barber shops, and other such businesses that existed before 1991 quickly gained private owners, usually the men and women who managed them under the communists. Other people formed upward of twenty thousand small firms, also mostly in the service sector.

Such "bottom-up" privatization would not have worked for the gigantic industrial enterprises that dominated the Soviet economy. Potential individual investors could not come up with anywhere near the necessary capital to buy these firms. And most were of dubious value because they would have had to be gutted and completely restructured before they could turn a profit. As a result, the government adopted a different approach to privatizing them, using a system of vouchers made available to the public. In 1992, all citizens got a voucher worth ten thousand rubles (then about twenty-five dollars), which they could sell, use to buy stock in privatized companies, or invest in larger funds that bought and managed shares

in those companies. Most chose the third option, which means that these new bodies, which are roughly equivalent to American mutual funds, became the owners of most of the stock that was offered for sale on the open market.

Shares were also made available to the firms' managers—in other words, to men and women who had been part of the old communist elite. The new owners/managers have thus enriched themselves and, in the process, have strengthened their links to the new state, which is not exactly what the orthodox economists had in mind when they urged the government to privatize.

Finally, shares in most enterprises being privatized were offered to foreign investors. At first, there was relatively little interest because the companies were inefficient at best and because Russian law limited how much of a stake foreigners could have in companies. After 1993, however, the investment and legal climates both improved, and foreigners pumped an average of $100 billion per year into Russia over the next five years. Outside investors, for instance, own about 90 percent of the shares of AO Volga, which produces a third of Russia's newsprint. The privatized firm is managed by Germans who are changing its operations so that it can export more of what it produces on foreign markets where it might earn more money.

Do not equate privatization with success for radical economic reform. Simply taking enterprises out of public ownership does not necessarily mean creating a competitive market economy. In part because managers were able to gain control of so many companies and because investment funds bought up most of the vouchers, there is a tremendous concentration of wealth in the Russian economy, which led to the creation of the powerful oligarchs and their conglomerates. And the oligarchs controlled the largest voucher funds.

Even shock therapy's strongest supporters acknowledge that in the short term it caused many people to lose their jobs or see their incomes shrink. However, few expected Russia to suffer as much as it has. The Russian economy deteriorated tremendously, with overall production declining by an average of more than 6 percent per year during the 1990s. The decline was particularly pronounced in heavy industry, which had been the mainstay of the old Soviet economy.

To cite but one example, the giant Uralmash heavy machinery factory lost more than twenty thousand jobs and came close to being shut down because there was no longer any real market for its products. Eventually Uralmash was swallowed up by one of the new conglomerates and is a thriving company today because it makes tools used in the booming oil industry (see discussion later in this chapter).

The Moscow State Circus

By 2007, most of the economy was at least nominally in private hands.

Then, that July, it was announced that the Great Moscow State Circus would be privatized. The circus in the Soviet Union, and now Russia, is very different from what most people in the West are used to. It operated in fancy, permanent arenas, and at least during the second half of the show, it usually featured (very) scantily dressed female performers.

By 2007, the Moscow circus was in trouble. It was nearly broke. It lost a lot of its top performers to foreign troupes such as the Cirque du Soleil. Many of those "defectors" came from families who had dominated circus life for generations.

The circus may once have been a symbol of a state enterprise that did well. Now, it reflects the fact that the state sector has all but disappeared.

The changes can be seen most graphically in the amazing decline in the value of the ruble. Under the Soviets, the ruble was not a convertible currency because the government artificially fixed its value at $1.60. When Chip was there in 1986, people could buy and sell rubles on the black market at about 20 rubles for a dollar. In mid-1997 it took 5,500 rubles to get a dollar, and when these lines were written, it was more than 32,000. (In practice, it was 32 to a dollar, because the Russians had introduced a new ruble that was worth 1,000 of the old ones on which these values were calculated.) Even today's ruble (most people still count in terms of the old one) is worth less than three American cents given the economic crisis and its shock to the oil-driven economy.

There were signs that the economy had reached rock bottom in 1997, but the country was shaken the next year by its worst financial crisis yet. The government had borrowed billions of dollars after 1991. For a variety of complicated economic reasons, Russia could not pay its debts and, for all intents and purposes, defaulted on the loans. The stock market lost half its value and the ruble fell by two-thirds. Two prime ministers were fired because they could not end the crisis. Finally, new loans and a new stabilization package imposed by Western governments and the International Monetary Fund slowed the decline.

Since then, there have been some promising economic trends. The value of the ruble has stabilized and risen a bit from time to time. Growth rates have averaged more than 5 percent in this decade and reached almost 7 percent in 2006. The upturn is most visible in the new middle class, which numbers at least 5 million people. Russia also currently has more billionaires than any other country, and

Muscovites buy more Mercedes than residents of any other city, though its overall sales are only about a tenth of those in the United States. Moscow's Mega Mall is the most visited shopping center in Europe.

But we should not make too much of this upturn for three reasons. First and foremost, it is not clear how much of a role the state has played in fostering it. There is no question that the stability of the Putin years has made the country more attractive to foreign investors, but it is difficult to see any direct connection between government policies and the better economic performance other than the fact that the state is playing more of a controlling role in what are nominally private companies.

That is the case, in part, because of the second cause for concern. Most of the improvement can be attributed to a single industry—petroleum. Because oil prices skyrocketed from the late 1990s until the onset of the current recession and because Russian supplies are stable and reliable, its petrochemical sector was enormously profitable. In 2006, oil and related products accounted for about half of the goods and services Russian firms sold abroad. Over the last decade, oil and gas prices fell before the current spike. On balance, then, Russian revenue from petrochemicals has fallen by as much as half over the last decade or so. Russia no longer has the petrodollars it did and may regret not using them to bolster other sectors of the economy when it had the opportunity.

Third, most Russians continue to suffer. The average person still makes about $250 a month, which makes buying a Mercedes or shopping at Ikea impossible. Even a rank-and-file judge only makes about $300 a month. The World Bank estimates that about 20 percent of the population lives in absolute poverty, which means their incomes fall below subsistence levels. Some Russian think tanks put the figure at closer to 30 percent. That's another way of saying that the bulk of the benefits from growth have gone to people near the top of those large conglomerates. In fact, it is estimated that they spirited about $24 billion dollars out of the country in 2003, a capital flight roughly equal to the amount of money foreigners invested in Russia that year.

Finally, Russia is frequently lumped with Brazil, India, China, and South Africa as one of the BRICS countries. We will explain where the term comes from and why it (or at least these countries) are important in Chapter 11. For now, it is enough to see that Russia gets into the top tier of such countries for very different reasons.

The first is its position as a superpower during the Cold War. The G-7 agreed to add the USSR in 1997, even though its economy was only roughly one-seventh the size of the American economy. In reality, the USSR and then Russia were always an odd match for the other seven.

Economic Liberalization
in Russia

Russia is often cited as a good example of liberal economic policy in action. After all, virtually all enterprises are now in private hands and, at least since 2000, the economy is doing reasonably well.

However, it is not that simple.

Privatization has not brought with it a competitive market, which is a key component of any liberal approach to economics. Rather, large conglomerates—many of which are run by oligarchs—control an immense share of the economy where there is no competition to speak of.

There are some signs of change. Russia now has about thirteen thousand people with MBA degrees who seem to be heading primarily toward new and more entrepreneurial businesses. For instance, the country's leading cell phone provider is not part of one of the conglomerates. Similarly, a Yale MBA started Russia's first American-style drug store, 36.6 (the "normal" temperature in centigrade). But on balance, the state and its allies control the key industries that will shape the core of the economy for the foreseeable future. ■

Second, because of its size and potential clout, it is one of the countries clamoring for the role of the G-8 to shift to a larger G-20 that includes the BRICS and other—if smaller—emerging economies. It was formed in 1999. Like the G-8, it has no staff of its own and rotates its presidency and meeting place among member states. There is reason to question whether Russia belongs. Of the members, it has the least diversified economy and one of the poorest populations. There is little doubt that the G-20 will come to rival the G-8 sooner rather than later.

Foreign Policy

One might have expected Russia to have similar difficulties with its foreign policy. After all, at the beginning of 1991 it was one of the world's two superpowers. A year later it was a relatively minor player in international affairs and a supplicant for economic aid. To make matters even worse, it had to develop relations with fourteen newly independent states that had been part of the Soviet Union, and which many Russians still felt were rightfully part of their country.

The Russians have occasionally given observers in the West reason for concern about their foreign policy. The ravings of politicians like Zhirinovsky have received a lot of attention in the press and among right-wing politicians on both sides of the Atlantic. Yeltsin's occasional anti-American statements and more frequent diplomatic gaffes worried people who saw him as the West's best hope for stability. And Russia unquestionably has been less than vigilant about the movement of nuclear technology across its borders and the disposal of nuclear waste, which has not allayed the concerns of observers.

Still, Russian foreign policy has been mostly pragmatic. Rhetoric aside, Yeltsin and his team adapted to their status as a middle-level power, developed reasonable relations with their neighbors, and began putting as much emphasis on economic as on geopolitical issues in their foreign policy. We can see this if we focus on relations with the United States.

It was hard for both Russian and American foreign policymakers to adapt to the new post-communist world, yet American leaders in the George H. W. Bush and the Clinton administrations took for granted that the United States needed to maintain a positive working relationship with the new Russian state. At first, they were genuinely enthusiastic about Yeltsin and his role in the collapse of communism. However, as Yeltsin's flaws became more obvious, American and European leaders sought to distance themselves from him even as they realized that the alternatives were worse.

They were not worried that Russia would pose the same kind of threat to the United States and its allies that the Soviet Union had. Indeed, the United States and Russia reached a series of agreements to dismantle more than a third of their nuclear arsenals and stop targeting each other. Moreover, the Russian government was so poor, and morale in the army was so low, that it could no longer be thought of as having a fighting force that could have an impact far beyond its borders.

Rather, the United States and its allies worried that instability in the region and aggression from Russia could exacerbate already difficult situations in such places as Chechnya, Yugoslavia, Georgia, and Moldova, and even as far away as the Indian subcontinent. They also had to pay attention to the fears of post-communist leaders in Eastern Europe, who were not convinced that Russia had given up all its designs on them. The United States and Russia have had a sometimes tense and sometimes cordial relationship in which the Americans have normally cast in their lot with Moscow despite some very important sources of friction. American support for Russia has included:

■ Aid in dismantling Russian nuclear equipment.

■ Incorporation of Russia as a permanent member of the G-7 (now, of course, G-8) annual summit.

- Provision of substantial economic aid and investment from the public, as well as from the private sector.

- Training and other assistance in developing democratic institutions.

Under Putin, Russian-American relations have been something like a political roller coaster. They took an unexpected turn for the better after 9/11. The Russians realized that they shared concerns about terrorism with the Americans when it emerged that al-Qaeda personnel had fought in Chechnya and that Chechens had participated alongside the Taliban during the war in Afghanistan. And Washington realized that it needed to use bases in several of the former Soviet republics, most notably Uzbekistan, all of which were, in turn, heavily dependent on Moscow for their defense. Not only did the United States and Russia cooperate in the initial stages of the war on terrorism, but their overall relations also improved. In particular, the two countries moved closer to an agreement on changes to the Anti-Ballistic Missile Treaty, which would allow the United States to move forward with its plans for a missile defense system.

In early 2003, however, the Russian-American relationship began to sour. Among other things, the Russian government did not share the American view that Iraq and Iran should be seen as targets in the war of terrorism.

Globalization
in Russia

Visitors to Moscow and St. Petersburg can be forgiven for thinking that globalization has taken firm root in Russia. Western chain stores and offices, gleaming new shopping centers featuring luxury goods, and thousands of BMWs and Mercedes are hard to miss.

But globalization's impact is more muted than those examples might suggest in two ways. First, compared to most countries there is less foreign investment in Russia as a whole. Thus, in 2010, direct foreign investment was down almost 14 percent to just under $14 billion compared to almost $105 billion in China where investment increased by almost 18 percent in that same year. Second, few people outside the biggest cities are enjoying the benefits (or enduring the consequences) of globalization. ■

It joined France and China in blocking United Nations Security Council approval for the invasion of Iraq. It should be pointed out, though, that even if Putin was as critical of the George W. Bush administration as French President Jacques Chirac was, Russia never drew the ferocious criticism that the United States leveled at France. In addition, there have been areas where Russia cooperated with the West, including the unsuccessful effort to convince North Korea to end its nuclear program.

THE MEDIA

Putin has perhaps been most severely and justly criticized for reasserting state control over the central organs of the mass media. Before Gorbachev came to power, the communists controlled everything that was legally printed, published, or broadcast. There was a tiny underground, or *samizdat*, press, but its circulation numbered in the tens of thousands at most.

Almost overnight, there was a revolution in the media that Soviet citizens had access to. One of the world's most closely controlled media became one of its most contentious. By 1988, almost anything that could be said was being said on the airwaves. New newspapers, magazines, and journals began publishing, many of which were critical of everything and everyone.

After 1991, the major media outlets passed into private hands. Not surprisingly, the most influential (and profitable) of them came under the control of the oligarchs. For instance, the two leading national television networks were run by Berezovsky and Gusinsky. And in Russia today, it is television that counts because newspaper circulation has plummeted given the rising cost of newsprint, journalists' salaries, and the like. Similarly, people with Internet access can get news from other, independent sources, but the best estimate is that well under 10 percent of the population is online. Television's impact became abundantly clear in the 1996 presidential campaign. As we saw earlier, Berezovsky and the other oligarchs orchestrated Yeltsin's reelection campaign largely by manipulating what was (and was not) presented on their channels.

Although there was some criticism of the obviously biased media, television did not become a major issue until the two network-owning oligarchs turned on Putin. He was able to use the power of the Kremlin to force them out of the television industry even before they were forced into exile. Ownership of the networks was transferred to other conglomerates sympathetic to the Putin administration. What that has meant is that the Kremlin has taken de facto control of television news, which is nearly as one-sided as it was before Gorbachev came to power.

The crackdown on free media continues. On August 16, 2007, the radio regulatory agency informed *Bolshoye Radio* that it would have to drop the BBC World Service or risk being shut down. The authorities told the last network to feature the BBC on the air that it had to produce all of its own content, even if the law officially required that only 82 percent of its content be original. The BBC is owned by the British government; it is known for its independence from political pressure and is arguably the most objective and highest quality radio news service in the world.

CONCLUSION: HALF-EMPTY OR HALF-FULL

Of all the countries covered in this book, Russia comes closest to reflecting the cliché about whether the glass is half-empty or half-full. This is the case because, even after more

than a generation of transition, it is impossible to predict whether Russia will develop a stable democracy and a prosperous market economy or not.

On the half-empty side are all the problems laid out in this chapter. Indeed, after analyzing the industrialized democracies in Part 2, it is hard not to be pessimistic given Russia's social, economic, and political difficulties, many of which have worsened since the breakup of the Soviet Union.

But, we should not ignore the "half-full" aspects of Russian life. It has had nine reasonably fair and competitive elections. There was a successful transition of power from Yeltsin to Putin. The oligarchs are slightly less powerful. There are signs that the economy has started to recover.

Nonetheless, there really is only one conclusion we can reach about Russia, one that will apply to many of the other countries we consider in the rest of this book: Transitions to democracy and market capitalism are rarely easy.

Looking FORWARD

AT THE END of Chapter 8, we actually anticipated what would be in this box and the next chapter. Because we could only consider current and former communist regimes, the countries to pick and the questions to ask were obvious.

Here we have explored the causes and consequences of the Soviet Union's collapse. In Chapter 10, we look at why the communist regime has survived in China, at least in name.

We say at least in name because we will see that little remains of egalitarianism and other Marxist goals other than control by the Chinese Communist Party. And we have already seen that Marx might not have been happy with its long-term stranglehold on power.

Indeed, in our teaching, we often ask students if China is still communist. We ask them to rename the regime. After we work through silly answers like "it's run by the Bobs," the students run out of ideas!

Key Terms

Concepts
democratic centralism
glasnost
near abroad
nomenklatura
oligarch
party of power
perestroika
power ministries

privatization
purges
shock therapy

People
Berezovsky, Boris
Brezhnev, Leonid
Chubais, Anatoly
Gorbachev, Mikhail
Khodorkovsky, Mikhail

Khrushchev, Nikita
Lenin, V. I.
Medvedev, Dmitri
Putin, Vladimir
Stalin, Joseph
Yeltsin, Boris
Zhirinovsky, Vladimir
Zyuganov, Gennady

Acronyms
CPRF
CPSU
KGB

Organizations, Places, and Events
Bolsheviks
Central Committee
Cheka

Comintern

Communist Party of the
   Russian Federation (CPRF)

Communist Party of the
   Soviet Union (CPSU)

Fatherland-All Russia

Federation Council

five-year plan

Gosplan

Just Russia

Liberal Democrats

Mensheviks

Our Home Is Russia

Politburo

provisional government

Russian Federation

secret speech

Secretariat

State Duma

Third International

Twentieth Party Congress

Union of Right Forces

United Russia

Yabloko

Useful Websites

Due to the shaky state of the Russian economy, many of the promising Internet portals created there a few years ago have fallen by the wayside. The best English-language entry point for Russian news and political sites is European Internet. Another good source of news is the Open Society Institute.

www.einnews.com/russia/

www.soros.org

Because of the difficulties Russians are having maintaining their own sites, especially their English-language mirrors:

www.cdi.org/russia/johnson

Some of the best entry points to things Russian are probably those maintained by American-based Russian studies centers, especially those at the universities of Michigan, Pittsburgh, and Washington.

www.ii.umich.edu/crees/resources/relatedunits

www.ucis.pitt.edu/reesweb

jsis.washington.edu/ellison/

A number of organizations and NGOs are doing analytical work and helping Russia develop. Two of the best are the Jamestown Foundation and the Initiative for Social Action and Renewal in Eurasia, with roots on the right and left wings, respectively.

www.jamestown.org

www.isar.org

Finally, the Carnegie Endowment for International Peace held a major international conference on "Russia—Ten Years After" in 2001, which is probably still the single best source in print or online on the transition.

www.carnegieendowment.org

Further Reading

Aron, Leon. *Yeltsin: A Revolutionary Life.* New York: St. Martin's Press, 2000. Perhaps the best biography of Russia's first president.

Goldman, Marshall. *Petrostate: Putin, Power, and the New Russia.* New York: Oxford University Press, 2008.

Gorbachev, Mikhail S. *Perestroika.* New York: Harper & Row, 1987. Despite what has happened to his reputation since then, an important and revealing book, especially about the reasons behind *perestroika* and new thinking.

Herspring, Dale, ed. *Putin's Russia: Past Imperfect, Future Uncertain.* Lanham, MD: Rowman & Littlefield, 2005. Not quite as well integrated as the McFaul volume, this is still an excellent and readable collection of essays.

Hough, Jerry, and Merle Fainsod. *How the Soviet Union Is Governed.* Cambridge, Mass.: Harvard University Press, 1979. The definitive text. Even though the Soviet Union is no more, this book is well worth reading because you cannot understand the post-communist transition without understanding what came before.

Mackenzie, David, and Michael W. Curran. *A History of the Soviet Union.* Belmont, CA: Wadsworth, 1991. One of the best of the brief textbooks on the entire Soviet period.

McFaul, Michael, Nikolai Petrov, and Andrei Ryabov. *Between Dictatorship and Democracy: Russian Post-Communist Political Reform.* Washington: Carnegie Endowment for International Peace, 2004. An excellent collection of integrated essays written by McFaul and a number of leading Russian experts.

Nolan, Peter. *China's Rise, Russia's Fall: Politics, Economics, and Planning in the Transition from Stalinism.* Houndsmill, U.K.: Macmillan, 1995 (distributed in the United States by St. Martin's Press). Probably has better coverage on China, but a good exploration of the uncertainties caused by the "stop-start" pattern of Russian reform.

Remington, Thomas. *Politics in Russia,* 6th ed. New York: Longman, 2009. The best short text on Russian politics.

Shevtsova, Lilia. *Putin's Russia.* Washington: Carnegie Endowment for International Peace. 2003. A very good overview of Putin's first term written by one of Russia's leading political scientists.

Shteyngart, Gary. *Absurdistan.* New York: Random House, 2007. A very fun novel about the transition in a fictional central Asian republic as told from the perspective of an American-educated Russian. Caution: contains lots of seemingly gratuitous sex.

Sixsmith, Martin *Putin's Oil*. London: Continuum, 2010. On the surface a book about the oil industry, but it goes much deeper into Russian politics. By a BBC reporter who has spent much of his career in Moscow.

Von Laue, Theodore. *Why Lenin? Why Stalin?* Philadelphia: Lippincott, 1971. A relatively old book, but still the best short source on why the revolution turned out as it did.

White, Stephen, Richard Rose, and Ian McAllister. *How Russia Votes*. Chatham, NJ: Chatham House, 1997. The first systematic study of Russian voters from 1991 on; also puts the country into a comparative perspective.

Black cat, white cat, what does it matter as long as the cat catches mice?

DENG XIAOPING

China

THE BASICS

China

Size	9,595,960 sq. km (a bit smaller than the United States)
Arable land	10%, down by one-fifth since 1949
Population	1.33 billion
Population growth rate	0.5%
Economic growth rate	9.1%
GNP per capita	$6,600
Currency	6.82 yuan renminbi = US$1
Life expectancy	75
Ethnic composition	92% Han Chinese
Capital	Beijing
Head of State	President Hu Jintao (2003)
Head of Government	Prime Minister Wen Jiabao (2003)

HU'S NOT ON FIRST[1]

One of the often misleading conclusions political scientists reached about communist countries is that they did not have a normal or routine way of choosing new leaders. Typically, the General Secretary of the Communist Party (as the office was formally known) stayed in power until he died. His death was followed by a power struggle that could drag on for years. In practice, most communist countries developed procedures whereby the party's leadership selected the next person in charge with a minimum of conflict, as we saw in Chapter 9 following the deaths of Brezhnev, Yuri Andropov, and Konstantin Chernenko.

In fact, China had worked out smooth mechanisms from one leader to the next, including a rule that only allowed a leader to serve two five-year terms. The current president, Hu Jintao, had been named Chairman of the **Chinese Communist Party (CCP)** in 2002 and president of the **People's Republic of China (PRC)** a year before

---

[1]Serious baseball fans will understand that this section's subtitle refers to Abbott and Costello's riotous and absurd routine, "Who's On First?" **www.baseball-almanac.com/humor4.shtml**. Who is on first. What plays second. Because is in left field. I leave the rest to your imagination. Or your browser.

Looking BACKWARD

BEFORE THE END of the Cold War, it seemed to many that communism was a major threat to the West. There were two communist countries that did pose a major challenge for the kinds of systems covered in Part 2.

That might seem silly today.

We have just seen how Russia collapsed to the point that it is barely a shadow of its former self and is no longer communist. But China retains a strong Marxist-Leninist regime. But, as we are about to see, just how communist it still is is an open question.

Another way of putting it is that the Soviet Union collapsed because it allowed political freedom without solving economic and social problems, because it put *glasnost* ahead of *perestroika*. China has followed what is, for all intents and purposes, an opposite path. It has emphasized reform in public policy and kept political reform to a minimum, especially when there seemed to be any chance that the Communist Party's monopoly in power could be challenged.

And that leads to another question that we will only be able to touch on: Can any communist or Marxist regime survive in this day and age?

Xi Jinping with Vladimir Putin shortly after he was named China's leader.

his predecessor was due to retire. In 2012 he is due to be replaced by **Xi Jinping** (1957–).

Xi was only 57 (young by Chinese standards) when he was selected. The key indicator that he was truly being groomed for the top spot was Xi's nomination to head the **Central Military Commission (CMC)** (www.globalsecurity.org/military/world/china/cmc.htm), a post that had preceded the elevation of his two predecessors to be head of the Party.

Now, struggles over the transition seem to be over. Xi will be a leader of a new but familiar sort. He is the son of a Politburo member who was a leading reformer and supported Deng Xiaoping. Like most of his contemporaries, Xi is a trained engineer and is apparently committed to economic reform. But, also like his contemporaries, he is a product of the Communist Party machine that is reluctant to give up control—at best.

He will also take power at a time of tremendous economic growth. It is expanding at the rate of over 9 percent per year, which means the economy as a whole will double in size in the next eight years if that rate continues. China, thus, clearly belongs in the BRICS category of states with booming economies, even if the growth rate slows down, as many predict. Overall, the Chinese economy is one of the strongest in the world; by some accounts it is the world's second largest. In time, it will join the world's leaders on a per capita basis as well. And, as the world's most populous country, it is already a major power and could conceivably be the most powerful before this century is over.

He will also take power at a critical time in Chinese political history. If the trends we will discuss below are at all accurate, it will become harder and harder for the Communist Party to maintain its stranglehold on political power that is central to its rule. With the spread of everything from private business to the Internet, it could well become impossible for the Party to retain its authoritarian state.

That is the key to this chapter. In other words, the Soviet Union may have fallen because it put political reform ahead of economic change. In China, the situation may well be reversed.

To complicate matters further, China's burgeoning economy is dominated by the Chinese Communist Party, which has run the country for more than sixty years. Unlike the Soviet leadership, the CCP has adopted a pragmatic economic stance once **Deng Xiaoping** came to power in the late 1970s. But unlike the Soviet example, the CCP has kept political reform to a minimum. In sum, China presents us with a pair of paradoxes.

Can communism survive? Many observers already think that China is communist in name only. That said, there are few signs that the CCP is going to give up its monopoly on power any time soon.

Similarly, will China become fully capitalist? To be sure it has one of the most dynamic economies in the world fueled by a new generation of entrepreneurs. However, many of the leading companies are still state owned, including quite a few that are controlled by the military. Corruption is also a concern, which is something we will see in the discussion of the Inspector Chen Cao mystery novels later in the chapter.

We should not exaggerate any of the problems facing China. To start with, the consolidation of power by **Hu Jintao** (1942–) in 2002 and 2003 marked one of the smoothest transitions in any communist country ever. Xi is unlikely to have any greater difficulty pursuing economic reform, if not sustaining political stability. China's history over the last two centuries has been among the most tumultuous on earth. Its divisions roiled the political water well into the 1980s. Now it has one of the world's most stable (if not the most democratic) regimes.

Chinese Names and Terms

Issues involving the Chinese language and names can easily confuse readers and, thus, should be clarified at the outset.

Chinese names are always rendered with the family name first. In other words, Barack Hussein Obama would be written or spoken Obama Barack Hussein.

Failure to remember this can be embarrassing. For example, the first time President Harry Truman met Chiang Kai-shek, he reportedly greeted him, "Glad to meet you Mr. Shek."

There are also two primary ways of transliterating Chinese terms. Almost everyone writing about China uses the pinyin system its leaders prefer. People in Taiwan and Hong Kong still use the Wade-Giles version. We have used pinyin for all names and terms other than those associated with Taiwan and the Nationalists who fled to Taiwan.

THINKING ABOUT CHINA

The Basics

China's most important characteristic is its size. The People's Republic of China is the world's most populous country, with more than 1.3 billion people or more than one-fifth of the global population. The government has engaged in largely successful attempts to limit population growth. Some 74 percent of women of childbearing age use contraceptives, compared with only 5 percent in Myanmar (formerly Burma) and 35 percent in India. Nonetheless, a baby is born somewhere in China every two seconds, and estimates now suggest that the Chinese population will reach 1.5 billion in the next fifty years.

China's huge population is stretching the country's limited natural resources. In all there are only about two acres of land—or one-eighth of the Asian average—per person, and only one-fourth of that is arable. There is also a severe water shortage for both human consumption and irrigation. On top of that, the limited land and water are being gobbled up by new housing and industrial development at an alarming rate.

Unlike Russia or the former Soviet Union, China has a relatively homogeneous population. More than nine in ten of its citizens are Han, or ethnically Chinese. The rest of the population consists of far smaller groups, but with the exception of the Tibetans and the Uighers (the spelling and to a lesser degree pronunciation of this term in English varies tremendously) minority nationalities have not been politically important.

Although there is a single written Chinese language, there are tremendous differences in the way it is spoken. Someone who speaks only Mandarin, for instance, cannot understand Cantonese and other southern dialects. Gradually, however, Mandarin is becoming the *lingua franca* and is now spoken by almost all educated people.

The two characters the Chinese use to denote their country (middle kingdom) tell us much about their country. Some sense of national superiority is a part of many cultures, but in the case of China, it has played an especially important role. It led Chinese leaders to try to close itself off from outside influence for much of the last millennium. As a result, a country that had been the intellectual and political leader of the world found itself unable to compete when Europeans arrived in earnest about 175 years ago.

In the meantime, China changed very little compared to the West. Examinations introduced more than two thousand years ago that tested a student's ability to memorize Confucian texts were still used to determine entry into the all-important civil service. Western values were disparaged barely a generation ago, when the CCP leadership launched an "antispiritual pollution campaign" that attacked people who used makeup or listened to rock and roll.

Whatever the communists and their predecessors may have wanted, recently China has changed dramatically. On balance, it remains a very poor country despite all the progress that has been made since the revolution in 1949 and the adoption of limited market reforms thirty years later. Per capita income calculated on a purchasing power parity (PPP) basis is more than six thousand dollars a year, but in real terms, more than half of the people live on barely more than one hundred dollars a month. Over the last few decades, at least 100 million people have moved from the desperately poor countryside to the cities, which offer the dream of wealth but often leave the young migrants in utter poverty.

At the same time, at least 100 million people should also be considered middle class by anyone's standards. Cities have skyscrapers, malls, and high tech businesses that have made many young Chinese wealthier than even the beneficiaries of reform in Russia.

The Chinese have made remarkable strides in overcoming the country's social and economic ills. Life expectancy has leapt to seventy-five years, far above the Asian average. Ninety percent of the population is literate, compared with the Asian average of 70 percent. Only 7 percent of Chinese children under 5—compared to 30 percent of India's—are born dangerously undersized.

We in the West probably overstate the degree to which China has become a global political and economic power. Overall, it has one of the top economies in the world; but its ranking pales when you calculate its wealth on a per capita basis. Its military is the largest in the world and has ambitious plans for developing new weapons to spread its influence. Yet, the **People's Liberation Army (PLA)** barely spends a tenth of what the United States does on its military. What's more, in early 2011 its leaders announced that China had no intention of challenging the United States—at least on the military front.

In short, China is in a time of transition. What will it be like as its position as one of the world's great powers solidifies? Will it become more democratic? And, most important of all, will the CCP survive as the dominant institution in the country?

Key Concepts and Questions

Xi and his colleagues will govern a China that is still officially communist, but it is very different from what we saw in the Soviet Union, even under Mikhail Gorbachev. The reformists in the former Soviet Union went a long way toward opening up their political system but foundered in their attempts to implement perestroika. The growing economic frustrations and the greater opportunities for people to participate politically, combined with ethnic and other tensions, put so much pressure on the regime that it collapsed.

The CCP's leaders, in contrast, have maintained a tight grip on political life. On those rare occasions when they have allowed a modicum of free expression, they clamped down as soon as the protests began to threaten the party's authority—as in Tiananmen Square in 1989 or with the public demonstrations of the Falun Gong since the late 1990s.

In the medium to long term, the question is whether the party can maintain its monopoly on political power. There are already signs that it is having trouble recruiting talented young members and that its organization is atrophying. More important, the economic reforms are transforming the lives of millions of people, who are growing used to making their own choices in the marketplace. So far, most Chinese have been willing to accept policies that limit their political freedom in exchange for economic improvement, but there is reason to believe that they will eventually demand political power as well.

Because only a handful of communist countries are left, what happens in China will go a long way toward determining what future Marxism has, if any. As the Chinese reform experience that began thirty years ago suggests, we will have to ask whether societies that maintain Leninist states, but allow their economies to become ever more capitalistic, will bear any real resemblance to the type of egalitarian and classless society Karl Marx envisioned even if the party retains its hold on political power.

From these broad concerns flow six more specific questions we will concentrate on here:

- Can the Chinese leadership realistically hope to limit the impact of the outside world on its economy? More generally, how can any leadership endure rapid change, especially one whose leaders want to maintain their hold on power?

- How has Chinese culture both helped and hindered reformers and hardliners alike? Today, that question has changed in subtle but important ways. As the Chinese people learn more about other cultures and have more money to spend, will they begin to demand political freedoms as well?

- Will the state continue to be able to put down protests that number 100 or so on a typical day?

- What will happen if the CCP continues to have trouble recruiting talented and dedicated members who could become its future leaders?

- Can any kind of regime survive if there is a sharp disconnect between two policy areas, in this case governance and economic reform?

- Xi and his colleagues are referred to as the "fifth generation" of leaders. How might they change Chinese political life?

THE EVOLUTION OF THE CHINESE STATE

As was the case with Russia, we cannot understand the reformist policies in China today or, for that matter, the more than sixty years of CCP rule without considering the impact of the country's past. We will see that its distinctive version of a Marxist-Leninist state is in part an outgrowth of historical trends that made China less than fertile ground for anything approaching orthodox Marxism. As in the Soviet Union, the CCP's commitment to Marxism was not one of the most important reasons it came to power. Indeed, as was also the case in the USSR, those other reasons go a long way toward explaining why China evolved as it did after the revolution.

The Broad Sweep of Chinese History

The historical roots of contemporary Chinese politics go back nearly three thousand years to the teachings of Confucius and other ancient scholars whose ideas have had a remarkable influence to this day (see Table 10.1). Commonly thought of as a religion in the West, **Confucianism** is actually more a code of social conduct that revolves around a few key principles. People should accept their place in the social hierarchy, the living should respect their ancestors, women their husbands, children their fathers, and everyone their social and political superiors 🌐 (**orpheus.ucsd .edu/chinesehistory**).

The Chinese also developed the world's first centralized state in the third century before the birth of Christ. The militaristic Qin (from which the English word *China* is derived) defeated most of the other regional kingdoms and established a single unified empire covering most of modern China. The Qin emperors were able to mobilize thousands of people to build canals, roads, and the first parts of the Great Wall.

The Qin and subsequent dynasties succeeded in large part because of the remarkable bureaucratic system. Two thousand years before Europeans even considered a civil service based on merit, the Chinese had a well-established bureaucracy. Senior officials who served the emperor were recruited based on their scores on competitive examinations that tested their understanding of Confucian texts. By the fourteenth century, at least forty thousand bureaucrats were responsible for collecting taxes and administering imperial law throughout the country. The civil servants often competed with local landlords who had their own armies. Nonetheless, the imperial bureaucracy was an indispensable part of a state that had to support more than forty cities of over one hundred thousand people, including several of more than a million as early as the seventeenth century.

When China had effective emperors, things went well. However, this was not always the case. China went through cycles in which a dynasty declined, rebellions broke out, and, eventually, a new group solidified its hold on the government, creating a new dynasty. In all, there were twenty-five of these dynastic changes in the two thousand years leading up to the collapse of the last one, the Qing, in 1911. The Qing was, in fact, led by Manchurians who took over in 1644. Quickly, however, they adopted the Chinese language and customs and ruled through the traditional imperial processes.

By the end of the eighteenth century, however, the Qing entered its period of decline. The population was growing faster than agricultural production, leaving an overstretched peasantry and an often hungry urban population. Peasant rebellions broke out over much of the country. More important were the cultural blinders that led the Manchus to look upon their adopted Chinese traditions as superior and to ignore the industrial revolution and the other trends that were transforming the West.

Early in the nineteenth century, Europe came crashing in. Though China never became a colony, European and American missionaries, traders, and soldiers gained considerable control over its affairs. The British, who had been smuggling opium into the country, defeated China in the first Opium War (1839–42). The country was then opened up to missionaries and merchants. During the 1850s, the loosely coordinated Taiping rebellion (led by a man who claimed to be Jesus's younger brother) broke out.

During the rest of the century, all the major European powers moved in. A few areas, like Hong Kong, passed directly into European hands. The Europeans took effective control of much of coastal China and imposed the

TABLE 10.1 Key Events in the Origins of the People's Republic of China

YEAR	EVENT
551 BC	Supposed birth of Confucius
221 BC	Start of Qin dynasty
1644	Start of Qing dynasty
1839–42	Opium War
1894–95	Sino-Japanese War
1898	Imperial reforms begin
1911	Overthrow of the Qing dynasty
1919	May Fourth Movement
1921	Formation of the CCP
1925	Death of Sun Yat-sen
1927	KMT attack on CCP
1931	Japanese invasion of Manchuria
1934–35	Long March
1949	CCP victory
	KMT flees to Taiwan

CCP, Chinese Communist Party; KMT, Kuomintang.

principle of **extraterritoriality**, which meant that their law, not China's, applied to the activities of the Europeans. Missionaries moved into much of the rest of the country, trying to convert the Chinese to Christianity.

The Chinese were humiliated. The government lost any semblance of authority, and the once proud and powerful civilization saw itself under the sway of Christians and capitalists. Parks in Shanghai, for instance, often bore the sign "No dogs or Chinese allowed."

Things came to a head after the Sino-Japanese War of 1894–95. Japan had been even more isolated from events in the West, but once Admiral Matthew Perry arrived in 1854, the Japanese embarked on a rapid and successful program of modernization. Even though the Chinese continued to look upon their neighbor to the East as a second-rate power, Japan was rapidly becoming one of the world's mightiest nations. After winning the war and seizing control of Taiwan and Korea, Japan gained concessions in China itself, thereby joining the Western powers in their *de facto* imperial control of much of the country.

By the end of the nineteenth century, Chinese leaders belatedly realized that they had to change. The educational system, for instance, was still based on the traditional Confucian curriculum, which left the country without the industrially and scientifically trained elite it would need to meet the challenge from the West.

The traditional examinations were discarded. Young people were sent abroad to learn about what **Chen Duxiu**, one of the founders of the CCP, called "Mr. Science and Mr. Democracy." Dissatisfaction with the imperial system grew. Young people adopted Western dress and Western values. Movements calling themselves democratic began to organize.

During the Hundred Days' Reform of 1898, the emperor issued decrees designed to modernize the education system, the economy, the military, and the bureaucracy. Instead, the reforms provoked resentment from the elite and were halted almost immediately following a coup that sent the emperor to prison and doomed any hopes that China would emulate the Japanese.

Some reform efforts did continue. But as in tsarist Russia, they came far too late. In fact, all the reform proposals did was further reveal China's weaknesses and heighten opposition to the imperial system. Universities that had so recently educated loyal Confucian scholars were now turning out revolutionaries.

A Failed Revolution

As was the case in Russia at the same time, China had more than its share of revolutionaries. Between May 1907 and April 1911, there were eleven failed coup attempts launched by the followers of **Sun Yat-sen** (1866–1925) alone.

Sun was one of the first Westernized intellectuals. While still in his twenties, he decided that the situation in China was so grim that he became a full-time revolutionary. In 1895, he was exiled for his role in an abortive plot against the government and spent most of the next sixteen years abroad. In 1905, a group of radicals studying in Tokyo elected him head of the Revolutionary Alliance, which soon became the **Kuomintang (KMT)**, or **Nationalist Party**.

On "double ten" day (October 10, 1911), yet another rebellion broke out, this time in Wuhan. Much to their surprise, the conspirators drove the governor general from the city and took it over. In Denver at the time, Sun decided to stay in the United States and finish his fund-raising tour rather than return to China for what he assumed would be another failure. This time, however, the rebellion spread throughout the country. When Sun finally returned in December, it was to take over as president of the new Republic of China.

As in Russia, toppling the old regime was one thing, but building a new one to take its place was quite another. The empire had fallen not because the revolutionaries were so strong, but because it was so weak. The revolutionaries had only their nationalism and their opposition to the imperial system in common. Within months their differences came to the fore, and central authority began to crumble once again. Unlike in Russia, however, it would be another forty years before a new regime was firmly in place.

In an attempt to save the revolution, Sun gave way to a **warlord**, General Yuan Shikai. Yuan was briefly able to bring the country together but his imperial pretensions simply spawned more rebellions. All hopes to unite China around a strong, authoritarian leader collapsed when Yuan died suddenly in 1916.

From then on, there was a central government nominally under the KMT. In reality, it never had control over much of the country. Instead, the warlords ran the regions they ruled with only the slightest concern for what the KMT wanted them to do or for modernizing the country. In short, the political situation remained as volatile as it had been a generation earlier.

The next major transition came in 1919 after the publication of the Treaty of Versailles. Like Japan, China had entered World War I on the Allied side on the assumption that Wilsonian principles of democracy and national self-determination would lead to the end of imperialism. Nothing of the sort happened. The German concessions were simply transferred to other Allied powers.

This proved to be the last straw for alienated, well-educated young Chinese. The day the treaty's provisions were announced, thousands of students took to the streets. Their **May Fourth Movement** quickly sounded broader themes against Confucianism, the education system, and the family. After May Fourth, the students and their supporters grew more political, but this particular movement, like so many before it, was poorly organized and gradually lost momentum.

China Stands Up

It was not surprising that many young people would turn to Marxism. Even though Marx argued that socialism could only develop after capitalism, his ideas now spoke to people who felt oppressed everywhere in part because Lenin had incorporated imperialism into Marxist analysis. Moreover, the radicalized Chinese students could easily relate to the Soviets' struggle against the Western European powers. In 1921, twelve delegates, representing fifty-seven members, met to form the CCP, first headed by Chen. The party was made up almost exclusively of young intellectuals and, like the rest of the international communist movement, it quickly fell under Moscow's direct control.

Oddly enough, the KMT also drew inspiration from the Bolsheviks, who were convinced that they were the faction Moscow should cast its lot with. KMT officers were trained by the Soviets and included **Chiang Kai-shek**, who would take over the party after Sun's death in 1925. Mikhail Borodin, the Comintern's agent in China, ordered the CCP to merge with the KMT to unify the country.

Meanwhile, the communists' influence expanded among industrial workers and became a major force within the KMT. Tensions between the CCP and the Nationalists mounted as the communists grew in strength and numbers as the center of gravity in the KMT shifted rightward. Chen and some of the other leaders urged an end to the united front, but Moscow prevailed.

Along with its communist allies, the KMT launched the Northern Expedition in 1926 in yet another attempt to unite the country under a single national government. Support for the CCP mushroomed. Workers threw open the gates of a number of cities as communist forces approached. Chen advocated arming workers and peasants under CCP leadership, but Borodin demurred again.

The conflict between the CCP and KMT finally came to a head in April 1927, when KMT forces attacked their supposed CCP allies in Shanghai. Nationalist troops slaughtered thousands of CCP members, including most of the leadership. Of the fifty thousand CCP members, only five thousand, including Chen, survived.

Just before the attack, one of the few party members from a peasant background, then little-known **Mao Zedong** (1893–1976), published a short pamphlet reporting on what he had found in his native Hunan province. Mao argued that, given China's overwhelmingly rural population and the KMT's control over most cities, the revolution had to be based on massive mobilization in the countryside and conducted as a guerrilla war.

Because of his peasant background and the time he had spent in the countryside during the 1920s, Mao was better able than the other surviving CCP leaders to draw two key lessons from the Shanghai massacre. First, revolution in China was not going to come through spontaneous uprisings in the cities. Second, it would take years to organize the only kind of revolution that could work: one based on the peasantry.

Ignoring Borodin's orders, Mao launched his first attacks on the city of Changsha that fall. The Autumn Harvest Uprising was quickly put down, and the CCP leadership was slow to come around to Mao's views. Mao persisted, establishing the first "base camp" along the Hunan-Jiangxi border.

The KMT responded by launching a series of campaigns to "exterminate the communist bandits." CCP forces survived the first four campaigns, but during the fifth they were surrounded by a massive force of KMT troops. Mao realized that conventional warfare was bound to fail, so in October 1934 a small group of communist soldiers launched a diversionary counterattack while the bulk of their forces, numbering about one hundred thousand, broke through the KMT cordon to the west.

Mao's bedraggled troops then embarked on what became the **Long March**, which lasted almost a year. CCP forces fought skirmishes every day and full-scale battles every few weeks against either the pursuing KMT or local

Mao Zedong and Zhou Enlai during the Long March.

warlords. The fighting and the difficulties of the march itself took a horrible toll. Only 10 percent of the troops who started out were still alive when the army arrived in Yanan in October 1935. Among the dead was one of Mao's sons.

Ironically, the Long March proved to be a stunning success for the CCP. All along the way, the party organized. Members talked about a China based on justice and equality. Unlike the bands of marauding soldiers who had come and gone over the centuries, they treated the peasants well. No men were conscripted and no women were abused. The CCP paid for the food and supplies it took. Where the party gained control, large estates were broken up and the land given to the peasants. Taxes were reduced and the arbitrary power of the landlords was eliminated.

In January 1936 the **Politburo** elected Mao chairman of the CCP, a post he would hold until his death forty years later. With this move, all notions that a Marxist revolution could be based on a large, urban proletariat disappeared. Although Mao always paid homage to Lenin, gone was the Bolshevik notion that a revolution could be carried out by a small vanguard party. In its place was the more populist **mass line**, which Mao described at length in 1943:

> In all practical work of our Party, all correct leadership is necessarily "from the masses, to the masses." This means take the ideas of the masses (scattered and unsystematic ideas) and concentrate them (through study turn them into concentrated and systematic ideas), then go to the masses and propagate and explain these ideas until the masses embrace them as their own, hold fast to them and translate them into action, and test the correctness of these ideas in such action. Then once again concentrate ideas from the masses and once again go to the masses so that the ideas are preserved and carried through. And so on, over and over again in an endless spiral, with the ideas becoming more correct, more vital, and richer each time.[2]

The Chinese revolution bore even less resemblance to Marx's expectations than the Russian one. Certainly, the CCP leadership was inspired by Marx's analyses, and Mao's writings were always couched in Marxist terms. Nonetheless, the CCP took even greater liberties with orthodox Marxism than the Bolsheviks. The Chinese communists made a remarkable contribution, turning Marxism into a philosophy that appealed to millions of peasants in Asia, Africa, and Latin America. Still, the fact that China was even more backward than Russia in 1917 meant that the kind of transition to socialism that Marx had in mind was impossible.

---

[2]Mao Zedong, "Some Questions Concerning Methods of Leadership," *Selected Works* 3 (Beijing: Foreign Language Press, 1943), 119.

The Chinese Revolution in Comparative Perspective

Unlike the former Soviet Union and most of Eastern Europe, communists came to power in China as a result of a massive popular revolution. However, this does not mean they did so in a way Karl Marx anticipated.

Rather, the revolution succeeded because the Chinese Communist Party could appeal both to the oppressed peasants and to people from other walks of life who wanted to resist the Japanese occupation. As a result, the CCP took China even further from orthodox Marxist expectations than the Soviets did. Over the years, the country was characterized by reliance on the mass line, emphasis on rural development, the central role attached to culture and ideology, and factionalism within the CCP itself.

It was thirty years before the party's leaders decided that those approaches could not pull the country out of its deeply rooted poverty and weakness. Thus, it was only after the death of Mao Zedong in 1976 that the first tentative steps toward economic, but not political, reform were taken.

There was yet another reason why the CCP ultimately won: its resistance against Japanese aggression once its troops occupied Manchuria and moved into the Chinese heartland after 1931. Chiang knew that the Chinese army was not capable of beating the Japanese and, so, he retreated to the south while trying to build a modern, more competitive army. During the Long March, however, the CCP decided that it would fight the invaders, something it set out to do as soon as the Yanan camp was established.

In late 1936 a group of disgruntled generals took Chiang prisoner. Communist leader **Zhou Enlai** (1899–1976) was consulted and called for Chiang's release in order to form a new united front to fight the Japanese. From 1937 to 1945, the KMT and CCP were ostensibly allies again. In practice, however, the KMT was always ambivalent about forming a united front. As a result, the CCP got most of the credit for spearheading the resistance. Adding nationalism and anti-imperialism to its message of social justice, the CCP became quite appealing in almost every social milieu.

The communist army grew from eighty thousand in 1939 to about nine hundred thousand regular troops and 2 million reserves by 1945. The CCP also gained considerable administrative experience in the one-fifth of the country it controlled.

Still, when World War II ended, the KMT seemed ahead. Its army was much larger, and it received millions of dollars of aid from the United States, whereas Joseph Stalin did little to help the CCP. But in early 1946 the disciplined communist army, headed by **Lin Biao**, gained control of Manchuria and started moving south. By the end of 1947, guerrilla war had given way to full-scale conventional combat, and the tide turned in favor of the CCP.

Less than two years later, the KMT had been routed. Only a few scattered troops were still fighting when Chiang and the Nationalist leadership fled to Taiwan. In October 1949, the communists proclaimed the creation of the PRC. The victory marked the end of one of the darkest periods in Chinese history, something Mao eloquently noted in a speech a week before the PRC was born:

> The Chinese have always been a great, courageous, and industrious nation; it is only in modern times that they have fallen behind. And that was due entirely to oppression and exploitation by foreign imperialism and domestic reactionary government. Ours will no longer be a nation subject to insult and humiliation. We have stood up.[3]

Factionalism

As we saw in the chapters on France, Germany, and Russia, the creation of a new regime does not mark the point at which we should stop examining its history. Rather, it makes sense to continue this discussion until at least a degree of stability and continuity in political decision making was achieved.

In China that took thirty years. In the interim, leadership shifted back and forth between more moderate, orthodox leaders and radicals who wanted to take the country toward socialism as quickly as possible. Twice, during the **Great Leap Forward** and the **Cultural Revolution**, the radicals under the leadership of Chairman Mao took the country to the brink of disaster. It was only with the death of Mao that the moderates gained definitive control of the party and state and set the country on the path of reform, which it has followed ever since (see Table 10.2).

The Chinese system closely resembled the Soviet state Gorbachev inherited, at least on paper. The CCP has a legal monopoly on political power and dominates all areas of policy making and implementation. It is also based on **democratic centralism**, which theoretically means that internal disagreements are kept to a minimum, if they are allowed to exist at all.

The CCP, however, was never able to escape those internal disagreements and, at times, has actually had loosely organized **factions** supporting different ideological

viewpoints and leaders. When the political pendulum swung most widely between them, the struggle led to attacks on key party and state institutions. It also propelled groups, including regional leaders and the military, onto political center stage. Most important, the struggle often led to the personalization of power around the "supreme leader"—even more than in the Soviet Union after Stalin's death.

The CCP did not start out divided. From 1949 until the late 1950s, whatever differences existed between the leaders had virtually no impact. Mao commanded the support of the entire party. Moreover, no one in the CCP questioned the assumption that they would establish a Soviet-style Marxist-Leninist regime as did every other communist country in the world.

So, the CCP announced a First Five-Year Plan in 1953 that channeled more than half the available investment funds into heavy industry. As in the Soviet Union, the heaviest burden fell on the peasants, who were driven into ever larger units and forced to sell their grain to the state at predetermined prices. Meanwhile, a constitution was promulgated in 1954 that centralized power even further and led to a rapid expansion of both state and party bureaucracies.

The PRC also quickly established an international role squarely within the Soviet-dominated communist movement. In 1950, without any apparent input from the Chinese, North Korean troops invaded the southern half of the Korean peninsula and occupied Seoul. The United States was able to convince the United Nations (UN) to send troops, dominated by the United States, into Korea. The Chinese had little option but to support their fellow communists in the

TABLE 10.2 Key Events in Chinese History since the Revolution

YEAR	EVENT
1949	CCP takes power
1956	De-Stalinization in Soviet Union begins Hundred Flowers Campaign
1957	Great Leap Forward
1960	Demotion of Mao Zedong
1965	Beginning of Cultural Revolution
1972	Opening to United States
1976	Deaths of Zhou Enlai and Mao Zedong; Formal end of Cultural Revolution
1978	Democracy Wall
1983	Antispiritual pollution campaign
1989	Democracy Movement and Tiananmen Square
1997	Reversion of Hong Kong to PRC; Death of Deng Xiaoping
2003	Hu Jintao becomes president
2012	Xi Jinping to become president while gradually assuming other posts

CCP, Chinese Communist Party; PRC, People's Republic of China.

---

[3]Cited in Witold Rodzinski, *The People's Republic of China: A Concise History*. New York: Free Press, 1988, 13.

north. As the UN troops approached the Yalu River, separating China and North Korea, the PRC sent in its troops and fought until the end of the war three years later.

This Soviet phase of the PRC's history was not to last long, however. Serious qualms about the Soviet Union and the relevance of the Soviet model lurked just below the surface. Nikita Khrushchev's "secret speech" in 1956 brought these concerns into the open. In it, he admitted that there could be multiple "roads to socialism," thereby opening the door for the CCP to pursue its own strategy. However, the Chinese leadership found the rest of the speech highly disconcerting. Its attack on Stalin's **cult of personality** did not sit well with a leadership that stressed Mao's thoughts and actions. More important at the time, the new openness of the world communist movement gave the CCP leadership an opportunity to vent its resentment toward the Soviets, which had been building since the days of Borodin.

Within months the Chinese and Soviets were taking verbal potshots at each other. Mao referred to Khrushchev's reforms as "goulash communism" that was taking Soviet-bloc countries further and further from Marxist goals. Most of the time, however, the early Sino-Soviet debate was couched in elliptical terms: with the Chinese attacking the Yugoslavs, when they really meant the Soviets, and the

Soviets doing the same thing with the Albanians, the only European Communist Party to ally with the PRC.

By the end of the decade, the Soviet Union had withdrawn its advisers and China stopped taking economic and military aid from it. During the late 1960s and the 1970s, there were skirmishes along the border separating China and Siberia. It was only in the late 1980s with the rise of reformist leaders in both countries that any substantial steps were taken toward healing the **Sino-Soviet split**.

For our purposes, the split was important because it allowed the CCP to develop its own policies and address its own problems, the most important of which was the factionalism that developed around both the ideology and, eventually, the role of Chairman Mao. From 1956 until the 1980s, Chinese politics was little more than a battle between two factions: the Maoists and the more moderate or orthodox Marxists.

The first open signs of the rift came with the **Hundred Flowers Campaign** in 1956. Intellectuals were given considerable freedom to express themselves, much as was the case during the "thaw" in the Soviet Union. Far more than the Soviets, the CCP traditionally relied on **campaigns** to mobilize the masses to meet its goals. Over the years, campaign goals ranged from eliminating flies and other pests to

Profiles
Mao Zedong

Mao was different from the sophisticated intellectuals who led the Chinese Communist Party (CCP) in its early years. His father was a reasonably successful peasant who ruled his family with an iron fist. Mao began working in the family fields at the age of six, but because his father wanted to make certain that at least one of his children could read and write enough to keep the books, he sent his son to school. The young Mao turned out to be an excellent student and graduated from teacher's training college in 1918. He then moved to Beijing, where he took a job at the university library under Li Dazhao, who, along with Chen Duxiu, was to found the CCP. Mao experienced May Fourth in Beijing and soon returned to his home region and began organizing.

Mao might never have become a major CCP leader were it not for the tragedies that hit the party in the 1920s and 1930s. The 1927 attack by the Kuomintang forced the CCP to adopt a peasant-based strategy—a decision that was confirmed by the Long March. Mao's leadership of the party was only once seriously questioned in the forty years between then and his death.

Mao Zedong addressing a crowd in Beijing shortly after taking power.

As more has been learned about Mao's personal life and the disruption caused by the Cultural Revolution, assessments of his historical role have become more critical. Nonetheless, he certainly will always be thought of as one of the most influential Marxist analysts and political leaders of the twentieth century. And there are still people who revere and love him, and not just in the older generations. ■

reshaping Chinese culture. In this campaign Mao used a traditional phrase—"Let a hundred flowers bloom and a thousand points of view contend"—in urging the people to speak their minds. They did just that in ways that soon worried Mao and the wing of the leadership that crystallized around him.

They therefore quickly brought the campaign to an end. The following year, Mao and his supporters moved in the opposite direction and called for a Great Leap Forward, through which the Chinese were to make rapid progress in the transition to socialism and communism. The new campaign was based on the assumption that they could do so if and only if the Chinese people threw all their energies into the effort. Therefore, the move toward collective agriculture was accelerated. An attempt was made to incorporate everyone in the process of industrialization—for instance, by building small backyard furnaces on the collective farms. Intellectuals, who in Mao's eyes had become suspect during the Hundred Flowers Campaign, were expected to engage in manual labor, which supposedly would bring them closer to the people. More generally, Maoists took the "red" side in the **red versus expert** debate in which the factions disagreed about the relative importance of ideological and technological factors in China's development.

The Great Leap Forward turned out to be a disaster. Industrial production declined precipitously. Experimental programs, like the one that called on farmers to build their own iron smelters, were abject failures. The situation in the countryside was particularly chaotic. In the harsh winter of 1958–59, at least a million people starved to death.

As the evidence about the failure of the Great Leap Forward began to pour in, the debates within the party heated up. Leading the charge was Peng Dehuai, head of the PLA and a Politburo member, who wrote a letter to Mao in July 1959 attacking the campaign. An enlarged Politburo met later that month to consider Peng's criticism. Mao threatened to go to the countryside and start another revolution if Peng's views prevailed, and he was able to summon up enough support to have Lin take Peng's place as head of the PLA.

Mao's victory was short lived. Within a year he had been forced to temporarily give up his position as chairman of the PRC and lost much of his influence in both the party and state bureaucracies. The more moderate wing of the leadership, led by **Liu Shaoqi**, who was named Mao's successor-designate, and Deng re-embarked on a more gradual and orthodox policy of industrial development during the first half of the 1960s.

For people likely to be reading this book, understanding the issues in the debate is less important than the fact that it was occurring at all. It marked the first time that Mao's leadership had been questioned, paving the way for the Cultural Revolution that was to do so much damage to the CCP and to China as a whole.

For someone who had been the architect of a popular revolution, there was good cause for Mao to show concern in the early 1960s. The CCP was becoming increasingly bureaucratic and displayed signs of developing the kind of conservative elitism of the Soviet Union under Leonid Brezhnev. Furthermore, there was a whole new generation of young people who had not experienced the trauma or the exhilaration of the revolutionary struggle. In short, Mao feared that China was becoming too self-satisfied and flabby.

The psychiatrist and historian Robert Lifton was the first of many observers to add Mao's aging and its effects on his personality to the factors leading to the Cultural Revolution. To such analysts, Mao mixed together concerns about his own mortality with those about the revolution that had been his life for almost a half-century. Another historian put it more bluntly and pejoratively: "Not only did his arrogance increase, his vanity did as well." In the end, we will never know how much of Mao's decision was a rational political response to the situation after the Great Leap Forward or how much of it was a quirk of an increasingly quirky personality. Nonetheless, almost immediately after his demotion, he turned to the main source of power he had left: the PLA.

With its support, Mao launched the Socialist Education Movement in 1963, which returned ideology and campaigns to center stage. Meanwhile, Lin used his position as head of the PLA to create a cult of personality around Mao that dwarfed anything orchestrated by Stalin and his henchmen. Every imaginable accomplishment was attributed to Mao. His position in Marxist philosophy was equated with that

Protesters during the Cultural Revolution.

of Marx and Lenin and enshrined as what came to be called Marxism–Leninism–Mao Zedong thought. The ridiculous turned to the absurd when a news story about the seventy-year-old Mao swimming six miles in an hour appeared on the front page of the PLA's daily newspaper.

In March 1966 Mao stepped up the pressure by attacking the Beijing party apparatus. Peng Zhen, then head of the Beijing party, was dismissed. In May 1966 Professor Nie Yuanzi put up the first *dazhibao*, (big-character poster) at Beijing University, urging revolutionary intellectuals to "go into battle" against the party bureaucracy. University officials quickly tore it down, but a few days later Mao publicly endorsed it.

Professor Nie's poster brought the conflict within the party into the open. Liu and Deng realized that their positions were in jeopardy and counterattacked. They organized work teams to go to the universities to criticize Nie and Mao and to enforce discipline.

Conflict
in China

China experienced more open conflict than any communist country, with the possible exception of Poland during the 1970s and 1980s. But Chinese conflict has been dramatically different from that in Poland in three important ways. First, it has, on occasion, turned violent. Second, some of it has been orchestrated from above as part of the factional dispute within the CCP itself. Third, even as dissatisfaction grew, there was little evidence that the protests and protesters would come together as a unified movement.

There has been less overt conflict in China since the **Tiananmen Square** demonstrations of 1989. Dissidents are occasionally arrested, but some of their colleagues are also occasionally released from prison. There have been press reports of strikes in many major cities, and there have also been violent outbursts in minority regions. The Chinese Communist Party (CCP) itself acknowledges that there are on average, two hundred protests a day, mostly in the countryside.

Undoubtedly, considerable resentment toward the CCP and its rule lurks just below the surface. Unlike Poland, China has not seen the development of an independent opposition movement with strong grassroots support. ■

Their efforts failed. University and middle school students formed groups of **Red Guards** to carry on the work of the Cultural Revolution. Within weeks they had paralyzed the nation's educational system. With Mao urging them to attack party members who also were **capitalist roaders** (those accused of opposing Mao), many of the Red Guards turned into vigilantes and vandals. Meanwhile, Mao attacked the CCP as "capitalist bureaucrats." In August 1966, Liu was officially labeled "the leading person in authority taking the capitalist road" and Deng "the number two person in authority taking the capitalist road." Liu, Deng, and thousands of others were arrested and sent either to prison or to the countryside. Liu would be the most famous of the countless thousands of Chinese citizens who died in this campaign. Deng, who was already in his mid-sixties, was forced to work as a machinist on a collective farm; one of his sons was either pushed or fell from a seventh-story window and has been confined to a wheelchair ever since (**www.morningsun.org/library**).

New radical groups emerged around the country. Most famous was the Shanghai commune, organized by three relatively unknown men—Zhang Chunqiao, Wang Hongwen, and Yao Wenyuan—who were quickly promoted to positions of national prominence and who joined Mao's wife, **Jiang Qing**, in eliminating anything Western and non-ideological from the theaters and airwaves.

"Seizures of power" took place all over the country. Jiang urged the Red Guards to use weapons to defend themselves if need be. Sometimes the violence was clearly aimed at political targets, but on all too many occasions, the young people were simply settling old scores or lashing out randomly at anyone who struck them as a symbol of the "bad" China.

Although it is hard to fathom just how disruptive the Cultural Revolution was, Harvard's Ross Terrill provides one insightful anecdote. It turns out that even trained circus horses were stripped of their lives of luxury and sent to work in the countryside. One group of horses was sent to a commune near a military base, where they worked dutifully until the bugles began to play, when they returned to the equine version of the capitalist road and performed a few of their old dance steps.[4]

By late 1967, it was clear even to Mao that things had gone too far and he called on the PLA to restore order. Red Guards were to merge into "three-in-one" committees with the PLA and politically acceptable CCP members. But in a country that large and in which conditions were so chaotic, the disruption continued.

Moreover, the party continued to tilt dramatically to the Left. Of the more moderate leaders, only Zhou

---

[4]Ross Terrill. *China in Our Times.* New York: Simon and Schuster, 1992, 65.

remained. To make matters even more complicated, Lin, who had been designated Mao's successor after Liu's fall, attempted a coup in 1971. Although details have never been made public, Lin had either come to oppose the Cultural Revolution or had grown tired of waiting his turn to replace Mao. Along with his wife, son, and other supporters from the PLA, Lin hatched a plot to kill Mao. The plot failed, and Lin died in a plane crash while trying to escape to the Soviet Union.

By then, order had been restored. The **Gang of Four**—as Jiang, Zhang, Yao, and Wang came to be known—still controlled cultural and educational affairs. The economy and administration, however, began to take center stage, and all but the most dedicated Maoists realized that China could not afford the disruption it had experienced since the late 1960s. This meant that, as the country's leading administrator and survivor, Zhou became more influential.

In 1973, Zhou announced that China would concentrate on the **four modernizations**—agriculture, industry, science, and the military—that have been the focus of the country's official policy goals ever since. Although already terminally ill, Zhou was still politically strong enough to bring Deng back from internal exile to become deputy prime minister later that year.

Zhou died in January 1976. On March 25, a Shanghai newspaper accused him of having been a capitalist roader—an accusation that evoked a tremendous response.

Memorial wreaths began to appear in Tiananmen Square and massive demonstrations were held in his honor until the authorities finally broke them up on April 4.

When Mao died the following September, the mourning paled in comparison. His positions in the party and government were taken over by Hua Guofeng, a political unknown who proved unable to end the struggle between Deng and the Gang of Four. In the short run, it seemed the Maoists would be the winners. Deng was demoted again, and Hua tried to drape himself in Mao's political mantle, even combing his hair the way the chairman had in order to emphasize the physical resemblance between the two men. Hua, however, was no friend of the Gang of Four. As a regional party official responsible for security in the late 1960s, he had seen the impact of their policies firsthand. Moreover, he realized that Jiang coveted his position. Therefore, he brought Deng back from political obscurity yet again and arrested the Gang of Four.

The Cultural Revolution was finally over, but its legacy remained. For a decade, scientific and industrial development had been put on hold. In addition, a generation of students had been unable to go to school, so the country lost their potential contributions to social, economic, and cultural development. Perhaps most important of all for the long term, the Cultural Revolution heightened the already substantial cynicism among large segments of the Chinese population.

Profiles
Zhou Enlai

Zhou was born in 1899. Unlike Mao's family, Zhou's was part of the gentry and his father had passed the traditional Confucian exams that determined entry into the bureaucracy. Like many privileged young people of his generation, Zhou went to Japan to study and returned to participate in the May Fourth Movement. He later continued his studies in France, where he became a Marxist.

Zhou's charm and sophistication enhanced the Chinese Communist Party's reputation with foreigners and Chinese intellectuals alike. Once the People's Republic was established, Zhou became prime minister, a post he held until his death. He was a conciliator, the one leading politician who held the respect of both factions and could sometimes build bridges between them.

Unfortunately, Zhou contracted cancer in the early 1970s and knew he would not live much longer.

Premier Zhou Enlai meeting and dining with President Richard Nixon's envoy, Henry Kissinger.

© Bettmann/CORBIS

Still, he was able to gain enough support to launch the four modernizations and bring Deng Xiaoping back into the leadership. ■

Since Mao's Death

Factionalism did not end with Mao's death. However, the conflict since then has not been as intense or disruptive.

By 1978, Maoism had been effectively destroyed with the arrest of the Gang of Four and the removal of Hua from office. Ever since, power has been in the hands of party officials who had been moderates before the Cultural Revolution; many had also been among its victims—if they were alive and politically active at the time—soon-to-be President Xi was only born in 1953. Not surprisingly, they have downplayed ideological goals and embarked instead on what has now been more than three decades of reform featuring the introduction of private ownership and freer markets in much of the Chinese economy. They have done little, however, to open up the political system. In fact, they have quickly brought the few even vaguely liberalizing political reforms to a halt as soon as any signs that they might challenge the party's hegemony appeared. The post–Cultural Revolution leadership has been more unified than at any time since the mid-1950s. Still, there has been considerable division within it over the nature and pace of reform.

Deng's role was critical, if always obscure, given that he championed both economic reform and continued party control. His critics said he was part of a "wind faction" that changed its direction with each shift in the political breeze. Whatever the details of what happened are, by the 1980s disruptive factionalism had disappeared most of the time because the moderate reformers and what were left of the hardliners found ways to coexist. That coexistence will be the subject of the rest of this chapter.

But the key point is that Deng, his colleagues, and their successors have all pointed China toward economic reform while maintaining firm party control of politics.

POLITICAL CULTURE AND PARTICIPATION

In previous chapters, political culture and participation were treated separately following the logic discussed in Chapter 1. Cultures generally reflect generations of political and other developments in the values of people living today. These values, in turn, help determine what those people do—and do not do—politically.

In China, the link between the two is far more complicated, and they feed off each other in ways we in the West are not accustomed to. Chinese political culture reflects the same long-term impact of history on people's values and assumptions about politics. However, as the discussion of the Cultural Revolution suggests, the culture itself has been politicized, especially when the Maoists actively tried to reshape it. Moreover, as in the Soviet Union before Gorbachev's time, the party has actively tried to manipulate political participation.

As with most of Chinese politics, much has changed since the death of Mao. Cultural campaigns are largely a thing of the past, and there are even competitive political contests in local elections in rural counties. However, it still makes sense to think of political culture and participation as more of a seamless web than it did for any of the liberal democracies covered in Part 2.

A Blank Slate? A Cultural Revolution?

Mao's greatest failures had their roots in his misunderstanding of his own people. He correctly realized that Chinese values would have to change if he and his colleagues were to succeed in implementing Marxist ideals. However, he incorrectly assumed that it would be relatively easy to do so. Shortly after coming to power, Mao wrote:

> **The two outstanding things about China's 600 million people are that they are "poor and blank." On a blank sheet of paper free from any blotches, the freshest and most beautiful characters can be written, the freshest and most beautiful pictures can be painted.[5]**

For dedicated Maoists, cultural change was the top priority because they believed that socialist institutions could only be built by a people committed to socialist values. Most orthodox and moderate party leaders differed only in degree, arguing that cultural change was but one of a series of priorities and ranked below economic growth in importance.

Despite the centrality of culture in Chinese politics, it is very hard to determine how much it has changed—if at all. Cultures are always difficult to chart because they include values and assumptions that people rarely think about and represent what amounts to their political "second nature." Political culture has also traditionally been documented using public opinion polls and more in-depth observations of what people think and do by journalists and anthropologists. In China, public opinion polling is in its infancy, and very few of the published results touch on issues of culture and change. We have access to some first-rate anthropological studies and journalistic accounts, but even these barely scratch the surface of a complex question about a complex society. Therefore, everything that follows in this section should be read with even more skepticism than usual.

In one sense, Mao was right about the Chinese people being a blank slate. Prior to 1949, Chinese peasants, who made up the overwhelming majority of the population, were not politically involved other than paying taxes and

---

[5]Cited in Terrill. *China in Our Times*, 1.

getting caught up in the occasional war. Politics was something that concerned the landlords and magistrates, a view reinforced by Confucian values stressing group loyalty, conflict avoidance, and acceptance of one's place in the social hierarchy.

But this does not mean that they had no political values. We also know from the history of dynastic change and peasant rebellions that this neo-Confucian culture did not always "work." Violent uprisings occurred for much the same reasons they did in other countries with a tradition of peasant unrest. Usually people tolerated the system. However, if a large number of peasants in a given area came to the conclusion that the local scholar-gentry elite was not performing adequately, respect for authority disappeared, and pent-up anger erupted into violence.

There is considerable evidence that much of this cultural tradition persisted into the communist period. Studies carried out in some isolated rural areas suggested that peasants still generally deferred to the authority of local leaders and that loyalty was rather easily transferred from the pre-1949 elites to CCP officials. Thus, many students and intellectuals who were "sent down" to the countryside during the Cultural Revolution expressed surprise at the willingness of the peasantry to accept them, even though they did not contribute much labor and stretched scarce local resources.

Reports persist, too, of the sense of resignation and the sullen anger that seem always to have been a part of peasant, and now working-class, life in China. During the immediate postrevolutionary, Great Leap Forward, and Cultural Revolution periods, there were numerous accounts of peasants using the official ideology of the campaign as a cover to settle old scores with other peasants or their former landlords. Some research on the events since the Democracy Movement of 1989 uncovered what can only be called urban thugs, who used demonstrations as a pretext for vandalism and intimidation. Finally, the Western press includes periodic reports of protest movements, especially in ethnic minority and other rural areas. Most have been quickly put down, often with some violence on the part of the authorities.

The early CCP tried to replace the culture it inherited with a value system based on four main elements:

■ *Collectivism.* Chinese culture has traditionally revolved around group loyalties to one's family or village. The CCP wanted to see that loyalty transferred to a broader and more inclusive institution—the party state. From at least the time of the Hundred Flowers Campaign on, however, this transition clearly has been an especially hard one for intellectuals and others to accept because they are increasingly tempted by individualism as the society and economy modernize.

■ *Struggle and activism.* Traditional values revolved around harmony and acceptance of the status quo. As part of Mao's notion of the mass line, the CCP wanted the Chinese people to participate in what the leadership understood would be a bumpy transition to socialism. However, the party also saw participation not as something people did for themselves but as part of the collectivist goal of serving the people and fighting selfish tendencies.

■ *Egalitarianism and populism.* Hierarchy was one of the key organizing principles in Chinese society prior to 1949. The CCP tried to end what it saw as the irrational subordination not only of the working class and peasantry but of women and younger people as well. Even recent policies that have created an extremely wealthy minority are justified as leading to a more egalitarian future. Abolishing hierarchy does not, however, lead to a more individualistic society, but rather, again, to one in which people voluntarily serve the country as a whole. It should be pointed out that the CCP also reinforced hierarchical traditions with its imposition of a Leninist-Stalinist-style party state, which certainly minimized the degree to which egalitarian or populist goals could be reached or even pursued.

■ *Self-reliance.* Finally, the Chinese tried to break with the traditional values that left most people dependent on the elite, waiting for instructions and leadership from above. Instead, the CCP tried to convince people that together they could control their own destinies. Over the years, self-reliance has taken on many forms, ranging from the extreme, failed campaign for self-sufficiency during the Great Leap Forward to the ongoing efforts to modernize China with as little interference from abroad as possible.

Especially in the early years, the party relied on two main techniques for speeding up cultural change. The first was the state domination of all key agents of political socialization except for the family. As in the former Soviet Union, the CCP has total control over the education system and the legally tolerated mass media. It even tried to undermine the power of the family by shifting many child-rearing activities to the *danwei*, or **unit**—the basic body assuring work, housing, and welfare to which most urban Chinese were assigned before the economic reforms took hold.

The CCP also relied on mass campaigns more than the communist parties did in the former Soviet bloc. From the 1950s through the 1970s, the CCP initiated countless campaigns to rid the country of physical and social "evils," from flies to homosexuality. The great movements, from the Hundred Flowers Campaign to the Cultural Revolution itself, were efforts in which party leaders argued that success hinged on maximum participation for two reasons. First, in the absence of a large, trained, and reliable bureaucracy, the people were normally needed to implement any kind of sweeping reform. Second, and more important for our purposes, the campaigns included political study sessions in which people were brought together to discuss the problem at hand and some relevant texts by Mao, and thereby deepen their understanding of and commitment to Marxism–Leninism–Mao Zedong thought.

Typical of the Maoist-era campaigns was the Socialist Education Movement. After the failure of the Great Leap Forward, Mao was deeply concerned about what he believed to be the corruption and demoralization of rural party **cadres** or full-time party members. Mao and his followers prepared a statement about rural conditions that required cadres to participate in productive labor. As in most campaigns, this document was discussed in study groups around the country, and Maoist sympathizers used it to foster popular criticism of the cadres and to put pressure on them to adopt a more Maoist point of view.

Neither the campaigns nor the broader efforts to create a "new socialist man" were very successful. There was a lot of cynical and self-interested participation in them. Many of the 17 million young people sent down during the Cultural Revolution came to resent their exile and the system that sent them there, as did the peasants whose lives were disrupted by their arrival.

These efforts, however, do seem to have been far more successful than their equivalents in the former Soviet Union. There, for example, university students were required to take classes in Marxism–Leninism, but these were treated as boring requirements by both the faculty who taught them and the students Chip saw who slept or knitted during them. In China, a far larger proportion of the party members who led the "education" and the average citizens who "learned" from them appeared to have taken those exercises more seriously. As a result, the CCP probably did succeed in forging a regime that was seen as legitimate by most people at least until the Cultural Revolution.

This blend of traditional and newer cultural values was evident even in the Democracy Movement of 1989 in which students and others occupied Tiananmen Square in the heart of Beijing and similar locations in cities throughout the country. The protesters worked on the assumption that democratic institutions could *and should* be built within the existing socialist order. Unlike many of their counterparts in the Soviet Union and Eastern Europe, the students who first occupied Tiananmen Square cast their demands in patriotic terms, arguing that socialist democracy required the elite to be open to criticism from the people. After they were attacked by the PLA and hundreds of them died, many became deeply disillusioned with the regime, although that has not resulted in a massive protest movement—at least not yet.

We should not make too much of either the CCP's commitment to cultural change or the degree of legitimacy it has enjoyed. That can easily be seen in its failed attempts to "reinvent" one of the most important lingering aspects of traditional thought and action: the role of women. Of all the countries covered in this book, the PRC made the most concerted efforts to improve the status of women. Women played a vital role in the revolution, prompting Mao to stress how they "held up half the sky." The 1950 Law on Marriage and other early decrees gave women legal equality and outlawed a series of traditional practices, including foot binding.

The CCP has not engaged in this kind of consciousness raising and gender reform since Mao's death, except for its largely successful campaign to limit most families to having only one child. As in the former Soviet Union, women in China continue to occupy secondary positions in everything from the politics of the household to the politics of the Politburo. In fact, only a few women have played a significant role in the CCP elite, most of whom were the wives of even more prominent men, including Mao and Zhou.

Currently, there are signs that the condition of women may actually be worsening. Women are being discriminated against more in hiring, housing, and the distribution of land. At a recent job fair to recruit government officials, fully 80 percent of the positions were only available to men. Women who are hired are routinely required to promise that they will not marry for at least three years. Furthermore, women are again being bought and sold as wives, a practice that was outlawed in the 1950s.

The party has also drastically scaled back its efforts to reshape public opinion and the political culture since the death of Mao. Deng's sense of pragmatism, according to which the people were exhorted to "seek truth from facts," left little room for the kind of ideological education Mao favored. The party has loosened its controls somewhat in recent years, allowing a wider range of views to be expressed in the media and schools and, more important, permitting foreign music, films, and news into China on a scale that would have been unimaginable a generation ago. Add to that the fact that pirated DVDs and computer software are readily available in the cities and you find that the party cannot hope to dominate public opinion as fully as it did before reform began in earnest.

Some party leaders are deeply concerned that the spread of Western pop culture and personal computers is creating a population more concerned with self-interest than collectivism. The modernization of the country opens the door to a greater diversity of interests and some of the new groups, such as the urban entrepreneurs and international traders, are beginning to band together to promote their professional interests. As the number of people who work outside the centrally planned economy continues to grow, the unit is becoming less and less of a factor in their lives.

Half the Sky: Women in Chinese Politics

In Chapter 8, we made the first of several references to *Half the Sky* by Nicholas Kristof and Sheryl WuDunn. We noted then that their title is borrowed from a statement that Mao quoted to justify the egalitarian moves referred to in the text.

However, all the signs suggest that Mao overstated his case. To be sure, abuses such as foot binding were eliminated and it became easier for women to get a divorce. Some would even argue that the one child per family law has eased the burden on women.

There are some areas in which the status of women has improved. About 100 of the richest 1,000 people in China are women, including two of the country's five billionaires. Yet even here the Chinese do not fare all that well. Only about 20 percent of its businesses are owned by women, which is about two-thirds of the global average.

The political situation is not even that good. There are no women on the Standing Committee of the Politburo, which is arguably the most powerful single political body in the country. Only 3 of the 27 cabinet ministers in late 2010 were women. It is hard to tell whether the CCP or the lingering impact of traditional culture bears the most responsibility here. Nonetheless, it is clear that there is a glass ceiling in Chinese politics that few women can get through. Thus, there are many women in lower-level positions, but next to none of them make it to the top.

As part of its effort to maintain control, the CCP has tried to keep access to western sources of information on the Internet to a minimum. Such giants as Microsoft and Google have agreed to block access to many websites the authorities find objectionable. The party has tried to ban Twitter and other social networking software. However, one Chinese scholar recently argued that their efforts may be in vain. Over 17 million people regularly use homegrown microblog technology, more than in any other country in the world (see the chapter on Iran for an example of how the new media can disrupt an authoritarian state's political life).

In some respects, then, the cultural unity that may have existed before the Cultural Revolution has disappeared. We have no way of knowing how much dissatisfaction there is with either the party elite or the regime as a whole. There clearly are pockets of discontent scattered throughout the country—among young intellectuals and business executives who have been "winners" during the reform years, and among manual workers, poor peasants, and ethnic minorities whose conditions have at best barely improved. Although there is more open protest than there was a generation ago, it undoubtedly lags behind public opinion. There

is now an active core of dissidents at home. More important may be their colleagues who live abroad but still manage to make some of their views known to friends and relatives still living in China.

Participation from the Top Down

People studying comparative politics in the West often conclude that political participation is largely from the bottom up. In the industrialized democracies, most of the civic engagement we focus on takes place because individual citizens choose to get involved most often to express their point of view on who should govern or what policies they should adopt.

This was not the case in the former communist regimes in the Soviet bloc, nor is it the case in China today. The Chinese authorities include democracy and the mass line in their rhetoric. And average citizens actually participate in political life more than their counterparts in the West. However, little of that involvement actually plays a role in shaping public policy. Rather, some political scientists call it "mobilized" participation because the CCP determines what people should do and then turns them out to meet the regime's goals.

Although they are sometimes consulted before decisions are made, their activity normally involves carrying out policies that have already been approved farther up the political hierarchy. This was especially true during the Maoist years, during which the campaigns were a routine fact of life. Politics affected all aspects of people's lives. Almost everyone in urban areas was assigned to units, which were dominated by local party representatives. Much the same was true of the people's communes in rural areas, which were much like state and collective farms in the Soviet Union.

In October 2007, the party claimed it had about 73 million members or nearly 10 percent of the adult population, which is actually a rather high proportion by Western standards (**www.chinatoday.com/org/cpc/**). Here, too, we should not read too much into these data because most party members do political work that is determined by the cadres. Most of their work, too, involves the routine implementation of policy decisions made by their superiors. And, as in the former Soviet bloc, many people join the party because it has been the one and only way to get ahead in all areas of Chinese society until quite recently.

There is less top-down activity now than there was during the Maoist years. As noted earlier, major campaigns are a thing of the past. The party has had trouble recruiting reliable and competent members now that private enterprise holds out opportunities to gain wealth and influence. The units are far less influential; in fact, many urban residents are no longer part of a unit at all, but instead find work, housing, and other services on the open market. In rural areas, the communes have been abolished and replaced with what amounts to private farms and looser forms of social control, which we will discuss in the public policy section. Finally, the party itself is trying to recruit members from the new generation of consumer savvy business leaders who share most of the values and styles of those who have chosen not to join.

From the Bottom Up?

There is also fragmentary evidence that some Chinese engage in more of the kinds of political participation we focus on in the West. The most important is based on elections in rural areas in which more than one candidate has been allowed to run since 1987. The CCP is still the only organization that can nominate candidates. Nonetheless, voters often now have choices for members of the governing bodies that replaced the people's communes. Economic liberalization has also given people more of an ability to make the decisions that shape their economic lives, which, if Western theorists are correct, could be translated into demands for more influence over their political lives as well (http://chinaelectionsblog.net/).

Those rural voters have been the subject of some empirical research. Polling is in its infancy in China, but surveys conducted in Beijing and in four rural counties in the late 1990s have shown that substantial numbers of people engage in voluntary political activity, some of which puts demands on policymakers. Unfortunately, the systematic evidence that is publicly available is more than 15 years old.

In the rural poll, respondents were asked if they had done any of the following (see Table 10.3):

- Attended local party meetings.
- Attended official village meetings.
- Worked with others to help solve a local problem.
- Expressed their opinion to a party cadre.
- Tried to contact and influence a local government official.

The results surprised the American scholars who helped direct the research. In fact, the numbers compare quite favorably with those in Western democracies, though we should take Chinese polling results with a hefty grain of salt.

In this decade, there is also considerable evidence that the authorities are willing to consider new, but still limited, forms of participation at the provincial and local levels. Most modernizing regions have active chambers of commerce. In other words, entrepreneurs in state and privately owned enterprises (we will distinguish between the two in the public policy section) are most likely to articulate their positions on key issues and have them heard. Some party organizations now allow more than one candidate to run for office both in internal and government contests. However, James Freuwirth, who has done the most research on the subject, says the authorities are trying to get "feedback but not pushback." In other words, they feel they need to know what people think and want, but they also want to avoid anything that smacks of western-style democracy.

Moreover, with but one exception, the same factors contribute to participation in China as in the West. For example, men participate more than women; young people are less active than their elders; and, as in most countries, the more educated people are, the more likely they are to be involved in political life. The one somewhat worrying difference is that CCP members are much more likely to get involved than the rest of society, which may limit the impact of this small rural groundswell of political participation in the future.

Dissent

As first noted in the section on political culture, there has been more active dissent by small and isolated groups of factory workers, peasants, Tibetans, Uighers, and other ethnic minorities. Few of these events were short-lived local movements. In fact, the skimpy available evidence suggests that the party rarely hesitated to put them down—although it used force less blatantly than it did in the 1950s. There have been three coordinated movements since the late 1970s. Although they never threatened the regime, aspects of each indicate that it may not be as powerful as some of its critics believe or even warrant being called totalitarian. The same can be said of isolated, uncoordinated protests that the CCP has to deal with apparently on a daily basis.

Democracy Wall

The first was the **Democracy Wall** in 1978. Initially, Deng and his colleagues allowed a degree of political freedom. With government approval, people put up big-character posters, first on the so-called Democracy Wall in Beijing, and then elsewhere in the country. Many were simply critical of how socialism was being implemented. Others went further and advocated a wider variety of reforms, ranging from freedom of speech to a multiparty system.

The man who became the most prominent of the dissidents, **Wei Jingsheng**, then a twenty-five-year-old

TABLE 10.3 Political Participation in Rural China

NUMBER OF ACTIVITIES	ALL FORMS (%)	DEMANDING FORMS ONLY (%)
0	41	66
1	31	22
2 or more	28	12

Source: Adapted from M. Kent Jennings, "Political Participation in the Chinese Countryside," *American Political Science Review*, 91 (June 1997), tables 2 and 3.

Students at Beijing's Central Academy of Fine Arts putting the finishing touches on the "Goddess of Democracy," modeled after the Statue of Liberty.

AP Images

electrician, described democracy as the fifth modernization to accompany Zhou and Deng's four. For instance, he wrote:

> We hold that people should not give any political leader unconditional trust. Does Deng Xiaoping want democracy? No, he does not. We cannot help asking: What do you think democracy means? If the people do not have a right to express their views freely, how can one speak of democracy? If refusing to allow other people to criticize those in power is your idea of democracy, then what is the difference between this and what Mao euphemistically called the "dictatorship of the proletariat"?[6]

Soon, Deng's patience ran out and the government prohibited all posters and publications that criticized socialism. The leaders were arrested, including Wei, who was sentenced to fifteen years in prison.

The Democracy Movement

For the next decade, visible dissent came only from isolated individuals, most notably the world-renowned astrophysicist **Fang Lizhi**. Fang was a brilliant physics student who graduated from Beijing University at the age of twenty and who was immediately assigned to work for the prestigious Academy of Science's Institute of Modern Physics. He later taught at the University of Science and Technology. Though he thought of himself as a loyal party member, he got into political trouble during the Great Leap Forward and the Cultural Revolution. Fang was able to keep his job, but he had to publish his scholarly works under a pseudonym and was never allowed to occupy the administrative posts his colleagues elected him to. In short, he was an unusual person to spark the second wave of organized dissent.

Beginning in 1978, Fang took advantage of his professional reputation and the relaxed political controls to begin speaking out on broader political issues. For example, he included the following remarks in a 1985 speech:

> There is a social malaise in our country today, and the primary reason for it is the poor example set by Party members. Unethical behavior by Party leaders is especially to blame. This is a situation that clearly calls for action on the part of intellectuals. We Communist Party members should be open to different ways of thinking. We should be open to different cultures and willing to adopt the elements of those cultures that are clearly superior. We must not be afraid to speak openly about these things. In fact, it is our duty.[7]

Fang soon ran afoul of the authorities and was silenced for most of the 1980s.

In 1989, the situation changed dramatically with the emergence of the **Democracy Movement**, the first large, reasonably well-organized protest movement against the CCP and its policies. As with the demonstrations in 1976, the Democracy Movement began with spontaneous protests following the death of a respected reformist leader—Hu Yaobang. Within hours of his death, big-character posters appeared on the walls of Beijing University. That evening, the highly connected graduate students in its Department of Communist Party History bicycled into Tiananmen Square to place a wreath in his memory. Two days later, five hundred students marched to Tiananmen Square to lay more wreaths. Each day brought larger and more militant demonstrations. The police did not intervene.

Within a week, younger students came to dominate the movement. Unlike the graduate students, they had few memories of the Cultural Revolution, took the new openness for granted, and assumed that they could take the

---

[6]Orville Schell. *Mandate of Heaven.* New York: Simon and Schuster, 1994, 29.

[7]Orville Schell. *Discos and Democracy.* New York: Anchor Books, 1989, 131–33.

Profiles
Liu Xiaobo

The Democracy movement in China gained an unexpected boost when the writer and professor Liu Xiaobo was awarded the Nobel Peace prize for 2010. Liu is a human rights activist who was in prison when he was selected.

The Nobel committee knew that the choice would be controversial, but not how virulent the Chinese reaction would be. Despite international opposition, they refused to release Liu or allow his wife to attend the award ceremony. Even the Soviet Union allowed the wife of imprisoned awardee Andrei Sakharov to attend the ceremony in 1975. ■

Kyodo via AP Images

by the political reforms undertaken under his leadership in Moscow. The demonstrations continued after he left. A small group of students began a hunger strike. By May 17, an estimated 2 million people filled Tiananmen Square in the largest demonstration since the Cultural Revolution.

On May 20, the hard-liners began a counterattack, seizing control of the party leadership. By the end of the month, they had replaced Zhao with **Jiang Zemin**, the mayor of Shanghai, who was squarely in their camp. The standoff continued for two more weeks. Finally, on the night of June 3–4, PLA soldiers stormed the square. No one knows how many people were killed, but estimates run as high as four thousand. Many student leaders fled the country. Even though they took no part in the movement, Fang and his wife had to take refuge in the American Embassy, where they remained for almost a year before he was allowed to emigrate and resume his professional career in the United States. In the days and months after the crackdown, the hard-liners solidified their hold on power and made the open expression of dissent impossible. Most movement leaders who stayed in China were arrested.

Falun Gong

In recent years, possibly the most dangerous dissent as far as the party is concerned came from a most unusual and seemingly apolitical source: **Falun Gong**. Falun Gong is one of those organizations that is hard to fit into Western conceptual frameworks. On one level, it is merely a version of *qigong*, which is a set of physical exercises that practitioners believe lead to spiritual and physical well-being. On another level, it is inspired by Buddhism and, thus, has many aspects of a religion. On yet another level, the very fact that it existed as an autonomous organization with as many as 50 million practitioners meant that the party leaders viewed it with caution—at best.

Falun Gong was founded in 1992 by a minor railway official, Li Hongzhi, who had no particular expertise in either medicine or religion. Nonetheless, the movement and its program of exercise and meditation quickly took hold—especially among middle-aged, middle-class Chinese, many of whom had been victims of the Cultural Revolution and were not thriving as a result of economic reform. The movement also spread through its effective use of the Internet. Although its sites are no longer easily accessible in China itself, Falun Gong adherents abroad now e-mail material from the sites, which Chinese can routinely receive online.

As long as Falun Gong adherents simply went to parks to perform their exercises, the regime tolerated them. However, on April 25, 1999, ten thousand of them held a peaceful demonstration in Tiananmen Square. By mid-2000, Falun Gong had held more and larger illegal rallies. Falun Gong members claimed that their meetings were not political at all. The authorities viewed things otherwise, just as they have

protest to a new level. On the night of April 21–22, ten thousand of them marched into the square—and stayed. A day later, their ranks had swollen to one hundred thousand.

On April 27, the students planned another massive march. This time the government tried to block them. The students demonstrated anyway, and their courage inspired an estimated two hundred thousand Beijing residents to join them.

At that point, both the government and the students were still looking for a mutually acceptable solution, but they kept talking past each other. In early May, the movement spread beyond Beijing to other major cities. Journalists defied party discipline and began reporting what they saw. The students who remained in the square proved to be an embarrassment during Gorbachev's visit to Beijing by making it clear that they were inspired in large measure

Democratization
in China

China is one of two or three countries covered in this book (Iraq and possibly Iran being the others) in which we cannot realistically talk about democratization. Western journalists and human rights advocates seize on whatever evidence they can find of hostility to the Chinese Communist Party, such as the 1998 attempt by dissidents to register their own opposition party, as signs of prodemocratic sentiment. In fact, there is little or no evidence to suggest that any significant democratization is occurring "below the surface."

What will happen in the long term is less than clear. Political scientists are not naïve enough to assume that the emergence of capitalistic forces in the economy will necessarily lead to democratic political movements as well. What is more, the regime still seems to be able to quash embryonic movements that spring up, such as the attempt to register an independent democratic party. Still, it is by no means certain that the regime will be able to stave off such efforts in the future or that it will not try to preempt them with gradual, pragmatic reforms of its own. ■

any attempt to create an independent body that lies outside their monopoly of sources of political power. That July they outlawed Falun Gong, claiming it was an "evil cult."

Falun Gong does have some cult-like tendencies, and its belief that ritualistic exercise and meditation can cure disease is certainly unusual by Western standards. Nonetheless, it is part of a venerable Chinese spiritual tradition whose beliefs are no more dangerous or cultish than those of, for instance, Christian Science.

Nonetheless, the authorities cracked down. Li went into exile and now runs the movement from New York. The party sent at least five thousand members to labor camps for "reeducation" and arrested several hundred more. A few dozen members committed suicide while in prison. As recently as 2007, there were press accounts of Falun Gong adherents being arrested, persecuted, and even executed for their beliefs.

Although the movement is not as visible in China as it was a decade ago, it still is repressed. Thus, 117 people in the single province of Jiangsu were brought before the authorities because of their alleged involvement in Falun Gong. More than half had their homes ransacked and/or went to prison. Fourteen claim to have been brainwashed; three were killed.

For our purposes, the key to Falun Gong is not what it does or does not believe in. Rather, it lies in the way the authorities respond to it. As the religious sociologist, Richard Madsen puts it, "[a]ny organization like Falun Gong, no matter what the content of its ideology, would be a threat to the communist regime."[8] The fact is that a well-organized group beyond the control of the party is an obvious source of concern for the party elite, who know that the CCP is nowhere near as powerful or popular as it once was.

Finally, there is what, for lack of a better term, is often called disorganized dissent. The individual events are themselves often coordinated at a city or provincial level. What is critical here is that little or nothing ties them to the kinds of broader and even national movements we have just considered.

Typical of this sort of protest was one that broke out at the Hohhot Nationality Movement in Mongolia in late May 2011.[9] Hohhot is a city of about 2.5 million people on the edge of the grass and desert that dominate Inner Mongolia. Despite its location, 87 percent of its population is Han Chinese, thus coming from the PRC's dominant ethnic group.

The protesters were doubly suspect not only because they questioned the party's hegemony but almost all of them were ethnic Mongolians. As one of them put it in expressing his anger, "First, they shut down our Internet, then they interrupted our cellphone service, and finally they imprisoned us at school. The students are afraid, but more than that, they are angry." Their colleagues at Inner Mongolia University threw their Chinese language textbooks out classroom windows before they were locked down on campus.

In fact, the protests seem to have begun after two Mongolians were run over and killed by drivers who were Han Chinese. The state responded in its typical approach of combining positive inducements (carrots) with repression (sticks). By the end of May, they had offered millions of dollars in economic help for the impoverished region, plus another half billion dollars to support Mongolian culture and provide financial aid for Mongolian students. At the same time, they arrested the protests' ringleaders, shut down parks and other public spaces protesters congregated in, and threatened to fire any public sector employee who joined the demonstrations. Students who sent text and other messages on Chinese social media sites were brought in for questioning by the police.

It is not as if the 2,000 or so students in Hohhot were unique. The unsystematically gathered evidence available to us suggests that sentiments like the one quoted here from one of the protesters are quite widely held. The hard part is turning what happens in places like Hohhot into national movements like those discussed above.

---

[8]Richard Madsen. "Understanding Falun Gong." *Current History* 99 September 2000.

[9]Andrew Jacobs, "China Extends Hand and Fist to Protesters." *New York Times.* 2 June 2011, A6

THE PARTY STATE

The Leninist State: Chinese Style

The one common denominator in Chinese politics since 1949 has been the unchallenged rule by the CCP. Despite all the forces that are changing the face of China, the party remains quite close to the Leninist model laid out in Chapter 8 and has been able to resist pressure for political reform.

Like all other communist parties that joined the Comintern in the 1920s, the CCP endorsed democratic centralism and the Bolshevik revolutionary strategy. This means that, although the PRC has a government and a constitution—the most recent version having been adopted in 1982—the state is not where real power lies. Despite some minor exceptions, which we will encounter later in this section, the party still calls all the political—if not the economic—shots.

The PRC is officially governed by a massive National People's Congress of well over two thousand members. But, like the Supreme Soviet prior to Gorbachev, the Congress meets infrequently and serves primarily as a rubber stamp for decisions made elsewhere. Similarly, the president and prime minister are powerful primarily because they hold positions at the top of the CCP, not because of their formal government offices.

The only significant structural difference between the PRC and other communist governments is the somewhat larger role given to provincial and local authorities in China. Even that should hardly be surprising given China's size and its relatively poorly developed communications infrastructure until the last few years.

As in the former Soviet Union, real power lies in the party. The 1982 constitution dropped Article 2, the PRC's equivalent of the Soviet Article 6, which gave the party a monopoly on power. This made little difference in practice, given Deng's continued endorsement of party control.

The CCP enrolls a slightly smaller proportion of the total population than did the Communist Party of the Soviet Union (CPSU). However, it is still a huge organization. Its more than 70 million members mean that the CCP is larger than all but twenty-two countries! The dominance of the party unit in determining where people lived and worked into the 1980s gave it at least as much control as the CPSU had before the reforms of the Gorbachev era.

Chinese Variations on a Theme

There are, however, some ways in which today's CCP is different from the Soviet model as well as reasons to believe that the party may be weakening. One of the often misleading conclusions political scientists reached about communist countries is that they did not have a normal or routine way of choosing new leaders. In practice, most communist countries developed procedures whereby the party's leadership selected the next person in charge with a minimum of conflict, as we saw in Chapter 9 following the deaths of Brezhnev, Yuri Andropov, and Konstantin Chernenko.

In fact, China had worked out smooth mechanisms from one leader to the next including a rule that only allowed a leader to serve two five-year terms. The next leader who will almost certainly be president of the country, head of the CCP, and commander of the military will be Xi Jinping .

Like most current CCP leaders, Xi is an engineer. What sets him apart from his contemporaries a bit is that his father, Xi Zhongxun, was a senior party official under Deng after his release from forced labor following the Cultural Revolution. That makes him part of what the Chinese call the "princeling party" to describe children of the party elite. In late 2010, he was named head of the Central Military Commission (CMC), which means he will almost certainly replace President Hu when his second term ends in 2013 🌐 (**www.globalsecurity.org/military /world/china/cmc.htm**).

There was some debate among experts on Chinese politics over how well the system worked in 2004 when Jiang Zemin finished handing over power to Hu, since there were rumors that they two did not get along. No such debate is expected now given Xi's pedigree and the early announcement of his appointment.

People are already talking about him as the first member of a fifth generation of party leaders (after Mao, Deng, Jiang, and Hu). He will be the first leader born after the revolution, yet he has the closest ties to the revolutionary leadership—his father joined the Communist Youth League at age 13. Many of his contemporaries studied abroad, and it may well be that they are more open minded than the fourth generation. Given that Xi did all of his university studies in China and has spent his entire career in the party bureaucracy, it remains to be seen how flexible he will be.

A New Kind of Party?

Today's generation of pragmatic leaders has tried to change the party's composition. They are trying to recruit university graduates and technicians whose expertise, and not their class background or ideological commitment, is seen as necessary if the party is to lead the way toward further modernization. That pattern is also seen in decisions about whom to promote.

Thirty years ago, the party would have had little difficulty finding ideologically dedicated members and future leaders because party membership was the one and only way to reach the top of Chinese society. Now this has begun to change. With private businesses employing more and more well-educated young people, the CCP is no longer the only "game in town," and the party is finding it harder and harder to recruit the kinds of cadres it wants.

This helps explain why the party announced in 2001 that it would allow capitalists to join. In 2001, party officials estimated that 113,000 CCP members already owned businesses, but they had all formed their firms after they had joined. Three years later it was estimated that between a quarter and a third of all Chinese entrepreneurs were CCP members.

Some hard-liners objected. A regional party official said that "if these people really join the party they will use their strength to first seize power within the party and to change the party's nature." Another put it far more bluntly: "Capitalists in the Communist Party? You've got to be kidding."

Party membership is still a requirement for a political career. However, for many apolitical young people who are more concerned with making money, there is no need to belong to the CCP. For them the often petty administrative work new party members are assigned can be an unwelcome burden. Nonetheless, there seems to be no turning back for a party that will have to adapt to China's changing social and economic realities if it is to survive. And the young party recruits Rob Gifford interviewed still believe that membership enhances one's career, even in the private sector.

But as we will see in the next section on public policy, even the distinction between the public and private sector has been blurred. Many supposedly state-owned companies act like private firms and, more important, even the private firms retain close links to the party, which offers them a degree of legal and political protection.

The Road to Power

The CCP leadership still controls all major appointments in the government and in the party itself. Like the CPSU, it has a *nomenklatura*. The Chinese were among the first communist governments to separate party and state leadership below the national level. In practice, however, this has yet to make much of a difference because the party elite still controls appointments to both.

Power is officially lodged in the party Congress, which normally meets every five years and selects the **Central Committee** that supposedly manages party affairs until its next session. Practically speaking, the Congress and Central Committee are powerless. As in the old Soviet Union, neither body has much influence. Democratic centralism still operates. Party Congress delegates are co-opted from above and its meetings have done little more than ratify decisions already made by the elite.

The Central Committee, too, exercises little day-to-day power. Unlike the former CPSU, there is not much continuity in its membership, with a turnover rate of about 50 percent at each of the most recent Congresses. The Central Committee is a massive body that meets only a few times a year because well over half its members live outside Beijing. Although its plenums have often been the site of acrimonious debate over most of the major policy initiatives undertaken since 1978, the final decisions are invariably made higher up.

As was the case in the CPSU, power is concentrated in the very small political elite, at the heart of which is the Politburo (26 members in June 2011) and its **Standing Committee** (9 members), all of whom are senior party leaders. The Politburo includes top state officials as well, such as the premier or the chair of the State Planning Commission. Unlike the CPSU, the Politburo's day-to-day work is the responsibility of its smaller Standing Committee (see Figure 10.1). We (perhaps) gained a unique glimpse into the inner workings of the party with the publication of the *Tiananmen Square Papers* in early 2001.[10] Three prominent American sinologists were given copies of what they were told were transcripts of secret meetings of the party's leadership held during the Tiananmen crisis in 1989. Initially, the three doubted that the documents were authentic. However, after months of study and queries of colleagues around the world, they decided that they probably were legitimate and decided to publish them. The papers reveal a leadership that was deeply divided between reformers and hard-liners, though it is safe to say that similar transcripts from meetings during the first days of the Cultural Revolution would show far more acrimony. In the end, Deng had the last word and cast his lot with the hard-liners and their desire to force the students and their supporters out of Tiananmen Square. No one knows how much debate there is about more normal political issues. The one thing we can say with a reasonable degree of certainty is that the president does seem able to prevail if he voices his viewpoint strongly enough. That said, the conventional wisdom has it that Hu is more of a consensus builder than any of his predecessors. No one knows if that will be true of Xi, but his whole career has been built as a team player.

There is one other key way in which the CCP is different from the old CPSU. When Deng was in power, he exercised power largely from behind the scenes, perhaps because he and other key leaders were very old. Although Deng was able to urge his colleagues into formal retirement with him in the 1980s, they continued to run the country through the

---

[10]Liang Zheng, Andrew Nathan, Perry Link, and Orville Schell, eds. *The Tiananmen Square Papers: The Chinese Leadership's Decision to Use Force Against Their Own People—In Their Own Words.* New York: Public Affairs, 2001.

FIGURE 10.1 Decision Making in China

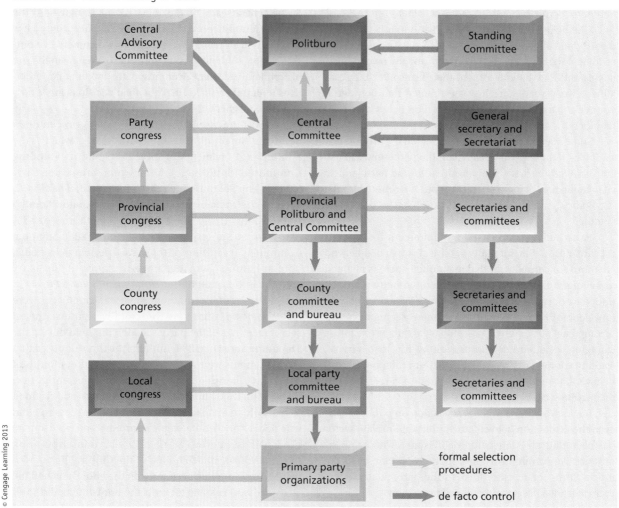

Central Advisory Commission (CAC), which was set up in 1982. In theory, the CAC existed only to advise the Politburo and the rest of the official leadership. In fact, its members remained the most powerful people in the country and made all the important decisions.

With most of its members either deceased or too ill to work even on a part-time basis, the CAC was abolished at the Fourteenth Party Congress in 1992. Although the CAC, therefore, existed for only a decade, it had the impact of delaying the real assertion of power by Jiang and other supposed leaders who were then widely—and accurately—seen as little more than puppets of their elders. It is hard to tell if "behind the scenes" leaders still have that much influence. What is clear is that no person has the power or authority that Mao or Deng wielded.

There are also growing signs that the party's organization is neither as rigid nor as powerful as the Leninist model or Figure 10.1 might suggest. If anything, the Chinese

tradition of authoritarian rule has been reinforced under the CCP, with its emphasis on the top twenty-five to thirty-five officials and the "core leader" at any one time. As in the old Soviet bloc, these officials have been able to concentrate power through their personal networks and the *nomenklatura* system. These general tendencies are probably even more pronounced in China with its system of *kou*, or policy gateways, which coordinate decision making in four key sectors: party organization, government administration, state security, and foreign affairs.

Conversely, there are powerful pressures toward decentralization and the weakening of the party's power in general that Kenneth Lieberthal has labeled "fragmented authoritarianism." Until recently, both Chinese tradition and democratic centralism led people to pass unsolved problems upward in the party hierarchy. As we saw with the distinction between political "thumbs" and "fingers" in Chapters 8, highly centralized decision making does not work all that well in a complex society in which people at the "bottom" have to take initiative or act quickly. It should also be remembered that some of China's provinces have more people than do most European countries. What's more, many politicians, including Deng, Jiang, and Hu, established their credentials by working successfully at the provincial level.

There also are growing signs of nepotism and corruption within the CCP that long antedate Xi's likely presidency. Of special concern is the fact that so many children of high-level party cadres have positioned themselves near the top of the political and economic hierarchies. Take, for instance, Deng's five children. Deng Pufang, crippled during the Cultural Revolution, heads the Chinese Federation for the Disabled. Deng Nan holds a critical position on the State Science and Technology Commission. Deng Lin is an accomplished artist, though many believe that the sixty thousand dollars she commands per painting or tapestry reflects her family name as much as her talent. Deng Rong was her father's secretary and interpreter, who many believe had the most influence over the aging leader. Finally, Deng Zhifang holds an American PhD and is one of China's top entrepreneurs.

The strength of these families opens the door to a far broader, but harder to document, concern: corruption. The press is filled with reports of new millionaires living luxuriously at least partially as the result of illegal activities. Bribes are an accepted part of doing business in the new China. Corruption within the police force is known as the "three chaoses"—for the acceptance of bribes, the unauthorized imposition of fines, and the illegal sharing of license and other fees by the men and women who collect them.

Finally, there is the PLA. As we saw in Chapter 9, the Soviet army stayed away from political controversies until the 1991 coup, at which time it proved incapable of intervening politically in any kind of unified manner. The PLA, in contrast, has been an important political actor since the Long March. At that point, the party and the army were one and the same. Many party leaders, including Deng, started their careers in the PLA, and army leaders have always held prominent positions in the CCP leadership. Membership on the party's CMC has similarly been a sign of political power within the CCP as well as in the PLA.

The PLA became part of the factional struggles in the 1960s, when Lin Biao was its leader. The PLA was far less political in the years between Lin's death and the Democracy Movement of 1989. During the 1980s the army was as divided as the party as a whole. Some leaders sided with the reformers. Press reports during spring 1989 suggested that the PLA was so deeply split that units controlled by the rival factions came close to fighting each other. In the end, most of the leading PLA officers came down on the side of the hard-liners.

The PLA is important because it has an independent power base. It is far less subject to control through the normal mechanisms of party oversight than was the case for the old Soviet army. And it has had a tremendous vested interest in the future of economic reform because it runs dozens of enterprises, some of which have been converted from military to consumer-oriented production and some of which have been accused of using what amounts to slave or sweatshop labor.

PUBLIC POLICY: *PERESTROIKA* WITHOUT *GLASNOST*

Since the late 1970s, the CCP has followed a political and economic strategy that is almost exactly the opposite of the one we saw in Gorbachev's Soviet Union. There the CPSU loosened political controls but dithered when it came to economic reforms. The combination of political liberalization and frustration with the accelerating economic decline opened the political floodgates that destroyed the USSR.

As we have just seen, there has been no significant liberalization of the political system. However, economic policy has changed so much that it is difficult to speak of China as a socialist state.

Economic Reform

The economy is the centerpiece of any socialist country's public policy. Concern about inequality sparked support for socialism in the first place, and socialist policymakers of all stripes have accorded the state a more central role in economic management than we find in the capitalist societies with the strongest *dirigiste* traditions.

In China today, we also have to focus on the economy because Deng and his colleagues led the country away from socialist principles, albeit always rationalizing their actions in the name of socialism. In so doing, they presided over one of the most dramatic periods of growth in world history, which some analysts believe will make China one of the world's leading economic powers in the near future.

When Mao died, China's economy was not in good shape, though it was doing better than might have been expected given the political turmoil of the Cultural Revolution. Industrial production had grown by an average of 9 percent per year from 1957 to 1976, and most factories were not targeted during the upheaval. During normal times, no one starved and everyone had access to at least an elementary education and rudimentary health care.

There were signs, however, that China would soon face many of the same problems the Soviet Union did during the Brezhnev years: a shortage of investment in everything

Profiles
Deng Xiaoping

Like Zhou Enlai, Deng was born into an elite family and spent his youth studying the Confucian classics. In 1920, at the age of sixteen, he went on a work-study program to Paris, where, among other things, he joined the European branch of the Chinese Communist Party (CCP) that Zhou had formed, worked in a factory, and developed a lifelong love of croissants. Later in that same decade, he again studied in Paris.

On his return to China, he joined Mao Zedong in his effort to organize in the countryside and took part in the Long March. He became a leading CCP military figure and by the 1940s was political commissar of the People's Liberation Army (PLA).

After the CCP came to power, he held a number of positions in the party hierarchy and gradually cast his lot with Liu Shaoqi and others seeking a more pragmatic approach to economic policy. For this he was purged during the Cultural Revolution and, again, following Mao's death.

He returned to office for a third time in 1978 and guided Chinese political life until his death. He never officially held a high position (he was never more than vice premier of China and vice president of

Deng Xiaoping in 1985—as usual, smoking a cigarette.

the Chinese Bridge Club), but like many of his generation, he exercised power from behind the scenes. He resigned from his last government position in 1989, made his last tour of the country in 1992, and died of Parkinson's disease in 1997. ■

---

but heavy industry, a slow rate of technological innovation, an emphasis on the quantity rather than the quality of production, the inability to respond to consumer preferences, supply bottlenecks, irrational prices, and insufficient food production. China had poor communication and transportation networks. The shortage of trained managers had been worsened by the Maoist policy of recruiting cadres on the basis of class background and ideological stance rather than professional competence.

Most important, China remained one of the world's poorest countries and had taken only minor steps toward improving the living conditions of its people. The problems were, if anything, worse in China than in most other poor countries. Mao had all but completely closed its borders, limiting foreign trade to the single city of Guangdong (Canton). No foreign aid or loans were accepted.

The first signs of change came in 1972, when Zhou announced that China would pursue the four modernizations. It would be another six years before the leftists would

finally be defeated and Deng would solidify his hold on power. Since then, the CCP has enacted a series of sweeping reforms guided by three very non-Marxist principles:

- Private property can play a useful role in a socialist economy.
- Market forces should be used to allocate goods and services and to determine prices.
- Material incentives, including higher wages, personal profit, and the accumulation of wealth, should be the main way to boost productivity and efficiency.

As Table 10.4 shows, recent Chinese economic growth has been remarkable, certainly faster than in any other country covered in this book. But western observers often get the nature of Chinese growth wrong, if not its pace. China has not become a capitalist country, if by that we mean one run by unregulated and privately owned companies. Chinese companies are far more competitive than

TABLE 10.4 Economic Growth in China: Annual Rates of Change

SECTOR	1980–1990 (%)	1990–1999 (%)	2001-2007 (%)
Gross domestic product	10.2	10.7	10.1
Industry	11.1	14.4	12.2
Exports	11.5	12.2	20.5

Source: *World Bank, World Development Report, 1998, 1999, 2010,* www.worldbank.org accessed December 12, 2010.

they were in Mao's day, and many are major players in the global marketplace. It has become a major exporter of everything from motorcycles to computer routers to low cost textiles. However, as we hope to show in a series of examples as well as with hard data, China also has its share of problems.

First, its growth is very uneven. It is concentrated in areas near major cities which, in turn, are not far from the coast. Much of the countryside and much of the interior of the country remain very poor; living conditions have not changed much—if at all—in those regions. The growth in and around cities like Beijing or Shanghai is spectacular, as many of us saw in television coverage of the 2008 Olympic games. Nonetheless, as we will also see in India, there still remain huge pockets of poverty and unemployment even in the booming cities.

Second, it has avoided reforms that would be likely to threaten its hold on power. As we will see, China does have privately owned companies, but the party's influence is never far away. Some of the most dynamic companies are still state-owned. Private sector firms have had to put on a **red hat** and accept the presence of party units inside the firm, many of which make the decisions that count—and are a source of widespread corruption. Even Walmart was forced to accept party-controlled unions before it was allowed to open its first stores in China, something it has not been willing to do anywhere else in the world.

Third, some economists think China is courting long-term difficulties. Of course, its insertion into the international economy has come as quickly as any country's in the world. At the same time, it has put its emphasis on savings at home to promote exports and foreign investment. That means that few Chinese have enjoyed all the benefits of the hard work they have put in. What, the critics ask, will happen when Chinese consumers demand something like a "fair share" of the growth?

Agriculture

Though it receives the least attention today, the first (and arguably most important) reforms came in agriculture. During the 1980s, the Maoist-era communes were dismantled and replaced by the household responsibility system. The party divided collective farms into small plots, which were worked by families that, for all practical purposes, owned their land. The state also reduced the amount farmers had to sell to it and allowed the market to determine almost all agricultural prices.

The agricultural reforms proved highly successful. Production increased by more than 10 percent per year during the 1980s. Some former peasants are now extremely well off, especially those who live in areas where they can readily sell their produce in the burgeoning urban markets. Overall, the gap between urban and rural standards of living was cut by about 30 percent.

Today, the picture for agriculture and farmers no longer seems all that rosy. Reports of Mercedes-driving peasant entrepreneurs turned out to be exaggerated. Most peasants make less than one hundred dollars a month. That makes even a menial job in a sweatshop attractive because most people make about twice that amount in the cities. As a result, young people are leaving the countryside in droves and heading for glamorous seeming places like Shanghai—though their own lives there are not likely to be very glamorous.

Private Enterprise

Even more dramatic has been the development of private businesses, some owned by the Chinese themselves and others by foreign investors. Indeed, it is the growth of this sector that has led observers to claim that China could soon become the largest economy in the world in absolute if not per capita terms.

The regime moved gradually until it was clear that private enterprise would contribute to its broader goal of modernization. As in the former Soviet Union, privately owned enterprises started out as small, service-oriented firms mostly in the retail trades. Until the late 1980s, they accounted for less than 1 percent of industrial output. Today their earnings are far greater than those of the state-owned enterprises and more and more of them are also being based on such market principles as profit and loss.

Beginning at about that time, the boom in the private sector began in earnest. The original legislation restricted private firms to eight employees, a figure that has never been seriously enforced. In 1988, the National People's Congress officially created a new category of "private business" to regulate the somewhat larger firms outside the state sector. In 1980, there were only 1,500 entrepreneurial firms in all of China; a decade later there were about 400,000. One million new businesses were registered in 2006 alone. In late 2010, the official Chinese news agency estimated that the value of all private enterprise had reached $1.4 trillion.

Urban co-ops, service organizations, and rural industries together employ about two-thirds of all nonagricultural labor. Privately owned village industries alone employ at least 100 million people, more than the entire public sector. Most importantly, the private firms are far more dynamic and profitable than the state-owned ones and thus attract the attention of the reformers, who are, above all else, interested in maximizing the rate of economic growth.

There was some concern that the hard-liners would slow the pace of economic reform in the wake of the events in Tiananmen Square in 1989. By mid-1992, however, it had become increasingly clear that Deng was throwing his lot in with the reformers. That summer, after visiting a steel factory, he complained that the party had not adequately responded to calls for more rapid economic change. Local officials seized the opportunity and even horse racing tracks were privatized.

The key to the initial success of the reforms is the way the leadership opened the economy to foreign investment. Even before Mao's death, the policies promoting economic self-sufficiency were eased. Foreign aid and investment came to be seen as ways of speeding up modernization. To facilitate—and control—foreign entry into the Chinese market, four **special economic zones (SEZs)** were created in 1979. In these regions, foreign investors were offered preferential tax rates and other incentives. Five years later, Hainan Island and fourteen more cities became SEZs as well. By the mid-1990s, market mechanisms and foreign investment had spread to most of urban China, blurring the distinction between the SEZs and the rest of the country.

Joint ventures have been established in dozens of industries and have turned China into a leading exporter of textiles and other low-tech products. It has also made some, albeit more limited, progress in developing high-tech goods, including rockets for launching satellites.

Typical of the new breed of private companies is Huawei Technologies based in Shenzen, one of the original SEZs. The company was founded in 1988 by a former sergeant in the PLA. At the time, it merely sold telephone equipment made in Hong Kong. Today, it makes world-class computer routers and telecommunications switches and competes effectively with global giants, Cisco, Siemens, and Alcatel. It employs eighty-seven thousand people worldwide, and its 2007 sales topped $12 billion, almost two-thirds of its revenue coming from overseas. In 2010 it joined *Fortune Magazine's* list of the top 500 global corporations.

Obviously, more than high-tech industries are involved. China is accused by both manufacturers and trade unions in the West of allowing factories that are little better than the sweatshops of early twentieth century New York or Manchester. Not only are workers poorly paid, but quality control of the production process is also minimal, at best. For example, China is the leading exporter of toys, which came to light in 2007 when millions of them had to be pulled from the American market because the manufacturers had used lead paint. In 2010, it had to withdraw millions of units of contaminated baby formula from western markets.

More typical of Chinese development is its motorcycle industry. Many Asians are earning more money. However, buying a car is still out of the question. Upgrading from a bicycle to a motorcycle is, however, economically feasible. In 1993, Yin Mingshan took advantage of the new laws to create a motorcycle repair shop with nine employees, the maximum allowed at the time. Today, his company, Lifan, employs almost ten thousand people and has an annual turnover of almost $1 billion. This does not, of course, come from motorcycle repairs. Lifan makes and sells upward of seven hundred thousand motorcycles in more than one hundred countries. It now also makes trucks and small cars. AIG (the financial conglomerate that contributed so much to the global economic crisis) now owns 25 percent of the company.

In all, Chinese companies make about 15 million motorcycles a year and accounts for about half of the world market. Companies like Lifan are often accused of simply copying designs from Honda or other Japanese companies. The fact remains, however, that they can translate their lower production costs into a market advantage, something we will see in Part 4 in our discussions of import substitution in the Global South.

By contrast, the state-owned enterprises (SOEs) lagged behind for most of the reform period. Most had been monopolies and models of inefficiency. However, in the late 1990s the authorities began to issue new rules requiring the SOEs to operate more under market conditions, which streamlined some of their operations. In October 2001, the government announced that it planned to sell about $3 billion worth of stock in them, but this amounts to only a tiny fraction of the still-nationalized sector of the economy. In 2010, the top three Chinese firms on the *Fortune* list were all state-owned but run in ways that allow them to compete globally, which they increasingly have to do whether the authorities want them to or not. In fact, as we noted above, it is actually hard to tell the private firms and the SOEs apart. As noted above, the party still maintains tremendous influence over the private sector; in fact, children of the party elite own and run many of them. In fact, on a practical level, it may not make much difference who officially owns an enterprise because the CCP still calls most of the shots. It is by no means clear that this will continue to be so as the market expands. It is clear that the CCP is not interested in relinquishing political power, though it may have no choice as the private sector grows.

But there is no question that the dynamism of both enabled China to withstand the "great recession" and maintain its position as the fastest growing economy in the world.

The government is planning to rein in the easy lending policies of both state-controlled and privately owned banks in 2011 to counter the threat of inflation. One of the upshots of the party's continued leverage over both sectors has been the rise of corruption. We can never pin down just how much corruption there is. However, an average of 15,000 party officials have been accused of malfeasance each year. Over the thirty-year period of the reforms, no more than three percent of them spent even a day in prison. The best source on corruption probably comes from fiction, especially the novels by Qiu Xiaolong which combine crime solving with insights into the pervasive influence of less-than-honest leaders.

The Rule of 72

Economic growth has an impact much like that of compound interest on your savings account. This year's interest builds on what you made in previous years as well as on the money you deposit.

It turns out that if you divide the growth rate in a savings account—or the gross national product—in a given year into 72, that tells you how many years it will take to double your account or the overall economy, assuming that growth rates remain the same.

With average growth rates of about 10 percent for the last two decades, that means that it will only take about seven years for the Chinese economy as a whole to double and fifteen years for it to quadruple.

The fallout from Tiananmen Square never extended to foreign investors. Investment grew steadily—from about $5 billion in 1987 to $27 billion in 1993 to $60 billion in 1999 and then to $82 billion in the first three quarters of 2010. Over half of it came from Hong Kong, Macao, and other overseas Chinese communities. Taiwan, which is still officially at war with the mainland, accounts for about 10 percent of the investment, as does South Korea, which has also had a hostile political relationship with the PRC.

On a tangible level, most people eat better because better quality food is available, often at lower prices than before the reforms. Some 80 million peasants have been able to leave the land and take more lucrative jobs in new rural enterprises. The urban standard of living has improved even faster, although there is still plenty of poverty in the cities as well as in the countryside.

Moreover, it is commonly believed that the *guanxi* (people with connections) benefit the most from the reforms. Such beliefs cannot be supported by hard evidence, though the frequent reports of official corruption suggest that they contain more than a grain of truth.

We should add one last caveat here. The very success of the reforms is worsening China's already fragile environment. Even its successful population control program is waning; the birth rate has already risen 0.2 percent since the 1980s, which will add another 15 million people each year to the total population. Increased agricultural production and industrialization have cost the country more than a million acres of arable land a year. Peasants who are trying to maximize their income have turned to cash crops such as tobacco instead of following their traditional crop rotation practices, which replenished the soil with needed nutrients.

In sum, China may not catch up with the United States for decades, but one of the goals it has set for itself, reaching what the leadership calls "reasonable prosperity," certainly seems to be in reach. And if and when it happens, one of the main causes will be the way the CCP has changed its priorities since the death of Mao.

Economic Liberalization
in China

Western journalists often hold China up as an example of how helpful it can be to shift to a market economy. Although such benefits are easy to see, we should also point out that China has not made the transition from a planned to an open economy as quickly or as fully as many of the Eastern European countries. There has been no shock therapy and Western economic theorists have had little or no influence on Chinese decision makers.

Rather, the leadership has shifted toward a market economy in a series of gradual and measured moves. Some of the steps—for example, the family responsibility system in agriculture, the first privately owned "cooperatives" in the service sector, and the creation of the original special economic zones—were risky. But, none is likely to prove riskier than the one the leadership is still resisting—privatizing the "commanding heights" of the economy, much of which is still state-owned.

Nonetheless, private enterprise seems there to stay. Although it may not be an important example, when journalist Rob Gifford went to a small city in the Gobi Desert, every room in his hotel had broadband. People he met took him to an An Li meeting. It took him a while to figure out what that was because they were having trouble pronouncing *Amway*. ■

Foreign Policy

Chinese foreign policy has also undergone profound changes that have brought the country closer to the international mainstream. Nonetheless, when *The Economist* carried a lengthy survey about the growth of China in December 2010, it was about the military, not the economy.

At times, relations have also been rocky with its neighbors and with the United States. In the first months of the Bush presidency, China reacted angrily after it shot down an American spy plane over Hainan Island in 2001. And the Chinese government still resists international pressure to improve its human rights record. Today, the Obama administration and other western officials take China to task for its failure to meet international economic norms and rein in North Korea and its nuclear weapons program.

That was not the case for most of the time Mao was in power; the PRC pursued the kind of foreign policy Marxist theory would lead us to expect. It supported Third World militants who fought against the vestiges of colonialism. China also was the first country with ties to the Global South to deploy nuclear weapons, and it consistently has been a major supplier of arms, especially to the Middle East.

The PRC consistently attacked the United States and other capitalist powers for trying to maintain their political and economic hold on the countries that we used to call the Third World, even after they achieved formal independence (see Part 4). Given its role in Korea, Vietnam, and elsewhere, and its failure to recognize the PRC, the United States has been a frequent target of Chinese criticisms. Most of the time, this conflict was purely rhetorical. Their two armies did fight in Korea. After that, the two countries only came close to war in 1958 during the dispute over Quemoy and Matsu, two tiny islands in the Taiwan Straits.

The rivalry came to the fore in the late 1950s when the Chinese decided that the Soviets had turned their backs on Marx and revolution. Tensions between the two reached a peak in 1969 when the rhetorical battles escalated into skirmishes along their border. Sino-Soviet relations remained highly strained until the collapse of the USSR.

Under Mao, Chinese foreign policy could best be described as rigidly independent and self-sufficient for two main reasons. First, the Chinese assumed that they would continue to face a hostile world and would not be able to get significant help from the outside. Second, the Maoist model provided an alternative approach to development. If the party was able to mobilize the masses, China could modernize using its own resources.

By the 1970s, both of those assumptions had been proven false, something best seen in China's relations with the United States. The Cultural Revolution taught the leadership something it probably should have learned from the Great Leap Forward. Mass mobilization and commitment to socialism were not the best way to industrialize the country. Also, geopolitical realities had changed. In particular, President Richard Nixon and Secretary of State Henry Kissinger were willing to overlook ideological differences if they could forge alliances that advanced what they took to be the national interest of the United States. China, in short, presented such an opportunity because of its hostility toward the Soviets.

Signs that things might improve began to appear in the early 1970s. An American graduate student was allowed into the country to claim the body of his recently deceased aunt, Anna Louise Strong, who had spent most of the period since the 1930s in China as a "friend" of the revolution. In 1972, an American table tennis team played in China, lending its name to what soon came to be called "Ping Pong diplomacy." Later that year, Kissinger made a secret trip to China. At that meeting, he, Zhou, and perhaps Mao reached a quick agreement that the two countries could and should reestablish diplomatic and other relations. Before the year was out, President Nixon had visited China and, virtually overnight, two of the world's worst enemies became practically the closest of friends.

Relations between the two countries continued to improve. The United States reversed its long-standing opposition to PRC membership in the UN. Formal diplomatic relations were resumed during Jimmy Carter's administration. Currently, no non-Asian country has more invested in China than the United States, and only Japan has more extensive bilateral trade.

Relations between China and the United States continue to be less than smooth. American leaders have been highly critical of China's human rights record. Critics were most vocal in the aftermath of the Tiananmen Square clampdown, but the rhetorical decibel levels have risen almost any time Washington had to make a decision regarding trade or other relations with China, including allegations about what amount to slave labor in factories owned by the PLA. Today, American critics focus on everything from the Chinese arms build up to its role in such troubled countries as Sudan. By contrast, the Chinese object to American criticism of its human rights record and to what they see as meddling in East Asian affairs. China also holds more of the American debt than any other country.

There are areas of deep disagreement between China and the West in general. The most famous was its refusal to endorse the American and British plan to invade Iraq. Less visible, but potentially more important for China, has been its reluctance to endorse UN involvement in Darfur because it plans to develop and purchase much needed oil from Sudan, the government that has been accused of genocide in its western provinces.

On the other side of the coin, there have been recent signs that Chinese-American and Western relations could improve.

To begin with, entry into the WTO will force China to open its markets more for outside investment, including from the United States. What's more, the decision to grant Beijing the 2008 Olympics brought with it pressure to open its political and social systems. If this happens, it should satisfy some of Beijing's critics in Washington. Finally, the events of 9/11 drew the two countries somewhat closer together because of the Chinese concern that al-Qaeda and other militants were training potential terrorists among China's Muslim minority groups.

China was a major participant in the six party talks that convinced the North Koreans to suspend their nuclear weapons and power program in 2007 and has worked closely with its partners since North Korea's nuclear test in 2009. China and the other parties did not always agree, but there is little doubt that the PRC put significant pressure on the regime in Pyongyang.

It is not simply Chinese-American relations that have normalized since the end of the Cultural Revolution. China has successfully negotiated the return of Hong Kong from Britain and improved relations with most of its neighbors. Given the size of its army and the sophistication of its weapons, China is certain to remain a regional, but not a global, military power. And if current trends continue, it will become a global economic force as well.

To give you a sense of how far geopolitical trends have changed in recent years, a group of American defense department officials are experimenting with a new way of thinking about foreign policy in general. No country fits their still unfinished model more than China in its relations with its neighbors and the world's other major powers. Traditionally, we have thought about international relations in terms of three broad patterns, each of which occurs at a different time from the others.

Peace—Conflict—War

Now, these people argue, we live in a different world. Again, there are three main "states" of international relation. Now, however we are often in each of them at the same time depending on the issue.

Cooperation—Competition—Conflict

Thus, China tends to cooperate on regional security issues, especially North Korea. It both cooperates and competes with those same countries on economic issues. It is in conflict with the United States, in particular over Sudan and Darfur. Note, too, that these defense intellectuals did not include war in the second list because they are convinced that war between any of the world's major powers and China is not on the horizon.

Globalization *in China*

China is often held up as the political "poster child" of globalization.

No other country has moved so strongly or so quickly onto the global economic stage. Its foreign trade has increased at a faster rate than the economy as a whole, which itself is growing extremely rapidly, as we saw. Some argue that China will become one of the world's economic giants long before the middle of this century.

It is not just the economy. About a million Chinese have studied at Western universities and returned. Western pop culture can be found in all cities—often in bootleg versions. On the other hand, some Chinese films have become cult hits in the West.

But, it must be recalled that only a small portion of the Chinese population is part of this immersion in global markets and culture. And, the regime still tightly restricts access to political information and opinions coming from the outside. ■

THE MEDIA

There is probably no better indicator of the limits to liberalization in China than the regime's continued leverage over the mass media, which is the primary way people learn about political events. As in the Soviet Union before Gorbachev came to power, the party has long determined who is on the air, what is written in the newspapers, and so on. Some journalists did speak their minds in the weeks before the 1989 crackdown in Tiananmen Square, but they all subsequently lost their jobs. As noted previously in the chapter, a few independent journals have been able to publish for brief periods, but their circulation has always been extremely small.

The best evidence that the CCP is trying to hold onto these levers of power lies in its policies regarding information technology. In 1989, students used fax machines to keep in touch with each other and with their colleagues studying in the West. Since then, people have tried to feed information into China via the Internet and satellite TV. Until recently, however, the regime has been remarkably successful at blocking access to foreign-based political websites, most recently Wikipedia. Private citizens are technically not allowed to own satellite dishes. Cable operators provide as many as thirty foreign channels to their subscribers, including some international news channels. However, cable reaches a very small proportion of the country. As recently as 2002, an Internet service provider was convicted for piping political news into the country via e-mail, which is less susceptible to the filtering technology that keeps people from accessing websites. But change is afoot, most notably in a deal announced in October 2001 that gave Time Warner the first franchise for a foreign company to operate a cable system in the country. Since then, access to cable has spread as has ownership of less-than-legal satellite dishes, most of which can receive signals from stations in Taiwan and Hong Kong. One recent report also suggested that the most technologically sophisticated of the 100 million Internet users have found ways to circumvent the blocks that supposedly keep them from accessing foreign sites.

China is also the world's leader in sale of pirated films, music, and software (not to mention purses and golf clubs). Most Western pop culture is available almost as soon as it is released in Hollywood or London. The underground media community also produces counterfeit as well as real versions of popular Western media, including at least eight fake versions of Harry Potter books with such titles as *Harry Potter and the Chinese Overseas Students at the Hogwarts School of Witchcraft and Wizardry.*

As a result, it seems unlikely that the CCP will be able to slow down an already opening media world. However, if the consumers only want to read real Harry Potter books or watch videos of the Harry Potter movies, maybe the authorities do not need to worry that much. At least not yet.

CONCLUSION: KADAN AND KARAOKE OR COMMUNISM?

The dramatic changes that have swept through the communist world since 1989 have made it abundantly clear that political scientists are not very good at predicting concrete events. This does not mean, however, that we cannot at least anticipate broad future trends.

In this sense, China provides us with a good illustration of the reasons most Marxist-Leninist regimes collapsed and the few remaining ones face uncertain futures. The pressures from an ever more sophisticated and impatient population and these countries' increasing incorporation in global economic and cultural life weakened all communist states. Some, like the Soviet Union, collapsed in part because the CPSU proved unwilling or unable to apply enough force to stay in power. In China, however, repression has helped keep the CCP in power, at least for now.

But the genie probably cannot be kept in the bottle forever. The Tiananmen Square crackdown in 1989 showed that desperate leaders can still suppress dissident movements, even ones with widespread mass and elite support. Nevertheless, it seems highly unlikely that such movements can be suppressed indefinitely. In part, this reflects the social changes that are leading to a more educated, sophisticated, and ultimately demanding population.

The "thumbs" of the command economies in the few remaining communist countries are also imperiled. Again, we do not know precisely what their economic future holds. No one knows if socialist goals of equality, justice, and dignity can be attained using a market-based economy. No one knows either how far communist elites are willing to go in sacrificing their political and economic power in exchange for economic growth. All we can conclude—and it is a very important conclusion—is that they will have to move away from thumbs and toward "fingers," a move that will have political as well as economic repercussions sooner rather than later.

As with protest from below, the obsolescence of command economies has two sources. First, domestic changes have eroded the ways in which central planning worked in the previous stages of development. Second, and in the long run more important, the global economy has had an inescapable impact on these systems. For good or ill, as long as they retain centralized planning, the communist regimes are simply not going to be competitive in the world marketplace.

Again, communist regimes such as the one in China may hang on to power for some years to come. If they do, they will have to be very different from the powerful ones that hostile analysts once called totalitarian. We could continue to examine more statistics and other "hard" evidence that illustrate these points. However, in closing, it might make more sense to consider two trends, one from the mid-1990s and one from today.

The first is a 1990 report on current fads. One of them was the Kadan (the closest Chinese equivalent of Cardin) Model Training School. Apparently, the school had a long waiting list of young people willing to pay the princely sum of forty-two dollars a semester to strive for a new version of the Chinese dream: wealth and fame. Such private training schools that teach everything from modeling to accounting to foreign languages have sprung up around the country to meet the demands of a growing generation of young people who are aware of the outside world and want to be a part of it. The modeling schools, of course, have a unique Chinese twist: Both men and women stagger around trying to learn how to walk in high heels. Still, all the aspiring models shared a common goal that one male student expressed well: "I came because I have a dream. I love this. I would love to travel around the world and be the best model of the century."[11]

---

[11]James Steingold. "China in High Heels: A Wobbly School for Models," *New York Times*, August 8, 1990, A5.

For good or ill, the Kadan school seems to be long gone. Today, the closest equivalent is the nationwide explosion in the number of karaoke bars. Almost every major hotel and even mid-sized city has one. They are places where hard-driving businessmen (rarely women) get together after work. They are shown into a room reserved for them with a "hostess" who plies them with drinks. After a while, they start singing songs from Taiwan and force their Western visitors to do the same for top forty hits from their own countries. Of course, the hostesses are available for other activities for an additional price.

It is not clear how important either Kadan was or karaoke is now. The question we leave you with is simple. Can a regime that has allowed its citizens this much leeway outside the political arena retain its lock on those questions that are the real subject of this book?

Looking FORWARD

IN PART 3, we have seen two countries in which the stakes of politics are dramatically higher than in the industrialized democracies.

We are about to shift gears again and consider what most political scientists now call the Global South. As we will see in the next chapter, no term does a good job of describing the mostly poor counties of Latin America, Africa, and Asia, many of which only gained independence since World War II.

We will examine a part of the world that has as many as four billion residents (if you include China), most of which have weak states and ethnic conflict to go along with poverty.

Some, often called the BRICS, are beginning to make their influence felt in global politics because of their size and their mostly newfound wealth. Most, however, continue to struggle for reasons that will begin to become clear in the next chapter.

Key Terms

Concepts
cadre
campaign
capitalist roader
Confucianism
cult of personality
democratic centralism
extraterritoriality
faction
four modernizations
mass line
nomenklatura
red hat
unit
warlord

People
Chen Duxiu
Chiang Kai-shek

Deng Xiaoping
Fang Lizhi
Hu Jintao
Jiang Qing
Jiang Zemin
Lin Biao
Liu Shaoqi
Mao Zedong
Sun Yat-sen
Wei Jingsheng
Zhou Enlai
Xi Jinping

Acronyms
CAC
CCP
CMC
KMT
PLA

PRC
SEZ

Organizations, Places, and Events
Central Advisory Committee (CAC)
Central Committee
Central Military Commission (CMC)
Chinese Communist Party (CCP)
Cultural Revolution
Democracy Movement
Democracy Wall
Falun Gong
Gang of Four
Great Leap Forward

Hundred Flowers Campaign
Kuomintang (KMT)
Long March
May Fourth Movement
Nationalist Party
People's Liberation Army (PLA)
People's Republic of China (PRC)
Politburo
Red Guard
red hat
red versus expert
Sino-Soviet split
special economic zone (SEZ)
Standing Committee
Tiananmen Square

🌐 Useful Websites

The Internet itself in China is controversial because the Chinese authorities have tried to block access to overseas sites that carry material critical of the PRC. That is becoming increasingly difficult as the number of regular Internet users approaches 10 percent of the adult population and enterprising Web surfers find ways to get around the firewalls the CCP's censors create. The government itself has created a portal with links to state agencies that have English language sites.

www.china.org.cn/english

There are also a number of non-Chinese portals that maintain good resources on Chinese politics and society, including links to other good sites. The University of Heidelberg in Germany continues to operate the Virtual Library site on China. London's Royal Society for International Affairs (Chatham House) not only has links but reports emanating from its highly respected projects on China. Finally, Professor William Joseph of Wellesley College has one of the largest and most frequently updated sites on China.

sun.sino.uni-heidelberg.de/e-index.html

www.chathamhouse.org.uk/research/asia/current _projects/china_project/

http://www.wellesley.edu/Polisci/wj/chinesepolitics/

Finally, there are some far more specialized sites. The Chinese Leadership Monitor publishes regular reports and updates on the country's elite. Chinese Military Power does the same for national security issues.

www.hoover.org/publications/clm

www.comw.org/cmp/

Further Reading

Blecher, Marc. *China Against the Tides: Restructuring Through Revolution, Radicalism, and Reform.* London: Pinter, 1997. The best recent overview of Chinese politics since the revolution, written by one of the few scholars who is still even somewhat sympathetic to socialism and Mao Zedong.

Gifford, Rob. *China Road: A Journey into the Future of a Rising Power.* New York: Random House, 2007. The best recent book on change in China; written to appeal to a general audience.

Gilley, Brian. *Tiger on the Brink: Jiang Zemin and China's New Elite.* Berkeley: University of California Press, 1998. A biography of the former Chinese leader; also a first-rate analysis of Chinese politics in the post-Deng era.

Lampton, David. *Same Bed Different Dreams: Managing U.S.-China Relations 1989–2000.* Berkeley: University of California Press, 2001. Although focused on foreign policy, a valuable resource on Chinese domestic politics as well.

Lee, Jennifer 8. *The Fortune Cookie Chronicles.* New York: 12 Books, 2008. Yes 8 is really her middle name. This is a book about Chinese and Chinese-American food, but I use it to help students take a step back from fortune cookies and General Tso's chicken (neither are Chinese) and have fun look at some of the most important issues in Chinese culture.

Lieberthal, Kenneth. *Governing China: From Revolution Through Reform.* New York: Norton, 1995. A comprehensive overview of Chinese politics that is especially good at illuminating the informal power relations, which may well be more important than the formal rules and procedures.

Lifton, Robert Jay. *Revolutionary Immortality: Mao Tsetung and the Chinese Cultural Revolution.* New York: Norton, 1976. A biography of Mao by this generation's leading psychological analyst of political affairs.

Mcgregor, Richard. *The Party.* New York: Harper-Collins, 2010. The best recent book on the CCP, which was written by an Australian journalist who has spent years in China.

Nathan, Andrew. *China's Transition.* New York: Columbia University Press, 1997. Mostly a collection of essays by an American academic who has long criticized the CCP for its human rights record. Unlike Blecher's book, it is quite hostile to the Beijing regime.

Qiu Xialong. *The Mao Case.* New York: St. Martins, 2009. The most recent of a series of mystery novels that are highly political and fun.

Saich, Tony. *Governance in China.* London: Palgrave, 2004. The best new overview of Chinese politics, including many of the author's personal experiences over the last thirty years.

Snow, Edgar. *Red Star over China.* New York: Random House, 1938. The best account of the early years of the revolution, written by an American who spent much of that period with the CCP and Mao.

Zhao Ziyang, Bao Pu, Renee Chiang, and Adi Ignatius. *Prisoner of the State: The Secret Journal of Premier Zhao Ziyang.* New York: Simon and Schuster, 2009. The best "insider" account of the CCP decision to repress the Tiananmen decisions based on the diaries of the leading reformist of the time.

The Global South

REUTERS/Desmond Boylan

CHAPTER 11

The Global South

THE GLOBAL SOUTH

Look for a moment at either the basic table that begins this chapter or the one on the inside front cover of the book. The one here contrasts what the United Nations considers the least developed countries with the most affluent ones. The one on the inside cover breaks similar data from the World Bank down by country. The two tables are based on slightly different ways of gathering and calculating the data, hence the slight differences in the two.

Both inexorably lead to the same conclusion. No other part of the world is in such deep trouble.

Poverty

As we will see in the next section, there is no commonly accepted name for the countries covered in Part 4—including the one we will use, **Global South**—let alone a consensus on how to analyze data about them. Nonetheless, one fact screams out at us from either of these tables. Another requires a little more digging.

The first is the relative poverty of the least developed countries. The Human Development Index is based on average income, years of schooling, and life expectancy. We think we would all agree that they would have to be at least a part of any definition of development.

THE BASICS

Contrasts Between the Richest and Poorest Countries

	LIFE EXPECTANCY (YEARS)	AVERAGE YEARS OF SCHOOLING (%)	GROSS DOMESTIC PRODUCT PER CAPITA (GNP)	HDI SCORE[a]
Lowest	57	3.5	1,393	0.39
Highest	83	11/3	37,225	0.87

[a]HDI, Human Development Index, is a statistical measure converting the information from the first three columns in the table to ranges from 0 (least developed) to 1 (most developed).

Source: United Nations Development Program, *Human Development Report: 2010*. http://hdr.undp.org/. Accessed June 2, 2011)

Looking BACKWARD

IN PART 3, we argued that the political stakes are much higher in the current and former communist countries than in the established democracies. We hope we made that case.

In Chapter 8, we also hinted at the fact the countries and concepts in Part 4 will show us parts of the world in which the stakes are higher yet. Over 140 countries could be included in Part 4, so it is impossible for any five of them to reflect them all. However, as we will see, the stakes are far higher than we saw in Part 3.

These countries, too, are struggling to find their way in an increasingly globalizing world. Most are also having trouble establishing and sustaining a democracy.

But we will add four themes that are far more important than in any of the countries we could have included in Part 2. First, with but a few exceptions, these countries are much poorer and much more devastated by problems they can't address because they lack the resources. For perhaps the most tragic example, see the table and discussion of HIV/AIDS that follows. Second, they have been wracked by conflict. Much of it is ethnic, linguistic, religious, or racial in origin. Those issues are far harder to reach compromises on than even the budget debate that is taking a terrible toll on the United States as we write. Third, almost all of these countries were subject to colonial rule and are still more deeply influenced by the North than anything we have seen, something former Tanzanian president Nyerere humorously refers to in the passage that begins this chapter. Finally, we will have to consider the idea of a failed state that cannot carry out such basic functions as maintaining law and order. To be sure, Russia and China had periods in which the state lost much of its capacity to govern. And none of the countries we will see here are "classic" failed states, although Mexico may become one because of the violence caused by its drug cartels.

First and foremost is poverty. Here, the most striking difference is in income. In the richest countries, people make almost 30 times as much as their fellow humans. To cite but two examples of countries covered in this book and which are neither the richest or the poorest in the world, the accounting methods the UN uses show that the United States has a GNP per capita of over $47,000 while the average Nigerian makes little more than $1,000. The World Bank uses Purchasing Power Party as its accounting tool. It is rapidly becoming the norm and tends to shrink the differences because many goods (purchasing power) are actually cheaper in the Global South. Still, the differences are enormous. The same is true if you use the other two indicators in the HDI. People in the North have a lot more education and live a lot longer than those in the South.

The second statistic is not shown in the basic data table in this chapter for the simple reason that the UN didn't collect it. Nonetheless, the fact of the matter is that most of the world's people live in what all observers agree are less developed countries. That figure is about three-fifths of the world's population if one does not include China but leaps to four in five if one does.

To be sure there are the BRICS countries or emerging markets that are both large and have been able to grow at a rapid rate for a generation or so. They are also clamoring for a place among the world's decision makers, whether in the G-20 or demanding to have leader of either the World Bank or International Monetary Fund come from one of them. The term BRIC (without the "s") was coined by bankers at Goldman-Sachs to cover Brazil, Russia, India, and China. Some pundits have added South Africa to the list. As we saw in Chapter 9, Russia may or may not belong. Still, these are all countries that have made tremendous economic and political strides.

But—and this is a huge but—they are still predominantly poor. We will see in the chapter on India, at least 300 million people live in absolute poverty, which means they are too poor to buy adequate food, in a country that now has a middle class that probably numbers more than 100 million.

The reality of life for the average resident of any of the countries covered in Part 4 is bleak. Just about half of the world's population survives on about $2 a day. No cell phone. No cable TV. Often no electricity. Or running water.

Or indoor plumbing. And the economic crisis of the last few years has made things worse. As we will see throughout the rest of this book, most of the countries we will be covering are so poor and so dependent on wealthier ones for their economic well being that it could not be otherwise. Take, for instance, this statement from MercyCorps, one of the leading **nongovernmental organizations (NGOs)** that provides humanitarian and development aid.

> **For families in places like the Central African Republic and Indonesia, rising prices for things like food and fuel can be catastrophic. It's difficult for most of us to imagine: When we're asked to pay more at the grocery store, it's hard for us—but for those living on just $1 a day, it can be a matter of life and death.** (www.mercycorps.org)

But for these countries, poverty is just the tip of the iceberg. What we will see are multiple crises, all of which make the stakes of political life for the people living in the world's poorest countries far higher than what we saw in either Parts 2 or 3.

In Chapter 5 on France, we used the term *syndrome* to describe the interrelated set of political and other problems that led to the collapse of the Third and Fourth Republics. For the Global South, using the term *syndrome* requires discussing issues that stretch beyond the political and, in fact, cover all of society.

The crisis of the last few years has only made a difficult situation worse. Because we will be discussing almost 150 countries in this part of the book, there is far more diversity in what we will cover in Part 4 than in Parts 2 or 3. Still, with but a few exceptions (including India, which is the focus of the next chapter), the vulnerability of the Global South have made the impact of the crisis far worse than anything we have seen so far.

In fact, it may be the case that politics is not the most important issue on which we should focus. To sum up the data in the basic table in a different and more down to earth way, if the West catches a cold, the Third World catches pneumonia.

The journalist Thomas Friedman titled his recent book *Hot, Flat, and Crowded.* Friedman has built his career writing mostly about the positive aspects of globalization. This time, he looks at its downside:

- *Hot.* Global warming and climate change in genera will almost certainly affect us all. The impact is somewhat harder to predict for the countries in the South, this time including Australia and New Zealand. Some island countries could end up largely under water. The desertification that has plagued central Africa for decades could well accelerate. Unpredictable epidemics related to climate change will certainly hit the rest of the South harder than anywhere else.

- *Flat.* Friedman is known for writing about how "flat" the world has become. It is not flatter physically, of course. It *is* "flatter" in terms of the speed at which international commerce is growing and making our world ever more interconnected. As we will see, with

A refugee camp in Darfur.

AP Images

but few exceptions, **globalization** is making the gap between rich and poor countries wider, not narrower.

■ *Crowded.* Population growth is one of the most serious problems confronting the South. In the richest countries covered in the basics table, the birth rate is well under two, which means that their population would decline without immigration. In some countries in the Global South, the population growth rate is as high as 4 percent per year, which means that the number of people there would double in about a generation. The population crisis is magnified by the fact that most countries have seen massive migration to their cities by people who are desperate for work. Mumbai in India, Mexico City, and Lagos in Nigeria all have populations in excess of 15 million. Add to that the up to 40 million people who flee conflict each year and end up in refugee camps, and it is hard *not* to see that "crowded" can be a political time bomb.

Although the most widely recognized authorities talk about the ostensibly nonpolitical issues among what Paul Collier calls "the bottom billion," politics is part of the syndrome in three ways.

First, as Friedman suggests with "crowdedness," the social and economic issues discussed so far can be a conflict waiting to erupt. They, in turn, are made potentially even more dangerous by the fact that all of the countries included in our discussion and almost all of the others we could have included are faced with what we call **identity**-based conflicts that pit people of different racial, religious, linguistic, and ethnic backgrounds against each.

Second, it should come as no surprise given what we have seen so far that most of these countries have weak or even failing states. The weakest of all, such as Sudan or Somalia, cannot assure basic governance outside the major urban areas and not always there. Even in relatively well-off countries, such as Mexico, national governments lack the human and economic resources needed to define and implement public policy, something we are seeing today in the, so far, vain attempt by the Mexican government to confront its country's drug cartels.

Third, we are beginning to learn about the status of women in these countries. In their pathbreaking book, *Half the Sky*, Nicholas Kristof and Sheryl WuDunn discuss the plight of women and girls who have either been enslaved or turned into sex workers. Put simply, most women in the Global South earn even less than the $2 a day that is the regional norm.

The picture has been quite depressing. However, the election of Barack Obama was met with tremendous enthusiasm throughout the Third World. There were huge rallies on election night in his father's home country of Kenya. At least six candidates for local office in Brazil changed their name to Barack Obama after he was nominated in an attempt to enhance their appeal. All seem to have lost. To be fair, the George W. Bush administration had significantly expanded foreign aid funding by the United States but people throughout the Global South understood that the new administration would be much more sympathetic to all of their needs. Two years into his term, it is too early to tell how much Obama will be able to accomplish given all the other issues on his agenda. However, the fact that he unexpectedly won the Nobel Peace Prize just as we were finishing the last edition of this book may augur good things to come.

The Arab Spring

In the first half of 2011, the world was shocked by a series of protests in the Middle East and North Africa. The so-called Arab Spring is still going on as we write. And none of the countries we will focus on are in the affected region. Nonetheless, because it was so surprising and in some ways so violent, it is worth exploring briefly to give us all a frame of reference for the rest of Part 4.

The countries embroiled by the Arab Spring are not necessarily among the poorest. Bahrain and Libya, for instance, are among the world's leading oil exporters, although others (Egypt, Tunisia, Yemen, and Syria) do not have a significant domestic petrochemical industry.

The one common denominator they shared was at least thirty years of rule by a single dictator (in Syria, a dictator and his son) who came to power in the first place through mechanisms that no one could confuse with democracy. Start with two quite different examples.

In Egypt, Hosni Mubarak (1928–) became president following the assassination of his predecessor, Anwar Sadat, in 1981. Muslim extremists who rejected his peace agreement with Israel had killed Sadat. At least some of the assassins' colleagues ended up in al-Qaeda. Like his fellow rulers in the region, Mubarak's government was both corrupt and authoritarian. He, his family, and the rest of his entourage amassed a huge fortune, most of which was sent abroad to secret banks accounts. Mubarak often talked about democratization, but in fact cracked down hard on the Muslim Brotherhood and other potential Islamic dissidents. He also condoned repression of the Coptic Christian community, which makes up about 10 percent of the Egyptian population.

At first, the protests were all but completely non-violent until the police tried to suppress them. Soon, the police (long a tool of the regime) were forced to hand over law enforcement responsibilities to the far more popular military. Less than a month after the protests began, Mubarak resigned and moved to one of his villas. He has since been indicted for the murder of political prisoners and others. The 83 year old former president is standing trial.

Muammar al-Qadaffi (his name is rendered in English in several ways—this is the one used by *The New York Times*) has been president of Libya since 1969. Qadaffi (1942–) seized power of this oil-rich country and set it on a path that turned it into a pariah for most countries covered in Part 2 and, later, Part 3. He was always one of the fiercest critics of Israel. More important for our purposes, he made Libya into one of the world's leading states condoning, if not downright supporting, terrorism. The Libyans most (in) famous act in this regard was the 1988 bombing of Pan Am Flight 103 over Lockerbie, Scotland. Qadaffi ended up in the international community's "better" graces in recent years because the regime seemed to moderate and everyone coveted Libya's oil. Nonetheless, by late 2010, many Libyans had had enough of the aging dictator. Protests broke out in early 2011 primarily in the regions least under the control of Qadaffi's tribe/ethnic group. The protests soon turned into a civil war with NATO launching air strikes to help force Qadaffi out of office or out of the country. As of this writing, it is by no means clear whether he will be able to hold on or if the dissidents can force him out.

Elsewhere, the protests were no less brutal, even if their leaders might have been less colorful. Only in Tunisia can we say that the upheaval might be close to over. Still, that country lacks a viable permanent government and is often caught up with the flow of refugees trying to flee Libya. In oil-rich Bahrain, protests led by the Shi'ite majority continue to threaten the Sunni led monarchy (we will distinguish between Shi'ites and Sunnis in both Chapters 13 and 14). In Yemen, peaceful protests seem to be turning into a civil war. Just before we finished writing, the longtime ruler of the Arab world's poorest country, Ali Abdullah Saleh, was wounded in the first direct attack on his palace. He went to Saudi Arabia "for medical attention," and it is by no means certain if he will ever return to his country.

We know the least about the movement in Syria where the regime led by Bashar al-Assad has banned all foreign journalists from coming to the country to report. All the signs are that at least 1,000 people were killed by the police and army in the first 5 months of 2011.

We will not return to the Arab Spring until the conclusion of the book in Chapter 17. For now, it is enough to see that non-democratic and often illegitimate rule, poverty, the uneven distribution of income and wealth, and identity-based differences can turn seemingly stable countries into powder kegs virtually over night.

What's In a Name

It's not just the people in the Global South who can't agree. Academics, who argue about almost everything, can't even agree on what to call this part of the world. Sometimes debates among academics help clarify matters; sometimes they do not. Debates over what to call the Global South have been particularly intense but *not* particularly helpful.

Over the years, each of the following terms has been in vogue: *developing, underdeveloped, less developed, Third World*, and *the Global South*. All were tried as part of the search for a term that would convey the plight of most of these countries in a nonpejorative manner.

Although it is currently out of favor, the term the *Third World* may be the easiest to understand at this point. It was coined more than a half-century ago by a French analyst who wished to distinguish the countries shaking off colonial rule from the Western democracies (First World) and the members of the Soviet bloc (Second World).

The Global South is currently in vogue and we will use that term most of the time. We will use some of the other labels from time to time as well in order to make the prose flow more smoothly.

THINKING ABOUT THE GLOBAL SOUTH

It is easy to convince students in countries like the United States that they should understand politics in other liberal democracies because doing so can tell them a lot about their own state and its institutions, values, and problems. At first glance, it is less obvious why we should worry about the rest of the world because countries like Nigeria and so many others have so little in common with the West.

In fact, the Global South is vitally important to us all. As we will see in more detail in the final chapter, we live in an interdependent world in which everything that happens affects everyone and everything else. Nowhere is this easier to see than in the speed with which the United States and its allies launched massive attacks against Afghanistan in the weeks following the 9/11 terrorism attacks.

But there is another, perhaps more important, reason. To a degree few of us in the West want to acknowledge, the South has also been a place where the rich countries exported their problems and waged their battles. It was there that Europeans and Americans established most of their colonies. More recently, almost all the wars during the Cold War and post–Cold War periods have occurred in Asia, Africa, or Latin America, often as a product of First and Second World disputes.

The events of 9/11 also drove home the fact that many of these conflicts have a direct impact on life in Europe and North America. This is true only in part because the North is subject to attack by terrorists today and may also be vulnerable to attacks by more conventional forces tomorrow.

Even before 9/11, the South was important because we in the North are dependent on it. Most of our natural resources and more and more of our relatively unsophisticated manufactured goods come from there. As the **Organization of Petroleum Exporting Countries (OPEC)** oil embargo of 1973–74 and the periodic oil price shocks since then have shown, when Southern commodity producers are able to band together, they can wreak havoc on Northern economies.

In short, we ignore the Global South at our peril. The failure to take its problems seriously has kept us from seeing two seemingly contradictory trends that together comprise a single dilemma. First, we have been slow to acknowledge the role of the rich and powerful countries in creating and sustaining the economic and political woes in the South. Second, we have been even more reluctant to come to grips with the fact that few countries in the Global South can solve their problems without significant support from the North.

Key Concepts and Questions

As was the case in Chapter 8, we will be dramatic shifting intellectual gears here. We will be able to use the same basic framework developed in Figure 1.1 in the next five chapters. However, as this discussion has already suggested, we will have to go further and ask four more questions that help us understand why so many Southern countries face such serious difficulties:

- Why are global forces so much more influential there than in the rest of the world and how do they contribute to poverty? This starts with the legacy of imperialism but continues to this day even though most of the Global South has been independent for more than a half century. While political independence is the rule rather than the exception in all but a tiny group of tiny places that are still under colonial rule, governments in the Global South are less and less masters of their own destinies, less and less able to enact and implement their own policies.

- Why have most of them failed to develop? That includes examining the strategies that have been tried and found wanting and other new ones that show some promise in pulling the South out of poverty.

- Why are so many of these countries deeply divided? We have used terms such as identity, ethnicity, language, race, and tribal a bit too loosely so far. They are better illustrated with concrete examples, which means we will only reach somewhat definitive answers in the concluding chapter.

- Why are many of their states weak if not failed? Like so much included in Part 4, "failed state" is a loaded term. We lack a good definition of what it means, but it will become clear sooner rather than later that much of the South is closer to the failed than to the successful end of any spectrum measure of state effectiveness we might consider using.

There is another question lurking below the surface that affects an author more than a reader: How can we accurately represent the diversity in well over 140 countries? For example, some of these countries are so poor that any discussion of their political or economic conditions will bring tears to the eyes of even the most dispassionate observer. Others, especially the BRICS, have made tremendous strides in recent years and are as well off as Spain or Portugal was a generation ago.

The Basics Again

Although few of these countries are going through the wrenching changes we saw in Russia, the stakes of politics are, if anything, higher because of their poverty, the impact of globalization, weak states, environmental threats, and identity-based conflict. We have touched on most of these in the introduction to this chapter, but it is worth spending a little more time on a more detailed examination of some of them.

Poverty

Whatever term one chooses to call it, most of the definitions and lists of countries in the Global South overlap significantly because they all have one key criterion in common: poverty. The Global South includes all of the world's poorest states. As the map at the beginning of this chapter shows, it covers all of Africa and Latin America and much of South and Southeast Asia. GNP per capita in the richest countries is almost thirty times larger than in the poorest, which also have almost four times as many people.

What does that mean tangibly in people's everyday lives? The richest countries consume nearly twenty times more energy than the poorest. In the United States, only about 6 out of every 1,000 babies die in infancy (and it only ranks thirty-third from the top). For the world as a whole, that number is between 42 and 49 out of 1,000 depending on whose statistics you use. Angola has the worst infant mortality rate—180 out of 1,000. In other words, 18 percent of the babies born in that country will not live to age one.

The average adult in Angola cannot expect to celebrate his or her fortieth birthday. Most Americans will reach eighty. Most American children today will reach 100. In the Global South as a whole, the lack of access to safe drinking water is the most frequent—and avoidable—cause of death for more than forty thousand children daily. The United States does not even bother gathering this statistic for its population.

There is one doctor for every 500 Americans, as opposed to one for every 25,000 people in Freetown, Sierra Leone's capital city. In the poorest regions, there is one doctor for every 285,000 people.

As is the case with almost every indicator of social and economic well-being, Africans face the most appalling medical conditions. Indeed, as Table 11.1 shows, the AIDS epidemic is more widespread in Africa than anywhere else. Of the estimated 40 million people infected with HIV worldwide, fully 25 million live in sub-Saharan Africa. Between 1981 and 2003, 12 million children in that part of the world were orphaned because they lost both of their parents to AIDS. Because governments and people there cannot afford the "cocktails" of antiretroviral drugs that can keep many patients with HIV alive. Even though the cost of the generic versions of them is down to less than $300 a year in most parts of the world, death rates dwarf those in any other region because even that sum exceeds what the countries where most AIDS victims live can afford.

In Africa and Asia, less than half of the people can read and write. Nonetheless, most of these countries have to cope with a "brain drain" because highly educated young people emigrate to Europe and North America because of the widespread unemployment among university graduates and others at home.

It is not just in the poorest Third World countries that people suffer. In South Korea and Brazil the infant mortality rate is, respectively, three and six times that of the United States. In each of these countries, only three-fourths of the people have access to safe water and there are only about one-third as many physicians on a per capita basis as in Europe and the United States.

There is no commonly agreed-on measure of the level of a country's wealth or development. GNP, for example,

has properly been criticized for missing the noneconomic side of a country's quality of life. This chapter's basic table, therefore, presents the scores on the UNDP's Human Development Index (HDI), which combines data on GNP with those on literacy and life expectancy. The fact remains, however, that the same depressing picture of the South emerges no matter which of the available indices we choose.

In the Global South, almost 70 percent of the rural population lives below the poverty line. For the region as a whole, more than a third of the rural population does not get enough to eat. And the number of poor people in the countryside has increased by 40 percent over the past quarter century.

The expansion of world trade has brought with it unprecedented levels of debt. At the height of the international **debt crisis** in the 1980s and 1990s, Argentina owed Northern banks and governments over $60 billion. For Brazil and Mexico, that figure was well over $100 billion. At the end of the 1990s, the Third World owed Northern banks, governments, and international financial institutions more than $2.8 trillion or more than $400 per person. In the mid-1990s countries as different as Brazil, Cameroon, Guatemala, India, Kenya, and Madagascar all paid more in interest on their loans than they did on social services.

To make matters even worse, the odds of catching up with the advanced countries are low—at best. Although the newly industrializing countries and some others have done quite well in recent years, per capita GNP in all the low- and middle-income countries is less than 10 percent of that in those covered in Part 2. And, perhaps most depressing of all, because the poorest and richest countries both grew at a rate of 2.4 percent per year during the 1990s, the gap between them did not narrow at all. Things have improved a bit since then, but the economic crisis seems likely to widen the gap between rich and poor at least in the short term.

They are also deeply in debt. Table 11.2 shows the share of GNP that countries owed to foreign banks, governments, and international financial institutions during the years when things were at their worst. They have improved some, but American, Canadian, and British readers will note just

TABLE 11.1 Estimated HIV/AIDS Cases and Deaths, 2007

REGION	PEOPLE LIVING WITH HIV/AIDS	PEOPLE NEWLY INFECTED	ADULT PREVALENCE (IN %)	ADULT DEATHS
Sub-Saharan Africa	22.0 million	1.9 million	5.0	1.5 million
North Africa and Middle East	380,000	40,000	0.3	27,000
Asia	5 million	380,000	0.3	380,000
Oceania	74,000	13,00	0.4	1,000
Latin America	1.7 million	140,000	0.5	63,000
Caribbean	230,000	20,000	1.1	14,000
East Europe and Central Asia	1.5 million	110,000	0.8	858,000
North America, Western and Central Europe	2 million	81,000	0.4	31,000

Source: www.avert.org/worldstats. Accessed July 2009

TABLE 11.2 Debt as a Proportion of Gross National Product

REGION	1981 (%)	1991 (%)	1998 (%)
Sub-Saharan Africa	28.6	107.9	71.8
East Asia and Pacific	16.9	28.2	84.8
South Asia	17.0	35.6	29.0
Middle East and North Africa	31.0	58.8	34.7
Latin America and Caribbean	35.5	41.3	69.0

Source: Data for 1981 and 1991 adapted from R. J. Barry Jones, *Globalization and Interdependence in the International Political Economy* (London: Pinter, 1995), 159. Data for 1998 from World Bank, *World Development Report, 2000*, www.worldbank.org, accessed Nov. 9, 2001.

how low our respective indebtedness is despite the intensity of our domestic debates, not to mention our ability to repay them.

Most lack anything approaching a diversified economy. They tend, instead, to rely on the export of a few primary commodities, such as oil in Iraq and Nigeria, or coffee and cotton in Nicaragua. Often, prices for these commodities fluctuate. When they fall sharply, there is little hard currency available to pay for food, manufactured goods, or other needed imports. Northern banks and companies refuse to accept money issued by these countries because it is not readily convertible into Northern currencies, they have to use dollars, euros, yen, and pounds to pay for those imports.

Environmental Threats

The rapidly growing population of the Global South magnifies the difficulties it faces. The population in the poorest countries is increasing at three-and-a-half times the rate in the richest ones. Even this figure underestimates the problem because population growth is exponential; it builds on itself like compound interest on a savings account. At 0.6 percent, it will take 120 years for the population of the richest countries to double, a rate they can easily absorb given projected rates of economic growth. At 2 percent, which is the norm in the poorest countries, it will take about 35 years for the population to double. In Sierra Leone, where the annual increase tops 4 percent, it will not even take a generation. Egypt, with its already overstretched economy and ecosystem, adds a million people to its population every nine months.

Poverty and population growth are combining to produce an ecological time bomb. Population growth puts demands on most environments that after centuries of Northern influence can often provide little more than a marginal existence. Poverty, in turn, has made people desperate, willing to trade their environmental future for food for themselves and their families today. Thus, many—perhaps most—of the people who slash and burn the trees in the Amazon rain forests are peasants who can provide for their families only by farming that land. In Asia and Africa, about 15 percent of the land has been severely damaged. Everywhere, development is putting marginally adequate water supplies and irrigation systems at risk. In short, throughout the Third World, human action is threatening what environmentalists call the **carrying capacity** of the land.

Identity and Conflict

These problems have been compounded by racial, linguistic, ethnic, and religious conflict. This is especially true in Africa and Asia, where the colonial powers paid little or no attention to traditional alignments when they drew boundaries during the nineteenth century, most of which are still in effect. This is less true in the Americas, though almost all those countries have significant minorities of "Indians" and people of African descent.

When political scientists started studying the Global South—or whatever we choose to call it—in the 1950s, most of them assumed that the spread of the mass media and Western culture would gradually erode people's attachment to what were then viewed as "primitive" identities. They were wrong. If anything, these identities have become much more important, both in and of themselves, and as a source of conflict within and between countries. There will be plenty of examples of identity-based conflict to follow, but none rival the genocide in Rwanda.

On April 6, 1994, an airplane carrying the presidents of Rwanda and Burundi was shot down, killing all aboard. This incident set off waves of violence between the majority Hutu and minority Tutsi populations in both countries, which Philip Gourevitch chillingly describes in the opening of his award-winning book on the genocide that followed:

> **Decimation means the killing of every tenth person in a population and in the spring and early summer of 1994 a program of massacres decimated the Republic of Rwanda. Although the killing was low-tech—performed largely by machete—it was carried out at dazzling speed; of an original population of about seven and a half million, at least eight hundred thousand were killed in just a hundred days. Rwandans often speak of a million deaths, and they may be right. The dead of Rwanda accumulated at nearly three times the rate of Jewish dead during the Holocaust. It was the most efficient mass killing since the atomic bombings of Hiroshima and Nagasaki.[1]**

Rwanda is not alone. At any time, there are twenty to forty wars being fought in the Global South, almost all of which have ethnic origins. That has even become at least partially true for the wars the United States began for other reasons in Iraq and Afghanistan since 9/11. Although few societies have had to deal with a conflict anywhere near as bloody as that in Rwanda, all are bitter and intense. In this decade, the most violent examples have been in Darfur and the Democratic Republic of the Congo where upward of 10 percent of their populations have been forced to flee and as many as 5 percent have been killed in the most affected regions.

Globalization

Yet another defining characteristic of the South is the role global forces continue to play in shaping what citizens and leaders alike can do. As this book's subtitle suggests,

---

[1]Philip Gourevitch, *We Wish to Inform You That Tomorrow We Will Be Killed with Our Families: Stories from Rwanda* (New York: Farrar, Straus and Giroux, 1998), frontispiece.

The crushed skull of a genocide victim is laid into one of the many mass graves to be found in Rwanda ... and in other places where ethnic conflict has disrupted the peace in the Third World.

global forces are limiting states' ability to maneuver. This is especially true of the Third World for the reasons former Tanzanian president Julius Nyerere pithily laid out in the sentence that begins this chapter. It may be an exaggeration to say that decisions made in Washington, D.C., are more important to Tanzanians than those made in Dar es Salaam, their capital city. Tanzania *is* a sovereign country that passes its own laws, issues its own decrees, and reaches its own judicial decisions. However, what happens in places like Tanzania is largely determined elsewhere—sometimes by force, sometimes as a result of subtle and often unintended consequences of actions by power holders in our increasingly interdependent world.

These relationships are hard to document, and their impact varies from country to country and from time to time. Nonetheless, they cannot be ignored, however incomplete our understanding of them may be. Whether they like it or not, almost all countries in the Global South are now being integrated into the world's economic and cultural systems. However, they are not being brought in as equals. The most obvious of these links are economic. In the section on public policy later in the chapter, we will explore how their

governments try to cope with global economic forces. Here, we will look only at the common difficulties most of them face that also extend far beyond the economy.

Global links antedate colonialism, but the imperial ones are most important for our purposes because they went a long way toward shaping today's political arrangements. Formal colonialism is long gone. However, the former colonial powers still have considerable economic leverage. In the 1970s and 1980s, radical social scientists popularized the idea of **dependency** to describe a situation in which the legal ties of colonialism gave way to informal mechanisms of economic control. Such ideas are far less popular in academic and political circles today than they were a generation ago. The shifting tides of political fashion, however, have not changed the reality of economic weakness in the South and economic strength in the North.

Multinational corporations (MNCs) headquartered in the North still dominate the more modern sectors of the economy (see Table 11.3). Such companies have always repatriated the bulk of their profits back to their home countries. In recent years, they have tended to relocate operations that require the lowest-skilled labor and produce the

If the World Had 100 People

The World Game was an educational organization that helped people understand what it means to live in an interdependent world. Its college version involved laying a massive map of the world on a gymnasium floor on which 100 people make some basic decisions about allocating the world's natural and human resources. The basic characteristics of these 100 people reflect current global demographic trends:

- 51 are female
- 57 are Asians
- 14 are from the Western Hemisphere
- 70 are non-white
- 30 are Christian
- 70 are illiterate
- 50 suffer from malnutrition
- 80 live in substandard housing
- 6, all from the United States, own half the wealth
- One has a college education
- None owns a computer

Unfortunately, the World Game stopped updating any of its projects in 1999. Therefore the data shown here are somewhat dated. For instance, as many as two people out of the one hundred would now have a computer. But the stark contrasts remain.

TABLE 11.3 The Leading Multinational Corporations by Country of Origin

COUNTRY	NUMBER OF MULTINATIONAL CORPORATIONS
United States	18
China	4
Japan	4
Germany	5
France	6
Great Britain	4
Italy	2
Switzerland	1
South Korea	3

Source: Adapted from "The Fortune Global Five Hundred: The World's Largest Corporations," *Fortune*, http://money.cnn.com/magazines/fortune/global500/2009/snapshots/10461.html. (Accessed June 2, 2009).

most pollution to the South. To be sure, many of the people who work for these companies are better off than they would have been otherwise, and most MNCs do contribute to local economic growth. At the same time, however, these countries are ever more at the mercy of institutions and events outside their borders. The largest of these companies are massive, controlling resources that make them richer than many Southern countries themselves. And as the table also shows, they all have their headquarters in Western Europe, North America, Japan, China, and South Korea. MNCs are often criticized for exploiting the workers and other resources they use in the Third World. In recent years, however, many have adopted corporate responsibility policies that guarantee above-market wages, protect the local environment, and help build the local infrastructure (see, for instance, 🌐 **www.timberland.com/timberlandserve/ timberlandserve_index.jsp**).

Some countries have been able to retain a substantial degree of control especially over their natural resources. The most obvious and spectacular example of this is the OPEC cartel, which forced worldwide oil prices sharply upward in the 1970s and brought untold riches to its member nations. But OPEC is very much the exception to the rule of economic as well as political power remaining concentrated in the North.

Finally, there has been a marked shift in global economic preferences that began prior to the end of the Cold War and has accelerated since then. As was the case in the countries we saw in Parts 2 and 3, almost all Northern governments, MNCs, and independent agencies have opted for liberal, market-oriented development strategies, which the Southern countries have "had" to adopt as well. The word *had* is in quotes because no one put a gun to the head of leaders in the Global South. Nonetheless, as we will see in the country chapters that follow, they had little choice but

to open their borders to trade and investment from abroad, export goods for which there is a niche in the global market, and reduce public ownership and other forms of state intervention.

Supporters of this approach, known as **structural adjustment**, assume that in the long run these countries will find areas of comparative advantage that spark sustained growth. In the shorter term, however, these trends are widening the gaps between the rich and poor within these countries and between themselves and the countries of the more affluent North.

Just as important, though perhaps even harder to pin down, is the growing spread of a common culture, also dominated by the North, especially by the United States. Such ties have existed since colonial times, with the spread of Western religions, languages, and media figuring most prominently in what many in the Third World see as the cultural subjugation of their peoples.

The Structure of Part 4

In order to simplify things, we decided to pick five larger but otherwise representative countries from the Global South in Part 4: India, Iran, Iraq, Nigeria, and Mexico. Among other things, you will find that global issues get a lot more attention and institutional arrangements get a lot less than anything we saw in Parts 2 and 3.

THE EVOLUTION OF POLITICS IN THE GLOBAL SOUTH

Imperialism and Its Legacy

With but a handful of exceptions, today's states in Asia, Africa, and Latin America all have their most lasting roots in **imperialism**. Almost all of them were ruled by white men from Europe and North America. Even the few countries that retained their legal independence (see Chapter 10 on China or 13 on Iran) were not able to escape the corrosive effects of Northern economics and culture.

From the sixteenth through the nineteenth centuries, statesmen, entrepreneurs, missionaries, and adventurers flocked to the Americas, Africa, and most of Asia in pursuit of what the British called the three g's: God, gold, and glory. In virtually every case, the colonizers looked down on the cultures they encountered and ignored the wishes of the people they subjugated. Boundaries were drawn to suit the colonizers' wishes—boundaries that often divided existing political units and lumped traditional adversaries together.

There were three distinct phases to European colonial expansion. The first came in the sixteenth and seventeenth centuries, when the Portuguese, Spanish, Dutch, British, and French carved up the Americas. These same countries also established beachheads in Africa to support their expanding commercial networks in India and the Americas, including the infamous slave trade. The second wave came mostly in the nineteenth century, when the forts and trading posts were transformed into full-blown colonies in Africa and much of Asia. The third came after World War I when the allies divided up the remnants of the Ottoman Empire (see Table 11.4).

The colonizers were convinced that they had encountered primitive peoples. This prompted the arrogance of what Rudyard Kipling called "the white man's burden," according to which everything Western was superior while everything in the indigenous culture was inferior:

> **Take up the White Man's burden—**
> **Send forth the best ye breed—**
> **Go, bind your sons to exile**
> **To serve your captives' need;**
> **To wait, in heavy harness,**
> **On fluttered folk and wild—**
> **Your new-caught, sullen peoples,**
> **Half devil and half child.**

Given this arrogance and these cultural blinders, the imperialists undermined some highly sophisticated civilizations: the Aztecs, Incas, and Mayans in the Americas; the great kingdoms of precolonial Africa; and the various cultures of India and China. Most of the new colonies had relatively unsophisticated **subsistence economies**. They were not affluent societies, but most produced enough food and other goods to meet basic survival needs.

But the colonizers wanted their newly acquired possessions to make a profit. Therefore, they introduced commercial agriculture based on one or a handful of crops to be exported back to the home country. The Central American countries became known as "banana republics" because of

TABLE 11.4 Key Events in the History of the Third World

YEAR	EVENT
1450 on	Exploration and then colonization of the New World
1600 on	Slave trade
1776	United States declares independence
1810–30	Most of Central and South America gains independence
1867	India formally taken over by British government
1880s	"Scramble for Africa"
1919	German colonies pass to Allied powers as League of Nations mandates
Late 1940s	India and other countries gain independence
1960s	Most remaining colonies gain independence
Mid-1970s	Portuguese African empire collapses
1997	Hong Kong reverts to China

the way United Fruit and other North American companies concentrated production. Massive coffee and tea plantations were built in the Central Highlands of Kenya. Cotton was sent back to factories in Britain, destroying long-established Indian spinning and weaving industries. Most tragically of all, regions that had previously been self-supporting now had to import food and other vital commodities.

Minerals, oil, and other natural resources were added to the colonies' list of exports. Eventually there was some industrialization. Nevertheless, the general situation remained the same. Decisions about what to grow, mine, or build were mostly made in Europe and North America. Almost all of the profits from what these businesses made went back to their home countries.

Despite these common trends, there was also a great deal of variation in European and North American colonialism that largely coincided with the time a given region was taken over. In North America, the colonists gained control of relatively sparsely settled lands and then proceeded to wipe out most of the indigenous population. Where large numbers of native peoples survived, they were integrated into the newly dominant Spanish or Portuguese cultures in Central and South America. There also was, of course, the forced relocation of millions of Africans, who were brought to the Americas and Caribbean islands as slaves. During the nineteenth century, colonization primarily occurred in Africa and South Asia. There, the colonial powers encountered a more serious "numbers problem." Because there were many more Africans and Asians than Europeans, the colonial powers could not hope to govern their new conquests on their own. Therefore, they had to incorporate growing numbers of "locals" into a system of government that the British called **indirect rule**.

Independence

There were three waves of decolonization. The first began during the 1770s, when thirteen of the colonies in British North America became the United States. It spread through most of the rest of the Western Hemisphere over the next half-century. In every one of these cases, however, it was not the native peoples—the directly colonized—who rose up and won their independence, but the descendants of the colonizers who had migrated from Europe.

Although one author has described the United States as the "first new nation," most accounts of this first wave of decolonization are restricted to the Spanish and Portuguese colonies in the Caribbean and in Central and South America. Independence came early there in large part because of the growing domestic weakness of Spain and Portugal, which left them unable to maintain their hold over the colonies.

As Chapter 16 will make clear, these revolutions settled little. Most of the newly independent countries suffered through at least another century of turmoil in which rival elites vied for power. Meanwhile, they remained on the bottom rung of the capitalist world economy, with Britain and the United States taking over the Spanish and Portuguese economic roles and managing the trade of food and other primary products and, later, low-quality industrial goods. Many nominally independent Central American states soon had to deal with the United States as a military as well as an economic power because it sent in the Marines whenever it felt that its financial or security interests were imperiled.

The second wave was also confined to a single region: the Middle East. After World War I, the Ottoman Empire collapsed, and some countries gained at least nominal independence. Others, such as Iraq, passed under British or French control, though most of them had become somewhat independent before World War II broke out.

The third wave occurred during the second half of the twentieth century. By the beginning of World War II, there was substantial anticolonial protest in most of Asia and Africa, the best known of which was the nonviolent movement led by Mohandas Gandhi in India. As we will see in the next chapter, Gandhi and his allies pressured the British into agreeing to grant India its independence after the war in exchange for its at least tacit support during the war. Despite some false starts, the British lived up to their word, and India and Pakistan became independent states within the British Commonwealth of Nations in 1947.

Over the next quarter-century, most of the remaining colonies gained their independence. Sometimes the colonial powers hung on, and independence required a protracted revolutionary struggle, as in Vietnam and Algeria. At others, independence came rather easily, as in Nigeria. By the late 1970s, this last wave of decolonization was all but complete. Today, Europe and the United States have only a few, mostly tiny outposts left.

In a few former colonies, such as India, Israel, Vietnam, and Algeria, independence occurred following a protracted struggle that engaged much of the population. When freedom did come, these new states found themselves with a large proportion of their populations committed to the new regime, which was led by the same groups that had led the protests against colonial rule. This unity eroded with time, but it gave these countries a host of advantages to start with, including a well-trained and respected elite that enjoyed quite a bit of legitimacy.

Most of the other former colonies were not as fortunate. By the late 1950s, it had become clear to most Europeans that their empires could not survive. Although independence itself therefore came more easily in most of Africa and the Middle East, its very ease obscured problems that were to plague these countries almost immediately thereafter. In particular, they lacked either the trained leadership or the unity and commitment on the part of much of the population that figured so prominently in India's nonviolent Congress or Algeria's violent National Liberation Front. In fact, as we will see in Chapter 14 on Iraq, independence often came without any significant development of national identity. The new leaders had support only among either the small Westernized elite or their own regional or ethnic constituencies. In other words, they took over countries that had weak institutions and limited support from the population as a whole. The effects of that were quick to appear once the exhilaration of independence wore off.

Postcolonial Problems

At first, there was tremendous optimism about these new countries. Most had internationally respected leaders presiding over institutions patterned after those in London, Paris, and Washington. Political scientists and political leaders assumed that what they mistook as the enthusiasm of the newly independent peoples, along with aid from the outside, would lead to a rapid improvement in the quality of life and the development of strong, democratic states. This is not what happened.

Almost all of the new governments degenerated into military, single-party, or other forms of authoritarian rule. Many faced bloody civil wars when the antagonisms between the ethnic groups that the colonial powers had forced to live together came to the political surface. Regional conflicts often turned into proxy battles between the superpowers, thereby worsening an already difficult situation.

In many former colonies, ethnic, religious, linguistic, and racial tensions disrupted political life and eroded what little sense of national identification and commitment had been built during the years before independence. Far from being helpful, Northern governments and businesses imposed their economic, and sometimes political, will. Meanwhile, the lack of experience of the new leaders and shortage of resources available to them made maintaining order difficult and left reaching broader social and economic goals nearly impossible. Under the circumstances, it is hardly surprising that the business elite, political leaders, military officers, and others who felt they had much to lose proved willing to toss out the seemingly democratic institutions most of these countries inherited from their erstwhile colonial masters.

POLITICAL CULTURE IN THE GLOBAL SOUTH

In Part 2, we saw that a political culture based on a common identity, shared values, and a sense of legitimacy plays a vital role in sustaining the established liberal democracies. In Part 3, we saw how hard it is for the former communist countries to develop similar attitudes and beliefs. Here, we will encounter even starker evidence of what happens when a country's political culture includes divisions over basic attitudes about the country's existence and the rules of the political game.

Identity

We cannot blame colonialism for all of the cultural problems in the Global South, especially as colonial rule recedes into history. However, imperialism remains an important long-term cause of the lack of a national identity.

In Part 2, we saw that most people in the liberal democracies define themselves politically first and foremost in national terms. In large part because of the way the colonial conquerors established borders in Africa and most of Asia, this is hard for people there to do.

In West Africa, for instance, different ethnic groups live in what amount to bands stretching east and west that parallel the Atlantic coast. In the 1880s and 1890s, however, the Europeans established colonial boundaries that ran from north to south, thereby splitting many ethnic, religious, and linguistic groups into several jurisdictions.

In other words, most Third World countries are artificial entities, with little or nothing that psychologically holds their inhabitants together. To be sure, soccer fans have been treated to the antics of wildly enthusiastic Africans at recent World Cups and Olympics. However, international soccer is one of the few things that lead them to think of themselves as Nigerians, Ivoiriens, or whatever. More often, their political views are derived from their regional or ethnic identities (see for instance ✐ **www.sfcg.org/programmes/cgp/the-team.html**).

The lack of a common national identity is a major cause of the divisions that have wracked most Southern countries. Preexisting ethnic divisions, worsened by the colonial powers' arbitrary drawing of national boundaries, have exacted a terrible cost by diverting scarce resources that could otherwise be used for economic and social development. Dozens of African countries have endured bloody civil wars. Even where wars have not occurred, there has been intense conflict, as we will see in Chapters 12 through 16.

As ethnic conflict erupted in much of the Third World, political scientists began to explore the resilience of the supposedly weak "traditional" societies. Among other things, they found that many institutions reinforcing older values persisted. For example, many countries still have strong informal **patron-client relations** that have their roots in feudalism. As in Europe during the Middle Ages or in the Mafia today, people are tied together in hierarchical relationships in which they have mutual responsibilities and obligations. Lords, bosses, and patrons are more powerful than their clients. Nonetheless, all are tied together through

financial, military, and cultural bonds that have proven remarkably hard to break.

Similarly, the assumption that the new nations would become more secular as they modernized has proved unfounded. If anything, religion has become more important and divisive. Such is the case in much of West Africa, where long-standing ethnic conflicts are exacerbated by the fact that adherents of traditional religions, Christians, and Muslim were forced together into the same geopolitical units. In other cases, such as India, the conflict is between religious, ethnic, and linguistic groups that have been at odds for centuries. Finally, contrary to what scholars initially expected, there has been a tremendous upsurge in **fundamentalism**, especially among Muslims who fear that modernity in the guise of Westernization is a threat to what they hold dear and is anything but a step forward.

In some instances, most notably in the Middle East, political cultures have evolved in ways that have left people and leaders strongly preferring *not* to develop along Western lines. The Islamic Republic that overthrew the shah and has ruled Iran since the 1979 revolution in many rejects everything Western and modern. The shah's grandiose industrial and commercial projects and his increasingly cosmopolitan society have given way to more traditional customs, including the strict application of Islamic law and the removal of women from much of public life.

It is not just the case in Iran. Throughout the Muslim world, more and more women are wearing the veil that is widely viewed in the West as a symbol of their lower status in Islamic society. More generally, Muslim peoples are coming to see their religion and the broader values and lifestyle it embraces as something to have pride in and even as something far superior to industrialization, democracy, and Western culture.

In short, rapid change can be a disruptive force. This is true not only in the poorest countries. As we saw in Part 2, many people are struggling to keep up with the technological revolution and with other economic changes sweeping the industrialized democracies. However, social and economic change has been particularly disruptive in the Global South precisely because so many of the "new" ideas are Western and require the shedding or, at least, alteration of long-standing values and practices.

Although it is hard to generalize, no doubt one of the by-products of cultural change has been additional demands placed on governments. To some degree, this simply reflects the fact that more people have the time and skills needed to organize politically and to put pressure on whoever is governing them. To some degree, too, it reflects the fact that changing social, economic, and political conditions have touched raw political nerves. Worldwide, new groups have been spawned all along the political spectrum—if it still makes sense to speak of a single political spectrum—including many that want to slow down and others who want to speed up the pace of change. In turn, groups have formed within elites that are increasingly committed to retaining the status quo, and with it, their own power and privileges.

To make sense of these rather abstract points, briefly consider two examples, the first of which we will return to in more detail in the next chapter. In India, a Hindu is born into one of four castes or into the so-called untouchables. These groups, in turn, are subdivided into smaller communities, or *jati*, usually on the basis of their member families' traditional occupations (e.g., grocer, tanner, or teacher).

The communities remain important despite many attempts to remove at least the worst of the discriminatory practices untouchables have been subjected to merely because their ancestors held jobs in which they dealt with animals, dead people, or human excrement. As India has become more urbanized and industrialized, the historical link between *jati* and profession has declined, and some of the restrictions it imposed on people such as who they can marry or who can prepare their food are no longer as important. However, caste and *jati* remain extremely significant politically because the patron-client and other relationships that keep them so strong are also the mainstays of the political party organizations at the all-important state level.

In other words, some Hindus have modified their cultural norms because they have had to. After all, it is very hard to tell the *jati* of the cooks who prepared their food when a meal is served on an airplane! But these values have not disappeared. In some politically important respects, they are, if anything, stronger in ways that tend to deepen divisions and hinder the prospects for either national unity or democracy.

The second example, of course, is the terrorist attacks on the World Trade Center and the Pentagon on 9/11. They obviously did not reflect a traditional division within a state. Rather, they forced us all to confront just how far some people are prepared to take their hatred of the United States and Western civilization. Analysts are still debating how much American foreign policy toward Israel, for instance, led to the attacks and how much they reflect what Samuel Huntington called a "clash of civilizations." Although it will probably be years before political scientists and historians reach a consensus on the causes of 9/11, these kinds of factors have to be included in any explanatory mix of such tragic events and of contemporary terrorism in general.

A Lack of Legitimacy

Finally, few Southern regimes enjoy much legitimacy. There is little of the tolerance of, trust in, or satisfaction with the regime that we find in the liberal democracies. It remains an open question whether a democracy needs such a culture. (Also see the conclusion to this chapter.) But clearly the cultural shifts, as well as those in the patterns of political participation we are about to discuss, have heightened *in*tolerance, *mis*trust, and *dis*satisfaction.

POLITICAL PARTICIPATION IN THE GLOBAL SOUTH

We can divide political participation into two main types: activities that provide support for the authorities and those that place demands on them. In Part 2, we saw that people in the industrialized democracies resort to the kinds of demands that could threaten the existence of the regime only under the most unusual of circumstances. What's more, they frequently engage in "supportive" participation that, at least indirectly, bolsters the regime. There may not be a lot of political content to such acts as singing the national anthem before a baseball game or a soccer match. Nonetheless, such symbolic forms of participation reflect the widespread support accorded the regime, if not the specific men and women who are in office at the time.

Conflict
in the Global South

The first and most obvious conclusion to be drawn from this chapter is that there is more conflict in the South than in either the liberal democracies or most of the current and former communist countries. In many cases, conflict targets not only the government of the day and its policies but also the regime. In some, the existence of the nation-state itself has been put in jeopardy. The conflict is all the more remarkable because, in the more authoritarian states, protesters run a major risk by signing a petition, let alone taking to the streets, something we saw in most of the countries many of whose people took part in the Arab Spring.

Not all are revolutions or civil wars waiting to happen. Still, even in the most stable of them, such as India, deaths during election campaigns are common enough that they rarely draw more than a passing note in the press. ■

Political participation is very different in most of the Global South. There are political parties, such as Mexico's *Partido Acción Nacional* (PAN), that try to forge broad coalitions around a few key ideological positions. Similarly, India has trade unions, women's movements, and other interest groups reminiscent of those in the industrialized democracies.

However, do not read too much into such examples. Even in countries with reasonably open political systems, there is less of a balance between supporting and demanding participation than we find in the industrialized democracies. Over the years, such countries have come to face more and more pressure "from below," which has led to massive waves of protest and, far too often, revolution.

In countries with authoritarian regimes, the patterns of political participation are more reminiscent of what we saw in the former Soviet Union. In the West, we tend to think of participation as a "bottom up" phenomenon, in which citizens participate voluntarily in order to have their views heard by those above them. But this is not always the case in the Global South. In countries with single-party or military governments, much of the participation comes from the "top down." For example, in Iraq before and after the first Gulf War, there were large demonstrations in support of the government's intransigence toward the United States, but most commentators wrote them off because they were orchestrated by Saddam Hussein's regime.

It is a mistake, however, to write such participation off as merely cynical manipulation of the masses by the elite. Like the demonstrations in favor of Mao Zedong at the height of China's Cultural Revolution, these activities often reflect genuine enthusiasm and add to the commitment of the people involved.

Similarly, there are many examples akin to the Chinese Communist Party's campaigns in which the state mobilizes people in an attempt to build support for policies that its weak and unreliable bureaucracy cannot implement on its own. These, too, may be portrayed as cynical and manipulative efforts by the state, as in the literacy campaigns of the Iraqi and Nicaraguan governments in the 1980s. In other cases, however, even the most skeptical analysts acknowledge that such campaigns can have a significant and positive impact. Nigeria has few programs it can point to for building bridges across communal lines. However, its National Youth Service Corps sends teams of young people for more or less compulsory service after graduating from college to work in economic and other developmental projects outside their home states. If nothing else, people in the regions where the volunteers work gain some positive exposure to members of groups toward whom they may harbor antagonistic relations.

As we have already suggested, patron-client relations are now more important in the Global South than in the countries considered in Parts 2 and 3 in large part because capitalism and the changes that came in its wake have not gone as far as political scientists first thought they would in destroying traditional social structures. Thus, Mexico's *Partido Revolucionario Institucional* (PRI) remained in power for more than seventy years not because of its ideology or accomplishments but because it built a client-based machine that could turn out—and, if need be, manufacture—the vote through the distribution of jobs and other benefits. Similarly, it has been a long time since India's Congress Party was nationalist or socialist in orientation or ideology. It, too, survives largely as an organization of ambitious politicians tied together by their desire for power. In perhaps the most blatant example of "clientelism," there were so many members of the Iraqi elite from Saddam Hussein's hometown that the government decreed that people should no longer include the part of their names that indicated where their family was from, thereby making the number of al-Tikritis in the ruling circles less obvious.

Perhaps most important of all is the degree to which political participation is based on **communal groups**. As has been the case with much of political life in the Global South, political scientists have sought nonpejorative terms to describe these trends. Terms like parochial or tribal, which were once in vogue, have now been rejected in favor of less telling but more neutral ones like communal.

Whatever term we use, much of political life revolves around religious, ethnic, linguistic, racial, and other "communities." To be sure, there is some of that in the West, including the all-but-total loyalty of African Americans to the Democratic Party in the United States. However, such trends pale in comparison with what we will see in the rest of Part 4. For instance, it is very hard to assemble a table of Indian election returns like the ones given in Part 2 because only three parties run candidates nationwide. Instead, much of the vote goes to parties that operate only in the one state where their linguistic or religious constituency is clustered. Similarly, the strongest opposition to the former regime in Iraq came from the Kurdish and Shiite communities, which objected not so much to Saddam Hussein's religious or foreign policies as to the fact that their people had been systematically discriminated against after the Baath Party took power in 1969. Even in relatively homogeneous Mexico, the on-again-off-again rebellion in the southernmost and poorest state, Chiapas, which broke out in early 1994, has ethnic overtones in that many rebels come from Indian groups that have never been assimilated into the dominant Spanish culture.

There is one final form of political participation that political scientists are just beginning to pay attention to: the role of nongovernmental organizations (NGOs). As their name suggests, NGOs are unofficial bodies that operate in less developed (and other) countries, though many of them are organized internationally and are composed of people, many of whom are not from the country in which they work. The most visible NGOs, such as *Médecins sans Frontières* (Doctors without Borders) and Save the Children, are not very political. They concentrate instead on humanitarian relief during what are euphemistically called "complex emergencies." Increasingly, however, even the most apolitical NGOs are recognizing that their work invariably brings them into political life. Those that concentrate on development or conflict resolution gladly acknowledge their political role. For countries in which both the state and the formal international community lack resources and credibility, NGOs can play a vital role in efforts to modernize the economy or build civil society from the grassroots level up ✐ (**www.ngo.org**).

Women and Politics in the Global South

As part of the new interest in the role of women in political science, their involvement—and often lack thereof—is getting renewed attention. Of course, there are women who play prominent roles in these countries, such as Dilma Rousseff who took office as President of Brazil in January 2011. But they are still few and far between.

More important is the fact that the problems buffeting the Global South normally hit women harder than men. Most domestic chores are "women's work." At times it is also getting harder to do, as in the regions bordering the Sahel desert where women often have to walk for miles daily to find enough firewood to cook with (no man would do this).

Far too many women and teenage girls are raped, and many are bought and sold into slavery. Teenage pregnancy rates are amazingly high, as is the incidence of often crippling diseases that go along with childbirth among girls who are not physically mature enough to bear a child. Girls spend less time at school. In poor families, it is not uncommon for fathers to force daughters to quit school and go to work, as prostitutes or otherwise.

In their path-breaking book on women in the South, *Half the Sky*, Nicholas Kristof and Sheryl WuDunn acknowledge that there are all kinds of things worth doing to help liberate women in South America, Africa, and Asia. But as they see it, assuring girls good health care and a quality education are the linchpins because those give them a chance to carve out a successful life for themselves. In particular in the conclusion, we will also explore how microcredit or small loans made to poor women also has the potential to give them the skills needed to pull themselves out of what all too often are generations of poverty.

WEAK AND FAILED STATES

In Parts 2 and 3, the industrialized democracies and the current and former communist regimes were defined in large part in terms of institutional features they shared. There are no such political common denominators for the Third World. In fact, we can identify five main types of states found there.

Democracies

There are a handful of established democracies in the Third World. In addition to India, they include Costa Rica, most of the island states in the Caribbean, and several of the smallest and newest African states.

Some observers add a few others, like Mexico, that have maintained some democratic features for many years. But Mexico cannot be said to guarantee basic individual freedoms, competitive elections, or the rule of law. Similarly, many of us would like to label South Africa as democratic given the remarkable changes there since Nelson Mandela's release from prison in 1990. However, it is far from certain that its multiracial democracy will survive the many social and economic problems facing the country.

Many countries have taken steps toward democracy since the late 1980s. Indeed, 1990 marked the first time that every country in South America had a government chosen through reasonably free and competitive elections, which most have sustained since then. Democratization has occurred more slowly in Africa and most of Asia, but moves in that direction are occurring there as well.

We will return to the issue of democratization as a central theme in the country chapters to follow. Here, it is enough to note that democratic regimes of the sort discussed in Part 2 are very much the exception to the rule and that most of those that do exist are fragile, to say the least.

Single-Party Regimes

Most of the new nations adopted liberal constitutions with multiparty systems patterned after those of their colonizers. Few lasted.

Especially in Africa, the struggle for independence was typically dominated by a single movement, which became the most powerful party after the transfer of power. Often, this group quickly abandoned the liberal democratic constitution and made itself the only legal party. In some cases, there were elaborate and plausible justifications for such a move. The late President Nyerere of Tanzania likened competitive party systems to a soccer game in which a lot of energy is expended for only a goal or two—energy a new and poor country like his could not afford. More often, the shift to a single-party regime was little more than a power play by one faction in the country's elite, often representing a single ethnic or religious group.

In Tanzania, attempts were made by the leaders of the Tanzanian African National Union (TANU) to expand party participation and internal competition in ways that resemble primaries in the Democratic or Republican parties in the United States. In most countries, however, the single party has amounted to little more than political window dressing for a dictatorship. None of the countries considered in the rest of Part 4 currently has a classic single-party regime. Iraq started that way under the Baath Party, but as Saddam consolidated his personal power, the party lost its influence as an independent force. Similarly, in Mexico, although other parties existed, the PRI controlled the Mexican state and dominated policy making for almost the entire twentieth century before it was finally defeated in 2000.

Military Regimes

Multiparty regimes have also frequently succumbed to military coups. Even though wars between states have been relatively rare—there were very few in South America, for instance, during the twentieth century—the military has played a prominent political role just about everywhere. The military has seen itself as having a dual role: to protect the country not only from external threats but also from civil unrest. From the military's perspective, multiparty regimes have turned chaotic far too often. Throughout Africa and South America, the twin fears of instability and communist insurrection led the military to seize power time and time again. Consider Nigeria. Under its first two republics (1960–66 and 1979–83), the political parties were organized almost exclusively along ethnic lines, making effective government all but impossible. The ensuing instability prompted the military to intervene to quell ethnic protest and political corruption. As has also often been the case elsewhere, not only has the military overthrown civilian governments, but one group of soldiers has also overthrown another on five occasions there as well.

Some military leaders have tried to do more than simply maintain law and order or enrich themselves. During the late 1970s and early 1980s, many political scientists and other observers believed that, for good or ill, these were the only kinds of regimes that could start Southern countries on the road to development. By the end of the decade, however, such governments were in trouble everywhere. Economic growth slowed, making the uneven distribution of its benefits a more significant political issue. Protest over economic conditions combined with opposition to human rights abuses to create powerful movements that removed the military from power throughout South America and, to a lesser degree, in the rest of the Third World.

Sani Abacha, military leader of Nigeria from 1993 to 1998.

Personal Dictatorships

Perhaps the most tragic form of government in the Third World is personal dictatorship, such as those run by the Somozas in Nicaragua, Mobutu Sese Seko in Zaire, Muammar Qadaffi in Libya, Ferdinand and Imelda Marcos in the Philippines, Robert Mugabe in Zimbabwe, and, in the case we will consider in detail in Chapter 14, Saddam Hussein in Iraq. Some times, these rulers came to power through military coups. At others, they were able to consolidate their control after more or less open elections. Almost always, they were able to stay in power because they developed networks of supporters who took control of much of the country.

The Somozas of Nicaragua are a painfully typical example, even if they disappeared from the political scene nearly 40 years ago. For all intents and purposes, the United States put the "dynasty's" founder, Anastasio Somoza, into power in 1937. A succession of American administrations had believed that this tiny Central American country was vital to the national security interests of the United States and so had periodically sent in the Marines in to keep people it opposed from taking power. During the 1930s, the Marines were used to help defeat a rebellion led by Augusto Cesar Sandino, whose primary goal was to force the United States out of his country.

Afterward, the Americans made the young Somoza head of the country's National Guard, in large part because he had been educated in the United States and spoke English. Thus began four and a half decades of arbitrary and often brutal rule by the first Somoza and by his two sons, Luis and Anastasio. The Somozas did not tolerate any opposition to their rule, and routinely killed dissidents. The National Guard was given free reign to use strong-arm political opponents and engage in a wide variety of corrupt activities, including prostitution and gambling. The Somozas stuffed their own pockets. By the 1970s, they owned the country's airports, electrical system, cigarette and match companies, a Mercedes-Benz dealership, and as much as half of the land. After the 1972 earthquake that devastated the capital city of Managua, Anastasio Somoza kept most of the millions of dollars in foreign aid sent to rebuild the city, claiming that the weather was warm, so people really did not need houses.

The Somozas are not alone. Mobutu, the former president of Zaire (now the Democratic Republic of the Congo [DRC]), built dozens of palaces for himself even though a third or more of his people were starving. After her husband was overthrown, people around the world were shocked by Imelda Marcos's collection of thousands of pairs of shoes. Dozens of former dictators, like former Haitian ruler Jean-Claude Duvalier, led lives of luxury in exile after being forced from power. Saddam and his family had dozens of palaces scattered around the country, many of which, ironically, housed the American-led occupation forces.

Relatively few of these rulers made it to the end of the twentieth century. The Somozas, for example, were finally overthrown in 1979 by revolutionaries inspired by the memory of Sandino. "People power" brought the Marcoses down eight years later. Mobutu was forced into exile and died in 1997. Unfortunately, their successors have not had an easy time of it. Typically, the new leaders took office only to find the treasury looted, the country's natural resources depleted, and the people extremely impatient. In other words, the dictators' impact on their countries continued long after they were thrown out of office.

Failed States

In the parts of the Global South most affected by communal violence, we can barely speak of sovereign states. In fact, observers are beginning to call them **failed states** because the government has lost the ability to exercise the most basic functions. All have governments and officials, but they resemble the Wizard of Oz more than leaders of an effective state. Once we get past the uniforms and the trappings of office, we can see that the leaders are little more than figureheads for a state that at best can control only a tiny fraction of its crime or other problems.

For reasons of space, we will not cover any definitively failed states in this book. However, some observers are convinced that Mexico could become one if its struggle with the drug cartels continues to deteriorate. In other words, in Chapter 16, we will see some of the dynamics that have led to the collapse of governments in such countries as Sierra Leone, the DRC, Burundi, Rwanda, and Somalia.

States and Power

Of the three types of states considered in this book, those in the Global South face the most daunting problems and so are most in need of a reasonably strong state. But few have one. At first glance, this might come as a surprise. After all, the stories we see in the news often stress the apparent power of their authoritarian rulers. This certainly was the case in accounts of Saddam Hussein after the invasion of Kuwait in 1990, the Nigerian regime that executed Ken Saro-Wiwa and other environmental activists in 1995, and the Taliban in Afghanistan.

But few have been able to do much more than maintain law and order by suppressing dissent, and many have not even accomplished that. There are some exceptions, such as in India, whose state-sponsored "green revolution" has improved agricultural output so much over the past generation that the country no longer has to import food. Far more common, though, is the disheartening history of Nigeria, where the average citizen is worse off than forty years ago despite the billions of dollars the government has earned from the sale of oil.

In the chapters that follow, we will see evidence of this weakness in three overlapping ways. The first is as a by-product of their poverty. No government in a country with a GNP of less than two thousand dollars per year will have much money to devote to education or health care. The lack of resources also leaves such a country with a weak infrastructure because it cannot afford to pave roads or lay cables or erect cell phone towers for modern telecommunications systems.

More than just a lack of money is involved. In the poorest countries, the government may not "reach" everyone in the ways we in the North take for granted, including enforcing the law and collecting taxes. These states tend to be short on human resources. For example, at the time of independence, there were only thirteen university graduates in all of what is now the DRC. Although there have been marked advances since then in education, life expectancy, and other areas of social life, none of these countries benefit from the kind of highly trained workforce that could produce the coalitions of business, government, and bureaucratic elites that have been so important in Europe, Japan, and elsewhere.

Second, many Third World countries have had trouble developing regimes that last for more than a few years. As we saw in Parts 2 and 3, it takes both time and a degree of political success to develop strong institutions that are not dependent on the power or personality of individual leaders. Time allows people to establish routines and expectations for the institutions that govern them. Success helps build legitimacy.

But this has not happened in most of the Global South. In part, the failure to develop effective states reflects the fact that most African and Asian countries are still new. More important, all have had to face heavy demands in a very short period of time. Many people expect what happened over two or three centuries in the West to be squeezed into two or three decades. Put simply, people run out of patience with states that are not providing results fast enough.

Weak institutions are a particular problem in countries that have had a personal or military dictatorship for an extended time. For reasons we do not fully understand, these kinds of leaders tend not to concentrate on building institutions that will function effectively after they depart the scene.

Third, many Southern countries with weak states are also plagued by widespread corruption, which extends far beyond the loss of scarce resource that leaders like the Marcoses, Somozas, Duvaliers, or Saddam Husseins spirited out of their countries. The corruption often extends far into the bureaucracy, especially in countries that lack a strong legal system and other institutions that could keep state employees in check. Thus, in Nigeria, civil servants are frequently referred to as *lootocrats* or *kleptocrats*.

Finally, think about what Ian Bremmer calls the "J curve" of state development. Authoritarian states such as those discussed below allow leaders to rule all but arbitrarily until they decide to or are forced to liberalize. It is at that point that they tend to face the most difficult moments, including political violence.

PUBLIC POLICY: THE MYTHS AND REALITIES OF DEVELOPMENT

Given the poverty described previously, it is hardly surprising that attempts to foster and speed economic development have been at the heart of most public policy making in the Global South. It should also come as no surprise that the inability to make much progress on this front is seen as yet another example of the weakness of the states that rule at least three-fifths of the world's population.

Timing is essential. Economic and political development in Western Europe and North America took the better part of three centuries. In the few cases in which it happened more quickly (Imperial Germany and Meiji Japan), it still took decades and required severe repression.

Most Southern countries—including those in Latin America that have been independent since the nineteenth century—embarked on their own developmental odysseys only recently and under much less promising circumstances. Britain, France, and the United States industrialized at a time when they already were the world's dominant economic and military powers and thus were largely free to marshal needed resources as their leaders saw fit. Quite the opposite is the case today. Most countries are playing a game of political and economic catch-up in which they lag way behind the North and have few opportunities to close the gap.

To make matters even more difficult, there is no agreement about what *development* itself means. Some observers argue that it involves creating an urban, industrial economy that would turn, say, India or Mexico into a carbon copy of Germany or Japan. Others doubt that there is such a "linear" or common path to development and that countries in the South will have to devise their own ways of sustaining growth, adding to their wealth, and improving their people's standard of living. And in recent years, some observers have questioned how much Southern countries should be allowed to develop given the pressures economic growth places on our fragile ecosystem.

In any case, they have adopted two general development strategies. The first—import substitution—was most popular from the 1950s into the 1980s. Since then, it has been all but completely abandoned in favor of the more market-oriented structural adjustment.

Import Substitution

Import substitution was designed to do just what the term suggests. If a country could replace expensive imported products with goods made locally, it would conserve much of its hard currency and other scarce resources, which could then be used to speed up development of its own industrial base.

It is easiest to see why such approaches were popular by first exploring **dependency theory**, which suggests why countries were eager to pursue what amounted to economic nationalism. Dependency theorists divide the world in two. On one side are the wealthy, capitalist nations of the North. On the other are the poor, underdeveloped countries that remain victims and de facto colonies of the North, whatever their legal status. In other words, dependency theorists focus on the economic rather than the political implications of imperialism and stress how the regions that became the Third World were forced into the global capitalist system.

From this point of view, capitalists restructured local economies for the worse. Instead of encouraging them to grow food or manufacture commodities for domestic consumption, the imperial powers forced their colonies to produce a few primary products for export: coffee and tea in Kenya, bananas in Guatemala, copper in Chile, and so on. In turn, the colonies, and then the new nations, provided markets for the North's finished goods, which earned massive profits for the already rich countries.

Dependency theorists do not deny that there has been considerable industrialization in the South in recent decades. Rather, they argue that such development has left them even more dependent on the North than ever before. The latter's banks and governments provide aid, but they invariably attach strings to it. These same institutions have issued loans that have left many governments owing hundreds of billions of dollars they cannot afford to repay. Northern corporations decide much of what is to be produced and ensure that the lion's share of the profits go back to their headquarters and shareholders.

As they see it, most Third World countries are left with narrowly based economies that are highly vulnerable to the vagaries of the international market. The industrial development that has taken place benefits only a tiny proportion of the population and has often left everyone else worse off. Foreign investment is increasingly oriented toward industries the Northern countries no longer want because they degrade the environment or cost too much in salaries and benefits. Most important, decision-making power remains overwhelmingly in foreign hands.

Leaders who accepted all or part of this explanation adopted policies that sought to reduce such dependency by strengthening their own economy—and their control over it. Most tried to develop a manufacturing base independent of the multinationals in such vital areas as steel, automobiles, clothing, and agricultural equipment. This involved, among other things, erecting tariff and other barriers to trade that made it more difficult for foreign goods and businesses to penetrate their markets. This way they could protect their own fledgling manufacturers from competition from cheaper and higher quality imports. Most set up publicly owned or controlled companies, often called **parastatals**, through which the government could steer the development of a domestic industrial base.

Of the countries covered here, India most consistently pursued import substitution. For the first thirty-five years after its independence in 1947, it enacted steep tariffs and passed other laws that made it hard for foreign companies to invest there and impossible for them to buy more than a minority share in an Indian corporation. Available resources were concentrated on Indian manufacturers, most of which were government owned or controlled. The goods they made were rarely competitive in open markets, which meant that India could not export much and that its overall growth rate remained low, but at least it controlled its own development, however limited that development was.

Many countries stuck with import substitution well into the 1980s. By then, however, two things had happened

Man carrying a dead child after the explosion of the Union Carbide plant in Bhopal, India in 1984.

that undermined support for it just about everywhere. First, it had become clear that the countries using it were growing far more slowly than those that had aggressively tried to build niches for themselves in global markets. In India, it was derisively known as the "Hindu rate of growth"—steady, but very slow.

It was at about this time that observers began noticing the Newly Industrializing Countries (NICs) and their often spectacular development record. Indians, for instance, had to acknowledge that they were far worse off than the Taiwanese, who had been as poor as they were in the 1940s. In short, India may have charted its own development. The problem was that there was just too little of it until the last few years.

Second, geopolitical changes all but forced Third World countries to become more active participants in the global economic system. The most important events in this respect, again, were the OPEC-induced "price shocks" of 1973 and 1979. Most countries in the Global South traditionally have to import not only oil but dozens of other products that are made using petroleum and its byproducts. Also they have had to pay for these goods in dollars or other **hard currencies**. At best, this meant that they had to export more to earn that money, which, in turn, implied meeting global price and quality standards. At worst, they had to borrow even more from Northern banks, governments, and international organizations, which left many of them so deeply in debt that there seemed no way they could ever pay back even the interest on the loans, let alone the principal.

In other words, dependency theory may have taken scholars and policymakers a long way toward explaining why the South was in such dire economic straits. Indeed, the debt crisis and the other post-OPEC difficulties

reinforced many of its conclusions about the power of the North. But, when conditions worsened in the 1980s, and the end of the Cold War removed socialism as an attractive option for leaders around the world, the political momentum shifted toward a dramatically different approach to development.

Structural Adjustment

Most economists now prefer a more conservative approach to economic growth known as **structural adjustment**. They are convinced that the best hope for the South lies in integrating themselves into the global economy as quickly and as fully as possible. This can be achieved by following a mix of policies designed to open up the domestic economy to imports and investments, reduce government spending and national debt, slash inflation, restore macroeconomic equilibrium, and sell off state-owned enterprises. Few Southern governments have eagerly embraced structural adjustment, However, most have been convinced, and in some cases compelled, to do so by Northern governments and the international financial institutions, as we will see in the next two sections.

Studies conducted by the World Bank divided Southern countries according to the degree to which they were "outward" or trade oriented. Contrary to dependency theory's predictions, the countries that traded the most—that is, the countries that played by the rules of the capitalist economic game—grew the fastest. From 1973 to 1985, these countries grew, on average, 7.7 percent per year overall and 10 percent per year in manufacturing. By contrast, the least trade-oriented states grew by only 2.5 percent overall and 3.1 percent in manufacturing.

The evolution of South Korea is instructive. Prior to the Asian economic crisis in 1997, it grew at a rate that exceeded even Japan's and was one of the most trade-oriented countries in the world. At first, the growth was concentrated in low-quality, low-tech industries in ways that mirrored what the dependency theorists would lead us to expect. During the 1970s, however, the nature of that growth changed. Korean companies started making steel, automobiles, and electronic goods, including most of our cell phones, and became major players in global markets.

There are many reasons why the South Korean economy boomed that had little to do with structural adjustment, including its then strong and often repressive state. Nonetheless, high on any list of explanations for its success has to be the way Korean companies, with the encouragement of the state, learned to operate effectively in international markets.

Structural adjustment's supporters may tend to exaggerate its benefits and ignore its shortcomings, including the fact that it does little to help the plight of the poor.

A new office complex in Bangalore, India, which has become a center for high-tech development.

Wilfried MAISY/REA/Redux Wilfried MAISY/REA/Redux

Nonetheless, they are correct in their basic assertion that the countries that have grown the fastest since the 1980s were those that, as the term itself suggests, adjusted their policies to the realities of global economic conditions.

Structural adjustment may not be the panacea its supporters think it is. However, there is no escaping the fact that it is now being followed almost everywhere. As with any major shift in public policy, there are many reasons leaders throughout South America, Africa, and Asia have turned to it. None, however, is more important than the fact that most loans and aid have been made contingent on its adoption.

The International Financial Institutions

The three international financial institutions are central to any discussion about development. The **International Monetary Fund (IMF)** (**www.imf.org**), the **World Bank** (**www.worldbank.org**), and the **World Trade Organization (WTO)** (**www.wto.org**) have been critical forces in the shift toward structural adjustment. The three are often called the Bretton Woods organizations because the first steps toward creating them occurred at a 1944 meeting at that New Hampshire resort.

Originally, the institutions were designed to spur economic recovery and stabilization in the war-torn countries of Europe and Asia. However, once Europe recovered and as more and more countries gained their independence, their focus turned to the Global South and, after 1989, the former communist world.

In recent years, these organizations have become more controversial than anyone could have imagined when they were created. Each of their major meetings since the protests against the WTO in Seattle in 1999 has been disrupted by demonstrators who accuse them international financial institutions of everything from destroying the environment to reinforcing poverty and sexism in the Third World and beyond.

The World Bank (officially the International Bank for Reconstruction and Development) is the largest—and perhaps the least well understood—of the three. Today, it primarily makes loans and also issues a smaller number of direct grants to developing countries. Some of its funds come from member countries, but most now come from the private financial market. It is controlled through a system of weighted voting in which the countries that contribute the most funds (the richest ones) have by far the greatest influence. Early on, the World Bank supported many large-scale industrial projects that were consistent with import substitution, but as it has moved increasingly into the private financial sector, it has also made more of its loans along strictly commercial lines. This orientation is one of the reasons anti-globalization critics have attacked the Bank's policies. Those criticisms reached a peak when Paul Wolfowitz, a key right-wing Republican in the United States, served as its president from 2005 to 2007. However, its supporters point to changes in the World Bank's family of institutions, including the creation of units to promote the environment, post-conflict reconstruction, environmental protection, and the reduction of poverty.

The first major protest against the World Trade Organization and globalization in Seattle. Dozens more have since been held.

Economic Liberalization
in the Global South

Structural adjustment is, in fact, little more than another term for liberalization. Unlike the former communist countries, however, the emphasis in the Global South has not been primarily on privatizing publicly owned corporations. This has occurred in countries like Mexico, which had a large and inefficient state sector, but most international banks and agencies have insisted that governments there get their countries' macroeconomic life in order in two other ways: reducing inflation and cutting the national debt. Doing so will enable them to participate more effectively in the international economy. This may make good sense from the perspective of classical economics. Yet it is less clear whether these countries can use structural adjustment either to catch up with the North or to close the gap between their own rich and poor citizens' policies.

Finally, it has to be stressed that few countries have adopted structural adjustment policies voluntarily. There are exceptions—for example, Chile under General Augusto Pinochet. For most countries, however, liberalization has been urged if not forced on them by Northern governments, banks, and agencies that made adopting structural adjustment a precondition for receiving aid and other forms of support. ■

The IMF, by contrast, is far more squarely in the structural adjustment camp. It was created at the same time as the World Bank, and the headquarters of the two organizations are located across the street from each other in Washington, D.C. The IMF was originally designed primarily to stabilize international monetary flows at a time when other currencies were fixed to the value of the American dollar, which, in turn, was determined to be worth an arbitrary amount for an ounce of gold. In the early 1970s, this system collapsed because of problems facing troubled economies in the Global South and, later, the former Soviet bloc. It is governed in roughly the same way as the World Bank, though the rich countries have even more voting power in the IMF. In recent decades the IMF has insisted on **conditionality**, or the acceptance of structural adjustment and other "conditions," before granting a country a loan. Thus, far more than the World Bank, it has been directly responsible for the often grudging adoption of these policies, something we will see most clearly in Mexico and Nigeria.

The IMF is going through its share of internal problems as we write. Its Chief Executive Officer, Dominique Strauss-Kahn, resigned in May 2011 after he was indicted for attempted rape and sexual assault in a New York City hotel. Members of the G-20 wanted the post to go to one of the emerging economies and not to another European who have always held the job. (Americans have always run the World Bank). In June, the French finance minister, Christine Lagarde, got the job making her the first woman to hold a job leading either of the Washington-based IFIs, as they are not always so affectionately known. Whatever happens in the short run, it is only a matter of time before someone from an emerging market runs one of the IFIs.

The WTO is the newest of the three organizations. Originally, the negotiators at Bretton Woods hoped to create a permanent institution that would work to reduce tariffs and otherwise open up international trade. For reasons we do not need to get into here, that organization was not created at the time. Instead, the far looser General Agreement on Tariffs and Trade (GATT) was formed in 1947. Its original agreement and subsequent "rounds" of negotiations gradually lowered tariffs and eased other restrictions on trade around the world. Finally, the leaders of over 130 countries agreed to form the permanent WTO in 1994 and granted it powers to enforce rules that would further free trade and resolve commercial disputes among member states. In other words, the WTO, too, is a strong supporter of structural adjustment and related policies. With China's and Taiwan's accession to membership in 2001, all the world's major economies other than Russia are members.

Foreign Aid

Long before the colonies began declaring their independence after World War II, it was clear that they would not be able to develop on their own. Therefore, the leading industrial nations—which, of course, included the leading colonial powers—realized that they would have to help.

The same sort of naïve assumptions we saw regarding state building also existed for economic development. The hope was that a limited amount of money and material aid would lead to what analysts at the time called an economic "takeoff" that would propel these countries to modern industrialized capitalist economies. However, this occurred only in a tiny handful of them. There are many reasons why this was the case, a number of which have to do with the internal politics of the countries themselves. But the overarching reason was a function of the way the distribution of **foreign aid** evolved after the 1950s. There are several kinds of foreign aid. Northern governments make some grants and loans directly to Southern governments. In recent years, international agencies have become more involved, most notably in providing loans both for long-term investment and to help countries work their way out of the **debt trap**. In a sense, MNCs also offer a form of aid when they invest in the Third World and create jobs and other indirect economic benefits. Finally, the past few years have seen a growing role for nonprofit NGOs, some of which have been attempting to counter what they see as the negative impact of aid from these other sources.

Foreign aid as we know it today began with the Colombo Plan. Signed in 1950, it committed the British government to providing developmental assistance to its former colonies in South and Southeast Asia. Soon, the United States (1951) and Japan (1954) signed on. Since then, most of the industrialized democracies have been providing some developmental assistance, which, at one point, they agreed should equal at least 0.7 percent of their GNP each year.

However, few of the industrialized democracies come close to reaching that goal. As Table 11.5 shows, only five of the world's richest twenty-two countries reached that 0.7 percent goal in 2008, all of which are fairly small and can thus have only a limited impact. The United States is the world's largest donor in absolute terms, and its contributions have increased since the terrorist attacks of 2001, as have almost all of the Organization for Economic Co-operation and Development (OECD) member states. Nonetheless, it ranks last in the column that measures the share of GNP it contributes. Also the top four recipients of American aid in this decade were Egypt, Russia, Israel, and Pakistan, not to mention Iraq and Afghanistan, which were chosen because of their strategic importance to Washington more than their economic need. But it should be pointed out that all the major donors concentrate their aid on former colonies and other countries deemed critical to their national interest. Citing the demands of their own economic downturn, Italy decided to cut all aid to The Global Fund to Fight AIDS, Tuberculosis, and Malaria while Spain and the Netherlands cut theirs substantially in 2011.

To be fair, Table 11.5 does not include sources of aid and investment that come from the private sector. Reliable statistics on that score are only available for the United States where corporations and NGOs provide at least twice the amount of aid made available by the government.

There are also serious criticisms of the nature of the aid itself that parallel those of the international financial institutions. Too much aid, it is said, goes for large-scale industrial projects that cannot be readily maintained and operated using domestic resources. Similarly, little of the aid is used to help people in the recipient countries develop the skills and other resources that will help them achieve some degree of self-sustained development,

thereby reducing the need for aid. Recipient countries are expected to use the grants or loans to buy material or hire consultants from the donor country. Also a surprising amount of the aid is aimed not at civilian but at military development whose benefits for the economy as a whole are limited. Finally, once all financial transfers and other economic costs, such as agricultural subsidies in Northern countries, are taken into account, the Third World probably contributes more to the affluence of the industrialized democracies than vice versa.

Microcredit

There is one promising long-term sign in what has so far been a relatively disheartening saga: **microcredit**. Some people in the poorest countries established their own small-scale financial institutions that enable them to determine and implement more of their own development policies and thus avoid the problems associated with foreign aid. In one form or another, each of these financial institutions tries to mobilize local people.

The first and best known of these institutions is Bangladesh's Grameen Bank ✎ (**www.grameen-info .org**). The bank was founded in 1976 by Muhammad Yunus,

TABLE 11.5 Foreign Aid: The Major Donors, 2008

COUNTRY	OVERSEAS DIRECT ASSISTANCE[a]	OVERSEAS DIRECT ASSISTANCE[b]
Sweden	4,729	0.98
Luxembourg	408	0.92
Norway	3,967	0.88
Denmark	2,876	0.82
Netherlands	695	0.80
Ireland	1,325	0.58
Belgium	2,381	0.47
United Kingdom	11,408	0.43
Finland	1,139	0.43
Spain	6,686	0.43
Austria	1,681	0.42
Switzerland	2,015	0.41
France	10,957	0.39
Germany	13,910	0.38
Australia	2,386	0.34
Canada	4,725	0.32
New Zealand	346	0.30
Portugal	614	0.27
Japan	9.362	0.20
Italy	4,444	0.20
Greece	693	0.18
United States	26,008	0.18

[a]In millions of dollars.

[b]As a percentage of gross national product.

Source: Adapted from www.oecd.org.

an economics professor at Chittagong University. Unlike most Western experts, Yunus was convinced that average Bangladeshi peasants could use banking services to create businesses they could run and profit from themselves. The success of the Grameen Bank and projects based on it around the world was honored when Yunus was awarded the Nobel Peace Prize in 2006 🌐 (**nobelprize.org /nobel_prizes/peace/laureates/2006/**).

The Grameen Bank's principles are simple and clear. As Yunus put it just as it was beginning to gain notoriety a decade ago:

Their [the peasants'] poverty was not a personal problem due to laziness or lack of intelligence, but a structural one: lack of capital. We do not need to teach them how to survive: they know this already. Giving the poor credit allows them to put into practice the skills they already know. And the cash they earn is then a tool, a key that unlocks a host of other problems.[2]

The Grameen Bank lends money only to destitute people. By mid-2008, the bank had made seven and a half million loans to people living in more than two-thirds of Bangladesh's villages. Ninety-four percent of its clients are women because they are better credit risks than men. To obtain a loan, a borrower has to pass a test on how the bank works and has to join a group of fellow borrowers who provide support, but also, if necessary, apply pressure to the grantee to repay the loan. The bank does not provide business training, but it does expect its borrowers to abide by "sixteen decisions," including a pledge to send their children to school and not to pay dowries when their daughters marry. Loans are for a year and may be renewed and extended for up to five years. Repayments are made at weekly meetings in which eight to ten of the loan groups gather.

In one typical case, a villager could not afford to feed her three children and her blind, unemployed husband. After overcoming her husband's objections, she passed the bank's test, got her loan, and bought a calf. Within a year, she used money from the sale of the cow to pay off the loan. She then took out another loan, with which she bought another calf and land for banana plants. Within five years, her farm had grown to include a rice paddy, goats, ducks, and chickens. Her family ate three meals a day, and she could afford to send her children to high school. As she put it, "You ask me what I think of Grameen? Grameen is like my mother. She has given me new life."

This is not an isolated example. A World Bank study found that over 95 percent of Grameen loans were repaid on time. Even more impressively, within five years, half of the borrowers were above the poverty line, and another quarter were close to it. The Grameen Bank's operations have expanded, and it now gives three-hundred-dollar home mortgages to families who have taken out and repaid at least three loans. It also has begun giving its village leaders cell phones, which serve as the only local pay phones. Also, in 1999, the bank became Bangladesh's leading Internet service provider—on the profits from its cell phone business.

Most of the countries in the world now have some type of microcredit projects, including the United States. In 2006, over two thousand people from 110 countries met in Washington for the second Microcredit summit 🌐 (**www .microcreditsummit.org**). At the first summit five years previously, then American Senator Hillary Clinton and World Bank president James Wolfensohn shared the stage with women from around the world who had taken major strides to improve their living conditions through microcredit

Profiles
Bono

Aging rock stars rarely find a place in political science textbooks.

Bono is an exception.

Born Paul David Hewson, Bono has been the lead singer for U2 since he formed the band's predecessor as a teenager in 1975. In this decade, Bono has become the most visible champion for development aid in the Third World along with the academic, Jeffrey Sachs. ■

Bono smiles into the camera at a meeting with politicians of the Social Democratic Party (SPD) in Berlin on May 14, 2007. He urged Germany to push for more aid to Africa in the next G-8 summit.

---

[2]Quoted in Alan Jolis, "The Good Banker," *Independent on Sunday Magazine.* 5 May 1996, 15–16.

Grameen Communications

Muhammad Yunus with a typical group of Grameen Bank clients.

programs. Attendees pledged to reach 175 million of the world's poorest people by 2007.

Microcredit is not the only innovative program that is seeking ways to blend the benefits of the market with the hope of raising at least a billion people out of poverty permanently. For instance, the late C. K. Prahalad not only wrote about but helped fund projects that would entice major multinational companies to develop products that would not only sell to and empower what he calls the "bottom of the pyramid" but make money for those companies as well. A visit to the website set up in his memory and to continue his mission will also show you what a program based on MNCs' desire for profit can accomplish (**www .bus.umich.edu/prahalad/**).

THE MEDIA

The media, too, are different in the poorest parts of the world in ways that reflect many of the broader themes of this chapter.

Because of poverty, relatively few people have access to television, which has become the primary source of political information in the rest of the world. Indeed, in 1985, when an American peace group wanted to do a global televised presentation of its annual award, it encountered what seemed to be an insurmountable obstacle. Tanzania, where one of the recipients lived, had no television at all. But it is not just television. Whereas two out of three Americans

have access to the Internet at home, that figure is more like one in three thousand in the South.

Many Third World countries also do not have a free press available to their citizens who can read or afford to buy a newspaper or magazine. The authoritarian regimes, in particular, are quite effective when it comes to censoring the news.

There are, however, a number of changes afoot. In the 1990s, a major breakthrough occurred for the world's poorest people who do not have electricity when a British inventor developed an affordable radio that uses a hand crank to generate its own power. They have become so popular that National Public Radio sells them to its American listeners who can use them when their power goes out (**shop.npr.org**). In the first decade of this century, Michael Negroponte, founder of the innovative Media Lab at MIT, committed himself to developing a laptop that would have wireless Internet access and have a hand crank and other tools for people who do not have electricity—all for one hundred dollars or less (**www.laptop.org**). People in the North who want one for themselves have to buy two, one of which will be donated somewhere in the Global South.

Last but by no means least, the mass media have often been used to foment ethnic conflict, most notably in the lead up to the 1994 genocide in Rwanda. Some NGOs like Search for Common Ground (**www.sfcg.org**) have tried to counter those trends by producing radio programs that document interethnic healing in deeply divided societies, including some that helped ease tensions in Sierra Leone.

Globalization and the Global South

Westerners often think of globalization in their own terms. For the optimists, it is bringing unprecedented riches, instant communication, and affordable global travel. For the pessimists, it is eroding working class jobs and harming the environment.

When we shift our attention to the Global South, the picture looks less clear—from either an optimistic or a pessimistic perspective. Globalization is drawing more and more people into international networks, commercial and otherwise. However, there are still upward of a billion people whose lives are barely touched by global forces. Moreover, a case can be made that globalization is contributing to a growing gap between rich and poor and is reinforcing traditional values and religions, thereby sparking conflict the Third World can ill afford. ▪

CONCLUSION: DEMOCRATIZATION

A generation ago, an introductory chapter on the Global South would have ended with a recap of its economic or environmental woes. It would have been even more depressing than this one, given the rampant and deepening poverty, the debt crisis, violence, and environmental degradation. Today, those problems remain, and most of them are as serious as they ever have been. Nevertheless, we can end this chapter on a slightly more upbeat note.

For the past decade or so, the most exciting trend in the South has been democratization. In 1990, all the Latin American countries south of Mexico had a democratically elected government—the first time this had ever happened—and most have kept those regimes. At the end of the decade, the Nigerian military turned control of the country over to a fourth republic and a few other African governments are experimenting with competitive elections, the first time the momentum had swung in that direction since the early 1960s. A number of the previously authoritarian regimes in East Asia have taken substantial, though still incomplete, steps toward democracy, including the Philippines and South Korea.

Democracy may well be taking root in places that were as far from it as one could imagine a decade or so ago. South Africa, in particular, has made remarkable strides in moving from apartheid to majority rule. Most remarkably, the core leaders of the old Afrikaner regime made their peace (albeit reluctantly) with the African National Congress and served in the government of former president Nelson Mandela for two years before quitting in May 1996. The fledgling South African democracy also made great strides with its Truth and Reconciliation Commission that began the process of healing the wounds of the apartheid era.

For over a decade, political scientists have been focusing more of their attention on why some democracies survive and thrive while others do not. Although they are far from reaching anything like definitive conclusions, they have come to six preliminary ones that offer some reason for hope.

First, much will depend on the attitudes and behavior of average citizens, many of whom are less than forgiving toward dictatorial regimes that have done little or nothing to improve basic standards of living. The experience of South Africa today and India over most of the past sixty years suggests that people may come to support a regime and temper their own demands, not out of a general commitment to democracy but because they are convinced that it is working. In other words, short-term pragmatic considerations, which states may actually be able to do something about, can be as important in building a basis for democracy as the forging of the more difficult-to-achieve sense of commitment to the abstract principles and procedures underlying it.

Second, for this kind of "pragmatic support" to build, the state has to be reasonably effective. One of the misreadings of contemporary and historical trends that has come with the rightward shift in recent years has been the assumption that if the state merely "gets out of people's lives" things will improve. But the historical record reviewed in Part 2 reveals something quite different. Democratic regimes succeeded in part because their states were capable of making tough decisions about the allocation of resources, the shape of institutions, and the handling of disorder.

Third, timing is important. The first years of any regime are critical because it is new and fragile. Therefore, it seems to be the case that if a democracy can get through the first few elections and, as we saw with France's Fifth Republic, if it can survive the transition from its first leadership to the opposition, it is usually much stronger and more likely to endure.

Fourth, there is a link between democracy and capitalism. However, it certainly is not as simple or as automatic as the advocates of structural adjustment would lead us to believe. Markets are not natural phenomena but have to be created and sustained, reinforcing the importance of a reasonably strong state. Also, the purported benefits of markets do not come quickly—if they come at all—whereas, as the history of all democratic regimes suggests, people tend to be impatient and to expect dramatic improvements in the short run. There is also evidence that democracy may have a good chance of succeeding only after societies have reached a certain level of wealth. The most recent research has put that figure at a per capita income of about five thousand dollars per year, which is well above what most LDCs can dream of.

Fifth, for all the reasons discussed previously, international factors will become more and more important as the world continues to "shrink" (see Chapter 17). There is growing awareness that Northern policy toward the South should be made with more long-term goals regarding development and democracy in mind, which might mean sacrificing some shorter-term profits or market share. However, there are stronger signs that the shift toward market-based policies will continue, which might actually worsen conditions for most people in the politically all-important short run.

Finally, we should definitely *not* expect the democracies that might emerge in the Third World to resemble those in the West. As we saw in Part 2, the Western democracies developed as a result of a long historical process that cannot be replicated because conditions are so dramatically different today. Indeed, it may well be that democracy in the Third World will not be much like what we saw in Part 2 at all.

At this point, the best way to think about these hypotheses is to consider Iraq and Afghanistan. One of the reasons (but by no means the only one) the United States and some of its allies went to war with both countries was to create democracies. For good or ill that has not happened, in large part because of problems associated with these six conclusions.

Looking FORWARD

OBVIOUSLY, IT IS time to put some "flesh on the bones" of what has of necessity been a rapid-fire overview of the Global South. As noted in the text, we chose the five countries because they are large enough to make a difference and because they each illustrate something different and significant about the South.

Here is a list of the themes we will be emphasizing in the next five chapters.

Chapter 12, India. How has the world's second largest country built and sustained a democracy? How did one of the world's poorest countries become one of the BRICS?

Chapter 13, Iran. Why did Iran adopt one of the world's last theocratic regimes? Why has the Islamic Republic put other goals (perhaps including making nuclear weapons) ahead of economic development and the well-being of its people?

Chapter 14, Iraq. Iraq is a classic artificial country put together for reasons that were more important to the British than those who became Iraqis. How did that lack of an auspicious start help lead to authoritarian rule by Saddam Hussein and his Baath party? What difference has its three wars (and occupation by the United States and its allies) had on Iraqi prospects for stability or prosperity?

Chapter 15, Nigeria. Of the five countries in Part 4, Nigeria has had the most tumultuous history, including at least five coups (it depends on how you count) and four republics. Why has this oil-rich but ethnically divided country had so much trouble on almost all policy fronts?

Chapter 16, Mexico. Mexico spent the first century of its independence in an intermittent civil war that then gave way to seventy years of uninterrupted rule by a single party, the PRI. Three questions emerge. First, why did the PRI hold on to power for so long only to lose in 2000? Why has Mexico had so much trouble developing? Finally, why do some observers think that Mexico could become a failed state sooner rather than later?

Key Terms

Concepts

carrying capacity
communal group
conditionality
debt crisis
debt trap
dependency
dependency theory
failed state
foreign aid
fundamentalism
Global South
globalization
hard currency

Human Development Index (HDI)
identity
imperialism
import substitution
indirect rule
microcredit
newly industrialized country (NIC)
parastatal
patron-client relations
structural adjustment
subsistence economy
Third World

Acronyms

HDI
IMF
MNC
NGO
NIC
OPEC
WTO

Organizations, Places, and Events

International Monetary Fund (IMF)

Multinational corporation (MNC)
nongovernmental organization (NGO)
Organization of Petroleum Exporting Countries (OPEC)
World Bank
World Trade Organization (WTO)

🌐 Useful Websites

There are not many websites on the Third World, per se. There are, however, many good ones that touch on much of what is covered in this chapter. The best of these is the new site on globalization created by the Center for Strategic and International Studies in Washington.

www.globalization101.org

The Virtual Library also has good sites on sustainable development and on microcredit.

www.ulb.ac.be/ceese/meta/sustvl.html

www.gdrc.org/icm/

The Center for World Indigenous Studies focuses on the status of ethnic minorities in the Third World. The Third World Network is a good, left-of-center source for news and analysis on development issues.

www.cwis.org

www.twnside.org.sg

Many international organizations and NGOs issue regular reports filled with analysis and data, including the World Bank, the United Nations Development Program, and the World Resources Institute.

econ.worldbank.org/wdr/

www.undp.org

www.wri.org

Further Reading

Beah, Ishmael. *A Long Way Gone.* New York: Susan Crichton Books/Farrar Strauss Giroux, 2007. The best book on child soldiers and maybe the best book to start with in thinking about the less developed world.

Collier, Paul. *The Bottom Billion.* New York: Oxford University Press, 2008. A great overview of problems facing the Third World.

Easterly, William. *The Elusive Quest for Growth.* Boston: MIT Press, 2001. An exploration of how the conventional wisdom and policy on development have evolved over the years and the costs associated with those changes, by a leading World Bank economist.

Fisher, Julie. *Non-Governments: NGOs and the Political Development of the Third World.* West Hartford, CT: Kumarian Press, 1997. By far the best source on NGOs, by a woman who combines the insights of an academic with the enthusiasm of an activist.

Friedman, Thomas. *Hot, Flat, and Crowded.* New York: Farrar, Strauss, Giroux, 2008. The most recent book by the prolific columnist and author. This one does the most with the downside of globalization for the LDCs.

Ghani, Ashraf, and Clare Lockhart. *Fixing Failed States.* New York: Oxford University Press, 2008. The best book on governance in the Global South.

Haynes, Jeff. *Third World Politics: A Concise Introduction.* London: Blackwell, 1996. A basic text organized conceptually that goes beyond the basic issues to get at such themes as gender and the environment.

Huntington, Samuel P. *The Clash of Civilizations: Remaking the World Order.* New York: Simon & Schuster, 1996. A highly controversial book, by one of the most respected (and conservative) analysts of the Third World, that focuses essentially on cultural arguments in anticipating the next round of global conflict, domestically and internationally.

Isbister, John. *Promises Not Kept: Poverty and the Betrayal of Third World Development*, 6th ed. Bloomfield, CT: Kumarian Press, 2003. The best overview of the dilemmas facing Southern countries trying to develop economically and politically.

Kaplan, Robert. *The Coming Anarchy: Shattering the Dreams of the Post–Cold War.* New York: Random House, 2000. A depressing, journalistic account of looming conflict and its implications. This book is a collection of short essays, but interested readers with time would do well to consult his longer *The Ends of the Earth.*

Kristof, Nicholas and Sheryl WuDunn. *Half the Sky: Turning Oppression into Opportunity for Women Worldwide.* New York: Knopf, 2009. By far the best general book on the status of women in the Global South.

Power, Samantha. *A Problem from Hell*: America and the Age of Genocide. New York: Basic Books, 2002. By far the most important and depressing book on genocide and why the United States has been among the slowest countries to respond.

Prahalad, C. K. *The Fortune at the Bottom of the Pyramid.* Philadelphia: Wharton School Press, 2006. Not an easy read, but the best book on the role of the private sector in fighting poverty.

Przeworski, Adam. *Sustainable Democracy.* New York: Cambridge University Press, 1995. Probably the best book written so far on the subject. Actually written by a committee of twenty-one well-known social scientists who combine a lot of important ideas about democratization and economics in the "east" and "south" into 112 pages. A difficult read, but well worth it.

Sachs, Jeffrey. *The End of Poverty.* New York: Penguin, 2005. Perhaps not the best book on new plans to end poverty in the Global South, but most readable by far. Foreword by Bono.

Taras, Raymond, and Rajat Ganguly. *Understanding Ethnic Conflict: The International Dimension.* New York: Longman, 2002. An excellent overview of the way ethnic conflict hinders many countries in the Global South and beyond.

World Bank. *World Development Report.* Published annually, the best single source of statistics on development issues as well as a topic considered in depth each year.

12

India

As Indian citizens, we subsist on a regular diet of caste massacres and nuclear tests, mosque breakings and fashion shows, church bombings and expanded cell phone networks, bonded labour and the digital revolution, female infanticide and the NASDAQ revolt, husbands who continue to burn their wives for dowry, and our delectable stockpile of Miss Worlds.... What's hard to reconcile oneself to, both personally and politically, is the schizophrenic nature of it.

ARUNDHATI ROY

THE BASICS

India

Size	3,287,590 sq. km (About 1.3 times the size of the United States)
Population	1.17 billion; growing at the rate of 1% per year
GNP per capita	$3,280
Growth rate	7.4% (2009)
Currency	47 rupees = US$1
Ethnic groups	72% Indo-Aryan, 25% Dravidian, 3% other
Religion	81% Hindu, 12% Muslim, 2% Christian, 2% Sikh, 2% other
Capital	New Delhi
Head of State	President Pratibha Patil (2007–)
Head of Government	Prime Minister Manmohan Singh (2004–)

NO CRISIS HERE

In mid-2011, most of the world was still mired in the worst recession since the great depression of the 1930s.

Not India.

To be sure, the economy slowed down. Growth in gross national product was 7.4 percent, down two percentage points from two years earlier. Still, after decades of stagnation India's economy was growing so fast that it is one of the five major emerging markets in large countries—along with Brazil, Russia, South Africa, and China.

India now has a middle class of about 100 million people who can afford to buy televisions, refrigerators, and one of the small locally manufactured, no-frills automobiles. Few Indians can afford a Mercedes or a Lexus. However, many are able to purchase a Tata Nano or one of the other two 4-passenger cars that typically come without air conditioning or a radio but sell for the equivalent of $2,500. The Nano was introduced in April 2009. By the time the car officially went on sale that July, more than 200,000 of them had already been sold.

Even some of the most traditional practices in Indian society are catching up with the times. For generations, upper- and middle-class Indians have had arranged marriages. In the past, parents of the potential bride and

Looking BACKWARD

IN CHAPTER 8 and several others, we claimed that the political stakes are much higher in the current and former communist countries. Until Part 3, you had to take that as a leap of faith. In Part 3, we hope we showed that we are right for the countries that used to claim that they were ruled using the philosophy of Karl Marx and his disciples and in the few remaining countries that still do so.

In Chapter 11, we claimed that the stakes are even higher in the Global South than they are in a country like Russia or China. Now, we have to make that less of a leap of faith on your part. We start with India because it is among the most successful of the Southern countries. It has had a functioning democracy for all but two of its more than 50 years as an independent country. In the last decade, its economy has also boomed after years of stagnation.

In short, India may not be our best example of what's wrong about politics and everything else in the Global South. In fact, India is one of its few success stories. Still, you will not have to read between the lines to see just how much India has had to overcome.

---

groom would meet and agree to the wedding before the couple themselves met. Now, it is common for prospective brides to put videos of their cooking or sewing skills on services like "Star Wedding," which its owners call the wedding version of You Tube. Many poorer women are insisting that their husbands-to-be guarantee that the new family will have a toilet before they agree to wed.

India is also enjoying a rare period of political stability. In 2009, Congress and its allies won 262 of 550 seats in the all-powerful **Lok Sabha**, or the lower house of parliament. Enough independents voted for Prime Minister Manmohan Singh that he enjoys a comfortable majority, a rare outcome in recent Indian elections. Perhaps even more important,

the conservative, Hindu-based **Bharatiya Janata Party (BJP)** suffered a terrible defeat, winning only a quarter of the popular vote and losing more than 10 percent of its seats (**www.indian-elections.com**).

Not all is well with India. Indians are poor. Using the World Bank's measure—earning less than $1.25 per day—almost half a billion Indians live in absolute poverty.

There has been a lot of progress. Hindustan Unilever started selling soap, toothpaste, and other personal care products in 2000. By 2006, its products reached one hundred thousand villages and it hoped to have five hundred thousand customers by the end of 2010. The workforce is overwhelmingly composed of women, most of whom are

One of the first Tata Nanos to hit the road in India.

AP Images

illiterate (see the discussion of microcredit in Chapter 11), Indian merchandisers have learned to sell in small quantities that poor people can actually afford; shampoo, for instance, is sold in a small bottle that has just enough to wash a single person's hair once ✦ (**www.bus.umich .edu/prahalad/**).

India also has had its share of political tensions based on language and religion best seen by the fact that what many people see as a fundamentalist party regularly wins more than a quarter of the vote. India is the world's largest democracy, but upward of a thousand people are killed in each campaign. As we will see, the most common kind of violence is between Hindus and Muslims. It includes not only India's on-again off-again rivalry with its neighbor Pakistan, but occasional outbursts of communal violence between Hindus and Muslims inside India itself. Although Muslims make up only 12 percent of the population, there are more Muslims in India than in any country other than Indonesia and Pakistan.

Yet, India is an exception given what we will see in the rest of Part 4. It is solidly democratic. Its regime has troubles, but it is hard to argue that it is less democratic than Poland or Belarus or the other countries we could have covered in Part 3. As political scientists, we tend to equate democracy with countries in the West. India will show us that that trend may be changing. We still do no want to count India as one of the liberal democracies. But it is close....

India is also one of BRICS countries along with Brazil, Russia, South Africa, and China. That also means that it will be an economic force to be reckoned with in the next decades. It is frankly too early to determine what will happen, but it will be interesting.

THINKING ABOUT INDIA

As the statement by Arundhati Roy that begins this chapter suggests, India is a country of contrasts, if not contradictions. It is one of the most diverse countries in the world, however one chooses to define *diverse*. It is also changing as fast or faster than all but a handful of much smaller countries.

The Basics

A Nation of Contrasts

Depending on your perspective, India is one of the most backward or one of the most promising countries on earth. It is one of the poorest countries, yet it is also the world's tenth largest industrial power. Only the United States and Russia have more scientists and engineers. About 60 percent of Indians are illiterate, yet rural India is connected by a network of satellite stations that have brought television to more than 80 percent of its seven hundred thousand villages.

India was the home of the most famous and influential pacifist, yet it has one of the largest armies in the world and is one of but nine countries—as far as we know—to have nuclear weapons. A founder of the nonaligned movement that tried to avoid taking sides during the Cold War, India nevertheless fought several wars with its neighbor and fellow nuclear power Pakistan and also imposed an economic and military blockade on Nepal, and sent fifty thousand troops to protect the Tamil minority in neighboring Sri Lanka between 1987 and 1990.

Size and Diversity

Another striking thing about India is its size and diversity. Only China has more people. Seven of its states have more inhabitants than Britain or France. Despite its family planning program, India adds the equivalent of Argentina to its population each year. A decade ago the total topped a billion people.

India's diversity is most evident in the languages its people speak. Nearly 60 percent of the population speaks one of the Indo-Aryan languages used mostly in northern India. The 30 percent of the people who live in the south mostly speak one of the Dravidian languages, which are completely different from those used in the north. About 5 percent of the people (mostly Sikhs) speak Punjabi, an offspring of Farsi and Urdu, the dominant languages of Iran and Pakistan, respectively.

India's constitution lists fourteen "principal languages" (see Table 12.1). In fact, the situation is far more complicated because there are hundreds of dialects subsumed in these linguistic families, and as many as 100 million people

TABLE 12.1 India's Principal Language Groups

LANGUAGE	POPULATION (%)	WHERE SPEAKERS ARE CONCENTRATED
Assamese	1.4	Assam
Bengali	7.6	West Bengal
Gujarati	4.9	Gujarat, Bengal
Hindi	38.6	Bihar, Haryana, Himachal Pradesh, Rajasthan, Uttar Pradesh, Delhi
Kannada	3.9	Karnataka
Kashmiri	0.5	Jammu and Kashmir
Malayalam	3.8	Kerala
Marathi	7.2	Maharashtra
Oriya	3.3	Orissa
Punjabi	2.7	Punjab
Tamil	6.5	Tamil Nadu
Telegu	7.9	Andhra Pradesh
Urdu	5.2	Most Hindi-speaking regions

Source: Adapted from Robert W. Stern, *Changing India* (New York: Cambridge University Press, 1993), 19.

speak languages that do not figure on the list. As in much of South Asia and Africa, the only language educated Indians have in common is English. Thus, the language of the colonizer has become the lingua franca in much of business and government.

The government has drawn the twenty-eight state and seven union territory boundaries so that each has a dominant language and culture. Nonetheless, they all have large minorities that have played a significant and often violent role in local as well as national political life.

India also has three main religious groups. Slightly over 80 percent of the population is Hindu, but each major regional/linguistic group follows a different version of the religion. As noted earlier, about 12 percent are Muslim, but they run the full range of belief from fundamentalists to highly assimilated and secularized people who have, for all intents and purposes, stopped practicing their religion. Most of the rest are Sikhs. Their religion has at its roots in an attempt to blend Hindu and Muslim traditions, emphasizing peacefulness and other worldliness, but Sikhs are now known for their ferocious fighting ability and their dissatisfaction with their status in Punjab.

Like language, religion has been politically important since the Muslims first arrived as part of the **Mughal** conquest. Independent India came into existence amid communal violence as millions of Muslims tried to escape India for Pakistan and millions of Hindus fled in the other direction. In the 1980s, the most difficult problem involved Sikhs, who sought their own homeland and who saw the national government attack their holiest shrine, the Golden Temple at Amritsar, and kill thousands of their most militant leaders. Since then, violence has most often occurred along religious lines, as in the case of the conflict over the temple/mosque site at **Ayodhya**, which we will examine in more detail later. Here, it is enough to note that the attempt by Hindus to build a new temple there led to riots in which thousands of Hindus and Muslims have been killed throughout the northern part of India over the last twenty years.

Finally, India is divided along **caste** lines. Historians trace the caste system back nearly four thousand years, when in all likelihood the lighter-skinned Aryans established it to minimize "mingling" with the darker-skinned Dravidians. There are four main castes. The Brahmans historically were the priests and the most prestigious caste, the Kshatriyas were rulers and soldiers, and the Vaisyas were merchants. These three upper castes are often referred to as "twice born," reflecting the belief that they are farther along in the Hindu cycle of death and reincarnation. The lowest caste, Sudras, traditionally were farmers but did "respectable" enough work to warrant their inclusion in the caste system. Below them are the **untouchables**, or dalits, who are outside the caste system altogether because their ancestors were sullied by their occupations as scavengers and collectors of "night soil." About 20 percent of the population is outside the caste system either because they are Muslims or members of other minority groups that were never part of this unusual pattern of social organization.

Each caste, in turn, is broken into hundreds of sub-castes known as *jati*. The castes and jati have elaborate rules for most social situations, including such things as what clothes to wear and what food to eat. Until very recently, people rarely broke out of those restrictions.

The constitution officially abolished the status of "outcaste" and outlawed discrimination against untouchables and tribals. In practice, caste remains a volatile political issue. Discrimination against those at the bottom of the hierarchy is still as pervasive as racism is in the United States or Western Europe. In the summer of 1990, for instance, Prime Minister V. P. Singh proposed reserving about a quarter of all new positions in the civil service for members of the lower or "scheduled" castes in an Indian version of American affirmative action. The proposal so incensed upper-caste young people that they staged demonstrations at which some burned themselves alive.

Poverty

The most important fact of life in India is poverty. It is so widespread and has proved so difficult to eradicate that we will devote much of the public policy section to it. As the table on the inside front cover shows, India's average per capita GNP is a bit more than $3,000 per year, making it the second poorest country covered in this book. Despite recent gains, the gap between India and other countries that started out as poorly as it did, such as China, continues to grow.

Fifty Indian babies out of one hundred born in 2010 died before reaching the age of five, and overall life expectancy is just over 60 years. For most people, health care is rudimentary at best. Although the "green revolution" of the 1960s all but eliminated mass starvation, most Indians eat a diet that does not quite meet the minimal caloric intake needed for a healthy life. And in 1998, a doubling in the price of onions took millions of people to the brink of starvation and cost the then ruling BJP (**www.bjp.org**) control of three states.

The statistics only tell part of the story of Indian poverty. The cities are crowded and filthy, as portrayed powerfully by the Nobel Prize-winning Indian-Caribbean writer V. S. Naipaul in describing Bombay during his second visit to India in the late 1980s. Things have not changed much since then:

> **Traffic into the city moved slowly because of the crowd. When at certain intersections, the traffic was halted, the pavements seethed all the more, and such a torrent of people swept across the road, in such a**

bouncing froth of light-weight clothes, it seemed that some kind of invisible sluicegate had been opened, and that if it wasn't closed again, the flow of road-crossers would spread everywhere, and the beaten-up red buses and yellow-and-black taxis would be quite becalmed, each at the center of a human eddy.

With me in the taxi were fumes and heat and din. Bombay continued to define itself: Bombay flats on either side of the road now, concrete buildings mildewed at their upper levels by the Bombay weather, excessive sun, excessive rain, excessive heat; grimy at the lower levels, as if from the crowds at pavement level, and as if that human grime was working its way up, tidemark by tidemark, to meet the mildew.[1]

Key Concepts and Questions

Because India is the first country considered in Part 4, this section of the chapter will address general questions related to the entire Global South along with specific ones about India alone.

- What are the country's political origins?
- How do its people participate politically?
- How is the country governed?
- How has the government coped with poverty and unemployment?
- How and why has democracy endured in India but not in most other Southern countries?
- Why is ethnicity based on religion, language, caste, and the like so important in India, as it is in most of the Global South?
- Why has India—like most Southern countries—had trouble stimulating and sustaining rapid economic growth?

Like most of the South, India suffered from centuries of occupation and colonization, first under the Mughals and later under the British. Its experience with imperialism was typical in many ways. Foreigners made all the decisions that mattered, which, among other things, served to destroy much of the country's economic base.

However, in other ways India's experience was unusual. The British never directly ruled the entire country. Moreover, they allowed a massive independence movement to develop following the creation of the **Indian National Congress** (www.aicc.org.in) in 1885. As a result, the Indian regime that gained its independence in 1947 had widespread popular support and experienced leaders who were committed to democracy. That group of leaders, headed by the first prime minister, **Jawaharlal Nehru** (1889–1964), gave the country a generation of stability that deepened popular support for democracy and that helped the country survive more serious conflict since the late 1960s.

India has been able to sustain its democracy in large part because its citizens supported it, especially during the country's critical formative years. Although we have to ask why this was the case, it is even more important to ask why there has been so much more protest in recent years than there was during the heyday of Nehru's rule.

When Nehru was prime minister, Congress was what political scientists call an inclusive party that found a way to appeal to people of all socioeconomic backgrounds and political beliefs. Once Nehru's daughter, **Indira Gandhi**, (1917–84) became prime minister two years after her father's death in 1964, the party system began to fragment. National opposition parties, including the predecessors of the BJP, began to gain strength by appealing to narrower segments of the electorate. More important, regional parties began scoring impressive victories, often winning control of state governments and electing up to half of the members of the lower house of parliament from "their" state. The fragmentation has not been just electoral. As noted previously, communal violence has been widespread since the late 1970s. Violent protests and riots occur on a regular basis, and disaffected members of minority ethnic groups assassinated both Indira Gandhi and her son **Rajiv Gandhi** (1944–91), who also served as prime minister.

Therefore, one obvious question to ask in terms of how India is governed is whether or not Indian democracy is cut from the same political cloth as the version we saw in Part 2. On paper, the answer is an obvious yes. India's institutions were patterned closely on Britain's parliamentary system and have changed surprisingly little since independence. In practice, however, democracy there has some decidedly Indian characteristics, starting with the dominant role Congress has played for most of India's history as an independent country. Under Indira Gandhi and her successors, Congress transformed political life by centralizing political power to the point that the Indian state can now be more repressive and certainly is more corrupt than anything we saw in the countries discussed in Part 2.

Finally, we have to ask why India's public policy has broken so sharply from the rest of the Global South. From independence until the late 1980s, India was one of the world's strongest supporters of import substitution and of the autarkic strategy of industrialization it led to. Since then, however, India has adopted the more liberal policies of structural adjustment, which has fueled so much of its recent growth.

---

[1]V. S. Naipaul, *India: A Million Mutinies Now* (New York: Viking, 1991), 1.

THE EVOLUTION OF INDIAN POLITICS

The Weight of History

As we have seen throughout this book, one cannot understand politics in any country without first knowing how it evolved over time (see Table 12.2). Most Southern countries have not been independent for long. But the impact of history is, if anything, more extensive than those that have a longer history as sovereign states because of the additional factor of colonialism, which did not figure prominently in most of the countries covered in Parts 2 and 3.

Exploring the evolution of India's politics means going back more than three thousand years. As early as 1500 BC, Aryans from the north began developing what became the Sanskrit language, Hindu religion, and the caste system. Many of the classics of Indian literature and culture antedate the birth of Christ. During the third century, the Mauryan Empire was able to unite almost the entire subcontinent during the reign of Ashoka, who remains an inspiration to many Hindus today.

Until 1000 or so, Indian culture flourished. The last thousand years have been a different story. For all but the past fifty years, most of India has been dominated by outsiders.

In the centuries after the death of the Prophet Muhammad, Muslim armies set out to conquer and convert the world. They got as far west as Spain and were gaining ground in France when they were beaten at the Battle of Tours. Their influence extended all the way to the Atlantic coast of Africa. And most important for our purposes here, the Muslims moved east as well, reaching far beyond India to the Philippines.

Beginning in the tenth century, Muslims made inroads into India, which they continued to expand over the next

TABLE 12.2 Key Events in Indian History Prior to Independence

YEAR	EVENT
Circa 1000	Beginning of Islamic impact
1556–1605	Mughal unification of much of the subcontinent
Circa 1600	First significant European impact
1707	Start of Mughal decline
1857	Sepoy mutiny
1858	Government of India Act
1885	Formation of Congress
1919	Jallianwala Bagh massacre
1920	Gandhi's first *satyagraha* campaign
1930	"March to the Sea" against the salt tax
1937	Elections
1939–45	World War II
1947	Independence

500 years. Although the Persian-based Mughals were able to gain control of most of India by the middle of the fifteenth century, they were never able to establish a central government for the subcontinent.

In 1526, some of the regional rulers turned to Babur, a descendant of the great Mongol warrior Chinghiz (Genghis) Khan. Babur took Delhi and was named the first *padishah*, or Mughal emperor, of India. It was only after the accession of Babur's grandson Akbar in 1556 that the Mughals consolidated their rule. Through a combination of negotiation and force, Akbar united most of the subcontinent and built an elaborate and efficient bureaucratic regime. This system was far superior to anything in Europe at the time and allowed the Mughals to run a region that already had over 100 million inhabitants.

The Mughals never managed to subdue all their opponents and almost always faced violent opposition, either from rival Muslim claimants to the throne or from Hindus and Sikhs struggling to regain control over their own land. More important for the long run, the Mughals never tried to change mass values, including religion, outside of their bastions in the north. As a result, Islam remained a minority religion and the Mughals adapted to local conditions and became every bit as much Indian as they were Muslim. Among other things, they did not seek to eliminate the caste system. In fact, because many *jati* seem to have converted to Islam en masse in an attempt to improve their social and economic lot in life, there are some castes in the Indian, Bangladeshi, and Pakistani Muslim communities despite Islam's emphasis on equality.

Toward the end of the seventeenth century, the last of the great Mughals, Alamgir, dedicated the last quarter-century of his life to uniting the subcontinent. He assembled an army of unprecedented proportions and traveled with it in a "moving capital" that was thirty miles in circumference and had five hundred thousand "residents." On average, one hundred thousand people died during each year of the campaign, which ultimately ended with the Mughals' conquest of the bulk of India in 1707. It proved, however, to be a Pyrrhic victory. Alamgir himself died two years later, leaving an overextended empire that quickly fell prey to infighting among the Mughals and opposition from the countryside.

British Colonialism

Ultimately, the greatest threat to Mughal rule came from a new source: Europe. Portuguese traders had established a beachhead in India as early as 1498. By the middle of the eighteenth century, British and French merchant companies, supported by private armies, operated from coastal bases. Gradually, the British emerged as the most powerful of the European forces in India, largely because of their victories in wars fought back in Europe.

From its base in Calcutta, the **British East India Company** began to expand. It should be stressed that this first stage in the British takeover was not carried out by a

The Enfield mutiny.

government, but by a private corporation—albeit one with strong state support. Thus, the architects of British colonial rule stressed profit rather than political conquest. At that time, the colonizers were more than willing to allow local rulers to remain in power if they helped the company's commercial operations. Indeed, their policy was to find or, if necessary, create a class of leaders who would be loyal to Britain and who could themselves profit from the trading networks the British established.

By the early nineteenth century, the company had spread itself too thin. There were years when it lost money and could not pay its debts to the English crown. Meanwhile, it also lost its monopoly over British trade to a new generation of merchants who undermined the weaving industry of Bengal by shipping Indian cotton to the new factories in northern England. In so doing, these merchants magnified the anger many Indians already felt, and fears of popular protest led the British to take more and more territory under their military "protection."

Tensions boiled over in 1857 when the British introduced the Enfield rifle for use by its army, which included a large number of Indian soldiers. The rifle used grease from cows and pigs, which offended Hindus and Muslims, respectively. In the first anticolonial mutiny, they killed a number of British soldiers, freed some prisoners, and captured Delhi at the cost of hundreds of British lives, including women and children.

The British fought back with what Stanley Wolpert calls "terrible racial ferocity."[2] Although the outcome was never

in doubt, the British wreaked savage vengeance on the Indian population, destroying the social bridges that had been built between themselves and the people. The mutiny also proved to be the death knell for this peculiar mix of state and private colonization.

On 2 August 1858, the British Parliament passed the **Government of India Act**, which transferred all the company's powers to the British crown. As the map in Figure 12.1 shows, the British never took direct control of the entire country, but even in the areas where "princely states" continued to exist, the British called the political shots. The British raj was an elaborate bureaucratic system that relied heavily on the cooperation of the Indian elite. It could hardly have been otherwise, given that Indians outnumbered the British by more than ten to one. Indeed, this was a problem colonial rulers faced everywhere, as we will see in the discussion of colonial rule in Nigeria and Mexico.

At the top of the raj was a secretary of state who was a member of the British cabinet in London and was responsible for Indian affairs. He, in turn, appointed a viceroy who served in India, usually for five years. The administration was dominated by the **Indian Civil Service**, which, despite its name, was chosen on the basis of competitive examinations given only in London until 1923.

The Struggle for Independence

As was the case throughout the empire, British colonial rule in India planted the seeds of its own destruction. Its oppression of the Indian people and, ironically, its use of Indian elites in business, education, civil administration,

---

[2]Stanley Wolpert, *A New History of India*, 3rd ed. (New York: Oxford University Press, 1989), 237.

FIGURE 12.1 British India circa 1900

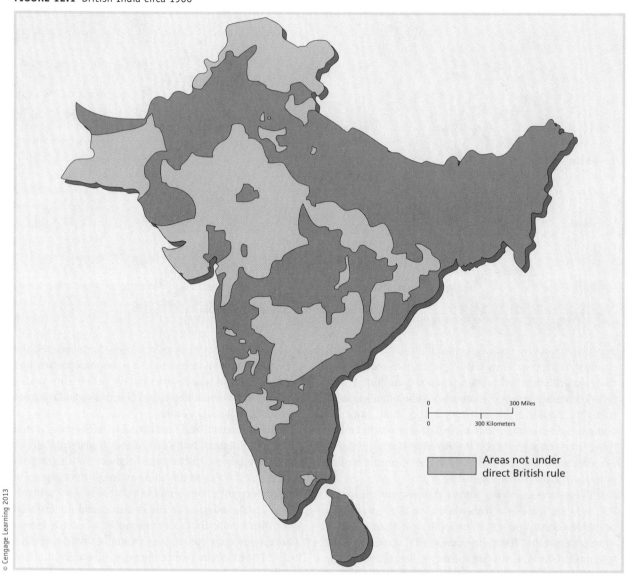

Areas not under
direct British rule

© Cengage Learning 2013

and the military created an ever growing body of people who objected to the raj. What makes India unique is the way this opposition to colonial rule came together in a mostly unified and nonviolent movement that achieved independence very early and that endowed the new state with a consensus its first generation of leaders could use to get the country off to a good start.

Opposition to British rule intensified after the Enfield mutiny. By the 1880s, a group of well-educated, upper-caste Indians began talking about *swaraj*, or self-rule. Some were merchants who had benefited from British rule but came to see how much they were discriminated against at the same time. Others were intellectuals who, ironically, had discovered their Hindu or Muslim roots while receiving a British education.

Frustrations with colonial rule came to a head in 1883 when the British enacted a new law that actually was designed to aid Indians by allowing some of them to serve on juries that tried Europeans. The one hundred thousand or so British then living in India forced the government to back down. As Wolpert, again, put it:

> **It soon became painfully clear to more and more middle-class Indians, however, that, no matter how well intentioned or powerful individual Englishmen might be, the system they served was fundamentally unresponsive and hostile to many basic Indian needs, aspirations, and desires.[3]**

---

[3]Wolpert, *New History*, 56.

In December 1885, seventy-three Indians met in Bombay to form the Indian National Congress. The Congress advocated *swaraj* and demanded that Indian Civil Service exams be given in India as well as in England so that Indians would have a better chance of gaining admission to the increasingly powerful service.

Meanwhile, the British raj became more ruthless and arbitrary. Costly wars were fought to conquer and then retain land on the frontiers of the subcontinent in what is Myanmar, Afghanistan, and Tibet. Then in 1905, the British decided to split Bengal into two. This action infuriated the nationalists, leading Congress to launch its first widespread protest movement: a boycott of British imports. The polite petitions and requests of Congress's first twenty years turned into the first steps of what would be a nationwide, nonviolent revolutionary movement. By 1908, imports had been cut by more than a quarter. Indians, instead, started buying the more expensive *swadeshi* ("of our country") cloth woven in new factories in Bombay and in other northern cities.

The British responded by arresting and prosecuting hundreds of Congress leaders, which further incensed younger activists, many of whom turned to violence. The adoption of what could only be called terrorist tactics split Congress and enabled the British to gain the upper hand.

World War I fueled hopes for independence among Indian leaders. Most agreed to support the British war effort on the assumption that doing so would enhance their chances for freedom. Those hopes were quickly dashed, however. Proposed political reforms died in the British House of Lords. Meanwhile, Indian soldiers were being killed by the thousands in distant lands while the economy suffered from the loss of its huge markets in Germany. To make matters worse, Indian troops, including Muslims, were used in the invasion of parts of the Ottoman Empire. The end of the war brought anything but the hoped-for transfer of power to Indian hands. All political meetings were banned, and in April 1919 troops led by Brigadier R. E. H. Dyer opened fire without warning on a group of Hindus at Jallianwala Bagh, killing four hundred and wounding more than one thousand. At that point, thousands more Indians joined the movement, demanding outright independence.

For the next twenty years, the Indian independence movement was to be dominated by Congress and its remarkable leader, **Mohandas Karamchand Gandhi** (1869–1948). In the early 1920s, Gandhi led a massive boycott of British goods that landed hundreds of Congress leaders in jail. By the end of 1921, it was clear that the boycott was not going to lead to independence any time soon. Frustration with the Gandhian approach set in, which led to violence between Hindus and Muslims that would culminate in the partition of the subcontinent into two countries in 1947. Meanwhile, Gandhi was sent to prison, where he served two years of a six-year term. After his release, Gandhi pulled back from active politics for the rest of the decade, claiming that India was not ready for a nonviolent movement.

Despite the failures of the 1920s, two important breakthroughs had occurred. First, until then Congress had been a movement of intellectual upper-caste leaders. Gandhi's personal integrity, simple life, and political strategy brought the broad masses of the Indian population into the struggle for independence. Second, new leaders emerged within Congress who added a more modern approach to Gandhi's traditional spiritualism. Most important of these was the young, British-educated Brahmin Jawaharlal Nehru, who by the end of the 1920s was already mayor of Allahabad and was exploring ways of combining socialist ideas with *satyagraha* and *ahimsa*. The independence movement took on new life in early 1930 when Gandhi proclaimed a salt boycott. Salt was one of the few commodities all Indians needed and it had been heavily taxed by the British. Gandhi and seventy-eight colleagues began a two-hundred-mile march to the sea, where they gathered salt as a symbol of their resistance against the British. The sight of the tiny sixty-one-year-old, half-naked man leading his band inspired millions of other Indians and led to yet another wave of arrests that included both Gandhi and Nehru.

Talks between the British and prominent Indians soon began, but Congress was excluded, which led to even more support for the opposition. Gandhi launched one of his famous fasts. More demonstrations occurred, culminating in the Government of India Act of 1935, which expanded the franchise and enabled Congress to take over eight provinces two years later.

The experience of governing frustrated Gandhi, Nehru, and their allies. In particular, they proved unable to maintain any semblance of intercommunal unity as Hindu and Muslim nationalists grew farther and farther apart.

World War II was to bring an end not only to British rule but also to Gandhi's dream of a united and peaceful India. When the war broke out, most Indians seemed to be either apathetic or to unenthusiastically support the Allies. Gandhi led thousands of protesters in a campaign demanding that the British "quit India." A few of his former rivals in Congress even collaborated with the Nazis.

The British sent a high-ranking delegation to stabilize the situation on the subcontinent, which everyone now acknowledged would gain independence after the war ended. However, negotiations between Congress and the Muslim League broke down, which also made it likely that colonial India would be divided into Hindu and Muslim states.

Talks about how to partition India began in earnest right after the war but got nowhere during 1945 and 1946. In February 1947, Prime Minister Clement Attlee told Parliament that Britain had decided to relinquish power to

Profiles
Mohandas Karamchand Gandhi

Mohandas Karamchand Gandhi was born in 1869. His family was reasonably upper-caste and his father was the chief minister of a small, unimportant princely state.

Like many privileged and ambitious Indians of his day, Gandhi studied in England. He then spent twenty years in South Africa, where he practiced law and served as the informal political advisor for the large Indian community there. In 1914 he returned to India and began pressing for independence. By 1920 he was already a prominent Congress leader and in the aftermath of the violence of the immediate post-war years, the other leaders made him their de facto leader, in part because he had such a broad appeal based on his commitment to nonviolence.

Gandhi was a remarkable man whose views, power, and impact cannot be summarized in a few sentences. He was one of the few truly charismatic leaders of the twentieth century, whose power stemmed not from his personality or oratory but from his conduct, in which every action was based on humility and principle.

Gandhi was a devout Hindu. Despite his worldly success, he lived the ascetic life of a Hindu *sadhu*, or holy man, wearing only plain white robes made of cloth he spun and wove himself. Gandhi and his family lived in rural communities known as ashrams, where they forswore almost all modern (that is, Western) human pleasures.

Personally, Gandhi rejected all forms of violence. Moreover, he realized that, given the British war machine, there was no way India could win its independence through the use of violence. In its place, Gandhi

Mohandas Gandhi in the simple clothing he always wore, even when, as in this case, he was meeting with top British officials.

offered a radically new strategy based on two Hindu concepts: *satyagraha* (holding fast to truth) and *ahimsa* (nonviolence toward all forms of life). Instead of violence, Gandhi offered fasts, boycotts, and marches. Instead of consumption of British goods, Gandhi offered self-reliance, especially the use of homespun cloth.

Because of his spirituality and devotion, he was known as the Mahatma, or "holy one." ■

"responsible Indian hands" by June of the following year. He dispatched Lord Louis Mountbatten, the dashing commander of British forces in Southeast Asia during the war and Queen Victoria's great-grandnephew, to be the last viceroy and to supervise the transition to independence.

Within weeks of his arrival, violence broke out throughout the country. Mountbatten helped convince the most important Indian leaders that the creation of a separate Muslim Pakistan was inevitable. Only Gandhi refused to accept partition, and he roamed the country trying to

quell the rioting. But the inevitable came sooner than anyone expected. By the summer of 1947, Great Britain, the Indian National Congress, and the Muslim League agreed to make about 80 percent of the colony part of a new and independent India and to turn the rest into Pakistan, itself divided in two parts in the northwestern and northeastern (now Bangladesh) corners of the subcontinent.

Even though the new countries were to be overwhelmingly Hindu and Muslim, respectively, as many as 50 million people were caught within the borders of the "other" country. Within days, most of them started to flee in both directions. The outbursts of communal violence that accompanied the refugee movement continued beyond August 15, 1947, the day India and Pakistan both formally gained their independence.

All this happened over Gandhi's objections. He began yet another fast to try to get people to end the violence. From almost everyone's perspective, however, Gandhi and his ideals were a thing of the past. The demands of governing independent India seemed to call for more pragmatic leaders such as Nehru. Gandhi accused Congress of corruption and its leaders of engaging in power politics. He even went so far as to demand that the venerable organization be dissolved.

Meanwhile, because of his support for all Indians, including outcastes, Muslims, and Sikhs, Gandhi had earned the enmity of militant Hindus. On January 30, 1948, a member of one of one of the militant Hindu groups assassinated him while he was on his way to lead a prayer meeting. That evening, Nehru announced during a national radio broadcast that "the light has gone out of our lives and there is darkness everywhere." Though Nehru was only talking about one man, his words were prophetic, because the assassination also marked the death of Gandhi's principles (see Table 12.3).

The New Republic

The movement for Indian independence was not as unified, principled, or nonviolent as Gandhi would have wanted. However, it did have two legacies that helped the Nehru-led republic maintain its democratic regime and make progress on a number of social and economic fronts in its first twenty years of independence. In fact, no other Third World country has started with so much working in its favor.

Because of the tactics Congress followed and because the independence movement lasted so long and developed as it did, there was a strong sense of national identity. This identification with India was a highly positive one, which for most people probably was as important as any religious, ethnic, caste, or linguistic attachment. People had little trouble thinking of themselves as both Indian and, say, a lower-caste Hindu, which was rarely the case in the other new countries of Africa and Asia.

The new country had a strong and popular political party in charge. In the early elections, Congress got the lion's share of the votes and seats in the Lok Sabha. Even more important, because of the way the independence movement had developed, Congress also set about forging coalitions with other parties and organizations as part of the consensus building that was at the heart of Nehruvian values (see Table 12.4). Congress sought to be an inclusive political party. As we will see, although the party had opposition, it also included groups representing all the major ideological and social groups in Indian society. Thus, when problems arose, Congress was able to take positions that would appeal to the disaffected groups, if not co-opt them into the party altogether.

Centralization and Fragmentation

Indian political life has changed dramatically since Nehru died, which is why the historical section of this chapter includes some quite recent events. Indeed, some observers argue that politics in India has changed so much that we can almost think of it as having created a new regime in

TABLE 12.3 Key Events in Indian History since Independence

YEAR	EVENT
1947	Independence
1950	Constitution goes into effect
1964	Jawaharlal Nehru dies, replaced by Lal Bahadur Shastri
1966	Shastri dies, replaced by Indira Gandhi
1975	Emergency Rule begins
1977	Emergency Rule ends; first non-Congress government
1979	Congress returns to power
1984	Indira Gandhi assassinated; Rajiv Gandhi succeeds her
1989	Second non-Congress government
1991	Rajiv Gandhi assassinated; P. V. Narasimha Rao becomes prime minister
1996	Congress suffers its worst electoral defeat; BJP comes in first
1998	BJP elected; nuclear weapons tested
1999	BJP government reelected
2004	Congress returns to power
2009	Congress reelected massively

TABLE 12.4 Indian Prime Ministers

NAME	YEARS IN OFFICE
Jawaharlal Nehru	1947–64
Lal Bahadur Shastri	1964–66
Indira Gandhi	1966–77
Morarji Desai	1977–79
Charan Singh	1979–80
Indira Gandhi	1980–84
Rajiv Gandhi	1984–89
V. P. Singh	1989–90
Chandra Shekhar	1990–91
P. V. Narasimha Rao	1991–96
H. D. Deve Gowda	1996–98
Atal Bihari Vajpayee	1998–2004
Manmohan Singh	2004–

the 1990s, even though the core institutions have not been substantially altered.

This political change started with the concentration of power in fewer and fewer hands under Indira Gandhi. Nehru was one of the last pre-independence stalwarts, and there was no obvious candidate to succeed him. Congress leaders—known as the **Syndicate**—turned to Lal Bahadur Shastri. However, he never gained more than the grudging support of his colleagues and had not left much of a mark on political life before he died suddenly in 1966.

This time conflict between the party's left and right wings became public. In the end, the conservative Syndicate chose Nehru's daughter, Indira Gandhi (no relation to Mohandas), to be prime minister. They assumed that, as a woman with little political experience, she would be more easily manipulated than any of the other contenders. Perhaps because she had begun her political career at the top and so had never developed strong ties to average Indians or to local political elites, Gandhi adopted an authoritarian leadership style that alienated many of her colleagues. Within a matter of months, Congress split when the business-oriented **Morarji Desai** formed a rival faction.

After an election victory in 1971, Gandhi announced a series of bold new economic initiatives. Land was given to the peasantry, coal mines were nationalized, and harsh new taxes were imposed on the rural and industrial elite. The Fifth Five-Year Plan called for the "removal of poverty" and the "attainment of self-reliance."

Not everyone was happy with Gandhi's policies or her heavy-handed rule, which included appointing her son Sanjay as head of the new state automobile enterprise, thereby catapulting him onto political center stage. Protests against inflation and corruption within Congress became more frequent and strident. Desai became the focal point of an increasingly unified opposition.

Then, on June 12, 1975, the Allahabad High Court found Gandhi guilty of two counts of illegal campaign practices during the 1971 election. Technically, Indian law required her to resign, but Gandhi gave no indication that she would do so. Politicians around the country urged her to step aside temporarily until her legal predicament was resolved. She did nothing of the sort.

Instead, on June 26, Gandhi invoked the constitution's provision for **Emergency Rule**. Civil liberties were suspended. Press censorship was imposed. Twenty-six political groups were banned and all major opposition leaders were arrested. In July, the remaining Members of Parliament (MPs) passed a law extending Emergency Rule indefinitely, enacted constitutional amendments that banned any legal challenges to it, and retroactively cleared Gandhi of any wrongdoing. Parliamentary elections were "postponed" until 1977.

Democracy was in jeopardy. On January 18, 1977, however, Gandhi suddenly ended Emergency Rule, released all political prisoners, and called for national elections in March.

The opposition that bore the brunt of the repression under Emergency Rule was now more united than ever around Desai, the Gandhian socialist Jayaprakash Narayan, and other anti-Indira leaders at both the national and state levels. Their new **Janata** Party beat Congress by 10 percent in the popular vote and won an overwhelming majority of the seats in the Lok Sabha.

But the Janata coalition was a "negative" majority united only in its opposition to what one historian has called the "Indira Raj." Within two years it collapsed. New elections were held, which Congress won, bringing Gandhi back to power. Her second term in office was just as tumultuous as her first. Hopes for radical economic reform disappeared. Many states elected legislatures hostile to central rule, and in a number of cases she dissolved those governments and replaced their leaders with officials loyal to herself.

Gandhi's biggest problem was the increase in ethnic hostility toward what opponents saw as her centralized and authoritarian rule, especially in Punjab. As we will see in more detail later, there was growing and widespread protest from Sikhs, who had begun demanding independence from India and who often used violence in pursuit of their political goals. In May 1984, she imposed martial law in Punjab. The next month Indian troops attacked the Golden Temple in Amritsar, leaving it in ruins and killing hundreds of militant Sikh activists. Finally, on October 31, Sikh members of her own bodyguard assassinated the prime minister, setting off yet another wave of violence with Hindus taking revenge against Sikhs living outside Punjab.

Gandhi's domination of Indian politics for nearly a generation remains a subject of controversy to this day. There is, however, one point on which her supporters and critics agree. She ended Congress's role as a consensus builder. Instead, she centralized power within the party, driving out politicians who either rejected her vision of India's future or who balked at the concentration of power in her hands. And as a result, for the first time in Indian history, a strong opposition was created that was capable of governing as well as winning elections.

She had been grooming her son Sanjay to succeed her, but he was tragically killed in an airplane accident. Consequently, her other, and previously apolitical, son, Rajiv, became the heir apparent. No one was surprised when he became prime minister and immediately called for new elections while sympathy for his mother remained high. Rajiv proved to be an effective campaigner, building support around his youth and his image as "Mr. Clean" in an otherwise corrupt political system. Congress won an unprecedented 80 percent of the seats in the Lok Sabha.

Congress's victory marked the entry of a new generation of leaders into Indian politics. Rajiv Gandhi and his closest advisers were young, well-educated, Westernized, and affluent. They did not share the older generation's commitment to economic planning and democratic socialism, but instead were highly impressed with the market economies in the Western countries where they had studied and worked. At first, then, they seemed to be ideal candidates to implement an Indian version of structural adjustment.

In his five years in office, Rajiv Gandhi did introduce the first market-oriented reforms. However, his reputation for honesty was undermined by the Bofors scandal in which the government and the Congress party machine were implicated in a kickback scheme in their dealings with a Swedish arms manufacturer. Moreover, to keep itself in power, the government had to resort to the same kind of centralizing tactics that had gotten Indira Gandhi into so much trouble.

In 1989, Rajiv Gandhi's term came to an end. Congress was still the only party with a truly national base, but it could not beat another loose opposition coalition, the **Janata Dal**. As in 1977, the Janata Dal was another "negative coalition," brought together in opposition to the incumbent government but with little or no agreement about what it should do if and when it won.

Coalition Politics

In one key respect, the 1989 election marked the last major turning point in Indian politics. With it, Congress lost its traditional role as a hegemonic party because it could no longer build anything approaching a nationwide consensus. Since then, India has been governed by broad-based coalitions because no national party has any realistic chance of winning either a majority of the vote or of the seats in the Lok Sabha. Furthermore, the balance of power is held by politicians with regional, ethnic, or caste bases of support, a point we will return to in the section on political parties.

The Janata Dal coalition elected in 1989 lasted only months, and after two more weak governments fell, early elections were scheduled for 1991. The polls again showed that Congress was in trouble, though no single party mounted a serious challenge.

In the middle of the two-week voting period, Rajiv Gandhi was assassinated by Tamil extremists. The elections

Profiles
The Nehru Clan

No democracy has ever had one family exert as much influence as the Nehru-Gandhi clan in India.

The patriarch, Jawaharlal Nehru, was one of the two most important leaders of the independence movement, and he also served as prime minister during the new country's first, critical years. His daughter, Indira, was as influential (although often less constructively so) from the time she became prime minister in 1966 until her assassination in 1984. At that point, her elder son, Rajiv, became prime minister, but only because his younger brother Sanjay had been killed in an airplane crash.

Formally, the Nehru-Gandhi clan has been out of office since Rajiv's assassination in 1991. Instead, they exert power from (barely) behind the scenes. His Italian-born widow, Sonia, became leader of the Congress Party in 1999. That year, she presided over its third consecutive defeat at the polls. In 2004, she led the party to victory and then surprised the country by declining the prime ministry. Her political future—and that of her children—is uncertain. ■

Jawaharlal Nehru, India's first prime minister, holding his grandson Rajiv Gandhi on his knee. Gandhi eventually succeeded his mother and became the third family member to hold India's highest office.

© Bettmann/CORBIS

were postponed, and Congress desperately sought a new leader. Rajiv's Italian-born widow, Sonia, turned down an offer to run for prime minister and, thus, keep the dynasty alive. Thus, the party had to turn to the seventy-year-old former foreign minister **P. V. Narasimha Rao** (1921–2004), a long-time party loyalist.

When the elections were finally completed, Congress won, though it fell sixteen seats short of an overall majority. The BJP came in second, well ahead of Janata Dal and the regional parties. Narasimha Rao proceeded to form a coalition government with a few of the minor parties. No one expected the new government to do very well given the problems it inherited. Surprisingly, however, it lasted its entire five-year term, during which time it accelerated the pace of economic reform. It was not a strong government, though, being tainted by corruption (Narasimha Rao was sent to jail after he left office) and internal bickering, and it did little to address the country's other problems. It was thus hardly surprising that Rao and Congress went down to a crashing defeat in 1996.

As had the case the other two times Congress lost, a divided coalition won in 1996. This time the erstwhile opposition turned to H. D. Deve Gowda, a little-known politician from the southern state of Karnataka, who was the first prime minister who did not speak Hindi.

Like all of his non-Congress predecessors, Deve Gowda headed an unwieldy coalition consisting of thirteen political parties. Therefore, no one was surprised when it collapsed after less than a year, as did the government of his successor, Inder Gujral.

Early elections were held again in 1998, which cemented coalition politics, though with a new and—for some—worrisome twist. This time the BJP came in a strong first and was able to form a government with twelve other parties under Prime Minister **Atal Bihari Vajpayee** (1924–). Many observers feared that the BJP would stress its fundamentalist Hindu roots and deepen the divisions and intolerance that had marked Indian politics for the preceding generation. However, Vajpayee and his colleagues understood that they had to govern from the center, both to retain the support of their coalition partners and to have any hope of gaining new voters for the BJP.

Congress was able to convince enough of the BJP's partners to defect that it lost a vote of confidence by one vote in March 1999. When early elections were held yet again in September, the BJP's coalition increased its support in the Lok Sabha following a disastrous showing by Congress, now led by **Sonia Gandhi**. Vajpayee was able to put together an even broader coalition of twenty-four parties, which allowed it to remain in office until the end of the parliamentary term in 2004.

That year, Congress scored a surprising but limited victory. Forty-two parties won at least a single seat. The two leading parties barely won half of the 543 elected seats (two members from the Anglo-English community are appointed). Prime Minister **Manmohan Singh** became head of a coalition of thirteen parties, only five of which had ten or more MPs. Then, as we saw earlier, Congress was returned to office in 2009 with an even stronger majority coalition.

Democratization in India

India is one of the few Southern countries that has been able to sustain a democratic regime for an extended period of time. The reasons for this are not clear, largely because we do not understand how democratization works anywhere all that well. Nonetheless, two main factors seem to stand out. First, India's independence movement and first governments were able to build a strong sense of national identification and support for the new state. Second, despite the difficulties of recent years, the government has functioned reasonably well and has avoided the kind of serious centrifugal conflict that has disrupted political life in so many other Third World countries. ∎

POLITICAL CULTURE

The historical section of this chapter was longer than most because it was only in the past few years that the basic contours of contemporary Indian politics were set.

As far as political culture is concerned, this long history combines with the diversity of India in two ways that might seem contradictory at first glance. On the one hand, the growing identification with region, caste, and religion has spawned considerable conflict, some of which has turned violent. On the other hand, ever since independence, there has always been widespread identification with and support for the Indian regime. A generation ago, many observers thought that the growing intolerance might tear India apart. Now, however, there is general agreement that Indian democracy is secure.

We will explore these two points in this section, and each will appear in one form or another throughout the rest of the chapter. Keep in mind, however, that because public opinion polling is not very well developed, it is easier to see these points in what we know about the way Indians act than in what we can guess about the way they think.

Challenges to Culture and Country

As we saw earlier, Indira Gandhi's eighteen years in and out of office marked a major turning point in Indian politics as consensus and coalition building gave way to more centralized power and adversarial politics. This new political style has been echoed in a culture marked by division and conflict.

By far the most important manifestation of this cultural division has been the rise of regional identification and, with it, periodic demands for the creation of new states along ethnic or religious lines and even for secession from India itself. This topic is important enough that we will defer dealing with it until the section on public policy. Here it is enough to note that in such different regions as Assam, Kashmir, Tamil Nadu, Punjab, and Gujarat the growth in ethnic and regional identification has presented the central state with serious challenges since the 1970s. In the late 1990s, according to one study, as many as 200 of India's 534 districts (the administrative unit below the state level) were experiencing intense conflict.

Next to the growth of regional identification, the most disruptive force has been the rebirth of religious fundamentalism, especially among Hindus. As remarkable as it may seem, many Hindus think of themselves as an oppressed group, even though they make up more than 80 percent of the total population. Politically organized Hindu groups have existed since the creation of the **Rashtriya Swayamsevak Sangh (RSS)** in the early twentieth century. The RSS and similar organizations have become an important and troubling force on the Indian political landscape. In some states, Hindu groups are pressing for reforms that would put the secular commitment of the country's founders into question, including special provisions on divorce and other legal issues for Muslims. Because the growth of Hindu nationalism has been inextricably intertwined with the meteoric rise of the BJP in the 1980s, we will defer dealing with it, too, in more detail until we cover the party system.

Last but by no means least, we cannot ignore the continued importance of caste. Although the constitution and subsequent legislation banned discrimination against *dalits* and other backward castes and tribes, it continues to have a major impact on people's daily lives—from what they do for a living to whom they vote for.

Recall that the fifty thousand or so castes and *jati* are social structures that reflect centuries-old social, racial, and economic divisions. For Hindus, caste is not merely a social category one is born into. It has a religious side as well that carries with it duties and devotions commensurate with one's position in the hierarchy. Caste can still spark protest if members believe that their interests are in jeopardy.

For instance, the creation of the reserved-places scheme for untouchables, members of scheduled tribes, and lower castes touched off massive protests among the upper castes, which included the ritual suicide of hundreds of young Brahmins. More recently, a mere typographical error led to rioting. In 1994 an official document included "Gond-Gowari" instead of "Gond, Gowari," which legally meant that there was no Gowari caste eligible for the set-aside jobs. Furious Gowaris protested in the state of Maharashtra, where most of them lived. By the time the rioting ended a few weeks later, at least 113 Gowaris had died.

Support for the Regime

Despite the aforementioned conflict, there is compelling evidence that most Indians are satisfied with the regime. India has held fourteen national and countless state and local elections since 1947, and only once—during Emergency Rule—did the democratic process fail to hold. In that case, the Indian people repudiated Indira Gandhi and Congress at the first opportunity.

Elections are remarkable events. Every time Indians go to the polls, it is the largest event ever organized by humans. Turnout has averaged 57 percent in each national election, which is a bit higher than that in the United States. But in India, over half of the electorate cannot read enough to comprehend a ballot and has to rely on pictures to identify which party and candidate they prefer. In fact, the poorest Indians vote at a rate higher than the national average. Generally, poorly educated Indians are remarkably well informed about the issues and the politicians before they go to the polls.

In a survey conducted in the mid-1990s, almost seven in ten respondents thought that parties and elections made government function better, as opposed to only a little more than four in ten in 1971. Similarly, six in ten agreed that voting made a difference and, again, the poorest voters were disproportionately likely to take that point of view.

Indian voters have a penchant for electing movie stars, former bandits, and politicians who have previously been convicted of corruption. That said, they also have reelected only about half of the incumbents in most recent elections, compared with an average of about 90 percent in elections for the House of Representatives in the United States with the exception of unusual years like 2010.

Most political scientists are convinced that this supportive side of Indian political culture exists because of the way Indian democracy was created and evolved. Dozens of events, from the way independence was forged to India's ability to build and test nuclear weapons, have added to the pride most Indians feel for their country. Perhaps more than any other public in the world today, they have no trouble combining a positive identification with the nation-state and those with their caste, religion, or ethnicity.

Congress's remarkable leadership in the years before 1947 did a lot to create both this sense of Indian identity and the consensus regarding certain broad public policy goals before independence was achieved. In short, nation building occurred along with and, in some ways, even ahead of state building. This fact undoubtedly helped India survive the first years after the communal strife of partition, when many observers doubted that an egalitarian democratic political system could be grafted onto a society that was both deeply divided and rigidly hierarchical. Some observers, too, thought that elements of Hindu culture, including its emphasis on harmony, pluralism, and spiritual rather than worldly matters, helped smooth the process. Whatever the exact constellation of causes, there is considerable evidence that by the late 1960s India had developed the kind of political culture that helps sustain democracy in Britain and the United States.

The Challenge of Modernization

One other cultural question looms on India's horizon, and it is applicable to many rapidly changing countries in the South. Will India's culture evolve as the country's economy grows and develops more of a Western-style middle class?

There is some evidence that Indians will adapt quite easily. In 2007, almost 7 percent of the population owned a car. Close to two hundred million people had access to cable or satellite television service. Middle-class Indians have become the world's biggest market for blenders, which they use to grind the chilies and other spices they need to make their traditional dishes. Similarly, it seems to take only about six weeks to train English-speaking Indians to sound as if they are from Birmingham, England, or Birmingham, Alabama, so that they can work in call centers that handle routine requests for businesses in Europe and North America.

As rural India has become wealthier, more and more consumer goods have become available. Younger people are, of course, the ones most attracted by these new luxuries. This does not mean, however, that traditional values have disappeared. For example, even though the government ruled dowries illegal years ago, many couples who clamor for Western products at the same time submit to arranged marriages with dowries that can top $6,000 and include a television, refrigerator, or motor scooter.

Worrisome signs of the persistence of traditional values involve the treatment of girls and women. In most parts of India, male babies still are prized whereas girls are seen as a burden, and not only because their parents will have to pay dowries to get them married. Medical care for girls has always been worse because parents do not seek treatment for them as often. If there is a food shortage, boys are more likely to be fed and girls are allowed to starve. The now widespread use of ultrasound tests for pregnant women has added a new twist to the discrimination against girls. There are only about 850 live births of girl babies for every 1,000 boys because parents often choose to abort a fetus if they know it is a girl.

It is too early to tell what the overall impact of economic growth on cultural values will be. There have been some protests against the presence of Western institutions, including, as surprising as it may seem, Coca-Cola's sponsorship of international sporting events. However, there has been little of the open and visceral rejection of Western culture we see in much of the Global South even among the overwhelming majority of India's 150 million Muslims.

POLITICAL PARTICIPATION

The tensions between age-old traditions and modern democratic practices extend beyond the political culture to the day-to-day behavior of India's people and the organizations they form. As in any long-standing democracy, this, in turn, means focusing on political parties and elections. As we explore political participation here, you will see yet again the interplay between the two and the challenges they pose.

The End of the Congress System

A handful of democracies exist in which a single party has dominated political life for an extended period of time: the Social Democrats in Sweden since the depression, the Christian Democrats in postwar Italy, and the Liberal Democratic Party in Japan. India's Congress was one of them. Although never able to win an outright majority at the polls, it routinely took advantage of India's British-style single-member-district electoral system and the division of its opponents to win overwhelming majorities in the Lok Sabha until the onset of coalition politics in 1989 🖘 (www.aicc.org.in).

Congress was successful then for the same reasons it had been prior to independence. Paradoxically, it both stood by its basic principles and proved to be remarkably flexible in dealing with allies and potential adversaries. Of all the democracies covered in this book, India is the one in which class has played the least important role, even during Indira Gandhi's most radical years. Rather, the Indian party system and politics in general involve many different, overlapping cleavages. As a result, a party that hopes to win enough votes to govern has to be able to balance the interests and demands of enough of the groups spawned by India's many divisions to forge a majority coalition in the Lok Sabha.

Nehru's Congress party did that extremely well. However, the fragile balance that gave the party its hegemonic power was not to survive the leadership struggle after the unexpected death of Prime Minister Shastri in 1966.

As we have seen, Indira Gandhi challenged the Syndicate and won, but her victory had tremendous costs for Congress.

TABLE 12.5 Congress's Share of the Vote and Seats in the Lok Sabha, 1952–91

YEAR	PERCENTAGE OF VOTE	NUMBER OF SEATS
1952	45.0	364
1957	47.8	371
1962	44.7	361
1967	40.8	283
1971	43.7	352
1977	34.5	154
1980	43.7	353
1984	48.1	415
1989	39.5	197
1991	36.0	226

Over the next decade, the Congress system fell apart in three ways. Its share of the vote declined, its organization deteriorated, and it faced new opposition (see Table 12.5).

The decline began with the 1967 elections in which Congress's majority in the Lok Sabha was reduced to 54 percent. Congress also lost six states, in each case as a result of its inability to respond to local pressures. Those defeats, combined with the initial signs of Gandhi's heavy-handed leadership, provoked the first post-independence split within the party. Gandhi was unwilling to become a pawn of the powerful factional leaders in Congress. Her relationship with them worsened and the tensions erupted during the 1969 election for the largely symbolic presidency. Against the wishes of the Syndicate, Gandhi supported the incumbent, V. V. Giri, who was running as an independent. The Syndicate then threw her out of the party. Congress MPs, however, voted overwhelmingly in her favor.

Despite her personal victory, the party split, ironically, during the one-hundredth anniversary of Mohandas Gandhi's birth. Now there were two Congress parties: the Syndicate's Congress (O for organization) and Indira Gandhi's Congress (I for Indira). Congress (I) now lacked a working parliamentary majority, and the Gandhi government stayed in power only through the support of former opposition parties, including the communists and Tamil nationalists.

In 1971, Gandhi dissolved the Lok Sabha and called for new elections. In the campaign, it became clear that Congress (I) was going to be a new kind of party in at least two respects. First, it ran on a far more radical platform to appeal to the poor and disadvantaged, especially the scheduled castes, youth, and Muslims. Second, the party was personalized around Gandhi's rule in ways never before seen in Indian politics. Not only did Gandhi centralize her power in the new party, but the opposition also made her the focal point of its campaign, with the slogan *Indira hatao* (Indira out of power) as its centerpiece.

Gandhi confounded the experts by winning 44 percent of the vote and 352 of 518 seats. State legislative elections the following year gave Congress (I) even wider margins of victory. Gandhi and Congress (I) won in large part because the opposition was so divided and ineffective, which was also typically the case in other countries in which a single party dominated for a long period of time.

From that point on, because of Gandhi's performance as prime minister and as head of the Congress, the other faction soon disappeared (so we can drop the I) and contributed to the collapse of the party system as it had existed since independence. Perhaps the most damaging of her actions was the imposition of Emergency Rule. Almost

Indian election officials counting the vote in May 1996. Because so many Indians are illiterate, ballots have pictures as well as words to identify each candidate's party affiliation.

AP Images

as important was the prominence given her younger son, Sanjay, who was widely viewed as little more than a power-hungry young man. Sanjay pushed such controversial policies as family planning and forced sterilization. He also controlled access to his mother, the "household" of personal advisers to the prime minister, the Youth Congress, and much of the government's repressive apparatus.

In 1977, Gandhi made yet another of the mistakes that plagued her final decade. She decided to end Emergency Rule and hold new elections on the assumption that she would win again.

This time she got it wrong. There was widespread opposition to Emergency Rule, her policies, and Sanjay's style. More MPs quit Congress, including Jagjivan Ram, a senior cabinet member, Congress leader, and the most prominent untouchable in political life. Meanwhile, Morarji Desai forged the Janata Party, a coalition of four opposition groups.

Congress was routed, dropping to 34.5 percent of the vote. Both Indira and Sanjay Gandhi lost their seats. Janata and its allies won a clear majority with 298 MPs. Desai's government brought Indira Gandhi to trial and sent her to prison for a brief period. Quickly, however, it became clear that nothing held Janata together other than its desire to drive Gandhi from office. By 1979 the coalition had fallen apart, and the following year Prime Minister Charan Singh realized his minority government could not survive and called for new elections.

For the first time, an Indian election had turned into a personalized contest focused on the three main candidates for the prime ministry: Singh, Ram, and Gandhi. This time support swung to Congress, which won about 43 percent of the vote and an overwhelming two-thirds majority in the Lok Sabha. As in 1972, victory at the national level was followed by more successes at the state level.

But all was not well with Congress. Gandhi had taken the party even farther to the Left. She also insisted on personal loyalty to herself, her family, and the rest of her inner circle. After Sanjay died in June 1980, Indira Gandhi tapped her elder son, Rajiv, who until then had shown no interest in national affairs.

But Rajiv Gandhi quickly took to political life, and by 1982 he had established himself as his mother's likely successor, a job he took on following her assassination. He hoped to modernize the country by breaking away from many of the traditional political practices and economic policies Congress had followed since independence in favor of a more pragmatic approach emphasizing modern management systems. Indeed, he used the one-hundredth anniversary of the founding of Congress to launch an attack against what the party had become, at least implicitly, criticizing both his mother and the remaining party oligarchs.

As we will see in the policy section, most of those reforms never got beyond the drawing board. Gandhi suffered a series of defeats in state elections. Moreover, the new government faced unprecedented challenges from dissidents in a number of states. Finally, Gandhi's reputation for honesty wore off as his government was implicated in scandals much like those that had tarnished his mother's reputation.

In short, Gandhi and his advisers quickly realized that despite the magnitude of their victory in 1984, their hold on power was tenuous at best. They stopped taking risks in terms of both policy making and reforming the Congress Party. In fact, by 1989 he was running Congress in much the same way his mother had—with an iron fist. Further, the party itself had lost virtually all the enthusiasm for and commitment to social change that had characterized it during his grandfather's time. The deterioration of Congress's fortunes continued after his death, despite the surprisingly effective leadership initially exercised by Narasimha Rao. As we saw previously, even he could not stem the public's dissatisfaction with the party and it went down to another crushing defeat in 1996.

The defeat and corruption charges Rao was facing forced him from the party leadership. He was replaced by seventy-eight-year-old Sitaram Kesri. Kesri was responsible for bringing down the Gujral government, which necessitated the 1998 elections in which Congress saw its seat total decline once again (see Table 12.6). The party lost despite the fact that Rajiv's widow, Sonia, finally joined and campaigned actively on its behalf.

Sonia Gandhi then became party president and led its 1999 election campaign, but everything went wrong that possibly could have. The fact that she was born and raised in Italy (though she had become an Indian citizen in 1983) cost her votes. So, too, did a series of tactical blunders that convinced many voters she would not be as effective a leader as the BJP's Vajpayee.

Much to the surprise of most observers, Gandhi proved to be an outstanding campaigner during the 2004 and 2009 election campaigns and led her party to victory without dramatically altering its decades-old stance as a secular organization in favor of economic reform. Those elections are important enough that we will consider them separately after discussing the other parties.

It is enough now to note that the very non-charismatic Singh has been in charge for two successful elections in a row. That said, Sonia Gandhi is the real force in Congress, and she has children waiting in the wings. . . .

TABLE 12.6 Seats in the Lok Sabha: Major Parties and Their Allies, 1996–99

PARTY GROUP	1996	1998	1999
Congress and allies	139	148	134
BJP and allies	186	251	296
United Front	111	97	—
Others	98	51	107

Note: The first three rows include only major political parties and minor parties that had firm alliances with them. Other winning candidates are included in the "Others" category. Also, seven seats were not filled following the 1999 election.

The Bharatiya Janata Party

Twenty years ago the BJP would not have featured prominently in a book like this. It had topped 10 percent of the vote in 1989 and won eighty-five seats, but few serious observers thought it could do much better, let alone temporarily become India's largest party (**www.bjp.org**).

Although the BJP itself is a rather new party, its roots lie in the revival of organized Hindu fundamentalism that began with the formation of the RSS in 1925. It was a disgruntled RSS member who assassinated Mohandas Gandhi in 1948. In the 1950s and 1960s, the RSS led campaigns opposing the slaughter of cows, the presence of Christian missionaries, and other alleged evils.

It also had a political party, the Jan Sangh, that won more than 7 percent of the vote only one time and was part of the Janata coalition in 1977 and 1979. Jan Sangh left Janata and ran on its own under the new BJP label in 1984, winning exactly the same percentage of the vote as in 1971.

The party was beginning to score major breakthroughs in the northern "cow belt," where it won control of four states during the 1970s. There it did particularly well among young men from upper castes who felt threatened by affirmative action and other programs they believed would undermine their social status and economic power.

The BJP's symbolic breakthrough occurred as the result of a clash centered on the disputed mosque/temple in Ayodhya. The building had been a mosque, which some Muslims claim had been built by the first Mughal conqueror, Babur, during the sixteenth century. Some devout Hindus disputed that claim, arguing that the site was the birthplace of one of their major gods, Lord Ram, which made it one of the holiest places in their tradition.

Not surprisingly, the building had long been a source of contention between Hindus and Muslims. For most of the past century or so, however, a *modus vivendi* had been worked out in which Muslims used it on Fridays and Hindus were free to pray there during the rest of the week.

Controversy broke out in 1986 after a judge's ruling closed the building to everyone. The rapidly growing Vishwa Hindu Parishad (VHP), or Worldwide Hindu Brotherhood, which made the freeing of such properties its highest priority, entered the scene. It routinely gathered one hundred thousand devout Hindus along the banks of the river next to the temple/mosque. Within two years, the VHP had mustered enough support to convince a judge to open the facility only to Hindus. This, in turn, led to Muslim counterprotests. In one typical incident, a riot broke out in 1989 after the VHP announced that it would add on to the building using specially consecrated bricks. More than 150 people were killed.

Later that year, Congress was defeated and replaced by a government that convinced the VHP to postpone construction of the new addition. Pressures around Ayodhya then eased until a Hindu mob destroyed the mosque and started building a new temple in December 1992. The violence soon spread far from Ayodhya. Hindu revivalist movements, such as the Shiv Sena in Mumbai, took to the streets, demanding vengeance and attacking Muslims who obviously had nothing to do with the situation in Ayodhya. At least 1,700 died in Mumbai alone.

Evidence of the destruction at Ayodhya mosque/temple, which has been in dispute between Hindus and Muslims for a generation.

DOUG CURRAN/Staff/AFP/Getty Images

The BJP and related organizations had thus built a base of support reminiscent of France's National Front. Its leaders had taken extreme positions and used what can only be described as thinly veiled racist rhetoric.

Most notorious on that score has been the BJP's ally the Shiv Sena, and its leader, Bal Thackeray (1926–), a cartoonist and former gang leader 🔗 (**www.shivsena .org**). Thackeray is the former mayor of Mumbai, the most important politician in Maharashtra, and a vital cog in the BJP machine. He rose to prominence by, among other things, refusing to allow Kentucky Fried Chicken to open restaurants in Maharashtra because there had been some minor health code violations in KFC restaurants elsewhere in the country. It was hard, however, to raise too much of a fuss about a restaurant using excess amounts of MSG or having a dead fly in the batter when street vendors in the same neighborhood were selling cucumbers soaked in water that came from open sewers. Thackeray's supporters charged (with some degree of accuracy) that the grain needed to raise KFC's chickens would be better put to use directly in feeding people. Most observers, though, were convinced that his real anger was rooted in the fact that the chain was foreign and that its parent company, PepsiCo, did business in Pakistan.

It is easy to not take such actions seriously. However, Shiv Sena and other groups loosely affiliated with the BJP are responsible for widespread violence against Muslims, Sikhs, Christians, and other minorities. They maintain paramilitary organizations, some of which are armed and can mobilize tens of thousands of activists for major protests such as those over Ayodhya.

The BJP also has a strong nationalist streak. Some of its more extreme leaders have argued against economic reforms because they will open the country up to foreign economic and cultural influences. And few analysts who were familiar with the BJP were surprised when the Vajpayee government tested nuclear weapons in 1998 because such plans had long been a part of the party's platform.

In power, however, the BJP proved to be far more moderate, in large part because it had to be to retain the support of its coalition partners. Vajpayee's government continued the liberal economic reforms to be detailed later in this chapter. It did not propose legislation that would make India into a Hindu country or in any significant way undermine the commitment to secularism expressed in the constitution. In fact, it took a strong nationalist stance only in regard to relations with Pakistan—including its testing of nuclear weapons—and the related issue of Kashmir. But even there, the BJP did not act in dramatically different ways than a Congress-led government would have.

The Other Parties

It is impossible to cover all the other Indian political parties in an introductory text because there are so many of them. Thirty-seven of them won 209 seats in 2009 (along with nine independents). To complicate matters further,

Bal Thackeray, along with other right-wing Hindu activists, at a meeting during the 1996 election campaign in which the Hindu BJP party came in first.

AP Images

they change so frequently that it is impossible to present the kind of tables used in previous chapters to document election results. What is more, almost all of them operate within a single state or appeal only to a single ethnic, linguistic, or religious group. This is true even of those whose name or ideology might suggest a national appeal.

Things have not always been this way. Under Nehru, several opposition parties enjoyed nationwide support, including the Communist Party of India and the socialists on the Left, and the Jan Sangh and Swatantra on the traditionalist Right. As noted above, however, Congress had factions of its own with similar beliefs. Moreover, Congress found it fairly easy to adopt at least some of the opposition's goals, as in the redrawing of the internal boundaries so that each major linguistic group was predominant in at least one state.

During the 1960s, however, more and more politicians left Congress to form new parties, of which only the regional ones prospered at the time. More important, these politicians went through a radical transformation of their own. Most were arrested during Emergency Rule, which served only to harden their opposition. It also led them to the realization that whatever their many differences, they had to work together. As a result, most of the former Congress politicians, plus some of the others from the original opposition, formed Janata in 1977. As we saw earlier, these groups had only one thing in common—opposition to Congress.

These small parties can be divided into two main types:

- *The remnants of the traditional left.* Two parties call themselves communist: the traditional, orthodox Communist Party of India (CPI), which has seen its support dwindle to less than 3 percent of the national vote, and the more radical Communist Party of India-Marxist (CPM), which has support primarily in the state of West Bengal, where it is the largest party. There are also some even weaker socialist parties. In practice, these are all regional parties with no illusions about winning votes nationwide. Their support, however, was needed to keep the Singh government elected in 2004 in power until Congress' sweeping victory in 2009.

- *Regional parties.* Every state that has been subject to ethnic, linguistic, or religious unrest has spawned at least one political party that claims to speak for those interests, including the Akali Dal in Punjab, the DMK and AIADMK in Tamil Nadu, the National Conference in Jammu and Kashmir, and the Telegu Desam in Andhra Pradesh.

By 2004, most of these groups had aligned themselves as part of coalitions with either Congress or the BJP, which won sixty-seven and thirty-seven seats, respectively, from them. Another seventy-four members of the Lok Sabha were elected from the extremely loose All India Forward Bloc.

The Elections of 2004 and 2009

As the 2004 election neared, all the signs pointed to a fourth straight victory by the BJP and its partners in the National Democratic Alliance. Vajpayee's government had muted some of its more nationalistic stands. Polls showed it had gained support among all groups other than the *dalits*, scheduled tribes, and Muslims who had always been put off by what most of their voters saw as Hindu fundamentalism. The government even expected to benefit from India's victory against arch rival Pakistan in that winter's test match series in cricket.

Congress did find a winning issue by appealing to the 300 million people who lived in chronic poverty. The lucky people who, for instance, got high-tech jobs outsourced from the West numbered barely a million at a time when 9 million young people were entering the workforce each year, most of whom ended up unemployed. Sonia Gandhi and her party appealed to this largely rural bloc of voters who passed below the pundits' and pollsters' radar screens. When the votes were counted, Congress and its formal allies won thirty-two more seats than the BJP but fell short of a majority (see Table 12.7). Because it could count on support from the Left Front, Congress immediately set out to form a new government. The only surprise was Gandhi's decision not to take the prime ministry, which left the job to Singh, who had been the architect of Congress' first economic reforms in the early 1990s and to whom we will return later.

TABLE 12.7 The Indian Elections of 2004 and 2009

PARTY	VOTE 2004 (%)	SEATS IN LOK SABHA 2004	VOTE 2009 (%)	SEATS IN LOK SABHA 2009
BJP	22.2	138	18.8	116
BJP allies	13.1	47	5.8	43
Congress	26.8	145	28.55	206
Congress allies	7.8	70	8.7	56
Left Front	7.6	59	21.5	79
Minor parties and Independents	22.5	78	6.5	16

The 2009 election was even more of a rout than Table 12.7 suggests because dozens of leftist and minor party members of the Lok Sabha supported the new Singh government giving it an overwhelming majority. By summer 2009, more than enough left-wing and independent deputies supported the government giving it an unassailable edge over the BJP and the rest of the opposition, which should guarantee another five years of Congress rule and continuity in the economic and other reform policies to be discussed in the public policy section. As such, it brings to an end (at least for now) a period of weak governments and frequent elections.

Interest Groups

Because India has been a functioning democracy for more than sixty years, it has the range of interest groups we saw in the countries covered in Part 2—and then some. However, this does not mean that they look and act the same as those in the West.

India has an extensive labor movement that seeks to improve the lot of mostly manual workers. India, in fact, has more than twenty-five thousand unions because the labor law allows any group of seven or more workers to organize one. Nevertheless, only about 10 million people are unionized. Moreover, the unions themselves are fragmented. Most major unions are extensions of political parties rather than autonomous organizations such as the American AFL-CIO or French CFDT. Congress controls the Indian National Trades Union Congress (INTUC). The All-Indian Trades Union Congress (AITUC) is associated with one of

Cricket and the 2004 Election

The passions of Indian politics were on center stage during the winter of 2004 when India began a series of six five-day cricket test matches of six hours each (with additional time for lunch and tea) in Pakistan.

This sport, bequeathed to the subcontinent by their common British colonizer, produces more excitement and more animosity than any American Super Bowl or NCAA Final Four. Analogies are often drawn between cricket and war because both can only have one winner and must thus have one loser (critics of cricket lament that wars often do not last as long as a test match, which they think drags on interminably).

The 2004 test series turned out to be quite different. To be sure, Indian and Pakistani fans painted their faces and cheered against each other as vehemently as ever. However, the hundreds of thousands of Indian fans who traveled to Pakistan for the matches that often ended up as ties found an unexpected welcome from Pakistanis once they left the stadiums.

Overall, cricketers are trying to build bridges between the two countries. In 2003, they fielded a joint team to play (and wallop) New Zealand in a one-day exhibition match. Two of their national stars had a daily television program during a recent series when India played (and was walloped by) Australia.

Scott Barbour/Staff/Getty Images Sport/Getty Image

Indian and Pakistani cricket fans seek reconciliation during the 2004–05 Test Match series.

the communist parties, and the Congress of Indian Trades Union (CITU) is linked to the other. What's more, few of the unions seem to be gaining strength. The one exception may be the Bharatiya Mazdoor Sangh (BMS), which is associated with the BJP.

The unions have a limited impact, too, because they primarily cover workers in the "organized" sector of the economy, in which people are employed for cash wages. Virtually unrepresented are the poorest people, who work in the "informal economy," who do not earn regular wages, and who are more desperately in need of help. Perhaps most important, when unions have chosen to strike, they have rarely been able to overcome the resistance of either the state or private employers.

Similarly, India has no shortage of business associations. The most important of these is the Federation of Indian Chambers of Commerce, which represents some forty thousand enterprises. Unlike the unions, business groups do not have formal ties to parties but have historically supported the conservative wing of Congress and its right-wing rivals. Individual business leaders also gain some leverage because of the substantial contributions they make to individual candidates.

Like the unions, business has not been particularly powerful in India. This lack of influence reflects, in part, the traditional Brahmin disdain for commerce. It also grows out of Congress's preference for socialist policies in the years before Rajiv Gandhi came to power. Primarily, though, business traditionally has been weak because the modern sector of the economy has been dominated by the state. This situation is changing as India opens up its economy, but it is too early to tell how the new generation of entrepreneurs will align themselves politically.

Both business and labor are far less important than the religious, linguistic, and ethnic groups that have gained newfound influence over the past quarter-century. Consider just one example: protest in Assam.

Assam is a poor state in the northeastern part of the country. During the 1950s and 1960s, its fortunes improved when the tea it produces became a significant moneymaker in global markets. But its economy was always fragile and native Assamese never constituted more than a bare majority of the state's population.

In the 1970s, tensions began to mount after significant numbers of Hindus and Muslims fled into the state from war-ravaged and even more impoverished Bangladesh. Predictably, there was widespread concern among the Assamese that they would become a minority in their own state. Thus, the 1970s saw the emergence of a number of organizations that sought to mobilize Assamese worried about their future.

In 1978, eleven organizations came together to form the All Assam Gana Sangram Parishad (AAGSP) or Popular

Conflict
in India

At first glance, it might seem as if India's democracy is threatened by the conflicts that kill at least a thousand people during each election campaign. In practice, however, overall conflict is not that serious in view of the size of the Indian population. Nor does it have as serious implications as the disputes we will see in the next two chapters, largely because even the most outspoken critics of the current government accept the basic "rules of the game" in India. ■

Movement Front. The AAGSP protested the continued immigration of Bengalis from both India and Bangladesh. The All Assam Students' Union even went so far as to demand the expulsion of all foreigners.

The issue was hardly new. Attempts to block the immigration of Muslim Bengalis dated back at least to 1926. But it was a particularly charged issue in the 1970s when the redrawing of Assam's borders reduced the state in size. The various groups launched a campaign to remove non-Assamese from the list of registered voters, a figure some estimated to be 7 million. They also organized massive protest movements that all too frequently launched savage attacks on Muslim Bengalis. In February 1983, a crowd of about 12,000 Assamese killed an estimated 1,400 Bengalis in what became known as the Nellie Massacre. In all, well over 10,000 people died before an agreement was reached in early 1985 between the Assamese leadership and Rajiv Gandhi's government. Less violence occurs now, but a number of farmers and business leaders have raised private armies because neither the central nor the state government can ensure law and order.

Today it is not at all clear how far such protest movements can or will go. Thus far the violence has been contained in the sense that it has not led to serious calls for a new regime or the breakup of India itself. Whether this will remain the case is anybody's guess, especially if the recent pattern of weak coalition governments and sociopolitical fragmentation continues.

Women in Indian Politics

There are plenty of women who have risen to the top of Indian politics and not just Indira and Sonia Gandhi. The current president, Pratibha Patil, for example, is the first woman to hold that post. Although the presidency is largely symbolic, her election is a sign that women are now playing a more prominent role. A number of women have been chief ministers in some states. Feminists should not be too excited by that trend since at least one of them, Phoolan Devi, was a former bandit and ex-convict who became popular politically largely because of her checkered past.

Women are underrepresented in Indian politics. India ranks 97th in the world (tied with Jordan). Less than 10.5 percent of the current Lok Sabha members are women.

There is a small feminist movement, but most observers think that middle class women may lead liberated lives before they get married. But once they are married, they fall back into the traditional pattern of male dominance and, in some cases, control by their mothers-in-law.

Indian women have plenty to be concerned about. Above, we saw that dowries are still the norm. So, too, is everything from wife beating and other forms of violence to unequal pay.

All this is the case despite the fact that the Constitution grants equal rights for all women.

THE INDIAN STATE

India has more than its share of problems, most of which are typical of the Global South. It is unique, however, in that it has kept its democracy alive—if not always flourishing— for more than a half-century. Accordingly, the section on the state will be longer and more detailed than the comparable ones for Iran, Iraq, Nigeria, and Mexico, where the personality of individual leaders is often more important than institutions in determining what the state does.

India's democracy has endured in large part because Indians have adapted European institutions and practices to create a political hybrid that in some ways very much resembles and in others markedly differs from British-style parliamentary democracy (see Figure 12.2).

The Constitution

Like the leaders of most of the new states in Asia and Africa, India's founders gained independence under a system they inherited from their colonial masters. They confirmed that

FIGURE 12.2 Decision Making in India

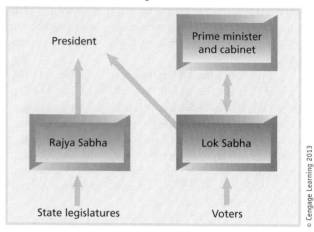

© Cengage Learning 2013

legacy when they wrote their own constitution, which went into effect in January 1950 (**indiacode.nic.in/coiweb/welcome.html**).

Yet it is not a carbon copy of the British constitution. For one thing, it is written. Indeed, with nearly four hundred articles and eight schedules, the Indian constitution is one of the longest in the world. And because it can be amended by a simple majority vote in both houses of parliament, it is among the easiest to change. In fact, as of mid-2009, it had been amended ninety-four times but not once since 2006.

The constitution defines India as a secular republic, to ensure a degree of religious and political freedom to the roughly 20 percent of the population that is not Hindu. It also guarantees an extensive list of civil liberties and forbids discrimination along religious, caste, racial, and gender lines.

Although it allows the prime minister to exercise emergency powers during a crisis, these provisions have only been used once, in 1975, as we saw earlier. During the nearly two years of Emergency Rule, the constitution was drastically amended. After the 1977 elections, however, the Desai government repealed most of those amendments and limited the conditions under which emergency powers could be used to an invasion from abroad or an armed rebellion at home.

As with most recently formed states, India has no king or queen. Instead, a president plays the symbolic role of head of state, much as we saw in Germany. Most presidents have readily accepted their secondary role; the exception was Zail Singh, who frequently complained that Rajiv Gandhi failed to keep him informed about government policies and plans. The president has had a substantial political impact only during the brief periods when there was no majority party or coalition. At those times, the president played the role expected of him, helping to find a prime ministerial candidate who might forge a majority coalition or, if that proved impossible, paving the way for the dissolution of the Lok Sabha and for new parliamentary elections.

Parliament

As in Britain, the key to power in India lies in the lower house of parliament, the Lok Sabha. All but two of its 543 members represent single-member constituencies in which elections follow the same kind of **first-past-the-post**, or winner-take-all, system used in the United States and Great Britain. It should be noted, though, that given the size of the Indian population, the average MP represents close to 2 million people 🐭 (**loksabha.nic.in**).

The upper house, or **Rajya Sabha** (House of the States), has 250 members. Of those, twelve represent the artistic and intellectual community and are appointed by the president. The rest are elected by the state legislative assemblies, making the Rajya Sabha much like the Bundesrat in Germany in the way it is chosen, though it is nowhere near as powerful.

Nominally, the president appoints the prime minister, but in reality he has little or no leeway, because the prime minister must be the head of the majority party or coalition in the Lok Sabha 🐭 (**parliamentofindia.nic.in**). As in Britain, the prime minister appoints the other members of the Council of Ministers, all of whom must already be MPs or must win election to it in a by-election within six months. Of the council members, the prime minister will invite somewhere between twelve and eighteen to join the cabinet. And because a group even that size can be ungainly, there is normally a smaller group of cabinet members and other informal advisers (e.g., the "household" of Indira Gandhi's years) who wield the most power.

The decision-making process is very similar to that in Britain. The cabinet initiates almost all significant legislation 🐭 (**pmindia.nic.in**). Other business, including private-member bills, receives less than a day's attention per week when the Lok Sabha is in session.

Bills receive the same three readings they do in Britain. The most important is the second, when the Lok Sabha votes on the principles of the legislation after it has been examined by the relevant committee. Voting is almost always along party lines, which all but ensures that the government's legislative proposals are passed, except during periods when there is no clear majority.

Party discipline in the Lok Sabha has not been enforced quite as strictly as it is in Britain's House of Commons because the parties themselves are often in flux. Thus, until recently, it was not uncommon for an individual MP to quit his or her party and join a new one during the middle of a term. These defections caused so much uncertainty at both the federal and state level that current legislation requires MPs who quit their party to leave parliament as well unless one-third of their delegation joins them. Not surprisingly, these rather draconian rules have led to a sharp reduction in the number of defections and to less uncertainty in the Lok Sabha.

Once passed by the Lok Sabha, a bill is sent to the Rajya Sabha. If the two houses do not agree, a variety of consultative mechanisms are used to iron out the differences. If they cannot do so, the two houses meet together and vote on the bill—a vote the Lok Sabha invariably wins, given its more than two-to-one size advantage.

On balance, though, the Lok Sabha is even weaker than the House of Commons as a legislative body. To begin with, there is far more turnover, which leaves the Lok Sabha with fewer experienced members than lower houses in most liberal democracies. Even more than in Britain, MPs lack the staff, offices, and other facilities that would enhance their ability to assume an effective oversight role. Finally, and most important, the opposition has been so fragmented that it has been hard for it to effectively utilize question time and other mechanisms that give oppositions elsewhere a modicum of leverage over the majority party and the executive.

The Bureaucracy

Another British inheritance that is a cornerstone of the state is the **Indian Administrative Service (IAS)**, which sits atop the country's gigantic bureaucracy. The British established the Indian Civil Service in the nineteenth century, and over the last half-century of colonial rule more and more positions in it were filled by Indians.

After independence, the service was renamed, but little else changed. The Union Public Service Commission 🐭 (**www.upsc.gov.in**) supervises annual examinations through which about 150 extremely talented young men and women are admitted into the IAS and a few other top civil service corps. In all, this bureaucratic elite has about four thousand members, and thus constitutes only a tiny fraction of a civil service that employs something approaching fifteen million people.

The rest of the civil service is a different story. Below the IAS level, the bureaucracy is generally seen as overstaffed and inefficient. Although bureaucrats have job security, their salaries are quite low. Many, therefore, tend not to work very hard. Many take bribes. Informal groups of fixers act as intermediaries (paid, of course) between average citizens and the bureaucracy. For instance, it is often only through these intermediaries that villagers gain access to development assistance. In short, in contrast to the impersonal, legally structured civil services in the advanced industrialized democracies, power in the Indian civil service—and, hence, in the effectiveness of policy implementation—revolves around personal connections, which are typically based on family, caste, or religion.

Federalism

The British were never able to bring all of India under a single, centralized government. Their successors never tried. A series of "reorganizations" since the constitution went into effect have left India with the states mentioned above. Their respective boundaries are drawn so that one major linguistic group predominates in each of them ✍ (**http://www .india.gov.in/knowindia/state_uts.php**). Some of the states are the size of a major European country.

Each has a government patterned after the national one. A governor appointed by the central government is the official head of state. Real power, however, is supposed to lie with a legislature (bicameral in some but not all) and a council of state ministers responsible to the lower house. The exact names of these bodies vary from state to state and language to language. What matters here is not how these state governments are structured or what powers they do or do not have. Rather, the states are of interest because they demonstrate the importance of caste and other informal social relationships in political life.

At first, Congress dominated at the state level as well, not losing control anywhere until 1967. Since then, its support has declined even more rapidly in the states than in New Delhi. But even this picture is misleading because much of state politics is not about ideological issues. Rather, the competition is mostly between factions based on **patron-client relations**.

Patrons can be party, caste, or religious leaders (they, of course, overlap), who offer their clients jobs, infrastructural projects, or other benefits in exchange for votes. Local patrons tend to be clients of more prominent leaders who weave the networks together into what are all but ideology-free factions. Above all, factional leaders want and need to win to obtain the resources and benefits that keep their clients loyal. So they can seem quite fickle, casting their lot with one party or leader today but shifting to another tomorrow. Robert Stern has described this process well for Congress, and his analysis applies to most of the other parties:

> Parties or factions, unburdened by ideological commitment, inclined to promote middle-class welfare, purposeful primarily in winning elections and positioned to deliver the goods to its voters, the Congresses have patched together their pluralities and majorities from India's vast heterogeneity. Here from one village, there from another. Here from one jati or jati subgroup, there from their rivals. From a state coalition here that depends on the support of dominant and twice-born jatis, from another there dependent on the support of other backward classes. The myriad, separate cost-benefit calculations that have held the Congresses together in fragments and factions can, however, undo them in fragments and factions. Factions want to know what's in it for them.[4]

The combination of factional politics with growing linguistic, religious, and ethnic tensions has also made most states hard to govern. Few elect clear and disciplined majorities to their lower houses, which means that state governments have often been unstable. Moreover, all too many factional leaders have condoned the use of violence, engaged in corruption, and relied on organized criminals (it is worth noting that *thug* is one of many English words of Indian origin) in seeking power.

In part to maintain their own power, central governments controlled both by Congress and its opposition have been increasingly willing to suspend normal state politics and to use Article 356 of the Constitution to impose **President's Rule**, the state-level equivalent of the federal emergency powers. The most recent use of these provisions came in January 2009, when the chief minister of Jharkhand failed to win a by-election as required by the constitution for him to be legally allowed to stay in office. The state assembly was put in what one newspaper called "a state of suspended animation." The decision to impose central control also reflected the continued influence of the Maoist insurgency by the Naxalites, which claimed about one thousand lives nationwide in 2008.

In December 2003, the federal and state governments reached an agreement that should sharply curtail the use of this practice. The prime minister agreed to apply it as a last resort and only if constitutional mechanisms completely broke down. The government would also have to get prior agreement from the Lok Sabha if it was in session (or have it ratify its decision when it next met) and fully explain its reasons for resorting to President's Rule.

PUBLIC POLICY

The continuity of India's democracy may be unusual by Third World standards. The travails it has encountered with its public policies are not.

As is the case in most of the Global South, the weakness of India's state is evident in virtually any policy area in which the domestic and global forces summarized in the figure on the inside front cover come into play. Lacking economic and other resources to start with, India faces increasing pressures from groups in its own society and from the outside, most notably as the global economy impinges ever more on it. The two sets of pressures are easiest to see

---

[4]Robert Stern, *Changing India* (New York: Cambridge University Press, 1991), 189.

in successive governments' attempts to confront ethnic, linguistic, religious, and caste-based conflict and to speed up economic growth.

Confronting Communal Violence

The issue of ethnic conflict crops up in a number of places in this chapter, as it will throughout Part 4. What is important to see at this juncture is that violence resulting from such conflict, and the state's reaction to it, have become an all but permanent part of the Indian political landscape. Certainly ethnic conflict contributed to the rise of the BJP and the regional parties. Alternatives involving, for instance, strengthening federal institutions, which seemed plausible a generation ago, would now be much harder to implement given the resentments that have built up over the years. In other words, India will doubtlessly face serious ethnic tensions for years to come, in large part because of the policies pursued by national and, to a lesser degree, state governments since Indira Gandhi's time.

In the first years after independence, Indian governments did fairly well in settling communal conflict short of violence because they followed two key principles, the second of which is less important today. First, all governments have been committed to maintaining the unity of India. Second, the government tried to work out accommodations with linguistic groups desiring more autonomy. However, given its commitment to India being a secular state, the leadership was unwilling to allow religious groups to stake territorial political claims, prompting unrest in many states and union territories. Although specific policies have varied from state to state and group to group, it is safe to say that, on balance, the net effect of public policy since the mid-1970s has been to exacerbate—not ease— ethnic, religious, and linguistic tensions.

During the Nehru years, Delhi redrew some state borders so that each major linguistic group would have a state it could govern. Once those states were created or restructured in the mid-1960s, however, the government faced an impasse because the remaining issues generally involved conflict within individual states, pitting the majority linguistic or religious group against a minority or, as in Assam, minorities. Furthermore, these more difficult issues emerged at the same time that Congress's majority was eroding. Therefore, unlike in the 1950s and 1960s, the party had to pay more attention to holding on to its core constituencies, which included key groups that were hostile to further accommodation with minorities.

Ethnic conflict worsened under Indira Gandhi, with her contradictory desires to control as many states as possible but to do so with as weak leaders as possible. As Paul Brass put it,

> [The] relentless, unprincipled intervention by the center in state politics has been the primary cause of the troubles in Punjab and elsewhere in India since Indira Gandhi's rise to power. A structural problem arises from the tensions produced by the centralizing drives of the Indian state in a society where the predominant long-term social, economic, and political tendencies are towards pluralism, regionalism, and decentralization.[5]

To see the general patterns of ethnic conflict and the way public policies contributed to it, we will focus on Punjab, Kashmir, Gujarat, and the terrorist attacks on Mumbai.

Punjab

Punjab lies along the Pakistani border. Communal violence there in the 1980s was the most disruptive of any such outbursts since partition. The original state of Punjab was ethnically mixed. In 1951, a little over half of its 16 million people were Hindus, but it also had the country's largest concentration of Sikhs. By the 1960s, they were the only large ethnic group that did not have its own state (www .sikhnet.com).

Negotiations to create a majority Sikh state were complicated by the fact that they are a religious as well as a linguistic group, and granting them a state would call the commitment to a secular India into question. Nonetheless, an agreement was finally reached to split Punjab, creating a new state with the same name whose population was about 60 percent Sikh. Some difficulties remained, including the status of Chandigarh, which was to serve as a shared capital for Punjab and the other new state. Still, most people expected this to be another of the largely successful settlements that had marked the history of ethnic conflict in India up to that point. This was not to happen. Observers are still having a hard time disentangling all the reasons protest increased. Most, though, cite two main factors.

The first was the social and economic changes that swept Punjab and left many members of its Sikh majority dissatisfied. Punjab had been one of the poorest regions in the country. However, the state-sponsored green revolution and the hard work of thousands of Punjabis had turned it into one of the richest. When this happened, some Sikhs began to fear that their traditional culture and values would be lost. Others remained dissatisfied that the state borders were redrawn. To make a long story short, a new generation of militants emerged, the most audacious of whom was a young cleric, **Jarnail Singh Bhindranwale**.

---

[5]Paul Brass, "The Punjab Crisis and the Unity of India," in *India's Democracy: An Analysis of Changing State-Society Relations.* Edited by Atul Kolhi (Princeton, NJ: Princeton University Press, 1990), 212.

Most Sikhs rejected the extremists' call for an independent Sikh state. Nonetheless, tensions mounted as more Sikhs came to demand a larger slice of the political and economic pie, including, for instance, a greater share of water from the rivers that flowed through the state. In addition, a Sikh party, the **Akali Dal**, mounted a serious challenge to Congress's domination of state politics. Finally, employing a strategy that has become quite common in the South as a whole, Bhindranwale and other leaders used the mass media to spread their message, including their growing hatred of a central government that they thought was ever more pro-Hindu and anti-Sikh.

Second, after Indira Gandhi took office, the government became far less accommodating. And after the creation of the new Punjab, the government rejected further Sikh demands. Gandhi never dealt gently with people who disagreed with her. She took a particularly hard line toward Punjab because the Sikhs and the Akali Dal had been among the most vocal opponents of Emergency Rule.

As support for the Akali Dal grew in the late 1970s, Congress tacitly supported Bhindranwale and other Sikh extremists who were critical of the party. But this support backfired on Congress once it returned to power. More and more Sikhs endorsed a 1973 agreement that would have drastically reduced Delhi's power in favor of the states. It never went into effect. More seriously, Sikhs launched attacks against Hindus, some of whom assaulted Sikhs in retaliation. Meanwhile, Bhindranwale and other extremists gained more and more influence, especially among young men.

In 1981, Bhindranwale was accused of murder. Two years later, when it seemed as if the government might finally take him into custody, Bhindranwale and his supporters occupied the Golden Temple in Amritsar, the Sikhs' holiest shrine.

In a typically opportunistic move, Gandhi overthrew the elected Akali Dal state government and imposed President's Rule. Nonetheless, violence continued. Clashes between Sikhs and Hindus threatened to undermine Congress's electoral base among Hindus outside Punjab, who were frustrated by the government's inability to protect their coreligionists. Congress also had lost contacts and relationships within the Sikh community that it might have used to defuse the increasingly tense situation.

In March 1984, the All India Sikh Student Federation (AISSF) was officially abolished. One hundred fifty companies of police troops were stationed in Punjab, including ninety at the Golden Temple alone. In response, still active AISSF members occupied more temples. Meanwhile, in neighboring Haryana, the Congress chief minister at the very least condoned organized mob violence against Sikhs who lived in his state.

Finally, in June Gandhi ordered troops to storm the temple. Bhindranwale and at least five hundred of his supporters, as well as eighty-three soldiers, were killed. The surviving Sikh leaders, including most prominent Akali Dal officials, were arrested. Sikh soldiers in other units mutinied and rioted in the most serious breach of army discipline since independence.

Then in October, Sikh members of her own security detail assassinated Gandhi. The assassination was followed by nights of rioting in which Hindus killed hundreds of Sikhs in Delhi and other cities. These were innocent people who had nothing to do with Gandhi's murder and probably did not support Sikh secession.

In short, Indira Gandhi had acted very differently from her father, who typically took powerful politicians from the states and incorporated them into the national elite. His daughter did everything possible in Punjab and elsewhere to undercut popular local politicians and to replace them with weak chief ministers who were personally and politically beholden to her. When the crisis came and unifying leadership was needed both in New Delhi and in Chandigarh, there was none to be had.

As was the case in most public policy areas, Rajiv Gandhi set out to do things differently. Almost immediately upon taking office, he began negotiations with the Akali Dal. The two sides eventually reached an agreement that, among other things, would have returned Chandigarh to Punjab and given the state some control over the vital water resources its farmers claimed they needed.

In 1987, however, Gandhi backed down. He played the Hindu trump card in the 1989 campaign in ways designed to maximize his party's support among orthodox Hindus, who were expected to be the swing vote and thus the key to victory. On television, Congress frequently showed footage of Indira Gandhi's funeral pyre with a sobbing Rajiv standing nearby, the implication being that the Sikhs were to blame. In his own constituency, he was challenged by his brother's widow, Maneka, herself half-Sikh. One of Congress's most widely used slogans during the campaign was "the daughter of a Sikh, traitor to the nation." Put simply, his Hindu constituents throughout northern India were not prepared to go along with such sweeping concessions to the Sikhs.

The violence continued, albeit at something less than the levels of the early 1980s. The situation in Punjab was so intense following Rajiv Gandhi's assassination during the 1991 campaign that elections there had to be put off for months. In the last few years, support for Sikh independence has diminished considerably. Indeed, the most significant protests of the early 2000s in the state came from the BJP, which objected to special benefits supposedly given to Sikhs. Sikh nationalists as such did not launch counterdemonstrations and the whole question of secession has disappeared from mainstream politics, though many Sikhs

The Golden Temple, the holiest shrine in the Sikh religion. It was the site of a bloody 1984 attack by government forces against nationalist rebels.

remain resentful of what they claim to be several hundred thousands of their compatriots who have been killed by Indian authorities and as many as fifty thousand who have been imprisoned since 1984. To cite but the most recent example, in May 2009, rioters protesting against a shoot-out at a Sikh temple in Austria burned buses and destroyed ATMs in a number of cities.

Kashmir

Over the last decade, the most serious communal conflict has been in the state of Jammu and Kashmir, the status of which has been in dispute since independence. Conflict there is also important because the region was a site of tension between India and Pakistan following the 9/11 attacks on the United States and could well have led to war between the two rivals.

Kashmir was one of the princely states that were not officially under British rule. Its leaders had to choose to join either India or Pakistan. Geography made that choice easy in most cases, but that decision was anything but easy for what officially became the state of Jammu and Kashmir, which lies in northwestern India along the Pakistani border (**www.jammu-kashmir.com/index.html**). It has a substantial Muslim majority, which would lead one to expect that it would have gone to Pakistan. However, its prince was a Hindu who wanted to be in India. In the months after independence, Pakistani troops invaded part of the state and forced the maharajah to flee. He then asked for support from Indian troops, at which point the state formally joined India. Nehru's government agreed to hold a referendum on which country the state should definitively

join, but it was never held because Pakistan continued to occupy part of it.

War broke out again in 1965, and Jammu and Kashmir were battlegrounds in the 1971 war that led to the independence of Bangladesh. Afterward, the two sides agreed to a de facto division of the state into regions controlled by India and Pakistan on each side of the last positions their troops had occupied, now dubbed the Line of Control.

Over the next few years, opposition to remaining part of India grew among Muslims. Some wanted to join Pakistan, and others wanted to create their own country. Tensions reached a peak when many Muslims became convinced that the 1987 state election had been rigged against them.

At about the same time, some militant Muslims went to Pakistan, where they were trained as fighters (many Indians would say terrorists). In 1989, the most recent wave of fighting broke out when militant Muslims and allies from abroad started launching attacks on Indian targets. According to Indian sources, over 35,000 people have been killed since then. The Pakistanis put the number at 70,000. One count in 1996 found ninety-four armed groups operating in the Kashmir Valley alone. Some 350,000 Indian troops were based in the state and faced an equally large force of Pakistanis in the land they occupied and just across the border in Pakistan proper.

The two sides could not even agree on who did what. Pakistan claimed that it gave only "moral and diplomatic support" to the Kashmiris, and India accused Pakistan of sponsoring "cross-border terrorism." One thing is clear. During the 1990s and the first years of the twenty-first century the opposition became more Islamic than nationalistic and began attracting other *jihadis* who had fought against the Soviets in neighboring Afghanistan.

The outside world paid relatively little attention to the on-again off-again fighting in the region until India and Pakistan both tested nuclear weapons in 1998. At that point, observers realized that the fighting in this disputed state could set off a devastating regional nuclear conflagration. This was readily apparent in May 1999, when Indian artillery began shelling Pakistani positions across the Line of Control, claiming that the government had infiltrated regular troops into the Pakistani region, a charge the government vehemently denied. Tensions were defused when Pakistan submitted to pressure from the United States and redeployed some of its troops.

Jammu and Kashmir finally made the world's headlines after the 9/11 terrorist attacks. Pakistan quickly agreed to become a major force in the American-led war against terrorism. Tensions with India remained high, however. This led the Vajpayee government to accuse the then government of General Pervez Musharraf of hypocrisy. On the one hand, it claimed to oppose the terrorism of al-Qaeda and the Taliban. On the other, it continued to support it in Kashmir. The worst fighting in more than a year began in October 2001 when India started shelling Pakistani positions. Tensions mounted ever further following an attack on the Indian parliament building in December, for which Vajpayee's government blamed Pakistani and Kashmiri militants. For the rest of 2001 and the first weeks of 2002, rarely a day went by without at least one violent death. More troops massed along the Line of Control, and yet another war between India and Pakistan seemed possible.

A brief glimmer of hope occurred in late 2003 and early 2004 when both governments floated peace proposals as part of a general rapprochement between the two countries. Neither succeeded. The most important source of optimism today is the work of Indian and foreign nongovernmental organizations (NGOs) who have been working to get the two sides to the negotiating table.

The most impressive of these has been run by the Washington-based International Center for Religion and Diplomacy 🔖 (**www.icrd.org/projects.html#kashmir**). Since 2001, it has sent teams of clergy and laypeople to Kashmir to work on both sides of the Line of Control. By the summer of 2004, it had conducted reconciliation seminars that more than three hundred local Muslim, Hindu, and Buddhist leaders have attended. It helped some of those young men and women establish reconciliation centers in Jammu and Srinagar, which are the winter and summer capitals of the state respectively. Perhaps most significantly, it identified and helped train a group of leaders who are interested in building bridges between the two communities.

In early 2005, the two governments also forged some small and largely symbolic agreements, the most important of which established bus lines that would carry people across

Next-generation Kashmiri leaders discussing reconciliation at a seminar organized by the International Center for Religion and Diplomacy.

the Line of Control. This may not seem like a major step forward, but any agreement after more than a half-century of frustration has to be taken as a serious move by both sides.

There has been less violence since then. Still, protests flare regularly, most recently when Indians proposed giving a large swath of Muslim-controlled land for a Hindu temple. As we will see, there is reason to believe that at least some of the terrorists who attacked Mumbai in late 2008 were either from Kashmir or had fought there.

Gujarat

The most vicious fighting in the 2000s has occurred in the state of Gujarat, which also borders Pakistan and the Arabian Sea more than five hundred miles southwest of Punjab. Its population pretty much matches that of the country's profile as a whole. Almost 90 percent of all Gujaratis are Hindus; not quite 10 percent are Muslim.

Gujarat is also one of the richest states in India. Its gross state product may be as much as twenty times that of the country as a whole. It accounts for 20 percent of India's industrial production and almost half of its exports even though Gujaratis only make up about 5 percent of the population.

The peak of the violence between Hindus and Muslims there lasted from 2002 until late 2004 and left almost 800 Muslims and 250 Hindus dead. Well over 200 people are still listed as missing. Some advocacy groups put the death toll at closer to 2,000.

The violence began to escalate on February 27, 2002, when a Muslim mob allegedly burned fifty-eight Hindus to death while they were riding in a train. Most were women and children. The state's BJP government at best turned a blind eye to a campaign of ethnic cleansing in which tens of thousands of Muslims were forced to flee their homes for hastily constructed refugee camps.

Attacks by Muslims against Hindus and Hindus against Muslims roiled about 60 percent of the state's twenty-six districts. By the middle of 2002, the violence had become so intense that almost as many Hindus as Muslims were homeless. The police did little to try to end the violence, which also got relatively little attention at first from the national government.

Most of the blame for the riots was placed on the VHP and other groups connected to the BJP. Finally, in 2004 an independent commission determined that the initial fire in Godhra was probably accidental in origin. The state government resigned, and when the national government finally allowed a new ballot, the BJP was returned to power in a landslide.

The disturbances in Gujarat did not last as long as those in Punjab or Kashmir. As in those two states, there have been sporadic protests since then, including a demonstration after police officers killed an election worker who was monitoring a polling place in 2009.

However, because militant Hindus were at the heart of the violence, they are often seen as the largest threat to democracy of them all. As Martha Nussbaum put it, "Hindus in India have internalized a historical narrative according to which they are a pure and peaceful civilization that has been conquered again and again. When people murder people who have been their neighbors for years, something has gone wrong at a deeper level."[6]

Mumbai

India and the world woke up on November 27, 2008, to one of the most devastating terrorist attacks anywhere and at any time. India had terrorist attacks before, but none matched this one either in terms of the carnage it left or in the audacity of the attack.

Some of the details are still murky in summer 2011. About fifteen Muslims terrorists, from some combination of India, Kashmir, and Pakistan, came ashore at the port of Mumbai in rubber dinghies. Mumbai is one of the world's most densely populated cities, historically known for its overcrowding, filth, traffic jams, and poverty. Today, it is also at the forefront of India's economic boom to be discussed in the next section.

The terrorists attacked a number of high profile targets, including a luxury hotel, the city's main commuter railroad station, and an orthodox Jewish center. It seems (this is one of the murky details) that their assault was well planned and highly coordinated. When the siege ended three days later with the death or capture of all the terrorists, at least 101 were dead and almost 300 wounded. The terrorists seem to have singled out holders of American and British passports.

After the attacks, the Indian and Pakistani governments hurled verbal attacks at each other, though there were few signs that the crisis could take the countries closer to war again.

After a few weeks, the Pakistani government acknowledged that the sole survivor was Pakistani, the plot was at least partially planned in Pakistan, and at least some of the terrorists were part of Lashkar-e-Taibi, a militant Muslim group that has been active in India, Pakistan, and Kashmir since 2000, if not before. It has long been on the list of terrorist organizations that most Western governments maintain. The survivor was found guilty and sentenced to death in 2010. His case is currently under appeal.

Stimulating the Economy

Prior to the mid-1980s, Indian governments pursued import substitution and central planning of a largely state-owned and state-controlled economy to spur growth and reduce poverty. Since then, a combination of outside pressures and domestic frustration with what the Indians themselves often called the "Hindu rate of growth" led Rajiv Gandhi and his successors to reconsider the social democratic goals and practices that their predecessors had taken for granted. Though less dramatically than has Mexico (see Chapter 16), India has opened its economy to the global market. So far, growth has increased by about 7 percent a year in this century. Like China, it has largely escaped the current economic crisis. Its growth rate has largely held steady and actually rose slight to 7.4 percent in 2010. That said, no major dent has been put in the poverty rate and other social problems. In fact, the United Nations Development Project's Human Development Report (HDR) for 2010 ranked India just 118th in the world although it has made significant progress since the economic reforms.

But unlike China, the state has not been a major stimulus for change. It has changed laws that, for instance, prohibited foreigners from owning India-based companies. But more important, the boom of the last 20 years has almost completely been driven by entrepreneurs in the private sector.

For example, consider the case of Gurgaon, which is about 15 miles from New Delhi. The city barely existed 30 years ago. Now it has well over a million people. As Jim Yardley of *The New York Times* put it:

> There are 26 shopping malls, even golf courses and luxury shops selling Chanel and Louis Vuitton, Mercedes-Benzes and BMW's shimmer in automobile showrooms. Apartment towers are sprouting like concrete wees, and a futuristic hub called Cyber City houses many of the world's most respected corporations.[7]

But not all is well in Gurgaon. It has no sewer system, reliable electrical service, sidewalks, decent roads, adequate parking, or a public transportation system, all of which are

---

[6]Martha C. Nussbaum, *The Clash Within: Democracy, Religious Violence, and India's Future* (Cambridge: Harvard/Belknap, 2007), 6 and 48.

[7]Jim Yardley, "Where Growth and Dysfunction Have No Boundaries." *New York Times*, June 9, 201, p. A1.

normally services provided by the state. In the boom cities of today's India, that public sector is just not up to speed.

Indian economic policy from independence through the 1980s was not an abject disaster. There was enough growth to create a new middle class. The **green revolution** introduced high-yield crops that all but eliminated famine, if not hunger and malnutrition. In some technological areas, India is a world leader. It has tested nuclear weapons and medium-range ballistic missiles, and its computer software is among the best in the world. Further, India has been among the most successful Third World countries in using modern telecommunications technology to reach the residents of its villages, who would otherwise be isolated from the outside world.

On balance, though, the Indian economy did not fare very well, especially when compared with countries like South Korea, which were almost as poor as India at the end of World War II. Table 12.8 presents comparative data on economic growth for India and some other Southern countries in the mid-1980s that had roughly equal economic conditions in the immediate post-war years.

Two seemingly contradictory trends emerge from these data. India's economy grew by an average of nearly 2 percent per capita per year during that period ending in the late 1980s. The growth was concentrated in the industrial sector, which the import substitution policy made the top priority. But India did not do very well in relative terms. Of the countries included in the table, none had a slower rate of growth and only China had a lower GNP per capita. India's economic plight seems all the worse because a number of countries that were equally poor in the early 1950s far outperformed it.

Poverty

This relative failure of India's economy is not simply a statistical artifact. It has had tangible and politically significant costs, most notably the inability of the Indian government to do much to alleviate the wrenching poverty in which so much of its population lives.

TABLE 12.8 Selected Economic Indicators: India and Comparable Countries before Structural Adjustment

COUNTRY	GROSS NATIONAL PRODUCT, 1987 ($)	AVERAGE ANNUAL GROWTH 1965–87 (%)
India	300	1.8
Brazil	2,020	4.1
China	290	5.2
Indonesia	450	4.5
Mexico	1,830	2.5
Pakistan	350	2.5
South Korea	2,690	6.4
Thailand	850	3.9
Turkey	1,210	2.6

Most mainstream scholars today estimate that at least 300 million Indians are poor, a number greater than the total population of every country on earth except for China. Of the 20 to 30 million Indians born each year, well over half are born into poverty. The bottom 10 percent of the population controls 3 percent of the income; the top 10 percent makes ten times that.

One recent study defined poverty Indian style as not having access to adequate food, clothing, and shelter. By that standard, about one-sixth of the population lives in what is called ultrapoverty, meaning their incomes fall more than 25 percent below the level needed to obtain those basics. Many of the poor are homeless; the best off live in substandard housing, with dozens of families crammed into teeming tenements. Many are malnourished, and those who do get the minimum daily caloric intake needed to sustain a healthy life survive primarily on grains. A missed day or two of work can leave a family without money for food. Health care for the poor is virtually nonexistent and life expectancy for those in poverty barely tops fifty years.

Poverty, of course, is not randomly distributed. The lower castes and *dalits* are most likely to be poor. There are still about six hundred thousand families of outcaste origin who make a living, such as it is, emptying latrines and chamber pots. Poverty is worse in rural areas though the gap between them is much smaller than it once was. There are thousands of villages without safe drinking water, roads that are passable in all weather, or rudimentary health care services.

Women bear the heaviest costs of poverty. In poor families, they are responsible for all household tasks, which in rural areas can include the time-consuming and physically draining search for firewood. In urban areas, women are much less likely to receive health care or an education than are men. In the states of Bihar and Rajasthan, for instance, about 38 percent of the population is literate. Overall, not even one-fourth of India's women are literate, and in the poorest, rural areas, only about 2 percent of all women can read and write, thus depriving them of one of the skills they could use to pull themselves out of poverty.

The government has enjoyed some success in reducing poverty. Between 1970 and 1990, the poverty rate was cut by about one-fourth. Still, as a result of continued population growth, the number of poor people actually increased during those same years.

The government also devised a number of successful and innovative approaches to help people improve their lives. The Integrated Rural Development Program (IRDP) was created to give villagers low-level technology and other new skills. For instance, in a number of villages, "night soil" gatherers were taught how to harness the methane contained in human waste to generate electricity to fuel small-scale industrial facilities. In all, the IRDP reached about 27 million rural families, spending an average of about $500 on each. But this gave no more than 10 percent of the rural poor the ability to escape poverty—assuming the program worked perfectly, which, of course, it did not.

Finally, India's record pales in comparison with most other large Southern countries. India has been able to reduce the size of the population below the poverty line by about 1 percent per year, which is better than Colombia, Morocco, and Sri Lanka have done. But most other countries that started at similar rates of development have done far better, including Indonesia, which is reducing its poor population by about 2.5 percent per year. On another indicator of poverty—reducing the mortality rate for children under five years of age—India ranks last in this same sample of countries. It has been able to reduce that number by almost 2 percent per year, but Morocco and Colombia both top 5 percent.

The Nehruvian Model and India's Economic Woes

India's continued poverty obviously has many causes, the most important of which is the broader economic policy of import substitution pursued from 1947 until the mid-1980s. Nehru and his colleagues had been deeply influenced by the British Fabian movement and its democratic version of socialism. This led them to focus on a strong public sector to steer development and to generate a more just and egalitarian society.

The Industrial Policy Resolution of 1948 called for a mixed economy, with government ownership of all munitions, atomic energy, and railroad enterprises. The resolution also gave the government the sole right to start new ventures in such key sectors as iron and steel, telecommunications, aircraft, and shipbuilding. Eighteen other industries were to remain in private hands but subject to government control and regulation.

Under the leadership of one of Nehru's closest advisers, P. C. Mahalanobis, these "commanding heights" of the economy were to be managed using five-year plans that were more controlling than the French plans but less so than the Soviets' before Gorbachev. At the heart of the system was what the Indians call the **permit raj**, an elaborate system of tariffs, licenses, and other regulations that kept most imports out and made the ones that did get in so expensive that next to no one could afford them. In this manner, it protected publicly and privately owned firms alike, which continued making the same old products in the same old way and earning the same all-but-guaranteed rate of profit year after year.

Over time, most Indian business leaders came to accept the planning system because it guaranteed reasonable profits and an advanced standard of living for those working in the modern sector of the economy. Wages in that sector averaged about 70 percent higher than those in the rest of the country.

High tariffs and other regulations also protected domestic industry. In 1985, rates ranged from 107 percent on capital goods to 140 percent on most manufactured products. In addition, most industrial goods could be imported only by what the government called "actual users." But even that was not always possible because, for instance, automobile, truck, and bus manufacturers were not allowed to import tires.

There is little question that these economic policies met their initial goals, as India did become reasonably self-sufficient. In 1984 the import of finished goods accounted for only 8 percent of its gross domestic product, compared with an average of over 19 percent in other LDCs. India developed a substantial industrial base with limited interference from or obligations to other countries. But isolation also had its costs. The absence of internal competition was one of many causes of corruption and inefficiency. More important, the economy did not benefit from the capital, technology, and other resources more trade could have provided—admittedly, at the cost of considerable domestic control. Most significant of all, the Indian economy was falling ever farther behind those of many other Southern countries.

Liberalization

By the early 1980s there was a growing consensus that import substitution and related policies were retarding overall growth by depriving the economy of the stimuli a more open market could provide. Since then, India has gradually opened its economy and adopted other promarket policies supported by international financial institutions and multinational corporations. It has not done so as quickly as Mexico, nor has international pressure on it to change been as direct. Nonetheless, India's policies in the new century are a far cry from what they were when Rajiv Gandhi took office in 1984.

There are many reasons why he began to tilt the balance away from state ownership, planning, and control. In part, the new policies reflected his own background, which included university study in the West and a career that began in business. In part, they grew out of pressures in the global economy that inflicted a heavy price on countries that tried to resist the trend toward more open markets and relatively unrestricted international trade.

In contrast, countries like South Korea were growing far more rapidly because they took advantage of some niches in the emerging global marketplace. This is not to say that their economies were trouble free, but following international economic trends seemed to bring them significant economic payoffs. Gandhi and his youthful colleagues wanted to take India in that same direction. During his five years in office, the proposed reforms were implemented incrementally. The forces behind liberalization gained even more support after 1989 and the collapse of the Soviet bloc. Reform

Economic Liberalization
in India

India has gradually liberalized its economic policy, although government approval is needed for most direct foreign investment, and the elaborate system of rules and regulations of the permit raj remain largely in place for the big corporations protected during the years of import substitution. Thus, foreigners may own as much as three-fourths of the shares in a privately owned bank but only 20 percent in those that are publicly traded.

Central to this gradual process of liberalization has been current Prime Minister Manmohan Singh (1932–). The Oxford-educated economist was named minister of finance in 1991 after a long career in academe and the civil service. After leaving office, he served in the largely ceremonial Rajya Sabha and was a powerful behind-the-scenes advisor to Congress's economic policy makers.

As noted previously, he was a surprise choice when his colleagues in Congress chose him to be prime minister in 2004 after their presumptive selection, Sonia Gandhi decided not to take the position. ■

The most visible change has come in information technology. Because its economic borders historically were so closed, India had not developed a competitive domestic computer industry even though it had long been a world leader in software development. With the newly open economy, it offered outside investors a pool of skilled and low-paid labor, and it held out the promise of a massive new market at some point in the future. "Silicon valleys" have developed around Bangalore in the south and Hyderabad in the north.

In 2011, there were more than ten thousand extremely wealthy people whose fortunes were based in information technology in the Bangalore area alone. More than one-fourth of all outsourced offshore jobs from the United States have ended up in India with almost half of them in the IT sector.

The government has also encouraged more exports so that India can earn hard currency to buy the goods it has to import. Since the 1990s, exports have grown at the average rate of 20 percent per year, although the country still imports about $100 billion worth of goods and services more than it exports. The biggest growth area, not surprisingly, is in information services.

The government has also steered some of its revenues from taxes on the new firms to address the isolation of poor villages. Pilot programs have been conducted in some desperately poor regions near Bangalore in which solar power is introduced and people are trained to use telephone and computer systems. The knowledge center in the town of

efforts peaked early in the Narasimha Rao government, in which reformers like Singh and P. Chidambaram (with his Harvard MBA) were given the key economic ministries.

Recently, barriers to outside investment have been cut on the assumption that capital and competition from abroad will give a much needed boost to domestic industries that stagnated under the protection of import substitution. Foreign direct investment has mushroomed in India even though the government limits the portion of a firm that can be owned by non-Indians. Thus, in 2008, people from outside of India (including a large number of expatriates) invested $27 billion in the country. By contrast, that figure was only $13 million in 1981 and $121 million in 1989. The government has sold parts of many state-owned industries, including the automobile manufacture, Maruti Udyog, which is now controlled by Suzuki. Air India and Indian Airlines merged in 2011 when the state owned 51 percent of each of them. They are scheduled for privatization at some point in the not so distant future.

Prime Minister Manmohan Singh, the surprise choice to lead the government following Congress's surprise victory in 2004.

Embalm brought more than six hundred new users to the Internet, which saved them significant amounts of time and money that they would have had to expend on travel to find out such basic things as market prices for their crops.

India has not gone as far in terms of economic reform as some of the other LDCs because of domestic political pressures. Recall that the Gandhi and Narasimha Rao governments were not terribly popular and were beholden to traditional politicians and conservative social groups within Congress. As a result, as the costs of economic reform mounted for everyone, from the poor to the economically powerful, their governments backed down. Further, the two coalition governments that succeeded them were far weaker and were all but paralyzed as far as economic reform was concerned. Finally, the BJP continued the process of reform, but it has not been willing to speed it up, especially when it comes to eliminating the permit raj. Still, in early 2004, the government issued new rules allowing foreigners to own as much as 74 percent of private banks, petrochemical companies, and scientific and other scholarly journals.

It is all continuing during Singh's second five-year term as prime minister. The very fact that Singh was one of the architects of the initial liberalization projects in the 1990s indicated that the rules and regulations that limit the role of market forces would continue to be weakened, and possibly even eliminated now that he has won that second term with what seems like an unassailable majority in the Lok Sabha.

Globalization
in India

India is often portrayed in the English-speaking world as one of the most striking examples of how globalization can reshape a country. That has especially been the case in the last decade with the growth of its "silicon valleys" and the export of many Western technology jobs to them.

However, it should be noted that India as a whole has not been all that deeply affected by these globalizing developments. It has opened its economic borders more slowly than many countries and continues to try to protect domestic industries, albeit less than previous Indian governments did. To cite but one example, its overall export totals are only about one-eighth those of the Chinese. China ranks third in the world in gross exports. India is twenty-eighth. ■

THE MEDIA

As befits its tumultuous and divided political system, India has a lively mass media. Even though barely half of the population is literate, the country has more than two thousand daily newspapers, which are among the cheapest in the world. The papers, of course, are published in dozens of languages, and 12 million out of each day's circulation of 68 million are in English. They cover the entire political spectrum, with many of the best papers featuring well-respected reputations for their investigative journalism. Although political news dominates the printed press, the fastest growing newspapers are the ones that concentrate on financial news; their circulations have tripled since the introduction of economic liberalization.

Until recently, television and radio were completely state owned. Since the mid-1990s, however, cable and satellite television have been introduced, and one journalist estimates that more than 200 million people have access to one or the other. These people can now watch both the BBC World News and Rupert Murdoch's Star service and, thus, get differing perspectives on political events. A nationwide network of satellite dishes brings television service to most villages, where the whole community watches together on its one screen.

CONCLUSION: DEMOCRACY IN INDIA AND THE THIRD WORLD

However serious its difficulties, India is not likely to suffer the fate of the Soviet Union or Yugoslavia, or even see its democracy succumb. It is risky to predict anything during these times of such rapid and unanticipated political change; nevertheless, this conclusion seems warranted if we place India in a broader comparative and theoretical perspective.

Over the past decade, political scientists have spent a lot of time investigating why some democracies succeed and others collapse. Although these studies are controversial, two themes appear time and time again in the. First, the more legitimate the regime, the less likely it is to collapse. Second, the more effective the government, the more likely it is to retain that legitimacy and, more generally, to survive. These may not seem like particularly profound conclusions, but if we shift from abstract theory to two comparisons, the reasons we can be reasonably optimistic about India's political future become clearer.

In examining the Soviet Union and the broader collapse of communism in Europe, we saw the dramatic interplay between policy failure and the loss of legitimacy. We may lack systematic evidence that would allow us to directly compare their experiences with India's, but the impressionistic indications available to us reveal a very different situation in the latter country. The Indian government has been more successful in at least some policy areas (e.g., liberalization) than any European communist regime was. And although its population is increasingly angry and polarized, most Indians still view the regime as legitimate. Perhaps most important, Indians on the whole seem to lack the kind of repressed rage ready to erupt when political straitjackets are removed, as happened when *glasnost* was instituted in the Soviet Union and Eastern Europe.

The other comparison is between India and the rest of the Third World. No matter how dire India's situation might have seemed in this chapter, it is in relatively good shape on two levels. First, India's economic performance and, of even more consequence, its economic potential are both superior to most of what we will see in the chapters on Mexico, Iran, Iraq, and Nigeria. Second, its regime has been more effective and retains more legitimacy than most others, some of which are wracked with basic divisions over whether the country itself should even exist.

Whether India is a relative success or a failure in comparative terms should not obscure the most important points for American or European students to learn about this or most other LDCs. First, these are incredibly poor countries that lack some of the basic resources and amenities we take for granted, such as primary education, rudimentary health care, safe drinking water, and shelter. Second, poverty is but one of many factors that make these countries much harder to govern, whatever the strengths or weaknesses of the people who end up trying to lead them.

Looking FORWARD

WE HAVE ASKED you to take one last intellectual leap of faith here. In Chapter 11, we argued that India has been more successful economically and in sustaining its democracy than most other countries in the Global South. Given what we saw especially in the first half of this chapter, that might seem like a preposterous claim.

But as we consider the four other countries in the following chapters, we might end up convincing you.

We turn next to Iran. Unlike India, it was never formally a colony, although much of its territory was occupied for brief but significant periods that proved critical for the evolution of Iranian politics. Until 1979,

Iran was technically a monarchy ruled from the 1920s until 1979 by the Pahlavi dynasty. It was secular and pro-Western. Tehran was a cosmopolitan city. But the Shah's regime was also a brutal one. It was overthrown in 1979 by groups that turned the country into one of the last theocracies, the Islamic Republic.

We will cast some doubt on criticisms of the Ayatollahs' rule made by the United States and its allies. There should be no doubt, nonetheless, that the current regime is dictatorial at best and sometime seems guilty of supporting terrorists and others who might attack the United States or Israel.

Key Terms

Concepts	People	Acronyms	
caste	Bhindranwale, Jarnail	BJP	green revolution
dalit	Singh	IAS	Indian Administrative
Emergency Rule	Desai, Morarji	LDC	Service (IAS)
first-past-the-post	Gandhi, Indira	RSS	Indian Civil Service
jati	Gandhi, Mohandas		Indian National Congress
less developed country	Karamchand	**Organizations, Places, and**	Janata
(LDC)	Gandhi, Rajiv	**Events**	Janata Dal
patron-client relations	Gandhi, Sonia	Akali Dal	Lok Sabha
permit raj	Narasimha Rao, P. V.	Ayodhya	Mughal
President's Rule	Nehru, Jawaharlal	Bharatiya Janata Party	Rajya Sabha
swaraj	Singh, Manmohan	(BJP)	Rashtriya Swayamsevak
untouchable	Vajpayee, Atal Bihari	British East India Company	Sangh (RSS)
		Government of India Act	Syndicate

〰 Useful Websites

As one might expect of a country with such a large high-tech community and such a large diaspora, there are several good portals on Indian affairs, all of which have links to political sites and news feeds. Among the best are:

www.outlookindia.com

www.indiainfo.com

Asianinfo.org is a general site, but it is more focused on making information on Asia (including India) available to the rest of the world.

www.asianinfo.org/asianinfo/india/politics.htm

The Indian government maintains an excellent site about the parliament, federal agencies, and most state governments.

Indiaimage.nic.in

Finally, there are some good sites on Indian politics, including the one run by the government, the Virtual Library, and an India-based site that has material on elections, parties, and public opinion polls. Indian Elections has good, if often too-detailed, data on election results at the national and state level.

www.india.gov.in

http://www.vl-site.org/india/index.html

www.indian-elections.com

Further Reading

Brass, Paul. *The Politics of India since Independence.* New York: Cambridge University Press, 2008. The most detailed of the texts on Indian politics. It is especially good on ethnic issues.

Das, Gundcharan. *India Unbound.* New York: Knopf, 2000. A personal and analytical account of India's economic and political transformations by one of the country's leading entrepreneurs.

Dukes, Edward. *Despite the Gods.* New York: Doubleday, 2007. The best recent book on Indian economic growth despite the restrictions imposed by its spiritual traditions.

Giridharadas, Anand. *India Calling: An Intimate Portrait of a Nation's Remaking.* New York: Times Books, 2011. The best and most recent of a series of books on India's economic renewal by one of its leading architects.

Gupta, Bhabani Sen. *Rajiv Gandhi: A Political Study.* New Delhi: Konark, 1989. A highly critical but also highly insightful biography that takes Gandhi up to the end of his term as prime minister.

Hansen, Thomas. *Wages of Violence: Naming and Identity in Postcolonial Bombay.* Princeton, NJ: Princeton University Press, 2001. A systematic analysis of ethnicity in Bombay, written by a social anthropologist.

Jeffrey, Robin. *What's Happening to India?* 2nd ed. London: Macmillan, 1994. A book primarily about Sikhs and Punjab, but of more general interest as well.

Kochanek, Stanley and Robert Hardgrave. *India: Government and Politics in a Developing Nation*, 7th ed. Belmont CA: Cengage, 2008. The best—and now perhaps only—full-length text on Indian politics.

Kohli, Atul. *India's Democracy: An Analysis of Changing State-Society Relations.* Princeton, NJ: Princeton University Press, 1990.

———, ed. *Democracy and Discontent: India's Growing Crisis of Government.* New York: Cambridge University Press, 1990. Two works that focus on ethnicity and other problems imperiling Indian democracy.

Meredith, Robyn. *The Elephant and the Dragon: The Rise of India and China and What It Means for All of Us.* New York: W. W. Norton, 2008. Best easy-to-read treatment of the way India is changing. Pretty good on China, too, but not quite the best book on that country.

Nussbaum, Martha C. *The Clash Within: Democracy, Religious Violence, and India's Future.* Cambridge: Harvard/Belknap, 2007. An interesting and provocative new book that likens the violence in Gujarat and elsewhere to genocide.

Roy, Arundhati. *Power Politics.* Boston: South End Press, 2001. An impassioned plea against dams, globalization, and their impact on India by a leading architect and writer who gained notoriety after this book was published for criticizing the war against terrorism in Afghanistan.

Schofield, Victoria. *Kashmir in Conflict: India, Pakistan, and the Unending War.* New York: I. B. Taurus, 2003.

Varadarajan, Siddharth, ed. *Gujarat: The Making of a Tragedy.* New York: Penguin, 2002. An in-depth analysis of why Gujarat joined Kashmir as one of the two most explosive states in recent years.

Wolpert, Stanley. *A New History of India*, 3rd ed. New York: Oxford University Press, 1989. The best single-volume history of India.

13

Your task is very difficult. Not even Iranians understand Iran.

ANONYMOUS IRANIAN PROFESSOR

Iran

THE BASICS

Iran

Size	1,648 sq. km. Roughly the size of Alaska
Population	77 million
Age distribution	21% under 15 years old
Ethnic distribution	Persian (51%), Azeri (24%), Kurds (7%), Arabs (3%), Others (15%)
Religion	Shiite Muslim (89%), Sunni Muslim (9%), Other (2%)
GNP per capita	$10,900
Growth GNP	1.5%
Poverty rate	18% (estimate)
Literacy rate	77%
Currency	9,900 rial = US$1 (2008)
Head of State	Mahmoud Ahmadinejad (2005–)

THE LOOMING CRISIS

No chapter will illustrate the overlap between international relations and comparative politics more than this one. Ever since the creation of the **Islamic Revolution** in 1979, Iran has faced domestic challenges with domestic and international roots that more often than not reinforce each other and have taken on new meaning in the last two or three years.

The stakes of Iranian politics have changed. If this chapter had been written in the summer of 2009, it would have focused on the election that year and the **Green Movement** or **Revolution** it provoked, which we will consider in detail in the section on political participation.

A year and a half later, the best way to begin a chapter on Iran is to briefly consider the three overlapping international and domestic issues confronting **Mahmoud Ahmadinejad** (1956–) as his second and final term reaches its halfway point.

First, relations between Iran and most western democracies have been strained since the revolution. There was already resentment toward the West dating back more than a century. Then, supporters of the new regime occupied the American embassy and held fifty two of its diplomats hostage for 444 days. The two countries broke off diplomatic relations. Since then dozens of other issues

Looking BACKWARD

WE JUST FINISHED a chapter on India, which is arguably the most successful democracy outside of the countries covered in Part 2. It is also booming economically to the point that Goldman Sachs economists coined the term BRICS (Brazil, Russia, India, China, and South Africa), which are by far the most important "emerging markets" and of the size and clout to be on the verge of getting spots among the world's major powers.

We will see something very different in Iran. Other than some hints of electoral competition a generation ago, Iran has almost no democratic history. And, despite its oil and other resources, its economy has languished at least since the Islamic Revolution of 1979. Finally, because of its human rights record and alleged plans to build a nuclear arsenal, it is considered a pariah or rogue state by most of the other countries covered in this book.

have made normal relationships impossible, including Iran's support for radicals in Palestine and Ahmadinejad's Holocaust denial.

Since Ahmadinejad took over the presidency in 2005, the most vexing issue has been what the West alleges is Iran's plan to build nuclear weapons. Iran acknowledges that it has a nuclear program but insists it is to generate electricity not build bombs. Until Iran gets to the point of being able to join the "nuclear club," we will not be able to say definitively what its goals are.

Second, doubts and worries about Iran's nuclear ambitions have led the United States to wage a campaign to get its allies and the United Nations to impose **sanctions** on Iraq. Sanctions are coercive economic policies that are designed to deter a country from engaging in policies its adversaries do not like by coercing or forcing it to change its behavior.

The sanctions have not had the impact the United States would have liked. Some countries—including Russia and China—have not participated in the sanctions regime at all.[1]

Third, by 2006 or 2007 it was clear that the sanctions were hurting the Iranian economy, most notably because they blocked the sale of about half of its oil abroad. Iran had used its massive oil exports to fund the government and keep prices artificially low. Now, the **subsidy** policy was putting Iran in a financial crisis far worse than anything we saw in Parts 2 and 3.

Therefore, in 2010 the government embarked on a program of subsidy reform. Within six years (for most

products), the market would determine the price of goods that everyone would pay. Poorer Iranians would get checks to help defray the rise in the cost of basic commodities. Wealthier Iranians would not. One of the products whose price would rise the most is oil. That will also affect truck and taxi drivers who have to buy a lot of gas.

Put simply, Iran currently faces three crises all of which are directly or indirectly caused by its unusual public policy since the revolution.

THINKING ABOUT IRAN

Persia versus Iran

Iran, usually known as Persia (in the West at least) until 1935, is one of the world's oldest countries. In one form or another, a country with one or the other of those two names has existed for more than 2,500 years from the time it was created by its first great emperors, Darius and Cyrus.

The name Persia comes from the region's dominant language, Farsi. **Reza Shah**, the first of the two **Pahlavi** monarchs, officially changed the country's name to Iran (in common use there already), a term whose origins are the same as the word *Aryan*, which he wanted to stress as a critical part of the country's origins.

Over time, modernizers like the Pahlavis stressed the country's Persian roots over its more recent affiliation with the Shiite sect of Islam. That, of course, changed with the Islamic Revolution, which turned the emphasis back to religion. That said, Iran is not an overwhelmingly Persian country because they make up less than 60 percent of the

---

[1]Note that in international relations, regime has a very different meaning from the one we introduced in Chapter 1.

population. Almost a quarter are Azeris. The rest come from a number of ethnic groups, including Kurds and Arabs, none of which make up more than 8 percent of the population. This ethnic diversity is reflected in the fact that not even three in five Iranians are native Farsi speakers. As we will see later, more than 2,500 years of common history have enabled Iranians to overcome these ethnic differences and develop a strong sense of national identity.

Shiite versus Sunni

As already noted, Iran is an Islamic republic that is governed according to Muslim principles largely as interpreted by clerics. As such, it is one of the few theocracies left in the world today, where **Sharia** (Muslim law) is far more influential than, say, in Nigeria, as we will see in Chapter 15.

As is the case with all of the world's major religions, Islam has been divided into rival sects over the centuries. Most Muslims are **Sunnis**, who make up the majority of the population in every Muslim country other than Iran, Iraq, and Bahrain (there is some dispute about Lebanon). Iran and now Iraq are dominated by **Shiites** who are widely and often mistakenly viewed as the most militant and fanatical believers in their faith. However, almost all followers of al-Qaeda and related groups are Sunnis, not Shiites.

The origins of the Sunni/Shiite split date from the early years of Islam. When the Prophet Muhammad died in 632, he had not designated a successor to head the rapidly expanding faith and empire he had created. Almost immediately, his followers split into two groups. Those who became Sunnis felt that the most prominent members of the community should select the new leader, or caliph, on the basis of personal attributes such as piety, wisdom, morality, leadership ability, and competence. Others, however, contended that the leadership of the Islamic community should stay in the prophet's family. They also believed that Muhammad had designated his cousin, son-in-law, and close companion, Ali, to be his successor. They were called Shiites or Shi'a, a word derived from the expression "Shi'at Ali," or "the partisans of Ali."

Although the Sunni won the argument, Ali was eventually elected to the caliphate in 656 after the death of Uthman, the third caliph. Muawiyah, Uthman's nephew and governor of Syria, refused to accept this choice. Eventually he prevailed and established the Damascus-based Umayyad dynasty (661–750).

The Shiites never recognized Umayyad rule, continuing to claim that only direct descendants of Ali had the right to govern the Islamic community. In 680, Ali's second son, Hussein, led a group of his followers in an armed uprising against Umayyad rule. Hussein was defeated and killed at Karbala in what is now southern Iraq. The story of Hussein's defeat lies at the heart of Shiite culture, especially its emphasis on martyrdom and sacrifice. In the following centuries, what initially had been limited to a disagreement over who

should succeed the Prophet became a full-fledged religious and political schism that continues to be felt throughout the Muslim world.

A Note on Transliteration

Rendering Iranian terms in English is a problem, as it is for all languages that do not use the Roman alphabet. The task is particularly difficult in the case of Iran because scholars, the American government, journalists, and others use multiple conventions in transliterating names and terms. We have chosen not to use the system favored by most scholars and government officials in which names, in particular, are shown in complicated forms. We have decided to adopt the transliteration scheme used by the *New York Times*, *Washington Post*, and other Western press services because they are far simpler and, frankly, easier to follow. Of course, they do not always use the same names, so we had to make a lot of judgment calls....

For our purposes, Shiite beliefs differ most importantly from the more widely practiced Sunni version of Islam in two main ways. First, Shiites have an established clergy and stress the importance of theological training among those who reach the top of their hierarchy, the ayatollahs. It is easy for outsiders to see the differences within the Shiite clergy. Regardless of rank, direct descendants of the Prophet's family who are members of the clergy are allowed to wear black turbans. It is also not uncommon to see articles about their claim to power with titles such as "revolt among the black turbans." Second, as is often missed by Western observers, Shiites have long tolerated and even encouraged debate over the interpretation of key principles from the Quran, Hadith, and Sharia. Iran is not only one of the few Islamic countries in which Shiites constitute an overwhelming majority of the population, it was the only one in which they dominated the government until their Iraqi co-religionists came to power in Iraq following the ouster of Saddam Hussein (see Chapter 14).

Many conventional interpretations of Shiism overstate its **fundamentalism**. Before the Islamic Revolution of 1979, the Shiite clergy largely shunned politics, arguing for an Islamic equivalent of the Western principle of separation of church and state. Last but by no means least, Shiism is not monolithic. In fact, the community has actively encouraged debate between leading clerics about the true meaning of the faith, which has traditionally made the Shiite community as intellectually open as any major religious group in the world.

Since the Iranian revolution and the rise of terrorism, however, many in the West have used the term fundamentalist to refer to groups like the Iranian leadership. Observers latched on to that term as they struggled to understand why millions of people were turning to traditional interpretations of religion after years in which the trend had been toward a more secular and Western approach to life.

But more recently, some scholars have stopped using the term fundamentalist in this context because it tends to blend together so many very different viewpoints. The word was initially coined to describe American Protestants who adopted a literal interpretation of the Bible. In that sense, Osama bin Laden, the Taliban, and many of the early leaders of the Islamic revolution in Iran could well be considered fundamentalists. However, others, including the reformers in Iran, are better thought of as **Islamicists**, meaning those who are trying to find a way to blend the tenets of their faith with the needs and complexities of a modern, industrialized, and globalizing world.

The same should probably be said even more strongly for another commonly used label, fanatics. It is true that some of the people we will encounter in this chapter and the next hold extreme views and, like many of their colleagues throughout the Muslim world, are deeply angry about the impact of the West in general and the United States in particular. But fanaticism is a pejorative word, one that could be used to describe anyone who deeply espouses and publicly demonstrates unusual beliefs.

Personally, we do not use either fundamentalist or fanatic because we find that they tend to obscure the complexities of life in a country like Iran and make it harder to understand a regime like the one Saddam Hussein led in Iraq for almost a quarter-century. Moreover, thinking in these terms can drive us into what psychologists call the **image of the enemy**, which leads us to view people we disagree with as completely evil and unacceptable.

We are as critical as anyone of the intolerance, violence, and brutality that has been carried out in the name of "God the most compassionate." However, words like fundamentalist and fanatic can hinder our perception of a lot of complicated trends that we need to understand if we are to deal with the vitally important challenges posed by countries like Iran.

Persia versus Shiism

In short, Iran has two powerful traditions, Persia and Shiism. Over the last century, its leadership has fought over which one would be the most important in shaping political life.

As we will see in the section on Iranian history, the Pahlavis and other modernizers wanted to downplay the role of Islam and thus stressed the more secular aspects of Persian history, ranging from the poetry of its intellectuals to the world-famous wine made from Shiraz grapes. By contrast, the clergy emphasized the country's Shiite tradition and the role of faith, especially in the impoverished rural areas of the country and, later, in the slums of Tehran and other big cities.

Arab and Muslim

Westerners often make the mistake of equating Arabs and Muslims. They are definitely not one and the same. Arabs are an ethnic group that constitutes the bulk of the population from Morocco in the west to Iraq in the east. Not all Arabs are Muslims. Large numbers of Lebanese and Palestinians, in particular, are Christians, as was Tariq Aziz, one of the leaders of Saddam Hussein's regime in Iraq.

And by no means are all Muslims Arabs. Most Iranians are Persians who have a different heritage from Arabs and do not speak Arabic. Overall, Islam spread as far as Western Africa (see Chapter 15 on Nigeria) and the Philippines. In fact, the countries with the largest Muslim populations, India, Pakistan, and Indonesia, have no Arabs to speak of.

Social and Economic Conditions

Iran has tremendous economic potential because it sits atop almost 100 billion barrels of proven oil reserves. Even though a growing number of countries now refuse to buy oil from Iran, it still produces almost 4 million barrels a day, much of which finds its way onto the global market.

However, oil has not produced the level of wealth in Iran that one finds in Saudi Arabia, Kuwait, and the other oil-producing states on the Persian Gulf. Hard statistics are hard to come by, but the Central Intelligence Agency (CIA) estimates that gross domestic product per capita is only about $11,000 a year. Additionally, the distribution of income and wealth is highly skewed toward a rather small upper middle class that coexists with as much as 20 percent of the population living in poverty.

As we will see later in the chapter, President Khatami's government sought to introduce market reforms to make the economy more efficient and remove the structural problems created both under the shah and during the early years of the Islamic Republic. Iran has also lost some of its brightest, best-educated, young professionals who have emigrated for political or economic reasons since the 1970s.

Finally, it should be noted that Iran has the youngest population of any country covered in this book. In the early years of the Islamic Republic, the leadership encouraged people to have as many children as possible to boost the size of the country's population (again see the basics box). Because the population explosion has been an unexpected burden on economy with an inflation rate of about 15 percent, the government has now encouraged the use of birth control to limit the expansion in the number of young people. The emphasis on youth is also reflected in the fact that authorities lowered the voting age for a while to 15, which was almost certainly the youngest in the world. It has since been raised to 18 again.

The Status of Women

One of the most controversial issues involving Iran is the status of women. Islamic scholars and clerics disagree about what women should be allowed to do. It is safe to say that the Iranian authorities have limited women's rights as much or more than any Islamic regime other than the one led by Saudi Arabia or the Taliban in Afghanistan before it was overthrown after the terrorist attacks of 9/11.

The restrictions imposed on women in Iran after 1979 came after more than half a century of relative openness for them in the workplace and in society 🌐 (www.stophonourkillings.com). More than half of the university students were—and still are—women. Trendy stores in chic neighborhoods of Tehran sold clothes and other goods that one could buy in Paris or London or New York.

But after the Islamic Revolution, everything changed. Stonings and other executions were far more frequent. Women had to wear at least a head scarf and veil, and the regime preferred that they add a *manteau* (coat) that covered their entire bodies. Things got to the point that women who ran up the stairs in the few remaining coed schools were often arrested because parts of their ankles showed. By the late 1990s, at least some middle-class women were testing the rules by wearing makeup under their *manteaux* or allowing wisps of hair to appear from around their head scarves. At the time, women were not allowed into the stadiums where soccer-crazed men watched Iranian teams play, so some disguised themselves as men (*manteaux* do have their advantages in that respect) and sneaked in.

As the *Reading Lolita* box points out, middle-class and educated Iranian women have increasingly found ways to work around the restrictions placed on them by the regime. But there is no denying that those limitations are as great in Iran as in any country in the world and that many women chafe under them.

There is no better example of the ambiguities in Iranian policies toward women than the cases of two very prominent women:

In 2003, **Shirin Ebadi** was awarded the Nobel Peace Prize. She studied law before the fall of the shah and soon became a judge, but she had been a loyal supporter of the revolution in its early days. Within a few years, the authorities thwarted her career as a judge because they believed that women should not be allowed to interpret Islamic law. She then decided to defend cases of alleged human rights abuse. In 2003, she was awarded the Nobel Peace Prize. As a devout Muslim, she covered herself in public in Iran, but did not when accepting the Nobel Prize as a sign that many Iranian women sought change. 🌐 (nobelprize.org/nobel_prizes/peace/laureates/2003/ebadi-lecture.html).

Four years later, an American scholar who was born and raised in Iran was imprisoned for almost seven months. Haleh Esfandiari is head of Middle Eastern studies at the

Reading Lolita in Tehran/Lipstick Jihad

Analysts in the West have spent the nearly thirty years since the Islamic Revolution trying to make sense of the status of women in Iran. Two very different and very nonacademic books have shed a lot of light on what has happened—for good and for ill. Both are memoirs, though by of women of different generations and sensitivities.

The first is Azar Nafizi's *Reading Lolita in Tehran*. Vladimir Nabokov's *Lolita* would be a controversial book anywhere because it deals with a middle-aged teacher's obsession and affair with a thirteen-year-old student. But nowhere is it more controversial than in Iran, where women face as much discrimination as they do anywhere in the world. Nafisi is an American-educated literature professor who went back to Iran at the time of the revolution and taught at a number of universities. Eventually, she lost her job because she would not conform to clothing and other restrictions. In the year before her family decided to return to the United States, she taught an independent study course in her own home for her best women students. The curriculum included *Lolita*, but that's not what her book is about. Instead, she chronicles how these young women handled themselves in public and in private, where they took off their veils and *manteaux* to reveal Western clothing, makeup, and anything but traditional Iranian values.

Lipstick Jihad is a very different book. Its author, Azadeh Moaveni, was a young journalist who had dual Iranian and American citizenship. She was studying in Egypt just as the reform period under Mohammad Khatami was coming to an end. She also found that she was one of the few Americans who could actually go to cover events in Iran because she had both citizenships. Her book focuses on the culture shock that hit a totally Westernized young woman professionally and personally. Among other things, she was shocked that most people she met did not fast during Ramadan.

nonpartisan Woodrow Wilson Institute for Scholars funded by the American government. In December 2006, she went to visit her ninety-three-year-old mother, who had stayed behind in Tehran when most of the family emigrated to the United States. On her way to the airport to return to Washington on December 30, Esfandiari was arrested. Over the next few months, the government accused her of being part of a group of spies Washington had sent to undermine the regime. No one in the United States bought that story.[2] Finally, in September 2007, she was released and soon allowed to leave the country, but only after her mother and the rest her family put up more than three hundred thousand dollars in "bail."

Key Concepts and Questions

To understand Iran, we need to explore certain key questions that arise everywhere in the Global South. But, in so doing, we will also see issues that are specific to Iran and, at most, a handful of other countries.

- How do countries that were never formally colonized deal with the legacy of imperialism, which has been a central feature of Iranian political life since long before the 1979 revolution?

- Why is Iran having a hard time developing its economy, especially in view of the fact that it has so much oil and other natural resources?

- Why is Iran one of the few countries left in the world that is run by its religious leaders?

- What is the importance of charismatic leadership? The Ayatollah Khomeini was certainly charismatic, if an austere and dour cleric can ever be seen as charismatic. What about President Ahmadinejad? Khomeini is long dead. Ahmadinejad will leave office in about two years. Will his successor be charismatic? Does it matter?

- How does the isolation it has experienced since the 1979 revolution affect the way the Iranian government is structured and limit the prospects for democracy?

THE EVOLUTION OF THE IRANIAN STATE

Before Islam

Many features of politics in Iran today have important roots that go back more than 2,500 years (see Table 13.1). Although we do not have the time or space to discuss that

---

[2]Glenn Kessler, "Iran Signals Readiness to Cooperate." *The Washington Post*, September 25, 2003, A18, A26.

TABLE 13.1 Turning Points in Iranian History before 1900

YEAR	EVENT
550 BC	Cyrus comes to power
332 BC	Defeat by Alexander the Great
560 AD	Accession of Khosrow I
638	Arab victory; introduction of Islam
1219	Invasion by Mongols
1501	First Safavid shah named
1896	Assassination of Nasir ed-Din Shah

entire history, we will highlight some key themes from the thousand years before the Arabs conquered the country and converted Iranians to Islam 🌐 (**www.iranchamber.com/history/historic_periods.php**).

Iran's origins are both religious and political in nature. They begin with the Prophet Zoroaster, who lived sometime between the ninth and seventh centuries before the birth of Christ and created one of the world's first monotheistic religions, which took root among most of the people in what is now Iran. A political evolution began somewhat later and dates from the accession of Cyrus the Great to the Persian throne of Medes in 550 BC. At that time, the people who lived on the Fars plain were taking up agriculture and moving into fixed settlements that required protection. By the time the next ruler, Darius, died in 521, he had expanded that Empire as far as parts of today's Bulgaria and Greece in the northwest, Libya in the southwest, and India and Pakistan in the east. It was not only the size of the empire that made this expansion successful; Cyrus and his successors, Darius and Xerxes, drew on Zoroastrian traditions that required just rulers to establish a positive working relationship with those they governed. In other words, they could not rule solely by force.

Their power was not to last, however. In 332 BC, the Macedonian Alexander the Great defeated the Persians and occupied their large and glorious capital, Persepolis. Shortly after Alexander's death, the nomadic Parthians—an Aryan tribe (another source of the name Iran)—began to settle in the area and adopted Persian culture. By 163 BC, they were able to establish enough power to wall Persia off from the Roman Empire and restore a degree of independence. The Parthians stayed in power for almost four hundred years until their rule disintegrated in tribal fighting. The struggle culminated not in a war but in a personal struggle between the last Parthian, Adravan, and his challenger, Ardeshir. Once the latter killed the former, he was able to establish the Sassanian dynasty that ruled Persia from 208 to 637. Most important for our purposes, like the Parthians, the Sassanians adopted most of what was by then a millennium-old Persian culture and style of rule. That said, one of their key innovations was to begin calling the ruler *shahinshah*, or "king of kings." The last of the great Sassanian shahs, Khosrow I, took power in 560. He restored Persian power and began to move its influence and borders westward again. He also built a new capital at Ctesiphon, where the floor of his immense palace was covered with a remarkable ninety-foot-square carpet dubbed the "Spring of Khosrow."

The Arrival and Consolidation of Islam

Khosrow's power would not last long either. The Christian Byzantines fought back and forced him to flee in 626, which effectively shattered the Sassanian state. But it would not be the Byzantines who would dominate Persia.

At that same moment, a new religion, Islam, was taking root on the Arabian Peninsula. Following the Prophet's death on June 8, 632, his followers fanned out in all directions to convert people to the new faith. Previously, Persians had never had any reason to fear the relatively underdeveloped Arabs. Thus, when their far larger and far better equipped army faced the Muslims at Qadisiya just west of the Euphrates in present-day Iraq, they expected a swift and easy victory. But when the battle began in 637 after four months of negotiations, the dispirited Sassanian troops crumbled. The next year, the Arabs occupied Ctesiphon. In a sign of things to come, they shipped the Spring of Khosrow back to Mecca, where they cut it into pieces.

Incorporating Islam into Persian culture was not very difficult given the Zoroastrian belief in a single God who led the struggle between good and evil. However, Persians had a hard time adjusting to the fact that they were now a far less important power and that their tradition of strong kings had been undermined by subordination to the temporal and spiritual leaders of Arab-based Islam. Persians did help make the Islamic Middle East one of the cultural centers of the world during the early centuries of the last millennium. However, Persia itself fell into decline in part because Islam downplayed the role of kingship, which had been at the heart of its culture since the time of Cyrus and Darius.

As we saw previously, the Islamic world split between Shiite and Sunni in the decades after the Prophet's death. However, it would be eight hundred years before the Persians became the first people to accept Shiism en masse—and then only following another debacle that would shape Persian values for centuries to come.

In 1219, the Mongol army led by Chinghiz (Genghis) Khan overran Persia. Among other atrocities, the Mongols decapitated and disemboweled every resident of Naishapur, then one of Persia's intellectual centers. Chinghiz's grandson, Hulagu, returned to Persia to rampage 40 years later and remained to rule much of the region as an independent Mongol territory. The last invasion from the northeast came under Tamerlane, who called himself a Tatar rather than a Mongol, in 1394. These repeated invasions gave birth to an understandable fear of outside intervention that has endured ever since.

During this time, some Iranians created the sufi mystical tradition, in which holy men whipped up religious frenzy throughout the region, promising that the faithful would reach communion with God. One of the sufi orders,

Courtesy of Search for Common Ground

The ruin of the ancient city of Persepolis.

the Safavid, came to the fore under Junayd, who also turned it from a religious into a political movement as well. In 1501, forces loyal to his grandson, Ismail, took control of the city of Tabriz and proclaimed their leader **shah**. Ismail and his followers fought back repeated attacks from the Sunni Ottoman Empire founded by the Turks who originally came from what is now Western China and Mongolia. As they solidified their rule over a land that is about 20 percent larger than today's Iran, they also turned to Shiism, in part to set themselves apart from the Ottomans and Arabs.

For the next four hundred years, the Safavid and, later, Qajar, dynasties combined the traditional Persian commitments to strong kingship with Shiite beliefs in faith and obedience to rule the country. Unlike earlier periods, however, their approach to governing produced stagnation, not the kind of growth and domination that had been so much a part of Persian history in early centuries.

During that time, the Persian kings came to emphasize the authoritarian nature of their rule. To cite but one example, Abbas Shah was convinced that his closest advisors were conspiring with his sons against him. So, he ordered one of his sons killed in 1615 and another blinded six years later. His successors may not have been quite as ruthless. Nonetheless, they continued to build a regime in which monarchs with absolute power dominated a hierarchical society where religion was central and social and economic change all but impossible to achieve. Authoritarian rule was reinforced by Shiism, which provides tremendous respect to the most learned scholars, especially those who are descendents of the Prophet.

The combination of the tradition of Persian kingship and Shiite Islam produced a strain in the country's culture that called for charismatic leadership from the king but required that his rule be just and in keeping with religious beliefs. By the end of the nineteenth century, the inability of generations of kings to live up to that ideal did the traditional line of dynasties in.

The shahs of that era were not wholly without accomplishments. If nothing else, they were among the few rulers in what is today's Global South who were able to prevent direct colonial rule. The Qajars, in particular, could put together a reasonably integrated state by building networks of local warlords and potentates out of which grew at least a rudimentary sense of national identity.

Nonetheless, by the late nineteenth century, like many other cultures in Asia and Africa, Persia found itself torn between its own traditions and the growing pressures from the West. Although Iran escaped direct colonial rule, that does not mean that pressures from the West had little or no impact. To begin with, many middle-class Iranians studied and later did business in Europe and North America. Foreign companies developed a presence in the country long before oil became its leading export, often as a result of direct grants or concessions handed to them by the Qajars.

TABLE 13.2 Iran: 1900–1979

YEAR	EVENT
1905	Start of Constitutional Revolution
1911	End of Constitutional Revolution
1925	Reza Khan becomes shah
1941	Mohammad Reza Pahlavi becomes shah
1953	Overthrow of Mossadeq government
1979	Islamic Revolution

Russian military advisors provided the only semblance of training and discipline to the army. Most telling of all, the military and economic power of the West drove home just how weak the Qajar dynasty had become.

Opposition to the regime built throughout the society. Orthodox Shiites objected to secularization. The *bazaaris*, or small businessmen who owned stalls and shops in the country's marketplaces, wanted the opportunity to make more money while reducing competition from outsiders. The growing secular middle class wanted political reforms that would lead to the rule of law, if not to democracy itself (see Table 13.2).

The last decade of the nineteenth and first decade of the twentieth centuries were troubled years for Iran. There were protests against almost all aspects of Qajar rule, including an extremely unpopular ban against smoking tobacco. In 1896, the aging (and most thought incompetent) Nasir ed-Din Shah was assassinated.

The most important of the protests was the **Constitutional Revolution** of 1905 to 1911. It succeeded at first because it promised all things to all people, including firming up the legal status of Islam, strengthening the state, instituting economic reforms, and codifying the legal system. On January 12, 1906, a huge protest convinced Muzaffar ed-Din Shah to dismiss his prime minister, give up absolute rule, and call the first equivalent of a parliament.

Unfortunately, the situation degenerated in the months that followed, culminating in June when soldiers fired on demonstrators and killed a cleric. As many as twenty thousand protesters then fled inside the walls of the British embassy. But the situation was thrown into turmoil again when the shah died and was replaced by his son, Muhammad Ali, who was described by one American advisor as "perhaps the most perverted, cowardly, and vice-ridden monster that had disgraced the throne of Persia in many generations."[3] The king finally dismissed his prime minister, created the **Majlis**, and accepted the Constitution of 1906.

---

[3]W. William Schuster, *The Strangling of Persia*, cited in Sandra Mackey, *The Iranians: Persia, Islam, and the Soul of a Nation* (New York: Plume, 1996), 149.

In the end, the secularized and Westernized portion of the Iranian population was the most pleased with the constitutional reforms. By 1907, proclerical forces were already attacking the Constitution in the Majlis, insisting, for instance, that a council of clerics get the right to review all legislation passed by the parliament.

In the meantime, the Russians and British had divided the increasingly ungovernable country into two zones of influence. On June 23, 1908, Russian-led troops attacked and destroyed the Sepahsalar Mosque, which had been the symbolic home of the protest movements of the preceding two years. For the next three years, Russian troops reinforced those of the shah until December 24, 1911, when the shah dissolved the Majlis.

The Last Shahs

The defeat of the Constitutional Revolution did not restore the shah to anything approaching full power. He controlled Tehran and a few other cities, but tribal leaders ran the rest of the country, to the degree that it was run at all.

British influence increased as well. Following its navy's decision to switch from coal to oil to fuel its ships, Iran's oil became a vital resource. As a result, the British all but formally occupied the southern part of the country while the Russians took over the north, leaving Iranians in de facto

Reza Khan Shah and Mohammad Reza Shah at the former's coronation.

control of a narrow strip in the center that did not include Tehran or most other major cities.

The situation deteriorated even further after the Bolshevik Revolution when Marxists briefly set up a Soviet Republic in the Gilan region of northern Iran. This event produced a massive reaction that, in the short run, led to the defeat of the Marxist republic and, in the longer term, produced the first serious nationalist movement in modern Iranian history.

Central to that nationalism was a mid-level officer, Reza Khan, who would establish Iran's final dynasty a decade later. Born in 1878, he quickly rose in the ranks of the Cossack troops (named for their Russian leaders), becoming their leader in the city of Hamadan. After defeating the Soviet republic, he led three thousand Cossacks into Tehran and occupied the city. He also subdued many of the tribal leaders who were still in charge in most of rural Iran. The British, meanwhile, were convinced that this tall, tough soldier could bring order to the country and threw their support behind him. For the next four years, Reza Khan was the de facto leader of the country, but it was only on October 31, 1925, that he had himself crowned shah and chose the dynastic name Pahlavi, after the language spoken before Persia was defeated by the Arabs.

The first Pahlavi shah took power in the name of nationalism and Shiism. However, he soon turned his back on Islam and focused his attention on modernizing his poor and weak country. The shah set out to change the Iranian landscape. His government built the first national railroad system, introduced the first modern factories, and expropriated land from rural elites. The Majlis continued to exist, but it did little more than rubber-stamp decisions made by the monarch.

Perhaps most drastically, the shah turned on the clerics. He took two steps that proved later to be symbolically important to orthodox Muslims. Women were no longer allowed to wear the veil and men had to shave their beards. He closed religious schools, replacing them with free, state-run institutions that stressed science and other modern topics.

The Pahlavi regime also stressed the country's Persian origins and its historical glories before the arrival of Islam. He even changed the name of the country from Persia to Iran on the dubious historical claim that it was the legitimate name because it was the one used under Cyrus and Darius.

Reza Shah played the traditional Iranian "game" of protecting territorial integrity through a complicated pattern of international alliances. In the 1930s, because of his support for the Nazis' Aryan policies, he cast Iran's lot with Germany. After Germany attacked the Soviet Union in 1941, the British decided that they could not run the risk that the Iranian oil fields could come under Nazi control. Therefore,

Dmitri Kessel/Time Life Pictures/Getty Images

on August 25, 1941, the British navy captured southern Iran and the Soviets marched into the north. Saying he could not remain at the head of a country under foreign occupation, the shah abdicated less than a month later and went into exile.

Assessments of his generation in power are mixed. There is little doubt that Reza Shah brought much needed social and economic change to a country he seemed to treat as a personal fiefdom. That said, he definitely lost touch with most of the people, provoking widespread anger because he failed to live up to the Persian tradition of "just rule."

Mohammad Reza Shah replaced his father. Born in 1919, the new shah was not quite twenty-two years old and was thought to be a playboy who preferred dancing and drinking in Europe to the affairs of state. And, indeed, the new shah did little to alter his reputation for the first twelve years he sat on the Peacock Throne.

The shah faced daunting challenges once World War II ended. Surprisingly, the easiest came when diplomatic pressure from the United States and United Kingdom led the Soviets to withdraw from northern Iran. In 1949, the growing communist party (Tudeh) tried to assassinate him. One bullet hit his cheekbone and emerged under his nose. Three more went through his hat. Somehow he survived.

When the charismatic **Mohammad Mossadeq** was prime minister from 1951 to 1953, the shah's political future was even more severely challenged than his physical survival had been in 1949. Over the shah's objections, the prime minister led a campaign to nationalize the Anglo-Iranian Oil Company (AIOC), of which the British owned 51 percent. AIOC was a visible symbol of the degree to which foreigners controlled the country. To cite but one example, Iran earned more from the export of carpets than it did from the much more valuable oil. Mossadeq himself was part of a broad coalition of political groups known as the National Front, which included many of the early non-religious leaders of the Islamic Republic as well as the more politicized clerics of the time. On taking office, he ordered all British employees of AIOC to leave the country. Because Iran did not have workers who could run the production and refinery facilities, chaos ensued. In July 1952, the Majlis granted Mossadeq emergency powers in a law including nineteen clauses that enumerated areas in which he was authorized to act.

The nineteenth was simply "et cetera."

Mossadeq overstretched his capacities when he lost the support of the clerics and the Tudeh. He also generated opposition when he dissolved the upper house of the Parliament, suspended the supreme court, confiscated royal property, and expanded the scope of martial law. The shah then tried to fire the prime minister, who refused to resign.

At that point, the United States intervened, largely through the actions of Kermit Roosevelt (son of President Theodore Roosevelt), who was CIA station chief in Tehran. Fighting broke out, killing at least three hundred. The shah fled to Rome. Finally, the United States succeeded in forcing Mossadeq to resign, which paved the way for the shah to return.

The coup against Mossadeq was at most a short-term and Pyrrhic victory for the United States and the shah. It would only contribute to the anti-Western and anti-American sentiments that boiled over during the revolution of the 1970s and in the early years of the Islamic Republic. In other words, the return of the shah to power laid the groundwork for his defeat a quarter-century later.

Some observers think that the shah took his survival from the attack in 1949 as a sign that he had a divine right to rule and to do so in an absolutist manner. Moreover, he governed in a way that reflected his lack of trust, even in the men who were supposedly his most valued advisors. Consequently, he provoked more intense opposition than his father ever had seen.

First he alienated the Shiite clerics. Despite the stereotypes that have arisen since the 1979 revolution, most Shiite scholars and clergymen have traditionally shunned politics, especially those who teach at such centers of the faith as Qom in Iran and Najaf in Iraq. That situation changed in the 1960s once the shah instituted the **White Revolution** and created the notoriously brutal **SAVAK** to enforce his rule.

The White Revolution began in 1963 and was a revolution in name only. In truth, it was yet another attempt to both modernize the country and increase the shah's power. As was the case under his father, this shah made the clergy an important target of the reforms. He gave the peasants land that belonged to the clerics and reduced the clerical impact on daily life in general. Women's rights were extended, and the training and equipment provided for the growing military were upgraded.

SAVAK was formed in 1957; it is a Farsi acronym for Intelligence and Security Organization of the Country. It not only arrested and tortured dissidents at home, but it spied on and even killed students and others living abroad who dared to oppose the shah.

But the most important change in the 1960s and 1970s came from the religious community, especially from **Ayatollah Ruhollah Khomeini** (1902–89). Khomeini had long been one of the leading clerics in Qom. The tall, austere Khomeini built his reputation and his **charisma** largely because he was seen as a religious leader who was above politics and was exceptionally learned in the legal aspects of Islam. When he gained the title of ayatollah in 1960 he was not actively involved in political life. That would change in a matter of months.

The White Revolution proved to be the last straw for Khomeini. Given the regime's opposition to Islam, he

Profiles
Mohammad Reza Shah

Mohammad Reza Shah, the last Pahlavi king, was born in 1919, two years before his father became ruler of Iran. He received his initial education in Switzerland but later graduated from a military academy in Tehran.

His first years on the throne were marked by turmoil. Communists tried to assassinate him in 1949. In 1951, he fled the country and the reform government of Muhammad Mossadeq and could return only after the Central Intelligence Agency (CIA) orchestrated a coup d'état that forced the nationalist prime minister from office.

By the 1960s, the shah had solidified his rule and embarked on the White Revolution designed to continue the secularization and modernization begun by his father. He provoked even more opposition from both the secular Left and the religious Right and was forced from office and the country in 1979. He died of cancer the following year (persepolis.free.fr/iran/personalities/shah.html).

A soldier bends to kiss the feet of Mohammad Reza Shah as he leaves the country in 1979.

argued that one could no longer separate state and religion and that clerics had an obligation to see to it that Islamic principles were upheld in Iran. In so doing, he shifted the center of gravity of opposition to the shah from the secular left to the followers of orthodox Shiite Islam.

The repression followed quickly. On March 22, 1963, the shah's troops broke into the most famous theological school in Qom and killed two unarmed students. The students who escaped immediately went to Khomeini's house because he was already the symbolic heart of the opposition. When he went to preach at that same school on June 3, the authorities cut off power throughout the city. The next day, Khomeini joined the ranks of over sixty clerics who had been arrested. His followers rioted after he was detained, and it took the imposition of martial law in a number of cities to end the disturbances.

Khomeini was released from prison the following spring. The shah and his supporters tried to convince him to stay out of political life, but he always gave what became his standard response: "All of Islam is politics." Do note that this was a massive change for the Shiite clergy, which had largely been apolitical during Iran's earlier conflicts. In November 1964, he was arrested again, put on an airplane and sent into exile in Iraq, and later moved to the outskirts of Paris. For the next fifteen years, his teaching and preaching galvanized opposition to the shah. Even though he was ignored by the official media, his supporters were able to smuggle in audiotapes of his messages, which circulated among the faithful throughout the country.

More than religion was involved in the downfall of the shah. In fact, the unintended consequences of land reform may have done him the most harm. Most peasants were illiterate and ill-prepared to run the farms they were given. Many, for instance, had to take out huge loans that they could not repay, lost their land, and ended up flocking to the cities, where they lived under appalling conditions in the slums of south Tehran and other urban areas. Tehran's population doubled in the 1970s, and urban dwellers reached half the total population of the country in 1979. In other words, the rapid rate of overall economic growth, the foreign investment, the skyscrapers and mansions built in north Tehran provided a misleading picture of how successful and popular the shah was.

But the shah failed to see that his reforms and his power were little more than an illusion. He became increasingly distant from the population as a whole, continued with his economic reforms, and concentrated more and more power in his own hands. All opposition political parties were abolished. The SAVAK kept track of the opposition at home and abroad and is widely believed to have assassinated a number of leading dissidents and tortured thousands more at its infamous and enormous Evin Prison.

Profiles
Ayatollah Ruhollah Khomeini

The Ayatollah Ruhollah Khomeini was born in 1902 in the isolated town of Khomein. As was the norm in those days, he did not have a last, or family, name, something Reza Khan Shah imposed on the country in 1926, at which point Khomeini became known as Ruhollah Mustafavi. His father, also a cleric, was killed when Ruhollah was a baby, and the boy (whose name means "soul of God") reportedly finished his first reading of the Quran when he was only seven.

In Shiism, an ayatollah has reached the highest level of spiritual awareness. Those who are descended from the Prophet are allowed to wear a black turban; others wear a white one. In Iran, they also usually use their hometown as their family name, which is why he became known as Ayatollah Khomeini rather than Mustafavi.

Khomeini emerged as a leader for two main reasons. First, he developed the notion that senior clerics had the obligation and right to rule to maintain the Islamic nature of Iran because of their spiritual expertise. Second, he became one of the leaders of the

Ayatollah Khomeini addresses an audience in the airport building in Tehran, Iran, February 1, 1979, after his arrival from fourteen years of exile.

opposition to the increasingly secular regime of the shah, especially after Khomeini was forced into exile, first in Iraq and later in France.

As **supreme leader** of the Islamic Republic, Khomeini struck a stern and often angry pose in both his dealings with his own people and with the United States (**www.asiasource.org/society/khomeini.cfm**). ■

The regime also got into trouble because of its alliance with the United States. With the overthrow of Mossadeq, the United States and the CIA became the main focus of anti-imperialist sentiment. Yet the shah forged a close alliance with the United States and used the country's newfound oil wealth after the Organization of Petroleum Exporting Countries' (OPEC) oil embargo quadrupled prices in 1973–74 to buy billions of dollars worth of weapons. Americans doing business in Iran did not help their country's image because they acted as if they ruled it and failed to even notice that their drinking or sexual openness insulted the sensitivities of many Iranians.

The Islamic Republic

The rest of the chapter will deal with the institutions and policies of the Islamic Republic. However, because there are so many misconceptions about the Islamic Republic, especially since the death of Ayatollah Khomeini, it is important that we review its history here and now. Everything covered in this brief review will reappear in the second, more analytical half of the chapter.

Some scholars talk about four periods or even four republics that coincide with the influence of the four men

who have dominated political life in post-revolutionary Iran (see Table 13.3).

The first period, not surprisingly, covers the decade when Khomeini was supreme leader. Despite the initial popularity of the revolution and Khomeini himself, these were not easy years. To begin with, the coalition of individuals, groups, and organizations that toppled the shah was too diverse to govern. Early on, Khomeini issued declarations about having an open government in which the clerics might not play the dominant role. He also ruled alongside prominent politicians who had opposed the shah and did

TABLE 13.3 Key Events in the Islamic Republic

YEAR	EVENT
1979	Khomeini becomes supreme leader
1980–88	War with Iran
1989	Death of Khomeini
1997	Election of Khatami
2004	Victory by conservatives in Majlis election
2005	Election of Ahmadinejad
2009	Reelection of Ahmadinejad

not share his conception of an Islamic state, including Abolhassan Bani-Sadr and Sadeq Gotzbadeh.

Quickly, and in ways reminiscent of Joseph Stalin's or Saddam Hussein's purges (see Chapters 9 and 14), people from every other major political faction were purged and removed from office. Some prominent politicians, including Bani-Sadr, were accused of crimes and executed as were thousands of supporters of rival political movements ranging from the communists to moderate Muslims.

By the early 1980s, there was little doubt that Khomeini had created an Islamic republic. Members of the laity continued to hold important positions in the Majlis, the bureaucracy, and the executive, but all decisions that mattered were made by senior clerics. Khomeini's power was reinforced by three of the most important events of his decade in power:

The first was the 444-day occupation of the U.S. embassy by a group of young Islamic militants, often described as "students," that began on November 4, 1979. These young people had occupied the embassy earlier and been denounced then by both Khomeini and the revolution's secular leaders, which led them to withdraw.

After the first occupation, the United States allowed the dying shah to enter the country for medical treatment. That act deepened anti-American sentiment and led to the second occupation of the embassy. This time, Khomeini and other hard-line leaders gave the action at least their tacit approval.

The occupation had a dual impact. First, it deepened the divide between Washington and Tehran, which has been hostile—at best—ever since. Second, it made it easier for Ayatollah Khomeini and his allies to remove more moderate and secular leaders from power. Virtually none of them remained in prominent positions by the time the hostages were released the day President Ronald Reagan was inaugurated in 1981.

The second event was the long and brutal war Iran fought with Iraq from 1980 to 1988. Ayatollah Khomeini was not the only ruler to come to power in the region in 1979. That year, the longtime second-in-command in Iraq, Saddam Hussein, forced his mentor and predecessor from power (see Chapter 14). The two new rulers viewed each other as threats both to their respective regimes and to their hopes for hegemony in the troubled Persian Gulf region and the Middle East as a whole (**www.crimesofwar.org/thebook/iran-iraq-war.html**).

The eight years of fighting turned into little more than a stalemate. The front lines barely moved inside the borders of either country. Yet by the time the two sides accepted a cease-fire there were more than five hundred thousand killed and wounded on each side. The war also solidified American hostility toward the Islamic republic, which led it to give at least indirect support to Saddam's regime, something most American policymakers came to regret following the Iraqi invasion of Kuwait in 1990.

Most scholars add a third trend to this first period. The dangers imposed by the war led Ayatollah Khomeini and his colleagues to increase the level of repression against potential as well as real opponents. On one level, that introduced new institutions like the **Iranian Revolutionary Guard Corps (IRGC)**, which sought to supplant the less than loyal military inherited from the shah. Even more worrisome is

Mohammad Sayad/AP Images

An Iranian protester sets fire to a United States' flag, while other demonstrators give a clenched fist salute during an anti-American protest in Tehran, Monday, November 5, 1979. The demonstration came after students stormed the United States Embassy in Tehran and held the staff hostage against the deportation of the former Shah of Iran from the United States.

the fact that the regime imprisoned or executed thousands of people in an attempt to solidify support for the regime and its war with Iraq.

The second period coincides with the death of Ayatollah Khomeini and the election of **Ayatollah Hashemi Rafsanjani** (1934–) as president. Although **Ayatollah Ali Khamenei** (1939–) replaced Khomeini as supreme leader (a post he still holds), the balance of power shifted to the more moderate Rafsanjani, one of the clerics who led the Islamic revolution to power in the early 1980s. Rafsanjani had also been seriously wounded in an assassination attempt and, if for no other reason, was held in high esteem. What's more, Khamenei was not a senior religious leader and lacked the moral authority Khomeini had. In fact, Khamenei only became an ayatollah just before Khomeini died so he could be eligible to succeed him.

Unlike Khomeini, Rafsanjani was and still is a pragmatist who has always wanted to concentrate on Iran's mounting domestic policy concerns. Chief among them was reforming the slumping economy hurt both by the theological commitments of the new regime and the costs of the war with Iraq, which included a boycott by the United States and some of its allies. It should be noted that Rafsanjani and many of his colleagues became extremely wealthy men through their control of the shah's former property and other assets, which will be discussed in the policy section. That has led to accusations of corruption and to a drop in support of this second generation of clerical leaders.

Rafsanjani had widespread support because he had the backing of the vast majority of the conservative clerics of which he was ostensibly one. In 1989, for instance, he won

the presidential election with over 95 percent of the vote; four years later, he got more than two-thirds of the ballot in his bid for reelection.

Khamenei is far more conservative and has tried to keep the spirit of the revolution and the purity of the theocracy alive. He has consistently made statements that are far more hostile to the United States and Israel than the first two presidents who served with him. That said, there was relatively little political reform under Rafsanjani. Some changes were made to the Constitution in 1989 that slightly shifted the balance of political power away from the clerics, but significant reform came only under Rafsanjani's successor, Mohammad Khatami, who was elected in 1997 when Rafsanjani was constitutionally barred from seeking a third term.

Although a cleric himself, Khatami was widely known as a moderate who had, among other things, fought against censorship when he was a newspaper editor. During his election campaign, he supported more rights for women and members of religious and ethnic minority groups and stressed the importance of strengthening civil society. Therefore, many observers expected him to lose to the more conservative cleric, Ali-Akbar Nateq-Nouri, who had been the speaker of the Majlis and had the implicit support of Khamenei.

In fact, the election was a landslide, with Khatami winning more than two-thirds of the vote and almost four times that gained by Nouri. Reformists did even better in the 2000 legislative election, winning 189 of the 290 seats. When Khatami ran for reelection the next year, he won 78 percent of the vote against what amounted to only token opposition from nine other candidates, only two of whom won more than 1 percent of the vote. Khatami and the moderates did

Former president Mohammad Khatami.

particularly well among women and young people, which were the social groups who chafed the most under authoritarian rule and a stagnating economy.

During the first six years of his presidency, Khatami introduced a number of reforms. It became easier for people to organize political groups, there was less press censorship, and some open protests were permitted. The government also began to try to improve relations with the United States and other less antagonistic Western powers and even allowed inspections of its nuclear facilities by the International Atomic Energy Agency.

What appears to be a very different fourth period began in 2003 when Khamenei and his more conservative colleagues began to reassert the influence of those who favored retaining the goals and values of the first years of the Islamic republic. In particular, forces loyal to the clerics struck back at the limited political reforms of the first Khatami years. For example, armed thugs operating with government support routinely attacked demonstrators. Most important of all, the clerics refused to allow about 2,500 moderates and reformists to run in the 2004 Majlis election, thereby guaranteeing a conservative landslide. The conservative ascendancy continued with the surprise election of Ahmadinejad over the far more widely known Rafsanjani when Khatami had to step down in 2005. As we will see later, Ahmadinejad is probably more conservative than the Supreme Leader and, while devout, is the first person from outside the clergy to hold a key post in Iran since the early 1980s.

The repression extended into the elite. Khatami was banned from traveling abroad. Rafsanjani's son was arrested for his part in the Green Movement to be discussed below.

Since then, Iran has become far more conservative and hostile to both the West and reform at home. Ahmadinejad has presided over a country with ever worsening economic problems but has focused his attention elsewhere. Along with Supreme Leader Khamenei, the Iranian authorities have stepped up their criticisms of Israel. They have also rejected all pressure from the West to abandon their nuclear program and even acknowledge that it could lead to the manufacture of atomic bombs. And, as the protests after the 2009 election shows, power may be shifting somewhat away from the clergy to the revolutionary guard, a trend that does not augur well for democracy in any way, shape, or form.

THE PEOPLE AND POLITICS

In other chapters, we discussed political culture and then political participation in a fairly linear way. We can't do that here. Because culture and participation are so inextricably intertwined in Iran, it makes more sense to start with a most recent crisis and then work back to culture and more conventional forms of participation.

TABLE 13.4 2009 Presidential Election

CANDIDATE	FIRST BALLOT (%)
Mahmoud Ahmadinejad	62.6
Mir Hossein Mousavi	33.8
Others and invalid votes	4.6

President Ahmadinejad ran for reelection in June 2009. While there is some dispute about the outcome, most outside observers think that President Ahmadinejad actually lost and certainly did not come close to the 62 percent of the vote as it was officially reported (see Table 13.4).

Most members of the opposition, including former President **Mohammad Khatami** (1943–) opted not to run and united behind **Mir Hossein Mousavi**, who had impeccable revolutionary credentials and was deemed the most electable of Ahmadinejad's rivals. He had been prime minister in the 1980s before that post was abolished. Both he and his wife are from minority ethnic groups.

Most observers in Iran were convinced that Mousavi had won and that Ahmadinejad stole the election. The authorities refused to authorize a recount of the vote, let alone a return to the polls. President Obama, who had come to power holding out an olive branch to Tehran vigorously opposed the actions of the authorities. The possibilities of meaningful negotiations on Iran's nuclear program, and almost everything else, all but disappeared.

The people who supported Mousavi and the other opposition candidates were furious. Demonstrations of massive and unprecedented proportions were held over the following few weeks. The government took a hard line, and a series of religious and civil authorities determined that the election had been run fairly and that the results were more or less accurate.

After that, all hell broke loose, setting Iranian domestic politics and Iranian-Western relations back to a state where they were as bleak as they have been in many years. Many middle class and young Iranians, who never liked Ahmadinejad to begin with, refused to accept the results of the elections and launched a spontaneous wave of protests that is called either the **Green Revolution** or **Movement**.

Over the next two weeks, daily protests occurred with hundreds of thousands of participants. The notoriously vicious *basij*, or semi-legal vigilantes affiliated with the Revolutionary Guard, in particular cracked down. Hundreds of protesters were killed, including the recent college graduate and previously apolitical Neda Agha-Soltan, who became a global celebrity after her killing was shown on television worldwide.

Walter Bieri/AP Images

People protesting the death of Neda Soltani who was killed in the demonstrations after the 2009 presidential election.

We prefer the term Green Movement because it never came close to threatening the regime, which one would expect of a full-fledged revolution. Instead, the movement was always defined in ways that supported the Islamic republic in principle but rejected the practices of the current leaders. Indeed, the very use of the term "green" says a lot. It is the dominant color in the Iranian flag and is also commonly associated with Islam in general. Thus, the movement was called green because participants dressed in green as a sign of their piety and their acceptance of the regime.

It was also a new kind of social movement in which participants relied heavily on such social media software as Twitter and Facebook to organize their demonstrations. Iranians living in the diaspora also participated in the planning to such an extent that Western analysts had a hard time telling which tweets came from Los Angeles and which from Tehran.

For good or ill, the movement was short lived. As a *New Yorker* reporter who was one of the few Western journalists allowed into Iran put it, "repression works." The government and the revolutionary guard found ways to keep demonstrators out of the broad boulevards that allowed large numbers of people to gather. Many participants in

the movement were arrested. There was talk of thousands killed. Those who survived were the subjects of show trials that were reminiscent of those in the Soviet Union under Stalin. Even an Imam who blogged ended up in court where he confessed to crimes that he did not commit but that the state alleged.

In short, the statement that begins this chapter is worth keeping squarely in mind as we head into the nuts and bolts about this confusing country. As is the case with all of the chapters on countries in this book, our primary objective is to describe and explain basic patterns in their political systems. This chapter has a second, and more focused, purpose. For most of the quarter-century since the overthrow of the shah, Western observers have portrayed Iran as a ruthless dictatorship, something President George W. Bush encapsulated as part of the "axis of evil" in his State of the Union speech in 2002. We will try to show next that the realities of Iranian political life are far more nuanced. To be sure, the banning of reformist candidates in the 2004 election and the crackdown since 2009 show a regime that is not very liberal. However, we will also see that it has provided more opportunities for public participation and has allowed more debate and division than popular depictions of it in the West might lead us to expect.

No one has defined this complex situation better than the British political scientist, Ali Ansari:

Far from the monolithic totalitarian state described by some commentators, Iran's politics reflect an intensely complex, highly plural dynamic characteristic of a state in transition that incorporates the contradictions and instabilities inherent in such a process. Democratizing moderates confront authoritarian conservatives; a secularizing, intensely nationalistic society sits uneasily next to the sanctimonious piety of the hard-line establishment.[4]

Political Culture

For all practical purposes, foreign political scientists and other scholars have not been able to do field research in Iran since 1979. Among other things, that means that there are tremendous gaps in what we know about the country, especially its political culture, which can only be analyzed through in-depth and direct observation of the link between people's core beliefs and their political behavior.

The lack of information, of course, has not kept academics and journalists from speculating about this vitally important topic. Nonetheless, any statement that tries to assess the importance of particular values with any degree of precision needs to be taken with many grains of intellectual salt. One thing is clear. Iran does not have a homogeneous political culture. Its history has left the Iranian people quite nationalistic, perhaps increasingly so. Both its long history as an independent country and its troubles of the last century have given Iranians a stronger sense of national identity than most people in the Global South have. After that, however, any sense of homogeneity disappears in a welter of somewhat overlapping subcultures, the size and importance of which are hard to define.

The division into subcultures is even true of religion. Although most Iranians are Shiites, they approach their faith in a number of ways. A goodly number of people support the conservative and even puritanical version of Islam adopted by the clerics who proved victorious after the overthrow of the shah. But there is also an Islamic Left, which is best reflected today in the reformist groups. Finally, there are Iranians like Azar Nafisi and most of her students, who are secular and do such forbidden things as drink alcohol, wear makeup, and watch foreign television shows and films, albeit in the privacy of their own homes.

The religious subcultures also overlap with ones that grow out of the country's social and economic divisions. Orthodox Shiites are found most commonly in rural and poor areas. The bazaaris have mostly cast their lot with clerics like Rafsanjani who have supported them, for instance, against foreign competition. Well-educated and affluent Iranians are most likely to have had ongoing contacts with the West and to be secular.

The Lizard

One of the ways Iranians can express their dissatisfaction is through film, and no better example exists than *The Lizard (Marmoulak)*, produced in 2004 with the approval of the authorities.

The film's lead character (Reza played by famous comic actor Parvis Pathui), is in jail yet again as a chronic thief. He then finds himself in a hospital ward in a bed next to a *mullah* (we are not told why they are in the same prison hospital). When the mullah goes to take a shower, leaving his robes behind, Reza dons them and walks out of the prison. After all, who would question a mullah in a theocracy?

He tries to hail a cab. Because most people do not like mullahs, no one picks him up until one cabbie stops for him—and drives twenty miles in the wrong direction.

At the end of the film, Reza is trying to get out of the country and finds himself in a village near one of Iran's borders. Worshipers at a local mosque see him (still in mullah's robes, of course) and demand that he come lead Friday prayers. He does his best, but, as is often the case in modern Iran, people fall asleep as soon as he starts his sermon.

The most significant wild card in Iranian culture will be how today's youth evolves. Three in ten Iranians are under twenty; almost two-thirds of the population is under thirty. These people have at most hazy memories of the revolution and its early years. Instead, they have grown up in difficult economic times in which about half of the younger members of the workforce are unemployed at any one time. The protest movements that have burst onto the scene on several occasions since the mid-1990s were composed all but exclusively of dissatisfied young people of all social classes, but especially university students.

The protests after the 2009 election may have marked a turning point in this respect. This time, the protesters came from all walks of urban Iranian society. For an overwhelmingly Muslim country, Iran is surprising liberal, although it is very far from being a democracy. As we will see in the next two sections, some dissent is allowed some of the time and Iranians have voted in regular, reasonably fair, and competitive elections, although the degree to which they are fair and competitive has varied considerably over the past twenty-five years.

[4]Ali Ansari, "Continuous Regime Change from Within," *Washington Quarterly, 26* (Autumn 2003): 53

These differing and even conflicting values are reflected in Iranian attitudes toward the United States. Many Iranians despise the United States—and the West as a whole—for the way it treated Iran and its resources until the overthrow of the shah and for its opposition to the regime's politics since then. But others are fascinated by American culture, especially those aspects of it that are formally forbidden by the clerics. In fact, one public opinion poll conducted in 2007 showed that Iranians were more pro-American than citizens in any other country in the Middle East.

This evidence is highly speculative. However, Western doctors, scientists, filmmakers, and others who have been able to participate in cultural exchanges and to visit Iran have been amazed at how warmly they have been welcomed by their Iranian colleagues. Although that may not tell us a lot about Iranian culture as a whole, it nonetheless suggests that stereotypes of unified hostility toward the West are not accurate.

Protest and Challenges to the Islamic Republic

Unlike Iraq, Iran has had an often vibrant and visible opposition for much of the period since the Islamic revolution. As we saw, the coalition that overthrew the shah was quite diverse, and it took several years before the clerics could completely solidify their rule and remove most members of the Islamic left from office.

But other perspectives never disappeared, and by the mid-1990s significant protest movements began to occur. Most notable were two "spasms of unrest"[5] in 1999 and 2003 in addition to the Green Movement. All were brutally put down by the regime. But, the fact that they existed at all is one of those nuances a western student of Iranian politics has to keep in mind.

The protests in 1999 tell us the most about how limited the opposition was before the Green Movement and has become again today. There is some uncertainty about how large they were. Supporters claim that the students and their allies gained control of some cities for two days. What is clear is that tens of thousands of students at most of the country's universities held rallies at which both Khatami and Khamenei were criticized for their failure to enact pro-democratic reforms. Then, on July 9, the authorities allowed *basijis*, to attack a dormitory. At least one person was killed and several others were hurled out of fourth-story windows. Larger protests followed in the next few days, but they quickly lost momentum as the regime made it clear it would use arrests and the *basijis* to quell the protests.

The 2003 demonstrations started in a more mundane way as students complained about the high costs of tuition. But they evolved in two respects that were quite different from those of four years earlier. First, they began to draw some working-class youth who were frustrated by unemployment and poverty, which is the lot of as much as 40 percent of the population. Second, they gained a lot more international attention, both from the George W. Bush administration and from the television and radio stations set up by the Iranian exile community in southern California where about a half million of them live. Again, the government quickly cracked down.

We should not read too much into these protests. The Bush administration and the émigrés saw them as signs of an imminent revolution, yet there is no reason to believe that such is the case (but also see the conclusion to this chapter). The links between the university students and other young people are limited. And, while the few available public opinion polls show widespread support for reform, almost everyone wants it to occur within the framework of the system created in 1979. Indeed, most dissidents who have been interviewed by Western television networks and newspapers insist that their country has been through too much turmoil since the revolution and that any regime change would almost certainly make a bad situation worse.

Elections and the Ayatollahs' Democracy

The best new book on Iran is Hooman Majd's *The Ayatollahs' Democracy*. Majd is an Iranian-American journalist known mostly for his work for the *New York Times.* He is also former President Khatami's cousin, which means he has tremendous contacts among the reformers.

Majd's sentiments clearly lie with the reformers, but he makes the case that some leaders of the 1979 protests wanted to create what they saw as an Islamic—or perhaps better, Persian—form of democracy. As we will see in the rest of the chapter, the senior clergy would call all of the major shots but there would also be a role for citizens as well. In short, as we will see more clearly in the section on the state, Iran has a hybrid system in which a strong authoritarian regime permits a noticeable albeit varying amount of democracy.

It may well be that events in much of North Africa in early 2011 (see Chapter 11) will leave at least some of the countries involved in the Arab Spring dramatically more democratic than Iran. However, that doesn't take away from the that when we teach about Iran, our students are most surprised by the fact that Iran has one of the freest electoral systems in the Middle East. Far more common are countries such as Saudi Arabia, which has had no elections at all, or Kuwait, where the suffrage is strictly limited.

Iranians have voted in nine presidential and seven Majlis elections since the revolution. All citizens over the age of fifteen were eligible to vote until the voting age was raised to eighteen following the 2005 presidential election.

---

[5]"Thanks, but Please Don't Support Us: Iranian Protest," *The Economist*, 21 June 2003, 38.

TABLE 13.5 Majlis Election 2008

ROUGH COALITION	SEATS
Regime supporters	230
Reformists	46
Independents and Others	71

There are also dozens of political parties, most of which are tiny and poorly organized. In 2004, one authoritative source listed thirty-four of the parties along with their websites, but put them all in the "minor party" category. In practice, Majlis candidates run their own campaigns as what Americans would call independents, but they make it clear where they stand in relation to the broad ideological groupings in the population as a whole, most of which deal with the pace and extent of political reform (see Table 13.5).

The weakness of the parties is an all but inevitable outgrowth of the fact that there are still clear limits on who can play an active role in political life. They are also weak because of the way Majlis elections are conducted. That also means that we cannot build a table that examines election results over an extended period of time because the parties reflected in Table 13.5 would be so different from those even four years earlier.

The country is divided into twenty-eight constituencies, which are allocated seats on the basis of their populations. Candidates who wish to run put their name forward to a subcommittee of the **Guardian Council**. Even at their best before 2004, Iranian elections cannot be considered democratic because the unelected Guardian Council has to approve all candidates. In some elections, it has simply screened out candidates who were too radical in one form or another and those who had no chance whatsoever of winning. In the 1992 and 1996 elections, the council kept about a third of those who wanted to run off the ballot. In 2000, it was far more lenient, doing so for only 11 percent of the candidates, including just a handful of prominent reformers.

In the run-up to the 2008 election, more than 7,000 people indicated they were willing to run for the 290 seats in the eighth Majlis. The council then determined who should be allowed to run using criteria developed in the Constitution and later electoral laws. Some are straightforward: Candidates must be under seventy-five, and those running for the first time must have the equivalent of a university degree. Men who did not meet those criteria but were already members of the Majlis before the current law went into effect could continue to run and serve. All must have a "belief in and commitment in practice to Islam and the sacred system of the Islamic Republic of Iran." Unlike 2000, when the Guardian Council interpreted that rule quite loosely and allowed many popular reformists to run and win, in the next two elections they denied more than two thousand candidates the right to run, most of whom were reformists.

Elections are officially held on a nonpartisan basis. When they arrive at the polls, voters see a ballot with a long list of names without any partisan identification. Furthermore, the official election campaign is only a week long. Many typical campaign tactics in the West, such as putting up posters are forbidden. Candidates are allowed to hand out campaign literature, but no piece of paper can be larger than roughly four by six inches. Candidates are allowed to circulate lists of colleagues they support to help voters reach decisions.

Voting occurs in two rounds. Any candidate who wins with a plurality of at least 25 percent of the vote at the first ballot is declared a winner. That was the case for three-quarters of the seats in 2004 and 2008 A second round is held several months later for the undecided seats, at which time only the top two remaining candidates can run, as is the case in France (see Chapter 5).

The last two Majlis elections did not bode well for democracy. In 2004, all but sixty-four seats were decided at the first round, and the vast majority of the victors were conservatives. Turnout nationwide was 51 percent, but it was much lower in the urban areas where the reformists have the most support. Barely a quarter of the residents of the Tehran metropolitan region voted, and the conservatives swept all thirty of its seats. The most reliable estimate is that the reformists elected as few as thirty candidates.

Four years later, the Guardian Council again sharply limited the number of reformists allowed to run for the Majlis. To no one's surprise, reformists won under 20 percent of the seats. Turnout was only 47 percent, the lowest under the Islamic Republic.

At this point, there is no political party that officially supports the conservative clerics. After the revolution, they created the Islamic Republican Party, which was a bastion of supporters of the new regime, but it was disbanded at Khomeini's urging in 1987. The closest the conservatives have to a party is the *ruhaniyat*, or Militant Clergy Association. Its members include former President Rafsanjani and Ali-Akbar Nadeq-Nouri, the former speaker of the Majlis who lost to Khatami in 1997.

The Khomeini government had previously abolished the National Front and other groups that were part of the revolutionary coalition. Some of them, including the communists and the Islamic *Mujahadin e-Qalq*, still exist underground but have at most a limited impact. There are also dozens of political parties and other organizations in the exile community that dream of a return to open political activity inside Iran.

The same is true of the reformists. They created the **Second of Khordad Movement** (named for the day of Khatami's first, landslide election—Khordad is a month in the Iranian calendar). In 2009, its leaders were candidate Mousavi and Mehdi Karroubi, who was twice president of the Majlis and is rumored to want to run when Ahmadinejad has to leave office. The movement and others like it are largely moribund and will probably stay that way until the 2013 campaign, if they revive at all.

As noted at the beginning of the chapter, the 2005 presidential election was expected to be much like the one for the Majlis the year before. As of early March 2005, no candidate had formally declared his intention to run even though the vote was less than three and a half months away. The reformists tentatively planned to present a ticket with outgoing President Khatami's brother as the vice presidential candidate. However, in an interview with CBS News' *60 Minutes* on February 27, 2005, he was all but certain that the Guardian Council would keep them off the ballot—and it did. Earlier in the year, the Guardian Council overturned a court ruling that women who met all the qualifications for the presidency should be allowed to run by interpreting the Constitution such that only men could be candidates.

That left the field to clerics and others who were committed to maintaining the core values of the Islamic republic. Although Rafsanjani easily took the lead at the first ballot, almost all voters for the eliminated candidates voted for Ahmadinejad, who became the first noncleric to occupy the presidency.

The more important presidential elections are held under a slightly different system. Anyone can declare his (not her) candidacy. The numbers often reach into the hundreds because the government actually pays candidates to run, not the other way around. The Guardian Council again has the responsibility to determine who legally can run for the office. Unlike the last two contests for the Majlis, it eliminated candidates who had next to no chance of doing well, thereby giving voters a reasonable chance to sift through the claims of a handful of nominees during an election period that is as short and as officially nonpartisan as those leading up to votes for the Majlis. More important, it denied the right to run to many known reformers.

In many respects, the 2009 election turned out to be an important turning point in Iranian politics. The conservative Militant Clergy Association did not make its position clear during the campaign, and Rafsanjani criticized the way the vote was held and counted during the weeks of protests afterward. Another smaller group, the Militant Clergy Society, actually came out against Ahmadinejad. The protests mentioned previously show how divided the country is. How that plays itself out in day-to-day politics is anybody's guess.

Conflict
in Iran

Iran has been beset by conflict for a century or more. In the first years of the twenty-first century, much of the conflict revolves around the differences between religious conservatives and reformers. Reformers probably have more public support, especially among young people. However, conservative clerics control enough of the country's critical political positions that they were able to ensure victories in the most recent elections.

The most recent form of conflict has been a series of squirt gun fights among young people. They claim they are not being political. However, a number of the participants have been arrested and hardline critics worry that this could turn into an opening "salvo" for the next presidential election. ∎

Women in Iranian Politics

The chapter on Iran in the seventh edition started with the death of Neda and the broader protest of which it was a party. And more generally, the role of women has featured more prominently here than in any other chapter in this book except for the conclusion.

The status of women in Iranian politics is more limited than in any of the other countries we have considered. They have been able to vote since 1963 but the Guardian Council has kept most women from running for the Majlis and other high-level offices since the revolution. Currently, there are 8 women in the parliament, down from a high of 13 in the one elected in 2000. Needless to say, Iran ranks very near the bottom of the Interparliamentary Union's list of countries with women in parliament. Except for the countries that ban them outright, Iran ranks fourth worst.

It is not just in politics that women's rights are severely limited. Men can have several wives and are not legally obligated to tell any of them about the existence of others. Some examples are more humorous, if not absurd. In June 2011, FIFA (the governing body of world soccer) banned the Iranian national women's team from qualification rounds for the Olympics because the players wore headscarves deemed to be a violation of FIFA uniform rules.

What might be called a feminist movement exists almost completely underground. The one exception was the wave of protests, especially the one following the 2009 presidential election in which thousands of Iranian women clamored for what they saw as their rightful place in the "public space."

THE IRANIAN STATE

The not so democratic nature of Iranian politics is even easier to see in the way its state operates. We can look at this briefly, because many of its features have been discussed already.

The revolutionary leaders wrote a Constitution shortly after taking power in 1979. Some significant amendments were added in 1989 (e.g., abolishing the prime ministry) but its basic features have remained the same since the revolution 🖱 (The constitution can be found at **iranonline .com/iran/iran-info/government/constitution.html** and more general information is at **parstimes.com/gov_iran .html** but beware that semi-official and official Iranian sites tend to disappear).

On the one hand, by relying on elections using universal suffrage to elect the Majlis and president, this Constitution is by far the most democratic one Iran has ever had. On the other hand, it was written to ensure that ultimate authority rested in the hands of senior Shiite clerics through a series of unelected and often repressive institutions. Over the years, the clerics have certainly lost some prestige and possibly some of their power. The last two sets of elections, however, suggest that they have no intention of going into a permanent political decline. Indeed, how the balance between the elected and authoritarian elements of the state evolves will largely determine the political direction the country takes.

The order in which this section is written is a telling statement about Iranian politics. Had it been written in 2000, the elected parts of the state might have come first. Many signs indicated that the rule of law and other aspects of democracy were gaining support under the leadership of President Khatami. But writing in the aftermath of the last presidential election, it is clear that Supreme Leader Khamenei, the Guardian Council, the Revolutionary Guard, and other unelected and more conservative components of the Iranian state have reasserted their influence and that the future of reform and of the elected parts of the state are very much in doubt.

The Unelected Components

For all intents and purposes, Iran has two chief executives. On the one hand, there is an elected president as we have already seen. On the other, there is a supreme leader, a senior cleric named for life by other senior clerics, who has veto power over almost everything elected officials want to do.

The rationale for the position of supreme leader lies in the writings of Ayatollah Khomeini. As his opposition to the shah intensified, Khomeini added political recommendations to his preaching, most notably in a series of nineteen lectures he delivered in Najaf, Iraq, in early 1970. These were subsequently published as *Velayat-e Faqi*, or the **Guardianship of the Jurist**.

Profiles
Ayatollah Ali Khamenei

Supreme Leader Ali Khamenei was born in the provincial city of Mashhad in 1939 and began his theological studies in elementary school. At eighteen he moved to the holy city of Najaf in Iraq, but returned to Qom the following year to continue his studies under Khomeini and others.

He joined the growing Islamic resistance to the shah in the early 1960s and was arrested with many others in 1963. After his release, he continued to teach and preach. He was arrested again in 1977. After his subsequent release, he helped found the Combatant Clerics Association, which became the Islamic Revolutionary Party after the fall of the shah.

Following the assassination of President Muhammad Ali Rajai in 1981, Ayatollah Khamenei was elected to that post with about 95 percent of the vote. He was named an ayatollah in early 1989, which made him eligible to replace Ayatollah Khomeini when he died later that year. ∎

Vahid Salemi/AP Images

Supreme Leader Ayatollah Ali Khamenei.

As noted previously, for most of the history of Shiism, its clerics shunned direct political involvement. Most argued that until the twelfth imam reappears it is inappropriate for members of the clergy to take part in mundane political affairs.

Khomeini, in other words, caused a major shift in Shiite thinking by arguing that a senior cleric had a moral responsibility to provide leadership in political as well as religious matters. Because the jurist carried with him the ethical concern about faith and justice, he would be a more legitimate ruler than anyone drawn from the secular community.

The supreme leader is appointed by the **Assembly of Experts**, a body of senior clerics who are elected by the people. The leader then serves for life. For the decade he served, the charismatic Khomeini was the dominant personality in the entire political system. At first, Khamenei had much less power and prestige than his predecessor. As is almost always the case for leaders who follow a charismatic figure, he failed to command the same degree of authority. It did not help that Khamenei was a relatively minor cleric at the time of his selection. In fact, he was made an ayatollah just a few weeks before Khomeini's death, and his appointment drew some criticism from more senior colleagues. By the end of the 1990s, though, his prestige had grown and, more important, he became the focal figure for conservatives who resisted the reformist movement that was based among President Khatami's supporters.

The supreme leader has immense legal and de facto power. He controls the military, much of the media, the judiciary, and the clerical hierarchy. Both Khomeini and Khamenei have spoken out on any issue they deemed important and, thus, largely set the agenda for the country as a whole.

The most powerful theological body is the Guardian Council. It consists of six senior clerics appointed by the supreme leader and six judges named by the Majlis from a list compiled by the Supreme Judicial Council, the members of which are appointed by the supreme leader. In the aftermath of the 2009 election, the American press often referred to it as the main legislative body. Although that may not constitutionally be the case, the Majlis can do little without the council's approval.

Today, the Guardian Council is composed overwhelmingly of men who support the conservative and theocratic elements of the regime. It has to approve all legislation and has blocked reform proposals on numerous occasions. One example occurred when it vetoed the loosening of restrictions on the media in the late 1990s. It also has to approve all candidacies for presidential and Majlis elections. As noted a few paragraphs ago, it was the body responsible for barring thousands of candidates in 2004 and 2008, thereby ensuring conservative landslides.

Although the council is one of the more conservative components of the state, it does not always live up to that reputation. In May 2004, it approved a bill to ban the use of torture in Iranian prisons, which had been widely used in the first years after the revolution and has not been uncommon in recent years, if statements by dissidents are to be believed.

To help resolve the frequent conflicts between the Majlis and the Guardian Council, Khomeini created the **Expediency Council** in 1988. It is a senior advisory board whose members are appointed by the supreme leader for five-year terms. All major factions are included, but Khamenei's followers currently have an overwhelming majority. That said, it is led by former President Rafsanjani who has become an increasingly outspoken critic of the leadership.

The Expediency Council meets with the leaders of the other two appointed bodies and generally tries to anticipate procedural and other problems not foreseen by the Constitution. The fact that it and the Guardian Council are currently headed by former President Rafsanjani suggests these bodies are important indeed, even if their formal powers are not all that clearly defined. Their role may become even more critical and harder to predict now that Rafsanjani has criticized the way the 2009 election was conducted, which led to his daughter's brief arrest.

The judiciary is probably more important than its equivalents in most Southern countries. In addition to the kinds of criminal and civil courts one finds in most countries, Iran also has clerical courts with vast powers not only to adjudicate but also to prosecute cases involving Islam.

The Constitution adopted a highly restrictive version of Sharia. Offenses, such as adultery or homosexuality, may lead to the death penalty. The courts may impose stoning or amputating fingers as punishments for various crimes. And, initially at least, banks were not allowed to charge interest. The courts have loosened up a bit as the regime has solidified, but it is still one of the major conservative forces in the country.

The final unelected institution is the IRGC. As noted earlier, it was created because Khomeini and his colleagues doubted the loyalty and competence of the military they inherited from the Shah's regime. The IRGC has since become a linchpin of the regime, especially because it served as Ahmadinejad's political base. Despite loose ties with clerics, the Revolutionary Guard is one of the most conservative elements of the regime and is widely rumored to manage the *basij* vigilante groups that were so in evidence in putting down the demonstrations after the 2009 election. The IRGC also plays a major role in managing the economy.

Democratization
in Iran

The uncertainties about democratization in Iran are reflected in the two types of state institutions. On the one hand are the offices that are directly elected by the people and that seemed to be gaining in importance under President Khatami. On the other hand, however, with the resurgence of the conservative clerics before and after the 2004 election, nonelected and nondemocratic institutions regained their central place in Iranian politics. It seems likely that these institutions will keep their influence until the next round of elections are held in 2012 and 2013, if not longer. It is not clear, however, if that can remain the case indefinitely. ■

Profiles
Mahmoud Ahmadinejad

Mahmoud Ahmadinejad comes from a humble background. His father was a blacksmith who always struggled to earn a living. After moving to Tehran when Mahmoud was a child, he changed the family to one that reflects piety.

Mahmoud earned degrees in engineering (including a PhD after his political career had taken off) and joined an ultraorthodox and conservative student movement before the 1979 revolution. Shortly after he was elected, some of the former hostages at the United States embassy claim that he was one of the leaders of the "student" militants. The State Department conducted an inquiry into those claims, but it was inconclusive.

Ahmadinejad is not a cleric, but he is as conservative on religious and political issues as Supreme Leader Ali Khamenei. There is little humorous about Ahmadinejad. However, after he spoke at Columbia University in 2007 and said there are no gays in Iran, Saturday Night Live went after him. The skit featured an Ahmadinejad look-alike who acted in a way that fits most stereotypes of gay men including wearing a red sleeveless dress and heels. In its first week on YouTube it was viewed more than a million times. NBC insisted that it be removed from it and other sites for copyright reasons, but there are still copies of it out there on the Web. Because they are there illegally, you will have to find one on your own. ■

President Ahmadinejad speaking at Columbia University.

The Elected Institutions

Since the death of Ayatollah Khomeini, the most visible politician in day-to-day politics has been the president. For reasons noted earlier, there could well be a shift away from presidential power if another lay president has to work with a senior ayatollah.

The president is directly elected. Since 1979, Iran has had six presidents (see Table 13.6). The first two are barely worth mentioning. Abolhassan Bani-Sadr, an Islamic leftist, was removed from power by Khomeini within a year of taking office. He remains a part of the opposition living in exile. He was succeeded by Muhammad Ali Rajai, who was assassinated the following year. After that, three clerics were president: Khamenei, Rafsanjani, and Khatami. In a surprise to many, Ahmadinejad was elected in 2005 despite not being a cleric. That said, he may be more religious than his three predecessors.

TABLE 13.6 Presidents of Iran since 1979

NAME	YEARS IN OFFICE
Abolhassan Bani-Sadr	1979–80
Muhammad Ali Rajai	1980–81
Ali Khamenei	1981–89
Hashemi Rafsanjani	1989–97
Mohammad Khatami	1997–2005
Mahmoud Ahmadinejad	2005–

The other important elected institution is the Majlis, whose formal title is the Islamic Consultative Assembly. The title suggests right away that it is not a parliament with formal decision making authority. The Majlis can force individual ministers and governments out of office through the kind of votes of confidence we saw in Part 2. However, given the dominance of conservatives following the last two elections, that seems highly unlikely.

The Routinization of Charisma

More than a century ago, Max Weber introduced the term *charisma* into the social sciences. By invoking a concept with powerful religious overtones, Weber wanted us to realize that there are a few political leaders who have remarkable personal gifts that lead people to follow them all but unquestioningly. That was certainly the case for Ayatollah Khomeini and several other leaders we encountered in previous chapters.

However, Weber also warned that charisma was the most fleeting form of rule, one that rarely survived the initial leader's departure from the political scene. As we saw in Chapter 5 on France, a few leaders have been able to "routinize" their charisma so that less magnetic successors could govern almost as effectively. So far, that seems to be the case in Iran.

That said, it should be pointed out that the generation of clerics and lay politicians that was swept into power along with Khomeini are disappearing from the political scene. Anyone who studied with Khomeini in Qom, for instance, would now be well into his sixties or older. Whether the next generation will be able to sustain the authority the clerical leadership still holds is anybody's guess.

Ahmadinejad versus Khamenei

In Chapter 11, we talked about how power is often fluid in the Global South because institutions are much less important in determining who does what, where, when, and how than they are in countries covered in Parts 3 and, especially, 2. In Iran since the 2009 election, that has been most visible in the often open rivalry between President Ahmadinejad and Supreme Leader Khamenei. There is nothing unusual about such a split. Khamenei certainly found much of what President Khatami did distasteful. In the case of his disagreements with Ahmadinejad, the dispute probably runs deeper, and it involves two men who have been traditionally associated with the same political camp.

Four examples stand out.

- **The aftermath of 2009.** Supreme Leader Khamenei is generally known as a hard liner. However, after the 2009 presidential election and the demonstrations, he apparently came to the conclusion that President Ahmadinejad had gone too far in rigging the vote count or putting down the Green Movement or both. Officially, the Supreme Leader stood by the president, for instance insinuating that the protesters were supporting a dictatorship during a Friday prayer service after the movement broke out. By the middle of June, the demonstrations were so large, enough prominent people had been arrested including perhaps the losing candidate, and the allegations of ballot box stuffing were so specific that Khamenei had to convene a clerical conference. By the end of June, Khamenei had refused to compromise with the opposition and called on Iranians to abide by the official tally of the votes. Nonetheless, his differences with the president were out in the open.

- **Resignation of Vice President**. In 2009, Khamenei forced Ahmadinejad to fire his senior vice president, Esfandiar Rahim Mashale, who the president had recently appointed. Mashale may be more moderate than most of his fellow leaders, having once said that Iranians and Israelis are friends. Khamenei's letter to Ahmadinejad stated that the appointment was "against your interest and the interests of the government. It is necessary to announce the cancellation of this appointment." Khamenei's decision may have been fueled by the fact that Mashale is not a cleric and has been rumored to want to succeed Ahmadinejad who is legally barred from running for a third term.

- **Who is too secular?** Ahmadinejad is seen as a religious as well as a political hard liner in the West. That said, the president has done a number of things that rankled the most devout members of Iranian society. One of the most surprising of those actions was to allow women to attend soccer matches, which had been a male preserve since the revolution. The key here may be the lingering impact of Mashale was often considered to be too secular because he sponsored a Western pop music festival, relaxed rules on head coverings for women, and was often seen in the company of a good-looking actress.

- **The curious case of the former but still Intelligence Minister**. In April 2011, the president tried to dismiss the Intelligence Minister, Heydar Moslehi. In most countries, that would not stir up a controversy because the chief executive of the government has the right to hire and fire officials. As is often the case, Ahmadinejad asked for and got a letter of resignation from Moslehi, who certainly did not want to quit. Iran is different in that the Supreme Leader has the final say on most personnel matters, including cabinet appointments. He forced the president to reinstate the minister, at which point Ahmadinejad began a brief boycott of cabinet meetings. Moslehi missed more than his share as well, apparently because no one bothered to tell him when and where they were to be held. That same spring, the Supreme Leader only allowed one of three women named by the president to take their seats in the cabinet.

The Supreme Leader and president do agree on most broad policy initiatives including the nuclear program and purging secular professors and other intellectual leaders. But their differences are no doubt important as well.

PUBLIC POLICY

In the next chapter, we will see that Saddam Hussein's three wars all but destroyed the Iraqi government's hopes of pursuing any coherent domestic public policies. Although Iran was certainly hampered by the costs of its war with Iraq and from its isolation by much of the West, it has been able to develop and implement social and economic policies at home to this day.

Faith and Gender

During the 1990s, the late Samuel Huntington created a wave of controversy with his idea of a clash of civilizations. As he saw it, the post–Cold War world would not be tranquil because it would give rise to conflicts among followers of the world's major cultural traditions. As he saw it, too, none would be more severe than that between the Muslim world and the West. The terrorist attacks of 2001, the wars in Afghanistan and Iraq, and the renewed hostilities between Israelis and Palestinians have sparked more interest in, and criticism of, Huntington's thesis.

Most political scientists, however, believe that his argument is too simplistic. From their perspective, none of his "civilizations" are coherent culturally nor do their states act uniformly in international politics.

Nonetheless, if there is a country that comes close to meeting what Huntington had in mind, it is Iran. It is one of a mere handful of countries that is run by religious leaders. Nowhere is their impact clearer and the prospects for reform more uncertain than in the policies regarding women. As we saw in the introduction to this chapter, the regime has enacted policies that even antifeminists in the West would find unacceptable. Women who commit adultery can legally be stoned to death. After a divorce, husbands almost always get custody of the former couple's children.

But, as is the case with almost every subject in this chapter, the status of women is much more complicated than one might think at first glance. Women make up only about 10 percent of the workforce, but that is a higher percentage than in most other countries in the Middle East. Female students outnumber men in Iranian universities.

The Economy

Perhaps the most important issue for the long-term future of the Islamic republic is the weak state of the economy. Iran is by no means a poor country. Its per capita income of almost eleven thousand dollars a year in purchasing parity terms makes it almost as wealthy as Mexico or Russia.

But as we hinted at in the introduction, even that figure masks a number of serious problems. Much of Iran's wealth is the result of a single industry: oil. It has 7 percent of the world's proven oil reserves and only Russia has a larger untapped supply of natural gas. The spike in oil prices after the 9/11 terrorist attacks is largely responsible for Iran's growth rate, which stood at about 7 percent for most of the first years of this century. As is true in Russia and Nigeria as well, dependence on the export of a single commodity is not a recipe for economic success in the long term. It may prove to be what economists call the "Dutch disease," a term based on the Netherlands' unhealthy reliance on the export of tulip bulbs three hundred or more years ago.

Yet, even if the tulip analogy is not completely accurate, the Iranian economy faces problems that are political in origin. The sudden drop in its oil sales caused by the economic sanctions has taken a toll. That is why the government was all but forced to introduce subsidy reform.

Put frankly, in the current context, there is relatively little the Iranian government can do to jump start the economy. It has a host of problems above and beyond the impact of sanctions. For the long term, the key is to create jobs for the hundreds of thousands of young people who join the work force every year and have next to no chance of finding a steady job.

Even at its peak, the oil boom did not help address the poverty, inflation, and youth unemployment. To find work for all of its young people, Iran needs to add eight hundred thousand jobs a year, a figure it has never come close to meeting. The standard of living of most Iranians is below what it was in 1979. The inflation rate routinely hovers close to 20 percent. Even oil production is only about two-thirds what it was under the shah.

The economy has problems for two reasons that are currently beyond the government's control. It still suffers from the cost of the war with Iraq (see Chapter 14). And, although some Western countries have expanded their trade ties with Iran, the United States reinforced its sanctions in October 2007, thus further depriving the country of what had been its leading economic supporter under the shah.

There are also some public policy concerns shared by analysts of almost all ideological stripes. They do not agree on what the problems are or what should be done about them, but they do agree that the state's economic priorities for the last quarter-century have been largely misguided.

Especially during periods when the conservative clerics have been dominant, the economy has not been at the top of the leadership's list of priorities. When asked by an assistant about the difficult state of the economy, Ayatollah Khomeini once said, "This revolution was not about the price of watermelons." Like Nigeria (see Chapter 15), Iran is a major oil exporter but has to ration gasoline sales to its own citizens.

In short, economic growth and prosperity have never been the most important goal of the conservatives. Yet, the conservative government wields impressive economic clout that adds to the complexity of Iranian politics. Depending on how one counts, the state owns or controls as much as 80 percent of the economy, far more than is the case in any other country covered in this book.

Profiles
Shirin Ebadi

The hopes for human rights and an improvement in the status of women in Iran were given a major and unexpected boost when Shirin Ebadi was named the Nobel Peace Prize winner in 2003. She was a surprise pick because Ebadi was little known outside of Iran. British bookies, at least, expected the gravely ill Pope John Paul II to win the award.

Ebadi is, however, widely known in Iran. She was the first female judge in Iran but was forced to resign after the 1979 revolution on the assumption that women should not be permitted to interpret Islamic law. Since then, she has been a champion of human rights and democracy. After being forced out of the judiciary, she became a professor and set up an organization that tried to reform laws on inheritance and divorce and defended dissidents, and she was banned from practicing law in 2000 for her political beliefs and activities.

The Nobel Prize committee said in announcing her award, "As a lawyer, judge, lecturer, writer and activist, she has spoken out clearly and strongly in her country, Iran, and far beyond its borders." And, in a rare political statement, the committee also made it

The Nobel Peace Prize winner and human rights lawyer, Shirin Ebadi.

clear that its choice was designed to aid the movement for democracy and human rights in Iran.

In the first hours after the announcement, no mention of Ebadi's honor was made in the state-run Iranian media. When informed of her award, Ebadi said, "I'm a Muslim, so you can be a Muslim and support democracy. It's very good for human rights in Iran, especially for children's rights in Iran. I hope I can be useful." ▪

Iran's private sector was never a model of either efficiency or transparency under the shah. After 1979, the new leaders confiscated the property of the shah's family and almost every other industrial leader who had cooperated with the old regime. Those resources were turned into **bonyads**, a form of Islamic charity that the clerics control. The evidence is sketchy, but it seems certain that the *bonyads* are corrupt money losers for the most part. Some even charge that former President Rafsanjani has become the wealthiest man in Iran because of the money he rakes off from them. Ultimate responsibility for what they do and how they operate rests with the supreme leader, not the marketplace.

The potential for growth is there. However, there are few incentives to work for it because the constitution denies the government the right to privatize many state-run enterprises. The government has been willing to issue low-interest loans and grant so-called "justice shares" in state-run enterprises. These developments should not be scoffed at since almost $3 billion worth of shares have been handed out, which have already resulted in over $50 million in dividends. Similarly, when the Khouzestan Steel Company was privatized in

August 2007, 5 percent of its stock sold within minutes of its initial public offering (IPO).

Yet, as one economist put it recently,

> **This government believes in supply side economics. It knows there is excess capacity in the country that could be harnessed with a cash injection. Unfortunately, the business climate is so bad that people only want to invest in hard assets such as property—and that fuels inflation.[6]**

The leadership has also been reluctant to open the economy to outside investment or involvement. In 2002, the government signed a contract with a Turkish firm to run the Imam Khomeini International Airport in Tehran. When the company arrived to set up operations, it found that the government had decided to break the contract, arguing that foreign management of the airport would be an insult to Iranian national pride.

---

[6] Cited in Angus McDowell, "Immunising the Economy Faced with Further Sanctions and a Confrontation with the United States." *Middle East Economic Digest, 51* (24 August 2007).

Economic Liberalization
in Iran

Of all the countries covered in this book, Iran has the smallest private sector. Its major firms also operate all or mostly beyond the control of the state. The government itself does not formally own much of the economy, but its control of the *bonyads*, Islamic charities, and other seemingly private enterprises leaves it with de facto control of about 80 percent of it. That said, Iran does have a long tradition of private enterprise, though many of its entrepreneurs fled after 1979. If the leadership allows the economy to open up more to foreign investment, the involvement of the Iranian diaspora and others could give a major boost to what is a largely moribund economy. ∎

Two years later, following the conservatives' electoral victory, the Majlis passed legislation making it harder for foreign firms to invest in Iranian enterprises. The election of Ahmadinejad also did not bode well for the economy because, as he once claimed, he knows nothing about economics.

Iran and the United States: Toward the Next War?

Ever since the 1979 revolution, Iran and the United States have had sharply different interests and have pursued seemingly incompatible goals in their foreign policies, which is part of the reason why Iran is included in a book like this. Iranian hostility toward the United States dates back at least to the 1953 overthrow of the Mossadeq government, which was more than partially orchestrated by the CIA. It intensified along with opposition to the shah, who was widely seen—and resented—as a tool of Washington's Cold War politics. For many Iranians, the Carter administration's decision to allow the shah to come to the United States for medical treatment was the last straw.

But Iranian hostility toward the United States has deeper roots. Today, many of the conservative clerics think the United States would like nothing more than to provoke a regime change. Under Republican and Democratic administrations alike, American governments have never minced words in objecting to Iranian support for the Palestinians and its belief that the state of Israel should not be allowed to exist,

something President Ahmadinejad restated as recently as his visit to New York in 2007. Since then, Iran has continued to support Hezbollah and other groups that oppose Israel.

There have been five particularly difficult periods in Iran's relations with the United States. The first began with the occupation of the American embassy on November 4, 1979. The hostage crisis of course infuriated most Americans and their government, an anger that was reinforced by Iranian action and rhetoric during the fifteen months the standoff endured. It was at this time that Khomeini and his colleagues' language was most inflammatory, including calling the American government "the great Satan." Even its few humanitarian gestures, such as releasing the women and people of color it held, were accompanied by self-serving and anti-American statements. The authorities reacted to the failed attempt by American forces to rescue the hostages in mid-1980 as yet more evidence of Washington's evil designs on Tehran. Finally, many saw the timing of Iran's releasing the hostages the day President Reagan was inaugurated as a sign of their hatred of President Carter, whose chances for reelection were destroyed by a crisis he was unable to solve.

Iranians also demonstrated their profound dislike of the United States during an eight-year war with Iraq, which will be discussed in more detail in Chapter 14. The United States never officially supported Iraq and never harbored any illusions about the nature of Saddam's regime. Nevertheless, its antipathy toward Iran led the Reagan administration to rebuild its relationship with Iraq, much of it done, ironically, by the same Donald Rumsfeld who would be the chief architect of Saddam's defeat two decades later. Khomeini's government kept up its anti-American rhetoric, especially during the second half of the war in response to two American actions it found particularly reprehensible. First, the United States "reflagged" Kuwaiti and other tankers that shipped oil from the Middle East to the West in 1986. The tankers sported American flags, which meant that they could and would be defended by the U.S. Navy. When some of the tankers were attacked, the U.S. Navy fought a series of skirmishes with the small Iranian fleet. Then, as the war was drawing to a close in the summer of 1988, the *USS Vincennes* mistakenly shot down an Iranian airliner, killing all 290 people aboard.

Second, the one exception to this track record of hostility was the secret negotiations and deals between the United States and Iran that Americans known as the Iran-Contra affair. Officially, the United States claimed it would never negotiate with terrorists and was pressuring its allies not to supply arms to Iran. However, in a series of secret deals, the United States supplied Iran with missiles and other arms, initially to win the release of Americans held hostage in Lebanon and later to provide funds for the Contras fighting a civil war in Nicaragua, which Congress had explicitly banned. When the affair became public in 1987, President Reagan claimed he was hoping to build support among moderates in the Iranian regime, despite the little evidence of support there to be had.

The third episode came in the aftermath of the terrorist attacks on the United States on 9/11. This time, relations deteriorated largely because of decisions made in Washington rather than in Tehran. In fact, under the Clinton administration, relations between the United States and Iran had actually eased a bit despite the fact that the United States passed a law in 1995 prohibiting American companies and their subsidiaries from doing business with it. The United States indicated its approval of the reform efforts made by President Khatami and urged his government to go farther and faster.

But after 9/11, President George W. Bush sought to link Iran to al-Qaeda and the global terrorist network, even though little evidence existed of any link between the two. If anything, Iran played a minor, but constructive, role in the defeat of the Taliban in Afghanistan and did nothing to oppose the war that toppled Saddam's government. Its diplomats even tried to defuse tensions between the American occupation forces and supporters of radical Shiite clerics in the spring of 2004.

Fourth, President Bush included Iran with Iraq and North Korea as part of the axis of evil in his 2002 State of the Union address and stepped up his anti-Iranian rhetoric, especially regarding its nuclear energy and weapons program and its alleged support for terrorist activities carried out by Hezbollah, Hamas, and Islamic Jihad against Israel.

Evidence on both accusations is mixed. There is little doubt that Iran has supported Israel's opponents, including providing funds and training for some groups that commit acts of terrorism. That said, its links to al-Qaeda are far less certain and probably not very extensive. To begin with, most al-Qaeda members are Sunni, not Shiites. Furthermore, some Iranian officials suggested that they helped the United States by closing its borders so alleged terrorists could not cross into Iran and even turned over a few that had somehow managed to do so.

Similar ambiguity exists about Iran's nuclear weapons program. There is no doubt that the nation has long been working to enhance its nuclear capacities, including developing the ability to produce the enriched plutonium that would be needed for manufacturing weapons. The Iranians, however, claim that the program is designed only to provide electricity. The United States is skeptical because, given its vast oil and natural gas reserves, it is hard to see why Iran needs nuclear energy for that purpose. Tensions eased a bit in late 2004 when the British, French, and German governments convinced Iran to suspend its enrichment activities. Even though Iran initially agreed to the suspension, its acceptance was always conditional.

In February 2005, tensions eased a bit again. At a summit of NATO leaders in Europe, President Bush announced that it was preposterous for people to think that the United States had plans to attack Iran. But he almost immediately qualified that remark by saying all options remained on the table.

On his return from the summit, the president sent out trial balloons suggesting that the United States might join the European effort to use economic and other incentives to convince Iran to abandon any of its plans that could lead it to build nuclear weapons, although analysts close to the Bush administration voiced doubts that a diplomatic solution could work.

Iran's response was similarly mixed. It insisted it had the right to enrich uranium for what it continued to claim was a nuclear energy program. And, within days of the NATO summit, it signed an agreement with Russia that would provide precisely the kind of uranium the United States and the major European powers were most worried about.

The final difficult period is the one we have been going through since mid-2009. The Obama administration came to office opposed both to Iran's nuclear weapons program and committed to reducing the hostility between the two countries. Many of us with links to the Obama transition team argued that it had to take a hard line on the nuclear weapons issue but that it was also time to try a different approach with Tehran given the fact that thirty years of conflict had not improved the situation for either party. Also, the National Intelligence Estimate in 2007 had cast doubt on how committed Iran was to a nuclear weapons rather than a nuclear energy strategy. Unfortunately, the election in Iran and the protests that followed have made any rapprochement between Washington and Tehran all the more difficult.

Relations between the two countries are bad not only because they have conflicting interests but conflicting values as well. Both have engaged in a practice psychologists call the image of the enemy. One side views the other in stereotypical terms, typically stressing what it sees as the negative characteristics of the other. Use of terms like "axis of evil" or "the great Satan" only deepen already deep divisions and lead to misperceptions and mistakes in judgment about the other side's behavior and the intentions underlying it. Most problematical of all, when both sides invoke the image of the enemy each waits for the other to take the first steps to improve the relationship, which means that it almost never happens.

At the end of his term in office, President Bush was probably engaging in more of this form of behavior than was the Iranian government. It had almost nothing positive to say about events in Tehran, and in so doing missed such important trends as Iranians' understandable concerns about ensuring their national security in a hostile world. There has been one area in which some progress has been made through what the conflict resolution community calls track-two diplomacy. Such negotiations involve private citizens who have no official authority and cannot represent their governments in discussions that could lead to binding treaties or other agreements. Instead, track-two processes can involve people with close ties to decision makers or simply try to improve the relationships among people in the societies involved at a time when formal, traditional diplomatic initiatives are not likely to prove fruitful.

There was, in practice, very little track-two contact between Americans and Iranians before the late 1990s. It was very difficult for people to get permission to visit the other's country, and there were relatively few contacts between people from the two societies, except through Iranian émigrés, who are for the most part vocal opponents of the Islamic republic.

The first significant opportunities for track-two work began after newly elected President Khatami called for a "dialogue of civilizations." Search for Common Ground, an organization founded with the purpose of finding cooperative rather than adversarial ways to resolve conflict, has been a leader in those efforts ever since 🖋 (www.sfcg.org). In 1998, it arranged for the American national wrestling team to participate in a major international tournament, the first time the American flag had been displayed by Americans in Iran since the hostage crisis. The American athletes were greeted warmly by the Iranian wrestlers and by the huge crowd that turned out for the event; wrestling is one of the two most popular sports in Iran.

Since then, other athletic opportunities have been seized, including a soccer match between the two national teams that was watched by over one hundred thousand fans, all men. Search for Common Ground and other NGOs have also arranged exchanges of scientists, filmmakers, and artists, arranged for the Iranian ambassador to the United Nations to meet with two leading Republican members of Congress, and helped host an Iranian cultural festival and the visit of a leading ayatollah to Washington. In 2004, at the request of Iranian officials, Search for Common Ground sent a group of American educators to Tehran to begin negotiations on long-term exchanges of students and faculty.

But, as we write in 2011, war seems as likely as peace. As we have seen, tensions between the United States and Iran have ebbed and flowed since the hostage crisis. The Obama administration is not rattling sabers as much as its predecessor. Nonetheless, it has been vocal in its opposition to the Iranian nuclear program and its rejection of the results of the presidential election.

In 2007 and 2008, there were serious concerns that the United States would launch preemptive strikes against Iran, presumably through heavy bombing. That did not happen and may not do so in the next years. On the American side, the military is stretched so thin in Iraq and Afghanistan that it is hard to see how it could mount an all-out assault on Iran. That fact does not rule out a strategic bombing campaign against alleged nuclear and other strategic sites. However, the failure of such bombings to win wars in Bosnia, Kosovo, Iraq, Afghanistan, and perhaps now Libya suggests that any

Globalization
in Iran

Iran is one of the few countries in which globalization is not primarily an economic issue. To be sure, the government is eager to see restrictions on its sales abroad end, especially given the on-and-off but still dramatic rise in oil prices since the start of the Iraq war in 2003. However, it is probably the case that its overall isolation from the rest of the world will prove a more vexing problem. The conservatives' recapture of control of the presidency in 2005 had led to more radical rhetoric, if not more radical policies, toward the West. That said, the authorities will have a harder and harder time keeping Western influences out of the country, influences that have already had a profound impact on at least the younger members of the middle class. ▪

such effort is likely to come up short from Washington's perspective.

Much hinges on two things. First, how quickly will the United States withdraw from Afghanistan and Iraq? Second, what, if anything, will the Iranians do to provoke American anger, which, of course, includes building a bomb?

THE MEDIA

Iran's official media are all but completely controlled. The country's television and radio stations are all owned and run by the state, and the clerics have an obvious vested interest in their programming.

At times, the government has allowed critics to publish newspapers and magazines. But they tend to crack down whenever these publications are perceived as having gone too far. Since 2000, the government has shut down almost all of them, and virtually no dissenting periodicals were being published in 2011.

CONCLUSION: UNCERTAINTY

There is more uncertainty about the future of politics in Iran than in any of the countries we have considered so far in this book.

One seemingly minor example from the summer of 2004 suggests how hard it is to predict anything about Iran these days. Just six years earlier, the American national wrestling team took part in an international championship in Tehran, a visit that was taken as a sign that the government was seeking an opening to its longtime enemy in Washington. But just before the opening ceremony at the 2004 Olympics, two-time world judo champion, Arash Miresmaeili, announced that he would forfeit his opening match against an Israeli judoka, thereby giving up any chance of winning an expected gold medal. Miresmaeili minced no words: "Although I have trained for months and was in good shape I refused to fight my Israeli opponent to sympathize with the suffering of the People of Palestine and I do not feel upset at all."[7]

---

[7]Michelle Kaufman, "Politics, Not Sports, Come First for Iranian Athlete," *Washington Post*, August 10, 2004, D12.

Some of the uncertainty regarding Iran's future is domestic in origin. There is every indication that the power struggle between the orthodox and moderate factions will continue even though the conservatives seem to have won resounding victories of late. What is not clear is who is likely to win in the medium to long term. The conservatives will likely win the next Majlis and presidential elections. However, the reformers are too numerous and too influential to give up and simply disappear.

The other major uncertainty is at least as important. How will the United States deal with Iran during the remainder of the Obama administration? As suggested previously, this could well be the next major foreign policy decision facing the United States.

As mentioned earlier, our best suggestion is to pay attention—and, we would add, get involved.

Atta Kenare/AFP/Getty Images

An American and an Iranian wrestle in a 1998 international tournament in Tehran. The American wrestlers were able to participate in the event because of the work of Search for Common Ground, the world's largest nongovernmental organization working on conflict resolution.

Looking FORWARD

WE NOW TURN our attention to two other countries whose political lives have been marred by violence and instability—Iraq and Nigeria. The two countries have shown that instability in different ways.

In Iraq, Saddam Hussein's all but totalitarian regime led the country into three wars, one with Iran and two with allied coalitions led by the United States. As almost all readers will know already, the third war brought down Saddam and eventually led to his execution. But the war solved little. The US-led forces occupied Iraq beginning

in 2003 and the last American troops are due to be withdrawn about the time this book is published. The wars and the invasion/occupation have left a country that just might be able to govern itself and then only if it is lucky.

Nigeria has not been through wars with its neighbors or anyone else. But it has had four periods of military rule and only now may have created a republic that can endure and govern. Successive Nigerian regimes have had corrupt leaders and squandered one of the country's few assets—its oil.

Key Terms

Concepts

charisma

fundamentalism

Guardianship of the Jurist

image of the enemy

Islamicists

Pahlavi

sanctions

Shah

Sharia

Shiite

subsidy

Sunni

People

Ahmadinejad, Mahmoud

Ebadi, Shirin

Khamenei, Ayatollah Ali

Khatami, Mohammad

Khomeini, Ayatollah Ruhollah

Mossadeq, Mohammad

Mousavi, Mir Hossein

Rafsanjani, Ayatollah Hashemi

Shah, Mohammad Reza

Shah, Reza

Acronyms

IRGC

SAVAK

Organizations, Places, and Events

Assembly of Experts

basij

bonyad

Constitutional Revolution

Expediency Council

Guardian Council

Iranian Revolutionary Guard Corps (IRGC)

Islamic Revolution

Majlis

Second of Khordad Movement

supreme leader

White Revolution

Useful Websites

There are not a lot of reliable websites that provide information on Iran. The Iranians themselves have very few sites with information in English, and most Westerners treat them with skepticism because they are directly or indirectly controlled by the government. However, there are four Western sites that provide good sets of links to sites on Iran as well as news feeds on a daily basis.

The Middle East Research Information Project (MERIP) is a somewhat left-of-center publication. The website includes its own material plus op-ed pieces and other items that originally appeared elsewhere. Columbia University's School of International and Political Affairs is also one of many sites that provides in-depth news on the country. Finally, the Iran Chamber is one of the best general portals for information on Iranian life in general and not just politics.

www.merip.org

gulf2000.columbia.edu/iran.shtml

www.daraee.com/iran.html

www.iranfocus.com/modules/news

www.iranchamber.com

Search for Common Ground maintains a website not only on its own initiatives on U.S.–Iranian relations but most other track-two projects currently underway.

www.sfcg.org

Further Reading

Brumberg, Daniel. *Reinventing Khomeini: The Struggle for Reform in Iran.* Chicago: University of Chicago Press, 2001. An intriguing analysis of how Khomeini's political persona was created and how competing politicians have tried to adapt it since his death.

Ebadi, Shirin. *Iran Awakening: A Memoir of Revolution and Hope.* New York: Random House, 2006. By the Nobel Peace Prize–winning jurist.

Ignatius, David. *The Increment.* New York: W. W. Norton, 2009. A novel by the *Washington Post*'s best foreign policy editorial writer. Examines both the American intelligence community and the Iranian nuclear program better than any academic has.

Keddie, Nikki. *Modern Iran: Roots and Results of Revolution.* New Haven, CT: Yale University Press, 2003. Probably the best book on Iran by an academic historian; covers the period from the late eighteenth century to the present.

Mackey, Sandra. *The Iranians: Persia, Islam, and the Soul of a Nation.* New York: Plume, 1996. The best single overview of the broad sweep of Iranian history and culture.

Majd, Hooman. *The Ayatollahs' Democracy.* New York: W. W. Norton, 2010. By a cousin of Former President Khatami. Immensely readable.

Moaveni, Azadeh. *Lipstick Jihad. A Memoir of Growing Up Iranian in the United States and American in Iran.* New York: Public Affairs, 2005. A very funny and insightful book by an American journalist of Iranian origins who goes to Iran to cover events in her "home" country while still in her twenties.

Nafisi, Azar. *Reading Lolita in Tehran.* New York: Random House, 2003. A stunning look at gender and politics in contemporary Iran through the lens of a small, informal American literature seminar run by a former Iranian professor.

Pollack, Kenneth. *The Persian Puzzle.* New York: Century Books, 2004. By the provocative author of one of the best books on why the United States should have gone to war with Iraq. He argues the opposite here.

Roy, Olivier. *The Failure of Political Islam.* Cambridge: Harvard University Press, 2001. This controversial book argues that the attempt to build a political agenda on the basis of Islamic principles cannot consistently be done. Covers much more than Iran.

Sciolino, Elaine. *Persian Mirrors: The Elusive Face of Iran.* New York: Touchstone, 2000. The most readable overview of Iran written by the veteran *New York Times* correspondent who has spent a lot of time covering Iran.

Takeyh, Ray. *Guardians of the Revolution: Iran and the World in the Age of the Ayatollahs.* New York: Oxford University Press, 2009. Probably the best book by a policy wonk on Iran. Very readable.

14

Iraq

THE BASICS

Iraq

Size	437,009 sq. km. Roughly twice the size of Idaho
Population	28.9 million with at least 2 million in exile
Ethnic groups	Arabs 75–80%, Kurds 15–20%, Others 5%
Religious groups	Muslims 97%, Others 3%
GDP per capita	$4,000
Currency	1,178 new Iraqi dinars = US$1
Capital	Baghdad
Prime Minister	Nouri al-Maliki (2006–)
President	Jalal Talabani (2005–)

WHAT IF YOU HELD AN ELECTION AND NOBODY WON?

In fall 2010, Iraq held its second election after **Saddam Hussein's** (1936–2006) regime was overthrown during the American-led invasion of the country (we will deal with Saddam's impact later). The 2010 election occurred almost a year after it was originally scheduled. And, as we write more than six months later, a government has just taken office.

Within a month of the election, it was clear that incumbent Prime Minister **Nuri al-Maliki** (1950–) would remain in office despite the fact that his party came in a close second in the election (see the section on parties and elections below). But it took about six months for al-Maliki to put together a coalition that had to include Kurdish members (again, see below). As late as February 2011, a year after the election, the "partners" had not agreed on who should serve in several key ministries, including national security, defense, and the interior (including the police), which the prime minister retrained on an acting basis.

To say the least, Iraq is a troubled country and since the 2003 invasion and occupation, it has become the best example in this book of a **failed state** which, for all intents and purposes, cannot maintain order let alone provide its people with social services they desperately need.

Looking BACKWARD

IRAQ IS AMAZINGLY different from the other countries we have seen and will see.

It has fought three wars in just a bit more than thirty years, the last of which led to a regime change and American occupation. However tumultuous Iran has been at times, it pales in comparison with Iraq.

But some of the same questions we've seen in Part 4 are important here, especially as the United States continues its departure. In particular, what can be done to build a democratic regime in a deeply divided country? Indeed, some observers wonder if you can do it at all.

The election shows us that even in post-Saddam Iraq, much of the uncertainty has to do with the ethnic and religious nature of Iraqi politics, especially its divisions between Kurds, Shiites, and Sunni Muslims, which we will explain in the next section. The election and the wars that gave rise to it lead us already to two broad conclusions that will shape this chapter.

First, this will be the most inconclusive and controversial chapter in *Comparative Politics.*

It will be inconclusive because the war is still going on even though all American combat forces have left the country as will most or all of the rest of them by the time this book

is published. That does not mean that all is well in Iraq. The transition to a new government that might bring stability, let alone democracy, will not be completed soon.

It will be controversial because people inside Iraq and abroad still disagree strongly about the proper path that should be followed. We both opposed the war even though we despised Saddam's regime and were glad to see it go. However, the **George W. Bush** administration did not convince us that an invasion was either needed or justified as part of the American response to 9/11. Chip has many friends in the military who have served as many as four tours in Iraq. They did their duty valiantly but came home with grave

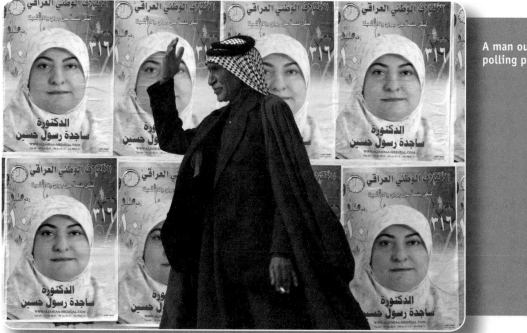

A man outside an Iraq polling place in 2010.

AP Photo/Alaa al-Marjani

doubts about this war and questions about how best to deal with terrorists or insurgents who, after all, are quite different from each other. In other words, we agree with Thomas Ricks of the Center for a New American Security who titled his first book on Iraq, *Fiasco*. Little has gone as planned in either Baghdad or Washington. In short, our main goal in writing this chapter is not come down for or against a war that occurred almost a decade ago. Rather we want to share with the readers our own uncertainties, both about politics in Iraq and how the rest of the world has chosen to deal with it.

The war was extremely controversial in the United States, the United Kingdom, and other countries that joined what Bush called the "coalition of the willing." The growing opposition to the war in Britain was the main reason Prime Minister Tony Blair had to resign in summer 2007. In the United States, dissatisfaction with the war turned Bush into one of the most unpopular presidents ever. Put simply, the United States and its allies were not prepared to fight what colleagues in the conflict resolution field call an asymmetric war against insurgents who did not wear uniforms and blended back into their communities quickly and easily.

Because Iraq does raise so many raw nerves, this chapter has to be organized differently from most of the others. Because the coalition of the willing did impose a regime change on Iraq, we will have to work our way twice through Iraqi politics, treating the regimes before and after the fall of Saddam separately in much the same way we did for the Soviet Union and, then, Russia.

Wherever one stands on the role of the United States and its consequences, we have to start by considering Iraq's difficulties in the context of its recent wars, most notably the one initiated by the United States and its allies in 2003. Iraq fought Iran to a bloody stalemate in the 1980 and lost to the U.S.-led coalition in the Gulf War of 1991. The third war led to the collapse of Saddam Hussein's Baathist regime, and eventually to his arrest and execution.

Although few people shed a tear for one of the most despotic leaders of our time, the speedy American victory on the battlefield gave way to a prolonged insurgency that left 160,000 American troops in the country six years after President Bush declared that major combat operations had ended. More than 4,400 American troops have been killed. No one really knows how many Iraqis have died, but most estimates start at ten times that number.

The bottom line is that the country is still in the middle of a civil war, albeit one that is not as deadly as it was just a few years ago. More than 2 million people fled the country because of it. Particularly dangerous were neighborhoods in which Sunni and Shiites (see the section on the basics) had lived together for generations, but experienced ethnic cleansing in which members of whichever group was in the minority was forced out of the neighborhood and some of its members were killed. On most days suicide bombers still blow up their cars and kill dozens of people in Baghdad and other cities in central and southern Iraq. Many Iraqis have electricity for no more than four hours a day. The overall

AP Images

Saddam Hussein is led into a courtroom on Thursday, 1 July 2004, at Camp Victory, a former Saddam palace on the outskirts of Baghdad.

infrastructure of roads, utilities, schools, hospitals, and more is in far worse shape than it was before the war began.

Just before President George W. Bush left office, the United States and Iraq signed a Status of Forces Agreement (SOFA) that called for the removal of all American combat forces. As many as fifty thousand troops remain as we write in June 2011, but they are only being used in support and training missions and are due to leave by the end of the year ✐ (http://www.cfr.org/iraq/us-security-agreements-iraq/p16448).

By early 2011, the security situation *had* improved, especially in the so-called **Sunni Triangle** that was at the heart of the insurgency and home to al-Qaeda in Iraq. Few Americans are being killed; only six died in January 2011. Iraqis, however, are only marginally safer. On January 27, 2011, alone, 87 Iraqi civilians were killed in a series of bombings.

That leads to a second broad conclusion that echoes one we reached for Iran. Given the three wars, occupation, and insurgency, it is impossible to understand Iraqi politics without considering its dramatically changing role in the international system. So, again, we will break down the artificial barrier between international relations and comparative politics.

THINKING ABOUT IRAQ

If we could go back in time and conduct a poll in July 1990, we would undoubtedly learn that most Westerners did not know who Saddam Hussein was or where Iraq is located. That was the case even though Iran and Iraq had just ended an eight-year war that killed at least half a million people in each country.

Ever since, Iraq has been on center stage. The sudden upsurge of interest in this previously little-known country began because of Iraq's invasion of its small, oil-rich neighbor, Kuwait, on August 2, 1990. In an unprecedented display of cooperation, most of the international community, including both superpowers and several Arab states, denounced Iraq's actions and demanded its withdrawal. After Iraq refused to do so and the United Nations (UN) approved an international military response, President George H. W. Bush ordered the international coalition he led into the **Gulf War**, which resulted in the defeat of Iraq on the battlefield but not the overthrow of Saddam's regime, which, in the end, turned out to be the key issue for the George W. Bush administration.

The Basics

Any discussion of Iraqi politics must begin with the legacy of more than thirty years of brutal rule by the **Baath Party** and the man who was its undisputed leader from 1979

until 2003, Saddam. As in Joseph Stalin's Soviet Union, a totalitarian regime was established by a narrowly based party that claimed to speak for the masses but that, in fact, represented little more than a tiny group of activists who were never able to develop much genuine popular support.

Individual and minority rights were subordinated to the "needs" of the state, which the party claimed it represented. Dissidents were systematically denounced as "traitors" and "enemies of the state," and the most prominent of them were executed after well-publicized show trials that succeeded in instilling massive fear of the regime.

However, as in any country, we cannot understand Iraq's politics without first considering some of the country's social and economic features because those characteristics shaped many of the issues Iraq faced during Saddam's years in power and the difficulties it confronts today.

Economic Potential

One of the tragedies of Iraqi politics is that its current plight was by no means inevitable. Different policy choices could have led to very different outcomes, including prosperity for most Iraqis.

By Southern standards, Iraq has tremendous resources. There are over 100 billion proven barrels of oil (one barrel holds forty-two U.S. gallons) under its soil, which represents 15 percent of all known Middle Eastern reserves. Only Saudi Arabia has more. Many geologists believe that Iraq has more undiscovered oil than any other country in the region.

Iraq also has significant agricultural potential, despite a southwestern region that is a desert and the high salt content of the soil elsewhere. There are surprisingly fertile areas in the Kurdish regions of the north and along the banks of the Tigris and Euphrates rivers, which provide ample water for irrigation and the generation of electricity.

Iraq's other major resource is its population. With almost 30 million people, it is relatively large compared to Saudi Arabia and the smaller Gulf states and can therefore support a diversified and integrated economy. Moreover, Iraq's labor force is relatively skilled and well educated by regional standards.

As a result, Iraq could easily be an economically successful country. In fact, in the mid-1970s, following the worldwide quadrupling of oil prices, many observers predicted that it would emerge as the economic powerhouse of the Arab world. Although some of this newfound wealth was used to modernize the country's infrastructure and provide Iraqis with an enhanced standard of living, the staggering increase in oil revenues mostly enabled the regime to buy sophisticated weapons to both strengthen its political control and to build up the military.

Diversity

Iraq's population is more than 95 percent Muslim. Behind this apparent homogeneity lies a sharp distinction between Sunni and Shiite Muslims and between Arabs and Kurds.

Iraqi population statistics are notoriously inaccurate. Nonetheless, the best guess is that approximately 60 percent of the population is **Shiite** and approximately 35 percent is **Sunni**, with the majority of them being **Kurds**.

The origins of the Sunni-Shiite rivalry dates back to the dawn of Islamic history. The prophet Muhammad died in 632 without naming a successor to head the rapidly expanding Muslim faith and empire he had created. Almost immediately, his followers split into two camps. The one that became the Sunni believed that the most prominent members of the community should select the new leader, or caliph, on the basis of personal attributes such as piety, wisdom, morality, leadership ability, and general competence. Others, however, contended that the leadership of the Islamic world should stay in the prophet's family. They believed that Muhammed had wanted his cousin, son-in-law, and close companion, Ali, to be his successor. They were called Shiites, a word derived from *Shi'at Ali* which means "the partisans of Ali" (**http://www.uga.edu/islam/**) and the terms Shiite and Shi'a are used more or less interchangeably.

Although the soon-to-be Sunni won the argument, Ali was eventually elected to the caliphate in 656 after the death of Uthman, the third caliph. However, Muawiyah, Uthman's nephew and governor of Syria, refused to accept this decision. Eventually, Muawiyah prevailed and established the Damascus-based Umayyad dynasty (661–750).

The Shiites never recognized Umayyad rule and continued to claim that only the descendants of Ali had the right to govern the Islamic community. In 680 Ali's second son, Hussein, led a group of his followers in an armed uprising against the Umayyad dynasty. Despite his bravery and courage, Hussein was defeated and killed at Kerbala in what is now southern Iraq.

The story of Hussein's defeat lies at the heart of Shiite culture, especially its emphasis on martyrdom. To the Shiites, who rapidly became the most important minority sect within Islam, the battle of Kerbala symbolizes worldly injustice and the triumph of the forces of evil over the forces of good. More significantly, the defeat widened the gulf between the two main Islamic sects. In the following centuries, what initially had been limited to a disagreement over who should succeed the prophet became a full-fledged religious and political schism that continues to be felt throughout the Muslim world.

In addition to the Sunni-Shiite split, Iraqis are also divided into two main ethnic groups: Arabs and Kurds (see Figure 14.1). About 75 percent of Iraq's population is Arab—that is, people who speak Arabic and identify with

FIGURE 14.1 Distribution of Ethnic Groups in Iraq

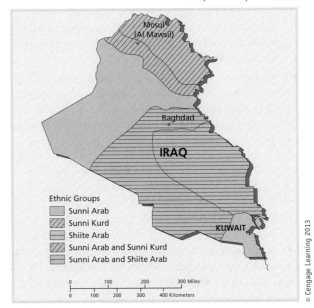

Arab culture. The Kurds, who represent 20 percent of the population, speak Kurdish, which has nothing in common with Arabic. Kurds also have their own history and modes of social and political organization. Indeed, they have less in common with Iraq's Arab majority than they do with other Kurdish communities in Turkey, Iran, Syria, and the former Soviet Union. In fact, Kurds are the largest ethnic group in the world without their own state.

Key Concepts and Questions

As noted in Chapter 11, most countries in the Global South struggle with three related problems: economic development, ethnic tensions, and limited prospects for democratization. These are key issues in Iraqi politics as well. However, given the discussion so far, it should be clear that we need to focus on other questions in addition. In particular:

- Why did Iraq end up with a totalitarian regime in the first place?

- How were Saddam and the men around him able to create such a powerful regime?

- How were they able to sustain it despite all the setbacks during the two decades before the 2003 war?

- What are the prospects for the new Iraqi state that emerged fitfully in the aftermath of the 2003 war?

- How much of Iraq's political culture is an outgrowth of its own history rather than the impact of outsiders?

- Along those same lines, Iraq is the best example we have of the impact of globalization. To be sure, we think of globalization primarily in economic or cultural terms, but it is also geopolitical and reflects the might the United States exercises throughout the world. In that sense, is globalization helping or hurting Iraq today?

■ Our study of Iraq will show us just how difficult it is to build a state or a nation more clearly than our analysis of any other country covered in this book other than perhaps Mexico. Why is that the case? What difference does it make?

THE EVOLUTION OF THE IRAQI STATE

In European liberal democracies, the development of the state was a mostly indigenous process that spanned hundreds of years. Consequently, when the twentieth century began, most Europeans already thought of themselves as belonging to a "nation" or "state"—a group of people bound together by a common history, a shared culture, a sense of collective identity, or a willingness to live together and be governed by at least a reasonably effective state.

By contrast, few countries covered in Part 4 are more than a half-century old in their current form, and imperialist powers often arbitrarily imposed their boundaries. As a result, countries like Iraq have had to simultaneously address both state and **nation building** under less than auspicious circumstances. As in so many countries (Iran being a partial exception), outside influence has been there from the beginning and continues to this day.

Urban civilization began some six thousand years ago in the city-state of Sumer in what is now southern Iraq 🌐 (**www.al-bab.com/arab/countries/iraq/history .htm**). The Sumerians were the first to invent writing by drawing pictures on clay tablets, and also invented irrigation, literature, mathematics, architecture, metal working, transportation (they built the first wheeled chariot), and astronomy (they produced the first reasonably accurate calendars). Their successors added to those accomplishments—most notably the Babylonians, who produced the Code of Hammurabi, the first complete legal framework. After their region of Mesopotamia was incorporated into the Muslim empire during the seventh century, its fame and prosperity reached new heights. Baghdad was the seat of the Abbassid dynasty (750–1258), during which time Islamic civilization reached its peak while Europe still lived in the Dark Ages.

Given its strategic location on the eastern flank of the Arab world and its defenseless borders, Iraq was always coveted by foreign powers that sought to dominate the region. Its period as one of the leading cultural centers in the world came to an end when the Mongols invaded Baghdad in 1258, destroyed it, and slaughtered one hundred thousand Iraqis. A century and a half later, in 1394, the invading Tatars reportedly built a pyramid with the skulls of their unfortunate victims in the small provincial town of Tikrit, where Saddam Hussein was born 543 years later.

Even this brief overview should illuminate the illustrious early history of the area that is now Iraq. Yet Iraq as a distinct political unit is barely eighty years old. Until World War I broke out, "Iraq" was nothing more than an ill-defined region on the edge of the **Ottoman Empire**.

In 1914, the already weakened Ottoman authorities made what turned out to be a disastrous choice when they entered World War I, siding with Germany and the Austro-Hungarian Empire against France, Britain, and Russia. During the war, the Ottoman Empire collapsed, which gave Britain and France the opportunity to divide its former Arab provinces between themselves. They created entirely new countries, the borders of which were drawn to fit Britain's and France's colonial ambitions and did not reflect the distribution of religious, ethnic, and linguistic groups or the wishes of the populations involved. Iraq was one of them (see Table 14.1).

In 1916, when most of the Arab world was still under Ottoman control, British officials struck a deal with a group of local leaders. In an attempt to facilitate the allied war effort, they promised to support the creation of one large Arab state after the war if the Arabs rose up against the Ottomans. The Arabs lived up to their side of the bargain, but the British did not. By 1920, Arabs found themselves living in separate countries under regimes installed and controlled by either France or Britain. Understandably, the Arabs felt betrayed. To complicate matters for the future, no Kurdish state was created.

The British imposed a constitutional monarchy on Iraq, which was a political system entirely alien to the area's customs and traditions. They then added insult to injury by selecting a foreigner to be Iraq's first king. **Faisal I** was a member of the prestigious and pro-British Hashemite family, whose roots lay not in Iraq but in the western part of what is now Saudi Arabia.

From the beginning, therefore, the Iraqi government lacked legitimacy. It also had to contend with the

TABLE 14.1 Key Events in Iraqi History

YEAR	EVENT
1919	Treaty of Versailles, giving Britain control over Iraq
1932	Nominal independence
1958	Overthrow of monarchy
1963	First, short-lived seizure of power by Baath Party
1968	Definitive seizure of power by Baath Party
1979	Saddam Hussein takes control

heterogeneity of Iraq's population. When the British created Iraq, they brought together disparate ethnic, religious, and tribal groups, none of whom considered themselves "Iraqi" nor wanted to become part of the new country. In fact, some of the groups artificially stitched together by the British had a long history of mutual distrust and hostility. Thus, it was not easy to forge a cohesive political community out of a patchwork of rival groups that shared neither a common heritage nor a willingness to live together, something we will also see in the next chapter on Nigeria.

During the 1920s and 1930s, the task of the new regime was made even more difficult by the presence of rebellious Kurdish and Shiite tribes and by traditional feelings of distrust toward any central authority.

In 1932, Iraq became formally independent, although British advisers continued to exert tremendous influence over the kingdom. The minority Sunni Arabs controlled every regime after Iraq gained its independence until the defeat of Saddam. Their domination was part of the legacy of the Sunni-ruled Ottoman Empire, which systematically discriminated against Shiites. It continued under the monarchy, when Shiites and Kurds were forced into the new state against their will.

After twenty-six years under the monarchy, a group of military officers overthrew it but retained Sunni control. In retrospect, the demise of the monarchy seemed all but inevitable, considering its narrow base of support, the poor quality of the men at the helm, its perceived subservience to British interests, and its unwillingness or inability to reduce glaring social inequalities and to reach out to a rapidly growing and politicized middle class.

The decisive moment in the downfall of the monarchy came after the spread of pan-Arab, socialist ideologies in the army's ranks. Riding a wave of popular discontent, Arab nationalist officers, led by General Qasim, organized a successful coup and in 1958 established the first republican regime in the country's short history. It proved to be a republic in name only. The country was ruled by heavy-handed army officers for most of the first decade after the overthrow of the monarchy. In 1963, the Baath Party overthrew the officers then in power, but was itself forced out in a matter of months.

In July 1968, the Baath came back to power. This time, the Baathists were determined to stay in control, and they rapidly moved to eliminate everyone else from positions of influence (see Table 14.2). Eleven years later, Saddam forced his predecessor, **Ahmad Hassan al-Bakr**, into retirement. He announced his ascension to the presidency at a meeting of the Central Committee of the Baath party, after which almost a third of its members were summarily executed.

Afterward, he consolidated his own power along with that of the party to the point that it was all but impossible to separate the two, as we will see in the rest of this section. The

TABLE 14.2 Key Events in Iraq since the Baath Took Power

YEAR	EVENT
1968	Baath Party seizes power
1970	Government signs autonomy agreement with Kurds
1972	Kurdish autonomy agreement collapses
	War breaks out in north between Baghdad and Kurdish separatists
1975	Iran and Iraq agree on Kurds and Shatt al-Arab waterway
	Kurdish uprising collapses
	Deportation and resettlement of Kurds
1979	Saddam Hussein becomes president
1980–88	Iran-Iraq War, including use of chemical weapons against Kurdish civilians
1990	Invasion of Kuwait, Operation Desert Shield
1991	Gulf War
1995	Saddam's son-in-law and former minister of industry, Hussein Kamel al-Majids defects to Jordan
	Referendum gives Saddam Hussein another term
1996	Hussein Kamel al-Majid is pardoned, returns to Iraq, is killed
	Saddam launches attack on Kurdish enclave in north
	Assassination attempt on Saddam Hussein's son, Uday
1998	Crisis between Iraq and the West over United Nations' weapons inspections
	Four-day bombing campaign of Iraq by American and British forces
1999	Continued U.S. and U.K. bombing in response to Iraqi violations of 1991 cease-fire terms
2003	U.S.-led invasion topples Baath regime

dictatorship of the Baath Party gave way to personal rule by Saddam. Indeed, the state became little more than a tool Saddam, his family, and the rest of his entourage used to reinforce their hold on the country.

IRAQ UNDER SADDAM

The first of the two historical sections of the chapter covers the period of Baath rule. After all, it has only been out of power for less than a decade. The rest of the chapter concentrates on the tumultuous years since 2003. Some subsections—including the next one—cover both periods.

Cultural Traditions

Pluralism

Iraq's history produced a culture that political scientists believe hinders the development of a stable, effective, and popular regime, let alone a democracy. Even without the years of repression under the Baath, Iraq would have had a hard time creating any sense of national unity. That said, we cannot underestimate the impact of the regime they built. Indeed, Iraq shows us better than any other country in this book, other than perhaps Nigeria (see Chapter 15), that state and nation building are very different phenomena.

As in most of the South, religious and ethnic divisions acted as a brake on the development of an Iraqi national identity. Instead, older, parochial identities thwarted government efforts to promote any sense of Iraqi nationalism. After all, Iraq was little more than an artificial conglomerate of tribes, clans, and religious and ethnic groups that had lived in isolation from one another for centuries, had no tradition of political cooperation, and shared a long history of mutual distrust.

The sharply differentiated religious and ethnic communities were reluctant to give up their distinctive character for an Iraqi identity mostly concocted by British colonial officers. Although religious and ethnic cleavages did not always preclude cooperation between Sunni and Shiites or between Arabs and Kurds, they did make nation building more difficult than in any of the other countries considered in Part 4.

The Baath regime understood the need to defuse tensions among Iraq's ethnic and religious communities. Accordingly, it tried to convince Iraqis that a common identity rooted in the country's Mesopotamian heritage transcends its religious and ethnic divisions. Its propaganda portrayed modern-day Iraqis as direct descendants of the ancient Sumerians, Akkadians, and Babylonians. In addition, it invested huge sums of money in the rebuilding of Babylon and in archaeological excavations intended to showcase the country's pre-Islamic past.

However, these efforts failed because many Iraqis continued to identify primarily with their clan, ethnic, and religious groups. This is by no means uncommon in the Third World, but in Iraq, the way in which parochialism played itself out at both the mass and elite levels put exceptional burdens on the former regime and seems likely to do so under any government.

That means that the differences between Kurds and Arabs and Shiites and Sunni are a central element in Iraqi political culture. Those differences surged to the surface in the months after the U.S.-led invasion in 2003, but have been part of the country's political landscape for many generations.

The inability of Arabs and Kurds to coexist peacefully has always been a major problem for Iraqi leaders. Given the development of a Kurdish nationalist movement at the turn of the twentieth century and the lip service paid by the Great Powers to the principle of self-determination after World War I, the Kurds had hoped that the postwar settlement would see the establishment of a Kurdish state. Instead, as noted previously, the Kurds found themselves scattered across five countries, none of which they could call their own.

Most Kurds never accepted the crushing of their nationalist aspirations. Consequently, their relationship with successive Iraqi governments has been stormy. Kurdish uprisings have punctuated Iraqi political life since the mid-1920s. In turn, the Iraqi central authorities have always seen Kurdish aspirations for autonomy as a threat to the country's very existence. The fact that Kurdish insurgents were supported by Iran, the United States, and other outsiders did little to ease the tension between them and Iraq's Arab majority. Thus, at the height of the Iran-Iraq War, one of the two main Iraqi Kurdish organizations, the **Patriotic Union of Kurdistan (PUK)**, cooperated with the Iranian army and helped it seize a number of villages in Iraqi Kurdistan.

Much of the blame for Arab-Kurdish hostility also lies in a succession of Iraqi governments that never made a sincere effort to meet even limited Kurdish demands.

Kurdish refugees, once across the lone footbridge into Cukurca, Turkey, wash themselves and their belongings, April 7, 1991, while thousands wait on the Iraqi side to be given permission to cross the border.

In 1970, for instance, Kurdish leaders and Saddam reached an agreement granting administrative autonomy to Iraqi Kurdistan, the teaching of Kurdish in schools, the use of Kurdish as the official language in the north, and the increased representation of Kurds in state institutions. A year after signing the agreement, however, it became clear that the Baath leadership had no intention of living up to it. And, as many Westerners learned in the run up to the first invasion of Iraq, the authorities in Baghdad used chemical and biological weapons against its own Kurdish citizens during the war with Iran. Even today, the Kurdish-Arab split remains important. Many Kurds are unwilling to live under a government dominated by Arabs and want at least autonomy over their own region if not outright independence. Meeting Kurdish demands for more freedom from Baghdad while maintaining the territorial integrity of Iraq has been a major challenge for the old and new regime alike, especially because the Kurds have been outside Baghdad's control since the Gulf War of 1991 and have something approaching autonomy today.

The split between the Arab Shiite and Sunni communities is likely to prove even more intense as the United States and Iraqi authorities try to reconstruct the country. Their antagonism stems more from political, social, and economic differences than from theological disagreements. There are differences of faith, as there are between Catholics and Protestants in Northern Ireland. However, religion has become more a symbol of communal identity and a way for Shiites to express their grievances over the inequalities in wealth and power that have characterized Iraq since its formation.

In the late 1960s, there was not a single Shiite on the **Revolutionary Command Council (RCC)**, which officially sat atop the Baath Party. By the late 1980s, however, more than 25 percent of the RCC members and close to 30 percent of all party leaders were Shiites. They were represented in numbers roughly proportional to their share of the population at lower levels of the bureaucracy. Yet Shiites' sense that they were discriminated against erupted in the first months after Saddam's overthrow in one phase of the insurgency led by the cleric, **Muqtada al-Sadr** (1973–).

The Shiites' sense of deprivation has also been fueled by the perception that their community has been discriminated against economically. Living conditions in the predominantly Shiite south were so miserable in the 1940s and 1950s that tens of thousands of Shiite peasants migrated to Baghdad every year, where they formed the nucleus of a rapidly developing urban proletariat in what used to be known as Saddam City and is now Sadr City. Not surprisingly, a neighborhood that has been beset with intercommunal violence since 2003.

The Baath regime worsened the already deep division between the two sects. Initially this occurred because of the party's militantly secular orientation, which antagonized religious minded Shiites and by its long-standing rivalry with the Communist Party, which traditionally had recruited heavily among Shiites. Tensions deepened following the creation of a distinctly Shiite underground movement, al-Da'wa al-Islamiyya (the Islamic Call), which supported the establishment of an Islamic regime and is also the movement al-Maliki joined as a young man.

The Baath government responded in a particularly brutal manner to break the hold of religious leaders in the Shiite holy cities of Kerbala and Najaf. Clerics and theology students suspected of being affiliated with al-Da'wa were arrested and as many as forty thousand of them were deported to Iran.

The outbreak of the Iran-Iraq War, however, forced the regime to reconsider its strategy toward the Shiites. The fear that they might defect and support their coreligionists to the east led Saddam to temper his repression with various measures designed to win them over, including bringing a large number of them into the nominally governing RCC.

But the moderation was not to last. When Shiites finally rose up in the wake of the first Gulf War, the authorities' brutal response only heightened their antagonism toward Baghdad. To flee the government, many Shiite rebels took refuge in the southern marshes, which were a vital part of the regional economy. Saddam had the marshes drained to flush out the rebels, which only reinforced the hatred many in the region felt toward the Sunni-led regime.

A Culture of Secrecy and Fear

Iraq has often been described as having an inward looking and secretive culture, which stems in part from the centuries of isolation after the Mongol and subsequent invasions. Mass and elite concerns about foreigners included not only the West, but relations with two neighbors, Turkey and Iran. Neither is an Arab country. Both have vastly larger populations. In past centuries, empires based in those countries invaded and occupied at least parts of modern day Iraq long before the British arrived.

That means that today's Iraqis inherited reasonable worries about their security, some of which are centuries old. For instance, many Kurds still believe that Britain's decision to cede the Mosul region to Iraq in the early 1920s was illegal. Eighty percent of Iraq's water supply comes from Turkey and Syria, where the Tigris and Euphrates have their origins. Turkey's pro-Western government allowed allied bombers to launch attacks from bases there during the first Gulf War. Saddam's regime had similar worries about Iran, epitomized by the dispute over the Shatt al-Arab River in southeastern Iraq, which we will see in more detail later in the chapter as we consider the events that gave rise to the Iran-Iraq War.

Some Iraqis, too, are concerned with what they see as the Western desire to dominate the region. They have not forgotten Britain's broken promises to Arab nationalists after World War I and continue to resent the way colonial officials drew the country's borders. They remember, too, that Britain was the real power behind the monarchy and that it manipulated Iraqi affairs to further its colonial interests.

The bitterness toward Britain in particular and the West in general was compounded by the decisive role that Western countries played in the creation of Israel. To this day, many Iraqis regard Israel as an artificial entity imposed by the colonial powers to divide and weaken the Arab world.

After the Baath secured power, it actively encouraged distrust of the West. Saddam and his colleagues sought to limit the access of foreign visitors to Iraq, and those who were allowed in could not travel freely or easily come into contact with average Iraqis. Any Iraqis who did were likely to have a "visit" from one of the security forces that could put their careers—and even their lives—in jeopardy.

A Tradition of Political Violence

The last aspect of Iraqi popular culture is a propensity for violence. As early as the seventh century, the area was known for its turbulent nature, which coexists uneasily with its tradition of authoritarian rule.

Conflict
in Iraq

Conflict is the name of the game in Iraqi politics. Under Saddam Hussein, conflict from below was largely suppressed. However, as the insurgency after the end of major combat operations in April 2003 has shown, conflict among and within the three main religious and ethnic communities discussed in this section is likely to haunt Iraqi politics for years to come.

Very little is being done to address the root causes of the conflict. Those of us in the conflict resolution community think it will be decades before the Kurdish versus Arab and Sunni versus Shiite disputes can be overcome, even if Iraqi and American forces can definitively put down the insurrection that broke out within days of the overthrow of Saddam's regime. ■

During the 1940s and 1950s, the uneven distribution of wealth and the politicization of a new generation of Iraqis dissatisfied with the authoritarian nature of the monarchy resulted in social and political upheaval. In July 1958, widespread popular discontent with the monarchy exploded in a particularly bloody fashion that led to its destruction.

The aftermath of the revolution was no more peaceful. In March 1959, local army commanders rose up against the government of General Qasim in the northern city of Mosul. For three days, the city was engulfed in violence and bloodshed. Old personal grudges and family feuds were settled. Qasim's supporters were summarily executed. When it became clear that the coup had failed, the government allowed the Communist Party to go on a rampage and avenge the earlier killings.

When the Baath Party overthrew Qasim in 1963, his downfall turned into a gruesome spectacle. His bullet-ridden corpse, for example, was shown for several days on television.

When the Baath Party finally solidified their power in 1968, the government was able to put a lid on most public forms of violence—other than those it carried out itself. Nonetheless, when they fell, the conflict burst back into the open again and, along with the Kurdish/Arab divide, could well imperil the future of Iraq for decades to come.

Political Participation under the Baath

Public involvement in political life under Saddam was much like that in the Soviet Union before Mikhail Gorbachev opened up the system. There were no opportunities for Iraqi citizens to express their opinions, especially those that were at odds with the regime.

Instead, to the degree that members of the public were engaged in political life, they were coerced into doing so by the Baathist authorities. For instance, massive demonstrations were held in favor of the wars the government fought before it was toppled, but few people joined them voluntarily.

We can see the lack of real democratic political participation in the last two presidential elections under Saddam's reign. In 1995, 99.47 percent of the population went to the polls, and, of them, 99.96 percent voted for Saddam. In other words, no more than three thousand people did not vote and no more than another three thousand cast a ballot against Saddam. The regime outdid itself seven years later when it reported a 100 percent turnout and that all 100 percent of them had voted for Saddam. That may not have been terribly surprising since participation was mandatory and voters had to show their ballots to poll watchers before casting them.

The limits on "demanding" public participation were also evident in the extreme weakness of the Iraqi opposition.

It had no open support inside the country and given the repressive power of the regime (see the next section) it was forced to operate from abroad. Many of those groups were funded by the United States, Iran, and other opponents of the Baath Party that further undercut their potential support at home, something we saw in the difficulties Iraqi governments have had establishing themselves since 2003. In fact, most prominent politicians today spent upwards of a decade in exile, which limits their understanding of day-to-day life under Saddam.

The little opposition that existed was highly fragmented. Some of these divisions reflect the country's ethnic and religious cleavages. Thus, the most outspoken critics of the regime were Kurds or Shiites. The one exception was the Iraqi Communist Party, which protested the regime in all parts of Iraq, but like the Tudeh in Iran, it had been all but completely destroyed by the 1990s.

After the first Gulf War, there was a Western-led attempt to create a broadly based opposition coalition—the **Iraqi National Congress (INC)**, which was headed by Adnan Chalabi and all but completely funded by the United States. Chalabi, a Shiite, has since been accused of secretly passing information to the Iranian government and is all but completely discredited in Iraq and the United States outside of neo-conservative circles. The second-largest group was the Iraqi National Accord, led by **Ayad Alawi**, who became the interim prime minister as the United States began the transfer of power to Iraqis in 2004 and remains a leading political figure today.

The State Under Saddam

Most countries in the Global South have governmental institutions that are elaborately laid out in their constitutions. In some cases, such as India, those provisions define political life roughly to the degree that they do in industrialized democracies. In many others, however, power rests primarily with a single leader or a small group that is not constrained by constitutional language or conventional laws. That was certainly true in Iraq, which was dominated by one man and his entourage for a quarter century.

A Party State

As in the Soviet Union, we have to start any discussion of Saddam's state with the single party that controlled everything. The Baath Party was founded in the early 1940s by two French-educated Syrian teachers: Michel Aflaq, a Greek Orthodox Christian, and Salah al-Din al-Bitar, a Sunni Muslim. Soon afterward, the party established branches in Iraq, Jordan, and Lebanon.

Its ideology was always an ill-defined mixture of pan-Arabism and non-Marxist socialism. The key to its political philosophy was the premise that nation-states in the Arab world were artificial entities created by colonial powers that wanted to divide and weaken the region. Therefore, the party's founders argued that only the unification of the various Arab states would enable them to overcome underdevelopment and foreign domination, something they believed the British and French had promised during World War I. Their goals were reflected in the very name of the party, which means resurgence or renaissance.

Because Baathist leaders saw Arab countries as no more than parts of a wider Arab nation, the party's highest decision-making body, the National Command, was a supranational institution. Subordinated to it were the party's Regional Commands, which made up the leadership of the Baath in each country.

However, the notion that the Baath was a party that transcended existing state boundaries soon became a fiction, as country-based organizations asserted their independence from the National Command. In 1966, an important split took place between the Syrian and Iraqi branches. From then on Syria and Iraq each had their own "National Command" that put national interests well above those of the "Arab nation."

After the Baath Party seized control in Baghdad in 1968, anyone who posed a potential threat to its monopoly of power was retired, jailed, executed, dismissed, or reassigned to less-influential positions. All strategic positions in the state machinery were given to trusted or long-standing party members.

Saddam, then head of the party's security apparatus, orchestrated and directed this thorough "Baathization" of the state. At the same time, he revamped the Baath itself, transforming it from a small, underground party into a mass-based organization. Full membership was reserved for individuals who, after years of service, finally proved their dedication to the regime. Membership in the party was for life and resignation was punishable by death.

Like other totalitarian parties, the Baath relied on indoctrination to foster a sense of Iraqi nationalism and unconditional loyalty. The party tightly controlled the media, all school curricula, and entry into the teaching profession.

Thus, in the mid-1980s, when Iraq's leadership courted U.S. support in its war with Iran, teachers in Baghdad's schools taught their students that Americans were friends of the Iraqi people and that American visitors deserved a particularly warm welcome. During the 1990–91 Gulf crisis, the same teachers taught children that Americans were imperialists bent on dominating the Middle East and destroying Iraq.

The Baath also helped the authorities control the population. It could do so because it literally was everywhere—from small "cells" in neighborhoods and villages all the way up to the national leadership. Party units were called "divisions" in towns or urban neighborhoods, "sections," which combined several divisions in a city or a region, and "branches" for the eighteen provinces plus three for Baghdad.

The party had units in factories, universities, and government offices. It monitored the activities of journalists, lawyers, doctors, peasants, and workers through unions and professional organizations that it controlled. Party members reported on their colleagues' and superiors' performance and loyalty.

Therefore, there were really two distinct chains of authority in the Iraqi state: the official, bureaucratic one and the one associated with the Baath Party. State and party were often played off against one another in an attempt to weaken both and to diminish the possibility that either could provide the regime with potential enemies that had a power base strong enough to threaten it. The confusion and delays that this generated are consequences of a system that valued political control over efficiency.

As such, two parts of the former Iraqi state—the Council of Ministers (or cabinet) and the National Assembly—might seem familiar at first glance because they have the same names as institutions found in democratic systems. In fact, they had little in common with their Western counterparts because they had next to no influence over policy making.

The cabinet did little more than implement policies that had already been adopted by the president and the RCC. The National Assembly's 250 members were only allowed to run for election after being handpicked by a committee controlled by Saddam. In practice, all power was concentrated in the hands of the Baath party leadership. After he took control, the distinction between the party and his personal power all but disappeared.

The Cult of Personality

As was also the case in most totalitarian regimes, power was concentrated in the hands of a single leader in what is referred to as a **cult of personality**. When *New York Times* correspondent Elaine Sciolino arrived in Iraq after the invasion of Kuwait in 1990, she asked her taxicab driver what he thought about Saddam. His answer was short but to the point. He tapped the dashboard of his car and said, "this is car, but if Saddam Hussein says it is bicycle, it is bicycle." In October 1991, Izzat Ibrahim, then vice chairman of the RCC, summed it up even more briefly: "Saddam Hussein is Iraq, and Iraq is Saddam Hussein."

Throughout the country, huge billboards portrayed him in different guises: Saddam in a military uniform, Saddam in a tailor-made Italian suit, Saddam praying, Saddam wearing a Bedouin headdress and robe, Saddam as a shepherd tending his flock, or Saddam wearing the green fatigues favored by Baath leaders. His portrait was everywhere: in taxicabs, in stores, in government buildings, in homes (especially those of government employees), and in bus windows. There were Saddam t-shirts, watches with his face on the dial, and notebooks and calendars adorned with his image. Throughout the country, one found placards with quotes attributed to Saddam and others praising the president.

In the mid-1980s one of the jokes making the rounds about the regime went like this:

> **"What is the population of Iraq?"**
> **"Twenty-eight million."**
> **"Fourteen million Iraqis and fourteen million pictures of Saddam Hussein."**

Saddam's birthday was a national holiday. School children memorized his sayings as well as poems and songs exalting him. News broadcasts focused on his activities. Television anchors read the dozens of congratulatory telegrams sent to him every day by government officials, artists, and leaders of professional, women's, and youth associations.

The most striking example of the personality cult is probably the set of two monuments called "Hands of Victory" that he had built to celebrate Iraq's "victory" over Iran. These identical sculptures are at opposite ends of a huge field in Baghdad. Each consists of two enormous, twenty-ton bronze forearms, which are giant replicas of Saddam's. The arms burst from the ground, each holding a giant sword. When they meet, the swords and the arms form an arch. Next to the base of the arches are some five thousand battle-scarred helmets of dead Iranian soldiers. The symbolism is obvious: Iraq's victory was achieved through the military genius and valiant leadership of Saddam, who will continue to lead his nation to ever greater triumphs.

The cult of personality reinforced two opposing images of Saddam: as benefactor and as ruthless leader. Thus, welfare programs and development projects were portrayed as personal gifts that Saddam bestowed on his people. In the 1970s and 1980s, for instance, he frequently handed out television sets while visiting Kurdish or Shiite villages. But if Saddam was the one who handed out benefits, he also was the one who handed out punishment. After the village of Dujayl, known to be a hotbed of Shiite fundamentalism, was the site of an assassination attempt against Saddam, he ordered it razed. Almost immediately afterward, the government rebuilt it.

Through such displays, Saddam projected the image of a leader who was omnipresent, omnipotent, and omniscient. The message sent through such dramatic and seemingly contradictory actions was simple: Saddam alone decided who would live and who would die. And although

Profiles
Saddam Hussein

Saddam Hussein was born in 1937 and grew up in Tikrit, a poor city one hundred miles north of Baghdad. His mother was a widow, and there are rumors that he was abused by several of the relatives who helped raise him. Saddam moved to Baghdad in 1955 and quickly became active in politics. He was wounded in the Baathists' attempt to assassinate Qasim in 1959 and fled to Cairo, where he studied law but never earned a degree. He returned to Iraq when the Baath Party first came to power in 1963.

After the Baath seized power for good in July 1968, he served as second-in-command to the new president, Major General Ahmad Hassan al-Bakr. In practice, however, he quickly became the driving force behind the new regime, and by the mid-1970s he had emerged as the de facto leader of Iraq. In July 1979 he forced al-Bakr to resign and assumed the presidency himself. Through repeated purges of the ruling elite, he rapidly turned Iraqi politics into one-man rule. He has been aptly described by *New York Times* columnist Thomas Friedman as a thirteenth-century tyrant whose unrelenting desire to acquire weapons of mass destruction make him the archetypical twenty-first-century threat.

He was captured by American troops on December 12, 2003 and hung on December 30, 2006. ▓

A best-selling watch during the 1991 war, with Saddam Hussein pictured on the dial. Many wrist- and pocket-watches, as well as a wide selection of Saddam t-shirts, were available.

© Ceerwan Aziz/Reuters/Corbis

many of the stories circulating in Iraq and in the Arab world about his brutality were true, many more were concocted to add to his aura of invincibility.

The Informal Chain of Command

Saddam Hussein's ability to stay in power rested largely on his personal control over a vast network of subordinates who managed the party and state. Trusted aides who reported directly to him and who were kept relatively uninformed of each other's activities headed every institution that mattered. In so doing, Saddam made it unlikely that he would ever face a serious challenge from inside the government.

The influence of any member of the elite was primarily a function of personal access to the leader. Thus, men who did not belong to any of the official government bodies but who were close to Saddam often exerted more power than those who held formal positions. Real authority was exercised through a series of concentric circles all centered on Saddam. The personalization of power, and the fluidity of institutional arrangements it implies, makes it all but impossible to present the kind of diagram of decision making included in the other chapters of this book.

The inner circle, made up of Saddam's relatives, largely ran Iraq from behind the scenes. In 1990, this group included eight of his family members: his two sons, **Uday** and **Qusay**, both of whom were killed by American forces in 2003; three cousins on his father's side, two of whom were also his sons-in-law; and three half brothers.

However, the number of reliable family members declined significantly as a result of disputes among them. Although there are several such examples, one stands out. In August 1995 Saddam Hussein's two sons-in-law, who had been number two in the regime and head of his personal security guard, respectively, defected to Jordan, where they called for the overthrow of their father-in-law. When they finally returned to Baghdad after being granted a presidential pardon, they were killed along with all those who had shared their brief exile except for Saddam's two daughters, who, with their mother, were placed under house arrest.

A second circle consisted of a handful of Saddam's close associates, who had been connected to him since the Baath's underground days. Although these men had some real influence, they lacked any kind of independent power base and owed everything to Saddam. This circle included Vice President Taha Yassin Ramadan, Foreign Minister Tariq Aziz, and others who were not as visible to observers in the West.

A third circle was composed of Saddam's relatives and others who hailed from his hometown, Tikrit. It used to be customary for last names to refer to a person's place of origin, as in "Saddam Hussein al-Tikriti" (that is, "from Tikrit"). In 1976, the Baath Party suddenly abolished this practice on the grounds that it encouraged people to think of themselves not as Iraqis but as members of the parochial groups discussed previously. Many observers believe that the real reason behind the decision was that the leadership did not want to call attention to the fact that an embarrassingly large proportion of the political establishment had roots in Tikrit and were related to Saddam.

Other Institutions

Early in the Baath regime, one institution did matter: the RCC. Like a communist country's central committee, the RCC was the highest de facto authority. It was chaired by Saddam who was also president of the republic, commander in chief of the armed forces, and secretary general of the Baath Party.

The RCC functioned as a collective decision-making body during much of the decade after the Baath Party seized power. The situation changed dramatically in July 1979 when Saddam forced al-Bakr out. By 1982, the new president had removed all RCC members with an independent base of support and replaced them with people who were personally loyal to him. During the next twenty years, he reduced the size and influence of the RCC.

One of the most important challenges facing the RCC and the party as a whole was control over the military. Considering its tradition of intervention in Iraqi politics, the leadership's suspicion was not unjustified.

The importance of the military was reflected in the composition of the first RCC, the five members of which were all career officers and in the domination of the initial Baathist cabinet by individuals closely associated with prominent military figures. From the very moment the new

regime assumed power, therefore, civilian party activists were fearful of the power that senior military commanders wielded in the state bureaucracy. Turf battles between the civilian and the military wings of the party were compounded by ideological differences between the two groups, with the professional soldiers tending to be more moderate and pragmatic than the more doctrinaire and ideologically oriented Baathists. Only days after the 1968 coup, the civilian wing of the party, led by Saddam, moved to neutralize the most prominent military figures. Within a few years, most of them were removed from positions of influence in the government and were replaced by party functionaries. Significantly, the proportion of army officers in the RCC declined from 100 percent in the immediate aftermath of the 1968 coup to 40 percent in the second RCC established in November 1969. In the late 1970s and early 1980s, it fell to about 20 percent.

The armed forces were subjected to repeated purges as scores of officers were dismissed, forced to retire, and even executed. Political loyalty to the regime became a much more important consideration than professional competence in determining promotions. Only party members were allowed into the military academies. Soldiers were told that belonging to non-Baathist organizations was a crime punishable by death.

The outbreak of the war with Iran in 1980 revived latent animosities between the political and military leaderships. After Iraqi forces suffered serious defeats in 1982, senior army commanders were reported to be highly resentful of the excessive centralization of decision making in Saddam's hands. After an aborted attempt to force him to step down

The monumental arches reportedly modeled after Saddam Hussein's forearms. Oddly, they were one of the few Baath-era monuments the United States did not tear down.

© Independent Picture Service/Alamy

in 1982, he launched a purge of the military and executed scores of high-ranking officers whom he suspected of conspiring to remove him.

In an attempt to undermine the ability of army officers to develop their own power bases, the government sped up their rotation from one military branch to another. As a lesson to their colleagues, officers blamed for defeats on the battlefield were executed for treason. In several instances, successful officers were summoned to Baghdad after being told that they were going to be awarded medals for their performance at the front. Upon reaching the capital, they were arrested, and some were executed.

Saddam also tried to buy the officer corps' loyalty. Military spending was increased. Officers were given special privileges, including better housing, higher salaries, and access to government-controlled stores filled with imported goods unavailable to most Iraqis.

This mixture of carrot and stick, combined with the frightening prospect of an Iranian victory, succeeded in ensuring the army's loyalty throughout the war. Yet after it ended in 1988, there were once again rumors of coup attempts, followed by the execution of dozens of officers.

With Iraq's defeat in 1991, many analysts hoped that the military might finally topple the regime. Saddam understood the threat and took steps to foil possible coup attempts. He appointed a new army chief of staff, replaced the heads of the air force and the elite **Republican Guard**, and sped up the rotation of senior military commanders even more.

Despite these and other precautionary measures, four officers in the Republican Guard attempted a coup in June 1992. Shortly afterward, two hundred officers were purged, many of whom were executed. During the course of the next decade, reports and rumors of attempted coups surfaced on a regular basis. The most serious took place in mid-1995 and was organized by a senior general who had been close to Saddam. Afterward, the general's mutilated body was delivered to his family, which was one of Saddam's favorite ways of publicizing the cost of "treason."

The last major component of the regime was its collection of intelligence agencies that rivaled those of any other totalitarian regime in terms of their reach and brutality. The secret police was made up of not one but four distinct organizations. The most powerful was the General Intelligence Apparatus, which grew out of the Baathist secret police created by Saddam when the party was still underground. It handled both internal security and overseas operations but focused on monitoring the army, the bureaucracy, the Baath Party, and the "popular organizations" affiliated to it. The General Security Directorate was primarily in charge of domestic operations. Military Intelligence was set up to spy on the Iraqi armed forces, gather intelligence on foreign countries, monitor the activities of Iraqis living abroad, and arrange assassinations of Iraqi dissidents in exile. Finally,

Special Security was based at the presidential palace and provided Saddam with information on key government officials.

The fact that there were this many security agencies points to the leadership's obsession with political control. It also reflects Saddam's reliance on divide-and-rule tactics as a way of preventing any single institution from becoming a threat to his personal power. Thus, the various intelligence agencies were given overlapping responsibilities, and they were instructed to spy not only on the population, the bureaucracy, the party, the army, and foreign countries, but also on one another.

Public Policy

Because of its oil, Iraq has a greater economic potential than most Third World countries. Unfortunately, Iraq's resources were squandered by a leadership that chose to use them to try to make Iraq the most powerful country in the Arab world. To fulfill this ambition, Saddam Hussein led Iraq into the disastrous wars that cost him his regime and his life. Thus, Iraqis have suffered not only defeat in war but also continued poverty, both of which could have been avoided if Saddam had been less aggressive and intransigent.

Economic Reform

When the Baath Party seized power in 1968, its ambiguous socialist rhetoric did not include a strategy for stimulating economic growth. Yet the absence of a concrete economic agenda did not really disturb the new elite, whose first priority was neither economic nor social, but political.

During the Baath's first decade in power, the leadership used economic policy primarily as a tool to consolidate power. It is in this light that we should examine the tremendous increase in the state's economic role before the wars eliminated any chance of reform in domestic policy.

By the late 1970s, about 25 percent of the economically active population worked in government-related jobs. The leadership used the public sector as an employer of last resort in an attempt to bolster popular support. At the same time, the nationalization of many key businesses, the tightening of state regulations over industry and trade, and the extensive land reform measures of 1970 were also designed to increase the regime's control over the population.

The expansion of the public sector, however, was expensive. Financing it was made possible by the quadrupling of oil prices in 1973 and the nationalization of the oil industry the year before. The regime suddenly found itself the beneficiary of unprecedented oil revenues. It used them not only to increase state control but also to modernize the country and to extend basic social services to most of the population.

During the 1970s and 1980s, the state's modernizing policies radically changed the face of Iraq. In two short decades the country's infrastructure was improved. Modern highways, bridges, airports, and hotels were built. Irrigation systems were developed, and electricity and running water were expanded in rural areas whose residents could only have dreamed of having such services just a few years earlier. Suddenly, people in the countryside had television sets and refrigerators, sometimes handed out by the government. The fact that much of the country's infrastructure was destroyed during the first two wars should not keep us from seeing how much the Baath rulers were able to accomplish.

Oil revenues also enabled the Baath leadership to provide the population with an impressive array of social services. Poverty was reduced considerably. University graduates were guaranteed a job in the bureaucracy. The middle class grew. The state made large tracts of government-owned land available at low prices. Unemployment all but disappeared. Legislation was enacted to benefit workers. Rent controls were put into effect to guarantee access to housing. Basic commodities were heavily subsidized by the state.

The leadership also improved the condition of women in a country in which they traditionally have suffered fewer social restrictions than in the rest of the Persian Gulf region. Daycare centers were built. New laws banned discrimination against women in the workplace, guaranteed them the same salaries as men, and mandated paid maternity leave. By the late 1970s these measures had yielded significant results, with more women employed in the professions and the civil service than ever before. Further, following the outbreak of the war with Iran, women joined the labor force to replace men sent to the front.

The state also sought to improve educational and health services, which it provided free of charge. The government spent an unprecedented amount of money to train nurses and physicians, and it expanded the number of clinics and hospitals in rural areas that had been neglected by earlier governments. These efforts produced significant improvements in public health. Iraqis born in 1984 could expect to live an average of eight to nine years longer than those born two decades earlier. Meanwhile, infant mortality rates decreased from 140 to 80 per 1,000 live births between 1960 and 1981. Schools, universities, and technical institutes were built or expanded. The number of primary school graduates doubled between 1973 and 1979. During the same period, the number of who finished secondary schools tripled, and the number of university and technical institute degree holders jumped to eighteen thousand a year. The efforts made at the level of secondary education were particularly remarkable because the percentage of the eligible Iraqis enrolled in secondary schools rose from 38 percent in 1976 to 67 percent in 1984.

Realizing that adult illiteracy remained high, the government also launched a literacy campaign in 1978. In its characteristically heavy-handed way, the regime forced all illiterates between the ages of fifteen and forty-five to participate. Public buildings were put at the disposal of the campaign, and efforts were made to reach the most remote corners of the country. Marsh dwellers were forced to attend "floating schools," while nomads were assigned to "traveling schools." To facilitate participation by mothers, hundreds of new nurseries were built. This massive effort paid off. Many women received their first formal education. Within just a few years, hundreds of thousands of Iraqis learned to read and write.

Thus, during its first decade in power, the Baath contributed substantially to the socioeconomic development of Iraq. Unfortunately, these results were achieved through rigid repression and systematic political indoctrination akin to that practiced by the Soviets under Stalin. Moreover, Saddam could have improved the living standards of his people even more had it not been for his diversion of Iraq's resources to the development of the agencies of repression and a massive arms buildup that consumed more than 40 percent of the budget from the 1980s onward.

Most important, the prosperity of the 1970s had been due not to an increase in productivity or to a diversification or expansion of the economy, but to the massive injection of oil revenues. Oil money, however, could not compensate indefinitely for the structural weaknesses of the economy that were increasingly apparent by the end of the decade.

In an effort to address these problems and improve economic performance, the authorities moved toward economic liberalization when Saddam became president. Many farms and state-owned service industries were sold. The government encouraged foreign investment and reduced the bureaucracy's cumbersome controls.

Unfortunately, economic liberalization primarily benefited a group of speculators with connections to the regime. Industrial production stagnated, shortages of essential goods plagued the country, and black markets in consumer goods and currencies flourished.

Even more important, after the invasion of Kuwait, it was impossible to talk about any kind of coherent economic policy in Iraq. Almost all disposable income went to the military. Iraq also had to endure the sanctions mentioned in the introduction that largely kept it out of global markets and sharply limited the amount of oil it could sell. Last but by no means least, Saddam and his entourage diverted as much as half of the income that was brought in through the UN oil for food program to the pocketbooks of the elite.

Iraq's Wars: Political Suicide

The subordination of Iraq's welfare to Saddam's personal ambitions was not limited to domestic policy. Even more important were the decisions that took the country to war three times in fifteen years (see Table 14.3).

The Iran-Iraq War

Iran and Iraq had long been rivals. To some extent, this stems from the religious and ethnic differences discussed earlier. However, tensions between the two countries also exist because of their competition for power in the Persian Gulf and the Middle East as a whole.

Until the late 1960s, the British military presence in the Gulf had helped prevent the hostility between the two countries from degenerating into open warfare. However, when the British announced that they would withdraw their military forces east of Suez by 1971, the rivalry between Iran and Iraq intensified.

By that time, Iran was the more powerful of the two. Its population was about three times and its area almost four times that of Iraq. It was also wealthier and more developed. Perhaps most important of all, the shah had benefited from military and economic support from a succession of American administrations that decided to use his regime as the pillar of its policy in the Gulf.

In the late 1960s, the shah rekindled a long-standing border dispute with Iraq. Since 1937, the internationally recognized border between the two countries had been the Iranian bank of the Shatt al-Arab River, which gave Iraq exclusive control over it. In 1969, the shah unilaterally abrogated that treaty and announced that Iran would now recognize the border along the middle of the waterway's main channel, in effect claiming sovereignty over half the river.

Tensions continued to build. In 1970, an Iranian-sponsored coup was foiled in Baghdad. Meanwhile, with support from the United States, the shah began to project himself as the strongman of the Gulf. In November 1971, Iran occupied three islands strategically located at the entrance of the Strait of Hormuz off the coast of the United Arab Emirates (UAE). In retaliation, Iraq cut off diplomatic relations with Tehran.

Much more threatening to Baghdad, however, was Iranian support for a Kurdish uprising in Iraq. The rebellion threatened the new Baathist government, which led it to make a major concession to Iran. At an **Organization for Petroleum Exporting Countries (OPEC)** meeting in Algiers in March 1975, Saddam negotiated an agreement with the shah that called for an end to Iranian support for the Iraqi Kurds in exchange for Baghdad's recognition of Iran's claim to half of the Shatt al-Arab.

In 1979, however, Iranian-Iraqi relations took a turn for the worse. The overthrow of the shah and the establishment of the Islamic Republic headed by Ayatollah Ruhollah Khomeini created an entirely new situation in the Persian Gulf (see Chapter 13). Soon, Iraqi authorities were accusing the Islamic Republic of interference—claims that were not unfounded. Meddling by Tehran was threatening to the Baath because Iraqi Shiites were increasingly alienated from the government in Baghdad. Yet despite clear evidence of Iranian involvement, it is hard to accept Iraq's claim that it started the Iran-Iraq War in self-defense. In many ways it was little more than a bid for regional hegemony by Saddam.

The 1979 Camp David Accords and Egyptian President Anwar Sadat's peace treaty with Israel left Egypt—traditionally the most influential country in Arab politics—ostracized by the rest of the Arab world. Saddam, who had led the opposition to the normalization of relations between Israel and Egypt, must have realized that oil-rich Iraq now had a unique opportunity to establish itself as a leading Arab power. He also had to have noticed the effects of the ongoing revolutionary turmoil in Tehran. The Iranian officer corps had been decimated in the wave of purges and executions that followed the shah's downfall. Given reports about the declining morale in the Iranian military, Saddam assumed that a sudden Iraqi attack could provoke the fall of the Iranian government. Whatever the exact set of motivations, the Iraqi army did invade Iran in September 1980. Unfortunately for Iraq, the Iranian army did not disintegrate, and the Islamic Republic in Tehran survived by gaining the enthusiastic support of most Iranians who rallied around the regime. Far from being the short campaign that Saddam envisioned, the war turned into a protracted and bloody stalemate.

It lasted eight years and was the deadliest conflict in the history of the modern Middle East. As many as a million Iraqis and Iranians died. Hundreds of thousands more were disabled. Virtually no Iraqi family was spared. All too many parents had several children die at the front.

It was also one of the most futile conflicts in history. It was largely caused by the personal hatred between two tyrants, each aspiring for regional leadership and imbued with a messianic conception of himself. Saddam saw Khomeini's revolutionary zeal and mixture of religion and

TABLE 14.3 Iraq's First Two Wars Under Saddam Hussein: A Chronology

1980	Iraq invades Iran
1982	Iran drives Iraqi army back into Iraq
	Saddam expresses willingness to end conflict, but Iran refuses
1984	Iraq restores diplomatic relations with United States
1986	Iranian troops capture Fao Peninsula
1988	Cease-fire with Iran is signed
1990	Iraq invades Kuwait
	United Nations Security Council authorizes anti-Iraq coalition
1991	Gulf War

politics as a dangerous threat that could be eliminated only through the annihilation of the man and the regime he had created. Khomeini, in turn, perceived Saddam as the archetypical modernizing, secular leader who had betrayed Islam and who had to be eradicated. Khomeini also had personal accounts to settle with Saddam. At the shah's request, Saddam had Khomeini expelled from the Shiite holy city of Najaf in 1978, where he had lived and taught for fourteen years. By 1981, Khomeini had made the ouster of Saddam from power one of the preconditions for a cease-fire. His refusal to compromise combined with Saddam's equally adamant refusal to step down, largely explains why the war lasted so long.

To justify this senseless and increasingly bloody war, both regimes engaged in extravagant and self-serving rhetoric. Thus, Baghdad described the war as a valiant defense of the "Arab homeland" against the "fanatic Persians," the "Persian racists," or the "fire-eating Persians." For its part, Tehran portrayed the war as a jihad against "Baathist infidels" who had betrayed Islam and were oppressing Iran's Shiite brethren in Iraq.

After eight years of fighting, Iranian and Iraqi forces were stuck almost exactly where they had been when the war started. Neither country had achieved its aims. Exhausted and lacking viable alternatives, the Islamic Republic finally agreed to sign a cease-fire for which Iraq had long been pleading.

The First Gulf War

Upon seizing power, the Baath immediately launched a propaganda campaign against Israel and the United States. Then, in 1972, feeling increasingly threatened by the pro-Western

Women in Iraqi Politics

Oddly enough, women have not been discriminated against to the same extent and in the same ways as those in Iran since 1979. As noted earlier, even under the Baath, women were heavily represented in higher education and the professions.

But politics at the highest level remains a man's "game." The new regime established a goal (some say quota) that 30 percent of all legislative candidates should be women. So far, the plateau has not been reached, and few of the women who have run have been taken seriously. That is especially true in rural areas where female candidates rarely appear in public, which, of course, makes it hard for them to campaign. A few women candidates were killed, perhaps by Islamists who objected to seeing photographs of them. Perhaps because of pressure from the United States and Iraqi officials, it actually ranks 39th on the Interparliamentary Union's list of women in the lower house of parliament, which puts it 30 places ahead of the United States.

There is a small feminist movement in Iraq, but many critics believe it was inspired and is led by American feminists. That strikes us both as highly unlikely.

regime of the shah, Iraq signed a Treaty of Friendship and Cooperation with the Soviet Union. This development caused alarm in Washington, where it was interpreted as a sign that Iraq had become a Soviet puppet, giving it a foothold in the strategically important and oil-rich Gulf region.

Saddam Hussein and his family during happier times. The photo includes his two brothers-in-law, who defected in 1995 and then were killed the following February.

AP Images

Meanwhile, Baghdad also offered support to extremist Palestinian factions and adopted a confrontational stance toward the moderate, pro-Western Arab states in the Gulf.

From the mid-1970s onward, however, Iraq's relations with the Arab Gulf states improved because it distanced itself from the Soviet Union after the latter's invasion of Afghanistan in 1979. It also developed closer ties with a few Western European countries—in particular, France, which became its major arms supplier.

The outbreak of the war changed things even more. Desperate for financial, political, and military support from Arab and Western states, Iraq toned down its militant rhetoric and began portraying itself as a bulwark against Iran's attempt to export its revolution to the Arab world. Within a few months, Egypt, Jordan, Saudi Arabia, and the smaller Gulf states cast their lot with Iraq. Weapons, spare parts, munitions, military advisers, and migrant workers began to flow into the country. Even more decisive was the $40 billion in aid for Iraq's war effort sent by the Gulf states.

Relations with the United States improved. The Reagan administration was interested in improving relations with Baghdad out of fear that an Iranian victory would result in the spread of Khomeini's version of Islam throughout the Arab world. The United States provided a limited amount of ostensibly nonmilitary aid, although the computers it sent, for instance, could be used for military as well as civilian purposes. By 1987 Baghdad had become the world's largest recipient of U.S. agricultural loans, the biggest single overseas buyer of American rice, and one of the largest importers of American wheat and corn. Washington also supplied intelligence data on the movement of Iranian troops.

When hostilities between Iran and Iraq came to an end in 1988, the prevailing view was that Iraq was now led by a reformed, moderate, and pragmatic regime. Further, from Washington's perspective, Iraq was seen as a necessary counterweight to Iran. For the next two years, Western governments were willing to turn a blind eye to the continuing repression and human rights violations in Iraq and the mounting indications that the country was still expansionist.

But only for two years. In 1990, Iraq made a new bid for leadership of the Arab world. As in the past, this was most evident in the upsurge in anti-Western and anti-Israeli rhetoric.

At a meeting of Arab states that February, Saddam gave his most virulent anti-American speech in more than a decade. He pointed out that the end of the Cold War had left the United States in an unprecedented position to exert power over Arab states and to encourage Israeli aggression against them.

Barely a month later, an Iranian-born journalist working for a British magazine was arrested while investigating an explosion at a missile plant near Baghdad. Accused of spying for Israel and forced into making a confession, he was tried, convicted, and hanged within a week. Throughout that spring, evidence mounted that Iraq was trying to smuggle in nuclear weapons technology from the West, accelerate the development of biological and chemical weapons facilities, and build a long-range artillery piece dubbed the "Supergun." In April, fearful that Israel was planning strikes against Iraqi nuclear or chemical operations, as it had done ten years previously, Saddam made a fiery speech claiming that if Israel attacked Iraq, Baghdad would retaliate with a chemical attack that would "burn half of Israel."

Saddam Hussein reserved his sharpest attacks for the Gulf states. For eight years, he argued, Iraq had shed "rivers of blood" to protect the Gulf dynasties and the "Arab homeland" against Khomeini's revolutionary zeal. Yet, despite Baghdad's repeated requests, the oil-rich Arab states remained unwilling to cancel Iraq's war debt or provide it with funds to rebuild its economy. Such intransigence, Saddam contended, was an insult to Iraq and its war dead.

Meanwhile, Kuwait and the United Arab Emirates continued to exceed their oil production quotas as determined by OPEC, driving down prices and depriving Iraq of much-needed revenues. Saddam claimed that excess pumping by the Gulf states had already cost Iraq $84 billion, which he took to be evidence that the small Gulf states were engaged in a plot against the country hatched by "imperialist and Zionist forces." Infuriated by what he saw as the arrogance of the Gulf rulers, Saddam pressed them even harder, asking for $30 billion in additional grants.

He also charged Kuwait with stealing Iraq's oil by pumping from the Rumaila field, which lies mostly beneath Iraqi territory but stretches just across the border into Kuwait. Iraq also revived its old demand to be given or leased the two Kuwaiti islands of Warbah and Bubiyan to give it a deep-water port. The Kuwaiti emir failed to take the threats seriously and worded his refusal of Saddam's demands in language that was highly critical of Iraq. This, combined with his belief that the United States would not be able to reverse an Iraqi takeover of Kuwait, sealed the tiny nation's fate. He appears to have believed that Saudi Arabia would never allow U.S. troops on Saudi soil, leaving the United States with no way of forcing Iraq out of Kuwait.

On August 2, 1990, one hundred thousand Iraqi troops invaded Kuwait and took over the country in a mere six hours. By seizing its neighbor, Iraq would not only automatically eliminate its debt to it but also suddenly control about 20 percent of the world's proven oil reserves. Kuwait's wealth also would enable Iraq to repay its debt to Western European countries and to launch ambitious new development programs. Iraq's regional position also would be greatly enhanced by the annexation of Kuwait, which he could present as a successful "reconquest" of lands that Iraq

Globalization
and Iraq

Iraq is one of the few countries where the impact of globalization has been felt more as a result of political than economic forces.

Of course, globalization has had an economic impact. The United Nations imposed sanctions before the first Gulf War that continued for the most part until the 2003 defeat, which meant that most Iraqis did not have access, for instance, to adequate medical care. Many, too, had at most marginally acceptable diets. Estimates vary, but somewhere between a hundred thousand and a million Iraqis died because of easily treatable diseases and malnutrition during that twelve-year period.

Today, Iraq is not fully a part of the global system, especially economically. For instance, as early as 2007, National Public Radio reported that Iraqis had to import everything from disposable cigarette lighters to water pumps. By contrast, it exports little other than oil. ■

had long claimed were rightly its own. Finally, by providing Iraq with a major port on the Gulf, the takeover of Kuwait would reduce its economic and military vulnerability.

Yet, despite what he may have expected, the international community responded with an unusual degree of unity and demanded the immediate, unconditional withdrawal of Iraqi forces from Kuwait. Far from limiting itself to a verbal condemnation, the United States took the lead in the international campaign. To Saddam's even greater surprise, the Soviet Union joined Washington in condemning Baghdad. France, the European country closest to Iraq, also insisted on an Iraqi withdrawal. The Arabs were split. Saddam, who had hoped that the Arab world would rally behind him, suddenly faced an alliance that included several key Arab states, including Egypt and Syria. Over three-quarters of a million allied troops, including more than five hundred thousand Americans, were sent to the region as part of **Operation Desert Shield** in an attempt to convince Iraq to pull out of Kuwait.

Saddam still could have backed down. Instead, he decided to leave his forces in Kuwait, confident that the United States would not go to war over the emirate, that Arab states would never dare ally with the United States against "Brotherly Iraq," and that, if they did, people throughout the Arab world would rise up in Baghdad's defense. He turned out to be wrong on all three counts.

Repeated attempts to reach a negotiated settlement failed in part because of Saddam's belief in the primacy of coercion and intimidation over diplomacy and negotiation.

Iraqis examining a ruined cruise missile during the Gulf War.

AP Photo/Salah Nasrawi

Unlike those who see the use of force as a last resort, the Baathist leaders saw concessions as a sign of weakness and accordingly believed that compromise should be resisted unless one has absolutely no other option.

The United States launched **Operation Desert Storm** on January 17, 1991. They were backed by a broad coalition of the world's most powerful nations, including many in the Gulf region. Arabs throughout the region did not rise up in defense of Iraq. By early March, less than a year after Iraqi tanks had rolled into Kuwait and only forty days after the beginning of the war, Iraq had been transformed from a major regional power into a devastated country, subject to the dictates of the UN and the U.S.-led coalition.

After that, the Iraqi regime at best grudgingly complied with UN resolutions that compelled it to disclose and dismantle its weapons of mass destruction. It allegedly tried to assassinate former U.S. president George H. W. Bush during his visit to Kuwait in April 1993. It interfered repeatedly with the work of inspection teams sent to monitor Iraqi compliance with UN resolutions. And, it continued to support terror as an instrument of state policy and failed to cease its brutal repression of the Iraqi people as required by UN Security Council Resolution 688.

When Iraqi forces withdrew from Kuwait and surrendered several days later, the Allies were faced with a choice. They could suspend their own offensive operations, or they could push on to Baghdad and force Saddam Hussein from power.

President Bush and his colleagues chose the first option. There are three generally accepted reasons for their decision. First, the mandate given for the use of force by the coalition was limited to freeing Kuwait, and Bush, therefore, did not feel he had the legal authority to continue the fight. Second, Bush's advisors told him that a drive to capture Baghdad would be far bloodier than the war had been so far, which had claimed fewer than two hundred American lives, many of them through accidents or friendly fire. From what we have seen since the end of major hostilities in May 2003, the first President Bush's advisors were probably correct. Third, and probably most important, the Bush administration expected Kurds and Shiites, if not Sunni Arabs, to rise up and topple the regime.

Bush's hoped-for rebellions did break out, but they did not have the results he wanted. Saddam's forces responded with the kind of brutality the world had come to expect of his government. Iraqi troops battled Kurdish insurgents and recovered large parts of their region until allied forces returned to create safe havens and turned the area into an autonomous region that largely remained beyond Baghdad's control for the rest of his rule. If anything, Iraqi troops were even crueler in the south. Among other things, they drained the swamps, which were a vital part of the ecology and economy on which millions of Shiites depended.

Eventually, a bombing campaign forced the regime's troops to leave the region. A no-fly zone was established over the Shiite and Kurdish regions where Iraqi military planes could no longer operate.

Nonetheless, Saddam remained in power. His military, of course, was much weaker, but there seemed to be few signs that he could be overthrown, despite explicit attempts by the West to create a viable opposition in the exile community.

The first Gulf War accomplished little more than restoring the independence of Kuwait. It would be another dozen years before the United States decided to end Baath Rule and embark on the transition to a new regime.

After the war, the West pursued what international relations scholars call a policy of containment. Economic sanctions remained in place, denying Iraq the ability to sell oil or buy almost anything in global markets. Those rules were eased a bit in 1996 when Iraq was permitted to sell a limited amount of oil, ostensibly to buy food, medicine, and other humanitarian supplies (see Table 14.4).

Allied forces also flew hundreds of thousands of sorties over Iraqi airspace. Any time an Iraqi antiaircraft locked onto an allied aircraft, the allied plane would launch tons of bombs, even though there was next to no chance that the Iraqi batteries could hit one of the planes.

Of all the issues troubling Iraq's relations with the rest of the world, nothing was more important or more indicative of the cat-and-mouse game the regime played with the international community about its **weapons of mass destruction (WMD)** program. The **United Nations Special Commission (UNSCOM)** was created in the wake of the Gulf War to monitor Iraq's compliance with

TABLE 14.4 Wars in Iraq: 1990–2009

YEAR	EVENT
1990	Iraq occupies Kuwait
1991	First Gulf War
1992	Iraqis allegedly try to assassinate former U.S. President George H. W. Bush
1994	Iraq drains the marshes in the south
1996	Oil for food program authorized by the United Nations
1997–98	UNSCOM forced to leave
1999	Bombings of Iraqi
2001	9/11 terrorist attacks
2002	George W. Bush implicates Iraq in his "axis of evil" State of the Union speech
2003	U.S.-led invasion topples Saddam Hussein's regime; insurgency breaks out almost immediately and continues
2005	Constitution drafted and first elections held
2007	American surge of additional troops
2009	Start of American withdrawal

United Nations Special Commission (UNSCOM) inspectors examine suspected chemical and biological warheads.

the cease-fire resolution that called for the elimination of its WMD programs. According to the terms of this resolution, the embargo on Iraq would be lifted once UNSCOM certified that Iraq had fully disarmed. UNSCOM relied on spot inspections of sites suspected of being locations where WMD were manufactured or stored. Once inspected, these sites would remain closely monitored using sophisticated surveillance equipment.

Between 1991 and 1998, UNSCOM proved quite effective. Tons of chemical and biological weapons were located and destroyed. Still, in late 1998, most experts thought that Iraq was still hiding some stockpiles. That December, Baghdad stopped cooperating with UNSCOM. It claimed that some of UNSCOM's members, including the commission's leader, Australian diplomat Richard Butler, were American agents (which could possibly have been true). In addition, the regime argued that, even if UNSCOM certified that all Iraqi WMD had been eliminated, the United States would still refuse to lift the sanctions on Iraq as long as Saddam remained in power.

The Iraqi government's refusal to allow UNSCOM to operate prompted a four-day bombing campaign by American and British forces. Shortly thereafter, Baghdad announced that UNSCOM inspectors would never be allowed back into the country. The UN Security Council and the Iraqi government were unable to agree on a new way of inspecting that either could accept 🌐 (**www.un.org/Depts/ unscom**).

When UNSCOM was forced out, many outside observers thought that Iraq still possessed some chemical and biological weapons, had the capacity to make many more of them quickly, and that its ongoing nuclear program had led Iraq to be dangerously close to developing a nuclear bomb. Saddam said nothing to indicate otherwise, which, as we will see, contributed heavily to his ultimate defeat.

But, it is safe to say that Iraq was not seen as one of the world's most dangerous places until 9/11. And even then, the reaction that led to war came only from Washington and London, not the other major Western capitals.

Meanwhile, the coalition formed in 1991 had already begun to unravel. Some of the allies thought the policy of containment was working well enough that Iraq was no longer a threat to its neighbors or anyone else. Others, most notably France and Russia, wanted to ease or even eliminate sanctions because of their economic ties to Iraq that had been interrupted following the invasion of Kuwait.

The Final War

The terrorist attacks on the World Trade Center and the Pentagon changed everything as far as the George W. Bush administration was concerned. It had already been critical of what it saw as the weakness of many previous policies, including the containment of Iraq. But the day before the attacks, there was no reason to believe that major changes in the way the United States dealt with Iraq were forthcoming.

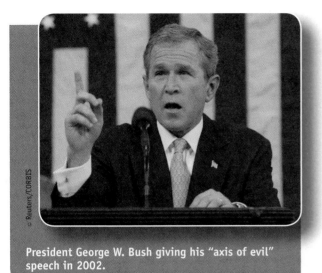

President George W. Bush giving his "axis of evil" speech in 2002.

© Reuters/CORBIS

Bush's response to the attacks was surprising, at least to his critics. After a few hours of uncertainty, his first public statements on and after 9/11 reflected a resolve and a firmness few thought he could muster. That was evident in the massive support given to the decision to go to war to topple the Taliban regime and undermine the al-Qaeda networks it harbored less than a month after 9/11.

There are also rumors that President Bush and Vice President Dick Cheney decided on the night of 9/11 or the next morning that war with Iraq was all but inevitable. As the stories go, it seems that both assumed that no war against terrorism could be won as long as Saddam and the Baath regime remained in power.

We may never know when the most critical decisions about Iraq were made. Nonetheless, it was clear by the time that Bush gave his 2002 State of the Union speech that Iraq was his highest priority. Bush certainly did not mince his words when discussing North Korea, Iran, and Iraq, which he labeled an "axis of evil." Regarding Iraq, he stated:

> Iraq continues to flaunt its hostility toward America and to support terror. The Iraqi regime has plotted to develop anthrax, and nerve gas, and nuclear weapons for over a decade. This is a regime that has already used poison to murder thousands of its own citizens—leaving the bodies of mothers huddled over their dead children. This is a regime that agreed to international inspections—then kicked out the inspectors. This is a regime that has something to hide from the civilized world.
>
> States like these, and their terrorist allies, constitute an axis of evil, arming to threaten the peace of the world. By seeking weapons of mass destruction, these regimes pose a grave and growing danger. They could provide these arms to terrorists, giving

them the means to match their hatred. They could attack our allies or attempt to blackmail the United States. In any of these cases, the price of indifference would be catastrophic.

As Bush's speech indicated, American accusations about Iraq revolved around three main themes.

- Iraq still had a stockpile of WMD. It may have had fewer than it did a decade earlier, but it not only had weapons but had the capacity to add new ones to its arsenal, possibly including primitive nuclear bombs.

- It had close ties to terrorist organizations that it had frequently supported over the years and to which it could supply such weapons.

- Therefore, Iraq was a threat not only to the existence of Israel and the stability of the Middle East but to global security in general.

Each of those claims was questioned by Bush's critics in the United States, Iraq, and beyond.

Even if Iraq had weapons of mass destruction, its stockpiles were far below 1990 and 1991 levels. It was also not clear that the material it had tried to buy illegally abroad were for these and other weapons programs. But perhaps most important of all, there were no signs that Iraq had any plans to transfer those weapons to terrorist or other dangerous organizations.

There was no doubt that Iraq had supported and harbored some militant Palestinian terrorists who were committed to destroying the state of Israel, but these were not the people or organizations who were responsible for the 9/11 attacks. There were reports that one of the leaders of the hijackings had met with Iraqi intelligence officials in the Czech Republic, but that was never confirmed. What is more, the kinds of people who joined al-Qaeda networks were highly critical of secular leaders like Saddam.

Few observers doubted that Saddam still harbored hopes that Iraq could become a regional power. However, most intelligence reports indicated that Iraq's military capacity had been seriously eroded by the 1991 war and its aftermath and probably did not pose a serious threat to its neighbors, let alone Israel and the rest of the world.

It is beyond the scope of this book to speculate on why the Bush administration continued to rely on the worst possible estimates of Iraqi capabilities and intentions (though see any of the books listed in the Further Reading section at the end of the chapter). Neither the Bush administration nor the authorities in Baghdad showed any serious interest in cooperation or even negotiation.

Tensions continued to mount. In May 2002, the United States prevented $5 billion of humanitarian aid and other supplies from entering Iraq. Four months later, Bush used his address to the General Assembly of the UN to attack

AP Images

On December 2 2003, U.S. helicopters flew over the area as workers dismantle one of the four giant bronze busts of Saddam Hussein that long dominated Baghdad's skyline, in yet another move aimed at eradicating the former leader's influence in Baghdad.

what he called the "grave and gathering danger" of Iraq. He charged that if the UN did not do so, it would become "irrelevant."

A month later, the U.S. Congress overwhelmingly voted to authorize the use of force in Iraq if need be. In November, the UN Security Council passed Resolution 1441, which found Iraq to be in "material breach" of its resolutions on WMD, and inspectors were allowed into the country once again. In early December, Iraq submitted an all but indecipherable report that claimed it had no such weapons.

Just before Christmas 2002, President Bush authorized sending troops to the region, a force that reached two hundred thousand by March 2003. But this time, the coalition did not hold. During late February and the first half of March, the United States and Great Britain lobbied for a new UN resolution allowing the use of force. In order for the resolution to pass, they needed nine of the fifteen members of the Security Council to vote in favor of using force; they would also have to convince every permanent member of the Security Council not to veto the action. France, Germany, Russia, China, and others refused to back sending troops at that time. Furthermore, all but Germany had veto power in the Security Council and made it clear that they would block any authorization of the use of force until and unless it was completely clear that inspectors could not defuse the crisis. Bush would not wait nor would Saddam. In early 2003, the United States was leading a much smaller coalition than it had twelve years earlier. The only other major power willing to commit a significant number of troops was the United Kingdom.

When it became clear that they would not come close to getting the necessary votes, the United States abandoned its campaign at the UN on March 14. Three days later, the British ambassador declared diplomatic efforts had failed. Bush gave Saddam and his family forty-eight hours to leave the country. They did not.

Two days later, on March 20, the military offensive dubbed **Operation Iraqi Freedom** began without UN authorization. It started with three days of air attacks on Baghdad and other high-priority targets aimed at "decapitating" the Iraqi leadership. Unlike the first Gulf War, the air-only phase of this struggle was very brief. On March 21, troops began to move toward Baghdad, which fell on April 9. On May 1, after flying a plane onto an aircraft carrier himself, Bush declared the end of major combat operations.

Little did he know....

THE NEW IRAQ

The end of the formal war did not turn out the way the Bush administration had expected. Its leaders assumed that American and allied troops would be cheered as liberators and that they could all but immediately begin the transition to a new and more democratic Iraq.

It did not happen.

Instead, several insurgencies broke out against the American occupiers, including one by a group that called itself al-Qaeda in Iraq. There was also widespread violence between Sunni and Shia in those rare places where they lived near each other, such as the Sadr City neighborhood of Baghdad, which had previously been known as Saddam City.

The one thing the war and occupation did produce was a change in regimes. It, too, did not go smoothly, as we are about to see. The United States did not expect to have trouble administering Iraq, and therefore, it was ill prepared to deal with everything from the country's devastated infrastructure to the insurgency, let alone state building.

None of this surprised the NGOs who had been warning the administration about what might happen after victory on the battlefield. Many senior military planners also realized how much trouble the United States might be in for. For whatever reason, the administration chose not to listen, not only to the NGO community but also to the advice of some senior officers and diplomats who had doubts about the ease with which the coalition would manage the postwar transition.

It did not start out all that badly. After a few missteps, the United States appointed a veteran diplomat, **Paul Bremer**, to head the civil administration in Iraq. Ironically, the headquarters of Bremer's operation was in one of Saddam's lavish palaces, newly dubbed the Green Zone. Virtually nothing he and his team tried seemed to work. It may well be that someone far more competent than Bremer would have come up against the same obstacles on which we will spend a lot more time here.

From the beginning, it was clear that the occupation forces were in for a hard time. At first, they faced widespread lawlessness that included looting of banks and even of historical treasures from Baghdad's museums. British and other troops in the Shiite south faced less widespread, but still serious, discontent. Only in the Kurdish-dominated north were things reasonably calm. The occupation forces

also tried to track down, capture, or kill the remaining leaders from the old regime. After Baghdad fell, the U.S. Department of Defense issued its "deck of cards" that listed the top fifty-two leaders still at large. Saddam, of course, was the ace of spades 🌐 (**www.defenselink.mil/news /Apr2003/pipc10042003.html**).

The cards were not just a publicity stunt. They were given to American troops in the field so that they would have a reasonable chance of identifying Baathists on the run—they would learn the faces by playing cards, which is a time-honored pastime of bored, off-duty soldiers. This was the one area where the occupation forces were reasonably successful, although the hunt absorbed tremendous amounts of time and energy.

The toll taken on the Baath regime truly was enormous. All but four of the "cards" were captured; many have been executed. To cite but the most obvious examples, Saddam's two sons were surrounded on 22 July 2003 and killed. Saddam was captured in an underground hideout that December. It took three years before he was convicted and hung at the end of December 2006.

On the three other fronts, the occupation forces and civil administrators had a harder time.

Regime Change

Whatever else one might think of his policies, President Bush got one thing right. He provoked the most abrupt regime change (his term, as well as ours) we will see in this book.

There have been others. But in Russia, the change took a few years and a few referenda. In South Africa (an online chapter), it also took time and occurred largely through the cooperation between the apartheid regime and its foes.

In this case, however, regime change occurred virtually overnight, was imposed from abroad, and led to a leadership that had few ties to the Iraqi people.

Political scientists who study democratization would argue that this was almost exactly the wrong way to do things.

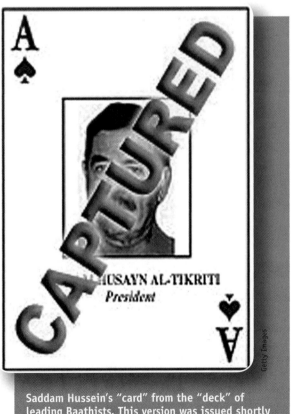

Saddam Hussein's "card" from the "deck" of leading Baathists. This version was issued shortly after his capture.

First, in part because of the civil unrest and in part because of the extent of the destruction, it took much longer than expected to rebuild even the most basic components of Iraq's infrastructure. In late 2004, when Baghdad's main electrical generation plant was returned to Iraqi control, the city still did not have a reliable electrical supply. It did not have it yet in summer 2011. Equipment destined for rebuilding the power plants and the grid either disappeared or was destroyed.

Second, the United States was never able to find any WMD or even any evidence that the government had been working on them in the months before the invasion. At the end of 2004, the State Department announced that the search was over. One of the consequences of that was that the United States and the occupation lost ever more credibility in world opinion.

The Three Block and Long War

The American military began worrying about protracted conflicts in places like Iraq in the 1990s.

Toward the end of the decade, General Charles Krulak, commandant of the Marine Corps, began writing about a three-block war in which Marines and soldiers would confront armed resistance, peacekeeping operations, and reconstruction challenges in the same neighborhood at the same time. A few years later, the Defense Science Board issued a report suggesting that any such set of operations was likely to take at least a decade to finish.

In more recent years, the idea has been taken on by General **David Petraeus** and the COIN (Counterinsurgency) policy he champions which downplays the use of force and emphasizes winning the hearts and minds of the people in general.

Iraq was the first test case.

The third and most vexing problem facing the occupation and the new government was the insurrection, which we will discuss in the section on political participation.

At this point, we can best pursue our analysis of Iraq using the systems model that we have used in all other chapters and which will show just how fragile Iraq is more than eight years after the invasion and occupation.

Culture and Participation in Iraq

Political Culture

It is less than a decade since Saddam and his regime collapsed. In other words, we should not expect Iraq's political culture to have changed all that much so quickly.

For good or ill, the neo-cons in the Bush administration thought that the Iraqi culture harbored a lot of anti-Saddam sentiment that was waiting to "come out" and would make his overthrow popular and ease what they expected to be a short Allied occupation.

That may have been true in one sense. Saddam was widely disliked by many in Iraq. Yet, the invasion and overthrow of the regime exacerbated the ethnic and religious differences. The Kurds, in particular, had already established an autonomous region in the north and participate only episodically in national politics.

The Insurgency

Secretary Rumsfeld's belief that the Iraqis would embrace the American troops as liberators and that only a skeletal force would remain for only a short while evaporated within days.

Within a few weeks a more or less organized insurgency took shape. Perhaps it would be better to put the term in the plural, insurgencies. The most difficult of them all was centered among the Sunni. Some were Saddam loyalists. Others were frustrated by the fact that they would certainly lose power under a Shiite-led government. Others yet may not even have been Iraqis but were at least loosely tied to al-Qaeda.

The insurgents established strongholds throughout the so-called Sunni Triangle in central Iraq. From them, it launched attacks on American forces and on targets thought to be collaborating with the occupiers. The insurgents who had been Saddamists often took their weapons with them when the regime changed. To that end, most observers now think that the U.S. made a mistake by dismantling the army rather than just purging its most senior leaders with the closest ties to the Baath.

Insurgents who did not have access to such weapons relied on more primitive ones that came to be known as improvised explosive devices (IEDs). They would plant them near roads the Americans used to send convoys with troops and goods and set them off in a seemingly random manner.

More systematic fighting occurred in some of them, especially in Falluja in al-Anbar province west of Baghdad. It was all but totally controlled by the insurgents under al-Qaeda control. The Americans decided they had to wrest control of the city that sat on a major road out of the country. Therefore, in 2004, it launched a campaign to do just that. Exact statistics are hard to come by. However, most observers estimate that over half the buildings in the city were damaged or destroyed. Casualty statistics are even harder to obtain because it was impossible to tell who was an insurgent and who was a civilian caught in the battle, but the number of dead certainly numbered in the thousands. At the same time, there is evidence of an Anbar Awakening,

MOHAMMED AMEEN/Reuters/Landov

Photo of the destroyed United Nations headquarters in Iraq.

especially after al-Qaeda in Iraq demanded the right to marry the daughter of local sheikhs.

If anything, the insurgency may have made Iraq's tribal loyalties even more important, perhaps eclipsing the religious divisions. In the 2010 election, tribal blocs won critical votes, especially in the Sunni Triangle. What remains to be seen is whether they will become supporters of reconciliation across the secular divide or continue to fragment the country.

There was a smaller and less vexing uprising among Shiites, especially those loyal to Moqtada al-Sadr (1973–). Al-Sadr is a relatively young cleric, a direct descendent of the Prophet, and the son and son in-law of leading religious leaders. His father was killed by Saddam's security forces.

Although not yet a senior leader, al-Sadr was the first well-known Shiite to oppose the U.S.-led occupation and demanded that all foreign forces leave. "His" insurrection began with a dispute over the Imam Ali Mosque in Najaf. It is one of the holiest places for the Shia because it contains the tomb of Ali, who was the spiritual founder of the sect. The fighting escalated in 2004 and 2005 when his so-called

Mahdi Army[1] attacked coalition forces and seized control of parts of cities with large Shiite populations, including Sadr City, which was named for his father.

Because of his own support and the reputation of his family, he also has close ties to the now dominant Shiite

---

[1] In Shiism, Mahdi is revered as the twelfth imam who disappeared. Both branches of Islam assert that when he reappears in some form through a descendent of the Prophet's wife, all will be resolved. Al-Sadr is part of that lineage. The cult of the twelfth imam is particular powerful among the Shiites.

Shiite cleric Moqtada al-Sadr leads Friday prayers in the town of Kufa, some 160 km south of Baghdad on 16 April 2004 at the height of Shite resistance to the U.S.-led occupation.

politicians, including Prime Minister al-Maliki (see below). In 2007, he left Iraq for Iran to pursue studies he needed to become an ayatollah. The Iranian connection worried American authorities since it led to fears that Iran might be involved in all parts of the insurgency.

In 2008, he told most of his supporters to disarm, but he did maintain a small, elite force that could serve as the core of a new Mahdi Army. In 2010, he returned to Iraq to play a more active role in politics and continue his studies. Again, he has called for American withdrawal and urged all Iraqis to vote for candidates who share that position.

COIN

In an odd—but important—twist of fate, the difficulties the U.S. faced in Iraq and Afghanistan have led to a profound shift in military thinking. It is popularly associated with General David Petraeus, but in fact it is rippling throughout the ranks of serving officers if not all politicians.

Petraeus rose to prominence when he commanded the 101st Airborne in the early days of the Occupation. He experimented with novel techniques, some of which he had developed more than a decade earlier while serving in Bosnia. One marine who served with him in the 101st summed up his approach as "make mama happy."

Make no mistake about it. COIN is a military strategy. But it downplays the use of force and emphasizes winning the support of at least some of the members and supporters of an insurgency. It is conducted by men and women who have chosen to put themselves in harm's way. But it should be understood that it also involves trying to win over the support of at least some of the members and supporters of an insurgency.

The current military doctrine on COIN was written when Petraeus came back to head the United States Command and General Staff College at Fort Leavenworth, which all army majors must complete before being promoted to colonel. He has had ample opportunity to put his ideas into practice as head of the allied forces in Iraq, the United States Central Command, and, more recently, as commander of ISAF (International Security Assistance Force) in Afghanistan.

COIN has had more success in Iraq than in Afghanistan—at least so far. Nonetheless, it is hard to argue that it did not play a major role in defusing the insurrections in Iraq. A then-colonel has written that COIN provided the "tipping point" that eased conditions in al-Anbar province, then the most dangerous place in the Sunni Triangle.

"Normal" Participation: The 2010 Election

There are some signs that the reforms imposed by the United States are bearing fruit. The emphasis should be on "some." We will see those both here and in the section on the state below.

As we saw earlier, the 2010 election did not unfold smoothly. It took place months late and it took yet more months before the new government took shape. It did not have thousands of people holding up their ink-stained fingers indicating that they had voted and could not vote again as was the case four years earlier. Also, some 500 candidates mostly Sunni were barred from running because

Another Sad Story

The history of Iraq since the fall of the monarchy is littered with tragic stories. Now, they tend to involve Americans as well as Iraqis.

Here's another one that also illustrates what COIN is all about.

Captain Travis Patriquin had risen through the enlisted ranks and become an officer. Somehow, along the way, he learned Dari, Pashtun, and Arabic.

Captain Patriquin rises to importance here because he wrote a power point presentation that summarized his work with dissidents in al-Anbar and revolves around building trust with local leaders and drinking a lot of tea with them. It is not a flashy slide presentation, consisting mostly of stick figures. But it went viral on the Web only after Patriquin was killed by an IED shortly after he posted the slides. With it, you can see all you need to know about the basics of COIN in about five minutes.

🌐 abcnews.go.com/images/us/how_to_win _in_anbar_v4.pdf

of their alleged connection to the Baathist regime. Another three who were allowed to run and won were not allowed to take their seats.

However, the 2010 election did show the electorate falling into broad categories that could well endure (see Table 14.5). These are not political parties as we know them in the west. Rather, they are loose coalitions which means they could fall apart at any time. In fact, the coalitions are so loose that different sources provide different figures for something like Table 14.5. There is agreement that the first two coalitions won 91 and 89 of the seats, respectively, with the others and independents winning the rest yet holding the balance of power.

- **Iraqi National Movement (Iraqiya).** This group largely supports former interim prime minister Ayad Allawi who is a secular Shiite. More important, it is the one major political grouping that has attracted the relatively few Sunni who have chosen to take part in electoral politics. It has closer links to Iraqi domestic groups than the State of Law, at least in part because Allawi stayed in the country and was even briefly a Baath party member.

- **State of Law.** This is a largely Shiite organization that strongly supports Nuri al-Maliki and has its origins in the exile opposition. Al-Maliki is typical. He began his political life in the underground *Dawa* movement and went into exile shortly after Saddam solidified his control in 1979. He returned after the American invasion toppled the old regime. Unlike Allawi, al-Maliki is seen as a divisive figure, leading several American Senators, including future Secretary of State Hillary Rodham Clinton, to call for his ouster in 2007.

- **National Iraqi Alliance.** This group was also close to the outgoing prime minister. It was an all but exclusively Shiite coalition and included all the major orthodox Shiite factions, but its supporters were close to al-Sadr. It initially won 70 seats in 2010 but fell apart when al-Sadr withdrew his support.

- **Kurdish Alliance** As always, the Kurdish community remains internally divided, most notably between supporters of the Barzani and Talibani families/clans. Since the creation of a largely autonomous Kurdish region after the first Gulf War, the two factions have worked together reasonably well. The most recent Barzani leader helped broker the agreement that made the 2010 election possible, while his Talibani equivalent is in his second term as president of the entire country.

- **Voters loyal to al-Sadr.** This group does not figure separately in Table 14.5 and did not have any formal organization, but most of "its" candidates ran on lists favorable to al-Maliki. It remains to be seen how much of a hold al-Sadr will hold over these officials, but it seems that candidates loyal to him won about 40 seats.

In short, the 2010 election left Iraq short of a majority and even shorter of a democracy. However, the fact that election occurred at all is a sign of progress since the American-led invasion.

Iraq As a Failed State?

In the seventh edition of this book, we referred to Iraq as a failed state. As we have noted throughout Part 4, that is a controversial term in part because no one has agreed upon a common definition of what it means. At most, there is a broad consensus that a failed state cannot carry out the basic functions of governing, however they are defined in a given time or place.

This certainly has been true of Iraq, which has been occupied and essentially deprived of its sovereignty for the

TABLE 14.5 The Iraqi Election of 2010

NAME OF COALITION	SEATS
Iraqiya	91
Rule of Law	89
National Iraqi Alliance	70
Kurdish Alliance	51
Others	24

Vietnam and Iraq

Many critics of the war in the United States drew parallels between our involvement in Iraq and Vietnam forty years earlier.

The two are similar in that massive numbers of American troops were engaged in both.

However, there was one important difference. The United States "inherited" the Vietnam conflict from the French after their defeat in 1954.

By contrast, the war in Iraq and the insurgency that followed would not have happened without the American decision to invade.

For at least some critics of the war, that means that the United States had an added responsibility, not just to leave but to do so in a way that does not make conditions in Iraq worse.

To echo the Hippocratic oath that all physicians sign, Americans have to try to find a way to "do no harm."

better part of a decade. Polls, including those conducted by the American government, show that most Iraqis think that Washington still calls the shots and that they want American troops to leave as soon as possible.

As the transition to Iraqi sovereignty continues, it is by no means clear that its state can guarantee the rule of law and other provisions that are at the heart of any stable system, democratic or not.

Two seemingly contradictory trends stand out. As above, we will concentrate on the second because it is more of a key to Iraq's future.

Continuing Violence

The insurgency is not what it was a few short years ago. Iraqi civilians still have to dodge IEDs and other explosives left near major buildings, but it is nothing like what we saw two or three years earlier. Instead, Iraqis, who will be largely responsible for their own security beginning in January 2012, should be looking over their political shoulders and seeing what has been happening as part of the Arab Spring, which is nowhere near resolution yet.

The effects of this Arab Spring are already being felt in Iraq. If they hit Iraq as hard as any of the other countries involved so far, it would not turn out to be a hard state to topple, once the Americans leave.

The Emerging State

A new state does seem to be emerging in Iraq. That is surprising to us because of our depiction of it two years ago. We tried to convey to readers that Iraq had at least two struggles to deal with either of which could do the still fragile state in. First, after totally decapitating the Baath regime, Iraq has few domestic resources to draw on and does not have a reliable police force, military, or many of the other trappings of a successful state. Second, it found itself in the not historically atypical position of having a new regime imposed from abroad. These two challenges are easiest to see in faulty historical analogies made by the Bush administration, some of which have been repeated under Obama.

However it turns out, the linchpin of the new state will be its Council of Representatives. It has 325 members who pass all laws and oversee the executive. It is eventually to be joined by a Council of Union, which will represent the regions. The Constitution leaves it to the elected Council to define and create this second house. So far, it has failed to do so.

Far more important will be the largely behind the scenes political trends. In Germany (see Chapter 6) and Japan (online chapter), the United States occupied defeated countries and helped them build democratic regimes for the first time—and do so surprisingly quickly. However much President Bush cited those experiences, they had little in common with Iraq after Saddam. First, almost everyone in Germany and Japan acknowledged how dreadful their defeated regimes had been and the need for their societies to undergo profound change. Second, the occupation authorities drew heavily on leaders who had spent the war years at home and could therefore build bases of support. Third, virtually everyone in Germany and Japan agreed that their country, as such, should continue to exist.

Instead, the United States is relying on a group of politicians who had been part of the opposition to Saddam but lived in exile in London, Washington, and other Western cities. For the first year after Saddam's fall, the United States, with minimal support from the other coalition members or the UN, ruled Iraq directly through the **Coalition Provisional Authority (CPA)**. Its two leaders, General Jay Garner and Ambassador Bremer, did not distinguish themselves. More important, many thought that the Americans, who governed from the Green Zone, looked more like colonial powers than liberators. In short, the United States never won the "hearts and minds" of more than a small percentage of the Iraqi people.

After consulting fairly widely, the CPA appointed an Interim Governing Council in June 2003 that, in turn, appointed a cabinet in September. The CPA wanted to create a body that was broadly representative of Iraq's three main ethnic groups and ideological factions. But there was little illusion that the council was an independent body. Its main job was to draft an interim Constitution, which went into effect in March 2004, and to pave the way for the creation of an **interim government** to which the CPA transferred at least legal sovereignty on June 30, 2004.

At that point, Bremer left. Michael Negroponte, the leading American civilian official, became the new ambassador. Negroponte had been the U.S. ambassador to the UN and became Director of National of Intelligence in April 2005 and Deputy Secretary of State two years later.

In most respects, however, the handover of sovereignty was more symbolic than real. Virtually none of the members of the interim government were critical of the United States. And, more important, the fact that this government is being put together under the eye of almost 160,000 occupying troops makes any real claims for its independence more than a little illusory.

What emerged by the summer of 2004 was a regime that had little legitimacy and was divided among the country's three main religious and ethnic groups. It came as no surprise that the Shiites would dominate the new government, given their majority status in the population. The Kurds, who had been largely outside of Baghdad's control since the first Gulf War, continued to govern their region as if it were an all but independent country even if one of their main leaders, Jalal Talabani, is the president of the new Iraq.

In 2005 and 2010, elections to the Council of Representatives were held, which led to the ambiguous outcomes described above. Despite the fact that it is not working very well, the new state may be working well *enough* to ensure stability after the last Allied troops are gone, something we dare not say about Afghanistan.

With the change of administrations in Washington in 2009, the United States again committed itself to leaving Iraq. As noted above, combat forces have all left and the remaining troops only perform advisory functions and have next to no presence in Iraqi cities. On August 31, 2010, Operation Iraqi Freedom officially came to an end. In short, Iraq is once again becoming a sovereign state. The question is, will the Iraqis be able to make it work?

The new Iraq defines itself as Muslim, democratic, and federal. For our purposes, that last term is probably the most important. The federal nature of the new state gives significant powers to the eighteen provinces, as well as to the central government, although it is too early to tell how that will evolve in the long term.

Otherwise Iraq has a fairly standard parliamentary system. Real power lies with the prime minister, who is the leader of the largest group in parliament and stays in power only if he retains the support of the majority. There is a president (currently a leading Kurdish politician), but he is largely a figurehead.

As we saw earlier, the 2010 election ended in a virtual tie. In the end, a deal was brokered to allow al-Maliki to stay on as prime minister while Allawi became head of a policy council that has yet to take shape. The thirty-three cabinet posts have been roughly split between supporters of the two men with a few Kurds as well. It does not help that these al-Maliki and Allawi barely speak to each other.

In sum, the Iraqi state is tenuous to say the least. The key thing to understand about the state is that it is only a few years old. Everything could change. By the time you read these words, things *might* be different. Something approaching a sovereign Iraqi state is taking form.

Public Policy: It's All About Oil

Unlike every other chapter in this book, this one does not have an extended sections on either the state or public policy. Having gotten this far, you should probably have already figured out why that is the case. It is a significant stretch of the imagination to say that Iraq has the resources to make public policy except in one area—the way it deals with its massive oil reserves.

Beyond oil, there has been some progress. The number of Internet connections and cell phones has grown by at least a factor of 40 since 2003. Nonetheless, the overall balance sheet for public policy reform is less than ideal. To cite but two examples, much of the country still does not have reliable electrical service; some urban areas get less than three hours a day. Also, as much as half the population does not have a full time job.

But Iraq does have oil. The Rumaila oilfield near Basra in the south is apparently the world's second largest. And that doesn't count unconfirmed supplies, which foreign firms are desperately searching for.

It is true that the petrochemical industry was neglected under Saddam—or worse. At the end of the first Gulf war, forces loyal to Saddam burned down many key facilities in the Shiite-dominated south.

During the years of sanctions, Iraq could not sell oil abroad above a limited amount, which was supposed to be used to purchase food, medicine, and other vital supplies. In reality, Saddam and his colleagues skimmed off most of those funds.

After the invasion and occupation, the United States largely dominated the oil industry and most business went to American firms, including Haliburton, once run by former Vice President Cheney. Now, the Iraqi government is diversifying its international partners. It recently signed a contract with BP to provide technical assistance at Rumaila. The Chinese state-owned oil company seems ready to sign contracts with its Iraqi equivalent to buy large quantities of oil, which as we saw in Chapter 10 it desperately needs.

The government plans to increase production from 2.5 million to 12 million barrels a day. That is more than Saudi Arabia produces, but it will take the better part of a decade for Iraq to reach that level. Put simply, oil could again become the resource that allows Iraq to develop a more diverse set of public policies. It is clear that it was mismanaged under the Baath. But as with the state, only time will tell if these hopes will turn into reality.

Southern fields are still full of land mines, another one of Saddam's legacies. There is even opposition to foreign involvement in Iraqi oil, especially from people who support Ayad Allawi, who could potentially be the next prime minister. Everything from political violence to a shortage of ports on the Gulf will impede its progress.

THE MEDIA

Under Saddam, the regime had total control of the mass media. This power was not limited to the regime's domination of newspapers, radio, and television news. Foreign newspapers and magazines were banned, and it was illegal for Iraqis to watch television or listen to unapproved radio programs beamed in from abroad. Iraqis began tuning in to networks like al-Jazeera (**www.aljazeera.com**), based in the UAE, in the last few years, although one suspects that anyone who had a satellite dish did so with the knowledge and acceptance of the authorities.

A lot of this has changed since Saddam was ousted. There are now at least one hundred privately owned newspapers and almost as many radio and television stations. The American authorities claim that these are all privately owned and independently run, which does generally seem to be the case.

However, none of those media outlets are more than slightly critical of the new regime. The creation of a truly free and vibrant press will be a major challenge for the regime that comes to power when, and if, al-Maliki falls.

The United States and its allies have tried to create a domestic media service that supports the new government. However, most of those attempts have not met with much success—other than in televising the matches of the country's surprisingly successful national soccer team.

CONCLUSION: FIASCO REVISITED

People close to former Secretary of Defense Donald Rumsfeld referred to the initial invasion as employing "shock and awe." Eight years after the invasion, the real shock and awe is that Iraq remains in deep trouble. The key problem is that Sunni Arabs have felt excluded from and oppressed by the new regime. A few Sunni politicians and religious leaders have cooperated with the new government. A somewhat larger number have cooperated to try to put down al-Qaeda in Iraq. However, most prominent Sunni Arabs have all but boycotted the new regime until the 2010 election.

Not all Shiites are happy with it either. The government and its American supervisors tried to dismantle the remaining militias, including those run by Shiites as well as the ones that led the Sunni resistance. In early 2011, the members of parliament and armed citizens closest to al-Sadr were giving the government only grudging support, even though they were part of the governing coalition.

There is no question that things are better on the personal security front in much of the country, especially in the north and the south. And the counterinsurgency operation, with its emphasis on winning the hearts of minds of current and potential insurgents, has made huge strides most notably in al-Anbar province, which was a stronghold of al-Qaeda in Iraq.

Looking FORWARD

IRAQ ACTUALLY ENDS the tragic stories we have to cover. Nigeria has had more than its share of ethnic conflict and Mexico's economy has not grown as much as was expected a generation ago. However, neither's problems come close to Iraq's. It is important to note, too, that progress has been made there, most notably through the impact of now Head of the CIA David Petraeus and his remarkable team. Do not get us wrong. We will find plenty of problems in the last two "country" chapters and the conclusion. But Iraq has been a trouble spot since we were in graduate school in the 1970s and 1980s respectively.

Key Terms

Concepts	People		Organizations, Places, and Events
cult of personality	Alawi, Ayad	Hussein, Uday	Baath Party
failed state	Al-Bakr, Ahmad Hassan	Petraeus, David	Coalition Provisional
Kurds	Al-Malaki, Nuri	**Acronyms**	Authority (CPA)
nation building	Al-Sadr, Moqtada	CPA	Gulf War
Shiite	Bremer, Paul	INC	interim government
Sunni	Bush, George W.	OPEC	Iraqi National Congress
Surge	Faisal I	PUK	(INC)
weapons of mass destruction (WMD)	Hussein, Qusay	RCC	Operation Desert Shield
	Hussein, Saddam	UNSCOM	
		WMD	

Operation Desert Storm

Operation Iraqi Freedom

Organization of Petroleum
Exporting Countries
(OPEC)

Ottoman Empire

Patriotic Union of Kurdistan
(PUK)

Republican Guard

Revolutionary Command
Council (RCC)

Sunni Triangle

United Nations Special
Commission
(UNSCOM)

Useful Websites

During this time of transition, websites on Iraq are likely to change more rapidly than those listed in other chapters in this book. There will, for example, be sites created for the transitional government and permanent regime that follows it. So do not be surprised if some of these links no longer work.

The best source on the Middle East in general and Iraq is one of them. The University of Texas recently stopped its MENIC project, which was also the virtual library site for the region. The site maintained by Columbia University's Middle East and Jewish Studies Program is almost as good.

www.columbia.edu/cu/lweb/indiv/mideast/cuvlm/Iraq.html

Arabic News is one of several good sites that offer news feeds for the Middle East. Al-Jazeera translated much of its feed into English.

www.arabicnews.com

www.aljazeera.com

The Middle East Research and Information Project (MERIP) is a nonpartisan, Washington-based think tank that focuses on Iraq and the Gulf region as a whole. Its site includes its own reports and links to other good information.

www.merip.org

The Council on Foreign Relations has probably done the most consistent and unbiased work on Iraq since 9/11. Its website archives almost everything its scholars have written, but its URL has changed a number of times. Your best bet is to go to the Council's home page and navigate from there.

www.cfr.org

Further Reading

Baker, James, and Lee Hamilton, eds. *The Iraq Study Group Report*. Washington, D.C.: United States Institute for Peace, 2007. The report of this quasi-official and bipartisan body whose recommendations were only partially accepted by the Bush administration.

Filkins, Dexter. *The Forever War*. New York: Knopf, 2008. The best book that tries to analyze Iraq and Afghanistan together.

Karsh, Efraim, and Inari Rautsi. *Saddam Hussein: A Political Biography*. New York: Free Press, 1991. One of the best of many books on Iraq that appeared after the invasion of Kuwait, this one focuses on Saddam himself.

al-Khalil, Samir. *Republic of Fear: The Inside Story of Saddam's Iraq*. New York: Pantheon Books, 1990. A masterly treatment of the origins and functioning of Baathist totalitarianism in Iraq. A difficult but powerful and rewarding book.

Marr, Phebe. *The Modern History of Iraq*. Boulder, CO: Westview Press, 1985. One of the best brief histories of Iraq in this century; part of a series of such books published by Westview.

Pollack, Kenneth. *The Threatening Storm*. New York: Random House/Council on Foreign Relations, 2002. By far the best book by a liberal and veteran Iraq watcher on why war was inevitable. Pollack has since written about why some of his analysis was wrong, especially on WMD issues. His article on that is listed in the InfoTrac College Edition Sources section.

Packer, George. *The Assassin's Gate*. New York: Farrar, Straus, and Giroux, 2005. Along with the Ricks book mentioned next, the best account of postwar Iraq by an American.

Ricks, Thomas. *Fiasco*. New York: Penguin, 2006. *The Gamble*. New York: Penguin, 2009. Probably the best journalistic accounts of why the invasion fell apart and the relative success of the surge.

Sciolino, Elaine. *The Outlaw State: Saddam Hussein's Quest for Power and the Gulf Crisis*. New York: Wiley, 1991. Probably the most accessible general introduction to contemporary Iraq and the Gulf War. A pleasure to read.

Shabar, Ariel. *My Father's Paradise: A Son's Search for His Jewish Past in Kurdish Iraq*. Chapel Hill: Alongquin Books of Chapel Hill, 2008. The author is the son of Jew born in Kurdistan who later emigrated to Israel and then the United States. Not very political but great on the Kurds, Muslims, and Jews alike.

United States Army. *Counterinsurgency Manual*. http://www.fas.org/irp/doddir/army/fm3-24.pdf.

Woodward, Bob. *State of Denial*. New York: Simon and Shuster, 2007. The last of his three books on American engagement in Iraq.

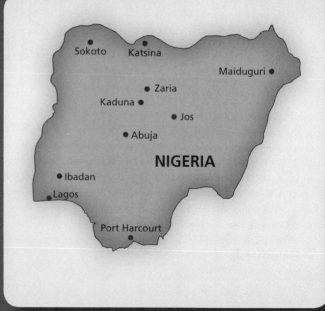

NIGERIA

Sokoto
Katsina
Maiduguri
Zaria
Kaduna
Jos
Abuja
Ibadan
Lagos
Port Harcourt

15

Nigeria

The trouble with Nigeria is simply and squarely a failure of leadership. There is nothing basically wrong with the Nigerian character. There is nothing wrong with the Nigerian land or climate or water or air or anything else.

CHINUA ACHEBE

GOODLUCK, JONATHAN

On April 8, 2011, Nigeria held its fourth national election since the military yet again handed power back to civilians. The incumbent president had the unlikely name of **Jonathan Goodluck** (1957–). He grew up in the Niger Delta in the southern part of the country, where his family made canoes. Unlike most members of his family, he went to school and ultimately earned a PhD in biology from the University of Port Harcourt, which is not far from his home village.

He was also a politician with a good bit of good luck. Already vice president, Jonathan became acting president in early 2010 when his predecessor, **Umaru Musa Yar'Adua** (1953–2010), had to leave the country for medical treatment. When Yar'Adua died later in the year, Jonathan formally assumed the presidency.

Jonathan is an unusual politician by Nigerian standards. He has a Facebook page with more "friends" than British Prime Minister Cameron, Germany Chancellor Merkel, and South African President Zuma *combined*. He is also renowned for his hats, only one of which adorns the photo shown on page 436.

Therefore, to the surprise of few, he won more than 58 percent of the vote in what was one of the fairest elections

THE BASICS	
Nigeria	
Size	823,770 sq. km (about twice the size of California)
Population	155 million (estimated)
Population growth	1.9%
GDP per capita PPP	$2,400
Growth GDP	6.8%
Currency	118 naira = US$1
Major religions	50% Muslim, 40% Christian, 10% indigenous religions
Literacy	68%
Life expectancy	47 years

Looking BACKWARD

THROUGHOUT PART 4, we have argued that there is no country that is typical of the Global South. While most countries in Asia, Africa, and Latin America are hampered by an often toxic combination of ethnic divisions, poverty, and weak or failed states, no two are alike. In fact, the first three countries we've seen could be considered idiosyncratic. India has made great strides on all three fronts. Iran is a rare example of a country in which religious leaders are dominant politically as well as theologically. Iraq is one of a handful of countries that has been at war for a generation and has been occupied by a foreign power.

Now, we turn to two countries in which the balance between ethnicity, underdevelopment, and a weak and—even failing—state feed off each other in seemingly pernicious ways. In this chapter, we will consider Nigeria, which has tried four republics and experienced three periods of military rule, has to balance off hundreds of ethnic groups, and remains mired in poverty despite being blessed with massive oil reserves.

in the more than sixty years that Nigeria has been independent. Earlier that April, his **People's Democratic Party (PDP)** did lose votes but still won a majority in the House of Representatives and the Senate that represents the states.

But he also had a triple dose of bad luck.

First, he is a southerner. As we will soon see, Nigeria is deeply divided along ethnic and religious lines. There is an unspoken agreement that the presidency should rotate between the largely Muslim north and the heavily Christian south. Yar'Adua was a Muslim. He was under 60 years old when he was elected to his second term; and many pundits assumed that the presidency would stay in the north until he had to leave office because of term limits. After his untimely death, many northerners thought they had the "right" to choose the next president.

Jonathan's problems began with his predecessor. Yar'Adua was elected to succeed **Olusegun Obasanjo** (1937–) as head of the country's fourth republic. Obasanjo had actually run the country twice, first as a military dictator and then as an elected president. The transfer of power from Obasanjo to Yar'Adua marked the first time that a republican regime in Nigeria had done so. That was the good news.

Goodluck Jonathan with Barack Obama at the White House.

AP Photo/Pablo Martinez Monsivais

The bad news is at least as clear. While Jonathan and the PDP swept the south, the Muslim-dominated parties did the same in the north. For years, deep ethnic conflict has been a common theme in Nigeria and has led to political violence that has been far more than intermittent and extends beyond disputes between Muslims and Christians. Indeed, as the presidential campaign was heating up in early 2011, violence broke out in Jonathan's home state of Bayelsa where he had been governor before going to Abuja, the national capital, as vice president. There had been widespread violence there and in other oil producing states in the Niger Delta, which a 2009 amnesty apparently did little to calm.

It wasn't just Bayelsa. In 2009, a previously little known sect, Boko Haram (loosely translated as Taliban), killed hundreds of what it considered to be less-than-observant Muslims. That took away press coverage of the Movement for the Emancipation of the Niger Delta (MEND), the most recent group trying to wrest control of oil production and the environmental problems it generates, from the central government.

Second, as we will see in more detail later, Nigeria has suffered from more than its share of corruption. During the campaign it was also revealed that millions of *naira* (the Nigerian currency) slated for hospitals, schools, and other development projects "disappeared" into private hands. It, of course, is impossible to measure the extent of corruption with any degree of precision.

Third, even before the recession began in 2008, Nigeria was one of the poorest countries in the world and, by far, the most disadvantaged one included in *Comparative Politics*. It need not have turned out that way; in fact, Nigeria should be at least the wealthiest country in Africa. It is the biggest producer of oil and natural gas on the continent and is in the top fifteen in the world, ranking barely below Kuwait and Iraq. It ranks even higher when it comes to proven oil reserves.

Nigeria has been deeply affected by the economic crisis despite its abundance of oil. A drought threatened to kill thousands already suffering from malnutrition. As we will see, ethnic strife broke out in the oil fields in the south and among factions in the Muslim community in the north. We will return to both of these protest movements later in this chapter.

For now, it is enough to see that Jonathan's election and the three main problems he inherited illustrate how the central dilemmas in Nigerian politics can be seen through the lens of a single paradox. On the one hand, they do not seem to suggest that Nigeria is on the verge of falling apart or becoming a failed state. The fact that it survived the shift from one leader to another should not be scoffed at. On the other hand, the ethnic and economic problems plaguing the country has it on most lists of countries that could lapse into a bloody civil war sometime in the next decade or two.

Bodies of men killed during rioting in Northern Nigeria in July 2009.

THINKING ABOUT NIGERIA

Nigeria has a lot going for it. Almost one in every five Africans is Nigerian. The country is blessed with some of the most fertile soil on the continent. Compared with the rest of Africa, it has a well-educated population—at least 2 million citizens have university degrees. Most important of all, those oil and gas deposits have brought it more money than most other African nations can dream of.

Other than the oil, those assets were available before Nigeria gained its independence in 1960. Therefore, most observers expected Nigeria to help lead the continent in building strong states, democratic regimes, and modern economies.

Yet, as the world-renowned novelist Chinua Achebe suggests in the statement that begins the chapter, Nigeria has had more than its share of trouble. Whether run by civilians or the military, the state has never lived up to expectations. There have been times, as during the civil war of 1967–70 over **Biafra**, when it could be argued that there was no viable Nigerian government, if by that we mean a unit that can maintain basic law and order.

Those troubles begin with the basic social and economic conditions under which Nigerian citizens and their leaders live.

Poverty

Despite all of its resources, Nigeria remains desperately poor. According to almost every indicator, it ranks among the poorest quarter of the countries in the world.

From 1965 until 1980, Nigeria's gross national product (GNP) grew by an average of 6.9 percent per year because of the income it was able to realize from some low-level industrial development and oil exports. From 1980 to 1987, however, the economy shrank by more than 40 percent because its industries ceased being productive and oil prices collapsed. In the decade between 1992 and 2002, the shrinkage continued at a pace of about half a percent per year. Growth has picked up in this decade, but not enough to make Nigeria anywhere near as well off as the other countries considered in this book.

These economic ups and downs have taken a human toll. When oil prices were at their peak in the early 1980s, GNP per capita averaged around $700 per year. By 1990 it had been cut by more than half. Today, it is little more than $300 in absolute terms. Even at the more generous purchasing power parity (PPP) rate, it is barely $2,400. Although there has been some improvement in the way people live, the average Nigerian still leads an appallingly difficult life.

About 9 percent of all Nigerian children do not reach the age of one; fourteen percent die before their fifth birthday. Most of those children succumb to malnutrition or diarrhea that could easily be treated or prevented if the country could afford basic medications that are sold over the counter in the West.

Nigerians who survive childhood can expect to live less than fifty years. The average Nigerian consumes only between 85 and 90 percent of the calories required to maintain a healthy life, a figure that has actually declined from 95 percent in the mid-1960s. Only 20 percent have access to safe drinking water. There are only 0.28 doctors per thousand Nigerians. In Mexico, the comparable figure is 1.5. There are almost as many Nigerian-born physicians practicing medicine in the United States as in Nigeria itself. About two-thirds of the population is literate, but barely three in five women can read and write.

Population statistics in Nigeria are notoriously unreliable, though it now seems that about half of its population lives in cities. Those cities are booming as millions of young people flee the countryside seeking jobs. The population of Lagos, for instance, reached 1 million by the mid-1970s, and many people were surprised when the 2006 census showed it "only" had 8 million people. Its metropolitan area is estimated to have nearly 17 million people today, which would make its region the largest city on the planet.

Lagos also provides a good picture of the twin realities of urban life in many countries in the Global South. Miles of shantytowns surround a central city of wide boulevards and gleaming skyscrapers that remind one of New York or London. For most urban Nigerians, the shantytown is reality, with ethnically segregated neighborhoods; houses without running water, electricity, or sewers; dead-end jobs, if they have jobs at all; endless traffic jams (called "go slows"); and conflicts with people from different ethnic groups who live in other neighborhoods.

Nigerians are also in more or less constant danger of famine. In 2009, the *Washington Post* reported that almost 40 percent of Nigerian children are malnourished. Two-thirds of the population is what the United Nations calls food insecure. The year before, when food prices soared, there was fear of rioting in many cities. The government agreed to import more food and then had to renege on its promise because it would take longer to bring food into the country than to grow it at home in a country that has millions of acres of land that could grow crops with only minimal irrigation. Seven percent of that land is currently farmed.

Pedestrians and shoppers make their way through a crowded street in Lagos.

As is the case in most of Africa, Nigeria has to cope with population growth of monstrous proportions. During much of the 1980s it averaged over 3 percent per year. About 45 percent of the Nigerian population is under fifteen, while only 3 percent is over sixty-five. At the current average growth rate of 2 percent, the population will double every thirty-six years. At that rate, Nigeria will have nearly 400 million inhabitants by the middle of the twenty-first century. That would be more than the United States and roughly one-and-a-half times the total African population today. Such population pressures are likely to make Nigeria poorer as it is forced to spread its already limited resources even further.

Ethnicity

In Nigeria, no other political force comes close to ethnicity in importance. In all, Nigeria has about four hundred ethnic groups, each of which has its own language and customs.

Politically, the three largest ones matter the most. The largest of these are the **Hausa-Fulani**, who live in the north and are mostly orthodox Muslims. The Fulani, who had Northern African or Arabic roots, gradually moved into the north and, beginning in 1804, gained control of the region and its predominantly Hausa-speaking population. Since then, the two have intermarried to the point that they are virtually indistinguishable. The region to the west of the Niger and Benue rivers is dominated by the **Yoruba**, that on the east by the **Igbo** (sometimes called the Ibo by American analysts). Many Yoruba and Igbo have converted to Christianity, but there are sizable Muslim and non-Christian minorities among the Yoruba. Together, they account for 60 to 65 percent of the population and have produced many of the country's leading politicians.

In the center of the country lies the **middle belt**, where no single ethnic group or religion dominates. As a result, this region has produced more than its share of nationally oriented leaders. In an attempt to create a symbol of national unity during the 1980s, the government moved the capital from Lagos, in the heart of Yoruba territory, to a new city in the middle belt, Abuja.

About half the country is Muslim and 40 percent is Christian. The rest of the population practices religions that antedate the arrival of the Arabs and Europeans. Interethnic difficulties begin with the seemingly simple question of the way people communicate with each other. In the rather homogeneous rural areas, almost everyone still uses the local group's traditional language. The elite usually speak English, which is the official language of the national government and most mass media. In the cities, where poorly educated people from different groups have to communicate with each other, new languages have

emerged that combine simple English terms and African grammatical structures. Then *Washington Post* correspondent Blaine Harden provides the following example from a rap song about corrupt politicians: "If him bring you money, take am and chop. Make you no vote for am," which means, "If he tries to buy your vote, take the money and buy food. Then vote for somebody else." *Chop-chop politics* is the common Nigerian term to describe what Americans call log-rolling or pork-barrel politics.

As we will see in the rest of the chapter, Nigeria's ethnic problems go far beyond the trouble people have in communicating with each other. More than anything else, ethnicity structures life where people live, what they believe in, how they conduct their lives, how jobs are allocated, and who they support politically. And, more than any other factor, ethnicity has made democratic government difficult and led to the coups of 1966, 1983, and 1993, countless riots, and the civil war of 1967–70.

Finally, Nigeria has one of the world's highest rates of HIV infection. The best estimate is that 3.6 percent of the population is HIV positive, including eight hundred thousand children. Two hundred twenty thousand people died of it in 2009. The struggle against HIV/AIDS has been hampered by two main problems. First, Nigeria's health care system in general is among the worst in the world. Second, HIV/AIDS carries a greater social stigma in Nigeria than in most other countries. Indeed, the situation was so bad that the government could not meet a minimal goal of treating ten thousand people in one hundred hospitals in the late 1990s and early 2000s (**www.nigeria-aids.org**).

High-Stakes Politics

These problems and more have turned politics in Nigeria into a very high-stakes game. More people have been killed by repressive regimes elsewhere. Nonetheless, its politics is highly charged because people have great and growing expectations about what their government could and should do, expectations that leaders are rarely able to meet.

In Chapter 5, we saw that Third and Fourth Republic France suffered from a complex syndrome that left it unable to effectively meet the country's domestic and international challenges. Even more, Nigeria has seemed locked in a deteriorating spiral of social, economic, and political difficulties that, at best, reinforce and, at worst, feed off each other.

The most obvious manifestation of Nigeria's ills is the alternation between civilian and military governments, none of which have been able to make much headway on any front. Whatever institutional forms it takes, Nigerian politics is a struggle in which all the key groups desperately want to win or, at the very least, keep their adversaries from winning. The spoils of office are high, as the rampant corruption attests. No officials seem able to make decisions primarily based on national interests.

The uncertainties of Nigerian political life also make this country harder to study than most of the others covered in this book. Because of the shifts back and forth between civilian and military rule, Nigeria has very few established institutions to structure political life, no matter who is in power. As a result, the sections on the state and parties will be shorter than those in other chapters. On the other hand, the next major section on the history of the alternation between civilian and military rule has to be relatively long because without understanding those twists and turns you will not be able to understand why the stakes of politics are so high.

Key Concepts and Questions

In short, we will be asking two sets of questions about Nigerian politics. The first will mirror those posed in the chapters on other countries in Part 4. The others will focus on conditions unique to Nigeria.

- How is the legacy of colonization still reflected in Nigerian politics?

- What role does ethnicity play in reinforcing the country's difficulties?

- Why does Nigeria remain one of the poorest countries in the world despite its massive oil and natural gas reserves?

- How have the frequent shifts from civilian to military rule and back again exacerbated the country's many social and economic problems?

THE EVOLUTION OF THE NIGERIAN STATE

Critics are quick to point to the flaws in and corruption of Nigeria's post-independence leaders in assessing the country's problems. To a large extent they are right because leaders of all political stripes have made damaging mistakes, many of which seem, in retrospect, to have been easily avoidable. However, the incompetence or venality of these men is by no means the entire story. Whatever the leaders of independent Nigeria had been like, they would have faced a tremendous burden of problems inherited from colonial times. In that history, three trends have played an important role in the shaping of modern Nigeria and continue to trouble it today:

- The slave trade cost the Nigerians and their fellow Africans countless millions of people from the sixteenth through the nineteenth centuries.

- Colonization disrupted traditional social and political systems when Europeans created new borders that suited their own purposes but did not take existing regional alilgnments into account.

- Moreover, the very drawing of the boundaries, as well as the nature of colonial administration, made ethnic conflict all but inevitable after independence. The anticolonial struggle, the political arrangements made at the time the former colonies became independent states, and the largely informal pattern of neocolonial relations that was established afterward left the new state in a poor position to develop politically, socially, and economically.

Before the British

For many years, the conventional wisdom held that precolonial Africa was "primitive" and lacked anything approaching civilization or government. That was not the case (africanhistory.about.com). A number of rather advanced civilizations existed in what is today's Nigeria. None had a written language, but, otherwise, many of them had well-developed political, cultural, and economic systems.

Outside influence in Nigerian life actually began before the Europeans arrived in the late fifteenth century. The spread of both the Sahara Desert and Islam brought the Hausa-speaking peoples into contact with the Arab world about a thousand years ago, when it, not Europe, was the center of world civilization. By the thirteenth century, most Hausa had converted to Islam.

By the thirteenth century, a king, or *mai*, had been able to consolidate his rule over a wide region, bringing together dozens of Hausa states. Although the regime's power ebbed and flowed over the centuries, it had well-developed bureaucratic, judicial, and imperial institutions. Political control was further centralized in the early nineteenth century when Usman Dan Fodio led a Fulani takeover of the northern region, established a caliphate under Islamic law, and transformed the old Hausa states into emirates.

These emirates were part of an elaborate trading network that extended at least as far as Baghdad. When the British arrived, they found extensive mines, factories that made elaborate ceramics, and over thirty types of cloth sold by merchants who had established sophisticated financial and monetary systems.

The Yoruba developed a very different—but no less complex—political system. One man, Oduduwa, brought together the thirteen settlements of Ile-Ife and created the first Yoruba kingdom—and with it, the first real sense of being Yoruba. Over the centuries, people spread out from Ile-Ife and established at least sixteen other kingdoms, all patterned along the same basic lines. By the end of the eighteenth century, a single kingdom covered what is now the Yoruba regions of Nigeria and virtually the entire country of Benin.

The Igbo had a different, but still elaborate, social and political system. Little attempt was made to forge a centralized regime. Instead, individual villages were largely self-governing, though all used essentially the same practices. The Igbo had a widely accepted, if unwritten, constitution, specifying clearly defined policy-making, administrative, judicial, and military roles. The society, brilliantly described by Chinua Achebe in *Things Fall Apart*, was based on households led by men. Power and prestige went to those elders who had accumulated the most wealth, shown the most bravery in battle, and demonstrated the strongest commitment to the village's values. In short, life among the Igbo was based more on merit and less on the accident of birth than it was for the British who colonized them.

The Portuguese began the European impact on what is Nigeria today in the late fifteenth century when its explorers landed on the coast and its merchants started exchanging gold for slaves. The slave trade began to take a significant toll during the seventeenth century when huge sugar plantations were established on the Caribbean Islands, which could not survive without imported labor. At that point, British, French, Dutch, Spanish, and Swedish "merchants" joined the Portuguese, and by the middle of the eighteenth century, the booming slave trade was centered along what is now the Nigerian coast.

The Europeans did not establish many permanent settlements at that time. African rulers were too strong and malaria and other diseases too deadly. Instead, they traded with African merchants, who were rich and powerful enough to kidnap or purchase millions of people. In exchange, the merchants obtained textiles, firearms, liquor, iron, salt, and tools.

At least two hundred thousand slaves a year were sent westward from 1827 to 1834 from one port alone, the Bight of Bonny. No one knows for sure how many people were enslaved before the practice was finally ended in Brazil in the 1880s, but the most reliable estimates range from 11 to 20 million. Of those, upward of 1 million were Nigerian. But the cost of slavery cannot be measured simply in numbers of people alone. As Richard Olaniyan has put it,

> In assessing the impact of the Atlantic slave trade on the Nigerian societies, it is strongly tempting to think largely of the quantifiable, tangible costs—the number of prime-age individuals forcibly removed, for example—leaving aside the intangible social, psychological and political effects. Both the victims and the beneficiaries of the nefarious traffic suffered from it; as Professor Ryder holds, "on those who lived by it as well as those who suffered it the slave trade wrought havoc and debasement."[1]

But the costs of slavery went much deeper. At the same historical moment when new discoveries sparked by human initiative and curiosity were propelling European civilization forward, African development was being stunted as generations of its best and brightest youth were ripped out of society and sold into slavery.

Migration Today

In a curious twist of fate, U.S. immigration officials announced in early 2005 that more Africans voluntarily moved to the United States in the 1990s than came to the Americas during any decade of the slave trade. The current wave of migrants, which is obvious to anyone who lives in or near a major metropolitan area in the United States, Canada, or Europe, reflects a desire by young Africans to escape the poverty and underemployment that they assume would be their lot back home.

Colonization

The slave trade wound down after its abolition in the British Empire in 1833 and in the United States after the Civil War. That did not mean that European involvement in Africa ended.

Quite the contrary.

The industrial revolution and the rise of capitalism led Britain and the other European powers to seek new supplies of raw materials and markets for finished goods (see Table 15.1). In Nigeria, the most important product exported

TABLE 15.1 Events in Nigeria before Independence

YEAR	EVENT
Eleventh century	Arrival of Arabs
Sixteenth century	Beginning of slave trade
1884–85	Berlin Conference on Africa
1914	Unification of Nigeria as a single colony
1920	Creation of National Congress of British West Africa
1923	Formation of Nigerian National Democratic Party
1938	Nigerian Youth Charter issued
1948	Nigerianization of civil service begins
1951 and 1954	Interim constitutions go into effect
1960	Independence

[1] Richard Olaniyan, "The Atlantic Slave Trade," in Richard Olaniyan, ed., *Nigerian History and Culture*. (London: Longman, 1985), 120.

was palm oil, which was used to lubricate the machines in the new British factories. Between 1814 and 1834, annual sales of palm oil grew from 450 to 14,000 tons per year.

The end of the slave trade and the beginning of new relationships with the West elicited more resistance from African traders and rulers, leading the British to establish a permanent colony at Lagos and a base at Lokoja where the Niger and Benue rivers come together. A more permanent European presence was also made easier when it was discovered that quinine cured malaria. Still, there was little thought of colonizing all of Nigeria or the rest of Africa. Instead, in 1865, a British parliamentary commission went so far as to advocate phasing out all British activity along the Nigerian coast.

The European geopolitical situation changed all that. The 1870s were a tumultuous time in Europe. The newly unified Germany and Italy disrupted the balance of power that had been so delicately carved out after the Napoleonic Wars ended in 1815. Those pent-up pressures had to be released somewhere, and that somewhere turned out to be Africa, setting off what is commonly known as the "scramble for Africa."

Explorers and soldiers spread all over the continent staking claims to territories for their governments back in Europe. Often, representatives of two or more countries claimed the same places. The German government convened the International Berlin West Africa Conference, which lasted from November 1884 to February 1885. For all intents and purposes, the Berlin Conference finalized the carving up of the continent that was already well under way.

More than the pursuit of national glory and the balance of power, economics was at the heart of the colonization of Africa. The businesses spawned by the industrial revolution needed new markets to keep expanding. That led them to erect stiff tariff barriers to protect their own industries and to seek colonial markets in which they would have the exclusive right to sell manufactured goods.

Meanwhile, missionaries were appalled by the values and customs of the Africans they encountered. The new sense of nationalism combined with the Europeans' moral certainty to create an unfortunate blend of arrogance and ignorance. The Europeans failed to even notice that there were well-developed—albeit very different—civilizations all over the continent, prompting religious and educational leaders to try to convert the "heathens."

The British conquest of Nigeria was conducted from its existing coastal enclaves. They launched pacification campaigns to destroy the power of local leaders and, in the process, undermine popular belief in the various indigenous cultures. Though vastly outnumbered, the British were aided by their technical superiority and by the divisions among the Africans that made any kind of unified resistance impossible. Thus, the British manipulated warfare taking place among the Yoruba to take over the western region and establish a protectorate in Ibadan in 1893.

The British also used economic pretexts to justify their actions. In 1885, they fabricated a charge of obstructing free trade against Jaja of Opobo, a merchant and strongman. Jaja was arrested, paving the way for British occupation of the territory previously under his control. By 1902, the British had solidified their hold over what is now eastern and western Nigeria. The British also took over the north during that same period. Here the central character was an adventurer and trader, Sir George Goldie. At age thirty, Goldie first visited the north, realized that there was too much competition among the British traders already operating there, and brought them all together into the United African Company (UAC). Goldie also was a fierce nationalist who feared that France had designs on the north. In short, Goldie realized that British trade and political control had to go hand in hand. His quest for "gold" and "glory" led him to convince the Foreign Office to appoint him chief agent and vice-consul of the Niger, which allowed him to offer British military protection on behalf of the UAC. By the time of the Berlin Conference, Goldie had negotiated more than two hundred treaties, which the British government used as the basis for its claim to the north.

In reality, British rule was anything but secure away from the towns and the navigable rivers. Over the next fifteen years, they overcame stiff, if sporadic, resistance and gradually extended their control over more and more of the region. Finally, in 1906, British forces destroyed the remnants of the Fulani Empire and established British authority in the north. Eight years later the British combined the north with the south and east to create the single entity that came to be called Nigeria. This was not even an African word, but one coined by the British. It was, in short, an artificial name to describe an artificial entity that had nothing in common with traditional regional alignments.

Colonial Rule

In comparison to other colonized countries, British rule in Nigeria, where there were very few European settlers, was relatively benign. Nonetheless, colonization had a devastating impact. As Basil Davidson put it,

> **All the systems, in essential ways, operated with the same assumptions and for the same purposes.**[2]

Each of them was racist and exploitative. They used colonial power to treat Africans as inferior to Europeans, justifying this by a whole range of myths about a supposed

---

[2] Basil Davidson, *Modern Africa* (New York: Longman, 1983), 4.

"white superiority." The purpose of using colonial power in this way was to make Africans serve the interests of European colony-owners.

Things Fall Apart

The cultural, economic, and political disruption caused by colonialism went a lot further in Nigeria than it did in either India or Iraq. No one has shown that any better than Chinua Achebe in *Things Fall Apart*. Most of us would not want to have lived in traditional Igbo society. Women were second-class citizens. Twins were killed.

But it was also a society with a distinctive culture and values in which people led lives of dignity as portrayed in the successes and failures of Okonkwo, the novel's protagonist and his village's leader.

Toward the end of the book, British missionaries arrive and try to convert the residents of his village. They start with its weakest links, including one of Okonkwo's children who could not or would not live up to the culture's demand that men prove themselves as warriors. The first missionary is relatively kind, but soon he is replaced by a less tolerant and less patient colleague who tries to convert the village in a far less tactful manner.

Seeing his way of life slipping away, Okonkwo ultimately kills the minister, knowing full well that his act will bring British soldiers in. He knows, too, that not only his life, but the way of life of his people, are about to be destroyed, Okonkwo kills himself in a final act of desperation. The novel ends with a British soldier writing his memoirs, tentatively titled *The Pacification of the Primitive Tribes of the Lower Niger*.

In 1914, the British created a single Nigerian colony but administered the north and south separately until the very end of the colonial period. Thus began the often conscious practice of deepening already existing divisions, thereby magnifying the problems the Africans would have to deal with once the country gained its independence. As one expert put it, "If the British 'created' Nigeria, British colonial policy largely contributed to its remaining a mere geographical expression."

In the north, the British relied on **indirect rule**, in which local leaders continued to govern subject only to the limited supervision of imperial officials. In the south, they established a traditional colonial regime in which expatriate British bureaucrats governed directly. Even there, the British had to depend on local officials since they were vastly outnumbered. As late as 1938, there were no more than 1,500 British administrators in the entire colony.

Frederick Lugard, the first British governor of northern Nigeria, referred to this as a **dual mandate**. On the one hand, colonial administrators had to serve the interests of imperialists and industrialists back home. On the other hand, they had to promote members of the "native races" for many clerical and other administrative positions. The British chose to rule through traditional local leaders, most of whom they created, "kings" and "emirs" in the north and "chiefs" in the south. But it cannot be stressed strongly enough that these local leaders had no role in determining colonial policies, which were set by white men in London and Lagos.

There was one area in which colonial rule did benefit Nigerian society: education. Missionaries opened schools that were funded by grants from the British government. By 1926, there were about 4,000 elementary and 18 secondary schools. Of those, however, only 125 of the elementary and none of the secondary schools were in the north. In 1934, the first "higher college" that concentrated on technical education was opened, followed by a full-fledged university in Ibadan in 1948.

Only a tiny fraction of the colonial population received even an elementary education. Nonetheless, the establishment of a rudimentary system at the secondary and university level had two important and unintended side effects that were to hasten independence and a third that would trouble the new country. First, it created a new elite, separate from the traditional authorities, who would form the core of the independence movement. Second, the growing number of literate Nigerians made it possible for an active and often critical press to appear. Lastly, the unequal attendance at English-style schools gave advantages to those groups that sent the most children to them. Southerners—especially those from the southeast—went to school at much higher rates than northerners. When the new Nigerian government needed bureaucrats literate in English and familiar with Western-style administration, southerners filled most of the jobs, which bred considerable resentment in the north.

Economically, the picture was decidedly less positive. The British assumed from the beginning that their colonies would pay for themselves while aiding industrial development at home. That was not possible given the economic systems the British inherited with the consolidation of colonial rule. Therefore, as in India, they embarked on a series of changes that "undeveloped" Nigeria. Up to that point, Nigeria had produced enough food to feed its people and had the trade and manufacturing networks noted earlier. The British destroyed almost all of that. They introduced cash crops for export to help cover the costs of administering the colony. Each region specialized in a different crop: palm oil in the east, cocoa in the west, and peanuts in the north. As a result, Nigerian agriculture no longer produced enough for local consumption, and the colony had to begin importing food.

To make matters worse for Nigerians, the new Royal Niger Company was awarded a monopoly on trade and the profit that accrued from it. The British seized the tin mines in the Jos plateau that Nigerians had worked for more than two thousand years. The British expanded their operations, introduced modern machinery, and by 1928 were employing upwards of forty thousand Nigerians, but now the Nigerians were poorly paid wage laborers, not independent producers.

Taxes and customs duties were imposed on imported goods. Economic policy made Nigeria dependent on Great Britain and at the same time heightened the regional differences within the colony. Thus, people began to consciously define themselves as Yoruba or Igbo or northerners. That sense of self-identification was especially pronounced in the north, where development lagged and more and more people began to fear becoming permanently poorer as well as politically weaker than residents of the south.

Independence

However powerful and destructive it may have been, British colonialism began sowing the seeds of its own destruction virtually from the beginning, just as it had in India. The British may have conquered Nigeria, but they could not keep it in submission forever. If nothing else, there were too few British and too many Nigerians. In addition to expanding education, their "civilizing" mission also led Nigerians not just to read and write and pray to the Christian God, but to learn about what the British claimed to be their values, including freedom and democracy.

From the moment the unified colony of Nigeria was created, events began to unfold that would lead to independence barely a half-century later. The start of the drive toward independence came with World War I. The British imposed heavy taxes on its African colonies to help pay for the war. Some Nigerians were drafted into the British army, where most served as porters. The war and the reasons the British gave for fighting it do not have much of an impact on the Africans who served in the army. On the other hand, they did help a few members of the still tiny educated elite see the contradiction between the colonizers' democratic principles and the harsh realities of their rule.

Meanwhile, the vastly outnumbered British found they had to rely on Africans more and more in administering Nigeria. No Africans occupied decision-making positions during the interwar period, but the colonial rulers had to employ thousands of interpreters, clerks, and police officers.

Colonial rule in the 1920s had an unintended side effect that did neither the British nor the Nigerians much good in the long run. Because the British were convinced that most Africans lived in tribes, indirect rule would rest on the power of chiefs. Therefore, they created them in areas where none had previously existed. Gradually, the practice took hold. Chiefs began to consolidate their authority over communities that came to see themselves as unified peoples.

With time, those tribes became vehicles Africans could use to see and defend their common interests and, later, serve as the base of support for the parties that were to steer the path to independence and the tumultuous politics afterward. At about this time, organized opposition to colonial rule appeared. In the first years of the last century, the American Marcus Garvey and others created a pan-African movement designed to bring Africans and African Americans together to work for common goals, including colonial independence.

During the 1920s, pan-Africanism gradually gave way to the idea of a West African and then Nigerian nationalism. In 1920, the **National Congress of British West Africa (NCBWA)** was formed by representatives from all the British colonies in the region. As with the other early African efforts, the NCBWA advocated limited reforms, such as the granting of some African representation in the colonial assemblies the British created.

The first purely Nigerian political movement emerged with the formation of the **Nigerian National Democratic Party (NNDP)** by **Herbert Macaulay** in 1923 (1864–1946) who is frequently seen as the founder of Nigerian nationalism. For the most part, the NNDP and groups like it gained their support from the still small group of Western-educated lawyers, teachers, and merchants in Lagos. Only a few members of the old elite like Sir **Ahmadu Bello** (1909–66), the Sardauna (ruler) of Sokoto, supported these movements and thus helped build bridges between the new and traditional elites.

Although Macaulay took a more militant line than earlier opponents of colonial rule, his movement stopped short of demanding independence. During the 1930s, support for Nigerian political groups began to broaden with the formation of the **Nigerian Youth Movement (NYM)**. Now critics went beyond attacking specific colonial institutions, such as the educational system that did not provide Africans with the skills that would allow them to become leaders, and began talking about a united and free Nigeria.

In 1938, the NYM issued the Nigerian Youth Charter, which was the first call for self-government. The document was largely ignored by the British, but it heartened and radicalized the educated elite, which now included a growing number of young people living outside of Lagos. Perceptive British observers also realized that irreversible changes were occurring in Nigeria and many other colonies that, sooner or later, would lead to the end of colonial rule.

Dissatisfaction continued to mount. Colonial rule had made Nigerians dependent on international markets. That was tolerable as long as the outside world was paying reasonable prices for Nigerian goods. But after the October 1929 stock market crash in New York, the demand for colonial goods evaporated. That left not just the Nigerian elite but also workers more painfully aware of what colonial rule was costing them. Nigerians paid nearly £1 million in taxes in 1934, but only about a quarter of the colonial budget went to social service, educational, or economic programs that would benefit them.

World War II made independence inevitable. This time, around one hundred thousand Nigerians served in the British army. Many saw combat. Unlike their parents in 1914, these soldiers returned with a heightened desire for independence, democracy, and equality—all those things they supposedly had been fighting for. The war that had begun as an antifascist struggle became an anticolonial and antiracist one as well. In 1944, Macaulay and **Nnamdi Azikiwe** (1904–96) formed the **National Council of Nigeria and the Cameroons (NCNC)**, which went beyond the small steps advocated by earlier nationalists and demanded independence. As Azikiwe, who was to become the most important nationalist leader during the next generation, put it,

> **We who live in this blessed country know that until we are in control of political power, we would continue to be the footstool of imperialist nations. We are fed up with being governed as a crown colony. We are nauseated by the existence of an untrammeled bureaucracy which is a challenge to our manhood.[3]**

Meanwhile, the social changes that had begun before the war continued at an ever more rapid pace. The closure of many European and American markets deepened poverty in the countryside. The cities filled with un- and underemployed young men. Meanwhile, hundreds of new schools and a few universities were opened. Trade unions were formed. All were to become fertile ground for nationalist organizers over the next fifteen years.

Events outside Nigeria also hastened independence. In 1941, American President Franklin Delano Roosevelt and British Prime Minister Winston Churchill issued the Atlantic Charter, which declared that the Allies would "respect the right of all peoples to choose the form of government under which they will live" after the war. Shortly after the war, Britain granted India, Pakistan, Burma, and Ceylon (now Sri Lanka) independence. Those landmark events gave the Nigerians new hope for their own future, especially because it was more developed than Sri Lanka. In addition, the war had weakened the British, leading many politicians to conclude that they could no longer afford the empire. In 1946, the new Labour government committed itself to reforms that would give colonies like Nigeria "responsible government" without either defining what that meant or establishing a timetable for the transition to self-government.

Nigerians joined their fellow Africans in stepping up the pressure for independence sooner rather than later. Everywhere on the continent, nationalist movements garnered new support and radicalized their demands. Nigerian leaders raised the stakes by demanding meaningful political power immediately and independence in the not very distant future. They recognized that if they were to build a mass movement that would extend beyond the urban intellectuals, it would be easiest to do so on a regional level, which led to the formation of parties that recruited support largely along ethnic lines. Nationalist leaders also were able to gather support among the "old boy" networks of high school and university graduates and the ethnic associations that emerged among the new urban migrants who sought to live and socialize with people like themselves. They also used a relatively free press to publicize their attacks on British policy and to claim that they would do a better job if they were in charge of an independent Nigeria.

The British did not reject their demands out of hand. Instead, as early as 1946, they helped the transition to self-government by promulgating a constitution that established elected assemblies in each region, solidifying the borders that would later create problems for the independent Nigeria. In 1948, the British started the "Nigerianization" of the civil service. By the early 1950s, they had decided that they were going to have to speed up the transition to self-government, and therefore helped the Nigerians write two more constitutions, which allowed each region to elect its own representatives and draft its own laws, gave them equal representation in the national legislature, and established a federal structure in which the national government shared power with the three regions.

Elsewhere, the drive toward freedom was moving even faster, especially after Ghana (formerly the Gold Coast) became sub-Saharan Africa's first independent state in 1957. Throughout this period, representatives of the British government and all the major Nigerian forces met to negotiate further constitutional reforms. By that time, electoral politics had already taken on a decidedly regional and ethnic tone. The NCNC organized the Igbo, including some in the neighboring French colony of the Cameroons. The relatively conservative **Northern People's Congress (NPC)** and more radical **Northern Elements Progressive Union (NEPU)**

---

[3] Cited in Davidson, *Modern Africa*, 73.

did well among the Hausa-Fulani. The **Action Group (AG)** dominated among the Yoruba, while the **United Middle Belt Congress (UMBC)** organized the various groups in the center of the country.

A federal election under universal suffrage (except for women in the north) was held in 1959. Final provisions for independence called for representation to be determined on the basis of population, which was to work to the benefit of the north that then accounted for about 40 to 45 percent of the total population.

Nigeria finally became an independent country within the British Commonwealth of Nations on October 1, 1960 with **Tafawa Balewa** (1912-66) as prime minister and Azikiwe as governor-general. Azikiwe would later become the symbolic president when Nigeria declared itself a republic three years later.

But as independence neared, two of the problems of high-stakes politics emerged as well. In their desire to spur development and to gain the support of voters, politicians began dispensing "favors," the first step toward the corruption that no Nigerian regime has been able to overcome. Similarly, the evolution of shared power within a largely regional framework intensified the already serious ethnic differences. Until it became clear that Nigeria was going to become independent, its people had a common enemy: the British. But once independence was assured, their internal differences began taking center stage. By the time independence officially came, Nigeria was united in name only.

The First Republic

Like most former British colonies, Nigeria inherited a traditional parliamentary system based on the Westminster model. It had a bicameral parliament, but only the lower chamber, the House of Representatives, was directly elected and had any real power. Executive authority was vested in a cabinet and prime minister drawn from the ranks of the parliamentary majority. The government could remain in office until its five-year term ended as long as it maintained the support or confidence of that majority (see Table 15.2). There also was a ceremonial but powerless head of state: the governor-general until 1963, and the president thereafter.

The new Nigerian regime differed from classical parliamentary arrangements in only one significant way. It was a federal system in which the national government shared power with three (later four) regional governments whose boundaries roughly coincided with the territories in which the largest ethnic groups lived. These governments, too, were structured along classical parliamentary lines. The creation of a federal system marked the early recognition that high-stakes politics in this highly diverse country

TABLE 15.2 Nigerian Regimes and Leaders since Independence

YEARS	HEAD OF STATE	TYPE OF REGIME
1960–66	Tafawa Balewa	First Republic
1966	J. T. U. Aguiyi Ironsi	Military
1966–75	Yakubu Gowon	Military
1975–76	Murtala Muhammed	Military
1976–79	Olusegun Obasanjo	Military
1979–83	Shehu Shagari	Second Republic
1984–85	Muhammadu Buhari	Military
1985–93	Ibrahim Babangida	Military
1993	Ernest Shonekan	Third Republic and Military
1993–98	Sani Abacha	Military
1998–99	Abdulsalami Abubakar	Military
1999–2007	Olusegun Obasanjo	Fourth Republic
2007–2010	Umaru Yar'Adua	Fourth Republic
2010–	Goodluck Jonathan	Fourth Republic

would make governing from the center impossible without fanning ethnic tensions that long antedated the arrival of the British.

In retrospect, it is easy to see why that type of system did not work. In parliamentary regimes, politics tends to be adversarial, pitting a unified majority against an equally united opposition. It "works" in a country like Great Britain because everyone accepts the rules of the game, and the ideological differences between government and opposition are limited. The opposition accepts the fact that it is not going to have much influence on the shaping of legislation and that its main role is to criticize the government to try to turn the tables at the next election.

In Nigeria, those conditions were certainly not met. Early public opinion polls demonstrated considerable hope for the new regime. Subsequent events, however, showed that whatever legitimacy the regime started with evaporated quickly.

Instead, political life turned into a vicious circle. Politicians were convinced that every contest was a zero-sum game and worried that the costs of losing were potentially catastrophic for themselves and their supporters. The government feared that losing would entail far more than simply spending a few years out of office. The opposition, in turn, resented its powerlessness and grew more convinced that the incumbents would do everything possible to stay in control.

It was clear that politics was going to have a strong ethnic base. The main parties produced the four main leaders of those years—Nnamdi Azikiwe (NCNC), **Obafemi Awolowo** (AG), **Aminu Kano** (NEPU), and Sir Ahmadu Bello (NPC). Although they all tried to gain support throughout the country, they enjoyed next to no success outside their own ethnic community. The very confusing material on parties

TABLE 15.3 Political Parties and Leaders in the First and Second Republics

	FIRST REPUBLIC	SECOND REPUBLIC	
REGION	PARTY	PARTY	ORIGINAL LEADER
North	Northern People's Congress (NPC)	National Party of Nigeria	Ahmadu Bello
West	Action Group (AG)	United Party of Nigeria (UPN)	Tafawa Balewa
East	National Council of Nigeria and the Cameroons (NCNC)	Nigerian People's Party (NPP)	Nnamdi Azikiwe

and elections in the first two republics is summarized in Tables 15.3 through 15.5. Each party won overhelmingly in its "home" region. The Muslim-based NPC came in way ahead of the other parties but fell nineteen seats short of an absolute majority and therefore had to form a coalition with the Igbo-based NCNC, with which it had formed a loose alliance.

In other words, the first government of the new Nigeria represented some of its groups, but only some of them. From the beginning, democracy was on shaky ground. At the regional level, Nigeria was a collection of one-party fiefdoms where leaders bullied their opponents, which only served to heighten ethnic conflict and raise the stakes of national politics.

The new state had a lot of responsibility and a lot of resources to distribute, including the aid money that poured in after independence. Each faction sought to control the government so that it could distribute the lion's share of those resources to itself and its clients. Meanwhile, politicians began making choices about where they were going to operate. The most powerful northern politician, Ahmadu Bello, chose to stay home and serve as premier of the northern region, while his deputy, Balewa, became prime minister of the federal government. Awolowo (1909–87), the AG's leader, decided to lead the opposition in Lagos, leaving Chief Samuel Ladoke Akintola to head the regional government in the west. Azikiwe left the east to become the governor-general and then president.

Only one thing united these politicians: the pursuit of power. Leading politicians became enthralled with the wealth, status, and privileges that holding office offered. To make matters more complicated, although the north dominated politically, it lagged economically. Traditional Islamic rulers and values remained important, which led to limited educational development (only 2.5 percent of northern children were attending school), the exclusion of women from civil and economic life, and something approaching the rejection of "modern" society. Yet, the south feared and resented the north's political power.

The first crisis occurred in the west. Awolowo had gradually moved to the Left and began criticizing the fancy lifestyles politicians were beginning to lead. In the process he threatened and alienated both the national government and the regional one headed by his colleague and now-rival Akintola. Awolowo provoked a confrontation within the AG that culminated in the regional assembly's vote of no confidence in the Akintola government. Four days later, the federal government declared a state of emergency in the region. Akintola was returned to office, and Awolowo was arrested on trumped-up charges of treason and sentenced to ten years in prison. The AG was irrevocably split.

Those same problems burst back onto the political scene shortly thereafter when the government tried to conduct a census in 1963. In most countries, a census does not provoke deep divisions. In Nigeria, it was controversial because the results would determine how many seats in parliament each region would be given and how government revenues and outside development aid would be distributed.

Consequently, each region's leadership doctored the census results. Preliminary counts showed that the populations of the east and west grew by 72.2 percent and 69.5 percent, respectively, in the ten years since the last census had been conducted. Demographers easily showed that such growth was impossible given the rate at which women can physically bear children. Meanwhile, the north reported a more or less accurate increase of 33.6 percent, which meant it would see some of its political power eroded. Therefore, northern officials mysteriously "found" 8.5 million people who had been left out of the initial count, which restored them to the same share of the population they had had before the census began. The government threw these figures out and tried again the next year. The results were no different. But because the northern-dominated leadership then used the wildly inaccurate results in allocating seats for that year's parliamentary elections, the census did little more than fuel the antagonism between north and south.

The census debacle fed the next crisis over the parliamentary and regional elections of 1964 and 1965. On the surface, the party system seemed to be realigning into two broad coalitions. On the one hand, the losers in the previous crisis—the NCNC and Awolowo's wing of the AG—came together with some minor groups to form the slightly left-of-center United Progressive Grand Alliance (UPGA). Meanwhile, the NPC allied with Akintola and others in the southern minority who themselves had created a slightly more conservative NNDP.

In fact, the two were little more than collections of separate, ethnically based organizations, each of which was dominant in its own region. The politicians expressed lofty goals during the campaign. In reality, it was marked by fraud, intimidation, and violence which made a mockery of the democratic process.

Even though a candidate needed the support of only two fellow citizens to get on the ballot, sixty-one seats in the north went uncontested because NPC operatives "convinced" their opponents to withdraw. Violence during the campaign was so widespread that the vote had to be delayed in fifty-nine constituencies. Contests in many others were rigged to such a degree that district-by-district results were never published and would not have been believed had they been. In the end, the NPC-led coalition swept to victory, winning 198 of the 253 seats contested in the first round of voting. Although it did poorly in elections to fill the remaining fifty-nine seats, it still had an overwhelming majority.

The results confirmed the regionalization of Nigerian politics. The NPC won 162 of 167 seats in the north and none anywhere else. All the NNDP victories were in the west, where it won 36 of 57 seats. The opposition carried every seat in the east, in the new midwestern state, and in Lagos. President Azikiwe called on his adversary, Prime Minister Balewa, to form a new government.

Regional elections in the west proved to be the last straw. The campaign was so violent that the federal government banned all public gatherings and sent half the federal police force into the region. When results came in, they showed an overwhelming NNDP (Akintola) victory, even though most experts thought the UPGA (Awolowo) had actually won. Akintola returned to power and turned on his opponents, ordering the assassination of two popular UPGA organizers. The UPGA, in turn, decided that it had no legal way to redress its grievances, so it, too, turned to violence, which included "wetting" its opponents by drenching them with gasoline and setting them on fire. On the

night of January 14, 1966, Akintola met with Ahmadu Bello and Balewa in a desperate attempt to try to restore order. By morning, the military had intervened, overthrown the republic, and killed all three of them.

Military Rule I

What happened that night is, unfortunately, not uncommon in the Global South. At one point or another, well over half of the sub-Saharan African countries have had military rulers, and almost all of the rest have had some other type of authoritarian regime.

Nigeria's case was typical, too, in that the military had two reasons for intervening. The obvious one was the one they spoke about: the need to restore order. But there were ethnic reasons as well, for the Nigerian military was by no means neutral in the ethno-partisan battle that was the downfall of the republic.

Like everything else in Nigeria, the army changed rapidly after independence. In 1960, 90 percent of its officers were British expatriates. By 1966, 90 percent were Africans. Most of the officers, in other words, were young and had risen through the ranks very quickly. A disproportionate number of them, too, were Igbo and resented the way easterners were being treated.

After some initial confusion, Major General J. T. U. **Aguiyi Ironsi**, an Igbo, took control of the new military regime. He moved quickly against corrupt officials and promised a rapid return to civilian rule. Ironsi also suppressed civil liberties and established a **Supreme Military Council (SMC)** and a **Federal Executive Council (FEC)** of

Four starving Biafran children sit and lie around a bowl of food in the dirt during the Nigerian-Biafran civil war.

Hulton Archive/Getty Images

leading civilian civil servants that were to govern the country for the next thirteen years.

On May 24, 1966, however, Ironsi made a terrible mistake. He announced plans for a new, centralized constitution. This confirmed northerners' worst fears that the coup had been carried out to secure Igbo control over the entire country. Hundreds of Igbos, who had been recruited to live in northern cities because of their education, were killed in rioting there. In July, another set of officers staged another coup that brought Lieutenant Colonel Yakubu Gowon (1934–) to power. Gowon was chosen in part because he was a "compromise" ethnically. He was a northerner but a Christian.

Now the task was not simply containing the conflict but keeping the country itself intact. The first serious talk of secession came from the north, but the second coup ended it. The SMC divided the country into twelve states in an attempt to reduce ethnic and regional polarization, but nothing Gowon and his supporters did could stem the anger and violence.

The eastern region's governor and military commander, Colonel Chukwuemeka Ojukwu, refused to recognize Gowon's government and demanded more autonomy for his region. More riots broke out. A million Igbo refugees hastily returned to their region, and Ojukwu ordered all noneasterners to leave.

The east then created the independent Republic of Biafra, plunging Nigeria into a bloody civil war. Over the next thirty months, hundreds of thousands of Nigerians died before federal troops finally put down the revolt.

In sharp contrast with the events of the preceding decade, Gowon and the SMC were generous in victory. He announced that the military would remain in power another six years and then hand the government back to civilians. Moreover, oil revenues, especially after the price increases following the 1973–74 Organization of Petroleum Exporting Countries (OPEC) embargo, left the government with unprecedented resources to use in smoothing the reintegration of the east. Nigeria began to cultivate its image as a continental leader, even entertaining some global pretensions, including the possibility of building an atomic bomb.

By 1974, it had become clear that things were not going well. Many officers proved to be as corrupt and arrogant as their civilian predecessors. In October, Gowon announced that the return to civilian rule would be postponed indefinitely.

Finally, nine years to the day after he seized power, Gowon was overthrown in a bloodless coup and replaced by General Murtala Muhammed and a group of fellow officers who claimed they were committed to reform. The first day he was in power, Murtala removed the twelve state governors. He then quickly moved on to fire ten thousand government officials and 150 officers. On October 1, 1975, he took the most important step of all, outlining a four-year plan for the restoration of democracy. Unfortunately, Murtala also incurred the wrath of many of his fellow officers, who assassinated him in early 1976.

He was replaced by Lieutenant General Obasanjo, who continued preparations for the return to civilian rule. Over the next three years, Obasanjo was a model of integrity and made certain that progress toward the new regime went smoothly. Freedom of the press and other liberties were extended, a new constitution was drafted, and seven more states were created ostensibly again to ease ethnic tensions. A powerful Federal Electoral Commission (FEDECO) was established to remove the conduct of elections and the counting of ballots from the partisan process. In July 1978, civilians replaced military officers as governors of the now nineteen states. In l979, Obasanjo gracefully gave up power.

The Second Republic

Like the Gaullists in France, Obasanjo and his colleagues tried to draft a constitution that they felt would give the country the best chance of avoiding a repeat of the catastrophe of 1966. Parliamentary institutions were rejected in favor of a presidential system modeled on the one in the United States.

Obasanjo and those in agreement with him hoped that a directly elected president would provide the country with an office around which unity could be rebuilt. The president and vice president would be eligible to serve two four-year terms. In a measure designed to break down the ethnic stranglehold on the parties, they decided that a candidate needed to win a majority of the vote and at least a quarter of the ballots cast in at least two-thirds of the states to get elected.

The president appointed a cabinet that was neither drawn from nor responsible to the Parliament, which had two houses with equal powers. The House of Representatives would have 449 members elected from single-member districts drawn up on a one-person-one-vote basis, although, of course, no census had been conducted to provide accurate population figures. There would also be a senate, with ninety-five members, five from each state.

FEDECO had to officially license all parties. All First Republic parties were banned. To be licensed, a new party had to demonstrate that it had a national and not just a regional organization.

Problems began before the new republic came into existence. The military government waited until September 1979 to lift its ban on partisan politics. That meant that the new organizations would only have three months to organize, establish national offices, and file the required papers with FEDECO.

Not surprisingly, only nineteen of the fifty or so potential parties were able to comply; of those, only five were eventually licensed. Not surprisingly, too, four of them were similar to First Republic parties in large part because only the surviving politicians had well-established networks that would allow them to put together even the semblance of a national organization in so short a period. Thus, the **National Party of Nigeria (NPN)** succeeded the NPC and was based largely in the north and led by **Shehu Shagari**, a former First Republic minister. Awolowo headed the **United Party of Nigeria (UPN)**, whose Yoruba base coincided with that of his faction of the old AG. Azikiwe headed an Igbo-based replacement for the NCDC, the **Nigerian People's Party (NPP)**. The **People's Redemption Party (PRP)** appealed to the same radical minority in the north as the old NEPU. Only the small Great Nigerian People's Party (GNPP), itself the result of a schism within the NPP, had no clear First Republic roots. Each party tried to broaden its base of support, and each had some success in doing so. Nonetheless, because they had so little time to prepare for the first elections, all the politicians found it easy to return to the rhetoric of First Republic days.

Five separate elections for state and federal offices were held in July and August 1979 (see Tables 15.4 and 15.5). Although there were quite a few charges of fraud and unfair campaign practices, the first elections were conducted relatively freely and honestly. The NPN won 37.8 percent of the house and 37.4 percent of the senate vote, respectively. Its candidate, Shagari, won 33.8 percent of the presidential vote, 4.6 percentage points more than his chief rival, Chief Awolowo.

The ethnic tensions that plagued the first republic were rekindled before the second officially began. Awolowo challenged the results, claiming that because Shagari had won only 25 percent of the vote in twelve of the nineteen states, he had not met the constitutional requirements for victory. FEDECO ruled that Shagari had won the 25 percent in

TABLE 15.5 Seats in Parliament: 1979–83

PARTY	HOUSE OF REPRESENTATIVES	SENATE
GNPP	43	8
UPN	111	28
NPN	168	36
PRP	49	7
NPP	78	16
Total	449	95

GNPP; NPN, National Party of Nigeria; NPP, Nigerian People's Party; PRP, People's Redemption Party; UPN, United Party of Nigeria.

twelve and two-thirds states, thereby giving him the minimum required.

Dissatisfaction with the new regime spread quickly once it became clear that politicians were not going to be any more honest this time. Ministers were accused of accepting bribes. A governor was arrested for allegedly trying to smuggle millions of naira to his private British bank account. The national telecommunications center was burned down to keep evidence about fraud and mismanagement from being made public.

Meanwhile, world oil prices collapsed again. Well over 90 percent of Nigeria's foreign earnings came from oil sales, so when its income dropped by nearly 60 percent from 1980 to 1983, the government found itself in desperate straits. The federal and state governments no longer had enough money to pay civil service salaries or complete development projects. "Still," as Larry Diamond put it, "the politicians and contractors continued to bribe, steal, smuggle, and speculate, accumulating vast illicit fortunes and displaying them lavishly in stunning disregard for public sensitivities. By its third anniversary, disenchantment with the Second Republic was acute, overt, and remarkably broad-based."[4]

The second round of elections was held in 1983. All observers assumed that they would be a make-it-or-break-it event for the republic. Unfortunately, the campaign proved even more violent and fraudulent than the previous one. There was blatant manipulation of the voter registration lists, which showed an unbelievable 34 percent increase in the size of the electorate in just four years, most of which occurred in the north. Meanwhile, millions of names were missing altogether from the registers in the south and east.

Both Awolowo and Azikiwe insisted on running for president. Most observers expected that the divided opposition would guarantee Shagari's reelection. But, fearing the worst, the NPN passed out thousands of already completed ballots,

TABLE 15.4 Presidential Elections in the Nigerian Second Republic

NAME	PARTY	PERCENT OF VOTE 1979	PERCENT OF VOTE 1983
Shagari, Shehu	NPN	33.8	47.5
Awolowo, Obafemi	UPN	29.2	37.1
Azikiwe, Nnamdi	NPP	16.7	14.0
Kano, Aminu	PRP	10.3	–
Yusuf, Hassan	PRP	–	3.8
Ibrahim, Izzat	GNPP	10.0	2.5
Braithwaite, Tunji	NAP	–	1.1

GNPP; NPN, National Party of Nigeria; NPP, Nigerian People's Party; PRP, People's Redemption Party; UPN, United Party of Nigeria.

---

[4] Larry Diamond, "Nigeria: Pluralism, Statism, and the Struggle for Democracy," in Larry Diamond, Juan J. Linz, and Seymour Martin Lipset , eds., *Democracy in Developing Countries, vol. 2, Africa* (Boulder, CO: Lynne Rienner, 1988), 53.

bribed election officials, and refused to allow opposition poll watchers to do their jobs. When the votes were counted, Shagari and the NPN had won a landslide victory. The official—and unbelievable—figures gave him nearly 48 percent of the presidential vote, an almost 50 percent improvement over his 1979 tally. Even more amazingly, not only did all the corrupt NPN incumbent governors win, but the party also won six more states, giving it control of thirteen in all. And, despite all the evidence of growing dissatisfaction with the government and the NPN, it turned its slim plurality into a two-thirds majority in the House of Representatives. To no one's surprise, the military stepped in again on New Year's Eve 1983. Like its predecessor, the Second Republic was not to survive its second election.

Military Rule II

At first, the military coup was widely accepted as inevitable given the level of corruption. As a former army leader put it, "[d]emocracy had been in jeopardy for the past four years. It died with the election. The army only buried it."

The new military regime, led by Muhammadu Buhari, was a lot like the old one. The SMC was reconstituted. The military rulers cracked down, arresting hundreds of civil servants and politicians, including the president, vice president, and numerous ministers and governors. Soldiers found vast quantities of cash in the homes and offices of those arrested, lending even more credibility to the rumors of corruption in high places.

Decree Number 2 gave the government broad powers to arrest anyone thought to be a security risk. The military interpreted this to mean anyone who criticized the regime. Decree Number 3 established military tribunals to try former politicians and government officials. Decree Number 4 banned any publication or broadcast that inaccurately criticized any government official or policy.

Support for the regime was not to last. It soon became clear that the officers were far less vigilant in prosecuting former NPN leaders than other politicians. Moreover, the economy continued to founder as the oil-induced crisis sent unemployment, inflation, and the foreign debt skyrocketing. And the government gave indications that it would not prepare a transition back to democracy.

Few were surprised when Buhari was overthrown in 1985 in yet another coup led by General **Ibrahim Babangida** (1941–), who was the first general who actually assumed the title of president. In his first months in power, Babangida sent mixed messages. On the one hand, he immediately repealed Decree Number 4 and declared that his government "does not intend to lead a country where individuals are under the fear of expressing themselves." Journalists were released from jail, and

the detention centers created to hold those arrested under Buhari were opened for public inspection. On the other hand, Babangida continued the crackdown, banning serving politicians from public life for a decade. Babangida renamed the SMC the **Armed Forces Ruling Council (AFRC)**, but in practice there was little difference between the two.

Then, in 1986, the regime embarked on two new directions that made Babangida's rule seem much like Obasanjo's. First, the AFRC accepted a new economic policy of **structural adjustment**, including fiscal austerity and support for markets and other capitalist practices. Second, it announced a phased transition back to democracy to be completed by 1990. Both will be discussed in the section on public policy.

The latter was greeted skeptically by critics who had come to doubt any general's commitment to civilian rule. Their suspicions grew as the government announced a series of delays to its plans to hand over power. Nevertheless, the military plugged ahead with its reform effort, guiding a constituent assembly through the process of writing a constitution for a third republic. The next year, it began rebuilding the political parties. All politicians who held office in the First and Second republics were prohibited from running in at least the first round of elections. Thirteen groups asked to be certified as political parties, but all were rejected. Instead, the government created two new ones, the **National Republican Convention (NRC)** and **Social Democratic Party (SDP)**, which were, in Babangida's own terms, "one a little to the left, and the other a little to the right of center."

Once presidential elections were finally scheduled for 1993, both parties nominated rich business leaders with close ties to the military regime to be their candidates. And despite the regime's attempt to cast politics in national and economic terms, ethnicity remained on center stage. The NRC's candidate, Bashir Tofa, a Hausa-Fulani banker, chose an Igbo Christian as his running mate. The SDP, in turn, nominated Yoruba **Moshood Abiola** (1937–96), a well-known shipping magnate, publisher, and owner of soccer teams. Because he was a Muslim, the SDP thought Abiola might have an appeal in the north as well.

Neither candidate would have made an American campaign manager happy. Tofa was so unknown he did not even appear in Nigeria's *Who's Who*. His commitment to democracy was suspect because he had publicly urged Babangida to stay in power until the turn of the century. Abiola was better known than Tofa, in part because of Afro-Beat star Fela Kuti's song about him and the publicity he received in 1992 for demanding that Britain and the other colonial powers pay reparations for the damage they did to Nigeria and the rest of Africa.

The election campaign had little of the violence that marred previous contests. But that is about the only positive thing that one can say about it. Only about 30 percent of the population turned out to vote. Voting patterns once again broke along ethnic lines, as Abiola ran far better in the east and west and Tofa in the north.

Unofficial results showed that Abiola won easily with 55 percent of the vote. But even before the election took place, a shadowy group close to Babangida—the Association for a Better Nigeria—called on the general to stay in power. As the results began coming in, the association went to court, citing rampant corruption in an attempt to get the publication of election returns overturned.

Finally, on June 23, the military nullified the election. It issued a decree claiming, "These steps were taken to save our judiciary from being ridiculed and politicized locally and internationally." Babangida insisted the military still intended to return the country to democratic and civilian rule in August, but it was hard to see how that could happen.

In turn, Abiola and his supporters went to court and took to the airwaves to defend what they clearly saw as a victory at the polls and to proclaim their boycott of any subsequent reruns at the polls. More protests took place, especially in Lagos, Abiola's base of support. On August 26, Babangida decided to forgo another election and turned power over to a handpicked civilian government headed by Ernest Shonekan, the former chief executive officer of Nigeria's largest business conglomerate. Although Shonekan claimed otherwise, he was little more than Babangida's puppet.

This attempt at civilian rule was to last eighty-three days, which makes it hard to even talk about a third republic. In November, the Supreme Court ruled that the Shonekan government had been put in office illegally. Within days, he was forced out of power by yet another military leader, **Sani Abacha**, who had been a coconspirator with Babangida in 1983 but had since become one of his fiercest critics.

Military Rule III

Abacha appointed a number of civilians to his cabinet, including Abiola's running mate, a leading civil rights lawyer, and the editor of the largest independent newspaper. Nonetheless, Abacha's rule turned out to be the most repressive and the most corrupt in Nigerian history.

In the summer of 1994, Abiola declared himself president. The government responded by arresting him and dozens of others. Abacha declared that "choosing the path of confrontation and subversion at this time of our national history will not be tolerated. Such acts will be sternly punished." All civilian political organizations were officially disbanded by the Provisional Ruling Council, which was made up exclusively of officers.

Opposition continued with a long series of strikes, concentrated in the petroleum industry and located mostly in the southwestern part of the country where Abiola was born and raised. The regime cracked down on dissidents—real and imagined—culminating in the execution of the writer and environmental activist **Ken Saro-Wiwa** in 1995.

Then the government cracked down harder than ever to keep its real and potential opposition cowed. In late summer 1995, Abacha purged the cabinet and fired leaders of the trade unions, the military, and all other government institutions except for the elementary school system.

More worrisome for most was the repression of dissidents, including the Nobel Prize–winning author Wole Soyinka, who had his passport seized and was forced into exile. Other government opponents, like radical lawyer Gani Fawehinmi, spent time in jail under a new law that allowed the government to imprison people without trial. Detainees included leaders of the National Democratic Coalition and the Campaign for Democracy as well as former President Obasanjo, who was sentenced to death shortly before the military government fell.

The government gained some international support for sending its troops to neighboring countries on peacekeeping missions, but took more criticism for its human rights and economic policies. It got to the point that a joke circulated about how Abacha's Nigeria exported what it did not have (pro-democratic troops) and imported what it already had (oil). At the same time, the military was losing its grip on power, which came to an end in 1998 when Abacha died under mysterious circumstances.

The Fourth Republic

After Abacha died, the presidency was given to yet another general, **Abdulsalami Abubakar**. In the face of considerable pressure at home and from abroad, Abubakar announced plans for a speedy return to democratic rule.

We could consider here why military rule unraveled under Abacha and how that helped pave the way for the creation of the Fourth Republic. But it makes more sense to see those details in the context of the broader prospects for democratization included in the section on public policy.

Weeks of uncertainty ended with the election of Obasanjo as president. He took office with more popular support and enthusiasm than the country had seen since the first heady days after independence. Interviews with average Nigerian citizens by Western journalists showed widespread support for democracy and the new president.

Though once a military dictator, Obasanjo had become one of the continent's leading advocates for

Profiles
Sani Abacha

Sani Abacha was the military ruler of Nigeria from 1993 until his death in 1998. He was born in the northern city of Kano in 1943. After graduating from high school, he joined the army and received further training at some of the most prestigious military academies in Great Britain. He then rose through the ranks very quickly and was promoted to general in 1980, at which point he received further training in Monterey, California.

There is some debate about his role in General Ibrahim Babangida's coup in 1983 or in his subsequent government. By the early 1990s, Abacha had certainly become one of the regime's most vocal "insider" critics. When the 1993 election led to another coup, he was the obvious person to lead the next military government.

His was probably the most ruthless and certainly the most corrupt of Nigeria's military governments. It is estimated that Abacha's family alone spirited $5 billion out of the country, a sum probably equaled by what his colleagues stole. Abacha died at his villa in June 1998. Rumors about his death still circulate. The most credible one is that he suffered a heart attack after taking Viagra as part of an encounter with four Indian prostitutes.

His legacy endures. One of the most popular Nigerian Web scams comes from someone claiming to be his widow who seeks help in obtaining their funds, which are supposedly frozen in foreign bank accounts. ■

Nigerian President General Sani Abacha at the airport of Abuja shortly before he died of cardiac arrest.

reform and democracy in the twenty years after he had turned over power to the civilian leaders of the second republic. He was one of the founders of Transparency International (www.transparency.org), a leading NGO that advocates openness in government.

In his first term in office, Obasanjo offered evidence for optimists and pessimists alike. Several northern states adopted Sharia, the Islamic legal system, despite opposition from the non-Muslim half of the population. The army bloodily suppressed ethnic fighting in the state of Benue. Rioting in Lagos resulted in hundreds of deaths. The Miss World pageant, scheduled for the Muslim-dominated city of Kaduna, was forced out of Nigeria by protesters who believed that a beauty contest was an insult to Islam.

Corruption remains so widespread that civil servants are often referred to as lootocrats. In short, the old problems continue in the new Nigeria.

Optimists saw hope in the fact that ethnic divisions had not played much of a role in either the 1993 or 2003 elections. There was hope, too, in the formation of the New Partnership for African Development by the Nigerian, Algerian, and South African presidents.

In 2011, Nigeria finds itself at a critical turning point in its hopes to solidify a fourth and lasting republic. As noted earlier, Yar'Adua was elected to replace Obasanjo in 2007, marking the first time that one elected president who replaced another lasted more than a few months in office. But his long and fatal illness brought the relatively unknown

Jonathan to power at a time when the country seemingly needed more veteran and visible leadership. A little more than a year into his presidency, however, things seem to be going reasonably well.

POLITICAL CULTURE AND PARTICIPATION

Any country's political culture reflects the impact of its history on the way people think about politics and society as a whole. In Nigeria's case, the lack of unity and support for the regime and, at times, for the very existence of Nigeria, have plagued it since independence. If anything, the actions of the elites since then have left the country more polarized than it was fifty years ago.

Mass Political Culture

As is the case in most of the Global South, there have been no systematic studies of Nigerian culture even though most scholars are convinced that it is one of the most important causes of its fluid, unstable politics. Because of the lack of systematic studies, all we can do here is outline the broad themes they point to.

First and most obviously, there is little that Nigerians like about their political system. Things did not start that way. Polls conducted in the early 1960s suggested that Nigerians had a greater sense of national identity and pride than did most people in what we then called the Third World. One 1962 survey, for example, found that only 16 percent of those sampled had trouble thinking of Nigeria in national terms. Similarly, three-quarters of that same sample felt that Nigeria had "made progress" over the previous five years, and two-thirds thought it would continue to do so in the five years to come.

A survey conducted forty years later found that 68 percent of Nigerians believed that "democracy is preferable to any other kind of government." The same poll reported that half of all Nigerians supported a free market economy while 41 percent thought the government should plan production and the distribution of goods and services. However, neither the early optimism nor the more recent sentiments in favor of democracy have turned into sustained support for any of the country's regimes. If anything, Nigerians have grown more skeptical and cynical. A recent poll showed that 20 percent of Nigerians thought that in "some circumstances, a non-democratic government can be preferable."

Part of the problem is that Nigeria is one of the most fragmented countries in the world. Naive observers assumed that ethnic identifications would give way to a national one soon after independence, not just in Nigeria but in the newly independent states in general. That has not been the case. If anything, ethnicity has become more, not less, important.

The limited evidence available to us suggests that most Nigerians do think of themselves as Nigerians. However, their ethnic identification matters more than their Nigerian identification, both as a source of pride (e.g., we Igbo) and, even more important, as a source of dislike and division (e.g., you Yoruba).

The three largest groups have virtually nothing in common politically, socially, or historically. The overwhelming majority of Nigerians only speak their "home" language, and if they learn another, it is invariably English and not one of the other indigenous tongues. The different groups live separately, either in their traditional regions or in ethnic enclaves referred to as *sabon gari*, literally "strangers' quarters."

Closely paralleling ethnicity is religion. Religion is nowhere near as important as ethnicity in most of the south, where, for instance, Yoruba Muslims tend to act politically as Yorubas more often than as Muslims. In the north, however, it is hard to disentangle the impact of religion and ethnicity because so much of Hausa-Fulani culture is defined in terms of Islam. Traditional political and religious officials (who are often one and the same) have resisted attempts to "Westernize" the region, often with considerable success. Women in the north have voted only under limited circumstances and then only in voting booths that are separate from and perpendicular to those for men. The northern desire to use a separate legal system based on Sharia, or Islamic law, held up the drafting of the constitutions for every republic, although northern states have been allowed to implement versions of it since Obasanjo returned to power.

Finally, there is the region itself, which transcends both religion and ethnicity in even broader fears the north has about the south and vice versa. As we saw earlier, many northerners are afraid that southern (or modern) cultural values and economic practices will undermine their way of life. Southerners, by contrast, fear that a northern majority could seize power and leave them a permanent and aggrieved minority.

Nigeria is by no means the only country divided along these kinds of lines. The problem is that Nigeria is not just fragmented, it is polarized as well. Under the best of circumstances, it is hard for people to reach compromises about identity-based issues. The use of Sharia in some parts of a country but not in others is seen as a win-lose conflict. Any concession is viewed by many as a total defeat. In Nigeria, the politicians who have fanned the flames of ethnic, religious, and regional hatred also failed to address the country's social and economic shortcomings. Therefore, it was just a matter of time before the violence that had been primarily orchestrated by the elites started breaking out among an increasingly embittered public.

The importance of this alienation has been magnified by other aspects of Nigerian political culture, not the least of which has been the failure of class issues to take root. Most Nigerians are extremely poor, one of the few things most of them share. Moreover, the gap between rich and poor has grown dramatically, in particular as the corrupt political elite siphoned off public funds to support its lavish lifestyle. Had economic issues become more important in defining basic values and assumptions about politics, Nigeria might have found itself in a better position to mute the divisions along ethnic, religious, and regional lines.

There are also sharp differences between rural and urban cultures. In the countryside, where about half of all Nigerians still live, many "traditional" structures and values remain strong. In particular, rural elites have found it relatively easy to turn the power the British handed them as emirs or chiefs into powerful patron-client relations.

In a 1988 study of politics in rural Nigeria, William Miles showed that the traditional distinction between nobles and commoners has been carried over into the politics of modern Nigeria. Virtually everyone seems to accept the hierarchical relationships in which clients defer to their patrons—and not just politically.

Moreover, most seem to reject such notions as "all men are created equal" or a world in which one's rank or status does not matter. To the degree that it is understood, democracy is sharply at odds with values that remain strong in most areas of rural Nigeria. One herder defined democracy this way in talking with Miles: "Men wander around like cattle, without any direction. They make all kinds of excited noises, but there's no sense to it. Each goes his own way, lost, until there's no more herd."[5]

In addition, illiteracy remains highest in the countryside. Not surprisingly, local studies have shown that most rural residents have at best a fuzzy idea of what national political processes and issues are all about. For instance, on the morning after the 1983 coup, Nigerian radio began playing Western classical music, which residents in one typical village assume is military music because it is only played before the announcement of a coup.

When the announcement itself was made, it was in English, which very few people in the countryside understand. Only two days later was it broadcast in Hausa. Perhaps because of their isolation, rural residents rarely get deeply involved in national politics. Rather, they tend either to follow the initiatives of their local patrons or be swayed by the outsiders who appear during crises or election campaigns.

The ever-growing cities are a different story altogether. There, observers find highly politicized people who seem willing to take a stand on almost any issue at almost any time. They also find large numbers of highly dissatisfied people, alienated from a government that cannot provide jobs, housing, or health care.

That cynicism is not simply an urban phenomenon. The peasants Miles lived with were convinced that politicians are by their very nature dishonest and that it makes no sense whatsoever to trust them. And because cultures change slowly under the best of circumstances, it seems unlikely that these values will erode any time soon.

"The Station"

Some people are trying to break down the barriers among Nigerians. One intriguing effort is "The Station," which was finishing its first year on national television as these lines were written. Produced by Search for Common Ground, "The Station" revolves around the work of journalists at Nigeria's and Africa's first 24/7 news channel. In all, 1,800 Nigerians have been involved in producing the series. The following photo is a scene in which an anchor (in tie) and producer (in a sport shirt) discuss plans for that evening's broadcast.

Search for Common Ground is the world's largest producer of conflict-resolution soap operas. None beat the viewer or listener over the head with their political message. They simply show people solving their everyday problems (www.sfcg.org/programmes/cgp/cgp_station2.html).

Courtesy of Search for Common Ground

Screenshot from "The Station," a program about a television station that was "designed" to be the first 24/7 all-news network in Africa. The series (as opposed to the fictitious station) addresses almost all of the issues facing Africans in Nigeria and beyond.

[5] William Miles, *Elections in Nigeria: A Grassroots Perspective* (Boulder, CO: Lynn Rienner, 1988), 86.

Elite Culture

In every country, elites think and act differently from average citizens. In few places, however, are the differences as pronounced and as potentially politically explosive as they are in Nigeria.

The political and economic elite there has been what amounts to a bourgeois class, if not quite in the way Karl Marx had in mind. Its wealth stems from its control of the state. This situation has given rise to a category of political and bureaucratic officials who have used their positions for personal gain and who, like the European bourgeoisie Marx wrote about, have been able to protect their wealth and power under civilian and military rule alike.

Consequently, with few exceptions, members of the Nigerian elite were willing to violate the rules of the democratic game under the first three republics and overstepped normal bounds of authority when the military was in power. That greed and the willingness to subvert the democratic process that went along with it were shared by the elite as a whole and were not the province of any particular ethnic, religious, or regional group.

Women and Politics in Nigeria

Women play a relatively minor role in Nigerian politics.

In 2007 (2011 figures are not available yet) there were only 26 women in the two houses of the legislature, up from 15 in the one elected in 2003. The International Parliamentary Union uses slightly different criteria and ranks Nigeria 113th of the 129 countries for which it has adequate data.

There are a number of reasons why this is the case. In the Muslim-dominated north, few women are able to even exercise their right to vote, which they only gained definitively in 1976. Similarly, elections are expensive affairs, and few women have access to the supply of money needed to win.

There is a women's movement. The most prominent of its organizations is Women's Rights Advancement and Protection Alternative (WRAPA). Formed in 1999, WRAPA casts its net widely to cover all areas of public and private life in which women are discriminated against.

Nonelectoral Participation

If we looked at culture alone, it would be tempting to conclude that Nigeria is a disastrous civil war or revolution waiting to happen. Yet ironically, neither seems imminent in Nigeria today because of the long history of military rule, which has provided little outlet for protest and has prevented any widespread expectations that mass involvement can accomplish much. Thus, although there have been episodes of spontaneous, violent protest, they have been few and far between in comparison with India or many other ethnically divided societies.

In 2011, political life is particularly strained in the religiously mixed regions in the north, which we will return to at the end of the chapter, and in the oil-rich Niger Delta, which is where Jonathan grew up. The delta is particularly problematic because it is home to Nigeria's one source of wealth.

Chevron and the Role of Multinationals

Above and beyond its relationship with Movement for the Emancipation of the Niger Delta (MEND) and the Nigerian petrochemical industry, Chevron illustrates the dilemmas facing many multinational corporations (MNCs).

It is one of the world's seven or eight leading oil companies. Most of its production is in countries where pipelines run through troubled territory. However one wishes to judge the company's motivation, it has become a leading promoter of conflict resolution, social and economic development, and a sustainable environment in countries like Nigeria.

Since 2001, it has donated an average of $140 million a year to projects in the Niger Delta. It has also become a leading funder of alternative energy research worldwide.

Some analysts think Chevron is just trying to make itself look good. Go to (www.chevron.com) and make your own decisions.

For at least twenty years, the center of the oil-producing region in the Niger Delta has been a political hotspot. Ogoni activists, including Saro-Wiwa, were executed for their opposition to alleged environmental devastation and human rights abuses by Abacha's regime in the 1990s.

More recently, opponents of the oil industry have come together as MEND. MEND members have been accused of everything from siphoning oil from the pipelines to destroying the infrastructure that allows multinational corporations to get the oil to market.

In 2010, MEND agreed to a cease fire in which its militants would take courses in conflict resolution. In practice, most of the fighters were so poorly educated that they could not complete the exams they were given at the end of course

And the violence continued. Young men enrolled in the program get stipends of about $400 a month which is six times the average regional salary, which only serves to magnify tensions. Once the 2011 elections loomed on the horizon, the demand for young men to violently support

Conflict
in Nigeria

Almost every instance of protest politics in Nigeria since independence has revolved around religious, linguistic, and regional issues. No single incident reflects that fact better than a bizarre series of protests that broke out in the northern city of Kaduna in November 2002 that ultimately killed more than one hundred people and injured five hundred more.

For reasons that defy belief, the leaders of the Miss World Pageant decided to hold the 2002 finals in this city populated largely by devout Muslims. Many of the residents were deeply offended by the notion of scantily clad young women parading across the stage of their local civic center. Anger mounted when an English-language newspaper jokingly criticized the anti–Miss World activists by writing that the Prophet Muhammad would probably have chosen a woman like one of these for his wife.

The protests started out calmly enough. Crowds chanted *Allahu Akhbar* (God is great) or "Miss World is sin." Quickly, and without much warning, things turned violent. People the mob thought were Christians were pulled from cars, beaten, and often killed. Churches were burned; Christians later retaliated and burned mosques.

The organizers of the Miss World contest moved it to London. A Muslim Turk won.

One of the few recent incidents of conflict that did not involve ethnicity occurred in the summer of 2004 when urban residents, who are pretty much the only people who own cars, rioted after the government announced that gasoline prices would be set by the market and not fixed at an arbitrarily low level by the government. ∎

In July 2009, MEND's leader was in prison when his supporters supposedly set fire to a pier Chevron and other oil companies used in Lagos. This came at a time when MEND and the government were negotiating for the leader's release and MEND's handing over its weapons.

Just as tensions with MEND seemed to be easing, a new conflict broke out in the north. A hitherto unknown group, Boko Haram, staged a series of attacks, most notably in Maiduguri where upward of one hundred civilians were killed. Boko Haram is thought to be close to the Taliban and other Muslim extremists. Its leader, Mohammad Yusuf, was apparently captured and killed shortly thereafter. Boko Haram may prove to be a fleeting phenomenon, but conflicts among Muslims in the north and between them and the more secular Igbo and Yoruba in the south could prove to be important schisms in a country that is already divided enough. As this book went to press, Boko Haram had taken responsibility for blowing up the UN's building in Abuja in August 2011, killing at least 21 people.

Most of the largest and often violent protests that have wracked Nigeria in the last generation have occurred in the cities, although, ominously, there are now more in rural areas. In 2004, violence broke out in the northern city of Kano, resulting in the destruction of many churches. In the early 1990s, rioters in Lagos burned cars, looted stores, and trashed government offices to protest the government's acceptance of an austerity program imposed by the **International Monetary Fund (IMF)** to be discussed in the public policy section. In urban areas, we also find a wide variety of groups representing doctors, lawyers, students, and more. Informal groups of business leaders or ethnic associations seem to be far more influential, in large part because they can work more effectively within the patron-client networks revolving around religious, linguistic, and regional affiliations that still largely dominate Nigerian politics.

Though they have been few and far between, there have also been a number of interest groups that were not organized along ethnic lines. In particular, they had an important role in pushing for legal and constitutional reform when military rule began to weaken after the execution of Saro-Wiwa and his colleagues. Thus, the sixty-three human rights organizations that made up the Transition Monitoring Group (TMG) brought to light a number of violations of the electoral law during the 1999 legislative and presidential campaign.

Political Parties and Elections

Political parties and competitive elections are accorded a privileged place in theories of democracy. Their very existence is part of the definition of liberal democracy itself.

politicians increased. In the words of Allen Onyema who supervised the course, "Politicians are ready to recruit them. Election year is coming. Even Obubra (where the courses were held), the boys are receiving calls to do one thing or another."[6]

---

[6] "Nigeria's Restive Delta." *The Economist.* January 1, 2011, 57–8.

How they operate in practice goes a long way in determining whether or not democracy will endure.

At this point, it should come as no surprise that at least until 1999, political parties and elections instead contributed to Nigeria's problems because they magnified existing ethnic tensions. Therefore, after the ill-fated presidential election of 1993, the Abacha government banned all partisan activity. Indeed, it was only after his death in June 1998 that the government authorized the creation of new political parties.

Unlike the parties created along with the Second Republic, the parties that sprang to life in late 1998 had little in common with previous institutions. In all, nine political parties gained legal recognition. Each tried to ensure victory in one area of the country and gather at least some support elsewhere. Thus, the successful parties tended to be large coalitions. Of the nine, only three did well enough in state and local elections to be eligible to run in the 1999 legislative and presidential elections.

The two most prominent of them had close links to the military. Obasanjo and others who had come to oppose the Abacha government in the mid-1990s (though only after many of them had been sent to prison) formed the PDP. The smaller **All Nigeria People's Party (ANPP)** was led by politicians who were close to Abacha. Only the small **Action Congress (AC)** had anything approaching unambiguous democratic credentials because it was led by people who had been close to Abiola and to Atiku Abubakar, who ran against Yar'Adua in 2007 despite his having been Obasanjo's vice president for eight years.

Perhaps even more significantly, all the parties had loose but noticeable links to the ethnically based parties that dated back to the First Republic. Although he is a Yoruba, Obasanjo's PDP's roots could be traced back to the dominant Muslim-based parties of the north from the 1960s onward. Similarly, the ANPP had an Igbo stronghold, whereas the AC drew support from a handful of Igbo and the bulk of the Yoruba population. That said, all of the parties are doing a bit better than their predecessors in building support across ethnic lines.

They have to have expanded their base beyond their core ethnic constituency. No presidential candidate can win in an election unless he or she has won at least one-fourth of the votes in two-thirds of the states. As we saw previously, officials in the second republic manipulated a similar requirement to ensure a victory in 1979. So far, that has not been a problem in the fourth republic.

More worrisome is the fact that it is hard to tell where the parties stand on national issues, even after the four national elections since 1999, because their goals and ideologies are rarely mentioned in their own literature or in the press. To complicate things further, sixty-three parties were officially registered for the 2011 campaign for the House of Representatives, although not all were planning to run candidates and only a handful could be taken seriously (detailed final results were not available as of this writing). The seventeen minor party candidates barely won 10 percent of the vote in the presidential campaign, and only three captured a state with one of them proving victorious in just a single state.

Obasanjo, Yar'Adua, and Jonathan were candidates of the PDP (all party websites can accessed at the official Electoral Commission site 🖰 **www.inecnigeria.org/index. php?do=political&id=34**). Their party claims to support a market-based economy but has also pioneered a national health service that would eventually cover all Nigerians.

The ANPP is, in reality, a northern and thus Muslim-based party, which controls six states in the Hausa-Fulani region. It has close links with the former military rulers who grew up in the north, including Muhammadu Buhari, who was its standard bearer in 2007 and 2011.

The AC came in a weak third in 2007 and fourth in 2011. Its candidates, Abubakar and Ribadu, received well under 10 percent of the vote. Its legislative candidates fared marginally better. Although it is the only truly left-of-center party in Nigeria, it seems unlikely to win power any time soon.

Table 15.6 sums up the results of the 1999, 2003, 2007, and 2011 elections, which do not and cannot show how much fraud occurred each time. All the signs are that Yar'Adua won the 2007 election but could not have won as many votes as the official tally suggests. The same is probably true of Jonathan as well.

More worrisome is the fact that elections are becoming more ethnic again. Jonathan carried every southern state but next to none in the north.

As we have seen in previous chapters in Part 4 and will see in the one that follows, election results are often subject to tampering. As many Americans suspected in Florida in 2000, the same can happen in industrialized democracies.

But not on this scale.

THE NIGERIAN STATE

Of the countries we have considered so far in Part 4, Nigeria comes closest to being a failed state without having been defeated in a war. That might seem surprising at first glance. After all, military rulers ran the country with an iron fist for many years. They tolerated little or no organized opposition. Thus, when Abacha and his colleagues seized power in November 1993, they dissolved Parliament and all the other governmental institutions

TABLE 15.6 Elections in Nigeria: 1999, 2003, 2007, and 2011

	HOUSE OF REPRESENTATIVES SEATS	PRESIDENTIAL VOTE	HOUSE OF REPRESENTATIVES SEATS	PRESIDENTIAL VOTE	HOUSE OF REPRESENTATIVES SEATS	PRESIDENTIAL VOTE	PRESIDENTIAL VOTE
PARTY	1999		2003		2007		2011
PDP	206	63	223	63	263	69.8	58.9
APP/ANPP	74	37	96	32	63	18.7	32.0
Action Congress	68	—	34	—	30	7.5	5.4
Others	12	—	7	—	4	4.0	4.7

APP/ANPP, All Nigeria Peoples Party; PDP, People's Democratic Party.

Note: The APP and ANPP ran a single candidate for president in 1999 and Action Congress did not run one in 2003.

that would have been part of the Third Republic. In other words, with the exception of the civil service, the institutions of Nigerian government have rarely lasted more than a few years, and, at any given moment, their structures and operations have reflected the views of whichever group happened to be in power. Yet civil servants are often underpaid, and when they do get their salaries, the money is not enough to live on. As a result, many are corrupt.

Whoever is in charge, the weakness of the state is obvious. Neither the military nor civilian authorities have been able to ensure basic law and order in Lagos and other cities. Foreign diplomats and business executives rarely leave their homes without armed escorts. It is not just the rich and powerful who live in fear for their lives. The bodies of people killed in traffic accidents are frequently left by the side of the road because the officials who are supposed to collect them are afraid of being attacked by gang members or being held until they pay a bribe to the police.

To complicate matters further, the Nigerian state does not have many resources. A full 82 percent of its revenue comes from either the sale of oil or taxes on the profits made by multinational petroleum companies. Although such statistics are reflected in the country's poverty, they also mean that winning control of government is more of a high-stakes contest than it would be in any of the countries covered earlier in this book. In Nigeria, control of the state allows the leadership to put friends, relatives, and clients on government and corporate payrolls and to direct development projects to favored villages and neighborhoods.

The Nigeria State Today

By creating the Fourth Republic, President Obasanjo and his colleagues hoped to end nearly half a century in which Nigeria had a weak, corrupt, and often repressive state and replace it with one that is both more effective and

responsive to the expectations of most of Nigeria's people. The initial signs were not all that encouraging. For example, the new constitution was not published until after the 1999 legislative elections took place, and many of its provisions were not known until after Obasanjo was inaugurated. In the years since then, however, the new institutions have at least demonstrated considerable staying power if not the capacity to create a state that can enact and implement public policy nationwide (**www.nigeria.gov.ng**).

The centerpiece of the new state is its American-style presidency, which is not responsible to the National Assembly (**www.nigeria-law.org/ConstitutionOfThe-FederalRepublicOfNigeria.htm**). It, in turn, has two houses, a 360-member House of Representatives elected from single-member districts and a 109-member Senate composed of three people elected from each state plus a single member from the capital region of Abuja.

For the moment, at least, the presidency is the most important institution, largely because of Obasanjo's pre-eminence as both a current and former leader. How that will translate into authority for Jonathan remains to be seen.

The president is responsible for managing the day-to-day operations of the state and is also commander in chief of the armed forces, an important power in a country with such a long history of coups and military rule. As is the case in most such systems, the president is not a member of the legislature, but he (or she, presumably, at some point in the future) can make statements to it at the request of either body.

The president can only serve two terms. The Senate rejected a proposed constitutional amendment that would have allowed Obasanjo to run for a third in 2007. It is not clear if Jonathan's first year on the job would have counted as a term, but he has already declared that he will not run for re-election in part to resume the alternation between northern and southern leadership in the PCP.

The National Assembly's powers are quite similar to those of the Congress in the United States. Each house must agree on the same version of a bill before it is submitted to the president. Although the president does not have a formal veto power, he must give his assent before a bill becomes law. If he refuses to do so or fails to act within thirty days, the bill is returned to the legislature. If each house passes it again with at least a two-thirds majority, it becomes law without any further action by the president.

The constitution also put in place a fairly standard judicial system for a country with strong Anglo-American legal roots. It retains the previous regimes' network of local and state courts and reinforces the power of a Supreme Court whose authority was often honored in the breach during Nigeria's first thirty years of independence. The one important new feature is an appellate court for Sharia law in Abuja and any individual state that chooses to create one. If a case involves issues that touch on Islam, either the plaintiff or the defendant can refer it to these religious courts rather than to a civil one.

The Personalization of Power

As is the case in much of the Global South, one should not read too much into the formal language of the constitution and other legal documents because individual leaders can bend them to their own "needs" with far more

Profiles
Olusegun Obasanjo

Olusegun Obasanjo was born in 1937 in Abeokuta in the largely Yoruba region in the southwest. Like many soldiers of his generation, he won swift promotion in part because, after independence, Nigerians had to replace the British expatriate officers who had run the military during the colonial era.

At age thirty-three, he was already a general and was the officer who accepted the surrender of Biafran forces that ended the bloody civil war. Six years later, he was part of the group that staged a military coup that made him the country's de facto ruler for the next three years.

Unlike most other military rulers around the world, Obasanjo relatively willingly and relatively graciously presided over the return to civilian rule with the creation of the Second Republic in 1979, at which point he retired from active political life and returned to his home region to set up a poultry and pig farm.

He never fully withdrew from politics, serving on a number of ad hoc groups dealing with broader African issues, including apartheid in South Africa. He also was the founding president of Transparency International.

In 1995, he and forty-three other former soldiers were arrested by the Abacha government. Obasanjo was sentenced to death and expected to be executed before Abacha suddenly died in 1998 and all political prisoners were released. He instantly became the favorite to win the presidency of the new republic, an election he won in a landslide the next year.

Nigerian President Olusegun Obasanjo, *left*, shakes hands with outgoing military ruler Gen. Abdulsalami Abubakar after a ceremony to hand over power to civilian rule in Abuja, Nigeria, on Saturday, May 29, 1999. Promising that "we shall not fail," Obasanjo became Nigeria's first civilian president in fifteen years, ending a string of military regimes that crippled this west African nation.

Most observers think that Obasanjo was one of the most honest and effective elected leaders in recent African history. His critics, on the other hand, point to the fact that at least ten thousand Nigerians died because of their politics in the first term of his presidency and also because of accusations of corruption among the people surrounding the president. ◼

impunity than one finds at least in the countries covered in Part 2. That emphasis on the individual politician may turn out well when he or she is someone of integrity and talent, as seemed to be the case for President Obasanjo. But it also opens the door for abuse of power when the person involved lacks either the ethical principles or the ability he and a handful of other Nigerian politicians have demonstrated over the years. Obasanjo himself understood the stakes he faced, especially the fact that his task included making certain that the military could never come back to power. As he stated shortly after his first election, "We need someone who can act as a bridge for a gradual disengagement of the military. If we don't have someone who can understand them, then I think we will have problems."

In Chapter 5, we saw the importance of "routinizing" the charisma of someone like President Charles de Gaulle. It is by no means clear that Obasanjo did so anywhere near as well as his all but equally tall French counterpart. Failure to routinize charisma in France would have been devastating in the early 1960s; its implications are far less obvious for Nigeria in the early twenty-first century.

In short, doubts persist about the ability of a less respected official such as Jonathan to run the country. He both won the election after a disputed ballot and is not highly thought of in the political community. If and when the economic crisis eases, he may have a chance to complete what Obasanjo only seems to have started.

Corruption

The weakness of the Nigerian state is most evident in the corruption that has plagued the country since independence. Of course, there is much we do not know about the magnitude of the problem because allegedly corrupt officials rarely talk about their ill-gotten gains. There is no doubt, however, that it is widespread. Accordingly, there was little surprise when a 1996 poll of international business executives rated Nigeria the most corrupt country in the world. Along those same lines, President Obasanjo built much of his political base for his return to power as head of Transparency International.

Corruption in Nigeria takes many forms. In 1995, *60 Minutes* broadcast a program on scams run by Nigerian "businessmen" seeking investment capital from naive, rich foreigners. Charges (a euphemism for bribes) are exacted for ignoring environmental regulations on imported goods or even getting a boarding pass for an airplane flight. The customs system is notorious. According to one importer, "No one pays the full customs duty. The going rate is to pay the customs officer a third of the difference between the official rate of duty and what you actually pay in duty (usually nothing)."

Under military rule, the government encouraged foreign investment, but official approval for a contract typically came only when the officers in charge got their "personal interests" satisfied: cars, offshore bank accounts, tuition fees for their children's schooling abroad, and the like.

In 1992, the Nigerian National Petroleum Company (NNPC) had a gap of $2.7 billion—equal to 10 percent of the country's total gross national product (GNP)—between what international experts say it earned and what it claims it took in. The assumption is that the money was diverted to the military leaders' offshore bank accounts.

The corruption in Nigeria is further typified in the actions of the most recent governments to retrieve money allegedly spirited abroad by the Abacha family. Before he turned power over to Obasanjo, Abubakar obtained about $750 million from those accounts. The Obasanjo government convinced Swiss banking authorities to freeze more than $600 million in Abacha deposits and to return nearly $140 million. Banks on the island of Jersey have given $149 million back to the Nigerian government. If government estimates are correct, the Abachas still have $3 billion in foreign bank accounts, and who knows how much other members of the former military regime have in addition.

Some critics suggest that Obasanjo himself was not immune to the lures of corruption. But whatever his role, it was nothing compared to that of his predecessors.

The Obasanjo government did try to reduce corruption. The ninety-three top generals who served under Abacha were replaced as soon as Obasanjo took office. He also revoked all appointments and contracts made by the military after January 1, 1999. During his October 1999 visit to Washington and in almost all his other public statements for domestic as well as international audiences, he stressed the new regime's commitment to honesty.

An investigation in 2004 caused the American company Halliburton to fire several of its top executives in Nigeria. A white paper—a document that outlines what the government intends to do—issued at about the same time charged 130 contractors, including a former presidential advisor, of accepting over 7 billion naira for projects that were never completed. Meanwhile, the National Electrical Power Authority set up a series of anticorruption committees at its offices across the country and fired more than 100 employees charged with corruption.

In this decade, corruption remained a common feature in Nigerian politics. To cite but one example, the House and Senate failed to pass a bill that would have tightened the country's money laundering legislation, a failure to act that was condemned by the Financial Action Task Force, arguably the most important intergovernmental organization fighting official corruption.

Federalism

Another important part of the Nigerian state is its federal structure. At independence, the country was divided into three regions in a way that maximized the influence of the leading ethnic groups. Since then, the country has been subdivided in an attempt to blunt the impact of ethnic conflict. The result is thirty-six states and 449 municipalities, which, as in India, means that every substantial ethnic group can control the government of its "home" territory.

On one level, the creation of so many local government bodies has been a success. If nothing else, having so many smaller states has made local politics less a part of the all-or-nothing game played at the national level. The 1999 constitution did lay out some powers that states would exercise on their end and twelve they were to share with Abuja. Little scholarly research has been done on the impact of those changes.

In other ways, however, the federal system has been an impediment to democracy and stability. There has always been considerable uncertainty about what the respective responsibilities of the central and regional authorities should be. If nothing else, the inevitable duplication of services between the two levels drains the resources of this country that is so poor to begin with.

But most important of all, **federalism** has reinforced ethnicity as the most disruptive force in Nigerian political life. At the same time that it created places where each of the major ethnic groups could govern, it has made ethnic identity the most important stepping-stone to political power under both civilian and military rule.

PUBLIC POLICY

Two issues have dominated policymaking in Nigeria since independence: **democratization** and development. No Nigerian government—civilian or military—has made much lasting progress on either front, giving rise to the widespread futility and dissatisfaction that characterizes political life there today.

Democratization

With the partial exception of Iraq under American occupation, Nigeria is the only country discussed in Part 4 that has explicitly tried to build a democracy after years of authoritarian rule. And it has made three attempts to do so. In that sense, Nigeria is like much of Africa, which has lagged behind the rest of the world in creating democratic regimes. In fact, some would argue that no African country has fared worse at it than Nigeria.

The difficulties start with the First Republic during the years after independence. Development economists often refer to factories that are built by outsiders and then handed over to countries covered in Part 4 as turnkey operations because their managers literally only have to "turn the key" to get them to work. Such facilities are rarely successful because the designers have not adapted the facility to local conditions. If nothing else, they have not trained technicians who can keep the factory working when, as inevitably happens, something breaks down.

In that sense, the First Republic, like most of the initial African regimes, was a "turnkey government." The Second

Profiles
Umaru Yar'Adua

The post military regime in Nigeria has had three presidents.

Olusegun Obasanjo was known as Baba because of the respect he drew throughout the country. His successor, known for his timidity, was often called Baba Go Slow. President Yar'Adua had impeccable political credentials in this violent and unstable country. His family had long been prominent in politics in the north.

Yet, they were unable to avoid controversy. His older brother, for instance, died in prison in 1997.

Yar'Adua's years in office were characterized by a lack of innovation. Perhaps the best that can be said for his government is that it marked the peaceful transition from a Christian to a Muslim leader. Until his death just about halfway through his first term, he had not recovered from the scandals surrounding his election or from Obasanjo's shadow. Also, the economic crisis limited his ability to implement new public policies to address poverty or the many other problems Nigeria faces. ■

Republic was, by contrast, "homegrown," but it fared no better, not surviving its second election. Since then, there have been two more attempts to build a democracy, both of which we will explore in some detail here, because they show us the difficulties of doing so in a country as divided as Nigeria.

Babangida's Failure

After he seized power in 1985, General Babangida decided to make democratization the centerpiece of what he claimed would be a brief period of military rule. Many observers are convinced that he was never strongly committed to democracy or civilian government. Researchers have yet to get access to documentary and other evidence about what really happened, so we simply do not know how seriously to take those charges. Here, we have chosen to take his government at its word because even given the best assumptions about their motivations, the failure of democratization in the late 1980s and early 1990s tells us a lot about both Nigeria and the Global South as a whole.

Babangida endorsed what he called the custodial theory, which holds that military government can be justified only on a temporary basis and only to prepare for the return to civilian rule.

One of the first things his government did was to assess what had gone wrong in the First and Second Republics, in particular the way that ethnicity gave rise to conflict and corruption. The seventeen-member team he designated to create the Third Republic therefore sought to engineer institutions through which a more cooperative, if not consensual, politics could operate. They started by banning all leading politicians and parties from the First and Second republics on the assumption that they had twice demonstrated that they could not run the country. Then they laid out a phased transition that was scheduled to last four years. During that time, the next generation of politicians who lacked practical experience would learn on the job at the local level.

Just as important was the conclusion that the party and electoral systems had to be rebuilt from scratch. The government would license new political parties that could not succeed with narrowly based, ethnic support. The federal government would also fund the parties so that they would not be dependent on local bosses or corrupt officials. A neutral federal election commission would be set up to regulate the conduct of elections. In March 1987, the bureau submitted its report to the military authorities who accepted its basic provisions but pushed the planned date for the elections from 1990 to 1992.

Later that year, the government issued decrees setting up the official plans for the transition. Realizing that democracy requires a more tolerant population than Nigeria had, the government created a Directorate for Social Mobilization whose head described its mission: "If you want democratic government to be sustained over time, then the people have to be enlightened, mobilized, and properly educated."

The problems with the plan surfaced almost immediately. The government rejected all thirteen of the potential parties that emerged from grassroots organizational efforts and created two of its own practically out of thin air. Then it rejected the presidential candidates the two parties initially nominated, which sent them back to the drawing boards.

When the 1993 presidential election actually occurred, it was the most honest and least violent in Nigerian history up to that point. Nonetheless, the government rejected the results and arrested the apparent winner, Abiola, thereby setting in motion the events that culminated in the coup led by Abacha later that fall.

Abubakar and Obasanjo

A more successful so far, at least move toward democracy began in 1999 as we saw previously. Ironically, this shift occurred with far less prior planning and only after Abacha's sudden death the year before.

After Saro-Wiwa and his colleagues were executed in 1995, about forty countries withdrew their ambassadors from Abuja. Leaders throughout the Western world threatened to cancel all pending trade and aid deals, although in the end only military and certain other kinds of assistance were cut. Along with the international pressure, new protest groups developed at home, sparked by the repression, the corruption, and the country's ongoing economic difficulties. Much of the protest focused on the release of Abiola and the establishment of the government that had been elected in 1993.

No one knows what would have happened had Abacha and Abiola not both died in rapid succession in 1998. Their deaths, however, opened the door to a remarkably rapid chain of events that made the Fourth Republic possible less than a year later.

Abacha's successor, General Abubakar, made it clear that he was not planning to perpetuate military rule and announced a timetable for the recreation of political parties and the holding of elections. At the Economic Council of West African States (ECOWAS) summit in late 1998, he announced that this was the one and only time that he would be addressing the delegates. In the end, Abubakar held true to his word and retired on May 29, 1999.

The election and reelection of Obasanjo in 1999 and 2003 seemingly provide evidence for the beginnings of stability, if not national unity. For instance, President Obasanjo made a speech extolling it at the celebration marking the two hundredth anniversary of the accomplishments of Islamic scholar and warrior Usman Dan

Fodio. Less than a week later, a group of northern governors issued a statement pledging loyalty to Nigeria as a single nation.

The regime faced its first serious test in the 2007 election. As the campaign drew near, the potential candidate most frequently discussed was Babangida. In fact, he did not run, but the candidate who came in second was a former military leader. The criticisms of the election and its outcome have not helped the long-term prospects for democracy especially because the victor, Yar'Adua, had been part of the elite since childhood.

The three years Yar'Adua was officially in power did not produce much other than the fact that the new republic survived the transition to a second president—and now a third. The next real test of the Fourth Republic will come when Jonathan's term ends in 2015. Two questions stand out above all the others. Will the PDP be able to continue its alternation between northern and southern leaders? Will Nigeria find itself in a position in which some other party could win or will it continue what looks like its drift toward a one party dominant state.

Economic Development and Structural Adjustment

As has been suggested throughout this chapter, the Nigerian economy is in shambles. Although there have been periods when it grew at a respectable rate and the future seemed promising, the country has not been able to take any significant steps that would dramatically improve the living conditions of its impoverished population. Moreover, its economy has declined dramatically on and off for many years, and the signs currently point to an uncertain and unpromising future.

In many respects, Nigeria has a typical economy for a country in the Global South. Most Nigerians live in utter poverty. Also, like most countries in the Third World, Nigeria's economy is largely based on the export of "primary" products and the import of some food, most manufactured goods, and almost all investment capital. That pattern invariably leaves it vulnerable because it is so reliant on at most a few commodities whose prices fluctuate on world markets.

Even the statistics are suspect. Officially, GDP per capita is about $2,500 a year. But if one includes the "informal" economy or the black market in goods and labor it could be almost twice that. What is not open to question is the degree to which the division between rich and poor shapes the country.

In Nigeria's case, the situation might not seem so bad given its oil reserves. Indeed, many observers expected oil revenues to turn Nigeria into one of Africa's, and perhaps even the world's, leading economic powers. But most of Nigeria's attempts at development have fallen flat on their face. The economy went into a tailspin in the mid-1980s from which it has yet to recover, despite having adopted the structural-adjustment policies all but forced on Nigeria by the IMF, **World Bank**, and other financial institutions.

In part, that economic failure reflects the corruption and mismanagement discussed earlier. It also results from forces beyond the Nigerian government's control. Until the start of the crisis that led to the invasion of Iraq, oil prices had not stayed anywhere near as high as they were after the price shocks of 1973 and 1979. In 1989 alone, for example, the price of oil on the spot market dropped from about twenty-one to fourteen dollars a barrel in one six-month period. That decline cost the Nigerian government almost a third of the export revenues it had been counting on to pay for its imports and to finance industrial and other development projects.

The decline in oil prices produced a crisis of massive proportions. In the second half of the 1980s alone, plummeting prices led to a more than 80 percent fall in GNP and only rebounded slightly in the early 1990s. Graphing oil-price changes is like drawing the side view of a roller coaster. The price went from $21 a barrel in 1996 to about $12 in 1998. In 2000 it rose to over $30 a barrel, but by 2001 it was down to $16. The war against terrorism caused prices to increase to almost $150 a barrel in 2008, which produced a spike in Nigerian economic growth. Nonetheless, production was hampered by strikes brought on by government attempts to raise gasoline prices and violence in the delta region, which led Shell and Total to shut down oil production operations for extended periods because of threats to their facilities and personnel. To make matters more confusing, oil prices have continued to fluctuate and were at $100 a barrel as a result of the political turmoil in the Middle East when we drafted this chapter in May 2011.

The official exchange rate of the naira has never been a good indicator of its real value because most urban Nigerians choose to trade on the black market. In other words, the naira could well be worth quite a bit less than the official exchange rate listed in the Basics Box at the beginning of the chapter.

Whichever version you wish to rely on, the naira's value dropped by about half in the 1980s, a decline that continued through the 1990s. In October 1999, the U.S. dollar was worth 95 naira on the open market; the official exchange rate was 50 to the dollar. This gap allowed military government insiders to buy naira at the official rate and sell them on the black market to earn quick and guaranteed profits. Since 2003, the exchange rate has stabilized at between 120 and 140 naira per dollar.

Democratization
in Nigeria

Nigeria is one of many countries that has tried to make the transition from authoritarian to democratic rule, though few have had as many frustrations along the way.

Although many of the signs are positive for the Fourth Republic, it still has many hurdles to get past before we can feel reasonably certain that it will endure. To begin with, its first and highly popular leader, Olusegun Obasanjo, had to leave office because of term limits. Second, Obasanjo's successors lack his charisma or track record. Third, it is by no means certain that the military will stay as politically neutral as it has been since Obasanjo took office. Fourth, neither the election of Umaru Yar'Adua nor that of Goodluck Jonathan involved the transition to an opposition leader, which is an important step in solidifying any democracy. Finally, it is hard to imagine democracy gaining widespread public support unless the government can address many of the social and economic problems that plague the country. ■

The fall and subsequent re-equilibration of the value of the currency were due to reforms demanded by the IMF and to a 2002 crackdown on banks' international exchange business that may help the Nigerian economy in the years to come. Still, the overall drop in the naira's value is one of the reasons why the country's total debt had gone up by about 1,000 percent during the last twenty years. Politically, it created real problems for the leaders trying to manage the economy and maintain international support for Nigeria.

These are not just statistical abstractions. At the everyday level, the economic changes took a terrible toll on people's lives. The cost of basic foodstuffs increased by a minimum of 250 percent in the second half of the 1980s alone. The price of imported goods rose even faster.

Until the late 1980s Nigerian leaders, civilian and military alike, pursued the then popular development strategy of import substitution. In the 1960s and 1970s they focused on developing Nigeria's industrial base so it could reduce its dependence on imported goods. That, in turn, meant relying heavily on foreign aid and loans for the investment capital that Nigeria could not provide on its own. Thus, right after independence, the U.S. government gave Nigeria a $225 million grant for roads, water supply, and education.

Over the years, Nigeria received considerable aid from both governmental and private sources, which it used to help build universities, factories, and modern urban amenities in its major cities. Typical was the Delta steel complex in Aladja in Bendel state, which opened in 1982. Creating a locally run integrated steel and iron industry has always been a high priority for the Nigerian or any Southern government because they are components of almost all modern industrial products. The Aladja mill was to provide steel rods and other products for factories that would produce finished "rolling" steel. The Nigerian government played a major role in this and other development projects. Normally, it was the recipient of the foreign aid or loans. Either on its own or through the more than ninety partially private and partially public organizations known as **parastatals**, it determined how and where those funds would be invested.

Typical, too, is the fact that the Aladja mill did not live up to expectations. It never operated at more than 20 percent of capacity, which means that other factories that depended on its products were underutilized as well. Another project, the Adjaokuta steel mill, was projected to be Africa's largest steel factory when it was conceived in the boom years of the 1970s, but it was a decade late in coming on line and ended up costing $4 billion more than originally budgeted.

There are lots of reasons for the problems with the iron, steel, and most other industrial sectors. Skilled labor is in short supply. Replacement parts and repairs are too expensive. Nigeria's legendary corruption extends into the economic arena as well as the political. There has also been far less foreign aid than Nigerians expected, far less than the 0.7 percent of GNP annually that the Organisation for Economic Co-operation and Development (OECD) countries initially pledged for the developing world as a whole in 1970.

Whatever the reasons, the bottom line is clear. Two decades after these ambitious projects were conceived, Nigeria could not meet its own industrial demand. In iron and steel, that shortfall reached about 6 million metric tons in 1990, but even if all its plants that were either in operation or under construction worked at full capacity, it would only have been able to produce 1.3 million metric tons. The same was true in every other industrial sector.

Problems existed with agriculture as well. As noted previously, until colonization, the territory that became Nigeria could easily feed its people. Colonial Nigeria was a major exporter of agricultural products. But after independence, Nigerian officials emphasized industrial development at the expense of agriculture. In the 1980s, agricultural products made up only 3 percent of total exports. Moreover, Nigeria also was heavily dependent on imported food. Despite the grandiose "Operation Feed the Nation" (1976–79) and "Green Revolution" (1979–83) schemes, most farmers still use traditional agricultural techniques.

Even though there are now more roads into farming regions and there are more support services, irrigation, and machinery available to farmers, agricultural production has not increased appreciably. Furthermore, there is very little quality control in what is produced and marketed. And as with everything else in Nigerian life, corrupt trading practices take a lot of the potential profit and best produce out of the market.

In keeping with its general policy of **import substitution**, the Shagari government introduced higher tariffs in 1982 and other policies that would make imports more expensive and thus give a boost to domestic producers. Economic conditions did not improve, which was one of the reasons why the military stepped in the next year. The new Buhari administration strengthened the existing import restrictions and offered businesses incentives to encourage them to buy needed goods domestically.

Government spending was cut and new projects frozen, which led to the layoff of thousands of workers. Meanwhile, the price of oil continued to plummet. As it did, the country's debt spiraled upward, at which point the international financial institutions that "owned" the debt stepped in. The Buhari government had to apply to the IMF's Extended Fund Facility for a loan to cover its immediate problems and restructure its long-term debt. The IMF agreed to grant the money and negotiate new terms for the outstanding loans only if the government agreed to a very different set of macroeconomic policies, conditions that have come to be known as *conditionality*. The IMF's conditions were part of the reason for Babangida's 1985 coup, leading the new government to declare an economic state of emergency that October. A massive public debate ensued. Ultimately, the government decided to reject the IMF loans under the proposed terms, but it did agree to do whatever was necessary to restructure Nigeria's economy in a more profitable direction, which, in the end, meant acceding to northern demands.

Late that year, Babangida announced a two-year **structural adjustment** program, which has been extended in one form or another ever since. Its goal was to expand exports other than oil, reduce the import of goods that could be manufactured locally, achieve self-sufficiency in food production, and, most notably, increase the role of the private sector. Tariffs were reduced and import-license procedures

simplified or, in some cases, eliminated altogether. In 1986 alone, seventeen parastatals were privatized, and by 1990, sixteen more had been as well. Another thirty have been sold since then.

There is more investment capital available. Foreign investors can now own a 50 percent share of existing enterprises and a controlling ownership or, in some cases, even total ownership of new ones. In summer 2010, for instance, the government announced plans to attract $10 billion in foreign investment to take over the decrepit electrical generation industry. That same year, the government began negotiations to sell the Nigerian National Petroleum Company which has a monopoly in the domestic market. In all, dozens of industries from cement to the national airlines and a number of banks are at least in the process of being sold.

So far, structural adjustment's record is mixed. At first glance, things are improving. GDP doubled between 2005 and 2010 without counting the underground economy.

On balance, however, the transition has been difficult. Debt remains high, and interest on those loans continues to eat up about a third of the government's annual budget. The official inflation rate increased from 12 percent in 1987 to nearly 50 percent in 1989 before it began to level off at about 12 percent again early in this century. That did not help unemployment, which has finally leveled off at about 5 percent. Most important of all, whatever the benefits of structural adjustment, economic control has shifted either outside the country altogether or to a small, increasingly wealthy domestic elite. Economic inequalities have increased, and structural-adjustment plans in general provide few, if any, incentives for the beneficiaries of economic growth to deal with poverty and other social problems.

Progress under structural adjustment or any other economic strategy was also hindered by the bribes and other corrupt practices that remained central feature of Nigerian political life, even after Obasanjo was elected. Thus, in 2001, the Nigerian authorities were able to meet but four of the eleven conditions laid out by the IMF in granting the country a loan three years earlier.

In the end, real and sustained growth may require Nigeria to end its economic dependence. Obasanjo's team tried to do that with limited success. Yar'Adua's administration did not do as well. It is too early to tell if Jonathan's team will fare any better.

THE MEDIA

As is the case almost everywhere, most Nigerians learn about political life primarily through the mass media. For most of its history, Nigeria has had a reasonably free press.

Economic Liberalization and Globalization

in Nigeria

Nigeria shares many of the problems that all less developed countries are facing as they struggle to integrate their economies into the increasingly interdependent world economy. That has been true since before Nigeria gained its independence, but it has become particularly burdensome in the last twenty years, when the debt crisis and other problems led international financial leaders to require that governments adopt structural adjustment plans in order to receive loans and aid. These programs typically include reductions in tariffs, the encouragement of foreign investment, the greater use of markets in domestic economic life, privatization of state-owned enterprises, and fiscal restraint on the part of the government.

The logic behind structural adjustment is that, in time, Southern economies will find profitable niches that will stimulate rapid growth in general. The problem is "in time." So far, the benefits of structural adjustment have gone to relatively few Nigerians, most of whom were wealthy to begin with.

In other words, the gap between rich and poor has widened considerably in the last generation. There is no better example of this than the riots that occurred when the government tried to change gasoline prices so that they better reflected market conditions. In fact, the protests were so intense that the government had to cancel many of the increases it had intended to implement. ■

Its hundreds of newspapers and magazines reflect a wide range of opinions on almost every issue. To be sure, the various military regimes cracked down on the press and even closed some outlets at moments of the highest tensions, as was the case after Saro-Wiwa was executed. But in general Nigerians have had access to a free press.

The problem is that relatively few Nigerians are literate enough to read a newspaper or wealthy enough to afford to buy one. Therefore, the key to feedback in Nigeria is radio and television, which civilian and military authorities have tried to control through the Nigerian Broadcast Commission (NBC).

Since the creation of the Fourth Republic, the NBC has struggled to find a balance between a desire to foster national unity and the new constitution's provision that states could establish and even own radio and television stations, which most of them now have done. The contradiction between those two positions became clear in 2001 when the state of Zamfara created a radio station, Voice of Islam, that infuriated Christians already worried about what they saw as the extreme use of Sharia in the state. Zamfara's leadership, for example, had authorized the beating of a woman who conceived a child out of wedlock and banned women's soccer as un-Islamic. The media, especially television has spread largely through cable and satellite services, but their impact is limited by the fact that there is a total of 7 million sets of any kind in the country.

CONCLUSION: THE IMAM AND THE PASTOR

At this point you might well be asking a question that has lurked below the surface throughout this chapter. Why should there even be a Nigeria? After all, Nigeria as we know it began as an artificial creation of the colonial powers, and its history has at best been a rocky one ever since. It has never come close to creating an effective government or a modern economy despite all the human and natural resources Achebe alluded to in the statement that begins this chapter. In other words, it may well be the case that the Nigerian people would be better off if the country split up into at least three parts representing the main geographic and ethnic divisions of the First Republic.

But there is some hopeful news.

In the late 1980s, Pastor James Wuye and Imam Muhammad Ashafa ran rival militias in the northern city of Kaduna, which is one of the few places were Muslims and Christians live side by side. It is also where the initial rounds of the Miss World contest were held in 2002.

Early in this century, the two men decided that their rivalry no longer made sense. They began reconciling their personal differences and then embarked on a larger project on interfaith understanding, that resulted in the highly acclaimed film, "The Imam and the Pastor," at least some of which is available for free on the Internet (**www.fltfilms. org.uk/imam.html**). Like "The Station" mentioned earlier, this film is a sign of what could go right in Nigeria.

We can only hope so.

Looking FORWARD

WE ONLY HAVE one more chapter on a single country to go.

As we noted in Chapter 11, it is impossible to represent the entire Global South with only five countries. However, as we have seen so far, each chapter adds something important—if not always typical—to our understanding.

In Chapter 16, we will see that Mexico has some unusual characteristics, not the least of which is its close relationship with the United States, which some would say is too close. But, we will also see that in its own way, Mexico shares two key features with Nigeria. First, it has long struggled and is still struggling to create a viable and durable democracy. Second, it has had to bow to pressure from the United States and the rest of the international financial community and shift away from an economy based on import substitution to one that relies on markets through structural adjustment.

Key Terms

Concepts

democratization
dual mandate
federalism
Hausa-Fulani
Igbo
import substitution
indirect rule
middle belt
parastatal
structural adjustment
Yoruba

People

Abacha, Sani
Abiola, Moshood
Abubakar, Abdulsalami
Awolowo, Obafemi
Azikiwe, Nnamdi
Babangida, Ibrahim
Balewa, Tafawa
Bello, Ahmadu
Ironsi, Aguiyi
Jonathan, Goodluck
Kano, Aminu
Macaulay, Herbert
Obasanjo, Olusegun
Saro-Wiwa, Ken
Shagari, Shehu
Yar'Adua, Umaru Musa

Acronyms

AC
AFRC
AG
ANPP
FEC
IMF
NCBWA
NCNC
NEPU
NNDP
NPC
NPN
NPP
NRC
NYM
PDP
PRP
SDP
SMC
UMBC
UPN

Organizations, Places, and Events

Action Congress (AC)
Action Group (AG)
All Nigeria People's Party (ANPP)
Armed Forces Ruling Council (AFRC)
Biafra
Federal Executive Council (FEC)
International Monetary Fund (IMF)
National Congress of British West Africa (NCBWA)
National Council of Nigeria and the Cameroons (NCNC)
National Party of Nigeria (NPN)
Nigerian National Democratic Party (NNDP)
Nigerian People's Party (NPP)
Nigerian Republican Convention (NRC)
Nigerian Youth Movement (NYM)
Northern Elements Progressive Union (NEPU)
Northern People's Congress (NPC)
People's Democratic Party (PDP)
People's Redemption Party (PRP)
Social Democratic Party (SDP)
Supreme Military Council (SMC)
United Middle Belt Congress (UMBC)
United Party of Nigeria (UPN)
World Bank

Useful Websites

The Nigerian government now has a very good portal with links to its main offices and departments:

www.nigeria.gov.ng

The Library of Congress has commissioned a series of country studies over the years, all of which are now available online. One of the most useful and most recent is:

countrystudies.us/nigeria

There are now a number of portals that include general information about Nigeria and its politics. These include:

www.nigeriamasterweb.com/Politics.html

www.nigeriaworld.com

There are also a number of sources of news on Africa, including Nigeria. The first to be owned by Africans based in the United States is:

www.usafricaonline.com

Further Reading

Aborisade, Oladimeji, and Robert Mundt. *Politics in Nigeria,* 2nd ed. New York: Addison-Wesley, 2002. The best text-book on Nigeria.

Achebe, Chinua. *The Trouble with Nigeria.* London: Heinemann, 1984. Although very dated, this book addresses many of the problems Nigeria still faces today, especially its leadership.

Campbell, John. *Nigeria: Dancing on the Brink.* Boulder CO: Rowman & Littlefield, 2010. By far the best recent book that was written for a general audience.

Davidson, Basil. *Modern Africa.* New York: Longman, 1983. One of the best overviews of modern African history that puts Nigeria in perspective.

Dike, Victor. *Nigeria and the Politics of Unreason.* London: Adonis-Abbey, 2003. One of the highly critical books on the Obasanjo government.

International Crisis Group. The International Crisis Group does the best research on crisis burdened countries. Its work on Nigeria is state of the art. Go to the website, *www.crisisgroup.org,* and then navigate to Nigeria.

Maier, Karl. *This House Has Fallen.* Boulder, CO: Westview, 2000. An outstanding account of military rule in the 1990s.

Schwab, Peter. *Designing West Africa.* London: Palgrave, 2004. This book provides a historical overview for most major West African countries and thus puts Nigeria in perspective.

CHAPTER 16

Mexico

Our evidence does not support the conclusion that Mexican society is deeply divided along the lines usually associated with profound political cleavages.

JOSEPH L. KLESNER

A POTENTIALLY DEVASTATING CRISIS?

We began every other chapter with a quote we knew we believed in. We are not sure about this one. Joseph Klesner is an expert on Mexico and therefore knows a lot more about the country than we do. But from the vantage point of mid-2011 his words only ring partially true, for reasons that had not arisen when he wrote that sentence a few years ago, because Mexico comes closer to being a **failed state** than any of the countries we cover.

We revised this chapter after Chip returned from a conference with senior officers at the Special Operations Command (SOCOM) where we were asked to look at the implications of migration and related issues for Mexico for the next decade or so. Our conclusions were fairly bleak and very typical. Mexico faces a series of problems it *may* not be able to handle, and it *may* turn into a failed state for four main reasons.

First, there is the economic crisis. As the Basics box shows, Mexico is relatively prosperous compared to other countries in the Global South. However, its economic prospects today do not seem so promising. There is debate over whether the **North American Free Trade Agreement (NAFTA)** has

THE BASICS	
Mexico	
Size	1,972,550 sq. km (roughly three times the size of Texas)
Population	114 million
GNP per capita	$13,800
GNP growth rate	5% (2010)
Out migration	3.24 people per 1,000 per year
Currency	12 peso = US$1
Religion	76% Catholic, 6% Protestant, 17% Unspecified or None
Capital	Mexico City, Federal District
President	Felipe Calderón (2006–)

Looking BACKWARD

MEXICO IS THE final country we will consider. It is a good country to end Part 4 with because it allows us to see most of the themes of the last five chapters one more time.

It has much in common with those other countries except for disruptive identity based conflict. Like them, it is still quite poor and has had to shift its economic policies under pressure from the International Financial Institutions. There are questions about the effectiveness of its state. Indeed, it may be closer to a failed state than all but Nigeria. As with all the others, it lives in the shadow of the rest of the world. In this case, the impact of global forces will be a bit different because Mexico is primarily influenced by a single country—the United States. In short our final country will cover much of the ground dealt with in the previous four chapters.

helped or hurt Mexico. There is little doubt that it has caused dislocations at home that both added to the pressure to emigrate and helped fuel the drug wars.

Second, the United States can't be kept out of a chapter on Mexico. Indeed, of all the countries covered in *Comparative Politics*, no other is as interconnected with and dependent on a single neighbor than Mexico.

Mexico's second largest source of foreign income comes in the form of remittances from its citizens living in the United States, amounting to about $25 billion in 2008. That figure dropped 14 percent in 2010 and 2011 because the American recession hit Mexicans living and working there particularly hard. There are even some signs that unemployed Mexicans in the United States are returning home (there are no figures about how many) to a country that already has a moderate unemployment rate and where almost 15 percent of the population lives below the poverty line as defined by lacking adequate access to a nutritious diet.

Third, Mexico's government is currently paralyzed. In 2000, **Vicente Fox** (1942–) of the **National Action Party (PAN)** became the first president elected from the opposition after more than seventy years of rule by the **Institutional Revolutionary Party (PRI)**. Many outside Mexico saw this as a welcome change. However, Fox never had a majority in Congress, which limited his ability to

Members of a Mexican drug cartel at their arraignment.

ALFREDO ESTRELLA/AFP/Getty Images

enact sweeping reforms. The same is true of his fellow PAN member **Felipe Calderón** (1962–), who replaced him in 2006 because elected officials in Mexico are only allowed to serve one term. A new president will be elected in 2012; he (there are next to no women who could conceivably win) will face a similarly divided government. In short, Mexico now has something akin to the gridlock that often keeps an American president and Congress from passing sweeping legislation.

Finally, Mexico also faces violent fighting between drug cartels and the authorities. The death toll in the drug wars is now at least 40,000. Ironically, most of the weapons the cartels used were smuggled in from the United States—there is only one legal gun store in all of Mexico.

The country has long been a conduit for the trafficking of drugs and immigrants from all of Central and South America to the United States. In the last few years, the drug trade has begun to tear Mexico apart. About 70 percent of the illegal drugs entering the United States come by way of Mexico, although few were produced there. That trade is controlled by a handful of powerful cartels , which are at war with each other and the government.

Mexico has a lot going for it. It ranks seventh in the world in oil production, pumping in excess of a billion barrels a day more than Nigeria. Petroleum products account for as much as 40 percent of its gross national product (GNP). As former foreign minister Jorge Castañeda points out in his recent book, *Mañana Forever?*, overall living standards have risen rapidly since NAFTA.

Thinking About Mexico

Most readers of this book live in the United States. That means that most will be more interested in Mexico than any other country in the Global South. But just because people in the United States and Mexico share a long border, that does not mean that Americans know much about their southern neighbor. That ignorance often leads to stereotypical images about what Mexico is like and what public policy toward it should be.

The Basics

Poverty

Mexico is not as poor as most counties that could have been included in Part 4. Although it is not one of the BRICS countries, the World Bank ranks Mexico's economy ahead of Russia's. It has a middle class whose lifestyle rivals that of the United States. Similarly, it is one of the world's fifteen leading industrial powers.

For much of the past forty years, stagnation rather than growth has been the economic norm. Thus, growth averaged only about 1 percent per year in the 1980s, though it is higher now, especially since NAFTA went into effect in 1994. By contrast, inflation typically topped 50 percent per year in the 1980s and stood at nearly 30 percent before the government began to get it under control in the late 1990s.

This translates into continued poverty for many Mexicans. Housing and health care are not very good. More than 20 percent of Mexicans do not have access to either safe drinking water or indoor plumbing. Many Mexicans cannot find jobs that provide themselves and their families with more than a subsistence income, which contributes to the steady flow of immigrants to the United States. In the decade after NAFTA went into effect, the number of people in extreme poverty (income that is 25 percent below the poverty line) grew from 17 to 26 million. Eight percent of the population lives on less than the equivalent of $2 a day today. The cities are overcrowded, and Mexico City is so polluted that most experts doubt that its air can ever be made safe to breathe again.

Mexico's economic difficulties are compounded by its massive debt. Like many Third World countries, Mexico borrowed heavily during the 1960s and 1970s on the assumption that it could use oil revenues to pay back the banks and governments that had issued the loans. When prices fell after the oil crisis of 1979, Mexico's debt skyrocketed, reaching more than $100 billion in the late 1980s. Although it declined somewhat in the early 1990s, total debt leaped back toward late 1980s levels as a result of the peso crisis in 1995. For the bulk of this century it has been $210 billion a year.

But things are changing and Mexico is growing rapidly. As Castañeda tells us, about half of all Mexicans own their homes. The spread of other middle class consumer goods is continuing at about that same pace. So is the number of children graduating from high school and university. The distribution of income is probably not as skewed as it was.

Diversity

Mexico is also a remarkably diverse country, which may not be apparent to generations of Americans raised on Westerns with their scenes of an arid, wide-open country of mountains and deserts. That image applies only to the northern part of the country. Southern coastal regions are hot and humid, but as you move inland and into the mountains, the climate turns more temperate.

The stereotypes are right in one respect: Mexico is a rugged country. Between the mountains, deserts, and jungles, only about 12 percent of its land is arable, and much of that land is marginal at best. But Mexico does have natural resources in two areas: minerals and petroleum. Mining became an important industry the day the Aztecs greeted Hernán Cortés and his fellow Spaniards with what seemed like mountains of gold artifacts. In the twentieth century, the discovery of substantial petroleum reserves turned Mexico into one of the world's leading oil and natural gas producers.

The Mexican population is also extremely diverse. Relatively few Spanish women came to New Spain, as Mexico was called after the conquest in the sixteenth century. Moreover, unlike the situation in the British colonies to the north, the Spaniards did not kill off most of the people they encountered. In short, marriages and non-marital sexual relations between Spanish men and Indian women were common, so that now the largest group of Mexicans are **mestizos**—part Indian and part white. A substantial number of blacks also were brought to Mexico as slaves, especially in the state of Veracruz along the Gulf coast, which many observers think still feels more Caribbean than Mexican.

Mexican Names and Places

There are two linguistic issues to keep in mind while studying Mexico.

First, names. As in most Spanish-speaking countries, Mexican names have the following structure: first or Christian name, father's family name, mother's maiden name. Some Mexicans (e.g., President Felipe Calderón) do not routinely include their mother's family name. It can be confusing, but it will be clear which is which from the usage below. If there are three names, it is the middle one that denotes the family, as in Carlos Salinas de Gortari.

And, like most writers, we will regretfully use the term American to refer to the United States. Anyone who lives in either North or South America is, of course, an American. However, given the way the English language has evolved there is no other stylistically acceptable adjective to describe things and people from the United States.

Currently, terms like Indian or *mestizo* are not often used to describe people's physical appearance. Instead, they refer to the culture they were raised in. The very term "Indian" is controversial. Some scholars refuse to use it, preferring the not dramatically better term "indigenous." Whichever term you use, Mexicans, like Brazilians, are a racial mélange. To complicate matters further, the term Indian is primarily used politically to describe the 5 percent or so of the population that only speaks an indigenous language and are thus not very well integrated into what is predominantly a Spanish-speaking culture. Whatever you choose to call them, Mexicans pay more attention and place more value on their origins than do most people.

The very name Mexico is derived from either Mexica, one of the Aztec tribes, or Mexitl, an Aztec epithet for God. Native influences can be seen in everything from the way many Mexicans dress, to the food they eat, to the way they practice Catholicism.

Big Brother *Is* Watching

All countries in the Global South have had a long and not always pleasant relationship with one or more of the industrialized democracies. The one between Mexico and the United States is unusual in two ways. First, the United States never colonized Mexico, although it did seize one-third of its territory after the Mexican-American War of 1848. Second, the United States exerts more influence over Mexico than any single country has on any of the others covered in this book.

The two countries really are not as "close" as the length of their borders might imply. The United States and Canada share the world's longest unguarded border at least until the aftermath of 9/11. As the seemingly never-ending controversy over immigration reform suggests, the U.S.-Mexican border, in contrast, is one of the most closely patrolled because of the flow of illegal immigrants and drugs heading north. Indeed, some pundits refer to it as the border between the first and third worlds. U.S. concern about the porousness of the frontier only heightened after the 9/11 terrorist attacks, even though neither Mexico nor the border had anything to do with what happened.

The United States and Mexico are increasingly dependent on each other economically. Mexico is the United States' third leading trading partner, trailing only Canada and China. The United States is even more important for Mexico because two-thirds of all Mexican exports are sent north. Even prior to NAFTA, there was significant U.S. investment, especially in the *maquiladora* factories that dot the border and produce goods for foreign markets using low-priced Mexican labor. They have now spread to much of the country as a result of the trade agreement.

More important politically is the migration of Mexicans to the United States. There is nothing new to this. The American Southwest has long been a "safety valve" providing jobs for unemployed Mexicans, who, had they not traveled north, might have fomented protest at home. The Department of Homeland Security estimates that there could be as many as 11 million Mexicans living legally or illegally in the United States, and they send about $20 billion a year back to family members at home, adding more money to the economy than Mexico makes from its agricultural exports.

Many people in the United States believe that Mexican immigrants are a burden, a belief that led to the passage of the **Immigration Reform and Control Act** of 1986 and California's restrictive Proposition 187, which denied illegal aliens access to public service in 1994. Many Americans, too, are worried that the presence of so many Spanish-speaking immigrants (not all of whom are from Mexico, of course) is diluting and threatening American culture.

Both Presidents George W. Bush and Barack Obama wanted to regularize the status of illegal aliens, none of which have come close to passage largely because of opposition from members of Congress from border states with large numbers of immigrants.

American fears notwithstanding, the United States is by far the more powerful partner in this highly unequal relationship. For the two centuries that Mexico has been an independent country, the United States has exerted a massive and often unwanted influence on its politics. This began with the first U.S. ambassador to Mexico, Joel Poinsett, who insisted that the new Mexican government heed Washington's wishes. Incidentally, Poinsett brought back from Mexico the Christmas plant that bears his family name, the poinsettia.

As recently as 1914, American troops invaded Mexico. And although the United States no longer engages in that kind of direct intervention, its indirect leverage—ranging from the tens of billions of dollars Mexico had to borrow in recent years to the impact of its popular culture—may be no less overwhelming. Many Mexicans speak of their "dependent psychology," or the sense that the American big brother is always watching. With its wealth and freedom, the United States is highly regarded by most average Mexicans. At the same time, many are envious of what North Americans have and resent their often arrogant, high-handed interference in Mexican affairs.

A typical lineup of cars waiting to cross the border between Mexico and the United States just south of San Diego. Delays can last as long as four hours.

Key Concepts and Questions

The most important question about Mexican politics cannot be answered yet. As these lines were written, Mexico was nearing the end of the *sexeño* or six-year term of its second non-PRI president in almost a century. President Fox had initiated sweeping reforms, many of which died in Congress. President Calderón faces a similar predicament especially after the PRI made gains in the 2009 mid-term legislative elections. Nonetheless, they each tried to shift the center of gravity of Mexican politics and reinforced the following five questions as central to its future. The question we cannot answer is what happens after the next election. As of July 2011, the list of candidates is fluid, but it does appear that the PRI is likely to win. Other key questions include:

- Why did the PRI win so consistently, and how could it stay in power for so long?
- How and why did forces undermining PRI rule emerge?
- Why did three successive administrations in the 1980s and 1990s embrace **structural adjustment** as fully as any leadership in the Global South?
- How much have those reforms addressed Mexico's poverty and other pressing needs?
- How have the events of the last few decades affected Mexico's all-important relationship with the United States?

THE EVOLUTION OF MEXICAN POLITICS

The evolution of Mexican politics has a lot in common with most other Central and South American countries—Spanish or Portuguese colonization, independence in the early nineteenth century, and a rather tumultuous history afterward (see Table 16.1). There is one way in which Mexico's political history is dramatically different. As should be clear already, the United States has had a massive impact on Mexico at least since its first years as an independent country (**www.mexconnect.com/mex_/history/historyindex.html**).

The Colonial Era

There is much uncertainty about the Indians who inhabited what is now Mexico before the Spaniards arrived. A thousand years ago the Mayans who lived along the Gulf coast had one of the most advanced civilizations in the world, but by the sixteenth century it had already begun to decline for reasons no one fully understands. By that time, the Aztecs had come to dominate dozens of other tribes from their capital of Tenochtitlán (now Mexico City). They

TABLE 16.1 Key Events in Mexican History

YEAR	EVENT
1519	Arrival of Hernán Cortés
1810	Declaration of Independence
1836	Loss of Texas
1848	Mexican-American War
1864	Emperor Maximilian installed
1876	Beginning of Porfirio Díaz's reign
1910	Revolution
1929	Formation of PNR, which renames itself PRI in 1946
1934	Election of Lázaro Cárdenas

were able to establish a centralized empire with an elaborate system of courts, tax collectors, and political-military administrators.

Ironically, the Aztecs believed that white gods in strange ships would one day appear on their shores. Despite fierce resistance from Moctezuma (Mexicans prefer this spelling rather than Montezuma as usually used in English) and, later, his nephew Cuauhtémoc, Cortés was able to use his superior weaponry (with the help of some diseases) to defeat the Aztecs and gradually extend Spanish control over a territory that stretched from what is now northern California well into Central America.

Spanish colonial practices differed dramatically from those of the British. The Spaniards encountered well-established civilizations, not nomadic tribes. They thus had to incorporate the native population into the colonial system in an elaborate hierarchy that placed native Spaniards at the top, their mixed offspring below them, and the massive indigenous population at the bottom. New Spain became part of an exploitative mercantilist empire that sent resources back to Spain but gave little politically or economically to the colonies. The Spaniards also brought the Catholic Church, which, in addition to trying to convert the natives, became an integral part of the colony's government. Perhaps most important, New Spain lacked the degree of self-government that was well established in British North America long before the Revolutionary War. Hints of problems to come appeared under Spanish rule. The church, for example, ended up owning one-third of the country while forcing Catholicism on virtually the entire population. Similarly, by the seventeenth century, huge estates, or *haciendas,* had been formed. Land originally given to the Indians was seized, and the prior owners became indentured servants to their Spanish overlords.

Ultimately, the Spanish were not very effective colonial administrators and were never able to secure their rule throughout the country. Nonetheless, late in the seventeenth century they tried to take firmer control of the colonies, thereby antagonizing the growing Mexican-born elite.

Independence

Although Americans tend not to think about it in this way, the thirteen colonies gained their independence in large part because the British were preoccupied elsewhere and could not commit the resources needed to hold onto a distant, troublesome, and not very important part of their empire. Independence for Spain's American colonies, too, became possible when Spain was weakened by the Napoleonic wars that swept Europe in the early nineteenth century. As a result, Spain could not or would not pay the price to hold onto its colonies in the Americas.

In Mexico, the bloody, decade-long struggle for independence began in 1810 when the *mestizo* priest Miguel Hidalgo y Castillo first proclaimed independence and raised an army of more than one hundred thousand people. Hidalgo proved to be something less than a brilliant military strategist when his forces were slaughtered at Guanajuato. Within a year he was captured and executed, a fate that befell many others who took up the cause before the decade was out. But Hidalgo's forces were never fully defeated, and those who survived took to the countryside and kept fighting.

In the end, it was the lay and clerical elite that finally forged an independent Mexico. They decided that they might be able to maintain their wealth and power against Hidalgo's successors if it was independent. But their victory settled very little.

For more than a hundred years, Mexico careened from crisis to crisis and from *caudillo* (strongman) to caudillo while its social and economic problems festered. To solve them, Mexico needed outside help, but this was not forthcoming due to the tumult of the next century. No historical figure exemplifies independent Mexico's difficulties any better than one of its first leaders, Augustin de Iturbide. Iturbide was a rather unscrupulous opportunist who manipulated Spanish emissaries into granting Mexico its independence and making him the head of the first government. But pressures quickly mounted. When Spain rejected the agreement that gave Mexico its independence because the Mexican government was bankrupt, Iturbide responded by having himself declared Emperor Augustin I. In fact, Iturbide only knew how to rule as a dictator, and by the end of 1823, he had been overthrown. It should be pointed out that U.S. intervention in Mexican politics began in these years, too, when its emissary, Poinsett, made it abundantly clear that the Monroe administration did not approve of the Iturbide regime and left it financially ruined.

The most important political figure over the next thirty years was General **Antonio López de Santa Anna**, best known in the United States for his victory at the Alamo at San Antonio, Texas, in 1836. At home, Santa Anna has a considerably worse reputation, which Daniel Levy and Gabriel Székely describe as follows:

> **In 1848, Mexico's most despised, traitorous, duplicitous native son presided over the loss of roughly half of Mexico's territory in a war with the United States. Santa Anna's most consistent preoccupation was self interest. Among his favorite self-designations were Most Serene Highness, Father of the Country, Savior, and Perpetual Victor. It is a sad commentary on Mexico's political instability from the 1820s to the 1950s that the last title had some validity. Almost no one could establish a viable government and a viable economic base.[1]**

Santa Anna first appeared on the political scene in 1823 when he forced Iturbide into exile and then had him executed when he tried to return. Santa Anna dominated Mexican politics for the quarter-century that followed. Most of the time he operated behind the scenes as a series of weak elected presidents and military officers tried to govern. Meanwhile, the country was torn by conflict, largely over the economic and other powers of the church.

Santa Anna held on to power primarily because of his reputation for defending Mexico's threatened sovereignty, though it must be said that he was not very good at it. He led Mexican troops in overcoming Spanish forces attempting to regain their lost colony in 1830, but after that he fared less well. Despite having defeated the Americans at the Alamo, he proved unable to win the war and keep Texas from gaining its independence. He also could not prevent the United States from seizing Texas and most of northern Mexico during the Mexican-American War in 1848. After the war, Santa Anna was exiled to Jamaica. Remarkably, he was asked back five years later to help restore order. This time he sold parts of what are now Arizona and New Mexico to the United States and used the money to support his repressive regime for two more years before the liberals finally overthrew him and exiled him for good.

For their part, the liberals were unable to secure their hold over the country. Nonetheless, they tried to promulgate a new constitution in 1857, launching the period of—and the war for—reform. In particular, they stripped the church of virtually all its wealth and civil power. In 1861, liberal forces led by General Benito Juárez entered Mexico City and took control of the country.

They were not, however, able to enact many of their reforms. The years of war, intrigue, and chaos had taken their toll. Moreover, now that the American Civil War was under way, the United States could not afford to continue supporting Juárez. British, Spanish, and French forces saw this as an ideal opportunity to intervene, ostensibly to extract payment for their financial losses. At first, Mexican forces defeated the invaders at Puebla in 1862. But the Europeans eventually forced Juárez out of Mexico City and in 1864 installed the Austrian prince Maximilian and his Belgian wife, Carlotta, as emperor and empress. Quickly, the puppet emperor and the French forces that really held power realized that there were few riches to be had and that the Mexicans were not going to accept new foreign rulers. Within three years, Juárez was back in Mexico City. Maximilian was executed and Carlotta was sent into exile.

By the time of the 1871 election, political leaders were looking for someone to replace the aging and less than effective Juárez. Attention shifted to one of his most successful generals, **Porfirio Díaz** (1830–1915), whose campaign for the presidency was based on the idea that no president should be allowed to be reelected. When no one won a majority of the votes, the nation turned to Juárez yet again. But he died the next year, touching off another period of violence and instability that culminated in a coup by Díaz in 1876.

Thus began the longest period of dictatorship in Mexican history, led, ironically, by the man who had introduced the principle of **non-reelection** to political life. To his credit, Díaz brought more than thirty years of stable government after a half-century of chaos. With the stability came considerable foreign investment and the first steps in the development of a modern economic infrastructure. Thousands of miles of railroads were built, as were oil refineries, sugar mills, and electrical generation facilities. Nevertheless, growth came with a price. Order in the countryside was maintained by the ruthless mercenary *rurales*. Perhaps as many as 5 million peasants were forced back into servitude on the *haciendas*, many of which were now owned by foreigners. Perhaps most important, the poor benefited little from the country's economic progress.

The Revolution

By the early 1900s, Diaz's rule had touched off the same kind of broad-based opposition that toppled earlier strongmen. In the countryside, loosely coordinated bands of peasants took up arms, including groups headed by the legendary Emiliano Zapata (1879–1919) and Pancho Villa (1878–1923). In the cities, liberals, too, found themselves increasingly frustrated. In 1910, the anti-Díaz forces found a rallying point in the meek Francisco Madero, who wrote *The Presidential Succession of 1910* in which he pointedly used Díaz's own theme of effective suffrage and non-reelection against the aging dictator. Meanwhile, the new labor movement organized a series of crippling and often violent strikes in the mines and mills.

---

[1] Daniel Levy and Gabriel Székely, *Mexico: Paradoxes of Stability and Change*, 2nd ed. (Boulder, CO: Westview Press, 1987), 23.

All the tensions came to a head with the 1910 presidential election. Madero easily won the nomination of his newly created Anti-Reelectionist Party. As the campaign neared its end, however, Madero was arrested on trumped-up sedition charges. Díaz was declared the winner even though there was considerable evidence that the election was rigged.

Right after the election, Madero's family bribed the government to secure his release on the condition that he would stay out of Mexico City. He took to the countryside, gathering supporters and evidence about electoral fraud along the way. On October 25, Madero and his growing band of supporters issued the Plan de San Luis Potosí, which was a de facto call for rebellion against the Díaz dictatorship.

Madero received strong support from the United States and from populist leaders like Zapata and Villa. In early 1911, he left his base in Texas and started a war against a surprisingly weak federal army, which ended with the agreement that Díaz would abdicate and be replaced by Madero.

The revolution, however, was far from over. Madero proved to be a weak leader, and he quickly lost the support of most of the other populist leaders, including Zapata, who rebelled only two and a half weeks after the new president was inaugurated.

Madero's rule came to an end after the so-called Ten Tragic Days and the coup staged by General Victoriano Huerta in February 1913. Pitched fighting broke out between forces loyal to Díaz and to Madero. After his initial military leader was wounded, Madero appointed the untrustworthy Huerta as his new commander in chief. Before the ten days were over, Huerta had defeated both Díaz and Madero. Madero was arrested on February 18, resigned the next day, and was shot three days later. U.S. Ambassador Henry Lane Wilson played a major role in all of these events.

Despite the American machinations, Huerta, too, was not to survive. A number of regional leaders, including Venustiano Carranza, refused to accept his presidency and took up arms along with Villa and others. Meanwhile, the Woodrow Wilson administration in Washington grew increasingly concerned with the European influence in Mexico—especially in the oil industry—and ended up attacking as well, occupying Veracruz for most of 1914. Between them, the U.S. invaders and Mexican rebels drove Huerta from office before the year was out, leaving yet another power vacuum in the capital. Marauding armies ravaged the countryside, ultimately resulting in the deaths of about 1.5 million people in a country that at the time had only 14 million inhabitants.

By 1916, Carranza, Zapata, and Villa were all forming armies of landless peasants, poor industrial workers, and others whose grievances were unmet and whose lives had been disrupted if not destroyed. Finally, by mid-1916, Carranza had defeated both Villa and Zapata and occupied Mexico City, forcing President Wilson to recognize his government. That fall, elections were held to choose a new constitutional assembly, which brought the bloodiest six years of the country's bloodiest century to an end.

Institutionalizing the Revolution

On several occasions in the course of this book, we have seen that new constitutions do not necessarily lead to sweeping political change. That was also the case in Mexico. Given the instability and violence of its history in the century after 1810, there was no reason to believe that the new constitution of 1917 would fare very well.

Surprisingly, the constitution has lasted and has structured Mexican political life ever since. None of the problems have disappeared, but Mexico has largely been spared the widespread violence that characterized its first century of independence and plagues many other countries in the Global South today.

The new constitution drew heavily on the principles underlying the largely ineffective but popular 1857 document. The president and most other officeholders were denied the right to run for reelection. The power of the church was sharply limited. Foreigners were no longer allowed to own Mexican land or mineral resources. Articles 27 and 123 legalized the breakup of the largest haciendas, though not without compensation for their owners.

At first, there did not seem to be much of a chance that this constitution would be any more successful than earlier ones. Carranza understood the importance of enacting reforms but proved reluctant to put them into effect. Moreover, the new regime was quickly beset by many of the same problems as the old one, and its leaders proved only marginally less corrupt than their predecessors. The Carranza government turned on its opponents, assassinating Zapata in 1919 after luring him to a meeting supposedly to discuss peace. Zapata's forces, in turn, assassinated President Carranza the following year.

Carranza was succeeded by another general, Alvaro Obregón, who had risen to prominence by defeating Villa in 1915. Obregón undertook an ambitious program to expand public education and attempted to implement land reform, though only about 3 million acres of land, about half of which was arable, was turned over to the peasantry. After putting down a rebellion by Huerta's forces in 1923, Obregón turned power over to President-elect Plutarco Elías Calles when his term ended in 1924. Calles, in turn, attacked the church, provoking a right-wing and clerical counterrevolution from 1926 to 1929. Then the succession issue reared its ugly head once again. Without Calles's support, Obregón chose to run for the presidency in 1928 in clear violation of Article 23. He won the almost certainly rigged election anyway, but he, too, was assassinated before he could assume office for a second term.

Calles displayed an all-too-rare sense of tact and commitment to democratic practices, and, for once, an assassination did not lead to further violence. More important, having realized that presidential succession was not going to be possible, Calles and his supporters found another way to provide continuity from one presidency to the next: create a political party that could control the nomination and hence the election of the next president. The first convention of their National Revolutionary Party (PNR) was held in 1929, and after several name changes, it became the PRI in 1946. Until 1934, Calles and the men who succeeded him put the brakes on social reform. The redistribution of land, in particular, ground to a halt even though Mexico still had the largest number of rich landowners in the world. In short, despite the revolution, most Mexicans still lived in misery, albeit less violent misery.

These were important years, nonetheless, precisely because Calles and his colleagues accomplished something that had eluded their predecessors: regularizing how succession would occur.

Although the specifics continued to change over the next decade or so, the basic principles were set by the end of the 1920s. The single party would control access to all political offices, but the various groups within the party would all win some of them. Because no president could serve more than a single term, the outgoing president would consult widely within the party, but he would ultimately select the candidate to succeed himself.

Cárdenas and His Legacy

The Great Depression that began with the U.S. stock market crash in October 1929 hit Mexico hard and led to new protest and another wave of reform. Disgruntled party leaders convinced Calles (who remained the behind-the-scenes kingmaker) not to select another conservative as the presidential candidate in 1934, but to turn instead to the populist Indian and minister of war **Lázaro Cárdenas** (1895–1970).

Cárdenas had learned how to reach out to the masses when he was governor of Michoacán in the 1920s. He drew heavily on populist themes in blaming Mexico's problems on capitalism at home and abroad. In this, he was not terribly different from many of his contemporaries. Unlike them, however, he was able to translate the rhetoric into concrete accomplishments. The highlight of his *sexeño* was agrarian reform, in which his government redistributed more land than all his predecessors combined. In all, about fifteen thousand villages and a quarter of the population benefited from the reform. Roughly half the cropland was taken from the *haciendados* and given not to individual peasants but to collective or cooperative farms known as *ejidos*. Typically, an individual family farmed but did not own its plot of land, and the *ejido* could take it back if it were inefficiently or dishonestly run.

Cárdenas is also known for nationalizing the oil industry. Mexico produced about a quarter of the world's oil in the 1920s, most of which was controlled by foreign firms despite the earlier nationalization of other natural resources. In 1938, Mexico took over the oil wells and refineries, placing them under the control of a single nationalized firm, **PEMEX**. This was not simply a nationalist act. Until the 1950s, about three-quarters of the oil was sold to businesses at subsidized prices, which helped make rapid industrialization and economic growth possible.

Cárdenas was by no means the radical revolutionary the American press often portrayed him to be. However, he was not all that democratic a president either. The radical policy initiatives came from the government, and not as a result of pressures from below. Potential opponents, including former president Calles and a top labor leader, were exiled to the United States. Moreover, it was during the Cárdenas presidency that the party established an official trade union, the **Confederation of Mexican Workers (CTM)**, and two peasant organizations, which became the main cogs in the PRI's corporatist machine.

Problems mounted during the second half of his presidency. The nationalizations cost the Mexican government considerable support from Britain, the United States, and other countries. Most ominously of all, the reforms provoked enough opposition at home that there was talk of another armed uprising. Perhaps as a result, Cárdenas slowed down the pace of reform and turned his attention to building the party and planning for his own succession, choosing the moderate Catholic minister of war Manuel Avila Camacho instead of another reformer. Unlike many of his predecessors, Cárdenas withdrew from politics after he left office, thereby starting a practice that all subsequent Mexican presidents have followed.

Cárdenas's reforms were by no means an unqualified success. Land redistribution did little to eliminate poverty or inequality. The *haciendados*, for instance, were able to use loopholes in the law to hold onto almost all of the most productive land. Still, considerable progress was made toward some of the goals espoused during the revolution, and Cárdenas richly deserves his reputation as one of the most revered leaders in Mexican history.

Cárdenas's retirement is normally viewed as the end of the revolutionary period in Mexican history. Since then, Mexican politics has been dominated by conservatives, most acting in the name of a revolution now more than ninety years in the past. The key to this process is what Fox's first foreign minister and political scientist, Jorge Castañeda, calls the "peaceful and well-choreographed transfer of power."[2]

---

[2] Jorge Castañeda, *Perpetuating Power: How Mexican Presidents Were Chosen* (New York: Free Press, 2000), xi.

His retirement set the stage for the beginning of what political scientists call the pendulum effect. The PRI was still the only party that mattered, but it had its own left and right wings. There was an unwritten rule that power would swing between the two factions primarily through the choice of a new president.

An Institutional Revolutionary Party

It was through this process that Mexico's revolution was institutionalized. Since 1940, Mexico has had eleven presidents (see Table 16.2). The first two, Manuel Avila Camacho and Miguel Alemán, were far more conservative than Cárdenas. Avila Camacho successfully cooled revolutionary enthusiasm and is known today mostly for introducing the country's first social security system. Alemán, in particular, shifted away from Cárdenas's policies and leadership style. Placing land reform on the back burner, he pursued rapid economic growth through industrialization, assuming that such progress would eventually provide a better standard of living for all Mexicans through what is called the trickle-down theory. The Alemánista model was not based on market forces. Rather, his approach stressed state ownership of a few key industries such as PEMEX and substantial state control over the private sector, which was largely controlled by the PRI.

He was followed by the rather bland Adolfo Ruiz Cortines, who claimed to try to strike a balance between the Cárdenistas and Alemánistas but who is often called

TABLE 16.2 Presidents of Mexico

NAME	START OF TERM
Venustiano Carranza	1917
Adolfo de la Huerta	1920
Alvaro Obregón	1920
Plutarco Elías Calles	1924
Emilio Portes Gil	1928
Pascual Ortiz Rubio	1930
Abelardo Rodriguez	1932
Lázaro Cárdenas	1934
Manuel Avila Camacho	1940
Miguel Alemán	1946
Adolfo Ruiz Cortines	1952
Adolfo López Mateos	1958
Gustavo Díaz Ordaz	1964
Luis Echeverría	1970
Jose López Portillo	1976
Miguel de la Madrid	1982
Carlos Salinas de Gortari	1988
Ernesto Zedillo	1994
Vicente Fox	2000
Felipe Calderón	2006

the Mexican Eisenhower because so little happened during his administration. Then, in 1958, the pendulum swung marginally leftward with the next three presidents, Adolfo López Mateos, Gustavo Díaz Ordaz, and Luis Echeverría. Although López Mateos called himself a leftist "within the revolution," there was not much substance to his leftism. Echeverría tried to limit the cost of food and housing and to increase government control over some key industrial sectors. But, on balance, all three stuck with the Alemánista approach to economic development. Even more important for our purposes, each proved willing to repress groups that raised objections to PRI rule, including the bloody crackdown on student demonstrators in 1968.

Many Western countries experienced major turmoil in 1968 as we saw in Chapter 5 on France. The same was true in Mexico. Although many of the protesters involved in the demonstrations that swept the country that year returned to the PRI fold as adults, widespread disillusionment with the party set in for the first time. From then on, the PRI faced growing pressures for reform from outside the core of the system it had controlled for so long.

Under Echeverría, too, economic problems began to mount. Growth slowed, debt accumulated, and the peso had to be devalued. His successor, Jose López Portillo, stabilized the economy for most of his administration. The effects of the post–OPEC slump had begun to wear off, and economic growth picked up again. Political freedoms were expanded, making his one of the most open administrations since the revolution.

But the turnaround came in large part because López Portillo was able to impose wage controls and other austerity measures that kept labor costs down and increased the profits of middle-class and foreign investors. Moreover, there was ever more corruption, and reports began to implicate the office of the president.

It was at the end of López Portillo's presidency that the Alemánista model collapsed. With the steep drop in oil prices, Mexican debt skyrocketed from not quite $49 billion in 1980 to over $72 billion the following year. The government had to cut its budget and subsidies to industry and consumers alike. Conflict over wages and prices broke out, as government, business, and labor all found themselves strapped. The flight of capital out of the country accelerated.

The government had no choice but to turn to the International Monetary Fund (IMF) and private banks for $8 billion in loans. These agencies, of course, attached conditions to them, including pressuring the Mexican government to shift away from its state-dominated approach to economic development.

As it had done so many times in the past, the PRI followed the shifting political and economic winds, and in 1982 nominated a new kind of presidential candidate,

Miguel de la Madrid (1934–). Previously, most prominent PRI politicians had built their careers in the military, labor, or the interior ministry. De la Madrid represented a new generation of politicians, dubbed the *tecnicos*, most of whom had studied business or economics at prestigious American universities and had previously worked in one of the economic ministries. He spoke of "moral renovation," democratic reform, and a shift toward a more market-based economy but only made progress in the latter. Foreign investment was encouraged. Public enterprises were sold off, especially those that were losing money. Public subsidies were cut, and thousands of bureaucrats were fired. Unfortunately, because interest rates remained high and the price of oil low, very little economic growth occurred, especially after the middle of his term.

Midterm congressional and state elections showed that the PRI's electoral grip was loosening. The conservative, business-oriented PAN grew rapidly, won some local elections, and probably won two governorships that the PRI managed to hold onto through fraud.

Nonetheless, the de la Madrid administration continued to pay lip service to democratic and economic reform, which it claimed to have fostered with the selection of another young *tecnico*, **Carlos Salinas de Gortari** (1948–), as presidential candidate for 1988—an election he won only through fraud and deceit. Salinas continued the generational change begun under de la Madrid. Eight of his twenty-two cabinet secretaries, for instance, had advanced degrees in economics or management and were in their early forties or younger, earning them the nickname "smurfs" to contrast them to the older "dinosaurs." The new market-oriented policies de la Madrid and Salinas so enthusiastically endorsed were as far removed as one could get from the egalitarian ideals of the revolution or of the Cárdenas years. So, too, was the corruption and the repression that some observers believe included the use of torture and occasional killings by the authorities. The Salinas administration was able to keep a lid on the most serious problems. However, his retirement opened the proverbial floodgates.

Ernesto Zedillo (1951–) almost certainly won the 1994 presidential election legitimately. As soon as he took office, however, he was greeted by another financial crisis that required even more foreign loans. Soon, scandals reached the top ranks of the party, including the Salinas family. His government's and the PRI's popularity plummeted.

The most important event demonstrating that Mexico was nearing the end of a political era came with the 1997 congressional election. The PRI only won 38 percent of the vote and 48 percent of the seats. **Cuauhtémoc Cárdenas** (1934–) of the **Party of the Democratic Revolution (PRD)** was chosen mayor of Mexico City in the first election for that post.

An Intriguing Parallel

This overview of Mexican presidencies since 1940 allows us to see a country whose evolution in some respects parallels that of the Soviet Union prior to Mikhail Gorbachev. To be sure, the two countries had very different institutional arrangements, and Mexico never had anything approaching Stalinism. Nonetheless, the five most important themes in Mexican politics after Lázaro Cárdenas mirror those we saw in the Soviet Union under Leonid Brezhnev, Yuri Andropov, and Konstantin Chernenko.

First, the Mexican system was stable. No leader has been willing to pursue policies that might undermine the regime or even provoke serious opposition.

Second, as the regime grew more stable and the PRI solidified its rule, social reform and the other goals of the revolution receded from center stage.

Third is the elitism of the Mexican state, although it fell far short of the CPSU on this front.

Fourth, the stranglehold on power was accompanied by quite a bit of corruption, though in the Mexican case it went far beyond the opulent living conditions of its equivalent in the nomenklatura.

Fifth, like the centralized planning of the command economy, the Alemánista model of state sponsored development no longer seemed to work very well.

Then came the 2000 election. This time, the electoral reforms (to be discussed in the section on political parties) had progressed too far for the PRI to be able to easily steal another victory. Fox won the presidency handily, but his supporters fell far short of a majority in the Chamber of Deputies and trailed the PRI in the less powerful Senate, which brought on what is now more than a decade of legislative paralysis. We will defer discussing this, too, until later in the chapter.

POLITICAL CULTURE IN MEXICO

Mexico has an important place in the history of scholarship on political culture. It was the only Third World country included in Gabriel Almond and Sidney Verba's pathbreaking study of the relationship between culture and democracy whose findings were discussed in the chapters on Britain and Germany. Since then, unfortunately, the study of Mexican political culture has gone into eclipse. This is probably the case because the liberal democratic biases in traditional studies of political culture make Mexico hard to understand in at least two respects. First, analyses based on individual attitudes about authority and the regime have not yielded useful descriptions of Mexican culture itself. Second, to the degree that we understand it, political culture in Mexico has not been as important as those in Britain or the United States in determining what is politically acceptable.

As we have repeatedly argued, political culture is one of the most imprecise terms in comparative politics. However, it is hard to deny the importance of the values that follow. Thus, it would be a serious intellectual mistake to avoid Mexican political culture on two levels. To begin with, when viewed in ways akin to what anthropologists mean by "culture," it was a major force sustaining PRI rule. In addition, we will also see that social and economic changes eroded some of these traditional values, and helped produce the more democratic Mexico that elected Fox and Calderón.

General Trends

Although the recent evidence is skimpy, it makes sense to focus on the following seven values, knowing full that none are held universally and that political scientists don't agree about all of them.

First, in stark contrast to Iraq, there is a very strong sense of national identity among almost all Mexicans. There is a common language, mass culture, and history from which only a few non-Spanish speaking Indians are excluded. And, even they share a common religion that, despite the anticlericalism of many Mexican regimes, is a powerful unifying force.

This national identity rests, too, on what some scholars have more speculatively seen as the blending of Spanish and Aztec cultures starting in the sixteenth century. Both had strong doses of authoritarianism and corruption that became part of the Mexican political landscape from the beginning.

Second, in many, often surprising, respects, most Mexicans believe that the regime is legitimate. In particular, the revolution of 1910–17 remains a source of pride for most Mexicans no matter how they react to the way its institutionalizers ruled in its name. And, the more populist and revolutionary figures in Mexico's past—Hidalgo, Juárez, Zapata, Villa, and Cárdenas—are still widely viewed as heroes. The term revolution is used to describe almost anything positive, and the PRI tried to associate everything it does with a revolutionary mythology. Nationally approved textbooks speak positively of revolutions in the Soviet Union and Cuba, not because the PRI is in any way Marxist but because this helps to legitimize Mexico's own revolution by linking it to "great revolutions" elsewhere.

Although anthropologists warn us not to exaggerate their importance, there have been trends toward authoritarian leadership throughout Mexican history. The revolutionary process, with its frequent turns to charismatic

TABLE 16.3 Satisfaction with Democracy and Respect for Human Rights*

COUNTRY/REGION	SATISFACTION WITH DEMOCRACY	RESPECT FOR HUMAN RIGHTS
Mexico	37	43
Advanced Democracies	63	74
Latin America and Caribbean	53	41
Africa	50	54
East Asia	45	59
Post-Communist Societies	35	45

*Percentage saying they were very or somewhat satisfied with democracy, and human rights matters a lot or some.

Source: Adapted from Alejandro Moreno and Patricia Mendez, "Attitudes toward Democracy: Mexico in Comparative Perspective." *International Journal of Comparative Sociology 29* (December 2002), 350–369.

and, according to some, even messianic leaders, has at the very least reinforced those broader cultural traditions. Undoubtedly, all this made it easier for the PRI to build support for a strong presidency that, though shorn of the messianic, repressive, and even charismatic aspects, is highly reminiscent of these deeply rooted leadership styles.

Third, there are concerns about how strongly Mexicans support democracy. The World Values Survey, which tracks people's commitment to democracy and other beliefs around the world. As Table 16.3 suggests, Mexicans tend to have less respect for either democracy or human rights than people in all major parts of the world except for the post communist societies.

Fourth, despite its often violent history—or perhaps because of it—Castañeda claims that Mexicans tend to be conflict averse. As we will see on several occasions, including in the section on political parties, Mexicans prefer to avoid a fight. One piece of "evidence" Castañeda cites is their dismal record in competitive sports.

Fifth, there are deeply ambivalent feelings about the United States that are powerful enough that they should be considered as part of its culture. We will wait to discuss this in depth until the section on U.S.-Mexican relations toward the end of the chapter. Here it is enough to note that, on the one hand, most Mexicans are drawn to things American ranging from their love of American values to their love of baseball. On the other hand—and not surprisingly—most Mexicans resent what they see as American interference from the days of Poinsett on.

Sixth, along with most of Latin America, Mexico is also known for male dominance in all areas of life, not just politics. Historians debate why this exists. Some cite the Spanish *conquistadors*, and others stress aspects of precolonial social structures. Whatever the cause, women have historically played a relatively minor role in Mexican politics—they only got the right to vote in federal elections in 1953—which many observers are convinced is a sign of how strong values associated with machismo still are.

But as is so often the case with stereotypes, the reality is much more complicated. As Mexico urbanizes, as women get more education, enter the formal or wage-based workforce (they currently make up only one-third of it), and as social conditions deteriorate, more and more women are beginning to reject the macho side of Mexican culture and to demand a more equal role in social, economic, and cultural as well as political life.

Seventh, Mexican society is also noted for strong **patron-client relations**, or *camarillas*. The PRI in particular drew heavily on networks that bound the party elite to vote-mobilizing and patronage-dispensing organizations all around the country. As we will see in the next section, the influence of the *camarillas* has eroded, taking with it much of the support for the PRI.

Beyond the Broad Themes

Along with these general trends, we can talk about at least four distinct Mexican political subcultures.

First, there are some people—certainly less than 10 percent of the total population—who would be what Almond and Verba labeled parochials. Most of them are rural Indians who, as noted earlier, do not speak Spanish well, are not integrated into the dominant national culture, and have not traditionally been active in politics. However, small groups of them have been involved in on-again/off-again uprisings in such poor states as Chiapas and Guerrero, which surrounds Acapulco.

Second, impressionistic evidence suggests that most Mexicans are what Almond and Verba called "subjects." That is, they are reasonably aware of what the government is doing. But these Mexicans probably are not as disinterested in the system or as unaware of their potential to influence decisions as are archetypical subjects. Rather, they tolerate the system, assuming or knowing that there is little they can do to change what they take to be a powerful, corrupt, or evil government. In one observer's words, they are "stoically fatalistic." They are disproportionately older, poorly educated, rural, lower class, and female—precisely those groups that have benefited very little from the system and have the least well-developed ideas about alternatives to it.

Third, there are also quite a few people who clearly supported the PRI and the system as a whole, just as there were in Brezhnev's Soviet Union. Some Mexicans undoubtedly still believe in the revolution and the party's commitment to carrying out its ideals. But they are few and far between. Rather, the PRI's supporters tend to be those people who benefited from it.

Finally, there is an emerging anti-PRI subculture. The regime always had its critics. Although very few people were willing to take up arms, anti-PRI opposition grew from the 1960s onward.

Most scholars also are convinced that broad-based support for the regime as a whole is eroding. This is not to suggest that cultural change is putting it in jeopardy. Indeed, there are no signs from the first eleven years that the PAN has been in power that it intends any sort of drastic constitutional reform, which it could not get passed even if it wanted to.

POLITICAL PARTICIPATION

Democratic Rights, Sort Of

A generation ago, the focus here would have been on how the PRI was able to manipulate the way people participated in political life. Then, as now, there were few legal restrictions on what people could do. The Mexican constitution grants the basic freedoms of a liberal democracy including the right to vote to everyone over eighteen. There is little or no interference with an individual's ability to exercise a religion, travel, own property, or choose a school for his or her children. There is also open and heated debate in the press and the legislature on almost every significant issue.

That said, the PRI, at least, violated human rights more than we would expect in a true democracy. Strikes by railroad engineers in the 1950s and by telephone workers in the 1970s were forcibly suppressed. The government expelled peasants from land they had occupied. Most notoriously, government forces killed at least three hundred students in the so-called Tlatelolco massacre of 1968. During the infamous "battle of the streets" in 1980, Mexico City police officials "convinced" dissidents that their demonstrations clogged traffic and posed a danger to public safety, and so had to be stopped. Everyone understood that traffic was not the real problem and that if the protesters did not accept this ruse, the police would be willing to use more drastic means. Some even claim that elements of the PRI were responsible for the assassination of its own candidate in the early stages of the 1994 presidential election. Because the government had been willing to resort to violence so often, even veiled threats of coercion worked until recently.

In comparative terms, however, the Mexican regime was not all that repressive after the revolution was institutionalized. Instead, the PRI was able to maintain its power by turning the clientelistic networks into an umbrella organization that shaped what people did politically most of the time. It usually did not have to rely on force to keep the opposition at bay and out of office. If it needed to, it could simply stuff the ballot box or resort to other forms of fraud to ensure that it "won" every election that mattered.

It is because of this distinction between the relative freedom of individual expression and the sharply limited opportunities to turn dissent into political power that

Democratization
in Mexico

Under the PRI, Mexico was what political scientists call a "semiauthoritarian state." It had the trappings of democracy, including competitive elections and constitutional guarantees of basic civil liberties. In practice, access to power was highly limited because power itself was concentrated in very few hands, mostly those of the national PRI leadership, which was a self-perpetuating oligarchy. There were concerns, too, about how much those civil liberties were honored, especially with the upsurge in crime and corruption involving the police in recent years.

As a result, the 2000 election that swept the PRI from power for the first time since the 1920s marked a sea change in Mexican politics. However, it will take years of expanding democratic practices before we can state that Mexico has become truly democratic with any degree of certainty. ■

political scientists were reluctant to call Mexico a democracy prior to 2000 and perhaps even to this day. To be sure, civil society has grown considerably over the past generation. The PRI was also forced to accept reforms designed to make elections fairer and vote counts more honest and transparent. Together, these changes produced a political landslide. In 1976, the PRI won 85 percent of the vote in the Chamber of Deputies election; it only won 39 percent in 2009.

It is because of the changes to be discussed next that political scientists are now more willing to think of Mexico as at least on its way to democracy.

The PRI and Its Hold on Power

Mexico was sometimes called "semi-democratic" because the PRI violated democratic principles to keep itself in power. Elections were always officially competitive. However, everything from the PRI's willingness to buy votes to its stuffing of ballot boxes made it impossible to think of Mexico as anything like the kind of democracy we see in a country like India, let alone the countries discussed in Part 2 (www.pri.org.mx).

The PRI is also a different kind of political party from any of those covered in the chapters on functioning democracies. Although the PRI has a formal institutional structure and holds regular meetings at which national issues are debated, it is not a classical democratic party whose main goal is to build support for a particular viewpoint at the polls. (For this entire section, see Tables 16.4–6.)

Instead, the PRI is an elaborate network of *camarillas* enrolling as many as 10 million members. These patrons and their clients are drawn to politics less by their ideological views than by their desire for power and, sometimes, wealth. The first part of this section focuses on the way the PRI *used* to work, and we will conclude with the challenges to change it has faced since 2000 if not before.

At the grassroots level, the PRI's organizers rarely talk about the "high politics" of government or national issues. Votes were won—or manufactured—in ways reminiscent of an American urban political machine of the early twentieth century. Votes were often bought either directly or through the provision of benefits to a given neighborhood, village, or social group. Fully 5 percent of the people who took part in the first-ever primary election to choose the PRI's candidate for the 2000 presidential campaign admitted to pollsters that they had been paid for their votes. Loyal and effective party workers were rewarded with jobs that are abundantly available given the rules on non-reelection.

The PRI probably won most of its elections fairly. But it was also able to win even when it stood a chance of losing. Because the party also controlled the **Federal Election Commission (CFE)**, which was responsible for counting and validating election returns, it was easy for it to manipulate the results. Polling places were moved during the middle of election day. Mysteriously, only likely PRI voters knew where they had gone. Some people voted more than once, and PRI supporters stuffed the ballot box with fistfuls of premarked

TABLE 16.4 Mexican Chamber of Deputies Election Results, 1976–2009*

YEAR	PRI	PAN	PRD AND ITS PREDECESSORS	OTHERS
1976	85.2	8.9	–	5.9
1979	74.2	11.4	5.3	9.0
1982	69.3	17.5	4.4	8.6
1985	68.2	16.3	3.4	12.2
1988	50.4	18.0	4.5	27.3
1991	61.4	17.7	8.3	12.6
1994	50.3	26.8	16.7	6.2
1997	38.0	25.8	25.0	11.2
2000	36.9	36.9	18.7	6.1
2003	48.0	23.1	17.6	11.3
2006	28.2	33.4	29.0	6.7
2009	39.3	28.7	12.9	22.1

*All numbers are percentage of valid votes. PAN, National Action Party; PRD, Party of the Democratic Revolution; PRI, Institutional Revolutionary Party.

votes. The vote count often bore little or no resemblance to the actual tally. Once the votes were in, *alquimia electoral*—literally, **electoral alchemy**—took place. A few days later, the CFE would report the official results, which were widely viewed as fraudulent. As one "elected" PRI governor put it, "If it is fraud, it is patriotic fraud."

Electoral swindles became a serious political issue in 1988 when, it is all but universally assumed, the PRI stole the presidential election. From 1985 to 1988, the opposition staged over nine hundred demonstrations to protest the cheating. After the 1989 municipal elections, opposition groups seized over a hundred town halls to protest alleged electoral fraud. At least twenty protesters were killed. After that, elections were conducted more honestly, but the corruption hardly disappeared. In the months before the 1991 elections, about 8 percent of the registered voters discovered that the CFE "lost" their enrollment cards. In the state of Guanajuato, Fox, then the PAN's gubernatorial candidate, claimed that more PRI votes were cast than there were registered voters at several hundred polling stations. He also alleged that voting credentials were withheld from his supporters and used by others to cast multiple ballots for his PRI opponent. In this case, the corruption was so blatant that the PRI candidate had to step aside and cede the state to the opposition.

That said, the PRI campaigns before 2000 were not merely pork barrel politics in action. In addition, the PRI also used them to legitimize its rule, not simply by maximizing its vote but also by building broader awareness and support. In 1982, de la Madrid made nearly two thousand campaign appearances. PRI symbols were everywhere—on posters, walls, t-shirts, and plastic shopping bags. Party leaders in Oaxaca gave prizes to workers who did the most to make the party known. Opposition parties had neither the money nor the activists to match PRI's efforts (see Tables 16.5 and 16.6).

The bottom line is that the PRI always won until the 1997 congressional election and had never lost a presidential election. Prior to 1988 it never won less than 72 percent of the reported presidential vote or less than 65 percent of that for the Chamber of Deputies. Through the 1985 elections, it never lost a governorship and failed to win only a single Senate seat. Even after its support began to erode, it

TABLE 16.5 The 2000 Mexican Election

CANDIDATE	VOTE FOR PRESIDENT (%)
Vicente Fox (PAN)	42.5
Francisco Labastida (PRI)	36.1
Cuauhtémoc Cárdenas (PRD)	16.6
Other/spoiled ballots	4.8

PAN, National Action Party; PRD, Party of the Democratic Revolution; PRI, Institutional Revolutionary Party.

TABLE 16.6 The 2006 Presidential Election

CANDIDATE	VOTE (%)
Felipe Calderón (PAN)	36.7
Andres Manuel López Obrador (PRD)	36.1
Roberto Madrazo (PRI)	22.7
Others and nullified votes	4.5

PAN, National Action Party; PRD, Party of the Democratic Revolution; PRI, Institutional Revolutionary Party.

was still able to maintain control of more than 95 percent of the country's two thousand municipalities.

Like Germany, Mexico now has an electoral law that combines single-member districts and proportional representation for the Chamber of Deputies. Out of a total of five hundred seats, three hundred are elected from single-member districts. The rest are drawn from party lists following a complex formula that brings each party's total representation closer to its share of the vote. Prior to 1997, no opposition party ever won more than nine single-member districts, which meant that the proportional side of the voting had no practical effect because the PRI had already won an overwhelming majority before the last two hundred were allocated. By the mid-1990s, the PRI had been forced to accept sweeping reforms that made the 1997 elections by far the most honest since the revolution. A truly independent **Federal Electoral Institute (IFE)** was created to supervise the balloting. Voters were issued registration cards with their pictures on them. Workers at polling places were given at least rudimentary training, and independent observers monitored the voting at most of them. Most important, the IFE developed a mechanism for reporting the vote tallies the same night as the election, leaving the ruling party with little time to engage in electoral shenanigans.

This new sense of fairness, combined with the social and economic problems facing the country, produced the most dramatic changes in Mexican electoral history. In 1997, the PRI lost its majority in the Chamber of Deputies. The PRI was still the largest party, but the PAN and PRD together won significantly more votes and slightly more seats.

The first election of the twenty-first century finally saw the PRI defeated (see Tables 16.5 and 16.6). The campaign went badly for the PRI from the beginning. The outgoing president, Zedillo, did not handpick his successor, although it was fairly clear that he supported Francisco Labastida, who ultimately won the nomination. Labastida turned out to be a lackluster candidate who had to support an administration that had had little success in dealing with Mexico's economic difficulties or with the rebellion in Chiapas, both of which reached crisis proportions in the first days after Zedillo took office. As we will see, the PRI also faced a formidable opponent in Fox, who had been on the political scene for more than a decade. Although many observers called Fox's victory an upset, it probably was not, because the polls showed that voters were looking for change.

Even before its partial defeat in 1997, the PRI had weakened considerably. In part, this reflected the changes in the electoral system that made voting more honest, gave opposition parties more seats, and offered people more of an incentive to vote for them.

Most important of all, its base of support was rooted in Mexico's version of **corporatism**, which had been eroding for decades. In Germany, we saw that corporatism was used to smooth economic policy making. In Mexico, the PRI used it, instead, to secure its control.

Recall that an official trade union and two peasant organizations were created during the Cárdenas administration. Afterwards, others were formed for railroad, electrical, and telecommunications workers. Even journalists and photographers had their official PRI associations. Until recently, nearly all workers or peasants belonged to one or another of these quasi-official organizations, which blanketed Mexican society and played an important role in solidifying PRI support in three main ways.

First, they provided Mexicans with tangible benefits that some theorists think are more powerful than the attitudes we normally associate with legitimacy. For example, more than two million families benefited from land redistribution during the 1950s alone. Government sponsored health care programs are often administered through these organizations. Photographers could buy inexpensive film only through their professional—and PRI-sponsored—association. Rest assured that the PRI made certain that people remembered who was responsible for providing such benefits.

Second, by tying poor and powerless Mexicans to the regime, the PRI was able to reduce the amount and severity of the protest it might otherwise have faced. Put simply, these organizations provided another example of the "causal arrow" running "downward" from state to society.

Third, these organizations gave the PRI a pool from which to recruit grassroots leaders. This, in turn, meant that workers or peasants who saw themselves as potential leaders built their careers more by being part of the PRI machine than by being advocates for those they supposedly represented.

The PRI's hold on these organizations and their control of their constituents began to erode as the economic crisis deepened and its own policies became more market oriented. In the late 1980s, in particular, the CTM called strikes at some of the *maquiladora* factories, apparently against government wishes. More important, the PRI found it harder to incorporate well-educated urban voters into its networks.

By early 2002, the PRI had begun something of a political comeback. It staged a hotly contested election for its new leader in which Roberto Madrazo edged out Beatriz Paredes in a ballot that was open to all Mexican voters. After forming broader alliances than ever before, the PRI won close to half of the vote in the 2003 election for the Chamber of Deputies and continued to do well in state elections through 2004. But, then, as we saw earlier, the bottom fell out for the PRI, culminating in Madrazo's disastrous campaign in 2006.

That said, the legislative elections that year and in 2009 saw a surprising recovery by the PRI. It is now the largest party in Congress by far, which allows it to block most of Calderón's legislation should it choose to do so. Whether that translates into victory at the end of his *sexeño* will not be clear until 2012. At any rate, it is hard to see the PRI returning to its position of all but total control at any point in the foreseeable future.

As we write, the PRI and the unions are at odds. The party's congressional leadership seems willing to strip the CTM of its collective bargaining and other rights. For instance, party leaders proposed a ban on temporary and part-time work along with the elimination of probationary contracts. Despite the close ties some CTM leaders have to the PRI, the union rejected the bill out of hand. Protests by the unions and their supporters blocked the proposed legislation in April 2011 because it probably would have made the unions weaker than they ever had been since they were legalized in 1917. In the end, at least two things are clear. First, the PRI and its affiliated organizations are no longer on the left, however one defines the term. Second, the PRI's organizational might is largely a thing of the past.

All this suggests that the PRI entered the twenty-first century in trouble and will continue to have difficulties regardless of what happens in 2012. After more than seventy years in power, it has to forge a new identity for itself as a competitive party that is at least sometimes in opposition, that has close ties with business, and is committed to integrating Mexico into the international economy. This means, in turn, that it will have to develop new ideals and policy proposals it can use to rebuild support. And perhaps most damaging of all, it has to do so with a declining base of support among the most traditional voters.

The Other Parties

The PAN

Unlike the former Soviet Union, Mexico has always had more than one party. However, no opposition group posed a credible threat to the PRI until 1988. Some parties that were supposedly in opposition were actually funded by the PRI in a peculiar attempt to give the outside world the impression that Mexico was a viable democracy.

As late as the mid-1980s, only one opposition party mattered: the PAN. It was formed in 1939, mostly by people

Conflict
in Mexico

Observers who call Mexico democratic often cite the relative lack of violent, antisystem conflict to support their claim. It is true that by the Global South's standards Mexico has relatively little "outside-the-system" protest and little of the racial, linguistic, and ethnic strife that is so common in the Third World.

However, there are two countertrends. First, there has not been very much of it in part because the state has made it hard for potential opponents to organize, let alone express their discontent. Second, the amount of dissatisfaction with the PRI regime had been mounting for years, whether measured in the number of attacks by guerrillas in Chiapas or Guerrero or in the number of votes won by opposition parties. ■

most charismatic leader Mexico has had since Cárdenas. He had a broad appeal because he could present himself as an earthy farmer (he has been known to give the finger to PRI politicians) and a savvy business executive given his U.S. education and career at Coca-Cola. And in 2000, he decided to try to unify the opposition by appealing both to the Left and to traditionally conservative PAN supporters. He did this, for instance, by agreeing with Mexico's small Green Party to form the Alliance for Change and by associating himself with left-of-center intellectuals such as Jorge Castañeda and Adolfo Aguilar Zinser, who became his foreign minister and chief economic adviser, respectively, for the first years of his term in office. Electoral reforms in the 1990s also gave candidates ample public funds, which meant that the telegenic Fox had plenty of money to run Mexico's first "modern" campaign.

The bottom line is that Fox scored a resounding victory. He won an overwhelming majority among those who claimed that their primary reason for voting was to produce change. He also did extremely well among middle-class voters, women, and others who are at the core of the growing civil society. Finally, he convinced about 30 percent of the people who had voted for Cárdenas in 1994 to switch,

drawn from the Catholic Church and the business community who found Cárdenas's reforms too radical. Its support was concentrated in the north and other relatively affluent areas. There were questions, too, about whether the PAN was one of the parties that accepted support from the PRI (www.pan.org.mx).

By the 1980s, however, the PAN had become a viable opposition party though it was still too weak to mount a credible challenge to the PRI nationally. Nonetheless, it had staked out a strongly pro-business position and gained some verbal support from the Reagan administration. Most important, it had demonstrated that it could consistently win one vote out of six, even according to the official figures.

The PAN's first real breakthrough came with the 1983 local elections, when its candidate was elected governor of Baja California Norte. Its progress was blunted somewhat by the PRD's arrival on the scene (see the next section), though even then the PAN's vote at worst held steady and, given the fraud that year, probably increased marginally.

The PAN has been the biggest beneficiary of anti-PRI sentiment since then. It won a full quarter of the vote in 1994 and 1997, which set the stage for its breakthrough in 2000 and the election of Calderón six years later.

The PAN's success had a lot to do with the personality of former President Fox. The six-foot, five-inch Fox is the

November 20, 2006 rally of political supporters of Andrés Manuel López Obrador in Mexico City.

thereby eliminating the possibility that the PRI could sneak into power against a divided opposition.

The PAN did poorly in the 2003 legislative elections in part because of the gridlock in policy making discussed below. Still, it remained the second strongest party in an election that made it clear that no single party was soon likely to win a majority on its own.

Indeed, as the 2006 presidential campaign opened, it seemed that the PAN would lose to the PRD or the PRI (see Table 16.6). The PRD's candidate, **Andrés Manuel López Obrador**, began the race with a significant lead in the polls until Calderón nosed ahead in most surveys during the few weeks of the campaign.

The election results were so close that both Calderón and López Obrador declared themselves the winner. Two winners are not better than one, and eventually Calderón was declared the victor. Despite his victory, things do not look good for the PAN at least in the short run. Indeed, the setback in the 2009 legislative elections makes it clear that the party is not likely to gain a majority at that level any time soon.

The PRD

In 1988, it looked as if the more serious challenge to the PRI's hegemony would come from a new and unlikely source—Cuauhtémoc Cárdenas, son of the last radical president, who had named him for the symbol of Indian resistance to the Spanish conquest. The elder Cárdenas had criticized the PRI's conservative, antirevolutionary turn in diaries that were published after his death in 1970, which served to crystallize left-wing dissatisfaction with the government. This dissatisfaction continued to mount, especially after de la Madrid introduced his "liberal" reforms in the 1980s. Meanwhile, the younger Cárdenas emerged as the leading advocate of this new Left.

In 1986, many of the leftists organized their own faction within the PRI. As soon as Carlos Salinas's nomination was made public, Cárdenas and labor leader Porfirio Muñoz Ledo dropped out of the PRI to form the PRD. Cárdenas declared his own presidential candidacy and stressed many of the same populist themes raised by his father nearly a half-century earlier.

Profiles
Vicente Fox Quesada

Vicente Fox's victory removed the PRI from office for the first time in seventy-one years. Born in 1942 to a wealthy farmer and a devout Catholic, Fox was educated at a Catholic university in Mexico City and then at Harvard. He returned home to work for Coca-Cola, helping the company beat out Pepsi for the number one spot in the Mexican soft drink market. Today, he manages a 1,200-acre ranch where he grows vegetables and raises cattle and ostriches for export. When he ran for president, he was divorced, but shortly after taking office he married his public relations advisor.

Fox is a political veteran. He was first elected to the Chamber of Deputies in 1988. He ran for governor of Guanajuato in 1991 and probably would have won had the votes been counted honestly. He did win the seat four years later and almost immediately began his campaign for the presidency.

Fox is both charismatic and controversial. Although he claims to admire "third way" politicians such as Bill Clinton and Tony Blair, Fox has strong right-wing roots. He also tries to strike an earthy, populist tone despite his family's wealth. He was also close to President George W. Bush. He arrived in Washington for a state visit on September 4, 2001. Immigration reform was on the agenda but never got anywhere after the attacks on New York and Washington a week later.

AP Images

Vicente Fox holding a press conference wearing traditional Indian clothing.

He rarely wears a suit, preferring blue jeans and a belt with a massive buckle bearing his name. He also does not shy away from controversial statements. During the campaign, he even made personal attacks on his opponents that would have been considered unacceptable in most democracies. ■

The PRD did surprisingly well in 1988. Cárdenas "lost" only because of the most extensive voting fraud in Mexican history. Almost all outside observers were convinced that he won a plurality of the vote, but the PRI "manufactured" or "discovered" enough votes to deny him victory.

The PRD may have come closer to winning in 2006. In fact, its candidate, Andres Manuel López Obrador, to this day claims he won. The official tally gave Calderón the win by less than half a percentage point. López Obrador disputed the government's refusal to count nine percent of the ballots, most of which the PRD's candidate claimed would have gone to him.

It stumbled badly in 2009. Despite its reputation for honesty, the PRD got caught up in its share of scandals. A videotape shows many of its top leaders gambling at a high stakes table in Las Vegas. As we will see in the policy section, a number of its officials (including Cuautemóc Cardenas's son) are alleged to have ties to the drug cartels. Last, but by no means least, several PRI activists infiltrated the party and ran under its banner that year. All in all, it lost about a third of its vote and came in a distant third.

Since then, the PRI has adopted new welfare and social service programs that have eaten away at some of the PRD's support. Perhaps more important and paradoxically, the PRI seems to have built bridges to the PAN and the business community which, frankly, have been in the works since the days of de la Madrid.

Toward a Three Party System?

In this book, we have seen many kinds of party systems. The Mexican one is unique in that it has three parties each of which could conceivably win most elections, but none of which can win a majority. As political scientists point out, this can be the worst of all possible worlds as far as governing is concerned for two reasons. First, it tends to lead to gridlock in policy making. Second, it encourages parties not to take risks or strong positions on controversial issues to the point that the first PAN government passed a constitutional amendment banning negative campaigning. In short, it is both hard to produce a partisan realignment or take major new policy initiatives when three roughly equal parties vie for power.

We write barely a year before the 2012 election, when, of course, outgoing president Calderon cannot run. In typical Mexican fashion, it will be months before the candidates are known. In the United States, we will also have a presidential election that year, and no one could tell who the Republican challenger to President Obama would be a year before that party's nominee is determined. Therefore, it should not come as a surprise that we cannot predict what will happen in Mexico with any certainty.

If the early polls are to be believed, the PRI's candidate will win easily. One reliable survey had him or her (for the first time, there is a potential female candidate who could win) show the PRI outpolling the PAN by about two to one. The PAN, in turn, leads the PRD by about that same amount. Note, however, that about a third of the voters claimed not to have made up their minds.

Civil Society in Mexico

Much about electoral politics in Mexico remains uncertain, including whether a permanent realignment away from the PRI is taking place. What we can say with some certainty is that Mexico is unlikely to return to corporatist, *camarilla*-based PRI dominance. This will probably be the case even if the PRI wins in 2012. Rather, this style of politics is not likely to succeed because of the changes in Mexican society that have led to the emergence of a viable civil society.

We could list the dozens of human rights, environmental, labor, and other associations that have made the front pages since the 1980s as evidence of this trend. Given the macho aspect of Mexican culture, however, there probably is no better single example demonstrating how much the country is changing than its burgeoning women's movement.

The modern Mexican women's movement is new. In the 1960s and 1970s, it was limited almost exclusively to

Cuauhtémoc Cárdenas, former mayor of Mexico City and one of the founders of the PRD.

wealthy, educated women who had been influenced by feminists from the United States and Europe.

Since the late 1980s, it has broadened its appeal considerably. It started with one of those "historical accidents," which so often play an important role in political change. In 1975, Mexico City hosted a United Nations-sponsored conference to kick off International Women's Year, itself the beginning of a decade-long effort. It was hard for either the foreign participants or Mexican women to ignore the inequalities between men and women in Mexico when such an event was taking place there.

About that time, the earlier, rather elitist, women's movement began to give way to what has been called "popular feminism," which organizes poor and middle-class women in both the cities and the countryside. There is no single popular feminist movement. Rather, it consists primarily of organizations that come together mostly around local and national issues, ranging from reproductive rights to the lack of potable water or decent schools in small towns.

These organizations combined protests over the kinds of issues we see in feminist movements in most countries (e.g., abortion, violence against women, and unequal pay), with concerns for the poor in general. Meanwhile, the economic changes of the past generation have created more employment opportunities for women at all levels, from manual and clerical workers to corporate executives. No one knows how strong these loosely organized movements are. Nonetheless, it does seem safe to assume that, as Mexico democratizes and as economic developments further erode traditional social structures, women's groups will grow dramatically. As strong as the women's movement has become, it should be noted that the PAN remains quite conservative on such issues, strongly opposing both legalized abortion and gay rights. Therefore, feminists are likely to shift their support ever more to the PRD whose legislative assembly passed a law in Mexico City in 2007 to permit abortion during the first twelve weeks of pregnancy.

Women and Politics in Mexico

The early feminist movement in Mexico got a boost when United Nations held its conference to start International Women's Year there. But it is safe to say that women are just now coming to play mainstream roles in political life.

Thus, both the PRI and the PAN named women to lead their delegations in the Chamber of Deputies in 2009. The PRI's choice, Beatriz Paredes, is one of the handful of candidates being mentioned as a 2012 presidential candidate.

Calderón has named three women to key positions in his cabinet, including foreign relations, energy, and education. Some observers think that the central role of women is now so firmly established that the conservative Calderón's equally conservative wife, Margarita Zavala, does not bristle when she is called a feminist.

Discrimination remains. The business tycoon, Jorge Hank Rhon, once declared that women were his favorite animal without jeopardizing his career. A prominent woman doctor was offered a job at half the salary as the man she would replace even though the two had virtually identical resumes. Many businesses still have unwritten rules against hiring young married women out of fear that they would lose them to motherhood.

About the only feminist issue that reaches the front pages is abortion. In 2008, the Supreme Court ruled that decision making on abortion should be left to the states. Most now allow abortion under some circumstances, but only Mexico City allows it "on demand." More important, just as is the case north of the border, very few states provide extensive abortion services. Also, few enforce the laws on their books. For good or ill, doctors who conduct safe but illegal abortions are rarely prosecuted.

Mexico City passed a law in 2009 permitting gay marriage and adoption. The next year, the Supreme Court ruled that all states had to enforce the law despite objections from Calderón and the Church. Other bills on civil unions are working their way through about 20 percent of the states.

THE MEXICAN STATE

This section has two main goals.

First, it describes the way the state operated under the PRI and changed under Fox and Calderón. It should be pointed out from the outset that there have been no basic changes in state structures and procedures since Fox took office on November 30, 2000. Nor did either PAN president give many signs that he wanted to change the formal rules of the game. Besides, both lacked the votes in Congress they needed to pass constitutional amendments. There is little doubt that the government is more open under PAN rule, but it remains to be seen how much of a long-term difference this will make in terms of holding it accountable, changing policies, and the like.

Second, the material on the Mexican state will also provide a final example of the fact that constitutional theory and political reality are often not the same. As the revolution was drawing to a close in 1917, the men who would later form the PRI wrote a constitution that they supposedly patterned after the one used in the United States. Indeed, there are a fair number of parallels between the two—at least on paper. Like the United States, Mexico has a bicameral legislature. Both are federal systems in which state and national governments are supposed to share power. Both call for the clear separation of powers, so that the legislative, executive, and judicial branches of the national government can "check and balance" each other. 🖉 (**historicaltextarchive.com/sections. php?op=viewarticle&artid=93**).

In practice, the Mexican state has not been anything like the American. The constitution is not a sham. It was written with the best of revolutionary attention. But as the aforementioned dinosaurs took control of the PRI, the constitution and political reality had less and less in common.

Non-Reelection and Presidential Domination

As in the USSR, control of policy making was held in relatively few hands as long as the PRI had its monopoly on power. Rank and file PRI activists and elected officials had little influence over who made those decisions, let alone what they decided to do (see Figure 16.1).

The PRI's hegemony itself had two essential and overlapping components above and beyond its ability to "win" every election that mattered, neither of which has changed with the election of a non-PRI government. The first is the principle of non-reelection; the second is the concentration of power in the hands of the president.

The principle of non-reelection, which operates at practically every level of government, means that a new president works with inexperienced members of Congress and state officeholders, many of whom were also dependent on him for their positions. The president also appoints people to all key bureaucratic and judicial positions upon taking office. In other words, any new president can bring

FIGURE 16.1 Traditional Decision Making in Mexico

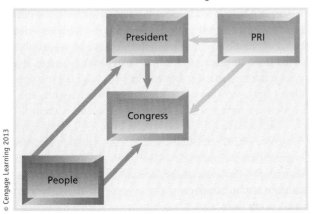

© Cengage Learning 2013

in a whole new team and embark in new policy directions in ways that happen only during rare periods of realignment in more fully democratic systems. The way the PRI used the system to reward its friends and punish its enemies gave it a compliant Congress and state governments for almost all of its more than seventy years in office.

The principle of non-reelection has another, equally important implication. Like everyone else, presidents cannot stand for reelection and are expected to leave political life completely at the end of their term. As Frank Brandenburg pithily put it, Mexico has been able to "avoid personal dictatorship by retiring their dictators every six years."[3]

No recent president has been anything like omnipotent. That said, any Mexican president is far more influential than his American counterpart, who, as we saw in Chapter 3, has little more than the power to persuade people who do not have to agree with him.

The constitution gives the president considerable leverage. He is allowed to initiate legislation, and virtually all bills of any importance begin life in the executive branch. He can issue decrees on a wide variety of subjects, including the way a law is implemented, the transfer of funds from one account to another, and even the authorization of expenditures above original appropriations. But the president's real sources of power are informal.

Although there was considerable variation in the way PRI presidents led, they all followed a common pattern driven by the constraints of the single, six-year term. For all intents and purposes, the president's term began before he took office, with the election campaign in which the candidate started to lay out his own agenda and style. Upon taking office, the president enjoyed a period of consolidation that lasted as long as a year and a half, during which he put his own team in place. It was primarily in the next two years or so that the president could implement substantial new policies of his own. In the last two years, his attention had to turn to the succession, and even before the election occurred, power began to shift to the next president.

Presidential domination hinged on the way he was selected. Because the president's political life ends with the end of his single term, the only chance he has to influence politics after his retirement was through the selection of his successor. Until Zedillo's administration, the outgoing president chose the next PRI candidate from the cabinet secretaries in office during the middle of his *sexeño*. The president was thus drawn from a very small and narrow pool of candidates. Beginning in the 1980s, most of them were relatively young men who were sons of PRI politicians, Mexico City–based, American-educated, and

---

[3] Frank Brandenburg, *The Making of Modern Mexico* (Englewood Cliffs, NJ: Prentice-Hall, 1964), 141.

part of the outgoing president's personal network of supporters. Salinas, for example, had been associated with de la Madrid since his student days, when he took a course from the future president.

A little more than a year before the election, the party chair (himself a client of the president) released a list of about a half dozen possible candidates to the press, beginning what was known as *el dezdado* or the "fingering" of the candidate. Supposedly, the list was the result of a wide consultation within the party, which rarely happened, so that it could be subjected to broader scrutiny in the population as a whole (which it was not). Within a few months, the president made his final choice known (he usually knew it before the short list was proposed), and all the other potential candidates jumped on his bandwagon. Only then did the party hold a convention to officially nominate the president's choice. The president-designate then began his campaign by exercising the first of his many informal powers: determining who the party's candidates for the Chamber of Deputies and the Senate would be.

The system of all but total presidential dominance may not continue even if the PRI returns to office. In March 1999, President Zedillo announced that he would not personally designate his successor. Instead, the PRI would hold an American-style campaign with debates among the contenders and then a primary election. Jorge Castañeda, who also published a book on presidential transitions shortly before being named foreign minister by Fox, claims that Zedillo made it abundantly clear that he wanted Labastida to win the nomination and that, as a result, the party machine fell into step behind his candidacy.

All three major parties now hold primary elections, and it is likely that neither Calderón nor López Obrador would have won their party's nomination under the old, behind-closed-doors system. In 2006, Madrazo used his position as President of the PRI to solidify his position as the frontrunner and won the primary easily when his main competitor had to withdraw because of corruption allegations.

The incoming president still has tremendous latitude in filling other posts. The president directly appoints thousands of people to positions in the twenty-four cabinet-level departments and the hundreds of quasi-independent agencies and public corporations. Normally, only about 35 percent of those appointees held high office in any prior administration, thereby providing the new president with an ample opportunity to assert his independence.

The Cabinet, the Bureaucracy, and the Judiciary

The president's appointive power extends to the entire state, which means he has tremendous leverage over the way policy is implemented as well. Under the PRI, most important positions in the cabinet and bureaucracy were filled either from his personal *camarilla* or from a small group of other politicians who had the new president's trust. Others were chosen less on the basis of their positions on the issues the new government would face than on their personal connections (**www.mexonline.com/mexagncy.htm**).

What this meant was that the government was based on patron-client relations even more than the society as a whole. Virtually everyone in office owed his or her job to someone higher up in the hierarchy and, thus, ultimately, to the president. Ambitious politicians enhanced their careers by exchanging favors with their patrons and clients, not by campaigning on their record or the issues.

There had been some changes over the years. At first, the PRI was little more than a loose coalition of revolutionary leaders held together by military officers turned politicians. Not surprisingly, the most important cabinet position and the source of future presidents was the minister of defense. As the regime became institutionalized, the center of gravity shifted to **Gobernación**, the ministry responsible for internal security and public administration. With the growth in the foreign debt and the emergence of other complex economic issues, the *tecnicos* came to dominate the PRI, and the various economic ministries became the most important stepping-stone. But this should not obscure the basic point. The *tecnicos*, like everyone else, rose to positions of prominence because of their personal connections in the shifting PRI constellation of patron-client relations.

Fox tried to break this pattern. His original cabinet consisted of prominent politicians and business leaders, many of whom had spent years opposing the PRI. Many of them, however, did not have a long prior history in the PAN or with Fox himself. Many of the others, including Castañeda, left the cabinet during the middle of the term, and Fox had trouble forging a coherent team to lead his administration. Calderón's initial cabinet was made up mostly of academics, other pro-business experts, and a handful of prominent PAN leaders, some of whom also served under Fox.

Remember that the entire government bureaucracy, which employs about one out of every five Mexicans, was also part of the PRI machine. The Mexican bureaucracy bears less resemblance to a classic civil service than any of the others considered in this book. No country in Latin America has traditionally had a strong, professional civil service that is recruited on the basis of merit, that willingly serves any government no matter what its ideology, and that provides career-long opportunities to the men and women who join it. Mexico's, however, may be the least professional of them all.

Individual civil servants tend to move from agency to agency with their bosses, who, in turn, move more frequently than politicians in other Latin American country. As with the Congress, there is so much turnover that it is hard for anyone to develop the expertise that comes from years of experience.

These bureaucratic weaknesses may not have been a serious problem when the demands on Mexican government were not very great. Now, however, they are a major contributor to Mexico's woes.

Presidents Fox and Calderón faced another constraint that has limited what they could accomplish. Some people around Fox wanted him to purge the civil service of PRI loyalists who did not share the new president's commitment to reform. However, the PAN had—and still has—few experienced men and women who could effectively fill senior executive positions. Therefore, he opted to keep much of the civil service in place, in essence choosing a hefty dose of corruption over inexperience.

Mexico also has a Supreme Court with the power (on paper) of judicial review. But, unlike its counterpart in Washington, it almost never overruled an important government action or policy under the PRI. That was the case because even the judiciary is subject to presidential control. Today, judges are nominated by the president and must be approved by the Senate. They can serve one fifteen-year term, although many resign each time the presidency changes hands giving the new chief executive yet another way to shape the state. The court has been somewhat more assertive and independent since the 1990s, including its decisions certifying that Calderón had won in 2006.

Congress and the Legislative Process

As noted earlier, the constitution established a bicameral legislature. Members of the Chamber of Deputies are elected for three-year terms. Senate terms last six years, with half its members chosen every three years.

Although the Congress has to approve all legislation, it has rarely been more than a rubber stamp. There is no Mexican version of cabinet responsibility that obliged the PRI's members in the Chamber of Deputies and Senate to fall in line behind their president, but they consistently did so because of the way power politics worked.

The roots of congressional weakness lie in the same peculiarities of Mexican presidential rule that have been at the heart of this section so far. Members of each house can serve only a single term. Therefore, it is impossible for them to develop the expertise or the seniority that make U.S. congressional committee chairs, for instance, so important.

Even more important, PRI members of Congress were subservient to the president, who selected its nominees. In the longer run, career advancement came only from building personal connections with more influential power brokers, not from making one's own mark in the legislature. Moreover, with the rise of the *tecnicos*, a congressional seat was no longer much of a stepping-stone for reaching the elite. Most members, instead, were PRI loyalists whose seats were rewards for years of party work.

As a result, prior to 1997, all significant legislation was initiated by the president and passed the Congress as easily as in parliamentary systems. Thus, the PRI voted as a bloc to confirm the questionable results of the 1988 election. The next year, it again voted unanimously to endorse President Salinas's bill to privatize the banks.

The 1997 election changed all that. Even though the PRI still held the presidency and a majority in the Senate, the PAN and the PRD held the balance of power in the Chamber. Because they did not agree on much and were not able to develop an alternative to the PRI's program, Mexico developed its own version of gridlock that students of the U.S. Congress would find familiar. And this remains the case today despite the two PAN presidential victories. There still is no majority party in either house, and the country has no tradition of compromise decision making. President Fox did allow congressional committees to gain a bit more autonomy and party discipline was relaxed somewhat. But as we will soon see, critics blame the PAN presidents' inability to build coalitions across party lines for their limited accomplishments.

The Federal System

Much the same can be said for state and local governments. Mexico is a federal country, officially known as the United Mexican States. The country is divided into thirty-one states plus the Federal District (Mexico City). The states, in turn, are subdivided into more than two thousand municipalities, which are more like American counties than cities. Each state has a governor and unicameral legislature. Each municipality has a mayor and municipal council.

In practice, the states and municipalities had little or no power because the PRI dominated there as well. At the time of the 2000 election, the PAN and PRD only controlled 15 percent of the municipalities and a third of the governorships. In other words, state and local governments were for all intents and purposes another appendage of presidential power. Not only did the president select the PRI's candidates, but he could also remove governors or mayors from office. Again, as with the members of Congress, governors and mayors could build their careers only by strengthening their position in the PRI machine. In short, it did not pay to rock the party boat. In addition, every national ministry maintained a federal delegate in each state to deal with overlapping jurisdictions and to make certain that the president's preferences were carried out.

Here, too, there were changes afoot even before 2000. By the mid-1990s, it was no longer surprising when the PRI lost a state or local election. By far the most important example was the succession of PRD victories in Mexico City, which gave it control over the Federal District in which roughly one out of every six Mexicans lives. The PAN, too, has taken more or less permanent control of a number of northern states. And its governors, in particular, have begun trying to promote investment there, reflecting the party's roots in the business community and their proximity to the United States.

The Military

There is only one area in which the PRI's long-term control of the government won nearly universal approval—curbing the political power of the military. The military repeatedly intervened in Mexican politics well into the twentieth century. Similarly, it remains an important and often uncontrollable political force in much of Latin America.

In Mexico today, however, the military has been effectively depoliticized.

The original PRI leaders were all generals, and in 1946 Alemán became the first civilian president in thirty years. However, over the past half-century, the military has been turned into a relatively disciplined force with a professional officer corps. It plays a role in issues of defense and national security, including the drug wars. But, otherwise, unlike what we saw in Iraq or Nigeria, it stays out of politics.

There is, however, one reason to worry about the role the military might play in the future. There have been some claims that some high-ranking officers are close to some of the drug cartels although the police force is much more deeply involved (see the section on drug-related violence below). In fact, in the last five years, the military has largely taken over the law enforcement side of the war on drugs. The concern is that if the problems discussed at the beginning of the chapter worsen and the state seems to be failing, the military might feel obligated to step in.

Corporatism and Corruption

Mexican politicians have never stressed individualism or the need to give the people access to the decision-making process. Rather, the emphasis has been on integrating groups in a version of corporatism which has little in common with what we saw in France and Germany.

As we saw earlier, the government created or legitimized organizations that at first glance look similar to the interest groups we find in industrialized democracies but whose primary function was to keep the PRI in power. As such, they are part of the elaborate spoils system that is responsible for much of Mexico's corruption. Every political system has some degree of corruption. It is, however, an especially serious problem in Mexico, where it is built into the very logic of the system. It is impossible to determine exactly how much corruption there is in Mexico or any other country for that matter. Most analysts believe there are few totally honest PRI officials anywhere in the country.

In one remarkable study, Transparency International surveyed 15,000 Mexican homes on their experience with bribery. Transparency asked whether or not the respondents had had to "grease the palms" of public servants in accessing a wide variety of services. Just over 10 percent of them said they had done so, paying what amounted to a hidden "tax" of about 14 percent of GNP. Particularly shocking was its finding that there were only three states in which less than half of the drivers pulled over for routine violations claim that they did *not* pay bribes to avoid being fined or jailed.

Racketeering and embezzlement are commonplace. Before oil prices plummeted the last time, PEMEX officials routinely accepted kickbacks from their suppliers, many of which they partially owned. Petrochemical union officials, in turn, demanded a share of workers' salaries as a condition of employment. The best estimate is that over the past half-century elites siphoned off about $90 billion for their foreign bank accounts and investments, a sum roughly equal to the total Mexican debt.

Recent presidents have tried to crack down on some of these practices. De la Madrid had Echeverría's minister of agriculture arrested and the former head of PEMEX imprisoned. The former police chief of Mexico City was accused of involvement in the narcotics trade and, possibly, in the death of a U.S. Drug Enforcement Agency officer.

Similarly, Salinas ordered the arrest of four leading stockbrokers, one of whom was among the PRI's leading contributors. He also released more than four hundred political prisoners the government had never even acknowledged it held.

The crackdown went further under Zedillo. Dozens of people at or near the top of the PRI hierarchy were implicated, including Salinas's brother, who was accused of ordering the assassination of the PRI's secretary general, Jose Ruiz Massieu. This, and allegations that the family had made tens of millions of dollars, forced former president Salinas into exile. Another of his brothers was murdered in December 2004 under mysterious circumstances.

Even more appalling may be the case of another member of the PRI elite, Carlos Hank Gonzales, who played a critical role in getting Zedillo the PRI nomination. Hank had used his years in public life to become a billionaire, stating that "a politician who is poor is a poor politician."

His son, Jorge Hank Rhon, was caught trying to import ivory and skins of endangered species. In 2004, he carried on the family dynasty by being elected mayor of Tijuana despite allegations that he ordered the murder of the cardinal of Guadalajara and is personally involved in the drug trade. The younger Hank is one of the richest men in Mexico, running a company that owns amusement parks, race tracks, pet stores, a mall, and hotels in nineteen Mexican states and eleven other countries. Although rumors swirl about his corruption, nothing has been proven.

The *Economist's* depiction of the PRI "dinosaurs" who are still prominent in Mexican political life.

Needless to say, the likes of Salinas and the Hanks could only have gotten away with it because of their connections. Zedillo may have been more committed than his predecessors were to the eradication of corruption. However, with the exception of Salinas, no president has broken the unwritten rule that no member of the top elite can be indicted.

Under the two PAN presidents, an attempt has been made to weaken the ties between the state and the private sector in the hope that it would weaken corruption. That does not mean that corruption has disappeared. The emphasis has shifted to alleged formal and informal ties to the violent drug cartels to be covered.

The Fox and Calderón Presidencies: An Assessment

It makes sense to end this section with an assessment of the first PAN presidencies for two reasons. First, they illustrate just how powerful the informal workings of Mexican politics still are. Second, the problems Fox and Calderón faced are, in turn, a good introduction to its policy dilemmas, which will be the focus of the rest of the chapter.

Evaluations of the PAN presidencies are mixed. Critics felt they were not very effective leaders, especially in dealing with the opposition, which is, of course, something none of their predecessors had had to do. Fox's supporters cite problems largely beyond his control, most notably the economic downturn that began just as he took office, the effects of the terrorism attacks on 9/11, and the renewed controversy over immigration in the United States. Calderón has been saddled with the violence surrounding the drug trade which he almost certainly had nothing to do with starting.

We will consider the external constraints and their impact on public policy in the next section. Here, it is enough to note that the Fox administration struggled through the first real change in political dynamics in Mexico since the 1920s. His was a minority presidency with minority support in the Congress. He, thus, needed the negotiating and bargaining skills an American president has to rely on to bring people on various points of the political spectrum together.

The key point is that we should not be surprised that Fox and Calderón, were not very good at that. They had little or no experience in using such skills. Instead, they rose to power in part because of their intransigent opposition to the PRI, with which they now had to cooperate if anything was to be accomplished in the legislative arena.

In other areas, they were more successful. Most Mexicans now understand that divided government will not lead to chaos and that the regime can live with policy-making gridlock, at least in the short run. Put in terms used throughout the book, the difficulties since 2000 do not seem to place the regime in jeopardy in any way.

For now.

In a worst case scenario, Mexico *could* become a failed state ten or twenty years from now. The country itself almost certainly would not fall apart, but its regime could. Military, nationalist, and left-wing populist leaders are among the possibilities we should be concerned about.

PUBLIC POLICY

Debt and Development

Had this book been written forty years ago, we probably would have focused on import substitution and the so-called "Mexican miracle," which turned into a house of cards with debt crisis. Its stable government had smoothed the transition from revolutionary egalitarianism to state-sponsored industrialization. An annual average growth rate of 6.5 percent was being translated into new enterprises, some owned by the state and some by the private sector, and into an improved standard of living for most people. Moreover, Mexico seemed to be breaking the bonds of dependency by building its own industrial base and relying less on imports.

The Mexican model of stable development is long gone. The sharp decline in oil prices in the early 1980s sparked a general downturn that left no part of the economy untouched. Even more important, the last three PRI presidents could no longer keep the economy largely closed to foreign involvement and had to adopt new policies more in keeping with the structural adjustment policies demanded by the World Bank, IMF, and other northern financial institutions.

Early Success

Industrialization was aided in the 1940s by high wartime demand for Mexican manufactured goods, minerals, and labor in the United States. More important for our purposes, it also was the product of a series of government policies that development economists call **import substitution**.

Despite the government's revolutionary origins and the huge role it was to play in industrial development, this was not a socialist policy. Rather, the government saw public ownership as providing it with leverage over the economy, which it could use to stimulate growth. The government stepped in where the private sector could not or would not act—for instance, in extending the railroad, highway, electricity, and telephone networks or in keeping troubled industries afloat. Rarely did it take private enterprises over for ideological reasons.

We should not underestimate the state's power because it did incorporate most of the major privately owned industries into the corporatist system. At the same time, this made most of their owners and employees almost as dependent on the state as they would have been had their industries been publicly owned.

At the heart of these efforts was NAFINSA, the National Development Bank, which supplied about half the total investment funds. Much of that money went to the public sector, beginning with the nationalization of the railroads and PEMEX in the 1930s. The expansion of the state sector

continued over the decades. By the end of the 1970s, the government owned all or part of more than a thousand companies, including smelters, sugar refineries, hotels, grocery stores, and even a shampoo factory. The wave of nationalizations ended in 1982 after the banks were taken over during the last weeks of López Portillo's presidency.

Taxes were kept low, and the prices of such key commodities as oil were subsidized to spur investment. Tariffs, in contrast, were kept high, averaging about 45 percent of the cost of the product being imported. Almost 95 percent of all imported goods required expensive government licenses and, as with everything else involving the state, entailed lots of red tape and substantial bribes.

The combined public and private sector efforts paid off. The economy as a whole grew by more than 6 percent per year from 1940 to 1980. Industrial production rose even faster, averaging nearly 9 percent for most of the 1960s. Agriculture's share of total production dropped from 25 percent to 11 percent, while that of manufacturing rose from 25 percent to 34 percent. Development was concentrated in labor-intensive, low-technology industries, such as food, tobacco, textiles, machinery, iron and steel, and chemicals. Exports grew tenfold, and manufactured goods came to account for a quarter of the total. The peso was one of the world's most stable currencies because the government kept it pegged at 12.5 to the dollar from 1954 to 1976. All this growth occurred without much of the inflation that was plaguing many other Latin American economies.

Don't let this picture mislead you into thinking that everything was fine. Relatively little attention was paid to equality and social justice that had led to the revolution in the first place. Social service programs were limited at best. For example, there was no unemployment insurance of any kind. Mexico's income distribution was (and still is) highly skewed. Rapid industrialization brought with it traffic congestion and pollution.

The Crisis

Although few economists or politicians realized it at the time, the economic boom began to slow during the 1970s. Neither the private nor the public sector proved able to spark the next stage in Mexico's industrial revolution, in which it would make more sophisticated, higher technology products.

Moreover, at this point, the mismanagement of key industries became a problem. It was estimated, for instance, that PEMEX employed three or four times the number of workers it needed. Rapid population growth meant that more workers were entering the workforce than there were jobs for them. There was a dramatic increase in government spending brought on by the last wave of nationalizations and a belated attempt to deal with social problems. To make matters worse, government revenues did not keep up

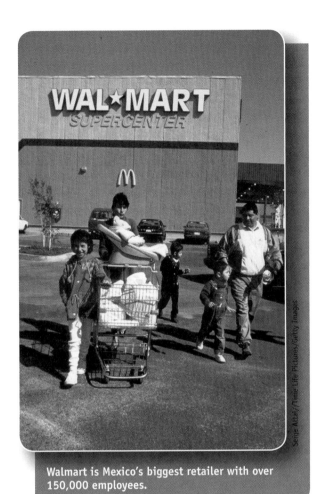

Walmart is Mexico's biggest retailer with over 150,000 employees.

with spending, creating budget deficits that, in turn, led to a rapidly rising national debt.

The budgetary and investment fund shortfalls were met through heavy borrowing, mostly from northern banks and governments. Because of the heavy debt load and ensuing political problems during prerevolutionary times, PRI governments had borrowed very little early on. In 1970, the total debt was only $6 billion. But by the beginning of the López Portillo presidency in 1976, the debt was already $26 billion, and it would reach $80 billion by the time he left office six years later. Ultimately, the total debt would reach a peak of more than $107 billion in 1987, making Mexico one of the most heavily indebted countries in the world, its debt accounting for 16 percent of its annual GNP in 1970. By 1987, its share was up to 70 percent.

The **debt crisis** was just the tip of the iceberg. Whether it wanted to or not, Mexico was being drawn into the global economy, which made it harder and harder to retain import substitution. The artificially low rate at which the peso was kept made it difficult for Mexico to import the new technologies it needed to continue its development. This, in turn,

made investment abroad ever more lucrative, leading to massive capital flight in the second half of the 1970s.

The government also made an extremely costly mistake. López Portillo based his economic strategy on the assumption that oil prices would remain high. The rapid price increases and supply uncertainties after the OPEC oil embargo of 1973–74 came just as Mexican production capacity increased. Then, after the Iranian revolution in 1979, oil prices shot up again. As a result, Mexico began selling massive amounts of oil. From 1979 to 1981 alone, Mexican oil revenues increased from $3.9 billion to $14.5 billion and accounted for almost 75 percent of all exports and for 45 percent of government revenues.

Oil revenues thus papered over many of the underlying economic problems. Nonetheless, budget deficits and overseas borrowing continued to mount. Increased imports of consumer goods outpaced the growth in exports. Inflation broke the 20 percent barrier for the first time. The low value of the peso and high interest rates abroad accelerated capital flight by the so-called *sacadolares* (dollar plunderers).

When oil prices began to fall in 1981, the government assumed that the decline would be temporary. It was wrong. By 1982, the Mexican economy was on the brink of collapse.

The government responded by closing the foreign exchange markets and nationalizing the banks. Still, the economy reeled out of control. By 1983, inflation had topped 100 percent, reaching a peak of 159 percent in 1987. The economy shrank for three of the five years from 1982 to 1986. The peso was allowed to float freely, and the exchange rate went from 56.5 pesos to the dollar in 1982 to 1,460 in 1987. This had devastating consequences for a country that was so dependent on imports, most of which had to be paid for in ever more expensive dollars. The economy suffered yet another jolt in 1985. A devastating earthquake in Mexico City cost the government somewhere between $4 and $5 billion, an amount it could not afford. Meanwhile, the price of a barrel of oil dropped another 50 percent, which cut export earnings from $16 billion in 1985 to only $9 billion the following year.

Reform

The onset of the economic crisis led to two fundamental shifts in Mexican politics: the election of de la Madrid and his government's commitment to debt reduction plans demanded by the country's international creditors.

Despite forty years of import substitution designed to maximize Mexican economic autonomy, the country found itself more dependent on the outside world than ever. Under the best of circumstances, Mexico would have had trouble competing in the global market with its inefficient industries, limited investment capital, and overvalued currency.

The crisis made this difficult situation all but intolerable. Moreover, it occurred at precisely the time that import substitution models were losing favor in international circles and being replaced by structural adjustment with its emphasis on unrestricted trade in free markets as the best "engine" for economic growth.

Thus, the policies pursued by the last Mexican governments of the twentieth century had a lot in common with what we saw in India and Nigeria. No foreign bank or government dictated what Mexican policy had to do. Rather, the size of the debt and the need for outside help in repaying it left the Mexican government in a far weaker position with far fewer options than it had had prior to 1982. It is only a slight exaggeration to say that the massive borrowing left the Mexican economy hostage to its creditors, who held the upper hand in negotiating deals to restructure the debt.

In short, the combination of the new leaders' values and the crisis conditions led to one of the most dramatic economic turnarounds in modern history. Quickly, the government adopted four overlapping policies that the Salinas and Zedillo continued and added to.

■ *Debt reduction.* Even before he took office, de la Madrid began negotiations with the IMF, the World Bank, northern governments, and private banks. The most sweeping measure was part of U.S. Secretary of the Treasury Nicholas Brady's multinational plan that consolidated some loans, turned others into bonds, and reduced Mexico's annual interest payments by

Economic Liberalization and Globalization
in Mexico

The trends buffeting Mexico are not unique. Indeed, as we saw in the previous two chapters, globalization is a major factor in political life in all of the Global South, and one of its most important effects has been movement toward a more liberal or market-oriented economy.

What makes Mexico unusual is the speed with which those forces hit the country and the directness with which its government reacted. Long one of the most autarkic of governments, the PRI all but overnight switched from import substitution to structural adjustment, rather than making the more typical and gradual transformation as we saw in Chapter 12 on India. ■

one-third. The agreement also offered incentives designed to keep up to $7 billion in capital in the country for future investment. Mexico still was paying an average of $10 billion a year in debt service, reducing the interest but not the principal on most of its loans. Mexico suffered a second fiscal crisis in the first weeks of Zedillo's term when investors removed about $5 billion in capital from the Mexican market, which sparked a run on the peso and forced Mexico to accept another expensive bailout package brokered by the United States. In other words, even with the Brady plan, past borrowing continued to plague the Mexican economy, forcing the government to take out yet more loans and siphoning off money it could have used for other, more productive purposes.

■ *Sharp cuts in government spending.* By early 1983, Mexico and the IMF had reached basic agreement on a severe austerity plan. Government spending would be sharply reduced to cut the deficit by half within three years. Subsidies would be cut and the prices charged by such government agencies as CONASUPO, which provided basic foodstuffs at below-market prices, would be increased. The Salinas and Zedillo administrations cut government spending and raised taxes even further. They were able to keep the deficit low (4 percent in 2003) and bring inflation under control. However, the social service programs, which were never very good to begin with, were seriously compromised.

■ *Privatization.* To give market forces a greater role in the Mexican economy, the government decided to give up much of its economic power by privatizing public enterprises, especially those that were a drain on public finances. In February 1985, the government announced that 237 parastatals would be sold, and privatization has continued apace. Of the 1,155 firms the government controlled in the mid-1980s, only about 100 remain in state hands today. The government does, however, retain control of some of the largest and most important ones, including most of PEMEX. The most significant privatization came in 1990 when the Salinas government returned the banks to private ownership. Actually, the first steps in that direction had begun within months of the initial nationalization, when the de la Madrid government allowed Mexican investors to buy 34 percent of the shares in any bank and foreign investors to purchase some nonvoting stock. With the 1990 decision, the state sold off most of its remaining stake in eighteen commercial banks, retaining only a limited, minority interest in some of them. The $6.5 billion it raised was supposed to be used to provide basic services, including drinking water, sewers, electricity, schools, housing, and health care, but little of it ended up there. All the signs are that PRI insiders were able to gain control of these companies and become wealthy overnight. Thus, Mexico had twenty-four billionaires in 2000, more than half of whom earned their wealth in the newly privatized banking system.

- *Opening up the economy.* The United States and the other creditors also insisted that Mexico open its economy to more foreign investment. This began as early as the 1980s, but reached its peak with the 1994 implementation of NAFTA, which officially removed all barriers to trade by 2010. The government also agreed to join General Agreement on Tariffs and Trade (GATT) and its successor, the World Trade Organization (WTO), the body that shapes international trade policy and requires free-market policies. Policies designed to make the economy more market oriented removed many of the rules on imports, which made it easier to acquire needed new technologies. Only 6 percent of imports now require government licenses. Tariffs have been reduced to an average of 10 percent, the lowest rate in Latin America.

In some ways, opening the economy has paid off. A mini-"silicon valley" was created in Guadalajara, where IBM, Hewlett-Packard, and other high-tech U.S. firms assemble computers for the Mexican export markets. Most of the new industrial development originally was concentrated in the north, where special laws had long allowed foreign firms to open *maquiladora* factories that use duty-free imported components, assemble intermediate or final products, and export what they manufacture. In 1990, more than fifteen hundred of them were shipping GI Joes and Barbie dolls, televisions, and automobiles for American and Japanese firms. The rules have since been loosened so that similar establishments can be opened elsewhere in the country. Mexico is attractive to foreign firms because wages are about an eighth of what they are north of the border. In fact, wage costs are so low that some Nissans built there are actually being shipped back to Japan. One American consultant estimated that it would make sense for any American firm that spends as little as 30 percent of its total budget on wages to relocate the manufacturing parts of its business to Mexico.

Under the PAN

It should come as no surprise that these trends have continued under the PAN's leadership. Since 2000, economists tend to rate the reforms fairly highly. Inflation is down, and, in some years, so is debt. Growth rates have often been respectable and there is a more visible middle class. Note, however, that the growth rate fell by two-thirds between 2006 and 2008 while the economy as a whole declined by about 7 percent in 2009. However, growth returned to about 5 percent in 2010 and should be about the same in 2011.

Scholars who focus on other issues, such as equity, are less optimistic. There has been something approaching a 50 percent decline in real wages. A total of 40 percent of the workforce is either unemployed or underemployed, and jobs have to be found for the million or so people who enter the workforce each year. About 40 percent of the population suffers from some form of malnutrition. Mexico's income distribution remains, in the World Bank's estimation, one of the world's worst.

At the same time that Mexico's yuppies are driving BMWs, downloading movies onto their home entertainment systems, and buying Pampers for their children, millions of poor people still lack indoor plumbing, hot water, health care, and adequate housing. The government tried to soften the impact of the economic reforms on the poor through the creation of the Program for National Solidarity (PRONASOL) and other welfare projects under de la Madrid and Salinas. In classic Mexican corporatist style, however, PRONASOL was administered through the president's office and was used as a way to solidify support for the PRI. In many people's eyes, it turned into little more than another body to distribute consumer goods to buy support for the PRI.

President Zedillo abandoned that approach, especially for the rural poor, when he created the *Progresa* program in 1997 which Fox renamed *Oportunidades* in 2002. There are two profound differences between it and traditional Mexican anti-poverty policy. First, the money comes in the form of cash transfers given directly given to mothers with children, giving women a degree of financial independence from their husbands. As we will see in the discussion of microcredit in the next chapter, there is a growing sense that women handle money more responsibly than men. *Oportunidades* provides enough money so that women now make about as much money as their husbands. Second, families receive the funds only if their children stay in school, the family gets regular medical care, and the mothers attend workshops on health, education, and financial priorities. About one fourth of all Mexican families are enrolled in the program. All in all, the number of rural Mexicans who lived in absolute poverty declined from 37.4 percent to 13.8 percent little more than a decade later. Though that reduction in poverty cannot be wholly attributed to *Oportunidades*, the improvement under the program has far outpaced the overall rate of growth. At least thirty other countries are experimenting with similar programs, and a pilot program has been established in New York City.

It also is not clear how much development the policies will lead to if by development we mean sustained, long-term growth. Some optimistic analysts think Mexico could be one of the next BRICS. Such development, however, works on the assumption that global markets will continue to grow and that trading patterns will favor a country with Mexico's location, pattern of industrial development, and labor force, none of which seems certain in these uncertain economic times. And even if Mexico does prosper, it is likely to have an exaggerated version of the distorted development we find in most of the supposedly successful economies in the Global South.

Meanwhile, the PAN continues privatizing industries, which often means foreign investment and at least partial ownership. Thus, in 2010, it announced plans to sell off much of the water industry, including pipelines, sewers, and dam construction. Similarly, the state is allowing foreign investment in the development of new oil fields. PEMEX alone could not afford to pay for them on its own. Nonetheless, the PRD claimed that the plan violated the law that nationalized the petrochemical industry. In other industries, privatizations that began earlier continued. For instance, all the freight rail lines linking Mexico to the United States are dominated by American firms, one of which has the distinctly un-Spanish name of Kansas City Southern de Mexico.

When all is said and done, only one thing is clear. Mexico is losing control of its development. It may turn out that the reforms lead to substantial growth and generate a lot of wealth. But much of it—and the concomitant political power—will lie in the hands of the foreign investors who supply the capital and the foreign bankers who attach conditions to their loans. For instance, Carlos Slim initially shared control of his telecommunications firms with American and European companies that provided his venture capital. The American government and private American firms are putting pressure on the government to allow outside investment in PEMEX **(www.pemex.com/ index.cfm)** and to increase the amount of oil it can sell in the United States, even though it is a symbol of Mexican national independence and pride. In 2008, Calderón said that core of PEMEX would not be privatized after a law was passed that allowed some foreign investment in the new oil fields mentioned earlier. Although the high-tech firms that have built factories in Guadalajara provide jobs and other benefits for people in the area, it is also true that the Americans control how those factories are run and repatriate almost all their profits back to the United States—just as they do with the *maquiladora*s along the border.

After more than a decade of NAFTA **(www.ustr .gov/Trade_Agreements/Regional/NAFTA/Section_Index .html)**, Mexican dependency on the United States has probably increased, although the impact of the trade agreement is a subject of tremendous controversy on both sides of the border. As NAFTA's supporters projected, trade between the United States and Mexico grew by a factor of four after the agreement went into effect. However, it also exacerbated differences within Mexico as the states closest to the U.S. border saw their economies expand while those elsewhere in the country grew poorer.

Profile
Carlos Slim

There is no better example of the new money in Mexico than Carlos Slim Helú (1940–) who is arguably the third richest person in the world.

Slim comes from good entrepreneurial stock. His father emigrated to Mexico from Lebanon (the family name was originally Salim) and established a small store. He soon started buying real estate.

After getting a degree in engineering, the younger Slim also went into business. He has been most active in telecommunications, controlling the leading landline, cell, and telephone equipment companies. In 2009, he loaned the financially troubled *New York Times* $250 million. He already owned almost 7 percent of the company; he could end up with 17 percent of it by 2015.

Slim is also a philanthropist supporting Mexico's largest technical university and development projects throughout Central and South America.

He is not without his critics, however. In 2011, for example, his company was accused of charging four times what it cost the firm to establish a cell

Carlos Slim, perhaps the world's third richest person.

phone account and it has something approaching a monopoly on the service. ∎

U.S.-Mexican Relations: Immigration and Drugs

In the first six editions of *Comparative Politics*, this section dealt almost exclusively with the immigration of Mexicans to the United States, legally and otherwise. The related issue of the drug wars was introduced in the seventh edition. Now, the two have to be given equal treatment.

In the United States, people are still worried mostly about illegal immigration from Mexico and other countries by way of Mexico. In March 2010, Arizona passed a highly restrictive law (SB 1070) limiting what illegal immigrants can do. At least five other states have bills closely patterned on Arizona's law pending.

Immigration *is* important to Mexicans. The United States has long offered an economic safety valve, employing workers who could not find work at home. In the state of Michoacán alone, migrants send about $2.5 billion a year to relatives back home. Nationally, the figure is ten times that amount even though the totals have been down so far in this decade because tens of thousands of Mexicans have returned home and the number of Mexicans who are trying to "go North" is down to a trickle. In fact, most of those who do so are trying to flee the drug cartels, not trying to find a better job to make more money.

In the last few years, however, Mexican attention has shifted to the difficulties involved in emigrating, the dislocations caused by NAFTA, and the drug violence that grows out of all three. Most of the thousands of weapons seized by the Mexican authorities come from the United States. After all, as mentioned earlier, Mexico has one legal gun store—and only law enforcement officials can shop there!

Imbalance of Power

Ever since 1821, the United States has had a tremendous influence on the way Mexicans live. Mexico retains considerable freedom to act as it wants in global affairs. Certain aspects of U.S.-Mexican relations can even work to the detriment of Americans. For example, many workers in heavy industry have seen their jobs move to Mexico. Nonetheless, when all is said and done, the relationship is much the same as it has always been. The United States rarely tries to dictate Mexican domestic or foreign policy. Because of its size, wealth, and geopolitical power, Mexican policy makers follow U.S. wishes more often than not, especially when the issue at hand matters a lot to their counterparts in Washington.

Mexican foreign policy involves far more than its relations with the United States. However, the U.S. shapes Mexican affairs to a degree that far exceeds the impact of any one country on any other considered in this book. One former U.S. ambassador recently remarked that he had once apologized to the Mexican foreign minister for having to raise a trivial matter. The minister told him not to worry because about 85 percent of his time was devoted to U.S.-Mexican relations anyway.

Avocados?

On July 14, 2004, the *Washington Post* and the *New York Times* both ran a full page ad by the Association of Producers and Exporters of Avocados from Michoacán. Their concern was that only thirty-one states in the United States allowed Mexican-grown Hass avocados to be imported during six months of the year. The rest banned them altogether.

The Mexicans claimed that California avocado growers were limiting the import of the Mexican salad ingredient to protect their own market, especially since their fruit cost American consumers 50 percent more than the Mexican version. The point here is not to debate the relative quality of the two types of avocados, but to see the importance of trade issues in the U.S.-Mexican relationship. *The law has since been relaxed some, and the Mexicans are now using more pesticides to meet American import restrictions.* Exports have been growing at about 6 percent per year, but barriers to trade still exist.

Similarly, when U.S. officials visit Mexico, they can count on working with the country's most important leaders. Conversely, when Mexican leaders come to the United States, they normally spend the bulk of their time with relatively low-ranking officials, such as the undersecretary of state for Latin American affairs.

Recent U.S.-Mexican relations have been fairly peaceful and even cooperative, but historically there have been moments of intense tension and conflict. U.S. intervention affected the course of the Mexican revolutions of 1810 and 1910 and almost everything in between. As the nationalist journalist Gastón Garcia Cantú put it:

> **From the end of the eighteenth century through 1918, there were 285 invasions, incidents of intimidation, challenges, bombardments of ports, and subtractions of territory out of which seven American states were carved. No people in the world have had their territory, wealth, and security as plundered by anybody as Mexico has by the United States.[4]**

With the consolidation of the PRI regime, relations improved to the point that the United States no longer contemplated direct intervention in Mexican affairs. Still, by the time Cárdenas took over in 1934, U.S. interests controlled more of the Mexican economy than ever. His reforms did strain relations some, but not as much as they might have a generation earlier, in large part because the United States

---

[4] Cited in Robert Pastor and Jorge Castañeda, *Limits to Friendship: The United States and Mexico* (New York: Vintage Books, 1988), 123.

faced far more serious threats elsewhere. Given Mexico's stable, non-communist regime, it receded from center stage in U.S. foreign policy concerns.

This is not to say that tensions completely disappeared. Mexico frequently criticized U.S. foreign policy, especially interventions in Latin America prompted by U.S. fears of communism. Mexico opposed the overthrow of leftist governments in Guatemala in 1954 and Chile in 1973. It similarly supported Cuba's right to have a communist government while opposing such U.S. attempts to topple it as the Bay of Pigs invasion in 1961. The Mexicans were among the first to break with the Somoza family dictatorship and to support the leftist Sandinistas in Nicaragua. Later, they were among the most strident critics of the Reagan administration's support for the Contra counterrevolutionary movement after the Sandinistas won.

Antagonisms between the two countries increased during the 1980s. In part, this had to do with the Mexican economic crisis and its resentment toward the U.S. role in forcing debt negotiations and other policy shifts discussed above. In part, too, it had to do with the Reagan administration's dissatisfaction with Mexico's Central American policy and its open courtship of the PAN, which it saw as a conservative, procapitalist, and realistic alternative to the PRI.

U.S.-Mexican relations have improved considerably since the election of the PAN, whose promarket policies meshed nicely with those of the Reagan, Clinton, both Bush, and now the Obama administrations.

Improved relations, however, should not obscure the main point being made here. At all times this has been an unequal relationship, controlled by a United States that has actively pursued its own interests, often without paying much attention to what the Mexicans wanted.

American Fears of Mexico

In a peculiar way, many Americans live in fear of Mexico, as seen in the 2010 congressional election campaign and the ongoing debate over immigration reform in the United States.

To get a first glimpse of this fear, consider the following incident. During the summer of 1991, the U.S. Immigration and Naturalization Service began constructing a fourteen-foot-high wall along the border between San Diego and Tijuana. Ironically, the wall was made of metal slabs originally manufactured to serve as temporary runways during the Gulf War to liberate Kuwait. Even more ironically, at precisely that moment in history when we celebrated the collapse of a Berlin Wall built to keep East Germans from fleeing to freedom, the U.S. government was building what many Mexicans called a Berlin Wall to keep their

citizens out of the United States. In 2007, some Republican candidates wanted to build such a wall all the way from San Diego to the Gulf coast.

Just below the surface lie other fears—of drugs, of the economic drain many believe the Global South imposes on rich countries, of the global population explosion, and the like. On the other hand, these fears tend to blind people in the north to their own power and to their ability to determine what happens on the other side of the more often invisible wall that divides north from south.

Finally, there is a strong undercurrent of wariness regarding the United States, both in Mexican public opinion and in its official policy even under the PAN. On the one hand, Mexican leaders realize that they must get along with their powerful neighbor to the north, and life in the United States is attractive to most Mexicans. On the other hand, most Mexicans remain highly suspicious of U.S. policies and intentions. One 1980s poll found that 59 percent of Mexicans sampled thought of the United States as an "enemy country," and 47 percent claimed that their opinion of the United States had worsened during the 1980s.

Virtually no Mexicans take U.S. declarations that its policies are altruistic seriously. Instead, Mexican leaders realize that the U.S. presence and its influence over foreign policy are facts of life. Their protests and seeming intransigence have been on issues that are not terribly important or in ways that are not very threatening to the United States. In fact, to cynical observers, they have been designed to placate Mexican voters rather than to demonstrate any real Mexican autonomy.

Immigration

In recent years no issue has revealed the unequal power in U.S.-Mexican relations more than the migration of millions of Mexicans to the United States. No comprehensive reform on this issue is likely to pass, at least not until after the 2012 presidential elections in both countries.

Migration between the two countries is not a new phenomenon. People have been moving from Mexico to the United States since colonial times. It only became a serious political issue, however, after World War II. As we saw earlier, the United States actually encouraged Mexican migration during the war. However, with the defeat of Germany and Japan and the demobilization of millions of U.S. soldiers, the Mexicans became "excess" labor, and the United States began sending them home.

For the next forty years, U.S. policy followed a similar pattern. During times of economic expansion, immigration policies were loosened or U.S. officials turned a blind eye to the hiring of illegal or "undocumented" aliens. But when unemployment rose and Americans began to complain that illegal Mexicans were taking "their" jobs, the U.S. government tended to force the immigrants back out again.

Historically, there have been four major crackdowns—in 1947, 1954, 1964, and 1986. Whether economically justified or not, each was handled in a way that was bound to anger Mexicans. The 1954 program, for instance, was known as Operation Wetback and was directed by an army general as a military operation.

In 1986, Congress passed the Immigration Reform and Control Act, which created an amnesty program for Mexicans who had been in the United States illegally for five years, limited further immigration and for the first time, imposed penalties on U.S. employers who knowingly hired undocumented workers. The act, of course, applied to all illegal immigrants, but it was widely perceived as an anti-Mexican act because something on the order of two-thirds of all undocumented immigrants were Mexican.

A fifth possible crackdown is occurring as we write. In late 2006 and early 2007, immigration reform became a "hot button" issue in American politics. Ironically, Presidents Bush and Fox were close to an agreement in summer 2001, but the furor following the terrorist attacks made any liberalization impossible in the short run. In 2006, Bush proposed a bill that would allow some illegal immigrants to remain and eventually gain the right to earn United States citizenship. New immigrants would be allowed to enter for fixed terms and for jobs they already had been offered. At the same time, border controls would be reinforced to slow the entry of undocumented workers. By late 2007, conservative lawmakers had killed the bill and no new one has been put forward under President Obama.

Despite the law and the efforts of the Immigration and Naturalization Service (INS) to close the border, the flow of people continued until very recently. Before then, the INS stopped about 200,000 people a year trying to cross the border illegally, but to little or no avail. No one knows how many people paid "coyotes" to sneak them into the United States and, sometimes, find them a job. Not surprisingly, a huge black market in counterfeit and stolen "green cards" and other documents also sprang up.

Concerns now extend beyond immigration to its impact on U.S. society as a whole. Fears about the cost of providing them with welfare, education, and other social services, and about the "dilution" of American culture, were key reasons behind California's Proposition 187, which passed in a referendum in 1994 and denied illegal aliens access to public services. There have also been attempts to make English the only language to be used in official state business and in education. Young people who are not in the country legally cannot get financial aid or in-state tuition to help pay for a university education in all but a handful of states.

In recent years, the key policy shift has been Arizona's law mentioned earlier. It does not affect the border, which is a federal responsibility. However, it introduced draconian policies, including allowing (practically forcing) the police to check on someone's immigration status whenever they are picked up for even a minor traffic violation.

To most Mexicans, U.S. immigration policy is biased and shortsighted. They note that many Americans believe that the roots of migration begin with the lack of jobs in Mexico. Although most Mexicans will admit that migration strains U.S. educational, social service, and health care systems, they argue that U.S. politicians overstate the problem. They point out that few undocumented Mexicans

An undocumented Mexican immigrant working construction in the United States climbs a ladder to the top of a scaffolding with no safety equipment.

©iStockphoto.com/sandro gomes

are taking jobs from Americans. Instead, most work in jobs that Americans are no longer willing to take. They also point out that the migrants themselves are not the riffraff they are frequently portrayed as being in the media. The immigrants disproportionately come from the most talented and dynamic sectors of Mexican society and include ten to fifteen thousand professionals a year.

Similarly, they also note that the United States has never fully acknowledged the benefits it gets from the migration or the role that its businesses have played in perpetuating the problem by hiring people they know are in the country illegally. And they complain that the racism and indignity that everyone of Mexican origin is subjected to are not even on the U.S. policy-making agenda. Further, they charge that U.S. policy does not address the root cause of the problem, which lies in Mexico itself. The Mexican government would prefer not to have migration serve as a safety valve for the discontent that might erupt if the migrants had to stay at home and remain unemployed or underemployed. Instead, Mexican leaders would rather see the United States invest billions of dollars to provide more jobs in Mexico rather than trying to close the border.

Drugs

There is no question that the United States has a serious drug problem. There is also no question that many of the drugs Americans consume enter the country from Mexico.

Drugs became politically important in the last decade because of a combination of unemployment due to the effects of NAFTA and limitations on immigration. The drug trade is run by a series of cartels that have close ties with the police, army, and the government. In all, the cartels are estimated to control 90 percent or more of the sale of cocaine, methamphetamines, and synthetic drugs. As strange as it may seem, Mexico does not have a serious drug problem of its own, and few of the drugs it exports were grown or made in Mexico. Rather, they are imported across Mexico's porous border and then sent north across the only slightly porous one with the United States.

The cartels are at war with each other over which of them will be able to control the largest proportion of the trade. But in 2010 and 2011 they have also taken to killing innocent civilians who, for instance, might have been riding in a bus hijacked by a cartel. Others who are not killed are held for ransom that can reach hundreds of thousands of dollars. No one knows for sure how many people have died. Mass graves are discovered on a regular basis. The best guess is that the total exceeded 12,000 in 2010, 10 percent higher than the year before, and now totals over 40,000.

The cartels have close ties with each of the three major parties and fill their ranks with former police officers and military veterans. That makes a crackdown on them all the more difficult. The Mexican government claims it has confiscated more than 300,000 weapons in the last decade, most of which were smuggled into Mexico from Arizona, Texas, and other border states.

George Grayson has written two recent books on the cartels, the first of which deals with *La Familia*, which is based in Michoacán. It deserves our attention here because it is both one of the largest and most unusual of the cartels.

It is based in the port city of Lázaro Cárdenas, ironically named for the last great reformist PRI president. The port, and

Marijuana seized by Mexican authorities in 1996. Many Americans argue that the Mexican government is not doing enough in the war on drugs.

AP Images

much of the state, sit on the Pacific coast and contain a number of transportation links to the United States. In one form or another, La Familia has been around for years, but only went off on its own in 2006 when it burst on the scene by tossing five decapitated heads into a night club. In part because of its position on those trade routes, it has become a major player in the drug trade and in organized crime in general.

It probably has about 4,000 full-time members. In order to join, they have to pass an alcohol and drug rehabilitation program based on models developed by conservative American Evangelical Christians. It counts at least ten mayors and countless local officials, plus a member of the Chamber of Deputies in its ranks.

Its operations are extremely profitable. Despite its commitment to a drug-free organization, it controls most of the trade in the state as well as a huge share of exports to the United States. It has also set up "legitimate" businesses including hotels and restaurants. The Calderón government has sent at least 8,000 military and police personnel into the state with the twin, but contradictory, goals of wiping out and negotiating with La Familia, although it is hard to tell who it could negotiate with.

The United States is paying more attention. In fact, Grayson's book was written for an office at the United States Army War College. Most senior officers in the U.S. military who work on the cartels think a viable strategy has to address the root causes discussed earlier. Nonetheless, most American politicians continue to focus on "simply" stopping the flow of drugs across the border.

There is little doubt that American policy on this front is dated and inadequate. During the 1980s, the U.S. government decided that it would concentrate less on reducing the demand for drugs and more on cutting the supply in what the first Bush and Reagan administrations called the "war on drugs." And as with immigration, this has led some Americans to blame Mexico for much of the drug problem. Also, after the murder of DEA agent Salazar, U.S. officials were highly critical of Mexican authorities for their failure to do much about the problem and for their involvement in drug trafficking itself. Such criticisms surfaced again in the mid-1990s with the scandals implicating the Salinas, Hank, and other leading PRI families.

There is now considerable cooperation between policy makers and enforcement agencies on both sides of the border. The CIA, FBI, and other U.S. agencies train Mexican officials, though they are skeptical of the commitment south of the border.

In this case, the tension emerges less from misunderstanding than from the different national interests in the drug issue. As noted above, Mexico itself does not have much of a drug problem. Moreover, even though the money is never included in official statistics and is never taxed, the profits from the drug trade amount to at least $2 billion in additional income for Mexicans. In this regard, the Mexican government has good reason to resist Washington's more drastic and invasive demands.

As with immigration, the point is not that U.S. policy is wrong per se. Rather, the problem is that it has contributed to the weakening of Mexican sovereignty. The Mexican government really has had no choice but to allow the DEA to operate inside Mexican territory, something Americans cannot ever imagine allowing another government to do on their soil. The Mexicans have been able to block some U.S. proposals, including one that would have allowed Air Force jets to pursue drug suspects into Mexican airspace. However, U.S. policy makers have largely turned a deaf ear to Mexican requests to pursue policies that address Mexican needs, particularly ones that would provide marijuana and poppy growers with the opportunity to make a decent living raising other crops.

As Grayson and his colleagues at the war college realize, the problem is far more complex and reflects almost everything about the Mexican-U.S. relationship. Most important, as the drug cartels have moved into the southwest to get guns, they have brought their rivalries along with them. In short, although Mexico may not yet be a failed state, it may become one soon if these drug wars continue to escalate. At the very least it has what the late student of revolutions Crane Brinton called "dual sovereignty," which means that official authorities have to share power with rivals in much of a country.

THE MEDIA

The same ambiguity regarding democracy and Mexico that we have seen throughout this chapter exists with the press as well. Newspapers, magazines, and television stations are ostensibly free of government control. The mass market press, however, rarely took the PRI governments on, failing to report on electoral fraud and other flagrant violations of the law because the government had considerable leverage over it. The PRI, for example, had a virtual monopoly on the supply of newsprint. It supplied chronically underfunded and understaffed papers with substantial amounts of information that often found its way into their pages with next to no investigation by journalists. The largest newspaper chain and, until recently, the one television network with a national audience were controlled by PRI loyalists.

Despite the control it already had, PRI governments did clamp down, as when it engineered the firing of the editorial team at the independent and often critical magazine *Excelsior* in 1976. But, more often, the press censored itself. Mass circulation dailies and television news provided bland coverage and tended to avoid controversial stories altogether. Instead, they presented government proclamations and covered the actions of its leaders in ways that made them seem like little more than propaganda outlets for the PRI.

That said, pressures to open up the media have been building for years and have already had an impact. While there are more independent outlets, most of these still only reach the relatively well-educated and affluent. Now, of course, the PRI-dominated media are critical of the two PAN administrations. Similarly, the opening up of the economy and the technological revolution have brought in more media that are not controllable by the government, including satellite access to CNN and the U.S. networks' Spanish-language services.

CONCLUSION: MEXICO AND THE GLOBAL SOUTH

The most important theme in the last few pages is the erosion of national sovereignty. Countries like Mexico remain nominally sovereign, but its de facto erosion is occurring everywhere. It is especially evident in Mexico and the other countries covered in Part 4.

We do not want to overstate this point. Few countries are giving up their legal sovereignty. Still, the growing interdependence of the world's economic and other systems is sapping all countries of at least some of their ability to determine their own destinies. This trend is especially marked in the Global South where governments lack the wealth and other resources of the liberal democracies in the north.

It may be that this "globalization" is inevitable and irreversible. However, this should not keep us from thinking about the ways in which it is reinforcing existing imbalances in the distribution of wealth and power or from worrying about what the consequences could be as globalization continues, including a growing number of failed or failing states.

Key Terms

Concepts

camarilla
corporatism
debt crisis
electoral alchemy
failed state
import substitution
maquiladora
mestizo
non-reelection
patron-client relations
pendulum effect
sexeño
structural adjustment

People

Calderón, Felipe
Cárdenas, Cuauhtémoc
Cárdenas, Lázaro
de la Madrid, Miguel
Diaz, Porfirio
Fox, Vicente
Lopéz Obrador, Andrés
   Manuel
Salinas, Carlos de Gortari
Santa Anna, Antonio
   López de
Zedillo, Ernesto

Acronyms

CFE
CTM
IFE
NAFTA
PAN
PEMEX
PRD
PRI

Organizations

Confederation of Mexican
   Workers
Federal Election Commission
   (CFM)
Federal Electoral Institute
   (IFE)
Gobernación
Immigration Reform and
   Control Act
Institutional Revolutionary
   Party (PRI)
National Action Party (PAN)
North American Free Trade
   Agreement (NAFTA)
Party of the Democratic
   Revolution (PRD)

Useful Websites

There are plenty of websites on Mexican politics. The problem is that surprisingly few of them have English language material, including those of the Mexican government and political parties. The sites listed here all have at least some material in English.

The President's Office now has a fairly extensive website in English, though there is far more in Spanish. The Chamber of Deputies' site is only in Spanish, but we have included it anyway on the assumption that many readers of this book will speak some Spanish.

> www.presidencia.gob.mx
>
> http://www.diputados.gob.mx/inicio.htm

Washington's Center for Strategic and International Studies has a good site on the Americas in general.

> www.csis.org/americas

The left-of-center North American Conference on Latin America (NACLA) provides periodic analyses of events in Mexico and throughout the region.

> www.nacla.org

The Latin American Network Information Center (LANIC) at the University of Texas has the best set of links to all aspects of Mexican life for academic use. Alex López Ortiz maintains a remarkable database of online articles and other documents on Mexican politics at the University of Waterloo in Canada.

> lanic.utexas.edu/la/mexico/
>
> http://www.cs.uwaterloo.ca/~alopez-o/polind.html

Further Reading

Barkin, David. *Distorted Development: Mexico in the World Economy.* Boulder, CO: Westview Press, 1990. A first-rate analysis of the uneven and, in some ways, unhealthy way the Mexican economy has evolved.

Bazant, Jan. *A Concise History of Mexico: From Hidalgo to Cárdenas.* New York: Cambridge University Press, 1977. The best short history concentrating on the century and a half when Mexican politics was most turbulent.

Camp, Roderic Ai. *Politics in Mexico.* New York: Oxford University Press, 2006. The best short book introducing Mexican politics, for a mostly undergraduate audience.

Castañeda, Jorge. *Mañana Forever.* New York: Knopf, 2011. An overview by Mexico's preeminent political scientist, who was foreign minister in Fox's government.

Domínguez, Jorge, and James McCann. *Democratizing Mexico: Public Opinion and Electoral Choices.* Baltimore: Johns Hopkins University Press, 1996. The first thorough analysis of the subject in Mexico. Unfortunately, there is little on the events after 1991.

Grayson, George. *La Familia Drug Cartel.* Carlisle PA, Strategic Studies Institute/Army War College. The first of two books by a professor at William and Mary. A broader and more popular book is due out soon.

Haussman, Melissa. *Abortion Politics in North America.* Boulder, CO, 2005. Particularly useful because it contrasts Mexico with the United States and Canada.

Levy, Daniel C., and Gabriel Székely. *Mexico: Paradoxes of Stability and Change*, 2nd ed. Boulder, CO: Westview Press, 1987. A thorough account of the strengths and weaknesses of the Mexican system; still worth reading more than two decades after it was written.

Levy, Daniel C., and Kathleen Bruhn, with Emilio Zebadua. *Mexico: The Struggle for Democratic Development.* Berkeley: University of California Press, 2001. A good overview of Mexican history focusing on the obstacles preventing the development of democracy.

Morris, Stephen. *Political Corruption in Mexico: The Impact of Democratization.* Boulder, CO: 2009. The most rigorous examination of corruption in Mexico.

Shirk, David. *Mexico's New Politics: The PAN and Democratic Change.* Boulder, CO: Lynn Rienner, 2005. The best recent book on the transition since 2000.

Warnock, John. *The Other Mexico: The North American Triangle Completed.* Montreal: Black Rose Books, 1995. The best left-of-center critique of the PRI and structural adjustment.

Wright, Lawrence. "Slim's Time" *The New Yorker.* June 1, 2009. By the best journalist working on terrorism who also plays in a blues band.

Conclusion

17

Sometimes I wonder if we put all the problems on a circular board, all the proposed solutions on the outer wheel, and just spun away, and implement each solution wherever it stopped on the wheel, whether we wouldn't do as well.

RICHARD FEINBERG

Global Challenges and Domestic Responses

This book and this course are both almost over. But, if yours is like too many of the courses we took as students and have taught as professors, you are running out of time and your instructor will have to give this material short shrift. If so, that is unfortunate. You have the rest of your life in front of you (well, at least after the final exam) in which you will have to make choices about both global challenges and domestic responses as citizens.

KEY QUESTIONS: OH YEAH? HOW COME? SO WHAT?

One of the leading comparative politics scholars from our youth used to ask three simple questions that would send graduate students into a panic because they hadn't touched on at least one of them in their presentations: "Oh yeah?" "How come?" "So what?"

So far, we have focused on the first two. The facts and figures in the first sixteen chapters get at the "oh yeah" or factual part of the course. Because this is an introductory course, we shied away from exploring the often arcane theories academics have devised to explain that factual material that make up the "how come" question. But especially in Chapter 1, the chapters beginning each of the first four parts, and in the thematic boxes, we have identified at least some key explanations of political phenomena in a way we

hope makes sense to readers getting their first systematic exposure to comparative politics.

We have not paid much attention to the "so what" question. It may be the most important of the three because asking it turns the challenges and the countries you have already seen into real life concerns you will face for the rest of your lives. Therefore, it only makes sense to concentrate on that third question in ending the book.

As scholar-activists, we know we court the objection that we are trying to foist our views on you. That is definitely *not* our intention. This chapter is based in part on our experience working on and promoting peacebuilding and women's rights, respectively. However, it is written in such a way that you can easily reject or modify our point of view. Indeed, one of the conclusions we reached in writing this chapter was just how much our own views have changed in the thirty years we have worked together.

Besides, we don't always agree ourselves.

WHAT GOES AROUND COMES AROUND

This chapter will be different from the first sixteen because it is far more speculative. Peacebuilding and the status of women are but two of literally dozens of issues we could have chosen to highlight the speed at which the world is

Looking BACKWARD

CHAPTERS 1 THROUGH 16 are based at least somewhat on a fiction, that you can understand a country's politics on its own.

Not so.

During the lifetimes of our careers, comparative politics has changed. Chip started out as an area specialist who assumed you could extrapolate from the experience of a single country. By the time Melissa came along a decade later, we knew better.

You do need to understand the specifics of individual places and times and leaders. But, you also need to pull the pieces together. That requires comparison, which, in turn, requires concepts and theories.

We would have liked to have done more of that in the previous fifteen chapters. However, because instructors do not cover the same countries, we couldn't know exactly which chapters you were assigned. That makes comparative analysis difficult at best from a purely logistical standpoint.

Now, we *can* be comparative and draw on the inductive and deductive sides of comparative politics to help you reach conclusions that were not possible thus far. There are many ways of doing that. We were both, for example, trained to do "most different" studies in which one might contrast Mexico, the United States, and Canada in order to find at least some lowest common denominators of democracy. In the body of the book, we used a "most similar" design in which we tried to figure out what made industrial democracies, current and former communist regimes, and countries in the Global South different from each other.

Now, our challenge is to break out of both modes and look at comparative politics as a whole by making the book's subtitle more explicit. Increasingly, comparative politics has to focus on domestic responses to *global challenges*. We have argued throughout the book that the dramatic changes of our times are making the distinction between comparative politics and international relations increasingly irrelevant, if not misleading. We were able to see that most clearly with the European Union in Part 2 and the International Financial Institutions in Parts 3 and 4. Now, our challenge is to show that the global challenges of international relations are an integral part of comparative politics.

Domestic politics remains our focus. However, we cannot reach anything like clarity without considering international forces as an increasingly important source of what takes place within any country's borders.

---

changing. In so doing, we will also discuss how important **globalization** is in our lives and just how much we still have to learn about it.

Our analysis suggests that we need to view politics through a new and somewhat different lens. As we argued in Chapter 1, political scientists have always tried to find patterns in the way people govern themselves. But we are at a stage in human history that is reshaping our lives so much that we even have to expand what we mean by politics itself. There is politics whenever and wherever power is up for grabs. Many feminists, for instance, are concerned about the media's role in portraying the traditional nuclear family, which is not the statistical norm, as the "regular" type of family. In short, politics takes place as "close to home" as possible. It also is global in its reach in the increasing interconnection of the world in politics, law, economics, communications, business, and even popular culture.

We introduced **systems theory** in Chapter 1 not only because it provides a good model for describing how states operate. It also is important because it helps us understand global interconnections at all levels better than any other theory. We will argue that globalization leads us to consider new ways of thinking about political life. However, the discussion around Figures 17.1 and 17.2 will help you see why many of the colleagues we respect the most come to dramatically different conclusions than we do.

The Wheel of Fortune

In September 1983, The *Wheel of Fortune* made its prime time debut. Almost thirty years later is still on the air.

Cohosts Pat Sajak and Vanna White (who are still on the job) have contestants spin a large wheel. After it stops, the spinner can "buy" a vowel or "guess" at consonants all the while trying to fill in the blanks in a common name, title, or expression. That continues as long as the contestant has at least $250 in the "bank" and the wheel doesn't stop at "lose a turn" or "bankrupt" until someone solves the puzzle.

In those same thirty years, versions of the show have been produced in 43 other countries. To be honest, neither of us paid much attention to it until Chip found the statement by Richard Feinberg, a former member of Policy and Planning staff at the State Department, which begins the chapter.

At the time he wrote, the world seemed a lot like Pat and Vanna's wheel. Feinberg seems to be saying that the policy maker trying to forge a coherent policy has no better way of knowing where the political wheel will end up than does the contestant playing on television. In other words, more often than we may like, politics in the age of globalization may be just as random as the Wheel of Fortune.

His were tough years to be an international relations expert, especially one who focuses on economics, which makes it easy to sympathize with views like his. However, we will make the case that life under globalization is anything but random. It may be incredibly complicated, but there are patterns as we have learned from chaos, complexity, and systems theorists since the Wheel's heyday.

Systems Theory

Systems theory has largely lurked below the surface since Chapter 1. However, it is important here because it helps us see the patterns Feinberg's statement seems to miss because it draws our attention to the often convoluted **feedback** loops among the component parts of a country's political system (see Figure 1.1 on page 12). Among those loops are keys to understanding the interplay between international and domestic politics.

We noted in Chapter 1 that systems theory was popular among political scientists in the 1960s and 1970s. Then, because most scholars drew conservative conclusions based on their preoccupation with political instability, it fell out of favor. Systems theory may not still be a major model in political science, but most other disciplines, especially in the hard sciences, base almost everything on it. The very term "ecology," for instance, means the study of the whole or whole systems.

Systems theory and globalization both also help us see that power relations can evolve in three basic ways:

- **Stay in balance.** From this perspective, a system does not change much, in ways akin to the way a thermostat regulates the temperature in a house. For the people who brought systems theory into political science, this is the best they thought we could do.

- **Decay or degenerate.** Their experience—often firsthand—with totalitarianism led them to fear this type of system and search for ways of avoiding the political equivalent of a dysfunctional family.

- **Grow.** Business executives, in particular, tell us that systems can improve their performance with

time, whatever one means by "improve." This was the aspect missed by the men and women who pioneered the use of system theory in political science. It may also be what we need more of in this age of globalization.

WOMEN AND PEACEBUILDING

We decided to focus on women's issues and peacebuilding because we have done the most research on them and because we are actively involved in political movements in their support. But they are also useful because they are good intellectual springboards to see the impact globalization could and should have in our lives. We also decided to put these two issues at the heart of this chapter because we hope that one or both of them will introduce you to some new and, occasionally, unsettling ideas.

The Inherently Gendered Nature of Globalization

Feminist scholars studying international relations and the international political economy have a long record of theorizing about how gendered political interactions—where men and women play different roles based on historically embedded expectations in domestic politics—get reproduced in international institutions such as the **IFIs**, the **UN**, and other **International Organizations**. Shirin Rai and Georgina Waylen study the shift from "government" to "governance" in a globalized world in which "governance includes not just government or institutions but a set of gendered social relations reflecting but also constitutive of capital/labor/market interaction." That leads, in turn, to a "gendered system of rules and regulatory norms and mechanisms that are translated through the discourses of law and policy."

Neither the gendering of globally linked processes of politics, law, and economics nor the processes they describe are all that new. For example, they state that "the move from the Bretton Woods system…reveals the consolidation of rules and regulations securing neo-liberal policies…essential for the functioning of global capitalism."[1] The IFIs were created to help manage the capitalist system that ran amok during the Great Depression and helped produce totalitarianism and World War II. As they see it, capitalism requires a gendered division of labor, which we will see in the example of a Filipina domestic worker below.

Rai and Waylen see the gendered nature of globalization as literally built into the very logic of the system. There have long—perhaps always—been gendered roles

---

[1] Rai, Shirin and Georgina Waylen, eds. *Global Governance: Feminist Perspectives.* London: Palgrave 2008, 6–7. All quotations.

and gender-based distributions of power and authority in everything from families to national political systems. However, if feminist theorists are right, globalization marks the first time that the very nature of the international system *requires* a considerable degree of uneven division of resources and power along gender lines.

Like many feminist scholars, Waylen often crosses the boundaries between international relations and comparative politics where her work and that of her colleagues is also vitally important. But, because Melissa is a feminist comparativist, she is more interested in highlighting state features which are most conducive to producing women-friendly policy outcomes in some states and hindering them in others. Indeed, there is now a Feminist Institutionalism International Network, which highlights how domestic, international, and multilevel institutions typically reinforce gender norms but in rare instances can be changed by a critical mass of women's presence and influence.

In that light, consider Melissa's research on the comparative differences in reproductive policy in three very different federal systems in Mexico, the United States, and Canada, which have, respectively, the most to least powers centralized at the national level (see Chapters 3, 16, and the online one on Canada). In one of her other books, she has shown the importance of studying the interaction between the domestic institutions created under federalism and supranational institutions such as the UN, Inter-American (**www.cidh.oas.org/DefaultE.htm**) and European Courts of Human Rights (**www.echr.coe.int/echr/Homepage_En**).

Feminists are thus part of the growing number of political scientists who view the world using a **multilevel analysis** to understand the differential rate of interest group influence on international institutions across and within countries as well as over time. The multiple levels reflect the complex feedback loops mentioned at the beginning of the chapter. They, in turn, blur the distinction between comparative politics, international relations, and all the other subfields of political science.

One example of the ways multilevel analysis can help is by examining how San Francisco became the first city in the U.S. to adopt the UN Convention for the Elimination of all Forms of Discrimination against Women (CEDAW). This is a most interesting development since the U.S. Senate has not ratified this treaty. Even though President Jimmy Carter signed it in 1979 and it has had the support of Presidents Clinton, Bush, and Obama, it has never come to a vote in the Senate where the Constitution requires a two-thirds majority to ratify any treaty.

As feminists see it, CEDAW is needed everywhere, not just in cities like San Francisco. If anything, women in the Global South suffer worse forms of discrimination and have fewer resources to improve their condition. For instance, no one knows how many women are sold

as what amount to sex slaves. Hundreds of thousands of girls who are too young to bear children get pregnant and come down with debilitating and, at times, life-threatening diseases.

Probably the most recent significant international acknowledgement of the importance of women's concerns and the need to work in a synthesized manner to force recalcitrant states to abide by human rights concerns is the July 2010 creation of "UN Women," short for the UN Entity for Gender Equality and the Empowerment of Women. This agency, headed by former Chilean President Michelle Bachelet (a supporter of women's political and reproductive equality when in office), combines four previously separate divisions of women's policymaking in the UN (**www.unwomen.org**).

We often think that phenomena such as the forced labor of women happen "somewhere else." Not true. On the day we drafted this section, the *Washington Post* reported that a couple had been arrested in the city's suburbs for having held a Filipina woman in slave-like conditions for about a decade thereby violating federal laws prohibiting domestic servitude.[2] She was paid a pittance and rarely allowed out of the house. The "owner" (a retired doctor) claimed that he spent a lot of money on a small apartment in the Philippines where the woman's nine children lived. Unless the couple is convicted of human slavery which rarely happens in the United States, they will at most get a slap on the wrist from the judicial system.

There is more involved in the gendered role of women's labor than this one example suggests. The Philippines is the second-largest recipient of remittance funds sent by its citizens who work abroad, half of whom are in the U.S. Altogether, remittances accounted for 12.5 percent of Philippine GDP in 2007. In Latin America and the Caribbean, those funds make up more of GDP than foreign direct investment and foreign aid combined. Most migrant workers are women. Mexico is an exception with men making up the majority of the immigrants, legal and otherwise.

In other words, governments in the Global South send women workers abroad to earn wages that are much higher than they could hope to make in their home country. In effect, the GDP and tax base of these Southern countries rest on women's labor. That dependence also denies Global Southern governments an incentive to negotiate better working conditions for their laborers at home.

Women have thus become foot soldiers in the globalized world. While women's lack of control over their wages has not changed since the interconnection of global finance and politics early in the twentieth century, their

---

[2] June Q. Wu." "Woman Allegedly Held in Servitude." *Washington Post.* June 10, 2011, B1 and B8.

U.S. Secretary of State Hillary Clinton and German Chancellor Angela Merkel at the ceremony honoring the twentieth anniversary of the fall of the Berlin Wall.

AP Photo/Herbert Knosowski

participation in the global economy has. This is one of the most significant shifts in the creation of an ever more interconnected world. More women than men are part of this global, transient work force, both because they are not protected as well by national and international laws and because they are generally paid less. The gendered wage gap makes women more attractive to hire in "private" areas, such as the home, and makes the phenomenon somewhat lower on the radar screen of most mainstream politicians.

We need to add a caveat here. The women's movement against globalization has had a hard time picking up steam outside of feminist circles. That should not keep us from seeing the importance of its analysis or its practical efforts. Some of the most influential work by feminist scholars focuses on how globalization *has produced* some of the problems they describe and decry. Thus, they have tended to focus on the demand for migrant labor, as in the case of the Filipina maid, as a consequence of globalization. That said, its practical impact should not be scoffed at.

While feminists would argue that there is still plenty still to do, their pressures have led to some strengthening of most "receiving" countries' laws regarding immigrant workers.

Peacebuilding

Peacebuilding is one of the most casually applied terms in all of political science. It can refer to everything from what happens as a war is winding down to conscious efforts to create conditions in which we can avoid war in the first place.

As used by its practitioners, the term echoes one of the conclusions drawn from the women's movement—the centrality of multilevel governance. It is all but impossible to imagine reaching a peace agreement in any of the countries beset by conflict that doesn't involve the international community, business leaders, **NGOs**, and more to supplement the efforts of people from all sides that are direct participants in the dispute.

Like the status of women, interest in peacebuilding is not new. Its roots can be traced all the way back to most of the world's great theological traditions. It entered political thought no later than Immanuel Kant's 1795 essay "On Perpetual Peace," which over time ushered in the theory that democracies do not go to war with other democracies.

But modern peacebuilding also has newer and somewhat different roots. There is no agreed upon starting point. The best bet is the early 1980s when three then-unrelated events occurred. Roger Fisher and William Ury published *Getting to Yes*, which has sold well over two million copies and has been translated into dozens of languages. A group of professors at George Mason created what is now the School for Conflict Analysis and Resolution, which was the first degree granting program that combined conflict resolution and peacebuilding. Finally, a former Foreign Service Officer, John Marks, created Search for Common Ground (**www.sfcg.org**), which initially worked on easing Cold War tensions and now has programs in more than 30 countries.

Most people in the field today started our as mediators who rarely had to address explicitly political issues. Instead, they helped divorcing parents, tried to heal dysfunctional families, and assisted judges and lawyers so that they make more productive decisions. It is from their work that the term **win-win** was created. In essence, a win-win outcome benefits all participants, at least over time. There are no winners or losers, which have been a staple of political life throughout recorded history.

Soon, scholars and activists learned that mediation and the like were not enough. As we saw, for instance, with the Oslo Accord between Israel and the Palestinians, no single agreement alone could do the job. International and other political disputes often take a long time to settle and require a wide variety of tools if we are seeking long-term reconciliation among the disputants. Therefore, Search for Common Ground does everything from arranging citizen exchanges to making television and radio soap operas that touch on conflict-related themes.

Consider three examples of what the peacekeeping community is focusing on today.

First is a fundamental question that probably should have been asked long ago: What is a peaceful society? For traditional political scientists, peace is simply the absence of war. But as long ago as the seventeenth century, the philosopher Baruch Spinoza knew it was much more, which also made it hard to achieve. "Peace is not an absence of war, it is a virtue, a state of mind, a disposition for benevolence, confidence, justice."

The most recent attempt to determine what makes states peaceful has been conducted by the Institute for Economics and Peace and its Global Peace Index (GPI). Its creator, Steve Killelea, was motivated by the fact that so many of the projects he helped fund were destroyed in wars. But instead of trying to figure out why states fail, the

Institute has concentrated on why some succeed and are peaceful. Overall, island countries and democracies tend to fare well, although the United States comes in 82nd largely because it was fighting two wars in early 2011 and has a high rate of domestic violence and a large prison population, both of which are weighed heavily in the GPI (**www.visionofhumanity.org**). Some of the "leaders" are obvious. The Scandinavian countries have routinely been at or near the top. Some were not, including Japan, Germany, and Ireland, which fought bloody wars as recently as half a century ago. The Institute has also decided to look into the causal links that lead to peace. That work is just beginning.

Second, how do we attempt to address armed conflict once it breaks out? Here we do not have as clear an answer as we do for peaceful states themselves. The Alliance for Peacebuilding recently launched what will probably be a decade-long analysis of conflict from a systemic perspective. Most people in the peacebuilding field have had some exposure to systems theory and pay at least lip service to the current phrase that we need "whole of government" or "whole of society" approaches to all of our public policy problems.

That means exploring all the feedback loops connecting potential causes and effects of peacefulness. Then, where the team has accumulated enough data, it will begin to design projects using a whole systems model.

Third, the peacebuilding community has seen the importance of cooperation with what some of its members call "strange bedfellows." Thus, in South Africa the African National Congress went out of its way to work with the security services even before Nelson Mandela was released after twenty-seven years in prison. In the United States and other countries that had troops in Iraq and/or Afghanistan, that means the military.

American and allied troops who have served in either country have returned home with serious misgivings about their commanders' strategy and tactics. Among other things, they began seeking out ways the peacebuilding community could help. The peacebuilders were slow to respond. Most harbored suspicions, if not resentment, about the military.

But gradually invitations came in and the peacebuilders kept showing up. At first these were mostly "getting to know you" exercises. But, in due course, they began to find ways to communicate with and learn from people in uniform. There are formal ties that include regular visits to the Pentagon and military schools so that peacebuilders now meet military leaders almost as a matter of course. More important, perhaps, are informal discussions in which both sides can let their political "hair down" because they do not have a concrete goal for the meeting. The most recent for Chip occurred when he attended a fund-raiser for an environmental and arts center at Oberlin College where he went (see below). Among the other people there

Conflict and Globalization

The nature of conflict has changed with the pace of globalization.

Neither the peacebuilding nor the women's movements are new. The struggle for women's right to vote goes back at least a century and a half. People seeking ways to produce ongoing peace may go back even farther to the likes of Kant and Spinoza.

However, the *nature* of conflict has changed in recent years, in ways that the women's and peacebuilding movements both highlight. The women's movement led political scientists to begin studying excluded groups that lack meaningful access to the decision-making process. Peacebuilders have extended the scope of conflict studies beyond the geopolitical disputes of traditional international relations to include identity-based conflict that is based on race, ethnicity, religion, language, gender, and more. Such conflicts are particularly hard to resolve because they do not readily lend themselves to compromise and other techniques for settling disputes that do not entail the use of violence. ∎

was Col. Mark Mykelby, who had just written a paper on human security for the Chair of the Joint Chiefs of Staff that even the most progressive NGO activist could have written 🌐 (**http://www.wilsoncenter.org/events/docs/A%20 National%20Strategic%20Narrative.pdf**).

We should not downplay how difficult these relationships can be. Peacebuilders who were active in past antiwar movements are reluctant to work with current and retired soldiers. That said, unlike the case with the women's movement, the military has probably taken more steps than members of the peacebuilding community. There is no better evidence about how far they have come than a story Elizabeth Bumiller wrote in the *New York Times* in 2010.[3] It turns out that a colonel serving in Afghanistan had befriended Greg Mortenson, author of *Three Cups of Tea*, long before the book was severely criticized. The relationship between Mortenson and the military did not go very far until General David Petraeus' wife read the book. She shared it with the wives of two other senior officers who played a major role in shaping counterinsurgency strategy. They realized that building schools and eventually winning the hearts and minds of the citizenry could be even more important than killing suspected terrorists or scoring other battlefield victories.

Impact or the Lack Thereof

We would love to make the case that either of these movements has produced fundamental change in public policy priorities in any of the countries we have studied. That has not happened for two main reasons.

First, these are new fields, and as is often the case, they have often been ignored or even resisted by academic and other intellectual leaders. In academe, that often means that it is hard for young scholars to get tenure. It may be easier in women's studies, which has won an established spot for itself in most social science departments. It could well be harder in peacebuilding, where most academics have found their home in a handful of stand-alone departments.

Second, for good or ill, we also have not had tremendous access to policy makers. Here, the roles may well be reversed. Peacebuilders have actively sought a "seat at the table" with policy makers in most major capital cities. Women's activists have been able to do so largely on a case-by-case basis depending on the issue and the people in power. That may be changing, especially when countries such as Afghanistan and other governments in current and former combat zones realize that their future has to include empowering women 🌐 (**www.huntalternatives.org**).

---

[3] Elizabeth Bumiller, "Unlikely Tutor Giving Military Afghan Advice." *New York Times,* July 1, 2010, A1

GLOBALIZATION

The parts of women's studies and peacebuilding that we work in share at least one common point of departure— globalization—which we think is the key to understanding political life today. Globalization has been touted as a force that will help enrich the poor. It has also been denounced for everything from the destruction of traditional cultures to the continued poverty of billions of people.

As we see it, globalization is shaking up all areas of our lives. Although we won't add more linguistic confusion by doing so, we might be better off saying the world is globaliz*ing*. Globalization is well underway, but the forces producing it are far from complete—if they ever will be.

To see how important globalization and its concomitant impact on power relations are, consider four examples, although some readers will not take some of the third one as seriously as the others.

Economics

Globalization is not new economically. Some critics of the term properly point out that international trade actually consumed far more of the major powers' GNP in the early twentieth century than it does today. World War I slowed down international trade, as did a series of postwar tariffs that were designed to keep foreign goods out of the rich countries while maximizing their firms' ability to sell in poor colonial markets. In fact, many economists blame the American interwar tariff legislation for causing a global reaction against free trade that became one of the scapegoats seized upon by Hitler for invading Austria, Czechoslovakia, and Poland.

Today, the economic side of globalization is more extensive than anything experienced a century ago. If you had had the privilege of traveling from the United States or Canada to Europe over the span of the forty years as we have, you would have noticed the homogenization of goods and services on both sides of what the British call "the pond." Unlike the case in the 1970s, hip young people, especially, wear the same clothes and enjoy the same music as their "pond mates." That is less true if you go to the Global South. But even there, people tend to buy the same computers, using the same operating systems, and relying on the same social networking software. On that front, consider the role that Facebook, Twitter, and other social media played in getting protesters out on the streets for the postelection demonstrations in Iran in 2009 and in the Arab Spring of 2011.

Two economic issues that could have global repercussions filled the business pages of leading news papers around the world as were finishing this chapter. The United States and Greece (and potentially other EU member states that have adopted the euro) could go into default. Default is a complicated economic issues, but; it essentially means that neither country could pay its debts without more borrowing (U.S.) or a massive bailout from European and international governments and other financial institutions (Greece).

In other words, as we globalize, we are increasingly *dependent* on each other. At the national level, the North has to import much of its oil and other sources of energy, basic foodstuffs, and many other things including the rare earth materials without which there would be no laptops, cell phones, or other portable electronic devices. As we saw with the OPEC oil embargo of 1973–74, a disruption in the supply of any such good can wreak havoc throughout the entire global economy. To use a phrase we first raised in Chapter 4 on the UK, every country is less and less the master of its own economic destiny.

Despite these and other problems, we have created institutions whose initial role was to manage the recovery from World War II. Today, the IFIs, parts of the UN, and regional bodies have taken on the job of managing all or part of global economic affairs.

The Environment Writ Large

But globalization is not just economic. Nothing demonstrates that better than the environment. As with the economy, there are dozens of issues we could focus on. Indeed, in the months we were finishing this book, the combined tsunami and earthquake that destroyed the Fukushima Daiichi nuclear power complex in Japan dominated the world's environmental news. The accident raised doubts about nuclear power and prompted the German government to announce plans to phase out all of its plants over the next decade. As catastrophic as the Japanese disaster was, it was neither particularly political nor filled with global implications.

Therefore, we will focus instead on **climate change**, which is far more controversial. Almost all mainstream scientists agree that it is occurring and that it is largely caused by human actions, ranging from burning rain forests to allowing carbon dioxide emissions from automobiles to reach the upper reaches of the atmosphere. In simple terms, the gases get trapped and block heat generated on earth from escaping. Climate change is the key issue facing environmentalists today.

The controversy occurs on two levels. Experts cannot agree on how fast it is occurring or what exactly its effects will be. More extreme critics doubt that it is occurring, let alone that human waste is its key cause.

It is hard to date the start of the modern environmental movement in North America. It may be as old as the creation of the first national parks (Yellowstone and Banff in 1872 and 1885, respectively). At the very latest, it goes back to the 1962 publication of Rachel Carson's pathbreaking book, *Silent Spring*, that made Americans aware of environmental problems and led to bans on the use of DDT and dozens of other dangerous chemicals.

By the 1970s, attention to environmental problems had gone global. Everything from the rise of the European Green parties to the Chernobyl and other disasters made it clear to millions that environmental concerns could not be limited to a single nation or region.

In the 1980s, a number of scientific breakthroughs brought **global warming** and the broader issue of climate change onto center stage. For years, scientists had known that the average temperature of the earth had been rising—at least three quarters of a degree Fahrenheit in the twentieth century. Now, sophisticated computer models suggested that so-called greenhouse gases formed a layer in the upper atmosphere that blocked hot air from escaping the earth's natural "air conditioning" system. The scientific mainstream holds that the rise in greenhouse gases was caused by human waste far more than by any natural change in global temperatures that occur from time to time (think of the ice ages for example).

Their models predicted that some currently frigid places would get warmer and more livable. That would not be true of most of the planet. Seacoasts would be in danger of regular flooding. The Washington Mall would be permanently under water as would the Maldives Islands and their 300,000 inhabitants.

In time, climate change skeptics began to organize and drew on their strong support in the conservative and Evangelical communities. Mainstream scientists rejected criticisms as unfounded and, in some cases, dishonest.

On one level at least, the critics are right. It *is* impossible to say whether or not specific events are due to climate change. There is, however, little doubt that we have experienced unusually disruptive weather of late. In the last decade we have seen the two most damaging tsunamis in recorded history, unusually powerful tropical storms, extended periods of drought and flooding in much of the world, the worst outbreak of tornadoes in modern American history, and the rapid melting of the polar icecaps.

Interest in climate change got an unexpected boost when former Senator and Vice President **Al Gore** made a film and published a book that shared a single title, *An Inconvenient Truth*. Since Gore's book/film, the most important trend has been the work of the **International Panel on Climate Change (IPCC)** (www.ipcc.ch). The IPCC did not rely on the computer models that Gore and others had employed, but instead used empirical data gathered in research over the previous twenty years. It also had the backing of the United Nations which had created it in the first place.

The IPCC confirmed what Gore and so many others had claimed. Temperatures will rise by 1.5 to 2.5 degrees centigrade during the course of this century and have the kinds of consequences Gore warned of. Perhaps most importantly of all, the Panel claimed that if decisive action were not taken

AP Photo/AIR PHOTO SERVICE, File

Wreckage of the Fukushima Daiichi nuclear power plant in Japan following the 2011 earthquake and tsunami.

©iStockphoto.com/Brasil2

Burning the rain forest in the Amazon basin.

by 2030, there might be no turning back. If they are right, we can work for incremental change for now, but not for long. As one commission member put it "(a)daptation will only work if climate change is not too large and not too fast."

Perhaps more interesting is the fact that the bid to slow climate change has found new allies, including the American military. At least since the beginning of the wars in Afghanistan and Iraq, military leaders throughout the

Western World have become more interested in what they and the NGO community call **human security**. Put simply, neither a people nor a country can be secure militarily unless it is also secure economically, environmentally, and so on. In fact, that is the main point of the paper that Colonel Mykelby coauthored and why he was asked to speak at a fundraiser for an environmentally friendly campus construction project.

One of the other key outgrowths of our concern with global warming and other environmental threats is the phrase "think globally, act locally." At first, this was largely an empty slogan that prompted few people to do more than recycle their trash. That is beginning to change.

The colleges we attended, for example, have begun construction and renovation projects that will make one of them at least carbon neutral in the new few years. Colby College (Melissa) is like most relatively affluent liberal arts colleges. All new and renovated buildings meet at least the LEED Gold (the second highest) standard, which is hard to do when renovating a fifty-year-old residence hall (**www.usgbc.org/LEED**). It is also building an $11 million dollar plant to turn biomass into electricity. Oberlin (Chip) has been an environmental pioneer for many years. Its Lewis environmental center was a state-of-the-art classroom building when it was built a decade ago. It will be LEED platinum when renovations are completed. It already generates all of its own heat and electricity. A new residence hall, which is also LEED platinum, does not allow students to bring cars to campus.

At the political level, there have been some policy changes. The Kyoto Protocol (1997) required signatories, which were both affluent and major polluters, to reduce their CO_2 emissions to their 1990 levels by 2012. The United States was one of the countries that did not ratify it. As the IPCC has put it, even with full American participation, its response could easily prove to be too little too late. Substantial, but most would say inadequate, progress has been made through such agreements, including the increased use of hybrid cars and close to universal recycling in the North.

The bottom line is clear. Whatever we think about global warming or the other environmental challenges, it is hard to argue that we are *not* all interconnected through a single ecological system. That was driven home in a frivolous but revealing way in the first half of 2008. A container of rubber ducks was on a ship that set sail from Hong Kong on 29 January. Unfortunately for the ducks but fortunately for environmental watchdogs, the container fell overboard and sprang open. The "friendly floaters," as they were soon called, had landed on every inhabited continent other than Africa by the middle of May. They made it there by year's end.

Make no mistake about it. We are having trouble finding political solutions for such transnational problems. As we will see throughout the rest of the chapter, we face problems that are increasingly global, but most of us—Americans in particular—seem to look instinctively first for domestic solutions to them.

Society and Culture

We are making two key points about globalization. First, we have already seen how our interdependence makes political cooperation all the more important. But this discussion is also making a second point, which is harder to come to grips with. Globalization is affecting all aspect of our lives, and even those that seem distant from comparative politics have their share of political implications because they reflect the way power is shifting. To see that, consider the way we deal with how technology and popular culture are being transformed.

The Media and Beyond

Pundits often argue that the world is shrinking. Obviously, that is not true physically. Ottawa and Washington are as far apart now as they were when the two cities were founded more than 200 years ago. Yet, the world is shrinking culturally, and probably doing so more rapidly than it is either economically or environmentally even though no one knows how to measure any of these trends with any degree of precision.

At the heart of those changes are the media, which we dealt with in a narrower way in all the earlier chapters. As we saw then, most of us learn most of what we know and think about politics from the media. And, because media are changing so rapidly, only one thing is clear. The media and the technologies on which they depend are at the heart of globalization, for better or for worse.

Take a simple example. Chip's family got its first television when he was five or six—and, no, that was not in the fourteenth century. It was black and white. We can both remember the introduction of color television, telephones that you do not have to dial, and personal computers connected to the Internet that made it possible for us to write this book together without seeing each other face- to-face.

When Chip's family bought its first television, the national news was on for fifteen minutes a night. It was only with the Vietnam War when he was in college that filmed coverage of what was happening was shown *on the same day*. When Chip went to teach at Colby, he had a color television, and the town had a cable system with one station he couldn't get with a roof antenna (roof antenna, we hear you say?). The cable system did improve but was not available at all on the farm he bought a few years later. When he moved to Washington, it was television heaven. All the C-SPAN networks, the cable news channels, and an increasing number of foreign language feeds. Not to mention all the sports channels.

It isn't just the suburbs of Washington. In 2006, the Canadian government published a study that showed that more than 85 percent of all households there had either cable or satellite service. That number is growing everywhere, although in countries that entered the world of modern technology fairly late, satellite dishes outnumber cable boxes. And, as you also undoubtedly know better than we do, our technologies are "merging," so that televisions, computers, and cell phones increasingly act as one.

You should already be asking: What does this have to do with comparative politics? As with so much of this chapter, the answer is both very complicated and deceptively simple. As noted throughout the book, the media have replaced face-to-face discussion as our primary source of political information.

On the one hand, we have access to much more information that our parents' or grandparents' generation ever dreamed of. But the proliferation of new media is a mixed blessing. For instance, you can watch coverage of the same events in the Middle East on al-Jazeera and Alhurra because both stream on the Internet. If you do, you will often have trouble realizing they are covering the same story ✍ (**www .aljazeera.net** and **www.alhurra.com**). Al-Jazeera is owned by the government of Qatar and has often been accused of being a mouthpiece for radical Muslims. Alhurra was created by the United States government and is routinely accused of masking propaganda as news.

Together, they demonstrate the greatest difficulty in dealing with the new media. Which of the two should we believe? It could even be harder to answer that question in countries like Russia, China, and Iran where the state still tries to control the official media but more and more people have Internet access, illegal satellite dishes, and the like.

There is also evidence that fewer people rely on any country's equivalent of network television for information now that the electronic age offers viewers a host of alternatives. Similarly, most "serious" newspapers including the *New York Times,* the *Washington Post,* and *Le Monde* are in such serious financial difficulty that they might not survive. Perhaps more ominously, fewer and fewer people bother to watch the nightly news on *any* network.

Other critics worry about the lack of quality control and what they are convinced are mounting biases in the media. In the English-speaking world, many on the left complain about what they think are the conservative leanings of the various networks and newspapers owned by Rupert Murdoch (Fox and *The Wall Street Journal* in the United States). Conservatives complain about what they think are liberal biases on National Public Radio and the Public Broadcasting System in the U.S. or the BBC in Britain.

Media critics also claim that objectivity all but disappears the farther you move away from the mainstream media. That is especially true in the blogosphere, where virtually anyone can publish virtually everything.

For the purposes of this book, nothing is more revealing of both the potential and the pitfalls of the new media than Wikileaks, which is a loose but global collection of anonymous hackers and technologists headed by the Australian, Julian Assange. Wikileaks began posting material in 2006, but only gained notoriety when it started publishing previously secret United States government cables. It describes itself ✍ (**www.wikileaks.org**) as:

> **a non-profit media organization dedicated to bringing important news and information to the public. We provide an innovative, secure and anonymous way for independent sources around the world to leak information to our journalists. We publish material of ethical, political and historical significance while keeping the identity of our sources anonymous, thus providing a universal way for the revealing of suppressed and censored injustices.**

Its actions are controversial to say the least. Should all relevant information be published in the interests of transparency? Or should we keep secret classified material that can jeopardize the careers or even put the life of those named at risk?

None of this will be new to most readers of this book. Yet it is important to realize just how new the new media are.

Chip often uses the history of the personal computer and the Internet as an example. When he started teaching in 1975, neither was remotely imaginable. He used a terminal connected to a mainframe before buying a Mac right after they were introduced in 1984. That Mac had no hard drive and 128K of memory. A floppy disk could hold no more than a chapter's worth of a manuscript. Today, he writes on a MacBook Air that is a million times faster than his first Mac, does not even have a floppy drive, and cost less than half of what he paid for the first one—without considering the impact of inflation.

The same is true for the Internet. It was only in 1974 that Vinton Cerf and his colleagues invented the TCP/IP protocol that allowed computers to talk to each other, and it could only be used by people with Department of Defense affiliations. Fifteen years later Timothy Berners-Lee and his team developed a language that allowed any user to find material on the Web known as html. It did not have graphics (in fact, Chip gave a talk in 1995 about why one would never need a graphics browser like the one that had just been introduced as Netscape and is today's Firefox). High speed access, the wireless revolution, and the promise of the cloud all show how far we have come and how short our journey has been.

Pop Culture

Basketball is one of the few sports whose origins are known. In December 1891, William Naismith was looking for a way to keep his exercise class busy on a rainy day. He came up with the idea of nailing two peach baskets to the wall. Players had a simple goal—to throw a soccer ball into the basket. Over time, the game evolved and was standardized. The baskets gave way to rims and nets that hung ten feet from the floor. Dribbling, passing, and other techniques were introduced. By the 1930s, the game bore at least a passing resemblance to today's version but without jump shots, slam dunks, or the NBA.

It remained an American game until 1936 when it became an Olympic sport (the United States beat Canada in the only championship game played outdoors). No one had any idea how global it would become. For the next 35 years, American teams composed mostly of college players dominated international competition until the gold medal round of 1972 Olympics when the U.S lost a controversial game against the Soviet Union's de facto professionals. FIBA was lobbied to open its tournaments and the Olympics to professionals, which it did in 1989, thirteen years after it started separate competitions for women.

Since then, basketball has changed in a lot of ways that illustrate just how much the world has shrunk and is epitomized by a sharp erosion of American domination. The Soviet victory may have been a fluke, but "dream teamers" from the NBA could not stop the American decline. The U.S. lost quite badly at the 2002 FIBA world championship and the 2004 Olympics despite having some of the world's best players on the floor both times. The United States has done better since, but it is worth noting that the 2002 and 2006 FIBA all-tournament teams together had but one American. Of the nine "foreign" players, all but two ended up with distinguished careers in the NBA.

Basketball is globalized. Today, the NBA boasts players from all six inhabited continents. The opening day rosters for the 2010-11 season had eight-four foreign players from thirty-six countries. Many of them are stars, including Dirk Nowitzki (Germany) who guided the Dallas Mavericks to the 2011 NBA title.

The NBA has already played quite a few preseason and regular season games outside of the United States. Even though travel times would be enormous, the NBA is considering expansion at least to Europe and China. For our purposes, the popularity of the NBA abroad is best measured by attendance at games, television audiences, and NBA paraphernalia young people wear. Anywhere you travel in Europe, Africa, Asia, or South America, you see LeBron James and Michael Jordan t-shirts. You even see them in videos of child soldiers who are compelled to join civil wars and kill their fellow citizens—sometimes starting with their families. NBA games are shown regularly in twenty-five countries and on three continent-wide networks.

Even more surprising has been the spread of popular music including rap and hip-hop. Hip-Hop International stages contests among performers and crews around the world. As of summer 2011, it has chapters in thirty-one countries. Some, like Trinidad and Tobago, or even France, make some cultural sense. But Singapore and Malaysia?

More interesting for our purposes, Iran has its share of rappers, even though there is no legal way for young people to even listen to the music let alone imitate it. Iran now has two informal collections of rappers named for the postal codes of Tehran and Mashhad where most of them live. Many of them were active in the protests that followed the 2010 election and some even wrote protest songs.

The same is true of Libya where hip-hop and rap never make their way onto the state-run media. In some ways Libyan rap artists have gone farther than their Iranian counterparts. They see the struggle against now ousted President Gadaffi as something their music could and should be a part of. They have gone so far as to create their own website (www.enoughgaddafi.com).

The political future of the world almost certainly does not depend on the continued popularity of either basketball or hip-hop. Nonetheless, two potentially important political implications are embedded in each story. First, the two fads show us that the world is indeed shrinking. Second, they show us how quickly popular tastes (presumably including those about politics) can change.

The End of History or the Clash of Civilizations

Now it is time to take this narrative away from the media, basketball, and popular music and return to comparative politics as it is generally known. We start with a basic question that may well be impossible to answer. Is globalization making us more similar or more different politically? At first, political scientists seemed to make the same kind of naïve mistake they did about how independence from colonial rule and the first stages of economic development would erode traditional cultural values.

For example, in the early 1990s, Francis Fukuyama claimed that we had reached the end of history, by which he meant life-and-death political struggles. He had served in the George H. W. Bush administration and believed that the defeat of communism had removed the last great ideological divide that could give rise to global or even regional conflict. History would not end in the literal meaning of the term. There would still be events, some of which would be beyond our control. But, as he saw it, liberal democracy along the lines of what we saw in Part 2 had triumphed once and for all.

Subsequent events have led most observers to doubt Fukuyama's conclusion. By the time his book was published, the former Yugoslavia had fallen apart and many of the now-independent republics were at war with each other. The brutality mostly of the Serbs turned rape into an internationally recognized war crime, introduced the term ethnic cleansing, and helped lead to the creation of the International Criminal Court. Since then, there have been devastating wars in much of Africa and Asia.

The most important and controversial book questioning Fukuyama's thesis was written by someone who was also on the right side of the political spectrum and was Fukuyama's mentor and friend. Samuel Huntington was a life-long Democrat who was on the left on most domestic issues, but a conservative when it came to foreign policy. In fact, he was one of the architects of some of the most innovative (and some would say disastrous) strategies that the United States pursued in Vietnam.

His renown reached a new high with the publication of *The Clash of Civilizations* in 1996. He thought that far from nearing the end of history, we were entering a new era in which the divisions would be between civilizations or cultures. He identified seven of them and felt that what he called the Western and Muslim communities would be most likely to clash. As he saw it, the apparently unifying globalizing trends, such as those we have just discussed, were producing resistance from people in each of those "civilizations." who resisted change.

His critics suggest he made the world's cultures seem more homogeneous than they are. Return for a moment to hip-hop. Many French hip-hop stars are of North African origin. By contrast, many Muslim clerical leaders in France argue that all forms of music—including hip-hop—are *haram* or forbidden in the most literal interpretations of Islam.

In short, globalization is probably both bringing us closer and in some ways driving us farther apart. Both al Qaeda and the United States government use the Internet masterfully. But what two political groups could be more different despite their use of the same technology?

The last standing fragment of the World Trade Center towers in New York.

A newly arrived refugee family from the Sudan region of Darfur crosses into Chad on 27 January 2004 in the direction of the three improvised refugee camps in Tine, Chad. Something like 250,000 people have been killed. Ten times that number have been forced into exile (www .savedarfur. org).

Tiny Steps Toward Global Governance

In addition to what we have seen so far, we are beginning to adapt our institutions to better meet global needs. As strange as it may seem given what we wrote above, we have developed new structures that can help us deal with all the interconnections and complexity. We do not want to go too far too fast. None could be called mature. But as the examples below will show, they exist and they exist in large part because of globalization. They are, as the subtitle of this section suggests, tiny steps toward what might be called **global governance**.

The Private Sector

Almost all companies have a home country, but **multinational corporations (MNCs)** have sales, workers, and a management team, all of which straddle national boundaries. If you own a Mac, you might think of it as an American computer; after all, Apple's home office is in Cupertino, CA. But, most of the parts of your iMac, iPod, iPhone, or iPad were made in Asia and may not have even been assembled in California.

MNCs were sharply criticized a generation ago for exploiting workers and markets in the Global South. Undoubtedly, some of that still occurs. But many corporations follow corporate responsibility practices that stress doing well by the people you work with.

Among the most visible is Chevron. It has championed everything from the economic development of the countries it has production facilities in to environmental protection to hiring, training, and retaining a more diverse work force  (www.chevron.com and www.willyoujoinus.com). Its online material on the state of the energy industry is as critical of the field as anything we have seen in the corporate world.

In addition, there is the growing importance of international NGOs, whose work almost by definition crosses national boundaries, as is the case in the peacebuilding field. Chip's organization was created a decade ago to coordinate American-based NGOs working in the Global South. The Alliance for Peacebuilding could not be effective if it worked solely in the United States. It now has international members, its projects have international leaders, and the Alliance as a whole is part of regional and global networks of conflict resolvers.

If anything, the women's movement is even more global at least in its aspirations. Perhaps even more important is the fact that feminist analysts see part of what they are doing in supporting their sisters all over the world is combating globalization.

States and Regions

There has been tremendous growth in the use of regional and supranational organizations, which open the door to multilevel governance, and to support and criticism of them by pundits across the political spectrum. We saw the most important of them in the chapter on the **European Union** and some of the others in passing elsewhere.

More important for our purposes are agreements that are less comprehensive in scope and do not oblige member states to give up as much of their sovereignty. The most important of those we have seen is the **North American Free Trade Agreement (NAFTA)**. Since it went into effect in 1993, NAFTA permits far freer trade of goods and services among the United States, Mexico, and Canada.

It has also been quite successful, at least in those terms. As we saw in Chapter 16, Mexico has had an unprecedented spurt of growth since the agreement went into effect. Its benefits are evident in the fact that almost all Mexicans have at least one television and the number of illegal migrants to the United States has been cut dramatically.

Democratization and Globalization

In Chapter 7, we wrote about the democratic deficit in the European Union.

As the quintessential multilevel governance unit on the planet today, it shows us the difficulties we will face if and when we try to democratize the emerging institutions of global governance.

Its members work in more than twenty languages and its relatively weak legislature has 736 members. In short, it is hard for average voters to relate to an elected official who represents almost a million people.

It has been hard to democratize the EU. It will only be harder to do so globally. Most other international organizations do not have any sort of assembly even indirectly elected by rank-and-file voters. If they did, how could they keep the size manageable and escape the linguistic and cultural differences that force almost everyone to wear a head set?

In sum, it will never be easy to create democratic regional or global bodies even if we can harness the potential in some of the technologies that are likely to appear in the next few years. ■

However, like most regional trade agreements, it has also sparked controversy. For instance, American and Canadian trade unions complain that jobs their members used to hold are moving to Mexico where labor costs are not even one fourth of what they are north of either border. Similarly, environmentalists worry that looser Mexican laws allow polluting firms to move there and avoid tighter regulation in the United States and Canada.

Ultimately, the real importance supranational organizations like NAFTA is that they have had to create mechanisms for handling disputes between their members that often are housed outside that institution. Thus, American environmentalists have taken their dissatisfaction with a proposed pipeline to bring oil from Canadian oil sands into the United States to the World Trade Organization tribunal. The U.S. countered that this involved charges about barriers to trade that were not caused by tariffs and, thus, should be sent for resolution to NAFTA instead.

Whatever measure you choose to use, the European Union is by far the most advanced of these institutions perhaps because it has been built in stages since the early 1950s, most of which enhanced its ongoing authority and day-to-day power. We are not going to repeat what we saw in Chapter 7. However, it is important to stress that the EU is the one international organization to which national governments have ceded the most sovereignty. And while causal effects are hard to disentangle, we should also point out that Europe has not had a major international war since European unification began, the longest such period in recorded history.

Acting Globally

When the two of us first studied international relations in the 1960s and 1970s, respectively, the realists and other leading IR theorists made the assumption that the state was the norm and the most advanced political unit we could hope to create. In the last twenty to thirty years states and other institutions have taken some important first steps toward global governance, creating formal institutions and less formal agreements to handle international disputes in ways that largely rule out the threat of violence and war.

Critics of the United Nations still scoff at the idea that we can ever make transnational governance the norm. In fact, that may be true of what IR scholars call "high politics" or the geopolitical relationships between powers that can and still do take us to war more often than any of us would like.

The **United Nations** does give critics of globalization ample intellectual ammunition. Even to its supporters, the UN lacks everything from the legal authority to adequate funding to do what we *think* should be its most important task—preserving international security. Others point to what they see as the UN's inefficient and bloated bureaucracy.

This book is not the place to rehash those arguments other than to acknowledge that some of them are at least close to correct. The Security Council is often paralyzed by differences between two or more of its permanent members who have veto power over all of its actions. One could also argue that at least some of the BRICS should now have a permanent seat on the Council. Similarly, the UN does not have anywhere near enough money, for example, for its peacekeeping operations and often has to seek contributions from member states outside of its normal budgetary process. In other words, as currently constituted, the United Nations is probably not much of a first step toward a stable and legitimate form of global governance.

For the most part, the criticisms of the UN are not as accurate in assessing the more specialized institutions of what insiders call the UN family. To see what it has accomplished and what a more potent body someday could do, consider three examples from arguably the UN's least and most controversial arms.

We start with the international financial institutions that are part of the UN family even if they operate autonomously. Of the three, the World Trade Organization is the newest and most useful for our purposes. In all, 153 countries are members; and, once Russia completes its negotiations to join, it will include all of the world's major economic powers. The WTO is responsible for promoting a more open global economy, for instance, by reducing tariffs and other barrier to trade.

The WTO is central to understanding multilevel governance because it has a legal system that can hear complaints lodged by the WTO itself, regional bodies, and national governments. The WTO's judicial mechanisms come into play most often when a member state files a claim accusing another of violating the organization's provisions by hindering free trade. In a normal case, the countries discuss the issue among themselves, the WTO then names a panel, and, within a year, it issues a ruling. If the "losing" state chooses to file an appeal, the WTO has another three months before rendering its final decision. That country then has to implement the Dispute Settlement Body's decision within a reasonable amount of time. To cite but one example, Mexico had filed twenty-two cases, had been the respondent (defendant) in fourteen others, and acted as a third party in fifty-five more as of early 2011.

A second, less glamorous and less controversial body is the International Telecommunications Union. It was created in 1865 when the only available telecom was the now all but obsolete telegraph. It thus antedates the League of Nations and was seamlessly integrated into it and the UN when they were created after the two world wars. Gradually, it added telephones and parts of the computing world to its list of responsibilities. Its tasks may seem to be simple, but the details are often anything but straightforward. How, for instance, do you route telephone calls or mail to and from countries that do not have diplomatic relations. For instance, the union assigns international codes that allow us to directly "dial" anyone around the world.

If the ITU is the oldest member of the UN family, the **International Criminal Court (ICC)** is the newest. International law is one of oldest parts of international relations. The International Court of Justice was created in an earlier form in 1922, but it has been criticized for only hearing cases if all parties concerned are willing to submit to its jurisdiction. In the aftermath of World War II, the international community created ad hoc courts that could do so in cases against people accused of war crimes, most notably the Nuremberg trials in Germany and the International Criminal Tribunal for Yugoslavia (1993). Most of their functions were taken over by the ICC 🖱 (**www.icc-cpi.int**) in 1998. It was first global court to be created by a treaty and entered into effect when the 120th country ratified it.

The ICC has been in the news recently because former Yugoslav/Serbian General Ratko Mladic was finally captured and now faces trial before it. The ICC is by no means perfect; the United States, for instance, refused to ratify its creation. Nonetheless, it provides a vehicle through which the international community can deal with crimes against humanity that national governments cannot or will not address.

Globalization Revisited

At the very least, global and multi-level governance have found significant places on the world's political radar screen. We raised the examples used in this chapter because they illustrate what international relations scholars call **regimes**. Academics being academics, they don't use the term in the same way comparativists do. Instead, an international regime consists of "principles, norms, rules, and decision making procedures around which actor expectations converge in a given issue-area" that member states agree to follow. The late Headley Bull used the term "international society" instead, claiming that states which used regimes had found alternatives to war that (normally) would help them settle their disputes.

These kinds of institutions have gained new prominence, in part because of our growing awareness that most of the problems we face are global. The attempt to combat HIV/AIDS may be the best example, because most efforts today are run either by the UN, other transnational organizations, and NGOs. Even the United States, which chose to act largely on its own through the PEPFAR program, has realized it has to work with others.

By contrast, nothing shows the difficulty of seeking largely domestic solutions for global challenges more clearly than the attacks on New York and Washington on 9/11. Whatever you think of what happened in the weeks, months, and years that followed, it was clear from the beginning that the United States could not not respond to the attacks. The United States wanted to act on its own but found it difficult if not impossible to do so. It invoked the provisions of the NATO treaty that considered an attack on one signatory as an attack on all of them, making the force that invaded and occupied Afghanistan transnational from the beginning. It also could not change global airport security policies unilaterally. Most important of all, it could not end, let alone conduct, the "war on terror" all by itself.

Ratko Mladic on trial at the ICC.

AP Photo/Valerie Kuypers, Pool

But it is important to bear in mind that most major powers—*especially* the major powers—tried to chart their own responses, which can be seen in such mundane indicators as different policies about taking off shoes and belts at airports, screening laptops and electronic equipment, and the process for crossing borders themselves. We could add more examples but the point is clear. As much as circumstances seem to demand cooperative multinational and multilevel responses, states still seek unilateral responses first.

A New Way of Thinking

If we think about the changes since Chip finished the first edition of this book twenty years ago, it will be easy to see the progress we have made with multilevel and transnational governance. This was the first book in the field to even raise the international relations/comparative divide as a surmountable barrier. NAFTA was not yet a decade old. The euro had just been announced. Skeptics far outnumbered advocates on every type of issue covered in this section.

Systems theory and globalization help us see causal factors that are interdependent yet "feed off" each other. They can lead to what two professors at the Harvard Business School called *predictable surprises* or unintended consequences of seemingly isolated events that were anything but isolated or random. If we are right, they also lead us to see things that more conventional approaches do not handle anywhere near as well. We can get a first glimpse of that by briefly considering two of the most important predictable surprises of our lifetime.

The last few years of the Soviet Union show how quickly a seemingly strong and stable system can collapse. Chip took a group of students to the Soviet Union a year after Gorbachev became General Secretary of the CPSU. There were no signs that the country had less than six years to live. As we saw in Chapter 9, Gorbachev opened up the political system with all the best intentions. Little did he know that he would soon introduce reforms that would lead to the fragmentation of the party, the birth of organized dissent, the opening of the media, and the rebirth of ethnic nationalism and then tear the country apart.

That occurred because the Soviet Union faced a number of international and domestic difficulties that together had more of an impact than any of them would have had separately. Briefly consider four that were raised in Part 3. The Soviet Union was no longer as closed as we thought. Chip and his students were taken to a disco which, despite the censorship of the media, played all the world's top hits. The country was also facing growing economic pressure, not only from the West but from its own satellites. Again, the Soviets had a reasonably good idea of how badly off they were because of what they were learning about the rest of the world. At home, Gorbachev attempted to solve the problems incrementally, for example, by making people work harder by making it harder to buy alcohol. When that failed, he and his colleagues decided on a wholesale transformation of politics and society. That was all but unprecedented historically, and, not surprisingly, it failed and brought down the USSR with it.

Much more positive but no less surprising was the reconstruction of the western part of Germany after World War II. Frankly, the Americans and their allies knew no more about how to make sweeping reform than Gorbachev did forty years later. They did, however, learn some key lessons from what had not worked after World War I. What's more, they knew they had to all but totally rebuild a devastated Germany and integrate it into what became the Western alliance. All in all, they helped solidify a democratic regime within a decade of Hitler's death.

After World War II, the victorious allies did not and could not draw on globalization or systems theory, but Gorbachev and his team did. They realized that the Eastern European satellites no longer held much strategic value because NATO missiles could fly over them, hit their targets, and rarely take more than fifteen minutes to do so. Therefore, when those countries began their waves of anti-communist protests, he renounced the Brezhnev Doctrine that tied them to the USSR and, instead, allowed them to chart their own paths. He entitled his 1987 book *Perestroika: New Thinking for Our Country and the World.* Both the book and his memorable speech at the United Nations the next year showed him to be one of the world's first leaders to claim that no country could be secure unless all others were, too.

New Thinking and Paradigm Shifts

Gorbachev's fate also illustrates that changes in ways of thinking do not happen automatically. More often than not, they take place in fits and starts if they happen at all. They are difficult because they are the political equivalent of what scientists call a **paradigm shift**.

In 1962, the historian of science, Thomas Kuhn, revolutionized the way we thought about how we learn new things by publishing a book on scientific revolutions.

As he saw it, real progress does not come about through what he called "normal" science in which people work in their laboratories and publish their findings in obscure journals. Major leaps forward occurred when a scientific community adopted a new paradigm or theory that covered an entire discipline and that structured everything from normal science to textbooks for introductory courses.

Kuhn did not call them scientific revolutions by accident. It is not clear how much he was influenced by Karl Marx and others who thought about political revolution. Nonetheless, the pattern Kuhn laid out parallels Marx's theory of how political and economic revolutions occur and more of them fail.

First, discrepancies or anomalies appear in the old paradigm. Thus, when Galileo invented the telescope, he and his fellow scientists realized that their predictions about the movement of heavenly bodies were wrong. Second, because they all "knew" that the old paradigm was "correct," they started to squeeze the anomalies into it. In the case of heavenly bodies, they decided that they did curlicues so that predictions that the moon, the planets, the sun, and the other stars revolved around the earth still held. Third, Nicolaus Copernicus devised a new paradigm that held that the sun, rather than the earth, was the center of the solar system. The earth, the moon, and the other planets revolved around it. Fourth, like Gorbachev in the USSR, Copernicus launched an unintended political struggle over the heliocentric versus geocentric paradigms. Eventually, disciples of Copernicus won out, although he himself was long dead. Gorbachev is still alive, but his ideas are dead in his own country.

Implementing Systems Theory and Globalization

Throughout this chapter, we have seen plenty of evidence that it would behoove us all to consider what we will call "new thinking" based on systems theory and globalization. We are not saying that you should adopt it. Our analysis could well be wrong, as many of our friends point out. Or we could go Gorbachev's route and not only fail but also cause tremendous harm on our political "journey."

Chip still uses a statement by Albert Einstein as a springboard for such a discussion, even though the issue that inspired him disappeared with the collapse of the Soviet Union. In 1946, he sent a telegram urging American policy makers to stop the nuclear arms race before it truly got started. In it, he included the following sentence:

> **The unleashed power of the atom has changed everything save our modes of thinking and we thus drift toward unparalleled catastrophe.**

Remember that English was not Einstein's first language (it was actually his fourth). And as we both know, one is very careful about choosing words in a tongue that is not one's own

Einstein's statement has four interesting components. The first is at the end. The unparalleled catastrophe of an all-out nuclear war is not likely for now unless some other country develops an arsenal equivalent to that of the Soviet Union. Second, Einstein said "everything" had changed, not just warfare. Even then, he realized we were entering a new era, not just politically but in all areas of life. Einstein died before the word globalization was invented, but he knew

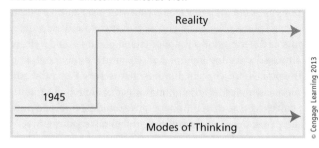

FIGURE 17.1 Einstein: A Literal View

that something like it was coming. Third, he went to say that everything had changed except for "our modes of thinking" or the values and assumptions that shape our lives. Finally, he used a remarkable verb to describe our condition that is powerful because it conveys weakness: drift. In old western movies, a drifter was a cowboy who rode aimlessly from town to town. A sailboat is adrift if there is not enough wind for it to move or be steered.

The colleagues Chip worked with diagrammed as we do in Figure 17.1. The unleashed power of the atom changed everything virtually overnight. The engineers who developed these figures called that a phase change in which something shifts all but instantaneously as water does when it boils or freezes. That led to the huge gap between the new reality and our relatively unchanged mode of thinking. Dealing with that gap meant something more dramatic than incremental change was needed in order to bring our thinking into line with the new reality.

When the Cold War ended, that figure as depicted ceased being useful. There was no single equivalent of 1945 when everything suddenly changed. Rather, whether one talks about the economy, the environment, technology, or hip-hop, the pace of change was different. We have redrawn Figure 17.2 with a diagonal line for the step function of Figure 17.1 to suggest that there was not one single defining moment. However, if either of us could really use the drawing tools on our computers, that line would have been an asymptotic curve that increases at a steeper and steeper rate over time. As NGOs like to put it, change is the only constant in life.

FIGURE 17.2 Einstein: An Expanded View

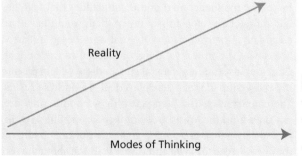

It actually is a better way to adapt and illustrate the initial rendering of the Einstein quote because it allows you to see the options we face. If the gap between reality and our ways of thinking is narrow, as at the left end of the curve, we can get away with incremental change. If, however, closing the gap requires a shift akin to those suggested at the right end of the chart, it takes something qualitatively different.

There are workshops that activists and teachers have developed over the years that try to define what new thinking is and what it might replace. All lead to conclusions much like those in Table 17.1. Again, do not think that we are trying to drum the second column into your head. Rather, read this table and the discussion that goes with it as food for thought about what our options might be.

If you have taken an international relations course, you have probably encountered ways of thinking that parallel the first column. Sometimes, they are presented as theory, sometimes as fact. We obviously think "theory" is a more accurate term.

Our dominant mode of thinking starts with the assumption that we live in a world of scarce resources. Because there is not enough of any vital resource to go around, we compete for them. Just as important, we see ourselves as independent or separate actors who could, and perhaps should, follow their self-interest. In the table we have it as putting "me" first. However, me is a metaphor that covers not just me literally, but all groups I am in that take part in those competitive relationships such as race, class, gender, or nation. As we have also seen time and time again, people in political life tend to think in terms of the short run. That is especially true of a country like the United States and other democracies where politics seems driven by very short election cycles. As we also saw, we tend to use the "image of the enemy" much of the time in which politics feels like a life-or-death struggle, which requires the use of power, which I exert over you, again using *I* and *you* in a broad sense. Under the circumstances, winning is important, but not losing is even more so. In fact, most political science defines power as my ability to get you to do something *you otherwise would not do.* Those five italicized words are critical. They imply that I have to force you, which I can do physically or in other ways, for instance, by deducting points from your grade if you hand your paper in late. In the end, not surprisingly, we think of conflict as something to be avoided because it has many negative consequences, including laying the groundwork for further disputes.

But what about basing thinking on systems theory and/or globalization? Those implications are summed up in the second column. It starts with the same assumption: we compete for scarce resources. But, in an interdependent world, our self-interests tend to converge over time for the simple reason that if I get "too much" at your expense, you will do your best to come back and get me. From this perspective, there are relatively few times when a political struggle has to result in winners and losers, as, for instance, may be the case with the debate over a woman's right to have an abortion. In almost every other case, we can envision a solution that all parties benefit from. If you and I realize that we share a long-term common interest, we can look at our differences in a new light. It makes absolutely no sense for me to treat you as an enemy (or vice versa) because this makes finding win-win solutions all but impossible. Rather, our challenge is to find a way to address our differences in a mutually acceptable way. Under those circumstances, I still engage in power but do so in a different way. Power is something I exert *with* you. In fact, in French, the word for power (*pouvoir*) simply means *to be able* when used as a verb. If I act in a way that tries to meet both of our shared interests, I can turn the system into one that improves over time. Conflict can actually even be a good thing.

Trying to determine how we could get from a political system based on the left column to one anchored on the right would take too much time in a book that is already too long. But, do think about what we have said in this section and in this chapter as a whole.

As we have also tried to point out throughout the book, we have just begun to think, let alone act, in those terms. But there are examples.

After years of repression and struggle, the leaders of the National Party and the African National Congress realized they had to live together. Otherwise, the country would slide into deeper difficulties and, perhaps, fall apart. At that point, then-president F. W. de Klerk, Nelson Mandela, and their colleagues began the negotiations that led to power sharing, the transition to democratic rule, the end of apartheid, the creation of the Truth and Reconciliation Commission, and a whole series of less visible bridges between the white and black communities.

Many cultures have experience with practices rooted in new thinking. Curiously, Afghanistan provides us with one. For centuries, Afghans have ended periods of turmoil by convening a *loya jirga*, in which tribal and other leaders

TABLE 17.1 Contrasting Values and Ways of Thinking

CURRENT VALUES	NEW THINKING
Scarce resources	Scarce resources
Separate	Interdependent
Short term	Long term
Self-interest = "me" first	Self-interest = good of the whole
We versus they, or enemy	We with they thinking
Power over	Power with
Power = force and violence	Power = cooperation, working together
Conflict is bad	Conflict can be good

come together and talk until they reach a consensus on what should happen next.

We are *not* by any stretch of the imagination trying to suggest that anything like that will become the norm anytime soon. Nonetheless, as we saw in the "evolution" sections in the preceding sixteen chapters, conventional wisdom can be changed and, indeed, must be changed when it has outlived its utility. Throughout history, whenever a crisis became so overwhelming that it threatened what people held dear, they have found a way to overcome it. This response never came easily and it inevitably involved shedding ways of thinking and acting that were so deeply ingrained that many people were not even aware that they existed. There have always been doubters, but the fact of the matter is that people changed, and in so doing they changed the institutions that governed them.

Conclusion: Students and Citizens

The hardest part of writing a book is coming up with the first few paragraphs and the last ones. The conclusion has been especially difficult in drafting the first eight editions of this book. We keep ending up at the same place.

You will leave this course and enter a world filled with global challenges. Whether you accept the arguments made in this chapter, you will be asked to help make decisions about the issues discussed throughout this book and this course.

Your challenge will be not just *whether* you get involved but *how* you do so. We are lucky. We chose jobs that allow us to integrate our profession and our politics. Not all of you will share that luck (if it is, indeed, luck). Nevertheless, the world will be placed in your hands as you get older and you will need to find some way to respond to this responsibility.

We both have step-grandchildren who give us tremendous joy. We also want to leave them a better and safer world. So, in the first year of his grandson's life, Chip is reminded in a new way of a mug his step-daughter gave him for Christmas just before the first edition of this book came out. In its short and simple way, it leaves you with the lesson it took us more than 500 pages to get to. Imagine a picture of a tabby cat holding up the world. The caption: Fragile. Handle With Care.

Key Terms

Concepts
climate change
feedback
globalization
global governance
global warming
human security
international financial
  institutions
international organization
multinational corporation

multilevel analysis
nongovernmental
  organization
paradigm shift
regime
supranational organization
systems theory
United Nations
win-win

People
Gore, Al

Acronyms
ICC
IFI
IO
IPCC
MNC
NAFTA
NGO

UN

**Organizations Places and
  Events**
European Union
International Criminal Court
International Panel on
  Climate Change
North American Free Trade
  Agreement
United Nations

🌐 Useful Websites

Globalization 101 is by far the best single site on globalization. It has links to material on most topics covered in this chapter—but not on peacebuilding. In keeping with the pace-of-change argument we have made, it has "moved" three times since it was created in 2000.
  www.globalization101.org
The International Panel on Climate Change not only does the best work but it has the best site on the topic.
  www.ipcc.ch
UN Women focuses on its own work, but it has plenty of links to other sites and covers a lot of ground.
  www.unwomen.org

The best site on peacebuilding is not the one maintained by the Alliance for Peacebuilding where Chip works. Rather, Beyond Intractability amounts to an online handbook on the subject.
  www.beyondintractability.org
The Institute for Peace and Economics conducts the annual Global Peace Index, which has a ton of good analysis as well as the results.
  www.visionofhumanity.org

Wikileaks has more on its website than you might expect, although little of the "juicy" material can be found there at this point because of legal proceedings against the organization.

www.wikileaks.org

A final, but not very political, website is maintained by the Institute for Global Ethics, which we mentioned at the start of the chapter.

www.globalethics.org

Further Reading

Collier, Paul, *The Bottom Billion*. New York: Oxford University Press, 2007. The best book on globalization, poverty, and their implications.

Friedman, Thomas P. *Hot, Flat, and Crowded*. New York: Farrar, Straus, and Giroux, 2009. Arguably the best and most optimistic book on globalization.

Fukuyama, Francis. *The End of History and the Last Man*. New York: Free Press, 1992. While we don't agree with Fukuyama in this book, he is arguably the most influential conservative thinker today.

Gore, Al. *An Inconvenient Truth*. New York: Rodale, 2006. Probably did more than anyone to popularize the idea of global warming. The video is also worth watching.

Hauss, Charles. *International Conflict Resolution, 2nd ed*. New York: Continuum, 2010. A good introduction to conflict resolution built around cases in which it has and has not worked.

Haussman, Melissa, Marian Sawer, and Jill Vickers, eds. *Federalism, Feminism and Multilevel Governance*. Furnham (UK): Ashgate, 2010. Like Rai and Whalen, the authors focus on multilevel issues but do so solely within federal systems.

Huntington, Samuel. *The Clash of Civilizations and the Remaking of World Order*. New York: Simon and Schuster, 1996. Another book we disagree with but it served as a lightning rod for political debate over the role of Islam and was published five years before 9/11.

Rai, Shirin, and Georgina Waylen, eds. *Global Governance: Feminist Perspectives*. London: Palgrave 2008. The most comprehensive book on global governance from a feminist perspective.

Waldrip, Mitchell. *Complexity: The Emerging Science at the Edge of Order and Chaos*. New York: Simon and Schuster, 1992. Still the best and most readable book on the subject.

Younge, Eric. *Who Are We—And Should It Matter in the 21st Century?* New York: Nation Books, 2011. The best book on the link between personal identity and cultural norms. Covers everything from Younge's life as a person born in Britain of West Indian origin to almost all of the countries covered in this book.

Glossary

Concepts, Organizations, Places, & Events

Action Congress (AC) Political party in Nigeria. Third in most recent election.

Action Group (AG) A Yoruba-based political party in post-independence Nigeria

Akali Dal The Sikh-based party in Punjab, India.

All Nigeria Middle Belt People's Party (ANPP) The leading opposition party in Nigeria today

Alliance Coalition of British Liberals and Social Democrats in the 1980s that became the Liberal Democrats of today.

American exceptionalism The theory that the United States occupies a special niche in the world in terms of its national credo, historical evolution, political and religious institutions, and unique origins.

Anticlerical The belief that there should be no link between church and state.

Armed Forces Ruling Council (AFRC) Formal title of the military government during the second period of military rule in Nigeria.

Assembly of Experts An informal body in Iran that has de facto veto power over all major political decisions.

Autogestion A version of self-managed socialism popular in France in the 1970s and 1980s.

Ayodhya Site of a disputed mosque/temple that sparked communal violence in India for much of the 1990s.

Baath Party Party in control of Iraq from the late 1960s until the U.S.-led invasion in 2002.

Backbenchers Members of a parliament who are not in the government or shadow cabinet.

Base Marxist term to describe class and other economic relations that define the "means of production" and the distribution of wealth and power.

Basic Law The German constitution.

Basij Semi-legal vigilantes in Iran

Beveridge Report Published in the 1940s; set the stage for the British welfare state.

Bharatiya Janata Party (BJP) The Hindu party that won the 1998 election; often referred to as fundamentalist.

Biafra A secessionist state in southeastern Nigeria.

Bloc vote French practice that requires a vote on an entire bill without amendments.

Bolsheviks Lenin's faction of the Russian Social Democratic Party; later came to mean anyone who subscribed to his views and/or organization.

Bonyad Islamic charities in Iran, many of which are controlled by the government.

Bourgeoisie Among other things, a Marxist term to describe the capitalist class.

British East India Company Private company that colonized much of India until the 1850s.

Broadening Support for expanding EU membership.

Bundesbank Germany's central bank, replaced by the European Central Bank in 1999.

Bundesrat The upper house of the German parliament.

Bundestag The lower house of the German parliament.

Bureaucracy The part of the government composed of technical experts and others who remain from administration to administration.

Cabinet responsibility Principle that requires a prime minister and government to retain the support of a parliamentary majority.

Cadre Term used to define the permanent, professional members of a party, especially in the communist world.

Camarilla In Mexico and elsewhere in Latin America, a politician's personal following in a patron-client relationship.

Campaign In China, policies in which the party seeks to reach its goals by mobilizing people.

Capitalism An economic system in which the means of production are privately owned and prices, wages, and profits are determined by private industry.

Capitalist roader Derogatory term used to label moderate CCP leaders during the Cultural Revolution.

Carrying capacity The amount of development an ecosystem can bear.

Castes Groups into which Hindu society is divided, each with its own distinctive rules for all areas of social behavior.

Catch-all parties Term devised in the 1960s to describe a new type of political party that plays down ideology in favor of slogans, telegenic candidates, and the like.

Central Advisory Committee (CAC) Informal group of senior Chinese Communist leaders in the 1980s.

Central Committee Supposedly the most important body in a communist party; its influence declined as it grew in size and the party needed daily leadership.

Central Military Commission (CMC) The political leadership of the Chinese military.

Chancellor democracy Germany's informal system of political domination by the prime minister.

Charisma A style of leadership that emphasizes the personal magnetism of a single individual.

Checks and balances In the United States, the informal designation of separation of powers.

Cheka The Soviet Union's first secret police.

Chinese Communist Party (CCP) The only legal party in China, which has run the country since 1949.

Christian Democratic Union (CDU) Germany's leading right-of-center party; similar parties exist elsewhere where there is a large Catholic population.

Civic culture Culture characterized by trust, legitimacy, and limited involvement, which some theorists believe is most conducive to democracy.

Civil society The web of membership in social and political groups that some analysts believe is needed to sustain democracy.

Cleavage Deep and long-lasting political divisions.

Climate change Also known as global warming or the greenhouse effect, in which the Earth's temperature increases incrementally due to carbon dioxide release.

Coalition An alliance of parties that are close enough to one another ideologically to stay together for the duration of a parliamentary term.

Coalition Provisional Authority (CPA) Official name of the U.S.-led occupation administration of Iraq.

Codecision A cooperation procedure that obliges the EU's Council and Commission to consult the Parliament in two stages and gives the Parliament more influence.

Codetermination German system that gives unions half the seats on boards of directors of all companies with more than two thousand employees.

Cohabitation In France, a period in which one party or coalition controls the Parliament and the other has the presidency.

Cold War Rivalry between the superpowers from the end of World War II to the collapse of the Soviet Union.

Collective responsibility The doctrine that all cabinet members must agree with all decisions.

Collectivist consensus Cross-party British support for the welfare state that lasted until the late 1970s.

Comintern The interwar coalition of communist parties directed from Moscow.

Command economy A centrally planned and controlled economy. This kind of economy operated in the former Soviet Union and other communist countries.

Commission, European The executive of the European Union.

Committee of Permanent Representatives European Union civil servants who are sent by and work for the member states rather than the EU itself.

Common Agricultural Policy (CAP) The EU's agricultural policy, blamed for many of its economic troubles and likely to be changed as it adds new members.

Common Foreign and Security Policy (CFSP) EU goal of creating a single foreign policy for its fifteen member states; one of the three pillars.

Common Market Colloquial name used to describe the European Union, especially in its early years.

Communal group Racial, ethnic, or linguistic groups that today are often the source of political violence.

Communism/Communist Has many meanings, but usually used to describe policies and institutions derived from the works of Marx, Engels, and Lenin that were adapted and used in such countries as China and the former Soviet Union.

Communist Party (PCF) French Communist Party.

Communist Party A political party inspired by Marxism-Leninism, usually as developed in the former Soviet Union.

Communist Party of the Russian Federation (CPRF) The new incarnation of the CPSU for Russia.

Communist Party of the Soviet Union (CPSU) The party that ran the Soviet Union until its collapse in 1991.

Compromise Decision-making procedure in which all sides make concessions in order to reach an agreement.

Concerted action Cooperation involving the government, business, and labor in Germany.

Conditionality The imposition of stipulations before the granting of loans by the IMF, World Bank, and other international financial institutions.

Confederation of British Industry (CBI) The leading British business interest group.

Confédération Française Démocratique du Travail/French Democratic Confederation of Labor (CFDT) Socialist leaning trade union federation in France. Once Catholic.

Confédération Générale du Travail/General Confederation of Labor (CGT) Trade union federation in France affiliated with the communist party.

Confederation of Mexican Workers (CTM) The trade union affiliated with the PRI

Confucianism Chinese philosophical and religious tradition stressing, among other things, order and hierarchy.

Consensus policy making Decision making procedures that emphasize win/win outcomes.

Conservative Party Britain's most important right-of-center party, in power more often than not for two centuries.

Constitution A basic political document that lays out the institutions and procedures a country follows.

Constitutional Council French council created in 1958 with the power to supervise elections and rule on the constitutionality of bills passed by the National Assembly before they formally become law.

Constitutional Revolution Begun in 1906, the first attempt to bring anything like democracy to Iran.

Constructive vote of no confidence In Germany, means that a chancellor can be removed in a vote of confidence only if the Bundestag also agrees on a replacement.

Contradictions Marxist notion that all societies based on inequality have built-in flaws that will eventually lead to their destruction.

Corporatism/corporatist In Europe, arrangements through which government, business, and labor leaders cooperatively set microeconomic or macroeconomic policy, normally outside of the regular electoral legislative process; in Mexico and elsewhere in the third world, another term to describe the way people are integrated into the system via patron-client relations.

Council of Ministers A generic term used to describe the cabinet in many countries.

Crisis A critical turning point.

Cult of personality In communist and other systems, the excessive adulation of a single leader.

Cultural Revolution The period of upheaval in China from the mid-1960s to the mid-1970s.

Dalit Term to describe untouchables in India.

Debt crisis The massive accumulation of loans taken out by third world countries and owed to northern banks and governments from the 1970s onward.

Debt trap The inability of third world countries to pay back their loans to northern creditors.

Decision making The way governments (or other bodies) make policies.

Deepening Expansion of the EU's powers.

Demand Inputs through which people and interest groups put pressure on the state for change.

Democracy/democratic A system of government in which sovereignty resides in the people.

Democracy Movement Protests by Chinese students and others that culminated in the Tiananmen Square disaster of 1989 in Beijing.

Democracy Wall Literally, a wall on which Chinese dissidents wrote "big-character posters" in the late 1970s.

Democratic centralism The Leninist organizational structure that concentrates power in the hands of the party elite.

Democratic deficit The lack of an effective democracy in the EU.

Democratic Party U.S. political party that is more likely to propose expansion of social service programs and tax rates that tend to demand more of richer Americans.

Democratization The process of developing democratic states.

Dependency/dependency theory A radical critique of mainstream economic theory that stresses the continued power the north has over the third world.

De-Stalinization The shift away from Stalinist policies and practices beginning with Khrushchev's secret speech in 1956.

Devolution The process of decentralizing power from national governments that stops short of federalism.

Dialectic The belief that change occurs in dramatic bursts from one type of society to another.

Dirigisme French belief in a centrally planned and managed economy.

Dual mandate In Nigeria and elsewhere, the notion that colonial powers had to rule on their own and through local leaders at the same time.

École Nationale d'Administration (ENA) *Grande école* for training France's bureaucratic elite

Electoral alchemy The way Mexican governments have used fraud to rig elections.

Electoral system Mechanisms through which votes are cast and tallied, and seats in the legislature are allotted.

Emergency Rule A provision in some constitutions that allows cabinets to rule in an all but dictatorial way for a brief period, as in India from 1975 to 1977.

Environment In systems theory, everything lying outside the political system.

EU Committee of Permanent Representatives (COREPER) In the EU, permanent representatives of the national governments.

Euro The new European currency, introduced in 1999.

European Central Bank (ECB) Leading bank for the EU, replaced national central banks.

European Coal and Steel Community (ECSC) One of the precursors of the European Union, formed in 1951.

European Community (EC) The formal name of what became the EU in the 1970s and 1980s.

European Court of Justice (ECJ) The EU's judicial body, with sweeping powers.

European Economic Community (EEC) The precursor of the EU.

European Monetary System (EMS) The first attempt to link the EU member states' currencies.

European Monetary Union (EMU) Created in 1998; includes a central bank and the euro.

European Parliament The EU's legislature.

European Union (EU) The current name of the "Common Market."

Euroskeptic People opposed to expansion of the EU's power.

Events of May 1968 French protest movements that almost toppled the Gaullist government.

Expediency Council A half lay and half clerical body designed to smooth relations between those two communities in Iran at the highest levels.

Extraterritoriality Portions of China, Japan, and Korea where European law operated during the late nineteenth and early twentieth centuries.

Faction A group organized on ideological or other lines operating inside a political party.

Failed state System in which the government loses the ability to provide even the most basic services.

Falsify testing/falsify Contradicting a theory by finding at least one example in which it does not hold true.

Falun Gong Chinese spiritual movement suppressed by the government since the late 1990s.

Fascism Right-wing regimes, often drawing on racist philosophies in countries such as Germany and Japan between the two world wars.

Fatherland-All Russia One of the leading opposition parties in Russia in the 1999 Duma elections.

Faulted society Germany from the late nineteenth century to the rise of Hitler, reflecting the unevenness of its social, economic, and political development.

Federal Constitutional Court (FCC) Constitutional court in Germany with significant powers of judicial review.

Federal Election Commission (CFE) The old (and corrupt) body that supervised elections in Mexico.

Federal Electoral Institute (IFE) Created before the 1997 election to provide more honest management of elections in Mexico than its predecessor, the Federal Election Commission.

Federal Executive Council of Nigeria (FEC) Leadershp of the first Nigerian republic.

Federal Republic of Germany (FRG) Formal name of the former West Germany and, now, the unified state.

Federalism/federal Constitutional practice in which subnational units are granted considerable power.

Federalist Papers Key documents written in support of the U.S. Constitution during the debate on ratification in the 1780s.

Federation Council The largely powerless upper house of the Russian parliament.

Federation of German Labour (DGB) The leading German trade union.

Feedback How events today are communicated to people later on and shape what people do later on.

Fifth Republic French regime since 1958.

First-past-the-post Electoral system based on single-member districts in which the candidate who receives the most votes wins.

Five-year plan In the former Soviet Union and other communist countries, the period for which Gosplan developed goals and quotas.

Force ouvrière Workers' Force, France's second largest and most dynamic trade union federation.

Foreign aid Money or goods provided by richer countries to help poorer ones develop.

Four modernizations A policy first introduced by Zhou Enlai and championed by Deng Xiaoping, focusing on developing industry, the military, agriculture, and science in China.

Fourth Republic Current Nigerian regime

Fourth Republic French regime from 1946–58.

Free Democratic Party (FDP) Germany's Liberal party.

Freedom Charter The ANC's proposals from the 1950s that led to its being banned.

Führer German term for "leader," used by Hitler.

Fundamentalism Religious beliefs of a literal nature that often lead to right-wing political views.

FY Fiscal year.

Gang of Four Radical leaders in China during the Cultural Revolution, led by Jiang Ching, Mao's wife.

Gaullists General term used to describe supporters of General Charles de Gaulle and the parties created to back his vision for the Fifth Republic.

General Intelligence Apparatus One of Iraq's main intelligence agencies.

General secretary Term used to denote the head of a communist party.

General Security Directorate One of Iraq's main intelligence agencies.

German Democratic Republic (DDR) Formal name of the former East Germany.

German question A series of questions used to study Germany's unique circumstances: why did Germany take so long to unite; why did the country's first attempts at democracy give way to Hitler; how did the division of Germany and other events after World War II help create the prosperous and stable democratic FRG in the west but also the stagnant and repressive DDR in the east; and why did unification occur with the end of the Cold War in Germany?

Glasnost Under Gorbachev, Soviet policies that opened up the political system and allowed for freedom of expression.

Global warming The well-supported theory that the earth is getting warmer due to the trapping of certain gases in the atmosphere.

Globalization Popular term used to describe how international economic, social, cultural, and technological forces are affecting events inside individual countries.

Global governance The goal--and to some degree the reality--of making political decisions internationally.

Global South The underdeveloped and largely poor countries in the world. Often called the third world.

Gobernación The ministry in charge of administration in Mexico; until recently, a post often held by politicians before becoming president.

Good Friday Agreement A practical peace agreement reached by the major parties in Northern Ireland with the British and Irish governments on, not surprisingly, Good Friday 1998.

Gosplan The Soviet central planning agency.

Governance The exercise of political authority and use of institutional resources to manage society's problems and affairs.

Government Either a generic term to describe the formal part of the state or the administration of the day.

Government of India Act The 1858 law that turned most of India into a formal British colony.

Gradualism The belief that change should occur slowly or incrementally.

Grand coalition A cabinet that includes all the major parties, not just a bare majority.

Grandes écoles Highly selective French universities that train top civil servants and, hence, much of the elite.

Grandeur Gaullist goal for France.

Great Leap Forward Failed Chinese campaign of the late 1950s to speed up development.

Great Reform Act Law passed in 1832 that expanded the suffrage; widely seen as a key step toward democracy in Britain.

Green Revolution In India and elsewhere, the technological improvements that drastically improved agricultural production and eliminated widespread starvation.

Greens Political parties that emphasize environmental and other "new" issues, and radical change. In Germany, the first major environmentally oriented party; a junior partner in government until 2006.

Gross domestic product (GDP) A measure of the total output of goods and services in a country.

Gross national product (GNP) The total value of the goods and services produced in a society.

Guardian Council The leading theological body in Iran for political purposes.

Guardianship of the Jurist Developed by Ayatollah Khomeini, supports the notion that senior clerics have the best capacity to rule in a Muslim society.

Gulf War The war between the UN coalition and Iraq following the latter's invasion of Kuwait in 1990.

Hard currency Currencies that can be traded openly on international markets.

Hausa-Fulani The leading Muslim group in northern Nigeria.

Historical materialism Marxist belief that the class divisions of a society determine everything else that matters.

House of Commons The all-important lower house of the British Parliament.

House of Lords The weaker upper house of the British Parliament, slated for reform or abolition.

Human Development Index (HDI) The UN's best indicator of social development.

Human security The belief that security includes all areas, not just the military.

Hundred Flowers Campaign Reformist Chinese campaign in the mid-1950s.

Identity How people define themselves in racial, linguistic, ethnic, or religious terms.

Igbo The leading ethnic group in southeastern Nigeria. Often also spelled Ibo.

Image of the enemy Psychological concept that focuses on stereotyping one's adversary.

Immigration Reform and Control Act U.S. law, passed in 1986, that limits the rights of immigrants, especially those from Mexico.

Imperialism The policy of colonizing other countries—literally, establishing empires.

Import substitution Development strategy that uses tariffs and other barriers to imports, and therefore stimulates domestic industries.

Incompatibility clause French constitutional provision that bars people from holding a seat both in the National Assembly and in a cabinet.

Incrementalism Used to describe policies that make limited, marginal, or minor changes in existing practices.

Indian Administrative Service (IAS) The bureaucratic elite today.

Indian Civil Service The bureaucratic elite during colonial rule.

Indian National Congress The leader of the struggle for India's independence and the dominant party since then.

Indirect rule British and other colonial procedures through which "natives" were used to carry out colonial rule.

Individualism The belief that emphasizes the role of the individual voter or consumer, typically associated with the rise of democracy in the West.

Industrialized democracy The richest countries with advanced economies and liberal states.

Input Support or demand from people to the state.

Institutional Revolutionary Party (PRI) The party that governed Mexico from 1927–2000.

Integrated elite In Japan, France, and Germany, refers to cooperation among government, business, and other interest groups.

Interest group An organization formed to work for the views of a relatively narrow group of people, such as a trade union or business association.

Intergovernmental Panel on Climate Change (IPCC) An international body working on the threat of climate change. Endorsed by the UN.

Interim government Generically, any government that serves for a brief period as part of a transition. In Iraq, the government chosen in the 2005 election whose one main mission was to draft a new constitution.

International Criminal Court (ICC) A new international tribunal that deals with alleged crimes against humanity.

International financial institutions (IFI) Transtional bodies that are charged with regulating trade and investment.

International Monetary Fund (IMF) International agency that provides loans and other forms of assistance to countries with fiscal problems.

International organizations (IO) Formal transnational governing institutions. Some, like the EU, have considerable power.

International political economy The network of economic activity that transcends national boundaries.

Interventionist state Governments in industrialized democracies that pursue an active economic policy.

Iranian Revolutionary Guard Corps (IRGC) Elite military unit set up after the 1979 revolution. Some claim it runs the country.

Iraqi National Congress (INC) The leading exile-based opposition group to Baath rule.

Iron triangle A variety of close relationships between business leaders, politicians, and civil servants.

Islamic Revolution The overthrow of Iran's monarchy under Shah Mohammad Reza Pahlavi and its replacement with an Islamic republic under Ayatollah Ruhollah Khomeini, the leader of the 1979 revolution.

Islamicists Muslims who are convinced that their faith should dominate politically.

Janata An early political party in India.

Janata Dal Loose coalitions that unseated Congress in the late 1970s and 1980s in India.

Jati In India, a subcaste with its own rules, customs, and so forth.

Judicial review Power held by courts in some countries that allows them to rule on the constitutional merits of laws and other policies.

Just Russia a Russian political party created in 2006 under Putin.

KGB Soviet secret police

Kuomintang (KMT) The Chinese Nationalist Party, which was nominally in power from 1911–49; now on Taiwan.

Kurds Minority ethnic group in Iraq and other countries in the region.

Labour Party The leading left-wing party in Britain, in power from 1997 to 2010.

Laissez-faire Economic policy that stresses a limited government role.

Länder (land) German states.

Law for Promoting Stability and Growth in the Economy Passed in 1967, a key provision in Germany's economic consensus.

Left Party A German political party formed in 2005 that brought together dissident SPD members and the remnants of the East German Communist Party.

Left Political groups favoring change, often of an egalitarian nature.

Legitimacy A key concept stressing the degree to which people accept and endorse their regime.

Less Developed Countries (LDC) A classification of countries marked by poverty; often the inability to forge functioning courts, bureaucracies, and other institutions; and have often experienced military coups and other forms of political upheaval that have sapped regimes of the popular support needed for the long-term strength.

Liberal Democratic Party In Britain, the number-three party and in some ways the most radical; in Russia, the neofascist and racist opposition party led by Vladimir Zhirinovsky.

Liberal In the United States, it refers to people who support the left and an interventionist government. Everywhere else in the world, however, it means opposition to government interference in the economy and any other area in which individuals can make decisions for themselves.

Lok Sabha The all-important lower house of the Indian parliament.

Long March Retreat by the CCP in the mid-1930s, which turned into one of its strengths in recruiting support.

Maastricht Treaty Created the EU and EMU; signed in 1992.

Magna Carta An English charter signed in 1215 that marks the first trend toward democratization.

Majlis The Iranian parliament.

Manifesto In Britain and other parliamentary systems, another term for a party's platform in an election campaign.

Maquiladora Factory in Mexico (initially on the U.S. border, now anywhere) that operates tax-free in manufacturing goods for export.

Marshall Plan U.S. funds provided for reconstruction of Europe after World War II.

Marxism-Leninism The philosophy adopted by ruling communist parties, which combined Marxist analysis with Leninist organizational structures and tactics.

Mass line Chinese Communist principle that stressed "learning from the masses."

May Fourth Movement Chinese protest movement triggered by opposition to the Treaty of Versailles; a major step on the path leading to the creation and victory of the CCP.

Means of production Marxist term designating the dominant way goods are created in a given society.

Member of Parliament (MP) Elected members of the British or other parliament.

Mensheviks The smaller and more moderate faction of the Russian Social Democratic Party before World War I.

Mestizo Term used to describe Mexicans of mixed racial origin.

Microcredit Lending and development strategy that stresses small loans for new businesses, developed by the Grameen Bank in Bangladesh.

Middle Belt Ethnically mixed region of central Nigeria where the capital, Abuja, was built.

Modell Deutschland Term used to describe the political approach to German economic growth after World War II.

Movement of French Enterprises (MEDEF) Leading French business association.

Mughals The Muslims who invaded and dominated India beginning in the sixteenth century.

Multilevel analysis A way of looking at politics that includes several layers of government at once.

Multilevel governance A form of decision making that involves national, regional, and/or local governments together.

Multinational corporation (MNC) Company operating across national boundaries.

Nation As used by political scientists, primarily a psychological term to describe attachment or identity rather than a geopolitical unit such as the state.

Nation building A process in which people develop a strong sense of identification with their country.

National Action Party (PAN) The leading right-of-center opposition party in Mexico.

National Assembly In France and South Africa, the lower house of parliament.

National Congress of British West Africa (NCBWA) One of the leading groups advocating Nigerian independence

National Council of Nigeria and the Cameroons (NCNC) An Igbo-based movement for Nigerian independence

National Democratic Party (NPD) Germany's most powerful neo-Nazi party since the end of World War II.

National Front (FN) France's racist right-wing party.

National Party of Nigeria (NPN) A Muslim-based political party during the Nigerian Second Republic

National Republican Convention (NRC) A leading independence movement in colonial Nigeria

National Socialist Democratic Workers Party (NSDAP) Political party of Hitler and the Nazis in Germany

Nationalist Party The Kuomintang, the ruling party in China before the CCP victory.

Nationalization Philosophies or attitudes that stress the importance of extending the power or support for a nation; government takeover of private business.

Nazis Hitler's party, which ruled Germany from 1933–45.

Near abroad Russian term to describe the other fourteen republics of the former Soviet Union.

New Left Radicals from the 1960s.

New Right Conservative political movements in industrialized democracies that have arisen since the 1960s and stress "traditional values," often with a racist overtone.

Newly industrialized countries (NIC) The handful of countries, such as South Korea, that have developed a strong industrial base and grown faster than most of the third world.

Nigerian National Democratic Party (NNDP) One of the regionally based political parties in post-independence Nigeria

Nigerian People's Party (NPP) One of the major parties in post-independence Nigeria

Nigerian Youth Movement (NYM) A leading pro-independence movement in colonial Nigeria

Nomenklatura The Soviet system of lists that facilitated the CPSU's appointment of trusted people to key positions, adopted by other communist regimes.

Nongovernmental organizations (NGO) Nonprofit, private groups that exert political influence around the world and are playing an increasingly important role in determining developmental and environmental policies.

Non-reelection Principle in Mexican political life that bars politicians from holding office for two consecutive terms.

North American Free Trade Agreement (NAFTA) Agreement linking the economies of Canada, Mexico, and the United States.

Northern Elements Progressive Union (NEPU) A left-of-center Muslim party in the Nigerian second republic

Northern People's Congress (NPC) One of the Muslim-based political parties during post-independence Nigeria

Oligarch Business and political leaders with what some think is undue influence in Russia.

Operation Desert Shield the mobilization of American troops into Saudi Arabia at the time of the Gulf War.

Operation Desert Storm the Persian Gulf War launched on 17 January 1991 by the United States against Iraq.

Operation Iraqi Freedom Official name of the American-led invasion of Iraq in 2003.

Organization of Petroleum Exporting Countries (OPEC) Cartel of oil-producing countries; responsible for the 1973–74 embargo.

Ossi German who grew up in the former East Germany.

Ottoman Empire Islamic empire based in present-day Turkey; collapsed with World War I.

Our Home Is Russia New political party chaired by former prime minister Viktor Chernomyrdin.

Output Public policy in systems theory.

Pacting A process in which leaders from opposing sides cooperate.

Pahlavi dynasty The father and son who ruled Iran for most of the twentieth century, until the revolution of 1979.

Pantouflage The French practice of leaving the bureaucracy to take positions in big business or politics.

Paradigm A theory that covers an entire discipline.

Paradigm shift A change in basic assumptions and theories in science, including political science.

Parastatal Companies owned or controlled by the state in the third world.

Parity Law Recent French legislation guaranteeing seats in the parliament for women.

Parliamentary party The members of parliament from a single party.

Party of Democratic Socialism (PDS) The successor to East Germany's Communist Party.

Party of the Democratic Revolution (PRD) The leading left-of-center opposition party in Mexico.

Party of power A kind of Russian political party created to support the current leadership.

Party state The notion that the CPSU and other ruling communist parties dominated their entire political systems.

Patriotic Union of Kurdistan (PUK) One of the leading Kurdish opposition groups in Iraq and beyond.

Patron-client relations Neofeudal relations in which "patrons" gain the support of "clients" through the mutual exchange of benefits and obligations.

PEMEX Mexico's nationalized petrochemical industry

Pendulum effect The notion that policies can shift from left to right as the balance of partisan power changes; in Mexico, reflects the fact that the PRI can move from one side to another on its own as circumstances warrant.

People's Democratic Party (PDP) The current ruling party in Nigeria

People's Liberation Army (PLA) China's military.

People's Redemption Party (PRP) A leading political party in Nigeria's second republic.

People's Republic of China (PRC) Official name of the Chinese state.

Perestroika Ill-fated program to reform the Soviet economy in the late 1980s.

Permit raj In India, the system of government rules and regulations that required state approval of most enterprises.

Politburo Generic term used to describe the leadership of communist parties.

Political culture Basic values and assumptions that people have toward authority, the political system, and other overarching themes in political life.

Political participation Opportunities for citizens to take part in their country's government, such as voting in competitive elections, joining interest groups, and engaging in protest.

Political party Organization that contests elections or otherwise contends for power.

Politics The process through which a community, state, or organization organizes and governs itself.

Positive-sum outcome Conflict resolution in which all parties benefit. Also known as win-win.

Postindustrial society Society in which the dominant industries are in the service and high-tech sectors.

Postmaterialism/postmaterialist Theory that young middle-class voters are likely to support environmentalism, feminism, and other "new" issues.

Power As conventionally defined, the ability to get someone to do something he or she otherwise would not do.

Power ministries The most important departments in the Russian government.

Prefect Until 1981, the central government appointee who really ran France's departments.

Presidential Rule In India, the government's power to remove elected state officials and replace them with appointees from Delhi.

Privatization/privatized The selling off of state-owned companies.

Proclerical The belief that the church should play a leading role in government.

Proletariat Marxist term for the working class.

Proportional representation (PR) Electoral system in which parties receive a number of seats in parliament proportionate to their share of the vote.

Provisional government Generic term used to describe temporary governments formed until a new constitution is written; also, the government in Russia between the two 1917 revolutions.

Public policy The decisions made by a state that define what it will do.

Purges The systematic removal of people from party, state, or other office; especially common in communist systems.

Qualified majority voting The EU voting system in which the Council of Ministers does not need to reach unanimity on most issues.

Radicals People to the left of center; in France, the liberals who were radical only in nineteenth-century terms, which is to say they favored democracy, capitalism, and anticlericalism.

Rajya Sabha The weaker upper house of the Indian parliament.

Rally for the Republic (RPR) The former name of the Gaullist Party in France.

Rashtriya Swayamsevah Sangh (RSS) A fundamentalist Hindu group and a precursor of the BJP.

Realignment A shift in the basic electoral balance of power in which substantial groups in a society change their longterm party identification.

Red Guard Radical students and other supporters of Mao Zedong during the Cultural Revolution.

Red hat A slang term used to describe CCP influence in formally privatized enterprises.

Red versus expert Debate in China pitting ideologues against supporters of economic development.

Regime The institutions and practices that endure from government to government, such as the constitutional order in a democracy.

Reparations Payments demanded of defeated powers after a war, especially important in Germany after World War I.

Republican Guard The elite military units in Iraq.

Republican party/Republican One of the two main contemporary political parties in the United States whose political platform is considered center-right and support business interests.

Revolutionary Command Council (RCC) The leadership of the rulng Baath Party in Iraq.

Right Political forces favoring the status quo or a return to earlier policies and values.

Rule of law In a democracy, the principle that legal rules rather than arbitrary and personal decisions determine what happens.

Russian Federation Formal name of Russia.

Sanctions Policies designed to limit or end trade with a country to help force it to change its policies.

Satellites The countries in eastern and central Europe that came under communist rule after World War II.

SAVAK Iranian intelligence service under the shah.

Second of Khordad Movement The political party organized to support the reform efforts of then-president Khatami in Iran. Named for the day he was first elected.

Secret speech Given by Khrushchev in 1957; seen as the start of the "thaw."

Secretariat Generic term used to denote the bureaucratic leaders of a communist party.

Senate Upper house of the legislature in the United States, France, Mexico, and South Africa.

Separation of powers Formal term for checks and balances in a system like that of the United States.

Sexeño The six-year term of a Mexican president.

Shadow cabinet In systems like Britain's, the official leadership of the opposition party that "shadows" the cabinet.

Shah Title of the rulers of Iran before the 1979 Islamic revolution.

Sharia Islamic legal code that many argue should supersede civil law in countries such as Iran and Nigeria.

Shiite Minority Muslim sect, usually seen as more militant than the Sunnis.

Shock therapy Policies in formerly communist countries that envisage as rapid a shift to a market economy as possible.

Single European Act (SEA) Act that created the truly common market in 1992.

Single-member district Electoral system in which only one representative is chosen from each constituency.

Sino-Soviet split Tensions between the USSR and China that rocked the communist world.

Social Democratic Party (SDP or SPD) Germany's left-of-center party, in power since 1997; Britain's former Social Democratic Party; also, one of the political parties in Nigeria during the very short-lived third republic.

Socialism A variety of beliefs in the public ownership of the means of production and an egalitarian distribution of wealth and income.

Socialist Party (PS) France's Socialist Party, created in 1971.

Solidarity The anticommunist union formed in Poland in the 1980s.

Special Economic Zones (SEZ) Cities and regions in China in which foreigners are allowed to invest.

Standing Committee The subcommittee that runs the Politburo in China.

State All individuals and institutions that make public policy, whether they are in the government or not.

State Duma The lower house of the Russian parliament.

Strong state One with the capacity and the political will to make and implement effective public policy.

Structural adjustment Development strategy that stresses integration into global markets, privatization, and so on. Supported by the World Bank, IMF, and other major northern financial institutions.

Subsidiarity In the EU, policy that devolves decision making to the lowest appropriate level.

Subsidy In Iran and elsewhere, policies that compensate or help individuals or groups overcome economic problems.

Subsistence economy One in which peasants predominate and grow food and other crops primarily for domestic consumption.

Suffrage The right to vote.

Sunni Majority Muslim sect, usually seen as more moderate than the Shiites.

Sunni triangle The region of Iraq in which Sunni Arabs make up the majority of the population.

Superstructure Marxist term for the government, religion, and other institutions whose primary role is to help support the dominance of the ruling class.

Support In systems analysis, popular input that tends to endorse the current leadership and its policies.

Supranational Authority that transcends national borders.

Supreme Leader Title given to the ayatollah who sits atop all Iranian political institutions.

Supreme Military Council (SMC) A title used during the two most important periods of military rule in Nigeria.

Surge Sending more troops into a military engagement, such as the U.S. surge launched in Iraq in 2007.

Swaraj The Indian movement for independence and self-rule.

Syndicate Indian Congress leaders who ended up opposing Indira Gandhi.

System A group of interacting, interrelated, or interdependent elements forming a complex whole–in comparative politics, inputs, decision making, outputs, feedback, and the environment within a state.

Systems theory A model for understanding political life examining how state's components interact over time and how nonpolitical and international forces shape what it can and cannot accomplish.

Tea Party Loosely organized American political movement which was largely responsible for GOP gains in the 2010 election.

Theory Explanatory statements, accepted principles, and methods of analysis.

Third International Moscow-dominated organization of communist parties around the world between the two world wars.

Third way A term used to describe the new and more central left-wing parties of the 1990s, most notably Britain's "New Labour."

Third world Informal term for the poorest countries in Asia, Africa, and Latin America.

Three line whip In a parliamentary system, statements to MPs that they must vote according to the party's wishes.

Three pillars Informal term denoting the main areas in which the EU has worked since the Maastricht Treaty.

Tiananmen Square Symbolic heart of Chinese politics; site in Beijing of protests and a massacre in 1989.

Tories Informal name for Britain's Conservative Party.

Totalitarian/totalitarianism Regime in which the state has all but total power.

Trades Union Congress (TUC) Britain's leading trade union confederation.

Treaty of Amsterdam Minor 1998 agreement that added some limited powers to the EU.

Treaty of Lisbon A 2007 EU treaty that balances big and small states, old and new members but does not serve as a constitution and has not been fully ratified by Fall 2009.

Treaty of Nice EU's December 2000 treaty that opened the door to the broadening of the EU in 2004 and 2007 and outlined provisional plans for reforming the EU's institutions so they could function effectively with as many as thirty members, including the possibility of enacting a constitution.

Treaty of Rome Created the EEC in 1957.

Treuhand The agency responsible for selling off formerly state-owned East German companies.

Tutelle In France, central government control over local authorities.

Twentieth Party Congress Occasion of Khrushchev's "secret speech" launching de-Stalinization.

Two-ballot system An election system in France in which any number of candidates can run at a first ballot, and if one of them wins a majority, he or she wins the seat. If not (which is usually the case), a second ballot is held one week later.

Two-party system Countries in which only two parties seriously compete for power.

U.K. United Kingdom.

Unanimity principle Formerly required for all decisions in the EU, now only for major new policies.

Union for a Popular Majority/Movement (UMP) Center-right French political party that was founded in 2002 and has an absolute majority in the National Assembly, a plurality in the Senate, and elected Nicolas Sarkozy as their candidate for president in 2007.

Union for French Democracy (UDF) The number-two right-of-center party in France under various names since 1962.

Union of Right Forces A Russian democratic opposition party associated with free market reforms and privatization.

Unit The basic body assuring work, housing, and welfare to which most urban Chinese were assigned before economic reforms took hold.

Unitary state Regimes in which subnational units have little or no power.

United Middle Belt Congress (UMBC) A powerful force during the Nigerian second republic.

United Nations (UN) The world's leading international organization.

United Party of Nigeria (UPN) The main Yoruba party in Nigeria's second republic.

United Russia The political party led by Russian president Vladimir Putin.

UNSCOM United Nations Special Commission that formerly conducted arms inspections in Iraq.

Untouchable Indians outside of and "below" the caste system; abolished legally with independence.

Vote of confidence In a parliamentary system, a vote in which the members express their support for (or opposition to) the government's policies; if it loses, the government must resign.

Warlord Prerevolutionary Chinese leaders who controlled a region or other relatively small part of the country; also a term used in other countries such as Afghanistan.

Warsaw Pact Alliance that was the communist world's equivalent of NATO.

Weapons of mass destruction (WMD) Biological, chemical, and nuclear weapons.

Weimar Republic Germany's first and failed attempt at democracy.

Westminster system Term used to describe the British parliamentary system and others based on it.

White paper In Britain and elsewhere, a government statement that outlines proposed legislation; the last stage before the submission of a formal bill.

White revolution The term used by the shah to describe reforms in Iran between the end of World War II and the downfall of his regime in 1979.

Win-win outcome Conflict resolution in which all parties benefit; also known as positive-sum game.

World Bank A major international lending agency for development projects based in Washington.

World Trade Organization (WTO) International organization with wide jurisdiction over trade issues; replaced the General Agreement on Tariffs and Trade.

Yaboloko One of the leading reformist parties in Russia.

Yoruba The leading ethnic group in southwestern Nigeria.

Zapatistas Informal name for Mexican revolutionaries in Chiapas.

Zero-sum game Political outcome in which one side wins and the other loses.

People

Abacha, Sani The military ruler of Nigeria until his death in 1998.

Abiola, Moshood The apparent winner of the 1993 Nigerian presidential election; died in prison of unexplained causes five years later.

Abubakar, Abdulsalami Interim military leader of Nigeria in 1998.

Adenauer, Konrad First chancellor of the German Federal Republic (West Germany).

Ahmadinejad, Mahmoud President of Iran.

Al-Bakr, Ahmed Hassan First Baath president of Iraq, replaced by Saddam Hussein in 1979.

Al-Malaki, Nuri Current Prime Minister of Iraq.

Alawi, Ayad Prime Minister of interim Iraqi government.

Al-Sadr, Moqtada An influential Shiite cleric in Iraq who led insurrections after Saddam Hussein's overthrow.

Awolowo, Obafem A leading Igbo politician and head of Biafra during the civil war in Nigeria in the late 1960s.

Azikiwe, Nnamdi The leading Yoruba politician in post-independence Nigeria.

Babangida, Ibrahim Military ruler of Nigeria in the 1990s and potential candidate in 1997.

Balewa Tafawa One of the leaders of early independent Nigeria; killed in the first coup.

Barroso, José Manuel The Brazilian-Portuguese eleventh President of the European Commission, since 2004.

Bello, Ahmaedu One of the leaders of early independent Nigeria; killed in the first coup.

Berezovsky, Boris Russian oligarch who put together United Russia.

Bhindranwale, Jarnail Singh Radical Sikh leader killed during the attack on the Golden Temple in 1984.

Bismarck, Otto von Chancellor and most important founder of unified Germany in the last half of the nineteenth century.

Blair, Tony British prime minister, 1997–2007, and architect of "New Labour."

Bové, José An outside-the-system French protester and well-known critic of globalization.

Brandt, Willy First Socialist chancellor of the German Federal Republic.

Bremer, Paul Administrator of Iraq under the American occupation.

Brown, Gordon Prime Minister of Great Britain from 2007 until 2010.

Brezhnev, Leonid General secretary of the CPSU, 1964–82; largely responsible for the stagnation of the USSR.

Bush, George W. 43rd President of the United States.

Calderón, Felipe Current Prime Minister of Mexico. Elected Mexico's president in 2006.

Cameron, David Leader of the British Conservative Party since 2006.

Cárdenas, Cuautémoc Son of Lazaro Cárdenas, founder of the PRD, and first elected mayor of Mexico City.

Cárdenas, Lazaro President of Mexico, 1934–40. The last radical reformer to hold the office.

Castro, Fidel President of Cuba since 1959.

Chen Duxiu Founder of the Chinese Communist Party.

Chiang Kai-shek Nationalist president of China before 1949 and later of the government in exile on Taiwan.

Chirac, Jacques Career French politician; president from 1995–2007.

Chubais, Anatoly Russian reformer committed to promarket policies and who created the Union of Right Forces.

Clegg, Nick Leader of British Liberal Party and current Deputy Prime Minister.

De Gaulle, Charles Hero of the French resistance against German occupation; founder and first president of the Fifth Republic.

De la Madrid, Miguel President of Mexico, 1982–88; introduced structural adjustment reforms.

Debré, Michel Primary architect of the constitution of France's Fifth Republic; also its first prime minister, from 1958–62.

Delors, Jacques Prominent French Socialist politician who was president of the European Commission, 1985–95.

Deng Xiaoping De facto ruler of China from the late 1970s to 1997.

Desai, Morarji First non-Congress prime minister of India.

Diaz, Porfirio Introduced the principle of nonreelection into Mexican politics; ironically, de facto dictator of the country for a quarter century in the late nineteenth and early twentieth centuries.

Ebadi, Shirin an Iranian woman who Won the Nobel Peace Prize for her work as a lawyer defending cases of alleged human rights abuses in Iran.

Engels, Friedrich With Karl Marx, the creator of communist theory.

Faisal I British-imposed king of newly independent Iraq after World War I.

Fang Lizhi Physicist and leading Chinese dissident, now living in exile in the United States.

Fillon, François Current Prime Minister of France.

Fischer, Joska Green member of parliament; foreign minister in the Schroeder government in Germany.

Fox, Vicente First non-PRI president of Mexico, elected in 2000.

Gandhi, Indira Prime minister of India, 1966–75 and 1979–84; daughter of Nehru and mother of Rajiv Gandhi; assassinated in 1984.

Gandhi, Mohandas Karamchand Leader of the Indian National Congress in the twenty years before independence.

Gandhi, Rajiv Prime minister of India, 1984–89; assassinated in 1991; son of Indira and grandson of Nehru.

Gandhi, Sonja Head of the Congress Party; turned down the prime ministry in 2004.

Giscard d'Estaing, Valery Moderate president of France, 1974–81.

Gorbachev, Mikhail Head of the CPSU and last president of the Soviet Union.

Gore, Al Former American Vice President. Author of *An Inconvenient Truth*.

Hitler, Adolf Nazi leader of the Third Reich, 1933–45.

Hobbes, Thomas British social theorist of the seventeenth century who emphasized a strong state.

Hu Jintao President of China.

Hussein, Qusay Younger son of Saddam Hussein; probably the second most powerful person in Iraq when his father was deposed in 2002; killed along with his brother by U.S. troops in 2003.

Hussein, Saddam President of Iraq from 1979–2002; captured in December 2003 and executed in 2006.

Hussein, Uday Elder son of Saddam Hussein; thought of as the heir apparent until he was seriously wounded in a 1996 assassination attempt; killed along with his brother by U.S. troops in 2003.

Ironsi, Aguiyi The military ruler of Nigeria during the Biafran war.

Jiang Qing Fourth (and last) wife of Mao Zedong and one of the leaders of the Gang of Four, a radical faction in the CCP during the Cultural Revolution.

Jiang Zemin Former President of China and successor to Deng Xiaoping.

Jonathan, Goodluck Current President of Nigeria.

Jospin, Lionel Socialist prime minister of France, 1997–2002.

Kano, Aminu A Muslim leader of early Nigeria.

Khamenei, Ayatollah Ali Supreme Leader of Iran since the death of Ayatollah Khomeini.

Khatami, Mohammad Reformist president of Iran, 1997–2005.

Khodorkovsky, Mikhail Russian tycoon arrested on corruption and tax evasion charges in 2003.

Khomeini, Ayatollah Ruhollah Muslim cleric who led the 1979 revolution in Iran and was leader of the country until his death in 1989.

Khrushchev, Nikita Successor of Josef Stalin as head of the CPSU and Soviet Union from 1953 until he was ousted in 1964.

Kohl, Helmut Longest-serving chancellor of Germany, 1982–98; oversaw unification.

Le Pen, Jean-Marie Founder and main leader of France's racist National Front.

Lenin, Vladimir Architect of the Bolshevik revolution and first leader of the Soviet Union.

Lin Biao Head of the PLA and designated successor to Mao Zedong; died in mysterious circumstances after a failed coup attempt in 1972.

Liu Shaoqi Moderate CCP politician and designated successor to Mao Zedong; died during the Cultural Revolution.

Locke, John Leading democratic and liberal theorist who stressed "life, liberty, and the pursuit of property."

Lopéz Obrador, Andres Manuel A Mexican politician who was the mayor of Mexico City from 2000 to 2005, before resigning to contend the 2006 presidential election representing the PRD.

Louis XIV French king from 1643 to his death in 1715, popularly known as the Sun King.

Macaulay, Herbert The most important leader of the struggle for independence in Nigeria.

Major, John Former Prime Minister of the United Kingdom and leader of the Conservative Party. He held these posts from 1990 to 1997.

Mao Zedong A Chinese revolutionary, political theorist and Communist leader. He led the People's Republic of China from its establishment in 1949 until his death in 1976.

Marx, Karl With Friedrich Engels, the leading nineteenth-century communist theorist.

Medvedev, Dmitri Third and current President of Russia.

Merkel, Angela Chancellor of Germany since 2006

Mitterrand, François Resuscitated the French Socialist Party; president, 1981–95.

Monnet, Jean Primary architect of the EU and the French planning system.

Mossadeq, Mohammad Left-of-center prime minister of Iran, overthrown in a CIA-led coup in 1954.

Mousavi, Mir Hossein an Iranian reformist politician who served as the fifth and last Prime Minister of the Islamic Republic of Iran from 1981 to 1989 and was a candidate for the 2009 presidential election.

Narasimha Rao, P. V. Prime minister of India, 1991–96.

Nehru, Jawaharlal Indian leader before independence, and prime minister, 1949–64.

Obasanjo, Olusegun President of Nigeria since 1999.

Petraeus, David U.S. General who took command of coalition forces in Iraq in 2007.

Pompidou, Georges Second president of the Fifth Republic of France, from 1969 until his death in 1974.

Putin, Vladimir President of Russia from 2000 to 2008. Odds on favorite to win the post again in 2012.

Rafsanjani, Ayatollah Hashemi Second president of Iran after the 1979 revolution.

Royal, Ségolène A prominent French politician who is a member of the French Socialist Party.

Salinas de Gortari, Carlos President of Mexico, 1988–94; continued structural adjustment reforms; currently living in exile because of his family's involvement in scandals.

Santa Anna, Antonio López de Nineteenth-century general and dictator responsible for Mexico's losing more than a third of its territory to the United States.

Sarkozy, Nicholas President of France since 2007.

Saro-Wiwa, Ken Nigerian activist executed by the military government in 1996.

Schmidt, Helmut Chancellor of West Germany, 1974–92.

Schröder, Gerhard SPD chancellor of Germany from 1998 to 2006.

Shagari, Shehu President of Nigeria; overthrown in 1983 coup.

Shah, Muhammad Reza The second and last Pahlevi shah of Iran; deposed in 1979.

Shah, Reza First Pahlevi shah of Iran.

Singh, Manhoman Prime minister of India since 2004.

Spaak, Paul-Henri Belgian politician who was one of the leading architects of the early Common Market.

Stalin, Joseph Leader of the CPSU and Soviet Union, 1924–53.

Sun Yat-sen President of China after the 1911 revolution.

Thatcher, Margaret Conservative and first woman prime minister of Great Britain, 1979–90.

Vajpayee, Atal Bihari BJP prime minister of India, 1998–99.

Walesa, Lech Most important leader of Solidarity and then president of Poland.

Wei Jingsheng Major Chinese dissident, now in exile in the United States.

Xi Jinping Likely next Head of the CCP and President of China.

Yar'Adua, Umaru Musa President of Nigeria since 2007.

Yeltsin, Boris Former reformist communist leader and president of Russia, 1991–2000.

Zedillo, Ernesto President of Mexico, 1994–2000.

Zhirinovsky, Vladimir Leader of the right-wing and racist Liberal Democratic Party in Russia.

Zhou Enlai Number two to Mao Zedong in China from 1949 until his death in 1975.

Zyuganov, Gennady Head of the Russian Communist Party.

Name Index

Italic page numbers refer to photographs, illustrations, tables, or figures. Boldfaced page numbers refer to biographical sketches.

A

Abacha, Sani, *317*, *446*, 452–**453**, *453*, 456, 461, 463, 468
Abbas Shah, 376
Abiola, Moshood, 451–452, 458, 463, 468
Abramovich, Roman, 253, 255
Abramowitz, Alan, 45, 53
Abubakar, Abdulsalami, *446*, 452, 458, 460, 463–464, 468
Achebe, Chinua, 435, 441, 443
Adenauer, Konrad, 150, *150*, 155–156, 171
Adravan, 374
Aflaq, Michel, 411
Agha-Soltan, Neda, *383*, *384*, 388
Aguilar Zinser, Adolfo, 487
Ahmadinejad, Mahmoud, 369–370, 374, *380*, *383*, 387–388, *391*, **391**, 391–392, 395, 399
Akbar, Emperor, 336
Akintola, Samuel Ladoke, 447, 448
Alamgir, 336
Alawi, Ayad, 411, 429, 431–432
al-Bakr, Ahmad Hassan, 407, **413**, 414, 432
Alemán, Miguel, 480, *480*
Alexander II, 230
Alexander III, 230
Alexander the Great, 374
Ali, 405
Ali, Muhammad, 376
al-Maliki, Nouri, 401, 409, 428–429, 431–432, 432
Almond, Gabriel, 24, 29, 52–53, 75, 77, 152, 481, 483
al-Qadaffi, Muammar, 305, 317, 522
al-Sadr, Muqtada, 409, 427, *428*, 429, 432
Anderson, J, *56*
Andropov, Yuri, 214, 235, 286, 365, 481
An Li, 293
Anne, Queen, 71
Ansari, Ali, 385

B

Babangida, Ibrahim, 451–**453**, 463, 466, 468
Babur, Emperor, 336, 349
Bachelet, Michelle, 514
Bagehot, Walter, 87–88
Balewa, Tafawa, 445–446, *446*, *447*, 448, 468
Balladur, Edouard, *123*
Balladur, Raymond, *117*
Bani-Sadr, Abolhassan, 381, 391, *391*
Bardes, Barbara A., *53*
Barnier, Michel, 186
Barr, R., *56*
Barre, Raymond, *117*, *123*
Barroso, Jose Manuel, *186*, 187, *188*, 196
Batista, Fulgencio, 204
Bayrou, François, 116
Becker, Wolfgang, 196, 202
Beethoven, Ludwig van, 152
Bell, Martin, 85
Bello, Ahmadu, 444, 446, *447*, 448, 468
Benn, Anthony Wedgwood, 81–82

Arbatov, Georgi, 201, 213
Ardagh, John, 106, 165
Ardeshir, 374
Argyris, Chris, 6
Aronowitz, Stanley, 47
Ashafa, Muhammad, 467
Ashdown, Paddy, 84
Ashton, Catherine, 177, 186
al-Assad, Bashar, 305
Assange, Julian, 521
Attlee, Clement, 74, *78*, 339
Aubry, Martine, **183**
Avila Camacho, Manuel, 479–480, *480*
Awolowo, Obafemi, 446–448, 450, 468
Azikiwe, Nnamdi, 445–448, *447*, 450, *450*, 468
Aziz, Tariq, 413

B (continued)

Bérégovoy, Pierre, *123*
Berezovsky, Boris, 248, 252, 260, 261
Berghahn, V. B., 148
Berg-Schlosser, Dirk, *153*
Berners-Lee, Timothy, 521
Bernstein, Richard, 106
Berra, Yogi, 225
Bettencourt, Liliane, 105
Beveridge, William, 74
Bhindranwale, Jarnail Singh, 357–358, 366
Biden, Joe, 6
bin Laden, Osama, 62, 372
Bismarck, Otto von, 145, 171
al-Bitar, Salah al-Din, 411
Blair, Tony, 30–31, 34, 68–69, *73*, 74, 78–80, 82–83, 88, 91–98, 100, 157, 226, 403, 488
Blow, Charles, 46
Boehner, John, *60*
Bogdanor, Vernon, **81**
Boldyrev, Yuri, 249
Bono (Hewson, Paul David), *325*, **325**
Borodin, Mikhail, 271
Bosman, Jean-Marc, 189
Bové, José, 121
Braithwaite, Tunji, *450*
Brandenburg, Frank, 491
Brandt, Willy, 150, *150*, 157, 163, 171
Brass, Paul, 357
Bremer, Paul, 425, 430, 432
Brezhnev, Leonid, 211–214, 222, *232*, 235, 250, 261, 275, 286, 365, 481, 527
Brokaw, Tom, 48
Brown, Gordon, 66–67, *73*, *78*, 80, **83**, *88*, 89, 92, 100, 226
Bruni, Carla, 104, 119
Brüning, Heinrich, 147–148
Buffet, Marie-Georges, *117*
Buhari, Muhammadu, *446*, 451
Bull, Headley, 526
Bumiller, Elizabeth, 517
Burnham, Walter Dean, 67
Bush, George H. W., 54, *56*, 168, 219, 259, 404, 421, 522

Bush, George W., 7, 22, 34, 39, 47–48, *50*, 51, 54–56, *56*, 61, 97, 135–136, 142, 191, 242, *243*, 259–260, 304, 384, 386, 396, 402–404, *421*, 422–424, *423*, 432, 475, 488, 503, 522
Butler, David, 86
Butler, Richard, 422

C

Caesar, Julius, 179
Calderón, Felipe, 471, 473–475, *480*, *485*, 486, 490, 492–493, 495, 506
Callaghan, James, 29, 76, *78*
Calles, Plutarco Elías, 478–479, *480*
Camacho, Manuel Avila, 479, 480
Cameron, David (prime minister), 6, 65–67, *78*, 80–**81**, *81*, *84*, 89, *90*, 96, *98*, 100, 112, 167, 175, 435
Cameron, David (professor), *130*, *135*, 175, 176
Cárdenas, Cuauhtémoc, 481, 488–489, *489*, 506
Cárdenas, Lázaro, *476*, 479, *480*, 481, 506
Carranza, Venustiano, 478, *480*
Carson, Rachel, 518
Carter, Jimmy, *56*, 514
Castañeda, Jorge, 473, 479, 482, 487, 501
Castro, Fidel, 204, *209*, 217, 222
Castro, Raoul, 217
Ceausescu, Elena, 213
Cecchini, Paolo, 193
Cerf, Vinton, 521
Chaban-Delmas, Jacques, *117*, *123*
Chalabi, Adnan, 411
Chamberlain, Neville, 74, 148
Charitonov, Nikolai, *247*
Charles, Prince, 88
Charles I, 71
Charles II, 71
Chavance, Bernard, *205*
Chen Duxiu, 270, 271, 274, **274**, 297

Subject Index

Italic page numbers refer to photographs, figures, and tables.